W9-BDM-555

# HISTORY OF THE 20TH CENTURY

# HISTORY OF THE

# 20<sup>TH</sup>

# CENTURY

## INTRODUCTION
## BY ALAN BULLOCK

derbibooks

First published in the United States of America 1976 by
Derbibooks and distributed by
Booksales Inc., 110 Enterprise Avenue
Seacausus, N.J. 07094

© 1968/69/70 BPC Publishing Ltd.

© 1973/74 Phoebus Publishing Company/BPC Publishing Ltd.

© 1976 This edition Phoebus Publishing Company/BPC Publishing Ltd.

This book is adapted from the 'History of the 20th Century' partwork
with additional material. It has been produced by Phoebus Publishing
Company in association with Octopus Books Limited.

ISBN 0 7064 0551 X

Produced by Mandarin Publishers Limited
22a Westlands Road, Quarry Bay, Hong Kong
Printed in Hong Kong

Credits: ½ title page: Syndication International; Title page: Camera Press
Ltd; Contents: Camera Press Ltd; Introduction: left to right, S C R Photo
Library, Communist Party Library, U S Army Dept., H.Cartier-Bresson—
Magnum, United Press International, Camera Press.

# Contents

# Introduction

Trying to write the history of a century while still in the middle of it is a bold undertaking. The difficulties are obvious. At best, it can only be a provisional account, subject to much later revision, particularly for the most recent years. Nonetheless, there are good reasons for making the attempt, despite the difficulties.

No one, to take the first, can hope to understand the times in which he lives unless he knows something of the history which lies behind the immediate news. Let me give an example suggested by a recent visit to Berlin. Hitler's and the Kaiser's former capital is to-day a city literally divided down the middle by the famous Wall. How did the Wall ever come to be built? Why is it that more than thirty years after the end of the war, British, American and French—not German—troops are still in occupation of West Berlin which remains virtually isolated except by air in the middle of a hostile country? Why is it that there are two German states, and that World War II was never ended with a German peace treaty? How could anyone hope to answer these questions, or explain why any change in the extraordinary situation of Berlin during the past thirty years might well have started—might still start—another war, without turning to the history of Europe since World War II, and indeed as far back as the Russian Revolution of 1917?

Secondly, if the historians will not make the attempt and set up critical standards,

then the field is left open for every sort of myth, half-truth, propaganda twist and downright lie. One has only to recall the use which totalitarian regimes, Hitler's and Stalin's for example, have made of such distorted versions of the recent past to realize what a powerful political force 'history' can become in unscrupulous hands.

Finally, by standing back from the changes and events which we have witnessed, in order to see them as history, we put them into the perspective of time. That not only makes it easier to understand and place them, but easier to retain one's balance in face of the flood of events and the fears they evoke. It requires strong nerves to live in the 20th century; to see what is going on around us as part of an historical process helps, I believe, to preserve a more detached and critical interest in what is happening than simply wondering whether one is going to survive.

Fortunately, since World War II, an increasing number of historians has been attracted to study the history of the 20th century: there are specialist journals, and many books about recent history, good, bad and indifferent, are published every year. But this is not much help to the general reader who needs, first of all, an introduction which, without confusing him with too much detail, will give him an overall view and enable him to find his bearings. That is the value of the present book. Apart from the intrinsic interest of the individual chapters,

it provides in effect a plan of the first seventy-six years of the century, allowing the reader to relate the different episodes to each other and then go on to dig more deeply into those which interest him most. By way of introduction, I want to suggest some of the characteristics which distinguish the history of the 20th from that of earlier centuries.

Let me begin with one of the most obvious, the astonishing increase in population. Up to the middle of the 18th century, the population of the world appears to have grown steadily but slowly. Then, between 1800 and 1900, it very nearly doubled, from an estimated 900 million to close on 1,700 million. The rate of increase in the 20th century has been even greater: more than double in the first seventy years (from 1,700 to 3,500 million), with a further increase by two-thirds again expected between 1970 and the year 2000. Anyone who ponders on the implications of these figures—the increased pressure on resources; the growth of urban populations (eleven cities with over a million inhabitants in 1900, ten times that number in 1970, nine of them with more than seven millions each); the much higher proportion of young people under the age of twenty in those countries where the population grows fastest—will find the key to much of this century's turbulent history.

A second characteristic which compounds the effects of the first is the accelerating rate of change which has accompanied the growth of population. In earlier centuries

change was slow and intermittent, allowing time for people to adjust themselves to it; to-day, it is continuous and makes incessant demands on human adaptability.

Both these characteristics, the huge rise in population and the speeding up of change, derive from and depend upon a third: men's increasing mastery of environment, their ability to control famine, flood and disease, to extend the span of human life and raise their standards of living, to annihilate distance, even to launch themselves into space. To take only two examples: conditions of life in the countryside have been transformed, and the back-breaking burden of work in earlier times lifted by the provision of cheap electric power and the invention of the tractor. Such examples can be multiplied many times over. Their combined effect would seem incredible to previous generations which had always to adapt themselves to their environment, without the power to change it, and were helpless in the face both of natural and of social disasters such as epidemics.

The benefits of technological advance were at first a monopoly of the industrialized countries of Europe and North America, which used them in the 19th century to establish a predominant position over the rest of the world, and within those countries of the governing and propertied classes. Two of the major themes of 20th-century history have been the double challenge to this monopoly, from within and from without. Within the industrialized countries, the challenge has come particularly from organized labour seeking to make the benefits of technology and economic growth more generally available to all classes of the population. The challenge from without has come with the revolt of the rest of the world against its economic and political subordination to Europe and North America. This challenge too has taken many forms, from Japan's dramatic assertion of her independence at the beginning of the century, to the break-up of the European colonial empires after World War II, the Chinese Revolution and

the demand of the underdeveloped countries of the Third World for economic aid as well as independence.

This double challenge reflects what has been called 'the revolution of rising expectations', the belief that the old restraints set by nature on higher standards of life, not just for the few, but for the many, have been—or could be—removed by science and technology. It also reflects another great change; the end of the parallel belief that it is part of the unquestioned order of things that power and wealth should be confined to a minority, whether a single class or a small group of nations. On both counts, one could put up a good argument for saying that the most powerful idea characteristic of the 20th century has been equality.

The great engine of equality has been the state, and it is no coincidence that the effective power of the state has been so greatly increased in this century. Although this is seen at its clearest in countries living under totalitarian regimes, where the state, controlled by a single party, regulates the whole of economic and social life, as well as politics and education, it has happened to some degree in every country, whether developed or undeveloped. In the process, a major new interest has been created, that of the bureaucracy itself, the growth of which Max Weber foresaw at the beginning of the century as the inescapable consequence of the highly organized life of modern society. Nor has this been limited to the nation state, for every international organization and big business as well, whether operating nationally or multinationally, have been unable to escape the same 'iron law' of increasing bureaucratization.

These are some of the characteristics which strike me looking back over the first seventy-six years of the 20th century. I could go on adding to the list: the changing relations between the sexes and between generations, the unparalleled importance which the 20th century attaches to education, and so on. Every reader can make his

own list as he reads the chapters that follow. I wish to end this introduction, however, with a different point.

If it is natural, in introducing a book about the 20th century, to single out features which seem to distinguish it from other centuries, it would be quite wrong to conclude from this that there is a cut-off point, a break with the past, around 1900 or 1914 or some other date, after which earlier history ceases to have any relevance. On the contrary, I believe that no one can study the history of the 20th century and not be struck by the continuities with the past— provided that he knows something of the history of other centuries besides the 20th. This is why I hope that the reader who goes on to read more about the history of his own times will not limit himself to that. If he does he is in danger of missing the most important lesson of an historical study, including that of the recent past—its continuity. No age, even one which has seen such great changes as ours, is self sufficient, but part of an historical process which reaches back even into the remote past. Anyone who reads what Thucydides and Euripides had to say about the contemporary world of ancient Greece, or Machiavelli and Shakespeare about the world in which they lived, will not be in danger of overestimating the originality of his own experience and will be better fitted to distinguish between what is unique about our own time and what has been part of human experience in many other periods of history besides this.

*Alan Bullock*

Alan Bullock.

Corfu,
April 1976.

  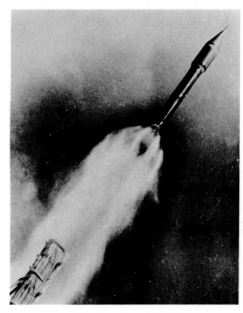

# Uneasy Splendour 1900-1914

## INTRODUCTION

The quarter century preceding the outbreak of the First World War has often been called an 'age of empires'. Imperialism as such was not, of course, an invention of the period. Extensive empires had been established in Asia a thousand years before the birth of Christ. The rise and decline of imperial dynasties provided the main subject-matter of the histories of the classical civilizations of the Mediterranean, India, China and the Islamic world. What was new about the imperialism of the late 19th century was its universality and its hard, competitive spirit. The dynamic expansionism of the Western imperialist powers made conflicting territorial rivalries rather than dynastic change the main motif of international history. Diplomats concerned themselves with problems of frontiers, buffer-states and 'spheres of influence'. Generals and admirals were obliged to balance the defence needs of the national homeland against the necessity of maintaining secure communications with distant colonies and vital trading partners. Politicians proclaimed imperial dominion to be essential for the power and prosperity of first-rank nations.

Journalists echoed and exaggerated their sentiments. Empire offered a few men a source of profit, many men a sense of mission and, to the anonymous everyman of Europe's slums, a source of pride. The façade of empire was massive and monolithic. Wealth and grandeur were symbolized by impressive public buildings, colourful pageants and all the paraphernalia of anthems, flags and festivals. Yet this imperialism contained within itself the most profound contradiction. At the same time as the railway, the steamship, the telegraph and the joint-stock trading company were making the great nations of the world more and more economically interdependent, politicians, publicists and teachers were emphasizing their differences and separateness. The tensions which arose from this inner contradiction were eventually to find their resolution in conflict.

It is tempting for the historian to simplify the task of description by assigning particular historical phenomena to general categories, to regard, for example, Britain and France as dominant empires, Spain and Austria-Hungary as declining empires or America and Japan as emerging empires. These judgments, however, obscure important distinctions. Also they do not necessarily give us a picture of the world as it was perceived by people living at the time.

In 1900 Great Britain was still, from a global point of view, the world's dominant power. It was, indeed, the only truly intercontinental power, with vast territories in North America, Africa, India and Australasia. A quarter of the world's land surface and a quarter of its population lay beneath the shadow of the Union Jack. While the white-settled regions of the empire advanced towards self-government, the rest were ruled by a system of benevolent and moderately competent despotism. British goods still dominated world trade, although the United States had already begun to out-produce her in coal and steel, and Germany had taken the lead in the development of the electrical and chemical industries. Britain's merchant marine accounted for nearly half the world's commercial tonnage. Britain's foreign investments extended far beyond her formal empire to give her a major stake in the prosperity of the United States, Argentina, Egypt and a dozen other nominally independent states. The British navy, which assured the security of international commerce, was still twice as large as the next largest fleet, even if the British army was humiliated by the guerrilla tactics of an amateur army of Boer farmers in South Africa. English had already become, as it was to remain, the international language of commerce, science and diplomacy. The British parliamentary form of government was widely admired, if less widely imitated.

*Left: The explosion of the US battleship* Maine *in Havana harbour provided an excuse for expansion; this painting shows US allies, Cuban cavalry, in a machete charge.* **Below:** *During this period in France, the day's prominent figures, often visited the demi-monde of casinos.*

B. Morganiès

8

*True to the extravagant nature of Japanese 'war art', this print extols Japanese superiority over the Russians. In fact, the bravery of the Russian soldier was remarkable. But he was let down by the blunders and inefficiency of his commanding officers. The Japanese soldier was also hardy, well-equipped, and well-trained. He considered it an honour to die for his Emperor*

France, Europe's only major republic, ruled an empire about half the size of Britain's, most of it concentrated in Africa and South-East Asia. Less industrialized than Britain, less populous than Germany, France still commanded a renowned army and possessed a capital city famous for its beauty and culture. Her great rival, Germany, has been regarded as a disruptive newcomer to the international scene. United as recently as 1870 Germany had proved itself a formidable industrial and military power. In the 1880's it had begun to carve out an empire in Africa and the Pacific. By the 1890's it had begun to challenge Britain as a major naval power. Germany's desire for 'a place in the sun' threatened to thrust her neighbours into the diplomatic shade.

Germany's allies, Austria-Hungary and Italy, were essentially satellites rather than equals. Austria-Hungary, ruled by an ageing and instinctively conservative emperor, was gravely weakened by the dissensions of rival ethnic groups. Italy, like Germany a new nation since 1870, was striving ineffectually to keep pace with the more industrialized imperialist powers. In 1896 her troops had suffered a mortifying defeat at the hands of Abyssinian irregulars at Adowa.

Ranged against the 'Triple Alliance' (formed in 1882) of Germany, Austria-Hungary and Italy were France, its ally Russia, and, from 1907 onwards, Great Britain, the powers of the 'Triple Entente'. Immense in area and population, Russia was widely regarded as the world's greatest military power. This illusion was to be shattered by the result of the Russo-Japanese war of 1904–5. A latecomer to industrialization, Russia was simply incapable of mobilizing its vast resources effectively.

Of the other European states none can be accounted as being of the first rank. Spain had been obliged to surrender Cuba, Puerto Rico, Guam and the Philippines to the tutelage of the United States after a short and decisive war in 1898. Portugal still clung to the shreds of a once-great empire in Africa, India and the Far East. The Netherlands, too, retained an avaricious grasp on the islands of South-East Asia while Belgium, a nation only since 1830, laid claim to the sprawling Congo basin through the person of its sovereign Leopold II. Scandinavia was, politically speaking, a backwater of no strategic significance. The independent nations of the Balkans, Serbia, Rumania, Bulgaria and Greece, which had all previously been part of the Ottoman Empire, were too preoccupied with squabbling with each other, with Austria-Hungary and with the remnants of the Ottoman Empire to assert themselves in wider spheres. Nevertheless, their strategic location at the junction of three great and mutually antagonistic land empires made their internal affairs a matter of more than purely local significance.

Of the non-European powers only two can be regarded as being of global stature—Japan and the United States. America, having become the world's leading industrial power, and having acquired overseas possessions by conquest, still kept itself aloof from foreign entanglements. Latin America, however, it regarded as its own special sphere of interest. The partition of Africa had strengthened American determination to insulate South America from European interference. This did not, however, preclude the possibility of direct armed interventions by the US itself, whether to squash revolutions or to support governments favourable to American interest. The most important single outcome of this style of diplomacy was the construction of an international canal to link the Atlantic and Pacific oceans through the Isthmus of Panama. Without the active encouragement of President Theodore Roosevelt and the direct support of the United States Navy it would have been impossible for the Panamanian revolutionaries to assert their independence from Colombia in 1903. Without the complicity of a Panamanian puppet-state it would not have been possible for the United States to lease and police the necessary 'Canal Zone'.

America's future Pacific rival, Japan, having transformed itself into Asia's only industrial state in less than half a century was seeking to assert itself on the Asian mainland as an equal with the great powers of Europe. Its alliance with Britain in 1902 signified its arrival as an independent state of international significance. Its victory over Russia in 1904–5 heralded a turning-point in world history. Its annexation of the Korean peninsula in 1905 marked the beginning of a long and expensive struggle to achieve economic hegemony in Eastern Asia by force of arms.

China, then as now the world's most populous state, was quite incapable of resisting Japanese expansionism. Humiliated in battle by her smaller but more advanced neighbour in 1894–95, she was wracked by internal disorders which the reactionary and ineffectual Manchu regime could neither control nor exploit to its own ends. The anti-foreign 'Boxer Rising' of 1900 ended with a reassertion of the military supremacy and commercial privileges of the great powers which effectively controlled the nation's coastal regions, customs service and main arteries of communication. Sun Yat-sen's nationalist revolution of 1911 expressed new aspirations for the Chinese people but failed to achieve anything for their material conditions or international status. Rather, it marked the boisterous prelude to almost half a century of further disorders and confusion.

Apart from a few traditional monarchies, such as Abyssinia, Siam and Persia, which remained nominally independent because they could offer little to justify the trouble and expense of conquest, or because it suited the great powers to let them survive as neutral zones, only one other power counted in the diplomatic world of 1900: the Ottoman Empire. Long stigmatized as 'the sick man of Europe', it had in fact successfully resisted many attempts to dismember its territories and had, with a certain measure of foreign aid, transformed itself from a traditional oriental despotism into a reasonably efficient autocracy on central European lines. In essence this meant that the arbitrary will of the sovereign was obeyed not just in the court and the capital but also in the more remote provinces of the empire as well. Yet the sickness of the Ottoman Empire was nonetheless real for all that. Distracted by religious and racial tensions, weakened by the loss of large tracts of territory in North Africa to Italy and in Europe to its former vassal states, the oldest and most extensive empire in the history of Islam was to collapse entirely under the onslaught of total war.

The most important single event to take place between 1900 and 1914 was the Russo-Japanese war of 1904–5. It began with a surprise naval attack on the Russian base at Port Arthur which resulted in the crippling of the Russian Pacific squadron, thus enabling the Japanese to land and supply their expeditionary force virtually unhindered. The land war consisted of two major engagements—the investment of Port Arthur, which fell after a protracted and bloody siege, and

*Below: The Habsburg empire was a sprawling conglomeration of many peoples. Some, like this Bosnian girl, might seem more in place in the Middle East than in central Europe. The girl is wearing the traditional Bosnian wedding-dress, and around her neck is her dowry in the form of a necklace*

the battle of Mukden, in which both sides suffered some 50,000 casualties. Having failed to trounce the Japanese by land, the Russians pinned all their hopes on their Baltic squadron which, after an epic voyage half-way round the world, was destroyed in the Straits of Tsushima in less than an hour. At this point the combatants accepted the mediation of President Roosevelt. Russia's newly-constructed Trans-Siberian Railway had proved totally inadequate to the task of supporting an effective military presence four thousand miles from her industrial and military heartland. Japan, too, was on the point of exhaustion, though this was less immediately apparent at the time. Contemporary statesmen were dazzled by her achievement. Russia, supposedly the world's greatest military power, had been defeated by a state which half a century before had been obliged to accept an almost tributary relationship towards the great Western powers.

The impact of the Russo-Japanese war was far-reaching. Nationalists throughout Asia were exhilarated by the victory of a non-European state over a European one. The myth of the invincibility of the white man had been convincingly destroyed. Western statesmen, by contrast, were less concerned at Japan's victory than at Russia's defeat, which stimulated German ambitions in Europe and contributed to the strengthening of the Anglo-French Entente as France sought to compensate for Russia's newly revealed impotence by adding Britain's naval strength to her anti-German alliance.

In Russia itself the war led to an abortive revolution. The Tsarist government, having hoped for a short victorious war to rally the nation behind the throne, found itself faced with strikes in the towns and riots in the countryside, as the twin burdens of inflation and conscription pushed the masses beyond the limits of their endurance. Taking advantage of this situation, bourgeois liberals demanded reforms which would pave the way to a Western-style democracy. At the same time radical agitators attempted to foment a full-scale revolution which would inaugurate the establishment of a socialist Utopia. By a

*Wilhelm and Edward VII enjoy a family party. Edward personified much of what Wilhelm liked and loathed about the British*

*'Dress rehearsal for 1917': Russian workers on strike in Moscow during 1905 revolution*

combination of brutal repression and grudging concessions the Tsarist regime reasserted its authority. The subsequent attempt to govern through a Duma or parliament was never more than half-hearted but a policy of land reform, aimed at creating a prosperous, conservative and loyal peasantry, did seem to promise some hope of stability in the countryside. In the event it was to take three years of carnage—from 1914-17—to squander the Tsardom's last reserves of authority and prestige.

Although the outcome of the Russo-Japanese war came as a shock to contemporaries, it was overshadowed by the threats to European peace implied by a series of diplomatic crises in North Africa, the Balkans and the Middle East. As the scope for colonial expansion narrowed, the significance of Europe's strategic fringe increased.

Efforts to establish a German presence in Morocco led to diplomatic rebuffs for her over an incident at Algeciras in 1905 and at Agadir in 1911. Her financial and technical support for a 'Berlin-to-Bagdad' railway was likewise viewed with suspicion. But it was Austria's 'forward policy' in the Balkans which was eventually to provoke the nemesis of the Central Powers. In 1908 she managed to bring off a major diplomatic coup by formally occupying the nominally Ottoman provinces of Bosnia and Herzegovina, which had, in practice, been under her control for thirty years. But the attempt to repeat her success in 1914 by humiliating Serbia was to escalate into a disastrous confrontation from which there was no retreat.

Since the 1890's she had striven to close the naval 'gap' between herself and Great Britain. This accelerated the pace of the already existing 'arms race', which had grown out of increasing speed of change in military technology, and the increasing governmental nervousness which this induced. The German naval building programme was interpreted by the British as a direct threat to the safety of her commerce and empire. In 1906 she retaliated by launching the first of a fleet of Dreadnoughts, the world's first all-big gun battleship. The result was a further vicious twist in the spiral of rising arms budgets. Fear, as ever, fed on itself and the search for security itself bred the conditions for its breakdown.

*The mailed fist at Agadir: German cartoon of Kaiser Wilhelm's arrogant intervention*

As the major European states became divided into mutually antagonistic blocs of mutually supportive powers, the likelihood of a general conflagration increased. At the same time as international co-operation was being extended through the success of such organizations as the International Postal Union, the Red Cross and the International Court of Justice, it was curtailed by the suspicion which Germany's military and industrial strength aroused among her apprehensive neighbours.

By 1900 the pace of social change was accelerating throughout the Western world under the impact of technology. Commentators, bemused by the doctrine of progress, had for more than half a century been accustomed to praise the astonishing discoveries and achievements of modern science, epitomized by such triumphs as the laying of submarine telegraph cables from England to America. Such accomplishments, however, had, until the closing decades of the 19th century, relatively little influence on the daily lives of ordinary people. By the 1880's this situation had begun to change as working men, united in ever stronger trade unions, began to exert political and economic pressure to secure for themselves an increasing proportion of the wealth that they produced. The result was an immense boost to the industries catering to mass needs and mass tastes and the adoption and development of new technologies which would increase their productivity and output. If the entrepreneurs of the mid-19th century had made their fortunes out of steel and coal, their successors made them out of cheap newspapers, canned foodstuffs, machine-made boots and mass-produced kitchenware. At the same time, and as part of the same process, the adoption of new technologies created entirely novel occupations such as the telephonist, the typist, the chauffeur and the electricity worker.

These changes took place against a background of rapid urbanization. In 1870 Germany had eight cities with a population of more than one hundred thousand; by 1900 it had forty-one such cities. In Russia the number of cities of comparable proportions rose from six to seventeen during the same period. In 1870 only London and Paris had a population of more than a million. By 1900 they had been joined by Berlin, Vienna, Moscow and

*Sir Edward Carson, the anti-Home Rule leader, signing the Ulster Covenant, 1912. The Ulster crisis led almost to the rejection of constitutional government itself, and threatened Britain with civil war*

St Petersburg in Europe, New York, Chicago and Philadelphia in the United States, Tokyo, Osaka and Calcutta in Asia, and Rio de Janeiro and Buenos Aires in Latin America. Change in the size and area of major cities was matched by changes in their structure and appearance brought about by the increasing availability of tram services, the extension of suburban railway lines and the proliferation of artificial lighting in homes, streets and public buildings.

Social change was by no means confined to the industrialized regions of the world; but the changes which were taking place in what has since become known as the developing world can be attributed less to the impact of technology than to the introduction and development of new forms of economic activity and organization, usually associated with the exploitation of primary products through systematic forestry, deep mining or plantation agriculture. As in the industrialized nations of the West this trend led to increased social and geographical mobility and the emergence of new occupational groups, such as clerks and dockers, the forerunners of an Afro-Asian proletariat.

Missionary activity was another significant factor in the promotion of social change. More important than spectacular struggles to abolish cannibalism or polygamy in remote islands of the Pacific were the widespread efforts being made, from the Guinea coast to China, to raise the standards of health and literacy of native peoples. In many countries of Asia and Africa mission schools laid the foundations of a national system of education and educated the first generations of nationalist leaders. Even where these activities provoked a hostile reaction they were not without significance, leading thoughtful Hindus and Muslims to re-examine their faiths and customs in the light of Western beliefs and values.

Change was a marked feature of both the developed and developing regions of the world, but there is little doubt that the contrast between their material circumstances was growing more rather than less glaring. By 1900 the European working man could expect to live roughly twice as long as an Asian peasant. In terms of bulk and nutrition his diet was probably superior and almost certainly more varied. His clothing and the furnishings of his home were likewise more plentiful—though often less pleasing to the eye. Access to railways and steamships also gave the Western worker the option of changing his fortunes by changing his country. The flow of migrants from Europe to North and South America, Australasia and South Africa continued unabated, until it was cut off by the tide of war in 1914. Almost half the natural increase in Europe's population was siphoned off in this way, relieving the pressure of jobs and housing in the rapidly expanding cities and, by their absence, improving the bargaining power of those left behind.

Another contrast between Europe and Asia is also striking. The bulk of the world's population lived under the rule of two sorts of regime—traditional autocracies or alien empires—neither of which expected the peoples in their charge to play any role other than that of obedient subject. Pseudo-parliamentary forms were observed in a number of 'progressive' colonies, a few modernizing monarchies and the more self-consciously republican republics of Latin America; but wherever they existed they served only to disguise the real structure of power and processes of decision-making. The ear of the sovereign or president, or of his most trusted minister, command of armed men or the possession of great landed wealth gave men a predominant political voice in every region of the world except North-West Europe, North America and the white-settled 'Dominions' of the British Empire. In these areas democratic sentiments and the power of organized labour had begun to challenge the established power of the wealthy and the privileged. The capacity to mobilize the votes and voices of ordinary men was becoming, for the first time in the history of the world, the most significant of political resources. Though the pace and extent of democratization varied from country to country the general trend in that direction throughout the developed world was both unmistakable and seemingly irresistible.

Associated with the trend towards mass participation in politics, partly as a cause and partly as a consequence, was a general tendency to enlarge the sphere of state action. More and more governments came to assume a range of functions which would have astounded the statesmen of a previous generation. Whereas the role of the state had once been virtually confined to the maintenance of law and order and the defence of the realm, it now came to be extended into such matters as education, housing, health and urban development, which had formerly been the concern of churches, guilds, municipalities and charitable organizations. By 1914 the citizen of an advanced European state could expect that the government would not only require him to obey its laws, pay its taxes and serve in its army, but would also regulate his conditions of work, educate his children and alleviate the threat of absolute destitution, if not actually guarantee him a modest affluence. The conception of welfare embodied by the state-sponsored services of the decade before the outbreak of the Great War was, by the standards of the late 20th century, at best a minimal one. Benefits were not generous, ameni-

*The rival fleet that alarmed Great Britain— German dreadnought battleships, in 1911*

ties were not luxurious, the system as a whole was by no means comprehensive. But the idea that the state should take positive steps to raise the condition of its citizens had taken firm root.

The extension of state functions had three important consequences. It led to a notable increase in the number of persons employed in the public service, whether as clerks, teachers, nurses or a hundred kinds of inspector and official. It necessitated and at the same time justified the diversion of a rising proportion of the national income into the coffers of the public treasury. And it reinforced the bonds of loyalty which tied the citizen to the state and strengthened his willingness to regard its purposes as his own and to accept its claim to command his life and property in time of war as entirely legitimate. In other words, bureaucratization enabled nationalism to withstand the challenge of socialism.

The socialist movement, born of the turmoil of 19th-century industrialism, proclaimed the international solidarity of working men, the unity of their common interests vis-à-vis one another and against their common enemy, the industrial and financial bourgeoisie. Socialists denied the overriding claims of the nation-state which, they alleged, governed only in the interests of the bourgeoisie, regardless of whether the form of government was nominally democratic or not. The prospect of bloody revolution, however, seemed less attractive to most thoughtful workers than the opportunities for piecemeal social improvement which were offered by parliamentary government and the state's acceptance of an ever-widening range of responsibilities.

The outbreak of the Great War tested ultimate allegiances. Socialist ideals were swept aside by socialist leaders who pledged both themselves and their followers to support with total loyalty the cause of their respective nations. Without the fervent support of the masses of ordinary men and women the Great War could never have begun, let alone continued for four years at the cost of forty million lives and the devastation of the world's richest continent. As the young Winston Churchill had prophesied to the House of Commons in 1901:

'Democracy is more vindictive than Cabinets. The wars of peoples will be more terrible than those of kings.'

# Europe:The World's Overlord

*Below: A leading world statesman of 1900, Great Britain's Lord Salisbury. He looked forward with mixed feelings to the new century, foreseeing danger in the rivalries of the great powers*
*Bottom: A half century earlier Karl Marx prophesied the impending destruction of the existing social order and the total re-organization of society in favour of the workers. For Marx's followers in 1900, the days of Salisbury and his kind were numbered*
*Right: Colonial rule at its worst. African women in chains in Leopold II's Congo. The ruthless exploitation of the Congo's vast resources was pursued regardless*

In May 1898 Lord Salisbury, the British prime minister, surveyed the world scene in a great speech in the Albert Hall in London. 'You may,' he said, 'roughly divide the nations of the world as the living and the dying. On one side you have great countries of enormous power growing in power every year, growing in wealth, growing in dominion, growing in the perfection of their organization. Railways have given to them the power to concentrate upon any one point the whole military force of their population and to assemble armies of a magnitude and power never dreamed of in the generations that have gone by. Science has placed in the hands of those armies weapons ever growing in their efficacy of destruction. . . . By the side of these splendid organizations, of which nothing seems to diminish the force and which present rival claims which the future may only be able by a bloody arbitrament to adjust . . . there are a number of communities which I can only describe as dying.'

These observations by one of Europe's most experienced statesmen provide as good a point as any from which to look at the world on the eve of the 20th century. It was a moment when the great powers of Europe dominated the world, but when their expansion was resulting in increasing rivalry between them.

seemed to offer an easy field of expansion for the European powers. The 'struggle for Africa', when Great Britain, France, Germany, and even individuals such as King Leopold II of the Belgians, tried to gain control of these vast regions by diplomacy, conquest, or treaties with African tribal leaders, was an important source of international tension in the 1890's.

There were various reasons for this expansionist activity by the European powers in the last quarter of the 19th century. Economic motives – the need for new fields for capital investment and new markets for manufactures, the hope for new sources of raw materials – were undoubtedly important. But there were other considerations. At least some of the leaders of imperialist activity were inspired by philanthropic motives, especially by the desire to end the slave trade, and by Christian

*British Museum*

*Above: Wishful thinking in Boxer propaganda: European soldiers retreat, pursued by the Boxers. Although primitive in its execution and message, this sort of propaganda was symptomatic of the hatred felt for the foreigner in Chinese society*

Yet there is in Lord Salisbury's speech more than just a statement about European world domination and about the dangers of imperial rivalries among the powers.

### The 'living' and the 'dying'

When Lord Salisbury made his speech, the strongest powers of Europe – Great Britain, France, and Germany – were undoubtedly 'living' and expanding. The United States, too, in the midst of a rapid economic development, based on the exploitation of vast untapped natural resources and on the reserves of manpower provided by a stream of immigrants from many parts of Europe, had established itself as a world power when it defeated Spain in 1898, freeing Cuba from Spanish rule and acquiring the Philippines. The emergence of the United States as a great power in the Pacific Ocean was paralleled by the still more startling appearance among the 'living' nations of a new great power, Japan. After some decades of intensive modernization and the adoption of Western economic and, superficially at least, political models, Japan defeated China in 1895, and was attempting to establish control over Korea.

When Lord Salisbury spoke of 'dying' nations, he had especially in mind the once-great empires of Turkey and China. The weakness of the central governments of these countries had enabled the Western powers to acquire great economic influence in their possessions and, in some cases – when, for example, the British occupied Egypt, and the French Tunisia, in the 1880's, and, later in 1911, the Italians conquered Libya – had led or was to lead to the actual occupation of their territory. It was to take successful revolutions in both Turkey and China to enable their governments to hold their own again; but in spite of episodes like the Boxer Rising against foreign influence in China, successful resistance to the Western powers still seemed, in 1900, a long way off.

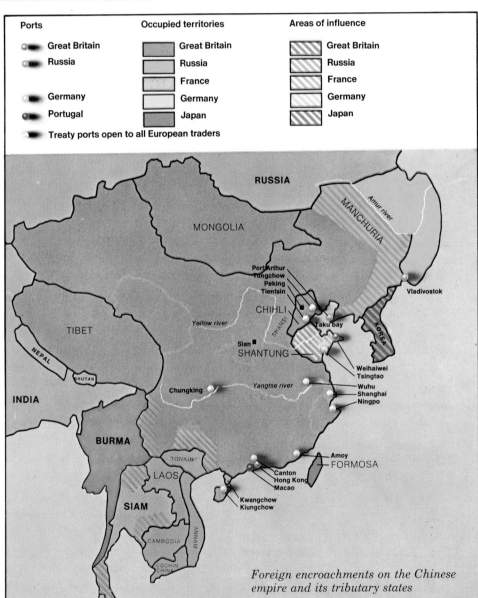

*Foreign encroachments on the Chinese empire and its tributary states*

| Ports | Occupied territories | Areas of influence |
|---|---|---|
| Great Britain | Great Britain | Great Britain |
| Russia | Russia | Russia |
| | France | France |
| Germany | Germany | Germany |
| Portugal | Japan | Japan |
| Treaty ports open to all European traders | | |

### Imperialist tensions and aims

If the weakness of some of the large states of the Middle and Far East provided a temptation to the great powers to intervene, there were other areas of the world which were still almost without state organization and which had had little contact with Western technology. Such areas – Africa is the obvious example –

missionary zeal. Moreover, the control over an area, once established, had its own consequences – the desire to control neighbouring districts in the interest of security, or the wish to forestall moves by other European powers and to protect strategic routes to existing imperial possessions. The British stayed in Egypt largely in order to safeguard the route to India; and the occupation of Egypt led in turn to a demand for the control of the Sudan and of parts of central and east Africa in order to protect Egypt's southern border and the sources of the Nile. Often motives of pure prestige and international status-seeking led to the acquisition of territory which offered little tangible profit. This was true of the German colonies in Africa and the Pacific.

By 1900 there were several ways in which the European powers controlled other parts of the world. In some countries influence was exercised without political control. Many Latin American countries, for example, depended on foreign investments and foreign technicians and were often dominated by European economic interests. In other countries, such as Egypt or the empire of Annam in French Indo-China, the existing state was controlled politically by a foreign power, but indirectly, its own social structure being left more or less intact. In China the independence of the government was limited by the British administration of the customs. Elsewhere again, colonial territories were under the direct rule of European administrators; in tropical Africa the arbitrary boundaries drawn up by the imperial powers to suit their administrative or diplomatic convenience have become the frontiers of independent states in our own day.

### The old empires
Alongside the new colonies the old empires still survived, even when the powers which had once conquered them no longer retained much international importance: Holland still possessed rich territories in the East Indies, and the Portuguese colonies in east and west Africa were coveted by both the Germans and the British. After the loss of Cuba and the Philippines, Spain had only small and unimportant colonies left. But Spanish settlers and Spanish culture had struck deep roots in the New World, and the Spanish element in Latin America survived the end of Spanish rule there.

The British empire also included territories which had been settled by men of British stock, and Great Britain alone of the imperial powers of the late 19th century had colonies in which there were deep cultural and national bonds between colonists and mother country. Canada, Australia, and New Zealand had by 1900 obtained a large measure of autonomy and self-government, and were sufficiently aware of the fact to thwart the attempt of the ambitious colonial secretary, Joseph Chamberlain, to create an imperial tariff union and a federation which would bind the colonies more closely to Great Britain. In fact, during the 20th century, the trend was to be towards looser and less formal links between Great Britain and the European-peopled colonies. In 1900, indeed, the weak point in Great Britain's empire was South Africa, where a bitter war was raging between Great Britain and the Boer (Dutch) settlers.

### The European powers
The period of European overseas expansion was a period of peace in Europe itself. The Franco-Prussian war of 1870 had established a new balance of power which in 1900 was only just beginning to be threatened by the tensions which were to lead to war in 1914. The most striking fact was the emergence of Germany as the strongest power on the continent. Her large and efficient army was backed by an industrial strength which was growing rapidly: Germany's coal production exceeded that of France and Belgium combined, and was soon to rival that of Great Britain. By 1900 Germany was neck and neck with Great Britain as the second iron and steel producer. German technical enterprise gave her a large share in 'the second industrial revolution' in the last years of the 19th and first decade of the 20th century. This revolution was based on electrical power and the internal combustion engine, and on the replacement by synthetic chemicals of many materials hitherto available only from natural sources at great expense in manpower and transport. The labour force for Germany's expansion was provided by a rapidly growing population: the German population rose from 41 million in 1870 to over 60 million in 1910, whereas the French population remained almost static at about 40 million.

Many people in Germany thought that, for all its success, the German empire did not yet have a position in the world commensurate to its strength. In 1898 the German government embarked on a programme of naval expansion. Although it was not for several years that the British became worried by this threat to their traditional naval hegemony, an important pressure group in Germany was spreading the idea that Germany should assume the role of a great naval power able to challenge Great Britain, and acquire the colonies which Germany had failed to win because its belated achievement of national unity had made it a late starter in the race for an empire. A great navy would be the symbol of Germany's greatness – though it was not always clear what aims beyond the expression of German power and prestige the German navy was to serve.

France, after the defeat of 1871 and the loss to Germany of Alsace and Lorraine, had made a surprising recovery. Her agricultural strength, her independence of imported food, her widespread foreign and colonial investments, and the brilliance of her intellectual and cultural life ensured her place among the great powers. Great Britain, too, as far as the world balance of power was concerned, still had enormous assets in spite of the fact that these were imperceptibly entering a relative decline after 1900. Her industrial wealth, her maritime power, the riches coming to London – one of the chief banking, insurance, and mercantile centres of the world – made Great Britain's claim to world power a real one. However, there were by 1900 many people who were anxious about the economic challenge from the industries of Germany and the United States and were demanding tariff barriers to protect British industry against the new and developing threat of an increasingly competitive world market.

### Nationalist rumblings
Among the remaining European countries which were generally regarded as great powers, one, the Austro-Hungarian empire, was already beginning to fit into the category of Lord Salisbury's dying nations, as its internal national problems became increasingly intractable, while another, Russia, faced enormous internal difficulties. It is true that Russia was rapidly becoming industrialized, and that the steady expansion across Siberia and central Asia, followed by the construction of the Trans-Siberian Railway, which reached its terminus on the Pacific in 1902, gave Russia a place among the imperialist powers, with ambitions to control Manchuria and north China. However, her defeat by Japan in 1905 did much to shake faith in Russia's strength, while the revolution of 1905 revealed the weakness of the Tsarist regime.

While the great nation-states of Europe were asserting their claim to rule the 'backward' peoples of Africa and Asia, the smaller nationalities of Europe were claiming the right to rule themselves. The example had been set by the countries which, in the course of the 19th century, had been freed from Turkish rule – Greeks, Serbs, Rumanians, Bulgarians – while the romantic Italian struggle for unification in the mid-century had aroused the sympathy of liberals everywhere. This example was followed not only in Europe: in China, the young Sun Yat-sen, later the leader of the Chinese revolution, was in the 1890's eagerly reading the works of Mazzini, the philosopher of the Italian national movement, and in India the moderate requests for autonomy put forward by the National Congress, founded in 1885, were giving way to angrier and more outspoken nationalist demands.

But it was in Europe itself that the disruptive force of nationalism was most apparent. True, Austria-Hungary had, in 1900, achieved an uneasy and temporary calm; but within a few years the Hungarians' demand to rule their half of the monarchy without interference from Vienna was followed by renewed agitation among the South Slav inhabitants of the monarchy – Serbs, Croats, and Slovenes. This was at a time when the rulers of the independent kingdom of Serbia were showing a new enthusiasm for the struggle of their fellow South Slavs for independence from Hungarian and German rule.

Elsewhere, too, national movements were causing growing anxiety. The Irish demand for Home Rule was a major issue in British politics; the Finns were able to use the crisis of the Russian revolution of 1905 to attain autonomy; the Poles under Russian and German rule were continuously working for independence, while the obstinate refusal of the inhabitants of Alsace and Lorraine to accept incorporation into the German empire meant that relations between Germany and France would continue to be strained.

These national aspirations created new sources of tension among the great powers. Serbia looked to Russia for aid in her fight against Austro-Hungarian domination, and events in the Balkans were, in the first decade of the century, to arouse as much anxiety and conflict as imperial rivalries outside Europe. Growing mutual suspicion found its expression in increased armaments and the preparation of plans for war, such as the famous German plan drawn up by General von Schlieffen for the invasion of France through Belgium.

Imperial rivalries and nationalist ambitions were leading to a re-grouping of the great powers and to a feeling that the balance of power on which the peace of Europe had rested since the 1870's was being upset. In 1902 Great Britain signed an alliance with Japan to protect her Far Eastern interests against Russia. Soon after, the British government settled its outstanding colonial differences, first with France in 1904, and then with France's ally, Russia, in 1907. These agreements

## The Power of the Powers, 1900

*Below:*
*Size in square miles of national states (green) related to the approximate size of overseas empires (yellow)*

| | | | |
|---|---|---|---|
| 1 | Great Britain | 120,979 | 10,500,000 |
| 2 | Russia | 8,660,395 | |
| 3 | France | 204,092 | 4,367,000 |
| 4 | USA | 2,939,000 | 620,000 |
| 5 | Germany | 208,830 | 1,000,000 |
| 6 | Austria-Hungary | 264,204 | |
| 7 | Italy | 110,646 | 185,000 |
| 8 | Japan | 147,655 | 14,000 |

*Below: Europe's dominant position in 1900*

- Areas directly ruled by nations of European stock
- Areas where European political, cultural, or technological influence is strong
- Areas still almost completely untouched by European influence: only Ethiopia in Africa, and Afghanistan and Tibet in Asia

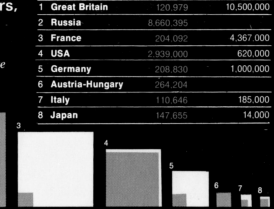

*The vital economic and military statistics expressed in three dimensions*

| | Austria-Hungary | France | Germany | Great Britain | Italy | Japan | Russia | USA |
|---|---|---|---|---|---|---|---|---|
| Population | 45,015,000 | 38,641,333 | 56,367,176 | 41,605,323 | 32,450,000 | 43,763,153 | 132,960,000 | 76,085,794 |
| Men in regular army | 397,316 | 589,541 | 585,266 | 280,733* | 261,728 | 273,268 | 860,000 | 70,802 |
| Annual iron & steel production (tons) | 2,580,000 | 3,250,000 | 13,790,000 | 13,860,000 | 500,000 | | 5,015,000 | 23,980,000 |
| Annual value of foreign trade (£) | 151,599,000 | 460,408,000 | 545,205,000 | 877,448,917 | 132,970,000 | 52,658,000 | 141,799,000 | 481,445,000 |
| Merchant fleet (net tonnage) | 313,698 | 1,037,720 | 1,941,645 | 9,304,108 | 945,000 | 796,930 | 633,820 | 5,524,218 |
| 1st class battleships† | | 13 | 14 | 38 | 9 | 6 | 13 | 17 |
| 2nd class battleships† | 6 | 10 | | 11 | 5 | | 10 | |

*Period of Boer War. Also includes Indian army †Built or under construction 1st December 1900

soon acquired a wider significance; Germany, with whom the British government had considered allying itself as recently as 1900, was becoming Great Britain's main rival; and Germany began to see in the new alignments a plan by Great Britain to encircle her with a ring of hostile powers.

### The spread of Marxism

Within the major countries of the world the development of industrial society had produced new stresses and new conflicts. Since 1870 the working classes of the West had become increasingly well-organized and were effectively agitating for an improvement of their lot. The introduction of a greatly enlarged franchise in most countries of Europe—though women as yet nowhere had the right to vote—meant that the working class was beginning to exert direct pressure on their governments. The ruling classes realized that measures of social reform were necessary if they were to remain in control. Schemes for social insurance had been introduced by the German government in the 1880's, and the Liberal administration in Great Britain after 1905 was to lay the foundations of the modern welfare state. Most civilized governments realized the necessity of introducing legal codes aimed at protecting the workers against the worst abuses of the industrial system.

These measures, and the official support given them by the Roman Catholic Church in an important statement of social policy by Pope Leo XIII in 1891, did not, however, check the development of a powerful socialist movement. The nature of the socialist parties depended on the industrial structure and political traditions of each country, but the strongest influence on the most powerful and best organized of them, the German Social Democratic Party, was the doctrine of Karl Marx (1818-1883). Marx's friend and collaborator, Friedrich Engels, had done much during the 1880's and 1890's to popularize his doctrines.

What stuck in people's minds was not so much the sophisticated economic and sociological analysis to be found in Marx's

Bibliothèque Nationale, Paris

writings but a few simplified ideas which seemed to offer the industrial workers not just hope of an immediate improvement in their condition, but ultimately a total reorganization of society in their favour. According to this doctrine, all history was the history of class struggles; and the stage was now being reached in advanced industrial societies when, in a final struggle, the proletariat would replace the bourgeoisie, just as earlier the bourgeoisie had replaced the feudal aristocracy. The triumph of the working class, therefore, was a matter of historical necessity; in the meantime the workers must cultivate a consciousness of their historical role.

### Socialist dilemma

The Marxist socialist parties were less revolutionary in practice than in theory, and were as concerned to win immediate gains—more wages or shorter hours—as to prepare for the revolution. In 1900 the international socialist movement was deeply divided on the question of how far it was legitimate to co-operate with other parties and concentrate on the achievement of short-term practical reforms. In Germany the discussion had been a theoretical one based on an attempt to revise some of Marx's doctrines, especially his belief that the proletariat was, in capitalist society, doomed to increasing poverty and misery (which in the prosperous Germany of the late 19th century was demonstrably untrue). In France the question had arisen of how far socialists should join with other democrats to defend the republican constitution or to carry out programmes of social reform. Although the official doctrine of the Marxists, accepted in theory by most of the socialist parties of Europe, was uncompromisingly revolutionary, in those states with a wide franchise and a degree of civil liberty, the socialists were increasingly reformist in their actions.

Marxist ideas were eagerly adopted even in those countries, like Russia, to which the Marxist analysis of historical development was not immediately applicable. In 1900 the Russian Social Democratic Labour Party was largely composed of exiles, Lenin among them, engaged in bitter doctrinal and tactical discussions with little contact or influence inside Russia itself. As yet, the ideas of Marx had not spread far beyond Europe, though a few Japanese, faced with a society which combined features of both feudalism and capitalism, were picking up some ideas from European socialists. In the United States it looked in 1900 as though a socialist party might develop, and in many industries violent labour unrest suggested that the class struggle was a reality. But Marxism in America never became the creed of more than a very small minority, partly because in an expanding and fluid society class barriers never became rigid, and the American worker did not feel, as his European comrades did, that he was condemned to permanent membership of the proletariat.

Marxism attracted the attention, if not the whole-hearted support, of a number of intellectuals, and its effects were felt

*Below: Top hat in the tropics. African notables in French-ruled Dahomey. Europe imposed her social and cultural standards as well as her rule. Left: Friedrich Nietzsche—prophet of the 20th century's complete rejection of 19th-century values and of a search for new codes of conduct*

Le Petit Journal Illustré (Snark)

beyond the sphere of politics. The idea, for example, that economic factors were at the root of all historical change suggested to historians many new ways of looking at the past and led to a new emphasis on social and economic history and on economic explanations of historical events. But there were in 1900 other important ideas in the air which were profoundly affecting men's outlook on the world.

Throughout the 19th century, a demand for the application of the principles of the natural sciences to all branches of life had been gathering strength. This 'positivism', together with the teachings of Darwin and his followers about the origins of man, had led to a prolonged debate about the truth of Christianity and the relation of science to religion. Politically, there had been an attack on the position and powers of the Church, especially in Roman Catholic countries; in France, for example, the Church was disestablished in 1905 and lost its state support and many of its privileges; in Italy, where the Pope had been finally deprived of his territorial possessions in 1870, the Vatican refused to have any relations with the state.

By 1900 the application of scientific principle to activities ranging from literary criticism to municipal government was widely accepted. It had given man in the Western world a new control over his environment, with the eradication or control of epidemics and improved medical knowledge and methods, rapid and efficient transportation, and speedy communications, and it had given, to the rich at least, an ease of living greater than ever before. Faith in scientific method and in human progress seemed to be justified, and for those who accepted this faith, no problems seemed insoluble. There seemed no reason why improvement of the physical conditions of life should not continue indefinitely, just as, with the spread of education and literacy, there seemed no reason why men's moral improvement should not match their physical progress.

### Nietzsche and the new outlook

Yet there were, at the end of the 19th century, influential voices criticizing the assumptions of the liberal rationalist outlook. Some sociologists and political thinkers were stressing the irrational element in political behaviour, and a whole new science of sociology was developing the suggestion that human conduct was very complex and not always governed by rational considerations. Philosophers such as Bergson were stressing the importance of intuition in understanding the world and suggesting that the flow of human consciousness could not be subjected to cut-and-dried scientific analysis. The writer whose message was most important for the development of this new outlook and was influencing all sorts of intellectual and artistic activity was Friedrich Nietzsche.

Nietzsche ceased writing in 1888, and although he lived till 1900, his last years were spent in complete mental breakdown. Few people had read his works during his active lifetime, but in the 1890's his ideas began to spread rapidly. It is impossible to summarize Nietzsche's unsystematic thought, but he was in fact preaching a complete rejection of the values of existing society and the need for a fresh set of values appropriate to the new age which he believed was coming. Nietzsche was, in short, a true prophet of the 20th century.

### Artistic revolution

The mood of protest to which Nietzsche appealed, the desire to find new forms of expression and new codes of behaviour, was present in much of the intellectual and artistic activity at the turn of the century. A revolt against the stuffiness and hypocrisy of the prosperous bourgeois world was expressed both by the dramas of Ibsen, with their relentless yet poetical and sympathetic demonstration of the dark passions and unavowed motives underlying provincial middle-class society and, in a different way, by the youth movements which were starting in Germany. These movements encouraged young people to throw off the constricting clothes of respectable society and the corrupt culture of cities and to seek a simple life closer to nature. This mood of protest also found expression in architecture and design. At a time when the houses and museums of the great cities of Europe had become cluttered with massive furniture, vast narrative and historical paintings, and endless bric-a-brac, reaction began to set in; a new respect for architectural materials was to lead in the early 20th century to the development of a new, simpler, international style of architecture and design.

Even the experiences of the imperialist activity of the late 19th century affected European modes of thought and expression, so that, while Europeans were trying to impose their standards on the countries of Asia and Africa, influences from the cultures of these areas were flowing back to Europe. Contact with other societies gave a new impetus to the study of anthropology. The art and music of exotic regions were making an impact on European taste: the French composer, Claude Debussy, for instance, heard music of the Far East at the Paris Exhibition in 1889; this contributed to his revolt against the academic music of his day, and helped to form his own particular style. Paul Gauguin went to the French colonies in the South Seas in search of new subjects for his painting. The collections of African sculpture shown in the museums of Paris and of Germany in the early years of the 20th century inspired young painters, notably Pablo Picasso, with a new vision of the human form.

Thus all over Europe, new ideas and new movements in the arts, not yet widely accepted but destined to dominate the consciousness of the first half of the 20th century, were already alive in 1900. A new awareness of the complexity of human nature – Sigmund Freud was studying nervous disorders in Vienna and completed *The Interpretation of Dreams* in 1899, even though few people read it – new ways of writing, composing, and painting intended to provide a more intense and direct expression of the artist's experience were all contributing to challenge the certainties of scientific rationalism, just as a generation earlier scientific rationalism had challenged the dogmas of revealed religion.

Thus, at the moment of Europe's apparent domination of the world, many of the assumptions and the self-confidence on which that domination had been based were already being criticized and undermined. Moreover, those features of European society in the 19th century to which liberals and progressives pointed with pride – representative government, a belief in the justice of national self-determination, the hope of a continuing rise in the standard of living through the application of scientific discoveries and technological improvements – were themselves within the next half-century to lead to the overthrow of European rule in the colonies. While it would be going too far to say that the main features of 20th-century development can all be observed in 1900, yet the movements predominant in Europe in 1900, imperialism, nationalism, Marxism, expressionism, and the rest, were those which by the 1970's were to affect the whole world.

*'Tahitians on the Beach' by Paul Gauguin. European artists were being influenced by the arts and subject matter of exotic regions which had come under Europe's political sway*

# The British Raj

The British ruled in India for only a third as long as the Romans ruled Britain. Yet they made a deep impact on the Indian way of life, drawing India inexorably into the orbit of the Western world. The period of direct British rule lasted only ninety years. Because it was so short a time, two dramatic moments stand out, and seem to dominate the British period. The first was the Indian mutiny in 1857, when the British reacted vigorously to a military revolt, and decided to impose direct rule from London. Before then the traders and officials of the East India Company had controlled both the commerce and politics of India. The second dramatic moment was when the Indian independence movement reached its climax ninety years later in anarchy and violence. The British then withdrew completely from the sub-continent. But the story of British India is much more than the story of preliminary panic and ultimate scuttle. There were many remarkable achievements under the British 'raj' during its ninety years. These achievements can be set against certain weaknesses and failures. But, even viewed in this light, they were nevertheless impressive.

In 1900 British imperial rule in India had reached its halfway mark. Yet there were few Indians, and probably no Englishmen, who would in that year have dared to prophesy that within half a century the whole complex, intricate and well-buttressed fabric of government would be no more. India in 1900 was Great Britain's largest imperial possession; yet less than 5,000 British officials were responsible for the well-being of 300 million Indians, guarding their frontiers, governing their countryside, and introducing them to the various skills and techniques of the industrial and commercial revolutions of the 19th century.

### Vaccination to education

In almost every other imperial possession in the world, both British and European empire-builders were confronted with chaos. Against the hostility of the native inhabitants and the ravages of tropical diseases the soldiers, missionaries, and administrators of five empires were struggling, many of them in vain. France, Portugal, Germany, Italy, and, since 1898, the United States, were caught in a costly battle with little or no economic reward. Each brought under its rule vast tracts of desert and jungle, and new, unwilling subjects, often in open revolt, against their masters. It was to warn the new American imperialists that Rudyard Kipling had

written his poem which explained the problems and the hardships of empire-building:

*Take up the White Man's burden—*
*No tawdry rule of kings,*
*But toil of serf and sweeper—*
*The tale of common things.*
*The ports ye shall not enter,*
*The roads ye shall not tread,*
*Go make them with your living,*
*And mark them with your dead.*

But in India such pessimism seemed quite unjustified. The rulers felt as confident as kings, and puzzled over Kipling's assertion that they should after all be toiling like serfs. The great ports which they did build—Bombay, Madras, Calcutta—had become the emporia of the eastern world. The Great Trunk Road, together with the world's largest railway network, provided them, their traders and their subjects, with a first-class transport system. For the British in India, the government which they had established seemed indestructible. They could not imagine that the Indians themselves might seek an end to foreign rule. 'We cannot foresee the time,' wrote Sir John Strachey, a leading administrator, 'in which the cessation of our rule would not be the signal for universal anarchy and ruin.' 'It was clear,' he continued, 'that the only hope for India is the long continuance of the benevolent but strong government of Englishmen.'

Almost alone of the world's imperial possessions, India lay serene in 1900. The era of conquest had ended fifty years before. Although the number of British officials was small, the web of their administration spread out over the sub-continent, along great river valleys, across burning deserts, and into jungle forests and mountain defiles. A European-style postal and telegraph system, a stable currency, and widespread imitation of Western behaviour made the large Indian cities appear as well-organized and familiar as Manchester or Birmingham. The British raj succeeded in creating a vast municipal structure, draining, watering, cleaning, lighting, and linking its cities. It repulsed all tribal attacks

*The state entry of the viceroy into Delhi, 1903. The viceroy lived in surroundings of the utmost splendour. But despite the glittering trappings of imperial pomp that surrounded him, the reins of real power were held in London. Indians might regard him as the supreme arbiter of their fortunes, but the British government saw him as their agent*

Mansell Collection

across the north-west frontier, and brought a measure of calm to frontier villages which had for centuries been the scenes of bloody tribal warfare.

Young civilian administrators, many just graduated from Oxford or Cambridge, brought justice and security to remote villages, which were once the scene of Muslim conquest or Hindu oppression. Taxes were collected effectively and without violence. These young officials sought to master the local languages, and ruled vast areas with ease and enthusiasm. One of them, John Beames, has left a terse account of his duties, which ranged 'from vaccination to education; from warding off a famine to counting the blankets of convicts in his jail; from taking a census to feeding an army on the march'.

### 'The glory of the empire'

The young district officer was on the lowest rung of the official hierarchy. Of all the officials in India, he was the closest to the Indian people. Very few Indian peasants, or *ryots*, as they were called, saw anyone more senior. To the peasant, it was the district officer who represented the British raj. Through him they paid their taxes, or obtained remission of taxation during

hard times. To him they took their problems of land ownership, field boundaries, and agricultural needs. He did his best to answer them. He gained his training as he went along. Cut off from the society of most other Englishmen, he learned to associate himself, at times without reserve, with the Indians among whom he worked. The district officer has been called 'the glory of the empire'. He was certainly its backbone, and without him the whole complex system could not have stood for long.

Although each of the seven British-ruled provinces of India had its own carefully drawn-up rules and regulations for local administration, the district officer often had to act by rule of thumb. In an emergency, such as a flood or famine, he was his own master and took full responsibility for whatever he might decide. Scrutinizing his work was the provincial government under which he served. Each of the seven provinces had its administrative chief, a governor in Bombay and Madras, a lieutenant-governor or a commissioner elsewhere. These senior officials presided over a series of departments responsible for finance, administration, public health, education, and law and order. Each province had its own traditional methods of

administration. Bombay had a reputation for adopting a severe and even callous attitude towards its peasantry. The Punjab on the contrary, was sympathetic towards the problem of peasant poverty. One governor of Bombay even taunted the governor of Madras for what he considered 'promiscuous charity' when the Madras officials decided to help the peasants financially during a famine year.

There was much rivalry between the provinces. But each was so vast that its administration needed no outside pressure or competitive stimuli to enable it to flourish. The departmental officials belonged, as it were, to a provincial club. They looked for inspiration and amusement to their respective provincial capitals. At Bombay, Madras, Calcutta, and Lucknow were centred four intricate systems of government. Each had its separate written code of administration and unwritten rules of behaviour. Each had its own traditions

*Two rulers: the imperious and dynamic Lord Curzon, viceroy of India with 300,000,000 subjects, and the Maharajah of Patiala, ruler of 1,600,000. Amenable Indian princes were favoured and flattered by the British rulers*

Martin Gilbert

carefully fostered since 1857. Each had the memories of former governors or lieutenant-governors who had brought prosperity or notoriety to their provinces.

Proud of their achievements, jealous of their neighbours, and conscious of their autonomy, the provincial governments had wide powers. Each could inaugurate agricultural reforms, stimulate the education of Indians, build canals, hospitals, or roads, and reward those who served them well. To be governor or lieutenant-governor of an Indian province was to hold a position of greater power than a cabinet minister in Great Britain, and to rule directly more people than did the British prime minister from whom such authority ultimately descended.

### The Lords of India

The district officials and provincial governments often worked in extremely hard climatic conditions. Each administrator accepted a thirty-year exile from England in order to create whatever he or his provincial government considered to be an enlightened policy. To him belonged the daily chores and vexations of governing an alien people and living 5,000 miles from home. But it was the viceroy who was the real ruler of India. He spent only four years in the sub-continent. His home and his political career lay in England. For him the viceroyalty was a short period of a wider life, and India a vivid but passing picture. Sent out by the British government, the viceroy was supreme for four years, and during these years could determine both the pace and internal change and the foreign policy of India. Resident in Calcutta or Simla, depending upon the season, the viceroy was the giant towards whom all provincial eyes were turned and from whom every favour came. He might only be a passing show, but in passing he dominated the lives of those for whom India was their life's work.

The viceroy was surrounded by a cumbersome and complex apparatus of government: an administrative council, government departments, and civil servants. He had his own ministers for every aspect of Indian administration. At his side, and as his subject, the commander-in-chief de-

ployed an army of 250,000 men. Seemingly the source of all power, the viceroy was also the focal point of all ambition. He could determine the future of men who had given as much as thirty years in the service of the sub-continent. He was the arbiter of promotion and honours. He was the man upon whom centred not only the administration of the government of India but also the frivolity of society and fashion. To his court flocked the native princes who, though 'sovereign' in their own native states, were in fact subject to continual viceregal scrutiny and ultimate control. To his court came those rich Englishmen who cared to visit India and could muster a letter of introduction, for the chance to sit at the viceregal table. His daily movements were the subject of newspaper comment; photographs of the tigers he shot found a place in a hundred albums; his letters and memoranda were daily printed by a private press; and special time-tables were produced whenever he travelled by train.

### The outsider

Yet what were the real powers of this man with his 700 servants and a salary nearly twice that of the prime minister of Great Britain? The pinnacle of Indian society, he was a man uprooted from the society of his friends and companions. He came to India as a stranger and left without necessarily having entered at all deeply into that alien world. However much he might be fascinated by India and however much of its atmosphere he might absorb, he was always considered an outsider by his subordinates. When he departed, the Government of India and the provincial governments turned to his successor and forgot the man who had sailed away. Vice-

*1 Maharajahs were socially acceptable; this one, the Maharajah of Kanwar, takes on the British in an egg and spoon race. 2 South African cartoon of Gokhale, the Indian nationalist leader. He is being presented with the brush, as a suggestion 'that he should sweep before his own door, having regard to the Depressed Classes of India'. 3 Lord Minto (second from left) with wife, daughter, and dead tiger*

roys could expect little appreciation for their service. The problems of India were so great—poverty so desperate, disease so virulent, famine so frequent—that within four years he could hardly hope to avoid some error of policy by which he would be judged by history, and by those few Indian civil servants who remembered his name.

### Responsibility without power

But it was not the weight of administrative responsibility, nor the crescendo of Indian claims, that made the viceroyalty onerous. It was the fact that, despite the glittering trappings of imperial power, real power lay elsewhere. For the viceroy was no more than the nominee and representative of the British government. He owed his position and thus his power to their patronage. He went out to India as an advocate of their policies. Every decision that he made, they could unmake; every appointment that he advised, they could query; every honour that he sought to grant, they could refuse. Nor were his powers limited only by the instructions given him when he went out to India. More vexatious, the policy of the 'home government' could and did change during his tenure of office, with the result that he could find himself the agent of a

policy in which he did not believe, expounding it to subordinate officials well aware of his predicament, arguing it with a secretary of state for India who, from the remote fastness of London, and with a British cabinet to support him, could say 'no' as often as he liked, and always get his way. Indians regarded the viceroy as the supreme arbiter of their fortunes; the British government regarded him as an agent of their own political aspirations.

The viceroy was expected to give a lead in the relations between British and Indian society. He could welcome any Indians he chose to his court, or he could refuse to dine with maharajahs. Aware of the swiftly mounting passion of Indian aspirations for a part in political life, he could decide which sections of Indian society should be drawn into the orbit of British administration. The old aristocracy of rajahs, princes, and chiefs had been favoured and flattered since the 1857 mutiny. As their loyalty seemed increasingly important in the face of growing nationalist agitation, they were consulted more often. But by 1900 the viceroy was forced to decide whether to widen the scope of his social and political contacts. Bombay social reformers, Bengali nationalists, and agitators were increasingly making their voices heard, not only by the viceroy, but by the millions over whom *he* was sovereign, and whose loyalty *they* sought to win.

A deeper malaise affected the government of India than the burden of conflicting loyalties and powers. In all these carefully balanced governmental hierarchies there was little room for dissent. The administrators tended to see themselves as a unified body of men, all rulers, all responsible, all viewing the Indians whom they ruled with an air of detachment, and even at times of superiority. There was none of the vigorous cut and thrust of parliamentary opposition known in Great Britain; none of the sharp excitement of political controversy that could lead to the overthrow of governments; none of the eagerness of men who, though powerless in opposition one day, could by their own exertions find themselves in power the next. It was a bold Indian civil servant who challenged his superiors on matters of high policy, and a lucky one whose challenge did not lead to his isolation and eclipse.

The hierarchy of government, except at the level of the district officer, looked inwards, and was over-conscious of its own importance. From the time of the mutiny the hierarchy had reinforced its own high opinions of itself. Turning away from close contact with Indians, following the shock of discovering that Indians could rebel, the majority looked askance at too much contact or co-operation. The hierarchy would administer and the Indian would obey.

### The curse of famine

One problem with which the British in India were confronted could not be overcome. This was the failure of the rains. The Indian peasant, with his tiny plot of land, depended upon the monsoon for his livelihood. Without adequate rain, his crops would fail, and when they failed, he could not pay the land revenue demanded of him, which usually amounted each year to over one third of the total value of his crops. If the peasant could not pay, he borrowed from the money-lender. The only security he could offer was the land itself. There thus developed in India a cruel and exacting domination by the money-lenders over the peasants, few of whom managed to avoid being indebted, and most of whom had grave difficulty in paying their annual revenue demand to the British. When the **rains failed, and the crops were burned by the powerful Indian sun, there was no reserve of food over vast areas,** and despite the excellent communication system grain was often slow in reaching the distressed districts. The result was famine.

Between 1866 and 1900 there were four major famines in India. In all, over nine million people died of starvation. Hardly any part of India was free from this curse. The Punjab, the Ganges Valley, Orissa, Madras, the Central Provinces, and parts of Bombay were all affected at different times. In some of the provinces the British policy was to rush food to the peasants, and to spend as much money as possible in trying to alleviate the famine conditions. But in other provinces the policy was the reverse. One famine administrator, Sir Richard Temple, took the view that the Indian peasants would profit by a certain amount of hardship, and that if they tasted the ravages of famine in one year they would work all the harder in the next. This was a harsh doctrine. But there were places in which it became law. Some people blamed the Indians for much of the misfortune that fell upon them. Thus a viceroy, Lord Curzon, wrote in 1900, at the height of one of the most severe famines in Indian history of 'the extraordinary apathy and indifference of representative natives. They leave the whole burden of the battle to be borne by the European officers, they do not visit the poor-houses . . . they decline to come forward with subscriptions; they illustrate irresponsibility and indifference in every possible way. It is a curious thing that the Hindu, who is so merciful and tender-hearted in a lot of stupid ways, such as saving the lives of pigeons, and peacocks, and monkeys, is almost completely callous as regards the sufferings or lives of his fellow-creatures'.

In their approach to famine one can see both the range of the problems with which the British officials were confronted in India, and also the wide variety of responses of which they were capable. Famine problems gave rise to a vast amount of correspondence, comment, and disagreement, reflecting both the difficulties and the limitations of British rule. The difference of approach is reflected in the following two examples. Of Captain Dunlop Smith, who had supervised famine relief in the Hissar region, an observer wrote that he 'is absolutely Prussian in his accurate and careful methods of organization. In fact he was treating the famine in his territory as a campaign or as a game of Kriegsspiel. One wall of his office was covered with an enormous map . . . every particle of relief work going on being accurately marked'. Dunlop Smith's great success was to persuade the richer Indians to play an active part in famine relief, and to bring enough of needed grain into his district to mitigate the effects of the famine.

Sir Richard Temple, when governor of Bombay, took another view of what should be done. When the Famine Commission enquiry of 1880 asked him whether a reduction of the land revenue demanded of the Indian peasant would not greatly increase the wealth of the peasant, and thus enable them to stand up more effectively when famine struck, he replied that 'there would not . . . be any use in that, because the assessment [over 40 per cent of the value of one year's crops] is so moderate as to impose no check on agricultural industry; indeed many think that the obligation to pay has a stimulating effect on the apathetic native character'. Both Sir Rich-

*Mahatma Gandhi, Indian nationalist leader. He was then a solicitor in South Africa*

ard Temple and Sir John Strachey felt that what the Indian peasant needed was the incentive of impending hardship. Lord Northbrook wrote privately in 1881: 'I have always had my suspicions that the land revenue has been over-assessed, and always treated with great suspicion the opinion of Sir John Strachey, who was all for screwing up the land revenue.'

The famines continued, and the heavy rate of land revenue which the British demanded remained the central figure of the peasant's life. Many administrators fought against it, but it was not significantly reduced until the 1920's. Famine itself continued to threaten the Indian peasant until the very end of British rule, for in 1943, famine in Bengal again killed over a million people. The poet, Clive Branson, then serving in the British army in Bengal, wrote to his wife:

*Come to me and I will show you,*
*Almost hidden in the shadow of an*
*  Indian night*
*Pavements strewn with human bodies*
*That with all the other shit*
*The authorities forget*
*Even to worry about . . .*

But the authorities were not normally negligent. The problem was too great for them, and they were unable to institute in India any system radically different from that which already existed. The bureaucracy was too vast, the chain of government too complex, the problems themselves on too massive a scale for the British to deal with them in anything but a marginal way. Sometimes an energetic viceroy like Lord Curzon might pester the **British government in London and the secretary of state for India in particular** for some major reform. But as one observer noted, the viceroy 'might as well have whistled jigs to milestones hoping to see them dance, as expect to get the Indian secretary of state to listen to words of commonsense'. And with greater bitterness the radical Wilfred Blunt wrote in his diary at the height of the 1900 famine: 'I suppose not a single official of all that have

*1 Britain's India was divided into areas of direct British rule and areas still controlled by native chiefs, the viceroy intervening in the event of misgovernment. 2 Areas affected by famine and plague – between 1866 and 1900, over nine million people died of starvation. 3 Structure of Indian administration*

fattened upon India will give over a third of his income – or a fourth, or a tenth part of it to benefit the people – this although they are subscribing and making the native subscribe to the South African war.' These were outspoken criticisms. They were also, in the main, unfair. With few exceptions, the provincial British officials

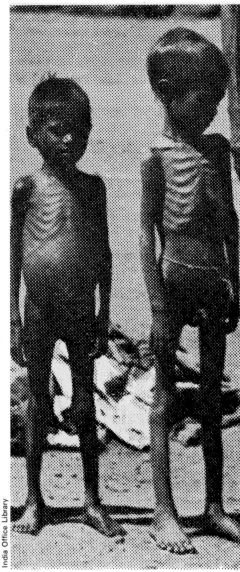

*Above: 'Distressed Natives of India': two Indian children suffering from the effects of a famine*

in India made considerable efforts to alleviate distress wherever they found it. But they could not move the government in London, or even, at times, the central Government of India to give them the support which they felt necessary.

The Government of India could not always set the priorities it wished, for among its burdens was one imposed upon it from London. Most British prime ministers were nervous of asking Parliament for the large sums of money needed for imperial wars; they knew that the House of Commons was not a persistent supporter of too much conquest and annexation. Successive British governments therefore prevailed on India to pay as much as possible of 'imperial' military expenditure. Much of the high cost of a series of British wars fell upon the Indian budget; and the money needed to conquer new territory or suppress rebellions was found, often with great difficulty, in the dwindling reserves of the already overtaxed Indian peasant. Wars in Abyssinia, Burma, China, Egypt, the Sudan, and Afghanistan were in large part paid for by the Government of India, as was the training, feeding, and transport of large numbers of British troops once they were east of Suez.

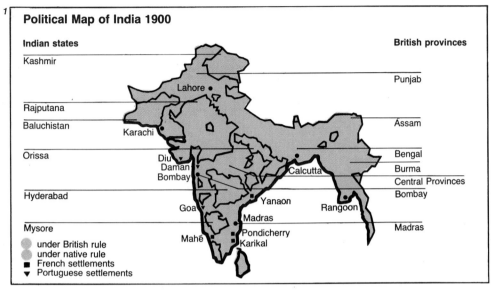

**Political Map of India 1900**

Indian states

Kashmir
Rajputana
Baluchistan
Orissa
Hyderabad
Mysore

Lahore
Karachi
Diu
Daman
Bombay
Goa
Mahé
Madras
Yanaon
Pondicherry
Karikal
Calcutta
Rangoon

British provinces

Punjab
Assam
Bengal
Burma
Central Provinces
Bombay
Madras

⬤ under British rule
⬤ under native rule
■ French settlements
▼ Portuguese settlements

India Office Library

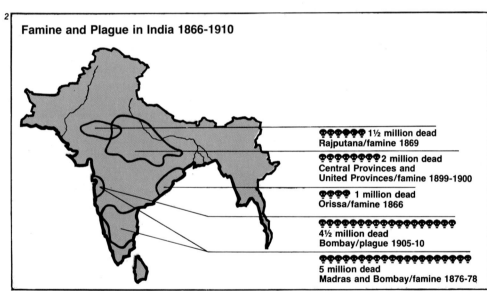

**Famine and Plague in India 1866-1910**

1½ million dead
Rajputana/famine 1869

2 million dead
Central Provinces and
United Provinces/famine 1899-1900

1 million dead
Orissa/famine 1866

4½ million dead
Bombay/plague 1905-10

5 million dead
Madras and Bombay/famine 1876-78

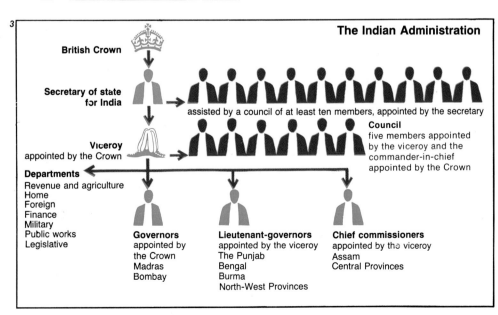

**The Indian Administration**

**British Crown**

**Secretary of state for India**

assisted by a council of at least ten members, appointed by the secretary

**Council**
five members appointed by the viceroy and the commander-in-chief appointed by the Crown

**Viceroy**
appointed by the Crown

**Departments**
Revenue and agriculture
Home
Foreign
Finance
Military
Public works
Legislative

**Governors**
appointed by the Crown
Madras
Bombay

**Lieutenant-governors**
appointed by the viceroy
The Punjab
Bengal
Burma
North-West Provinces

**Chief commissioners**
appointed by the viceroy
Assam
Central Provinces

What were the particular achievements 1 of the raj by the turn of the century? Certainly, as far as famine and finance were concerned, they had not mastered the problem. But in other spheres they could point to notable success. Barren tracts of country, particularly in the Punjab and Orissa, were irrigated by British engineers. Government-supervised model farms were established to enable the peasant to benefit from the new water supply. Laws were passed liberating the peasant from the more exorbitant demands of the money-lenders. In the cities, public works provided employment and slowly tackled the problems of drainage. Sanitation was as much a curse in the cities as famine was in the countryside. Insanitary conditions in Bombay led to the death of 4,500,000 people from plague in the five years before 1910. The problem of plague, like that of famine, was on such a massive scale that it would be naïve to expect the handful of men, without full support from London, to have worked miracles. Their daily routine was normally too exacting to encourage a far-sighted approach to major problems. And, in addition, the hierarchical system did little to encourage individual initiative.

Even by contemporaries at home the British in India were regarded with hostility. It was to defend them that Lieutenant Winston Churchill wrote to *The Times* in May 1898: '. . . I must deplore the bitter fact that his countrymen at home are inclined to regard the Anglo-Indian, be he soldier, trader, or administrator, as an object of aversion.' When the British official returned home after thirty years in India, he did not find much appreciation, if any, for what he had done or tried to do. For the British public, all Indian affairs were a bore. When the House of Commons debated the Indian budget, as it did each year, most members of parliament stayed away. Few people in Great Britain thought of India as anything more than a land of jungle and tigers, prosperous tea plantations, and gilded palaces, busy 'natives' and bejewelled maharajahs. They did not see the burning sun, the parched fields, the vast areas to be administered, the small number of administrators, the provincial govern-

*Below: Loyal subject: Indian with portraits of King George V and Queen Mary*

ments with their restricted and insufficient finance, the Indian peasant with his often minuscule plot of land and constant fears of debt and famine. Many of those who returned to Great Britain were gravely disappointed by their fellow-countrymen's complete lack of interest in the sub-continent. Instead of appreciation they discovered apathy.

## Stirrings of nationalism

Among the British achievements by 1900 was the opening up of wide opportunities in education for the Indian upper classes. A growing number of Indians had been educated at Indian universities which the British had founded and financed, or even at Oxford and Cambridge. These Indians were far from being uncritical supporters of the British raj. Indeed, many proved particularly vociferous advocates of Indian independence. Nearly all the British administrators, who had favoured the education of Indians along European lines, looked with horror at this rapid development of Indian nationalism. But there was also a British tradition which had looked forward to the rise of Indian self-consciousness. In 1833, speaking in the House of Commons, Macaulay had said: 'What is power worth if it is founded on vice, on ignorance, and on misery; if we can hold it only by violating the most sacred duties which as governors we owe to the governed, and which, as a people blessed with far more than an ordinary measure of political liberty and of intellectual light, we owe to a race debased by three thousand years of despotism and priest-craft? We are free, we are civilized, to little purpose, if we grudge to any portion of the human race an equal measure of freedom and civilization. Are we to keep the people of India ignorant in order that we may keep them submissive? Or do we think that we can give them knowledge without awakening ambition? Or do we mean to awaken ambition and to provide it with no legitimate vent?'

By 1900 Indian ambitions had certainly been awakened. A strong nationalist move-

ment had grown up in Bengal, and throughout the country Indians had begun to take a renewed pride in their ancient culture. Unfortunately, Indian national aspirations were not provided with a 'vent' sufficient to satisfy them. In 1910 the British government agreed to allow Indians to play a larger part in local government, and one Indian was even appointed to the viceroy's administrative council. But this was no longer enough. The nationalists now demanded the right fully to determine India's destiny. Extremists among them called for the immediate removal of British rule. The moderate nationalists urged their cause in pamphlets, newspapers, and public debates. The extremists used the weapons of terrorism. Many Muslims hoped British rule would continue. They agitated in order to obtain special privileges for the Muslim community. The Hindus, who outnumbered the Muslims by three to one, resented what they felt was British 'favouritism' for a rival religion, and pressed for greater Hindu privileges. It was among Hindus that the more violent nationalist agitation flourished.

Almost from the very moment in 1905 when the efficient, imperious and dynamic Curzon left India an era of violence opened. A bomb was thrown at the new viceroy, Lord Minto, but failed to explode until after he had passed. His successor was also the victim of an assassination attempt. At first the British officials argued that the outbreaks of violence were connected with the world-wide anarchist movement, denying that they had anything to do with Indian aspirations in particular. But by 1910 it had become clear that some Indians were now willing to kill, and to be killed, in order to free India from British rule. The first Englishman to be murdered by an Indian during this time was killed in London in 1909. The murderer was hanged, but not before the cabinet had debated the case, and both Lloyd George and Winston Churchill had shown some sympathy for the Indian, believing him to be a patriot, however misguided. Before his execution the Indian declared that 'just as the Ger-

East Indian Railway.

TIME TABLE.

SPECIAL TRAIN

FOR

HIS EXCELLENCY

THE RIGHT HONOURABLE
THE EARL OF MINTO,
*P. C., G. M. S. I., G. C. M. G., G. M. I. E.,*
VICEROY AND GOVERNOR-GENERAL OF INDIA,
THE COUNTESS OF MINTO
AND SUITE,
FROM
Jubbulpore to Howrah *en route* from Bombay on 21st and 22nd
November 1905.

| Distance from Jubbulpore. | Stations. | | Standard time. | Halts. | Remarks. |
|---|---|---|---|---|---|
| Miles. | | | A. M. | H. M. | |
| ...... | Jubbulpore | { arr. | 9 20 | } 0 30 | From G. I. P Ry. On 21st November 1905. Breakfast. |
| | | { dep. | 9 50 | | |
| | | | P. M. | | |
| 118 | Sutna | { arr. | 12 35 | } 0 8 | |
| | | { dep. | 12 43 | | |
| 166 | Manikpur | { arr. | 1 47 | } 0 30 | Lunch. |
| | | { dep. | 2 17 | | |
| 224 | Naini | { arr. | 3 34 | } 0 15 | Afternoon tea. |
| | | { dep. | 3 49 | | |
| 275 | Mirzapur | { arr. | 5 15 | } 0 8 | |
| | | { dep. | 5 23 | | |
| 315 | Moghal Sarai | { arr. | 6 15 | } 0 8 | |
| | | { dep. | 6 23 | | |
| 373 | Buxar | { arr. | 7 40 | } 1 0 | Dinner. |
| | | { dep. | 8 40 | | |

Martin Gilbert

man government have got no right to occupy this country, so the English people have got no right to occupy India, and it is perfectly justifiable on our part to kill any Englishman who is polluting our sacred land . . . I wish the English will sentence me to death, for in that case the vengeances of my countrymen will be all the more keen'. This appeal sent a thrill through the discontented of India. It became a clarion call to further protest.

### Imperishable empire

The serenity of British India was no more. Violence, demonstrations, and growing antagonism between the British and the Indian communities were to dominate the remaining forty years of empire. Yet the British achievement was a real one. A peasant society had been set on the road towards modernization and industrialization. A land where religious superstition had crippled individual incentive was now the scene of business activity and economic enterprise. A land of feudal maharajahs

who ruled over an apathetic people had become a land with a growing educated class no longer content to be treated as second-class citizens. The British had educated the Indians sufficiently for the Indians to wish to govern themselves. Whenever such a day comes, Macaulay had said in 1833, 'it will be the proudest day in English history. To have found a great people sunk in the lowest depths of slavery and superstition, to have so ruled them as to have made them desirous and capable of all the privileges of citizens, would indeed be a title to glory all our own. The sceptre may pass away from us. Unforeseen accidents may derange our most profound schemes of policy. Victory may be inconstant to our arms. But there are triumphs which are followed by no reverse. There is an empire exempt from all natural causes of decay. Those triumphs are the pacific triumphs of reason over barbarism; that empire is the imperishable empire of our arts and our morals, our literature, and our laws.'

*1 Bombay railway station. Striking symbol of the British raj, combining aspects of a medieval cathedral, an Oxford college, and an Italian palace, all in an oriental splendour. It also served the world's largest railway network. 2 The viceroy had special railway time-tables printed each time he travelled. This one was prepared for Lord Minto. 3 Part of menu for a St Andrew's Day celebration in Calcutta— far from the cold blasts of the Scottish winter. 4 King George V and Queen Mary at the 1911 Durbar, in which they received homage of the Indian princes. 5 A 19th-century Durbar. Indian and European notables wait for the march past*

Saint Andrew's Day
Celebration Dinner
Town Hall
Calcutta
30th November
1905.

NEMO ME IMPUNE LACESSIT

Martin Gilbert

Martin Gilbert

# Mass Society in Great Britain

Great Britain has been chosen as the most representative example of social change – but similar patterns can be discerned elsewhere, particularly in Germany and the United States.

It was in the 1890's and 1900's that many of the most familiar features of the contemporary social landscape first appeared. One year, 1896, stands out, indeed, as a birth year. Alfred Harmsworth founded the first really popular national newspaper, the *Daily Mail*. Guglielmo Marconi arrived in Great Britain with his pioneer wireless equipment to demonstrate to the post office how he could send signals by wireless for a hundred yards. The first moving picture show was presented in London's West End at the Regent Street Polytechnic and was so successful that it had to be transferred to the Empire Music Hall, Leicester Square. The British government recognized the existence of the motor car, and increased the speed limit on the roads from four miles per hour to twelve.

The full implications of each of these developments were not clear to people until the middle of the 20th century. Journalism was not transformed overnight by Harmsworth, who followed up the *Daily Mail* with the *Daily Mirror* in 1903. Wireless was for a long time thought of as a substitute for point-to-point communication by wire rather than as a medium of communication: indeed, the fact that broadcast messages could be picked up by people for whom they were not intended was thought to be a drawback rather than an advantage. It was not until 1908 that the first building specially designed for film shows was opened – not in the West End, but in Colne, Lancashire – although six years later there were 3,500 cinemas in Great Britain. As for motor cars, during the first decade of their existence they were thought of primarily as symbols of status. When J.H.Knight, 'a well-known scientific man . . . and one of the first to work at motor cars', spoke to the Camera Club of London in 1897 about 'two years' progress in mechanical traction', he raised a laugh by saying that he hoped as soon as possible to see the horse abolished or 'found only, perhaps, in the hunting field and the parks'. By 1904, when compulsory registration was introduced, there were 8,500 motor cars in the country, a figure which had risen to 132,000 ten years later.

While the full social and cultural implica-

tions of technical changes of this kind were not immediately apparent, there was some recognition by 1914 of 'problems' they created. In 1907 a writer in *Encore,* the music-hall journal, claimed that for several years he had been trying to point out 'to the profession that the greatest enemies the artistes had were the film merchants'. The battle of the media had thus started in the middle of a radiant 'golden age' of the theatre. Likewise in 1913, when the motor car was still a luxury, the London traffic branch of the board of trade directed attention to the 'traffic problem', particularly in London. 'Among the various phases of the London traffic problem, one most important feature is the daily movement of a very large section of the population from their residences within an area of thirty miles round London to places of business in Central London and back again. . . . There can no longer be any doubt about the gradual withdrawal of a large amount of traffic of all sorts from the railways to the roads, owing to the development of the motor vehicle. The convenience of the mechanically-propelled vehicle for passenger purposes rapidly asserted itself, and today it accounts for fully ninety-four per cent of the passenger vehicles met with on the roads round London . . . Street accidents are an unfortunate phase of the traffic problem and there is no hope that they can ever be entirely eliminated.'

### Pull of London

Other 'problems' to which national attention was being directed included the growth of London, its increasing pull on national life, and the threat it posed to the survival of older provincial cultures; the dangerous power of the press, particularly that section of the press which tried to reach 'the meanest capacity and the most uncultivated mind'; and the spread of 'spectatoritis' in sport, with its attendant challenge to amateurism, and the great burst of gambling associated with it. All these 'problems' were to be leading themes in the social history of Great Britain in the 'long week-end' between the two World Wars.

Yet there was more emphasis in Edwardian Great Britain itself on the unprecedented opportunities for businessmen in the 'consumer industries', as they were beginning to be called, than on the social problems they posed. There were two reasons for this. First, businessmen were beginning to count for more in Society, to be not only acceptable but welcome: even the King, it was said, might have been a businessman if he had been born in differ-

SHOULDER MUTTON 6

LEGS 7

J. Sainsbury

*Catering for the mass market. The meat department in Sainsburys, one of the new chain stores of the period*

ent circumstances. Second, there was a mass of more urgent social problems centred on the existence of poverty in the midst of plenty, terrifying poverty, the statistical details of which had been revealed by Charles Booth in his massive survey of London life and by Seebohm Rowntree in his book on provincial York.

### Pleasure ground or treasure house

While in retrospect Edwardian Britain, with its prelude in the 1890's, offers us ample evidence of the origins of 'mass society', it also offers us ample evidence, not of increasing social homogeneity, but of more marked and more disturbing social division. While we can trace back to the period, through the history of the market, the emergence of forces which were to pull the community together, we can also trace back the origins of 'the welfare state', which was designed through conscious policy to pull the community together in a different way. 'England must be less of a pleasure ground for the rich,' exclaimed Campbell-Bannerman, the Liberal prime minister in 1906, 'and more of a treasure house for the nation.' 'It is not about details that people care or are stirred,' wrote another Liberal leader, R.B.Haldane. 'What they seem to desire is that they should have something approaching equality of chance with those among whom they live.' For all the pressures towards mass society, they had not got very far by 1914, when the American ambassador could still write, with America, already far more of a mass society, in mind, that 'the sad thing in London is the servile class. Before the law the chimney sweep and the peer have exactly the same standing. . . . But there it stops. The serving class is what we should call abject. It does not occur to them that they might ever become or their descendents might become ladies and gentlemen'.

Changes within the market, influenced by technical discoveries, were in the long run to change the Edwardian pattern as much as changes in legislation or taxation, and it is significant that the term 'mass market' preceded more recent terms like 'mass communication' and 'mass culture' which were used for the first time only after the First World War. Moreover, there was a mass market in commodities like tea and bacon, before there was a mass market in ideas or entertainment. During the last twenty years of the 19th century commodities from abroad – not only tea and bacon, but frozen meat, canned foods, cheese, and vegetables – began to be distributed far more efficiently to 'ordinary people'. Between 1870 and 1900 the wholesale price of commodities fell by about forty per cent, while money wages rose by eleven per cent in the decade from 1880 to 1890 and by another eleven per cent in the decade from 1890 to 1900. Throughout this period chain stores, both provincial and metropolitan, like Maypole or Sainsbury's, established their position, and new department stores began to cater for a far wider and less rich clientèle than Harrods in London.

Although real wages actually fell in the decade from 1900 to 1910 – this was one of the main economic determinants of the social conflicts of the period – retailing developments continued, reaching their dramatic climax in 1910 when Gordon Selfridge 'made the experiment', as the *Economist* put it, 'of starting a big store at full speed' in Oxford Street. By then, there were large concentrations of company capital in the retail trade, many of the concentrations specializing in their own 'branded goods', which were known in all parts of the country. Thomas Lipton, for example, started as a Glasgow grocer without an assistant in 1876, had seventy shops in London alone by 1890, had converted

his business into a limited liability company in 1898 – with Asquith, the Duke of Fife, and Lord Rothschild among the original shareholders – and, after Edward VII came to the throne, basked in the favours of the court.

Throughout this period, despite the pressure on the wage packet as prices rose, working-class demand broadened in scope, and new 'expenses', in the words of Philip Snowden, the Labour leader, became conventional through 'the development of tramways, the coming of the halfpenny newspaper, the cheap but better-class music hall and the picture palace, the cheap periodicals and books'. He might have added to his list professional football which was increasingly attracting working-class supporters on Saturday afternoons. The Football League had been founded in 1888, and over 110,000 spectators watched the Cup Final in 1901 on the Crystal Palace ground.

### How to succeed in business

The kind of private businessman who could exploit openings in the new 'mass market' had to have other qualities besides the favourite Victorian virtue of hard work. He had to display genuine business imagination to make profits on a large scale, if need be by creating the sense of a market where there had been none before. Of course, without the favourable economic and social circumstances he would never have succeeded, and intelligent commentators were already aware of what these circumstances were.

First, there was the existence of a large and concentrated urban population. In 1911 only 21·9 per cent of the population of England and Wales lived in what the census called 'rural districts', and what was now called the Greater London area encompassed 7,250,000 inhabitants. The other great national 'conurbations' had all

taken shape. It was within these areas that there were the greatest opportunities for development in the retailing both of goods and of ideas and entertainment, and it was no coincidence, for example, that by 1914 Manchester had one cinema seat for every eight inhabitants, the highest density figure in the country. Second, there was the rise in spending money, checked though that rise was for large sections of the working classes in the period from 1900 to 1914. Third, and equally important, there was a rise in the amount of leisure time, as working hours were cut, sometimes by legislation, as in the coal mining industry, and sometimes by negotiation, as in the cotton industry. Fourth, there were great improvements in transport, as Philip Snowden had noted, facilitating cheap and easy travel from city centres to private homes: the building of London's electrified underground was one of the great achievements of the Edwardian period. Fifth, there was continuous incentive, in this phase of Great Britain's industrialization, to apply technology to the home, the office, the holiday resort, and the place of entertainment as well as to the factory. Sixth, there was unprecedented scope for an increase in the volume and the range of advertising, in newspapers and on the hoardings, in cigarette packets — forty per cent of the country's tobacco imports went into cigarette manufacture in 1914 as against only five per cent in 1890 — and in railway stations and on buses.

Most of these social and economic factors were related to each other. Thus, for example, the rise of the cheap, mass-circulation, national daily newspapers would have been impossible without revenue derived from advertising. Large-scale retailing would have been curbed had it not been for flamboyant showmanship on the part of retailers. It would have been difficult to develop the elaborate technical complex without the typewriter and the telephone. One thing was abundantly plain. Technology by itself was never enough, whether it was the technology of making soap or margarine or the technology of the camera, the gramophone, and the wireless set. What Gilbert Seldes has said of the cinema had more general, if not universal applicability. 'The moving picture had to be taken away from its inventors by aggressive and ignorant men without taste or tradition, but with a highly developed sense of business, before it could be transformed from a mechanical toy into a medium of the first popular art.'

Bibby's Annual

*Above:* The unemployed of the period, as illustrated in an article on unemployment in Bibby's Annual. *This article declared: 'These men should be made to feel . . . that their condition is a disgrace. . . . Teach them how to play, run, jump, sing; to get a move on things. Play is action, and all action is good.'* **Right:** *An advertisement for London's District Line, part of the cheap and efficient transport that was being provided from city centre to suburbs*

**Opposite page: Left:** *Road menders at their dinner hour. Compulsory education, the demands of trade unions, liberal legislation, and the mass production of cheap goods had barely reduced the gulf between the poorer classes born to penury and the privileged ones brought up only to luxury.* **Right:** *A lady of fashion at Ascot. Attending horse races was one of the favourite pursuits of the Edwardian upper classes, a small elite who flaunted their lace parasols, their motor cars, their country house parties, while most of Edward's subjects, underfed and unhealthy, had an unremittingly grey struggle trying to earn and scrape together the means for what was at best no more than the skimpiest livelihood*

DISTRICT Rly ELECTRIC TRAINS

London Transport Board

## The 'new' utopia

By no means all businessmen were 'aggressive and ignorant', but there were already many signs of divergence in Edwardian Britain between businessmen who believed confidently and exuberantly in 'turning the luxuries of today into the necessities of tomorrow', and social critics, particularly writers, who were anxious about 'the quality of life' in a 'mass society'. George Gissing, the novelist, had written scathingly in 1891, for example, about publishers and writers who treated publishing simply as a trade and their public simply as a market. One of his characters in *New Grub Street* quite deliberately sets out to appeal to 'the quarter-educated; that is to say, the great new generation that is being turned out by the board schools, the young men and women who can just read, but are incapable of sustained attention. People of this kind . . . want something to occupy them in trains and on buses and trams. As a rule they care for no newspapers except the Sunday ones; what they want is the lightest and frothiest of chit-chatty information – bits of stories, bits of description, bits of scandal, bits of jokes, bits of statistics, bits of foolery'. With this in mind, he insisted that all authors should write articles no more than two inches in length, with every inch broken up into at least two paragraphs.

Eighteen years later, when motor cars were, for the most part, still associated with luxury – and certainly not with 'mass consumption' – Charles Masterman, the Liberal social critic, looked forward with fear to a time when 'every man of a certain income has purchased a new car' and 'that definite increase of expenditure' would be accepted as 'normal'. 'Yet will life be happier and richer for such an acceptance?' he asked. In the same year, 1909, H.G.Wells painted an unforgettable picture of a young man working for his uncle on the selling of a patent medicine, Tono-Bungay. His 'special and distinctive duty' was 'to give Tono-Bungay substance and an outward and visible bottle, to translate my uncle's great imagination into the creation of case after case of labelled bottles of nonsense, and the punctual discharge of them by railroad, road, and steamer towards their ultimate goal in the Great Stomach of the People. By all modern standards the business was, as my uncle would say, "absolutely *bona fide*". We sold our stuff and got the money, and spent the money honestly in lies and clamour to sell more stuff. Section by section we spread it over the whole of the British Isles'.

Such *critiques* looked to the future, when there really was to be a mass market, spread over the whole of the British Isles, a mass communications system, a large part of it financed by advertising revenue, and a commercially managed mass culture. For the most part, however, the men of the early 20th century still lived in their own social 'sub-cultures' and could see only dimly into the future, employing the adjective 'new' with great alacrity to cover such diverse phenomena as the 'new art', 'new morality', 'new religion', 'new women', even 'new life', but never quite agreeing about just what the 'newness' consisted of and always arguing sharply about whether or not it was a 'good thing'. As changes took place they reacted to them piecemeal, expressing concern for Edward VII's safety after he had driven from London to Windsor *'en automobile'* in 1901, being shocked when a Sunderland footballer was transferred to Middlesbrough for the absurd sum of £1,000 in 1905, being suitably impressed when they entered one of the new plush 'picture palaces' or read about the yachting enterprises of Sir Thomas Lipton the chain grocer (he was knighted in 1898), and praising the patriotic initiative of the *Daily Mail* in 1910 (one year after a Frenchman, Louis Blériot, had flown the Channel) in offering a prize of £10,000 for a successful flight between London and Manchester.

There was, however, a marked change of mood between 1900 and 1914. G.M.Young, the great historian of 19th-century Great Britain, well expressed the feelings of his contemporaries – or rather those of them who were comfortably well-off – in 1900 when he said that 'we looked forward to leading, with some improvements, the sort of life our fathers had lived'. By 1914 this would have been a blatantly conservative reaction, above all a complacent reaction, in any section of the community. It was clear by then that the conditions of life had changed and were still changing, although more emphasis was placed on the social and political forces in society which were tearing it apart than on those social and economic forces which were already beginning to pull it together. Much of the assurance of 1900 had been undermined, and for all the sense of continuity, which loomed large in retrospect after the great divide of the First World War, there was also a sense of conflict.

H.G.Wells, prophet as well as critic, and a vigorous optimist about the shape of things to come, took account of the signs of the times in his *Modern Utopia*, published in 1905. All previous utopias, he argued, had been 'perfect and static states, a balance won for ever against the forces of unrest and disorder that inhere in things. One beheld a healthy and simple generation, enjoying the fruits of the earth in an atmosphere of virtue and happiness, to be followed by other virtuous, happy, and entirely similar generations until the Gods grew weary'. Wells no more liked this conception of a utopia than he liked the actual state of affairs in Edwardian Britain or the 'wasteful' state of affairs as it had been in Victorian Britain. He was exhilarated by the 'enormous and unprecedented facilities' for 'the spirit of innovation', and maintained that his modern utopia would have to be kinetic not static, 'not a permanent state but a hopeful stage, leading to a long ascent of stages'. One facet of this approach was that social relations within his utopia would depend not on each man's living 'according to his defined and understood grade' but on a dynamic conception of individuality. 'The fertilizing conflict of individualities is the ultimate meaning of the personal life, and all our utopias no more than schemes for bettering that interplay.'

All pictures of utopias tell us more about the society in which they were sketched than about ideal states of human existence. Wells was directing attention to the basic questions of whether continuing social change was in the interest of human welfare and, if it was not, whether there were means of planning that it should be. His optimism about what he called the coming Century of the Common Man was certainly not shared by all his contemporaries. In the very year that he was looking ahead to forces which would transform society, another extremely popular writer, Marie Corelli, a 'queen of the circulating libraries', was comparing British society with what it had been in the past and finding it wanting. 'Our evil star, the evil star of all empires, has long ago soared above the eastern edge; fully declared, it floods our heaven with such lurid brilliancy that we can scarce perceive any other luminary.

*GLC Photo Library*

*1 London's grim East End: a back street in Stepney, 1909. This was typical of the terrible poverty that lay at the base of Edwardian society. The rich and poor might have lived on different planets. 2 Marie Lloyd, a queen of mass entertainment, depicted on this song sheet for one of her 'hits'. This was the heyday of the music hall, but the cinema was becoming a significant rival. 3 Scene in the Bayswater Omnibus, painted by William Joy: the well-fed, well-dressed, middle-classes and the under-nourished, and harassed poor*

And its name is Mammon. Wealth in excess – wealth in chunks – wealth in great, awkward, unbecoming dabs, is plastered, as it were, by the merest haphazard toss of fortune's dice, on the backs of uncultured and illiterate persons, who, bowed down like asses beneath the golden burden, are asininely ignorant of its highest uses.' Whether or not the future lay with the

Common Man, the present lay with the millionaire. 'Men of high repute . . . are "shunted" as it were off the line to make way for the motor car traffic of plutocrats, who . . . manage to shout their income figures persistently in the ears of those whose high privilege it is to "give the lead" in social affairs.'

### 'Upsurge of elemental forces'

The language was colourful, even strident, yet every Edwardian with a conscience was forced to admit that his society was a society of picturesque contrasts. 'Public penury, private ostentation,' wrote Charles Masterman, 'that, perhaps, is the heart of the complaint'. On the one side there was the glittering West End, on the other side the bleak East End. On the one side there was the plutocrat, on the other side the pauper. On the one side there was the village hovel, on the other side the great estate. Not surprisingly the Edwardian period was characterized by the first serious political discussions of how to change Great Britain from pleasure-house for the few into treasure-house for the many, by Lloyd George's highly controversial budget of 1909, which he called 'a war budget . . . to wage implacable warfare against poverty and squalidness', and by the first welfare legislation to alleviate the social burdens of ill health and unemployment. Yet party politics could no more express, let alone satisfy, the aspirations of the dispossessed than it could express or satisfy the fierce aspirations of the militant suffragettes battling for the vote in the name of women's rights. The result was that between 1910 and 1914 there was relentless industrial warfare which showed the world how divided British society really was. The peak points of what contemporaries called a 'great upsurge of elemental forces' were the dock and railway strikes of 1911, the year of George V's coronation, the coal

strike of 1912, and the Port of London strike of the same year. It seemed, indeed, as one trade union leader put it, that 'the dispossessed and disinherited classes in various parts of the country were all simultaneously moved to assert their claims upon society'. There was even talk, just before the First World War broke out, of a civil war between labour and capital.

Labour and Capital were often spelt out during this period with capital letters, great anonymous forces in society moving sharply against each other in what John Galsworthy called 'inexorable Strife'. Another way of establishing the confrontation was to refer to 'the classes' and 'the masses'. This equally anonymous distinction was popularly said to have been made for the first time by Mr Gladstone, one of the great 19th-century heroes—and villains. It was a convenient sociological distinction relating not only to wages and profits, income and capital, or the structure of industry, but even more potently to privilege and power set against deprivation and subordination.

What made the late Edwardian period uniquely stormy was that large sections of 'the classes', with all their hereditary authority, were almost as discontented between 1910 and 1914 as the masses. They were suspicious of many of the social reforms, afraid of the increase in taxation, apprehensive about the check to the House of Lords, frightened of Irish Home Rule. Some among them were at least as tempted as trade union leaders were to pursue direct action to achieve their objectives, to challenge the authority of Parliament, even to break the law. 'Were there now to be *two* classes of citizens in the land,' asked Lloyd George, their chief *bête noire,* 'one class which could obey the laws if they liked; the *other* which must obey whether they liked it or not? A Law to ensure people against poverty and misery . . . was to be optional. Was the law for the preservation of game to be optional? Was the payment of rent to be optional?' Another of Galsworthy's *dicta,* this time from his *Silver Box*—'There's one law for the rich and another for the poor'—might well have been a text for Edwardian Britain.

Not until many of the Edwardian gulfs had been bridged could Great Britain be considered in any sense as a 'mass society', whether or not the term may properly be applied to what Wells would have called 'subsequent stages' in British social history. There was little mixing of social classes in Edwardian Britain, but rather, perhaps, a greater sense of common interest among those with property and among those without it. 'The rich,' said Masterman, 'despise the Working People; the Middle Classes fear them.' And the popular newspapers, revelling in gossip and 'stunts', far from unifying society, drew more sustained public attention to the facts of division. However eagerly we look back to the first fourteen years of the century, 'dear, dead days beyond recall', for the first signs of what are now familiar features of the social landscape, the landscape itself on closer view will appear more and more strange and alien to us.

## Mass society in USA and Europe

In the United States and in the more industrialized areas of Europe, society was evolving on similar lines to Great Britain. From Berlin to San Francisco, the revolution in transport not only changed travelling patterns; it brought into being new suburbs, and provided new experiences. The increasingly professional advertisements, the appearance of new and cheap consumer products, and their availability in the rapidly developing chain and department stores was revolutionizing purchasing habits. Many people found that their lives had become brighter and easier – but by no means all. The 19th-century legacy of extreme poverty was far from eradicated.

1 German advertisement, circa 1913, for the 'ideal family cine-camera' designed by Ludwig Hohlwein. The devastatingly smart family (note spats) gives the product an haute couture image
2 Eno's Fruit Salts advertisement of 1900. The incredibly romantic style of the advertisement is typical of the period, but it certainly does seem curiously at odds

with the product – a mild laxative
**3** The first incandescent gas mantle was produced in 1885, and by 1904 the streets of Britain were lit by gas. The company for which this poster was designed is still in existence
**4** United States: performance in 1913 of Made for Laughs, starring the Keystone Cops. Films were still silent, a pianist providing the musical accompaniment. America was already establishing herself as a large-scale film producer
**5** United States: crowning the numerous posters for music-hall performances are advertisements for Turkish cigarettes, and corsets ('For the Women of Fashion')
**6** France: inside a large department store. Painting by the French artist Valloton
**7** Italy: lives of the urban poor. Painting of a cheap dining-room in Milan
**8** France: suggested remedy for Paris traffic problems provided by a humorous French magazine. Traffic congestion was becoming an increasing problem in many of the world's capital cities
**9** Germany: advertisement for antiseptic – 'very agreeable to take!'

Gallery of Modern Art, Milan

L'Assiette au Beurre

Huntington Hartford

# Socialism:
# The 19th-Century Background

'Socialism, reduced to its simplest legal and practical expression,' George Bernard Shaw wrote at the end of the 19th century, 'means the complete discarding of the institution of private property by transforming it into public property and the division of the resultant income equally and indiscriminately among the entire population.' Put like that it seems simple, yet the vast literature to which socialists have treated the world shows wide divergencies of belief among them, both over ends and means. Most socialists have agreed, however, that they aim at a classless society, based on the public ownership of the essential means of production, including land, and that the best way to achieve this is by appealing to the exploited working class, whose historic mission it is to destroy the class system.

The words 'socialism' and 'socialist' were first used in France in the second quarter of the 19th century to describe the theory and the men opposed to a society run on a *laisser-faire*, or free-enterprise, basis by the ruling *bourgeoisie*, or middle class. The followers of Robert Owen (1771-1858), the pioneer of the English co-operative movement, officially adopted the name 'socialists' in 1841 and with them the word entered English political life.

The origins of socialist doctrine have sometimes been traced deep into history, but we may begin with the doctrines of the Frenchman, Babeuf (1760-97)–'Gracchus' Babeuf as he liked to call himself. In 1796 he took part in a plot to overthrow the French government. It failed and he was executed. Thirty years later, a devoted follower, Buonarroti, transmitted the legend and teaching of Babeuf to the next generation of revolutionaries in a book called *The Conspiracy for Equality*. Babeuf stressed that the French Revolution had failed to bring economic and social equality and that a revolution was still needed to found a social order based on them. But he lived in a pre-industrial society. Egalitarian ideas such as his still had to absorb the impact of the industrial revolution before they could be developed effectively into modern socialism.

One of the first men to see this was a French nobleman, Claude Saint-Simon (1776-1825). Saint-Simon's great contribution to socialist thought was to recognize that industrial and scientific advance made planned organization of the economy imperative. He was the first radical thinker to grasp the social implications of an economic organization based on factories

and great financial houses and to argue that social relationships adjusted themselves to economic evolution. He accepted Babeuf's belief that the state had an obligation to provide work for all and that all were obliged to work according to their powers. What he added was that the state must plan the means of production.

## The revolutionary pamphlet

1848 was a year of abortive liberal revolutions throughout Europe and of a great rising in Paris–the 'June Days'–which terrified middle-class liberals with the spectre of socialist revolution. It was also the year of the publication of the *Communist Manifesto*, the greatest pamphlet of the century. In it, the young German Karl Marx (1818-83) made a clean break with what he called the 'utopian socialism' of his predecessors. According to Marx, nothing was to be hoped from the enlightenment or goodwill of the *bourgeoisie*. Everything depended on the revolutionary role of the proletariat. Fortunately, the proletariat's success in this historic role was certain, he said, because it was dictated by the course of history itself. Marx called his own theories 'scientific socialism', in opposition to what he sneered at as 'utopian socialism'. Utopian socialists attacked industrial capitalism because it behaved in an immoral and unjust way towards the working class which produced its wealth; Marx contended not that capitalism was morally wrong, but that it was out of date and therefore historically doomed.

The distinction was, of course, not as neat as this sounds. There is plenty of moral indignation in the writings of Marx. Nevertheless, his central importance in the development of socialism lay in the appeal which his apparently scientific and sociological analysis made to a materialistically and deterministically minded age. He taught that the structure of property rights and class relationships upheld a particular political system and ideology which would be bound to change as the economic substructure of society changed. This was what most men took away from his teaching: the belief that men are impelled by historical necessity to adapt their institutions to the requirements of the methods of production. This theory was a great source of confidence to social revolutionaries, who could thus feel irresistibly carried forward to the socialist millennium, though Marx applied that view only to the broad, sweeping changes in history which individuals are powerless

to resist and he did not apply them to its detailed unfolding.

Marx claimed that his analysis of the liberal, capitalist politics and economics of 19th-century Europe showed that they no longer reflected the economic realities of an industrial economy. Capitalism had created in spite of itself the industrial army of the proletariat which would destroy it. The internal contradictions of capitalist society would weaken it and drive it from crisis to crisis until its exploited wage-slaves would be able to overthrow their exploiters. The haphazard tyranny of *laisser-faire* economics (which condemned so many of the workers to starvation and degradation) would be replaced by the planned regulation of the economy, first in the interests of the working class and then in those of society as a whole. Only then would the material abundance promised to mankind by the industrial and technological revolutions be realized and man live in a society of which he was the creator and master, not the victim. Then, for the first time, man would escape from the determination of History and would finally be in a position to control his own fate.

Gradually the views of Marx came to be held by the majority of socialists–or so they claimed. This did not happen quickly. The International Working Men's Association ('The First International'), founded by British trade union leaders in London in 1864, of which Marx became the secretary, only slowly evolved precise political programmes, but it provided the first focus for struggling socialist movements separated by national boundaries. By its mere existence it emphasized that the enemy of the proletariat, the *bourgeoisie*, was an international enemy.

After the Paris Commune of 1871 had frightened European governments into vigorous police action against subversive movements, this First International was gravely weakened. It came to an end, however, only because of Marx's determination to destroy it rather than see it fall under the influence of his opponents, the anarchists who followed Mikhail Bakunin (1814-76), the great Russian agitator. The First International nonetheless left behind two important legacies: the ideal of international socialist unity, and a scattering of socialists in many countries affiliated as branches of the International.

By the mid-1880's socialist prospects seemed again to be improving. This was largely because of industrialization. In Great Britain and Germany, trade unions

*Above:* Paris docks aflame. **Right:** Communards at a barricade. The French capital suffered a heavy toll in both lives and damage during the rise and fall of the Commune of Paris set up by dissidents protesting the peace terms accepted by Thiers following the Franco-Prussian War

grew rapidly among the unskilled masses of the new industrial society. But the possibility of universal suffrage in some countries spurred the formation of socialist political parties, too. The biggest was the massive, rich, and highly organized German Social Democratic Party (SPD). No other country had anything like this concentration of working-class power, which by 1900 had become a major feature of the German political scene. But everywhere socialists began to play an active political role.

Partly because of the absence of any international socialist organization, socialist movements had by now taken on different characteristics in different countries. Thus, for example, the German SPD was distinguished by its rigid adherence to Marxist principles and centralized discipline, while the French socialist movement was broken up into many groups, only one of which was dogmatically Marxist; others were inspired by non-Marxist socialism, or even by anarchism. The British workers, on the whole, looked to their trade unions and to pressure on their parliamentary rulers to bring them practical reform.

Such differences help to explain the caution with which national leaders of socialism approached the next attempt to focus their movement internationally. This was the Second International, founded at Paris in 1889. It was, however, not until 1900 that the International required

a permanent secretariat, the International Socialist Bureau, at Brussels.

By that date, the International had succeeded in solving the first great problem it faced, that of its attitude to the anarchists. It dealt with it by excluding them. Thereafter the Marxist SPD by its numbers, wealth, and theoretical prestige, more and more stamped the Second International with its own character. In 1900 the full effects of this were not apparent: the socialist movements of all countries enjoyed a large measure of freedom to interpret the recommendations of the International in a manner appropriate to their own local conditions. This flexibility was never wholly to be lost in practice — indeed, it was one cause of the great failure which disillusioned so many

socialists in 1914, the inability of the Second International to organize effective working-class opposition to war. But in 1900 this dismal future could not be seen. The success of the great May Day demonstrations, the frequent use of the strike weapon, the activity of socialists in parliaments where they could denounce the oppressive brutalities of capitalist governments – all these things made socialists confident that the future was, as Marx had asserted, inevitably theirs and that the International would progress from strength to strength. Only the 'revisionists' dared to suggest that Marx's predictions might already have been falsified and that the road to socialism might differ from the revolutionary one lauded in the congresses of the International.

# USA: The Years of Expansion

The long-deceased humorous magazine, *Life*, in the golden years before the Great Depression began in 1929, ran a series of drawings which were extremely popular. They appealed to the recurrent fad of nostalgia for the past and they were called 'The Gay Nineties'. The name was an odd misnomer. For the last decade of the 19th century, in the United States and in other countries, was on the whole far from gay. The periods of 'bad times', which had begun in 1873 all over western Europe and North America, culminated in 1893 in the United States in the greatest of all financial 'panics' up to that time. The American social structure was never to seem so threatened again until the 1929 Depression.

The 'nineties were certainly not gay, but they were extremely important for the future of American society. For one thing, it began to be noticed that the character of that society was changing. In 1893 a young historian, Frederick Jackson Turner, read a paper to the American Historical Association calling attention to 'the frontier'. Turner took his cue from an announcement of the Census Bureau of the United States government describing the census of 1890 and asserting that 'the frontier' was closed. What the Census Bureau meant, and what Turner meant, was not that the great western movement had ended, but that all over the United States the unsettled margins, east and west, had met. All of the United States was now organized and, in some degree, settled. All the present continental states existed except Oklahoma, New Mexico, and Arizona, which were still

'territories'. The great colonizing movement, which began with the first settlement on the Atlantic coast in the early 17th century, was formally over. (It was not, in fact, really over. Free settlement of the 'public lands' continued until 1916. But Turner was right in seeing the census of 1890 as a climacteric—the conclusion of the old agricultural and pastoral settlement of the United States.)

Since the 17th century, the settlers moving westward from the Atlantic coast and then, in the 19th century, those moving eastward from the Pacific coast, had exploited the resources of the nearly empty land. In the course of this movement, they had swept into the corners the Indian tribes. The last desperate Indian revolts were over. On the three million square miles of the continental United States, what Professor David Potter was to call a 'People of Plenty' had established itself and was on the way to being the richest society the world had ever seen.

Although the farmers and pastoralists of the 'nineties did not realize it, the high tide of this movement had passed. The climatic cycle for a while provided adequate rainfall, and not only cattle-raising but wheat-growing was profitable and easy. By 1890 this boom was over and the High Plains never knew again the confidence and optimism of the years of their first settlement. As an unknown poet of the period has put it:

*Across the plains where once there roamed*
  *The Indian and the Scout,*
*The Swede with alcoholic breath*
  *Sets rows of cabbage out.*

### The new agriculture

Even in fertile, well-watered, and intrinsically rich regions like Iowa and Illinois, the American farmer was suffering from a shift of 'the terms of trade'. He was now faced with competition from the Canadian prairies, from Argentina, and from Australia. He was also suffering from the protectionist policies of European nations which decided to save their farmers from the competition of American crops.

Then, farming was becoming more and more a capital intensive industry. The mobile pioneer, taking up his free or cheap land, building his log cabin or, farther west, his sod house, and creating a farm he could sell or leave to his children, was becoming increasingly a myth. The farmer now needed expensive farm equipment. He needed transport for his crops, and that meant that he was at the mercy of the railroads. He was also part of the world market, and that meant he was at the mercy of bankers, of commission merchants. West of the Missouri, on the High Plains, he was entirely dependent for the basic necessities of life on eastern industry. For example, wire and then barbed wire were indispensable to the working of his farm. Farm machinery was needed to make it profitable to work the Dakota farms in the very brief growing summer of about ninety days. There was next to no timber on the High Plains so wood had to be imported. More and more western states were one-crop economies, and so food, clothing, necessities, and the few luxuries had to be paid for in cash and brought in by railway.

*Position of the states of the High Plains*

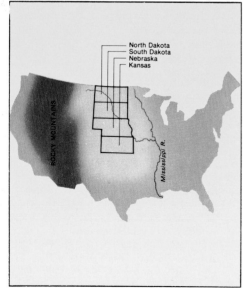

North Dakota
South Dakota
Nebraska
Kansas

ROCKY MOUNTAINS

Mississippi R.

*Unemployed march on Washington. Class war came in a violent form to the model republic*

Snark

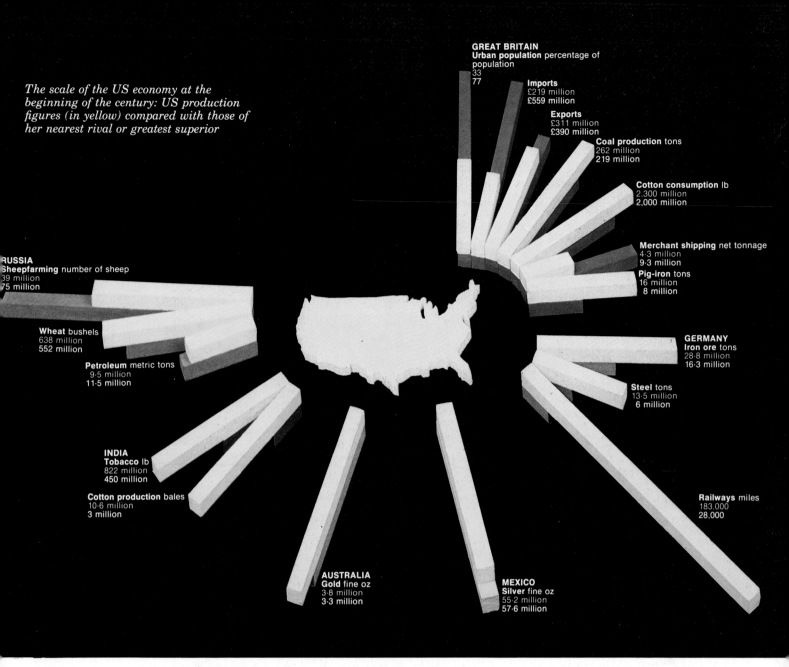

*The scale of the US economy at the beginning of the century: US production figures (in yellow) compared with those of her nearest rival or greatest superior*

**GREAT BRITAIN**
**Urban population** percentage of population
33
77

**Imports**
£219 million
£559 million

**Exports**
£311 million
£390 million

**Coal production** tons
262 million
219 million

**Cotton consumption** lb
2,300 million
2,000 million

**Merchant shipping** net tonnage
4·3 million
9·3 million

**Pig-iron** tons
16 million
8 million

**GERMANY**
**Iron ore** tons
28·8 million
16·3 million

**Steel** tons
13·5 million
6 million

**Railways** miles
183,000
28,000

**MEXICO**
**Silver** fine oz
55·2 million
57·6 million

**AUSTRALIA**
**Gold** fine oz
3·8 million
3·3 million

**Cotton production** bales
10·6 million
3 million

**INDIA**
**Tobacco** lb
822 million
450 million

**Petroleum** metric tons
9·5 million
11·5 million

**Wheat** bushels
638 million
552 million

**RUSSIA**
**Sheepfarming** number of sheep
39 million
75 million

All American settlers were, by definition, optimists, but in the last decade of the 19th century their optimism became very dim indeed. Without knowing exactly what was happening to him, the farmer believed he was getting a raw deal. The prices of what he sold oscillated, but mainly downward. The prices of what he bought — artificial prices kept up by high tariffs, as the farmer with some justice believed — did not fall. Debts contracted in the boom years had to be paid in the slump years. Life on the old frontier, and still more on the new frontier, was brutal and hard, especially for the women. It was a world angered by myth as well as by the realities of a changing position. The American farmer believed that he was being sacrificed to keep the United States on the gold standard at the behest of London bankers, especially the Rothschilds. And so anti-semitism entered the agricultural mentality.

*The new immigration*
It was not only the embattled farmer who was angry and alarmed. The class war had finally come in violent form to the model republic. Most of the working class in Europe had agreed with Lincoln that the United States was 'the last best hope of earth'. By the 'eighties, this was a belief held by a diminishing minority. In the great depression of the 'seventies, violence had broken out on an alarming scale. The long and dreary recovery did not diminish resentment or soothe frustration. 'The older American stocks', who had provided most of the skilled workers in the growing cities, were conscious that their role and their fortunes were changing. They were still providing the overwhelming proportion of the professional and managerial classes. But the labouring masses were coming increasingly from new types of European immigrants. Most settlers in the United States till the 1880's had come from northern and western Europe, principally the British Isles (including Ireland), Scandinavia, and Germany. Most of these immigrants had assets which made them adjust fairly quickly to the American way of life. Most were Protestants, although the majority of the Irish and a very large minority of the Germans were Catholics. Most were literate in their own native languages, if not in English. Some, especially the Irish, had a lively tradition of political action.

'The new immigration', as it was called, came from Italy, from Poland, largely from the horrible Polish ghettos, from the old Austro-Hungarian monarchy, and from Greece. These countries differed much more from the United States than did the countries of western Europe. It was a significant moment when the foreign press with the largest circulation became that printed in Yiddish and no longer that printed in German. Many of the new immigrants brought with them a tradition of anarchy or a tradition of hostility to government in general. The execution of the 'Chicago anarchists' in the 'eighties revealed to America and to Europe the changed situation. (The Chicago 'martyrs' are mentioned in the socialist song, 'The Red Flag'.) Most of the immigrants, even many of the Jews, were illiterate, and they crowded into racial ghettos in the great cities. They provided the labour force in the heavy industries, in coal-mining, and in steel. They provided the migrant farm workers on whom the American agricultural system more and more depended. And they came into a country in which the prospects for all Americans, and especially for the Negroes, were less rosy than they had been in the first two-thirds of the century. The great Homestead Strike near Pittsburgh in 1892, which took the form of a bloody civil war between the Pinkerton detectives hired by the Carnegie Steel Company and the embattled workers, emphasized the split in American society.

In the South there were also tensions. The recovery from the devastation of the Civil War was very slow indeed. The cotton farmers of the South suffered even more than the wheat farmers on the western plains from the oscillations of the world market. The emancipated Negro was neither a well-paid farmhand nor a peasant owner: he was a 'share-cropper' (a farm labourer who was paid not in cash but in a share of the crops). So were many of the poor whites. Both were victims of the war and of the new industrial and agricultural system. The South was now a colony of Northern finance – a colony administered by Southern leaders, but a colony all the same.

*Widening class divisions*
The polarity of the economy was also illustrated by the growth of the great corporations called, somewhat inexactly, 'trusts', of which the most famous or notorious, and certainly the most hated, was the Standard Oil Company. A Marxian could see the revolutionary crisis on the way, and many Marxians did see it. They were wrong about the end product, but not about the symptoms. The stage seemed set for a clash – perhaps a final clash – between the new masters of money and the mass of discontented, alarmed, and unhappy American poor and near-poor. The clash did come, but it took a different form from that foreseen by European and, indeed, by many American observers.

The threat of the clash, the appearance of such ominous signs as the march of Coxey's army of unemployed to Washington in 1894, a form of pressure on Congress for relief, alarmed, or excited the hopes of, spectators. In the South, the alarm of the ruling classes was caused mainly by the short-term alliance between poor whites and poor Negroes in the Populist Party. A real alliance between these two depressed groups would have been a threat to the established order all over the South. The Populists appealed also to the disgruntled farmers of the western states. The Populist platform in 1892, which called for the free and unlimited coinage of silver (a policy of inflation designed to enable debt-encumbered farmers to pay their eastern creditors), an eight-hour day for labour, public ownership of railways and telephones, and immigration restriction, was the most dramatic and doctrinaire platform which has ever won a large number of votes in the United States. The Populists threatened to take over the Democratic Party, or, at any rate, to permeate it and transform it into a radical combination of the discontented. At the same time, the middle classes were angered by their relative decline compared to the great new industrial magnates. The sight of the horrible new cities with the endemic graft and crime, the absence of any effective social communication between town and country, and especially between old and new classes, alarmed novelists like W.D.Howells. A hundred years after the United States had begun business under the new constitution, its future seemed more troubled than it had seemed in the late 18th century.

The reactions to this unpleasant dis-

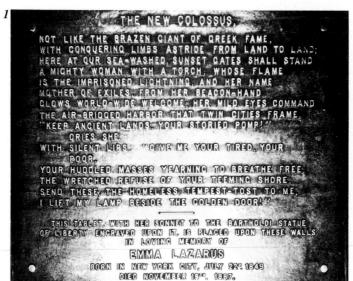

1 The dream which drew so many across the Atlantic in search of a new future: the inscription on USA's Statue of Liberty. 2 The new immigration – scene aboard an immigrant ship just after docking in the USA. 3 Crowded though a New York tenement block might be, families like this were better off in them than they had ever been in their homes in eastern Europe. 4 Most of the immigrants found themselves herded into new 'ghettos'. This is part of a Jewish ghetto in New York. 5 Children in New York's squalid East Side which was inhabited almost exclusively by new immigrants, arriving in their thousands at the turn of the 20th century

covery of the great schism in American life were various. Some were, in the strict sense of the term, reactionary. Thus, 'the American Protective Association' was a Protestant lobby against the menace of Rome. Hostility to Roman Catholics (it is illustrated in the letters and writings of the young Woodrow Wilson) was still extremely widespread. Many Protestants, deeply resenting the growth in power of Roman Catholic politicians, found it profitable to cater to the Protestant faction.

The reformers of this time, the 'Mugwumps', were themselves not free from anti-Catholic feeling. They attributed too

*Below : A girl at work in a South Carolina cotton mill in 1900. The industrial revolution had tapped an altogether fresh source by turning women into a pool of cheap labour*

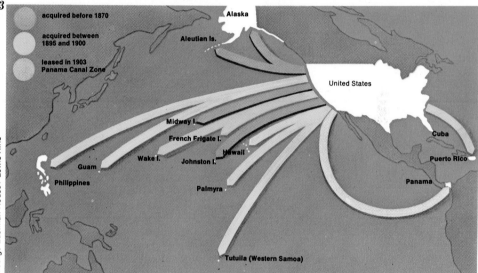

easily the demoralized political life of the great cities to Irish Catholic politicians, most of whom were Democrats. Young politicians like Henry Cabot Lodge catered, in public, to Irish hostility to Great Britain, and, in private, sneered at their supporters.

### 1896 — a watershed

The election of 1896 was a watershed, and a watershed of a kind not noticed at the time. The nomination of the young ex-Congressman, William Jennings Bryan, as the Democratic candidate overthrew the established order of that party. Bryan was known all over the Middle West as an eloquent speaker and he drew to himself a great deal of the discontent caused in the North and in the South by the economic crisis. He was eminently Protestant; he was a teetotaller; devoted to the old-time religion; by recent ancestry, from the South. Although his nomination at Chicago in 1896, after the famous speech in which he refused to 'crucify mankind upon a cross of gold', seemed a total surprise, it had in fact been as carefully worked for as was Senator Goldwater's nomination in 1964.

Bryan was a rural Populist and his nomination meant the alienation of most of the old and opulent Democratic families in the East. It alienated great city bosses like Senator Hill of New York; it alienated

*1 Bryan: 'You shall not crucify mankind upon a cross of gold.' 2 French caricature of McKinley at the time of the Spanish-American War. It was captioned: 'The age of chivalry is over . . . only blood and iron matter any more.' 3 The growth of America's empire as it expanded from Alaska in the north, purchased from Russia in* *1867, to Tutuila, the chief island in Western, or American Samoa, in the south. 4 No banker had ever been so powerful as J. P. Morgan. In this cartoon Morgan is saying to Neptune: 'You may as well slide off into the water, old chap. There isn't room for both of us here. I'll boss the ocean from now on.'*

*Below: The all-important election of 1896. McKinley's service in the American Civil War is cleverly exploited in his favour and he was to become and remain President until he was assassinated by an anarchist, Léon Czolgosz, in Buffalo, in 1901, where he was opening the first American exposition of the 20th century*

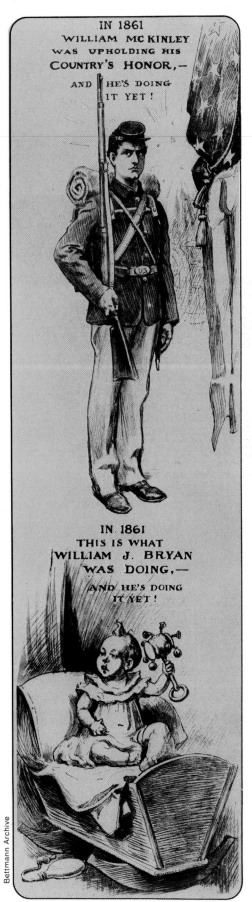

IN 1861
WILLIAM MC KINLEY
WAS UPHOLDING HIS
COUNTRY'S HONOR,—
AND HE'S DOING
IT YET!

IN 1861
THIS IS WHAT
WILLIAM J. BRYAN
WAS DOING,—
AND HE'S DOING
IT YET!

Bettmann Archive

Tammany Hall, the powerful Democratic Party organization in New York. Moreover, Bryan made no real attempt to win over the masses in the East; when he called it 'the enemy's country', he was referring not only to the rich and powerful, represented by cheering Yale students, but to the mass of the urban population. Any city was enemy country to Bryan.

All this meant that the campaign of 1896 failed on its Eastern wing. The quasi-revolutionary situation, which had frightened many of the rich, ceased to frighten them, as it was seen that Bryan was not, in fact, winning the depressed and angry population of the great cities. On the other hand, he *was* having unforeseen success with the masses of the Middle West, the West, and the South. The fears felt by the possessing classes were not all absurd.

The Republicans turned to a veteran politician, William McKinley, at that moment governor of Ohio after a long career in Congress. He was the opposite of the flamboyant and dramatic Bryan. He was a standard Republican presidential nominee of the dull generation after the Civil War, comparable to Hayes, to Garfield, to Harrison; but he was an extremely shrewd politician and much less the tool of the 'interests' or of his very formidable party manager, Mark Hanna, the great steel magnate from Cleveland, than either contemporary judgement or tradition has suggested.

But the coming of Mark Hanna to the front was another sign of the times. He was, for an American businessman, remarkably enlightened in his views of the industrial world. He despised people like Carnegie and Frick who quarrelled violently with their workers. He thought a great many businessmen were more frightened than hurt by organized labour. But he had no objections to frightening them. The Republican campaign of 1896 was the first campaign financed on a great scale by pressure put on big business. Mark Hanna 'assessed' the great business magnates and the great firms. He told them how much money they had to give to the Republican campaign fund.

Hanna was able to scare money out of rich Democrats as well, because behind Bryan's campaign lay the great force of agrarian radicalism. Bryan's fight for free silver was the last gasp of rural America before it was swallowed up by industrialism. It gained Bryan the financial support of the silver producers in the Rocky Mountain states, but it lost him the votes of urban workers, for whom it promised no relief, and of the business Democrats. Bryan and Populism were defeated in the 1896 election, although by only just over half a million votes.

Bryan still kept his hold on the faith of the Democratic Party, and indeed kept it for many years after that, with the result that the Democratic Party was no longer a serious opposition party with any real chance of wresting the federal government from the Republicans. Not until the Republican Party split in 1912 was a Democratic victory possible. Many of the Democrats who moved over to support McKinley in

1896 never moved back. From 1896 to 1912, the real political battles in the United States, including the battles of sections and of classes, took place inside the Republican Party. Some of the Populists who had been absorbed by the Democrats in 1896 drifted back to the Republican Party. In the South, both the Populists and the 'Bourbon' Democrats (the Southern agents of Northern business and the remnants of the old plantation class) were alarmed at the success which the Populists won by the use of the Negro vote. Both sides closed ranks to debar the Negro from the franchise to which he was constitutionally entitled, either by legal devices or by terror. The American Negro was now about to enter the lowest period of his sad post-'Emancipation' history.

*Prosperity and imperialism*

Two events extraneous to American internal history pushed on the decline of rural America. The first was the great increase of the gold supply as new gold came in from the Rand and from the Yukon. This was a shot in the arm for the stagnant capitalist system. Free silver was now irrelevant. And the United States suddenly found itself an imperial power. Cuba had again broken out in rebellion. The rebellion was in part caused by the collapse of the sugar market, itself caused in part by the tariff policies of the United States. The archaic Spanish government found it difficult to put down the rebellion: only in its methods of repression was Spain modern. It was the Spanish Marshal Weyler who invented 'concentration camps', the word and the thing. His methods, mild by modern standards, evoked a great deal of genuine and a great deal of bogus indignation. The Spanish-American War, when it came after the unexplained destruction of *USS Maine* in Havana harbour, could easily have been avoided. McKinley did sincerely try to avoid it: he was deeply pacific; but he was also a shrewd politician and he knew that resistance to the warmongers would politically be very expensive. The warmongers were young ambitious politicians like Theodore Roosevelt and Henry Cabot Lodge; they were newspaper owners like Joseph Pulitzer and William Randolph Hearst; they were politicians like Senator Donald Cameron and literary men like his wife's friend, Henry Adams. There were a great many young people who thought a war would be a great lark. When it came it was described by one of its makers as 'a splendid little war'.

At the end of this ignominious conflict, the United States had demonstrated to Europe not only that it had become a serious power with an important navy, but that it had become an imperial power. Cuba was formally 'freed'; Puerto Rico was

*The cotton exchange in New Orleans, painted by Degas. The cotton farmers of the South suffered severely from the oscillations of the world market. In fact the South became a colony of Northern finance — a colony administered by Southern leaders, but a colony all the same*

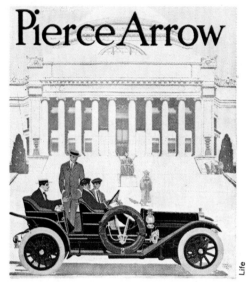

*Top left: The airplane in which Orville Wright made the first powered flight of fifty-nine seconds. Top right: Poster for an international shipping line. Above: Motoring for the rich. American luxury car advertisement*

annexed as a straight colony; and, across the Pacific, near the shores of China, the United States made itself the heir of Spain by annexing the Philippines. This involved them in a war with the Philippine rebels or patriots, and as the 19th century drew to a close, the country of the Declaration of Independence was involved in imposing its authority by force, 'puking up its principles', as the philosopher William James put it.

The annexation of the Philippines was justified on all sorts of absurd grounds. President McKinley announced that it was to bring Christianity to the islands, though most of the Filipinos already were Christians. The noisy young orator, Senator Beveridge of Indiana, preached the extension of the power of the Teutonic race over the lesser breeds. He also, with a curious lack of economic realism, saw the Philippines as a source of great wealth because of their role in the China trade. But without knowing it, the United States had given hostages to fortune that were literally to be taken in Bataan and Corregidor in 1942.

In 1898 the United States, which had for long been a kind of 'hermit' republic, became an imperial power of the normal type. It was soon involved in the politics of collapsing Manchu China. Naive Americans thought that the policy of secretary of state Hay, of an 'open door' in China, solved all the problems of that great country. This was an illusion. But all American imperial power was based on illusions.

Far more important, except for the distant future, than any imperial adventure, was the transformation of the economic position of the United States in the world. This was no illusion. The Standard Oil Company was the greatest of businesses, and its empire was far more real in Europe and in Asia than any empire of the political United States. Just as the new century began, the United States Steel Corporation was founded with a capitalization of a thousand million dollars, an unprecedented sum, equal to the annual revenue of Great Britain and equal to the total national debt of the United States. No man in history had ever been so rich as John D. Rockefeller; few have been so rich as Andrew Carnegie. No banker had ever been so powerful as J. Pierpont Morgan I. The centre of power in the capitalist world had moved west. True, the United States was still a debtor country, seeking capital in Europe, but it was a debtor on such a large scale that it was in fact more powerful than were its creditors.

The immense private wealth of the United States was now being turned to some public use. The great Rockefeller fortune was being spent largely, though far from completely, on philanthropic undertakings, mainly in the fields of education and medicine. The Carnegie fortune was being spent in the same way. The American universities quite suddenly came of age; some were now equal to the greatest universities of Europe, whether it was the oldest university, Harvard, or the new University of Chicago founded by John D. Rockefeller. The United States was now a great buyer of arts and of performers of the arts, if not yet a great producer of them.

### Roosevelt kicked upstairs

In 1900 McKinley was easily re-elected over Bryan, who fought on the issue of anti-imperialism, an issue which stirred only a few doctrinaire devotees of Jefferson. The American people, coming out of the long tunnel of the panic, forgetting in the typical national way the bleakness of the immediate past, entered on a new era of confident expansion. For reasons mainly concerned with New York politics, the chief hero of the Spanish war, young Colonel Theodore Roosevelt, who had become governor of New York in 1898, was kicked upstairs to be vice-presidential candidate. He found himself, as all vice-presidents do, helpless and powerless in Washington. McKinley, now a kind of national hero and certainly deserving a good deal of the affection which he inspired, went to Buffalo to open the first American exposition of the 20th century. He was shot by an anarchist with the extraordinarily un-American name of Léon Czolgosz.

Vice-president Roosevelt became, by this accident, the youngest man ever to enter the White House, and, by this accident, the United States entered the 20th century under a political leader who in ideas, action, manner, tastes, and social rank was quite unlike any other President since Lincoln. It was symbolic of the entry of the United States on to the world stage on which it was soon to be the most important actor.

*Bodies are added to the chassis of the 'Model T' Ford*

# Great Britain: Reform and Party Strife

*1 Rosebery: suggested 'Efficiency' as a Liberal slogan. 2 Balfour: Conservative leader. 3 Churchill: deserted the Conservatives in 1904. 4 Campbell-Bannerman: led Liberals to resounding victory in 1906. 5 Grey: he put the weight of the foreign office behind naval expansion. 6 Asquith: urbane leader of a radical government. 7 Lloyd George: intrepid opponent of the Lords, depicted in this contemporary photo-montage as the candidate of the working man*

Great Britain was the dominant power in the world in 1901, and London the dominant city. But this dominance was not a matter of military power, for the German army was recognized as the most efficient force in the world. Nor was it a matter of wealth in general, because the United States was already the leading industrial power.

Great Britain was the country that other nations wanted to imitate, or sometimes found themselves imitating without wanting to. Every government that wanted to be up-to-date had to have parliamentary institutions. The Tsar contemplated, although with distaste, the prospect of a Duma. Plans for reorganizing Turkey always included a national assembly. Inside Great Britain only two-thirds of the men, and none of the women, could vote. 'One man, one vote' was not so completely accepted an idea as Parliament, and even the word 'democracy' was not quite respectable. Yet the British machinery of democracy worked well enough to survive hostile foreign criticism.

The nation which Great Britain came closest to regarding with friendship in 1901 was the United States. By then Great Britain had come to accept the United States as the dominant power in the western hemisphere and to see that it was not worthwhile to quarrel with her. But even this was not really a relationship of equals. Rich Americans showed that they had 'arrived' by marrying their daughters into the British nobility or, in a few cases, moving to Great Britain. Waldorf Astor even joined the British nobility himself.

The flow of British capital to the United States was slackening, but Great Britain continued to be the banker for most of the developing world. Russia borrowed from France and the Balkans from Germany, but Australia, Argentina, and indeed most of Latin America, Canada, India, and South Africa got their money from London. The British were among the leaders in the competition to lend to China and obtain concessions from her, though other European powers were well represented.

## Conservative blunders and Liberal revival

Great Britain's enviable position had its weaknesses. The economy was growing very slowly, and has never again moved as sluggishly as it did between 1900 and 1914. Thirty per cent of the population lived on the edge of starvation. This had been the case for a long time, but Charles Booth (the sociologist, not the founder of the Salvation Army) and Benjamin Seebohm Rowntree had only recently brought the facts home to the comfortable classes. The force of this was driven home at the time of the Boer War, when the city poor turned out to be so underfed and unfit that they would not make good soldiers. Long before anyone took the German navy seriously, German education had attracted attention. Scientific and technical skill looked like being important in the new century, and English education neglected these subjects. A few school boards were setting up technical schools, but Latin and Greek were still considered the really important things to learn.

British political leaders did not ignore the situation. Lord Rosebery, the former Liberal prime minister, who was now in semi-retirement, said the party should take 'Efficiency' as its slogan. The idea did not catch on, and did not restore him to the party leadership. Balfour, the Conservative prime minister, produced an education act designed to set up secondary education on an adequate basis. Later critics said his act paid too much attention to grammar school education and starved the technical schools; but at the time what really caused trouble was the anger of the Nonconformists at the provisions of the act which transferred education from the boards to the county councils and gave more money to Church of England and Roman Catholic schools. The more determined refused to pay their rates, and the Liberal Party, which sympathized with their grievances, began to revive and reunite after the divisions caused by the Boer War.

What really restored the Liberal Party's fortunes was Joseph Chamberlain's decision to take up protection as the cure for the country's problems. Great Britain had enjoyed free trade since the repeal of the Corn Laws in 1846 and it had become a settled tradition. Chamberlain was the last man to be worried by such an obstacle. The self-governing colonies were protectionist, and at meetings of prime ministers of the empire they had asked Great Britain to join them in a system of Imperial Preference. When Chamberlain took up the crusade for protection, he hoped to defend British industry and also to unite the British empire into a tightly knit unit that could face any power in the world on equal terms.

But the Liberals replied that he could not help the exporters in the self-governing colonies unless he put customs duties on imports of food. Candidates held up 'big loaves' (the ordinary loaf of bread) and 'little loaves' (the very much smaller loaf which they said would be the result of protection) to their audiences. They also pointed out that British industry was so complex that almost every item imported was used by some manufacturer as the raw material out of which he made goods for export. Steel plates were a simple example: if they were taxed on entry British ship-builders would have to charge more and British shipping (over half the world tonnage) would lose its position of dominance.

Chamberlain was too wise to call himself a protectionist. He and his friends were Tariff Reformers, and in their slogan 'Tariff Reform means work for all' they showed they were facing the problem of unemploy-ment that had been nagging many people's consciences for the past dozen years. Unemployment was nothing new, but previously it had just been taken for granted. In the late 'eighties and the 'nineties (when the word was used for the first time) people began to wonder what could be done. Chamberlain claimed to have an answer.

## 1 Menu and budget of a labourer's family of four on an income of 15s a week

| | Breakfast | Dinner | Tea | Purchases for week | |
|---|---|---|---|---|---|
| Friday | Bread / butter / tea | Fish / bread / coffee | Bread / butter / tea-cake / tea | Friday | 1lb butter 1s 2d / 6lb sugar 10d / ¼lb tea 7d / 1 tin of condensed milk 3d / 1 bag of coals 1s 6d / 1qt paraffin 2½d / a week's new milk 1s / 1½st of flour 2s / yeast 1½d / 1 tablet soap 1d / 1lb soap 3d / ¼st soda 3d / 1lb fish 3d |
| Saturday | Bacon / bread / tea | Brawn / bread / butter / coffee | Bread / butter / tea-cake / tea | | |
| Sunday | Bread / butter / tea | Rabbit / potatoes / Yorkshire pudding | Bread / butter / currant cake / tea | | |
| Monday | Bread / bacon / tea | Rabbit / potatoes / bread | Bread / butter / tea-cake / tea | Saturday | Rabbit 1s 2d / ½st potatoes 3½d / papers 2d / sticks 1d / 1pt new milk 1½d / 4 eggs 3d / 1lb bacon 6d / ¼lb coffee 5d / ½lb brawn 3d |
| Tuesday | Bread / butter / tea | Meat pie / potatoes | Bread / butter / tea | Monday | Life insurance 8d / rent 3s 10½d |
| Wednesday | Bread / butter / tea | Pork chops / potatoes / bread | Bread / butter / tea-cake / tea | Tuesday | 1½lb beef 9d |
| | | | | Wednesday | ½lb pork chops 4d |
| Thursday | Bread / butter / tea | Bacon / bread / butter / coffee | Bread / butter / tea | Thursday | ½lb bacon 3d |

### Typical Sunday menu of a lower middle-class family with three servants

| | Breakfast | Dinner | Tea | Supper |
|---|---|---|---|---|
| Sunday | Porridge / eggs / bread / butter / milk / coffee / tea / cream | Mutton / cauliflower / bread sauce / potatoes / rhubarb / custard / blancmange / oranges / biscuits / tea | Potted meat sandwiches / bread / butter / cake / marmalade / tea / milk | Potted meat / cornflour mould / bread / cake / rhubarb / custard / cheese / hot milk |

Royal Academy of Art, London

## 2 Proportion of population living in poverty 1900

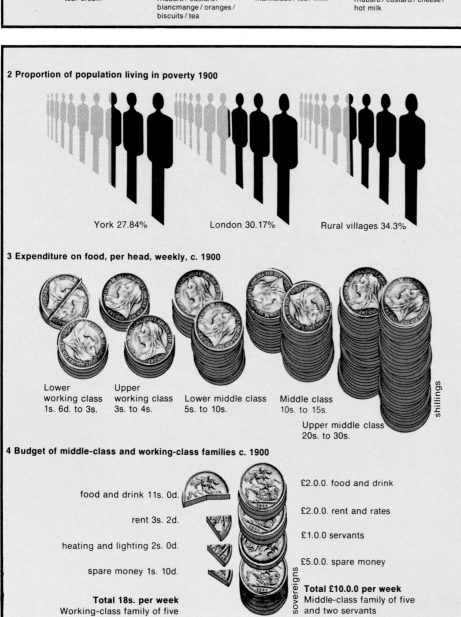

York 27.84%    London 30.17%    Rural villages 34.3%

## 3 Expenditure on food, per head, weekly, c. 1900

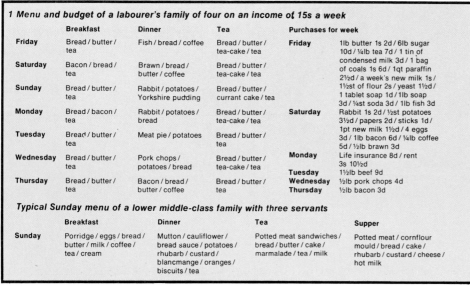

Lower working class 1s. 6d. to 3s.

Upper working class 3s. to 4s.

Lower middle class 5s. to 10s.

Middle class 10s. to 15s.

Upper middle class 20s. to 30s.

shillings

## 4 Budget of middle-class and working-class families c. 1900

food and drink 11s. 0d.

rent 3s. 2d.

heating and lighting 2s. 0d.

spare money 1s. 10d.

**Total 18s. per week**
Working-class family of five

£2.0.0. food and drink

£2.0.0. rent and rates

£1.0.0. servants

£5.0.0. spare money

**Total £10.0.0 per week**
Middle-class family of five and two servants

sovereigns

*Above: 'On Strike' by Hubert von Herkomer. Strikes were becoming ever more frequent. Irregular employment often caused workers and their families even greater misery than going on strike. Left: Statistics which lay bare the other side of the Edwardian glitter. The richest society in the world was upheld by the toils of the one-third of the population which lived in chronic poverty.*
*1 Typical menus in Edwardian Britain. For the working class, little variety, and never a sweet. For the middle class, a healthy, balanced diet. 2 Percentages of the population living at or below the 'subsistence level'. Benjamin Seebohm Rowntree's* Poverty: A Study of Town Life *(1901), pricked the Edwardian conscience with its revelations of the life of the poor in York. Charles Booth's* Life and Labours of the People of London *(1903) did the same for the capital.*
*3 Weekly expenditure on food per head in 1900. 4. Breakdown of weekly budget for a middle-class and working-class family in 1900. This striking disparity of incomes which is demonstrated here was an important factor in the rise of the Labour Party*

Campaign posters in the
great tariff debate which
split the Conservative
party and helped the Liberals
to their landslide electoral
victory in 1906

*Right:* Liberal poster shows
Joseph Chamberlain, the
Tory protectionist, crushing
the workers with his high
tariffs on imported goods.
Chamberlain, passed over for
the Conservative leadership
in 1902, resigned as colonial
secretary to press his
campaign for Tariff Reform.
But he aroused against his
party the deep-seated
English prejudice in favour of
free trade.

*Below:* Conservatives counter
the Liberal attack. Free trade
will depress home industry
and leave the population
without any means to buy
the cheap imported goods

FLATTENING HIM OUT, OR "BROADENING THE BASIS OF TAXATION."

"IF YOU ARE TO GIVE A PREFERENCE TO THE COLONIES YOU MUST PUT A TAX ON FOOD."
Mr J. CHAMBERLAIN. *House of Commons, May 28th 1903.*

TAXATION

"Mr BALFOUR AND THE TORY PARTY WANT TO "BROADEN THE BASIS OF TAXATION." This simply means, and CAN ONLY MEAN, making the poor pay more in the way of taxation. As a Tory paper said some time ago, "to broaden the basis of taxation, OF COURSE, means to place A LARGER SHARE UPON THE MASSES."

THE CONTINENTAL SUPPLY STORES UNLIMITED

A FREE TRADE FORECAST.

## Birth of the Labour Party

In some circumstances this approach might
have won over the relatively prosperous
members of the working class, who were
the only ones who had votes. Instead, two
events made the industrial working class
more anti-Conservative than ever before.
In 1901 the House of Lords gave judgement
in the Taff Vale case; taken with other
judicial decisions of the previous few years,
the effect was to make it possible for employers to recover from trade union funds
all the expenses incurred by a strike. The
trade unions asked the government to
restore the law to what everybody had
thought had been the position beforehand:
that a strike was a struggle in which both
sides paid their own costs. The government
set up a royal commission, but otherwise
did nothing.

The effect was to encourage the Labour
Representation Committee. In the 'nineties
the socialists in the Trades Union Congress
had been trying to persuade the less politic-

GLC Photo Library

Radio Times Hulton

**1**

**2**

**3**

ally-minded majority to set up a new political party which could co-operate with the recently established Independent Labour Party in promoting a socialist policy. By 1900 the TUC had been won over to the extent of agreeing to set up a Labour Representation Committee with the ILP, the Fabian Society, and the Social Democratic Federation. The vital TUC resolution spoke only of securing 'the return of an increased number of labour members'. For a good many trade unionists this meant they were tired of Liberal constituency parties which said they were friends of the working classes but never adopted working-class candidates. But a good many trade unionists were not interested in the LRC.

The Taff Vale decision changed all this. The number of trade unionists affiliated to the committee more than doubled. Herbert Gladstone, the Liberal Party whip, started discussions with Ramsay MacDonald, the secretary of the LRC, to arrange that Liberal and LRC candidates should not run against each other. This of course implied that the Liberals would revise the Taff Vale judgement.

The row over Taff Vale had a long-range effect, but at the time people were as excited about 'Chinese slavery'. To get the gold mines going again after the Boer War, Lord Milner, the British high commissioner, had brought in Chinese coolies to work on long-term contracts. Humanitarian feeling in Great Britain was aroused by the thought that the Chinese were being badly treated. Perhaps they were, but they did not complain, and Winston Churchill later admitted that to call it slavery was a 'terminological inexactitude' – the Conservatives suggested that 'lie' would have been shorter, but that was not what Churchill meant at all.

Workers in Great Britain had less humanitarian worries: they thought Chinese labour in the Transvaal might be a prelude to Chinese labour being brought to Great Britain and working for low wages. Apart from their low wages, their contracts meant

that they could not be formed into trade unions. David Lloyd George brought together the issues of inhumane treatment and of cheap labour when he asked if they were to have slavery on the hills of Wales.

Chamberlain's shift to protection divided the Conservatives badly. It was on this issue that Churchill crossed the floor of the House of Commons and joined the Liberals. Balfour managed to hold the party together by ingenious but demoralizing devices such as leading all his supporters out of the Commons rather than face a debate. But this could not go on. Balfour resigned on 4th December 1905 and left the opposition leader, Sir Henry Campbell-Bannerman, to form a government and ask for an election. Campbell-Bannerman had a moment of difficulty persuading Sir Edward Grey to accept the foreign office, because Grey at first thought Herbert Asquith ought to be the effective leader and Sir Henry ought to go to the House of Lords. But Asquith was much less inclined to make difficulties, and Grey gave way.

As soon as he was in office Grey had to make important decisions. The previous government had moved away from its proud isolation after the Boer War. First it made a treaty with Japan to guard the position in the Far East, and then made the *entente cordiale* with France. By 1905 this was beginning to alarm Germany, and in his first days of office Grey had to confirm that he stood by France. He explained the situation at this stage only to the prime minister, Asquith, and R.B.Haldane, the minister of war.

### The great landslide
Once the government was formed, it went forward to the election. The confidence of the protectionist wing of the Conservatives was entirely misplaced; their party won 245 seats fewer than in 1900, a larger drop than any party has suffered before or since. Four hundred Liberals (including 23 Lib-Labs who joined the Labour Party in 1909), 83 Home Rulers (Irish members advocating

*1 Elementary education was provided by the state for all children under twelve. In this Edwardian school boys and girls at their arithmetic. 2 A street in Lambeth. Weekly family income was often less than £1. 3 Inside one of the new labour exchanges set up by Churchill. Under the terms of the National Insurance Bill unemployed workers in certain trades who presented themselves at the exchange could get seven shillings a week when no other jobs were available. The other great radical innovation included in the bill was the provision of sickness benefits, national health insurance, for all wage-earners. 4 and 5 Election posters of 1910 attacking Lloyd George's 'People's Budget' of 1909. The Conservatives claimed that tariff reform would benefit the poor more than the social services set up in the budget and that the Liberal refusal to impose tariffs, 'to tax' the foreigner, was killing British prosperity. It was the working man who would suffer from increased taxation. In fact, Lloyd George's new taxes fell mainly on the rich*

a separate parliament for Ireland), and 30 LRC members were elected. Only 157 Conservatives were left.

The Liberals were a curious mixture. Some of them were like Broadbent in *John Bull's Other Island* — Shaw's play which made Edward VII laugh so much that he broke his chair:

'*Broadbent:* Of course there are some questions which touch the very foundation of morals; and on these I grant you even the closest relationship cannot excuse any compromise or laxity. For instance —

*Doyle* (impatiently): For instance, Home Rule, South Africa, Free Trade, and putting the Church schools on the Education Rate.'

But along with them were a few who called themselves socialists and several who would have been happy in the Labour Party (as the LRC called itself after the election) if it had not been a party for working-class members. From 1906 to 1914 the Labour Party looked very much like a pressure group inside the Liberal Party for getting trade unionists elected, and it had no real differences of principle with the government. The Labour Party's first demand was satisfied when the Taff Vale decision was reversed drastically by an act that laid down that trade unions could not be sued in court. The Liberals of the Broadbent school were relieved that free trade was safe and were glad to see self-government restored to the South African colonies, which went on to federate themselves in the Union of South Africa. But Home Rule had to wait, and when the government tried to satisfy the Nonconformists by

passing bills on education and on the licensing of public houses, the House of Lords which was nine-tenths Conservative rejected them. Lloyd George said the upper house was not the watchdog of the constitution, but Mr. Balfour's poodle; but it remained unshaken.

The Liberals who wanted government spending to be cut were glad to see that Lord Fisher was reorganizing the navy and Haldane was reorganizing the army in a way that reduced expenditure. They did not ask what the army was to do. Many years later Haldane put it down that he had thought 'we should have an expeditionary force sufficient in size and also in rapidity of mobilizing power to be able to go to the assistance of the French army in the·event of an attack on the northern or northeastern parts of France'. But this was not the sort of thing he could talk about in public.

Early in 1908 Sir Henry Campbell-Bannerman retired, and died almost immediately afterwards. Asquith duly succeeded him. Lloyd George took his place as chancellor of the exchequer and Churchill joined the cabinet as president of the Board of Trade. The changes strengthened the social reforming side of the government, and Asquith himself took the lead in this. Although he was prime minister, he brought forward the budget on which he had been working when Campbell-Bannerman retired: old age pensions of five shillings a week (prices were one-twelfth of today's level) were given to people who had reached the age of seventy, and unearned income was taxed at a higher rate than earned.

The House of Lords disapproved of the idea of pensions, but gave way because they traditionally did not interfere with legislation about money. The pensioners—who had been freed from fear of the work-house—were grateful, though apparently to Lloyd George rather than to Asquith. At the post office they said: '"God bless that Lord George" [for they could not believe one so powerful and munificent could be a plain 'Mr'] and "God bless *you*, miss" and there were flowers from their gardens and apples from their trees for the girl who merely handed them the money.

Apart from this the Lords kept up their blockade of Liberal legislation, and early in 1909 another problem came up. Grey and Haldane had their diplomatic and military problems with Germany, but what worried people in Great Britain was the German navy. By 1909 an agitation was building up; with the slogan 'we want eight and we won't wait', the supporters of a strong navy pressed for irresistible supremacy over Germany. They got their way, but the battleships had to be paid for.

Many of the supporters of a big navy were Tariff Reformers who felt certain that the cost of old age pensions and the new ships could be met only by imposing tariffs. Lloyd George had no intention of being caught in such a way. In his 1909 budget he expanded the revenue by introducing a graduated tax on really large incomes. This would do for the time being, but he also provided for the future by setting up taxes on increases in the value of land.

### Lords 'damn the consequences'

The additional revenue opened up the way to new social services without tariff reform. In addition, the taxes on land were seen as a direct attack on the House of Lords, which was largely made up of land-lords. The budget took a very long time to pass the Commons, and the Lords had time to grow increasingly determined. They were men with a high sense of their own dignity and were upset when Lloyd George attacked them in the everyday language of political abuse. In November they took Milner's advice to 'damn the consequences' and rejected the budget. The government had to have a general election if it was to raise money to run the country.

Rejecting individual bills was one thing, but the Lords had now claimed they could compel the government to have a general election whenever they chose. So there were two issues in the election: the budget, which the Conservatives said was not so good an idea as tariff reform, and the constitutional position of the Lords. In January 1910 the Conservatives won 273 seats and the Liberals 275 seats, but the government could count on another 40 Labour votes and could get 82 Irish votes, if it showed it was in earnest about the Lords. The

government committed itself to removing money bills from the Lords altogether and to laying down that any bill would become law if it were passed by the Commons three times in one session, no matter what the Lords did. The Irish could now support the Liberals in the knowledge that a Home Rule bill could not be destroyed by the Lords as Gladstone's bill had been in 1893.

In the summer of 1910 Edward VII died, and in the pause after this event there were private discussions between the parties. But the Conservatives were determined that the Lords should retain the power to throw out a Home Rule bill and the Liberals were equally determined they should not. The private talks drifted off into discussion of a very ambitious plan of Lloyd George's for a great Liberal-Conservative coalition which would deal with all the problems of the day on a basis of compromise. The party leaders might have accepted this, but even the most discreet of soundings showed that backbenchers were more rigidly attached to their principles.

So when Edward's successor George V had taken in the situation, Asquith asked him for secret assurances that, if there were another election and the Liberals won, he would create all the new peers the Liberals wanted. In the second 1910 election, held in December, the Conservatives suggested a referendum, stressed the attractions of tariff reform, promised that there would be a referendum on tariff reform and warned people of the danger of Home Rule. The Liberals stuck to the Parliament Bill and the misdeeds of the Lords. Several seats changed hands, but the net results showed no change from January (272 Conservatives, 272 Liberals, 84 Home Rulers and 42 Labour). The Parliament Bill passed the Commons, and Asquith announced that he had the King's promise to create peers. For this he was shouted down in the Commons by the Conservatives. It is not necessary to search for justification for this performance, nor possible to find any; the Conservatives were extremely angry at having lost three elections and simply wanted to express their feelings.

The rational Conservatives realized that the game was up. If the Parliament Bill were rejected, enough peers would be created to pass it, bring about Home Rule, disestablish the Church of England in Wales, and carry all the other Liberal measures. The less rational Conservatives thought Asquith was bluffing and would not create the peers. There was nothing in Asquith's character to justify this idea. He was sometimes lazy, but he was not a rash or an untruthful man. As the Parliament Bill came before the Lords the 'ditchers' (i.e. the peers who were ready to vote against the bill and die in the last ditch) already had more committed votes than the whole of the Liberal handful in the upper house. Moderate Conservatives, who at first had thought abstention would be enough, now had to find people to vote for the bill to avoid the creation of peers.

In the final debate in the Lords a great many sensible and a great many stupid things were said, but the decisive fact was

that 'every vote against the bill is a vote for a large and prompt creation of peers'. The bill passed by 131 votes to 114, which meant that about fifty bishops and Conservatives had voted with the government against their personal feelings on the bill.

The passage of the Parliament Act did not guarantee that Great Britain could solve the problems of the new century. All it did was to ensure that solutions could not be destroyed by a second chamber full of landlords who had great difficulty in adjusting themselves to modern society.

At the same time as the bill was going through the Lords Lloyd George was bringing another piece of modernizing legislation, the National Insurance Bill, through the Commons. The bill covered two quite distinct problems. It gave health insurance to all wage-earners: they paid a fourpenny weekly premium, increased by their employers and by the government so that they were getting 'ninepence for fourpence', and they became entitled to the services of doctors who had put their names on the 'panel' ready to treat national insurance patients. The bill also gave unemployment benefit to workers in certain trades that fluctuated with the trade cycle. If they went to the labour exchanges recently set up by Churchill, and thus proved that they were seeking work, they could get seven shillings a week when no jobs were available.

The unemployment side of the bill was not too difficult. It required the creation of a certain amount of new administrative machinery but did not encounter much opposition. Health insurance was another matter. The doctors said they would go on strike rather than enter such a scheme, and a good many women who employed servants declared that they would not lick stamps (as the scheme was contributory, unlike the old age pensions, employers had to provide stamps to show that contributions had been paid). The doctors were brought round by negotiations in which Lloyd George offered larger benefits for them than at first. The duchesses who held a much-publicized protest meeting at the Albert Hall were ignored.

As things turned out, this was the last piece of major legislation passed by the Liberals. Home Rule for Ireland took up a lot of time, because the House of Lords used its delaying powers to hold up the bill. Before it had become law, the 1914 war had broken out. All the same the Liberal government—in the event, the last Liberal government—had done a great deal for the country. It had set up the framework of the welfare state even if it had not brought about any noticeable reduction in inequality. It had defined the position of the House of Lords. It had handled South Africa in a way that meant she fought on the British side in the two World Wars. It had outbuilt Germany in the naval race. In 1911, or even in 1914, the Liberal Party seemed to stand on the threshold of an assured future.

But for all that it remained in office throughout the war and beyond, as the lamps began going out all over Europe, there was infinitely more at stake than the fate of the Liberal Party alone.

# Kaiser Wilhelm's Germany

When General von Caprivi assumed office in 1890 as the second chancellor of the German empire, he admitted publicly that he had merely obeyed his Kaiser's order as a soldier and had no programme to submit. Unaccustomed to public affairs, he was faced with a task of which he had no previous experience, even in the most general fashion. But Kaiser Wilhelm II, who had just celebrated his thirty-first birthday, told his new henchman bluntly: 'Don't worry – all statesmen cook with water, and it is I who take the responsibility.' He had shown the same self-confidence when he dismissed Bismarck, who for nearly thirty years had been the symbol of the foundation, rise, and security of the new Germany amid the diplomatic manoeuvres of the great powers. Kaiser Wilhelm II was impulsive, erratic, and just the sort of ruler many Germans wanted.

Bismarck's fall and Wilhelm II's foreign policy, which led to the isolation of Germany and eventually to the First World War, must not, however, be simply explained as the unfortunate consequences of personal misjudgement; they were rather the manifestations of a structural problem in the political system itself, the system that developed after the foundation of the empire in 1871. National unification, so long sought, was a sequel to the crushing of the liberal revolution of 1848 by conservative and reactionary elements: the princely courts, the military, and the bureaucracy. Bismarck and Prussia, the main supports and symbols of the old order, succeeded in creating the German national state by a revolution imposed from above.

It was a Prussian and authoritarian substitute for the liberal-democratic national state which had been striven for before 1848. But it satisfied the elementary desires of pro-unification citizens and succeeded at the same time in absorbing the middle-class liberal emancipation movement into the structure of a pseudo-constitutional semi-absolute, feudal, military, and bureaucratic state. The liberals capitulated to the oft-quoted words of Bismarck, that the great questions of the day would be solved not by speeches and majority resolutions, but by iron and blood. The German bourgeoisie, intoxicated by Bismarck's successes, submitted to a vulgar and cynical conception of *Realpolitik*, in which it was might that counted, not right or morality. From then onwards were to prevail those authoritarian, law-and-order, prestige notions which Thomas Mann, the writer, sarcastically castigated when he characterized the ideal German citizen as

'General Dr von Staat'. The cult of power and the spirit of submission were the two poles of this misconceived attitude.

Thus from its earliest beginnings the German empire was handicapped by gross tensions and structural defects that were superficially concealed by the glories of the *Gründerzeit* – as the prosperous period of the late 19th century, when innumerable companies were established, was called. These flaws prevented the development of a sound parliamentary system and responsible political parties. The authoritarian state, dominated by military officers and bureaucrats, rejected the co-operation of the masses of workers and their Social Democratic organizations and trades unions. The result was a deep discrepancy between the social structure and the political system, the latter taking little account of the social changes brought about by the industrial revolution. In fact, after the fall of Bismarck, there emerged a growing tendency to neutralize the problem by diverting the domestic pressures of social emancipation towards an imperialist expansion. The results of this extraordinary state of affairs were to be disastrous.

## Imperialist ambitions

In foreign affairs, too, the new unified German empire felt itself as a late-comer among the nations. Conservatives and liberals alike were convinced that Germany must as soon as possible catch up with the great powers both nationally and imperially, that Germany as a great power itself had a natural claim to hegemony over central Europe and to a fair share of the colonies into which much of the rest of the world was being divided. This idea of Germany as a national-imperialist state found its extreme expression in the founding of the Pan-German League in 1893. Though small in numbers, this was an active and influential association which fostered the colonial and imperialist ambitions that accompanied the expansion of German trade. Its military and political propaganda reached the height of its violence during the First World War. Even in the more moderate 'central European' idea the German claim to hegemony, shared by wide circles in the population, was bound to appear in time to Germany's neighbours as a dire threat to their existence.

Even intelligent men were affected by this atmosphere. The victorious campaign against France of 1871 and the rise of the new empire exposed the German intelligentsia and bourgeoisie (especially professors and teachers, civil servants, officers, and industrialists), more than in any other country, to the attractions of anti-democratic and anti-humanitarian ideologies. A leading historian like Heinrich von Treitschke could assert amid general applause that the individual citizen should sacrifice himself for the higher community of which he was a member and that he was not justified in resisting the authority of the state. The individual was degraded to the position of a mere chattel, material for the political power of the state and the people. Race-theorists and social hygienists intervened with demands that the state should breed the 'more valuable' and exterminate the 'inferior' elements in the population. It was to be a short step from this demand to the total subjection of the individual to the state and people exacted by the National Socialists.

The hectic nationalism of the Second Reich, incorporating and exaggerating the ancient Prussian ideals of discipline and obedience, was a rich soil for the growth of students' associations, patriotic clubs, military societies, and a host of other nationalist organizations. Even the Protestant churches, with their conservative and nationalist tendencies, helped to spread jingoist feelings. Ideas of national and imperial prestige concealed and compensated for the inferiority complex of a latecomer among nations and steered its social unrest—this was the period of economic crises, the *Kulturkampf* between state and Catholic church, anti-socialist legislation—into the channel of an ever-increasing antisemitism. Moreover, it fostered a cynical contempt for international legislation and agreements. The advocates of the powerstate countered the 'cowardly and sentimental' enthusiasm for internationalism with the idea of war as the renewer of life, with conflict as the supreme law. This unsubstantiated ideology of power and unity did not look for its historical basis in the free assent and choice of the citizen. Far from it—inescapable, inherited destiny, it was said, fettered each individual to the nation, whether he wanted to be or not. From this point it was a speedy transition to the 'blood and soil' theories of National Socialism. True, such sentiments were unable to dominate the political scene before 1914, but they were widespread among the people and were a potential danger for the future. Even the 'Germanic' content of Wagner's operas, which Hitler was to take under his wing, played a part in the transformation of public opinion.

The role played by the alleged militarism of the Germans is much disputed. It was certainly not a decisive role, if by militarism is meant military aggression. But it is true that the example and traditions of Prussia, a state which was to a large extent modelled on military lines, exercised a profound influence on the social structure and prestige of the Second Reich. The army was looked upon as the nation's school: the status of an officer in the reserve raised the social position of a civilian; military ways of thought dominated the political views of large sections of the community. Later, the aggressive ideology of National Socialism was to suit the militarist tendencies of the populace, and Hitler found it much easier than Mussolini did to win over the army to his cause. Nevertheless, speaking broadly, the importance of the Prussian military element in the German character, compared with Hitler's Austrian and pan-German concepts, must not be over-estimated. It was *against* the Prussian solution (i.e. a Bismarckian state that *excluded* a large part of the German nation, Austria), that Hitler's expansionist efforts were primarily directed. And it is no mere chance that the true precursors of the National Socialist Party arose at the beginning of the century, not in Prussia, but in Austria and Bohemia, where antisemitism and anti-Slav nationalism was specially violent, fostered by members of the middle and working classes and even of the clergy. Obscure sects in Vienna carried on a mystical 'Germanic' cult, in a region where, not Protestant and Prussian, but Roman Catholic and pan-German creeds were prevalent.

### The Kaiser's Huns
Over this country ruled a man whose light-minded self-confidence in military and foreign affairs, which had been held in check by Bismarck but which was now bolstered by Germany's growing economic strength and political importance, was made obvious to all the world in the summer of 1900. In his famous Bremerhaven speech to the German contingent being despatched to assist in the crushing of the Chinese Boxer Rising, Wilhelm II blared out: 'Give no quarter! Take no prisoners! Anybody who falls into your hands must be destroyed. Just as a thousand years ago Attila's Huns made a reputation for ruthless violence that still resounds through the ages, so let the name of Germans, through your actions in China, acquire a similar reputation that will last for a thousand years, so that never again will a Chinaman dare to look even askance at a German.'

Such was the origin of the term 'Huns' which was generally applied to Germans during the First World War. And barely a year after the China episode Wilhelm demonstrated his out-of-date autocratic feelings when, on the occasion of the inauguration of new barracks in March 1901, he proclaimed his soldiers to be the King of Prussia's bodyguards, in direct contravention of all democratic rights: 'And if the city of Berlin, once again as in 1848, rebels against the King with insolence and insubordination, then you, my grenadiers, are called upon to rout such insolent and insubordinate people at the point of the bayonet.'

Such speeches reveal the deep discrepancy between the semi-autocratic Wilhelmine system and the political and social realities of the times. A great modern state in which liberals and socialists were in the majority was being governed at the beginning of the 20th century according to the ideas and forms of a pre-industrial and pre-democratic autocracy. Wilhelmine Germany, though a great power, was not governed on a politically rational system capable of holding in check the Kaiser, the military, and the industrial imperialists.

Successive governments after Bismarck's departure were weak, devoid of thoughtful political leadership. The chancellor and his colleagues were dependent on the Emperor, not responsible to the Reichstag, and swayed by a public opinion that constantly and feverishly demanded that Germany, too, should enjoy the advantages already gained by the other powers. Economically Germany had recently attained the rank of the second industrial power in Europe, close behind Great Britain. But its political status depended on whether good relations with Great Britain and Russia, which were the basis of Bismarck's policy, could be maintained. The government's chief task should have been to prevent a coalition against Germany and, above all, to keep the peace.

Internally, the government's aim should have been to safeguard further development by modernizing the reactionary political system and by fostering parliamentarianism and democracy. In all these duties Wilhelmine Germany failed. Of course it was not simply and solely the fault of the talkative, boastful, vacillating Wilhelm. It was rather the mental and political climate of the period which made a character like Wilhelm II's at all possible. It is in the light of such conditions that one must give a verdict on the political events in Germany at the turn of the century, and it was these conditions chiefly that gave rise to the pre-war crises and ultimately to the outbreak of the First World War.

### Blunders and bravado
The first wrong decision, immediately after the fall of Bismarck, was the failure, in 1891, to renew the Reinsurance Treaty he had made with Russia. This failure left the way free for an alliance between Paris and Moscow—the alliance that was to form the nucleus for a coalition against Germany. Germany, involved in the conflicts of modern imperialism and trying to rival the established colonial powers, soon found itself in opposition to Great Britain. True, there was often much friction between London and Paris, some of it arising from quarrels over the division of the world into colonies. But the policy of Germany was such that in a few years her relations with Great Britain were badly strained by a series of actions in which once again the self-glorifying Kaiser played a prominent part, and the chance of exploiting Great Britain's quarrels with France was lost.

In January 1896 Wilhelm II, in a congratulatory telegram to President Kruger of the Transvaal, openly intervened in the Anglo-Boer conflict in distant Africa. Still more damaging was the interview the Kaiser gave to the London *Daily Telegraph* in October 1908, in which he vastly increased British distrust of Germany by accusing the British government, press, and people of rejecting the olive branch that he was proffering. His clumsiness aroused a storm of indignation even in Germany. But it showed more clearly than ever the flaws in a political system which could not give suitable advice to the monarch, and exercise proper control over him, and could guarantee neither political

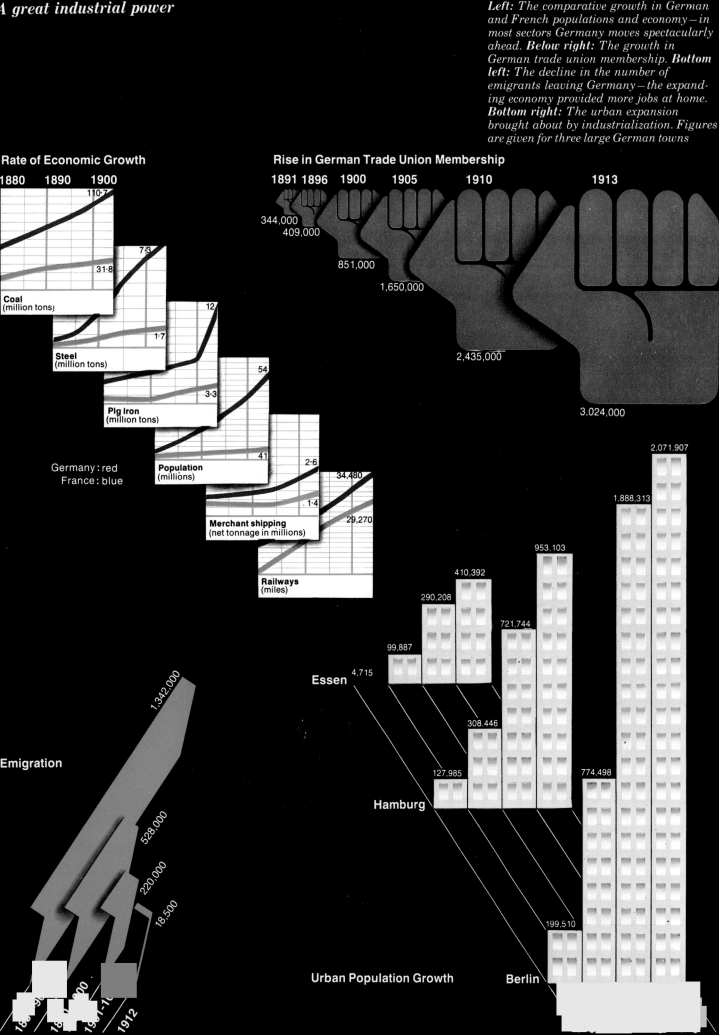

# A great industrial power

*Left: The comparative growth in German and French populations and economy—in most sectors Germany moves spectacularly ahead. Below right: The growth in German trade union membership. Bottom left: The decline in the number of emigrants leaving Germany—the expanding economy provided more jobs at home. Bottom right: The urban expansion brought about by industrialization. Figures are given for three large German towns*

## Rate of Economic Growth

1880    1890    1900

110·7

**Coal**
(million tons)

7·3

31·8

**Steel**
(million tons)

12

1·7

**Pig iron**
(million tons)

54

3·3

**Population**
(millions)

41

2·6

**Merchant shipping**
(net tonnage in millions)

34,480

1·4

29,270

**Railways**
(miles)

Germany : red
France : blue

## Rise in German Trade Union Membership

1891  1896   1900      1905        1910              1913

344,000

409,000

851,000

1,650,000

2,435,000

3,024,000

## Emigration

1,342,000

528,000

220,000

18,500

## Urban Population Growth

Essen    4,715    99,887    290,208    410,392    721,744    953,103

Hamburg    127,985    308,446    774,498

Berlin    199,510    1,888,313    2,071,907

responsibility at home nor well-considered policies abroad.

### Fear of 'encirclement'

The result was the road to isolation and a growing fear of 'encirclement'. Many Germans began to believe that in the long run the only way to assert itself in a 'world of enemies' was by a preventive war. The truth is that Germany's own policy, with its vacillations and uncertainties, and the ambition of the German expansionists, opened the way to a west-east counter-alliance. In the autumn of 1898 a colonial dispute in Africa brought France and Great Britain to the brink of war at Fashoda, but the agreement of 1904 whereby France gave up claims in Egypt and East Africa in return for a free hand in Morocco created the basis for the *entente cordiale*. Furthermore Russia, after its large-scale imperialistic advance towards the Far East was blocked by Japan in 1904-05, and now turned its attention again to Europe. The Balkans, too, were a powder magazine liable to explode any moment into a conflict with Austria-Hungary, which was Germany's sole ally apart from the very doubtful Italy. Finally, there was not a shadow of doubt as to France's wish to reverse the loss of Alsace-Lorraine.

Though Germany's situation worsened from year to year, there is no doubt that its interests lay wholly in the maintenance of peace. Nevertheless, self-confidence based on the easy victories of 1870 began to fill the minds of the Germans. They resolved to strengthen their defences in Europe and throughout the world, and, driven by longings for prestige, they became more and more sensitive in their dealings with the established powers who were more firmly seated in the saddle of imperialist politics. Thus German nationalism grew from year to year, and the vacillating and aimless policy of Wilhelm II was not calculated to guide the country into the channels of sober diplomacy and peaceful development. What was worse, as internal reform faltered, and the problems of democratizing the state and giving socialism its proper share in the government remained unsolved, outward pressures increased.

Two more wrong decisions hastened the fateful process. In Morocco Germany tried to block French colonial policy. The results were the Moroccan crises of 1905 and 1911, which brought Germany a further loss of prestige and increased its isolation. In its relations with Great Britain Germany announced its intention to launch a great navy in order to dispute Great Britain's naval supremacy. True, Germany was not increasing its armaments to a much greater extent than its neighbours. But in noisy pronouncements it boasted of its growing military might, thereby increasing the alarm of its potential opponents and provoking counter-measures. The clearest example of this mistaken attitude was the growth of the navy which Admiral von Tirpitz was carrying out at vast expense and with much braggadocio.

It has long ago been shown that Germany's fatal course in foreign affairs was accompanied by a still more damaging backwardness in its internal policies. The inability of the political system to adapt itself to inevitable change by reform, its complete involvement in Bismarckian ideas, in grotesque contrast with the economic development of the empire, were the chief causes of the decay of German politics after the turn of the century.

The mixture of helplessness and aggression that characterized Germany at this period was manifested also in the strategic planning of Count von Schlieffen, chief of the general staff. The essence of the

*Right: French view of Wilhelm. His pretensions as a warlord, his love of display and publicity, and his ambitions to find Germany 'a place in the sun' are all caricatured. Even his withered left arm has not escaped attention*
*Below: Military pageantry of the German empire: Prussian and Bavarian generals ride past in an imperial review*

French view of Wilhelm. His pretensions as a warlord, his love of display and publicity, and his ambitions to find Germany 'a place in the sun' are all caricatured. Even his withered left arm has not escaped attention

Schlieffen Plan, which envisaged a two-front war against France and Russia, considered inevitable at the time, consisted of a lightning stroke aimed at the occupation of France by means of an encircling attack from the north. The acceptance of this plan involved a march through Belgium, and at the same time it promoted the view that foreign policy must be determined by military necessity. From the fetters thus laid upon its foreign policy Germany was unable to free itself, when the final crisis came in 1914.

The internal problems of the Wilhelmine empire can be reduced to the single formula: vast material development leading to pressing demands, both at home and abroad. These problems had to be tackled by a regime that was both backward and immovable. And it was at its most reactionary in Prussia itself, which held the dominant position within the empire. Prussia comprised three-fifths of the Reich, its king was the German Emperor, its minister-president was the imperial chancellor. In Prussia a special three-class electoral system prevented the electorate from giving a unanimous vote on any particular issue, and, worst of all, it prevented the workers' movement (by now the strongest political force in the country) from being incor-

porated into the political system. The German monarchy was chained to an historical way of life that no longer corresponded to modern political and social forces. It was a sheer obstacle to the tendency of the times, the needs of which were progress and democracy in all walks of life.

In the eyes of the Western powers, Germany and its ally Austria presented the picture of a petrified, undemocratic structure. True, the German economy was highly prosperous, even under an antiquated mode of government. But while political modernization fell behind economic and social progress, the tensions between the various classes in the country grew under the personal rule of Wilhelm II until they were ready to explode. The reverses that the Kaiser's dilettante actions experienced —the worst being the *Daily Telegraph* affair—sobered him somewhat, but the cracks in the Kaiser-based structure became more and more apparent: the consequences were first war, then revolution.

There were indeed clear-sighted critics, not merely on the left, who pointed out the dangerous discrepancies and demanded an adaptation of the Bismarckian system to altered conditions. One such person was Friedrich Naumann, the liberal-socialist

politician, who had a scheme for a democratic monarchy. But it was pure illusion to imagine that slight modifications to the conservative empire of 1871 would enable it to solve the problems of a great modern state. The Reichstag, too, was a failure, inasmuch as its demands for reform and parliamentarianism were not forceful enough. The Social Democratic Party, though rapidly growing, was for the Kaiser, as for Bismarck, a movement of the 'enemies of the Reich' and 'unpatriotic rascals'. Even the liberals, who represented the wealthy industrialists, were refused full political representation.

The mass of the citizens of Germany willingly accepted a secondary role. For them the memory of the 1870 victory and Bismarck's foundation of the empire was still vivid, and they willingly conformed to the conservative Prussian form of government. They were intensively preoccupied with their economic progress and with their hopes and dreams of the expansion of German power within Europe. It was primacy in foreign affairs that they wanted: they forgot the demands of the constitutional liberal-democratic movement of 1848. But the foreign policy of Germany had now fallen far below the level to which Bismarck had raised it. Bismarck's share in the subsequent failure was his ruthless manipulation of an antiquated internal political system. The empire of 1871 had been based on the specific personal relations between Bismarck and Wilhelm I. When this association had gone, the German political system was left fully exposed to the defects in the imperial structure. It was unable to carry the burden of a complicated foreign policy towards West and East, nor could it resist either the demands of the German imperialists or the dynamism of the democratic movement towards emancipation.

### Bourgeois dreams

Wilhelm II's Germany, in both its strength and its weaknesses, was bolstered by the mentality of the German bourgeoisie, whose thoughts were permeated not so much by conscious aggressiveness towards other countries as by admiration for success. The dream of being ennobled, or at

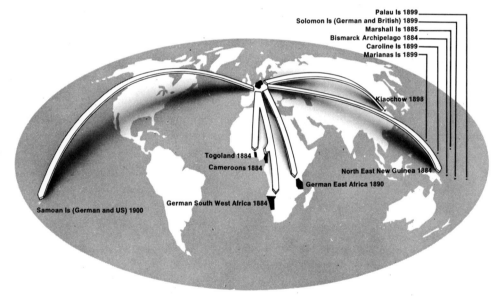

Palau Is 1899
Solomon Is (German and British) 1899
Marshall Is 1885
Bismarck Archipelago 1884
Caroline Is 1899
Marianas Is 1899

Kiaochow 1898

Togoland 1884
Cameroons 1884
North East New Guinea 1884
German East Africa 1890
German South West Africa 1884
Samoan Is (German and US) 1900

*Above: The Overseas expansion of the German empire. One way in which Germany expressed herself as a great power was by gaining colonies. But Germany was never satisfied with what she gained. By the time she set out to obtain 'a place in the sun' most of the best areas had been incorporated in the British and French empires. The frustration caused by Germany's second-class empire contributed to the aggressiveness of her foreign policy*
*Right: German officers—the elite of the German empire, who were looked up to by all classes. With the Prussian king as German Emperor and the Prussian minister-president as the imperial chancellor, German society was permeated by the ideals of Prussian militarism. The result was a stiff-necked conventionality and a disastrous narrowing of political and mental outlooks*

least of becoming an officer in the reserve, helped to mould the political views of the average citizen so as to accord with a semi-absolute monarchy and to break the spearhead of the liberals' struggle for liberty. Democratic socialism was looked upon as the enemy of the state, not its ally, and the middle classes helped to suppress it. Under the influence of the successful *Realpolitik* of 1866 and 1870-71 a foreign policy that brought military victories silenced demands for freedom in home affairs. In the security conferred by the Second Reich the chief concern of the bourgeoisie was money-making: expanding trade and a successful foreign policy were everything. Politics came to be synonymous with administration. In home affairs the best policy was good administration. Politics were best left to the professional civil servants, so that one could devote oneself wholly to business. Friedrich Meinecke, the historian, who had slowly progressed from Prussian conservatism to a democratic rationalism, summed

Zentral Bibliothek, Zurich

Snark

Südd. Verlag Munich

*Above left: 'The new Hercules'. Swiss cartoon of Wilhelm resisting the Social Democratic serpent. The Social Democratic Party was well-organized, but to Bismarck and Kaiser Wilhelm the Socialists were 'enemies of the Reich' and 'unpatriotic rascals'. Above: Five-mark stamp. Left: Officers' wives in regimental dress*

up the situation in his bitter words of 1945:

'Time and again, in the period when the empire was being founded, the bad side of Prussian militarism, so dangerous for the welfare of the whole community, retreated in face of the impressive demonstration of its power and discipline in the service of national unity. Militarism was endowed with an air of dedication. The Prussian lieutenant stalked through the land like a young god, the bourgeois lieutenant of reserve like a demi-god. One had to be a reserve officer to carry full weight in the upper-middle class, especially in the civil service. Militarism permeated the whole of bourgeois life, together with a conventional Prussianism and a naive and conceited admiration for the Prussian way of life. . . . This helps us to understand the effect of the maudlin Potsdam comedy of 21st March 1933, presented by Hitler to President Hindenburg before the coffin of Frederick the Great. National Socialism was to make its appearance on the stage of history as heir and propagator of all the best Prussian traditions.'

In Wilhelm II's Germany, then, lay all the elements and the roots of impending disaster. *(Translation)*

# World War I 1914-1918

## INTRODUCTION

Addressing an audience at the London Guildhall, on 9th July 1914, the British Chancellor, David Lloyd George, spoke eloquently of the improvement in international relations, especially Anglo-German relations, in recent months. 'The sky', he proclaimed, 'has never seemed more perfectly blue'. Even a crisis as alarming as the assassination of the Austrian Archduke, Franz Ferdinand and his wife, by Gavrilo Princip at Sarajevo in Bosnia on 30th June had not disturbed the prevailing optimism that the long era of international peace, dating from the Treaty of Berlin in 1878, would continue. Later historians have described the tensions underlying the apparent calm of Europe before 1914, how it had been divided into two 'armed camps' by 1907 with the Triple Alliance of the central powers, Germany, Austria-Hungary and Italy, matched by the Triple Entente of Britain, France and Tsarist Russia. The Balkan wars of 1912–13 were seen as an ominous portent. Such phenomena as the struggle for markets in strategic areas like the Middle East, North Africa and Latin America; the naval rivalry between Britain and Germany; the continuing tension between France and Germany along the Rhine; the conflict between Austrian expansionism and Balkan nationalism, supported by Russian Pan-Slavs, in South-East Europe—all these factors were cited by later writers to suggest a world plunging into turmoil at an ever-increasing speed. The war psychosis revealed by such alarmist literature as *How the Germans Took London* was also much quoted after 1918 to illustrate pre-war jingoism. 'Blood, blood was in the air', wrote the American, Mabel Dodge. This was not at all how most contemporaries saw things. The rush towards world war between 30th June and 4th August 1914 took almost everyone by surprise, despite the long and detailed preparations of most of the military chiefs. Germany had her own internal problems, notably the power of the Social Democrats in the Reichstag. France was involved in industrial unrest. Britain faced civil war over home rule for Ireland. Russia's ungovernability seemed as acute as ever.

Suddenly, a bewildering chain of events gave hideous reality to the previously theoretical time-tables of the various armies. Austria-Hungary's intransigent response to the Serbian note after the Sarajevo assassina-tion led to war between her and Serbia. Russia was inevitably sucked in to aid the Slav cause, thus bringing the alliance between Germany and Austria into play, and Germany declared war on Russia. In turn, France mobilized her reserves and declared war on Germany on 3rd August. After this, few seriously expected Britain to remain aloof, and Edward Grey, her foreign secretary, was able to use the German invasion of Belgium as a *casus belli*. By 5th August, of the major European powers, only Italy remained non-belligerent. The war, for which minute preparation had been made for twenty years, which public opinion never really expected to occur, had started. The prevailing view was that it would be short and sharp, like the Franco-Prussian war of 1870, with hostilities safely over by Christmas. In fact, war was to drag on for four terrible years and more, sucking in half the population of the globe.

The resources of the adversaries in August 1914 dictated their strategy. Germany had a massive, highly trained army, with reserves that would soon produce a military force of almost eight million men. They were backed by the most powerful economic machine in Europe, with huge mineral resources, a superb transport system and rapidly accelerating industrial production. Austria-Hungary was weaker and divided by ethnic rivalries, but it could bring over three million men to arms. Its chief of staff, von Hötzendorff, was already preparing his armies for swift offensives into Serbia. On the other hand, the Central Powers were facing attack on two fronts, and were at a disadvantage at sea where their supplies were vulnerable to naval blockade. They wanted above all a short, sharp contest: hence Germany's Schlieffen plan for invading France through Belgium. Against them, the Entente had more dispersed resources. Russia, with her population of 167 million, was hardly short of manpower, but the war with Japan in 1904–5 had shown up her military weaknesses. France's military capacity had been rapidly built up after the war of 1870–1, based on national conscription and much technical sophistication in fire power; but her economic reserves were relatively meagre, and her officer corps antiquated in ideas. Britain had the largest fleet in the world, and still claimed to be invincible. Yet her resources for a continental land war were uncertain: the mobiliz-ing of the British Expeditionary Force (B.E.F.) in August 1914, soon to see desperate action at Mons, was in itself a major triumph. The outcome of such a conflict was unpredictable in the extreme, but Britain and the Entente were perhaps the better equipped for a long drawn-out struggle.

The first two months of the war were dominated by the early German offensive into northern France. The initial German thrust along the Meuse and Somme almost ended the war at once; Paris was only forty miles away. The British retreated in disorder from Mons (24th August). But the desperate resistance of the French armies under Joffre and Gallieni from their *'points d'appui'* (strongholds) along the Marne in early September saved the Allied lines, and the Germans had to retreat. The battle of the Marne ensured a lasting war; in the long term it was also to ensure a German defeat. Meanwhile the B.E.F. salvaged its reputation by repelling the Germans at the first battle of Ypres (October–November), inflicting losses of perhaps 100,000 on Falkenhayn's troops. By the end of 1914, a bloody pattern of stalemate had developed along the western front, with German and Anglo-French armies confront-

*The orders of battle and campaign on the Eastern Front, August to December 1914*

*Members of the British Expeditionary Force pause in a French village in the course of one of their many exhausting marches. After his encounter with the British at Mons, Kluck gained a healthy respect for the fighting qualities of the British Expeditionary Force. He later described it as an 'incomparable army'*

ing each other in trenches on a line down from the Channel ports, along the Aisne, the Moselle and the Vosges mountains to the Swiss border.

On the eastern front, the position was equally unresolved. The early clashes between the German and Russian armies resulted in stupendous Russian losses; the vast defeat inflicted on the Russians at Tannenberg by Hindenburg and Ludendorff showed the ill-trained, immobile character of the Russian armies and the inadequacy of their generals, Samsonov and Rennenkampf. On the other hand, the Russians did inflict severe reverses on the Austrian III Army in Galicia, and captured the city of Lemberg. At the end of the year, there was a certain degree of stalemate here too, with the Germans reluctant to push much further east lest they weaken their position in the west. By the beginning of 1915, indeed, the war showed most movement beyond the confines of Europe. There were naval battles between German and British cruisers off the coast of Argentina and the Falkland Islands. There were assaults by British Empire troops against German colonies in East and South-West Africa, in Togoland and the Cameroons. In the Pacific, Japan joined the imperial countries, Australia and New Zealand, as belligerents. There were attacks on Samoa and New Guinea. Most significant of all, the expected entry of Turkey on the German side (5th November 1914) opened up a huge new theatre of war. The strategic importance of the Middle East (controlling the route to India), together with the great oil reserves of Mesopotamia and other Arab lands led to Anglo-French incursions there. In 1916 there was to be internal upheaval in the Turkish dominion as well, with Feisal and other Arab princes of the Hejaz rising up against Turkish rule, under the erratic inspiration of T. E. Lawrence. After twelve months there was fighting in every major area of the world except North America. This was indeed world war.

Inevitably, political and military leaders strove to find ways of by-passing the interminable stalemate in western Europe. There was scant prospect of breakthrough in France; the old orthodoxies of 'mobile war' were meaningless now, since machine-gun and artillery fire could easily hold off mass infantry assault, while the cavalry were almost useless. The most popular solution to trench warfare, canvassed by Lloyd George and Churchill in Britain, was to attack Germany and Austria in their 'soft underbelly'—in the Balkans and the eastern Mediterranean. These views were reinforced when Italy entered the war on the Entente side after the Treaty of London (April 1915), at first declaring war on Austria-Hungary alone. But attempts to fulfil a peripheral strategy by the 'easterners' were ill-conceived. The British expedition to the Dardanelles in 1915 was marked by a disastrous lack of co-ordination between the naval and land forces, and resulted in a humiliating withdrawal and the loss of about 200,000 allied troops. The result was to weaken severely the credibility of the 'easterners'; Churchill, in particular, was saddled with the responsibility for the Dardanelles fiasco, which diminished his military reputation for years to come. With the surrender (29th April) of an Anglo-Indian army of 13,000 to the Turks at Kut-el-Amara in Mesopotamia, the British position in the Near East, and the security of the route to India were imperilled.

For another eighteen months, the war dragged on with little real advantage accruing to either side. On the western front in 1915, new British initiatives at Neuve Chappelle, at Second Ypres and, worst of all, at Loos (15th September) were rebuffed, and undermined by lack of Anglo-French co-operation. The supplanting of Sir John French as British commander by General Haig, like the later replacement of Joffre from the French command, had little immediate effect. The main actions in France in 1916 were the bloody holocausts of Verdun and the Somme. Between February and December of that year, the French armies just held off tremendous German assaults on Verdun—but the French army was bled white, and the French became afflicted by a totally defensive mentality, symbolized by Pétain himself, the hero of Verdun. 'They shall not pass' was no motto for offensive warfare. The British attempt to assist the French with a summer offensive on the Somme (1st July) was a colossal tragedy —with over 60,000 casualties on the first day. Clearly there was no way through here. In the east, a major Russian offensive under Brusilov in eastern Galicia at first achieved a spectacular triumph in an assault around Lwow. The Austrians yielded massive territory, and lost 375,000 men as prisoners-of-war. Brusilov claimed that the war could now be rapidly won, though with Russian casualties already half a million, German reinforcements checked the Russian offensive in August. Meanwhile, in June, in the crucial naval encounter of the war, at the Battle of Jutland, the British Grand Fleet emerged with severe losses. Although its vaunted superiority was now open to serious question, the encounter meant that the German High Seas fleet did not venture forth again. The sole Allied diplomatic achieve-

ment proved equally fruitless. After the final surrender of Serbia, Rumania entered the war on the side of the Allies in August, but with scant reward. Its armies foolishly struck north, and were cut to pieces by Falkenhayn in Transylvania. Here again, peripheral offensives led only to the stalemate of attrition.

Attention focused increasingly on the psychological, social, economic and political resources of the various belligerent powers, for it was clear that in a total war, not merely armies, but also societies and civilizations were engaged in conflict. The First World War was the first to use mass psychological warfare—hence the importance of newspapers, censorship, and other methods of influencing mass opinion. Enthusiasm for the war was astonishingly persistent, despite the casualties. The French, including even long-standing socialists like Viviani, responded whole-heartedly to the cry of the *Union Sacrée*; pacifists were ruthlessly suppressed. Britain made extensive use of the control of information. Indeed, the impact of German 'zeppelin' raids and food shortages which led to rationing made the home population all the more devoted to the 'patriotic' cause. Stories about German atrocities were widely circulated, while the legendary heroism of Nurse Cavell, executed for helping Allied prisoners-of-war to escape, added to the prevalent belief in the 'frightfulness' of 'the Hun', the 'road hog of Europe', as Lloyd George called him. In Germany, with war on two fronts, opinion was no less nationalistic. Socialist critics such as the Spartacists headed by Rosa Luxembourg made little impact. German propaganda dwelt on the inhumanity of the British naval blockade, and on episodes like Britain's suppression of the Irish republican uprising in Dublin in Easter 1916. In all the major belligerent countries (except, significantly, Russia) war fever, not war weariness, was the rule. Equally uniform were the social and economic effects of total war. In all countries, 'war socialism' of a new kind resulted, with the 'autarky' of national self-sufficiency (shown in German *ersatz* products), new state controls on production, distribution and manpower, and a general drift towards collectivism. War was producing vast social changes—perhaps even making Marx's prophecies come true. It

*War takes wings: death falls from the air. 'Bombing by night' by François Flameng*

*Victim at Jutland—the German battle-cruiser* Seydlitz, *torn by a British shell*

brought new opportunities for women (who gained the vote in Britain at long last), and new social reforms in relation to housing, education and working conditions. Warfare and welfare went hand in hand. Wages went up, working hours went down, trade unions became more powerful. For millions of working men and women in Britain, France and Germany, it was a good war.

War also brought a new style of political leadership. The old boundaries between civilian and military authority largely disappeared. In Germany, a military dictatorship arose which made a mockery of the careful political balance that Bismarck had devised. By the end of 1916, Ludendorff and Hindenburg were virtual military dictators, dismissing two foreign secretaries and even the chancellor, Bethmann Hollwegg. In France, parliamentary liberties were preserved with difficulty. Joffre was dismissed as commander after Verdun, to be followed successively by Nivelle, Pétain and Foch. In November 1917, Georges Clemenceau, the very symbol of a French fight to a finish, became prime minister, with increased powers. In Britain, Lloyd George (previously a highly successful Minister of Munitions) succeeded Asquith as prime minister in December 1916: Asquith's reputation had been weakened earlier in the year by his mishandling of the Easter rebellion in Ireland. Lloyd George now set up a new War Cabinet of five to run the war. In each case, the executive triumphed over the legislative; party politics were eclipsed; a new type of politician-businessman of the type of Walter Rathenau and Sir Eric Geddes emerged. Under such leadership, the major belligerents seemed as committed as ever to unconditional victory.

Early in 1917, however, the war took a dramatic turn in the east. The overthrow of the hated Tsarist tyranny in Russia had long been expected; but it was the economic and social chaos which followed the checking of the Brusilov offensive that provided the final spark. There were widespread strikes, the virtual breakdown of government and the murder of the Tsar's sinister adviser, Rasputin. Nevertheless the overthrow of Tsar Nicholas and the proclamation of a new republic by the state Duma in February 1917 came like thunderbolts. The Tsar fled and was soon to

be murdered. During the spring and summer, various radical and socialist groups contended for power. Government, nominally in the hands of the Social Revolutionary, Kerensky, who was anxious to prosecute the war, really rested in the hands of the Petrograd 'soviet' of workers and soldiers' councils. Finally in the 'ten days' of October, the small Bolshevik wing of the Social Democratic party, under its relatively obscure leader, V. I. Lenin, recently returned from exile in Switzerland, seized power decisively. Kerensky's Provisional government was overthrown in favour of a new regime, controlled initially by the all-Russian Congress of Soviets and finally by the Central Committee of the Communist party. Lenin and Trotsky made clear their intention of withdrawing Russia from 'an imperialist war'.

At the same time, the war extended to the New World. Since August 1914, the United States had been firmly neutral. President Wilson had seen himself as the world's peacemaker, and had upheld America's traditional isolationism under the long-standing terms of the Monroe Doctrine. He fought, and narrowly won, the 1916 presidential election, as 'the man who kept us out of the war'. Yet the involvement of the US was inevitable. From 1914 on, the US shipped immense quantities of arms and other supplies to the British and French, apart from extending huge credit loans to them; in addition, American public opinion was largely pro-Allies. There were dangerous clashes with Germany on the high seas, like the sinking of the *Lusitania* in May 1915, with many Americans among the 1,200 who lost their lives. This was followed by the destruction of American merchant vessels by German U-boats. Nationalists like Theodore Roosevelt demanded American intervention; but a *casus belli* that affected American national and hemispheric security was needed. The all-out U-boat war proclaimed in early 1917, followed by an almost-incredible scheme (enclosed in the so-called Zimmerman telegram) to invade the US through Mexico, provided the stimulus. With only a few critics in the Mid-West, Wilson led an enthusiastic nation and Congress into war in April 1917. America's emergence as a world power was thus confirmed. The harnessing of America's immense resources on the Allied side meant that in the long term Germany's cause must be hopeless.

For much of 1917 and 1918 Germany attempted to secure a decisive advantage in Europe before the power of the United States was felt. There were still hopeful omens for the Kaiser. Although the British Third Army had captured Vimy Ridge, the new French offensive under Nivelle collapsed disastrously in April–May 1917 in the hills of Champagne near Rheims; Pétain had to assume command in order to restore discipline and morale after mutinies in the French armies. As a result, the French were unable to mount any offensive for many months afterwards. The British offensive, in the late summer under Haig at Passchendaele, fared even worse; about 300,000 men were lost, many of them drowned after torrential rain. The British army was equally incapable of mounting an offensive now, even with the mechanized 'tanks' at its disposal. (It was not until the battle of Cambrai in November that

mass tanks were successfully used for a break-through.) Further, incessant bitter conflicts between Lloyd George and Haig weakened the supreme command and led to recriminations about the shortage of reinforcements. In the south, high in the Julian Alps, the Italian army under Cadorna was ruthlessly crushed near Caporetto, and forced on to a desperate defensive. In the east, Germany had huge territorial gains in Poland and White Russia (imposed on the Russian negotiators by the Treaty of Brest Litovsk in March 1918). The overall military advantage still rested with Germany. Only in the Near East, where Allenby's empire troops conducted an efficient and controlled campaign against the Turks, capturing successively Gaza, Jaffa and finally Jerusalem, could the Allied forces claim any military successes. Elsewhere the outlook was grim.

On the other hand, the Germans found it difficult to deliver a 'knock-out blow' to Europe before the full impact of American strength was felt. Their main effort was in March 1918, when Ludendorff launched a massive offensive (the 'St Michael Plan') near Amiens and Arras, in northern France. The British were pushed back over the Somme and withdrew at Flesquières. They retreated in good order, however, while fatigue slowed up the German advance and no decisive gains were made. At sea, the British were able to protect their merchant vessels with the convoys which had been forced upon a reluctant Admiralty by Lloyd George. In the air, British and French planes had checked German armies with ground-strafing, and British bombers now launched

*The Brusilov Offensive. The main thrust towards Lutsk and Kovel sent the Austrians reeling, but Evert failed to attack on the West Front*

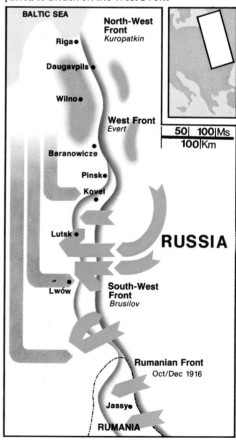

successful day and night raids on factories in the Ruhr. Most heartening of all was the fact that, by June 1918, American troops under Pershing's command, were crossing the Atlantic in vast strength; their first notable victory was won at Château Thierry (1st–2nd June).

The Turkish position in Palestine was crumbling fast. In the east, the position was obscure with 'Red' and 'White' Russian armies engaged in civil war; there could be no obvious German advantage here. Serious doubts arose about the continuing will to fight of Germany's Austrian allies, and there had been secret peace-feelers between British emissaries and the Austrian emperor, Karl. Worst of all, even Germany's own resolve to fight appeared to be weakening. The German population was suffering acutely from the Allied blockade of food supplies, and this was reflected in a 'peace' resolution in the Reichstag in July 1917. The Spartacist and Independent Socialist critics of the war were gaining ground. The scent of German defeat was in the air.

Nevertheless, in the summer of 1918 it was still widely believed that the war would drag on until 1920, when the full potential of American strength would be felt. Then, in August, a series of dramatic blows in different sectors knocked away the 'props' from under the Central Powers. Allenby, assisted by Lawrence and his Arab cohorts, swept on remorselessly towards Syria, decisively crushing the Turks at Megiddo (18th–20th September). The French general, Franchet d'Esprey, was equally victorious in Bulgaria; and at long last Anglo-French troops were able to break out of the bridgehead at Salonika in Greece. The Italians girded themselves for a new assault in the northern Appenines, and threw back the Austrian armies at Vittorio Veneto after ten days' fighting on the Piave. Germany's allies now melted away. Turkey and Bulgaria in turn were suing for peace. Austria-Hungary was likely to follow suit, for her ramshackle dominion was splitting up into its component ethnic parts, with new nationalist leaders, like the Czech Jan Masaryk, emerging in Slovak, Czech, Hungarian and Slav lands. Most decisive of all was the sudden collapse of Ludendorff's position on the western front after the German armies had failed to find a way through in May and June. Then on 8th August—known thereafter as 'Germany's black day'—British and empire troops, backed up by 600 tanks and covered by fighter planes, broke through near Amiens, crossed the Somme and pushed on towards the Rhine. The supposedly impregnable barrier of the Hindenburg line was breached in early September, with British assaults assisted by bad visibility. The German army was now in general retreat, many of the rank and file deserting to form soldiers' 'soviets' of their own. Austria-Hungary sued for peace on 27th October. The military outcome of the war was clear long before the final armistice on 11th November.

Peace negotiations between the Allied leaders, Wilson, Lloyd George and Clemenceau, had been started well before the hostilities in the west were over. In these they were, to some extent, guided by Wilson's idealistic 'Fourteen Points', which aimed at creating a world based on liberty, free trade and

*T. E. Lawrence created two myths. To Englishmen he became an ambiguous hero. To Arabs he offered a vision of unity that carried them to Damascus and helped Allenby defeat the Turks*

national self-determination. But negotiations had been pre-empted by the secret treaties of the war years—revealed to an astounded world by Lenin in January 1918. The Sykes-Picot treaty, for example, carved up much of the Middle East into British and French spheres of influence, the oil reserves of Syria being granted to France, those of Mesopotamia to Britain; meanwhile a 'Jewish national home' was mooted, to the fury of Arabs everywhere. *Realpolitik*, backed up by inflamed nationalism, would determine the course of the peacemakers: this was illustrated in miniature by the determination of 'Billy' Hughes of Australia to retain German New Guinea in defiance of world opinion. Woodrow Wilson's aims were ambiguous, for his idealistic commitment to the 'Fourteen Points' conflicted with a moral conviction that Germany and its rulers shared an ineradicable war guilt, and should be punished before the court of world opinion.

The Treaty of Versailles was the product of lengthy negotiations in January–July 1919. The attitudes of the peacemakers were more complex than has often been assumed. Although Clemenceau voiced French resolve that Germany should never again imperil French national security, he was also anxious to preserve the alliance with Britain. Lloyd George and Wilson were both trying to reconcile pledges to their electorates with modifications that would bring the pariah nations, Germany and Russia, into the comity of nations. The voice of moderation and appeasement at Versailles was particularly that of Lloyd George, and he was not wholly unsuccessful in his endeavours. The map of Europe was re-drawn on national lines after the collapse of the historic empires of Hohenzollern, Habsburg and Romanov. The financial penalties imposed on the defeated Germans were scaled down. But there were too many contradictory forces at work, too many nationalistic passions to satisfy. In the end, it was the frontier restrictions (like the loss of the Polish corridor, Danzig, the Saar and the Rhineland to non-German regimes), the reparations terms, the enforced disarmament and the war guilt riveted on Germany which were remembered—not that Germany could survive as a proud and powerful nation.

In the east, civil war raged on, with the White Russian minority receiving increasing aid from Britain and France. Peace was yet to be concluded with Austria and Bulgaria. In fact, the First World War was not formally concluded until the Treaty of Lausanne with Turkey (July 1923). For a time, in the eastern Mediterranean, an ambitious and expansionist Greece under premier Venizelos, was left in an illusory position of dominance. The age-old 'Eastern question' was born again.

Versailles was in few respects a durable settlement. Its great new instrument of order and redemption, the League of Nations, was crippled from the start, notably by Wilson's failure to persuade the American people to accept it and its covenant. Without America, the League faced a shadowy future. Disillusion set in even while the peacemakers were negotiating: the triumphant chauvinism of November 1918 did not last long. John Maynard Keynes started a flood of anti-war literature which undermined what little authority Versailles could claim. The critics of the 'system of Versailles' won the moral argument, and helped on the appeasement of the dictators in the 1920's and 1930's. Even after the loss of eight million lives and the disruption of hundreds of millions more, the same basic world survived. Later generations would face endless and terrible problems exorcizing the demons of that world.

# Why Europe Went to War

In 1911 G. P. Gooch, an English historian who had, until the previous year, been a Liberal MP, published a little book called *History of our Time 1885-1911*. It is still worth reading, not least because its closing sentences show an optimism about international affairs which has now all but disappeared. Although, the author noted, five million men were at that moment under arms in Europe, nevertheless he said, 'we can now look forward with something like confidence to the time when war between civilized nations will be considered as antiquated as a duel, and when the peacemakers shall be called the children of God'.

In those words spoke the proud, confident, liberal, humanitarian Europe which had been built over the previous half-century. Less than three years later it was blown to the winds, and we have never quite recovered it.

It is worthwhile to recall just how great a blow was given to this confidence by the scale of what followed. The war which began on 1st August 1914, when Germany declared war on Russia, was the first of several wars which were later to be lumped together as one—the 'Great War'. The struggle between Austria-Hungary and Serbia—the expression of a deeper conflict soon to erupt between Austria-Hungary and Russia—and the war between France and Germany which quickly followed had little logic to connect them: what had Vienna to do with Alsace, or Frenchmen with the fate of Serbia? That the British, too, should then join in seemed odd to many people on both sides of the Channel. And this was only the beginning. Japan, Turkey, China, Siam—the list of those at war was to grow until it included every major state and left unrepresented no part of the globe. Thirty-two 'victorious' nations were to be represented at the Peace Conference in 1919; some of them did not even exist in 1914 and twenty-two of them were non-European. By then, Baluchis and Vietnamese had been brought to fight in France, Americans and Japanese had gone to Vladivostok, Canadians to Archangel and Australians to Palestine, while Germans and British had slaughtered one another across the oceans of the world from the coasts of Chile to the Western Approaches. The fighting only ended when, in 1922, Greeks and Turks at last made peace.

This extraordinary explosion of violence was hardly foreseen in 1914. Though many people by then feared war, few envisaged so colossal a holocaust. In part, this was because, once started, the struggle developed its own, unforeseeable logic. The two sides were nearly balanced in strength at the outset and this led to efforts to mobilize a margin of superiority which would guarantee victory and to find new allies: this intensified and spread the war. Yet much of what followed was implicit in the state of the world and, above all, of its centre, Europe, on the eve of the outbreak.

The shock of the war soon provoked a hunt for those who were guilty of starting it. This was the earliest form of the search to explain so astonishing an event. It was to go on for many years. It came out most crudely in popular catch-phrases: 'Hang the Kaiser' in Great Britain had its equivalents in other countries. But some looked for guilty men at home. Even before 1914 radicals and pacifists were attacking the Liberal government and its foreign secretary, Sir Edward Grey, for committing the country to the side of France without authorization from Parliament. Another personal, but different, criticism was made of Grey by Germans: if only he had been more explicit (it was said), if only it had been made clear that Great Britain would enter a war between France and Germany, the German government would not have gone to war.

Some people preferred to blame whole groups of men. Germans blamed the British who, they said, grudged them their place in the sun; the British detected in Germans and German history a domineering tendency. Radicals and socialists attacked rather vaguely defined 'capitalists' who, it was alleged, either by so manipulating foreign policies as to safeguard their overseas investments and trade, or by encouraging the armaments which kept their factories working and paying large dividends, had pushed the world towards war. Whatever plausibility such arguments once had, historians have swung away both from them, and from large, schematic interpretations of the origins of the war in terms of economic interest.

We now prefer to place less emphasis on personal responsibility and policy except in the case of a few, clearly identifiable and delimited, crucial decisions. We need not go so far as to say that no one was ever personally responsible for anything decisive; the actions of Wilhelm II and his military advisers would by themselves make nonsense of such a view. Nevertheless, we admit that statesmen often have less freedom to act than they think, and that circumstances are as important in shaping their decisions as their own view of what they want. If we approach the world of 1914 in this way, what was there in its nature and structure which now appears, first, to have made war likely, and then so disastrous when it came?

## The diplomatic 'system'

The international system itself has been blamed. In an age of so much quarrelling and bickering, it may seem paradoxical to speak of a 'system'. Yet there was enough awareness of common principles and practice to make it possible to use this term. Diplomats everywhere understood one another in a sense in which, perhaps, they do not today, when deep ideological differences may separate them on fundamentals. The concept of national self-interest was the accepted basis of their business. This was tempered by a broad agreement that only vital threats to a nation's self-interest or a violent outrage to its dignity (whose preservation was a part of the national interest) could justify war between great powers. If war came, it was assumed, no power would ever seek to modify fundamentally the institutions of another – there would be, that is to say, no appeal to revolution as a weapon, and peace would eventually be made on the basis of a new adjustment of enduring interests.

This framework of common assumptions was reinforced by the fact that diplomatic business was then almost exclusively the affair of professional diplomats, who had evolved a very effective *esprit de corps* and skill. In 1914 they could look back to a long succession of tragedies averted and crises survived as evidence of the success of their methods. One towering fact stood out above all: since 1871 there had been no war between two European great powers and in this sense the Continent had enjoyed its longest period of peace since the Reformation.

The 'concert of Europe', as it had been called in the 19th century, was still a reality in that the European great powers had recently still tended to act in concert to avert threats to peace. They had done this successfully many times and, of course, to most statesmen it was only the European great powers which really mattered. This was not unreasonable. Portents of a very different future could already be discerned: there *had* been a war between Russia and Japan, and the United States *had* stripped Spain of her Caribbean and Pacific possessions. But these hints of a new era of global politics did not invalidate

*Right: Franz Josef of Austria-Hungary – symbol of the old order*

the achievement of the diplomats in Europe, because in 1914 it was still Europe which determined the fate of the world.

Yet this traditional diplomatic system has itself been blamed for the disaster. In one sense, this is a truism: war did break out in 1914 and the old diplomacy did not stop it. Many students of the crisis have concluded that the statesmen who were trying to deal with the crisis were too much imprisoned by their conventional assumption and too unwilling to step outside their usual framework of ideas to be able to dominate affairs as, perhaps, a Bismarck might have done. This is a charge which it is easier to make than to prove or disprove. What may fairly be observed is that conventional diplomacy assumed that the aims of the great powers were rational and moderate enough for negotiation to bring about their reconciliation one with another – and this was no longer possible when some of these powers had come to believe, as they had done by 1914, that their very existence was at stake.

Yet it is not usually on this basis that the old diplomacy has been attacked. More usually, it has been asserted that there was a defect in the international machine itself which made conflict in the end inevitable, and this has been identified as the 'nightmare of alliances' which Bismarck had so feared and which was an almost all-embracing reality in 1914. It had by then long been pointed out that the alliances introduced a dangerously mechanical and deterministic element into international life: once one cog began to turn, would not, in the end, the whole machine have to follow? Those who feared this thought mainly of two alliances: the Franco-Russian, signed in 1894, and the Triple Alliance of Germany, Austria-Hungary, and Italy, formed in 1882 and later modified and adhered to by Rumania. By them, it was said, Europe was divided into two armed camps, and the chance of war was immeasurably increased.

This is too simple. Qualifications are needed. The Triple Alliance, for example, was far from firm. Italy was not to enter the war on her allies' side in 1914 and by then it was well known in Vienna and Berlin that Rumania could not be depended upon. Both countries eventually went to war – but on the other side. The Franco-Russian treaty, too, had originally been made as a basis for co-operation against Great Britain. Its terms, so far as they concerned Germany, were consequential upon German action. Only if Germany attacked Russia was France to come to the aid of her ally; in the end the alliance never came into action at all because the Germans settled the question of France's involvement by attacking her. Similarly, the *entente cordiale* by no means pointed irresistibly towards a Franco-British alliance against Germany. In 1911, Agadir had certainly aroused feeling and had strengthened the informal ties between London and Paris. Yet this, too, was a paradoxical outcome, since the French government of the day was one which had hoped to cultivate better relations with Germany. By 1914 the British had got over their alarm at

the Germans' battleship-building, and down almost to the eve of the war Anglo-German relations were better than they had been for twenty years.

Nor did European alliances determine the extent of the conflict. Although the Great War was to be focused on Europe and make its impact on world history through the damage it did to Europe, it was to be a world-wide war. Great Britain's participation made this inevitable, but there were other reasons for it, too. Tradition, geography, and domestic politics all made it inconceivable that the United States should join in European quarrels in 1914, but two other non-European states – Japan and Turkey – did become involved.

Japan's position in 1914 cut right across the pattern of European alliances. She was the only formal ally of the British, who had turned to her because of their traditional fear of Russia in Asia and the threat to their interests posed by the seeming break-up of China. The alliance was crowned by the Japanese victory over Russia in 1905. Two years later, an Anglo-Russian convention attempted to clear up some of the delicate problems which still divided London and St Petersburg. Yet by 1914 the two states were bickering over Persia much as they had always done. It was not, in other words, formal alliances which brought about the paradoxical situation at the end of August 1914 in which Great Britain, Japan, and Russia stood on the same side as allies against Germany.

## Struggle for the Balkans

Turkey, too, was involved fundamentally and perhaps inevitably in the war, but hardly because of formal diplomacy. One possible name for the Great War would be the last war of the Turkish succession; eastern European history since the 17th century had been the story of attempts to allocate the booty and fill the vacuum left behind by the slow rolling-back of a Turkish power which had once embraced Hungary and lapped at the very walls of Vienna. The last stage in the dissolution of Turkey's European empire had opened in the Balkan Wars of 1912. The second

Balkan War made it clear that among the claimants to the Turkish succession – the 'new nations' which had appeared in the Balkans in the 19th century – quarrels were just as likely as between the Habsburg and Romanov dynasties which had for so long suspiciously watched one another's advances at Turkish expense.

Here, indeed, was a true seed of the war. Two great states sought power and influence in an area abandoned to feeble and bickering small states by the Turkish retreat. Inevitably, they had favourites and satellites. But Vienna and St Petersburg managed to co-operate or avoid conflict until the annexation of Bosnia-Herzegovina in 1908. Thereafter, to concern about prestige and influence in the Balkans was added fear for the Habsburg empire itself. Serbia, a Russian protégé, drew like a magnet the loyalty of the South Slav subjects of the Dual Monarchy in the recently annexed provinces. A reckoning with Serbia would have to come, it was felt in Vienna, and felt all the more strongly when Serbia gained more than a million and a half new subjects in the Balkan Wars. If the reckoning came, Russia would not be likely to leave Serbia unsupported

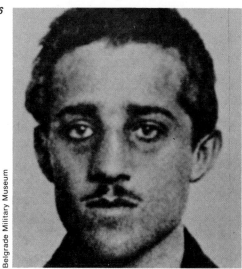

*Europe's heads of state in 1914. 1 Franz Josef of Austria-Hungary at a family wedding. 2 Kaiser Wilhelm II with the French General Foch. 3 Kaiser Wilhelm and George V of Great Britain. 4 President Poincaré (centre) of France visits Russia in 1914. 5 Kaiser Wilhelm jokes with a German general and the Austrian military attaché. 6 Gavrilo Princip, assassin of Archduke Franz Ferdinand and his wife at Sarajevo; their death led to the First World War*

in a second humiliation like that of 1909, when she had to recognize the Austro-Hungarian annexation.

Yet, Turkey's involvement at this level was remote and indirect: she was only to enter the war for very different reasons. Since 1900 German commercial and military influence had grown greatly in Constantinople. The Russians became more and more alarmed at the prospect of a re-invigorated Turkey under German influence. The old historic link between Berlin and St Petersburg, based on their common guilt in holding down the Poles, had begun to give way when Bismarck's successors decided to support the Dual Monarchy unconditionally against Russia (a crucial specific decision). It was killed by the fear of German power at the Straits. Russian hostility led the Turks to an alliance with Germany on 2nd August, 1914, the day after Germany declared war on Russia. It still took two months and the arrival of a German battle-cruiser (which guaranteed naval supremacy in the Black Sea) before Turkey took the plunge. And that meant the extension of the war to Egypt, Mesopotamia, and the Caucasus — theatres far from the provinces of Alsace and Lorraine, which had once seemed the greatest threat to European peace.

Thus, the part played in 1914 by formal alliances was small. The striking fact about the actual outbreak of war was the extent to which policy, in the end, was subordinated to questions of technique. What mattered were military plans and time-tables. In the end, the Franco-Russian alliance never came into operation at all, the entente proved too weak to take Great Britain into the war without the German invasion of Belgium, Germany's allies, Italy and Rumania, felt greater grievances against Vienna than against the entente and so stayed out, and, by a crowning irony, the contingency upon which the German-Austrian alliance had rested — a war between Russia and the Dual Monarchy — was the last and most superfluous link of all in the main chain of events. It was not until 6th August that those two empires went to war.

The failure of the diplomats, therefore, though real enough, was not pre-determined by the irresistible working of an alliance system which trapped them. Much in the traditional system, indeed, worked in precisely the opposite way in the twenty years before 1914. Not only had the well-tried resources of diplomacy avoided war over Fashoda, Morocco, Bosnia, and Agadir; they had also partitioned Africa peacefully and demarcated the interests of the powers in China. Even the aftermath of the Balkan Wars had again shown how the great powers could, if they wished, impose their will on the troublesome small.

### The failure of Liberalism

If we accept the fact that the alliances did not lead men willy-nilly into conflict, but that many different forces brought about this, we have a problem at a different level. When we have isolated the facts which made the last crucial decisions probable, and can understand the logic of the military and logistical planning which dominated the last weeks, it still remains astonishing that so many Europeans dreaded war so little and did so little to avert it. We have to explain why the comparatively few people who worked the machine should have felt so confident that their action would be endorsed by the millions they commanded.

This is all the harder to understand because the first years of this century were, for many people, the culmination of an era of liberal civilization and idealism. It had been marked by great optimism about the progressive enlightenment of international society. It was evidence of this which encouraged such men as Gooch — and there were many like him. The Hague Conferences had seemed to be the first steps towards disarmament and they had actually done something to regulate the conduct of war between civilized nations. An international peace movement existed and carried on a vigorous propaganda. The practice of international arbitration of disputes between two states had become more and more common. And even those who felt sceptical about such things could still comfort themselves with the thought that commercial and other economic ties made the disruption of international life by war between two major states almost unthinkable. Even the socialists felt confident: did not governments know that the workers of all countries would act, if necessary by strike action, to stop them going to war?

Or so it was hoped. Little attention was paid to what factors might qualify this optimism. The Second International, for example, could not actually organize collective action against war. All it could do was to conceal divisions between the socialists of different countries by vague formulae. In 1914 they meant nothing. One British socialist minister left the government and the Serbian and Russian socialists condemned the war. But that was all. As the German chancellor, Bethmann Hollweg, had hoped, Russian mobilization swung the SPD into line behind the imperial government. The socialist failure was, in a measure, symptomatic; it was only the most disillusioning of all the evidences of the helplessness of the pacifist and progressive forces so confident only a few years before. The force which overwhelmed them was old-fashioned patriotism.

This century, much more than the last, has been the great age of nationalism. More new countries have appeared since 1914 than ever before, and have been accepted as possessing the right to exist. The Great War was in this sense a great triumph of nationalism; it broke up historic and dynastic Europe to provide the new nations of the 1920's. But national feeling had already played a big part in mobilizing the psychological and emotional support which in some cases sustained and in some cases trapped governments in 1914. In every capital immense crowds greeted with enthusiasm the news that many of them were to be sent off to be killed.

Of course, the actual outbreak was a moment of excitement. Clearly, too, they did not know what was to come. By 1916 'war-weariness' and casualties would take

the steam out of patriotic enthusiasm everywhere. Yet even then there was little support anywhere for a peace that was less than victory. In retrospect this seems astonishing; no nation, after all, faced in the Great War what seemed to face Great Britain or Russia if they were defeated in 1940 or 1941. The explanation of desperation born of fear, therefore, is not enough. The strength of nationalism is the key to the inner nature of the Great War, the most popular war in history when it started, and the most democratic yet seen in the efforts it called forth as it went on.

This had not been easy to foresee. The behaviour of representative bodies is not a clear guide. The attitude of the Reichstag is not good evidence for the views of the German people and it is notable that the elections of 1914 in France (the only European great power where universal male suffrage actually worked) produced a chamber very hostile to the law of 1913 which imposed three years military service. On the other hand, the British Liberal government had more trouble with its internal and parliamentary critics than with the electorate when it undertook its great ship-building programmes.

The difficulty of knowing how to interpret such evidence as there is of mass opinion before 1914 has led to some attempts to blame the more strident examples of nationalism at that time on conscious propaganda. Some weight can be given to this, it is true. The British Navy League and the German *Flottenverein* had done much to excite popular interest in naval rivalry, for example. Winston Churchill's account of the years before 1914 in *The World Crisis* shows how wide an influence this exercised. Germans were encouraged by the publicity campaigns of their admiralty to believe that only a fleet could guarantee them British respect. This made Englishmen who had hardly given a thought to naval strategy uneasy; figures of comparative battleship strengths seemed easy to comprehend and were easy to

dramatize. In turn, British spokesmen used violent language which aroused in Germans fear of an attempt to 'Copenhagen' (the modern expression would be 'Pearl Harbor') the German fleet: that the British Admiralty might have similar fears was neither here nor there. Fear, indeed, some of it consciously inspired, must come high on the list of explanations of what happened in 1914. Fear of the consequences of a Russian victory provided the excuse German Social Democrats needed to fight for capitalist and imperialist Germany in 1914. But fear need not be the only source of acts of collective madness.

National feeling and xenophobia were, after all, not new. They had been shown more violently by the French against the British at the time of Fashoda and the Boer War than they were by the British against the Germans in 1914. What was new – or comparatively new – was the social context of nationalist feeling before 1914. Patriotism and jingoism were now widely shared, thanks to new technical and institutional facts. One of the most fundamental, paradoxically, was the immense spread of popular education since the mid-19th century. This had two important results. The first was that most education, because it was provided by the state, led

*Left: Bonds in Russian armaments companies, mainly issued before the First World War. After the end of the war, a view popular among radicals and socialists was that the armaments manufacturers helped bring about the war through their desire to sell more arms. Certainly the arms were there and ready to fight the most terrible war the world had ever known. But they were an effect rather than a cause. One of the main causes can be found in the attitudes not only of the half-educated but of the intellectuals. Below: Some of these fatal attitudes can be detected in the patriotism which supported an Empire Day celebration in the form of a great march in London, during May 1914*

*Top: This was, at its outset, perhaps the most popular war in history. Here, a German crowd greets the declaration of war by singing a patriotic song. Was one of the most enthusiastic members of the crowd Adolf Hitler (see inset face)? Certainly, like many others, he lost himself happily in a surge of warlike enthusiasm. Above: Admiral Fisher. When, in 1904, Fisher had repeatedly suggested to Edward VII the destruction of the German battle fleet in a surprise raid without the declaration of war, the King had replied: 'My God, Fisher, you must be mad.' Court circles were on the whole sympathetic to Kaiser Wilhelm and his rule*

to the spread of common attitudes and assumptions, many of them intimately linked with the nation and its symbols. Whether elementary education brought to the mass of the population the reading of patriotic poems and the singing of patriotic songs as in France and Germany, rituals about the national flag as in the United States, celebration of royal birthdays or glorification of the national past as in Great Britain, it was probably the most single powerful agency in spreading a conscious sense of national identity. And nations, traditionally, glorified their prowess in war.

The second important result was the spread of the ability to read. It is no accident that the sensational newspaper appeared in about 1900 in most western European countries as well as in the United States. Its pre-condition was a mass readership, and by that time this had been created by mass education. It was quickly associated with a stridently patriotic style of journalism, whose first-fruits were the excitement of American opinion against Spain in 1898 and the British hysteria over Mafeking. They could arouse popular excitement over international affairs, which had previously interested only a relatively small governing class.

One curious reflection of changing popular mentality was the growth of a new class of popular books about imaginary future wars. An able recent study has shown that between 1900, when there appeared *How the Germans Took London*, and 1914, when Conan Doyle's *Danger* gave a prescient account of the threat unrestricted submarine warfare would pose to Great Britain, there were something like 180 books published in the main European languages on this topic. This was roughly double the rate of the fourteen years before 1900. They were enthusiastically received everywhere.

In Germany, *Der Weltkrieg* (1904), which depicted a German conquest of Great Britain, was a best-seller. The greatest success of all was the English book of 1906, William Le Queux's *The Invasion of 1910*, which sold a million copies.

These books had great influence in forming the stereotyped ideas which filled most people's minds when they thought about international affairs. Many were zealously pushed by interested parties; Lord Roberts endorsed Le Queux's book as valuable support for the plea for compulsory military service. They also reflect shifts of opinion. In 1900 the 'enemy' in English books of this sort was still usually French. In 1903 came Erskine Childer's description of a German plan to invade England in *The Riddle of the Sands* and thereafter Germany was usually the danger which threatened. Such books prepared the popular mind for the fears and excitements which were first to sustain the big armament programmes and later to feed the hatreds used by the professional propagandists of the war years.

Another dangerous feature of pre-war society was its familiarity with violence. Most people saw something of it, if only by report. We must beware of being selective as we look back at the golden age which the years before 1914 sometimes appear to be. As J.M.Keynes, the economist, was to remark when the war was over, and the truth of his observation was obvious, the crust of civilization was very thin. In many countries there was a deep fear of revolution, which was strengthened by the social violence so common in the decade before the war. A great individual disturbance like the *Semana Trágica* in Barcelona in 1909, or the massacres attending the Russian revolution of 1905, did much to encourage such fears, but they were fed almost every day by a running current of social unrest and violence. Giovanni Giolitti, the liberal Italian prime minister, was accounted a great humanitarian idealist (or, alternatively, a poltroon) because he suggested that there might be some better way of dealing with Italy's social troubles than by force. Clemenceau made himself hated by French socialists by his ruthless strike-breaking, long before he was famous as the saviour of France. Even in Great Britain, the use of soldiers in support of the civil power was common in the years before the war.

Nor did all the violence or potential violence which faced governments come from social or economic grievance. The terrorism which broke out at Sarajevo had been for years a threat to the Habsburg empire. In Poland young revolutionaries held up post offices to obtain money for their cause. Nationalism, wherever state and nation did not coincide, was a far more violently disruptive force than class hatred. In 1914 the most striking example, indeed, was in Great Britain where the irreconcilability of two communities, the southern Irish and the Ulstermen, brought the country to the verge of civil war in 1914 and presented the world with the astonishing spectacle of leaders of the Conservative Party abetting armed resistance to laws made by Parliament.

### Fear of revolution

It has sometimes been suggested that fears and tensions arising from such sources led some people to welcome war as a means of avoiding revolution. There is something in this; certainly the Ulster crisis evaporated almost overnight when the outbreak of war removed the threat of Home Rule. It is also true that many people welcomed war through ignorance of what it would mean. This is not merely a matter of ignorance of what the results of the war would be but also of what its nature would be while it was going on. Soldiers, sailors, civilians alike all assumed, for example, that war would be short. Hardly any foresaw the destructive power of modern weapons and the casualties they would impose. That the internal combustion engine, barbed-wire, the machine-gun, and the aeroplane might revolutionize tactics was almost equally unforeseen. Above all, as the literature of imaginary wars shows, the inhumanity of 20th-century war was undreamed of. Only one writer, a Swiss, I.S.Bloch, correctly outlined the nature of the next war (one other writer, a man of genius, H.G.Wells, saw even farther ahead, and in 1913 already wrote about 'atomic bombs'). Most people assumed that war would be a sharp but short struggle of the armies and fleets.

Such ignorance made it easier for politicians to think war a simplifying release from problems otherwise almost insoluble. Revolutionaries in eastern Europe, too, sensing the damage war could do to the great empires they hated, thought the same. But it was not only ignorance of what war would bring that prepared people to accept it. One of the most surprising features of the reception of the news of the war was the enthusiasm shown not only

by the half-educated and xenophobic masses, but by intellectuals, too. It was a German economist and future minister of the Weimar republic, Walter Rathenau, who, even in 1918, remembered the outbreak as 'the ringing opening chord for an immortal song of sacrifice, loyalty, and heroism' and a great historian, Meinecke, who later looked back on it as a moment of 'profoundest joy'. A famous English example was the poet, Rupert Brooke. His enthusiastic and second-rate poem, 'Now, God be thanked Who has matched us with His hour', expresses an attitude shared by many of his contemporaries in all countries. In Italy many felt dismay at the prospect of neutrality.

Running through such responses to the war was a significant trait in pre-war culture which has too often been ignored. When it has been recognized, it has been explained as the creation of, rather than part of the background to, the Great War. This is the deliberate cultivation of values and qualities directly opposed to those of the dominant liberal civilization of the day. To the belief in reason inherited from the Enlightenment was opposed the glorification of unreason as the source of man's greatest triumphs; to liberal eulogies of the virtues of co-operation and negotiation as social techniques was opposed the teaching of those who saw conflict and violence as the dynamo of progress.

The roots of such cultural currents are very deep. The teachings of Karl Marx and Charles Darwin about the social and biological role of conflict must be counted among them. The much misunderstood but also much quoted writings of Friedrich Nietzsche were another. Some of the pioneers of the irrationalist wave, too, were not themselves aware of all the implications of what they were doing: Sigmund Freud's great onslaught on the primacy of reason was conducted in the name of scientific enquiry and therapeutic technique, and William James, whose philosophy of 'Pragmatism' won admirers in Europe in the early years of this century, was pursuing a healthy attempt to bring philosophy down to the firm earth of commonsense experience. Yet such sources fed a current deeply destructive of the assumptions of liberal civilization which made their work possible.

This came out clearly and explicitly in attempts to justify violence and irrationalism in moral or aesthetic terms. One spectacular example was the French engineer-turned-philosopher, Georges Sorel. His work, *Reflections on Violence* (1908), justified industrial action by the workers by a view of history which attributed all great achievements to violence and the heroic attitudes which were fed by struggle and myth. He despised the intellectuals and parliamentarians of his day who emasculated their civilization by directing its attention to material goals and to the rational settlement of disputes. In this he was like the Italian poet, Gabriele d'Annunzio, later to be identified by Lenin as the only true revolutionary in Italy. D'Annunzio had himself done very well out of the material goods of bourgeois society, but had joined the violent Italian nation-

alists to urge forward his countrymen to the invasion of Tripoli in 1911 as a step towards national regeneration by heroism and sacrifice.

A taste for violence was shared by other Italians. One of the oddest was the painter and poet, Marinetti, leader of the 'Futurists', who had already begun that attack on accepted aesthetic standards which culminated in Surrealism. The Tripoli adventure of 1911, he claimed, showed that the Italian government had at last become Futurist and his cultural pre-occupations increasingly drew him towards political themes. One Futurist's invention of the early weeks of the war, 'anti-neutralist' clothing, was, perhaps, only comic, but even such gestures as this registered the bankruptcy of traditional culture and traditional authority in the eyes of many of the young. The great liberal platitudes seemed to them to be cramping and stifling: they could not believe in them and strove to smash them. 'Merde à Versailles Pompei Bruges Oxford Nuremberg Toledo Benares!' proclaimed the French poet, Apollinaire, in a Futurist pamphlet. Cultural revolutionaries, like political ones, welcomed a war that promised to destroy the *status quo*.

Many middle-class people had expressed dissatisfaction with the materially satisfying but morally uninspiring world of the early 20th century. William James once said that humanity needed to find a 'moral equivalent of war' – an experience which promised the same demand for heroism, the same possibility of release from the humdrum and the conventional. In 1914 the behaviour even of thinking men throughout Europe showed how little progress had been made towards this elusive goal. The tired stuffiness of liberal civilization turned men against it, just as, paradoxically, did its material success.

It is not, therefore, in the diplomatic documents or the plans of the war offices that the whole story of the origins of the war can be found. When they have been ransacked, there still remain important questions about mass psychology and spiritual weariness to be answered before we can confidently say how so great a cataclysm came about. One participant, Winston Churchill, sketched briefly his own diagnosis in 1914 when he wrote: 'There was a strange temper in the air. Unsatisfied by material prosperity the nations turned restlessly towards strife internal or external'. It is only in this context that the automaton-like movements of the great military machines in the last crucial days can be understood, for it was only this temper that had prepared men, slowly, subtly, to accept such machines at all.

*Caricature by Dutch artist Raemaekers which appeared on the 4th August 1914. The socialist leader Liebknecht, dressed as Martin Luther, reproaches Kaiser Wilhelm for embarking on a war of aggression. But, in fact, the pacific doctrines of the large and highly organized socialist parties went for nothing. They were submerged in a great tide of patriotism*

*Above:* Kaiser Wilhelm II (fourth from right), surrounded by German generals. *Opposite:* **Top:** Troops of Belgium's neglected and poorly trained army. **Centre:** Austrian cavalry officers, the 'élite' of the Habsburg army. **Bottom:** Members of the British Expeditionary Force – well trained, well equipped, and the best marksmen of all

# The Military Balance

George Stephenson and General Lazare Carnot could well be called the grand-fathers, or perhaps the great grandfathers, of the European military system of 1914. From the French Revolution and from Carnot, who had built the armies Napoleon used, came the concept of the nation in arms—so-called, though it would be more accurate to call it the concept of 'the whole manpower of the nation in the army'. Under Napoleon this system had overwhelmed the armies of the old regime. To save themselves the other great continental powers had been forced to adopt it, but once peace was re-established, a military as well as a political reaction had set in, and armies had reverted to traditionalism and long-service professionalism.

In 1857 Prince Wilhelm, Regent of Prussia, appointed General Helmuth von Moltke chief of general staff of his army, and, in 1859, another reforming general, Albrecht von Roon, minister for war. Meeting bitter political opposition to army reform, Roon suggested the appointment of Bismarck as minister-president. Under these four, Wilhelm, soon King of Prussia, Bismarck, Moltke, and Roon, the nation in arms idea re-appeared in Prussia and there reached its prime. In 1866 the Prussians quickly and decisively defeated the old-style Austrian army, then, in 1870 at the head of the North German Con-federation, overwhelmed the French.

Roon in 1870 put 1,183,400 officers and men into the field. Moltke had been a pupil of Clausewitz, but he could not have handled effectively and rapidly an army of this size if there had not been two vital technical advances. First, the develop-ment of agriculture and industry had provided the means to feed, arm, and equip great numbers, and indeed produced the larger populations from which they sprang. Second, railways could now assemble this massed manpower along frontiers, supply it, and effect further strategic movements as needed. Impressed by the events of 1866 and 1870, the armies of continental Europe made haste to imitate the Prussian model.

The weapons of 1870 were a marked advance on those used in the Napoleonic Wars. By 1914 weapons had been further developed. Not at the pace to which we are accustomed today, but faster than at any previous time in history. The magazine rifle, the machine-gun, and the breech-loading quick-firing field gun, especially, had been perfected since 1870. But, partly because the internal combustion engine was still in its childhood, and much more because soldiers and statesmen in power

are inherently prejudiced against change, no new military system had appeared. Strategy remained a strategy dependent on railways. Movement at the 15-20 mph of the troop train became movement at the age-old 15-20 miles a day, normal march for men and horsedrawn transport, as soon as contact with the enemy became likely. Tactical theory, recoiling from the ugly lessons of 1870 and of the American Civil War of 1861-65, had gone into reverse, and reflected ideas that had already started to be out of date in the days of muzzle-loaders.

## The German Aufmarsch

The German empire, proclaimed in the Hall of Mirrors, Versailles in 1871, had in 1914 a population of over 65,000,000. In theory, except for the small number required by the navy, all fit men of military age belonged to the army. Called up each year, from the age of seventeen to twenty they were en-rolled in the *Landsturm,* Class I. At twenty those who were fit joined the active army for two-years' service, or the cavalry and horse artillery for three. Afterwards they went into the Reserve for five years (in the case of the cavalry and horse artillery for four years). In practice, the active army could only take about half the annual call-up, and the surplus, together with those excused for other reasons, was en-rolled in the *Ersatz* Reserve, receiving, at best, very limited training. From the age of twenty-seven to thirty-nine, all served in the *Landwehr,* then from thirty-nine to forty-five in the *Landsturm,* Class II.

The active army of twenty-five and a half army corps—each of two divisions—and eleven cavalry divisions was maintained at fifty to sixty per cent war strength. In addition, there were thirty-two reserve, seven *Ersatz* reserve and the equivalent of sixteen *Landwehr* divisions.

Mobilization was a vast and critical operation, during which the army would be largely ineffective as a fighting machine. Nor did it end there, for the army must be deployed, which in 1914 meant deploy-ment by rail. This operation, the *Auf-marsch,* was vital and planned with at least as much care as mobilization itself, for on it would hang the success of the opening campaign and, it was thought, of the war. Mobilization must be ordered in time so that the enemy could not establish a lead, and once ordered it led inevitably to the *Aufmarsch.* The armies could per-haps then be halted on the frontier, but the possibility was not seriously canvassed, and in 1914 mobilization spelled war.

Südd-Verlag, Munich

Der Welt Spiegel

Roger Viollet

## Schlieffen's strategy

To this pattern, almost standard in Europe, the Germans had made two exceptions. Seeking to achieve crushing superiority for a quick victory against France in a war on two fronts, General von Schlieffen, chief of the general staff from 1892 to 1905, had planned to use reserve and *Ersatz* reserve divisions in the opening battles, relying on the well-trained regular and reserve officers and on strong cadres of regular non-commissioned officers to make good the reserves' deficiencies of training. Secondly, six infantry brigades with attached cavalry, artillery, and pioneers were maintained in peace at war strength and quartered close to the Belgian frontier, ready to seize the Liège forts and open the way through Belgium to northern France as soon as war was declared.

The peacetime strength of the army in 1914 was 856,000. On mobilization, trained reserves would bring it up to 3,800,000, but in emergency a maximum of 8,500,000 could be called to the colours. Against France seven armies would be deployed, totalling thirty-four army corps—of which eleven were reserve formations—and four cavalry corps. In the east, the VIII Army—four army corps of which one was a reserve corps with cavalry and some *Landwehr*—comprised some 200,000 and would hold off the Russians as best it could. There were other garrisons, depots, and reserves, and in Schleswig-Holstein a reserve army corps was held back in case the British attempted a landing.

Despite their defeat in 1870, the French had given the Germans more than one sharp lesson about the power of the breech-loading rifle against men in the open, and in their training afterwards the Germans took modern fire power seriously. When the machine-gun was perfected, the Germans took it up more seriously than other armies. Schlieffen's strategic plan to envelop the French armies by a massive advance through Belgium stemmed from his realization that frontal attack would be costly and indecisive. Watching the German manoeuvres of 1895, an expert British observer wrote that the soldiers '. . . act like intelligent beings, who thoroughly understand their duty, and the fact speaks volumes for the way in which even privates are taught to use their initiative'.

But as the years passed, memories of 1870 faded and traditionalism and arrogance asserted themselves. The Germans remained good soldiers, but of the manoeuvres of 1911, Colonel Repington of *The Times* wrote, 'there is insufficient test of the initiative of commanders of any units large or small . . . The infantry lack dash and display no knowledge of the ground . . . offer vulnerable targets at medium ranges . . . are not trained to understand the connection between fire and movement and seem totally unaware of the effect of modern fire'.

In theory the vain and unstable Wilhelm II would be commander in war, and until 1908 he frequently spoke of actually doing so. He lacked his grandfather's serious interest in military affairs, revelling in display rather than warlike efficiency.

Schlieffen pandered to him with military spectacle, cavalry charges, and unrealistic victories in manoeuvres and war games. General von Moltke, nephew of the great Moltke and also a Helmuth, who became chief of general staff at the beginning of 1906, refused to do so. Artistic, doubting his own military ability, obsessed by fear of revolution, he had accepted the appointment in the belief that he would not be called upon to command in war. Lacking the conviction and force of character needed to carry through the Schlieffen Plan, he tampered with it, weakening the enveloping right wing, strengthening the holding left and the Eastern Front. In war games he accepted frontal offensives as practicable. In 1914 he was sixty-six, in poor health, past the work to which he had never been equal.

Below him came the army commanders: on the vital right wing, commanding the I, II and III Armies respectively, a trio of sixty-eight-year-olds, Generals von Kluck, von Bülow, and von Hausen, hard men, drivers—especially Kluck, brutal, a little brittle in crisis. Next came a trio of royals: the Duke of Württemberg commanding the IV Army; the Crown Prince, the V; Prince Rupprecht of Bavaria, the VI; then finally von Heeringen, sixty-four, ex-minister for war, the VII. In the Prussian tradition their chiefs of staff supported them with authority almost equal to theirs. Commanding the VIII Army in East Prussia was General von Prittwitz und Gaffron, sixty-six, fat, self-important, indolent, with connections so far proof against Moltke's wish to remove him. Major-General Ludendorff, forty-nine—his name was unadorned with the aristocratic von—was assistant chief of staff of the II Army, having lost the key post of head of the deployment section under Moltke for too much insistence on increasing the intake of the army.

The populations of France and the North Germany Confederation had in 1870 been approximately equal, but by 1914, while the population of the German empire had risen to over 65,000,000, that of France was still under 40,000,000. The disparity dominated French strategic thinking, and, with tragic irony, led to a military creed savagely extravagant of human life.

France had astonished the world with the speed of her recovery after 1870. She had re-organized her army on the Prussian model with short service and a powerful general staff. Where the loss of Alsace and Lorraine had laid open her eastern frontier, she had built a strong fortified line stretching from Belfort to Verdun. At the turn of the century the army had been racked and discredited by the Dreyfus Affair's outcome. In 1905 military service had been cut down to two years. Confronted with the rising menace of Germany, the prestige of the army and willingness to serve in it recovered, and in 1913 service was restored to three years. After that men served in the Reserve, the Territorial Army and the Territorial Reserve for varying periods up to the age of forty-eight.

In July 1914 the peace strength of the French army was 736,000. On mobilization it rose to 3,500,000, of which some 1,700,000 were in the field army of five armies, in all

twenty-one army corps, plus two colonial, three independent, ten cavalry, and twenty-five reserve divisions, the rest in territorials, garrisons, and depots. The five armies stretched from the Swiss frontier, where the 1st Army had its right at Belfort, to a third of the way along the Belgian frontier, where the left of the 5th was near Hirson. Beyond that was a cavalry corps of three divisions. A German offensive from Metz would thus be covered, but one through Belgium would meet only a weak cavalry screen.

## French élan

The French, however, had no intention of waiting for any offensive to develop, for the army had persuaded itself that the disasters of 1870 had been due to lack of offensive spirit on their side. Looking back to Napoleonic and even earlier battles, the army had become imbued with mystical faith in the attack, pressed home regardless of cost, as the answer to all military problems. To ensure its *élan*, when the Germans went sensibly into field grey, the French had retained the traditional long blue coats and bright red trousers of their infantry. More practical matters were neglected, and the French infantryman always wore his long coat and heavy military underwear, his boots were hard, and a load of sixty-six pounds was piled on him compared to the German's fifty-six.

For fire power, the French relied on the rifle and the 75-mm field gun, an outstanding weapon produced in large numbers. Machine-guns were neglected. As for tactics, 'Success depends,' said the manual of 1913, 'far more on forcefulness and tenacity than upon tactical skill.' Luckily the French soldier was not only brave but also adaptable and able to learn quickly, while the colonial empire, which during the war would supply 500,000 men, was available to replace some of the first shattering losses.

General Joffre, sixty-two, was vice-president of the war council, earmarked as commander-in-chief on an outbreak of war. He had been appointed in 1911, largely because the disciples of attack wished to get rid of his predecessor. Ponderous, very taciturn but a good listener, veteran of colonial service, he had no strong views on strategy or tactics, but was an engineer, and expert in military movement. He was to prove imperturbable and able in crisis, but did nothing before the war to check the ideas and plans that made crisis inevitable when war came. Galliéni, Joffre's superior in the colonies, more alert and realistic, had refused the appointment, and was now without military employment.

Of the army commanders, Lanrezac of the 5th Army, brilliant, pessimistic, impatient, and outspoken, was thought of by many as Joffre's eventual successor. Foch, responsible as commandant of the staff college for spreading the doctrine of attack, was a corps commander. Like Joffre he would be strong in crisis, and had in Weygand a chief of staff who could translate his wishes into clear orders. Pétain, out of favour for his realistic belief in fire power, commanded a division.

**Neutral Belgians: British 'mercenaries'**
Standing in the path of the main German thrust, Belgium deployed a field army of six infantry divisions totalling some 117,000 men, and three fortress garrisons, Antwerp, Liège, and Namur. Because Belgium was neutral, two infantry divisions faced France, one at Antwerp, Great Britain, one at Liège, Germany, with the rest in central reserve.

Relying on her neutrality, Belgium had neglected her army. Service in it was unpopular, training severely limited, morale poor, the officer corps seriously disunited. The fortresses were obsolete, improvements planned in 1882 were still incomplete and had by now been themselves overtaken by weapon development. There was one bright spot, however. King Albert, thirty-nine, was intelligent and brave, and he had great personal integrity. He did not control the army in peace, but when war came he found himself obliged by the constitution to command it.

| | Great Britain | France | Russia | Germany | Austria-Hungary | Turkey |
|---|---|---|---|---|---|---|
| Population | 46,407,037 | 39,601,509 | 167,000,000 | 65,000,000 | 49,882,231 | 21,373,900 |
| Soldiers available on mobilization | 711,000[1] | 3,500,000+ | 4,423,000[2] | 8,500,000[3] | 3,000,000+ | 360,000 |
| Merchant fleet (net steam tonnage) | 11,538,000 | 1,098,000 | (1913) 486,914 | 3,096,000 | (1912) 559,784 | (1911) 66,878 |
| Battleships (built and being built) | 64 | 28 | 16 | 40 | 16 | |
| Cruisers | 121 | 34 | 14 | 57 | 12 | |
| Submarines | 64 | 73 | 29 | 23 | 6 | |
| Annual value of foreign trade (£) | 1,223,152,000 | 424,000,000 | 190,247,000 | 1,030,380,000 | 198,712,000 | 67,472,000 |
| Annual steel production (tons) | 6,903,000 | 4,333,000 | 4,416,000 | 17,024,000 | 2,642,000 | |
| Railway mileage | 23,441 | 25,471 | 46,573 | 39,439 | 27,545 | 3,882 |

[1] Including empire  [2] Immediate mobilization  [3] Emergency maximum

The British, as is their habit, were in two minds about sending an army to the Continent at all. In 1908 Haldane had reorganized the British army, forming the units at home into an Expeditionary Force, six infantry and one cavalry division totalling some 160,000 men, capable of supporting either the garrisons of the empire or a Continental ally. In 1905 staff talks with the French had been authorized, but had languished until, early in 1911, the francophile Major-General Henry Wilson had come to the War Office as director of military operations. That August the crisis over Agadir had revealed an alarming divergence of war plans between the War Office, where Wilson had made detailed arrangements with the French for the deployment of the Expeditionary Force on the left of the 5th Army, and the Admiralty, which strongly opposed continental commitment of the army, though it did not have a properly worked out proposal to put in place of Henry Wilson's. The Council of Imperial Defence had deferred formal decision, but allowed the War Office to continue planning with the French.

When in 1914 war was declared, there were those who thought that the Expeditionary Force should remain in Great Britain, or should go direct to Belgium in fulfilment of the British guarantee of neutrality, but it was too late now to change, and on 6th August the cabinet decided that it should go to France as planned, but without two of its divisions which would for the present remain in Great Britain.

Although small, the British army was well-trained and equipped. On the South African veldt Boer bullets had taught it something of the reality of fire power. Now the marksmanship of the infantry was in an entirely different class from that of continental armies. The cavalry, too, were armed with a proper rifle, not the neglected carbine of continental cavalry, and knew how to use it, but there peacetime reaction was setting in and the glamorous, futile charge coming back into fashion.

Called by the Germans an army of mercenaries and, more flatteringly, a perfect thing apart, the British army was recruited from volunteers, who enlisted for seven years followed by five in the reserve. Each battalion at home found drafts for another in the overseas empire, so that its men were often raw and its numbers short. There were experienced men in the divisions that went to France, but to see them all as hardened professionals is a mistake; some were young soldiers, others reservists grown soft in civil life.

Continuing an old tradition in modern shape, the Territorial Force and the Yeomanry had been organized by Haldane into a second-line army of fourteen divisions, far from fully trained or equipped, but a good deal more effective than many realized. Beyond that there were the older reservists and the militia for replacements, and the distant imperial garrisons and armies of India and the dominions.

Field Marshal Sir John French, commander-in-chief, British Expeditionary Force, had been a successful cavalry commander in South Africa, but at sixty-two was showing his age. Lieutenant-General Sir Douglas Haig, commanding the 1st Corps, French's chief-of-staff in South Africa and Haldane's assistant in the subsequent reforms, was able and ambitious, but inflexible and wedded to cavalry doctrine. Kitchener, now secretary of state for war, a tremendous national figure, had flashes of insight amounting almost to genius but little appreciation of staff organization or civilian control. In general, British officers were efficient and devoted but narrow in outlook. However, a far higher proportion of them than of officers in France and Germany had experienced the reality of war.

### The armies in the East

With the main German strength committed in the west, the clash in the east would be between Austria-Hungary and Russia. Austria had been worsted by the French in 1859, and in 1866 trounced by Prussia. Since then the army had been reformed on the Prussian model, but not for forty-eight years tested in war.

The population, 50,000,000 in 1914, was a complex racial mixture. Germans were the ruling group in Austria, Magyars in Hungary; Poles in Austria and Croats in Hungary had special privileges; Ruthenes, Czechs, Slovaks, Slovenes, Serbs, Italians, and Rumanians were potentially disaffected. Languages, literacy, religions, and racial characteristics differed widely. Slav races formed two-thirds of the infantry, and the Germans in charge notoriously lacked the high martial seriousness of the Prussians. Yet, if the sottish chaos described by Jaroslav Hašek, a Czech writer, in *The Good Soldier Schweik,* typified one side of the coin, there was another: to many the army was an ideal of the empire as a supra-national society.

At the beginning of 1914 the peace strength of the Austro-Hungarian army was some 450,000. On mobilization it rose to over 3,000,000, of which some 1,800,000 formed the field army of six armies, in all sixteen army corps—mostly of three divisions, some of them reserve divisions—and eleven cavalry divisions. In a war against Serbia, the III, V, and VI Armies would be deployed in the south, according to Plan B (Balkans); but in a war against Russia and Serbia, Plan R, the III Army would be deployed northeast with I, II, and IV in the Galician plain beyond the Carpathian mountains. By ordering partial mobilization on 25th July the army was committed to Plan B, until the III Army could be recalled from the Serbian front.

General Conrad von Hötzendorf, chief of general staff, sixty-two, a cavalryman, hard working, spartan, a writer on tactics and training, was, like Foch, a firm apostle of the offensive. His recipe for victory against Russia was an early attack before the vast manpower of the enemy could be brought into action, but that plan was now seriously compromised by partial mobilization. Conrad would command the northern armies, General Potiorek, another spartan, keen, vain, incompetent, with powerful court connections, responsible for the muddle that had given the Sarajevo assassins their chance, would command against Serbia.

Although Russia went to war to rescue Serbia, the Serbian army, under Marshal Putnik, 190,000 strong, organized in three armies each little stronger than an Austrian corps, was in grave danger of being overwhelmed before help could become effective. Leaving delaying detachments on the frontier, it assembled in north Serbia, ready to deploy wherever the attack came. It had fought in the bitter Balkan Wars of 1912 and 1913. Its men were seasoned, inspired by fierce patriotism, and looked back undaunted on generations of relentless warfare. The prospect of engaging it in its native mountains might have given pause to better soldiers than Conrad and Potiorek.

*1 The imperturbable, ponderous, and taciturn Joffre—the French commander-in-chief. 2 Moltke—the German commander-in-chief. He was artistic, lacked force of character, and doubted his military ability. 3 French military dress of 1914: cavalry helmet, bayonets, képis, and bright red trousers. The French infantryman wore his long coat and heavy underwear even in the heat of August*

L'Illustration

Harlingue/Viollet

### The Russian masses

For Russia, whose population numbered 167,000,000, manpower seemed the least of her problems. Bad roads, scant railways, low industrial capacity, poor standards of education and literacy, and a grudging treasury limited the size and effectiveness of her army. Later it would appear that so

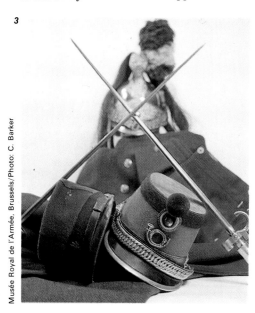

*In both east and west during 1914, the fortunes of the war ebbed and flowed to an extent perhaps unparalleled except in 1918. The Germans, having reached the Marne, were driven back into northernmost France and this was matched by the short-lived inroads of the Russians onto the 'sacred soil' of East Prussia. Below: German troops on the Eastern Front*

much of the Russian economy depended on sheer manual labour, that it would suffer disproportionately from withdrawal of manpower. For the moment, the great distances and bad communications slowed mobilization. Officer and non-commissioned officer cadres were weak in numbers and education, weapons, and equipment were in short supply, ammunition reserves set low, manufacture severely restricted.

Russia had fought Japan in Manchuria in 1904-05 and been badly worsted. Since then efforts had been made with the aid of large loans from France to modernize the army, but the combination of vast numbers and restricted resources had prevented it reaching the standard of Western armies of the day. In such choice as there was between quantity and quality, Russia had chosen quantity, instinctively believing that sheer numbers would bring victory. While a Russian division had sixteen battalions against a German division's twelve, its fighting power was only about half that of the German.

The peace strength of the Russian army was 1,423,000. On mobilization, three million men were called up at once, with 3,500,000 more to follow before the end of November. There were thirty-seven corps, mostly of two divisions, and in all seventy first-line divisions, nineteen independent brigades, thirty-five reserve divisions, twenty-four cavalry and Cossack divisions with twelve reserve.

It was planned to deploy thirty corps—ninety-five infantry and thirty-seven cavalry divisions, some 2,700,000 men—against Germany and Austria, but of these only fifty-two divisions could appear by the twenty-third day of mobilization (22nd

August). Two armies, the 1st and 2nd, would face East Prussia; three, the 5th, 3rd and 8th, Austria. Another, the 4th, would deploy against Germany (Plan G), if the main German strength came east, or against Austria (Plan A), if it struck west against France. Two more armies watched the Baltic and Caucasian flanks. General mobilization was ordered on 29th July, and on 6th August, deployment on Plan A.

General Sukhomlinov, minister for war since 1909, had been an energetic re-organizer, backed by the Tsar; he was corrupt, possibly pro-German, and a military reactionary, boasting that he had not read a manual for twenty-five years. Grand Duke Nicholas, commander-in-chief, fifty-eight, an imposing figure six-foot-six tall, was a champion of reform and opposed by Sukhomlinov. The jealousy of his nephew, the Tsar, had kept him from the Russo-Japanese War, depriving him of the chance to prove his worth as a commander, but also keeping him free of blame for the defeat. General Zhilinsky, commanding against East Prussia, had visited France in 1912 when chief of general staff, and had absorbed Foch's military beliefs, while also becoming personally committed to Russia's undertaking for an early advance against Germany.

Almost from the moment of declaration of war, France began to urge Russia to make this advance quickly and in strength. Russia responded gallantly, sacrificing her chance of massive deployment before action. Perhaps it need hardly be added that in Russia, as elsewhere, progressives and reactionaries were agreed on one thing, their faith in the offensive.

# The Reality of Total War

On 5th September 1917 Miss Barbara Adam, a twenty-year-old student at Cambridge University, married Captain Jack Wootton, aged twenty-six. According to the conventions of their era and class, neither was yet ready for marriage. It was simply because of the war that their families gave consent.

They had a twenty-four-hour honeymoon in the country and then a night at the Rubens Hotel, London, before Captain Wootton set off from Victoria Station to join his regiment at the front. Five weeks later, without his wife ever having seen him again, he died of wounds. The army sent his blood-stained kit to Mrs Wootton and she resumed her studies at Cambridge. She went on to make a considerable public career, ending as one of the first women to become a member of the House of Lords. She married again. Yet, describing her brief first marriage in her autobiography half a century later, she wrote that she still avoided any occasion for entering the Rubens Hotel.

In ordinary times, such a story would stand out as being especially tragic. But during the First World War it was routine; something of the kind happened to tens of thousands of couples. The most direct and most devastating result of the war was the wholesale killing of young men. Great Britain lost 680,000, France lost 1,300,000 and Germany lost 1,700,000. The point is not that the total numbers were particularly large—the warfare of the 1939-45 period accounted for many more deaths—but that the casualties were almost all of the same kind. It was as if some Pied Piper had travelled across Europe carrying off the young men.

There were so many widows and bereaved parents that, in Great Britain, a movement was started to make white the colour for mourning, lest the streets appear too gloomy. This did not catch on and the old mourning rituals were curtailed to a simple armband or dropped altogether. They never really returned. The Germans were rather more traditional. 'For weeks past the town [Berlin] seems to have been enveloped in an impenetrable veil of sadness, grey in grey, which no golden ray of sunlight seems to pierce, and which forms a fit setting for the white-faced, black-robed women who glide so sadly through the streets,' wrote Countess Evelyn Blücher, in her diary for 27th December 1915.

It would be false, however, to suppose that the mood in the combatant countries was one entirely of gloom. By 1916 the expectation cherished at the beginning by both sides, that the war would be a short one, had faded. But each side, convinced that it was fighting in self-defence against an evil enemy, was confident of ultimate victory. The roistering energies which over the previous period had revolutionized the European way of life were now turned inwards, to destruction. The war was not so much the end of 19th-century Europe as its consequence.

### Land of Hope and Glory

The deepest impact was upon Great Britain where the war acted as an accelerator and distorter of social changes which had already begun in the unstable Edwardian period.

The key decision, from which every other change derived, was the novel one of creating a mass British army on a scale comparable to the gigantic conscript forces on the mainland of Europe. That army was intended to end the war by overwhelming Germany on the Western Front. (Unfortunately neither its training nor its higher leadership matched the enthusiasm of its recruits.)

During the first two years of the war the whole resources of public propaganda were used to recruit the army. The country was saturated with patriotic appeals. 'Land of Hope and Glory' became a second national anthem. 'God Save the King' was introduced as a customary item in theatre and cinema performances, a custom which still survives. Kitchener's poster 'Your King and Country Need YOU', with its pointed finger, can still be counted as the most memorable piece of outdoor advertising ever designed. Every locality had its own recruiting committee. There were private-enterprise recruiters, notably the outrageous Horatio Bottomley. Some clergymen preached sermons urging young men to join the army. Music-hall stars ended performances with patriotic tableaux and appeals for recruits. Military bands paraded the streets and young men fell in behind them to march to the recruiting sergeant. 'We don't want to lose you, but

1 Horatio Bottomley, 1915. Popular jingoistic orator. He made patriotism pay, earning some £27,000 as a private enterprise recruiter.
2 Parisians queuing for coal in the Place de L'Opéra, March 1917. While their menfolk died women queued for the necessities of life. 3 A Hyde Park investiture. Widows and next of kin seen waiting to receive posthumous awards. There were very few families who did not know personal grief

Press Association

we think you ought to go' became an important popular song. The basic pay was a shilling a day, and many recruits did their first drills in public parks, with civilian spectators proudly looking on.

It became embarrassing to be a male civilian of military age. An admiral in Folkestone started a movement organizing girls to present white feathers to young men they saw in the streets in civilian dress. In one case, it was said, a winner of the VC got one while on leave. Some women went a stage farther. The romantic novelist, Baroness Orczy, founded the 'Women of England's Active Service League', every member of which pledged herself to have nothing to do with any man eligible to join up who had not done so. She aimed at 100,000 members; she actually achieved 10,000, and sent the names of all of them to the King.

The flaw, which by 1916 had become glaringly apparent, was that an army on such a scale required enormous industrial support to equip and clothe it. At least three civilian workers were required for every fighting soldier. By 1915 the shortage of artillery shells had become a national scandal and even so elementary a thing as soldiers' boots was presenting problems. Thousands of skilled workers had followed the band into the army and they were hard to replace.

### The government takes over

So, on a makeshift and temporary basis, began the characteristically 20th-century phenomenon of wholesale government direction of industry, Lloyd George as minister of munitions directing the initial stages. Until the war the condition of the economy had been considered hardly more the responsibility of the government than the weather. Even socialists had thought more about distributing wealth and resources than about managing them. Although after the war most of the controls were to be removed, the idea remained that the government was ultimately responsible for the economy.

To an increasing extent party politics and elections were to centre around economic questions. Unemployment between the wars was to become a political issue on a

scale which would previously have been impossible. Recruitment propaganda also had some influence in this direction. It was hinted, without any precise explanation of how it was to come about, that the military defeat of Germany would raise British living standards. The soldiers who came back tended to look to the politicians to raise them.

The aim in 1915 and 1916 was to create a tri-partnership of government, trade unions, and employers in which output, wages, and profits would be settled by negotiation instead of by the free play of the market. This had the incidental effect of increasing the size, status, and power of the unions. Instead of being pressure groups in the class war, they tended to become a recognized organ of the community, with rights and responsibilities to the whole nation as well as to their own members. Their membership rose dramatically, from 4,100,000 in 1914 to 6,500,000 in 1918; and when the soldiers returned it shot up to over 8,000,000. The effect was permanent (although numbers were to fall later) and it was one factor in the post-war displacement of the Liberal Party by the Labour Party.

By 1916 the war had become a way of life. The streets were curiously silent; the German bands and itinerant salesmen who in 1914 had enlivened them were now gone. There were short skirts and widows and multitudes of young men in uniform. For an army officer in uniform to have appeared in a tram or bus would in 1914 have been unknown; by 1916 it was commonplace for subalterns with their toothbrush moustaches to be handing their fares to girl conductors. Every issue of every newspaper carried lists of names of men who had been killed. Soldiers on leave sought to enjoy themselves before they died and nightclubs, previously furtive, almost unmentionable places, had become prominent features of the London scene. There were said to be 150 in Soho alone; in them the customers danced to the new jazz music which had just crossed the Atlantic. The older institution, the public house, had begun to decline; under emergency legislation the government had regulated the hours at which they could serve liquor and

*Top: 'A Land Girl Ploughing' by Cecil Allen. On the Continent the peasants' wives took over in the fields. The British were startled by the land girls, who worked as hired farm hands. By the end of 1917 there were 260,000 women, both part-time and full-time, who had joined the Land Army. Centre: Fashions rising to the occasion—a French reflection on German privations. Bottom: Boiling bones to extract the fats, Berlin 1917. War had become a way of life everywhere*

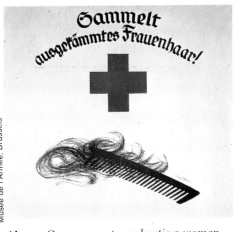

*Above: German poster exhorting women to save hair for making machine belting. Left: Berliners exchange firewood for potato peelings, Berlin 1917*

*Above: Substitute for rubber. Sprung metal 'tyres' on a German car. Right: Soup kitchen for Berliners 1917. Left: Parisians in a bread queue, 1917. Below: German poster appeals for aluminium, copper, brass, nickel, tin*

the phrase 'Time, gentlemen, please' had entered the language. The daytime thoughts of the nation were of the permanent battle which was being waged from trenches in France; sometimes the actual sound of the guns was so far-reaching that it could be heard by people in southern England as a distant thunder.

### Deadlock and disappointment

France and Germany, unlike Great Britain, had long prepared for the war in the sense that they had for generations run a system of universal military service and could, without improvisation, immediately mobilize a mass army. Neither, however, had reckoned on a long war. The German aim was a quick knock-out of France and then a switch of forces to the east to defeat the armies of archaic Tsarist Russia. The French, equally, had looked forward to dashing victories and the reconquest of the provinces of Alsace and Lorraine which they had lost to Germany forty-four years earlier. The outcome, a deadlock in France, was a disappointment to both sides.

The fighting on the Western Front was on French (and Belgian) soil, so that the French, unlike the Germans and the British, were on their home ground. Much of the industrial north-east of France was under German occupation. The result was that the French became less idealistic about the war than the British and Germans; they saw it as a plague rather than as an adventure. It was not until late 1917 that they found in Clemenceau an apt war-like leader. The French were drearily conscious of having been defeated in the initial battles of 1914, and by 1916 they feared that they were bleeding to death. The following year large segments of the French army were to mutiny in favour of a negotiated peace. German propaganda to the effect that Great Britain was willing to fight to the last Frenchman had its effect; the Germans actually subsidized the leading French left-wing paper, the *Bonnet Rouge*.

There was in France a special wartime drabness, save among the minority of industrial workers and their employers who made more money than ever before. In Paris the politicians quarrelled and at the front the soldiers died in thousands. Unlike the British and Germans, the French felt a widespread distrust of both politicians and generals, a distrust justified by some of the facts. There was no proper attempt at financial or industrial management. Since the richest industrial area was under German occupation, France had to rely upon imports from Great Britain, the United States, and Japan for the sinews of war and these were paid for by contracting debts. The internal debt also grew—in 1915 French revenue from taxes was actually lower than the ordinary peace-time level—and more and more paper money was printed. A crudely inefficient method was adopted by the government to finance munitions production. It lent capital, interest-free, to entrepreneurs; this, naturally, gave them enormous profits at the public expense. Few proper accounts were kept and by 1916 there was little reliable information on public finances.

The mass French army consisted largely of peasants conscripted from their small-holdings and sent to the front. The women left behind continued to work the holdings, but the total food output, in peacetime sufficient to meet French needs, fell sharply. By 1916 sugar had become a luxury, there were two meatless days a week, and restaurants were restricted to serving three courses. According to historic practice, the government concentrated on controlling the supply and price of bread, and success in this was the civil population's great palliative; no matter

*Workroom of a British war hospital supply depot, painted by J.B Davis*

what other hardships existed, there was bread for all. Other matters of price control and rationing were left to the departmental prefects, with the result that what supplies were available oscillated around France to the *départements* which momentarily allowed the highest prices.

Paris in the early 20th century was at its peak as the international capital for the arts, culture, and the amenities of luxurious living. Every cultivated European and American regarded Paris as in some way his spiritual home. The war, if anything, increased this prestige.

The war struck deeply into French family and social life. The depreciation in money — by 1916 the cost of living had risen by forty per cent — was beginning to wreck the *rentier* class which, by tradition, had its savings in fixed interest bonds. Secure employment as a public official had, until 1914, been the most respectable thing to which a Frenchman could aspire. By 1916 the officials were losing their social prestige and being overtaken by businessmen, a process which was to continue.

French war-weariness, which was already apparent in 1916, seemed to sap the spirit of the nation. In the occupied sector the people were cowed by strict German administration; there was no attempt at a resistance movement. Although eventually France emerged as a nominal victor, and got back her lost provinces, there remained a loss of national confidence and a deep-rooted distrust of war. The seeds of the disaster of 1940 were being sown.

*German appeal for acorns, chestnuts, 1917*

### Ersatz *coffee and 'means-test' clothes*

In Germany in 1916 something still remained of the elation caused by the great victories of 1914. With the United States not yet in the war and the Russian empire obviously crumbling, it was reasonable for Germans to expect victory. The strategy was to be defensive in the west until forces could be brought from the Russian front to overwhelm the French and the British.

The main effect of the war on the national life was, apart from the enormous casualties, the shortages caused by the British blockade. Bread rationing had started as early as January 1915, and there was an agonizing dilemma, whether to use scarce nitrates to fertilize agricultural land or to make explosives. Generally the claims of the explosives got priority and so agricultural production, which in any case was insufficient for the nation's needs, declined. Further difficulty came because of bad weather — the winter of 1916-17 was known as the 'turnip winter' because early frosts had spoiled the potato harvest.

German ingenuity concentrated on producing substitute — '*ersatz*' — foods and some, although they sound dreadful, were quite palatable. It was possible to make an eatable cake from clover meal and chestnut flour. '*Ersatz*' coffee, made from roasted barley, rye, chicory, and figs, became a national drink. Schoolchildren were lectured on the need for thorough mastication to prevent the substitutes from harming their digestions.

The virtual dictator of the German economy was the Jewish industrialist, Walther Rathenau, a brilliant administrator brought in by the war office to organize supplies for the army. Step by step Rathenau brought the principal industries under government control and set up an elaborate bureaucracy to run them. As in Great Britain, this was public control without public ownership, but Rathenau's methods were more thorough than those of the British; government 'kommissars' participated in the actual management of companies, and the plan allotted everyone his place. In 1916 the Rathenau machine had reached the peak of its efficiency and the whole of Germany was organized for fighting the war.

To accompany Rathenau's economic planning there were elaborate rationing schemes, with everyone ticketed and docketed for what he was entitled to receive. Clothes were distributed in part on a

'means-test' system — a customer had to prove to an official that he needed a new suit.

The political effect of the war was still, in 1916, to reinforce confidence in the German imperial system. Germany consisted of twenty-five states, each with its ruling dynasty, the whole under the dominance of the largest state, Prussia, of which the Kaiser was King. It was an authoritarian and hierarchical system with a strong infusion of democracy — the imperial parliament was elected on universal manhood suffrage. (In Great Britain only fifty-eight per cent of adult males had the right to vote.) Although a strong Social Democrat opposition existed in parliament, the imperial and hierarchical system worked because the average German worker trusted his social superiors and was willing to vote for them.

Even the Social Democrat deputies had voted in favour of war credits. The military victories had engendered further confidence in the system and war weariness had hardly begun. Shortages, hardships, and even casualty lists were tolerable as the price of a certain German victory.

Of course the vast self-confidence of 1916 turned out to be a mistake. Within two years the Kaiser and the authorities under him were simply to vanish from German politics. German success and German power proved to have been a delusion. The psychological shock was to be enormous and lasting and it helped to cause the strange and national mood in which so eccentric a figure as Hitler was able to rise to power.

### Debts and death

All the combatant countries financed the war by loans rather than by taxation. In Great Britain, for example, the highest wartime rate of income tax reached only 6s. in the pound. The theory was to lay the cost of the war upon the future generations it was being fought to protect. What it really meant was that, instead of being taxed outright, people subscribed to war loans and so received the right to an annual payment of interest.

After the war, France was to lessen the burden of debt by allowing the franc to depreciate in value. Germany got rid of it altogether in the great inflation of 1923. In Great Britain, however, where the value of money remained stable or even increased, the war debt was a continuing burden which contributed towards a sense of national ill-being and inability to afford costly projects, either for military defence or for the promotion of living standards.

But the greatest single effect of the war, clearly apparent in 1916, was the killing of young men. Public imaginations exaggerated the effect of the casualties far beyond statistical realities. In Great Britain and Germany, particularly, appeared a cult of youth which has continued ever since. There was impatience and even contempt for the past. Jeremy Bentham's plea that we should look to our ancestors, not for their wisdom, but for their follies became the fashionable mode of thought, and even half a century later it is still continuing.

# The Dardanelles Campaign

It is doubtful whether any single campaign of either of the two World Wars has aroused more attention and controversy than the ill-fated venture to force the Dardanelles in 1915. 'Nothing so distorted perspective, disturbed impartial judgement, and impaired the sense of strategic values as the operations on Gallipoli,' Sir Edward Grey has written. Lord Slim—who fought at Gallipoli, and was seriously wounded—has described the Gallipoli commanders in scathing terms as the worst since the Crimean War. The defenders of the enterprise—notably Winston Churchill, Sir Roger Keyes, and General Sir Ian Hamilton—have been no less vehement and there have been other commentators who have thrown a romantic pall over the campaign. 'The drama of the Gallipoli campaign,' wrote the British official historian, 'by reason of the beauty of its setting, the grandeur of its theme, and the unhappiness of its ending, will always rank amongst the world's classic tragedies.' He then went on to quote Aeschylus's words: 'What need to repine at fortune's frowns? The gain hath the advantage, and the loss does not bear down the scale.' Today, more than sixty years later, the Gallipoli controversies still rumble sulphurously, and the passions the campaign aroused have not yet been stilled.

## Amateurs in council

Few major campaigns have been initiated under stranger circumstances. The opening months of the war had imposed a strain upon the Liberal government from which it never really recovered. Asquith's leadership at the outbreak of war had been firm and decisive, but subsequently—whether from ill-health, as has been recently suggested by Lord Salter, or from other causes is immaterial in this narrative—his influence had been flaccid and irresolute. The creation of a War Council in November had not met the essential problem; the council met irregularly, its Service members were silent, and its manner of doing business was amateurish and unimpressive. As Winston Churchill commented in a memorandum circulated in July 1915: 'The governing instrument here has been unable to make up its mind except by very lengthy processes of argument and exhaustion, and that the divisions of opinion to be overcome, and the number of persons of consequence to be convinced, caused delays and compromises. We have always sent two-thirds of what was necessary a month too late.'

The military situation itself played a crucial part in what developed. The first

fury of the war had been spent, and the opposing lines writhed from the Channel to the Swiss frontier; Russia had reeled back from her advance on East Prussia; everywhere, the belligerents had failed to secure their primary objectives. Already, the character of the battle on the Western Front had become grimly evident, and by the end of 1914 Churchill (first lord of the Admiralty), Lord Fisher (first sea lord), Lloyd George (chancellor of the exchequer), and Sir Maurice Hankey (secretary to the War Council) were thinking in terms of using British force—and particularly sea power—in another sphere.

It was Churchill who emerged with the most attractive proposal. Since the early weeks of the war his restlessness had been unconcealed, and he had already proposed, at the first meeting of the War Council on 25th November, a naval attack on the Dardanelles, with the ultimate object of destroying the German warships, *Goeben* and *Breslau,* whose escape from British squadrons in the Mediterranean in August had been a decisive factor in bringing Turkey into the war at the beginning of November on the side of the Germans. The suggestion had been shelved, but the idea had been put forward, and Hankey is not alone in stressing the significance of this first airing of the plan.

Impatience with the lack of progress on the Western Front was now buttressed by an appeal from Russia for a 'demonstration' against Turkey, after a large Turkish army had advanced into the Caucasus. (By the time the appeal was received, the Turks had been defeated, but this was not known for some time in London.) Churchill at once revived the idea of an assault on the Dardanelles, and telegraphed to the British admiral—Carden—in command of the squadron standing off the western entrance of the Dardanelles about the possibilities of a purely naval assault. Admiral Carden replied cautiously to the effect that a gradual attack might succeed; Churchill pushed the issue, and Carden was instructed to submit his detailed plans; when these arrived, Churchill put the matter before the War Council.

The extent to which Churchill's service colleagues at the Admiralty were alarmed at this speed was not communicated to the ministers on the council, a fact which to a large degree absolves them from their collective responsibility. Churchill's account was brilliant and exciting, and on 15th January the War Council agreed that 'the Admiralty should prepare for a naval expedition in February to bombard and take

*Top: Assault by British Royal Naval Division on the Turkish lines. Above: HMS Cornwallis in action*

79

the Gallipoli peninsula, with Constantinople as its object'. Churchill took this as a definite decision; Asquith, however, considered that it was 'merely provisional, to prepare, but nothing more'; Admiral Sir Arthur Wilson, a member of the council, subsequently said that 'it was not my business. I was not in any way connected with the question, and it had never in any way officially been put before me'. Churchill's naval secretary considered that the naval members of the council 'only agreed to a purely naval operation on the understanding that we could always draw back – that there should be no question of what is known as forcing the Dardanelles'. Fisher, by this stage, was very alarmed indeed.

Quite apart from the matter of whether the navy had sufficient reserve of men and ships – even old ships, which was a major part of Churchill's scheme – to afford such an operation, the forcing of the Dardanelles had for long been regarded with apprehension by the navy, and Churchill himself had written in 1911 that 'it should be remembered that it is no longer possible to force the Dardanelles, and nobody would expose a modern fleet to such peril'. But Churchill – as his evidence to the Dardanelles Commission, only recently available for examination, clearly reveals – had been profoundly impressed by the effects of German artillery bombardments on the Belgian forts, and it was evident that the Turkish batteries were conspicuously sited, exposed, and equipped with obsolete equipment. And Churchill was not alone in rating Turkish military competence low. The admirals' doubts were put aside, Fisher swallowed his misgivings, and Carden prepared for the assault.

All this represented a considerable achievement for Churchill. There is no doubt that he forced the pace, that the initiative was solely his, and that his subsequent account in *The World Crisis* must be approached with great caution. A case in point is his version of the negotiations to persuade Lord Kitchener (secretary of state for war) to release the Regular 29th Division for the Eastern Mediterranean. The recently revealed minutes of the War

Council make it plain that Churchill had no intention of using the troops for the attack on the Dardanelles, but to employ them subsequently 'to reinforce our diplomacy' and garrison Constantinople. It was not surprising that Kitchener did not agree to send the division until March 10th.

The plans for the naval attack continued, and the British and Dominion (Australian and New Zealand) troops in Egypt were put on the alert. Carden opened his attack on 19th February, and had no difficulty in suppressing the outer forts at Sedd-el-Bahr and Kum Kale. The difficulties really began when the warships entered the Straits.

The intermediate and inner defences consisted of gun emplacements on the Gallipoli and Asiatic shores. These were supplemented by batteries capable of causing damage only to lightly armoured ships, and by mobile batteries. The Straits had been mined since the beginning of the war, but it was only in February and March that the lines of mines represented a serious menace. The attempts of the British minesweepers – East Coast fishing trawlers manned by civilian crews and commanded by a naval officer with no experience whatever of minesweeping – ended in complete failure. Marines went ashore at Kum Kale and Sedd-el-Bahr on several occasions, but early in March the resistance to these operations increased sharply.

Bad weather made the tasks of the warships and the hapless trawlers – barely able to make headway against the fierce Dardanelles current, operating under fire in wholly unfamiliar circumstances – even more difficult. Carden was an ailing man. The warships – with the exception of the brand-new battleship *Queen Elizabeth* – were old and in many cases in need of a refit. The standard of the officers was mixed. The Turkish resistance was more strenuous with every day that passed. The momentum of the advance faltered.

Urged on by Churchill, Carden decided to reverse his tactics; the fleet would silence the guns to allow the sweepers to clear the minefields. On the eve of the attack Carden collapsed and was replaced by Rear-Admiral Robeck.

By now, the soldiers were on the scene. Lieutenant-General Birdwood, a former military secretary to Kitchener now commanding the Anzacs in Egypt, had been sent by Kitchener to the Dardanelles to report on the situation. His reports were to the effect that military support was essential. Slowly a military force was gathered together, and General Sir Ian Hamilton was appointed commander-in-chief of what was called the Mediterranean Expeditionary Force, and which consisted at that moment of some 70,000 British, Dominion, and French troops. Hamilton was informed of his new appointment on 12th March; he left the next day – Friday, 13th March – with a scratch staff hastily gathered together, a series of instructions from Kitchener, and some meagre scraps of information about the area and the Turks. He arrived just in time for the *débâcle* of 18th March. Robeck lost three battleships sunk, and three crippled, out of nine; the minefields had not been touched.

Much ink has subsequently been spilled on the subject of what Robeck ought to have done. He did not know, of course, that the Turkish lack of heavy shells made their situation desperate. Even if he had, the fact remained that it was the mobile and minor batteries that were holding up the minesweepers. Roger Keyes's plan of using destroyers as minesweepers and storming the minefields was the only one that had a real chance of success, and it would have taken some time to prepare them.

The soldiers, however, were very willing to take over. On 22nd March Hamilton and Robeck agreed on a combined operation, and Hamilton sailed off to Alexandria to re-organize his scattered forces. 'No formal decision to make a land attack was even noted in the records of the Cabinet or the War Council,' as Churchill has written. '. . . This silent plunge into this vast military venture must be regarded as an extraordinary episode.' It was, however, no more extraordinary than the events that had preceded the crucial conference of 22nd March. Attempts by Hankey to obtain better information and an agreed assessment of the situation made no progress. 'The military operation appears, therefore, to be to a certain extent a gamble upon the supposed shortage of supplies and inferior fighting qualities of the Turkish armies,' he wrote in one of a series of prescient memoranda. But the War Council did not meet from the middle of March until two months later.

What subsequently happened was the direct result of the manner in which the British drifted haphazardly into a highly difficult amphibious operation. No calculation had been made of whether the British had the resources to undertake this operation. As Hankey wrote at the end of March: 'Up to the present time . . . no attempt has been made to estimate what force is required. We have merely said that so many troops are available and that they ought to be enough.' The state of affairs was subsequently well summarized by Sir William Robertson: 'The Secretary of State for War was aiming for decisive results on the Western Front. The First Lord of the

*Hamilton – 'He should have really taken command, which he has never yet done'*

*Liman von Sanders – he committed several major errors which might have been fatal*

*The landing at Suvla Bay, Gallipoli, 1915, painted by subaltern R.C.Lewis during the action, using the dye from cigarette packets*

Admiralty was advocating a military expedition to the Dardanelles. The Secretary of State for India was devoting his attention to a campaign in Mesopotamia. The Secretary of State for the Colonies was occupying himself with several small wars in Africa. And the Chancellor of the Exchequer was attempting to secure the removal of a large part of the British army from France to some Eastern Mediterranean theatre.'

One can sympathize with the cry of the GOC Egypt, Sir John Maxwell: 'Who is co-ordinating and directing this great combine?'

Furthermore, there was divided command in the eastern Mediterranean. Maxwell was in command in Egypt; Hamilton had his army; Robeck his ships. Before the campaign ended, there were further complications. Each commander fought for his own force and his own projects, and the limited supplies of men and material were distributed on an *ad hoc* and uncoordinated basis.

To all these difficulties, Hamilton added some of his own. His refusal to bring his administrative staff into the initial planning — and, indeed, into anything at all so long as he was commander-in-chief — had some easily foreseeable results. Security was non-existent. 'The attack was heralded as few have ever been,' the Australian military historian has written. 'No condition designed to proclaim it seems to have been omitted.' This was not Hamilton's fault, yet his protests were wholly ineffective.

His plan for landing on Gallipoli — Asia he ruled out entirely, over the strong arguments of Birdwood and Hunter-Weston, commanding the 29th Division — was imaginative and daring. The 29th Division was to land at five small beaches at the southern end of the peninsula; the Anzacs were to land farther to the north on the western shore, just above the jutting promontory of Gaba Tepe, and then to push overland to the eminence of Mal Tepe, overlooking the narrows. There were to be feint landings at Bulair, at the 'neck' of the peninsula, and (by the French) at Besika Bay, opposite the island of Tenedos. The French were also to make a real, but temporary, landing at Kum Kale, to protect the landing of the 29th Division.

Meanwhile, the Turks had been having their own problems. Until March the Turkish forces in the area had been scattered and few in number. In spite of the urgency of the situation, the Turks acted lethargically. When, on the morning of 26th March, General Liman von Sanders arrived to take command of the troops at the Dardanelles, the situation that faced him was grim indeed. In short, his task was to defend a coast-line of some 150 miles with a total force of 84,000 men, but an actual fighting strength of only about 62,000. His army had no aircraft, and was seriously deficient in artillery and equipment. The men themselves, for so long used to defeat, were the despair of the German officers, and it would have been difficult to see in these poorly equipped and ragged formations the army that was to rise to such heights of valour and resource.

Sanders has been fortunate to have been treated at his own valuation by the majority of British commentators. In fact, he committed several major errors which might have been fatal. He placed two divisions at the neck of the peninsula, two on the Asiatic shore, one to defend the entire southern Gallipoli peninsula, and a final division in reserve near Mal Tepe. The entire area south of the bald, dominant height of Achi Baba was defended by one regiment and one field battery, with the reserves placed several hours' marching away to the north. To the dismay of the Turkish officers, Sanders drew his forces back from the beaches and concentrated them inland. This, the Turks argued, overlooked the fact that on the whole of the peninsula there were barely half a dozen beaches on which the British could land; Sanders, like Hamilton, over-estimated the effects of naval bombardment on well dug-in troops. He was saved by the epic courage of the Turkish troops, good luck, and mismanagement by the enemy from losing the entire campaign on the first day.

It is impossible, even now, to contemplate the events of 25th April 1915, without emotion. The British and Dominion troops sailed from Mudros Harbour, in the island of Lemnos, in a blaze of excitement and ardour. 'Courage our youth will always have,' Lord Slim has written, 'but those young men had a vision strangely medieval, never, I think, to be renewed.' It was the baptism of fire for the Anzacs. It was also, in a real sense, the day on which Turkey began her emergence as a modern nation.

Three of the British landings at Helles were virtually unopposed. One was resisted, but the enemy defeated. But the fifth, at Sedd-el-Bahr, was a catastrophe. As the British came ashore, a torrent of fire was poured upon them as they waded through the water or sat helplessly jammed in open boats; others who attempted to land from a converted collier, the *River Clyde*, fared no better. In this crisis Hunter-Weston did not show himself to advantage. He was in a cruiser, barely five minutes' sailing from the disastrous beach, yet it was not until the day was well advanced that he was aware of what had occurred. The day ended with the British, exhausted and shaken, clinging to their positions.

The Anzacs had had a day of very mixed fortunes. They had been landed over a mile to the north of their intended position, in some confusion, to be faced with precipitous cliffs and plunging, scrub-covered gorges. As the first men moved inland, congestion built up at the tiny beach — Anzac Cove — which had to cope with all reinforcements and supplies. Only one battery of field artillery was landed all day, and units became hopelessly intermingled. As in the south, the maps were dangerously inaccurate. By mid-morning the Turks had begun to counter-attack and, spurred on by the then unknown Colonel Mustapha Kemal, these attacks developed in fury throughout the day. By evening, the Anzacs were pushed back to a firing-line which extended only a thousand yards inland at the farthest point; casualties had been heavy, and Birdwood's divisional commanders advised evacuation. In the event, although Birdwood reluctantly agreed, Hamilton ordered him to hang on. This was virtually the only initiative taken by Hamilton — on board the *Queen Eliza-*

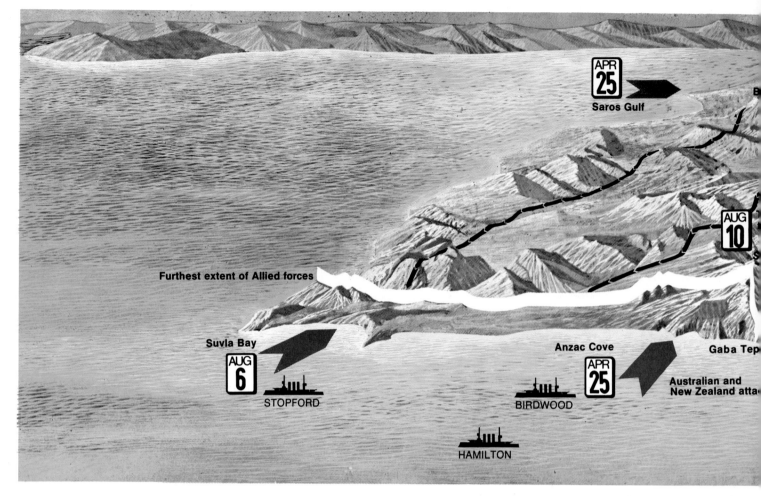

Labels on map: APR 25 Saros Gulf · AUG 10 · Furthest extent of Allied forces · Suvla Bay AUG 6 STOPFORD · Anzac Cove APR 25 · Gaba Tep · Australian and New Zealand atta· BIRDWOOD · HAMILTON

*The Gallipoli peninsula, seen from the west. On the map are marked the naval attack on 18th March, the landings on 25th April, the landing at Suvla Bay on 6th August, and the farthest extent of the Allied advances. The broken black lines show the direction of the Turkish thrusts against the Allies. The generals directed operations from ships offshore*

beth — throughout the day. As Birdwood wrote — some months later, 'he should have taken much more personal charge and *insisted* on things being done and really taken command, which he has never yet done'. Thus began the epic defence of Anzac, a fragment of cliff and gorge, overlooked by the enemy.

Hamilton pressed on at Helles, but although a limited advance was made, it was apparent by 8th May that the initial effort of his troops was spent. Casualties had been horrific — over 20,000 (of whom over 6,000 had been killed) out of a total force of 70,000 — and the medical and supply arrangements had completely collapsed under the wholly unexpected demands. The arrival of a German submarine and the sinking of three battleships — one by a Turkish torpedo-boat attack — deprived the army of the physical and psychological support of the guns of the fleet. Thus ended the first phase of the Gallipoli Campaign.

A week later the Liberal government fell, the first major casualty of the campaign, although there were other important contributory causes. Asquith formed a new coalition government in which Balfour, the former Conservative leader,

replaced Churchill as first lord of the Admiralty. An inner cabinet, from 7th June called the Dardanelles Committee, took over the conduct of operations, and a ministry of munitions was established. The new government resolved to support Hamilton, and more troops were dispatched. Hamilton continued to batter away at Helles throughout May and July until, in the memorable words of a British corporal, the battlefield 'looked like a midden and smelt like an opened cemetery'. Achi Baba still stood defiantly uncaptured, and the army was incapable of further sustained effort. To the shelling, the heat, and the harsh life of the trenches was now added the scourge of dysentery.

Hamilton now swung his assault north. A daring scheme for capturing the commanding heights of the Sari Bair range had been worked out at Anzac. Unfortunately, as in April, this was to develop into a joint operation as complex and dangerous as the first. The Anzacs, with British and Indian reinforcements, would break out of the Anzac position to the north, and scale the incredibly tangled gullies and ridges to the summit of the Sari Bair range by night after diversionary attacks at the south of the Anzac position and at Helles. At dawn on 6th August, a new Army Corps would be landed in Suvla Bay, which was thought to be sparsely defended and which lay to the north of Anzac, and, at first light, the Turkish positions at Anzac would be assaulted from front and rear. Some 63,000 Allied troops would be attacking an area defended by well under 30,000 Turks.

This time, the veil of secrecy that descended on the operation was so complete that senior commanders were not informed until very late. Sir Frederick Stopford, the commander of the 9th Corps, which was to land at Suvla, was allowed to amend his instructions so that his task was merely to get ashore and capture the bay. There was no co-ordination between General Stopford and Birdwood at Anzac, either before or during the action. Hamilton stayed at his headquarters for two vital days.

In the circumstances, the marvel was that the operation came so close to success. Sanders, once again, was outwitted by Hamilton. The night march from Anzac was a chaotic and frightening business, but by dawn on August 7th the New Zealanders were within a fraction of seizing the vital summit. The Suvla landing, although opposed by small units and something of a shambles in other respects, was successful. By the morning of August 7th the Turkish situation at Sari Bair was desperate, but the heat, the exhaustion and inexperience of the British, and dilatoriness by their commanders, saved Sanders; the Turks, as always, fought with frenzy and unheeding valour. It developed into a weird, ghastly battle. At Suvla, 9th Corps remained glued to the shore, and advanced only with timidity. At Anzac, the failures in advance planning and command meant that everything depended on the courage and initiative of the troops and their immediate officers; neither were lacking, and the fighting was intensely bitter, even by Gallipoli standards; but they were insufficient. Sanders gave command of the entire area to Kemal, who

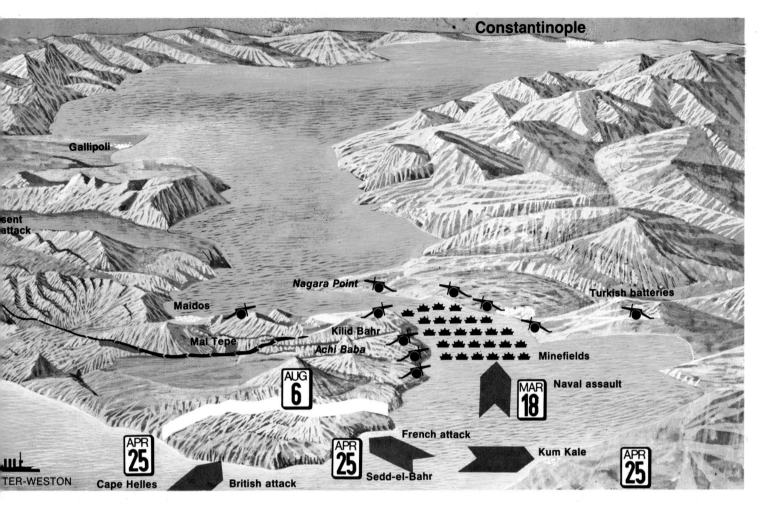

**Constantinople**

Gallipoli

sent attack

Nagara Point

Maidos

Kilid Bahr

Mal Tepe

Achi Baba

Turkish batteries

Minefields

AUG 6

MAR 18 — Naval assault

French attack

APR 25 — Cape Helles

British attack

APR 25 — Sedd-el-Bahr

Kum Kale

APR 25

TER-WESTON

checked the British at Suvla just as they were making a positive forward movement on the urgent commands of Hamilton, and at Sari Bair he launched a desperate attack at first light on August 10th that swept the Allies from the positions that had been won and held at a severely high cost. One British officer glimpsed the Dardanelles.

The rest was aftermath. Hamilton launched one last abortive attack at Suvla which was in terms of numbers the biggest battle of the campaign, but the issue had already been decided. At home, the many opponents of the venture became more vociferous and urgent; a new army was sent to Salonika; the Gallipoli fronts subsided into trench warfare; the weather got colder, and the decision of Bulgaria to enter the war meant that Austrian guns began to shell the exposed British lines with a new accuracy. In October Hamilton was recalled. His successor was Sir Charles

*Turkish prisoners. The Turks fought with frenzy and unheeding gallantry*

Monro, a man of a very different stamp, who recommended evacuation. Bluntly faced with the grim implications, the government became irresolute again. Kitchener went out to investigate, and was eventually persuaded of the necessity of withdrawal. Birdwood was in charge of the evacuation of Suvla and Anzac, which was brilliantly conducted, without a single casualty, on 19th-20th December.

The evacuation of Helles was now inevitable, and this was accomplished on 8th-9th January, again without loss of men, although that of stores and equipment was extensive. Thus, the campaign ended with a substantial triumph, an indication of what might have been achieved earlier.

The casualties were substantial. The first was the Asquith government, and, in particular, Churchill, whose removal from the Admiralty in May was a *sine qua non* for Conservative participation in the new

*The Dardanelles Campaign. Troops land a gun at what came to be called Anzac Cove*

Radio Times Hulton

coalition; it was many years before the shadow of Gallipoli was lifted from his reputation. Asquith's own prestige and position were badly shaken, as were those of Kitchener. The dream of a Balkan alliance against Germany was shattered, and Italy was the only Mediterranean nation that—in mid-May—joined the Allied cause. The British had acquired another vast commitment in Salonika. The Russian warm-sea outlet was irretrievably blocked. Compared with this last strategical disaster, the actual losses in battle or through disease—which are difficult to calculate on the Allied side but which were certainly over 200,000 (the Turkish are unknown, but must have been considerably greater, with a higher proportion of dead)—were perhaps of lesser significance. But, at the time, these loomed largest of all, and what appeared to many to be the futility of such sacrifice when the real battle was being fought almost within sight of the shores of Great Britain had an enduring effect. On 28th December the cabinet formally resolved that the Western Front would be the decisive theatre of the war. The stage was set for the vast killing-matches to come.

Had it all been loss? The enterprise came near to success on several occasions, but it is questionable whether even the capture of Gallipoli and the Straits would have had the decisive effects that appeared at the time. The entire operation grimly justified words written by Lloyd George before it had even been seriously considered: 'Expeditions which are decided upon and organised with insufficient care generally end disastrously.'

# Verdun and the Somme

The year 1916 was the watershed of the First World War. Beyond it all rivers ran in changed directions. It was the year that saw German hopes of outright victory vanish, and the Allied prospects of winning the war with their existing tactics and resources – without the United States – disappear. It was the last year in which Russia would be a powerful military force, and by the end of it Great Britain would have assumed the principal burden on the Western Front. It was also the last year in which the 'Old World' of pre-1914 still had a chance of surviving by means of a negotiated, 'stalemate' peace; it would have been as good a year as any to have ended the war. Finally, 1916 was the year of heavy guns, and – with the exception of the cataclysm of 1918 – the year that brought the highest casualty lists.

On land in 1916 there were two battles which more than any others came to symbolize the First World War for the post-war generation: Verdun and the Somme. Verdun was the occasion of Germany's only deviation – between 1915 and 1918 – from her profitable strategy of standing on the defensive in the west and letting the Allies waste themselves against an almost impregnable line at unimaginable cost.

By the end of 1915 deadlock had been reached along a static front stretching from Switzerland to the Channel. The Germans had failed, at the Marne battle, to win the war by one sledge-hammer blow against their numerically superior enemies, while suffering three-quarters of a million casualties. In attempting to repulse them from her soil, France had lost 300,000 killed and another 600,000 wounded, captured, and missing. Great Britain's naval might had proved impotent to wrest the Dardanelles from Turkey. Isolated Russia staggered on from defeat to defeat, yet still the Central powers could not bring the war to a decision in the limitless spaces of the east.

But on neither side had these early losses and disillusions impaired the will to fight on. Civilian resolution matched military morale. The opposing troops of France and Germany were no longer the green enthusiasts of 1914, nor yet the battle-weary veterans of 1917-18; they represented the best the war was to produce. In the munitions industries of both sides, artillery programmes had also reached a peak. In Great Britain Kitchener's army of conscripts was about to replace the lost 'First Hundred Thousand'.

On 2nd December, 1915, Joffre, the 'victor of the Marne', was appointed supreme commander of French military forces throughout the world. A sixty-three year-old engineer with little experience of handling infantry, he was now incomparably the most powerful figure on the Allied side and his new ascendancy enabled him to concentrate everything on the Western Front. Four days later Joffre held an historic conference of the Allied commanders at his HQ in Chantilly. From it sprang plans for a co-ordinated offensive by all the allies the following summer. By then, for the first time, there would be an abundance of men, heavy guns, and ammunition. The principal component of this offensive would be a Franco-British 'push' astride the river Somme. Forty French and twenty-five British divisions would be involved. There were no strategic objectives behind this sector of the front; Joffre's principal reason for selecting it was his instinct that he could be most assured of full British participation if they went over the top arm in arm with the French – 'bras dessus bras dessous'.

Sir Douglas Haig, who had also just taken over command of the British forces in France from General French, would have preferred to attack in Flanders (a preference which was to reassert itself with disastrous consequences a year later). However, after a meeting with Joffre on 29th December, he allowed himself to be won over to the Somme strategy. But on the other side of the lines, the chief of the German general staff, General Erich von Falkenhayn – a strange compound of ruthlessness and indecision – had his own plans. The Germans were to beat the Allies to the draw.

## To bleed France white

Prospects would never again seem so bright for German arms as at the close of 1915. In mid-December Falkenhayn prepared a lengthy memorandum for the Kaiser in which he argued that the only way to achieve victory was to cripple the Allies' main instrument, the French army, by luring it into the defence of an indefensible position. Verdun, perched precariously at the tip of a long salient, about 130 air miles south-east of where Joffre intended to attack on the Somme and just 150 miles due east of Paris, fulfilled all of Falkenhayn's requirements.

Verdun's history as a fortified camp stretched back to Roman times, when Attila had found it worth burning. In the 17th century Louis XIV's great martial engineer, Vauban, had made Verdun the most powerful fortress in his cordon protec-

*Südd-Verlag, Munich*

*Above:* French soldier wearing gas mask mounts guard at an entrance to Fort Souville, Verdun. The fort, part of the main French defence line on the east bank of the Meuse, consistently defied capture.
*Left:* The horror of Verdun. 'Hell', a painting by Georges Leroux. *Below:* Raemaekers cartoon. Crown Prince Wilhelm tells his father. 'We must have a higher pile to see Verdun'

ting France; in the Franco-Prussian War of 1870 it had been the last of the great French strongholds to fall, surviving Sedan, Metz, and Strasbourg. After 1870 it had become the key bastion in the chain of fortresses guarding France's frontier with Germany. In 1914, Verdun had provided an unshakable pivot for the French line, and without it Joffre might not have been able to stand on the Marne and save Paris.

From his knowledge both of her history and character, Falkenhayn calculated that France would be forced to defend this semi-sacred citadel to the last man. By menacing Verdun with a modest outlay of only nine divisions, he expected to draw the main weight of the French army into the salient, where German heavy artillery would grind it to pieces from three sides.

In Falkenhayn's own words, France was thus to be 'bled white'. It was a conception totally novel to the history of war and one that, in its very imagery, was symptomatic of that Great War where, in their callousness, leaders could regard human lives as mere corpuscles.

The V Army, commanded by the Kaiser's heir, the Crown Prince, was appointed to conduct the victorious operation. Day and night the great cannon and their copious munition trains now began to flow toward the V Army from all other German fronts. Aided by the railways behind their front and the national genius for organization, preparations moved with astonishing speed and secrecy. By the beginning of February 1916 more than 1,200 guns were in position – for an assault frontage of barely eight miles. More than 500 were 'heavies', including 13 of the 420mm 'Big Bertha mortars', the 'secret weapon' of 1914 which had shattered the supposedly impregnable Belgian forts. Never before had such a concentration of artillery been seen.

Verdun lay less than ten miles up the tortuous Meuse from the German lines. Most of its 15,000 inhabitants had departed when the war reached its gates in 1914, and its streets were now filled with troops, but this was nothing new for a city which had long been a garrison town.

In notable contrast to the featureless open country of Flanders and the Somme,

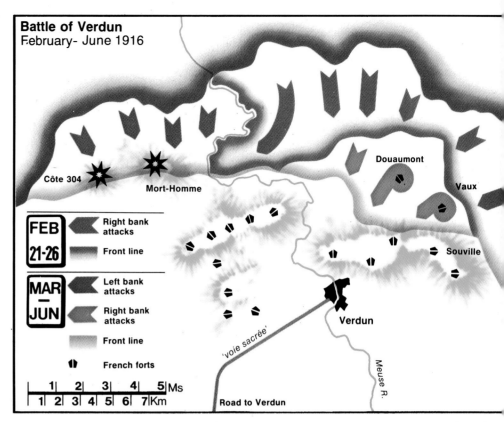

**Battle of Verdun**
February- June 1916

Douaumont

Côte 304

Mort-Homme

Vaux

Souville

| FEB 21-26 | ◣ Right bank attacks |
| | ◣ Front line |
| MAR – JUN | ◣ Left bank attacks |
| | ◣ Right bank attacks |
| | Front line |
| | ⬧ French forts |

Verdun

'voie sacrée'

Meuse R.

| 1| 2| 3| 4| 5| Ms |
| 1| 2| 3| 4| 5| 6| 7| Km |

Road to Verdun

Verdun was surrounded by interlocking patterns of steep hills and ridges which provided immensely strong natural lines of defence. The key heights were studded with three concentric rings of mighty underground forts, totalling no less than twenty major and forty intermediary works.

Each was superbly sited so that its guns could dislodge any enemy infantry appearing on the superstructure of its neighbour. With concrete carapaces eight feet thick, staunch enough to resist even the German 'Big Berthas', some of the major forts – such as Douaumont – were equipped with heavy artillery and machine-guns firing from retractable steel turrets. Outlying blockhouses linked by subterranean passages made them able to repel an attack from whatever direction it might come, and in their shell-proof cellars each could house as much as a battalion of infantry.

These forts lay between five and ten miles from Verdun itself. Between them and no man's land stretched a protective network of trenches, redoubts, and barbed wire such as was not to be found throughout the whole length of the Western Front. Verdun deserved its reputation as the world's most powerful fortress. In theory.

In fact – despite, or perhaps because of, its reputation – by February 1916, Verdun's defences were in a lamentable state. The fate of the Belgian forts had persuaded Joffre to evacuate the infantry garrisons from the Verdun forts, and remove many of their guns. The troops themselves had become slack, lulled by many months spent in so quiet and 'safe' a sector, whose deceptive calm was deepened by the influence of one of the nastiest, rainiest, foggiest, and most enervating climates in France. The French soldier has never been renowned for his ardour for digging in, and the forward lines of trenches at Verdun compared poorly with

the immensely deep earthworks the Germans had constructed at their key points on the Western Front. And, in contrast to the seventy-two battalions of élite storm troops, the Crown Prince held ready for the attack, the French trenches were manned by only thirty-four battalions, some of which were second-class units.

One outstanding French officer, Lieutenant Colonel Emile Driant, who commanded two battalions of *chasseurs* in the very tip of the salient, actually warned the French high command of the impending attack and the bad state of the Verdun defences. For this impertinence, his knuckles were severely rapped; the imperturbable Joffre paid little attention.

After a nine-day delay caused by bad weather (the first serious setback to German plans), the bombardment began at dawn on 21st February. For nine appalling hours it continued. Even on the shell-saturated Western Front nothing like it had ever been experienced. The poorly prepared French trenches were obliterated, many of their defenders buried alive. Among the units to bear the brunt of the shelling were Driant's *chasseurs*.

At 4 that afternoon the bombardment lifted and the first German assault troops moved forward out of their concealed positions. This was, in fact, only a strong patrol action, testing like a dentist's probe for the weakest areas of the French front. In most places it held. The next morning, the brutal bombardment began again. It seemed impossible that any human being could have survived in that methodically worked-over soil. Yet some had, and, with a heroic tenacity that was to immortalize the French defence during

*General Philippe Pétain in 1916. From warrior-hero he later turned defeatist*

L'Illustration

**Right:** *Verdun burning, 26th March 1916. A painting by François Flameng*

the long months ahead, they continued to face the unseen enemy from what remained of their trenches.

On the afternoon of 22nd February the Germans' first main infantry wave went in. The defenders' front line buckled. Driant was shot through the head while withdrawing the remnants of his *chasseurs*. Of these two battalions, 1,200 strong, a handful of officers and about 500 men, many of them wounded, were all that eventually straggled back to the rear. But the French resistance once again caused the German storm troops to be pulled back, to await a third softening-up bombardment the following morning.

On 23rd February, there were signs of mounting confusion and alarm at the various HQs before Verdun. Telephone lines were cut by the shelling; runners were not getting through; whole units were disappearing from the sight of their commanders. Order and counter-order were followed by the inevitable consequence. One by one the French batteries were falling silent, while others shelled their own positions, in the belief that these had already been abandoned to the enemy.

24th February was the day the dam burst. A fresh division, flung in piecemeal, broke under the bombardment, and the whole of the second line of the French defences fell within a matter of a few hours. During that disastrous day, German gains equalled those of the first three days put together. By the evening it looked as if the war had again become one of movement —for the first time since the Marne.

*Below: German troops at Verdun scramble up the soft earth of a devastated trench to launch a grenade attack*

Between the attackers and Verdun, however, there still lay the lines of the forts—above all, Douaumont, the strongest of them all, a solid bulwark of comfort behind the backs of the retreating *poilus*. Then, on 25th February, the Germans pulled off—almost in a fit of absent-mindedness—one of their greatest coups of the entire war. Acting on their own initiative, several small packets of the 24th Brandenburg Regiment, headed by a twenty-four-year-old lieutenant, Eugen Radtke (using infiltration tactics and armed with trench-clubs and pistols), worked their way into Douaumont without losing a man. To their astonishment, they discovered the world's most powerful fort to be virtually undefended.

In Germany church bells rang throughout the country to acclaim the capture of Douaumont. In France its surrender was rightly regarded as a national disaster of the first magnitude (later reckoned to have cost France the equivalent of 100,000 men). Through the streets of Verdun itself survivors of broken units ran shouting, *'Sauve qui peut!'*

At his headquarters in Chantilly even Joffre had at last become impressed by the urgency of events. To take over the imminently threatened sector, he dispatched Henri Philippe Pétain, France's outstanding expert in the art of the defensive. No general possessed the confidence of the *poilu* more than Pétain. Now—in tragic irony—this uniquely humanitarian leader was called upon to subject his men to what was becoming the most inhuman conflict of the whole war. Pétain's orders were to hold Verdun, 'whatever the cost'.

But the German attack was beginning to bog down. Losses had already been far

heavier than Falkenhayn had anticipated, many of them inflicted by flanking fire from French guns across the Meuse. The German lines looped across the river to the north of Verdun, and, from the very first, the Crown Prince had urged that his V Army be allowed to attack along both banks simultaneously. But Falkenhayn— determined to keep his own outlay of infantry in the 'bleeding white' strategy down to the barest minimum—had refused, restricting operations to the right bank. Now, to clear the menace of the French artillery, Falkenhayn reluctantly agreed to extend the offensive across to the left bank, releasing for this purpose another army corps from his tightly hoarded reserves. The deadly escalation of Verdun was under way.

### Mission of sacrifice

The lull before the next phase of the German offensive enabled Pétain to stabilize the front to an almost miraculous extent. He established a road artery to Verdun, later known as the Voie Sacrée, along which the whole lifeblood of France was to pour, to reinforce the threatened city; during the critical first week of March alone 190,000 men marched up it.

The Crown Prince now launched a new all-out attack along the left bank toward a small ridge called the Mort-Homme, which, with its sinister name, acquired from some long-forgotten tragedy of another age, was to be the centre of the most bitter, see-saw fighting for the better part of the next three months. On this one tiny sector a monotonous, deadly pattern was establishing that continued almost without let-up. It typified the whole battle of Verdun. After hours of saturating bombard-

ment, the German assault troops would surge forward to carry what remained of the French front line. There were no longer any trenches; what the Germans occupied were for the most part clusters of shell holes, where isolated groups of men lived and slept and died defending their 'position' with grenade and pick helve.

'You have a mission of sacrifice,' ran the typical orders that one French colonel gave to his men. 'Here is a post of honour where they want to attack. Every day you will have casualties . . . On the day they want to, they will massacre you to the last man, and it is your duty to fall.'

At Verdun most fell without ever having seen the enemy, under the murderous non-stop artillery bombardment, which came to characterize this battle perhaps more than any other. 'Verdun is terrible,' wrote French Sergeant-Major César Méléra, who was killed a fortnight before the armistice, 'because man is fighting against material, with the sensation of striking out at empty air . . .' Describing the effects of a bombardment, Paul Dubrulle, a thirty-four-year-old Jesuit serving as an infantry sergeant (also later killed), said: 'The most solid nerves cannot resist for long; the moment arrives where the blood mounts to the head; where fever burns the body and where the nerves, exhausted, become incapable of reacting . . . finally one abandons oneself to it, one has no longer even the strength to cover oneself with one's pack as protection against splinters, and one scarcely still has left the strength to pray to God.'

Despite the heroic sacrifices of Pétain's men, each day brought the sea of *Feldgrau* a few yards closer to Verdun. By the end of March, French losses totalled 89,000; but the attackers had also lost nearly 82,000 men. Even once they had taken the Mort-Homme, the Germans found themselves hamstrung by French guns on the Côte 304, another ridge still farther out on the flank. Like a surgeon treating galloping cancer, Falkenhayn's knife was enticed ever farther from the original point of application. More fresh German divisions were hurled into the battle – this time to seize Côte 304.

Not until May was the German 'clearing' operation on the left bank of the Meuse at last completed. The final push towards Verdun could begin. But the Crown Prince was now for calling off the offensive, and even Falkenhayn's enthusiasm was waning. The strategic significance of Verdun had long since passed out of sight; yet the battle had somehow achieved a demonic existence of its own, far beyond the control of generals of either nation. Honour had become involved to an extent which made disengagement impossible. On the French side, Pétain – affected (too deeply, according to Joffre) by the horrors he had witnessed – was promoted and replaced by two more ferocious figures: General Robert Nivelle and General Charles Mangin, nicknamed 'The Butcher'.

By now men had become almost conditioned to death at Verdun. 'One eats, one drinks beside the dead, one sleeps in the midst of the dying, one laughs and sings in the company of corpses,' wrote Georges Duhamel, the poet and dramatist, who was serving as a French army doctor. The highly compressed area of the battlefield itself had become a reeking open cemetery where 'you found the dead embedded in the walls of the trenches; heads, legs and half-bodies, just as they had been shovelled out of the way by the picks and shovels of the working party'. Conditions were no longer much better for the attacking Germans; as one soldier wrote home in April under the French counter-bombardment: 'Many would rather endure starvation than make dangerous expeditions for food.'

On 26th May a 'very excited' Joffre visited Haig at his HQ and appealed to him to advance the date of the Somme offensive. When Haig spoke of 15th August, Joffre shouted that 'The French Army would cease to exist if we did nothing by then.' Haig finally agreed to help by attacking on 1st July instead. Although Haig entertained vague hopes of a breakthrough to be exploited by cavalry, neither he nor Rawlinson – whose 4th Army were to fight the battle – had yet arrived at any higher strategic purpose than that of relieving Verdun and 'to kill as many Germans as possible' (Rawlinson).

Meanwhile, at Verdun the beginning of a torrid June brought the deadliest phase in the three-and-a-half-month battle, with the Germans throwing in a weight of attack comparable to that of February – but this time concentrated along a front only three, instead of eight, miles wide. The fighting reached Vaux, the second of the great forts, where 600 men under Major Sylvain Eugène Raynal in an epic defence held up the main thrust of the German V Army for a whole week until thirst forced them to surrender.

### The Suicide Club

Then, just as Vaux was falling, the first of the Allied summer offensives was unleashed. In the east, General Brusilov struck at the Austro-Hungarians with forty divisions, achieving a spectacular initial success. Falkenhayn was forced to transfer troops badly needed at Verdun to bolster up his sagging ally. Verdun was reprieved; although in fact it was not until 23rd June that the actual crisis was reached. On that day, using a deadly new gas called phosgene, the Crown Prince (reluctantly) attacked towards Fort Souville, astride the last ridge before Verdun. At one moment, machine-gun bullets were striking the city streets. Still the French held but there were ominous signs that morale was cracking. Just how much could a nation stand?

Two days later, however, the rumble of heavy British guns was heard in Verdun. Haig's five-day preliminary bombardment on the Somme had begun.

Because of her crippling losses at Verdun, the French contribution on the Somme had shrunk from forty to sixteen divisions, of which only five actually attacked on 1st July, compared with fourteen British divisions. Thus, for the first time, Great Britain was shouldering the main weight in a Western Front offensive. Of the British first-wave divisions, eleven were either Territorials or from Kitchener's 'New Armies'. Typical of the latter force was one battalion which had only three 'trained officers', including one who was stone deaf, another who suffered from a badly broken leg, and a sixty-three-year-old commanding officer who had retired before the Boer War. These new amateur units of 'civvies' had been trained to advance in rigid parade-ground formations that would have served well at Dettingen – straight lines two to three paces between each man, one hundred yards between each rank in the assault waves. In their rawness, their leaders did not trust them to attempt any of the more sophisticated tactics of infiltration such as the Germans and French had evolved at Verdun – despite a recommendation by Haig himself. French farmers were reluctant to allow their fields to be used for badly needed extra infantry training. But what 'K's' men lacked in expertise, they more than made up for in zeal and courage.

The Somme meanders through a flat, wide, and marshy valley. In the areas where the battle was to be fought, there are few geographical features of any note, except the high ground running south-east from Thiepval to Guillemont. This lay in German hands, and was the principal tactical objective for Rawlinson's 4th Army. The British, therefore, would everywhere be fighting uphill; whereas opposite General Fayolle's 6th Army, the French faced more or less level ground. The Germans had superb observation points gazing

*French troops attempt to take up position under fire in the Helby defile at Verdun*

*Haig: Architect of the 'Big Push'*

L'Illustration

down on the British lines, their excellence matched only by the depth of their fortifications.

In the nearly two years that they had sat on the Somme, they had excavated dugouts and vast dormitories out of the chalk as deep as forty feet below ground, comfortably safe from all but the heaviest British shell. Ironically, the British, by their policy of continual 'strafing' (in contrast to the prevalent German and French philosophy of 'live and let live'), had provoked the defenders to dig even deeper. When captured, the German dugouts astonished everybody by their depth and complexity. The German line on the Somme was, claims Churchill, 'undoubtedly the strongest and most perfectly defended position in the world'.

British security surrounding the Somme offensive was by no means perfect. Among other indiscretions, the press reported a speech made by a member of the government, Arthur Henderson, requesting workers in a munitions factory not to question why the Whitsun Bank Holiday was being suspended. In his diary for 10th June, Crown Prince Rupprecht, the German army group commander, wrote: '. . . This fact should speak volumes. It certainly does so speak, it contains the surest proof that there will be a great British offensive before long. . . .' Abundantly aware of just where the 'Big Push' was coming, for several weeks previously the German defenders had industriously practised rushing their machine-guns up from the dugouts. This had been perfected to a three-minute drill, which would give the Germans an ample margin on 'Z-day' between the lifting of the British barrage and the arrival of the attacking infantry.

For five days Rawlinson's artillery preparation blasted away without let-up (Haig would have preferred a short preliminary bombardment)—thereby dissipating what little element of surprise there still remained. By British standards of the day, it was a bombardment of unprecedented weight. Yet on their much wider front they could mount not nearly half as many heavy

guns as the French; and they had nothing to compare with the French 240-mm mortars and 400 'super-heavies' with which Foch (French northern army group commander) had equipped Fayolle. A depressing quantity of the British shells turned out to be dud; while defective American ammunition caused so many premature explosions that some of the 4.5 howitzer gun crews nicknamed themselves 'the Suicide Club'. The fire-plan also suffered from the same inflexibility which characterized the training of the new infantry. Through sheer weight of metal, large sections of the German front-line trenches were indeed obliterated, their skeleton outposts killed. But down below in the secure depths of the dugouts, the main body of the German defenders sat playing *Skat* while the shelling raged above.

The worst shortcoming of the five-day bombardment, however, was that it failed in its essential task of breaking up the barbed wire through which the British assault waves were to advance. Divisional commanders appear to have known this, but to have kept the knowledge to themselves. On the eve of the 'Big Push', Haig wrote in his diary with the misguided optimism that was to be found at almost every level prior to 1st July: 'The wire has never been so well cut, nor the Artillery preparation so thorough. I have seen personally all the Corps commanders and one and all are full of confidence. . . .'

At 0245 hours on 1st July a German listening post picked up a message from Rawlinson wishing his 4th Army 'Good Luck'. A little less than five hours later there was suddenly a strange silence as the British bombardment ended. Somewhere near a hundred thousand men left their trenches at this moment and moved forward at a steady walk. On their backs they carried their personal kit—including a spare pair of socks—water bottles, a day's rations, two gas masks, mess tins and field dressings, as well as rifle, bayonet, 220 rounds of ammunition, and an entrenching tool. Some also carried hand grenades or bombs for a trench mortar. The minimum load was 66lb; some men were laden with as much as 85 to 90lb. It was about to become a broiling hot day.

'. . . They got going without delay,' wrote the commanding officer of a battalion of the Royal Inniskilling Fusiliers;

'No fuss, no shouting, no running, everything solid and thorough—just like the men themselves. Here and there a boy would wave his hand to me as I shouted good luck to them through my megaphone. And all had a cheery face . . . Fancy advancing against heavy fire with a big roll of barbed wire on your shoulders! . . .'

Seen from the defenders' point of view, a German recorded that the moment the bombardment lifted:

'. . . Our men at once clambered up the steep shafts leading from the dug-outs to daylight and ran for the nearest shell craters. The machine-guns were pulled out of the dug-outs and hurriedly placed into position, their crews dragging the heavy ammunition boxes up the steps and out to the guns. A rough firing line was thus

rapidly established. As soon as in position, a series of extended lines of British infantry were seen moving forward from the British trenches. The first line appeared to continue without end to right and left. It was quickly followed by a second line, then a third and fourth. They came on at a steady easy pace as if expecting to find nothing alive in our front trenches. . . .'

Reading from left to right along the line, the British forces involved in the principal offensive were the 8th, 10th, 3rd, 15th, and 13th Corps, while below them on the river Somme itself came the French 20th and 35th Corps. General Hunter-Weston's 8th Corps had the most difficult task of all—the terrain was particularly difficult—and, because of its inexperience, it was the corps about which Haig had entertained the most doubts. With the 31st Division holding its left flank, the Yorks and Lancs were encouraged to see ahead of them numerous gaps in the wire opened up by the shelling. But at the moment of reaching them, they were scythed down by devastating machine-gun fire from the weapons which the Germans had rushed up from their dug-outs. It was an experience that was to be repeated innumerable times that day. By early afternoon the 31st Division had lost 3,600 officers and men, of whom only eight were prisoners.

Next to it, the 29th Division, recently returned from Gallipoli, had the task of rushing the 'Hawthorn Redoubt' after an immense mine had been detonated under it. But the mine had been timed to go off ten minutes before zero hour; giving the German machine-gunners plenty of time

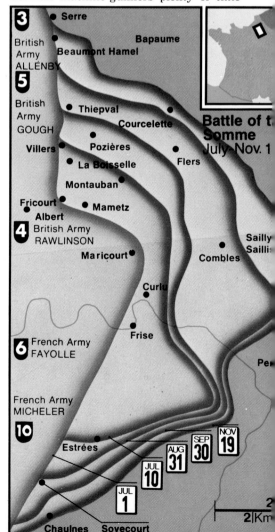

Battle of t. Somme
July–Nov. 1

*Painting of the Somme battlefield, Colincamps to Fouquevillers, from a German balloon*

the neighbouring English units. The division was left clinging precariously to the German front line.

On the 3rd Corps' front, the 8th Division was another unit to suffer appalling casualties in return for very little progress. It lost a shocking total of 1,927 officers and men killed; one of its battalions, the 2nd Middlesex, lost 22 officers and 601 men, another – the 8th Yorks and Lancs – 21 and 576 respectively, out of an average of 27-30 officers and roughly 700 men to a battalion.

Over the whole British front, only Congreve's 13th Corps, next door to the French, registered any notable success that day. Attacking through Montauban, it captured the entire HQ of the German 62nd Regiment; making a total bag of 1,882 prisoners (compared with the 8th Corps' 22). At Montauban, the cellars were found to be filled with German dead; apparently killed by the French heavy mortars.

### Fighting in hell

Indeed, for all the incredible fortitude of Kitchener's men, it was the French who won the laurels on 1st July. The terrain opposite them was admittedly much more favourable, the defences weaker; they had more and heavier guns, which had smashed up even some of the deepest enemy dugouts; their infantry moved with greater skill and flexibility; and they had the advantage of a certain degree of surprise. After the losses inflicted at Verdun, German intelligence could not believe that the French were capable of making a serious contribution on the Somme. To reinforce this belief, Foch cleverly delayed the French attack until several hours after the British.

By early afternoon, Fayolle's troops had taken 6,000 prisoners, destroyed the whole of the German 121st Division's artillery, and come close to making a breakthrough. Péronne itself was threatened. General Balfourier, commanding the 'Iron' (20th) Corps which had saved Verdun in February, urged Congreve on his left to join him in continuing the advance. But Congreve would budge no farther. Above him, Rawlinson was bent more on consolidation than exploitation. Thus Balfourier, with his left flank hanging in the air, was unable to advance either. It was not until 10 o'clock that night that Rawlinson made any attempt to push reserves up to the areas of least resistance. What prospect there had been of capitalizing on any success

to reoccupy the crater. Moving across no man's land the Royal Fusiliers could see ahead of them the bodies of their first waves festooning the uncut wire; all that came back from this one battalion was 120 men. The divisional commander, in a supreme understatement, noted that his men had been 'temporarily held up by some machine-guns', and pushed up another brigade; one battalion found itself so obstructed by the dead and the endless lines of wounded that it physically could not get forward. Attacking unsuccessfully but with fantastic courage at Beaumont-Hamel, the Newfoundlanders won their greatest battle honour: in a matter of minutes 710 men fell.

Also at Beaumont-Hamel, troops that had captured the Heidenkopf position were tragically shot down by the second wave, unaware that the German strong-point was already in British hands.

By nightfall, the 8th Corps alone had lost 14,000 officers and men without even broaching the main objective. It had taken only twenty-two prisoners. For the 10th, the 3rd, and part of 15th Corps the story of bloody failure was much the same:

'I get up from the ground and whistle,' recalled an officer commanding an Irish battalion in the second wave. 'The others rise. We move off with steady pace. I see rows upon rows of British soldiers lying dead, dying or wounded in no man's land. Here and there I see the hands thrown up and then a body flops on the ground. The bursting shells and smoke make visibility poor. We proceed. Again I look southward from a different angle and perceive heaped up masses of British corpses suspended on the German wire, while live men rush forward in orderly procession to swell the weight of numbers in the spider's web. . . .' The Highland Light Infantry went into battle behind their pipers. Swiftly their leading companies invested the German trenches, but while they were still exulting at their success, hidden German machine-guns opened fire. Within little more than

an hour of the beginning of the attack, half the HLI were killed or wounded, bringing the assault to a sudden halt.

Opposite Thiepval, the 36th (Ulster) Division came tantalizingly, tragically close to achieving success. Better trained than most of Rawlinson's units, the Inniskillings managed to advance a mile in the first hour of the attack, attaining the top of the ridge and capturing the Schwaben Redoubt, an important strongpoint in the German first-line. But, following the experiences of 1915 when so many field officers had been killed off, it was Haig's orders that no battalion commanding officers or second-in-commands should go in with their men in the first wave. Thus there was no one senior enough to consolidate the Ulstermen's fine success. Communications with the rear were appalling. Runners sent back for fresh orders never returned. Precious time was thrown away, while the Germans recovered their balance. When finally a reserve brigade was sent up to reinforce the Inniskillings, it too had no senior officers with it; with the result it advanced too fast, running into its own artillery barrage, where it lost something like two-thirds of its soldiers. That evening, of the 10th Corps' 9,000 losses, over half came from the Ulster Division – a fact which was long to cause bitterness against

*Australian Royal Field Artillery pass by 4.7 gun during the Somme battle*

*British go over the top in the Somme battle. Their dead bodies were to festoon the wire*

gained during the 1st July was swiftly lost; the Germans were soon replacing the machine-guns destroyed that day.

When the casualties were counted, the British figures came to 60,000, of which the dead numbered 20,000. Most of the slaughter had been accomplished by perhaps a hundred German machine-gun teams. 1st July was one of the blackest days in British history. Even at Verdun, the total French casualty list for the worst month barely exceeded what Great Britain had lost on that one day. Fayolle lost fewer men than the defending Germans.

Haig had no idea of the full extent of the British losses until 3rd July and neither he nor Rawlinson quite knew why some efforts had succeeded and others failed. On the 3rd Haig ordered Rawlinson to attack again; this time rightly trying to follow up the good results achieved on his southern sector. But the guns were now short of ammunition, and the losses on 1st July greatly reduced the strength of the new blows. That night it rained, and the next day 'walking, let alone fighting, became hellish'.

On 14th July, Rawlinson—chastened by the terrible casualties his army had suffered—decided to try something new. He would attack by night. Describing it caustically as 'an attack organized for amateurs by amateurs', the French predicted disaster. Haig, equally dubious, caused the attack to be postponed twenty-four hours—a delay that diminished the chances of success. Nevertheless, throwing in six brigades which totalled some 22,000 men, Rawlinson after a short hurricane bombardment punched out a salient four miles wide and a thousand yards deep, breaching the Germans' second line—and thereby briefly restoring the element of surprise to the Western Front. A French liaison officer telephoned the sceptical Balfourier: *'Ils ont osé. Ils ont réussi!'*

Once again, however, the fruits of victory were thrown away by poor communications and the painful slowness to react of the British command. As at Gallipoli, there was a horrifying absence of any sense of urgency. The cavalry were waiting in the wings, but too far back to be available to exploit any gains, and not until mid-afternoon that day was it decided to push up the already battle-weary 7th Infantry Division. Thus nine valuable hours were wasted, and darkness was falling when at

last the British cavalry and infantry reserves attacked. By then the shaken Germans had rallied.

Deeply disappointed, Haig now settled for a long-protracted 'battle of attrition'. Writing to the government, he declared his intention 'to maintain a steady pressure on Somme battle . . . proceeding thus, I expect to be able to maintain the offensive well into the Autumn. . . .' All through August and into September the bloody slogging match continued. As seen by the Australian official history, Haig's new technique 'merely appeared to be that of applying a battering-ram ten or fifteen times against the same part of the enemy's battle-front with the intention of penetrating for a mile, or possibly two . . . the claim that it was economic is entirely unjustified'. By the end of the summer, one level-headed Australian officer was writing '. . . we have just come out of a place so terrible that . . . a raving lunatic could never imagine the horror the last thirteen days. . . .'

Meanwhile, however, Verdun had been finally and definitively relieved by the dreadful British sacrifices on the Somme. On 11th July, one last desperate effort was mounted against Verdun, and a handful of Germans momentarily reached a height whence they could actually gaze down on Verdun's citadel. It was the high-water mark of the battle, and—though not apparent at the time—was perhaps the turning point, the Gettysburg of the First World War. Rapidly the tide now receded at Verdun, with Falkenhayn ordering the German army to assume the defensive all along the Western Front.

At the end of August Falkenhayn was replaced by the formidable combination of Hindenburg and Ludendorff.

Visiting the Somme, Ludendorff criticized the inflexibility of the defence there; '. . . Without doubt they fought too doggedly, clinging too resolutely to the mere holding of ground, with the result that the losses were heavy. . . . The Field Marshal and I could for the moment only ask that the front line should be held more lightly. . . .' It was a prelude to the strategic withdrawal to the 'Hindenburg Line' in the following spring.

### 'A pretty mechanical toy'

On the Somme, 15th September was to become a red-letter day in the history of warfare. Haig decided to throw into a third major attack the first fifty newly invented tanks. Rejected by Kitchener as 'a pretty mechanical toy but of very limited military value', the tank had been developed under the greatest secrecy and crews trained with similar security behind a vast secret enclosure near Thetford in Norfolk. Even the name 'tank' was intended to deceive

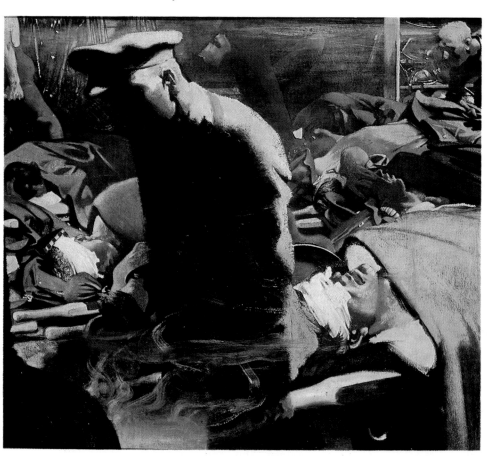

*Imperial War Museum*

*Painters capture the meaning of these sacrificial battles. **Above:** 'Paths of Glory' by C. Nevinson. **Below left:** 'Gassed and Wounded' by Eric Kennington*

the enemy. Its inventors begged the army not to employ the first machines, however, until they were technically more reliable; while even Asquith visiting the front on 6th September thought it: '. . . a mistake to put them into the battle of the Somme. They were built for the purpose of breaking an ordinary trench system with a normal artillery fire only, whereas on the Somme they will have to penetrate a terrific artillery barrage, and will have to operate in a broken country full of shell-craters . . .'

But Haig was determined. Historians will long continue to argue whether he was right or not; on Haig's side, the Cambrai raid the following year tends to prove that the surprise value of the tank had not entirely been thrown away, and undoubtedly, sooner or later, it would have had to be tried out under battle conditions.

On the day of the attack, only thirty-two of the original fifty tanks reached the assembly area in working order; twenty-four actually went into battle, and most of these broke down, became bogged, or were knocked out. At Flers the tank showed what it could do, and the infantry advanced cheering down the main street of the village behind four solitary machines. But once again poor communications between front and rear gave the Germans a chance to reorganize before success could be exploited. By the evening of the 15th all the tanks were either scattered or destroyed. With them vanished the last of Haig's three opportunities on the Somme; Montauban on 1st July, Rawlinson's night attack on the 14th, and Flers on 15th September.

Now the equinoctial rains turned the battlefield into a slippery bog. But, pressed by Joffre, Haig stuck out his Celtic jaw and soldiered on, in the mystic belief that — somehow, somewhere — an exhausted foe might suddenly break. The British army was equally exhausted. Conditions became even more appalling. In November, a soldier wrote: '. . . Whoever it is we are relieving, they have already gone. The trench is empty . . . Corpses lie along the parados, rotting in the wet; every now and then a booted foot appears jutting over the trench. The mud makes it all but impassable, and now, sunk in it up to the knees, I have the momentary terror of never being able to pull myself out . . . This is the very limit of endurance. . . .'

In a last attack on 13th November, shattered Beaumont-Hamel was finally captured. Having won the bloodily disputed high ground, the British were now fighting their way down into the valley beyond — condemning themselves to spend a winter in flooded trenches. Nothing of any strategic value had been attained. The 'Big Push' was over.

At Verdun in the autumn, Nivelle and Mangin recaptured forts Douaumont and Vaux in a series of brilliant counter-strokes — plus much of the territory gained so painfully by the Crown Prince's men. By Christmas 1916 both battles were finished. After ten terrible months Verdun had been saved. But at what a cost! Half the houses in the city itself had been destroyed by the long-range German guns, and nine of its neighbouring villages had vanished off the face of the earth. When the human casualties came to be added up, the French admitted to having lost 377,231 men, of whom 162,308 were listed as dead or missing. German losses amounted to no

less than 337,000. But, in fact, combined casualties may easily have totalled much more than 800,000.

What caused this imprecision about the slaughter at Verdun, as well as giving the battle its particularly atrocious character, was the fact that it all took place in so concentrated an area — little larger than the London parks. Many of the dead were never found, or are still being discovered to this day. One combatant recalled how 'the shells disinterred the bodies, then reinterred them, chopped them to pieces, played with them as a cat plays with a mouse'. Inside the great sombre *Ossuaire* at Verdun lie the bones of more than 100,000 unknown warriors.

On the Somme, the British had lost some 420,000 men; the French about 200,000 and the Germans probably about 450,000 — although a miasma of mendacity and error still surrounds the exact figures. On the battlefields of Verdun and the Somme, there also expired the last flickers of idealism; yet the war would go on.

The casualties of the two battles included among them the highest warlords on both sides. Falkenhayn had fallen; then Joffre, to be replaced (disastrously) by Nivelle, and Asquith by Lloyd George; a few months later Premier Briand's head would also topple. Because of the appalling extent to which Verdun had 'bled white' his own army, Falkenhayn's grim experiment had failed. Yet, in its longer-range effects, it contained an element of success. As Raymond Jubert, a young French ensign, wrote in prophetic despair before he was killed at Verdun: 'They will not be able to make us do it again another day; that would be to misconstrue the price of our effort. . . .' The excessive sacrifices of the French army at Verdun germinated the seeds of the mutinies that were to sprout in the summer of 1917, thereby making it finally plain that the war could no longer be won without American troops.

In many ways Verdun and Somme were the First World War in microcosm, with all its heroism and futility, its glorious and unspeakable horrors. They were indecisive battles in an indecisive war. Of the two, Verdun undoubtedly had the greater historical significance. Years after the 1918 Armistice this Pyrrhic victory of the 20th century continued to haunt the French nation. From the role the forts at Verdun had played, France's military leaders (headed by Pétain) drew the wrong conclusions, and the Maginot Line — with all its disastrous strategic consequences in 1940 — was born.

Spiritually, perhaps, the damage was even greater. More than three-quarters of the whole French army passed through the hell of Verdun — almost an entire generation of Frenchmen. Nobody knew this better than Pétain who, years after the war, remarked that at Verdun 'the constant vision of death had penetrated him (the French soldier) with a resignation which bordered on fatalism'.

For a symbol of what Verdun did to France, one need hardly search beyond the tragic figure of Pétain, the warrior-hero of 1916, the resigned defeatist of 1940.

# America Declares War

*American magazine illustration: New Year 1917 promises showers of Allied gold to America*

It was Lloyd George who once remarked that Europe slithered into war in 1914, and this applies equally to the entrance of the United States into the World War in 1917. Prior to these separate if similar *dénouements*, neither the Europeans nor the Americans quite knew what they were doing. As matters evolved, within weeks of the fateful date of the declaration of war on 6th April, President Woodrow

*Wild enthusiasm and waving flags on Broadway—America has entered the war*

Wilson was asking the belligerents for a peace without victory and hoping to achieve it through his efforts at mediation, while the United States remained outside the war as a neutral power. But then came a series of unexpected military, diplomatic, and political changes, none of them American in origin. Before long, Wilson, to use the description of Senator Henry Cabot Lodge, was 'in the grip of events'. On 6th April 1917 some of the election posters of November 1916 were still up on the billboards, and Americans could ponder the Democratic Party slogans which had helped re-elect the President: 'He Kept Us Out of War'; and 'War in the East, Peace in the West, Thank God for Wilson'. They were not, however, angry with Wilson, for they too had reacted to unforeseen events.

What were these events of early 1917 which moved the President and people? It is easy now to see that, given what had gone before, in January 1917 it would take only a few more blows from the German government to make America abandon her neutrality. Given that government's almost complete lack of understanding of the sensitivities of the American government and people, the wonder is that neutrality lasted as long as it did, that German blunders did not come sooner. It is also curious that Wilson and the American people believed in January 1917 that they still possessed freedom of manoeuvre. The

President early that month told his confidant Colonel House 'There will be no war'.

On 19th January 1917 the German government thoughtfully told Ambassador Johann von Bernstorff about the decision to resume unrestricted submarine warfare on 1st February but Bernstorff was to inform the American government, and duly did so, only on 31st January, at 4 pm. It was a crude beginning, this eight hours' notice. Bernstorff had done his best to prevent this stupidity, this tactic of loosing the submarines, which he knew would drive the Americans into war. It was not only the trans-Atlantic munitions trade, or the export of American food (harvests had been poor in 1916), that the Germans were seeking to prevent; they wanted to strangle British economic life by cutting off all imports. They did not have to use so thorough a submarine blockade, which would inevitably affront the Americans, Bernstorff thought. He had cabled his views, but the German leaders paid no attention.

Bernstorff meanwhile had lowered his stock with the American government and public, and with his own government (he deeply offended the Kaiser), by allowing a peccadillo to get into public print. On a vacation in the Adirondacks with a lady who often entertained him, he posed in a bathing suit for a photograph, with his arms intimately encircling two ladies similarly attired. At the very time when he

*A British cartoon showing the two faces of Wilson's policy of neutrality*

needed whatever personal influence and dignity he could muster, this photograph found its way into the hands of the Russian ambassador who passed it to the newspapers. Americans snickered at the Bathing Beauty Scandal. Bernstorff was a generally competent diplomat to whom both the American and German governments should have listened. Instead this 'good German' found himself ignored on public matters and laughed at over private ones. 'I am not surprised,' he said upon the break of diplomatic relations when he received his passports. 'My government will not be surprised either. The people in Berlin knew what was bound to happen if they took the action they have taken. There was nothing else left for the United States to do.' In despair he told a press conference that he was through with politics.

After · the formal break, two events followed which together pushed the country into war. The first was a clear-cut case of a German submarine sinking a passenger vessel with American citizens aboard. Wilson on 3rd February, when he informed Congress that he was breaking relations, had added that 'I refuse to believe that it is the intention of the German authorities to do in fact what they have warned us they will feel at liberty to do. . . . Only actual overt acts on their part can make me believe it even now'. For two weeks after resumption of unrestricted submarine warfare no incident occurred, no open violation of what Americans liked to believe was one of their principal neutral rights. There was no paralysis of shipping during the period, as American tonnage clearing United States ports dropped only from 1,019,396 in January to 847,786 in February. The day the fatal vessel, the 18,000-ton British liner *Laconia,* sailed from New York harbour, sixty-six ships of all nationalities were in the roadstead, loaded or loading for ports in the zone of war. Wilson spoke again to Congress on 26th February, reporting that 'The overt act which I have ventured to hope the German commanders would in fact avoid has not occurred'. That very moment, however, news of the sinking of the *Laconia* the day before was being flashed to Washington. It was whispered around the House chamber before the

President finished his speech, and printed in the country's newspapers the next day. Three Americans, including two women, had lost their lives. The deaths of the women were not pretty to contemplate: a torpedoing at night, a lifeboat half stove-in as it swung down over the careening hull, this fragile craft itself slowly sinking, Mrs Albert H.Hoy and her daughter Elizabeth standing waist deep in icy water throughout the long night.

This was interpreted as an open challenge, by the German government which authorized it, and by the American government and people who had brought themselves into a frame of mind to oppose it.

### The Zimmermann telegram

The second precipitating event came almost immediately when American newspapers on 1st March published the Zimmermann telegram. The *Laconia* disaster had proved that the Germans held no regard for international law and human rights. The Zimmermann telegram showed that they were guilty not merely of legal and moral turpitude but were enemies of the United States, willing to endanger the nation's very existence. In the annals of international stupidity during the 20th century, or any other century, this famous telegram hardly has an equal. It was a German proposal of an alliance to the government of Mexico (an alliance which was possibly to include the Japanese government as well). The Mexicans were to attack the United States during the hostilities now deemed imminent, in exchange for which the Germans promised a return of the 'lost territories' of the Mexican War of 1846-48: Texas, New Mexico, Arizona. The genesis of the proposal is now quite clear. The Americans had been giving Mexico much trouble in the past few years, even to the extent of sending in a punitive military expedition in 1916 under command of General Pershing. The Mexican regime of General Venustiano ('Don Venus') Carranza began to take interest in Mexican-German co-operation, and Don Venus in November made a suggestion, going so far as to offer submarine bases. An assistant in the German foreign office, one Kemnitz, turned the proposal into a project for an alliance. It was so preposterous a project that the German foreign secretary, Zimmermann, should have forgotten it. Instead he picked it up as a great idea.

Zimmermann sent his telegram to Mexico by several means, one of which was through the American embassy in Berlin and thence from Washington to Mexico City by Western Union. Ambassador Gerard transmitted this German message, in its original German code, as part of an arrangement which Colonel House had made, with Wilson's permission, for cable transmission of German messages pertaining to mediation. Ambassador Bernstorff had promised to use the arrangement only for peaceful purposes, but ·Zimmermann was not put off by that engagement.

The British government intercepted and decoded all three of Zimmermann's transmissions. Under the leadership of Admiral Sir William Reginald Hall, the

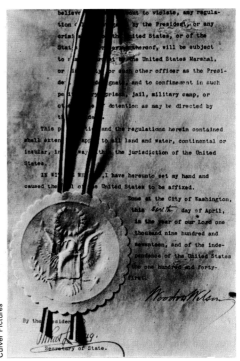

*The text of Wilson's declaration of war, forced on him by Germany's submarine warfare and the Zimmermann telegram*

Admiralty early in the war had set up a code and cipher-cracking operation, which triumphed with the deciphering of Zimmermann's idiotic telegram. Not wishing to show his knowledge of the German code, Hall at first was in a quandary about publishing, but ingenuity triumphed. One of his agents in Mexico City procured from the Mexican telegraph office a copy of the still-encoded telegram which Bernstorff had obtained from the American State Department and relayed from Washington. It contained certain small differences from the other intercepts, and upon publication the impression prevailed that someone had stolen or sold a decoded copy of the telegram, getting it from the German legation in Mexico City. The Germans reassured Hall that they were without suspicion by engaging in a lively inquiry with Eckhardt, the German minister in Mexico City, asking how many copies of the decode Eckhardt had made and who had handled them, using of course the same code which Hall had cracked. Hall found it amusing to read that Eckhardt tried to pass the blame off on to Bernstorff in Washington.

### No denial

Even after the cat was out of the bag, the telegram published in every American newspaper, it was still possible for Zimmermann in Berlin to quiet the uproar, or at the very least to make the Americans disclose how they obtained the telegram, by baldly denying that he had sent it. President Wilson himself, the author in 1918 of 'open diplomacy', once in a confidential conversation with Colonel House said, admittedly for House's ears only (and, as it turned out, for House's diary), that a man was justified in lying for two purposes, to protect the honour of a lady and to preserve secrets of state. Had Zimmermann but known it, he could have cited the President in support of a diplo-

The rest was anticlimax. The first Russian Revolution of March 1917 forced the abdication of the Tsar and the proclamation of a republic, and removed an embarrassing despotism from the ranks of the Allies, making it easier to say that the Allies were Democracy fighting the Central powers who represented Autocracy. About the same time, U-boats sank four American ships. The presidential decision to arm merchant ships, taken in mid-March, constituting a sort of armed neutrality, had no discernible effect on German policy. The President called a special session of Congress. On the evening of 2nd April 1917, Wilson went before both Houses, duly assembled in the Capitol building in Washington, and as the lights gleamed in the crowded chamber he asked his countrymen for what they were ready to give him. Many Senators had brought small American flags to the House chamber where the President spoke; during the course of his speech they clapped their hands and eagerly waved their flags to signify assent.

*Above: American soldiers, off to the Western Front, look back at New York. **Left:** Wilson asks Congress to declare war. **Below:** For Great Britain, America's declaration promised men—and hope*

matic denial. Secretary Lansing in Washington was certain that Zimmermann would lie his way out, and was incredulous to learn that the German foreign secretary almost at once admitted authorship in a burst of truthfulness which was as naïve as the composition which inspired it.

What could the American government do after the publication of the telegram on 1st March? If Wilson does not go to war now, Theodore Roosevelt wrote to Lodge, 'I shall skin him alive'. The 'Prussian Invasion Plot' was transparently clear. Newspapers in the hitherto isolationist Middle West acknowledged the end of neutrality. The Chicago *Tribune* warned its readers to realize now, 'without delay, that Germany recognizes us an enemy', and that the country no longer could hope to keep out of 'active participation in the present conflict'. The Cleveland *Plain Dealer* said there was 'neither virtue nor dignity' in refusing to fight now. The Oshkosh (Wisconsin) *Northwestern,* an authentic voice from the Middle West, said that the telegram had turned pacifists, critics and carpers into patriots overnight. Zimmermann, as Mrs Tuchman has written, 'shot an arrow in the air and brought down neutrality like a dead duck'.

*Bernstorff, discomfited by scandal*

## "We are coming, brothers, coming, A hundred thousand strong!"

# The New Military Balance

On 6th April 1917 the United States entered the First World War. At the beginning of June General John J. Pershing, the commander-in-chief of the American Expeditionary Force arrived in England for a four-day visit, and then went on to France to begin organizing his command. His reception by the British and French was warm to the point of hysteria: the King welcomed him, the crowds cheered and threw roses. The illustrated magazine *The London Graphic* caught the mood and the style of the time by surrounding a photograph of Pershing and his officers with a tabernacle in classical style, in which a luscious symbolic figure of a woman held a laurel wreath over Pershing's head; the caption read: 'Now is the winter of our discontent made glorious summer by this sun of (New) York.' (In fact, Pershing had been born in Linn County, Missouri.)

The hopes, the great expectations, that were aroused in the British and French peoples by American entry into the war were understandable. The spring and early summer of 1917 saw Allied fortunes at their lowest ebb. The year 1916 had ended with apparently nothing to show for colossal losses but small territorial gains on the Somme and the preservation of Verdun. The expulsion of the Germans from French soil seemed as difficult and as far off as ever. The very real and heavy damage done to German power by the Allied offensives in the late summer and autumn of 1916 was at that time hidden from view.

The third year of the war now unfolded for the Allies a prospect of catastrophe. On 1st February 1917 the Germans began unrestricted submarine warfare. The results of the first three months fully justified German calculations that before the end of the year Great Britain would be unable to prosecute the war because of lack of shipping to transport food, raw materials, and troops; the tonnage sunk rose from 470,000 in February to 837,000 in April. Admiral Jellicoe, the British first sea lord, believed that unless an answer to the submarine could be found – and in his estimation, none was in sight – the war was certainly lost. In March revolution exploded in Tsarist Russia and the Tsar Nicholas II abdicated. Although the Russian army had never fulfilled the hopes of 1914 that it would prove an irresistible steam-roller, it had nevertheless heavily engaged Germany's Austrian ally and brought her to the point of exhaustion, and had also drawn German resources away

from the Western Front. In 1916 General Alexey Brusilov's Offensive had inflicted a smashing defeat in the east on the Central powers. Now Russia was paralysed by revolution, no man could say what help she would bring.

Finally, at the end of April and the beginning of May 1917, the French army, under a new commander-in-chief, General Robert Nivelle, was crushingly, appallingly, repulsed in a general offensive on the Western Front which Nivelle had promised would lead to a swift breakthrough and a rapid, and victorious, end to the war. In the aftermath of this shattering disappointment, all the accumulated war weariness and exhaustion of the French nation exploded in widespread army mutinies and civil disorders. It was no wonder that the Allied leaders and peoples alike greeted the belligerency of the richest, most industrially powerful nation in the world, with all its unblooded manpower, with somewhat hysterical relief. America brought on to the Allied side a population of 93,400,000 and a steel production of 45,060,607 tons. The human resources went far to make up for the 180 million Russians now perhaps lost to the Allied cause. The industrial power was overwhelming; American steel production alone was nearly three times as great as that of Germany and Austria together. However, all this was only *potential*. How long would it be before American resources, human and industrial, were translated into vast, superbly-equipped armies on the Western Front able to crush down the exhausted and outmatched Germans? In view of the German submarine successes and the manifest unsteadiness of the French army and nation, would there even *be* a Western Front by the time the Americans had deployed their power?

Whatever its enormous long-term importance in 20th-century history, the American entry into the First World War in April 1917 in fact was in itself of far smaller strategic significance at the time than the cheering British and French crowds supposed. There was no progressive transformation of the war—no massive rescue operation. On the other hand, it is certain that without America, the Allies would have lost the war. The clue to this apparent paradox lies in the fact that American help *before* her entry into the war was more vital than many recognize; and American help *after* her entry rather less vital, at least for some fifteen months or so.

The German and Austrian war effort was

*Top: Tank Corps recruiting poster. At first the Americans tried to equip military units before sending them to France. Above: Appeal for the war loan. The American entry was greeted by the Allies with almost hysterical relief. Russia was undergoing revolution, German submarines threatened Great Britain's power to stay in the war, and the French army had been demoralized. Yet America's immediate military help was less than was generally realized*

TREAT 'EM ROUGH!

JOIN THE TANKS
United States Tank Corps

Huntingdon Hartford

BUY UNITED STATES GOVERNMEN
WAR SAVINGS STAMPS

W·S·S
For Sale Here

Your money back with interest from the UNITED STATES TREAS

Lords Gallery

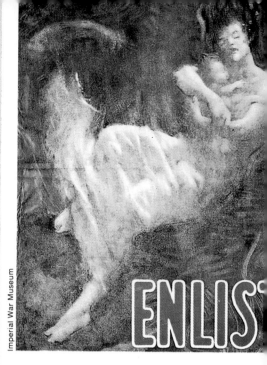

ENLIS

*Above:* American recruitment poster shows a drowned mother and child, supposed victims of a U-boat. *Left:* British tank passes US skyscraper in recruiting drive. *Right:* American soldiers embark at Southampton

entirely based on their own industries and technological skill. By the spring of 1915, after a temporary shortage of munitions, Germany had converted her vast chemical industry and her varied and highly modern engineering industries to the production of explosives, propellants, fuses, shells, ammunition, and weapons. Her machine-tool industry—the most modern and inventive in the world except for that of America—had no difficulty in equipping new munitions plants.

Great Britain and France, in sharp contrast, found when they tackled the problem of a massive expansion of war production that their industrial resources were largely out-of-date in equipment and techniques—and that they even lacked completely a whole range of the most modern kinds of industries. Thus, Great Britain and France before the war had been almost entirely dependent on Germany for chemical products, such as dyes, drugs, and photographic processing materials. It was plant that made dyes and drugs that could also easily make explosives. Great Britain had to create a chemical industry from scratch, based on seized German patents. While it was being built up, there was a bottleneck at the very base of shell manufacture—the propellant and the explosive.

British manufacturing industry was still largely mid-Victorian in its types of product, its methods of production, its skills and techniques. Mass-production plant, with lines of automatic or semi-automatic machines, producing all kinds of precision light-engineering work, was hardly known. Before 1914 Great Britain was dependent mostly on Germany, partly on America, for almost all the sophisticated products of the second phase of the industrial revolution—ball-bearings, magnetoes, sparking plugs, cameras, optical goods.

Great Britain therefore lacked both the general and the particular industries to sustain a modern war. Nor could her machine-tool industry equip the vast new

factories that had to be created. Machine-tools were—and are—the basic industry of modern technological growth; they are the machines which make machines. The British machine-tool industry was also essentially mid-Victorian; it was small-scale, it made a limited range of tools to order by almost craft methods in small workshops. For the 'modern' kind of automatic or semi-automatic machine for a production-line, it contented itself in peacetime by acting as a distribution agent for American and German imports.

France was in no better case. Thus, American resources and know-how were, from the end of 1914, absolutely essential to the survival of the Allies. It was to America—and to a lesser extent to Sweden and Switzerland—that they looked to supply the specialized sophisticated products that they had imported from Germany. It was on American industry that Great Britain especially depended for shells and other munitions during 1915 and 1916, while Great Britain was still painfully creating her chemical and munitions industries. Even in 1915 a third of all shells issued to the British army were made in North America. In 1916 the debut of the mass British armies in battle was only made possible by shells from America and Canada. As the history of the ministry of munitions expressed it: 'During the early part of 1915, in fact, overseas contractors assumed a place of utmost importance, since upon them the War Office was forced to depend for the bulk of the shell supplies required for the 1916 campaign.'

The Allies were just as dependent on America for their longer-term needs in constructing their own munitions industries. The essential basis of the whole vast programme of national munitions factories, on which Lloyd George's fame as minister of munitions hangs, was the American machine-tool and the American methods and organization it made possible. In 1916, when Great Britain's new war industries were at last getting into full production, *The Times* wrote: 'One of the new factories has grown up on a spot which last November was green fields. Now there are 25 acres covered with buildings packed with machinery. Most of the machines are of American make, and some are marvels of ingenuity.'

The extent of Allied dependence on American technology, and also of their purchases (at the cost of their accumulated overseas investments) is illustrated by the increase in production of certain American industries *before* America began her own war-production programme. Between 1914 and 1917, American exports of iron, steel, and their products to Europe rose four-fold; American explosives production grew ten times between 1913 and 1917. Bernard Baruch, chairman of the US war industries board, wrote: 'Cincinnati is the greatest machine tool manufacturing center in the world. In 1913 the total value of the annual product of the United States was about $50,000,000. During the war period preceding our entrance, our productive capacity was more than doubled, but the expansion took place largely in the out-

put of small and medium-sized machines—machines for the production of shells, rifles, fuses etc.'

It is therefore beyond question that without access to American resources, Great Britain and France would have lacked the material to sustain the war while their own industries were being created, and

could not have created the industries at all. This indeed was acknowledged by the British history of the ministry of munitions: 'Great Britain was practically dependent upon the United States of America for material for propellant manufacture, for a large proportion of her explosives material. She depended to a considerable

*Above left: 'This destroyer is needed to sink Hun submarines' reads the sign on the right. The destroyer was built in seventeen days. Above right: The American commanders of the army and the navy, General Pershing (on the left) and Admiral Sims (on the right)*

*Above: The first American prisoners to fall into German hands. Below: Loading a troopship for France. As the soldiers, fresh recruits for slaughter, tramp across the dock, girls in Red Cross uniform give each a last gift from the American people and wish them good luck*

extent upon the United States for shell steel and other steel . . . for machine tools.'

Thus America had proved a decisive influence on the course of the First World War long before her own entry into it.

However, by April 1917 the creation of the Allied — especially the British — war industries had been largely completed. Great Britain was now able to supply munitions freely to France and Italy. There was no longer so desperate or so large a need for American shells or machine-tools. The American declaration of war was therefore largely irrelevant and unimportant where Allied war production was concerned. Indeed, the flow of help was reversed once the American armies began to build up in France; it was France and Great Britain who largely equipped the American armies, as they were formed in France. The Americans made the capital mistake of deciding to produce their own designs of artillery pieces and aircraft, instead of adopting French or British designs for which many of their own factories were already producing ammunition or parts. The inevitable teething troubles of new designs were such that the American army received American guns just about in time to fire a salute in celebration of the armistice in November 1918. Not only this, but acute shortage of shipping space made it evidently more sensible to fill ships with men rather than guns, and then equip the men in Europe. So in the event the AEF was given French 75's for its field artillery, French 155-mm guns and howitzers for its medium artillery, and mostly British mortars. The British also supplied machine-guns, steel helmets, and even uniforms. The air component of the United States was equipped with French aircraft.

Obviously the prime fact about American *belligerency,* as opposed to mere industrial availability, was that United States armed forces would henceforth take part in the war. This indeed was the hope that inspired the civilian cheers, when the 1st Division, AEF, landed in France at the end of June 1917. These were the healthy men, from a nation twice as numerous as the British, or the French, who would take over the weight of the fighting from the tired, battle-shaken survivors of three terrible campaigns. Unfortunately, the American declaration of war was by no means followed by a breakneck expansion of the army and its swift deployment in France, such as the British had achieved in 1914-15. The 1st Division was not followed by the 2nd until September; by 31st October 1917 the AEF numbered only 6,064 officers and 80,969 men. Lloyd George has pointed out in his memoirs the poorness of the American performance compared with the British in creating an army: '. . . at the end of six months (after the outbreak of war) the British Expeditionary Force on the Western Front numbered 354,750. The First American Division was put into a quiet sector of the French front on 21st October 1917 — nearly seven months after the severance of diplomatic relations with Germany. The tide of American forces in France . . . mounted only in dribbling fashion during these early months. By the end of October

it was 87,000; by the end of November, 126,000; and at the beginning of 1918, 175,000. That was nine months after the entry of America into the war. At that stage in our own war effort we had already thrown 659,104 into the various war theatres.'

Thus the United States exerted no military effect at all on the critical year of 1917, when Russia subsided more and more from the war, when Pétain strove to quell the mutinies in the French army and keep it together until such time as the Americans should arrive in force, when the Italians suffered a catastrophic defeat at Caporetto, when the *only* Allied army still capable of an offensive — the British — slogged doggedly forward towards Passchendaele. And, the Germans hoped and expected, 1917 was to be the decisive and final year of the war. For it was their calculation that the American army, as a great force, would never arrive because the U-boats would have destroyed the shipping that might have carried it across the Atlantic; if in fact the war itself had not been ended by the U-boat blockade before the Americans were ready to cross. In 1917 the Americans provided hope, little else to the Allies.

The Americans are not to be entirely blamed for the extreme slowness of their military mobilization. The peacetime American army had been even smaller than the British, and far less prepared for modern war. Whereas the British had at least trained and prepared an expeditionary force of six divisions for a European campaign, and completed all the staff studies about organization and methods necessary for subsequent expansion, the Americans started absolutely from scratch in every way. For example, the size, or-

*American view of her sons — crusaders keeping the world free for democracy*

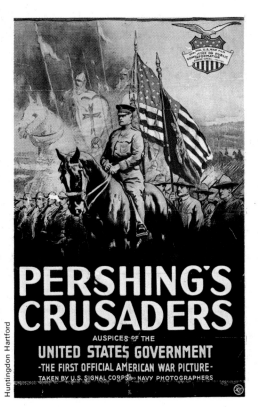

PERSHING'S CRUSADERS

AUSPICES OF THE

UNITED STATES GOVERNMENT

·THE FIRST OFFICIAL AMERICAN WAR PICTURE·

TAKEN BY U.S. SIGNAL CORPS·· NAVY PHOTOGRAPHERS

Huntingdon Hartford

Culver Pictures

*Industry steps up production for America's participation in the war — war workers making steel helmets for doughboys*

ganization, and ancillary services of the basic infantry division had to be worked out and decided upon, as well as of corps and armies. In peacetime the United States army had numbered 190,000 officers and men spread in small detachments across the face of America and her own overseas dependencies. The very size of America posed its own problems, for before troops could go aboard the troopships, they had to be concentrated and accommodated near the eastern seaboard. This meant a vast programme of camp construction, on top of other programmes for training camps and training facilities. In France itself port facilities had to be enormously extended, and lines of communication built up from the ports allotted to the Americans to their designated sector in the right-centre of the Allied line, in the Argonne. This entailed major construction work to increase the carrying capacity of the rail links. Colossal supply depots had to be constructed and filled in France. The British had found that supporting an army in another country over twenty-two miles of sea involved enormous rearward services; America had to make war across 3,000 miles of sea. The major bottleneck however was shipping; both for troops and cargoes. The United States mercantile marine had nothing like enough ships available to move the American army across the Atlantic.

Finally, there was a fundamental difference of views between Pershing on the one hand and Haig and Pétain on the other about the employment of American troops. Haig and Pétain at the beginning of 1918 were keenly aware that their armies were seriously under strength and without hope of adequate national reinforcements. They wanted American infantry to fill out their own divisions; they wanted help quickly. Pershing on the other hand (and his government) was resolved to build up a completely independent, self-contained American army in France, with its own divisions, corps, and armies. He was not prepared to see Americans swallowed up in Allied formations; he was prepared to wait, for months if need be, until all the artillery and supply services, the higher headquarters and staffs, necessary for an independent force were organized, trained, and equipped. Thus it was that when on 21st March 1918, the Germans launched the first and greatest of a series of titanic offensives on the Western Front, there was only one American division actually in the overstretched and outnumbered Allied line and three divisions in training areas.

The rate of the American build-up in France had been crucial to the calculations of the German high command in deciding on great offensives in the west in the spring of 1918. By November, 1917, when the German decision was taken, unrestricted U-boat warfare had failed in its object of knocking Great Britain out of the war; it had been beaten by the convoy system. Therefore, the Germans had to reckon on the entry into battle, sooner or later, of a mass and entirely fresh American army: certain defeat for Germany and her allies. Therefore, the war must be decided before that mass army arrived. Ludendorff told his colleagues: 'Our general situation requires that we should strike at the earliest moment, if possible at the end of February or beginning of March, before the Americans can throw strong forces into the scale.' In other words, since Russia had finally been knocked out of the war by the Treaty of Brest-Litovsk, the bulk of German strength could be concentrated on France and Great Britain before they could be rescued by their second great ally.

The crisis on the Western Front lasted from 21st March to 18th July, as the German onslaughts fell successively on different parts on the Allied front. Twice the British faced real danger of being driven into the Channel; once there was an acute risk of the French and British being separated; three times the French front was temporarily smashed and the French capital exposed again to possible occupation. In this largest, most violent, and most decisive campaign of the war, the American army played little part. Some units took part in the defence of the Amiens sector after 28th March; the 1st Division carried out a spirited counter-attack at Cantigny, near Montdidier, on 28th May; in June the 2nd Division helped the French block the German drive across the Marne, and launched a successful counterattack which led to the recapture of Belleau Wood; units of the 3rd and 42nd

*Big guns under construction. But the army only received the new American guns just before the armistice in November 1918*

Culver Pictures

Divisions fought defensively in the sector of Château-Thierry. These were very welcome, but hardly decisive contributions to a campaign against 192 German divisions.

What was far more important—indeed decisive—in terms of the issue of the war was the effect of the German offensive on the speed of the American build-up. A week after the Germans attacked on the Somme, on 28th March 1918, Pershing abandoned his somewhat deliberate and pedantic attempt to create an independent American army before entering the conflict, and offered Pétain as a temporary expedient all the troops he had, to use as Pétain wished. So the individual American units saw action under French or British corps and army command, not American. This immediate gesture was one sign of the American realization that the French and British might not last long enough to be rescued; that there was a need for desperate haste in getting American troops over to France and into battle. At the same time, Pershing still remained anxious that his Allies should not rob him of his own independent army by the feeding of Americans into their own divisions. It was only after long arguments between the Allied and American governments and commands, that it was finally agreed, at the beginning of June, that shipping space should be saved by bringing over men—infantry mostly—instead of complete divisions with all their space-occupying equipment. 170,000 combat troops were to come in June and 140,000 in July out of some 250,000 men ready to be transported in each of the two months. New divisions would be formed and equipped in France. These shipments of men were made possible by the British mercantile marine, made available as part of the bargain by the British government by cutting down British imports.

Whereas in March 84,000 Americans had crossed the Atlantic, 118,500 crossed in April, 246,000 in May, 278,800 in June, and 306,703 in July—nearly half of them in British ships. These figures, far higher than the German command had thought possible, spelt defeat for Germany.

On 15th-17th July the last phase of the great German 1918 offensive petered out in failure. On 18th July the French launched a surprise attack, led by massed tanks, from the Forest of Villers-Cotterêts. The attacking troops included two American divisions, each with a strength of 27,000 men, three times as large as a French or German division. The French attack marked the turn of the campaign; from then to the end of the war the Germans were to fight on the defensive.

It was now—and at very long last—that the American military presence in the war proved decisive. The great battles of March to July 1918, which the Allies had won virtually without American help, had left the British, French, and German armies all exhausted, with scant reserves and little hope of reinforcement from the homeland. For the original combatants of the war nothing remained but to break up divisions—to see their armies gradually decrease. A German battalion now numbered on average 660 men. The German

*'Five million American citizens become soldiers to defend the world's freedom'*

gamble on victory had failed: neither the German army nor the German people (hungry, miserable, and despairing after years of blockade) had any further hopes to clutch at. In August, when the British offensive on the Somme (some American units took part), confirmed that the Allies now possessed the initiative, and confirmed also that the morale and discipline of the German army was beginning to disintegrate, there were nearly 1,500,000 Americans in France. The only German reservoir of fresh manpower lay in the 300,000 youths of the 1919 class called up in June. Whereas Allied leaders were planning for a campaign in 1919, whose principal weight was to be borne by a hundred American divisions, for Germany's leaders another year of battle was absolutely unthinkable.

Thus it was that even in the last months of the war, it was the American military *potential*, advertised by their limited offensives at St Mihiel and in the Argonne, rather than the actual fighting achievements of American troops, that affected the outcome of the Great War in 1918. In point of fact, the brunt of the fighting from July to November 1918 was borne by the tired but still dogged British, who took 188,700 prisoners as against 196,000 taken by the French, Belgians, and Americans together.

The American role in the First World War was therefore decisive: decisive industrially between 1914 and 1917, decisive in terms of military potential from midsummer 1918 onwards. It illustrated two facts of enormous importance to the future balance of power in Europe: that Germany was militarily the equal of the British and French empires together; and that Great Britain, the 19th-century 'work-shop of the world', was no longer a first-rank industrial and technological power, no longer able to defend herself and her empire out of her own resources.

# The Bolshevik Revolution

The overthrow of the autocratic Tsarist regime in March (February by the Julian Calendar) 1917 was a great victory for the peoples of Russia. In alliance with the army, the working class of Russia fought for and won political freedom. The whole country was covered by a network of 'soviets' (councils) and of committees of soldiers and peasants. Power in the country was divided, but as early as June the Provisional Government had established a dictatorship with the help of the Mensheviks and Socialist Revolutionaries (SRs). Not a single one of the social aims of the revolution had been met. Neither the government of Prince Lvov nor Kerensky's government which followed it gave land to the peasants or rid them of their servitude to the landowners. Workers in the mills and factories continued to be cruelly exploited, their standard of living declined sharply, their wages were cut, and there was hunger in the towns. A country which had been exhausted by the First World War was now thirsting for peace, yet the Provisional Government's policy was to continue the war.

Russia was torn by violent contradictions. The progress of agriculture was held back by the fact that enormous areas remained in the hands of the landowners. At

*Below: The Bolshevik Colossus*

*The Tsarina's 'holy man', whose amazing sexual excesses had political repercussions*

the same time modern industry was developing in the country, with a high level of concentration of production and manpower. The urban working class which amounted to about 20,000,000 of the country's population of over 150,000,000, was organized into trade unions and had learned a great deal about political struggle in the first Russian revolution of 1905.

### The Bolshevik Party

The Bolshevik Party, led by Vladimir Ilyich Lenin, directed the struggle of the working class towards the acquisition of power, the solution of the land question, bringing the war to an end, establishing workers' control over production, and nationalizing banks and the more important branches of industry. But this struggle on the part of the workers and peasants came up against bitter resistance from representatives of the ruling classes.

In September 1917 the party of the Russian bourgeoisie, the Constitutional Democrats (Kadets), and the reactionary military circles led by General Kornilov tried to carry out a counter-revolutionary *putsch* and to set up a military dictatorship. In effect, this plot evoked general opposition among the people and rallied the revolutionary forces to the Bolshevik Party. At the beginning of September the Petrograd and Moscow soviets of workers' and peasants' deputies passed resolutions proposed by the Bolsheviks. The Moscow Soviet was led by one of the oldest members of the Bolshevik Party, V.P.Nogin, while L.D.Trotsky, who had only recently joined the Party, was elected chairman of the Petrograd Soviet.

The influence of the Bolsheviks in the soviets throughout the country spread rapidly in September and October. The Bolsheviks became the leading element in the soviets almost everywhere.

In the autumn of 1917 the revolution in Russia entered on its decisive stage.

All classes and all social groups in Russian society were drawn into the most far-reaching revolutionary crisis. It was a crisis affecting the whole nation, because it became apparent in all spheres of the nation's life, involving the working people, the ruling classes, and the political parties. With merciless precision Lenin revealed the inevitability of the collapse of a Russian economy dominated by the bourgeoisie and landowners and of the economic policy of the Provisional Government. It was not individual mistakes that brought the government to the brink of disaster. At a time when there was a tremendous growth in the revolutionary activity of the masses all efforts on the part of the Provisional Government to regulate economic life by reactionary bureaucratic means were doomed to failure. The government's whole policy was leading to famine and the disorganization of production, the destruction of economic contacts, and the creation of a state of chaos in the country. To carry out genuinely democratic measures for regulating the economy, to nationalize the banks and syndicates, and control production and demand would have meant taking a step forward – to socialism.

The collapse of the Provisional Government's food policy had an especially serious effect on the condition of the mass of ordinary people. Memories of the March days of 1917, which had started with food riots, were still very fresh in the people's minds. On the eve of the October Revolution the country's food situation worsened considerably as a result of the policy of the Kerensky government which paid no attention to the needs of the people.

The collapse of the Provisional Govern-

**Below left:** *March 1917. Revolutionary newspapers handed out.* **Below right:** *'Workers of all countries unite', Petrograd, May 1917.* **Bottom left:** *Funeral for 'Victims of the Revolution'; but only 200 people had died.* **Bottom right:** *Bust of Rasputin by Aronson*

ment's economic policy was seen in its most concentrated form in the breakdown of transport. This was the bloodstream sustaining the country's whole economic life and binding it together into a single organism, and it collapsed with tremendous speed. Towards the end of October 1917 the minister of transport, A.V.Liverovsky, admitted that the transport situation 'threatened to bring to a halt the major railroads which supplied the country with essential services'.

One very clear sign of the nationwide crisis was the break-up of the ruling parties of Socialist Revolutionaries (SRs) and the Social Democrats (Mensheviks). The formation of left-wing groups among the SRs and Mensheviks, the sharp intensification of conflicts between the leadership of these parties and the rank and file of their members and between the party headquarters and their local organizations, and the enforced rejection by the local committees of SRs and Mensheviks of the slogan of coalition with the bourgeoisie was the direct result of the collapse of those parties' reformist policy. On 4th November the soldiers' section of the All-Russian Central Executive Committee, led by SRs and Mensheviks, demanded peace and the transfer of land to the peasants, but proposed that power should be handed over to 'the democratic majority in the pre-parliament'—that spurious, representative body set up by the Provisional Government.

### Traitors to the revolution

From the middle of October 1917 open warfare on the part of all the working people against the Provisional Government became a daily occurrence in the nation's life. The workers everywhere were arming themselves, the number of workers' armed detachments—the Red Guards—increased rapidly, and they developed their contacts and their plans for common action with the garrisons in the major towns. The workers had a tremendously revolutionizing effect on the troops at the fronts, especially on the Western and Northern Fronts. Sailors of the Baltic Fleet declared the Kerensky government to be a government of betrayal of the revolution. Councils of workers' and soldiers' deputies, regimental and divisional committees, and peasants' organizations proclaimed at the numerous conferences they held that none of the tasks of the revolution could be solved without the overthrow of the Provisional Government and the transfer of power to the soviets. A resolution passed at a congress of soviets of the Vladimir province on 29th October declared the Provisional Government and all the parties which supported it to be traitors to the cause of revolution and all the soviets in the province to be in a state of open and determined warfare with the Provisional Government. This was only one of the moves in this general process of decisive and ruthless warfare between the people and the government. The same resolution was supported by the soviets in Moscow, Ivanovo-Voznesensk, Aleksandrov, Kovrov, Ryazan, and other towns. When a congress of soviets in the Ryazan province decided to hand

*Left:* A baker tramples on his old shop sign, 'By appointment to the Tsar' (Russian postcard 1917). *Right:* Lenin, on his way to Petrograd to direct the revolution

power over to the soviets immediately, Nikitin, the minister of the interior, demanded that armed force should be used against the people of Ryazan. On 31st October the minister cabled the commander of the Moscow military region: 'Impossible to take counteraction with resources of the civil authority.' But the military commander was also unable to render any assistance, because he had no dependable troops at his disposal. The soviet of the Moscow province proposed that all the soviets in the province should ignore the orders issued by the Provisional Government. The Vladivostok Soviet, some 6,000 miles from Moscow, issued instructions to the effect that failure to obey the soviet's orders would be regarded as a counter-revolutionary act. Soviets in the Urals declared that the main task was to overthrow the Provisional Government.

It was the industrial working class and its party which took the lead in this popular movement. Factory committees sprang up everywhere and quickly gathered strength, and they were everywhere dominated by the Bolsheviks. In Petrograd on 30th October-4th November there took place the first All-Russian Conference of Factory Committees. Ninety-six of the 167 delegates belonged to the Bolsheviks.

### Strikes and peasant revolt

The strike movement in the autumn of 1917 was closely connected with the soviets' struggle for power. There were strikes of metal-workers and woodworkers, of chemist-shop assistants and railway workers, of textile workers and miners. A general strike of 300,000 textile workers in the central industrial region (Moscow), which began on 3rd November, affected every branch of life in the region. The workers took control of the plants, occupied the telephone exchange, mounted guard over the warehouses and offices. It was more than a strike: the workers not only faced up directly to the problem of assuming power, they began to solve it. But in 1917 the strike was only one of many

weapons used by the proletariat in its struggle. The Red Guards and the workers' militia, the establishment of factory guards and workers' control, the factory committees and the bold acts of intervention in the management of industrial plants—all these forms of organization and means of struggle gave the working class tremendous possibilities for influencing the course of events and leading them on a nationwide scale.

The strength of the working-class movement was multiplied by virtue of the fact that the industrial workers exercised a tremendous influence over the peasantry and themselves received in return support in the form of a spreading peasant war against the landowners. In September and October 1917 there were something like 2,000 cases in which the peasants took political action, killing the landlords and seizing the land.

'If, in a country of peasants, after seven months of a democratic republic, things could come to the point of a peasant revolt, this demonstrates unquestionably the

*German cartoon: 'Russia'. Nicholas II is shown riding away with his enraged peasants chasing at his heels*

nationwide collapse of the revolution, the crisis it is in, which has reached unprecedented proportions, and the fact that the counter-revolutionary forces are reaching the limit of their resources,' Lenin wrote in mid-October 1917.

But the peasantry's official representative at the time was the All-Russian Council of Peasants' Deputies, which had been elected at the peasants' congress back in May and had long since lost any right to represent anybody. The executive committee of the All-Russian Council of Peasants' Deputies sanctioned punitive expeditions against the peasants, and supported the policy of hostility to the peasantry pursued by the government (in which the prime minister was the SR Kerensky and the minister of agriculture the SR Maslov). The peasant masses who had risen in revolt against the landowners took decisive action. In the main centres of peasant uprisings the struggle against the landowners acquired, under the influence of the industrial workers, both organization and a clear purpose. The 332 delegates to a peasant congress in the Tver province took a unanimous decision to hand over the land immediately to the management of land committees. The local land committees in the Tambov province seized land belonging to the Church and the landowners and rented it out to peasants who had very little or no land. Similar acts were repeated throughout the country.

### Government force

How did the Provisional Government reply to these demands by the peasants? It organized punitive expeditions and drew up various legislative proposals providing for eventual reforms, the aim of which was to 'pacify' the peasants and certainly not to satisfy their demand for the land.

The forces at the disposal of the Provisional Government for undertaking such punitive expeditions were limited, consisting mainly of Cossack and cavalry units. The actions undertaken by the peasants forced the Provisional Government to split up its troops between numerous areas in which there had been uprisings: in the Ryazan, Kursk, Tambov, Kiev, Tula, Saratov, Samara, Minsk, Kazan, Podolsk, Volhynia, and other provinces. Squadrons of Cossacks and cavalry detachments which were dispatched to particular districts became submerged in the vast sea of peasant revolt. Meanwhile, the provincial commissars of the Provisional Government demanded that soldiers be sent to *all* districts to suppress peasant disorders.

But even the local authorities soon realized the futility of using force against the peasantry. In the course of the peasant uprising even those land committees which supported the government's policy were forced to take over the property of the landowners and distribute it among the poorer peasants. The Kadets, the SRs, and the Mensheviks tried in every way to minimize the importance of the peasants' struggle, making out that it was just 'wild anarchy' and talking about 'pogroms' and 'disorders'. This falsification of the truth is disproved by the facts: in the main centres

of the uprising the peasants transferred the land to the poor peasants in an organized manner. In those places where the SR party obstructed the work of the peasant committees the movement did indeed assume anarchistic forms. But the peasants had thoroughly learned the lessons of the first Russian revolution of 1905. The more advanced forms of peasant protest and revolt (the seizure of arable land and landowners' property) were three or four times as widespread in 1917 as they had been in 1905-07. In the autumn of 1917 between

sixty and ninety per cent of all peasant actions included the seizure of land.

As for the proposed reforms, their essence is apparent from the final bill put forward by S.L. Maslov, the minister of agriculture. According to this bill, which was the most 'left-wing' for the Provisional Government, the landowners were to retain the right to own the land. The 'land-lease fund' to be set up under this bill was to take over only 'land not being cultivated by the resources of the owners'. The rent to be paid by the peasants was to go to the landowner.

*Above: The armband worn by the followers of Kornilov.* ***Right:*** *German cartoon, July 1917. Nicholas from his prison listens as Lloyd George, President Wilson of the United States, and Ribot, prime minister of France, exclaim: 'We never deal with an autocratic government, never.' Nicholas muses: 'Once these rascals were like brothers to me.'* ***Below:*** *Dutch drawing of Nicholas on his way to Siberia, where the Provisional Government sent him and his family in August 1917*

Historical Research Unit

The whole experience of the eight months during which the Provisional Government was in power demonstrated that without a further revolution the peasantry would not receive any land or rid itself of oppression by the landowners. It was this experience which pushed the peasantry to carry out an uprising which, when linked with the struggle of the industrial workers, created the most favourable conditions for the victory of the socialist revolution.

### The revolutionary structure

By November 1917 the Bolshevik Party had about 350,000 members. But its strength was to be measured rather by its influence over the many millions of people embraced by the soviets, the trade unions, the factory committees, and the soldiers' and peasants' committees. At a time when an armed revolt was developing on a nationwide scale the task of Lenin's revolutionary party was to take care of the political and military organization of the forces of revolt. At the centre of this preparatory work stood the working class. The Red Guards were acquiring fighting experience, were learning the tactics of street fighting, and were establishing and strengthening their contacts with the revolutionary units in the army. In the districts inhabited by other nationalities the Bolsheviks gained the support of the oppressed peoples, who saw in the victory of a socialist revolution a guarantee of national and social emancipation. Major centres of revolutionary struggle were set up in all these districts and they linked the national liberation movement with the workers' and peasants' movement, bringing Petrograd and Moscow together with the outlying regions in a single revolutionary front. One such centre in central Asia was Tashkent, which as early as September 1917 raised the banner of struggle against the Kerensky government. In the Trans-Caucasus the centre was the industrial city of Baku;

in the Ukraine Kharkov and the Donbass; in the Western territories of the country it was Minsk. The Bolsheviks were clearly the dominant force in the decisive places in the country: in the capital, in the industrial centres, on the Western and Northern Fronts, and in the major garrison towns in the interior. The seventy-five Bolshevik newspapers and periodicals which were published in all these regions were a very important organizing force.

The decision to work for an uprising, which was taken at the Sixth Congress of the Bolshevik Party in August 1917, was put consistently into practice. At a meeting on 23rd October, in which Lenin took part, the Central Committee of the Bolsheviks passed a resolution concerning the uprising. This decision did not set a date for the uprising, but it did stress that 'an armed uprising is inevitable and the time for it is fully ripe'. The Central Committee advised all the branches of the party to be guided by this fact and to consider and decide all practical issues with this in mind. The resolution was passed with Zinovyev and Kamenev voting against it. A week later Kamenev wrote an article opposing the decision in the Menshevik paper *Novaya Zhizn* (New Life). L.D. Trotsky voted in favour of the resolution on the uprising, but his later position amounted to delaying the beginning of the revolt until the All-Russian Congress of Soviets, which was to deal with the question of power. This attitude of Trotsky's was subjected to severe criticism by Lenin, who emphasized that to postpone the uprising until the Congress of Soviets would be to give the counter-revolutionary forces an opportunity of organizing themselves and dispersing the soviets.

On 29th October an enlarged session of the Central Committee of the Bolsheviks, attended by representatives of the Petrograd committee, the Bolsheviks' military organization, factory committees, and trade unions, approved the decision to organize an armed uprising and appointed from its number a Military-Revolutionary Centre composed of A.S.Bubnov, F.E. Dzerzhinsky, Y.M.Sverdlov, I.V.Stalin, and S.M.Uritsky. The leading spirit and organizer of the work of the Military-Revolutionary Committee was Yakov Sverdlov, a thirty-two-year-old Bolshevik who already had behind him seventeen years of revolutionary activity, prison, penal servitude, and seven escapes from deportation. This centre consisting of five men formed part of the Soviet's legal headquarters for the armed uprising – the Military-Revolutionary Committee of the

*Novosti*

*Gerard Oriol*

*Left: Women queuing for food in Moscow. The bread ration, a pound a day in the spring, was cut to half a pound just before the October revolution. Above right: Petrograd workers with an armoured car captured from Kerensky's troops. On the fatal night of 7th November, Kerensky was searching for loyal troops to support his government. Right: Red guards outside the Smolny Institute. Inside the hall on 7th November the Congress of Soviets was busy deciding the future course of the revolution*

*S.C.R. Photo Library*

Petrograd Soviet. A major part in the Committee was played by Bolsheviks N.I. Podvoysky and V.A.Antonov-Ovseyenko, and by the left-wing SR, P.E.Lazimir.

In late October provincial and district conferences and congresses of soviets, factory committees, and army and frontline committees took place throughout the country. History had never before seen such a mass mobilization of popular forces around the working class for a decisive attack on the capitalist system.

Meanwhile, the Provisional Government was trying to regain the initiative. On 1st November it dispersed the soviet in Kaluga, encircled Moscow and Minsk with Cossack troops, and tried to remove the revolutionary units of the capital's garrison from Petrograd. The only effect of these actions was that the revolutionary forces became even more active.

The Military-Revolutionary Committee appointed its own commissars to all units of the Petrograd garrison and to all the more important offices. The revolutionary troops and the Red Guards were brought to a state of readiness for battle. On 6th November the avalanche of popular wrath descended on the government which had betrayed the revolution. On that day the Central Committee of the Bolsheviks organized an alternative headquarters in the Peter and Paul Fortress and took decisions concerning the control of the postal and telegraph services, of the rail junction, and of the food supplies to the capital. The Petrograd garrison and the Red Guards went over to direct military action to bring about the immediate overthrow of the Provisional Government.

### The Congress of Soviets
The city of Petrograd is situated on a number of islands, joined together by bridges. Hence the great strategic importance of the bridges. During the day of 6th November units of the Red Guards seized practically all the bridges and defeated efforts on the part of the officer cadets to cut the working-class districts off from the centre. Revolutionary troops occupied the central telegraph office, the central news agency, and the Baltic (Finland) station. Ships of the Baltic Fleet put out from Helsingfors and Kronstadt to come to the help of revolutionary Petrograd.

On the evening of 6th November Lenin left his secret hiding place and arrived at the headquarters of the armed uprising, and under his leadership the uprising developed at much greater speed. Troops of the Military-Revolutionary Committee occupied, on the night of 6th-7th November and the following morning, the telephone exchange, a number of railway stations, and the State Bank. The capital of Russia was in the hands of a people in revolt.

On the morning of 7th November Lenin wrote his appeal *To the Citizens of Russia*, which announced the transfer of power in the state into the hands of the Military-Revolutionary Committee. This, the first document to emerge from the victorious revolution, was immediately printed and posted up in the streets of Petrograd.

At two thirty-five on the afternoon of the same day the Petrograd Soviet went into session. There Lenin proclaimed the victory of the socialist revolution. In a short, moving speech he defined the main tasks of the revolution: the setting up of a Soviet government, the dismantling of the old state administration and the organization of new, Soviet administration, the ending of the war, a just and immediate peace, the confiscation of the property of the landowners, and genuine workers' control over industrial production.

Throughout the day of 7th November meetings of the party factions from the Congress of Soviets were taking place in the Smolny Institute. Details of the party composition of the second All-Russian Congress of Soviets bear witness to the depth and the extent of the process of Bolshevization among the ordinary people. At the first Congress the Bolsheviks had accounted for only ten per cent of the delegates, but at the second Congress they embraced fifty-two per cent of the delegates. The Bolsheviks carried with them a large group of left-wing SRs – more than fifteen per cent of the delegates, whereas there had been no left-wing SRs at all at the first All-Russian Congress of Soviets. Mensheviks and right-wing SRs of all shades of opinion, who had unquestionably dominated the first Congress of Soviets (eighty-four per cent of the delegates), accounted for only twenty-six per cent of the delegates at the second Congress.

There is no need to produce any more precise evidence to demonstrate the extent to which the *petit-bourgeois* parties had disintegrated; the decline from eighty-four per cent in June 1917 to twenty-six per cent in October is sufficiently clear. All the same, the Bolsheviks did not try to antagonize or isolate the other parties which formed part of the soviets.

The first session of the second All-Russian Congress of Soviets began at 10.40 pm on 7th November and came to an end just after five next morning.

The white-pillared hall of the Smolny Institute was seething with people. Within its walls were to be found representatives of the whole of Russia, of her industrial centres and farming regions, national territories, Cossack regions, and of all the war fronts and garrisons in the interior. It was a representative assembly from the whole of Russia, which had to decide the future course of the revolution.

Sitting on the platform were the downcast leaders of the old Central Executive Committee – Bogdanov, Gots, Dan, Filippovsky – but this was their last appearance as leaders of the supreme organ of the soviets. It was, at the same time, an admission of defeat for their policy of resistance to the popular will and an admission of the legitimacy of the Congress, to which, by the very fact of the official opening, the old Executive Committee was handing over its very reduced authority.

The Congress elected a presidium from among the Bolsheviks and the left-wing SRs, and Dan and his friends departed. Then the work of the Congress began.

There was, in the long stream of speeches, in the heated dispute about the revolution which had taken place, and in the sharp conflict between the political parties, a certain strict logic and system which reflected the relationship of social forces in the vast country stretching out beyond the confines of the Smolny Institute.

The Provisional Government, meeting in the Winter Palace in the centre of Petrograd, was utterly isolated from the country. The palace was defended by detachments of officer cadets, Cossacks, and women's battalions. As the ring of rebel forces drew closer round the Winter Palace, and as the reports from the war fronts grew ever more hopeless, so the speeches of the more conciliatory statesmen became more nervous and their actions became more devoid of logic. By continually walking out of the congress and then coming back to it the Mensheviks and the right-wing SRs tried to disorganize its work. The result of their efforts was very painful for them.

After some noisy demonstrations and much hysterical shouting and appeals the right-wing SRs and Mensheviks succeeded in taking with them out of the congress an insignificant group of people – about fifty of the delegates. At the same time there took place a significant regrouping of forces at the congress. The number of SRs was reduced by seven, but the group of left-wing SRs increased to eighty-one. The Mensheviks disappeared altogether, but the group of Menshevik-internationalists rose to twenty-one. This means that many members of the faction of Mensheviks and SRs did not obey the decision of their leaders to leave the congress, but preferred to switch over to the left-wing groups.

At about ten in the evening of 7th November the revolutionary troops surrounding the Winter Palace went over to the attack for which the signal was a shot fired by the cruiser *Aurora*. The Winter Palace was taken. Antonov-Ovseyenko arrested the members of the Provisional Government and put them in charge of the Red Guards to be taken to the Peter and Paul Fortress.

### Pleading
Meanwhile, the forces of the counter-revolution – the Mensheviks, and right-wing SRs, pinned their hopes on the units at the front. During 6th and 7th November General Dukhonin from the General HQ and a representative of the war ministry, Tolstoy, sent messages from Petrograd demanding, begging, and pleading with the commanders of the fronts to send troops as quickly as possible to Petrograd to put down the uprising. The commanders of the South-Western and Rumanian Fronts, where the influence of the conciliators and nationalists seemed to be especially strong, declared that there were no units to be found which were suitable for the job of 'pacifying' Petrograd. And those regiments which they had succeeded by a trick in moving towards Petrograd were held up on the way by the railwaymen, the workers, and revolutionary soldiers. A strict revolutionary control was set up in Orsha, so that no trains were allowed through to Petrograd. The armoured trains which were sent off for Moscow were held

up in Minsk. Vyazma and Gomel not only refused to let troops through but even held up telegrams from the staff of the Western Front.

Contrary to the hopes of the forces of counter-revolution, the soldiers on all fronts came out in defence of the soviets.

At 5.17 am N.V.Krylenko, an officer and a Bolshevik, representing the revolutionary forces of the Northern Front, went up on to the platform of the congress to speak; he was staggering from fatigue. He was soon to be made supreme commander-in-chief of the Russian army. The congress listened with enthusiasm to his statement that a Military-Revolutionary Committee had been set up on the Northern Front, which had taken over the command and intended to prevent the movement of train-loads of counter-revolutionary troops in the direction of Petrograd. Delegations were continually arriving from the trains sent to Petrograd and declaring their support for the Petrograd garrison.

The first official state document of the socialist revolution—the *Appeal to the Workers, Soldiers, and Peasants*—was drawn up by Lenin. It proclaimed that the Congress of Soviets was taking power into its own hands and that all power throughout the country was passing into the hands of the soviets of workers', soldiers', and peasants' deputies. This was how the main question of the revolution was resolved legally—the soviets' power was established.

The most difficult problems, around which a bitter struggle had been fought throughout the eight months of the revolution—the questions of peace, land, workers' control, the self-determination of nations, the democratization of the army—were posed and decided openly and straightforwardly in that document.

The *Appeal to the Workers, Soldiers, and Peasants* was approved with only two opposing votes and twelve abstentions. This represented a complete victory for Lenin's idea of transferring all power to the soviets. The first decree approved by the second All-Russian Congress of Soviets was the decree concerning the peace.

### Peace

Certain critics were later to assert, quite unfairly, that Russia could have had peace even without the Bolshevik Revolution, and that if it did not come about it was only because of mistakes committed by the governments of the Entente powers and the Provisional Government who did not succeed in seizing the initiative in deciding the question of war or peace.

There can be no question but that the Provisional Government committed plenty of 'mistakes' of every kind. But it was by no means a matter of the weakness of certain individuals or of their personal mistakes. Those mistakes were dictated by the class nature of the policy of the Provisional Government, its loathing of the revolutionary movement and its fear in the face of that movement, and its dependence on the governments of the Entente powers. The growth of this dependence led even to the expulsion from the government of the war minister, A.I.Verkhovsky, who suggested

peace with the German bloc so as to concentrate forces against the revolution.

At 9 pm on 8th November the second session of the Congress of Soviets opened. Lenin went up on to the platform. 'Next Lenin, gripping the edge of the reading stand, letting his little winking eyes travel over the crowd as he stood there waiting, apparently oblivious to the long-rolling

*Two Soviet paintings of the revolution.* **Below:** *The signal for revolution—a shot is fired from the cruiser* Aurora. *The attack on the Winter Palace is to begin.* **Bottom:** *'The Inevitable' (by S.Lukin). The Winter Palace has been stormed. The members of the Provisional Government are under arrest. A Red Guard, one of the victors, stands in the throne-room of the Tsars*

ovation, which lasted several minutes'—recalls the American journalist John Reed.

'The question of peace is the burning
question, the most pressing question of
the present time,' Lenin began. The proletarian revolution was not decked out in the
flamboyant clothes of beautiful words, nor
was it concealed behind noisy manifestoes
and impossible promises. It got down in a
businesslike way to the great and difficult
job of liberating the peoples of Russia and
of the whole world from bloody slaughter.
There was a note of confidence and firmness
in the words of Lenin's decree, which
proposed that all the warring peoples and
their governments should enter immediately into talks concerning a just peace,
without annexations or indemnities.

The Decree on Peace gave legislative
form to new principles of foreign policy—
the principles of equality and respect for
the sovereignty of all peoples, the abandonment of secret diplomacy, and the co-
existence of different social systems. The
decree was addressed not only to the
governments but also to the peoples of the
warring nations.

The diplomatic representatives of the Entente powers tried to ignore the Decree on
Peace and pretend that the document 'did
not exist'. But the decree became the property of hundreds of millions of working

people. Evidence of this is to be found in
the strikes and demonstrations which
swept through many countries of the world
at the end of 1917 and in 1918.

The Decree on Peace was approved
unanimously by the congress.

The congress turned immediately to the
second question: the immediate abolition
of landlord property rights. The yearnings
of the people, their century-long dreams of
being free from the oppression of the land-
lords were expressed in the Decree on Land.

'Landlord property rights are abolished,
immediately and without any compensation,' the decree said. All land was declared
to be the property of the whole people. It
was made the duty of the local soviets to
draw up an accurate account of all property
and to organize the strictest revolutionary
protection for everything that was handed
over to the national economy. There was a
special point which proclaimed that the
land of the ordinary peasants and Cossacks would not be confiscated. Part of the
decree consisted of the peasants' demands,
drawn up on the basis of 242 local peasant
demands.

The Decree on Land was approved by a
general vote of the delegates, with only one
delegate voting against and eight abstain-
ing. Thus the Bolsheviks won a complete
victory on this cardinal question of the
revolution as well. The peasantry received
land from the hands of the victorious urban
working class. This turned the alliance between the proletariat and the peasantry
into a tremendous force promoting the further progress of the revolution. What the
proletariat had failed to achieve in 1905—
to unite its struggle for socialism with

the democratic movement of the peasantry
for land—was achieved triumphantly in
November 1917.

Since it was by its nature an expression
of revolutionary democracy, the Decree
on Land was put into practice by methods
which were both revolutionary and socialist. This is to say, it rid the land of the
survivals of serfdom more resolutely and
thoroughly than any bourgeois revolution
had yet done. By abolishing the private
ownership of land the Decree on Land·took
the first step towards the liquidation of
capitalist ownership of banks, industrial
undertakings, transport, and so on.

As a result of the agrarian reforms carried out on the basis of the Decree on Land
and the subsequent legislation the poor
and middle peasants received 540,000,000
acres of land. The big landowners, the
royal family and the Church lost all their
land—400,000,000 acres—and the rich
peasants (kulaks) lost 135,000,000 of the
216,000,000 they had owned in 1914.

This revolutionary redistribution of land
served as the basis for further reforms in
agriculture and for the development of a
socialist farming system.

### Bolshevik government
Since it enjoyed an overwhelming majority,
it was natural that Lenin's party should
form the new government. During the Congress the Central Committee of the Bolshevik Party had carried on intensive
negotiations with the left-wing SRs about
their participation in the government. The
left-wing SRs had been members of the
Military-Revolutionary Committee and
they had—though, it is true, not without

some hesitation—taken part in the armed uprising and supported the principal decisions taken by the Congress. But the left-wing SRs were too closely connected with their right-wing colleagues in the party and were too dependent on them in an ideological and organizational sense to be able to make up their minds immediately to join the Soviet government. It was a month later that they took this step.

At this point the Bolsheviks assumed the responsibility for forming a new government. 'We wanted a Soviet coalition government,' Lenin said. 'We did not exclude anyone from the Soviet. If they (the SRs and Mensheviks) did not wish to work together with us, so much the worse for them. The masses of the soldiers and peasants will not follow the Mensheviks and SRs.'

The decree which the Congress passed concerning the formation of a workers' and peasants' government headed by V.I.Lenin became in effect a constitutional document. It determined the name of the new government: the Soviet (Council) of People's Commissars, a name which reflected the fact that the new government was closely linked with the people and had developed out of the soviets. The decree laid down in general terms that the new government was subject to the control of the All-Russian Congress of Soviets and its Central Executive Committee. Thus the decree set out the constitutional principle regarding the responsibility of the workers' and peasants' government to the supreme bodies of the Soviet regime: the Congress of Soviets and the All-Russian Central Ex-

ecutive Committee, which had the right to remove people's commissars.

Once it had proved victorious in Petrograd the revolution spread quickly throughout the country. Immediately after Petrograd, the soviets were victorious in Moscow, where the battles for power were very violent and lasted for five days, ending on 16th November 1917 with the complete victory of the soviets.

In the course of three months the socialist revolution was victorious throughout the vast country, from the line of the Western Front to the shores of the Pacific Ocean and from the White Sea to the Black Sea. The ways in which the revolutionary power of the soviets was established varied greatly from place to place. In Smolensk, Voronezh, Kazan, Chernigov, Zhitomir, and Kiev the workers and peasants took power only after armed struggle with the counter-revolutionaries. In Minsk, Yaroslavl, Nizhny Novgorod, Samara, Kursk, and Perm the soviets came to power by peaceful means.

At the very beginning of its course the socialist revolution in Russia succeeded in doing what the Paris Commune tried but failed to do. The workers, peasants, and soldiers of Russia set up a new administration, formed their own government at the All-Russian Congress of Soviets, uniting millions of working people, resolved the questions of peace and land, and offered all the peoples of Russia the possibility of national independence.

Such was the victory of the Bolshevik Revolution.

*Below: Soldiers of the revolution, the ragged bootless men who enabled a relatively small party of 350,000 to gain control over a vast country of a hundred and fifty million people. This revolution was to change the face of the world and have a decisive influence on the fate of the whole of mankind. Bottom: 'Working people arise!' by Soviet painter V. Serov. The Bolsheviks exploited working class discontent with the war, and promised Russia's people what they wanted—land and peace. The revolution which aimed to achieve this was carried out almost without bloodshed*

Imperial War Museum

# Program for the Peace of the World

By PRESIDENT WILSON January 8, 1918

I. Open covenants of peace, openly arrived at, after which there shall be no private international understandings of any kind, but diplomacy shall proceed always frankly and in the public view.

II. Absolute freedom of navigation upon the seas, outside territorial waters, alike in peace and in war, except as the seas may be closed in whole or in part by international action for the enforcement of international covenants.

III. The removal, so far as possible, of all economic barriers and the establishment of an equality of trade conditions among all the nations consenting to the peace and associating themselves for its maintenance.

IV. Adequate guarantees given and taken that national armaments will reduce to the lowest point consistent with domestic safety.

V. Free, open-minded, and absolutely impartial adjustment of all colonial claims, based upon a strict observance of the principle that in determining all such questions of sovereignty the interests of the population concerned must have equal weight with the equitable claims of the government whose title is to be determined.

VI. The evacuation of all Russian territory and such a settlement of all questions affecting Russia as will secure the best and freest coöperation of the other nations of the world in obtaining for her an unhampered and unembarrassed opportunity for the independent determination of her own political development and national policy, and assure her of a sincere welcome into the society of free nations under institutions of her own choosing; and, more than a welcome, assistance also of every kind that she may need and may herself desire. The treatment accorded Russia by her sister nations in the months to come will be the acid test of their goodwill, of their comprehension of her needs as distinguished from their own interests, and of their intelligent and unselfish sympathy.

VII. Belgium, the whole world will agree, must be evacuated and restored, without any attempt to limit the sovereignty which she enjoys in common with all other free nations. No other single act will serve as this will serve to restore confidence among the nations in the law which they have themselves set and determined for the government of their relations with one another. Without this healing act the whole structure and validity of international law is forever impaired.

VIII. All French territory should be freed and the invaded portions restored, and the wrong done to France by Prussia in 1871 in the matter of Alsace-Lorraine, which has unsettled the peace of the world for nearly fifty years, should be righted, in order that peace may once more be made secure in the interest of all.

IX. A readjustment of the frontiers of Italy should be effected along clearly recognizable lines of nationality.

X. The people of Austria-Hungary, whose place among the nations we wish to see safeguarded and assured, should be accorded the freest opportunity of autonomous development.

XI. Rumania, Serbia and Montenegro should be evacuated; occupied territories restored; Serbia accorded free and secure access to the sea; and the relations of the several Balkan States to one another determined by friendly counsel along historically established lines of allegiance and nationality; and international guarantees of the political and economic independence and territorial integrity of the several Balkan States should be entered into.

XII. The Turkish portions of the present Ottoman Empire should be assured a secure sovereignty; but the other nationalities which are now under Turkish rule should be assured an undoubted security of life and an absolutely unmolested opportunity of autonomous development, and the Dardanelles should be permanently opened as a free passage to the ships and commerce of all nations under international guarantees.

XIII. An independent Polish State should be erected which should include the territories inhabited by indisputably Polish populations, which should be assured a free and secure access to the sea, and whose political and economic independence and territorial integrity should be guaranteed by international covenant.

XIV. A general association of nations must be formed under specific covenants for the purpose of affording mutual guarantees of political independence and territorial integrity to great and small States alike.

Kladderadatsch

# Darf Belgien Englands Aufmarschgebiet werden?

London
Dover
CANAL-TUNNEL
Calais
Holland
Rotterdam
Belgien
Antwerpen
Engl. Auf marsch Gebiet
Feindl. Aufmarsch am 8. Mobilm. Tag beendet.
Beginn des Einmarsches am 9. Mobilm. Tag
MÜNSTER
HAMM
ESSEN
Bochum
Leverkusen
KÖLN
Solingen
ELBERFELD
AACHEN
DÜREN
KREFELD
SIEGEN
Trier
Vernichtung der rheinisch-westfäl. Jndustrie droht vom 10. Mobilm. Tag an

= Rheinisch-westfäl. Jndustriegebiet

# War Weariness and Peace Overtures

Paul Popper

*Above: Kühlmann and his wife. He hoped to divide the Allies by negotiating separately with Great Britain. His unauthorized efforts only cemented British support for France and Italy. Far left: Sceptical German view of Wilson, May 1916. Wilson, a would-be peacemaker, strove to be 'neutral in thought and word'. But, this cartoon points out, Wilson's song of friendship to the German people is drowned by the organ of guns played by America – guns sold to the Allies. Left: Wilson's 'Fourteen Points' formulated the idealistic principles which Wilson had always felt should dominate peace negotiations. But the interest shown by the other powers in peace proposals was less idealistic. Below left: 'Must Belgium become open territory through which the English army can march on Germany?' German propaganda map showing how in ten days Great Britain could march through Belgium to attack the industrial heart of Germany. Belgium was the main stumbling block in peace negotiations. The Allies insisted that Belgium should be evacuated and fully restored by the Germans; the Germans insisted on remaining there*

The First World War affected the lives of ordinary men and women to a far greater degree than any war between supposedly civilized powers had ever done before. In the autumn of 1914 the hopes of a quick victory for either side faded, and from that moment the war machine clamoured for more men and more resources, a clamour which continued for almost four years. Millions of men were drafted into the armed forces. More millions, and women also, were directed into work on munitions or other industries essential for war. In most countries, profits and wages were regulated, more or less ineffectively. Prices rose as the governments poured out paper money, and supplies ran short. The free market which had brought prosperity in normal times now broke down. There was rationing of essential goods, particularly of foodstuffs. Very often there was a sharp reduction of the pre-war standard of life, and even so the rations were not supplied in full. Quite apart from the countless dead on the battlefields, the war brought hardship and sometimes starvation to the living.

There was social discontent and political unrest. The surprising thing is how slowly and how late this was translated into war weariness. For much of the period, men were demanding instead that the war should be waged more fiercely and more completely. The demagogues who called for aerial reprisals or the internment of enemy aliens evoked more response than did the few enlightened men who sought a way out. Equally surprising, the rulers of most countries, though usually of a conservative cast, showed little anxiety that the war would shake the fabric of society. On the contrary, they believed that failure to achieve a decisive victory would open the door to revolution. In the last year of the war, the prospect of revolution came to haunt Europe in the shape of Bolshevism, but even this only spurred the governments of the various belligerents to more violent efforts.

In the first two years of the war, peace overtures came from Woodrow Wilson, President of the one great neutral power, and not from any of the countries at war. Wilson strove to be 'neutral in thought and deed'. He refused to judge between the combatants, though his private sympathies were on the Allied side. His sole aim was to bring the belligerent countries to the conference table, and he therefore shrank from propounding terms of peace himself. His overtures were rebuffed by both sides. The Allies and the Central powers remained equally confident of victory, though they

did not know how to achieve it. Even the few who advocated compromise were fundamentally in disagreement. Compromise, it was agreed, meant an acceptance of the *status quo*, but each side had a different *status quo* in mind. On the Allied side, the *status quo* meant a return to the frontiers of 1914 with reparation for the devastated areas particularly in Belgium and northern France. For the Germans, the *status quo* meant the actual situation as established after their first victories: Germany would retain all she had conquered or at the very least be generously compensated for any territory from which she withdrew.

## A question of territory

Thus there were few peace overtures during this earlier period, because any common ground was lacking. The Germans made some cautious soundings of Russia in the hope of detaching her from the Allied side. Even here they were trapped by their own victories after the campaign of 1915. They would not surrender all the Russian territory they had overrun, and the Tsar Nicholas II was equally determined to liberate the soil of Holy Russia. In the autumn of 1916 the reactionary Russian ministers at last took alarm. They began to fear that war weariness was really beginning in Russia and were ready to respond when the Germans made overtures through Stockholm. At exactly this moment the German high command insisted on a declaration in favour of Polish independence. General Erich Ludendorff, the real director of the German high command, imagined, wrongly, that thousands of Poles would then join the German army. The Poland he proposed to recognize was entirely drawn from Russia's share of the partition. The negotiations with Russia naturally broke down. The Germans lost their chance of ending the war on the Eastern Front.

The topic of peace was first publicly aired in December 1916, though there was no serious intention behind it of ending the war. The impulse came from the renewed demand in German governing circles for unrestricted submarine warfare. The Germans had tried this earlier in 1915 and had then given it up when faced by American protests. Also they did not possess at that time enough submarines to make their threat effective. Now Ludendorff insisted once more. The German attack on Verdun had failed to produce a French collapse. The German armies had been heavily strained by the prolonged engagements on the Somme, and Ludendorff did not believe

that his armies could achieve a decisive victory in 1917. On the contrary he confessed that the Germans would have to stand on the defensive when he prepared a withdrawal to the Hindenburg Line. Ludendorff accepted, however, the claim of the German naval leaders that unrestricted submarine warfare would bring about the collapse of Great Britain. It might also provoke the United States into entering the war against Germany. Ludendorff did not care. He did not imagine that the Americans could develop any effective military strength, still less that this could be deployed on the European battlefield.

### Bethmann's Peace Note

Theobald Bethmann Hollweg, the German chancellor, was less confident. He had seen the brave hopes of German generals and admirals dashed time and again. He was anxious to stave off unrestricted submarine warfare, but this could be done only if he offered a firm prospect of ending the war on Germany's terms. On 12th December 1916 Bethmann therefore issued a Peace Note. This merely announced Germany's willingness to negotiate. There was no indication of the terms Germany would propose. Privately Bethmann intended that they should be those of victory: control of Belgium and north-east France for Germany. Even so, he imagined that war weariness in the Allied countries would produce some sort of favourable response. There had in fact been some discussion behind the scenes in Great Britain whether victory was possible. The people had not been consulted and were still not disillusioned. David Lloyd George, who had just become British prime minister, rejected Bethmann's Peace Note out of hand and answered by demanding the complete defeat of Germany, or, as it was called, the 'Knock Out Blow'.

President Wilson, like Bethmann, wanted to avoid a breach between Germany and the USA. He, too, recognized that negotiations for peace were the only way of achieving this. Despite the failure of Bethmann's Note, Wilson tried much the same tack. On 20th December he invited the contending powers to formulate their war aims: perhaps these 'would not prove irreconcilable'. The Germans failed to answer. They knew that their aims, if openly stated, would outrage Wilson and be the more likely to provoke him into war. The Allies, though offended at being put on the same moral level as the Germans, devised idealistic war aims which could not be denied Wilson's approval. The interchange had not much reality. Both sides were bidding for Wilson's favour, not trying to clear the way for negotiations. The Germans did not bid at all seriously. Even Bethmann had despaired of preventing the renewal of unrestricted submarine warfare and merely kept Wilson in play

*Left: A victim of the German blockade — a steamer torpedoed by a U-boat. In April 1917 the U-boats sunk 881,000 tons of Allied shipping. If this success had continued a few months longer, Germany might have won the war*

until the submarines were ready. The Allies picked out the more respectable bits of their aims, but there was a great deal more which they intended to demand and which they did not reveal to Wilson.

### Obstacles to peace

These first manoeuvres brought out the obstacles to a negotiated peace then or thereafter. Governments had to display a confidence of future victory in order to keep up the spirits of their peoples. If any country stated the terms which it expected would follow its victory, the opposing side was indignant and spurred to new efforts. If, on the other hand, a country tried to be moderate, the enemy regarded this as a confession that it foresaw defeat. More than this, negotiations were not needed to demonstrate that Belgium was the insuperable obstacle to a negotiated peace. The Germans were in possession and would insist on remaining there more or less openly. They even perversely used their own invasion of Belgium as proof that her neutrality was no protection for the Ruhr. They argued that what they had done in 1914, the British and French would do next time. The British, on their side, were equally adamant that Belgium must be evacuated and fully restored by the Germans. This was the ostensible reason why Great Britain had entered the war, and the British never wavered from it. The fumbling negotiations, far from making victory unnecessary, showed that nothing could be achieved without it.

### Social unrest

Even so, the idea of a compromise peace, however impractical, had been aired for the first time, and this was not without effect on the warring peoples. The early months of 1917 brought the first open signs of war weariness, though rarely in the clear form of a demand to end the war. Living conditions were at their worst during the hard winter of 1916-17. Food, clothes, and fuel ran short. There were strikes everywhere in factories and coal mines. In Germany there was a mutiny among the bored sailors who never left harbour. But there was still a margin for concession. Wages were increased. The trade unions were brought into partnership with government departments and the armed forces. Rationing did something to ensure that the reduced supplies went round more fairly.

In two great countries, the social unrest had political results. In Austria-Hungary, the Emperor Karl, who had succeeded to the throne in November 1916, tried to conciliate the nationalities of his nondescript empire. In Russia, the Tsar, Nicholas II, abdicated and a republic was proclaimed, in the belief that this would provide a government more worthy of the national confidence. It is sometimes said that the first Russian revolution of 1917 was made by the army and was against the war. On the contrary, the army was never in better spirits or better equipped. The revolution came after bread riots in Petrograd and took the army by surprise. The generals and the politicians who most favoured the war at first welcomed the overthrow of the Tsar as a preliminary to waging the war more effectively. Nevertheless, the people of Russia were now given a voice, at least in theory, and this voice was soon raised for peace.

The Emperor Karl and the democratic politicians in Russia both recognized that their countries would be ruined unless peace was made in the near future. Both made overtures for peace though they used different ways of doing it. Emperor Karl's way was by secret negotiations, a last splutter of old-style diplomacy. His brother-in-law, Prince Sixte of Bourbon-Parma, approached President Raymond Poincaré of France with terms which he thought the French might accept. Poincaré did not object to them, and Prince Sixte then showed them to Karl as official French demands. The most solid point in them was that France should recover Alsace and Lorraine. To this, Karl on his side made no objection. The British and French governments were now highly excited. They imagined that they were in sight of a separate peace with Austria-Hungary which would deprive Germany of her ally and perhaps even open a backdoor for the invasion of Germany.

In fact the whole affair was a muddle, as usually happens when amateurs dabble in diplomacy. Karl only meant to invite terms which he could show to his German ally. The British and French supposed that he was deserting his ally. There was a further difficulty. Great Britain and France were at war with Austria-Hungary only in theory. Their forces never clashed except for an occasional naval encounter in the Adriatic. Italy was the only Allied power seriously engaged against Austria-Hungary, and the Italian statesmen had no particular interest in securing Alsace and Lorraine for France. The Italians wanted South Tyrol and Trieste. In 1915 the Austrians had accepted war rather than surrender these territories, and their resolve was still unshaken.

However Lloyd George and Alexandre Ribot, the French premier, dangled peace with Austria-Hungary before the Italian foreign minister, Baron Sonnino, though they did not reveal Emperor Karl's so-called peace offer. Sonnino was unmoved. No peace without victory was his policy as it was that of his allies, except that in his case it was victory over Austria-Hungary, not over Germany, that he wanted. The Austrian peace offer, never very seri-

*British soldier examines French candlesticks once meant for Germany. Metal shortages hampered the German war effort and Allied blockades strangled the North Sea ports*

ously made, ran into the sands. Soon in any case the French decided that they would not welcome a peace which merely benefited Italy, while they went on fighting Germany. Only Lloyd George continued to pursue the dream of a separate peace with Austria-Hungary. General Smuts, for the British war cabinet, and Count Mensdorff, the Austrian diplomat, had long meetings in Switzerland. Their discussions always broke on the same point. Lloyd George wanted to be able to attack Germany through Austrian territory. The Austrians would only abandon their German ally after a general peace had been made. The Habsburg monarchy remained shackled to the war.

### Socialist efforts

The Russian search for peace was more open and created more stir in the world. Russia was now theoretically a democracy, and the Provisional Government sought to satisfy the wishes of the Russian people.

They abandoned the imperialist aims of tsardom which had been enshrined in the secret treaties and announced a programme of peace without annexations or indemnities. At the same time they remained loyal to their Western allies and desired a general peace, not merely Russia's withdrawal from the war. There were many in the West, particularly among the socialist parties, who desired the same thing. For the first time, public opinion in the West took the talk of peace seriously. Even in Germany there was a pull in the same direction. The moderate Russian socialists thought that peace without annexations or indemnities would prove irresistible, if socialists from all the warring countries combined to support it. They proposed a meeting of European socialists at Stockholm. The German socialists agreed to come. British and French socialists also wished to come, though their object was to show that Germany would not agree to the programme and thus to keep Russia in the

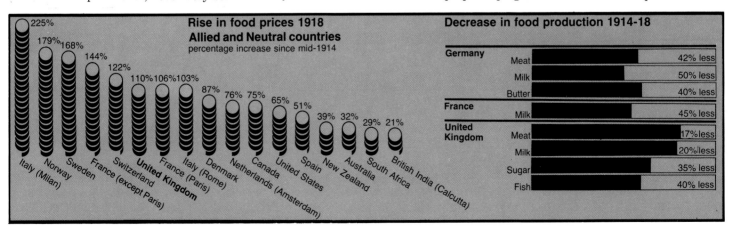

225% | 179% | 168% | 144% | 122% | 110% | 106% | 103% | 87% | 76% | 75% | 65% | 51% | 39% | 32% | 29% | 21%

**Rise in food prices 1918**
**Allied and Neutral countries**
percentage increase since mid-1914

Italy (Milan) | Norway | Sweden | France (except Paris) | Switzerland | **United Kingdom** | France (Paris) | Italy (Rome) | Denmark | Netherlands (Amsterdam) | Canada | United States | Spain | New Zealand | Australia | South Africa | British India (Calcutta)

**Decrease in food production 1914-18**

| | | |
|---|---|---|
| **Germany** | Meat | 42% less |
| | Milk | 50% less |
| | Butter | 40% less |
| **France** | Milk | 45% less |
| **United Kingdom** | Meat | 17% less |
| | Milk | 20% less |
| | Sugar | 35% less |
| | Fish | 40% less |

war, not to secure a real peace. The French government refused to allow their socialists to go. The British government reluctantly gave their socialists permission to attend the Stockholm conference. However, the British seamen, who were furiously anti-German because of the U-boat warfare, refused to convey the socialist delegates. The Stockholm conference was never held.

With this, the hope for a general peace without annexations or indemnities was dead. However, its influence went on rumbling. In Germany, Matthias Erzberger, a leader of the Centre Party, began to doubt whether Germany would win the war. He put forward a peace resolution in the Reichstag, and the Social Democrats supported him. Bethmann also welcomed the peace resolution as a means of restraining the high command. Instead, the high command secured his dismissal. When the peace resolution was passed by the Reichstag, George Michaelis, the new chancellor, endorsed it 'as I understand it'. What he understood was that it would not count as annexation for Germany to keep her present conquests nor would it count as indemnities if she were paid to leave them. When later Germany made peace with Russia and Rumania, it turned out that the Centre and the Social Democrats understood the peace resolution in the same sense. The peace resolution of the Reichstag had no effect in Allied countries. In Germany it helped to stem war weariness. Many Germans believed that the Reichstag had proposed idealistic peace terms and that the Allies had rejected them.

There was another remarkable overture for peace in 1917. The pope — Benedict XV — wanted to save the old order in Europe. Especially he wanted to save the Habsburg monarchy, the last surviving Roman Catholic power. Also he felt the socialist competition for peace. On 12th August 1917 the pope proposed peace to the warring powers in much the same vague terms as Woodrow Wilson had used earlier. The papal peace note envisaged a return to the *status quo* of 1914 and even mentioned the restoration of Belgian independence — not terms likely to please the Germans. The Western powers had promised Italy that they would not accept the help of the Vatican in peace negotiations. Arthur Balfour, the British foreign secretary, rashly asked for more precision in regard to Belgium. When France and Italy protested, he withdrew his enquiry. Nevertheless, the Vatican passed the enquiry on to the German government. The Germans, who meant to hang on to Belgium, gave an empty answer. The pope had failed to break the deadlock, like the socialists before him.

The German government was not wholly inactive. Richard von Kühlmann, who became secretary of state on 6th August, doubted whether Germany could win the war and was proud enough of his diplomatic skill to believe that he could end it. His aim was to divide the Allies by negotiating separately with one of them. There had already been some unofficial approaches from French politicians in the same direction. Joseph Caillaux, who had been prime minister before the war, gave re-peated hints that he was ready for a separate peace with Germany, though it is uncertain whether he actually attempted to negotiate with German representatives in Rome, while Germany and Italy were still not at war with each other. Aristide Briand, another former prime minister, also fancied that he could make a separate peace and perhaps recover Alsace, or part of it, at the same time. None of this was more than empty talk by out-of-work politicians. The French people, after all their sacrifices, would not accept peace without regaining Alsace and Lorraine. The Germans would not surrender the two provinces unless they were defeated.

Kühlmann thought in any case that it was a waste of time to negotiate with any French politician. In his opinion, it was British resolve which kept the war going. If the British were satisfied, the war would come to an end. Kühlmann therefore approached the British government through the King of Spain. He hinted, quite without authority, that the Germans might withdraw from Belgium if the British made a separate peace. The British, far from wanting to desert their allies, were afraid that France and Italy, both in a shaky position, might desert them. The British answered Kühlmann that they were prepared to discuss peace terms only if their allies were included. Kühlmann announced that Germany would never surrender Alsace and Lorraine. Lloyd George in return pledged that Great Britain would fight by the side of France until Alsace and Lorraine were recovered. The mere attempt to start discussions over peace terms thus, far from bringing understanding, drove the belligerents farther apart.

## Pressure from below
The fumblings towards negotiation, which had always been pretty futile, now came to an end and were not seriously resumed until the end of the war. There was, however, considerable pressure from below for some sort of action. Indeed 1917 was the great year of war weariness and even of revolt against war. This went farthest in Russia. Once the Provisional Government had failed to secure a peace without annexations or indemnities, its hold over the Russian people crumbled. It sought permission from its Western allies to make a separate peace. This was refused, for fear of the effect it would have on public opinion in France and Italy. For in these countries war weariness reached the level of action and resistance to war. In both countries discipline was breaking down in the armies, and order was breaking down behind the lines. In France, after the military failures under General Robert Nivelle in April 1917, most of the army refused to obey orders for any new offensive. At one time fifty-four divisions were in a state of mutiny. The more rebellious soldiers talked of marching on Paris and overthrowing the government. In Italy there was less open mutiny, but soldiers deserted their units and went home, where the police dared not arrest them and often did not want to. Thus, by the summer of 1917, the French army was incapable of fighting, and the Italian army was at little more than half its paper strength. The spirit in the factories was little better. In Turin and Milan, the workers were already planning to take over the factories for themselves as they did after the war.

Yet this discontent did not last. The war weariness gradually faded away, and there was a revival of national enthusiasm, though on a more cautious scale. General Henri-Philippe Pétain, who took command of the French armies in May 1917, assured the French soldiers that they would not be flung into more futile offensives and declared his intention of waiting for the Americans. When there was a governmental crisis in November, President Poincaré recognised that he must decide between Caillaux, the man of compromise peace, and Clemenceau, the man of more ruthless war. He chose Clemenceau as premier. From this moment, France was committed to the bitter end. Clemenceau arrested a few so-called pacifist agitators and arraigned Caillaux before the high court for correspondence with the enemy. These gestures were hardly necessary. There was still enough national enthusiasm to sustain Clemenceau, particularly with the Americans just over the horizon.

In Italy the national spirit was actually revived by a catastrophe — the great defeat of Caporetto. As the shattered Italian armies fell back behind the Piave, politicians of all parties rallied to the national cause. Disputes stopped in the factories. Soldiers went back to their units. The war actually became popular in Italy for the first time.

## Russian overtures
The Russian army, it seemed, was beyond saving. It began to break up after an unsuccessful offensive in July. The Russian people had become indifferent to the war. There was no mass movement to stop the war, but still less was there any mass support behind the Provisional Government. There was merely indifference, and this indifference enabled the Bolsheviks to seize power in November. Peace was the most urgent point in the Bolshevik programme. Lenin, the Bolshevik leader, believed that the people of every warring country would immediately respond to an appeal for peace if it were made firmly enough. The imperialist governments, as he called them, would have to conform, or they would be swept away by their angry proletariats.

On 8th November 1917 Lenin read the decree on peace to the All-Russian Soviet. It proposed immediate negotiations for 'a just and democratic peace' — with no annexations, no indemnities, and self-determination for every people, however long they had been ruled by another. An armistice of three months should be at once concluded on every front, so that negotiations should proceed. Here was certainly an overture for peace, the most practical and urgent made throughout the war. The German government responded. They welcomed an armistice on the Eastern Front, though they were not moved by the idealistic phrases.

The Western powers were more embarrassed. They wanted the Russians to go on

*Below: Bitter Dutch socialist cartoon on the Stockholm conference. Mars: 'I must see to it that the light does not reach him.'*
*Below centre: The wounded—victims of Europe's determination to continue the war.*
*Bottom: Swiss cartoon of Lenin, who called for 'open dealings', an end to secret diplomacy, and peace*

Musée de la Guerre, Paris

Imperial War Museum

fighting, not to make an armistice. They did not believe that the Germans would ever make peace on Lenin's principles, nor did they intend to do so themselves. Lloyd George and Clemenceau were both symbols of war to the end. If they now compromised, they would be replaced by more sincere peacemakers—Caillaux in France, Lord Lansdowne in England. The old theme was repeated that the only way of saving society and beating off socialist revolution was to carry the war to a victorious resolution. On 29th November the Allied supreme council gave a sharp and final negative to Lenin's Decree on Peace. From this moment the Bolsheviks were denounced as treacherous and disloyal, and their withdrawal was blamed for the continuance of the war. At the same time, anyone who proposed a compromise peace or even idealistic terms could be branded as a Bolshevik. This was a convenient arrangement, with rewarding results. War weariness became a symptom of Bolshevism. Most people disapproved of Bolshevism, which was supposed to maintain itself by Chinese methods of torture and to practise among other things the nationalization of women. Most people therefore did their best not to be war weary.

### Peace at Brest Litovsk
Peace negotiations between Germany and Soviet Russia were duly held. The Germans interpreted no annexations in the peculiar form that they should keep what they possessed. They also interpreted self-determination to mean that the inhabitants of the Russian territories occupied by German armies did not wish to be put under Bolshevik rule. Trotsky, who led the Soviet delegation, resolved to appeal from the German rulers to the German people. On 10th February 1918 he announced to the astonished conference: 'No war—no peace' and departed. The German and Austrian workers were now supposed to come to the aid of their Russian comrades. So at first they did. There was a renewed outbreak of strikes in both countries. Once more the strikers were mollified by increased wages and more food, itself looted from the Russian land. The strikes died away. On 3rd March 1918 the Soviet government reluctantly concluded with Germany and her allies the Peace of Brest Litovsk. This peace was not based on the principles which Lenin had laid down. The confident hope that idealistic terms would automatically end the war was dispelled.

With this, overtures for peace virtually came to an end. Some vague chat drifted on between British and German spokesmen at The Hague and between British and Austrian in Switzerland. An American, George Heron, also talked interminably to well-meaning Austrian professors who had no influence on their government. In July 1918 Kühlmann said in the Reichstag that the war would ultimately have to be ended by negotiations. For this he was dismissed from office by order of the high command. No one in the Allied countries went even as far as Kühlmann, though Lord Milner and perhaps others had the bright idea of buying Germany out of western Europe by

allowing her a free hand to dominate Russia. All such ideas were mere whimsy, another aspect of the anti-Bolshevism with which many Western statesmen were driving themselves demented.

War weariness, strangely enough, also declined. Food supplies improved in both Germany and Austria-Hungary, as the occupied Russian lands were more systematically looted. In many parts of Austria-Hungary there was a collapse of public order, or something near it. Deserters formed 'Green bands' and lived by terrorizing the countryside. These disturbances did not reach the industrial areas and had little effect on the Austro-Hungarian armies. In any case, with Russia out of the war, it did not much matter what happened in Austria-Hungary. Her armies in Italy could stand against the Italian forces which were in equally bad shape.

Both Germans and Allied peoples were shored up by the prospect of decisive victory. The Germans were inspired first by Ludendorff's offensives from March to July. During this period there was no war weariness in Germany—a clear indication that it sprang far more from boredom and discouragement than from hardship. During the same period the British and French people were actually stimulated by defeat. From the middle of July onwards they were inspired by victory. After 8th August the Allied armies rolled forwards. War weariness, though still there, was replaced by a confidence that the war would soon be over.

There were now peace overtures of a different kind. The earlier overtures had been political devices with which to embarrass the enemy or sometimes to placate a powerful neutral. At the end of September 1918 both Germany and Austria-Hungary made peace overtures with a genuine intention of ending the war. The two governments imagined that they were still free to choose: if the Allied terms were unsatisfactory, Germany and Austria-Hungary would go on with the war. This was an illusion. The two governments were making peace overtures only because they had lost the war. Moreover, as soon as the peace overtures became known, war weariness burst out. Later it was alleged that the German armies had been stabbed in the back. This was the reverse of the truth. Ludendorff confessed that the war was lost when he insisted on an immediate request for an armistice. Only then did political discontent blaze at home. Similarly, in Austria-Hungary the nationalities staked out their claim to independence only when the imperial government had begged for peace terms from President Wilson.

An ignorant, though rational, observer might assume that war weariness would provoke peace overtures. But, in the First World War, peace overtures, themselves usually a political manoeuvre, provoked war weariness, and when these overtures were rejected, enthusiasm for the war was revived. No doubt the people ought to have demanded an end to the war. In fact fiercer war was from first to last the popular cause.

# The Treaty of Versailles

The Germans surrendered to the Allies on 11th November 1918. Seven months later they signed the Treaty of Versailles, accepting new frontiers and stern penalties. During those seven months the victorious powers debated, both openly and secretly, every aspect of the future of Germany. Was it to be split up into small, separate states? Was it to be crippled economically? Was it to be deprived of territory? Was it to lose its empire in

*An appeal for pity in a German poster for 'Ludendorff's fund for disabled soldiers'. The cost of the war had been terrifying*

Africa and the Pacific? Was it to be prevented from ever having a powerful army, navy, or air force again? These were questions on which every public figure, and most private people, held strong opinions.

Yet the peace conference did not decide all of these issues. Many had been determined beforehand. During the war itself each side had worried continuously over the post-war settlement. Every nation had its dreams, its hopes, its secret agreements, and its publicly proclaimed aspirations. France was pledged to take back the provinces of Alsace and Lorraine which Germany had annexed in 1870. Great Britain

was determined to absorb as much of the German colonial empire as possible. As early as 1915 Italy had been promised Austrian, Turkish, and German territory in return for entering the war on the side of the Allies. Serbia was promised parts of Bosnia and Albania; Russia was promised Constantinople; the Jews were promised a 'National Home' in Palestine; the Arabs were promised independence from the Turks; and the Poles were offered the restoration of an independent Poland.

Woodrow Wilson, the President of the United States, had, in January 1918, offered *all* subject peoples the right of

Lu**n**rff-Spen für Krieg-beſchä**ig**

118

'self-determination'. This gave an impetus to many ambitious nationalists, to Czechs and Slovaks, to Serbs, Slovenes, and Croats, to Ukrainians, to the Baltic peoples, to the Rumanians inside Austria, to the Armenians inside Turkey, indeed, to a hundred groups, however small, who saw in 'self-determination' a chance, however slim, of statehood. Even the young Vietnamese Communist, Ho Chi-Minh, asked the Paris Peace Conference to liberate his people from the 'curse' of French imperial rule. But most of the small nationalities, like Ho Chi-Minh's, were doomed to be disappointed. Wilson's idealism shone like a beacon to the dispossessed; but to the French and the British, with their large empires and many subject peoples, and with their own hopes of territorial gain, 'self-determination' was a theme to be dampened down wherever it conflicted with their own ambitions.

### The 'war for human liberty'

Wilson believed that the war was the 'final war for human liberty'. He therefore wished to infuse the peace treaties with his own concept of liberty. For him, the central issue was that of national dignity: the right of people to be independent, with secure frontiers and unavaricious neighbours. When he spoke to Congress in February 1918 Wilson made it clear that, in his and the American view: 'Peoples are not to be handed about from one sovereignty to another by an international conference or an understanding between rivals and antagonists. National aspirations must be respected; peoples may now be dominated and governed only by their own consent. "Self-determination" is not a mere phrase. It is an imperative principle of action, which statesmen will henceforth ignore at their peril.'

Great Britain and France had little faith in self-determination. As a vague, idealistic liberal concept, they approved it in their public utterances; but during the heat of battle they had to consider other pressures besides liberal sentiment. At various moments in the war the Allied position was precarious. New allies had to be found. But neutrals do not easily agree to join in a war which they see to be one of terrible carnage, both on land and sea, involving the suspension of peaceful trade and industry, hardships in daily life, and, above all, the ever-present risk of defeat, occupation, humiliation, and national ruin.

The pledges made during the war had thus one dominating purpose, to persuade the uncommitted and the uncertain that it was in their full interest to support the Allied cause. Once that support had been forthcoming, the Allies could hardly go back on their promises. Where they did so, as in the case of Italy, they created a sense of grievance which had widespread repercussions. Italy had been promised, by Great Britain, France, and Russia, a share in any partitions of Turkish or German territory in Africa and the Near East. She was promised also the Austrian provinces of the Trentino, the South Tyrol, Gorizia, and Istria, the Dalmatian coast and control over Albania. But most of these pro-

mises were unfulfilled. Albania became fully independent. The Dalmatian coast went to Yugoslavia. Great Britain and France kept all Germany's African colonies for themselves, and gained all the benefits of the Turkish collapse. At the peace conference all Italy's protestations were in vain. Although she emerged from the peace treaties with her territory enlarged, she had become an unsatisfied nation, anxious to see a further revision of the treaty frontiers. Within a few years Mussolini was exploiting this sense of deprivation. He demanded the fulfilment of what Italy had been promised. But immediately the peace conference ended the world sought only to be done with alarms and crises, wars and arguments. At Paris, from January to June 1919, any claim could be made with impunity, for the six months of the conference was essentially a period when every nation pressed for as much as it dared to claim, and urged its claims with passion. But once the treaties were signed, any call for revision was made to seem an incitement to aggression, and the word 'revisionist' quickly became synonymous with 'troublemaker', even when the power demanding revision was a former ally.

In one case the war-time pledges could be easily ignored. For in 1917 the Russian Bolsheviks renounced the secret treaties and declared that they would not accept any of the territorial gains promised to Russia. As a result, the Anglo-French promise of Constantinople to the Tsar could lapse. But even so, the strategic waterway from the Black Sea to the Mediterranean was not to return easily into Turkish hands. From 1918 to 1924 the 'Zone of the Straits' was occupied by an Allied force, and for six years a British High Commissioner was the effective ruler of the former Turkish capital. Only the military successes of Kemal Ataturk made it possible for Turkey to retain Anatolia intact, and, although deprived of all her Arabian, Syrian, and Mesopotamian territory, to survive as a robust national state.

### The spoils of war

The secret treaties were not the only complications confronting the peace-makers when they reached Paris. Territory had changed hands at every stage of the war, and it proved difficult to dislodge claimants who were already in possession of what they claimed. During the conference Woodrow Wilson criticized the Australian Prime Minister, William Hughes, for insisting that Australia should keep control of German New Guinea, which Australian troops had occupied as early as 1914, within a month of the outbreak of war. Did Hughes really intend, questioned Wilson, to flout the opinion of the civilized world by annexing territory? Would she let it be said that she took part of the German empire as the spoils of war? Was Australia proposing to make a profit out of Germany's defeat, to impose her rule on aborigines, to take over valuable mineral rights, to extend her sovereignty as far north as the equator? To all of which Hughes replied acidly: 'That's about it, Mr President.'

The Australians were not alone in in-

*Gloom in Berlin. wretched civilians and demobilized men in the streets, June 1919*

sisting upon the maxim of 'what we have, we hold'. Japan pressed vigorously for control over the Chinese port of Tsingtao, a German possession which the Japanese had occupied in 1914, after a month's hard fighting. To the chagrin of the Japanese, the peace-makers forced them to return Tsingtao to China. As a result, the Japanese, like the Italians, felt cheated of a 'fruit' of victory, and looked for a chance to redress the balance. The Japanese invasion of China in 1937, like the Italian invasion of Albania in 1939, was in part a legacy of the frustrations of the peace conference. Other victor nations were less frustrated. No one dislodged the New Zealanders from German Samoa, the South Africans from German South West Africa, the British from German East Africa, or the Australians from New Guinea. Even the Japanese were allowed to retain control of most of Germany's vast Pacific island empire, which included over two thousand islands and covered three million square miles. Great Britain and France partitioned the German territories of Togoland and the Cameroons between them; the Italian occupation of the former Turkish Dodecanese Islands was made more secure; Cyprus, occupied by Great Britain under nominal Turkish suzerainty for forty years, was transformed into a permanent British possession. The areas of Turkey conquered in October 1918 remained firmly under the controlling hands of their conquerors – the British in Palestine, Transjordan, and Iraq, the French in Syria and Alexandretta, the Arabs in the Yemen and the Hejaz.

Such were the many territorial gains which were made during the course of the war. Most were criticized at the peace conference, particularly by Woodrow Wilson. But all survived the peace-making, and became a part of the new world order. Some even survived the Second World War; South Africa still rules German South West Africa; Australia still controls German New Guinea; New Zealand still occupies Samoa. Japanese control over Germany's Pacific Islands north of the equator passed, in 1945, not back to Germany, but on to the United States, the third imperial power to come into possession of the islands and atolls which stretch in a broad band out from the coast of China across three thousand miles of ocean.

### The new map of Europe

When the victor powers met in Paris they had to consider more than the promises which each ally had made, and the existence of new possessions which particular Allies had every intention of making permanent. They had also to take into account the people who, even before the war was ended, had proclaimed themselves independent. There were many such people, each determined to keep the territory which they claimed as the basis of permanent national frontiers. Thus the Czechs and Slovaks had declared their complete severance from Austria-Hungary before the Austro-Hungarian surrender; and they were insisting upon a new state which would include the historic frontiers of Bohemia, thereby placing over two million German-speaking people within their proposed territory. The South Slavs had also declared themselves an independent state, ruling over territory in which were to be found Hungarian, Italian, and Austrian minorities. These frontiers were of course still open to negotiation and change. But the Allies had for most of the war given support to all enemies of Austria-Hungary. In April 1915 they promised the future Serb state a part of the Adriatic coast and the Austro-Hungarian provinces of Bosnia and Dalmatia. They might strive to create 'ideal' frontiers, excluding minorities and satisfying conflicting claims and promises, but since the same territories were often occupied by different nationalities this was not easy, even from the viewpoint of abstract national geography.

As a result the frontiers in existence before the conference met tended to become the permanent ones. The pre-conference frontiers had been established by the subject peoples of Germany, Austria-Hungary, and Turkey. As the conference was made up of those who had fought these three empires in the war, the likelihood was that the pre-conference frontiers would, in the main, be allowed to survive—as indeed they were. When the Paris Peace Conference met a new map of Europe had already come into existence, drawn by new nations upon the ruins of the German, Austrian, and Turkish empires. The victor nations did not redraw the old map of Europe; instead, they fussed and argued over the new one. The conference obtained many marginal modifications; but the map which they saw in January was in most respects the same one which they were to agree upon in June.

Woodrow Wilson obtained some verbal changes in the war-time decisions. Instead of Germany's colonies being described as integral parts of the empires which conquered them, they were given the name of 'Mandates'. The new owners were then in theory responsible to the League of Nations, a world organization designed by Wilson to secure permanent peace and the just settlement of all international disputes, and which was transformed in 1945 into the United Nations. But the 'Mandates' remained securely under the powers who obtained them. The new League of Nations was also to safeguard the rights of minorities: and, this being

*Below:* 'The Surrender of the German High Seas Fleet'—part of the armistice agreement. *Above:* Advertisement for a bleach, typical of French feelings. Clemenceau uses it to wash out the Kaiser's crimes

*American signatures to the Treaty of Versailles (the American representatives signed it but Congress refused to ratify it). Wilson's utopian idealism left its mark on the final form of the treaty*

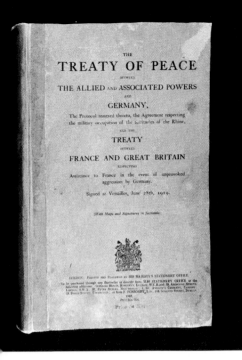

The transcript of the treaty sold in Great Britain. The British negotiators, in particular Lloyd George, had tried to temper the French demand for revenge and a crippled Germany—but in vain

British press poster after Versailles. The press had been a powerful agitator of patriotic emotion during the war. Its power to whip up hatred was less welcome to the men trying to create a fair peace

The stamp of a new nation—Czechoslovakia, which had declared its independence from the Habsburg empire during the last months of the war, and to whom the treaty gave generous frontiers

Imperial War Museum

so, minorities were allowed to remain in Poland, Czechoslovakia, Rumania, and Yugoslavia. Yet when persecution and discrimination began, the League was powerless to intervene.

### Conditions of armistice

The main barrier to a well-balanced treaty was built before the peace conference. When Germany, Austria, Bulgaria, and Turkey each surrendered, they did so by signing armistice agreements with the Allies. These agreements contained sets of conditions, on the acceptance of which the Allies agreed to stop the fighting. The armistice conditions were severe, and had to be carried out immediately. As a result of this, long before the Paris Peace Conference began, they had irrevocably altered the map, and the mood of Europe. Much of what politicians later denounced and historians criticized in the peace treaties was in fact created by the armistices.

The atmosphere at the time of the drafting of the armistice agreements was an atmosphere of war: the guns still roared, the fighting was still savage, the outcome was still uncertain. The terms were therefore harsh. It was necessary for the Allies to ensure that the armistice agreements were not tricks, brief halts engineered to obtain the breathing space necessary for recuperation and renewed fighting. Each armistice agreement was intended to make absolutely certain that the fighting capacity of the enemy was utterly broken. This they did. As a result, when the Paris Peace Conference opened, Germany, Austria, Bulgaria, and Turkey had already been treated with a severity which was both intentional, effective, and by its nature largely irrevocable.

The first armistice to be signed was with Bulgaria, on 29th September 1918. The Bulgarians were desperate for peace: their armies in Greece and Serbia were in retreat, while a large corps of Bulgarian mutineers was marching on Sofia, the capital. They therefore agreed to evacuate all Serbian and Greek territory which their troops still occupied, and which they had hitherto claimed for themselves. A month later, on 30th October, the Turks, two-thirds of whose Palestinian army had been taken prisoner, the remnant of which was in retreat, signed their armistice. They were obliged to accept the use of their capital, Constantinople, as an Allied naval base; to surrender the Black Sea port of Batum and the oilfields of Baku, both of which they were occupying; and to surrender all garrisons in Arabia, the Yemen, Syria, Mesopotamia, and Cilicia. The surrender of these garrisons was to be followed by immediate French and British occupation; the obvious prelude to political control.

On 3rd November the Austrians, beaten back on the Italian front, signed an armistice which was similarly decisive. Italian troops were allowed to occupy the territory which they claimed, and the Allies obtained the right to move at will along every line of communication throughout the Austro-Hungarian empire. The new nations had already proclaimed themselves. The Allied presence provided them with a firm guarantee that they would survive. They were thus two months old before the peace conference met.

### 'Reparation for damage done'

But it was towards Germany that the armistice was most severe. The total collapse of Bulgaria, Turkey, and Austria was taken for granted once the Allied military advances had begun. But Germany was believed to be stronger and more resilient than her allies. On 12th September, speaking at Manchester, Lloyd George, the British prime minister, insisted that 'Prussian military power must not only be beaten, but Germany herself must know that'. With the Allied armies reinforced by fresh, enthusiastic troops from the United States, and the German trench fortifications in Flanders broken, such a double aim seemed feasible. But a month later Sir Douglas Haig, the commander-in-chief of the British forces in France, sounded a warning note. On 19th October he returned to London from France to tell the war cabinet that all was not well. The American army, he claimed, 'is disorganized, ill-equipped, and ill-trained. . . . It has suffered severely through ignorance of modern war'. As for the French army, it seemed 'greatly worn out'. The British army, he concluded, 'is not sufficiently fresh or strong to force a decision by itself' and the war would go on, in Haig's view, well into 1919. All this pointed to the need for a severe armistice, which would deprive the Germans of any opportunity of hitting back once they had agreed to surrender. The war cabinet felt that if the armistice terms were comprehensive, they would serve as 'pledges for the fulfilment of our peace terms'.

On 11th November the fourth and last armistice of the war was signed. Germany accepted total defeat. Lloyd George's conditions were fulfilled: all military power was broken, and the German people were presented with a document both comprehensive and severe. Of the thirty-four clauses, the following give a picture of how much Germany had to agree to, not to make peace, but merely to bring an end to war.

*Right:* Versaillies, 28th June 1919. Painting by Sir William Orpen. German delegates (with their backs to the artist) Johannes Bell (seated) and Hermann Müller (standing) sign the treaty under the eyes of (seated, from left to right) Henry White, Lansing, Wilson, Clemenceau, Lloyd George, Bonar Law, Balfour, and Milner. *Left:* Whitehall: a crowd waits for news of the treaty

Immediate evacuation of the invaded countries — Belgium, France, Luxembourg, as well as Alsace-Lorraine.

Surrender in good condition by the German Armies of the following equipment —

  5,000 guns
  25,000 machine-guns
  3,000 trench mortars
  1,700 aeroplanes
  5,000 locomotives and 150,000 wagons,

in good working order, with all necessary spare parts and fittings, shall be delivered to the Associated Powers. . . . 5,000 motor lorries are also to be delivered in good condition.

To surrender . . . all submarines at present in existence . . . and

6 battle-cruisers
10 battleships
8 light cruisers
50 destroyers of the most
   modern types

Evacuation by the German Armies of the districts on the left bank of the Rhine. These districts . . . shall be administered . . . under the control of the Allied and United States Armies of Occupation.

By signing this armistice, Germany abandoned all hopes of territorial gain; even of retaining Alsace-Lorraine. She also agreed to accept a four-word financial condition: 'Reparation for damage done.' The interpretation of what was meant by these four words proved a major point of argument during the treaty negotiations, and poisoned the international atmosphere for twenty years, giving Adolf Hitler a powerful lever against the western democracies. The four words that the Germans, at the moment of defeat, accepted without discussion, were destined to provoke the most bitter discussion of the entire period between the two World Wars.

The idea of 'reparation for damage done' was not a new one. Germany had imposed such reparations on France in 1870, even though the fighting took place on French soil. Nor was there any doubt that the 'damage done' by Germany in France and Belgium was severe. Some small damage was done by Allied aeroplanes dropping bombs on Germany, but this was offset by the many more German air-raids, particularly on London, and by the German naval bombardment of undefended seaside towns on the east coast of Great Britain. The amount of damage done by Germany was immense, and little of it was made necessary by the dictates of war. In German-occupied France nearly 300,000 houses were completely destroyed. Six thousand factories were stripped of their machinery, which was sent to Germany. The textile mills of Lille and Sedan were smashed. Nearly 2,000 breweries were destroyed. In the coal mines around Roubaix and Tourcoing 112 mineshafts were blown in, and over 1,000 miles of underground galleries flooded or blocked. During their retreat, the Germans burned and looted on a massive scale, destroying over 1,000 miles of railway line, blowing up 1,000 bridges, looting thousands of houses, and stripping churches. During the four years of occupation the Germans took away half a million cows, half a million sheep, and over 300,000 horses and donkeys. These were the acts of vandals. And in the military sphere too it was France and Belgium, not Germany, that suffered most. After the war the French had to pull up over 300,000,000 metres of barbed wire, and fill in over 250,000,000 cubic metres of trenches. Much agricultural land was rendered useless because so many shells had fallen on it;

some remained dangerous for many years because of unexploded shells and the leakage of poison gas from unused canisters.

The British were equally determined to secure reparation. The Germans had torpedoed five hospital ships during the war; an action which inflamed the public and created an atmosphere in which the demand for high reparations flourished. The German U-boats had taken a cruel toll of merchant shipping. They had sunk thousands of unarmed ships mostly without warning. The British lost nearly 8,000,000 tons of commercial shipping; and many of the crews had been left to drown. Among the Allied nations, France, Italy, and the United States lost between them 2,000,000 tons of shipping; among neutrals Norway lost over 1,000,000 tons, Denmark, Holland, and Sweden over 200,000 tons each. No nation had been spared the deliberate terror of submarine war. The Allies had not, of course, sat idly by to watch these losses. The blockade of Germany was rigorously enforced, and as a result as many as 500,000 German civilians probably died of starvation. But in the moment of victory these victims of war's all-pervading cruelty did not seem to compensate for what the Allies had suffered. Nations use victory to settle the debt which they feel is owed to them; the other side of the account is ignored. The demand for reparations combined the physical damage that had been done with the psychological need to have tangible evidences in the form of gold, that the 'enemy' would make amends. Rudyard Kipling, who had lost a son in the fighting, expressed this feeling in a bitter poem (he wrote it in 1917 when the reparations issue was being discussed in public):

*These were our children who died for our
   lands: they were dear in our sight.*
*We have only the memory left of their home-
   treasured sayings and laughter.*
*The price of our loss shall be paid to our
   hands, not another's hereafter.*
*Neither the Alien nor Priest shall decide on
   it. That is our right.*
But who shall return us the children?

*That flesh we had nursed from the first in
   all clearness was given*
*To corruption unveiled and assailed by the
   malice of heaven*
*By the heart-shaking jests of Decay where it
   lolled on the wires —*
*To be blanched or gay-painted by fumes —
   to be cindered by fires —*
*To be senselessly tossed and retossed in
   stale mutilation*
*From crater to crater. For this we shall
   take expiation.*
But who shall return us the children?

### 'Squeeze the German lemon'

During the British general election held before the treaty negotiations began, the public cried out for heavy reparations. Almost every responsible politician tried to soften the public mood. But one, Sir Auckland Geddes, told an eager audience in London that 'we would squeeze the German lemon till the pips squeaked' and

even Lloyd George, tired out by the strains of electioneering, told a large meeting at Bristol that the Germans 'must pay to the uttermost farthing, and we shall search their pockets for it'. These were not his true views. He had begun, from the day the war ended, to adopt a moderate stance. He feared most of all that if Germany were humiliated too much by the treaty it would go Bolshevik, and not a single clause would be fulfilled, nor a penny of reparations paid.

In secret Lloyd George pressed his colleagues to adopt a certain leniency towards Germany, to send food to the starving millions in Germany and Austria, to think in terms of a peace free from vindictive clauses. But the public did not approve of such liberal sentiments. As Winston Churchill, who was then minister of munitions, recorded: 'The Prime Minister and his principal colleagues were astonished and to some extent overborne by the passions they encountered in the constituencies. The brave people whom nothing had daunted had suffered too much. Their unpent feelings were lashed by the popular press into fury. The crippled and mutilated soldiers darkened the streets. The returned prisoners told the hard tale of bonds and privation. Every cottage had its empty chair. Hatred of the beaten foe, thirst for his just punishment, rushed up from the heart of deeply injured millions. All who had done the least in the conflict were as might be expected the foremost in detailing the penalties of the vanquished. . . . In my own constituency of Dundee, respectable, orthodox, life-long Liberals demanded the sternest punishment for the broken enemy. All over the country the most bitter were the women, of whom seven millions were for the first time to vote. In this uprush and turmoil state policy and national dignity were speedily engulfed.'

Like Lloyd George, Churchill urged a moderate treaty. He too feared that harsh terms would force Germany into the Bolshevik embrace. But when Lloyd George reached Paris in January 1919, he found the French determined to obtain maximum reparations, and the sternest possible treaty.

At the peace conference Lloyd George was handicapped by the moods and utterances of the general election: the anti-German moods, continuing fierce, meant that in any moderation he urged he had to keep one eye on his own public opinion, which, when it felt that he was exercising undue leniency, could, and did, protest; while the bravado of the election speeches, vivid in French minds, meant that when Clemenceau, the French prime minister, urged severity he could always refer to Lloyd George's public statements as support for his own contentions. Although Lloyd George tried, throughout the negotiations, to control the evolution of the treaty, he began from a position of weakness from which he was unable fully to recover, and which obstructed many of his efforts to obtain a viable peace.

At Paris Lloyd George was the leading advocate of moderation. He sought to act as if he were above national antagonisms. He tried to be the arbiter of conflicting passions. But the House of Commons would not let him forget in what tone the election had been fought. When it became clear the reparations were being calculated on the basis of what Germany 'could' pay, rather than on what she 'ought' to pay, 370 Coalition Conservatives sent a petulant telegram, reminding him of what they and the electorate expected, and ending: 'Although we have the utmost confidence in your intention to fulfil your pledges to the country, may we, as we have to meet innumerable inquiries from our constituents, have your renewed assurance that you have in no way departed from your original intention?'

Within a week of receiving this challenge Lloyd George returned to London, and on 16th April 1919 rebuked the House of Commons for its impatience. He reminded MPs that he was having to settle the fate of five continents in Paris; that ten new states had to be brought into existence; that territorial, military, and economic questions had all to be decided upon, and that 'you are not going to solve these problems by telegram'. He reminded them that, even if mistakes were made, the League of Nations, which was being set up as part of the treaties, would be able to make the necessary adjustments later. He made it clear to his critics that if they insisted upon terms which the League were ultimately to judge unduly severe, those terms would be modified. For an hour Lloyd George cajoled, threatened, appealed to, and won over his listeners: '. . . and when enormous issues are dependent upon it, you require calm deliberation. I ask for it

for the rest of the journey. The journey is not at an end. It is full of perils, perils for this country, perils for all lands, perils for the people throughout the world. I beg, at any rate, that the men who are doing their best should be left in peace to do it, or that other men should be sent there. . . .

'We want a stern peace, because the occasion demands it. But its severity must be designed, not to gratify vengeance, but to vindicate justice. . . .

'[It is the duty of] statesmen in every land, of the Parliaments upon whose will those statesmen depend, of those who guide and direct the public opinion which is the making of all—not to soil this triumph of right by indulging in the angry passions of the moment, but to consecrate the sacrifice of millions to the permanent redemption of the human race from the scourge and agony of war.'

### Lloyd George as moderator

Lloyd George returned to Paris. But although he appeared to have convinced the House of Commons that leniency was needed, he was unable to convince the French. They made some concessions, abandoning their hopes for the creation of a separate Rhineland State, and for a Polish annexation of Danzig, but in general French desires were met. The treaty as finally published had a vindictive tone about it.

In a memorandum which Lloyd George wrote while at the peace conference, he declared that his concern was to create a peace for all time, not for a mere thirty years. A short peace might be possible if

punitive measures were taken against Germany. But unless the Germans were placated, they would go Bolshevik, and Russian Bolshevism would then have the advantage, according to Lloyd George, 'of the organizing gift of the most successful organizers of national resources in the world'. The initial shock of war would pass, and then, wrote Lloyd George: 'The maintenance of peace will depend upon there being no causes of exasperation constantly stirring up either the spirit of patriotism, of justice, or of fairplay to achieve redress. . . . Our Peace ought to be dictated by men who act in the spirit of judges sitting in a cause which does not personally engage their emotion or interests, and not in a spirit of a savage vendetta, which is not satisfied without mutilation and the infliction of pain and humiliation.'

This was utopian. Yet Lloyd George was convinced that he was right. He went on to criticize all clauses which might prove 'a constant source of irritation', and suggested that the sooner reparations disappeared the better. He deprecated putting Germany under alien rule, fearing that by doing so 'we shall strew Europe with Alsace-Lorraines'. He emphasized that the Germans were 'proud, intelligent, with great traditions', but that those under whose rule they would be placed by the treaty were 'races whom they regard as their inferiors, and some of whom, undoubtedly for the time being, merit that designation'. These arguments fell upon stony ground: the French could not understand Lloyd George's sudden conversion to

*The German delegation to Versailles. They had been forced to accept not only humiliating losses, but blame for causing the war*

Radio Times Hulton

what they could only describe as imbecilic pro-Germanism. Clemenceau replied icily to Lloyd George's memorandum that 'if the British are so anxious to appease Germany they should look . . . overseas . . . and make colonial, naval, or commercial concessions'. Lloyd George was particularly angered by Clemenceau's remark that the British were 'a maritime people who have not known invasion', and countered angrily that 'what France really cares for is that the Danzig Germans should be handed over to the Poles'.

These bitter exchanges were symptomatic of a growing rift in Anglo-French relations. For Clemenceau, the treaty was perhaps the best chance that France would have of designing effective protection against a Germany that was already almost twice as populous as France, and must therefore be shown by deliberate, harsh action that it would not pay to think of revenge. For Lloyd George, the treaty was an opportunity to arbitrate for Europe without rancour, and to create a continent whose future problems could be adjusted without malice. Great Britain, by supporting the League of Nations, would be willing to help in the process of adjustment. Clearly it was the treaty that would first need to be altered: Lloyd George did not fear that. For him the treaty was not a sacred instrument but a pliable one. It was obvious from his comments while it was being drafted that he would not be content to see it become the fixed rule of the new Europe.

At Paris Lloyd George opposed strenuously, but in vain, the transfer to Poland of areas predominantly German. His protest was a forceful one, yet it was not forceful enough to break the French desire for the reduction of German territory.

'I am strongly averse,' Lloyd George wrote, 'to transferring more Germans from German rule to the rule of some other nation than can possibly be helped. I cannot conceive any greater cause of future war than that the German people, who have certainly proved themselves one of the most vigorous and powerful nations in the world, should be surrounded by a number of small states, many of them consisting of people who have never previously set up a stable government for themselves, but each of them containing large masses of Germans clamouring for reunion with their native land. . . . [These proposals] must, in my judgement, lead sooner or later to a new war in Eastern Europe.'

The Treaty of Versailles was not as vindictive as France had hoped; nor was it as moderate as Lloyd George desired. It was certainly not as utopian as Woodrow Wilson envisaged. A study of its clauses reveals great concern for detail, an often punitive attitude, and very little account taken of the personal hardships and political discontent which the clauses might arouse. Thus Austria and Germany were forbidden, by Article 80, to unite, a future possibility which the British foreign secretary, A.J.Balfour, had regarded as a sensible solution which might soften the blow of defeat. Article 100 took away from Germany the entirely German city of Danzig, turning it into an isolated 'Free City' within the 'customs frontiers' of Poland, and depriving all its citizens of German nationality. Under Article 118 Germany renounced all her 'rights, titles and privileges . . . whatever their origin' outside Europe. This meant that even purely commercial concessions, freely negotiated before 1914, were lost. All Germany's colonies were taken from her, together with 'all movable and immovable property in such territories'; even the property of the German school at Shanghai was given to the French and Chinese governments. All pre-war German trading agreements were declared null and void, and the patient, innocent, costly efforts of German businessmen in China, Siam, Liberia, Egypt, and Morocco were entirely undone. Article 153 laid down that 'All property and possessions in Egypt of the German empire and the German states pass to the Egyptian government without payment'; and Article 156 transferred to Japan all German state submarine cables in China 'with all rights, privileges, and properties attaching thereto'.

The military clauses were as one would expect. The size of the German army was limited to 100,000 men. Germany was forbidden to import any arms or munitions. Compulsory military training was abolished. Universities and sporting clubs were forbidden to 'occupy themselves with any military matters'. They were specifically forbidden to instruct or exercise their members 'in the profession or use of arms'. All fortresses in the Rhineland were to be dismantled. At sea, Germany was restricted to six battleships, six light cruisers, twelve destroyers, and twelve torpedo boats. She was allowed not a single submarine. Her naval personnel were limited to 15,000 men. All warships under construction were to be broken up.

One clause was a dead letter from the moment it was signed. Under Article 227 the Allies announced the trial of the Kaiser 'for a supreme offence against international morality and the sanctity of treaties'. He was to be tried by five judges, an American, an Englishman, a Frenchman, an Italian, and a Japanese. It was their duty 'to fix the punishment which it considers should be imposed'. Despite the British public's keenness to 'hang the Kaiser', Lloyd George felt that such a solution was a mistake. When, therefore, the French began to demand the return of the Kaiser from Holland, Great Britain refused to give France any support. The Kaiser remained safely in exile, cultivating his garden.

## 'War guilt'

The most controversial clause in the Treaty of Versailles was Article 231, the notorious 'War Guilt' clause against which successive German governments argued in vain, and which even many British politicians thought too extreme. The Article read: 'The Allied and Associated Governments affirm and Germany accepts the responsibility of Germany and her allies for causing all the loss and damage to which the Allied and Associated Governments and their nationals have been subjected as a consequence of the war imposed upon them by the aggression of Germany and her allies.'

How had this clause come into being? What made the Allies so anxious to get Germany to accept responsibility for 'all the loss and damage'? Why was 'the aggression of Germany' referred to so bluntly?

The War Guilt clause originated before the end of the war. The Supreme War Council, meeting under the leadership of Clemenceau and Lloyd George at Versailles on 4th November 1918, had drafted a note to President Wilson, explaining to him the need for reparations from Germany. The note began: 'They (the Allied governments) understand that compensation will be made by Germany for all damage caused to the civilian population of the Allies by the invasion by Germany of Allied territory. . . .'

As Germany had never denied invading Belgium, Luxembourg, or France, this clause was a fair one: a statement of acknowledged fact. But someone at the meeting pointed out that as the clause stood, while Germany would have to pay for damage done from the Channel to the Vosges, there was nothing in this wording to enable any economic compensation to go to the non-continental allies, the USA, India, Australia, Canada, or even Great Britain, and that certainly the Dominions, who had played such a large part, not only in providing men but also materials, would resent their exclusion from money payments. The clause would therefore need redrafting. The new draft cut out 'the invasion by Germany of Allied territory' and replaced it by 'the aggression of Germany'. Aggression was a word that could cover a much wider sphere: it could be claimed that every aspect of war costs was involved. But it was also a condemnatory word. Invasion had been admitted; aggression had not. The justification in German eyes for the invasion was self-defence; aggression was a word pregnant with moral disapproval, allowing of no subtle interpretation; spelling, all too clearly, guilt.

Lloyd George's personal assistant recalled in 1931: 'I remember very distinctly discussing with L.G. the interpretation to be put upon the question of "restoration" or "reparations". His view was—"We must make it clear that we cannot charge Germany with the costs of the war. . . . She could not possibly pay it. But she must pay ample compensation for damage and that compensation must be equitably distributed among the Allies and not given entirely to France and Belgium. Devastated areas is only one item in war loss. Great Britain has probably spent more money on the war and incurred greater indirect losses in, for instance, shipping and trade, than France. She must have her fair share of the compensation."

'He then instructed me to prepare a form of words. . . . I did so. . . . I remember thinking, after the draft had been taken by L.G., that it did not cover adequately the point that compensation was due to all the Allies. . . . I therefore revised it to read "damage to the civilian population of the allies by the aggression of Germany by land, air and sea".'

Thus was written the clause which most aggravated Anglo-German relations between the wars, made the task of appeasement with Germany so difficult, and made the Germans feel that, whatever concessions Great Britain made, whatever gestures of friendship she volunteered, in reality her policy was dictated by an explicit belief in German guilt.

The reparations clauses were the most often criticized part of the treaty. Yet the total demand of £24,000,000,000 was whittled away at a series of international conferences, until finally, at Lausanne in 1932, reparations were brought to an end. Great Britain was paying off her war debts to the United States until the end of the 1960's; Germany stopped paying for the war over forty years ago.

### The new frontiers

The treaty's most lasting clauses were those which created new frontiers. They were also the most defensible. Many were established, not by Allied insistence, but as a result of plebiscites, in which the inhabitants were asked where they wanted to go. The plebiscites in East Prussia resulted in the province remaining entirely German. In two border areas of Austria the inhabitants voted to remain Austrian. The people of the Saar, after fifteen years of League of Nations supervision, voted to return to Germany, and were reincorporated into Hitler's Reich—this, his first territorial acquisition, was a positive gain made possible only because of the treaty which he was always denouncing. In Silesia the plebiscite results were indecisive. and

*Below: Germany's air fleet reduced to firewood—wooden propellers being sawn up after the planes were destroyed as the Treaty demanded*

this rich industrial region was therefore divided between Germany and Poland. The Danes of Schleswig voted to leave Germany: the sole plebiscite to go wholly against the German interest.

The lands which Germany lost outright were Alsace-Lorraine, a German war gain of 1871, and territory in the east which went to Poland. Germany had helped destroy Polish independence at the end of the 18th century, and had annexed Polish territory during the three partitions: now that territory was returned to the recreated Polish state, and with it a corridor which gave Poland an outlet on the Baltic Sea. The Germans later made a great fuss about this corridor. But its inhabitants were mostly Poles, and Poland, after over a hundred years of subjugation, was entitled to a measure of security.

The greatest frontier changes arose from the disintegration, in the last weeks of the war, of the Austro-Hungarian empire. Czechoslovakia had proclaimed itself an independent state; the treaties gave it a generous frontier. Yugoslavia did likewise, fulfilling the Slav dream of a new South Slav kingdom; and the Allies were again generous, though not allowing the port of Fiume to go to the new state. The Poles obtained territory from both Germany and Austria, and the Allies, eager to see Poland as a bastion between Bolshevik Russia and the west, encouraged an eastern frontier drawn very much at Russia's expense. Yet even here, Lloyd George was reluctant to see Poland push too far east or west, and it was left to Polish military action, not any Allied treaty, to secure parts of the Ukraine, Belorussia, and Lithuania for the new Poland. To Rumania the Allies allotted the primarily Rumanian districts of Austria-Hungary, principally Transsylvania. Bulgaria, an 'enemy' power, lost

her outlet on the Aegean Sea, which went to Greece; but her full independence, secured from Turkey not ten years before the war began, was not tampered with. Austria lost only one basically Austrian province, the South Tyrol, which went to Italy. The nation with the most convincing grievance was Hungary; large communities of Hungarians found themselves inside Czechoslovakia, Rumania, and Yugoslavia. But once again, Hungarian independence was secured, and although Hungary extended her frontiers when in alliance with Hitler, she returned to her 1919 borders in 1945; and they survive to this day.

What was the balance sheet of the peace treaties? Out of the collapse of the Austro-Hungarian empire emerged three independent states—Czechoslovakia, Hungary, and Austria; and three states gained from the old empire territory filled mostly with their fellow-countrymen—Poland, Yugoslavia, and Rumania. Two states, Austria and Hungary, felt deprived of territory; the other four were well satisfied.

Out of the collapse of the Ottoman empire emerged, after a brief period of British control, four independent states—Iraq, Transjordan, Saudi Arabia, and the Yemen. A fifth state, the Jewish national home in Palestine, remained under British rule for nearly thirty years, but was then partitioned between Arabs and Jews. The Armenians, too, were given a state of their own: but when the Turks destroyed it in 1922 the Allies did nothing to intervene. Over a million Armenians were murdered by the Turks during the war; but the Allies made no efforts to protect them after the war. Soviet Russia provided a haven for some, in the Soviet Republic of Armenia. Others fled to Europe as refugees, stateless, without a national patron.

Out of the collapse and Bolshevization of

Russia emerged four new independent states—Finland, Latvia, Lithuania, and Estonia. The Caucasian states also declared their independence; and the Allies encouraged Georgia to maintain its sovereignty. But when Stalin sent Soviet troops into the land of his birth, the Allies accepted the fall of Georgian independence.

### The German problem

Of the four empires shaken by the war only the German empire survived; it had lost one eastern province and restored Alsace-Lorraine to France, but its sovereignty was secure. As the Kaiser had abdicated before the end of the war, Germany became a republic; but alone of the defeated nations it preserved its territorial unity. The treaty restrictions were irksome, but made no serious inroads on national sovereignty, and, if anything, provided a powerful stimulus to German nationalism. The Treaty of Versailles may have created Hitler; it also preserved as a state the country in which he was to make his mark.

Neither the defeat of Germany nor the Treaty of Versailles solved the German problem. Germany was still the country with the largest population in Europe. The day after the treaty was signed Austen Chamberlain, the chancellor of the exchequer, wrote to his sister: 'So Peace is signed at last . . . Will the world have rest? . . .

'Even the old Germany would not, I think, rashly challenge a new war in the West, but the chaos on their Eastern frontier, and their hatred and contempt for the Poles, must be a dangerous temptation. . . .'

If the First World War was fought to prevent Germany from creating hegemony in Europe it failed. Germany was weakened, but not so weakened that it could not rise within a generation to threaten the balance of world power once again. The Empires of old Europe had been swept away. The provisions of the victorious peacemakers failed to fill the vacuum—millions had died in vain.

The shock of war made men think seriously of a new international system by which such disasters might be averted. The foundation of the League of Nations and the consequent revolutionizing of international relations meant no nation could any longer expect exemption from public debate on its foreign policy. The League was doomed to failure from its inception: Russia was never a member and America defected in 1919. Nevertheless, it did mean that international co-operation was at work, and within more modest limits the League was to prove capable of real successes.

*Below left: The League of Nations, 1920, and the building to house it, completed 1937. Below right: Nansen passport. This gave refugees a legal identity and the right to travel to look for work. Nansen was the first League of Nations Commissioner for Refugees. Bottom right: Punch cartoon: Dove of peace gapes at Wilson's olive branch. 'I want to please everybody; but isn't this a bit thick?'*

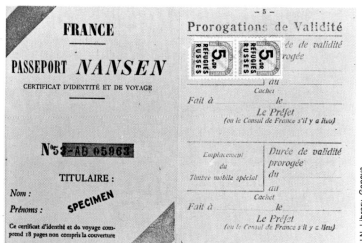

FRANCE

PASSEPORT NANSEN

CERTIFICAT D'IDENTITÉ ET DE VOYAGE

N°5 AD 05963

TITULAIRE :

Nom :

Prénoms :  SPECIMEN

Ce certificat d'identité et de voyage comprend 18 pages non compris la couverture

Prorogations de Validité

de validité prorogée

Fait à _____ le _____

Le Préfet
(ou le Consul de France s'il y a lieu)

Emplacement du Timbre mobile spécial

Durée de validité prorogée du _____ au _____

Cachet

Fait à _____ le _____

Le Préfet
(ou le Consul de France s'il y a lieu)

U.N. Library, Geneva

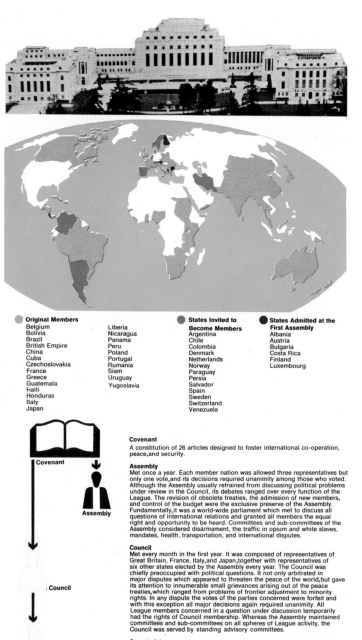

● Original Members
Belgium
Bolivia
Brazil
British Empire
China
Cuba
Czechoslovakia
France
Greece
Guatemala
Haiti
Honduras
Italy
Japan
Liberia
Nicaragua
Panama
Peru
Poland
Portugal
Rumania
Siam
Uruguay
Yugoslavia

● States Invited to Become Members
Argentina
Chile
Colombia
Denmark
Netherlands
Norway
Paraguay
Persia
Salvador
Spain
Sweden
Switzerland
Venezuela

● States Admitted at the First Assembly
Albania
Austria
Bulgaria
Costa Rica
Finland
Luxembourg

**Covenant**
A constitution of 26 articles designed to foster international co-operation, peace, and security.

**Assembly**
Met once a year. Each member nation was allowed three representatives but only one vote, and its decisions required unanimity among those who voted. Although the Assembly usually refrained from discussing political problems under review in the Council, its debates ranged over every function of the League. The revision of obsolete treaties, the admission of new members, and control of the budget were the exclusive preserve of the Assembly. Fundamentally, it was a world-wide parliament which met to discuss all questions of international relations and granted all members the equal right and opportunity to be heard. Committees and sub-committees of the Assembly considered disarmament, the traffic in opium and white slaves, mandates, health, transportation, and international disputes.

**Council**
Met every month in the first year. It was composed of representatives of Great Britain, France, Italy, and Japan, together with representatives of six other states elected by the Assembly every year. The Council was chiefly preoccupied with political questions. It not only arbitrated in major disputes which appeared to threaten the peace of the world, but gave its attention to innumerable small grievances arising out of the peace treaties, which ranged from problems of frontier adjustment to minority rights. In any dispute the votes of the parties concerned were forfeit and with this exception all major decisions again required unanimity. All League members concerned in a question under discussion temporarily had the rights of Council membership. Whereas the Assembly maintained committees and sub-committees on all spheres of League activity, the Council was served by standing advisory committees.

**Secretariat**
Prepared data for League conferences and committees, besides organizing and serving meetings of all League bodies. A connecting link between League organs and between these and member governments.

Punch

# The World after Versailles

*Below: Europe before 1914, dominated by Germany, Austria-Hungary, and Tsarist Russia. Right: Europe after the peace treaties. From the Austro-Hungarian empire have come three new states, Austria, Hungary, and Czechoslovakia. The Austrian-ruled South Slavs have joined the old kingdoms of Montenegro and Serbia in the new state of Yugoslavia. Italy and Rumania have gained large chunks of Austro-Hungarian territory. Poland has been re-formed from Russian, Austrian, and German territory. Amongst other changes, France has regained Alsace-Lorraine, and Greece has gained Bulgaria's Aegean coastline.*
*Bottom left: The break-up of the Turkish empire. Turkey kept only her northern, Turkish, territory. In Arabia the Hejaz and Yemen (and later Saudi-Arabia) became independent Arab kingdoms. Bottom right: What happened to Germany's colonies*

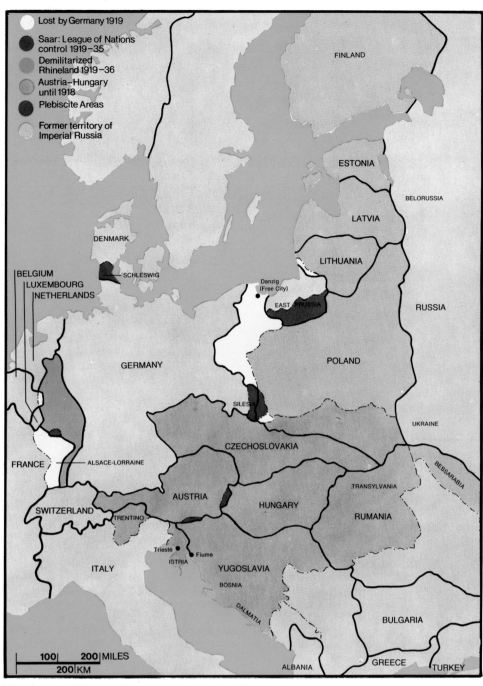

Legend:
- Lost by Germany 1919
- Saar: League of Nations control 1919–35
- Demilitarized Rhineland 1919–36
- Austria–Hungary until 1918
- Plebiscite Areas
- Former territory of Imperial Russia

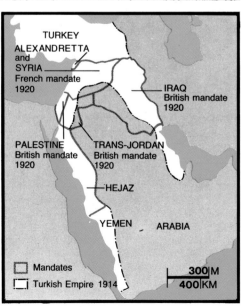

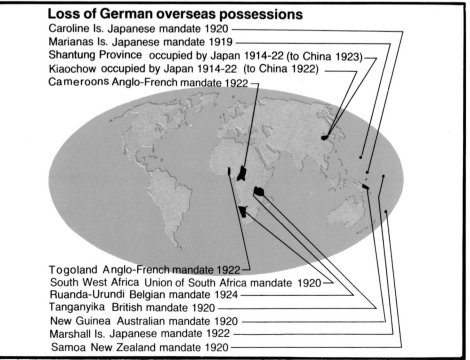

## Loss of German overseas possessions

Caroline Is. Japanese mandate 1920
Marianas Is. Japanese mandate 1919
Shantung Province occupied by Japan 1914-22 (to China 1923)
Kiaochow occupied by Japan 1914-22 (to China 1922)
Cameroons Anglo-French mandate 1922

Togoland Anglo-French mandate 1922
South West Africa Union of South Africa mandate 1920
Ruanda-Urundi Belgian mandate 1924
Tanganyika British mandate 1920
New Guinea Australian mandate 1920
Marshall Is. Japanese mandate 1922
Samoa New Zealand mandate 1920

# Fragile Peace 1918-1939

## INTRODUCTION

The world which emerged from the carnage of the Somme, Flanders and Gallipoli was a very different place from that which four years earlier had sent its children to die in their millions. The map of Europe was completely altered, partly by nationalist risings and partly by the disintegration of the two Central European Powers, Germany and Austria-Hungary, together with the American insistence that all had the right to national self-determination. Gone was the Austro-Hungarian Empire. In its place were a multitude of new states based on the old Empire's conflicting nationalities. Austria was left with little more than Vienna, an imperial capital without an Empire. In the east, Hungary staggered through a brief experiment in Soviet Socialism into the ruthless dictatorship of Admiral Horthy. To the north a new state, Czechoslovakia, had appeared, while beyond Hungary in the east and to the south, Rumania and Yugoslavia were created.

Germany, while not suffering the wholesale dismembering of Austria-Hungary, was also profoundly changed by the War. The Kaiser's German Reich was racked by internal dissention and violence, while the newly free nations like Czechoslovakia and Poland, as well as France, nibbled away at her borders. At home the German workers attempted to turn the Social Democratic coup of November 1918 into a fully fledged socialist revolution. For a brief moment, with Bavaria a separate socialist state and the revolutionaries of the *Spartakist Bund* on the streets of Berlin, it seemed that Germany might follow Russia, as Trotsky and Lenin confidently expected she would, and become the world's second socialist state. Their hopes, and the hopes of thousands of Germans, were crushed by the *Freikorps*, an élite right-wing militia, later the backbone of Hitler's SS and SA who, under the guise of restoring order, gave a grim warning of the future of Europe. Germany's wartime ally, Turkey, known as the 'sick man of Europe', saw the last vestiges of her once-great Ottoman Empire vanish.

On the surface the Allies, with the exception of Russia, came out of the War better than the Central Powers. The end of the Great War brought no peace to Russia. Britain and France poured money, arms and men into Russia in support of the 'White' armies who, led by Kolchak, Wrangel, Yudenich and Denikin, sought to restore their own versions of Tsarism. The war was to cost Russia dear; it has been argued that the exigencies of civil war led directly to the creation of the repressive state machine which was to assume such terrifying proportions under Stalin.

Beneath the surface, however, all was certainly not well with the Allies. Britain, France and Italy had come out of the First World War apparently united internally, and attempts in these countries to turn to socialism were short-lived and ineffectual; but a fundamental shift was taking place in the balance of power. Even before the war the US had been overtaking the old world industrial nations in output of iron and steel, coal and machinery, while her farms were feeding half of Europe. In the Far East Japan, with her vision of a non-Caucasian Empire controlling the Pacific shores of Asia, was emerging as a considerable industrial power.

This shift in the balance of power, particularly the emergence of the US as such an enormous force, was duplicated in a shift in cultural values. The war, and particularly the increase in the employment of women and higher wages, had led to a liberalization of morals. Skirts got shorter and hair was cropped in response to the practical demands of factory and field work, and the tragic brevity of so many young lives led to a literal interpretation of the saying 'eat, drink and be merry, for tomorrow we die'.

Nowhere was this new hedonism more pronounced than in the German Weimar Republic and in this tragic nation, racing towards Nazism, the whole madness and contradiction of Western Europe were symbolized. At the end of the war Germany faced economic ruin. The reparation payments demanded by the Treaty of Versailles placed an intolerable burden on her defeated economy. The Saar and the Ruhr, two of her great industrial areas, were placed outside her control, and large areas of her territory, both at home and overseas, had gone. This was reflected at home in massive inflation which wiped out the savings of the middle class and rendered the wages of the working class derisory. In 1918 a loaf of bread in Germany cost 0.63 marks; by January 1923 the same loaf cost 250 marks and by November of that year it cost a staggering 201 *million* marks. Yet through it all Germany, or at least its

*A delegate to the Second Congress of the Comintern addresses a Red Square rally*

wealthy youth, danced to Jazz, drank gin and sniffed cocaine, self-consciously abandoning the sexual puritanism which had characterized pre-war Germany.

Although Weimar was an extreme, the rest of Western Europe was not so very different. In the winter of 1920–21, unemployment in England reached 1½ million, many of them ex-soldiers who gave the unemployment demonstrations, which took place in every major town in England, a frightening new face as they marched in ranks behind the red flags and banners. The English Labour movement stood at a high point of unity, strength and militancy. Yet as unemployment rose through the 1920's, the old sectional divisions with in the working class reasserted themselves. Many of the Union leaders and a substantial section of the Labour Party feared that the rank-and-file committees of the war would turn into Marxist-orientated 'Soviets', and were anxious to avoid serious confrontation. While all sectors suffered a serious loss in wages, the miners came off worst. The industry, which had been effectively nationalized during the war, was returned to private hands, and the owners, pointing to the falling price of coal, cut wages. The miners threatened to strike and the TUC came to their aid. The Government backed down, and appointed a Royal Commission on the mines. The Samuel Committee reported on 10th March 1926. It criticized the owners and pointed to the terrible conditions in many pits, which had deteriorated during the war; it recommended changes in the ownership structure of the industry but it also demanded wage cuts. This was unacceptable to the miners and on 30th April they were locked out. Five weeks of negotiation followed. The TUC, although it had every sympathy with the miners, did not want to call a General Strike in their support; even when this had begun, and against the instructions of their members, they continued to negotiate. On the night of 2nd May, the printers at the *Daily Mail* newspaper refused to print an anti-strike editorial. Neither the Government nor the TUC were prepared or even able to back down, and on 3rd May the first and last General Strike in Britain began. It was over in nine days. The settlement, as far as the miners were concerned, was derisory.

In France and Italy the situation was even more disturbed, with the first open clashes between Left and Right on the streets of Paris. In Italy in September 1920, 500,000 engineering and steel workers took over their factories and, although their occupations were short-lived because the Socialist Party failed to support the workers, the spectre of Red Revolution had been raised, a spectre which was to provide the beginnings of support for Mussolini.

Benito Mussolini was an ex-revolutionary Socialist whose insistence that Italy should enter the war on the side of the Allies had separated him from his former left-wing comrades. By 1918 he had developed an ideology which he called Fascism, which elevated force above reason. He gathered around him a motley crowd of ex-soldiers, students and a few wealthy aristocrats. As was to be the case in Germany ten years later, the growing power of the Left in Italy caused a polarization of forces in which more and more of the

middle class were attracted to Mussolini's cause. In October 1922, in the face of government inefficiency and timidity, Mussolini's Fascists marched on Rome (although he himself stayed at home during the march), and formed a coalition of the Right, headed by Mussolini himself. The march on Rome was one of a series of displays of physical force by the Fascist militia which gradually removed effective power from parliament. Outside the capital Fascist squads burned Socialist and trade union halls, beat up and even murdered opponents, so that by 1924 the massive 65 per cent vote gained by the Fascists in the election was a foregone conclusion. In 1926 an attempt on Mussolini's life provided a pretext for all effective political opposition to be ended. Europe had its first Fascist dictatorship.

Through it all Europe danced to the tunes of America, the land of excitement and prosperity. It was the era of the 'bright young things', when a dance-craze like the Charleston, begun in America, could sweep the world in a matter of months; when Clara Bow with her painted mouth could invent 'It' and change a million womens' concepts of themselves, and when one-piece bathing costumes, Mack Sennett's beauties and Rudolph Valentino shocked the old and delighted and fascinated the young of half the world. But there was another side to this. Puritanism was still a force to be reckoned with, especially in middle America, as the trial in 1925 of Johnny Scopes, a Midwestern schoolteacher, for teaching Darwin's theory of Evolution, indicated. In January 1920 prohibition was introduced and added a new set of words to the English language, as well as providing a solid economic base for organized crime on a scale which dwarfed anything that had occurred when drinking alcohol was legal. If puritanism in these forms was at best eccentric and at worst involved only a few, there was a less pleasant aspect of the 'American dream'. The Ku Klux Klan was revived in 1915 and by 1923 was claiming a membership of five million. In May 1920 the campaign against trade unions and socialists, which had included some particularly bloody murders of Industrial Workers of the World (IWW) organizers, entered a new phase with the arrest of two mild Italian immigrants, Sacco and Vanzetti, charged with armed robbery and murder. They were to languish in jail for seven years until their execution in August 1927 amid international outcry.

Despite these ripples, there seemed little doubt that America was prospering. The great boom of the 'new era', so amply symbolized by Henry Ford, dominated the national scene, while the worsening economic and political situation in Europe was hidden by the prevailing doctrine of American isolationism. This had led to her withdrawal from the League of Nations in 1921, an economic policy of free-trade at home and high protective duties against foreign goods and the withdrawal of the last American troops from the Rhineland in March 1922 cut decisively the last direct military links with Western Europe.

Roaring or reactionary as they may have been for the Western world, the 1920's looked very different elsewhere. In the Soviet Union after the death of Lenin, the ruling Communist Party of the Soviet Union (CPSU) was

*Ireland 1922. British troops sorting through a burned-out customs house after a clash with rebels. As well as conventional troops, the British used the Royal Irish Constabulary, the 'Black and Tans', and the auxiliaries during the troubles*

divided as to who should be his heir, and the nation was economically ruined by the civil war. Out of the chaos emerged Joseph Stalin who, by a campaign of personal and political calumny, discredited his main opponents in the Party, especially Trotsky, and proceeded to elaborate and put into practice his personal interpretation of Communism: 'Socialism in one country'. For Lenin's heirs, with their increasingly 'national' view of Communism, the prime necessity was to create an industrial and self-sufficient nation. To achieve this they initiated a series of five-year plans for industry from the late 1920's onwards, accompanied by the enforced collectivization of the peasantry. Accompanying this period of industrialization Stalin sought to reinforce his control of the Party machinery by eliminating his former comrades including most of the 'old Bolsheviks', many of whom had taken a more active part in the revolution than Stalin himself. Gradually the 'purges' and show trials, the so-called 'revolution from above', extended down through the Party bureaucracy. By the mid-1930's nobody, even the most lowly worker or peasant, was safe from being denounced to the ever-growing secret police, especially if they had been members of the Party before Stalin's ascendancy. By the elimination of the old revolutionaries and the creation of thousands of new Party members, who were his creatures, Stalin sought simultaneously to eradicate potential opposition and also to mould the Party's history to his own needs. The plans and collectivization were ultimately successful, but at a terrible cost in human life and in the long term, perhaps even more tragically, at the cost of the revolution's vision of a new society.

At the end of the 1920's, conditions varied greatly from country to country. In Western Europe years of high unemployment and political violence presented a grim picture; in the Soviet Union the first five-year plan created work for all, but the hand of the state machine lay heavily on all sectors of society. Only in America did things look bright. All this was changed by the events on Wall Street of October and November 1929. After years of economic boom but widespread speculation in stocks, the bottom fell out of the share market in the last weeks of October. In a panic rush to sell, thousands of small speculators were ruined. It was not only small men who were affected. Throughout the administrations of Harding, Coolidge and Hoover, the Government and the big banks had stepped in and bolstered the market. They tried to do so again briefly in October 1929, but this time the task was too great.

The effects of the crash spread rapidly through the world as American loans were cut. In Germany and Austria the withdrawal of American support was disastrous. The mark collapsed again, as did the Austrian schilling, pushing up unemployment and reducing the purchasing power of wages and savings. By the summer of 1930 Britain was beginning to feel the pinch and, after a run on the London gold market, she went off the gold standard. France held out a little longer, but by the winter of 1932–33 the depression had set in there too. The shock waves spread well beyond Europe. Latin America had long been supported by American loans, often made with little purpose or security, and the withdrawal of these funds shattered the economies of those nations who depended primarily on the production of raw materials for export. The fate of countries like Brazil, where in 1932 a million bags of coffee were burned every month, was duplicated all over the world as nation after nation responded to the depression by increasing protective tariffs. Only Russia, isolated from the market forces of the West, remained unaffected.

The results of the crash were not simply economic. In many countries and to many people, the crash seemed like the final failure of capitalism to deal with its own problems. This was especially true of Germany. The Weimar Republic had tottered on through the 1920's barely coping with a series of economic disasters. Society had become increasingly polarized into two camps, the one of the Left and the other of Nazism. The NSDAP (German National Socialist Workers Party, universally shortened to 'Nazi') grew out of a motley collection of extreme right-wing groupings in Bavaria in the early 1920's. Despite a farcical attempt at a coup ('putsch') in Munich in 1923, and the imprisonment of its leaders, including Hitler, it was fast gaining political credence in Germany by the late 1920's. Its main support came from the urban middle class and the peasantry, who held the Left responsible for Germany's defeat in 1918, and whose political ideas amounted to little more than an explosive mixture of anti-Communism, anti-Semitism and fervent patriotism.

The reverberations of the Wall Street crash pushed the tottering Weimar Republic into oblivion, and to the middle class and the peasantry the choice seemed to be between Hitler and anarchy. At the last moment, the traditional conservatives threw their weight behind Hitler and entered a coalition with the NSDAP. From then on the process of 'Nazification' gradually, but often with extreme violence, replaced all the leading state and local officials with Nazi sympathizers. The burning of the Reichstag building was used by the Party as an excuse to outlaw the parties of the Left and most of the trade unions, as well as to bring the SA (Sturmabteilungen) and SS (Schutzstaffeln) on to the streets as 'volunteers' to maintain law and order. Coalition or not, parliamentary democracy was becoming irrelevant as power passed to the NSDAP outside the Reichstag. Following the Reichstag fire, civil liberties were suspended and in an atmosphere of hysteria whipped up by the Nazi Party the election was held on 5th March, from which most of Hitler's major opponents were excluded. The Party, however, still failed to secure a majority in the Reichstag. Then, on 23rd March, Hitler, with the support of all the middle class parties passed the Enabling Act which effectively made him dictator by giving the 'Government' the power to by-pass the Reichstag. On 2nd August 1934 when, following the death of Hindenberg, Hitler formally became head of the German State, this was simply a recognition of reality.

For a number of reasons Hitler's rise to power and the subsequent open violations of the Treaty of Versailles went unheeded by the major European powers. First, they had problems of their own. In Britain and France unemployment surged upwards and with this came a move towards polarization in politics, though not on the scale seen in Italy and Germany. In 1931 the Labour Party in Britain, which had been in power since 1929, entered a national Government with the opposition parties. This move split the Parliamentary and National Labour Parties, with many of the younger generation of the Left going into more or less open allegiance with the Communists. A tiny group of them, headed by Sir Oswald Mosley, moved to the Right. Although Mosley's power was never great, his 'blackshirts' were a constant reminder of the chaos into which Europe had plunged, as were the Labour League of Youth and the Young Communist League who opposed him. Similarly in France the Camelots du Roi and other extreme right-wing groups came into violent conflict with the Left in Paris.

There was another reason for ignoring the 'mad Corporal', as Hitler was known. The Great War had cost Britain and France appalling losses. Few families, especially in France, had not lost a relative in the mud of Flanders, and this led to a widespread anti-war feeling which was reflected in the actions of the politicians of Britain and France as well as in the Peace Pledge Union and other pacifist groups which mushroomed in the 1930's. On top of this was the feeling, rather later in the day, that the settlement of Versailles had been too harsh. These two sentiments together produced the policy of appeasement, of negotiation—anything rather than risk the slaughter of 1914–18 over again. America's isolationism and the enforced isolation of the Soviet Union further reinforced this policy by leaving Europe alone to deal with its problems.

Even in disregarding Germany while they sorted out their own problems, the Western nations were conspicuously unsuccessful in dealing with unemployment. Only in America, where the problem was one of enormous magnitude, did the depression produce any fundamental change. Following the crash, the situation in the United States worsened rapidly. Unemployment rose from the already high figure of $4\frac{1}{2}$ million in 1930 to nearly 13 million by 1933. Those most affected were the blacks and the poor white unskilled workers, but there were other factors which pauperized large sections still nominally in work, especially the small farmers. As prices fell it became less and less possible to produce at a profit. Worse was to come. Constant over-cropping in the Southern Great Plains caused soil erosion. In January 1933, after weeks of drought, high winds brought the first dust storms. A year later, in May 1934, an exceptionally bad storm blocked out the sun from Texas to Dakota. The dust clogged roads and homesteads and, crucially, it removed the top-soil.

Since the crash the Government had muddled on, while conditions worsened. In March 1933 Franklin D. Roosevelt was elected to the Presidency. In many ways he was an unlikely leader of the people, for he had been born into the American aristocracy and crippled by polio; yet during his famous first hundred days he initiated a massive programme of public works. Aided by a progressive and hard-working administration, the 'New Dealers', he transformed the American economy. However, mainly because of intense pressure at home, America remained firmly 'isolationist' in foreign policy. Roosevelt himself was a Wilsonian, believing America should play an international role, but as the 1930's wore on his anti-Fascist rhetoric grew more and more empty as it became increasingly obvious that America wanted to stay well clear of European affairs. Only in 1940, with the beginnings of 'lend lease', was Roosevelt able to gain enough support to begin America's decisive intervention in European problems.

Despite, or perhaps because of, her problems, America's entertainment industry still dominated the world. Hollywood, already a Mecca in the 1920's, reached new heights in the 1930's. The absurd doings of its stars and the glamour of its products at one and the same time preserved the 'American dream' and hid the harsh realities of American life. In music too the American product still dominated. The rough Jazz of the 1920's was gone, replaced by the less hedonistic and more sophisticated big band 'swing'. In the less popular arts, especially poetry and painting, a more sombre and often left-wing tone began to emerge. Gone were the gay excesses of

Dada. In their place came a new and violent Picasso with his distorted and tortured figures reflecting the agony of Europe. In poetry the elegant phraseology of the 1920's was replaced by simple and savage verses, often drawing on the culture of the poor for imagery and style.

This change in the high arts was a product of the worsening crisis in Europe. In Germany the Nazi Party, always anti-Semitic, intensified its campaign against the Jews. In March 1935 the notorious Nuremberg laws prohibiting sexual relations between 'Ayrian' and 'Non-Ayrian' people were passed, and in November 1938 the massive legalized pogrom —*Kristallnacht*—convinced even the most sceptical of Nazism's real intention towards racial minorities. But Hitler's intentions towards Europe had become clear before *Kristallnacht*. In March 1935 he had repudiated the Treaty of Versailles, introduced conscription and announced that the size of Germany's peacetime army was to be increased to half a million men. The new army soon had an opportunity of showing its teeth. Before the formal repudiation of the treaty the German armed forces had grown well beyond the size allowed by the Treaty of Versailles. This was achieved with the aid of the Soviet Union whose theorists argued that Fascism would, by destroying 'bourgeois democracy', hasten the socialist revolution in Europe.

Rearmament was crucial to Germany's 'economic miracle', especially after 1935; it also enabled Hitler to begin his campaign to 'right the wrongs of Versailles' and gain *lebensraum* for the master race which was to be the salvation of Europe. In March 1936, German troops reoccupied the demilitarized Rhineland without opposition. More sinister, however, was Hitler's march into Austria in March 1936, ostensibly to 'protect' the 'ten million Germans living on the borders of the Reich'. In the climate of appeasement the western democracies were unwilling to act, while Dollfuss's Fascist coup in February 1934 had effectively destroyed the parties of the Left and this left Austria defenceless.

It was not only in Central Europe that the forces of the Reich had been active. By the time Austria was annexed crack units of the German Army and Air Force had been gaining practical experience over the bloody fields of Spain for almost two years. Neutral in the Great War, a brief period of dictatorship in the 1920's had been followed by the emergence of a liberal democratic government and Spain had become a Republic in 1931. In July 1936 a group of army officers staged a coup in Spanish Morocco and then, supported initially by colonial troops and the Spanish Foreign Legion, invaded the south of Spain. Despite an international non-intervention agreement, both Italy and Germany poured arms and men into Spain, while the West stood by and watched the legitimate and democratically elected Government destroyed in a long and bloody war. Spain became a symbol, especially for the Left, of the fight against Fascism, and young men from all over the world volunteered to fight in the International Brigades against Franco. They fought with great courage against increasing odds—but courage was not enough. With less and less war material coming from Russia, their sole effective ally, and divided by internal disagreement, the Republican forces continually lost ground until Franco's troops entered Madrid in March 1939 to finish the war. For most of the supporters of the Republic the choice lay between flight into France, and imprisonment, torture and death under Franco. Hundreds of thousands fled, and an ever-dwindling number kept up raids into Spain over the Pyrenees until well into the 1950's.

Mussolini, to gain military glory, had actively supported Franco, but his main interests lay elsewhere—in building a new Roman Empire in Africa. In the autumn of 1935 Italy sent troops to East Africa and began the invasion of Abyssinia. The rationale for the invasion was a skirmish in the remote Oasis of Wal Wal between Italian and Abyssinian troops, but the reality had more to do with Mussolini's expansionist dreams. The war was short and bloody, and although Abyssinia held out longer than could have been expected, there was never any doubt that the Italian Army, equipped with all the paraphernalia of modern war and supported by aircraft, would ultimately win.

Those who died in Abyssinia were not the only victims of Mussolini's urge to conquer. From the incident at Wal Wal onwards the League of Nations had been discussing action against Italy for this aggression. Although sanctions against Italy were imposed on 11th October 1935 their only effect was to demonstrate the weakness of the League. Created by President Wilson in 1919 as an international forum where collective problems could be argued out and war avoided, the League was doomed to failure from the time of America's withdrawal from membership in 1921, while the Soviet Union had never been a member. The absence of these two great international powers rendered the League little more than a talking shop whose ineffectiveness was proved frequently during the 1930's.

Although Italy's invasion of Abyssinia was the final nail in the coffin of the League, it had been dealt a series of body blows earlier as a result of events in the Far East. Japan had emerged from the Great War as one of the victorious Allies, but the 1920's had seen her economy damaged and her plans for an Eastern Empire thwarted. Meanwhile China was racked by civil war between the War Lords in the north and the forces of Sun Yat-sen's Kuomintang in the south. The Kuomintang was composed of two main groups, the Nationalists and the Communists, but after the death of Sun Yat-sen, the Nationalists, led by Chiang Kai-shek, turned on their erstwhile allies. In a series of engagements ranging from fierce battles to simple pogroms, the Communists were apparently beaten, but under the leadership of Mao-Tse Tung they began the Long March from the south of China to the north, regrouping as they went, and there established a base from which they harried the Nationalist troops. Taking advantage of China's disorganization a clique of right-wing officers of the Japanese Imperial Army led an invasion of Manchuria in September 1931, against the express orders of the Emperor. However, once the invasion had begun, there could be no pulling back. Presented with a *fait accompli*, the Emperor supported the officers and the long and barbaric Japanese invasion of China began.

The West was outraged by the reports of the invasion of China, and particularly by the air raids on civilian towns, but attention was soon distracted from the Far East by a far more serious crisis which threatened to drag Europe into war. Since before the invasion of Austria, Hitler had made no secret of his intention of absorbing the German-speaking Sudetenland into Germany. In an attempt to prevent the situation from developing into a European war, Chamberlain flew to Berchtesgarten on 15th September 1938 to meet Hitler and solve the Czech 'problem'. Throughout the series of meetings which followed, at first between Chamberlain and Hitler and finally between all the major European leaders on 29th September, Europe waited for war. French reservists had been called up on 6th September, and on 22nd September France and Czechoslovsakia began to mobilize. On 27th September the Royal Navy was put on the alert, and in Russia thirty divisions of the Red Army began to move up. Then it all came to a halt. The Sudetenland was ceded to Germany.

It was a tenuous one-year peace. By the early 1930's a majority of British and a good number of French politicians had accepted that the Treaty of Versailles was over-harsh. This gave Hitler the excuse to begin his campaign of European expansion—'the righting of historic wrongs'—such as the reoccupation of the Rhineland, refusing reparations and building up the German armed forces. The invasions of Austria and Czechoslovakia were, however, very different. There was no way in which these could be justified by appeal to history. They were simple expansionism, the beginnings of a new German Empire in Europe. Munich seen at its best was a breathing space gained; at its worst it was the final signal to the 'mad corporal' that nothing could, and nobody would, stand in the way of his dream of increased *lebensraum* for the German people.

*Al Capone, the prominent gangster who made Chicago his private empire*

# The Post-War Slump

During the 1918 election, held immediately after the armistice with Germany that ended the fighting, Lloyd George spoke of making Great Britain into 'a fit country for heroes to live in'. When he proclaimed this objective it must have seemed a natural and attainable goal. Pre-war Great Britain had not been perfect, but improvement looked a fairly simple task on which all men of goodwill could agree.

It was particularly easy for men of goodwill to agree because it was taken for granted by practically everybody that the Germans were going to pay for it all. Sir Eric Geddes spoke of 'squeezing Germany till the pips squeaked'; Lloyd George was a little more cautious, but when he spoke of accepting the principle that Germany must pay, and said 'we shall search their pockets', he did nothing to warn his listeners that the Germans' pockets might be empty. The opposition parties did not plunge into the subject of 'making Germany pay' with the same gusto, though they certainly did not warn their listeners of the difficulties of extracting reparations.

The electorate was optimistic, unreasonable, and xenophobic: what it wanted to hear was 'Hang the Kaiser', 'Make Germany Pay', and 'Britain for the British'. Lloyd George began the campaign in a liberal frame of mind; but by the end he had adopted the popular slogans with a few verbal amendments which completely failed to warn the electorate that it was asking for too much.

In the election Lloyd George and his Conservative partners from the wartime coalition could draw on popular approval of their work in winning the war, a reaction against the Liberal government which had done badly in the opening years of the war, and a belief that a strong government was needed for the negotiations that were about to begin at Versailles. The coalition gained an enormous majority in the House of Commons (Coalition Unionists 339, Coalition Liberals 136 against

*Demonstration of the unemployed in the
Strand, 1922. Throughout the twenties
and thirties men were looking for work
and not finding it. In 1920 the unemployment figures rose to two million*

*Above: London society taking tea under the elms, 1919. (Magazine illustration.) Women vied for the attention of returning soldiers, for there were now many more young women than young men*

Independent Liberals 26, and Labour Party 59). But in a way the most surprising thing about the election was that the Liberals who followed Asquith out of office and the newly reorganized Labour Party polled almost half the votes cast.

### The hard-faced men

Despite this, Lloyd George's majority was too large for his own comfort. Before the election he had been comfortably balanced in the middle: if his Conservative allies had turned on him, there was always the possibility that he might have turned to the left and made an alliance with the Labour Party and the Asquithian Liberals. After the election the Conservatives had a majority; Bonar Law might say that Lloyd George could be prime minister for as long as he liked, but in fact he could only be prime minister as long as the Conservatives liked. He had as many Liberal supporters in the Commons as in the previous House, but they had been elected mainly because they had received the 'coupon' – a letter of approval from Lloyd George and Bonar Law – which freed them from the fear of Conservative opposition. If there were another election, they could expect to be opposed. Their prospects were dim.

The House of Commons elected in 1918 has never been very well thought of. Baldwin called the members 'hard-faced men who looked as if they had done well out of the war' and Lloyd George said that when he spoke he felt as though he had the Associated Chambers of Commerce behind him and the Trades Union Congress in front of him. This was natural enough: there were a couple of dozen more trade

unionists than in the previous Parliament, and there were perhaps a hundred more businessmen than previously. One of Lloyd George's contributions to the war effort was to bring businessmen into the work of running the administration of government, and it was natural that they now moved on to take a larger place in political life than before.

Lloyd George had probably struck a deadlier blow at the Liberal Party than he could possibly have realized when he brought the businessmen so firmly into the work of governing the country. Before the war businessmen had made up a good deal of the strength of the Liberal Party, and because they wanted to see things changed they had been allies of other groups that wanted change. The pre-war Liberal Party had looked rather like the Democratic Party in the United States, firmly attached to the capitalist system, but always ready to consider ways of making it less harsh if this could be managed without overthrowing the system. After 1918 the Liberal Party was much less ready to contemplate change, and the Labour Party was much more committed to changing the structure of society, by means of extensive nationalization.

The newly elected Conservative MPs were in a false position. Lloyd George had been elected on a platform that included a good deal of social reform; they were pledged to follow him, and they tended to see him as the great vote-winner responsible for their own success, but if it came to a choice between social reform and lower taxes they were going to choose lower taxes. During the election the question had been avoided by hoping for large reparations; as it became clearer and clearer that there were not going to be large reparations for a long time to come, the problem became harder to avoid.

Demobilization was carried out fairly successfully; at first the government tried an immensely complicated scheme which let skilled workers out first; as they were usually men who had been kept at work in factories as long as possible, the scheme looked rather like 'last in, first out'. The result was that mutinies broke out, and the government had to reconsider its approach. When a simpler 'first in, first out' scheme was tried, the soldiers accepted it peacefully, and the bulk of demobilization was over by the summer of 1919. The government was afraid that the soldiers might have difficulty finding jobs, and it provided a system of unemployment benefit to cushion the shock. This was a foundation of universal unemployment benefit, but at the time it was not needed.

### Post-war boom

After a few months of pause and demobilization, the economy launched itself into a post-war reconstruction boom. Soldiers found jobs easily, factories were sold, and new companies were floated at capital values which suggested that manufacturers expected a happy combination of wartime full order books and pre-war absence of controls, and prices resumed the steady upward course they had followed

since 1914. In these conditions trade unions could get pay increases, often without going on strike, and the country's difficulties appeared to be the pleasant difficulties that sometimes accompany a sudden rush of prosperity to the head.

The government did very little to hold this expansion in check. The budget con-

*Above: Mending roads – a government project to relieve the desperate plight of the unemployed. But the government had little real idea what course it should pursue*

tinued the war-time deficits, and this was natural because Great Britain was still maintaining a large army, part of which was occupying Germany. The housing problem which had been forcing itself on the attention of politicians before the war was now acute; Dr Christopher Addison, at the newly created Ministry of Health, was given responsibility for building more houses. But while it was a generous and humane step for the government to commit itself to providing houses, not much could be done immediately; the whole economy was going ahead so fast that the effect of Addison's attempt to build more houses was to drive up prices for everybody because the government was bidding against the private contractors. But although the Addison scheme came to an undistinguished end, the principle had been accepted and future governments had to work out better schemes.

### Two million unemployed

The period of explosive post-war prosperity lasted for a little over a year. When the war ended the government had refused to allow any further exports of gold to the United States. The result was that the pound, which had been worth $4·76 in 1918, fell in price to about $3·75. This fall was entirely natural and reasonable at the end of a war which had reduced Great Britain's foreign investments and had turned the United States into a leading creditor nation, but the Bank of England and most of the City of London were determined to bring the pound back to its pre-war level. When Montagu Norman became governor of the Bank of England in 1920, he moved decisively to put this programme into effect. In April the bank rate was raised to seven per cent, and was kept at this level for a year.

If any twelve-month period decided the pattern of British life between the wars, it was the year of Norman's seven per cent bank rate. The boom slowed down and came to a stop, the foreign exchange value of the pound went up, and unemployment rose to over 2,000,000. This crushing level of unemployment fell a little in the next few years, but throughout the 'twenties and 'thirties men were looking for work and not finding it.

The problem was two-fold. Markets for traditional British products, such as coal, cotton textiles, and ships, had disappeared during the war; other countries had built up industries of their own and no longer wanted British exports, and coal was beginning to be replaced by oil. According to the laws of economic theory the men who had lost their jobs should have gone off and found new ones. But the second part of the problem was that not many new jobs were appearing. High interest rates and the attempt to force the exchange rate up to the pre-war level had a discouraging effect on people who wanted to start new businesses; when new factories opened, they were often in London and south-east England, and the bulk of the post-war unemployed lived in Wales, Scotland, and the north of England.

London had its own difficulties. When the Poplar borough council tried to give poor relief to the unemployed in the borough at a more generous rate than the government thought proper, the councillors were told to make it up out of their own pockets. When they did not do so, they were sent to prison and for some weeks in the autumn of 1921 the government considered what to do. Eventually, the councillors were released, and expenses of poor relief were shared more evenly over London.

But although this cleared up a local difficulty, the prospects for finding a job by moving continued to be bad: a man out of work in Wales knew that he had a better chance of getting work if he went to

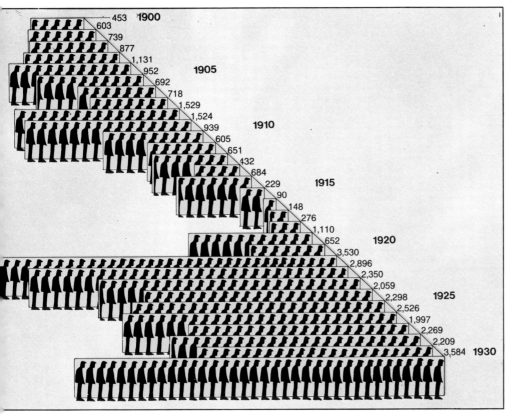

*Above:* Unemployment. (Statistics for 1900-15 are based on trade union returns, those for 1923-30 on figures for insured population.) *Below left:* Ex-service veterans turned 'hawkers' for lack of any other way to earn a living. *Below right:* The housing problem. There was an acute shortage of working-class homes even as drab and squalid as these

London, but he also knew that there was a considerable risk of finding himself out of work a long way from his home and friends. In these conditions it was natural for him to stay at home and hope that one day the mines would get back to pre-war prosperity. This was never very likely to happen: for one thing, so many more people were trying to find work in the mines in 1924 than before, and for another, other countries in Europe were developing their coal mines more efficiently.

Once the post-war reconstruction boom was over, there seemed to be about a million men to spare in England. The government expanded the 1911 Unemployment Insurance scheme to include more people during the war, gave unemployment benefit for some months to all ex-servicemen, and in 1920 insurance was extended to almost everybody. Even so, this was insurance for only fifteen weeks of unemployment in a year – the underlying idea was that people were out of work for a short time when moving from one job to another. The 1920 act was not designed for the long-term unemployment of the inter-war world, and perhaps no insurance scheme could be devised to deal with it. Variations were invented in the years to come, but the basic principle remained: insurance payments as a matter of right for a limited period of time, and then an appeal to the authorities for poor relief.

The modern economic theory is that, in circumstances like this, a government should spend generously and pump demand back into the economy. But in 1920 this idea was unheard-of; its inventor, John Maynard Keynes, had left the civil service, protesting violently at the Treaty of Versailles in his *Economic Consequences of the Peace*, but he had not yet worked out his new approach. The field was open to the budget-cutters, because the orthodox view was that a balanced budget would restore the health of the economy.

### The Geddes Axe

The government's economic policy consistently made matters worse. During the rapid expansion of 1919 and 1920 it had had a deficit on the budget, which meant

*The British cotton industry (poster 1924). The war added huge burdens, but these were not the root of British industry's malaise*

Museum of British Transport

Institute of Social History, Amsterdam

*Labour election poster, 1924. 'The Hope of the World—MacDonald the Peacemaker'. Ramsay MacDonald had never held any kind of office, but Conservative and Liberal failure to form a majority government led to his appointment as prime minister*

that inflation went ahead all the faster. When the economy slowed down to a crawl in 1921 the government appointed a committee under Sir Eric Geddes, who had recently retired from office, to investigate ways of cutting down expenditure. This was the first of many attempts in the next fifty years to reduce spending, and the government's approach was a little naïve. The Geddes Committee was asked to recommend steps to be taken, and when its report – so sweeping that it became known as the Geddes Axe – came out, the government declined to accept all its suggestions. Less was taken out of the education programme and the naval estimates than had been proposed, because the government could not give the committee complete control over its policy. But the Conservative backbenchers felt the government had let them down. Candidates had been elected at by-elections on an 'anti-waste' platform, which was intended to reduce government spending, and in the House of Commons they were led by Horatio Bottomley; before the war he had been on the left, asking for a 'businessman's government' as a way to push the old ruling class out of office, but after the war he was on the right, asking for a 'businessman's government' as a way to cut spending and taxation.

Lloyd George suggested from time to time between 1919 and 1922 that it would be a good idea to create a Centre Party. He was thinking of uniting his own Liberals with the main body of the Conservative Party to resist the Labour Party, who were more or less seriously called Bolsheviks by some people, and also to resist the Bottomley men as 'die-hards'. But the Conservative Party never really accepted this distinction between die-hards and the rest, and certainly did not intend to allow Lloyd George to create one. By 1921 a large number of Conservatives blamed the prime minister for some of the things they disliked about the post-war world.

Fisher's 1918 Education Act, which

raised the school-leaving age to fourteen and gave teachers higher pay, looked progressive to most people; the higher Tories disliked it because it meant more taxes, and because education would make the servant problem worse by giving children ideas above their station. The relaxation of British rule in India expressed in the Montagu-Chelmsford reforms, and made explicit when General Dyer was censured for killing off 300-400 Indians while suppressing a riot at Amritsar, also infuriated them. And Ireland was even worse.

At the end of the war the government had to face the fact that Home Rule had been put on the Statute Book at the beginning of the war. Lloyd George's coalition certainly was not going to allow Home Rule in the pre-war sense, which meant placing Ulster under Dublin, even for the relatively limited number of areas of government activity being transferred to an Irish parliament. So Northern Ireland got Home Rule for itself, and acquired certain limited powers.

There was no such quiet ending in the rest of Ireland. Almost all the seats outside Ulster had been won by Sinn Feiners in 1918, and instead of going to Westminster they set up a parliament of their own in Dublin. They wanted much more than Home Rule; they tried to ask for self-determination and the right to independence at Versailles, and when this failed Ireland began to drift to civil war. By modern standards it was a normal, even fairly civilized guerilla war; by late 19th-century standards it was a shocking reversion to barbarism. Civilians were shot for helping the rebels, and for co-operating with the government; Irish prisoners were shot while attempting to escape, and British officers were shot in front of their families. There were other familiar symptoms. Lloyd George said confidently: 'We have got murder by the throat'; the Irish looked for outside help, which they thought would come from the United States; and the people of Ireland suffered more than the people fighting on either side. Eventually, Lloyd George decided to make peace, and he moved cautiously in 1921, first winning Conservatives like Birkenhead to accept his point of view, and then getting the Irish to agree to remain inside the Commonwealth with Dominion status, as the Irish Free State, rather than insisting on independence.

This was perhaps the best settlement that could have been managed, but it infuriated the die-hards. At the 1921 party conference they were restrained from denouncing negotiations with the Irish only by appeals for loyalty to the leadership; this appeal could not be used again. The Conservatives were also annoyed by the way in which Lloyd George sold titles and honours. Selling honours was far from unheard-of; the Liberal and Conservative parties had been helping their finances for some years in this way. But they were selling on behalf of recognized party organizations, and were selling in relatively restricted quantities. When Lloyd George's agents went out, they looked for men with no particular political allegiance who would give money

*A miner's wife on a routine visit to the pawnshop. The miners were hit hard by the slump. Oil was replacing coal; other countries were developing their coal mines more efficiently; more men were seeking jobs in the mines and there were fewer jobs to be had. But since miners dreaded finding themselves out of work far from home and friends they stayed and hoped things would improve*

for a fund under their personal control.

But although there was a good case against some of the people Lloyd George ennobled, and although he gave more titles than any previous government had done in a comparable period of time, the real Conservative objection to the sale of honours was that it represented the triumph of businessmen who had done well during the war—the *nouveaux riches*. The 'new poor', as the people who felt less well-off after the war rather ostentatiously called themselves, resented the way that businessmen had taken charge during the war, and were now being accepted into the ruling class. The protests at the sale of honours concentrated on undesirable people getting titles in return for money (though the Conservative party funds shared the proceeds); there would have been irritation even if every peerage had gone to a businessman who had worked hard all through the war and never given a penny to the Lloyd George political fund. The rich as a class did not lose much ground to the poor, but the landed class lost ground to the new businessmen. In 1919 and 1920 there were enormous land sales as the old owners felt sure that there was not going to be a return to the days before the war; so many of Lloyd George's peers bought country houses at the time, though they did not try to keep up great estates and usually sold the farms off to the tenants.

### 'A great dynamic force'

After Ireland and the argument about honours, Lloyd George could survive only by convincing the Conservatives that without him they would be unable to resist the Labour Party. This argument was wearing thin, and in any case the Conservative backbenchers were no longer sure they cared to pay this price for resisting the Labour Party. In the summer of 1922 the government came very close to war with Turkey over the Middle East settlement. The cabinet might find this satisfactory, but the backbenchers had no desire for any more adventures or worse. In any case, they were rather pro-Turkish.

The cabinet might still have held its position, but only if no leading Conservative would oppose it. The day before the Conservative MPs were to meet and discuss the situation, Lord Beaverbrook persuaded Bonar Law to come out of retirement and lead the discontented backbenchers. On 19th October the Conservatives decided they no longer wanted Lloyd George, who was condemned in the meeting for being 'a great dynamic force'. There was no danger that his successors would be described in such terms.

# Germany: Failure of Democracy

In their periods of success, good fortune, and power, the Germans have always been ruled by men who held them, as a people, in profound contempt. Frederick the Great called them a nation of slaves; Bismarck, the creator of modern political Germany, said he could not stand them unless he had drunk at least one bottle of champagne; Kaiser Wilhelm's comments on his subjects were not always printable, and Hitler thought that the Germans were unworthy of his greatness. This contempt trickled down from the top to the broader levels beneath, especially after Germany's unification in 1871. Slaves must be disciplined, animals tamed. The vaunted discipline of the German army was ultimately aimed, in the words of one thinker in field-grey, at suppressing the *innere Schweinehund*, the swine within. For that reason, recruits had first to be stripped of their human dignity and then domesticated at wolf-hound level. Between 1871 and 1918, the sergeant-major was one of a trinity of officially sanctioned archetypes whose unquestioned power ate deeply into the life of every single German male, so long as conscription prevailed. The other two were the policeman and the school-master. The ubiquitous and inescapable presence of these pillars of German society showed that since unification by the Bismarckian formula of blackmail and coercion, Germans never ruled themselves, but only each other.

This atmosphere not only stifled all hope of self-government at the regional level, but prevented the development of voluntary support for government at the national level. Instead, the Second Reich was run under the sign of a narrow *esprit de corps*, pseudo-feudal and militaristic in character, through which the ruling élite was instinctively agreed, virtually without any conscious thought, on the techniques of holding down the rest. By the first decade of the present century the Social Democrats, once the party of revolution, had become so fully assimilated into the Bismarckian system, as inherited and presided over by Kaiser Wilhelm, that they formed its strongest political party. Yet where parliamentary control was minimal and ministerial responsibility unknown, the opposition had no hope of forming an alternative government and remained condemned to sterility.

*Chaos and hunger in Berlin—plundered shops characterize the period of German inflation. The army had to be called in to defend groceries as well as democracy*

On this dubious soil events in October and November 1918 planted the freest, most mature, and advanced form of government so far devised by the human mind: the republic. The French name their republics by simple numbers, whereas the first German Republic was named after an idyllic little provincial town, Weimar, a place largely untouched by the twentieth century and usually associated with the age of Goethe and Schiller. The Social Democrats, at last called upon to form not only a government, but an entirely new political structure, had chosen Weimar not primarily because they wanted to demonstrate how far they were from the spirit of Potsdam and Prussian Berlin. High among the attractions of that sleepy provincial town was the absence of an element that since November had dominated the streets of the German capital: the mutinous people, insubordinate soldiers and sailors, rebellious workers, those who had suffered the worst burdens of the war. These men and women wanted a genuine break with the discredited past, but, instead of providing leadership, the reluctant fathers of the Republic found it more prudent to escape from the turbulent masses. Yet, in the age of the telephone, there was little hope of keeping the spirit of Potsdam separate from that of Weimar. Speaking on one of history's most ominous hot lines, General Groener offered to put down the rebels in Berlin. The inevitable result was that the soldiers, sailors, and workers who in 1918 wanted a real revolution were quickly swept under the carpet with the broom so unhesitatingly provided by the army high command. The Weimar Republic was born not by a *coup d'état*, but by a *coup de téléphone*.

## The Right and the Left

The most widely accepted view of the Weimar Republic offered nowadays by historians in Germany and elsewhere is that the frail barge of state, once launched, instantly glided off towards the Right and the rapids of dictatorship. Through counter-revolution by telephone German democracy became a sham manipulated by the generals, bankers, industrialists, and the landowners from the far side of the river Elbe and reason. In this view, the Republic's drift towards the Right was accelerated by evil economic currents, financial helplessness, and social erosion until the fabric of democracy was torn apart by Adolf Hitler who owed his position to the generals, bankers, and the rest. But this was not the whole truth. The whole truth would

have to include the sweeping success in the 'twenties of a book entitled *The Kaiser Went, The Generals Remained*, written by an unusually courageous left-winger, Theodor Plivier. The title alone proclaims an undoubted and disastrous truth, but the mere fact that the book was published and sold was significant. The generals remained indeed, and it was they, together with their fellow-survivors from the Kaiser's day, who brought in Hitler, whatever some of them said afterwards. Yet Plivier's book, tearing off the camouflage behind which the survivors operated, was published, read, debated, condemned, and applauded until early in 1933 when the author's Berlin flat was smashed to pieces by Hitler's SA.

In other words, the true picture of the Weimar Republic must be bi-focal. Focus A consisted of the survivors of the Second Reich who gradually crept back into the bastions of their former power with their wealth and standards of conduct intact. Focus B was the minority with its bright aureola of liberty, change, progress, reform, and, above all else, debate. The German for focus is *Brennpunkt*, burning point. That these two central points of fire should glow side by side meant that for fourteen years either possibility, democracy or dictatorship, seemed potentially feasible. 'Nations,' Hugh Thomas wrote recently, 'achieve their identities from a study of their own history reasonably free of myth. Such is the mark of a civilized country.' It was just this sort of study by public debate blowing like a fresh breeze from every corner of Germany that was one of the most distinctive features of the Weimar Republic. The dispute raged between those proclaiming their versions of the German myths in academic lecture rooms, schools, and right-wing newspapers, while their opponents, inferior in number, superior in energy and intelligence, debunked the same fairy tales on lecture tours, in films, books, radio plays, and press campaigns in liberal newspapers. The myths propagated by the Right included the glory of war, the justification of Germany's war effort as one of self defence, the 'stab in the back', and the primacy of blood, irrationalism, capitalism, and the German race. The liberal case was presented not in the halls of the older universities, but in the open arenas of public opinion. It included anti-militarism, exposés of the ways and methods used by the ruling élite to keep Germany in the war during four years of false pretence, praise for the League of Nations, Europeanism,

534,910 Marks*

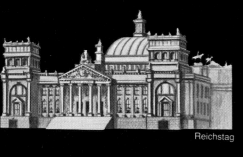

Reichstag

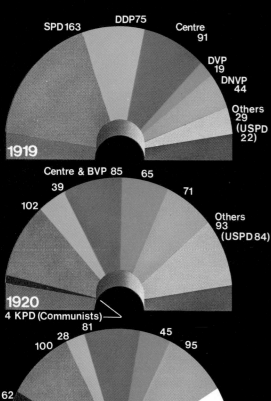

**SPD 163** **DDP 75** **Centre 91**

DVP 19
DNVP 44

Others 29
(USPD 22)

**1919**

Centre & BVP 85   65
39            71
102
Others 93
(USPD 84)

**1920**

4 KPD (Communists)

81         45
100  28         95
62
Others 29

**MAY 1924**

NSDAP 32 (Nazis)

88      51
131  32       103
45
14
Others 29

**DEC 1924**

25        78
153       45     73
12
54
Others 51

**1928**

| KPD | Kommunistische Partei Deutschlands (German Communist Party) |
|---|---|
| USPD | Unabhängige Sozialdemokratische Partei Deutschlands (Independent Social Democratic Party) |
| SPD | Sozialdemokratische Partei Deutschlands (Social Democratic Party) |
| DDP | Deutsche Demokratische Partei (German Democratic Party) |
| BVP | Bayrische Volkspartei (Bavarian People's Party) |
| DVP | Deutsche Volkspartei (German People's Party) |
| DNVP | Deutschnationale Volkspartei (German National People's Party) |
| NSDAP | Nationalsozialistische Deutsche Arbeiterpartei (National Socialist German Workers' Party — Nazis) |

## Inflation: retail prices

The cost of one loaf of bread in Berlin
1918 **0·63 Marks**

1922 **163·15 Marks**

January 1923
**250 Marks**

July 1923
**3,465 Marks**

September 1923
**1,512,000 Marks**

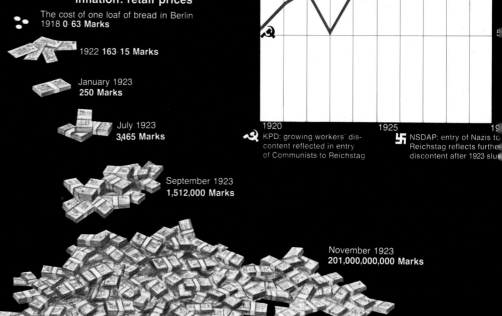

November 1923
**201,000,000,000 Marks**

## Inflation: exchange rates

Number of Marks to one Dollar

1913    1920    22    24    26    28

*Fixed at parity 4·20 gold Marks = $1
in November 1923

## Production of manufactured goods, 1920 -

1913

1920    1925    19

KPD: growing workers' discontent reflected in entry
of Communists to Reichstag

NSDAP: entry of Nazis to
Reichstag reflects furthe
discontent after 1923 slu

*Above left: Communist organization, 'International Red Aid', appeals for money for victims of 'proletarian class struggle'. 'Don't forget us', cries imprisoned Communist. Above right: Election poster. German Democratic Party claims it will send inflation up in smoke*

the equality of women, and recognition of the completeness of military defeat.

### Democracy in danger

While the respectable fathers of the Republic were engaged upon giving the infant Republic the breath of life, a state of siege had been declared in Berlin. From March to December 1919 the Social Democrats' new allies, the army high command, dealt with those who believed in revolution, for the nation of slaves had now produced its Spartacus—in the shape of not a single man but of a determined and, for German conditions, quite tough minority movement. The new liberators issued leaflets with screaming headlines like, 'All Power To The Workers And Soldiers Councils', 'Arm The Workers', and so on. On Christmas Day 1918 they occupied the building of *Vorwärts,* the official Socialist newspaper. The revolutionary sailors occupied the Kaiser's palace and vast stables. In the streets, soldiers tore off officers' epaulettes, badges of rank, and decorations. They waved red flags. In all parts of Berlin's west end there were spontaneous and improvised meetings where Spartacist and Independent Socialist speakers harangued mildly curious crowds of bystanders. It reminded one sceptical onlooker of Hyde Park on a Sunday afternoon. Meanwhile the shops were open, the

Christmas trade went on as usual, and electric trams clanked by on time. As in April 1945, the telephone service functioned. Would it have been possible to direct the popular élan into constructive channels, to lead the roused masses towards a place in the republican structure? The government Socialists, the Left majority, even before catching their trains to Weimar, decided otherwise and called in the army. Officers such as Colonel Reinhard picked the unemployed off the streets and defeated the Spartacists in a week, turning the Berlin rising into a royalist revolt, and issuing his orders in the name of 'His Majesty, our most gracious master'. The same colonel at the beginning of February sent a company of his regiment to Weimar to act as a guard of honour for the National Assembly, but the stage managers there had the sense to disarm them, or at least tell them to take off their steel helmets. If Germany missed its revolution, it certainly had its counter-revolution, its 'White Terror' organized at the request of the Majority Socialists by the Right. But despite several attempted coups, the survivors of the Kaiser's empire were incapable of grasping the reins of government, although the terror which they regarded as a necessary weapon went on in Germany to a greater or lesser degree until the mark was stabilized and

Hitler sent to prison in 1924. The right-wing violence of 1919-23 was terror without chivalry, for Germany's *ancien régime* wanted to terrorize, by the foulest means at its disposal, those holding inconvenient opinions. With the Spartacists out of the way, with Liebknecht and Rosa Luxemburg beaten to death for their Socialist beliefs, the men of the Reichswehr were able to take matters into their own hands. At Whitsun in 1920, for example, the well-known pacifist Hans Paasche was murdered by uniformed soldiers on his Pomeranian country estate. A week after the funeral of Rathenau, who was murdered in June 1922, the famous journalist Maximilian Harden, the champion of Bismarck, but enemy of the Kaiser's neo-Byzantine regime, was beaten up in the street. Bands of semi-demobbed soldiers, mercenaries on half pay acting on orders given by generals without lawful authority, roamed the countryside with black-lists of victims in their pockets.

The same illegal and invisible, but very real, leadership employed street-corner demagogues to make their contribution to creating an atmosphere of lawlessness, disintegration, and demoralization which the agitators of the Right judged they needed in order to discredit the Republic and restore their élite government to its former power. But the most effective weapon wielded by the Right was economic warfare and sabotage in the interior – inflation, unemployment, the deliberate refusal to stabilize the mark. When Ludendorff and Hitler set out on their putschist promenade through the streets of central Munich on 9th November 1923 they were both certain that all sense of public order and cohesion had been sufficiently undermined and corroded to give their coup a good chance of success. If the current image of the Weimar Republic as the prisoner of the old gang and its powerful agencies were wholly correct, instead of being only half correct, the Ludendorff-Hitler putsch must have succeeded.

### Reaction to terror

But it did not. 'White Terror' had not succeeded and the Republic was still intact. A movement within the German people had been roused by the 'White Terror' with which even so reactionary a soldier as the new head of the old army, General von Seeckt, found he had to reckon. Though statistics of voting trends show a swift decline of the Social Democrats, just as they show a marked resurgence on the Right, they do not show that the Social Democrats did infinitely better outside the government than inside. Nor do they show that, while the Left did not do so well in the Reich, it was more successful in, of all places, Prussia, including Berlin. Statistics indeed obscure the important fact that, as under the Kaiser, the German government lacked any 'formidable opposition' in the parliamentary sense. Some parties were in, others temporarily out. A group that might have been in office in May shivered in the cold in December. The only real opposition to this system came from the streets, after the putschist misfit Adolf Hitler emerged from Landsberg prison and looked round for allies and money for further agitation and for the organization of a new terror.

What statistics do not show is the encouraging fact that government by bloody murder and terror had, as a political notion, defeated its own purposes long before the Ludendorff-Hitler group crossed the bridge across the Isar on that November day in 1923. The ugly episode in the Ruhr after the Kapp Putsch in 1920 when the Reichswehr put against the wall and shot something like 2,000 non-violent workers, including boys of eighteen, was not quickly forgotten. Three years later a local schoolmaster who had taught some of the victims told a visitor that his boys had died shouting, 'Long live the new era'.

### Rathenau murdered

It is always difficult to agree on turning points in history, but it can be argued that the great turning point in Germany's post-1918 history came as a consequence of the murder of Walter Rathenau.

The date of the deed was the morning of 24th June 1922. By three o'clock the Reichstag was assembled and Chancellor Wirth rose from the government benches, next to Rathenau's chair, empty, draped in black, with a bunch of white roses lying on the table in front. Wirth's oration was a powerful indictment of the murder gangs, their henchmen and backers, and he announced that stringent measures would be taken for the protection of the Republic. The house dispersed, a good many deputies wondering whether the murder was the prelude to war within Germany. Would the Right march that night?

On the following day, a Sunday, there was a huge public rally in the Lustgarten flanking the Kaiser's Berlin palace. Beneath a fluttering sea of red and republican flags, some 200,000 people pressed and swayed against each other. 'The bitter feelings roused by the murder,' wrote a diarist, 'are deep and genuine, and so is the determination to back the Republic. All this is far more deep-seated than monarchical "patriotism" of pre-war days.'

The Reichstag held another session that Sunday and Wirth gave one of the greatest speeches of the Weimar Republic. Finally, the Reichstag held the funeral ceremony on 27th June. At twelve, the chancellor led Rathenau's mother into what had been the imperial box, still decorated with a crowned 'W'. The old lady 'pale as wax, a stony profile beneath the veils', seemed to preside over the muted ceremony with its speeches by President Ebert and others, its strains of Beethoven and Wagner, its stunned realization of its ultimate meaning. Then the coffin was carried outside, and presently the funeral cortege moved through the Brandenburg Gate. 'Lassalle's dream,' wrote the diarist, 'to enter Berlin through the Brandenburg Gate as President of the German Republic, has been realized by the Jew Rathenau through his martyr's death in the service of the German people.'

### Era of stability

Perhaps sentiment and funerals are not the stuff of politics, but Rathenau's funeral mobilized public opinion and showed the German people to each other in a new light. Though the 'White Terror' went on, the republican climate remained still unsafe for the enemies of the old gang, although on a diminishing scale. The impact of public opinion forced Seeckt, the uncrowned though undoubted leader of the militant and militaristic Right, to sit on the fence until, as Lloyd George said of Sir John Simon in 1915, 'the iron entered his soul'. When in September 1923 a Major Buchrucker tried to capture Berlin by a march on the capital from the fortress of Küstrin, he had reason to expect that Seeckt would give him his support. President Ebert, on the other hand, once again proclaiming a state of siege, had rather more solid reasons for thinking that the general would rally to the side of legal authority. Major Buchrucker had to call off his putsch at the last moment, only to find that his men went ahead all the same and caused the affair to collapse in public ridicule.

Seeckt also knew that interesting events were afoot in Munich, and had arranged for Frau von Seeckt to live in the Bavarian capital, start a political salon, and keep him informed. What he heard from this and other sources did not fill him with much sympathy for the Nazi movement as it then was and, on the whole, he inclined to doubt the chances of that particular plot – another reason why Ludendorff, Hitler, and Co. were in reality so many sitting ducks as they approached the Munich Feldherrenhalle en route for the ministry of war.

Seeckt, a disagreeable character, obtuse, narrow-minded, and charmless, wholeheartedly shared Frederick's and Wilhelm's estimate of the German people and therefore passed as a good patriot. However, he did not remain in command for long after the Munich Putsch and other Reichswehr debacles. He and his like appeared incongruous in the brighter era of stability, international understanding, and intellectual emancipation that eased the public atmosphere of the German Republic from 1924 onwards and gave people greater hope and confidence.

### The old gang withdraws

As Hitler sat and wrote in his Bavarian prison, the German Republic became almost a reality. Public opinion, an entirely new factor in German life, was on the side of the Republic. The old gang still remained in its bastions of power but was, in the Stresemann years between 1924-29, more circumscribed in power, less capable of resisting progressive labour legislation, less successful in selling to the German people the idea that military discipline and subordination were the only ways of life worthy of a German, and war the only solution for Germany's deprived position in Europe. The old gang did not give up, but, for five years, withdrew behind the scenes. A new generation grew up that individually if not, alas, collectively, remained immune from the old German power curse. This was the generation of the Scholls, of those who later became the younger opponents of the Nazis in power.

The transition from the period of terror to that of conciliation and reconstruction was, it must finally be stressed, not easy or uncomplicated. It was uphill work compared to which the labours of the legendary Sisiphus were child's play and those of Hercules amusing pastimes. Stresemann felt the incalculable strength of reactionary resistance every day of his life. Stresemann was one of that minority of Weimar Germans who made the long and dangerous journey from what we have called focus A to focus B, despite unceasing hostility at home and unimaginative lack of support abroad. German public opinion noted that he had become a name of European consequence, unsuccessful in detail, but accepted as a fighter for a better, more hopeful future. He died before the great counter-offensive from the German Right, which relied, as it had done before 1923, on economic distress, social corrosion, and compacted traditional values. Then the old German archetypes of the sergeant-major, the school-master, and the policeman were joined by a satanic synthesis of all three dressed in the black uniform of the SS man.

# Russia in the 1920's

By the end of 1920 the Bolsheviks were at long last real masters of ruined Russia. While fighting, their unity, ruthlessness, and political opportunism were the natural outcome of the circumstances. Now with peace returning Lenin had to create new circumstances to retain power. First, he decided to demobilize the majority of his peasant forces, in the face of strong opposition by the army leaders. He could not afford to antagonize the peasants by keeping them away from their land. Next, the peasants needed a stimulus to make profits out of their newly acquired land and it came in the form of the New Economic Policy (NEP) founded after the Kronstadt rebellion. The rising of this otherwise pro-revolutionary naval base made it quite clear to Lenin that the revolutionaries and the country were tired of 'war Communism', with its basis of sheer terror. It could not go on in peace-time.

Lenin therefore decided on a tactical withdrawal. The New Economic Policy was in fact a partial return to the capitalist system aimed at restoring the Russian economy and satisfying the Russian peasantry. Only by means of these ideological concessions could Lenin and the Bolsheviks retain power and remain masters of Russia. With the armies dissolved, only special security detachments were retained in order to maintain public order in the country. They were soon needed, to quell disturbances which flared up throughout

the country in 1921, when a drought added famine to the post-war chaos.

Once again, Bolshevik organizational talents and ruthlessness triumphed, with the help of International Red Cross relief missions. Only in 1924 and 1925 did the national economy really begin to pick up. But by then Lenin, whose will and skill kept the regime going against all odds, had died and the country was plunged into a leadership crisis which overshadowed all other events.

## Struggle for the succession

As soon as Lenin had won the Civil War and dealt successfully with the famine and economic difficulties, he was struck down by a series of strokes. Over the years 1922-24 he was in fact a dying man, but he made no clear provisions for a successor to take over in case the next stroke proved fatal. If anything, Lenin made sure that the succession crisis would be confused and prolonged. In 1923 he drew up a memorandum-testament which was to be made public on his death in which he described each contender for the leadership as quite incapable of guiding the Party singlehanded. He also turned against the undistinguished bureaucrat, Josef Stalin, and in a special codicil recommended that he be dismissed from his office as general secretary. But he took no step to assure anyone's succession. It is clear that he hoped for some kind of collective leadership, but

*Lenin recovering from his first stroke, with his wife Krupskaya, in Gorky, 1922*

without defining it further he created an impossible situation.

On 21st January 1924 Lenin finally died and the struggle for succession became acute. Trotsky, who probably overestimated his chances of being elected the new Party leader, had left Moscow three days before Lenin's death. It was repugnant to him to step immediately into the dead man's shoes, so he tried to keep in the background and did not even attend the funeral. The funeral ceremony was dominated by another contestant, the despised Georgian, Stalin, who began his own tactical moves to become Lenin's successor and seize the control of the Party.

It was obvious that Trotsky, who certainly had a strong claim to the leadership, had to be checked. Stalin's first astute move was to combine with two other contenders and leading Politburo members, Lev Kamenev and Grigori Zinovyev. This combination prevented Trotsky from becoming Lenin's successor as prime minister; instead Alexey Rykov, perhaps the most colourless of the Bolshevik leaders, was elected to this office. The same combination neutralized Trotsky in the collective Politburo, and helped Stalin in the Central Committee when Lenin's testament was read and discussed. Kamenev simply recommended that the part of the testament dealing with Stalin's dismissal be ignored and the Central Committee agreed. But the testament could not be published.

The next step of the triumvirate—Stalin, Kamenev, Zinovyev—was to oust Trotsky, who even after these checks seemed full of fight. Trotsky had come into conflict with Stalin before: first they quarrelled about

*Stalin, man of steel. At the time he was judged to be a 'grey blur'*

*Trotsky. There was a long-standing animosity between him and Stalin, but Trotsky was no match for the autocratic bureaurocrat*

the organization and tactics of the Red Army, then about intra-Party democracy. When Stalin became general secretary he quickly made it a habit to appoint secretaries at various levels directly from the secretariat instead of bidding the Party organizations to elect them. In May 1924, during the 13th Party Congress, Zinovyev compiled a whole list of these quarrels, presented them as Trotsky's conflicts with the Party and demanded a public apology from him. Trotsky refused to apologise and hit back. He published a pamphlet, *The Lessons of October,* in which he modestly showed himself to have been the mastermind of the 1917 *coup d'état,* but also demanded the revision of the Bolshevik Party's role. This public controversy had two-pronged effects. It harmed Kamenev and Zinovyev, who were known to have opposed the November uprising, but also, since Trotsky attacked 'the Party', it closed the ranks of the Party bureaucracy, and thus strengthened Stalin's hand.

The final showdown came in January 1925, when the Politburo forced Trotsky to resign as war minister; his supporters in the army also lost their jobs and Trotsky was effectively isolated. He nevertheless continued his unequal struggle against Stalin and was soon removed from the Politburo. In 1927, still loudly protesting, he was expelled from the Party and deported to Central Asia. Ultimately, he ended his days in exile in Mexico assassinated on Stalin's orders.

### Stalin eliminates his rivals

As soon as Trotsky was effectively out of the struggle the triumvirate collapsed. Stalin came to the conclusion that to eliminate his other rivals he would have to create his own faction rather than rely on alliances. In 1925 the Politburo was enlarged to ten members and Stalin's nominees, Molotov, Voroshilov, and Kalinin, joined this august body. With a majority in the Politburo, Stalin was ready to eliminate his former allies.

Stalin began to prepare his weapons in 1924. Both Kamenev and Zinovyev were internationally-minded Bolsheviks who believed in 'permanent revolution', a

theory propounded by Trotsky according to which world-wide revolution would usher in Communism sometime in the future. Zinovyev was the head of the Comintern, an international Communist organization which was supposed to help this revolution along, and he and Kamenev were active in international Communist circles. Stalin elaborated his own counter-theory, 'Socialism in one country', according to which Communism could be built without a world revolution in Soviet Russia.

Throughout 1924-27 the Comintern and its leaders, Zinovyev and Kamenev, suffered a series of setbacks. Every uprising they backed utterly failed, most notably the one in Germany. Stalin was able to exploit these failures in the intra-Party struggle; in addition his theory appealed to the nationalism of other Bolshevik leaders. Russian Communism would not depend on unsuccessful foreign Communists. Rykov, Tomsky, and Bukharin now joined Stalin's faction and Zinovyev and Kamenev were ousted in the same manner as Trotsky.

Stalin's theory of 'Socialism in one country' provided also the pretext on which the remaining Politburo rivals, who had just joined Stalin's faction, could be eradicated. The building of Communism in Soviet Russia presupposed swifter industrialization, and also modernized agriculture which ultimately meant the destruction of the peasantry. During the NEP period, farmers, especially the bigger ones – the kulaks –

flourished. Throughout the 1920's, Bukharin was in charge of agriculture and therefore could be made responsible for this development, and could be counted on to oppose any Party measures to upset his 'success' in this sector.

The Politburo and the Party discussed for a long time what could be done about the kulaks and a limited collectivization was thought inevitable. But no one thought of a wholesale onslaught on the peasantry who had only just started to produce enough grain to feed the country: it would have been another revolution. But by 1927, however, Stalin felt obliged to eliminate his remaining opponents and this was the only issue he could successfully exploit against them. As these discussions became public it was suddenly found that Soviet Russia would have a great grain deficiency. Stalin promptly accused the kulaks of sabotage and seized on this as a pretext for the forcible collectivization of Russian agriculture.

The last years of the 1920's were spent in enforcing the collectivization drive with special security detachments and deportations. In the Politburo these policies were opposed by Bukharin, Rykov, and Tomsky who now formed the so-called 'right opposition'. But Stalin was ready for them. In 1928 he strengthened his position in the Politburo still further by having Kuybyshev and Rudzutak elected to it. Kirov, Kaganovich, Andreyev, and Mikoyan became candidate-members, and Stalin had

*Travelling propaganda library leaving Petrograd, 1921*

Novosti

*Top left: A kulak laughs at the poor peasants' newspaper* Poverty's *news that kulaks have disappeared. The NEP encouraged capitalism.*
*Top right: Bolshevik cartoon attacks Mensheviks for organizing wage cuts with capitalists and suppressing workers. But the NEP itself allowed some return to capitalism.* **Above:** *Party card of Ordzhonikidze signed by Stalin. Party membership rose to over a million by 1930*

now achieved a position of complete control.

In 1929 the 'right opposition' tried in vain to unite all the discredited forces in the Party against Stalin's faction. But the Trotskyites and 'internationalists' were too demoralized to be anything but liabilities. Bukharin then tried a frontal attack within the Central Committee, but his criticism of Stalin's policies was rejected, all the opposition forces were lumped together and forced to resign from Party offices. They were next forced to recant, admit past errors and deviations, and submit to Party discipline. Trotsky refused outright and was promptly deported; the others chose to submit to avoid deportation and exile. But it was obvious that it was only a question of time before they would all be eliminated. Thus in 1929, Stalin finally achieved his ambition, became Lenin's successor as Party leader and thus ruler of the Soviet Union. He soon made it clear that he wanted absolute personal power. By 1930, he was able to achieve this ambition—the stage was set for police terror.

### External relations

Shortly after the coup, mainly as a protection against Allied pressures, Lenin created the Comintern, the new International of extreme left-wing parties. But Lenin's high hopes in this organization were soon

dashed. The social democratic parties not only refused to subscribe to Lenin's principles but gradually became the chief opponents of Communism. The successful revolutions planned by the Comintern parties were not realized and all that the Bolsheviks really achieved was to split the labour movement still further.

In 1918, after the collapse of the Central Powers, several ephemeral uprisings were staged in Germany, Austria, Bavaria, and Hungary. Though these revolts were badly organized and easily crushed, they nevertheless frightened the war-weary capitalist countries. Lenin used the Comintern and its reputation for trouble-making as a defence against Allied efforts to intervene directly in the Russian Civil War, but he never overcame the isolation in which the Bolsheviks landed themselves after 1917.

After the Civil War, Soviet Russia needed foreign aid and, clearly, as long as it maintained the Comintern, it could not get it from the victorious Western capitalist countries. Lenin therefore turned to Germany. In 1922 he scored his first diplomatic triumph when he concluded with Germany the Treaty of Rapallo, by which the two countries resumed diplomatic relations and agreed Germany should pay no reparations. The treaty also opened Soviet Russia to German investments, established mutual

trade, and brought German experts and advisers into Russia. The Soviet Union had no need of Western capitalism.

At the same time, the Bolsheviks made it clear that they considered the Germans only as temporary allies. While the Germans aided Russia economically and diplomatically, the Soviets prepared a Communist uprising there. The unsuccessful uprising in 1923 dangerously strained mutual relations, but the two 'defeated' powers had great need of each other, and they resumed normal relations after a cooling-off period of two years.

With a dependable and powerful ally Soviet Russia could afford to quarrel with Western capitalist countries. The commercial treaty with Great Britain in 1921 remained a dead letter. Great Britain's recognition of Russia in 1924 did nothing to halt Soviet subversion. Three years later a Soviet trade organization in London was found to be nothing but a cover for espionage. Great Britain broke relations—only to resume them again to counterbalance Germany's influence in Russia. France and the United States were not prepared to expose themselves to such strains, and had no official relations with Russia. Soviet foreign policy remained German-oriented until Stalin assumed personal control in the 1930's.

# Mussolini's Italy

The new ministry formed by Mussolini on 31st October 1922 reflected the ambiguous nature of Fascism's rise to power, halfway between a *coup d'état* and respect for traditional constitutional forms. It was a coalition cabinet in which practically all parliamentary forces were represented apart from the Communists and the Socialists, and in which the Fascists were in a clear minority. Mussolini reserved for himself the ministries of the interior and of foreign affairs in addition to the post of prime minister.

What really mattered now, however, were no longer delicate shifts in the parliamentary equilibrium, but the radically new political situation that had emerged in the country. The traditional parties had amply demonstrated their substantial impotence. They were condemned to suffer the growing imposition of that determined and violent minority which after creating a climate of civil war in the country, had illegally imposed an apparently lawful solution to the problem of government, and thus avoided presenting itself to moderate public opinion as a mere subversion faction.

The Italians were not, of course, generally aware that they had just started along the road to dictatorship. Even those who realized the intrinsically authoritarian nature of the Fascist movement, were for the most part sceptical about its ability to put down solid roots in the country and tended to consider it a temporary phenomenon of transition towards a new form of political organisation. Fascism was of a composite and contradictory nature, which prevented most people from spotting its essential characteristics in time. It was not for nothing that one of the leading lights of the Fascist movement, Dino Grandi, had been able to observe, about a year prior to the March on Rome, that it contained a little of everything: 'It includes the old Salandra follower, the Liberal Democrat, the Nationalist, the Monarchist, the Anarchist, the Republican, the absolute individualist, the relative individualist, the Syndicalist, the uneasy and the restless in temperament and habits, always ready to snatch the spoils from all parties.'

There was one single aspect which had increasingly made itself clear: its violently anti-Socialist and thus anti-proletarian nature. But this, during a phase of growing confusion inside the workers' movement and of aggressive bourgeois reaction, was an element of strength and stability for Fascism.

## Consolidation

Mussolini did not delay in making it clear to everyone that he considered himself not so much the head of a coalition based on parliamentary majority as the 'Duce' of a party which took upon itself privileges in the exercise of power. Two essential events at the beginning of 1923 sanctioned this route he had chosen: the constitution of the Grand Council of Fascism and the creation of the Volunteer Militia for National Security (MVSN).

The Grand Council, whose members were nominated by Mussolini from top-level Fascists, constituted the link at the top between the political will of the Fascist Party and the traditional state apparatus. It was this body which discussed and approved the general lines of government policy and the main legislative proposals which were then submitted for final drafting to the council of ministers and then to parliament. In this way, the task of initiating political and legislative activity was transferred from the normal organs of the constitutional state to a private group which represented the interests and aspirations of a mere faction, and which, as time went by, became increasingly subject to Mussolini's arbitrary decisions. The anomaly was even more glaring because the structures of the parliamentary and multi-party system remained in existence for some years.

With the transformation of the Fascist 'action squads' into a Militia recognised and subsidised by the state, violence in favour of a minority was finally institutionalised. This did not, even inside the opposition, arouse the dismay and indignation that might have been expected because it seemed like a return to legality, the squads which had struck terror into many regions of Italy as one of the main instruments of the triumph of Fascism — were dissolved, officially at least.

The government's first important measures in economic-social affairs went a long way to meet the aspirations of the financial and industrial world: the abolition of the requirement to supply the names and addresses of shareholders, a measure introduced in 1920 by Giolitti but which had not

*Right: An Italian girl proudly displays a portrait of Mussolini on her bathing costume.* ***Far Right:*** *Italian painting depicts Mussolini's bodyguard, all resembling him, daggers aloft in salute. The illusion of the Duce's infallibility and the state's power was maintained by the ritual hysteria of Fascist demonstrations*

Moro. Milan

*Left: Mussolini surveys a Roman crowd before addressing it, June, 1924. He liked to speak in front of statuary recalling former imperial glory. He affected to disdain adulation. But he was doubtless satisfied when the swelling chant of* Duce! Duce! Duce! *frequently drowned his histrionic and supposedly spontaneous speeches.* **Right:** *An Italian poster urges the destruction of Bolshevism. A Fascist tramples on the red flag*

yet come into effect; the transfer to private enterprise of the telephone network; the abolition of state monopoly on life insurance; the shelving of the enquiry into excess profits made during the war; the abolition of death duties within the family group and their reduction in other cases; the reduction of various direct taxes paid by the wealthy.

### Sudden crisis threatens

In the administrative field, in addition to various reforms of small practical effect to improve the effectiveness of the state apparatus, the government undertook a general reconstruction of the state bureaucracy. Naturally, it did not miss this opportunity to effect a dexterous, if limited, purge in the ranks of the administration.

Fascism had not yet captured all power; it exercised control through violence, and the constant threat of more violence, on the consensus of the traditional centre and rightwing political formations, within the parliamentary system. Mussolini was therefore faced by the problem of assuring a loyal and stable majority inside the Chamber. He dealt with this matter by extracting from the Chamber itself – highly disconcerted and skilfully manoeuvred by him with blandishments and veiled threats – a new electoral law, which stated that whichever party obtained the greatest number of votes, provided it was higher than 25 per cent of the total vote, would be entitled to two thirds of the seats. The Chamber was then dissolved and elections were set down for April 1924.

The result could not be in doubt. The government exerted every sort of pressure on the electorate, while in many areas of the country the violence of the Fascist squads was once again loosed against the opposition forces. Mussolini sponsored for the occasion a wide electoral coalition into which politicians of moderate and conservative views were dragooned alongside the predominant Fascists, their task being to attract the support of those vast sectors of bourgeois public opinion which were fervent supporters of a 'strong' government while repudiating the more extremist elements of Fascism.

The government 'electoral list' obtained nearly 65% of the votes. The remainder of the votes were divided between the most varied political formations which were therefore condemned to impotence on the parliamentary level, just as they had long since been rendered increasingly powerless on the general political level.

Then, at the very moment when Mussolini and Fascism appeared to be finally consolidated in power, crisis threatened.

A caricature of Mussolini from the clandestine Italian newspaper Becco Giallo *implying his complicity in Matteotti's murder. In fact, Matteotti was probably murdered by Fascist extremists without the Duce's knowledge*

On 30th May 1924 the Socialist deputy Giacomo Matteotti made an implacable speech in the new Chamber against the government and its head, denouncing among other things, with an abundance of details, the atmosphere of terror in which the elections had been held. On 10th June Matteotti was abducted in broad daylight in a Rome street by a band of Fascists forming part of the organisation which – under cover of the ministry of the interior – had long been taking care of 'punitive expeditions' against particularly prominent opponents. The disappearance of the Socialist deputy aroused an outburst of indignation even in many political circles until then decisively pro-Fascist: even though Matteotti's corpse remained undiscovered until several months later, it was immediately obvious that he had fallen the

*In an Italian cartoon by Giuseppe Scalarini, Bandi, a Fascist satrap, boasts his control of local government, judiciary, and police – won by liberal use of club and castor oil*

victim of an odious political crime. Mussolini's direct responsibility – in the sense of a precise order – for the abduction and killing of Matteotti has not been proved beyond doubt. That he was unaware of the project appears most improbable: moreover his moral responsibility for the crime cannot be denied and this was also the conviction of a great part of public opinion at the time.

A void yawned around Mussolini and for a short while his position seemed to be very shaky. But the wave of collective indignation aroused by an episode which in the eyes of many assumed the value of a symbol of the real nature of Fascism, could not by itself succeed in overthrowing a political system which did not hesitate to use violence to survive. There were no attempts to oppose violence with violence, or to overthrow Mussolini with an act of force, and even the vain attempts to organise strikes in some towns amounted to very little. The minority opposition in the Chamber chose the road of abstention, instead of giving battle. This was the so-called 'Aventine secession': the opposition deputies – including those of the Popular (Catholic) Party which had left the government team the previous year – decided not to participate in parliamentary affairs so long as law and order were not restored by the government. The Aventine deputies, firmly determined to avoid the use of any means which were not perfectly legal, hoped in this way to isolate the Fascist government and force it to withdraw under the pressure of public opinion. This was a mistake, because in this way they deprived themselves of the only means available to rid the country of Mussolini without overstepping legality: the intervention of the sovereign – who anyway should have dismissed the ministry on his own initiative, as the Constitution allowed him to do. But Victor Emmanuel III, as ever wavering and uncertain

in the face of a possible civil war, obstinately took refuge in constitutional legalism and refused to take any notice of any message from the opposition which did not reach him via parliament.

Mussolini was thus given time to pull himself together. By the end of the year, he was once again firmly in the saddle, to be met by a simmering revolt inside his own party. Turbulent extremist elements urged him to get rid of the opposition and the last remnants of constitutional liberalism, and set up a naked dictatorship. These extremists were particularly the provincial *'petit bourgeois'*, the original Fascist core who had hoped to prosper in public administration, and who after the March on Rome had been profoundly disappointed by the continuing persistence of the old ruling class in the posts of power.

### The Dictator emerges

On 3rd January 1925 Mussolini made the move which was finally to transform his regime into a real and true dictatorship. In a speech to the Chamber, he declared in defiant tones that he assumed entire responsibility for whatever had occurred till then: 'If Fascism has been a delinquent association, I am the head of this delinquent association!' The moment had come to break all restraints and to entrust to force the issue of a struggle between 'two irreducible elements'. Deeds immediately followed these words: dissolution of 'sub-

versive' organisations; closing down of opposition clubs; arrests and searches; the progressive smothering of the liberty of the press; ever increasing recourse to police repression and operations by the Fascist Militia. Then, in November 1926, liberty received its death-blow. Using as a pretext an attempt on Mussolini's life, whose circumstances have always remained wrapped in mystery, the government adopted a series of measures sanctioning the end of whatever autonomous political life still remained in Italy. All parties and associations pursuing activities judged to be contrary to the regime were dissolved; those papers which had not yet fallen into line were suppressed; the Aventine deputies were expelled from the Chamber; the death penalty was instituted for serious political offences; a special tribunal of army and militia officers was created and charged with trying even minor political offences—using the most expeditious procedure. Any form of opposition or criticism of the regime, however cautious and indirect, was now doomed to go underground.

The police regime thus 'created was harsh, but not inhuman or bloodthirsty, at least compared with other totalitarian regimes in this century. The death sentences pronounced by the special tribunal in peacetime—that is up to the end of 1940 —did not exceed ten, of which five were inflicted on Slav nationalists accused of acts of terrorism. There were over 4,000 prison sentences, sometimes very heavy ones, while for those members of the opposition judged to be less dangerous there was temporary banishment under police surveillance to some remote area like the small Mediterranean islands. There were never any true mass concentration camps or forced labour camps.

Clandestine opposition, which was fairly lively towards the end of the 'twenties and the beginning of the 'thirties before it was finally broken by police repression, came from two main sources: the Communist organisation which drew its support from among the working masses of the northern industrial centres, and the 'Giustizia e Libertà' groups, a new political movement mainly of democratic-radical intellectuals, founded in 1929 by Carlo Rosselli and led by him from exile in Paris. The internal clandestine opposition was naturally closely linked to the various exile groups abroad, especially in France. Without the talking-points, propaganda and direct action provided by the exiles' movement, the internal resistance, already operating in very difficult psychological and material

conditions, would certainly have been much weaker and more exposed to crises of discouragement and temptations of unconditional surrender. On the other hand, the internal resistance, even within its very restricted limitations, was indispensable to the anti-Fascist emigrés, as the concrete proof that their sacrifices were

not useless and that their hopes were not purely illusory.

### A badly-organized Party

Most Italians were not however affected by the action of militant anti-Fascism, just as the regime's police oppression did not intrude directly on those—the majority—

*Left: Toga-clad Fascists. They liked to flaunt their debt to Ancient Rome in their dress and behaviour just as they liked to recall its glories by sporting the legionary's dagger. 'Fascist' harks back to an Ancient Roman symbol of authority—the 'fasces', carried before the magistrates. Fascist's slogans included 'Believe! Obey! Fight!' and 'He who has steel has bread'. Right: Italian artist's idealized impression of a Blackshirt. There is little connection between this romantic hero and the violent thugs who helped Mussolini to power*

Collection Nizza

who limited their interests to the needs of daily life.

What made the Fascist dictatorship tolerable, even to those who were very far from approving its principles and its methods, was the regime's tendency to be satisfied more by appearances than by reality. This allowed most people to pre-serve their independence, despite Fascism's grandiloquent pretensions to control all aspects of public and private life. The state proclaimed itself totalitarian, but the Party, which should have constituted the main instrument for 'fascistifying' the country, became a heavy bureaucratic ap-paratus, deprived of all life by its rigidly centralised and authoritarian structure which did not permit any effective internal debate. Its essential role finally became to organise propaganda and spectacular and ostentatious ceremonies.

The amorphous character of the Party was further accentuated by the lack of selectivity in its recruitment. The Party was joined, automatically and indis-criminately, by all the young people be-longing to the Fascist youth organisations, membership of which was compulsory for all those attending primary and secondary schools. It is true that from 1925 access to the party by other categories of citizens was fairly rigorously limited, in order to avoid the risk of having the victor's chariot taken by assault by all the last-minute opportunists, but in 1932, on the tenth anniversary of the March on Rome, mem-bership of the National Fascist Party (PNF) was made open to all, except for notorious anti-Fascists. When shortly afterwards access to all public employment was made conditional on party membership, the transformation of the Party from a political organisation to a mere bureaucratic apparatus was finally sanctioned. If we add finally, that Mussolini always stressed the principle of the supremacy – in all vital political and administrative questions – of the traditional state organs over the Party organs, and that he rigorously stuck to this principle, this will give a clear idea of the reasons which prevented the Fascist Party from playing a really dynamic and creative role. It was only one of the instru-ments at the disposal of a minority for the authoritarian exercise of power.

The totalitarian pretensions of the Fas-cist regime also found themselves limited by the continued existence of two institu-tions which, though in different measure, had much deeper roots in Italian life: the monarchy and the Catholic Church.

Certainly, the advent of Fascism and the setting up of Mussolini's dictatorship had still more rigorously circumscribed the influence of the Crown over the country's political leadership. All decisions, even the most vital ones, were taken by Mussolini without obtaining the king's assent, though he kept the King scrupulously informed about the trend of the most important matters. But the monarchy continued to represent an autonomous pole of attraction for the citizens' loyalty – in particular the upper classes and the army – thus making less firm that monopoly of the Italians' political consciousness which was one of the aims of Fascist totalitarianism. This meant that the monarchy easily could – and in later years did – become the rallying point for malcontents and opponents of the regime, eventually constituting a mor-tal threat to Fascism.

In his relations with the Holy See, Musso-lini was able to profit from the gradual accommodation of the Church to the state,

*Left: Fascist rally in the Piazza Venezia, Rome, 1929. Mussolini was later to an-nounce the conquest of Abyssinia and Italy's entry into the Second World War from the balcony of the Palazzo Venezia, on the left*

Moro, Milan

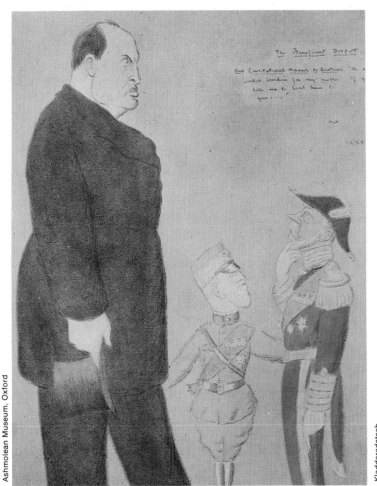

*Left:* '*The Beneficent Despot' by English caricaturist Sir Max Beerbohm. King Victor Emmanuel III of Italy introduces King George V of England to his monolithic prime minister, Mussolini, and remarks: 'he has worked wonders for my people. If you'd like me to lend him to you. . . .' **Right:** German cartoon deriding Italian Fascism, 1926. Victor Emmanuel honours ludicrous monument to new Roman Empire*

obvious signs of which had appeared during the last period of the liberal regime. Indeed, the belief that it would be even easier to reach an agreement with a Fascist government had been one of the reasons which had induced Pius XI and his advisers to assume a substantially benevolent attitude towards Mussolini.

On the 11th February 1929 Mussolini, on behalf of Italy, and Cardinal Gasparri, secretary of state on behalf of the Holy See, signed the Lateran Pacts, the so-called Conciliation. The government made many important concessions, giving the Catholic religion the position of official state religion and guaranteeing a particular position of privilege to the Church. Mussolini thus disarmed, without firing a shot, one of the most potentially dangerous opponents to the regime, and Fascism was assured of the adhesion of the Catholic masses under the leadership of a clergy which was in the majority substantially devoted to it. It was not by accident that the plebiscitary elections, which were held immediately after the Conciliation to elect a Chamber based on the new system of a single list of candidates chosen by the Party, were a clamorous success for Mussolini and Fascism, a success which could not be explained away exclusively in terms of the absolute lack of political freedom. A considerable number of the affirmative votes were genuine, and the contribution of the new Catholic votes was certainly not among the least decisive.

However, in the long run, the agreement with the Church also constituted an element of weakness for the regime. Once again, Fascism gave up even attempting to ensure the monopoly of consciences for itself and formally accepted to live alongside an institution of profoundly different ideological convictions and which because it was so firmly rooted in the very tissues of Italian life, could not but constitute a serious limitation to its totalitarian aspirations.

Fascism, once it had transformed itself into a dictatorship, endeavoured to provide itself with an economic-social theory of vaunted but substantially illusory originality, which disguised its anti-proletarian class structure, and contributed to reduce social tensions without eroding the privileged position of the economically dominant groups. The theory was that of the 'Corporate State', proposed as an improvement upon both the meanness of liberal and bourgeois individualism, and Socialist collectivism, and to be achieved by means of class collaboration rather than class warfare. The prospect could not but have a certain appeal, especially when the world economic depression after the 1929 crash had nakedly bared the grave contradictions of capitalism, while the Soviet Union's collectivist experiment appeared doomed to be wrecked by the violence and excesses of Stalinism.

The Corporate State was to see the harmonious blending of the opposed interests of capital and labour within the framework of corporations which, under the aegis of the state, were to act as places where their respective representatives could meet and reach mutual understanding, in accordance with their various productive sectors. Such a collaboration, presupposed, however, full parity between employers and workers, a parity which instead was in exact contradiction to what had been the historic function of Fascism.

The Fascist trades unions, the only ones allowed and recognised by the state, lacked any autonomy whatsoever and their leaders, imposed from above, rather than being representatives of the workers, were in fact Party and government officials. If to this is added the elimination of internal commissions inside the factories and the abolition of the right to strike, it is very easy to understand how precarious had become the condition of the workers when the care for their interests now depended on the goodwill of 'hierarchical superiors'. The latter, on their part, were far more the expression of the employing classes than of the working masses.

The economic crises of the 'thirties were part of a worldwide phenomenon, but Fascism must bear some responsibility for its effects in Italy. It had deprived the working class of its most effective instruments of defence while pretending to strengthen them. Fascist theory and organization was no foundation on which to build bridges across the Great Depression.

# The Ku Klux Klan

The political atmosphere of America in the 1920's was introverted, reactionary and materialist. The decade opened with a witch-hunt against anarchists and subversives. The worst was over by 1921, but in the next few years, minority opinions were in for a bad time. A great symbolic issue was the Scopes Trial of 1925 when a teacher was convicted of breaking a law of the state of Tennessee which forbade the teaching of the doctrine of evolution. Civilized America found the well-reported proceedings startling evidence of the backwardness of the legislation of Tennessee, and the rest of the world was contemptuous, but elsewhere other equally deplorable things were going on in American courts in the name of political orthodoxy. On the whole, the Supreme Court was successful in preventing gross infringement of constitutional liberties. Yet it was not its respect for legal and constitutional principle which attracted attention in the world outside, but the long drawn-out case of Sacco and Vanzetti. These two Italian immigrants, self-confessed anarchists, were tried and convicted of robbery and murder on very flimsy evidence, and, despite many appeals by prominent people in America and Europe, they were finally electrocuted in 1927. In this instance the Supreme Court was unable to get the case brought before it.

The 1920's was also to see the revival of the Ku Klux Klan, which added anti-semitism and anti-Catholicism to its defunct predecessors' racialism. The founder of the modern Klan, William Simmons, was a teacher of southern history who had dreamed since boyhood of leading a patriotic crusade against those forces he considered inimical to the American way of life.

When Simmons and sixteen followers reached the summit of Stone Mountain, Georgia, on a wild Thanksgiving night in 1915, they huddled around the comforting glow of a fiery cross and vowed to re-establish the 'Invisible Empire'. In a brief ceremony the muffled figures accorded new life to America's most infamous secret society. The Ku Klux Klan had been roused from protracted slumber.

The men who shortly began descending the granite mountainside could not have known that the next decade was to witness its greatest triumphs and its sudden, squalid disintegration.

Although the reanimated Klan retained the sinister hooded robes, the secrecy, and much of the weird ritual, the Kloran, or book of rules and rituals, indicates that it preserved very little of its former substance. The original Ku Klux Klan had been founded as little more than a friendly club in 1866. The founders, a group of bored Confederate troopers, felt the need for a club to recapture some wartime comradeship and excitement. They chose Kuklos, the Greek word for 'circle', as the name of the association, adding the word 'Klan' for its alliterative effect. When it was discovered that the accompanying robes, ritual, and terminology struck terror into the local Negro population the club began to assume a far wider political and social significance. In 1867 the 'Invisible Empire of the South' was established.

Existing basically to assert white supremacy and curb the activities of recently emancipated Negroes, the Klan devoted itself to restoring constitutional rights to white southerners, to the protection of southern womanhood, and the re-establishment of home rule. It played an important part in expelling those Yankee adventurers or 'Carpetbaggers' who had fallen upon a spent and exhausted south, solely in quest of loot.

Influenced by the success of the Klan, other similar societies spread rapidly through the former Confederacy. It has been estimated that during the late 1860's the majority of southern whites played some part in the Ku Klux Klan movement.

But the Klan soon lapsed into terrorism and Klan chapters became indistinguishable from predatory bands of outlaws. In 1869 the Imperial Wizard, General Nathan B. Forrest, disbanded the movement. But Klansmen persisted with acts of violence and the Grant administration responded with such measures as the drastic Ku Klux Klan Act of 1871, authorizing the President to suspend the writ of habeas corpus and suppress violence by military force. Although some 7,000 were indicted under various acts and 1,000 convictions secured, terrorism did not appreciably abate.

The new Knights of the Ku Klux Klan

***Below:*** *Ku Klux Klan initiation ceremony, 1915. Candidates kneel before an altar draped with the Stars and Stripes and surmounted by a fiery cross. Converts, many of startlingly feeble intelligence, were enveloped and overawed by a weird and meaningless code of rites, signs, signals and words*

established by William Simmons were as committed as their predecessors to maintaining white supremacy, but Simmons, as Imperial Wizard, insisted that foreigners, Jews and Catholics be excluded from their ranks. While appropriating much of the ritual of the original Klan, Simmons added some preposterous vocabulary of his own. His converts, largely of startlingly feeble intelligence, were enveloped and overawed by a weird and meaningless code of ceremonies, signs, signals and words. The Klansmen sang 'klodes', held 'klonversations', swore blood oaths, ignited crosses and whispered passwords.

The Klan had its own calendar. The Fourth of July, Independence Day, 1923 was 'The Dismal Day of the Weeping Week of the Hideous Month of the year of the Klan LVII'. Described by its new guiding spirit as a 'high class, mystic, social, patriotic society', the Klan was modelled along the lines of the federal union. The entire south, the 'Invisible Empire', was under the direction of an Imperial Wizard and each state constituted a realm under a Grand Dragon. Other administrative divisions included regional, county and local units bearing such titles as 'Giants', 'Cyclops', 'Titans', 'Hydras' and 'Furies'. The local 'dens' were governed by an 'Exalted Cyclops', whose administrative officers included 'Kludds', 'Kligrapps', 'Klabees', 'Kladds', 'Klexters', 'Klagaroes' and 'Klokanns'.

By 1920, Simmons had only succeeded in recruiting a few thousand subjects. It was to take the dynamic Mr Clark and Mrs Tyler, whom he met in the spring, to improve the fortunes of the 'Invisible Empire'. A couple of professional fund-raisers and publicity agents, they set about organizing the sale of Klan membership on a business-like basis. In parts of the country where white supremacy was the principal concern, recruiting stressed that aspect of the organization's crest. In other localities where anti-revolutionism, anti-Catholicism, or anti-Semitism were rife, they emphasized the Klan's Fundamentalist, Protestant character or its one hundred per cent Americanism. The systematizing of appeals to racial and religious intolerance certainly paid off.

Within a year Simmons could claim over 100,000 subjects. But the Klan's activities were being watched. The New York *World* had prepared a dossier on the organization and ran a story accusing it of responsibility for four killings, one mutilation, one branding with acid, forty-one floggings, twenty-seven tar-and-feather parties, five kidnappings, and forty-three threats to leave town. Not surprisingly, in October 1921 a Congressional investigation ensued, but it failed to elicit any legal evidence that the Klan's national organization had directed the outrages or approved them.

However, the circumstantial evidence, together with the New York *World's* revelation that Mr Clark and Mrs Tyler had recently been charged with 'disorderly conduct' and the possession of liquor, led to the growth of factionalism within the 'Invisible Empire'. From the exalted position of Kligrapp of the national organization, Dr Hiram Wesley Evans, Grand Dragon of the Realm of Indiana and a former dentist,

stripped Simmons of all power and appropriated his Wizardship in a sudden coup. Although provided with a $90,000 cash settlement by the Klan, Simmons persisted with attempts to organize rival enterprises. He spent his energies in vain, dying poor and disillusioned in 1945.

By 1923 Evans claimed a membership of five million, and the Klan decided to turn its hand to politics. The following year, at the Democratic national convention, Klan leaders successfully lobbied against a proposal that would have condemned their organization as un-American and campaigned for the nomination of William McAdoo over Al Smith. Smith symbolized everything abhorrent to the Klan, and although neither McAdoo nor Smith were eventually nominated, the Klan succeeded in bringing the proceedings to a stalemate. The compromise candidate, John W. Davis, was defeated at the elections in a year which should logically have seen a Democrat at the White House. Dr Evans, his Goblins, and Dragons had demonstrated their new-found strength and their political appetites were whetted.

But they had reckoned without the excesses of D. C. Stephenson, the Grandest Dragon of the Empire. 'I am the law in Indiana', he bragged and few disagreed. He owned the governor, the legislature, most of the representatives and both United States senators. Oversexed and bibulous, he craved money, power, and women. One unfortunate, Madge Oberholzer, resisted his blandishments. He assaulted her one night aboard a Chicago-bound train. Distraught, she swallowed six bichloride-of-mercury tablets. During the ensuing illness that preceded her death she managed to dictate an account of the incident to the prosecuting attorney, William H. Remy, one of the few officials that Stephenson did not control. She accused Stephenson of rape and mutilation and as a result the Grandest Dragon was tried and found guilty of murder in the second degree. The judge sentenced him to life imprisonment.

His conviction was a telling indictment of the Ku Klux Klan and it began to break up rapidly. But it died hard. In 1926–27 the Knights rallied to oppose Al Smith's nomination, and although they failed to do so, the religious hatred they stirred up undoubtedly conspired to prevent his winning the presidency.

The Klan's programme of hatred attracted a variety of sadists and perverts whose acts of violence aroused so much adverse public comment that the Klan was unable to survive Stephenson's conviction. By 1926, racked with internal strife, it began to lose its influence in an atmosphere of declining postwar hysteria and rising prosperity. By 1930 the 'Invisible Empire' was in ruins and only scattered cells of die-hards kept its memory alive, as they do today.

Salesmanship alone never accounted for the success of the Klan. It filled an urgent need in the southern psyche. In 1923 the United States was in a state of suspended emotion. The country had girded itself psychologically for mortal combat with the rapacious Hun and suddenly the enemy lay prostrate. A new enemy had to be found and pent-up jingoism released, so a treach-

erous fifth column was conveniently discovered in Catholics, Jews, Negroes and foreigners. Anything 'foreign' became synonymous with 'un-American'—especially the Catholic Church. Ruled by a foreign Pope in a foreign capital, it constituted a suitably insidious enemy whose activities could be depicted as a vast conspiracy against Protestant America. There was anyway a tradition of anti-foreignism and especially anti-Catholicism in the United States: it had been a major issue during the mass migrations from Europe, and before the immigration laws many Americans in the south and central west imagined they were about to be overrun by foreign hordes.

Other factors account for the resurgence of the Klan: post-war disillusion was rife and for many its reanimation brought purpose and excitement into their tedious and frequently repressed small-town lives. The Klan's aims were, moreover, well suited to their narrow puritan morality and the thousands who found its violent, crusading image secretly irresistible could point to its insistence on clean living and chastity and persuade themselves that membership constituted a moral obligation.

The Klan became the mouthpiece of small-time politicians and businessmen throughout the middle west and south who knew little and suspected much of anything they considered foreign. It made little headway in the big cities, but in towns and villages it came to dominate politics and commerce. Avowed Klansmen were elected county officials, legislators, and convention delegates and the Klan supported candidates and won governorships and seats in Congress. Two US senators from Georgia were probably members and the governor of Alabama and a senator from Texas certainly carried membership cards.

During its heyday in the 1920's the Ku Klux Klan served to reflect the post-war phobias and hatreds of a variety of fanatical patriots, religious fundamentalists, irrational nativists and white supremacists. Largely, however, it was embraced by well-intentioned but ignorant and xenophobic southern whites, who saw themselves as the rugged defenders of the American way of life.

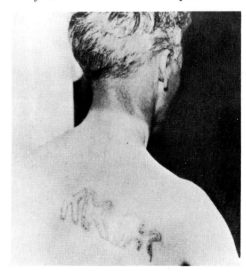

*Below: Klan revenge. A pastor who had angered local Klansmen bears a punitive brand. Many Klansmen were sadists and perverts*

# The Great Wall Street Crash

King Features Syndicate

*Above : Wall Street, October 1929. Relaxation as prices rally before plunging further. Everyone was sure of the 'fundamental soundness of the great mass of economic activities'. As many as a million people were involved in speculating. All through the summer of 1929 most of them made money.*
***Left:*** *The Stock Exchange (drawing by William Gropper). In the terrible weeks of late October the ticker tape spelt out ruin for thousands of Americans.*
***Below:*** *As the great bull market of the 'twenties roared on men raced to buy stocks, because they had heard the stock market was a place where people could get rich quick. Nothing warned them of impending disaster – except earlier, smaller, crashes. This American cartoon deplored the inability of small speculators to learn from their own mistakes: 'Never again – until the next time!'*

Culver Pictures

On 1st January 1929, the Coolidge bull market was at least four years old. The *New York Times* average of the prices of twenty-five representative industrial stocks which had stood at 110 at the beginning of 1924 had eased up to 135 at the beginning of 1925. At the close of trading on 2nd January 1929, it was at 338.35. Apart from mild setbacks, notably in early 1926 and early 1928, this climb had been almost uninterrupted. There were very few months when the averages did not show an improvement on the month preceding. There had been, in short, a speculative upsurge of unparalleled magnitude and duration.

In a market like that of 1929 there are three possible reasons why people buy stocks. One is for the old-fashioned purpose of sharing in the current income of an enterprise. Some eccentrics were undoubtedly so motivated in those days, although in the case of such a speculative favourite as Radio, which reached 505 on 3rd September 1929, up from 94½ in the preceding eighteen months, the desire for immediate income must have been fairly slight. The stock had never paid a dividend.

A second and far larger group of people were buying stocks because they had heard that the stock market was a place where people could get rich and they were righteously persuaded that their right to be rich was as good as the next person's. These were the innocent, although it was also their misfortune to believe – perhaps with some assistance from a customer's man – that they were really very wise. These buyers talked of the prospects for Steel, GM, United Corporation, and Blue Ridge with the familiarity of a friend and the unique unhesitating certainty, not of one who knows, but of one who doesn't know that he doesn't know.

Finally, stocks were being bought by those who knew that a boom was on but who intended to get out – or even, at a high level of professionalism, to go short – before the crash came. As 1929 wore along, it was this group that became increasingly nervous. The market was making phenomenal advances; one couldn't get out while there were still such gains to be made. But whenever there was upsetting news the market dropped sharply on large volume. Some *were* getting out.

Since capital gains were what counted, stocks were overwhelmingly being bought on margin. This meant that someone had to put up as a loan the part of the price which the purchaser wasn't paying. Since the stocks themselves were security for the loan, if the value of the stocks dropped, the creditors made calls for more margin – a higher cash payment, or further collateral security. If the debtor could not pay he would be forced to sell his shares. Forced sales of this kind could greatly accelerate any downward plunge of the market.

But despite a certain nervousness in February, confidence recovered in June, and prices started on their last great zoom. Every day the market went on to new highs. Margin accounts expanded enormously, and from all over the country – indeed from all over the world – money poured into New York to finance these transactions. During the summer brokers' loans increased at the rate of 400,000,000 dollars a month. By September they totalled more than 7,000,000,000 dollars.

Not everyone was playing the market as legend holds – the great majority of Americans were then as innocent of knowledge of how to buy a stock as they are today – but subsequent estimates have suggested that as many as a million people were involved in the speculation. During that summer, almost all of them made money. Never, before or since, have so many people so suddenly got so wonderfully rich.

## The shakes

On Saturday 19th October, Washington despatches reported that Secretary of Commerce Lamont was having trouble finding the $100,000 in government funds which would be required to pay the upkeep of the yacht *Corsair* which J.P.Morgan had just given to the government. There were other and more compelling indications of an unaccustomed stringency. The papers told of a very weak market the day before – there were heavy declines on late trading and the *New York Times* industrial average had dropped about seven points. Meanwhile, that day's market was behaving very badly. In the second heaviest Saturday's trading in history, 3,488,100 shares were changing hands. At the close of the day the *New York Times* industrial index was down twelve points.

On Sunday the break was front-page news – the *New York Times* headline read: 'Stocks driven down as wave of selling engulfs market.' The *New York Times* financial editor, who along with the editor of the *Commercial and Financial Chronicle* had never wavered in his conviction that the market had gone insane, suggested that, for the moment at least: 'Wall Street seemed to see the reality of things.' The news stories featured two other observations which were to become wonderfully familiar in the next fortnight. It was said that, at the end of Saturday's trading, an exceptionally large number of margin calls went out. It was predicted that, come the following week, 'organized support' could definitely be expected for the market.

### The market falters

Monday 21st October was another poor day. Sales totalled 6,091,870, the third greatest volume in history, and hundreds of thousands who were watching the market throughout the country made a disturbing discovery. There was no way of telling what was happening. Previously on big days of the bull market the ticker had often fallen behind, and one didn't discover until well after the market closed how much richer one had become. But with a falling market things were very different. Now one might be ruined, totally and forever, and not know it. And even if one were not ruined, there was a strong tendency to imagine it. From the opening on 21st October the ticker lagged and by noon it was an hour late. Not until an hour and forty minutes after the close of the market did it record the last transaction. Every ten minutes prices of selected stocks were printed on the bond ticker, but the wide divergence between these and the prices on the tape only added to the uneasiness – and to the growing conviction that it might be best to sell.

This conviction notwithstanding, the market closed well above its low for the day – the net loss on the New York Times industrial averages was only about six points – and on Tuesday there was a further, though rather shaky, gain. Possibly some credit for this improvement should go to Wall Street's cheery seers. On Monday in New York Professor Fisher said that the declines had represented only a 'shaking out of the lunatic fringe'. He went on to explain why he felt that the prices of stocks during the boom had not caught up with their real value. Among other things, the market had not yet reflected the beneficent effects of Prohibition, which had made the American worker 'more productive and dependable'.

By Wednesday 23rd October the effect of this cheer had been dissipated. Instead of further gains there were heavy losses. The opening was quiet enough, but toward mid-morning motor accessory stocks were sold heavily, and volume began to increase throughout the list. The last hour was quite phenomenal – 2,600,000 shares changed hands at rapidly declining prices. The New York Times industrial average for the day dropped from 415 to 384, giving up all of its gains since the end of the previous June. Again the ticker was far behind, and to add to the uncertainty an ice storm in the Middle West caused widespread disruption of communications. That afternoon and evening thousands of speculators decided to get out while – as they mistakenly supposed – the getting was good. Other thousands were told they would have no choice but to get out unless they provided more collateral security for, as the day's business came to an end, an unprecedented volume of margin calls went out.

New York, October 1929. A victim of plunging stock prices tries to raise some money to meet his margin calls. The Crash brought a rude awakening from dreams of wealth

Speaking in Washington, even Professor Fisher was fractionally less optimistic. He told a meeting of bankers that 'security values in most instances were not inflated'. However, he did not weaken on the unrealized efficiencies of Prohibition. There was, however, one bit of cheer. It was everywhere predicted that, on the morrow, the market would begin to receive 'organized support'.

Thursday 24th October is the first of the days which history – such as it is on the subject – identifies with the panic of 1929. Measured by disorder, fright, and confusion, it deserves to be so regarded. 12,894,650 shares changed hands that day, most of them at prices which shattered the dreams and the hopes of those who had owned them. Of all the mysteries of the stock exchange there is none so impenetrable as why there should be a buyer for everyone who seeks to sell. 24th October 1929 showed that what is mysterious is not inevitable. Often there were no buyers, and only after wide vertical declines would anyone bid.

The morning was the terrible time. The opening was unspectacular, and for a little prices were firm. Volume, however, was large and soon prices began to sag. Once again the ticker dropped behind the market. Prices fell farther and faster, and the ticker lagged more and more. By eleven o'clock what had been a market was only a wild scramble to sell. In the crowded board rooms across the country the ticker told of a frightful collapse. But the selected quotations coming in over the bond ticker also showed that current values were far below the ancient history of the tape. The uncertainty led more and more people to try to sell. Others, no longer able to respond to margin calls, were sold. By 11.30 unqualified panic was in control.

Outside on Broad Street a weird roar could be heard. A crowd gathered and Police Commissioner Grover Whalen despatched a special police detail to Wall Street to insure the peace. A workman appeared to accomplish some routine repairs atop one of the high buildings. The multitude, assuming he was a would-be suicide, waited impatiently for him to jump. At 12.30 the visitors' gallery of the Exchange was closed on the wild scenes below.

At noon, however, things took a turn for the better. At last came the long-awaited organized support. The heads of the National City Bank, Chase, Guaranty Trust, and Bankers Trust met with Thomas W. Lamont, the senior Morgan partner, at 23 Wall Street. All quickly agreed to come to the support of the market and to pool substantial resources for this purpose. Lamont then met with reporters and said: 'There has been a little distress selling on the Stock Exchange.' He added that this passing inconvenience was 'due to a technical situation rather than any fundamental cause,' and he told the newsmen the situation was 'susceptible to betterment'.

### The bankers intervene

Meanwhile, word had reached the Exchange floor that the bankers were meeting and succour was on the way. These were the nation's most potent financiers. Prices promptly firmed and rose. Then at 1.30 Richard Whitney, widely known as a floor broker for Morgan's, walked jauntily to the post where Steel was traded and left with the specialist an order for 10,000 shares at several points above the current bids. He continued the rounds with this largesse. Confidence was wonderfully revived, and the market actually boomed upward. In the last hour the selling orders which were still flooding in turned it soft again, but the net loss for the day – about twelve points on the *New York Times* industrial averages – was far less than the day before. Some issues, Steel among them, were actually higher on the day's trading.

However, this recovery was of distant interest to the tens of thousands who had sold or been sold out during the decline and whose dreams of opulence had gone glimmering along with most of their merchantable possessions. It was eight and a half minutes past seven that night before the ticker finished recording the day's misfortunes. In the board rooms speculators who had been sold out since early morning sat silently watching the tape. The habit of months or years, however idle it had now become, could not be broken at once. Then, as the final trades were registered, they made their way out into the night.

In Wall Street itself lights blazed from every office as clerks struggled to come abreast of the day's business. Messengers and board-room boys, caught up in the excitement and untroubled by losses, went skylarking through the streets until the police arrived to quell them. Representatives of thirty-five of the largest wire houses assembled at the offices of Hornblower and Weeks and told the press on departing that the market was 'fundamentally sound' and 'technically in better condition than it has been in months'. The host firm despatched a market letter which stated that 'commencing with today's trading the market should start laying the foundation for the constructive advance which we believe will characterize 1930'.

### Weekend calm

On Friday and Saturday trading continued heavy – just under six million on Friday and over two million at the short session on Saturday. Prices, on the whole, were steady – the averages were a trifle up on Friday but slid off on Saturday. It was thought that the bankers were able to dispose of most of the securities they had acquired while shoring up the market. Not only were things better, but everyone was clear that it was the banking leaders who had made them so. They had shown both their courage and their power, and the people applauded warmly and generously. Commenting on Friday's market the *New York Times* said: 'Secure in the knowledge that the most powerful banks in the country stood ready to prevent a recurrence [of panic] the financial community relaxed its anxiety yesterday.'

From other sources came statements of reassurance and even of self-congratulation. Colonel Leonard Ayres of Cleveland thought no other country could have survived such a crash so well. Eugene M. Stevens, the president of the Continental Illinois Bank, said: 'There is nothing in the business situation to justify any nervousness'; Walter Teagle said there had been no 'fundamental change' in the oil business to justify concern; Charles M.Schwab said that the steel business had been making 'fundamental progress' toward stability and added that this 'fundamentally sound condition' was responsible for the prosperity of the industry; Samuel Vauclain, chairman of the Baldwin Locomotive Works, declared that 'fundamentals are sound'; President Hoover said that 'the fundamental business of the country, that is production and distribution of commodities, is on a sound and prosperous basis'. A Boston investment trust took space in the *Wall Street Journal* to say, 'S-T-E-A-D-Y Everybody! Calm thinking is in order. Heed the words of America's greatest bankers'. A single dissonant note, though great in portent, went completely unnoticed. Speaking in Poughkeepsie, Governor Franklin D.Roosevelt criticized the 'fever of speculation'.

On Sunday there were sermons suggesting that a certain measure of divine retribution had been visited on the republic and that it had not been entirely unmerited. It was evident, however, that almost everyone believed that this heavenly knuckle-rapping was over and that speculation could be now resumed in earnest. The papers were full of the prospects for next week's market. Stocks, it was agreed, were again cheap and accordingly there would be a heavy rush to buy. Numerous stories from the brokerage houses, some of them possibly inspired, told of a fabulous volume of buying orders which was piling up in anticipation of the opening of the market. In a concerted advertising campaign in Monday's papers, stock-market firms urged the wisdom of buying stocks promptly. On Monday 28th October the real disaster began.

### The failure of 'organized support'

Trading on Monday, though in great volume, was smaller than on the previous Thursday – 9,212,800 as compared with the nearly thirteen million. But the sustained drop in prices was far more severe. The *New York Times* industrial average was down forty-nine points for the day. General Electric was off 47½; Westinghouse, 34½; Tel. & Tel., 34. Indeed, the decline on this one day was greater than that of all the preceding week of panic. Once again a late ticker left everyone in ignorance of what was happening save that it was bad.

At 1.10 there was a momentary respite – Charles E.Mitchell was detected going into Morgan's and the news ticker carried the magic word. Steel rallied and went from 193½ to 198. But this time Richard Whitney did not appear; 'organized support' was not forthcoming. Support, organized or otherwise, could no longer contend with the wild desire to sell. The market weakened again

and in the last hour three million shares changed hands at rapidly declining prices.

The bankers assembled once again in session from 4.30 to 6.30. They were described as having a 'philosophical attitude', and they told the press that the situation 'retained hopeful features'. But there was a more important clue to what was discussed for the two hours. It was explained at the conclusion that it was no part of the bankers' purpose to maintain any particular level of prices on the market. Their operations were confined to seeing that the market was orderly – that offers would be met by bids at some price, and that 'air holes', as Mr Lamont dubbed them, would not be allowed to appear in the market. Like many lesser men, Mr Lamont and his colleagues had obviously found themselves over-committed on promises. The time had come to go short on promises. It was also chilling news. To the man who held stock on margin, disaster wore only one face and that was falling prices. He wanted to be saved from disaster. Now he must comfort himself with the knowledge that his ruin would be accomplished in an orderly and becoming manner.

Tuesday 29th October, was the most devastating day in the history of the New York stock market, and it may have been the most devastating in the history of markets. Selling began at once and in huge volume. The air holes, which the bankers were to close, opened wide. Repeatedly and in many issues there was a plethora of selling orders and no buyers at all. Once again, of course, the ticker lagged – at the close it was two and a half hours behind. By then 16,410,030 shares had been known to have been traded – more than three times the number that had once been considered a fabulously big day. (On an average good day in 1923 sales were running about three million shares.) Despite a closing rally on dividend news, the losses were again appalling. The *New York Times* industrial averages were down forty-three points, cancelling all of the huge gains of the preceding twelve months. Losses on individual issues were far greater. By the end of trading, members were near collapse from strain and fatigue. Office staffs, already near the breaking point, now had to tackle the greatest volume of transactions yet. By now, also, there was no longer quite the same certainty that things would get better. Perhaps they would go on getting worse.

### Slaughter of the well-to-do

During the preceding week, the slaughter had been of the innocents. Now it was the well-to-do and the wealthy – the men of affairs and the professionals – who were experiencing the egalitarianism long supposed to be the first fruit of avarice. Where the board rooms were crowded the week before, now they were nearly empty. The new victims had facilities for suffering in private. The bankers met at noon and again in the evening of the 29th, but there was no suggestion that they were philosophical. In truth, their prestige had been falling even more disconcertingly than the market. During the day the rumour had swept the Exchange that, of all things, the 'organized support' was busy selling stocks, and Lamont met the press after the evening session with the trying assignment of denying that this was so. It remained for Mayor James J. Walker to come up with the only constructive proposal of the day. Addressing an audience of motion picture exhibitors, he asked them to 'show pictures that will reinstate courage and hope in the hearts of the people'.

On the Exchange itself a strong feeling was developing that courage and hope might best be reinstated if the market were closed and everyone were given a breathing spell. This simple and forthright thought derived impressive further support from the fact that everyone was badly in need of sleep. The difficulty was that the announcement of the closing of the Exchange might simply worsen the panic. At noon on 29th October the issue came to a head. So as not to attract attention, the members of the governing committee left the floor in twos and threes to attend a meeting; the meeting itself was held not in the regular room but in the office of the Stock Clearing Corporation below the trading floor. As the unfortunate Richard Whitney later described the session, the air quickly became blue with tobacco smoke as the tired and nervous brokers lit cigarettes, stubbed them out, and lit fresh ones. Everyone wanted a respite from the agony. Quite a few firms needed a few hours to ascertain whether they were still solvent.

But caution was on the side of keeping the market open at least until it could be closed on a note of strength and optimism. The decision was to carry on till things improved. Again the lights blazed all night. In one brokerage house an employee fainted from exhaustion, was revived, and promptly put back to work again.

Next day those imponderable forces were at work which bring salvation just when salvation seems impossible. Volume was still enormous, but prices were much better – the *New York Times* industrial average rose thirty-one points, and individual issues made excellent gains. Possibly it was the reassurances that accomplished the miracle – in any case these were forthcoming in volume. On the evening of the 29th, Julius Klein took to the radio to remind the country that President Hoover had said that the 'fundamental business of the country' was sound and prosperous. He added: 'The main point I want to make is the fundamental soundness of [the] great mass of economic activities'. On Wednesday Wadill Catchings, the head of Goldman, Sachs, announced on returning from a western trip that general business conditions were 'unquestionably fundamentally sound'. (The same, it subsequently developed, could not unquestionably be said for all of Goldman, Sachs.) Of more importance, perhaps, from Pocantico Hills came the first public statement from John D. Rockefeller in some decades: 'Believing that fundamental conditions of the country are sound . . . my son and I have for some days been purchasing sound common stock.'

Just before the Rockefeller statement arrived things looked good enough on the Exchange so that Richard Whitney felt safe in announcing that the market would not open until noon the following day (Thursday) and that on Friday and Saturday it would stay shut. The announcement was greeted by cheers. Nerves were clearly past the breaking point. On La Salle Street in Chicago a boy exploded a

firecracker. Like wildfire the rumour spread that gangsters whose margin accounts had been closed out were shooting up the street. Several squads of police arrived to make them take their losses like honest men. In New York the body of a commission merchant was fished out of the Hudson River. The pockets contained $9.40 in change and some margin calls.

### A special lunacy

No feature of the Great Crash was more remarkable than the way it passed from climax to anticlimax to destroy again and again the hope that the worst had passed. Even on the 30th the worst was still to come, although henceforth it came more slowly. Day after day during the next two weeks prices fell with monotonous regularity. At the close of trading on 29th October the *New York Times* industrial average stood at 275. In the rally of the next two days it gained more than fifty points, but by 13th November it was down to 224 for a further net loss of fifty points.

And these levels were wonderful compared with what were to follow. On 8th July 1932 the average of the closing levels of the *Times* industrials was 58.46. This was not much more than the amount by which the average dropped on the single day of 28th October, and considerably less than a quarter of the closing values on 29th October. But by then, of course, business conditions were no longer sound.

The question inevitably arises whether a similar cycle of speculation and collapse to that of October 1929 could again occur. The simple answer is: of course! Laws have been passed to outlaw some of the more egregious behaviour which contributed to the big bull market of the 'twenties. Nothing has been done about the seminal lunacy which possesses people who see a chance of becoming rich. On the assumption that history does not repeat itself precisely, we may never again see the particular lunacy of the late 'twenties. But if we survive to suffer such things, we can undoubtedly count on some variation. The time to worry will be when important people begin to explain that it cannot happen because conditions are fundamentally sound.

*Effects of the Crash in France: unemployed waiting for free hand-outs of soup*

*Alfred Hoffman of the United Textile Workers' Union flanked by bodyguards during the textile workers strike in Elizabethton, Tennessee, 1929. The Great Depression of the 1930's began before the stock market crash, with a series of strikes in the mills*

## Federal government finances

### Surplus or deficit
Figures in million dollars

## Developments on the stock exchange

Details of business failures, personal and government expenditure, and the stock market. In column one, business failures show a steep but not overwhelming rise. Diagrams in the second column show how personal finances went into the red as a result of the Depression in the early 'thirties when income (below) had dropped by over twenty-five per cent on the 1929 level.

The government however plunged into debit shortly after the Crash, as the diagrams in the third column show; its expenditure by far outstripped receipts (below). The fourth column shows how the stock market sales rose as people tried to cash in on the capital appreciation of stock — until confidence broke, and prices and the volume of transactions plunged

## Business failures

per 10,000 concerns

| | | | | | 154 |
| | | | 133 | CLOSED | CLOSED |
| | | 122 | CLOSED | CLOSED | CLOSED |
| 109 | 104 | CLOSED | CLOSED | CLOSED | 100 |
| 1928 | 1929 | 1930 | 1931 | 1932 | 1933 |

## Personal finances

### Net saving or borrowing
Figures in dollars per head

40
20
0
-20
-40

1928   1930   1932   1934

**Surplus or deficit** scale (right): 1,000 / 500 / 0 / -500 / -1,000 / -1,500 / -2,000 / -2,500 / -3,000 / -3,500

1928   1930   1932   1934

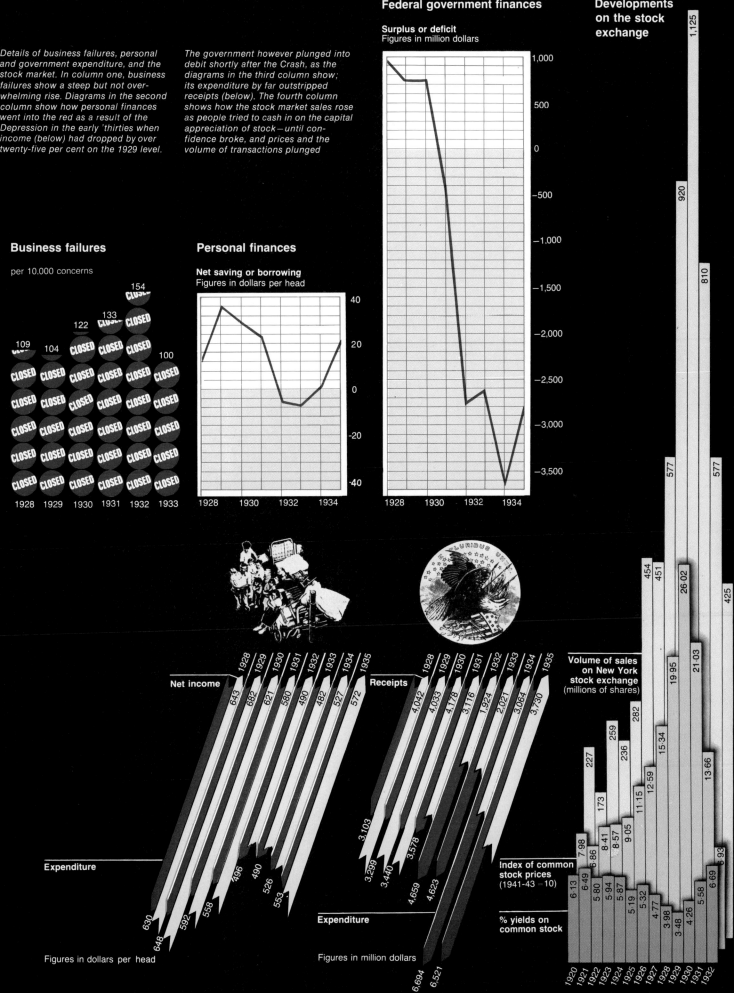

### Net income
Figures in dollars per head

| | 1928 | 1929 | 1930 | 1931 | 1932 | 1933 | 1934 | 1935 |
| Net income | 643 | 682 | 621 | 580 | 490 | 482 | 527 | 572 |
| Expenditure | 630 | 648 | 592 | 558 | 496 | 490 | 526 | 553 |

### Receipts
Figures in million dollars

| | 1928 | 1929 | 1930 | 1931 | 1932 | 1933 | 1934 | 1935 |
| Receipts | 4,042 | 4,033 | 4,178 | 3,116 | 1,924 | 2,021 | 3,064 | 3,730 |
| Expenditure | 3,103 | 3,299 | 3,440 | 3,578 | 4,659 | 4,623 | 6,694 | 6,521 |

### Volume of sales on New York stock exchange
(millions of shares)

### Index of common stock prices
(1941-43 = 10)

### % yields on common stock

| Year | Volume of sales | Index | % yields |
| 1920 | 227 | 7·98 | 6·13 |
| 1921 | 173 | 6·86 | 6·49 |
| 1922 | 259 | 8·41 | 5·80 |
| 1923 | 236 | 8·57 | 5·94 |
| 1924 | 282 | 9·05 | 5·87 |
| 1925 | 454 | 11·15 | 5·19 |
| 1926 | 451 | 12·59 | 5·32 |
| 1927 | 577 | 15·34 | 4·77 |
| 1928 | 920 | 19·95 | 3·98 |
| 1929 | 1,125 | 26·02 | 3·48 |
| 1930 | 810 | 21·03 | 4·26 |
| 1931 | 577 | 13·66 | 5·58 |
| 1932 | 425 | 6·93 | 6·69 |

# The New Deal

To those Americans who lived through it, the New Deal was one of the epics of history. To the great majority, then and since, it was a saga in which the new Beowulf, the new Ulysses, FDR, fared forth and slew all dragons, including, at last, the greatest Grendel of all, Nazism; and died, fitly, at the moment of victory. The essence of the New Deal was to be found in its chief's many eloquent utterances, like that which gave his saga its name: 'I pledge you, I pledge myself, to a new deal for the American people', or that from his first inaugural address: 'Let me assert my firm belief that the only thing we have to fear is fear itself. . . . The money changers have fled from their high seats in the temple of our civilization. We may now restore that temple to the ancient truths.'

One of his innumerable admirers summed it up: 'Roosevelt is the only President who has ever cared for people like us.' The poor took heart with his pledge.

The money changers and other supporters of the old deal took a very different view. To them, Roosevelt was a dangerous revolutionary who cut at the root of American liberty, justice, and sacred property; a dictator who overthrew the ancient Constitution; a persistent humbug and oath-breaker, who promised to keep the United States government solvent, the nation at peace, and did neither. Forgetting the extent to which big business had discredited itself in the Crash, they blamed Roosevelt for the disrepute into which Wall Street had fallen. They reviled him as a traitor to his class, and ostracized his supporters ('I still like Roosevelt, and think he's a champ; that's why the lady is a tramp!'). To them the New Deal was at best a fraud, at worst a conspiracy, probably Bolshevik-inspired.

Sober history cannot wholly endorse either of these apocalyptic visions, though it must take account of them, since they figured largely in the life and politics of the 'thirties, and figure now in folk memory. If nothing else, they are evidence of the intense emotional importance of the New Deal to its contemporaries. Finally, even the driest record will have to concede that this particular chapter in the history of the American people was indeed dominated by the figure of FDR. For good and ill his personality reached out to mark all parts and aspects of society indelibly.

*Left:* Roosevelt shaking hands with a West Virginian miner during his presidential campaign. He convinced millions of Americans reduced to misery by the Depression that he could and would do something to help them. *Above:* German cartoon—Roosevelt fighting the dragon of Prohibition. At the 1932 Democratic convention this was a bigger issue than the Depression. *Far left:* Roosevelt gives the victory sign, 1937—a symbol of the New Deal

"AND SO HE MAKES MUSIC WHEREVER HE GOES!"

## HOOVER CONCEDES DEFEAT

On the day of his inauguration—4th March 1933—he faced a crisis as grave as that which had faced Lincoln in 1861. That morning the banks of Chicago and New York—twin centres of American capitalism—closed their doors, following the example set during the previous month by all the other banks in the country. Badly-organized, the banking system had totally collapsed under the stress of withdrawals by panic-stricken depositors. Between twelve and fifteen million workers were unemployed—a quarter of the national labour force. Insurrection simmered throughout the farming regions, where farmers had seen the market prices of their produce fall by half and their incomes by two-thirds in three years, while the banks, desperate to save something from the impending wreck, foreclosed on farm mortgages far and wide. Industrial production was only working at some forty per cent of its potential. The machinery of relief (administered by states, cities, and private charity) had broken down, and starvation stalked the land. Many thought that revolution was imminent.

Hoover had asserted repeatedly that the root problem was one of confidence in the system, but he had proved unable to solve it. Roosevelt, the incarnation of abounding courage, gaiety, and energy, tackled it with superb effect from the first. 'We have nothing to fear but fear itself.' Before a week was out, the first half million letters of what proved, before long, to be a perpetual avalanche had descended on the White House, passionately thanking the President for a renewal of hope. But Roosevelt, again unlike Hoover, was not content to rely solely, or even mainly, on words. A year previously he had presciently stated 'the country needs, and, unless I mistake its temper, the country demands, bold, persistent experimentation.' Now he provided it. Congress was called into special session, lasting a now legendary hundred days, and, with a speed of which it had never before shown itself capable, and which it has seldom achieved since, whirled into law thirteen major measures, including an Emergency Banking Act, a Federal Relief Emergency Act, a National Industrial Recovery Act, an Agricultural Adjustment Act, an Emergency Farm Mortgage Act, and, to cheer everyone up, the end of Prohibition ('I think this would be a good time for beer,' said the President). Using to the hilt the powers given him under these laws Roosevelt proceeded to establish numerous executive agencies to carry out the programmes of rescue. There was the National

*Three cartoons from short-lived left-wing American periodical* Americana. **Top:** *Henry Morgenthau, Secretary of the Treasury, seen as 'on the fiddle' in government and business.* **Centre:** *'I must admit—he certainly can take it!' says Hoover of Roosevelt, under violent attack for New Deal policies.* **Bottom:** *Roosevelt forces big business through the eye of the New Deal needle, held up by Hugh 'Ironpants' Johnson, head of the National Recovery Administration*

Recovery Administration, the Agricultural Adjustment Administration, the Public Works Administration, the Civilian Conservation Corps, which was to take two and a half million jobless boys off the city streets to carry out huge afforestation programmes, and the Tennessee Valley Authority, which redeemed a vast area of ruined rural America while generating cheap electrical power from federally-built and operated dams.

The rescue work was successful; but the New Dealers, veterans of Theodore 'Teddy' Roosevelt's Progressivism as well as of Woodrow Wilson's New Freedom, seized the chance to push through reforms, many of which had been waiting for a generation. The banking system was reorganized, and control of the nation's financial destiny shifted from Wall Street to Washington. The farm programme of Henry Wallace, Secretary of Agriculture, was the product of a lifetime's study of agricultural problems, and led, though admittedly via many ups and downs, to the present permanent prosperity of the farm belt. By 1936 a system of federally-sponsored unemployment insurance and old age pensions had brought America into line with Europe; in 1938 a minimum wage and maximum hours law reinforced this accomplishment. The right of labour to its own organizations and to collective bargaining was finally established, though it took a series of bitter strikes for all its gains to be realized. A Securities and Exchange Commission cleaned up and supervised the stock market. Little was done directly for the negro, but much for the poor, among whom most negroes were counted. And though the New Deal did not, of itself, permanently solve America's worst economic problem, it did materially lessen it. The number of unemployed shrank by at least five million between 1933 and 1937; even the recession of the latter year did not entirely undo this good work.

### A drama of incompetence
The 1937 recession (touched off in part by the Administration's mistaken belief that inflation was becoming a danger) does, however, confront us with the limits of the New Deal's achievement. At times it can seem a drama of incompetence, played out against a back-drop of tragedy. It did not deserve the attacks of its selfish and stupid critics, mostly very rich men, who, it has been perceptively suggested, were in a condition of psychological shock at having been hurled from their honoured positions as priests of success. Nobody listened to them any more, and they could not bear it. Their state of mind, and the reasons for it, are brilliantly if unconsciously conveyed in the words of an advertising man who in 1934 remarked, apropos the troops of eager New Deal intellectuals who were remodelling the structure of the American economy, 'the day will come when, compared to the word "professor", the word "banker" will be a term of endearment'. But the professors themselves could not, as it turned out, provide complete solutions to the underlying problems. According to the most

# Depression and New Deal:
## facts and figures

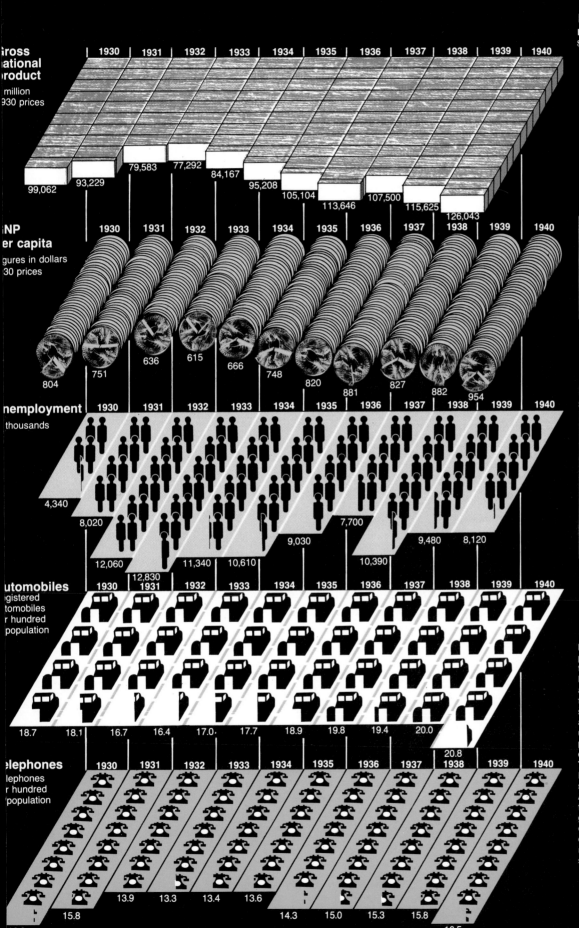

**Gross national product**

$ million
1930 prices

| 1930 | 1931 | 1932 | 1933 | 1934 | 1935 | 1936 | 1937 | 1938 | 1939 | 1940 |
|------|------|------|------|------|------|------|------|------|------|------|
| 99,062 | 93,229 | 79,583 | 77,292 | 84,167 | 95,208 | 105,104 | 113,646 | 107,500 | 115,625 | 126,043 |

**GNP per capita**

figures in dollars
1930 prices

| 1930 | 1931 | 1932 | 1933 | 1934 | 1935 | 1936 | 1937 | 1938 | 1939 | 1940 |
|------|------|------|------|------|------|------|------|------|------|------|
| 804 | 751 | 636 | 615 | 666 | 748 | 820 | 881 | 827 | 882 | 954 |

**Unemployment**

thousands

| 1930 | 1931 | 1932 | 1933 | 1934 | 1935 | 1936 | 1937 | 1938 | 1939 | 1940 |
|------|------|------|------|------|------|------|------|------|------|------|
| 4,340 | 8,020 | 12,060 | 12,830 | 11,340 | 10,610 | 9,030 | 7,700 | 10,390 | 9,480 | 8,120 |

**Automobiles**

registered automobiles per hundred population

| 1930 | 1931 | 1932 | 1933 | 1934 | 1935 | 1936 | 1937 | 1938 | 1939 | 1940 |
|------|------|------|------|------|------|------|------|------|------|------|
| 18.7 | 18.1 | 16.7 | 16.4 | 17.0 | 17.7 | 18.9 | 19.8 | 19.4 | 20.0 | 20.8 |

**Telephones**

telephones per hundred population

| 1930 | 1931 | 1932 | 1933 | 1934 | 1935 | 1936 | 1937 | 1938 | 1939 | 1940 |
|------|------|------|------|------|------|------|------|------|------|------|
| 16.3 | 15.8 | 13.9 | 13.3 | 13.4 | 13.6 | 14.3 | 15.0 | 15.3 | 15.8 | 16.5 |

## Federal government receipts and expenditure

$ thousand million

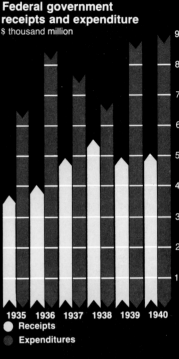

| 1935 | 1936 | 1937 | 1938 | 1939 | 1940 |

● Receipts
● Expenditures

## Federal government debt

$ thousand million

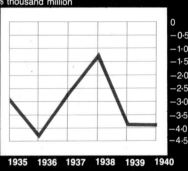

| 1935 | 1936 | 1937 | 1938 | 1939 | 1940 |

Diagrams show the effects of the Depression and the New Deal policies on the United States economy, 1930-40. **Left:** The New Deal raised both overall and individual production (top). Despite this, unemployment (centre) remained staggeringly high by modern standards, averaging some ten million annually until the end of the decade, when people were materially better off than ever before (below)

**Top and above:** The cost of the New Deal to the government. Government spending went some way to pulling America out of the Depression, but the fear of inflation in 1937 sparked off government deflationary measures and caused the recession of 1938. It was only the level of spending demanded by rearmament which finally brought a solid basis of prosperity after 1940.

cautious estimates, unemployment never ran at less than ten per cent of the labour force from 1933 to 1941; in most years it was far higher (nineteen per cent in 1938, for example). More open-minded than the doctrinaire businessmen of whom Herbert Hoover was such a perfect type, there were yet limits to the New Dealers' vision. The situation is summed up in Frances Perkins's grimly humorous tale, according to which, on their meeting in 1934, Roosevelt found J.M.Keynes too much of a mathematician, while Keynes found the President disappointingly illiterate in economics.

Roosevelt and many of those closest to him (notably Henry Morgenthau, his Secretary of the Treasury) were intellectually incapable of accepting the Keynesian idea of spending their way out of the Depression. Balancing the budget might be postponed, they felt, if it was pressingly necessary to do something for the poor; but balanced one day it would have to be, if not next year then the year after. The notion of deficit financing went flat against the grain of their common sense. So public expenditure, astronomical though it seemed, never rose high enough to accomplish the New Deal's main task and end the hard times. Insignificant funds were pumped into the construction industry, for example, although its decline had been one of the major causes of the Crash.

But Roosevelt's attachment to the superstition of a balanced budget, and his consequent inability to end unemployment, low prices, and the under-utilization of resources, were not merely children of economic backwardness. After all, in 1938 a theoretically anti-spending, anti-Roosevelt Congress made little difficulty about giving approval to the Administration's proposals for a 3,750 million-dollar emergency spending programme, and it was always far more rigid in its principles than the President, who consistently put the interests of what he called 'one-third of a nation ill-housed, ill-clad, ill-nourished' above petty consistency. Roosevelt refused to adopt a policy of deficit financing because any such whole-hog course went against his whole manner of government. During the early New Deal he had gained strength by refusing to commit himself wholly to any single programme or philosophy of government. At a time when even the experts, however cocksure, were not certain of their way, this was the course

*Left: 1. One of the friendly press conferences which were a feature of Roosevelt's presidency. Here, in August 1935, he jokes with newspaper correspondents in his garden. 2. 'Esquire's' comment on Roosevelt's fireside chats on the radio: 'Aw, gee, gran'pop, you're running over into Ed Wynn's program!' Ed Wynn was a popular comedian. 3. German view of American economy, 1934: US businessman says, 'Now we hold the world record in strikes, too.' Growing union militancy was threatening the authority of the bosses. 4. Leader of California cotton strike in 1938 displays his union card.*
*Right: Farm striker, Pennsylvania, 1938*

of wisdom. But by 1937 much more was known: the beneficial effect on the economy of large expenditures on public works was very evident. FDR should have derived a single policy from this experience, and stuck to it. He did not, being temperamentally averse to committing himself to one course—whether old-fashioned or progressive—and one set of advisers. In short, his addiction to 'bold and persistent experimentation' had become, by his second term, almost self-defeating.

### A bankrupt foreign policy

A similar pattern can be detected in his foreign policy. The failure of New Deal diplomacy, indeed, was almost unrelieved, whereas its domestic successes outweighed its shortcomings. By the familiar bitter humour of history the greater and later disaster—the Second World War—ended the Depression by forcing what amounted to a Keynesian solution of the economic difficulty. Nothing ever similarly redeemed the bankruptcy of United States

foreign policy. It did, it is true, evolve the so-called Good Neighbour Policy, by which the USA (temporarily, as it turned out) pledged itself not to impose its policies by force on its American neighbours. Secretary of State Cordell Hull, an old-style Wilsonian, pursued this design enthusiastically, with the warm support of his President, who was at heart of the same persuasion. But in no department of life was FDR's behaviour ever less than infinitely intricate; and if the Good Neighbour Policy reflected his simplicity, he more than made up by displaying, in all other diplomatic spheres, the full scope of his complexities.

It is true that he was faced with a highly intractable public opinion and some very recalcitrant politicians. For years he could make no headway against the general belief that intervention in the Great War had been a mistake. The tide of isolationism which flowed from this conviction reached its crest in the Nye Committee of 1934, which purported to show that America had fought because of a financiers' conspiracy, and in the Neutrality Acts of 1935 and 1937. The threat of renewed European conflict at first greatly strengthened Congress's determination to tie the President's hands. The illusion that America could steer clear of world war, and the determination that it should, remained extremely powerful until Pearl Harbour. Until that event Roosevelt found it extremely difficult to get the least concession to a more realistic view out of Congress.

Nor was Roosevelt's first major international démarche such a disaster as it seemed at the time. It had been part of Hoover's case that the Depression arose largely from causes outside the United States (and therefore, of course, outside his control). In accordance with this notion, he had earnestly sought to find a means of international co-operation to defeat the slump. The high point of this quest was to have been the London Economic Conference of 1933.

The 'brain trusters' did not accept this international theory of the Depression; they were rightly convinced that its roots were American, and consequently they fiercely resisted any plan likely to encumber America's attempts at recovery with foreign commitments. The President turned out to be the most intransigent economic nationalist of all. He sent a message to the conference announcing, in strong language, his refusal either to countenance an agreement to lower and co-ordinate tariffs, or to allow the conference to regulate international monetary relations. America must, at all costs, preserve the right to work out her own salvation, and, especially, her right to raise her own domestic prices—a measure which the 'brain trusters' were convinced was essential for recovery. This move was denounced at the time by everybody except Keynes. It wrecked the conference and implied the exclusion of America from the feeble attempts at international co-operation which marked the next stage of the slither into war. It is not clear that this mattered, and Keynes and the President were, on the economic issue, probably right. But there is no denying that the manner of his bombshell was a sign that Roosevelt was primarily thinking of domestic politics. It affronted all the leading friendly statesmen in the world, but helped to bolster the average American's belief that his country was in command of its destinies again; and that was undoubtedly Roosevelt's major purpose throughout 1933.

But in his second term this understandable respect for domestic priorities became pernicious. From time to time the President tried to warn his countrymen that they could not play ostrich forever. But when their strong resentment at this message became clear, he always backed down. And after his breach with Congress in 1938 he became not merely cautious, but craven. He was a Wilsonian by principle, and had early announced his intention of being a preaching President, like his cousin Theodore; but in the late 'thirties this mixture lost all dignity, as FDR hurled ineffective sermons against wickedness at the dictators, while making it plain that words would not be followed up by deeds. Not until 1940 did he nail his colours to the mast; and by then Hitler had done far more to educate the Americans than their President had ever tried.

### Roosevelt and the Supreme Court

If, domestically and diplomatically, the second term was far less successful than the first, the President must take some of the blame. The surliness on Capitol Hill was in large measure his own doing. He had been re-elected in 1936 by what was, up to that time, the largest majority of the popular vote in American history (27,476,673 to his opponent's 16,679,583) and carried every state save Vermont and Maine. His congressional majority swelled to record heights. Little wonder that he felt able to settle accounts with his enemies; and chief among them stood the nine justices of the Supreme Court—or at least the majority of them.

For the court, using recklessly a power that in the long run it could only vindicate by restraint, had struck down one after another of the statutes of the early New Deal. The National Industrial Recovery Act, the Agricultural Adjustment Act, the Bituminous Coal Conservation Act, the Municipal Bankruptcy Act, the New York State Minimum Wage Law for Women, the Frazier-Lemke Act (a measure for the relief of farm mortgagers) and a federal pensions law for railroad employees—all had been invalidated. The court did its best to discredit the Securities and Exchange Commission; it held its hand only over the Tennessee Valley Authority and monetary gold policy.

Such a challenge could not be overlooked, and in February 1937 Roosevelt launched his counterattack. He asked Congress for a law enabling the President to add justices to the court, up to six in number, if any justice of more than ten years' standing refused to retire at seventy. This proposal was eventually defeated ignominiously.

*Punch cartoon of 1937 sees Roosevelt on the roundabout of success—cheered on by the public—making unfair fun of the Supreme Court*

Roosevelt's failure was in large measure tactical. But it seems likely that even had he been less maladroit than he was, he would have been defeated. As Mr Dooley long ago remarked, the Supreme Court follows the election returns. Its majority was re-constituting itself on a pro-New Deal basis even before the President's intervention. By the summer the change had become manifest, and the pressing need for the so-called court-packing plan had disappeared. Roosevelt would not, at first, admit this, so his loss of face was even more complete than it need have been. By the autumn he was forced to recognize that in the course of the battle he had lost a large part of his influence with Congress. He had affronted the passionate conservatism that characterizes most Americans where their Constitution is concerned, and paid this crippling penalty.

Such are the difficulties of democratic leadership. But they cannot be allowed to dominate the New Deal picture or to determine our estimate of Roosevelt's success. In 1936 he proclaimed that 'to some generations much is given. Of other generations much is expected. This generation has a rendezvous with destiny'. When they reached that rendezvous, thanks to Roosevelt, the Americans were ready. He had restored, not only a large measure of the republic's prosperity, but all of its self-confidence. A deeply conservative, if always humane man, he had seen his task as, among other things, the rescue of the American middle way in an age of fascism and Communism; and he had seen that the presidency was an effective means to that end. He was the first fully modern President. He used the great crises which swept him into office to accustom the American people to look first to the White House for the solution of their political problems. The torrential activity of his first term greatly assisted this aim, and he furthered it with endless supplementary ingenuity. He was always news, always on the front pages of the newspapers whose reporters he cultivated at his twice-weekly press confer-

ences. In his 'fireside chats' on the radio he projected himself and his message into millions of homes. Most years, until the war, he made extensive tours through America, so that hundreds of thousands saw for themselves the big smile, the jauntily-cocked cigarette-holder, the pince-nez, straight nose, and jutting jaw made familiar by photographs and cartoons. During his presidency the legislative initiative passed irretrievably from the Capitol to the White House, and the Supreme Court fight, though at terrible cost to Roosevelt personally, re-established the constitutional convention that the Supreme Court must exercise judicial restraint, and not, for light causes, invalidate laws passed by Congress and President.

It is possible that any President elected in 1932—even Hoover, even a conservative Democrat—would have been forced, as Roosevelt was forced, into more or less appropriate remedies for the country's ills, and that, even had the Japanese left Pearl Harbour alone, politicians would eventually have caught up with the art of economics, and permitted the end of the Depression. If so, Roosevelt must be seen chiefly as an accelerator, for it is impossible to imagine any other American politician of his generation doing so much, so swiftly. But such observations would have seemed beside the point to the 'forgotten man' whom Roosevelt remembered. He suffered through eleven years of mass unemployment, not to mention a vast complexity of other social and political ills. He knew the profound humiliation of selling apples on the sidewalk, or of asking, in the words of that most depressing of all hit songs, 'Brother, can you spare a dime?' (Even in 1933 ten cents bought very little.) He would not have been comforted by suggestions that all would be well in the long run. In the long run we are all dead. The Great Depression may in the end come to seem the aberration of an age that knew not Keynes, insignificant beside the nuclear epoch, not at all the world-shattering thing men thought it at the time. Historians may amuse themselves by putting it 'into perspective' against the long vista of the USA's ever-mounting wealth and power, or the more sinister tale of American violence and intolerance. True understanding will scarcely be fostered by such exercises. To the men and women who endured it, the Depression was the most dreadful experience they were ever to know. Yet they paid triple sacrifice: on the battlefield, on the dole, and again in war. Roosevelt inspired them at last to hope that sacrifice was not in vain. That is the true measure of what the New Deal meant, and what it achieved.

*Above right: Billboard on Californian highway, about 1936, part of a national advertising campaign designed to help business out of the Depression. Below right: Drillers in action on Fort London Dam, Tennessee, one of the achievements of the Tennessee Valley Authority. Below far right: The Watts Bar Dam under construction on the Tennessee River, another TVA project*

# WORLD'S HIGHEST STANDARD OF LIVING

There's no way like the American Way

The use of this Poster Panel donated by Foster and Kleiser Company

# John Maynard Keynes

John Maynard Keynes (1884–1946) was one of the few men who understood something of the causes of the Depression which plagued Europe for almost all the inter-war years. He was therefore one of the very greatest of economists. But he was more than this, for as a prolific writer and a controversialist he became a major public figure; and one admirer suggested that future historians will know the mid-20th century as the 'Keynesian Period'.

Keynes taught economics at Cambridge, served in the Treasury during both world wars and was created Baron Keynes in 1942. His significance can only be understood against the economic conditions of the inter-war years, those troubled times during which Keynes produced his major work. Throughout the period the world economy was sick. The stability and prosperity of pre-war days receded further and further as statesmen wrestled with problems which they quite simply did not understand.

During the 1920's there was an uneasy patchwork of prosperity and depression. Great Britain, especially, suffered at this time because her major industries in the north of England, in Scotland, and in South Wales were in extreme difficulties. By contrast, America was prosperous, but few could see on what slender foundations this was based. Then, in the early 1930's, came the most catastrophic and widespread depression ever known. It engulfed nearly every country in the world. Banks shut their doors, businesses failed, production contracted, foreign trade shrank, the dole queues lengthened. The most obvious symptom of the economic malaise was unemployment. In Great Britain the number without work hardly dropped below one in ten throughout the inter-war years, and at the height of the Slump more than one in five had no job. In other countries, for example the United States, Germany, and Australia, the situation was even worse.

What help could the harassed politicians receive from economists and financial experts? What remedies were available for the pressing economic ills? Incredibly, the accepted economic doctrines were powerless. Economic science was based on out-of-date assumptions, and in the face of 20th-century problems it was irrelevant. In particular, the 'classical economists', as Keynes called them, had no answer to the unemployment problem. According to their theories unemployment should lead to falling wages and lower costs of production; in turn this would cause greater demand for the products of industry with consequent higher investment and employment. Thus the inexorable working of supply and demand, the iron law of the market place, would solve the problem. The government should not interfere. It should balance its budget and it should not spend money on public works to create employment (for this would simply divert funds from the private to the public sector and make no difference to total employment). Left to itself, the economy would always adjust to a situation of full employment.

But it so obviously did not; unemployment and unused industrial capacity became a permanent feature of life in the 1920's and 1930's. It was the genius of Keynes to tackle this dilemma successfully in a number of pioneering books. In the process he demolished the old orthodox economics and replaced it with a new system of economic theory. Keynes's theories dealt with the real world, a world in which trade union pressure might check wage reductions, in which tariffs might prevent the full working of international competition. In short, Keynes dealt with those institutional rigidities in economic life which a previous generation of economists had largely ignored.

Keynes was able to demonstrate theoretically how it was indeed possible to reach a situation of permanent unemployment, and, most important, he was able to draw policy conclusions from his analysis. Thus, it was due largely to the work of Keynes that economists could at last help statesmen to

*John Maynard Keynes (1924). He described his own writings as 'the croakings of a Cassandra, who could never influence the course of events in time'. But after the Second World War it was seen that he had diagnosed and offered a cure for that terrible economic illness, Depression*

come to grips with the problem of depression. The 'Keynesian Revolution' made economic theory once more a relevant and significant weapon in the fight against economic stagnation and decline.

For Keynes, the roots of depression lay in inadequate private demand. To create demand the people had to be given the means to spend. One conclusion to be drawn was that the dole ought not to be considered as purely a debit on the budget to be kept to a minimum but as the means by which demand could grow and stimulate supply. Moreover, a small demand meant that not enough would be invested to produce the quantity of goods needed to ensure full employment. Governments should therefore encourage more investment by lowering interest rates (a 'cheap money' policy) and they should also undertake an extensive programme of public works which would provide employment and generate greater demand for the products of industry. In this way a depression could be counteracted by a combination of both monetary policy and government spending. Significantly, Keynes titled his most important book *The General Theory of Employment, Interest and Money*. It was published in 1936.

The 'Keynesian Revolution' was therefore a revolution of theory and policy. At a time when the capitalist world appeared to be crumbling, Keynes gave it a blueprint for survival. The gulf between Keynes's proposals and the old laissez-faire tradition was enormous. Instead of government withdrawal, Keynes called for active government participation in economic life. Absurdly, some contemporaries thought this was dangerous socialism, and Roosevelt's New Deal policies, which were very much in line with Keynes's thinking, aroused similar fears among many people. In fact, Keynes was the apologist of a mixed economy, in which free enterprise co-existed with strong government activity.

Yet Keynes's message went largely unheeded before the Second World War. Many traditional economists and government officials opposed his ideas, and these theories have been a matter for keen debate and controversy ever since. But if the details of Keynes's analysis are still disputed, there can be no doubt about the importance of his work. If the world is now able to avoid the type of economic catastrophe that took place in the 1930's, and if governments can now pursue policies of full employment, this is due in no small measure to Keynes, who cut through the web of traditional economics, and helped us to understand the workings of the modern economy.

# Nazi Propaganda

It would be an unjustified simplification to identify National Socialist propaganda exclusively with Dr Joseph Goebbels, or vice versa. Goebbels was his master's voice, no more no less, though on occasions his voice was infinitely more cultivated, more articulate than Hitler's. Hitler's main gift lay in being able to project his personal mission: giving vent to the pent-up frustrations of his generation. That level the crippled Goebbels never reached. He could rouse the masses into hysteria, but he lacked Hitler's ability to drive them into action.

Goebbels' early tactics, after he had been appointed *Gauleiter* (Nazi regional supervisor) of Berlin late in 1926, followed closely the pattern set by Hitler. As Hitler had found in Munich, to conquer the city he had first of all to conquer the street; this meant provoking instant militant opposition from the Communists and the resulting clashes with them ensured the necessary free publicity for the Nazis, while at the same time drawing the attention of the 'respectable' middle classes to the existence of a party which in spite of its rowdyism was 'one of us' rather than the 'Reds'.

Though in a general sense Goebbels' adoption of Hitler's tactics proved their value, personally he found their appeals to the middle classes not always to his liking. Nor did Goebbels share Hitler's ideologically and pseudo-scientifically motivated anti-Semitism. When it proved wise and opportune to fall in with his master's wishes he did so, while at the same time the Jew was an ideal scapegoat to symbolize a bourgeois capitalist society he hated.

Like Hitler in his early days in Munich, Goebbels in Berlin had his Stormtroopers march provocatively through Berlin's industrial 'Red' north. The resulting violence between Nazis and Communists supplied him with that publicity in Berlin's press which Goebbels' own paper *Der Angriff* (The Attack) could as yet not adequately provide. Finally the murder of Horst Wessel, one of his Stormtroopers, and later that of Herbert Norkus, a Hitler Youth in his early teens, by Communists, gave to Goebbels the martyrs he needed and occasions for indulgence in impassioned semi-religious oratory. Horst Wessel, of course, was also the 'poet' of the rabble-rousing song which for twelve years was to be Germany's second national anthem. He became the sacrificial symbol of the Nazi movement with its emphasis upon national integration, upon the creation of a classless national community, the *Volksgemeinschaft,* a concept rooted deeply in German romantic thought.

*Left: German cartoon of 1933 sarcastically puts Hitler in lyrical setting for a spring-time address—in contrast to the violent nature of his message. Right: Nazi poster couples portrait of Bach with the slogan 'Cultivate German music at home'. At first, Nazi radio stressed German* kultur; *later propaganda was mixed with lighter entertainment*

## Building up the Party

Within a matter of months Goebbels succeeded in doubling Berlin's Party membership and in having it banned for eleven months for its strong-arm methods. This diverted his main efforts towards improving his paper which, within a year of his arrival in Berlin, began to pay for itself. Meanwhile Nazi membership continued to grow. In July 1927 the German railways had to lay on a special train for Berlin's Stormtroopers (officially forbidden and therefore out of uniform) to be transported to the Third Party Day of the NSDAP (Nazi Party) at Nuremberg. When they returned from the rally in full uniform Berlin's police offered additional publicity by arresting them *en masse* and transporting them in a convoy of open lorries, its passengers roaring Nazi songs, across the city, to the prison at Berlin's Alexanderplatz. By 31st March 1928 the ban was lifted and in the elections two months later, of 810,000 German voters casting their vote for the NSDAP, 39,000 were Berliners and one of the twelve Nazi members elected to the Reichstag was Goebbels himself.

The onset of the Depression late in 1929 radicalized German politics to a degree which could be compared only with the radical extremism the threat of revolution had brought to a number of German regions between 1919 and 1923. The landslide in favour of the Nazis in the elections of 1932 demonstrated the process of the erosion of the democratic parties at the centre, benefiting the extremes of both Right and Left. Hitler and his Munich entourage opened their second headquarters in Berlin. Whereas between 1926 and 1930 Goebbels had been basking in his own political glory, he was now gradually relegated to the position of just one of the more important luminaries in the Nazi firmament. In spite of his appointment by Hitler as chief of Nazi propaganda throughout Germany, Goebbels from now on had to compete with serious rivals: the Nazi press chief and later government spokesman Dr Otto Dietrich, and the shrewd commercial operator of the Nazi publishing house, the *Eher Verlag,*

Max Amann. Rivalries between these men were endemic throughout the twelve years of Hitler's rule and effectively restricted Goebbels' direct and personal control of the German press until late in the war. In spite of having married in Berlin a leading socialite divorcee to whom Hitler took a great personal liking, he found himself eclipsed by personalities like Göring and he did not regain popular prominence until after Germany's defeat at Stalingrad.

Still, two months after Hitler's assumption of power, Goebbels' running of the 1933 March elections amply demonstrated his propagandist talents. The Soviet Union had already used the radio as a political instrument, but it was Goebbels who was to use it as his special weapon. As in Germany broadcasting had always been subject to some degree of government control, Goebbels now systematically put Germany's broadcasting stations under Nazi control, purging those unwilling to comply with his directives and replacing them with his own men. Moreover, having discovered the political uses of the radio, he proved himself a superb practitioner in the art of political broadcasting. To be gripped by Hitler's oratory one really had to experience it at first hand. Over the radio Hitler's projection of his messianic mission frequently failed to come across. Goebbels, on the other hand, fascinated his audience by his stylistic brilliance, which yet retained a simplicity that made what he said understandable to all. Most important of all, he possessed a sense of humour which Hitler so lacked.

Shortly after the election of March 1933 Hitler decided to create a Ministry for Popular Enlightenment and Propaganda with Goebbels at its head. Within a space of eighteen months Goebbels centralized and controlled the main media capable of influencing public opinion: Party propaganda, broadcasting, films, theatre, and music.

Over the next six years by the versatile use of these instruments he created a cult from which Hitler the chancellor finally emerged as the Führer of Germany. It was due to Goebbels' efforts that—especially during the war—the majority of the German people, when dissatisfied with many aspects of the Nazi regime, made a clear and conscious distinction between 'the Party gang' and the Führer, a distinction which retained its currency almost to the last minute of Hitler's Germany.

## Master of the media

Three measures in particular enabled Goebbels to subject the German press to the direct control of the Nazi government. Firstly, he amalgamated the various German news agencies into one official German News Bureau, the DNB, and thus established a news monopoly. Secondly, by the promulgation of a law in October 1933 journalists were 'relieved of their responsibilities' towards their respective publishers. A German journalist henceforth was directly responsible to the state. The third measure was Goebbels' daily 'press conference' for German editors at the ministry of propaganda, introduced during the summer of 1933. These conferences were preceded daily by departmental conferences headed by Goebbels in which the news topics and the attitude to be taken to them was determined. Finally at the 'press conference' Germany's journalists were informed precisely what to take on each respective issue. Contravention of the propaganda ministry's directives could be prosecuted with the aid of a host of paragraphs of the German criminal law, culminating in a prosecution for treason.

While in the sector of the German press Goebbels' personal control was limited by the existence of Dietrich and Amann, in the realm of broadcasting Goebbels was sole master and director. As later there was to be a *Volkswagen* so now there was to

be a *Volksempfänger,* the people's radio receiver. Simple in design, its capacity was not restricted to the reception of German stations only. As a result between 1933 and 1939 wireless ownership in Germany quadrupled.

German radio programmes during 1933 and 1934 were heavily dominated by a mixture of Nazi propaganda and German *Kultur,* much at the expense of light entertainment. But as soon as Goebbels realized that even a German audience can get more than its fill of Beethoven, Wagner, and 'blood and soil' poetry, he was quick to reverse this policy by mixing indirect propaganda with popular entertainment and ignored the protests from vociferous National Socialist 'purists'. Nazi propaganda was not restricted to Germany only. In 1933 there was one German short-wave station broadcasting to regions outside Germany. Ten years later the number had increased to 130 stations broadcasting daily 279 news-bulletins in as many as fifty-three different languages.

Goebbels followed a similar course in his other exclusive domain: the German film industry. After an initial spate of pure propaganda films Goebbels again directed the industry's main effort towards the production of films offering light entertainment. For propaganda purposes the indirect rather than the direct approach was preferred. Propaganda films like the anti-British *Ohm Krüger,* the anti-Semitic *Jud Süss,* morale-sustaining efforts like *The Great King,* or *Kolberg,* or the pro-euthanasia film *Ich klage an* (I accuse) were exceptions rather than the rule. Goebbels himself preferred Emil Jannings in *The Blue Angel* to his role in *Ohm Krüger.*

That direct propaganda could also backfire was shown by the public response to *Ich klage an.* A good example is a diary entry of the present writer's brother when he was barely seventeen years old:

'This film portrays everything very

nicely. But reality is bound to look different. And who knows how far and how wide this kind of ascension can be extended, particularly when sanctioned by the law!'

This diary entry by a boy who was to be killed in action less than three years later clearly shows that not everything was received uncritically, and the public opinion reports of Himmler's Security Service (SD) provide abundant evidence that however wide the support for euthanasia *in principle* may have been, this support was regularly qualified by fears of its abuse.

Doubtless Goebbels' personal artistic tastes did not lack sophistication. Only after Hitler had cast his veto against 'modern art' did Goebbels abandon any public show of preference for German Expressionist painting, making amends for his 'ideological deviation', as Rosenberg called it, by organizing in 1937 a public exhibition of 'degenerate modern art'. Equally ambivalent was his attitude to the Nazi language purists whom he preferred to describe as 'volkish language acrobats'.

### The Nazi festivals

But the control of press, broadcasting, film, and the arts in general was only a relatively *negative* way of influencing the masses. To mobilize them fully needed more *positive,* more active devices, publicly expressing to the Germans themselves and to the world beyond its frontiers the national community in being. Apart from regular public collections such as the Winter Aid Fund, the year was divided up into public festivals, each of which culminated in some form of demonstration of the mobilization of the masses, whose participation could be ensured since most Germans, if not members of the Party, belonged to one of its many subsidiary organizations through which a certain degree of moral or sometimes direct coercion on the individual could be exercised.

The festival year began with the 30th

January, 'The Day of the Seizure of Power'. This was followed by the 'Day of the Commemoration of the Heroes' in March, and a month later by the celebration of Hitler's birthday on 20th April, again an occasion for military and Party parades. May Day was simply usurped by the Nazis from the Socialists. 1st May, 'The Day of Labour', was declared a public holiday by the Nazis (something which Weimar had forgotten to do) and has remained one ever since. The first 'Day of Labour' in 1933 was a major success for Goebbels as it was due to his personal persuasion that the as yet not outlawed trade unions participated in full. One and a half million workers turned up in Berlin alone, and together with 13,000 SA assembled at the Tempelhof field. Their songs, 3,000 flags, countless bands, with a Zeppelin flying overhead, all merged into one mass ovation for the 'new Germany'.

That event was Goebbels' own creation as was the organizational and propagandist feat of the Olympic Games three years later which seemed to affirm Nazi Germany's international respectability. He also took a leading part in the organization of the annual *Reichsparteitag*, the Party rally, at Nuremberg, but its 'artistic' direction lay in the hands of Hitler's architect, Albert Speer. The latter was not only entrusted with the design and construction of the assembly site and its buildings but also with the stage management of the event. Few who witnessed it have forgotten the dome of searchlights reaching 5,000 feet into the night sky, surrounding the field and its blocks of 110,000 Nazi local district leaders. Speer preferred this kind of design work to building in the massive and ornamental style demanded by Hitler. The conductor Wilhelm Furtwängler once remarked to Speer how marvellous it must be as an architect to build in such gigantic dimensions over so vast a scale. Speer replied: 'Imagine someone coming to you and saying "It is my irrevocable will that

*Members of the SA bawl out the Horst Wessel song after a rousing speech by Goebbels in Berlin's Lustgarten, August 1934. The SA provided Goebbels with the publicity he needed to double Berlin's Party membership*

as from now the Ninth is to be performed on the mouth organ only."'

The annual point of culmination of the Nazi mystique came on 9th November, on which the 'old fighters' commemorated their abortive putsch of 1923 by a ceremonial march through Munich. But for the continuous roll of muffled drums the city was silent. The route was flagged half-mast and lined by 'sacrificial' bowls of burning oil. The procession marched, keeping as near as possible to its original composition, along the same route taken in 1923 to the point where the police on that first march had opened fire. From there the column proceeded to the two specially built mausoleums in which rested the iron coffins of the sixteen dead. After homage had been paid to their sacrifice by Hitler the marchers and the masses lining the route regularly broke into the national anthem and the Horst Wessel song.

Since the entire population of any one city could not be at the place of Hitler's speech, during one of these festivals, Goebbels had loudspeakers erected on every street corner relaying the ceremonies and the speeches.

The war put an end to these annual mass displays. Goebbels personally disliked the outbreak of war, if for no other reason than the justified fear that it would bring into prominence the army's 'reactionary' generals, for whom, anti-bourgeois as he remained, he felt a hearty contempt. For another thing, as he said, 'a war does not happen to a clever man'. But once in it he was prepared to play his role to the full, though during the early years of Germany's military successes he stood, relatively speak-

# Ganz Deutschland hört den Führer

# mit dem Volksempfänger

ing, in the background. Personally he objected to Hitler's double policy of conducting a war and maintaining inside Germany almost peace-time conditions. He favoured an all-out utilization of Germany's resources of manpower and material. Once Germany had invaded Russia he propagated the official slogan of the 'Slav sub-human', but in the company of some of his subordinates and also in several memoranda addressed to Hitler he proposed a compromise peace with Stalin or alternatively the mobilization of the Russians themselves in a 'Crusade against Bolshevism'. Hitler remained unimpressed.

### Resistance at any price

Only when Germany's military and political ascendancy was diminishing did Goebbels' star begin to rise again. In the meantime he had helped to create a newspaper, modelled in lay-out on Great Britain's *Observer,* which was to act as Germany's intellectual show-case and was notable for its 'liberal' attitudes, compared with the rest of the German press. Every week, down to its last issue on 22nd April 1945, Goebbels contributed the leader to *Das Reich,* which had no dearth of able and prominent contributors. Theodor Heuss, the German Federal Republic's first President, was represented, as were many other staunch defenders of democratic principles in present day West Germany.

The change in the fortunes of war, the onset of the Allied air offensive against Germany, especially against Berlin, restored Goebbels' importance and brought him back to a position of prominence, which he had held before 1933 in Germany's capital and now attained throughout Germany. He was not a man to win the people's affection, nor did he court popularity, but between 1943 and 1945 he was certainly respected. Great Britain's reaction during the Blitz had taught him a lesson; like Churchill in 1940, so Goebbels from 1943 onwards preached blood, sweat, tears, and pessimism. And it was not nationalism, or fervent patriotism that dominated his performance. It was the sense of personal fulfilment so long denied him, the projection of the chaos of his innermost self which now supplied his essential driving force. Intellectually he was far too detached to be emotionally committed; he measured the degree of his success by the numbers he could emotionally commit to a cause which, when all is said and done, was no more to him than the vehicle of his personal ambition.

*Goebbels, himself a brilliant political broadcaster, used radio for mass propaganda on an unprecedented scale.* **Left:** *Advertisement for the* Volksempfänger, *the people's receiver. 'All Germany hears the Führer on the* Volksempfänger'. **Top right:** *Children's book illustration tries to bring children into contact with* Der Stürmer. *This newspaper, run by Julius Streicher, was an unofficial weapon of Nazi propaganda and included anti-Semitic material.* **Right:** *Dr Joseph Goebbels, who was appointed Minister of Popular Enlightenment and Propaganda shortly after the election of March 1933*

*Under the Nazis, life in Germany became increasingly militaristic. Goebbels made sure that it was also spectacular.*
*Far left: SA sports day: a change-over in a 4×100 relay in gas masks, 1935.*
*Left: Hitler Youth on parade during the Party rally in Nuremberg, 1938. Bottom left: End of the fifth anniversary of the Nazi take-over, 30th January 1938 – torch-light parade in Berlin's Wilhelmstrasse*

He shouted to his audience the call of the war of liberation of 1813:
'Now People rise
And Storm break loose!'
He did indeed achieve total mobilization of Germany's resources, but at a time when those of the Grand Coalition outstripped Germany's many times over. 'Faith can move mountains' he maintained. But in 1944, though Germany's output of arms of all kinds reached its highest peak ever, faith could perhaps prolong the war but not change its outcome. From the time he realized this the war was merely an opportunity to prolong his own existence.

As it became blatantly obvious that Germany was also at the end of her manpower resources, Goebbels, together with Himmler took up an idea first proposed by the chief of operations of the OKH (army high command), General Heusinger (a decade and a half later head of the Federal German Bundeswehr), to create a militia on the pattern of 1813. Nominally it was to include all male Germans between the ages of sixteen and sixty not serving in the armed forces already. As the Allies were to find out, in actual fact it included ten-year-olds and septuagenarians.

And so gradually Goebbels came to play on the last groove of his propaganda. He was trying to hold out at all costs, until a miracle would occur as it had done in the case of Frederick the Great and in the defence of the town of Kolberg against the French in 1806. Both subjects were turned into monumental propaganda films, the latter in colour. First the miracle was to be the V-weapons. When that miracle had evaporated the impending break-up of the enemy coalition was to be the next and also the final hope. In 1945 fanfares sounded again as a prelude to special victory announcements. Whereas between 1939 and 1943 they had announced the destruction of entire armies, in March 1945 they announced the destruction of a few Sherman tanks by the 'heroic action' of a Hitler Youth commando. 'Resistance at any price' was the headline of Goebbels' last leader in the last issue of *Das Reich*.

On 21st April 1945, a day before the publication of this leader Goebbels held his last inter-departmental conference with his subordinates. Like his master in the bunker of the chancellery he raved against the German people, its inability to live up to Nazi standards. He was about to leave his stunned audience, when at the door he suddenly turned around and exclaimed, 'But when we leave, the earth will tremble.' In the circumstances of that April in 1945 this was to prove, without doubt, to be an inflated self-assessment.

*Below: One of the occasions Goebbels organized so well: massed ranks of Nazis listen to Rudolf Hess at the annual Party rally in Speer's Luitpoldhalle, Nuremberg, 1934. The outbreak of war put an end to these annual displays, which had been occasions of great mass hysteria*

# The General Strike

Unwanted, unnecessary, yet perhaps inevitable, the only general strike in British history began in the early hours of Tuesday, 3rd May 1926 because a newspaper editor had written an inflammatory leading article and a prime minister had insisted on going to bed. 'We were in five minutes of a settlement,' said Ernest Bevin, one of the strikers' leaders, looking back years later when he was foreign secretary.

Yet although the strike might have been averted and nearly was, in a deeper sense it was unavoidable, then or later. It was something organized labour had to get out of its system: the last eruption of a syndicalist revolutionary philosophy of direct action that on and off had held the left wing in thrall for more than a century. It is, perhaps, characteristic of the British scene that when it came it was for quite other reasons than this and that those who organized and led it dreaded nothing more than that it should turn into an instrument of revolution in their hands.

Although the idea of a general strike had roots going back to Robert Owen's Grand National Consolidated Trade Union of the 1830's, to the Chartist movement, and to the recurring disillusion of workers with parliamentary progress, the General Strike of 1926 had a much more practical and immediate cause. It arose as a gesture of loyalty, never fully considered, foredoomed to failure from the start, but generous and noble in its purpose on the part of the great body of organized trade unionists in sympathy with those they believed to be the most ill-used among them – the miners.

The stage had been set a year earlier when the chancellor of the exchequer, Winston Churchill, aided, abetted, and perhaps deceived, in a field for which he had no great aptitude, by Montagu Norman, governor of the Bank of England, had put Great Britain back on the gold standard at the pre-war exchange rate of 4·86 dollars to the pound. This restored the prestige of the City as an international banking centre, but at a heavy cost to British industry, particularly coal mining whose selling prices in overseas markets were raised by ten per cent to a level where they could no longer compete. The coal owners sought to adjust the position by a cut in miners' wages. 'On grounds of social justice,' wrote the economist, Maynard Keynes, 'no case can be made for reducing the wages of the miners. They are the victims of the economic Juggernaut. They represent in the flesh the "fundamental adjustments" engineered by the Treasury and the Bank of England to satisfy the impatience of the City fathers to bridge the "moderate gap" between 4·40 dollars and 4·86.'

### The government wins time
One month after the return to the gold standard the coal owners gave notice to terminate existing wage agreements, cut wages and increase hours. Immediately the trade union movement which had recently voted new power to the TUC General Council to co-ordinate industrial action

*Left:* A convoy of Peerless armoured cars in London during the General Strike

*Above left:* Veteran syndicalist A.J.Cook, secretary of the Miners' Federation addressing strikers. The great body of trade unionists believed the miners to be the most ill-used among them. But in their sympathy they stumbled into a situation they could not manage. *Above right:* Emergency canteen in Hyde Park set up to feed the volunteers who answered the government's call for assistance. Even debutantes brewed tea. *Left:* Ernest Bevin, general secretary of the Transport and General Workers Union. 'We were in five minutes of a settlement,' he said, recalling the eve of the General Strike years later. *Below:* Volunteers unload milk churns in Hyde Park

E.T.U. College, Esher

*The General Strike by C.Rowe, 1953. With the passage of time the strike became part of the folklore of the labour movement. It came to be seen as an open conflict between bosses and workers, authority and idealism*

reacted in defence of the miners. Within a month it had considerable, but as it turned out, misleading success. Following the threat of a sympathetic strike by transport and other unions if the coal owners' demands were pressed the government approved a Royal Commission to consider proposals for re-organizing the industry and meanwhile provided a subsidy for the next nine months to keep wages at their existing level.

The belief that the power of industrial labour was now so strong that if the unions acted together they were bound to win was strengthened. In fact, it was the government that had won. What it had won was time. In the nine months' pause while the Royal Commission sat, a nation-wide organization – the organization for the maintenance of supplies – was set up to mobilize volunteers to keep essential services going in case of breakdown.

The Royal Commission with Sir Herbert Samuel, later Lord Samuel, as its chairman advocated many important changes in the coal industry. But they were for the future. There was no relief for the present. 'Not

a penny off the pay, not a minute on the day', declared the miners and on 30th April 1926 the miners stopped working following a national lock-out by the owners. At once, as they had done the previous year, the miners turned to the TUC General Council for support.

But although the miners' case had aroused such sympathy among the general body of ordinary trade unionists that the TUC was under great pressure to follow a militant course, its leaders were at this stage far from seriously preparing for a general strike. Misled by their previous success they believed that a threat of sympathetic strike action would of itself be sufficient to make the government ready to negotiate. Indeed, to such an extent were they convinced of this that at first no attempt was made to back up the promise of support for the miners by concrete plans for co-ordinated strike action – it was only when Ernest Bevin, the general secretary of the Transport and General Workers Union, insisted on the necessity for a joint command that this was done.

Thereafter strike plans proceeded rapidly – taking on their own momentum so that although no-one wanted a general strike nothing except an agreement by the government to reconsider the miners' case could stop it. On 1st May at a meeting of the executives of all trade unions affiliated to the TUC, delegates representing

3,650,000 organized workers, pledged support for strike action, although it was agreed that essential food and milk supplies should be maintained and that there should be no interruption in house and hospital building.

Meanwhile, representatives of the TUC had opened negotiations with the government. The government was divided. Some of its members, notably Churchill and Chamberlain, were all for a show-down with Labour. Others, including the prime minister and Lord Birkenhead, believed that every effort should be made to maintain industrial peace. On the night of 1st May it seemed that the peace-makers on both sides would win.

A formula was drafted by Birkenhead according to which in return for a withdrawal of lock-out notices the TUC would urge the miners to accept the Samuel Report even although it meant some temporary reduction in wages until the large-scale reconstruction of the industry recommended by the Report could be carried through. The TUC representatives thereupon retired to a room set aside for them in No. 11 Downing Street to meet the leaders of the Miners' Federation, while the cabinet committee waited at No. 10 for their answer.

The lull was shattered by a telephone call from the editor of the *Daily Mail*, Mr. Thomas Marlowe. He reported that the

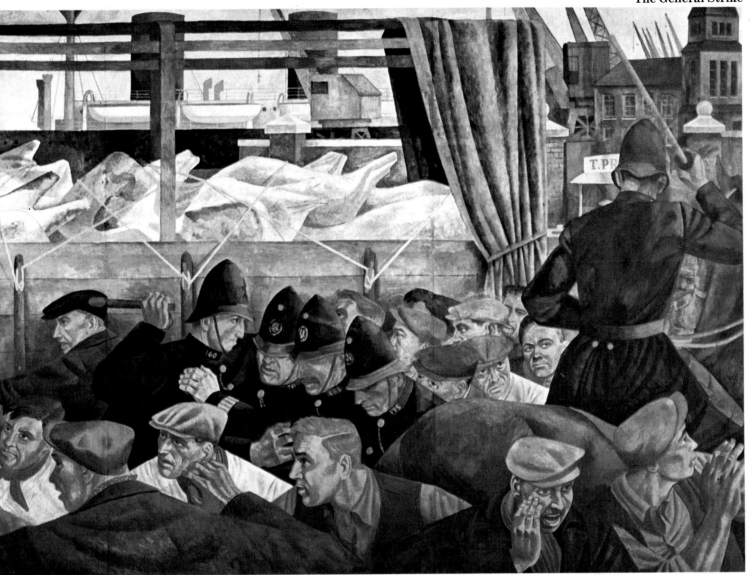

staff of the machine room at the *Mail* had refused to print an inflammatory leading article he had chosen to write at this particularly delicate stage in the negotiations. This denounced the TUC's plans for a sympathetic strike as a revolutionary act aimed at destroying the government and called upon all law-abiding men and women to resist. It was headed 'For King and Country'.

'A bloody good job,' said Lord Birkenhead when told of the printers' action. But other members of the cabinet took a different view. They prevailed and a letter signed by the prime minister was immediately dispatched to the TUC saying that in view of 'overt action' representing 'a gross interference with the freedom of the press' no further negotiations could take place unless this action was repudiated and all strike notices withdrawn.

The TUC members were flabbergasted. It was the first they had heard of the incident at the *Daily Mail*, which had been quite unofficial, and was condemned by the printers' own leaders. They had believed themselves to be on the edge of agreement. After a brief discussion Arthur Pugh, the chairman of the TUC, and Walter Citrine, the general secretary, hurried back to No. 10 to see the prime minister with a letter informing him that the *Daily Mail* printers had acted without any authority and assuring him of their conviction that peace

could still be secured between the two sides.

They arrived to find that the cabinet had dispersed and Mr. Baldwin had gone to bed leaving only a secretary to see them, although the prime minster had explicitly asked for a reply. It was the end of negotiations. Next day a state of emergency was declared. The strike that hardly anybody wanted began.

It lasted nine days—an appropriate time for it was to become a nine days' wonder to the rest of the world. All the workers called upon responded to the TUC's demand to withdraw their labour. On the other side thousands of ordinary people, including large numbers of undergraduates responded to the government's call for volunteers. Many of them had the time of their lives driving trains and buses. Society debutantes manned canteens to nourish them during their labours. But there was scarcely any violence. Instead, foreign correspondents who had arrived from all over the world to cover the start of a revolution could only report that in this curious country football matches were being organized between strikers and police.

Too late the trade union leaders realized that a general strike which must by its nature involve a total clash with the government had no chance of success unless it were in fact used as an instrument of revolution. And this was the last thing they wanted—or ever had wanted. When Mr.

Baldwin went to the radio to declare 'I am a man of peace. I am longing and working and praying for peace', and promised that if the strike were ended there would be no victimization or exploitation they were ready to believe him.

The strike was called off against the protests of the miners who believed themselves betrayed and who fought on alone for another six months before they, too, were driven back to work on the owners' terms. But in fact no other outcome was possible. Moved by a genuine loyalty to their fellow workers the trade unions had stumbled into a situation they could not manage with a weapon they dare not really use. They had no alternative but to disengage.

The strike left much bitterness behind it, especially when, despite Baldwin's promises, a new Trade Disputes Act was carried restricting powers the trade unions had previously enjoyed for many years. Nevertheless, it represented an important watershed in British industrial history. As both sides drew back from the chasm a new era of negotiation began: In the seven years before the General Strike nearly 28,000,000 days a year had been lost by strikes. In the seven years after, only 4,000,000 a year were lost. The General Strike had been in some ways a tragedy, in others almost a farce. But for a time at least it helped to make all sides of industry realize that conflict was out of date.

# Great Britain and the Depression

"BRITAIN'S HITLER"

*Above:* *A personable Oswald Mosley, young, ambitious, arrogant and ruthless, on the cover of the American magazine* Time, *March 1931; his practical impact was slight at the time.*

*Below:* *Labour election poster, 1929. Recently enfranchised young thing (in 1928 the vote was given to women under thirty) turns to Ramsay MacDonald in scorn of the 'old dears', Lloyd George and Baldwin, the Liberal and Conservative leaders. The 'flapper vote' is supposed to have benefited Labour in the 1929 election.*

*Opposite page:* *National government election poster issued by the Conservative Party. Originally a Conservative Party poster, this one was doctored for the 1931 election.*

THE NEW VOTER:—
"POOR OLD DEARS!
— ISN'T IT PATHETIC?"

The second Labour government took office in June 1929. Its ministers were mostly the same men of humble origin who had held office in the Labour government of 1924. Ramsay MacDonald, still the most respected and powerful figure in the Labour movement, was once again Prime Minister. Once again, Philip Snowden was his only possible chancellor of the exchequer. This time MacDonald did not make the mistake of acting as his own foreign secretary; instead, the Foreign Office went to the party secretary, Arthur Henderson. J.R. Clynes, MacDonald's immediate predecessor as chairman of the parliamentary party, became home secretary. The ebullient J.H.Thomas, whose reputation as a buffoon belied his real abilities as a negotiator, became lord privy seal, with the daunting responsibility of supervising and co-ordinating the government's unemployment policies.

If the leaders were the same, so were the led. The Labour Party was still a loose-knit coalition of groups and individuals, differing widely in background, temperament, and aspiration. It was held together by its commitment to public ownership, but it had no clear idea of the form public ownership would take, or of the principles which would govern its introduction in one industry rather than another. Its ideas about the part public ownership could play in solving the immediate problem of high and persistent unemployment, which had dominated British politics since the collapse of the post-war boom, were even more vague.

Most Labour men and women believed that the problem could not be solved at all until society had been transformed. To them, it was self-evident that unemployment was caused by capitalism, just as it was self-evident that war was caused by armaments. The only way to solve the unemployment problem was to abolish capitalism, just as the only way to prevent war was to disarm. But a minority government could hardly be expected to abolish capitalism. Hence, it could do nothing to solve the unemployment problem, apart from hoping that trade would revive, and trying to diminish the world economic instability which had caused Great Britain's trade to shrink in the first place.

At first, this gap between socialist rhetoric and economic reality did not seem to matter. During the first few months of 1929, trade did revive. By the summer, fewer people were out of work than there had been a year earlier. In these circumstances, it was reasonable to hope that the

trade cycle – which had been stuck in a downward phase for almost a decade – was at last moving upwards again, and that unemployment would return to normal proportions of its own accord. These hopes soon collapsed. In October 1929 came the famous Wall Street Crash; before long the world Depression had begun. The faltering British economy was dragged down with it. In March 1929, a total of 1,204,000 men and women were registered as unemployed. By March, 1930, the figure was 1,700,000. By July, it was over two million and by December it was two and a half million.

Even in retrospect, it is not at all clear whether this crisis could have been solved by any British government in isolation. The entire capitalist world was in chaos; and the British economy was uniquely dependent, then as now, on the ups and downs of world trade. It is by no means certain that the British economy could have been successfully insulated from the outside world, even if the British government had wished to do so – or that there was any real alternative to the orthodox wisdom of the Treasury and the Bank of England so long as the economy remained uninsulated.

What is certain is that Ramsay MacDonald and his cabinet were not prepared to do anything of the kind, or even to examine seriously the arguments of those who were. Thomas, the lord privy seal, had been given three assistants in his search for an unemployment policy – the sentimental and kind-hearted Socialist veteran, George Lansbury, who represented the left wing of the party in the cabinet, as first commissioner of works; Tom Johnston, the under-secretary of state for Scotland; and Sir Oswald Mosley, a wealthy baronet who had entered Parliament as a Conservative in 1918, and had been returned as Labour member for Smethwick in 1926. Mosley was young, ambitious, arrogant, and ruthless. He was also the most talented member of the government. He had been appointed to the sinecure office of chancellor of the Duchy of Lancaster; and with no departmental chores to tie him down, he was able to devote his talents to the plight of the unemployed.

The result was one of the greatest personal miscalculations in recent British history. Mosley soon became contemptuous of Thomas's bumbling, if well-meaning, inability to grasp the magnitude of the problem. With the help of his officials at the Treasury, and his parliamentary private secretary, John Strachey, he drew

Time-Life Inc.

Institute of Social History, Amsterdam

*National cabinet, 1931: (back) Cunliffe-Lister, Thomas, Reading, Chamberlain, Hoare, (front) Snowden, Baldwin, Macdonald, Samuel, Sankey*

*J.H. Thomas campaigning as National Labour candidate in 1931 election. He had to resign from cabinet in 1936 after a budget leak scandal*

up a memorandum, the central thesis of which was much influenced by the expansionist views of the Cambridge economist, J.M.Keynes. The existing administrative system, Mosley claimed, was too slow-moving to cope with the problem of mass unemployment. It was necessary to mobilize all the resources of government to deal with it, and this could only be done if the Prime Minister himself took charge. A new 'Prime Minister's department' should be set up to supervise a long-term programme of economic reconstruction, with an executive committee of ministers under the Prime Minister's chairmanship working alongside it.

The economic proposals contained in the Mosley memorandum were more sweeping than the administrative ones. Great Britain could only enjoy a standard of living capable of absorbing 'the great force of modern production', Mosley wrote, if she were 'insulated from the electric shocks of present world conditions'. It was useless to hope for an expansion of her export trade. The only long-term solution to the unemployment problem was to develop the home economy behind a protective barrier of import controls. Meanwhile, a great public works programme should be set on foot, to be financed by borrowing and to cost £200 million over the next three years. The suggestion that such a policy would cause a flight from the pound was nonsense. Confidence in sterling would be increased if unemployment were reduced and a systematic programme of reconstruction embarked upon.

For the first time, the government had been presented with a clear and coherent alternative to the deflationary doctrines of the Treasury and the Bank of England. But

*Above right: In a German cartoon of 1934 Sir Oswald Mosley administers a firm rebuff to Bolshevism and Jewry. **Right:** Casualty of clash between police and anti-fascists, south London, October 1937. **Below:** British anti-fascist pamphlet, 1934, typifies violent feelings sparked by British fascists. Later, Mosley's flirtations with Hitler and Mussolini made fascism an unpatriotic creed*

Kladderadatsch

Communist Party Library

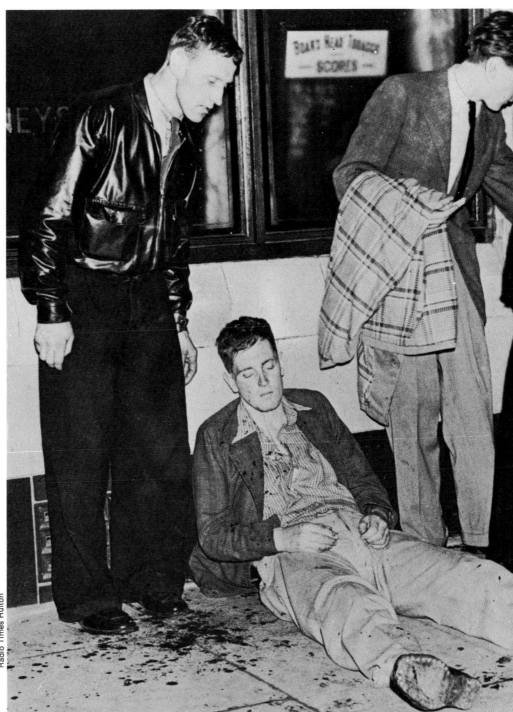

Radio Times Hulton

although MacDonald realized that the traditional orthodoxy of classical economics was inadequate, and although he liked Mosley personally and had gone out of his way to advance his career in Labour politics, he lacked the economic knowledge to counter the Treasury's objections to Mosley's proposals. He also lacked the will (and probably the political strength) to override Snowden's hostility to anything that smacked of fiscal irresponsibility. Snowden, like all chancellors of the exchequer in peace time, was the most powerful member of the government next to the Prime Minister himself; by this time he had become a rigid and unyielding exponent of Treasury doctrine at its bleakest. At the end of January 1930 a special cabinet committee, of which Snowden was a member, was set up to examine the Mosley memorandum. Not surprisingly, it reported against it; not surprisingly, the cabinet followed suit. On 20th May Mosley resigned. At a party meeting two days later, he moved a censure motion on the government's economic policy; and insisted on pressing it to a vote, in spite of an eloquent appeal from Arthur Henderson not to do so. His motion was defeated by 29 votes to 210, and within less than a year his career as a serious politician had come to an end. At the party conference in October he was elected to the national executive, but in February 1931 he announced that he was forming a new party to campaign for his views, and was expelled from the Labour Party for his pains.

Mosley's downfall brought no benefits to the government. MacDonald and his colleagues hung on for fifteen months after Mosley's resignation, desperately trying to find some way of halting the rise in unemployment without departing too far from fiscal orthodoxy, and succeeding in neither. The end came in August 1931. During the summer, Central Europe was convulsed by a series of monetary crises, culminating in a run on the mark, and the imposition of exchange controls by the German Reichsbank. This was followed by a run on sterling, as foreigners withdrew their money from London to meet the shortage of liquidity on the Continent. At the end of July, sterling was weakened still further by the report of the May Committee, which the government had set up a few months earlier under pressure from the Liberals to consider what economies might be made in public expenditure. The May Report was a savagely deflationary document, even by the standards of classical theory. It predicted a budget deficit of £120 million, and advocated sweeping cuts in public expenditure, including a reduction of twenty per cent in unemployment benefit.

### The economic dilemma

This was the last straw. The drain of funds from London became a flood. Before dispersing for their summer holidays, the cabinet had set up a special economy committee—consisting of MacDonald, Snowden, Henderson, Thomas, and William Graham, the president of the Board of Trade—to examine the proposals which the May Committee had made. A few days

after the House rose for the summer recess, it became clear that sterling would collapse altogether unless urgent action were taken. On the morning of 11th August, MacDonald arrived back in London on the overnight train from Scotland for consultations with Snowden and representatives of the Bank of England, and decided to summon the economy committee next day. It accepted the need to balance the budget and agreed that sweeping cuts would have to be made in public expenditure. At the same time, it turned down the Treasury's suggestion that unemployment benefit should be reduced by ten per cent, and rejected a revenue tariff—while nevertheless agreeing that a tariff was preferable to a cut in benefit.

In effect, the committee had ruled out all the possible solutions. In rejecting a revenue tariff, it had rejected the possibility of insulating the British economy

from the outside world, and with it all hope of solving the crisis by unorthodox methods. Yet in accepting the need to balance the budget, it had accepted the orthodox diagnosis: while in rejecting a cut in unemployment benefit, it had rejected the orthodox cure. For the point of balancing the budget was psychological, not economic. Its purpose was not to take purchasing power out of the economy, which was deflated enough already, but to restore confidence in sterling by demonstrating the government's determination to defend it. If this was to be done effectively, however, it was necessary, not merely to balance the budget, but to balance it in the way in which financial opinion wanted it to be balanced. In fact, financial opinion wanted it to be balanced by cutting unemployment benefit; and it soon became clear that confidence would not be restored if this were not done.

*Below: Salome's dance, 1931. 'King Herod' Henderson, Labour Party leader, approves sacrifice of Thomas and MacDonald. Maxton, left-wing Labour MP, wants the electorate as next offering. **Bottom:** MacDonald meets members of the press a week after his exclusion from the Labour Party. His action was regarded as betrayal by his former supporters*

On this rock, the government foundered. On 19th August the economy committee reported to the cabinet. Next day, it met a deputation from the TUC. It became clear that the TUC would oppose any major cuts in public expenditure, and that there was no hope whatever of persuading it to accept a reduction in unemployment benefit. It also became clear that it was impossible to remain on the gold standard or hold the existing parity of sterling without a loan from New York, and that no loan would be forthcoming unless unemployment benefit were cut. After five days of agonized debate, the cabinet voted by twelve to nine in favour of an economy programme slightly smaller than that originally proposed by the economy committee, but including a cut in unemployment benefit of ten per cent. The dissentients, however, included Henderson, Clynes, and Graham, and could count on the support of the TUC and probably of the parliamentary party as well. Obviously, the government could not continue.

After handing in his resignation, and that of his government, MacDonald was persuaded by the King to return to office as head of a National government representing all three political parties. He knew that this would be bitterly unpopular in the Labour movement, but saw no alternative if a complete collapse of the currency was to be averted. In any case, he did not expect the breach with the Labour movement to last. He believed that the National government would be a temporary expedient, and that it would be possible for him to return to his old party when the crisis was over. He also imagined that those of his former colleagues who had supported the economy programme while they were in office would go on supporting it after they left.

These hopes were disappointed. The Labour Party swung violently against the National government, and against MacDonald personally. Only a tiny handful of Labour MP's followed him, and most of the party became convinced that he had deliberately betrayed them. To make matters worse, the formation of the National government did not end the crisis after all. On 21st September Great Britain was forced off the gold standard, without the disastrous consequences which city opinion had predicted. A week later, MacDonald was expelled from the Labour Party, which he had done more than any other single person to create. A week after that, he succumbed to the mounting Conservative pressure to hold a general election, and seek a 'doctor's mandate' for the National government. The result was a catastrophic defeat for the Labour Party. It held only 46 seats, fewer than in 1918, while the government had a majority of 497. The temporary expedient had become a permanent fixture.

### MacDonald — a broken man
This was a catastrophe for MacDonald as well as for the Labour Party. He lingered on as Prime Minister for another four years, but he was a broken, isolated figure, and his powers waned fast. In his great days he had dominated the Labour movement as no one has dominated it since. Now he was vilified and hated, and his achievements were forgotten or passed over. In the miners' cottages in his old constituency of Aberavon, where his car had once been dragged through the streets by cheering crowds, his portrait was turned to the wall. His new colleagues had no love for him, and increasingly regarded him as an embarrassment. A faint shadow of the magnificent voice and presence still remained, but as time went on he began to lose the thread of his speeches and became increasingly painful to listen to. In cabinet, he could still discuss important business with force and authority. In public he seemed, while still in his late sixties, a tired and pathetic old man.

Moreover, he lacked a following. The National Labour Party (MacDonaldites) was an ineffective rump with no independent existence of its own. In 1932 the free-trade wing of the Liberal Party, led by Herbert Samuel, resigned from the government rather than accept an abandonment of free trade and the establishment of imperial preference. Thereafter, the government was to all intents and purposes a purely Conservative one, with MacDonald as its prisoner. In the last analysis, political power rested with Baldwin, while the driving force was provided by Snowden's successor as Chancellor of the Exchequer, the hard, narrow, but decisive Neville Chamberlain.

### Origins of the managed economy
Yet it was a different kind of Conservative government from the one which had returned to the gold standard in 1925, and unwittingly dealt a savage blow to the British economy in doing so. For 1931 was a greater watershed than most people realized at the time. Before then, people and politicians alike had been trying to go back to the past. Now they began, albeit in a confused and half-hearted way, to look to the future. In the 'twenties, few people disputed that Great Britain's troubles had been caused by the upheavals brought by the war, and only the odd Cassandra like Mosley or Keynes denied that the solution must lie in a return to the self-regulating world economy which had existed before 1914. These notions disappeared with the gold standard. After 1931, Great Britain had, in effect, a managed currency. Increasingly, she also had a managed economy, where the government takes measures to alter the course of the economy in the direction it thinks fit. Two such measures were the policy of cheap money (low interest rates), claimed as a way of stimulating economic recovery, and the imposition of tariffs, a constraint upon the working of free enterprise.

True, Great Britain's economic recovery was slow and patchy. The unemployment figures remained appallingly high; and an appalling price was paid for them in wasted resources and wasted lives. From August 1931 until January 1933 the total was nearly three million; and it did not fall below two million until July 1935. As late as July 1936 it was over one and a half million, while the proportion of insured workers was 12% as against 9.7% in May 1929. In the so-called distressed areas — the areas of the traditional staple industries of coal, shipbuilding, steel, and textiles, most of them heavily dependent on traditional export markets — the position was infinitely worse. In 1932, the unemployment percentage in Wales was over 36%, compared with under 14% in London and the South-East. In Merthyr in 1934 over 60% of the insured workers were unemployed; in Jarrow, almost 70%. In places like these, the 'thirties left a scar as deep and persistent as that left by the Hungry 'Forties in Southern Ireland. Even today it has by no means disappeared.

Great Britain's recovery, however, was no slower than that of most other industrial countries, and the methods used to promote it were not very different from theirs. The National government was drab and uninspiring. It contained no glittering figures, no brilliant phrasemakers, no strong men. Its social attitudes were in many ways reactionary; its treatment of the unemployed was mean-spirited. It had little to offer to idealistic young people, conscious of the growing threat of fascism in Central Europe and the misery of the distressed areas at home. Yet the fact remains that by introducing the techniques of economic management it made a decisive break with the past, and took a decisive step along the road which was to lead to the kind of economy which Great Britain has had since 1945. In doing so, it also helped to provide a pleasanter and more prosperous life for the great majority of the British people than they had ever enjoyed.

### A popular government
Perhaps for this reason, it held on to its popular support more successfully than any of its predecessors. In 1935, Ramsay MacDonald at last retired from the premiership, and Baldwin moved to No. 10. Shortly afterwards, there was a general election; and although the Labour opposition improved its position, the government still had a majority of 274. Two years later, Baldwin resigned in turn, and MacDonald left office altogether — to die at sea shortly afterwards. Chamberlain became Prime Minister, but the government went on much as before. All the evidence suggests that if a general election had been held in 1939 or 1940, the government would have been returned yet again. It fell in the end, not through electoral unpopularity, but because of a revolt by its supporters in the House of Commons. And this revolt was due, not to events at home, but to the failure of its foreign policy.

Strangely enough, the National government deserved its title, though not in the way its creators had intended. In personnel, it was overwhelmingly Conservative. In policy, it aimed, on the whole successfully, for the middle ground — for a consensus between liberal-minded men of goodwill. In home affairs this produced a broadly prosperous and contented society, though disfigured by terrible black spots. The tragedy was that in foreign affairs there was no middle ground available.

# China:The Long March

In 1935, by an extraordinary feat of arms known as the Long March, the Chinese Communist army, forced out of its stronghold in south China, retreated across the whole breadth of the country to the north-western province of Shensi. It appeared then to be a catastrophe for the Chinese Communist movement, and very probably the last despairing phase of its activity. Today, celebrated as the greatest triumph of its early struggles, the Long March has become a legend in Communist China. Whether it was more of a triumph than a catastrophe is debatable, but what is now

*Nationalist troops prepare to set out on a Communist extermination campaign. Their heavily-laden mule train typifies their traditional style of warfare which failed to eliminate Mao's elusive guerrillas*

certain is that the Long March was a factor that determined the entire subsequent history of China. As a result of it, the centre of revolutionary activity was removed from the south to the north for the first time since the overthrow of the Manchu dynasty. In the safety of the north the Communist Party built up its strength during the Japanese invasion until able to challenge and defeat the Nationalist government after the Second World War, and thus conquer the south and reunite the country with armies, which if still led by old time southern revolutionary leaders, were composed of northern recruits. This alliance contributed a greater unity to the revolutionary movement than was ever achieved by the Nationalist or Republican parties, which were always dominated by southern or south-eastern cliques.

On 12th April 1927 Chiang Kai-shek, commander-in-chief of the Nationalist army, staged a military coup in Shanghai and rounded up the Communist Party members and their followers who had, a month previously, seized the Chinese section of Shanghai from the troops of the northern warlord, Chang Tsung-chang. In July, after Chiang had set up a new Nationalist regime at Nanking, the former Nationalist government at Wuhan (which groups the three cities of Hankow, Wu Chang, and Han Yang) expelled the Communist members of the government, and later merged with Chiang's government in Nanking. This was the nadir of the fortunes of the Communist Party. Blaming the disasters on the leadership, a party meeting expelled the general secretary, Ch'en Tu-hsiu, from his post, and a few days later, on

31st July, elements of the army stationed at Nanchang, capital of Kiangsi province, mutinied against the Nationalist command, and declared themselves supporters of the Communist Party. The mutiny was led by Chu Teh, a general, and among his officers was Lin Piao, a young man who rose to a high position in the Chinese Communist regime before his death in 1971.

### From the barrel of a gun

The mutiny at Nanchang was a failure; after five days the Nationalist forces in the vicinity retook the city, and the new Red Army retreated southward, pursued by superior forces. 1st August 1927, the day after the insurrection, is now revered in China as the date of the foundation of the Red Army or, as it was re-named, the People's Liberation Army. From that day till the present time the Communist Party has never lacked armed forces under its own leadership. Power, as Mao Tse-tung re-marked, 'grows from the barrel of a gun', and on 1st August 1927, for the first time, the Communist leadership had had its own finger on the trigger of the gun. The con-sequences of this development were not apparent for several years. At first every-thing went badly for the new Red Army; it marched south and occupied the sea port of Swatow in September 1927, but was al-most immediately driven out with heavy losses. The failure of the Communist up-rising in Canton two months later was an-other serious reverse, after which, aban-doning the hope of seizing cities, the Red Army moved off into the interior of south China and became a wandering force har-ried and pursued by Nationalist and pro-vincial troops. Other misfortunes had befallen the party but Mao Tse-tung, orga-nizer of rural revolution in his native province of Hunan, had left Wuhan to raise an 'autumn harvest rising', and thus escaped the purge of the party when the Communists were expelled from the govern-ment. In September 1927 he and his ill-armed followers attempted to take Ch'ang-sha, the capital of Hunan, which he mistakenly believed to be poorly defended. They were heavily repulsed and he was nearly taken prisoner. The survivors fled to a remote mountain stronghold called Chingkangshan, on the border of Hunan and Kiangsi provinces. In April 1928 the wandering Red Army led by Chu Teh joined forces with Mao at Chingkangshan, a re-union now recalled as one of the great formative events in the history of the Chinese Communist Party.

### A disastrous direction

So indeed it proved to be. The region, an old bandit stronghold, lay on the border of two provinces, and was thus usually safe from punitive measures launched from either, since the provincial authorities rarely co-operated. Here Mao and Chu formed that political and military partner-ship which built up the remains of the Communist Party from new elements, in a new environment, and with new military tactics. The early leaders of the party were exclusively urban intellectuals, steeped in Russian teaching, and convinced that while

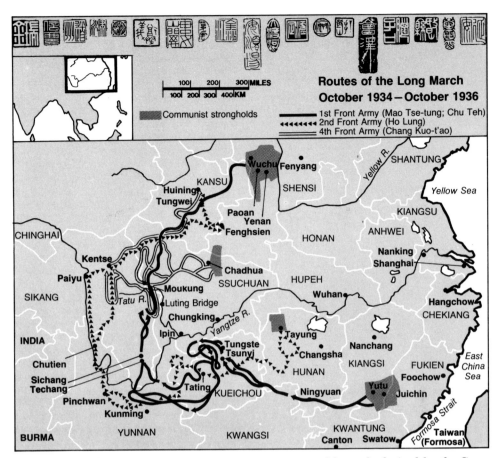

The Long March and key units participating, surmounted by seals devised by the Com-munists to commemorate the stages of the March. Scholars have been puzzled by the absence of a 3rd Front Army. The term 'Front' was adopted for widely separated forces and the independent Kiangsi-based 3rd Army could have simply been amalgamated with the other Kiangsi units into the 1st Front Army. Some marchers covered over 6,000 miles

the peasantry were a naturally conserva-tive force, the urban proletariat repre-sented the real source on which the Communist Party should draw for support. These leaders, from their secret hideouts in Shanghai, continued, with Russian ad-vice, to direct party policy, but in a disas-trous direction. They treated the movement which Mao and Chu were creating in the remote interior as a sideshow, a useful distraction, but one which could have no decisive impact. The revolution, they main-tained, must be based on large cities, and draw its strength from urban workers. How-ever this was a wholly unreal assessment in the China of the day. Urban industrial workers were few. In fact Shanghai was the only city where they were a significant force, and even there they had been crushed by Chiang Kai-shek's coup of April 1927. The peasantry were, on the other hand, oppressed by rack-renting absentee land-lords, harried by bandits, plundered by un-disciplined soldiery, and reduced to near-starvation by the vagaries of the rainfall. Their condition had been deteriorating for several years under the hapless regime of the warlords and they were in a revolu-tionary mood, only requiring leadership. This Mao and Chu supplied.

Mao Tse-tung conceived a new strategy, that of guerrilla warfare and reliance on the peasants for support. In return the Com-munists were requested to liberate the pea-sants from their landlords, suppress rural disorder, and defend the country from Nationalist forces. The peasants, hundreds

of millions of them, constituted the vast majority of the Chinese people; illiterate and ignorant to be sure, but nevertheless shrewd and enduring. If the Communist Party initially gained their confidence and support, it could build a movement com-manding overwhelming support; and it could hope to resist Nationalist attacks, since these were mounted by armies simi-larly composed of peasant soldiers, but who were conscripted and often treated with brutality by officers who cheated them of their pay. By 1929 the Red Army in Kiangsi had increased to 10,000 men and was grow-ing fast. It was possible to leave Chingkang-shan and occupy other rural areas. Chiang Kai-shek became aware of the renewed danger of Communist uprising, but in the years between 1927 and 1930 he was pre-occupied with subduing the remaining war-lords of north China, and then with the jealousies and intrigues of various factions within the Kuomintang, or Nationalist Party. Mao and Chu were left alone; had the party's leaders in Shanghai been wise enough to let them build up their reserves during this lull, their strength would have soon grown much greater, but the Moscow-inspired strategy of seizing large cities still dominated Shanghai's thinking. In July 1930 the central executive in Shanghai, under the leadership of Ch'ü Ch'iu-pai, a Moscow-trained intellectual, ordered Chu Teh to attack and invest Ch'angsha, the capital of Hunan province. Chu took Ch'angsha, and held it for ten days before being driven out with heavy losses. The policy of seizing large cities had once again failed. As a result of this defeat, the party ousted Ch'ü Ch'iu-pai and made Li Li-san its leader. He was also an urban-orientated revolutionary who had for years concentrated his work on trade union organization. Since at this time China's only developed trade unions, at Shanghai, had been crushed and infiltrated by Nationalist agents, there was little safe scope for him. Communist Party policy thus remained unrealistic and ineffective.

### Chiang's extermination campaigns
Towards the end of 1930 Chiang Kai-shek felt free to suppress the Communist insurrection in Kiangsi, which had so impertinently courted publicity with the abortive attack on Ch'angsha in July. The first Communist bandit extermination campaign – as it was styled – was launched in early December 1930. Chu and Mao met it with the now famous tactics, summed up by Mao's dictum, 'when the enemy advances we retreat, when he halts, we harry him, when he retreats, we pursue'. In other words the Red Army refused to meet superior forces in head-on combat, preferring to melt before the advance, and reform behind the enemy lines to cut his communications. Forced to halt, the Nationalist army was soon on the defensive in a hostile countryside where all intelligence was denied to them by the peasants, but freely supplied to the Red Army. When retreat was inevitable as winter closed in, the Communists struck, inflicting heavy losses on the Nationalists. The first extermination campaign had been ignominiously repulsed but Chiang Kai-shek was not deterred, nor did he learn from his failure. In February 1931 a second extermination campaign was mounted. It too, failed, and for the same reasons. By this time the Red Army, swollen by volunteers and Nationalist deserters, had attained a strength of 300,000 men. This was no mere bandit gang as Chiang liked to pretend; it was a very serious military challenge.

Still Chiang persisted. Although the menace of Japanese aggression was daily becoming more serious, he stood by his policy of 'internal pacification first, resistance to external attacks second'. So the third extermination campaign, employing still larger forces was launched in July 1931. It was brought to a halt by a Communist victory at Kaohsing in Kiangsi province just at the time news came through of the Japanese seizure of Manchuria and the setting up there of the puppet state of Manchukuo. As a major war with Japan now seemed imminent the anti-Communist campaign was called off and the Nationalist armies once more withdrew. Inspired by these victories, which had left it in control of a large part of Kiangsi province, the Communist Party in November 1931 set up its own provisional Soviet government of China at Juichin, a small city in Kiangsi. Li Li-san had been removed from the leadership in November 1930, and sent off to Moscow for 'retraining'. He remained there until 1945. Leadership was now in the hands of the 'returned students', a group of young men trained in Russia, and very

much influenced by their Russian mentors. Relations between the Shanghai leadership, which was constantly menaced by the risk of discovery or betrayal to the Nationalist police, and the Kiangsi Soviet, soon became strained. While the party's Shanghai leaders were forced underground Chu, Mao, and their followers lived at liberty in their own domain, three Nationalist invasions having been soundly repelled. They had organized a rudimentary, but effective government, which controlled a large army and a population of a million or more. By any standards the Kiangsi Soviet was now the centre and strength of the Communist Party in China. But Shanghai still tried to exercise control over it.

The real situation during the years 1932 until October 1934 remains very obscure. Today Chinese Communist historians not only insist that Mao Tse-tung led the party in these early formative days, but that he was unquestioned master of the Communist movement. But just how far he and Chu asserted their independent view, and how far Shanghai was able to override them, and did so, is a very intricate question on which source material is insufficient. It is at least clear that a struggle occurred, and that the decision of the Shanghai headquarters to move to Kiangsi early in 1933 was motivated partly by the need to assert authority in the real centre of power, and only in part due to the increasing risks of the 'underground' life in Shanghai. In February 1932 the Kiangsi Soviet, acting as a sovereign state, declared war on the Japanese empire. Although an empty gesture since Japanese troops were not within range of the Red Army, it proved politically effective, as a contrast to Chiang Kai-shek's policy of appeasing the invader with constant withdrawals and concessions. The Communists could now claim to be the patriotic party, and many Chinese, disgusted and alarmed with Chiang's policy, were more ready to give consideration to Communist claims and ideas.

### German military advice
The Shanghai central executive had hardly arrived in Juichin before Chiang launched his fourth extermination campaign, designed to be the final conclusive assault, and involving 250,000 Nationalist troops. It too failed although some early success was achieved over outlying Communist areas in Hunan and Hupeh provinces. But against the central hard core of Kiangsi, the attack was a total failure. Chiang lost three whole divisions, and two of their commanders were taken prisoner. It seems probable that despite this victory the newly-arrived central executive had come to assume greater power by the middle of the year. In his later writings Mao Tse-tung points to serious mistakes made in 1933 and early 1934, which necessitated the abandonment of the Kiangsi Soviet and the desperate retreat now known as the Long March. It is therefore evident that Mao did not claim to be the unquestioned leader at this time, indeed, he attributes the errors to those who opposed his views. There is, however, some reason to believe that this was not the real truth.

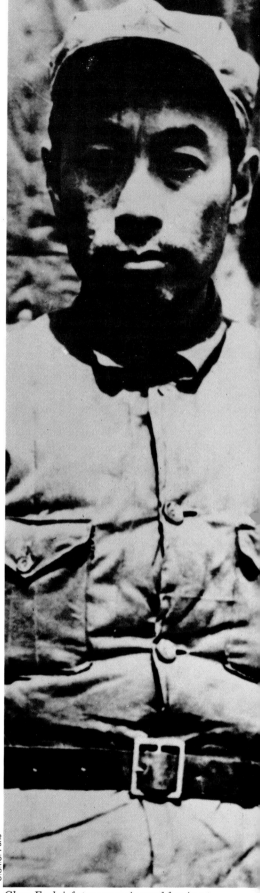

*Chou En-lai, future premier and foreign minister who marched with Mao*

Chiang Kai-shek had now enlisted the services of certain senior German officers, made available to him by the Nazi regime. General von Seeckt and General Wetzell became his advisers. They persuaded the Nationalist commander-in-chief to abandon frontal attacks, which had proved so costly and fruitless, and instead use his great superiority in numbers to blockade the whole Kiangsi Soviet, which was dependent on the importation of certain vital commodities, among them being salt. Blockhouses were built to guard every route, and reinforcements distributed in depth. It was planned to slowly strangle the Communist redoubt until it was too weak to resist a final assault. 700,000 men were deployed for this vast operation, but many of them, on the southern and south-western borders of the Communist area, came from provincial armies, less well equipped and of poorer fighting quality than Chiang's own regulars. The size and significance of these military activities was largely ignored by the world in general. Virtually no authentic news reached the world press from the Communist side; what was available tended to be ignored by news-papers in Shanghai which for the most part, although not much enamoured of the Nationalist regime, still preferred it to the Communists. Diplomatic missions in the Nationalist capital, Nanking, were well in-formed of the failures and weaknesses of the Chiang regime, but if they passed on this information to their governments, it was not disclosed to the public.

The fifth extermination campaign, using the new strategy of blockade, was launched in October 1933. In November a revolt occurred in the province of Fukien, which borders Kiangsi to the east and extends to

*Right:* Photograph taken of Mao Tse-tung during the Long March from Kiangsi to northern Shensi. Mao had led his men through Chiang's encircling troops, blockhouses, and barbed wire to start the Long March. Among his companions on the march were Chu Teh, future commander-in-chief of the Red Army and Chou En-lai, future premier and foreign minister.
*Below:* Chairman Mao on stamp, 1950. The Long March had not been in vain

the coast. The revolt involved the 19th Route Army, which had valiantly resisted the Japanese attack at Shanghai in 1932, but which had afterwards been transferred to Fukien by Chiang Kai-shek, who had not really wanted to challenge the Japanese militarily at that stage, and who, in any case, was becoming increasingly disturbed by the immense prestige which the 19th Route Army and its commander, Chang Fa-kuei, had reaped from its tenacious action at Shanghai, overwhelmingly supported as it had been by the Chinese educated classes. The 19th Route Army was well aware that it had been relegated to a region where it was not likely to make contact with Japanese forces. At this point many discontented politicians of a left-wing persuasion, although members of the Nationalist Party, hastened to Foochow where they proclaimed a new provisional government. They attempted to elicit the co-operation of the Kiangsi Soviet, but their overtures were scorned by the Communists. Mao Tse-tung and Communist historians have since attributed this serious error of judgement to the leadership of the 're-turned students'. It is not at all certain that even if this is so, Mao and others did not support the rebuff at that time. It was a grave mistake. Fukien has a coast and ports and from this region the Communists could have established better communications with the outside world besides importing arms and supplies. It is at least prob-

able that they could have absorbed the provisional government at Foochow and amalgamated the two movements. Had they done so the fifth extermination campaign would probably have failed, and the Communist movement would have been permanently established in the south.

### The gruelling march begins

As it was the Fukien movement collapsed in January 1934, unassisted by the Communists, who were now faced with Chiang's undivided strength, which was beginning to prevail. Mao has stated that under the leadership which he opposed, the tactics of guerrilla warfare were abandoned and plans to counter the Nationalist blockade by conventional warfare adopted – with disastrous results. There seems to be strong evidence that this was the case, and that in this year Mao's own authority was at a low ebb. In the summer of 1934 it became obvious that the blockade could not be lifted and that the choice lay between a break-out and ultimate extermination. It is, of course, now claimed that Mao was the originator of the plan to break out, and thus the Long March and its triumphant consequences are held to reveal his vision of the real road to victory. This is perhaps going somewhat beyond the known facts. It is not at all certain how the decision to retreat was arrived at, nor by whom. At that time it would certainly have needed to be a collective decision, for Mao was not

the master of the party, and the leadership itself was seriously discredited by failure. Probably their plight was so plain that no other decision was possible, and therefore no opposition or alternative put forward. What is certain is that it was a resolute, desperate venture, which at best only promised some hope of survival and from which few can have hoped to snatch victory. Mao has himself pointed out that a retreat is not itself a victory, even if its ultimate results can be exploited to transform defeat into triumph.

Communist historians and others who have since claimed Mao Tse-tung conceived the Long March also maintain that its ultimate destination of northern Shensi was selected in order to bring the Communists into touch with an area likely to be invaded by the Japanese. Chiang would thus find it very hard to continue attacks upon a patriotic party engaged in defending the country against alien invaders. There is some evidence for this intention; but in October 1934 when the Red Army and its dependants who were fit enough to make the march, left Kiangsi, their numbers had been reduced to approximately 100,000 in all and only the optimists could have felt confident that this small force could fight its way across China and survive in northern Shensi, a barren and harsh land. Many, even among the senior leaders were too sick to make the attempt. Ch'ü Ch'iu-pai, seriously ill with tuberculosis,

had to be left to make his way in secret to the comparative safety of Shanghai. He was arrested and shot by the Nationalists soon after the evacuation of Kiangsi.

The main body broke out of the blockaded area to the south-west, into the southern part of Hunan and then crossed into the backward province of Kweichow, traversing it to enter Yunnan, in the extreme south-west. This circuitous route to northern Shensi took the Red Army into territories ruled by backward and ill-armed warlords who had never so far admitted more than nominal allegiance to Nanking. They could offer no real resistance to the Red Army, and Chiang Kai-shek, relishing their plight, followed up with his regular troops rather slowly, in order to impose his own authority on the local warlords. His air force tried to bomb the Red Army, but with scant success. The Communists made few attempts to take cities, as the warlords concentrated their strength there to defend wealth and property, leaving the countryside to its fate. The Communist forces proved anything but a scourge: they treated the people with a restraint hitherto unknown in Chinese military annals and paid for supplies and porterage. Muleteers who accompanied the Communists could only complain of the inordinately long marches by which the Red Army proceeded to northern Shensi. The Communists never marched less than thirty or forty miles a day. My porter, who had been on the Long March, told me in

1936 that two years earlier the Red Army had crossed seventy miles over mountains and passes in twenty-four hours. It took us three days to cover the same ground.

Those who could not maintain these feats of endurance were left in the care of friendly peasants, to be concealed for years, if they lived. In later years the victorious Communists searched for lost children and relatives left en route. Some dramatic reunions were effected, but many were never traced. The policy of kind treatment to the peasantry paid off, and the very long distances marched confounded the tactics of the pursuers, who were never able to intercept the marchers. Taking a wide sweep through northern Kweichow and western Yunan the main body crossed the high Yangtze and penetrated into Sikang, the western province which is really eastern Tibet, but which had been under Chinese rule for a long period. Here, on 30th May 1935, the Red Army performed a celebrated feat of arms —the crossing of the Tatu river, a tributary of the Yangtze, at the Luting bridge. At this point the river flows in a deep gorge 100 metres wide, and was spanned by an ancient suspension bridge, typical of the region, made up of thirteen great iron chains pegged into the rocks on either side, and covered with planks. The defenders had removed the planks, but failed, or had not troubled to sever the chains. Covered by machine gun fire, twenty hand-picked men, armed with swords and hand grenades

*Red Army toiling over the Great Snow Mountains: recent painting by Ai Chung-hsin. The Long March is justly seen as an epic of human endurance*

swung along the chains and overpowered the defending guards. Only three of the attackers were killed. The planks were then replaced and the whole army crossed.

By the 12th June, after crossing the Great Snow Mountains (Tahsueh shan), the army reached a place called Moukung in Szechuan province. Here they encountered the Communist 4th Front Army, commanded by Chang Kuo-t'ao, who with Hsu Hsiang-ch'ien had some three years earlier set up a Soviet area in north-east Szechuan. Driven from the region, the 4th Front Army had moved south and west, and now met with Mao and Chu Teh and the 1st Front Army. A conference took place, but it soon appeared that Chang and Mao were not in agreement. Chang wanted to stay in Szechuan and set up another Soviet area; Mao wanted to press on to Shensi, nearer to the region where the coming war with Japan would be fought. The two armies agreed to proceed northwards, which meant crossing the grasslands of eastern Tibet, a vast swamp at a great altitude, bitterly cold, uninhabited, and roadless. The crossing of the grasslands from August—September 1935 is perhaps the most remarkable exploit of the Long March. The differences between Chang and Mao now led to a separ-

ation. On 18th September 1935 Mao went on into Kansu province defeating Nationalist troops who sought to bar the way, and after crossing the high Liup'anshan (Six Loop Mountains) descended into Shensi on 20th October, reaching the north Shensi Soviet area supervised by Kao Kang. This was the end of the Long March for the 1st Front Army.

Chang Kuo-t'ao had rejected this line of march. He recrossed the grasslands in September and attempted to establish himself in Szechuan. Failing in this, he crossed the grasslands for the third time in May 1936 and went on to north-western Kansu in an attempt to reach Sinkiang, which, as the great western province bordering on the USSR, he hoped would provide refuge. He failed, and in May 1937 was forced to seek safety with Mao in north Shensi. Not long afterwards Chang Kuo-t'ao deserted to the Nationalists, and in 1938 he was expelled from the party. He retired in old age to Hong Kong. Meanwhile the 2nd Front Army, originating in the separate Communist region on the Hunan-Hupeh border, had also carried out its Long March, rather further south and west than that of Mao and the 1st Front Army. It set out in November 1935 and Ho Lung its leader took the route through Kweichow and western Yunnan, crossing into Sikang over the high Yangtze at Chütien in May 1936. It then moved north to Szechuan and in forty days crossed the grasslands, finally making contact with the north Shensi 1st Front Army in October 1936. Its arrival boosted the strength of the combined Red Army to 80,000 men but of the 100,000 men of the 1st Front Army who had set out on their gruelling journey, not more than 30,000 had survived to reach north Shensi.

Chiang's hopes were dashed. The Red Army was once more established in a fixed base, this time at Yenan where it was well protected by a maze of barren mountains. War with Japan as everyone knew was imminent; it may well be that the successful conclusion of the Long March, or marches as they really were, constituted a contributory cause of the conflict. Japan had given Chiang the chance to exterminate the Red Army. He had failed, and the Japanese now had to contend with a menacing Communist presence on the flank of the provinces they planned to invade and occupy. Although Chiang was still planning more extermination campaigns he claimed the Long March as a great Nationalist victory, and it is indeed true that the Red Army had suffered heavy losses, but these were due far more to the rigours of nature than the prowess of the Nationalist forces. Chiang still refused to abandon his policy of suppressing internal rebellion before resisting foreign aggression. His attitude was soon, by the end of 1936, to precipitate the next Sino-Japanese crisis, which led to a truce between Nationalists and Communists, and directly to the Japanese invasion of July 1937.

*Left: Heroic end to journey which has become part of Chinese folklore: recent Chinese propagandist painting of Long March survivors in Yenan*

# The Spanish Civil War

The Spanish Civil War of 1936-39 was the fourth armed conflict fought out on Spanish soil in the 140 years since the beginning of the 19th century, and to a great extent the matters at stake in the 1930's were the same as those in the Carlist wars of the 1830's and the 1870's and in the Peninsular War, namely: the place of the Roman Catholic Church in society; the relation between the central province of Castile and the economically more advanced outlying regions of Catalonia and the Basque provinces; and the relation between classes. In the 20th century these old quarrels were exacerbated by the impact of modern technology—exemplified by the fact that the Andalusian upper class attributed the civil war to the telephone—and by the unfortunate coincidence that quarrelling erupted into conflict at an especially nervous moment in the history of Europe, so that other European countries, such as Great Britain, France, Russia, Germany, Italy, and Portugal became inevitably involved in varying degrees. Consequently although the war itself was a wholly Spanish affair in origin, it became an international crisis whose 'solution' was decided by external considerations.

The war began with a military conspiracy against the liberal government. A number of prominent right-wing officers, including most of those who had done well in the Moroccan wars of the 1920's, believed that the new, parliamentarily weak government of the Centre was only one step away from surrendering to just such a revolution as had occurred in Russia twenty years earlier. Most of the political Right and the old master classes of Spain generally were mesmerized by fear of another 'Russia'. They had for a time collaborated with the democratic Spanish Republic after the abdication of King Alfonso XIII in 1931 but now, with continuous verbal intransigence on the Left and much disorder in the streets, they believed that the Republican system of liberalism was doomed. Tacitly or actively the military conspiracy had the support of most of the Spanish middle-class, and of the Church. It was also supported by a small but growing semi-fascist party, the Falange, and the Carlist movement, a 19th-century survival which had re-established firm roots in parts of the rural north of Spain (particularly Navarre) during recent anti-clerical legislation.

On the other side, the liberal government was well intentioned and had much enlightened legislation to its credit in the early thirties. But its members were pitifully ignorant of economic management, often substituting rhetoric for policy. Furthermore, they were hemmed in on the Left by a large if divided Socialist Party (one branch of whose leadership, weary of

democratic compromises and frustrations was heading Leftwards) and by an immense if amorphous and anarchic-syndicalist labour movement which had poured scorn on, and had done its best to sabotage, democratic reform. They also had to contend with a Communist Party which, like the Falange on the Right, was small but increasing in numbers. The anarcho-syndicalists had no truck with the government of the liberals as they had had no truck with that of the King or the democratic Right. The Socialists and the Communists on the other hand nominally supported the government with whom indeed they had fought the previous general election. But they were not represented in the government.

The military conspiracy went off at half-cock. Spanish Morocco, the Canaries, Majorca, the north-west of Spain, Navarre, and large tracts of Old Castile and Aragón were quickly won by the rebels. But in the large cities such as Madrid, Barcelona, and Bilbao and most of the prosperous east, south, and the centre of the country, the rebels were quickly defeated by the government acting in conjunction with, or in many places displaced by, the working-class organizations.

### Orgy of killings

On both sides there then followed a ferocious purge. On the Right the army systematically sought to root out all possible government sympathizers, including on occasions even those who had simply voted for the Left in the preceding election. Many were arbitrarily shot, many more imprisoned for long periods. (Due to the unavailability of police or other records, it is impossible to make an accurate estimate of the numbers so killed, but the figure must have approached 50,000.) On the Left, the removal in many cities of the police and the army, who were compromised by the rebellion, permitted an unofficial but no less bloody persecution, sponsored by anarchists, or sections of the Communist and Socialist Parties. There were also as usual in such circumstances a very large number of outright criminals who seized on the occasion to settle old scores. In these massacres, the Church suffered particularly severely, many churches being burned and upwards of 6,000 priests, nuns, and monks being killed, including twelve bishops: in Barbastro province, Aragón, no less than eighty per cent of the priests died. Many of these killings were officially denounced by the government but they continued for weeks. Once again, it is hard to determine accurately the number of those who died, but they probably exceeded those killed behind the lines on the Right.

While political life more or less came to an end in the areas under military control, commerce and the economy being increasingly subordinated to the army, the government for a time lost control of the situation in the areas where the rising had been crushed. Here the working class organiza-

¡PUEBLOS DE LEVANTE!
Los hijos, las madres y las compañeras de los heroes de Madrid no deben perecer bajo la metralla y el fuego de los aviones fascistas.

¡Facilitad su evacuación! ¡Haced un hueco cariñoso!

PARTIDO COMUNISTA (S. E. de la I. C.)

*Above*: Communist Party poster calls on the people of south-eastern Spain to show compassion for civilians trapped in battle-torn Madrid, where the rebels were quickly defeated, by offering to take them in.
*Below*: Silhouetted against the sky, half-crouching Republican troops advance into battle—taken by Robert Capa, considered to be one of the greatest war photographers

Magnum Photo: Robert Capa

tions not only proceeded to wreak vengeance on their enemies but sought to carry out a full-blooded revolution. The government was thus powerless to act while the anarchists took over key industries in Barcelona, formed collectives on most large estates (sometimes in collaboration with the local Socialists) and organized militia

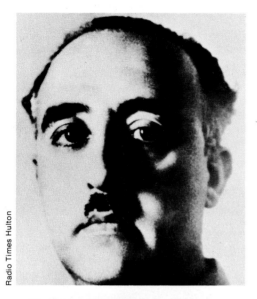

*Top left: General Francisco Franco, rebel leader and victor in the Spanish Civil War. He was determined to achieve complete military victory. Centre Left: Largo Caballero, Socialist Prime Minister. He refused to take office unless Communists joined the government. Left: Negrín, Caballero's successor as Prime Minister. He saw Spain's salvation in close cooperation with the USSR*

units to fight the rebels. Within weeks of the outbreak of the rebellion, both Catalonia and the Basque provinces had achieved autonomous regimes by their own declaration. Gradually however the coming of actual civil war forced an end to all such experimentation. Backed by the right wings of the Socialists and Communists in an uneasy and ephemeral alliance, the government began to resume command. The Socialist Largo Caballero became Prime Minister and the Communists entered the coalition cabinet, being later joined by representatives of anarchists, who were themselves prepared (unlike many of their followers) to postpone discussion of the exact nature of the social revolution to be enacted in Spain until after the end of the Civil War, and to support the Communists in their effort to organize a strong but conventional army out of the disorganized militias. Meantime the anarchists' insistence on collectivization antagonized many peasants and small shopkeepers who turned towards the one party prepared to defend them, namely the Communists, whose strength accordingly grew phenomenally, being afterwards also joined by many Socialists disgusted by the divisions and arguments in their own party and by nearly the whole of the Socialist youth movement.

### Help from Hitler

By this time straight-forward military questions were becoming paramount. To begin with the rebels had seemed certain to lose the war since they had failed in the capital, in the largest industrial centres, and two thirds of the population. Some of the cities where they had gained immediate victory such as Toledo, Seville, Granada, or Córdoba were isolated redoubts surrounded by a revolutionary countryside. The government had also won over many senior army officers and most of the admittedly small air force, and, after a revolution in the fleet, most of the rebel naval officers had been murdered. The rebellion, it seemed, was ill-starred. Its nominal leader, General Sanjurjo, had been killed in an air crash, most of the leaders of the Falange (including its chief, José Antonio Primo de Rivera) were in prison or had been shot, while the outstanding right-wing politician of the pre-war days, Calvo Sotelo, had been murdered a few days before the outbreak of open war. Nevertheless, General Mola, the leader of the military conspiracy, refused a telephoned offer of a compromise with the government and despatched a motley army, half conscripts, and half Carlist or Falangist volunteers, south from Burgos to Madrid. This force was held at the summit of the Guadarrama mountains by government

militias. But another force despatched by Mola did capture the summer resort of San Sebastián and thereby cut off the Basques from contact with relatively friendly France; while in the south General Franco, who had taken over command of the native troops and the Foreign Legion in Morocco, successfully transported a number of these crack units across the straits of Gibraltar, thereby turning the tide in Andalusia, relieving within a matter of weeks all the main rebel outposts there. He then despatched this so-called Army of Africa north to Badajoz and thence along the Tagus valley first to Toledo (relieved after a siege) and then to Madrid.

These events had not occurred, however, without the beginning of foreign intervention. While there was no explicit agreement on either side for military assistance from any foreign power before the war began, requests were quickly made by the generals for help from Mussolini, Hitler, and the Prime Minister of Portugal, Oliveira Salazar. At the same time the government urgently appealed for military material from France with whom they had an agreement to buy arms. Hitler sent a military mission and a number of transport aircraft which were of use in getting the Army of Africa across the Straits; Mussolini sent fighters, and Salazar agreed to provide every facility that the rebels needed – a great help in the early days. But France, worried by the possibility of involvement in a foreign adventure where she suspected that she could not count on the backing of Great Britain, was more circumspect. Further, the French government depended for its survival on the support of the Radical Party who were actively hostile to giving any help to the Spanish government. In consequence, France proposed an international scheme whereby all the European countries would undertake not to sell arms to Spain and to punish any of their nationals detected in so doing. Great Britain supported this scheme strongly and together with France persuaded all the European powers to accept it. A committee was set up in London to try and administer this interesting experiment in international control.

### A testing ground

The trouble with this plan, however, was that from the beginning neither Germany nor Italy had any intention of adhering to it. This was particularly true of Germany who had quickly discovered that Spanish minerals might, if successfully negotiated for, be of great importance in her own war preparations. Göring was also interested in providing a place for testing his 'young Luftwaffe' and other new elements of the German armed services. In consequence there was a regular flow of war material to the rebels from German ports for over two years, accompanied by a small number of military technicians, pilots, and tank crews. On several occasions these forces played critical parts. Mussolini also did his best, making up in quantity what he could not provide in quality. At one point there were 50,000 Italian servicemen in Spain – his motive for intervention being partly a strategic desire to present France with a further hostile frontier. He got no real advantage from the war, unlike the Germans, but it satisfied his ego to see Italy waving a big stick in the world again.

These developments soon became known though France, having earlier allowed a number of aircraft to proceed to Spain under André Malraux, the novelist and future minister of culture, pressed on with Great Britain in a desperate attempt to shore up non-intervention. 'Better a leaky dam than no dam at all' was the view of Anthony Eden, the British foreign minister, expressing the great hostility of British politicians to anything which might risk an expansion of the conflict (or of any conflict) and therefore increase the danger of a more general war. But no such comfortable formula was possible, for Russia was being pressed strongly by the world Communist parties to help Spain. Apparently against his better judgment Stalin did decide to send both men and material to help the government, for fear of being internationally outflanked on the Left by the Trotskyists who clamoured for intervention. The Communists also successfully organized the International Brigades of volunteers, not all of them being Communists, to fight alongside the government militias; and they acquitted themselves with great valour in several fierce battles. Hence the Spanish Civil War became more and more a European civil war fought out on Spanish soil: in one battle, Guadalajara, for instance left-wing Italian volunteers successfully turned back a regular Italian army force sent by Mussolini while German fought German in the environs of Madrid. In these circumstances the Non-Intervention Committee in London dithered on, listening to counter-charge and counter-charge by the German, Italian, and Russian representatives—all of whom lied.

General Franco's army had meanwhile reached the gates of Madrid. By means of a political manoeuvre scarcely less than a coup d'état, he had become head of state and head of the government of Nationalist Spain. As such he was recognized as the government of Spain by his German and Italian allies. All observers supposed that Madrid would soon fall, either to the four columns advancing on the city or by the action of a 'fifth column' of sympathizers within the city. It did not do so, due to the effective mobilization of the population of the capital, and to the last minute arrival of Russian aircraft, tanks, and advisers and the International Brigades. There were a series of indecisive battles around Madrid (Jarama, Guadalajara) from which General Franco gained ground but not the capital. In March he called off the offensive and turned to the north.

The campaign in the north occupied most of the rest of 1937. The Basque provinces and Asturias were finally reduced, providing Franco with rich mineral resources with which to bargain with Germany for arms supplies. Republican offensives at Brunete (near Madrid) and in Aragón ground to a halt. Despite the Republican control of much of the fleet, Franco's possession of the northern provinces, and his ability to rely on the German and Italian navies gave

him effective control of the sea, permitting aid from abroad to arrive effortlessly. The situation was different on the Republican side, where Russian aid had to traverse the difficult sea route through the Mediterranean, often meeting the attacks of disavowed Italian submarines. Some material was smuggled through from France but in keeping with the Non-Intervention Agreement she kept her southern frontier closed to the passage of arms for long periods. Short of food as well as of arms, it seemed only a matter of time before the government forces would collapse. There had also been continued difficulties behind the lines: fighting had broken out between Communists and anarchists in May; the Communists had carried out a purge of the revolutionary anti-Russian Communist Party the Partido Obrero de Unificación Marxista; and the Prime Minister, Largo Caballero, had been supplanted by the more moderate Dr Negrín, who was prepared to face the reality that the British and French boycott left him with no option but to remain on terms with Russia. Communist tactics in the army and in agriculture were depressing morale, while the anarchist dream

of immediate social revolution was inevitably stemmed by the need to harness industry and commerce to war. Even autonomous Catalonia was largely overcome by a centralizing government determined to sacrifice all to the priority of winning or at least sustaining the conflict. By this time, there were in effect two strong nation states at war rather than two Spanish parties. The difference between them was that while the government or the Left would perhaps have from 1937 onwards accepted some form of compromise peace, General Franco was determined on achieving nothing short of military victory. And in truth the only likely alternative to such a victory was an arbitrary dividing line, resulting in the quasi-permanent establishment of two Spains, on the model of the later divisions of Korea and Germany.

*Below: Italian troops in camouflaged capes. Mussolini sent 50,000 servicemen to Spain, making up in quantity what he could not provide in quality.*
*Bottom: Ground crew of the German Condor Legion arm a Heinkel III for a strike into Republican territory*

### Russian aid dwindles

The war dragged on throughout 1938 and into 1939. Two big government offensives at Teruel and on the Ebro river gained ground for a time but were ultimately repelled at great cost, Franco being enabled to cut the government territory in two by May 1938. In December 1939 Franco launched a major campaign against the government redoubt in Catalonia. By this time, partly thanks to the international situation after Munich, partly because of the greater difficulties of ensuring safe passage, Russian aid to the government had become a trickle. Normal commerce with government ports had declined because of Franco's blockade and because of air attacks on shipping. The food situation was bad. It had become evident to all, including the German government, that Great Britain (and in her train France) would never risk a general war over Spain, and particularly not over any breach of the Non-Intervention Agreement. Doubtless Great Britain should have taken a firm line and stated explicitly that continued German and Italian evasions of the agreement were making a mockery of all concerned; that therefore Great Britain would enable the Republic to buy arms freely on a commercial basis; and that further interference with British and other shipping on the high sea would not be brooked. Germany might then have backed down. But no such robustness was forthcoming. The consequences were that by the winter of 1938-39 with Barcelona and Catalonia threatened, the only real hope for the Republicans was the possibility of the outbreak of a general European war, over Czechoslovakia or Poland, in the course of which German aid to General Franco might have been expected to drop and perhaps a French or British expeditionary force, echoing the War of the Spanish Succession or the Napoleonic Wars, might have reappeared in Spain.

This, however, was not to be. Franco smashed Catalonia without a fight, and thousands of government troops were permitted to withdraw into France, along with the government itself. Dr Negrín flew back to the centre of Spain in February and began an investigation as to the possibility of continued resistance in the far from inconsiderable area, including the capital, left to his followers. Both he and the Communists supported, at least in their declarations, the aims of resistance to the bitter end, though some doubt must exist as to their real intentions since their preparations for such a heroic stand were not impressive. But this defiant declaration created such alarm that a conspiracy among many disgruntled liberals, anarchists, and members of the Socialist Party took shape within the government. They wrongly believed Negrín to be the tool of the Communist Party and feared that his intransigence coupled with that of the Communists was preventing the achievement of a compromise peace. In early March 1939, Colonel Casado rose against Negrín and the Communists in Madrid. There was much fighting. A civil war within the Civil War was thus the humiliating

culmination of so many months of sacrifice and endeavour. The Communists who had all along dominated the government army won the day in Madrid but in the rest of Spain widespread dissatisfaction with Negrín came to the surface and there was a mutiny in the fleet and a Falangist rising in Cartagena. Negrín and the leading Communists thereupon fled abroad, leaving Casado in control. Having shot his leading Communist opponents in the capital, Casado then turned to try and negotiate with Franco. But as Negrín could have told him Franco had no intention of effecting any compromise. Nor had he any need to do so. By that time Great Britain and France as well as Germany and Italy were ready to recognize him as the government of Spain. He had enough armaments from abroad to be able to contemplate a new offensive against Madrid without fear of resistance. Even while negotiations between himself and Casado were being fruitlessly pursued, the government armies began to melt away. In the end Casado, accompanied by such as could, made their escape from Spain by sea, and handed over Madrid without a fight. By 1st April 1939 rebel armies were in control in all the main cities of Spain. Some semi-guerrilla war went on for months in the Cantabrian mountains, but troubled no one.

### Victory, hunger, and misery

The main reasons for General Franco's victory were threefold: first he successfully galvanized the forces of the Right in Spain into accepting him as *Caudillo* (leader), and rallied behind him all the surviving right-wing politicians and groups. The Church with few exceptions (mostly in the ultra-religious Basque provinces, where most priests were Basque nationalists) rallied behind the rebels from the start of the war, being naturally horrified by the widespread massacres of their Republican counterparts and by the permanent closure of all churches save in the Basque area. The fascists of the Falange might perhaps have disputed Franco's leadership had more of their leaders survived the holocaust of the first days. But José Antonio Primo de Rivera, by far the most brilliant of them, was misguidedly shot after trial in a government gaol; as were, in even less edifying circumstances, most of his more able followers. This left a worthy but politically inexperienced Falangist from Santander, Manuel Hedilla, as the only possible rival to Franco. But he was gaoled by Franco after the latter had staged a merger of all the rebel parties, Carlists as well as Falangists, in a new movement with an ideology of almost insulting simplicity. In this the few surviving old Falangists were swamped by new recruits. This party never became a true fascist party, since it was always subservient to the Church and it never developed a semi-military organization. Much of the rebels' propaganda with its appeals to a heroic past, its stress on leadership, and insistence on a Spain untouched by 'internationalism' such as Jewry or liberalism or freemasonry was fascist in tone, but it scarcely went deeper than a justification for the persecution of

freemasons and liberals and similar groups.

On the other side, after the first hectic days of July 1936 there was never much trust between the different parties which made up the government coalition; neither Largo Caballero nor Negrín succeeded in establishing himself as the unquestioned national leader – though to be fair none of their possible rivals could have done any better. There was the paradox that the evident wisdom of the Communists' political proposals – a delay in the social revolution – was counterbalanced by their intolerance and cruelty towards opponents in a weaker position.

The second reason for Franco's victory was that since the war was fought in conventional terms, the generals had a slight edge over their opponents even though the People's Army on the government side was a remarkable achievement of swift organization. No serious effort was made to articulate anarchist discontent with a regular army structure into guerrilla activity on a large scale.

Finally, Franco received more regular and more substantial aid from Germany and Italy than the government did from Russia or from the international arms trade. This international assistance covered strategic goods as well as arms: government excesses in the first days of the Civil War antagonized international finance, and enabled Franco to receive credits from abroad, in particular from the Texas Oil Company which gambled on a rebel victory from the outset. The widespread sympathy which the government's cause excited on the Left in Europe and North America did, however, counterbalance this help.

The war was followed by a bloody proscription, when large numbers of government sympathizers were imprisoned and shot. The outbreak of the Second World War in September prevented any international finance being available for reconstruction in Spain and the succeeding years were therefore a time of hunger and misery.

*Top right: Spanish peasant woman surveys one of the war's many victims. The number of deaths in the Civil War is customarily held to be one million. The figure suits both victors and vanquished. The former can argue that they saved Spain from atheism and Communism at a cost of a million dead. The latter can allege that Franco climbed to power over a million corpses. It is more likely, however, that the total number of violent deaths in the Civil War was just over 400,000. Deaths from malnutrition, starvation, or disease directly attributable to the war may have amounted to over 100,000. Top far right: Last stand in Irún, September 1936. Taking the place of a dead comrade, a Republican sniper maintains fire on advancing rebels from a ruined farmhouse. Right: Welcome assistance for an elderly refugee. Terrified refugees were a frequent and harrowing sight all over Spain; thousands poured over the Pyrenees into France as the Nationalist armies established their hold over the country*

Keystone Press

# France and the Popular Front

The economic crisis which began in Wall Street in 1929 affected France later than other European countries, but with equal force. Men out of work, engineers as well as labourers, haunted the streets. The peasants' standard of living dropped; the industrial workers, forced to accept a reduction in working time, suffered a corresponding drop in wages. The crisis, which subsided a little in 1932, surged up again in 1933. It was in this atmosphere that a financial scandal, the Stavisky Affair, exploded. It was very clear that

*Léon Blum, France's first Socialist Prime Minister. As head of the Popular Front government he inherited a disturbed France besides a depressed economy*

Stavisky must have depended on the ineptitude or corruption of politicians then in power—mainly Radical deputies. Radical ministers, including the Prime Minister, were compelled to resign. The Right welcomed this opportunity to attack the moderates, and the Leagues, the militarily disciplined street-fighters of the fascist-inspired section of the Right, threatened to come out on the streets to force a semi-fascist take-over of the government.

On 6th February 1934 Edouard Daladier, one of the leaders of the Radical Party, formed a new government and presented his choice of ministers to the Chamber. On the same day the Leagues staged a massive demonstration in the Place de la Concorde, crying 'Down with the robbers', and threatened to march across the Seine to storm the Chamber of Deputies. Their way was barred by the police who opened fire, killing fourteen demonstrators. Over two thousand people were injured in the struggle, most of them policemen. Daladier, despite the opposition of the Right and the Communists, was supported by a majority in the Chamber, but when he was told on the following day that the demonstrations would be resumed with even more violence he resigned.

The provinces reacted sharply: the Left was eager to take up the challenge proffered by the Right. France was on the verge of civil war. A young Communist, at the time a school teacher in a provincial town, described in his novel *La Conspiration (The Conspiracy)* the atmosphere which hung over the country: 'It was a time which recalled the beginning of the Wars of Religion, when the barns of the Protestants went up in flames, when men travelled along the roads to fight. . . . Armed bands were formed, and through the towns marched processions of workers such as had not been seen for decades.'

In Paris the Communist organization of ex-servicemen, the ARAC (Association Républicaine des Anciens Combattants) had also threatened to demonstrate on 6th February; on the 8th it was still denouncing 'the ministry of the firing squads'; on the 9th it staged a demonstration in the Place de la République which was brutally suppressed. More lives were lost. On 12th February the CGT (Confédération Générale du Travail—a trade union federation) joined in the ferment of protest and called for a general strike. Most of the unions obeyed its call. On the same day, in Paris and the largest provincial towns, there were large-scale demonstrations demanding that the Republic should not be throttled nor public rights stifled. What had happened in Germany in 1933 was not going to be repeated in France if the people could prevent it.

The great surprise of 12th February was that the French Communist Party at last rallied to the 'defence of the Republic'. Until then, in the eyes of the Communist leaders, the Radical Socialist Daladier had been no better than the fascist Leagues. But Moscow suddenly realized the danger to which the USSR would be exposed by an alliance between a fascist government installed in Paris and the Nazi government in power in Berlin. Instructions were issued to the leaders of the French Communist Party to change their tactics. They were ordered to effect an entente with the Socialist Party and even with the Radical Party, and not only with their adherents and well-wishers but even with their leaders, who hitherto had been consistently vilified.

### The Left unites

On 12th February 1934, on the Cours de Vincennes, the Socialists found that the Communists who had shaken their fists at them only the day before were suddenly stretching out their hands to them with the cry of 'Unity!' In July 1934 they applauded the signing of the United Action Pact between the SFIO (Section Française de l'Internationale Ouvrière—the Socialist Party) and the Communist Party. But they were astounded a few weeks later to see a declaration signed by the authorized representatives of the Communist Party affirming its desire to extend the alliance to include the Radicals and the political organizations of the Left-inclined bourgeoisie.

This alliance, merging the ambitions of the proletariat with those of the middle class, could never have come about without the coincidence of three factors. The first was diplomatic. The USSR, apparently renouncing the position it had taken for fifteen years, rallied to the cause of collective security, and in May 1935 signed a pact with France, in which Stalin commented that he 'fully approved of the national defence policy adopted by France in order to maintain the armed forces at the level demanded by security'. The second factor was political. The League of the Croix de Feu was stepping up the frequency of its motorized rallies, which seemed to threaten a march on Paris. Its leader, Colonel de la Rocque, made menacing speeches in which he announced that the time for making a clean sweep was close at hand. At such a moment how could the Left risk a further split? Finally, there was a psychological factor. The masses had begun to mistrust the political parties as ineffectual and incapable. The action taken by the CGT and the recruitment of eminent intellectuals, hitherto uninterested, were restoring to the Left the intellectual and moral prestige it had lost.

### The masses march

The Popular Front, officially the 'Rassemblement Populaire', was more than a coalition of parties. It was the gathering together of a large number of organizations, differing in character and importance but all equally determined not to allow a fascist government to be set up in France. The executive committee of the Popular Front was composed of delegates from ten large organizations. Only four of these were political parties: the Communist Party, led by Maurice Thorez; the Socialist Party (SFIO) headed by Léon Blum; the Socialist-Republican Union (USR), composed of Socialists who had broken away from their party in 1905, 1920, and 1933;

*The 1930's in France saw the heyday of the fascist Leagues. Here Parisians read posters which announce the demonstration of 6th February 1934*

and the Radical Socialist Party, which had as its most prominent members Edouard Daladier, Edouard Herriot, and Camille Chautemps. The other six organizations were to arbitrate in possible conflicts between the four political parties. They included the CGT, led by Léon Jouhaux, and one other more Communist-inclined trade union organization; three left-wing intellectual groups; and the Mouvement d'Action Combattante (Movement for Fighting Action), an amalgamation of various left-wing organizations of ex-servicemen.

Originally the object of the alliance was to organize impressive mass demonstrations throughout the country on 14th July 1935, when the participants would swear to remain united in defence of democracy and for the dissolution of the 'turbulent Leagues'. But it swiftly became clear that the Popular Front represented more than an alliance of divided political groups. Marching shoulder to shoulder in processions which sometimes numbered hundreds of thousands of men, all with the same banners, the same words of command, the same enemies, the masses became aware of their strength, and of a sense of brotherhood. The processions were greeted as though it was carnival time. They relived in imagination the enthusiasm of the great days of the Revolution in 1789. So conscious of their power did they appear, escorted on either side by the disciplined forces of the trade unions and other organizations, that it seemed enough to display their strength: they did not need to use it.

After this great day it was unthinkable that any of the organizations who had formed the Popular Front should return to its old isolation. The National Committee decided unanimously to work out a common programme of action. It was not, however, until January 1936 that this made its appearance, after laborious discussions. The Radicals and Communists wanted a programme of demands moderate enough to avoid alarming the middle classes. Socialists of the SFIO and syndicalists in the CGT advocated a plan permitting structural economic reforms, particularly the nationalization of various industries. So as not to risk a rupture, they refrained from insisting on their demands. The programme as published was more of an election programme than a coherent plan.

## Elections

A general election was due to be held in 1936. The Popular Front did not approach it without apprehension. Members of the Leagues offered themselves for election in numerous constituencies. Were they going to enjoy a success like that of the National Socialists in Germany in September 1930? What would be the reaction of the rural districts which had been vigorously conditioned in certain regions by anti-parliamentary movements, especially that promoted by Dorgères, the leader of the 'Peasant Front'? At the first ballot there was some rivalry among the parties of the Popular Front. At the second ballot only the candidate who had headed the poll among the parties of the Left was to remain in the running, benefiting from the retirement of the other Left parties in accordance with the Popular Front programme, which had again become the common one. But would the candidates poorly placed in the first ballot agree to sacrifice themselves? Would the electors have the discipline to comply with the parties' instructions?

On the evening of the first ballot, on 26th April 1936, several certainties emerged: there had been no massive vote in favour of the candidates supported by the Leagues; in some regions even many of the peasants had voted Communist, the Communist Party increasing its vote from 783,000 in 1932 to 1,468,000 in 1936. But at the second ballot would this wave of votes towards the extreme Left bring with it a backlash of nervous electors towards the Right? No; on the evening of the 3rd May the Popular Front gained a total of 376 seats, composed of 72 Communists, 147 SFIO, 25 USR, 106 Radical Socialists, 26 Left Independents. It was much more than an absolute majority, and it was the first time in the history of the Third Republic that the Socialist Party (SFIO) had become the strongest party of the Left. But in spite of this big swing in representation, there was no change in the balance of political forces within the nation. In actual votes the parties of the Right and the Centre had only lost some 200,000 votes. That uneasy balance of strength which condemned the nation to permanent political instability still survived. On 4th May, Blum, who had not reckoned on so great an electoral success, claimed on behalf of the Socialist Party the right to be entrusted with the formation of the new government.

This right was not contested by the President of the Republic, Albert Lebrun, but the powers of the old Chamber did not expire till the end of the month. The country was faced with an interregnum of several weeks. Blum proposed to spend it quietly in forming his governmental team and in drawing up a plan of campaign against the capitalist reactions he foresaw.

The chief architect of the Popular Front had become the first Socialist and first Jewish Prime Minister of France. Yet Blum, an Alsatian, had made his name as a brilliant essayist, and literary and dramatic critic after graduating in law from the Sorbonne. He then entered active politics on the side of the Republican Dreyfusards during the Dreyfus affair. During the 1890's his criticisms appeared in the *Revue Blanche (White Revue)*, a review published by a select group of mainly Jewish intellectuals, including Proust. In 1901 he published a study on literature, aesthetics, and politics. His critical masterpiece, however, was a study on the French novelist Stendhal published in 1914. It was his association with Jean Jaurès, whom he greatly admired, which led to his joining the Socialist Party in 1899. In 1919 Blum was elected to the Chamber of Deputies and his first task was to reconstruct the Socialist Party after the split of December 1920 when the Communist section of it won a majority at the Congress of Tours and so inherited the party machinery, funds, and press. Blum, who ranks as the maker of the modern French Socialist Party and of its chief journal *Le Populaire (Voice of the People)*, led the opposition to the governments of both Millerand and Poincaré and in 1924 supported Herriot's Cartel des Gauches (Radical Coalition), though refusing to participate in the ministries of Herriot and Aristide Briand. In the elections of 1928 the Socialist Party won 104 seats in the Chamber, but Blum himself was defeated. A year later he was returned for Narbonne which also returned him in 1936, the year of his victory.

But an unexpected turn of events, unwished for by the leaders of the trade union movement, soured the achievement of the Socialist Party: a wave of stay-in strikes swept the country, starting with the metal industry in Paris and extending to other branches of industry and to commercial concerns, and overflowing into the provinces.

It was no trade union conspiracy. Active minorities, revolutionary trade unionists,

PARTI COMMUNISTE FRANÇAIS 120, rue Lafayette

*Above right: Communist election poster, 1937 stigmatizes French bankers for their preoccupation with speculation and profit terming them 'parasites of the Bourse'.*
*Above far right: Striking sawmill workers, Paris 1936. Devastating strikes swept France that year. Right: ARAC (Association Républicaine des Anciens Combattants) rally, Paris, February 1936. An ARAC demonstration in the Place de la Concorde on 9th February was brutally suppressed. Far right: In a French cartoon of 1937 the Republic, retreating before the clenched fist of Communism, draws back aghast from Hitler's gaping jaws. There appeared to be no middle way for France*

ute-Banque e la Nation

*Ces hommes ne représentent ni le travail créateur, ni l'honnêteté de l'épargne, ni la technique de la production ; ils ne sont que les parasites de la bourse, de la spéculation et du profit.*

MUNISTE

ECTIONS CANTONALES 1937 *Vu le candidat.*

David Seymour / Magnum

Snark / Spadem

# FRANÇAIS ALERTE !

# LE COMMUNISME A DÉJA MIS LE FEU AUX DEUX BOUTS DE L'EUROPE

anarchists, left-wing Socialists, Communists itching to act, took the lead in movements which spread in all directions. The people had shown its power during the elections: now it showed it again with devastating effect. With the exception of an inconsiderable minority of activists, none of the Socialists, probably, wanted these strikes. They were born of the joy of victory and the fear of losing its fruits. In the rapidity with which one led to another they recalled the days of the Terror in the countryside in the summer of 1789 when the peasants had revolted. The spectre they conjured from the shadows, militant trade unionism, seemed to announce to frightened employers that the day of the workers' liberation had arrived. The way in which the men on the shop floor acted, often going beyond the wishes of their leaders, was a foretaste of the events of May and June 1968. In truth, the fourth estate of the realm had risen, when it had been thought that it would agree to wait.

Simone Weil, a lecturer in philosophy who had chosen to become a worker, described the atmosphere in the occupied factories: 'The public and the bosses and Léon Blum himself and all those who are strangers to this life of slavery are in-

capable of understanding the decisive factor in this situation. This movement concerns something quite other than particular demands, however important these might be. If the government had been able to procure full and complete satisfaction for them the workers would have been much less happy. What counted was that after months, years, of bowing to everything, submitting, taking what came in silence, they dared at last to stand upright, to take their turn, to feel for a few days, men. Quite apart from their demands, this strike was in itself a joy. Pure, unadulterated joy.'

'An attack on the rights of property' was the employers' protest against the occupation of the factories. But was it prudent to risk incidents of violence and possibly start a full scale workers' revolt? Was it possible to remove the men from the works when stay-in strikes were increasing hourly? Wouldn't the strikers be less dangerous in the works than in the streets?

Revolution seemed to be at hand, but paradoxically, it was the leaders of the trade union movement who, in agreement with Blum and finally followed by the Communists, canalized the menacing flood between the dykes of legality, prevented it from disrupting public services and food supplies, and gave it moderate objectives — those which since 1920 the CGT had been asking the public authorities and the employers to implement.

It was in this feverish atmosphere that Blum formed his government on 4th June and presented it on the 5th to the Chamber of Deputies, which gave it its confidence by a majority of 384 votes. Blum immediately arranged for a meeting at the Hôtel Matignon, the official residence of the Prime Minister, between the delegates of the CGT and those of the employers. After several hours of difficult discussion an agreement was reached on the night of 7th-8th June. It comprised the following provisions: an all-round increase in wages of seven to fifteen per cent; the employers to respect the liberty of the trade unions; the election by the employees in individual concerns of representatives to deal with the management; the immediate establishment of collective labour contracts. Blum also promised Jouhaux, the secretary-general of the CGT, to bring before parliament bills establishing a forty hour week, instituting paid holidays, and outlining the legal framework of collective labour agreements.

The bills were approved before the end of the session. Under popular pressure, Blum had been forced to go much further in the social sphere than the Popular Front's programme had envisaged. Doubtless this was necessary if the force of a movement that went on for several more weeks before it was spent was to be cushioned. Certainly, had Blum been firmer, his popularity and that of the Popular Front would not have been so great as it was at the end of June, when millions of workers in the private sector were taking a holiday with pay for the first time in their lives.

## Léon Blum

Blum did not accept this governmental test without some apprehension. For years he had been opposed to any Socialist participation in the government. A subtle analyst, he drew a distinction between the seizure of power and the exercise of power. In the first case the Socialist Party would govern in revolutionary fashion; in the latter case it would manage bourgeois society conscientiously, while ensuring the continuity of the rule of law. He declared that he would never take it on himself to transform the exercise of power into the seizure of power. But he knew that not every member of the Socialist Party shared his views. At the Congress of Tours in December 1920 it was his intervention more than that of any other speaker that told against acceptance of Lenin's Twenty-One Conditions for membership of the Third International, but he had never abandoned hope that one day unity would be restored.

Having developed his intellectual outlook before the First World War, he remained a stranger and even an enemy to every attempt to modernize Socialist thought that had been made since 1919. For him the problems of property were fundamental; the Socialist Party ought not to compromise itself by setting up a regime that was halfway between capitalism and collectivism. What did he hope for, then? To inject into the political system as much social justice as it could stand. To show that the Socialist Party was capable of governing. To effect a reconciliation between the working classes and the nation as a whole. Had he the qualities that make for success? From time to time he put the question to himself. Was he as capable of taking action as he was of

summing up a situation? Had he around him the collaborators he needed? One could be an excellent speaker at a congress and a parliamentarian who could command a hearing and yet lack the qualities essential for a minister. Some of his choices proved to be excellent, others questionable. There was one fact that made him uneasy: though the Radical Party and the USR had agreed to collaborate in the government, the Communists refused categorically to do so; one of their spokesmen declared that they were reserving themselves for the 'Ministry of the Masses'. This upset the Socialists, especially as Communist influence within the CGT, whose membership had leaped up from one to five million in the space of a few weeks, was rapidly growing. Would not the Communist Party make use of the strength of the trade unions to oppose the Socialist Party, which it accused of softness?

And, in fact, from July onwards, difficulties began to multiply in ever increasing numbers.

## External troubles

When Blum came to power he realized the gravity of the German menace. A few weeks earlier, in March, Hitler had denounced the Locarno Pact and had remilitarized the Rhineland. Blum wanted above everything to restore the Entente Cordiale (1904), which had cooled after Laval's conciliatory attitude to Mussolini when he invaded Ethiopia. For him the first objective to strive for was common action by the two great democracies of the West. Only after that had been attained would he attend to the matter of imparting a military content to the Franco-Soviet alliance. This line of reasoning, which can be clearly traced in Blum's way of thinking, explains his attitude to the Spanish Civil War, which broke out on 17th July 1936. The French Popular Front had every reason to desire the victory of its counterpart in Spain

and to give whatever help it needed in the way of arms, munitions, and aircraft in order to obtain this victory. But when Blum discovered that Great Britain refused to intervene in conjunction with France, and that the Radical Party also favoured a policy of prudence, he found it impossible to plunge France into a hazardous adventure on its own. His way out of the difficulty was to propose a policy of non-intervention, and this was accepted by the USSR as well as by Germany and Italy. We know now that in spite of this, on becoming aware of Hitler's and Mussolini's bad faith, France did in fact supply arms and munitions to Republican Spain without being able to admit it. But at the time the workers' feelings were hurt by what seemed to be an attack on working-class solidarity. The Communists turned it into a weapon against Blum, and their campaign awakened protests from the CGT, where Jouhaux condemned the policy of non-intervention, and even from the SFIO, one of whose leaders, the left-wing Socialist Zyromski, made no effort to conceal his disapproval.

Blum's unwillingness to let France take the initiative was due not only to his aversion to cutting himself off from Great Britain but also to his discovery, on coming to power, of France's inferiority in modern armaments. After spending millions of francs on 'traditional' armaments, France was deficient in tanks and aircraft. Even though it was possible to believe that she still had a safety margin vis-à-vis Germany, she was being more and more dangerously outclassed, month by month. Blum, who had never ceased to preach disarmament, even unilateral disarmament, now brought about the adoption of an armament plan for which 550 million francs were made immediately available and for which further credits were envisaged in succeeding years. His government cannot honestly be blamed for having underestimated the needs of national defence. Blum went so far in this direction as to arouse the violent opposition of the extreme Left in the SFIO grouped around Marceau Pivert in the 'Gauche Révolutionnaire'. The result was a fresh secession in 1938.

These decisions of Blum's were not contested by the Communist Party—but this is not to say that it was satisfied with his foreign policy. It reproached him for his Spanish policy; it disapproved of the conversations which had been initiated with Dr Schacht, the German finance minister, and which, in the event, ended abruptly; it was annoyed especially by Blum's failure to conclude a military agreement with the USSR. Ten years later Blum gave the reason for his caution: a secret message from Beneš, the President of the Czechoslovakian Republic, received at the end of December 1936, had put him on his guard: 'His own intelligence service had informed him that the heads of the Soviet General

Bibliothèque Nationale, Paris

*Leagues on the march. Camelots du Roi (which means the King's newsvendors) with men of Solidarité Française. The Camelots, uniformed streetfighters, were recruited to sell Action Française's journal*

Staff were having suspicious negotiations with the Germans.'

In September 1936 the workers returned from their first paid holidays, and were no longer in holiday mood. They discovered that the rise in prices had eaten away part of their rise in wages. They went on strike again; but this time the enthusiastic jubilation of May and June had vanished. Slogans appeared in large numbers which contained criticism or a warning to the government: 'Blum à l'action' (Act, Blum); 'Des avions, des canons pour l'Espagne' (Aircraft and guns for Spain). The hopes of the workers, no doubt inordinate, had not been realized, and from the refuse heap of their disappointments sprang the poisonous flowers of defiance and doubt. Moreover, the 'great fear' experienced by the employers in 1935 was now a thing of the past, and some of them decided that the time had come to assert their own demands in industrial relations and recapture some of the ground they had yielded.

Precisely at this moment, after financial conversations with Washington and London, Blum decided on devaluation, euphemistically termed a 'currency alignment'. But devaluation came too late, and it was not drastic enough. Why had no action been taken earlier? Perhaps because the Communists had condemned such a measure in advance. Perhaps to avoid giving the impression that devaluation was the inevitable consequence of social legislation. Perhaps, above all, because Paris was unwilling to act without London and without Washington, and to obtain their agreement the French devaluation had to be less drastic than the devaluation of the pound in 1931 and that of the dollar in 1933.

Although insufficient, the devaluation of the franc made it possible for the economy to be set to rights that autumn. But it was compromised by the progressive adoption of a forty-hour week. The idea that a forty-hour week would solve the unemployment problem proved to be illusory. A lessening of the hours of work in the iron and steel industries or the building trade did not provide employment for redundant textile workers, and the vacancies on the railways were filled more by peasants leaving their villages than by unemployed industrial workers. Added to this, the reduction of working hours without a corresponding reduction of wages brought increased prices, which hampered the export trade. One critic wrote in 1938 that this 'absurd' law had 'reduced the productive capacity of France to the lowest level reached in the post-war period' and demanded the abolition of the 'law of national betrayal'.

### Failure

By January 1937 Blum realized that his governmental policy was meeting with such insoluble difficulties that he was compelled to order a pause in carrying out reforms that he still intended to make, such as introducing old age pensions. Doubtless he was inclined to the conclusion that he had inadvertently injected into the economic structure a larger dose of social justice than it was able to support at the time. But within the Popular Front and more particularly within the SFIO other militant members were drawing a different conclusion. To them the experiment seemed to be vitiated by the incompatibilities of Blum's policy. First, Blum was conducting simultaneously a foreign policy based on costly rearmament and an extremely expensive social policy. The French economy was too anaemic to bear this double burden. The second incompatibility was between a policy of interference in the social structure and a political and financial economy that was too respectful towards traditional arrangements. The nationalization of the Bank of France and the war industries, even when supplemented by the creation of the National Wheat Board, thanks to Georges Monnet, the young and energetic Minister of Agriculture in the Blum government, was not enough. The economy should have been controlled at every stage. The time for this had come in June 1936, and now the chance had been lost.

When, in June 1937, Blum, brought to bay by hopelessly complicated financial difficulties, tried to persuade parliament to adopt a programme of financial reform, he was thwarted by the veto of the Senate, in which Joseph Caillaux, chairman of the Financial Commission, chided Blum for attempting 'Rooseveltism for Lilliputians'.

Having twice failed to obtain a majority in the Senate, what more could Blum do, seeing that he was determined to respect the law? Before he could dissolve the Chamber of Deputies and seek a further mandate from the electorate confirming the confidence they had placed in the Popular Front a year before, he needed, according to the terms of the constitution, the authorization of the President of the Republic and of the Senate, and it was certain that neither was prepared to give it. In any case Blum was too well aware of the gravity of the international situation to plunge the country into a serious domestic crisis. Indeed, so strong was his sense of civic duty that he accepted the vice-chairmanship of the cabinet in the government formed by Camille Chautemps, a Radical Socialist senator who had the ear of the Senate. At the ensuing congress at Marseilles more than half the votes were against Socialist participation in this government. Far from confirming the cohesion of a Socialist Party proud of having done its work, the experiment of government had left its militant members uneasy and divided. They refused to admit that the Blum government had 'fallen for the same reasons as the others'.

From then on, the disintegration of the Popular Front began to gather speed. If the Communists believed that they could exert a greater influence on the Chautemps cabinet (in which they had offered, unsuccessfully, to participate) they were mistaken. Chautemps, without retracting the social reforms, tried to calm the anxiety of the well-to-do and to extend his majority towards the Right. But the Socialists had no intention of letting the Communists benefit from being the only party of the Left to return to opposition.

Such, then, were the conditions in which, after eight months of Chautemps government, Blum was induced to return to power, but they were very different from those he would have chosen. Convinced that the international situation would end in disaster (it was at this juncture that Hitler carried out his Anschluss with Austria), he tried to form a government ranging from Maurice Thorez the Communist to Louis Marin a leader of the Right, but the majority of the Right rejected his proposal. In order to fall in with the wishes of the SFIO and perhaps in the hope of restoring its fallen fortunes, Blum formed a second Popular Front government which included the young Mendès-France, now one of the most respected leaders of the Left in France. He brought in a programme of financial reforms which he did not hesitate to compare, ten years later, with the Russian Five-Year Plans and Göring's Four-Year Plan. Faced with war, he was reduced to adopting the idea of an intermediate scheme of partly Socialist economic organization that he had rejected a few years before.

This was how he hoped to deal with one of the two incompatible policies mentioned above, but though passed by the Chamber of Deputies, the project was thrown out by the Senate. Blum resigned. His second government had lasted from 13th March to 10th April 1938. He was to remain prominent in French politics, however, almost up until his death in 1950.

### The working masses fall away

Blum was succeeded by another Radical leader, Edouard Daladier, who was supposed at the time to enjoy the confidence of the General Staff. His government included some of the minority leaders (of the Right Centre, but not the Right): Georges Mandel and Paul Reynaud, but not Louis Marin. The SFIO refused to participate but did not refuse its votes, any more than the Communists. Daladier obtained the confidence of the Chamber by 575 votes to 5. The measures he took in the course of the summer to 'arrange' the forty-hour week and the laws-by-decree worked out in the early autumn brought about a sudden social tension. The Communists, who were very near to obtaining an absolute majority at the congress of the CGT in November 1938 and who refused to recognize the government's signature to the Munich agreement on Czechoslovakia, prevailed on the CGT to call for a general strike of protest on 30th November 1938, but this ended in utter failure. After this setback to its power and prestige, the CGT saw its effective strength dwindle as rapidly as they had risen in May and June 1936. The working masses, which Blum believed had been finally re-integrated within the nation, fell away again into a recession from which they were not to emerge until after the events of May and June 1940, during the period of the German occupation of France.

The Popular Front, which lasted only five years, nevertheless made deep impressions: it remains, for many, an ideal, for many others anathema. (Translation)

Simplicissimus ▽ David Seymour / Magnum ◁

*Above left: Intellectuals endorse the Popular Front. From right to left, Marcel Cachin, a leader of the French Communist Party; Jean-Richard Bloch, André Malraux, André Gide, Louis Aragon, French novelists; and Heinrich Mann, German writer and brother of Thomas Mann. Above: A German cartoon reflects on Blum's strike-torn year of office. Entering a nursery the Prime Minister exclaims 'For God's sake, have we got a sit-down strike here as well?' Left: On a French nationalist poster a Gaul wards off the insidious influences of Socialism, Nazism, Communism, and Freemasonry. Below: Léon Jouhaux, secretary-general of the CGT*

POUR ASSURER VOTRE SÉCURITÉ VOTEZ FRANÇAIS

Snark / Spadem ◁ René Dazy ▽

# Hitler's Germany

Nazi Germany's attempt to win absolute power within Europe was the mainspring of the Second World War. It was, however, on a grander scale, the continuation of that process by which the National Socialists had won power in Germany itself.

Hitler took office on 30th January 1933 not as dictator of Germany but as head of a coalition government in which the Nazis held only three out of eleven ministerial posts. The paradox of his career up to this point had been the combination of a movement built on a revolutionary appeal with the insistence that he meant to come to power by legal means. But once he had got his foot inside the door, Hitler had no intention at all of being bound by the rules of the conventional political game. He very soon showed that it was the façade of legality, not the revolutionary character of the Nazi movement, which was the sham.

The first step was the decree suspending all guarantees of individual liberty on the excuse that the Reichstag Fire on 27th February 1933 was in fact the sign for a Communist rising. Göring, placed in control of the Prussian police, enrolled 40,000 of the Nazis' strong-arm bands, the SA and the SS, as police auxiliaries. This gave them a legal immunity which they used to the full to arrest and beat up political opponents and Jews. The election on 5th March failed to produce the majority the Nazis had hoped for, but by eliminating the Communist deputies (most of whom were already in concentration camps) and pressuring the other parties, they obtained a clear vote for the so-called Enabling Law (23rd March 1933) which set aside the constitution and for four years empowered the chancellor, Hitler, to enact laws without parliamentary approval.

In the next few months the Nazis proceeded to carry out a political 'take-over' of Germany for which they coined the phrase *Gleichschaltung,* 'co-ordination'. Their political partners were not asked for their agreement but were ignored and elbowed out of the way. Theirs and all other political parties, as well as the trade unions, were abolished.

This was the Nazi revolution, and it was compounded of three elements. The first was the use the Nazis made of the legal authority to command the resources of the state and its administrative machine. This guaranteed to the Nazis control of the police, the neutrality of the armed forces, and the power, which they exercised without scruple, to dismiss any official suspected of opposition or even lukewarmness towards the new regime. The second was terrorism—not the breakdown of law and order, but something more shocking, its deliberate withdrawal. A free hand was given to the Nazi Stormtroopers to seize persons or property and do what they liked with them. The effect of this terrorism extended far beyond the numbers of those who actually suffered death, injury, or loss of property: it created an atmosphere of menace, a pervasive fear of violence which inhibited any thought of opposition. The compulsive power of terrorism was matched by the attractive power of propaganda drummed out by radio, press, and cinema, proclaiming a national rebirth of Germany. This was the third element. Propaganda produced on this scale and directed with the consummate skill of Goebbels was something new in politics, and it had a great impact on a people which had suffered for fifteen years from a deep sense of national humiliation. Most important of all was the impression of success which Goebbels' propaganda created: the Nazi band-wagon was on the move and anyone eager for power, position, and jobs (in a nation with six million unemployed) rushed to jump on it.

In every move they made, the Nazis showed the advantage enjoyed by a political movement which refused to be bound by any rules, which did not try to avoid but did everything it could to exploit surprise and shock, and instead of repudiating violence in the streets employed the threat of it to break down opposition. The result was that the stability of a society already weakened by the successive experiences of defeat, inflation, economic depression, and mass unemployment was profoundly shaken. But the Nazis' methods, if they repelled many, also attracted many, especially among the young, who felt a great sense of liberation at the promise of action after years of frustration.

The question Hitler had to answer in the summer of 1933 was how far he was prepared to let the revolutionary process continue before calling a halt. Was it to extend to the economic as well as the political institutions of the country? There had been a strong element of anti-capitalism in the Nazis' radicalism and there was now a demand to give expression to this in drastic

*Left: Hitler's face—a study in tyranny.* ***Below left:*** *Poster of the* Kraft durch Freude *(Strength through Joy) organization shows workers' housing estate. The organization regimented the leisure activities of lowly paid workers.* ***Below right:*** *Nuremberg Rally, 1938*

*Left: Arresting Communists, Berlin, 1933. The Nazis won popularity as bulwark against Bolshevism. **Right:** Hitler and group of admirers*

economic reforms. What Hitler saw, however, was that radical economic experiments would destroy any chance of co-operation from industry and business to end the depression, bring down the unemployment figures, and start rearming Germany. In July he told a meeting of Nazi provincial governors: 'The revolution is not a permanent state of affairs and it must not be allowed to develop into such a state . . . The ideas of the programme do not oblige us to act like fools and upset everything . . . Many more revolutions have been successful at the outset than have, when once successful, been arrested and brought to a standstill at the right moment.' By the end of the summer Hitler had made it quite clear that he chose close working relations with big business in preference to the Nazi enthusiasts who talked about 'the corporate development of the national economy' and who were now disowned or pushed into obscure positions.

Hitler's own wish, however, to halt the revolution, at least for the time being, encountered opposition in the Nazi movement, particularly in the brown shirt SA. The SA was a genuine mass movement with strong radical and anti-capitalist leanings, and attracted to it all those dissatisfied elements in the Party who felt they had been left out in the cold and who wanted no end to the revolution until they too had been provided for. And the SA did not lack a leader. Its chief of staff, Ernst Röhm, was the most independent of the Nazi leaders, a man who, having started Hitler on his career in politics in Munich, was not at all afraid to speak his mind.

This quarrel over the so-called 'Second Revolution' was the dominant issue in German politics between the summer of 1933 and the summer of 1934, and threatened to split the Nazi movement. In particular, Röhm and the SA leadership, which contained many who had been through the rough school of the Freikorps and were con-temptuous of the conservatism of the German officer corps, were incensed at not being allowed to take over and remodel the German army on revolutionary lines.

Hitler, as his subsequent behaviour showed, was as distrustful of the generals and contemptuous of their conservatism as Röhm, but in 1933 and 1934 he needed their support if he was to rebuild Germany's military strength and, more immediately, if he was to secure the succession to Hindenburg as head of state as well as head of the government. On their side, the generals were determined to resist any attempt by Röhm to incorporate the SA in the army and take it over.

The crisis reached its climax at the end of June 1934 when Hitler suddenly ordered the liquidation of the SA leadership on the pretext that they were planning a putsch. The purge, however, extended far beyond the SA. Amongst those summarily shot besides Röhm—all without any pretence of a trial—were General von Schleicher, Hitler's predecessor as chancellor, and Gregor Strasser, once Hitler's rival for the leadership of the Nazi Party. Hitler had not merely connived at murder, but ordered it to be carried out.

The generals, however, were satisfied to see the threat from the SA removed and when President Hindenburg died on 2nd August, there was no delay in announcing Hitler's succession as head of state, with the new title of Führer (leader) and Reich chancellor. The same day the officers and men of the German army took the oath to their new commander-in-chief, swearing allegiance not to the constitution or to the Fatherland, but to Hitler personally.

June 1934 was a major crisis, a crisis of the regime and the acid test of Hitler's leadership. In the weeks preceding the purge (for example, during his visit to Mussolini at Venice) Hitler gave every impression of being anxious and unsure of himself. This was the characteristic period of hesitation and weighing the odds which so often preceded one of his big decisions: equally characteristically, when the decision was made, it startled everyone by its boldness and brutality. Hitler repudiated the so-called 'Second Revolution' but he did so in such a radical way as to give no comfort at all to those who wanted to see the rule of law restored and a return to the conservative traditions of the German state.

### Nazification

In contrast to the tumultuous days of 1932 and 1933 and the crisis atmosphere of the summer of 1934, the next three and a half years, 1934 through 1937, saw political peace in Germany: no more elections, no more purges. This left the Nazis free to get on with the 're-modelling' of German society. Like other totalitarian creeds, Nazism was unwilling to leave any part of German life unorganized or to allow any group or individual to contract out. German men and women were to be as accountable for their thoughts and feelings as for their actions, and no claim of individual conscience was to be allowed to withstand the demands of the Party and the state.

Practice, of course, as in every form of society, totalitarian as well as democratic, was never so consistent as theory. In the first place, it is necessary to distinguish between the lengths to which the Nazis went in enforcing their style of government in the 1930's, during peace time, and in the 1940's, under war-time conditions. It is to the later period, for example, that the extermination camps, slave labour, and 'the final solution' of the so-called Jewish problem belong. There were concentration camps in Germany from the beginning of the Nazi period, but the total number of prisoners at the beginning of the war was roughly 25,000 compared with ten times that number a few years later.

Up to the outbreak of war, Germany was still open to visitors and foreign corres-

*Kladderadatsch*

*Left: Burning of 'degenerate' books by Nazi students, 1933. **Right:** Cartoon showing purified German poetry rising from the flames*

pondents in a way in which the Soviet Union has never been, and the Nazis showed themselves surprisingly sensitive to hostile comment from abroad, for example in their dealings with the Churches. This was an issue on which Hitler several times intervened personally to curb the zeal of those in the Party who wished to push their hostility to the Churches to the limit. Accordingly, Nazi practice towards the Churches was confused and inconsistent, marked by fundamental hostility in outlook and much petty local persecution (such as the expulsion of monks and nuns, the closing of churches, the imprisonment of pastors and priests) but still stopping short of the sweeping measures which some of the Party leaders would have liked.

Even setting aside considerations of expediency, it proved more difficult to translate totalitarian control into practice than is always recognized. It took time for Himmler and Heydrich to create the SS

*Below: Volunteer workers returning home by bicycle after work*

which was eventually to prove the most effective instrument for Hitler's purposes. One important reason for this was the clash of rival authorities which was characteristic of Nazi Germany from the very beginning. Its organization was anything but monolithic. After the summer of 1934 Hitler's authority at the top was uncontested, but right up to the top there was a fierce struggle for power. Hitler himself not only possessed no gift for administration; he was instinctively distrustful of creating settled administrative procedures which would limit his own arbitrary power of decision. Difficulties were to be met by emergency action, by creating special agencies, a method which led almost invariably to overlapping and conflict of authority, between ministries, between Party and state, between different Party organizations. Each minister and Party boss fought for his own hand, a situation which strengthened Hitler's own position — since each sought the Führer's favour against his rivals — but reduced the efficiency of operation and control.

Nonetheless, when all this is said, there is no doubt that between 1933 and 1939 the Nazis went a long way towards remoulding German life, not just German politics, on a totalitarian pattern. The key lay with the younger generation. In a speech on 6th November 1933, Hitler declared: 'When an opponent says, "I will not come over to your side", I calmly say, "Your child belongs to us already . . . you will pass on. Your descendants, however, now stand in the new camp. In a short time they will know nothing else but this new community." '

To make sure, a start was at once made on the nazification of the schools and universities. All teachers, from kindergarten to university, were compelled to join the National Socialist Teachers' League and to teach what they were told to. German universities, once famous for their scienti-

fic research, now became the homes of racist science. Outside the schools, independent youth organizations (including those of the Churches) were banned and all German boys and girls from the age of six were required to join the Hitler Youth. At eighteen boys were conscripted into labour service and the army, girls into farm and household service. Throughout these impressionable years they were subjected to continued indoctrination in the Nazi faith.

To make Nazi propaganda doubly effective and allow no independent voice to be heard, Goebbels was made minister of culture as well as propaganda. This gave him control over all the arts, literature, and the cinema, as well as the press. Nothing could be published without the consent of the Propaganda Ministry.

### 'Jews not wanted here'

A particular object for attack was anybody or anything Jewish. The Jew, according to Nazi teaching, was the source of all corruption and Germany must be purged of this racial poison, if not yet by physical extermination then by the complete exclusion of all Jews from German life. Jews (defined as anyone with a single Jewish grandparent) were excluded from all official posts (with loss of pension rights), from the professions, including teaching, medicine, and the law, from sport, and the arts. Holiday resorts, restaurants, and hotels were decorated with notices, 'Jews not wanted here', and any Nazi hooligan could beat up, evict, or rob a Jew with impunity. In 1935 the Nuremberg Laws prohibited marriage or any form of sexual intercourse between Jews and German nationals. Those who sought to escape abroad were only allowed to go after they had been deprived of their assets and property. Finally, after a young Polish Jew, driven off balance by the persecution of his people, had assassinated the German legation secretary in Paris, Ernst vom Rath, a deliberately organized attack (represented as a 'spontaneous' outburst of German anger) was made on Jewish synagogues and businesses throughout the country on the night of 9th-10th November 1938. The perpetrators of the attack went scot-free, while the Jews were fined a billion and a quarter marks and saw the insurance payments to which they were entitled confiscated by the state. This so-called 'Crystal Night' was followed by the forced sale of Jewish businesses and property, their eviction from their houses, wholesale arrests, and conscription for forced labour.

No Jew had any hope of protection by the courts. But it was unlikely that any German had more ground for hope if he became suspected of independent views or got involved in a dispute with state or Party officials. Not content with the *Gleichschaltung* of the judiciary and the ordinary courts, the Nazis set up special courts to try offences against the state, a category which could be enlarged at will. The orders and actions of the Gestapo *(Geheime Staatspolizei,* Secret State Police) were in any case not subject to the law. 'Protective custody' was the term cynically employed for those arbitrarily arrested and sent to concentration camps. One of the significant dates in the history of Nazi Germany was 17th June 1936 when Himmler was able to merge control of the two empires which he had built up, the police and the SS. So was created what German historians call 'the illegal executive', an agency with which the Führer, Hitler, responsible to no one but himself, could brush aside any limitation at all on his power to act outside or contrary to the law.

Terrorism and the secret police, like propaganda and censorship, were essential parts of the totalitarian society the Nazis were seeking to create. And they produced their familiar accompaniments of informers, persecution, and corruption. For those Germans who did not fall into line but stood out against the pressures to conform (and for all Jews) these were years marked by constant fear, often imprisonment and brutal treatment, sometimes death. But these people formed a minority and a small one at that. What counted with the majority was the Nazis' success. In a country which had suffered more severely from the Depression than any other in Europe, the Nazis could claim credit for cutting unemployment from six million to less than a million in four years, for raising national production more than one hundred per cent between 1932 and 1937, and for doubling the national income. This reconciled the millions of Germans who had lost, or feared to lose, their jobs to a regime which might have taken away some of their rights but had given them back security. In addition to security, the Nazis had

*Right: Poster urging return of Saar— worker heaves open gates of Saar to Nazi Germany. It was Hitler's last stop before resorting to force to reverse the Treaty of Versailles. Opposite: Nazis march past in snowstorm at political meeting near Saarbrücken on 7th March 1935, the day the Saar plebiscite returned the Saar to Germany*

given the German people back their pride in Germany as a great power. By the plebiscite of January 1935, Germany recovered the Saar. Two months later (March 1935) Hitler repudiated the military restrictions of the Treaty of Versailles, restored conscription, and announced that the German army would be raised to a peace-time strength of over half a million men. A year later (March 1936) German troops reoccupied the demilitarized Rhineland. The deeply felt national humiliation of the defeat and the 'Diktat' of Versailles had been removed, and there is no reason to doubt that the result of the plebiscite which followed (99 per cent voting and 98.8 of these voting in favour) represented overwhelming gratitude and approval for Hitler's restoration of Germany's status as the leading power of Central Europe.

Finally, it must be said that in abolishing the multiplicity of political parties, which had produced only a series of weak coalitions, and replacing them by a single strong government proclaiming national unity in contrast to sectional interests, the Nazis successfully appealed to the most deeply rooted political tradition in Germany, that of authoritarian government.

Once his power was established, Hitler showed little interest in the details of domestic administration, except when he had to intervene to settle a dispute. His attention was turned more and more to foreign policy and rearmament. The conquest of political power, even the remoulding of German society, were only stages on the way to his ultimate aim, the recreation of German national power, the reversal of the defeat of 1918.

It suited the Nazis in the early years of their regime when Germany was still un-

Institute of Social History, Amsterdam

3u Deutſchland

Central Press

prepared, to conceal this. Hitler never spoke without protesting his love of peace and reproaching the victorious powers of 1918 with the promises they had broken, particularly the promise to disarm. This, however, was the diplomatic equivalent of the tactics of 'legality' which he had practised in Germany before coming to power and was no more reliable a guide than 'legality' to his real aims in foreign policy.

By 1936 there was a change. The re-occupation of the Rhineland (March 1936) was a gamble: Hitler later called it the most nerve-wracking forty-eight hours of his life. But it was a gamble that came off and strengthened his belief that, if he played his cards with skill, limiting the issue at stake in each case, the Western powers would always draw back rather than risk a general war. From the summer of 1936 the political balance in Europe moved sharply in Germany's favour. The outbreak of the Spanish Civil War gave Hitler the opportunity to proclaim with redoubled effect Germany's role as the bulwark of Europe against Bolshevism. Italy, quarrelling with the Western powers over Abyssinia, was drawn into the Berlin-Rome Axis. France, divided by the Popular Front and by the Spanish Civil War, no longer had the will to maintain the system of alliances built up to contain Germany. Great Britain was reluctant to face the possibility of another war. The smaller countries began to gravitate to the new centre of power in Berlin and it was of German power that Hitler now began increasingly to speak.

There is no doubt from the evidence now available that accounts of German rearmament before the war were exaggerated. The programme took longer to produce results than was supposed and even in 1939 had not given Germany the military superiority commonly assumed. Most surprising of all is the fact that nothing like the full capacity of the German economy was devoted to war production before 1942. But the type of war for which Germany was preparing was very different from that which she had lost in 1914-18: it was a *Blitzkrieg,* a series of short campaigns in which surprise and an overwhelming initial blow would settle the issue before the victim had time to mobilize his resources or other powers to intervene. This is the

sort of war the German army fought in all its campaigns from 1939 to 1941, and it demanded a quite different pattern of rearmament, not long-term rearmament in depth, involving the whole of the economy, but concentration on a short-term superiority and the weapons which would give a quick victory. How nearly the plan worked can be seen from the history of 1939-41 when Germany's 'limited' rearmament programme produced an army capable of overrunning the greater part of Europe and very nearly defeating the Russians as well as the French.

It has often been said that Hitler was an opportunist in foreign policy. This is perfectly true, so far as tactics were concerned: he did not proceed by any timetable or 'blueprint of aggression', but kept his options open until the very last moment. Hitler, however, was able to take advantage of the opportunities offered by the mistakes of others because he alone among the European leaders of the 1930's knew what he wanted to achieve: the others only knew what they wanted to avoid.

Hitler set out the Nazi programme in *Mein Kampf:* not simply the restoration of Germany's 1914 frontiers but the conquest of living space *(Lebensraum)* in Eastern Europe from which the existing populations would be cleared by force and a Germanic empire established on a foundation of slave labour. These views have been treated as the fantasy of an unbalanced mind. But they cannot for that reason be dismissed. For not only did Hitler consistently repeat them in private talk for twenty years, but during the war he put them into practice in the most literal way, with the aid of Himmler and the SS, first in Poland, then in Russia.

### The 'Blitzkrieg' victories

What Hitler did not know was how he was going to achieve his objective, the order in which he would proceed, what opposition he would encounter. But from late 1937 onwards he was prepared to enlarge the risks he was ready to take. As part of the process he asserted stronger control over the two institutions which had been allowed to escape nazification, the army and the foreign office. Early in 1938 he seized an opportunity to get rid of Blomberg and Fritsch, the minister of war and com-

mander-in-chief of the army, suppressed the office of war minister altogether, and took over the high command of the armed forces (the OKW) as his own personal staff. Schacht, who had protested at the economic risks of the Nazis' rearmament programme, had already been allowed to go, leaving Göring to dominate the economic field, with a clear brief to prepare for war, and Neurath, whom Hindenburg had made foreign minister to safeguard the foreign service against Nazi influence, was replaced by Ribbentrop who for years had been pushing a radical Nazi policy in open rivalry with the more cautious official line of the foreign office.

The annexation of Austria which followed (March 1938) was an improvisation, but an improvisation which fitted in perfectly with Hitler's long-term programme and illustrates the relationship between this and the tactics of opportunism. Throughout the rest of 1938 and 1939, it was Hitler who forced the pace in foreign affairs, both externally by the demands he made on Czechoslovakia and Poland and internally by his determination to take risks which still, in 1938, alarmed the army leaders and led to the resignation of the army's chief-of-staff, General Beck. Neither in 1938 nor in 1939 did Hitler deliberately plan to start a general European war: in August 1939 he was convinced that the masterpiece of Nazi diplomacy, the Nazi-Soviet Pact, would remove any danger of Western intervention and either break the Poles' determination to resist or leave them isolated. But when his bluff failed, he steeled himself to gamble on the chances of a Blitzkrieg victory over Poland before the British and French could bring their forces to bear. The gamble came off and came off again, with the stakes increased, in Norway, the Low Countries, and France in 1940, against Yugoslavia, and almost against Russia the next year. By then the stakes had been raised to the point where failure meant the long-term, two-front war which Hitler had sworn to avoid, and for which Germany was ill-prepared.

The particular war which broke out in September 1939 was not inevitable – what event in history is? But it was no accident either. Nazism glorified force and conflict, and if one thing seemed certain in the later 1930's it was that this movement which had fastened its hold on Germany must, from the necessities of its own nature, seek to expand by force or the threat of force. Once Nazism – a philosophy of dynamism or nothing – came to a standstill and admitted limits to its expansion, it would lose its rationale and its appeal. The only question was whether the other powers would allow this expansion to take place without resistance or would oppose it. The Nazis themselves had always assumed that at some point they would meet opposition and had prepared to overcome it by force of arms. For this reason, while it is right to point to the differences between Nazi Germany up to September 1939 and after the outbreak of war, it is important to see the continuity between the two periods as well. What followed was a logical, if not inevitable, consequence of what went before.

# The Brink of War

The international conference at Munich on 29th September 1938 had a practical task: to 'solve' the problem of the three million German-speakers in Czechoslovakia and so to prevent a European war. Apparently it succeeded in this task. The Czechoslovak territory inhabited by the three million Germans was transferred to Germany; the Germans were satisfied; there was no war. The controversy which has raged over the conference from before it met until the present day sprang more from what it symbolized than from what it actually did. Those who welcomed the Munich conference and its outcome represented it as a victory for reason and conciliation in international affairs—appeasement as it was called at the time, 'jaw, not war', as Winston Churchill said of a later occasion. The opponents of Munich saw in it an abdication by the two democratic powers, France and Great Britain; a surrender to fear; or a sinister conspiracy to prepare for a Nazi war of conquest against Soviet Russia. Munich was all these things.

The problem of the German-speakers in Czechoslovakia was real. They had been a privileged people in the old Habsburg monarchy. They were a tolerated minority in Czechoslovakia. They were discontented and grew more so with the resurgence of national pride in Germany. No doubt Hitler encouraged their discontent, but he did not create it. Those in the West who called out, 'Stand by the Czechs', never explained what they would do with the Czechoslovak Germans. Partition seemed the obvious solution. In fact, as later events proved, Bohemia was the one area in Europe where partition would not work. Czechs and Germans were so intermingled that one or other had to dominate. Once Czech prestige was shattered, a German protectorate inevitably followed six months later, to the ruin of the Munich settlement. The Czechs themselves recognized that there was no room in Bohemia for both nationalities. When independent Czechoslovakia was restored at the end of the war, the Germans were expelled—a solution which is likely to prove final.

The timing of the Czech crisis was not determined by the Czechoslovak Germans or by Hitler. It was determined by the British government, and especially by Neville Chamberlain, the British Prime Minister. He wanted to restore tranquillity in Europe and believed that this could be done only if German grievances were met. Moreover they must be met willingly. Concessions must be offered to Germany, not extracted under threat of war. Until 1938 Hitler had been destroying one bit of the 1919 settlement after another, to the accompaniment of protests from the Western powers. This time Chamberlain meant to get in ahead of him. Hitler was to be satisfied almost before he had time to formulate grievances.

## Fear not reason

Chamberlain set himself two tasks. First, the French must be induced not to support their ally, Czechoslovakia. Second, the Czech government must be persuaded or compelled to yield to the German demands. He succeeded in both tasks, but not in the way that he intended. He had meant to use the argument of morality: that German grievances were justified and therefore must be redressed. Instead, as the months passed, he came to rely on practical arguments of force and fear. The French were driven to admit, with a reluctance which grew ever weaker, that they were unable to support Czechoslovakia. The Czechs were threatened with the horrors of war unless they gave way. When Chamberlain flew to Munich on his first visit to Hitler, it was not as the emissary of even-handed justice. He came in a desperate effort to avert a war which the Western powers dreaded. Thereafter fear, not reason, was his main argument, and the principal moral which the British drew from Munich was not that conciliation had triumphed, but that they must push on faster with rearmament.

At the Munich conference there was certainly an abdication by the Western powers. France especially had been the dominant power in Eastern Europe since the end of the First World War. Germany was disarmed; Soviet Russia was boycotted; all the new states of Eastern Europe were France's allies. She regarded these alliances as a source of strength. As soon as her allies made demands on her, she turned against them. France had been bled white in the first war, and Frenchmen were determined not to repeat the experience. They believed that they were secure behind their fortified frontier, the Maginot Line. Hence they did not care what happened beyond it. As to the British, they

*Left: A poster distributed throughout Czechoslovakia in 1938: 'We will all become soldiers if necessary.'*
*Czech morale remained high during the war of nerves conducted by Hitler.*
*Right: Britain's Prime Minister Neville Chamberlain arriving at Heston Airport, London, promising 'Peace in our time'*

Central Press

had always insisted that their interests stopped at the Rhine. Austen Chamberlain had said that no British grenadier would ever die for Danzig – or for anywhere else in Eastern Europe. The British recognized that German predominance would take the place of French. But this did not trouble them. Eastern Europe and the Balkans were no great prize economically. If they absorbed German energies and ambitions, it was all the more likely that Germany would leave Western Europe and the British Empire alone.

Fear of war was also a dominant motive at the Munich conference, but for the Western powers it was war that was feared rather than defeat. The French had confidence in their army, the British in their navy. But while they did not expect the Germans to defeat them, they doubted whether they could defeat Germany – except at a terrible price. There was no way in which the Western powers could give limited aid to the Czechs, as they might have done to the Spanish Republic. The facts of geography stood in the way. It was war on the largest scale or nothing. In those days, everyone believed that aerial bombardment would reduce the cities of Europe to ruin in a few weeks. European civilization would end. This was the peril which Chamberlain sought to avert.

The Czechs themselves shared this fear of war. President Beneš believed that Hitler was bluffing and would give way if faced with a firm united opposition. When Hitler did not give way, even Beneš in the last resort preferred surrender to war. The Czechs, Beneš held, were a small people, who must preserve their lives for a better future. Their country had been occupied before and they had survived. They would survive again. In a sense, his arguments were justified by events. The Czechs were abandoned by the Western powers. Their country fell under German tyranny for six years. But only one or perhaps two hundred thousand of them lost their lives. Prague, their capital was the only great city of Central Europe to remain undamaged in the Second World War, and Czechoslovakia re-emerged with unbroken spirit, at the end. In contrast, Poland was guaranteed by the Western powers, who went to war for her sake. As a result, six million Poles were killed. Warsaw was reduced to a heap of ruins, and Poland, though restored, lost much of her territory and of her independence.

### Was Munich a conspiracy?

Did more lie behind? Was the Munich conference not merely a surrender, an abandonment, or even a betrayal of Czechoslovakia? Was it also part of a deliberate attempt to promote a German hegemony and to clear the way for a German attack on Soviet Russia? This is a view strongly held by Soviet and other Communist-inclined historians. The Munich conference was certainly an assertion that Europe could settle its own affairs. Only the purely European powers – France, Germany, Great Britain, and Italy – were represented. The two world powers, Soviet Russia and the United States, were absent.

The United States had persistently refused to be involved in European conflicts ever since the end of the First World War. It is likely, too, that the Western powers welcomed the absence of any American representative. If one had attended the conference, he would have preached morality to others without being prepared to act on it himself. Great Britain and France looked forward to a time when there might be a great war and they would need American aid. Even with this in mind, they preferred not to be exposed to American reproaches before the time came for action.

Soviet Russia was a different matter. The Western powers never counted on Soviet aid. They did not believe, and quite rightly, that even if Soviet Russia entered a war against Germany she would be fighting either for democracy as they understood it or for the sanctity of treaties. After all, the settlement of 1919 had been made quite as much against Soviet Russia as against Germany, and the Russians would aim to take Germany's place in Eastern Europe, not to defend the independence of the small states. As well, the Western powers doubted whether Soviet Russia intended to fight Germany seriously or whether she was capable of doing so. They distrusted Soviet Russia quite as much as she distrusted them. Each side suspected the other of pushing it into the front line. Moreover, this was the period of Stalin's great purges. Nearly all the marshals and generals of the Red Army had been murdered or imprisoned. Under such circumstances, it was hard to believe that Soviet Russia could conduct a successful offensive. Geography stood in Russia's way even more than in theirs. Soviet Russia could not strike at Germany without crossing the territory of either Poland or Rumania. Both countries refused to allow the passage of Soviet troops – the Poles more rigorously than the Rumanians. The Western powers were supposed to be defending the rights of small nations and could hardly begin their campaign by trampling on the rights of Poland and Rumania.

'Twist the dagger out of that paw.' Soviet poster calls for a strong anti-fascist front

National Gallery of Prague

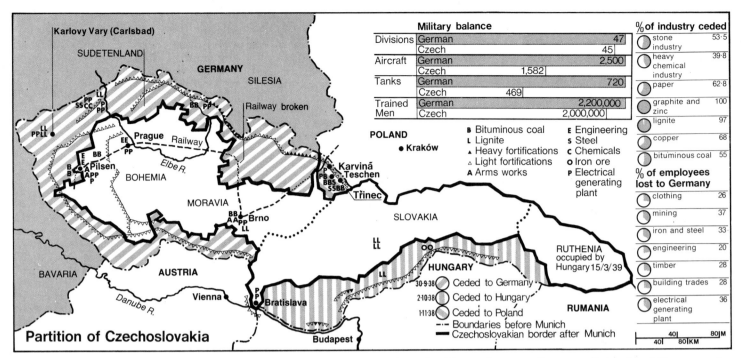

*How Czechoslovakia lost 33% of her population, her prime defences, and much of her industry to Germany. Poland and Hungary also shared in the post-Munich disintegration. As the military balance shows, the West sacrificed an ally with considerable military potential*

On paper, the Soviet government had a position of impregnable righteousness. According to the Czech-Soviet treaty of 1935, Soviet Russia was committed to supporting Czechoslovakia only if France did so first. The Soviet rulers surmised correctly that France would not honour her word. Therefore they were quite safe in declaring that they would honour theirs. Soviet leaders went further. They often hinted that they would be prepared to aid Czechoslovakia even if France did not act. But they would do this only if President Beneš and the Czechoslovak government asked them to do so. Here again the Soviet government was quite safe. The Czechoslovak government was predominantly right-wing, and President Beneš, though less on the Right, was determined not to fight with Soviet Russia as sole ally. This, he thought, would invite the fate of Republican Spain, and he was not far wrong. Hence we cannot tell what the Soviet government really intended to do. They could promise great things in the secure confidence that they would never be called on to fulfil their promises. Similarly, we do not know whether the Soviet government made any serious preparations for war. Most Western observers reported at the time that the Red Army had taken no measures of mobilization. Nowadays the Soviet spokesmen claim that the Red Army had mobilized thirty divisions. This, even if true, was a derisory force to use against Germany, and suggests that the Soviet government were intending only to seize some Polish territory. But as the Soviet government refuses to release evidence, all statements about its policy are guesswork.

We may dismiss one guess the other way round. Soviet writers then and later alleged that the Western powers aimed to switch German aggression eastwards, against Soviet Russia. Many Soviet writers even allege that the Western powers dreamed of joining in this aggression themselves. There is virtually no foundation for their

theory. The Communists imagined that everyone in the capitalist world was afraid of them and therefore wanted to destroy 'the workers' state'. In fact, Communism had lost its appeal. Soviet Russia was the best propaganda against Communism – it offered tyranny, starvation, inefficiency. No one in Western Europe feared Soviet Russia any more. Indeed, sensible English people regretted that Soviet Russia was so weak. In the end, German aggression was indeed switched. But it was switched from east to west by the Nazi-Soviet pact. It was not switched from west to east by the conference at Munich.

### The German view of Munich

One of the many obstacles to an understanding between West Germany and the Communist states of Eastern Europe is the Munich agreement. The Soviet bloc insisted that Bonn deny the validity of the agreement from the time of its signature. This demand may of course make political sense, although there are still two and a half million Sudeten refugees in West Germany clamouring for their national rights. But historically there can be no justification. Munich is as much 'a fact of history' (in Michael Stewart's words) as the Congress of Vienna: on both occasions great powers arrogantly and cruelly determined the fate of smaller nations.

Certainly the behaviour of the great

powers over Czechoslovakia deserves moral condemnation, but 'Munich' is the wrong label for it. Czechoslovakia's fate had been sealed well before the Munich conference. In fact the death sentence was passed after two important earlier meetings. The first was between Neville Chamberlain and Hitler in Berchtesgaden, the second between the British and French envoys and President Beneš in Prague during the night of 20th-21st September. This second occasion saw Czechoslovakia finally compelled to hand over to the Reich those provinces whose population was more than fifty per cent German. What followed ten days later in Munich was simply the formalizing of an already fully negotiated and legally binding agreement. This four-power summit conference was necessary only because a technical and procedural matter threatened the peace of Europe. But the myth now seems to have passed irrevocably into history that, faced with Hitler's threats of war, the Western powers yielded to him at Munich. The real situation was quite the opposite. Chamberlain and Daladier combined firmness with conciliation, peacemaking with a willingness to fight, and in so doing were able to avert European conflagration and save the Czech people and their beautiful capital from devastation and annihilation. Hitler had to be content to accept the Sudetenland by negotiation rather than take it by force. He was thus

*Chamberlain, Daladier, Hitler, Mussolini and Ciano, after signing the Munich agreement*

Keystone Press

Sphere

VHU, Prague

*1 German troops cross the Czech border
into the Sudetenland, 3rd October, in
accordance with the Munich agreement.
2 Czechs study maps of new frontiers.
3 Delighted Sudetens of Carlsbad give a
hero's welcome to their Nazi 'liberators'.
4 Hitler inspects Czech 'Maginot Line',
most of which was handed over at Munich.
5 Anti-tank barrier, part of the formidable defences whose loss put a virtual end
to Czechoslovakia as an independent power.*

denied the whole of Czechoslovakia and
his sense of defeat was shown by his angry
outburst: 'That fellow Chamberlain has
ruined my entry into Prague.'

Nevertheless the foundations for Czechoslovakia's demise had been laid, since six
months later Hitler was to march into
Prague without interference from the Western powers. On 20th September 1938
Czechoslovakia had been deserted by her
Western friends; a few days later she had
to surrender and hand over to a tyrannical,
fascist regime three and a half million of
her people (many of Czech origin), the
most modern defences in Europe, and the
best part of her industrial and economic
wealth. German pressure drove President
Beneš from his country and compelled the
Prague administration to subordinate both
its internal and external policies to the
wishes of the invader.

Two questions must now be asked. First,
was the peace of Europe worth such a
sacrifice? Second, why after betraying
Czechoslovakia in 1938 did Great Britain
and France in 1939 pledge their support to
Poland? For only a year earlier Poland had
joined Germany in claiming Czechoslovak
territory. Daladier and Bonnet were convinced that Hitler only used the Sudeten
problem as a pretext for annexing the
whole of Czechoslovakia. But the French
were still war-weary and their leaders
would not risk hostilities with Germany for
their smaller allies without an assurance of
British support. The British government
was equally aware of Hitler's aims but was

not ready to give help to France except as a last resort. Duff Cooper, who resigned as first lord of the Admiralty in protest against the Munich agreement, justified his acceptance of the 'betrayal' of Czechoslovakia on 20th September in the following words: 'I saw that if we were obliged to go to war it would be hard to have it said against us that we were fighting the principle of self-determination.' There is no doubt that, in the autumn of 1938, a very large proportion of the Sudeten Germans wished to be part of the fascist Reich. Under pressure Beneš had indeed promised them far-reaching autonomy, but too late: this would no longer satisfy them.

In many ways the Czechs had only themselves to blame for the turn of events. In the years after 1918 they had created a state dominated by a single nationality. In contrast to Switzerland they had ignored the rights of minority groups – Slovaks, Poles, Germans, and Hungarians. According to Lord Runciman, Czech rule over the Sudeten Germans was narrow-minded, tactless, and without understanding. The situation was aggravated by the world economic crisis for this hit Czechoslovakia hardest in its German provinces. By contrast neighbouring Germany was booming and this heightened temptation among the dissatisfied population. In the Sudetenland, as in Germany and Austria, a majority supported Hitler in 1938. It must not be forgotten, however, that they also wanted peace: it was a peaceful annexation of the Sudetenland that they hoped for.

### Chamberlain in the eyes of Germany

Except from Hitler's political opponents and victims, there has been no German criticism of Chamberlain either then or now. In fact, at the time, Munich's inhabitants gave him a standing ovation. But the policy of appeasement has certainly been a controversial issue, even in post-war German literature. As in Great Britain, historians and political scientists have been seeking the motives underlying Chamberlain's politics and many theories have been advanced. Among these are military weakness, political naivety, hopes for Anglo-German economic co-operation in southeast Europe, and rabid Tory anti-Communism (seeing fascist Germany as a possible bulwark against Bolshevism). In one of the most recent contributions to the debate, a young German scholar reaches this conclusion: 'There can be no moral condemnation of the British behaviour, for this would imply extraordinary foresight on the part of the British government. It would therefore be writing history backwards and make no contribution to understanding the past.'

There is little support for Chamberlain's policy from surviving members of Hitler's opposition. In the summer of 1938 Hitler's belligerency was alarming some circles of the army, foreign service, and government administration. They therefore considered a military coup to overthrow the Führer. In the absence of mass support, however, they felt that they must allow events to reach the brink of war before they could fasten any blame on Hitler. In consequence emissaries and messages were sent to No. 10 Downing Street requesting support. This was to be a public statement by the British government that any German attack on Czechoslovakia would be met by a declaration of war. The plotters hoped Hitler would lose prestige and that this would prepare the ground for them. But for various reasons Chamberlain refused to make the desired statement; in any case he could hardly have been expected to base his foreign policy on the uncertain plans of a group of conspirators. Nevertheless, in the last days before Munich, he did show the firmness they had wanted, for when he proposed the summit meeting he also put the British fleet on the alert. The move was entirely successful, as Hitler confided shortly afterwards to a colleague: 'Do you know why I finally yielded at Munich? I thought the Home Fleet might open fire.'

### The Danzig question

The Munich conference was supposed to inaugurate a new era in international relations. The 'slave treaty' of Versailles, as the Germans called it, was dead. A negotiated settlement had taken its place. Greater Germany had at last come into existence, and Hitler himself professed to be satisfied. He declared: 'I have no more territorial demands to make in Europe.' Nor was this mere pretence. Hitler formulated no plans for aggressive action during the winter of 1938-39. His generals were told to be ready 'to smash the remainder of the Czech state if it adopted an anti-German policy.' But this was no more than a precaution against the counter-offensive which Hitler half-expected from the Western powers. German expenditure on armaments was considerably reduced after Munich and remained at this lower level until the outbreak of war in September 1939 – clear indication that Hitler was not expecting a great war.

There was still one German grievance left over from Versailles which Hitler intended to remove. Danzig, though entirely German in population, was still a Free City, and the Polish Corridor still separated East Prussia from the rest of Germany. But Hitler did not anticipate conflict over these issues. Poland and Germany were on good terms, and Poland had been Germany's faithful jackal during the Czech crisis. Settlement seemed easy. With the creation of Gdynia, Poland was no longer dependent on Danzig as her only outlet to the world. Danzig could remain a free port for Poland and yet return to the Reich, as its inhabitants wanted. It should also be easy to arrange for German extra-territorial roads and railways across the Corridor. Friendship between Poland and Germany would then be secure, and the two could join in conquering the Ukraine from Soviet Russia.

Hitler did not understand Poland's policy of independence. Colonel Beck, the arrogant foreign minister of Poland, was determined to balance between Germany and Soviet Russia. He would not commit himself to either. He would certainly not enlist Soviet aid against Germany. Equally, he would not co-operate with Germany against Soviet Russia. Hitler wanted to get Danzig out of the way as the only stumbling block between Germany and Poland. For exactly this reason, Beck kept it in the way. Moreover, Beck had learned a lesson from the Czechoslovak affair. He believed that any negotiations or offers of compromise were a slippery slope to ruin. In his view a firm 'no' at the outset was the only safe course. He knew, too, that the Western powers sympathized with Germany over Danzig and would urge concession if they were consulted. He therefore did not consult them. Great Britain and France were assured that Polish relations with Germany were unclouded, while Beck was simultaneously showing a blank and uncomprehending face to Hitler's proposals for compromise.

### The limits of appeasement

The Western powers had given up Poland for lost. As Halifax, the British foreign secretary, said: 'Poland can only presumably fall more and more into the German sphere.' British and French statesmen assumed that Soviet Russia and Germany were irreconcilable. Russia would remain as a vague menace on Germany's eastern frontier, and, if Hitler were determined to go somewhere, it were better that he went east. The two Western countries were determined never to be involved again in 'an Eastern quarrel'. The British particularly were anxious to dodge out of the guarantee they had given to Czechoslovakia. Nor had they much faith in their French ally. France, once the advocate of resistance to Germany, now set the pace in appeasement. In December, Ribbentrop came to Paris. He and Bonnet signed a pact of friendship, in which France washed her hands of Eastern Europe—or that was what she seemed to have done.

The British did not like this. Their idea was to restrain France, not the other way round. Now they needed some other associate who would help to warn Hitler off

*1938 Czech Communist poster*

Photo: V. Chochola, Prague

Western Europe. In January 1939 Chamberlain and Halifax journeyed to Rome. Once more they urged Mussolini to play the moderating part which he had done at Munich. Mussolini was frightened. He knew that Italy was in no state for war and, more wisely than others, recognized that Great Britain might go to war if Hitler pressed too hard. From this moment he importuned Hitler for a firm written alliance – seemingly a move towards Germany. But in Mussolini's eyes, the essential clause of this alliance, finally concluded in May 1939, was that the two powers agreed not to start a general war before 1942 or 1943, and many things could happen before then.

The early months of 1939 saw everyone in a state of undefined apprehension. The British, alarmed by the deficiencies shown during the Czech crisis, were pushing on with their rearmament, a good deal faster indeed than the Germans were. Hitler snapped at every increase in British arms expenditure and complained that they were incompatible with the trust in his word which Chamberlain had professed at Munich. In his crude way, Hitler imagined that he would shake the British 'warmongers', from Churchill to Eden, if he denounced them. Instead he pushed up their reputation and began to shake Chamberlain's. London ran over with rumours of new German aggressions.

Then one came, though not at all as Hitler intended. Czecho-Slovakia, hyphenated since Munich, broke up. This was not altogether Hitler's doing. The Slovaks had always been discontented and could no longer be restrained when Czech prestige was shattered. They demanded first autonomy and then independence. The Czechs prepared to act against them. The Hungarians prepared to move in on the other

*Above: SA recruits in Memel following the city's return to Germany. Memel's population was predominantly German in origin and many were willing to fight for the Führer. In 1945 Memel was taken by Soviet troops and was renamed Klaipėda, in the Lithuanian Soviet Socialist Republic*

side. Hitler could allow neither course. He recognized the independence of Slovakia. Hácha, President of the Czech rump, appealed to Hitler for guidance. He came to Berlin and transformed Bohemia into a German protectorate. On 15th March 1939 German troops occupied Bohemia, and Hitler spent the night in Prague.

Nothing was changed except for the unfortunate Czechs, who received all the blessings of German rule – the secret police, persecution of Jews, and the loss of freedom. The British government rejoiced to be freed from 'the somewhat embarrassing commitment of a guarantee'. But British public opinion was in an uproar. Hitler was supposed to have gone back on his word. He was on the march to the domination of Europe. Neville Chamberlain, much against his will, had to speak words of protest and even of resistance. Secretly, Chamberlain, Halifax, and the rest wanted to settle with Hitler. They believed that war would achieve nothing except the ruin of Europe. But they needed to be stronger if they were to bargain at all and so became the prisoners of public opinion. As for the British people, this was the moment when most of them decided that the only thing to do with Hitler was to 'stop' him.

The British government were in a panic. They thought, quite wrongly, that Hitler was about to overrun the Balkans and Turkey. Any day the Middle East would be in danger. At precisely this moment, Tilea, the Rumanian minister, turned up with the news that German troops were about to enter Rumania. This was a totally false alarm. The British statesmen believed it. Helter-skelter, they tried to organize a peace front for joint resistance. The French agreed to join. The Russians agreed on condition all the others did. The Poles refused. They were still determined not to take sides. Negotiations over Danzig were becoming tenser as Beck kept up his negatives. But Hitler remained hopeful. As late as 25th March he issued a directive: 'The Führer *does not* wish to solve the Danzig question by force.'

Then came another alarm. There were reports, again unfounded, of German troop movements against Poland. These reports were fed to a British newspaper correspondent by German generals. Why? So that the British would resist Hitler? Or so that they would make the Poles give way? No one knows. At any rate, the correspondent was invited to attend the British cabinet. Chamberlain, convinced, wrote out with his own hand the offer of a British guarantee to Poland. Beck was conversing with the British ambassador when the message from London was brought in. He accepted the guarantee 'between two flicks of the ash from his cigarette'. It seemed to him to be a perfect solution. The British guarantee strengthened his hand against Germany. At the same time, it enabled him to refuse any co-operation with Soviet Russia. The British were entangled in 'an Eastern European quarrel' and yet could not appeal to Russia for aid. Poland would remain the dominant power in Eastern Europe, calling the tune on all sides.

When the British government came to

their senses, they did not like what they had done. By giving to Poland an unconditional guarantee, they had committed themselves over Danzig, a cause for which they did not care at all or on which they even agreed with Hitler. Colonel Beck visited London a few days later. The British then tried to modify their guarantee. Beck would not yield. With continued arrogance, he merely offered to make the guarantee mutual. He assured the British that they were in more danger from Hitler than he was. He said not a word of the deadlock over Danzig, and the British were taken in by his self-confidence. They even feared that, unless they stuck by Beck, he would take Poland into the German camp. Besides, British public opinion would not forgive them if they again ran away. Beck departed from London with the assurance that the guarantee would soon be turned into a formal alliance. Actually, this was delayed until 25th August, on the eve of war.

The British guarantee to Poland provoked Hitler instead of restraining him. He was still convinced that his opponents would give way – 'they are little worms. I saw them at Munich' – and so raised his bid. On 3rd April he told his generals to be ready for war with Poland in September, though he added an assurance that he would go to war only if Poland were isolated. On 28th April he denounced the Non-Aggression Pact with Poland of 1934 and the Anglo-German Naval Agreement of 1935. He still declared that he wanted agreement over Danzig and looked forward to friendship with the British later, when they too had given way over Danzig. Then, having stated his terms, Hitler withdrew into silence. There were no official exchanges between Germany and Great Britain until the middle of August, and none at all with Poland until the day war broke out.

### Alliance without risks?

This was a nerve-racking situation. Hitler had made no precise demands. He had merely stated his dissatisfaction and left others to remedy it. In 1938 the British knew how to do this, or so they thought: concessions from Czechoslovakia would do the trick. Now this road was barred, and Colonel Beck had made it clear that there would be no concessions from Poland. The British government threatened that they would not support him. No good. Beck had their guarantee and knew that they dared not go back on it. The British government had to make the gestures of preparing to resist Hitler, whether they intended to or not. A Ministry of Supply was solemnly instituted, though Chamberlain had earlier dismissed it as a measure of war. It was in fact instituted only in theory and did not operate before war broke out. Compulsory military service was introduced – again an empty gesture. The young conscripts would not make any significant contribution to the British Army until 1942.

The greatest gesture hung over the British government like a hideous black cloud – the proposal for an alliance with Soviet Russia. It would seem to have obvious advantages – a great power enlisted on the side of collective security, aiding Poland, and distracting Germany with an eastern front. The British Opposition clamoured for a Soviet alliance. So did the French, who, having been committed to the Polish guarantee without being consulted, now wanted someone else to fulfil their guarantee for them. But there were grave disadvantages also. The Poles would not make an alliance with Soviet Russia, and Beck insisted that he would reject Soviet assistance even if offered. Some members of the British government believed that Soviet Russia, bled by Stalin's purges, was too weak to fight. Others believed that she would not be a reliable ally. All were shocked at the idea of associating with Bolsheviks and regarded the prospect of Soviet victory, however remote, as even worse than that of a German one. Yet there was no escape. British public opinion wanted the Soviet alliance as the best means of deterring Hitler from war or of winning a war if it came. The French were determined to go forward. The British government therefore timidly set out on the quest for an alliance without risks, much as a man trying to go swimming without getting wet.

The basis of the British proposal, feebly dangled before the Soviet government time after time, was that Soviet Russia should provide aid 'if requested' or 'if desired'. Soviet aid was to be turned on and off like a tap. The Poles were to be allowed to turn the tap. Later the Baltic states were to be allowed to turn the tap. The British were to be allowed to turn the tap. But the Soviets were not to be allowed to turn the tap themselves. They were to stand by patiently, active or inactive according to the will of others. This was not an attractive proposition for the Russians. No one knows the original intentions of Stalin and his associates. Perhaps they hoped for a solid alliance with the Western powers. Perhaps they planned a deal with Hitler all along. Perhaps they intended to play with both sides and see what happened. Speculation is not rewarding and is made less so when the Soviet rulers are denounced for following the path of self-preservation like everyone else. The Bolsheviks lose either way: they are condemned as criminal monsters at one moment and expected to follow a more idealistic course than others at the next.

According to such evidence as exists, the Soviet government was anxious to conclude a firm alliance, and the British, when not evasive, were spinning things out. Each British subterfuge received a prompt Soviet answer. Then the British would take ten days or a fortnight devising another one. By the middle of May, negotiations had reached deadlock. The Russians would look at nothing except a straight defensive alliance. The British inserted the fatal 'if desired' into every draft. When this was rejected, they were ready to break off. Hitler had remained quiet, and perhaps there would be no trouble after all. The French were not so complacent. Failing all else, they would make a simple Franco-Soviet alliance without caring what happened to Poland. To prevent this, the British went reluctantly forward. This

*Südd-Verlag*

time they appeared to offer a pact of mutual security. But there were still problems. The Russians feared that Hitler would attack other countries before attacking them, and a glance at the map suggests that he could do nothing else. The Russians therefore demanded that 'indirect aggression', that is attack on some neighbouring country, should be regarded as attack upon themselves. They even demanded that peaceful surrender to Hitler by some small country should be treated as indirect aggression on themselves.

The British refused these Soviet proposals. They had made the cause of small countries their own. Besides, they suspected Soviet Russia as an imperialist power, with plans much like Hitler's. In that case, they should not have been seeking a Soviet alliance at all. Finally Molotov, now commissar for foreign affairs, suggested a way out. They should postpone the search for a political agreement and should hold military talks to consider how the alliance could work if it were ever made. The British jumped at this as an excuse for further delay. The French hoped to get military co-operation with Soviet Russia after all. The British and French governments appointed military delegations which departed on a slow boat for Leningrad. By the time they arrived all chance of a united front against Hitler had disappeared.

During the negotiations, both Russians and British had received offers from unofficial German sources. The Russians had

*Above: Local police remove customs barrier following Germany's annexation of Danzig, 1st September 1939—the day Poland was invaded. The Free City of Danzig had been under Polish economic domination*

indicated their willingness to renew trade relations with Germany. The British had gone further. Chamberlain's agents, though perhaps not Chamberlain himself, had displayed British anxiety to satisfy Hitler over Danzig, if only this could be done in a respectable peaceful way. Once Danzig was settled, Great Britain would forget her guarantee to Poland. She would give Germany a loan of one thousand million pounds. Happy relations would be restored.

By the beginning of August, Hitler knew that negotiations between Soviet Russia and the Western powers were stuck. He knew also that the British government would pay almost any price to avoid a war. He thought that the time had come for him to pull off his great stroke. The British people, he believed, were hoping for a Soviet alliance. If he could show that this hope was vain, the British would back down. He was right, or very nearly, about the British government. He failed to allow for the fact that the British people might have a will of their own. It was a very foolish proposition to suppose that Great Britain and France, without Soviet Russia, could do anything to aid Poland or indeed to deter Hitler in any way. But it was a proposition to which most British people were committed.

# World War II 1939-1945

## INTRODUCTION

At 11.15 a.m. on the 3rd September 1939, Neville Chamberlain, Prime Minister of Great Britain, broadcast to the nation. This was no clarion call to arms, but rather the voice of a tired, and suddenly much older, man telling the people of Britain that his hopes for peace had been dashed. 'I cannot believe', he said, 'that there is anything more or different I could have done. . . .' At 9 a.m. that morning an ultimatum demanding the withdrawal of German troops from Poland had been delivered by the British ambassador in Berlin; it had expired at 11 a.m. France declared war on Germany later that day; the Dominions followed Britain's lead very swiftly in this order: New Zealand (on 3rd September), South Africa (on 6th September), Canada and Australia (10th September).

For the second time in twenty-five years Britain was at war with Germany. The nation expected war, indeed it had done so for a year, but its ideas of what to expect were wrong. For the majority of people, war was a combination of Flanders mud and science fiction. The Great War had seen four years of immobile trench warfare, in which the civilian population outside the war zones had remained relatively unharmed. Now things would be different—or so people believed. It was expected that, within hours of the outbreak of war, massive bombing raids would be launched against the civilian centres; but apart from a false alarm in the afternoon of the 3rd, nothing happened—at least not in Britain.

In Poland, however, which had been invaded by Hitler's troops on 1st September, General Kluge's IV Army had cut through the Polish lines and was driving south through Lower Vistula towards Warsaw, while in the south the VII, X and XIV Armies were at Kracow. In three days Poland, the nation for which Britain and France had gone to war, was all but beaten in a totally new kind of war—the *Blitzkrieg*. This 'lightning war' was the complete antithesis of everything the Allied generals had learnt in 1914–18. Its essence was mobility. Using tanks and motorized transport with heavy air cover, the attacking forces made deep thrusts into the heart of enemy territory, while heavy bombing of military targets and communications disrupted the ability of the defenders to marshal their forces and launch a counter-attack. At the same time, bombing

raids on sections of the civilian population were carried out with the intention of creating demoralization and panic. It was a tactic which worked superbly well in Poland. The Polish Air Force was destroyed on the ground and the Polish Army, without air cover, was surrounded in a great north/south pincer movement and cut to pieces. By 27th September it was all over. On 17th September the Soviet Union, seeking to regain territory lost in 1918, had invaded from the east in agreement with Germany and reached Brest Litovsk with practically no resistance. On the following day the Polish Commander-in-Chief had fled to Rumania, leaving the Warsaw garrison to fight on for ten more days.

In the west the French had mounted a very minor attack into German territory to draw pressure off Poland, but it had failed. There simply was not time. The French, believing in trench warfare, had expected the Poles to hold out until the Spring, thus giving the Allies an opportunity to group their forces and attack Germany through 'neutral' Belgium. As it was, they did have to wait until the spring, but by then all thought of attack had been abandoned and the French army sat

securely entrenched in the Maginot Line, while some of their comrades and the British Expeditionary Force desperately tried to dig trenches along the Belgian border and extend the line to the coast. It seems almost incredible now that, even after the invasion of Poland, the British and French High Commands still thought in terms of static trench warfare, but the mentality of 1914–18 was not easily discarded. The Maginot line, a chain of forts and gun emplacements, was based entirely on the fact that the antiquated forts of Verdun had held against constant German attack in 1916. The Allies were not totally ill-equipped, for the French had tanks that were at least the equal of the Panzers. Yet these were scattered along the Line to plug gaps left by the infantry, instead of being grouped to repulse attack by enemy tanks.

Through the winter of 1939–40 Europe waited. Then, on 9th April 1940, the uneasy peace was broken; Germany invaded Norway and Denmark in order, according to Hitler, to prevent these two neutral countries from being occupied by an Anglo-French force. Denmark collapsed within twenty-four hours of the invasion but Norway, assisted by an

*Women as skilled machinists—a job regarded as 'man's work' before the war*

Anglo-French defence force, held out. Although the Germans swiftly gained control of Oslo, the British landed troops in north and central Norway on 14th April, and on 17th April further troops were landed at Andålsnes in an attempt to link up with Norwegian forces. Meanwhile, the Royal Navy carried out two daring raids on German warships in Narvik fjord and effectively isolated the German forces in northern Norway. However, elsewhere the tide of events was working against the Norwegians. The invasion and then the fall of France forced British and French withdrawal, and on 8th June the groups of Norwegians fighting in the mountains surrendered to the German Army.

While the war in the north held the attention of the watching world, the German Army launched a major two-pronged attack towards France on 10th May 1940. In the north, Bock's Army Group B struck through the Netherlands and Belgium, while in the south Runstedt's Army Group A came through Luxembourg into the Ardennes and raced for the sea. The British and French, believing the Ardennes to be unsuitable for tanks, rushed their armies north-eastwards into Belgium. It was a disastrous mistake and precisely the one the Germans had hoped they would make. Although deprived of air cover the northern armies held out well, but by the 12th May Runstedt's Panzers had reached the Meuse. From then on the Allied cause was all but lost. The British and French attempted to use what remained of their armour and air power in counter-attacking, but it was too late and, by the evening of 15th May, Gamelin admitted to Daladier that the French Army was broken and that he had no more reserves. The French tanks, the only ones in Europe of similar quality to the Panzers, were scattered, and what remained of them were withdrawing to defend Paris. The possibilities of a counter-attack were reduced by Churchill's decision not to commit any more squadrons of the Royal Air Force to France although he had, on 16th May, against the express wishes of Air Chief Marshal Dowding, indicated to the French government that additional R.A.F. support might be available. However, his subsequent decision not to send additional support was to cause bitterness in Anglo-French relations for many years after.

Once across the Meuse, the German army began its dash for the sea. By the evening of 20th May II Panzer Division had reached the shore, Reinhardt's forces were heading for St Omer and Rommel's for Arras. The élite of the Allied armies were trapped in the north and annihilation seemed certain until 24th May, when the German armour stopped short of the coast. A number of reasons have been suggested for this sudden halt; the crucial fact is that it allowed a valuable breathing space for the evacuation of the remaining, mainly British, armies from Dunkirk. Between 27th May and 3rd June, in a brilliant improvised operation, a mass of small boats took 338,226 Allied soldiers from the beaches of France.

The battle of France was over, and the Battle of Britain was about to begin. If Operation Sea Lion, Hitler's proposed invasion of Britain, was to succeed it was necessary that the Royal Air Force be destroyed. From early August 1940 the *Luftwaffe* began daylight raids on Fighter Command bases in southern and eastern England with this aim. From 16th to 23rd August the *Luftwaffe* pounded the fighter bases around London. The strategy was on the verge of success when Hitler, after a night raid by Bomber Command on Berlin, suddenly ordered the attack to be diverted to civilian targets, not only in revenge, but also in the belief (inspired by Göring's boasts) that, since Fighter ·Command was almost destroyed, all that remained necessary was the total demoralization of the civilian population.

These daylight raids on civilian centres reached their peak on 15th September, when the whole might of the *Luftwaffe* was flung against the south-east of England. All through the day and into the night wave after wave of bombers crossed the Channel coast; severe damage was caused and civilian casualties were high, but the German losses were enormous, and on 17th September Hitler postponed Operation Sea Lion indefinitely. This was the crucial point though few can have known it immediately. The Battle of Britain had been won. The *Luftwaffe* now switched its operations entirely to night attacks on civilian centres and these continued throughout the long winter of 1940–41. The losses suffered by the civilian population were terrible.

In the winter of 1940–41 the war was still a limited conflict involving only a small proportion of the world's population. The Soviet Union had so far taken very little part in the conflict and, more important for the Allied cause, the US remained neutral—although this neutrality grew more benevolent as time went on. On 21st September 1939 Roosevelt forced the Neutrality Act through Congress amid fierce debate. This was intended to aid the Allies directly, by facilitating the purchase of arms. It was followed, after the fall of France by the 'trading' of fifty obsolete destroyers for a number of British bases in the American hemisphere on ninety-three-year leases. American public opinion was not yet ready for full-scale involvement in the European conflict, but America had begun, through this introduction of Lend Lease in January 1941, to play an increasing part in the Allied war effort.

Although the war had not yet assumed world-wide proportions in early 1941, it was certainly spreading fast. Italy entered on the side of Germany on 10th June 1940, and thus extended the war to the Mediterranean and the Middle East. In August and September 1940 the Italians invaded first British Somaliland and then Egypt. The Duce did not have much success in either of these two campaigns, or in the Italian invasion of Greece in October. However, the fall of France released German troops to assist their allies, and an élite force, the Afrika Korps, under the command of Erwin Rommel, was sent to North Africa. At the same time Germany invaded Greece from Bulgaria, to end the Greek heroic resistance which until that point had not only repulsed invasion but had driven the Italians back into Albania. On 21st April 1941 the Greeks surrendered to Germany and four days later the last British troops were withdrawn from Greece. The same fate befell Crete in the following month.

Novosti

*Russian partisans in Belorussia. By 1943 the partisan movement was better organized, and the local population more prepared to help with the resistance; but the partisans were suspect to the Kremlin, and only twenty-five per cent of them were ever fully rehabilitated after the war*

During the spring and summer of 1941 Britain's efforts shifted to the defence of Egypt. From January 1941 to August 1942 the British 8th Army, which included a large number of Australian, New Zealand and Indian troops, fought a to-and-fro battle along the North African coast. At the end of August Rommel renewed his offensive at Alam Halfa in a further attempt to break through the Allied lines. The attack failed and the Allied forces, now strengthened by supplies from the US, who had entered the war in December 1941, regrouped and counter-attacked on 23rd October in the second Battle of El Alamein, and on 4th November broke through the German defences. It was a crucial victory. On 8th November Anglo-American forces landed in Morocco and Algeria. Rommel and the Axis forces were trapped, and it was only a matter of time before they were either captured or driven out of North Africa.

In the meantime, most of western and central Europe stayed uneasily under German occupation. From the first, two significant minorities emerged: those who were prepared to collaborate fully and those who were prepared to resist actively. The size of the first group has until recently been grossly underestimated. There were many with reasons other than simple expediency who co-operated with the invaders, as the size of the foreign units within the German army and Waffen SS shows. However, most of them co-operated simply to make life easier. At the other extreme were the various resistance movements. Initially in Europe these were ill-organized, and the British support agency, the Special Operations Executive (S.O.E.), had little success. With the entry of Russia into the war on the side of the Allies, the Communist Parties of Western Europe threw their strength into the resistance, and by the end of 1941, active opposition had become much more efficient, especially in eastern Europe.

There was a third minority, or rather group of minorities, for whom Nazism had been horrific from the onset. In western Europe Hitler's policy of anti-semitism led first to the registering of Jews and the systematic deprivation of their civil rights and then, from 1941 onwards, to their wholesale deportation to concentration camps. This was the 'final solution to the Jewish problem' and led to the mass slaughter of the Jewish population in occupied territories. Other minority groups, like the gypsies, suffered a similar fate. In addition, huge numbers of 'inferior racial groups', like Russians, Lithuanians and Poles, were transported about Europe as forced labour, and treated with appalling brutality.

Suddenly the scope of the war changed drastically. The Soviet Union had signed a non-aggression pact with Germany in 1939, and through the first year and a half of war these two unlikely friends had co-operated uneasily. In the summer of 1941 the pact was broken: on 22nd June, the German army crossed the Russian frontier and began Operation Barbarossa—the crusade against Bolshevism which Hitler had been promising since 1933. Initially the invasion seemed a repetition of Poland; despite advance warning from their espionage organization, the Russians were ill-prepared for the Red Army had lost many of its best officers in the purges of 1937–39. By 3rd July German forces had gone deep into Russia and General Halder was boasting that the campaign had succeeded. Two factors made this an empty boast, however. First, the Russians had enormous reserves of both manpower and production. Stalin's five-year plans had turned Russia into a major industrial nation and from July 1941 onwards this industry was moved to the east, where production could continue out of the range of German bombs. Secondly, Hitler had relied on a swift campaign and once the advance was halted, the geography and climate of Russia acted as weapons against the German army. Their lines of supplies were stretched across thousands of miles and constantly harried by guerrilla units, and the combination of winter and the heroism of the Russian forces led to the start of the retreat of the German army. With the thaw in the spring of 1942 the Red Army counter-attacked, though with disastrous results. Out-gunned by the German army, they fell back in disorder but were re-grouped around Stalingrad by General Chuikov. There followed weeks of hand-to-hand fighting as Soviet forces and civilians defended every inch of the city. Then, on 19th November 1942, the importance of the safe industrial plant and manpower reserves was shown by the Red Army's counter-attack in a wide pincer movement, utilizing new tanks and fresh men. By the end of November a quarter of a million German soldiers were trapped in Stalingrad, and although attempts were made to relieve them, it was hopeless.

Also at the end of 1941, the war extended to the Far East, and thus became a truly 'world war'. Japan's ambitions in the Far East were not a direct threat to the American mainland, and although American opinion was largely anti-Axis, any attempt to take America into the war would certainly have met with strong criticism. On 7th December, a Japanese force of 353 aircraft and five midget submarines attacked the base of the American Pacific Fleet at Pearl Harbour, in the Hawaiian Islands. It was not as crippling a blow to the US Navy in the Pacific as had been intended, and it was a disastrous political blunder. The attack on Pearl Harbour, Japan's involvement with the Axis and Hitler's entry into the war against America on Japan's request, invalidated any opposition to the US entering the war. From Pearl Harbour until the battle of Midway in June 1942, the Japanese swept all before them. By the end of December 1941, the Japanese had overwhelmed the Philippines, Wake Island and Guam. They had launched major attacks into Malaya, Thailand and Burma, and had taken Hong Kong by the end of the year, as well as dealing a major blow to British naval power by sinking the *Prince of Wales* and the *Repulse* off the coast of Malaya during air attacks in the Indian Ocean.

Japanese successes continued during the spring of 1942. In February Singapore fell and in March resistance in Java ended. Meanwhile, an Allied fleet suffered a serious defeat in the Java Sea at the end of February. In June 1942 the Japanese High Command was in a state of elation. Losses were much lower than they had expected and everywhere their forces seemed triumphant. They controlled a significant area of the Asian land mass and had apparent mastery of the air and sea over large areas of the Pacific. That position was decisively altered by the Battle of Midway. At the beginning of April, the Japanese decided to try and lure the US Pacific Fleet out of harbour and into a major sea battle. The US Intelligence had broken the Japanese codes, and on 14th May Admiral Nimitz, on the basis of information derived from the codes, decided that Midway was the object of Japanese planning. This led to vital re-grouping of the US Fleet. Even so, what followed was a tortured and complex battle in which luck on the part of the Americans and lack of judgment on the part of the Japanese were at least as important as any American tactical advantage. The apparent losses were not great, but the Japanese lost four major aircraft carriers to the dive-bombers of the *Enterprise* and *Yorktown*. This effectively restored the balance of naval power in the Pacific. More important, it was a major psychological victory for the US which was to stand it in good stead for the long and bitter battle of the Solomon Islands which began in the following August.

The battle of the Solomon Islands was the beginning of the long and bloody 'island-hopping' campaign. Slowly, American forces began to recapture the islands lost in the first months of the war in the Far East, but each island was a bloody battlefield, especially for the US Marines. By the middle of 1944, US forces were pressing home attacks on the Marianas Islands—Guam, Tinian and Saipan —whose capture would bring the Japanese homeland within reach of American bombers. The Japanese decided again to lure the Americans into a sea battle, and the resulting battle of the Philippine Sea was a disaster for the Imperial Navy. Although the fleets never sighted one another, and the battle was fought entirely by carrier-borne aircraft, it was a battle from which the Japanese never recovered.

In the western sector of the war, Britain and her Allies, reinforced by increasing numbers of American troops and aircraft, prepared to invade Europe. By 1943 the battle of the sea in this area was well on its way to being won. Despite terrible losses, the Royal Navy had all but destroyed the threat posed by German surface vessels by sinking some of the German navy's major ships, including the *Graf Spee* and the *Bismarck*. The war against the U-boats continued, however, and with America's entry into the war and the consequent enormous increase in Atlantic shipping, victory on this front became crucial. Events came to a climax during May and June 1942 when the Germans lost over fifty U-boats in two months. From then on the development of long-range land-based aircraft and above all the improvements in convoy escorting rapidly reduced the U-boat risk.

Further, the war was beginning to be pressed home on Germany and the occupied territories in Europe. From the first months of the war the R.A.F. had carried out raids on German cities and industrial areas. However, it was the development of the long-range, four-engine bombers, like the Halifax and the

*Towards victory in Burma. British troops take village on the road to Mandalay, in the Irrawaddy basin after fierce fighting, February 1945*

*Yalta, February 1945. The Crimean conference marked the high tide of Allied unity*

Lancaster, plus the arrival of the USAAF with B 17s and B 24s, at the end of 1942, which marked the beginning of the real bombing campaign. Although German attempts at retaliation with 'V' weapons caused some panic, these were pinpricks in comparison. In the course of the Second World War nearly six hundred thousand German civilians died in air raids, while the total British civilian losses for the same period were sixty-five thousand.

After the surrender of the Axis forces in North Africa on 13th May 1943, the Allied armies, under the Supreme Command of General Dwight D. Eisenhower, invaded Sicily and gained their first territory in the 'fortress of Europe'. Mussolini's regime had fallen on 24th July, but all was far from finished in Italy. At Quebec in August 1943, the Allies had designated Italy a 'secondary theatre'. Although Allied troops were on the mainland of Italy in September the withdrawal of some of their crack divisions from the Italian front prolonged the fighting. The German army retreated up Italy, fighting on through 1944 and into 1945, inflicting terrible casualties on the Allies, particularly during the two winters.

In June 1944 the curtain was raised on the final act. Public attention was focused on Normandy. On 6th June, after months of preparation, Operation Overlord, the Allied invasion of Europe, began. The Germans had expected an Allied invasion to come by the shortest route and land in northern France, an illusion fostered by the Allies with an elaborate dummy operation, which included bombing the wrong areas of France and leaking false information to German Intelligence. The invasion went almost entirely according to plan. Allied forces moved quickly inland and by the end of the first week a continuous bridgehead of sixty miles had been secured. German opposition was fierce. It was not until Operation Cobra, on 25th–31st July, that the real break-through came. On 31st July General Patton's 3rd Army broke through the German lines and, in a spectacular dash through Brittany, raced towards Le Mans and Chartres. The combined Allied armies now pushed on towards the Rhine, the British army taking the northern sector and the American army taking the southern one. But the disastrous failure at Arnhem in Holland slowed down their advance and made an early victory unlikely.

In mid-November the Allied armies launched their major offensive against the German border on a wide front. It failed, and in mid-December the German army counter-attacked in the Ardennes. Although the Allies were taken by surprise the German army could not sustain the attack, and Hitler's insistence that they fight to the last prevented an orderly retreat. Meanwhile, on the eastern front Zhukov, pushing through Poland, reached the Oder barely fifty miles from Berlin, in mid-January. In the west only the Rhine lay between the Allies and victory now. At the beginning of February the final assault was launched. Although the Americans were held at Cologne, another brilliant break-through by Patton's 3rd Army established the first bridgehead near Mainz on the night of 22nd February. The main attack was launched the following day, and headed by General Montgomery's 21st Army Group, crossed the Rhine further north. Resistance in the west now began to crumble, despite the Führer's orders to defend every inch of German soil. The unspoken hope of the German people was that the Allies would reach Berlin before the Russians. But this was not to be. On 16th April the Red Army started its final assault on Berlin, and by 25th April the city was completely encircled by Soviet troops. It was the end of the Axis dictators. In a shell-proof bunker beneath the Reich chancellery building on 30th April, Hitler committed suicide. Two days earlier Mussolini had been executed by Italian partisans. Their dreams of a Thousand-Year Reich and a fascist Europe lay in ruins.

But the war was not over. Even as Germany finally surrendered on 8th May, the Japanese were fighting a desperate retreat across Asia and the Pacific. In Burma, General Slim was slowly pushing the Japanese army out of its defences around Rangoon and preparing for a final assault down the Irrawaddy. In the Pacific the US Marines secured, at terrible cost, the vital air bases on Iwo Jima in March and by 7th April the bases were open to provide vital fighter cover for the bombing raids on Japan now beginning in earnest. It was not these raids, nor the desperate and bloody attack on Okinawa which were to end the war, but one weapon—the atomic bomb. On the morning of 6th August the 'Enola Gay', a specially converted B 29, took off from Tinian and dropped the first atomic bomb on Hiroshima. Descending by parachute the bomb exploded at approximately 1,850 feet, and killed 80,000 people, most of them within minutes. On 9th August a second bomb was dropped on Nagasaki. On 15th August the emperor of Japan surrendered unconditionally.

Peace had been won but at a terrifying price. Europe was in ruins. Her industries had been destroyed, converted to war production or worn out by six years of over-production, and she had lost thirty-three and a half million of her population. For western Europe, the only hope lay in massive American aid to reconstruct her industrial plant and this was forthcoming under the Marshall Plan. For eastern Europe, particularly countries like Hungary, which had fought on the side of Germany, there was no such hope. The Soviet Union had paid a higher price than any other nation for victory and intended, somehow, to get it back.

Although the leaders of the Nazi Party and the German war machine were brought to trial at Nuremberg, this seemed, even at the time, a futile gesture which could do little to atone for the terrible carnage of the war.

The victorious Allies seemed on the verge of division. The post-war policy of the Allied nations had been decided at a series of meetings, notably between Churchill, Roosevelt and Stalin at Yalta (4th–11th February 1945) and between Attlee, Truman and Stalin at Potsdam in the following July and August. Crucially for the future of the world in the second half of the 20th century, in Moscow in October 1944 Churchill and Stalin had agreed on spheres of influence in Europe and the Middle East. This was ratified at Yalta and at Potsdam, and effectively gave the Soviet Union control of most of Central and Eastern Europe in return for a Soviet pledge not to interfere elsewhere in Europe. The other great product of the wartime meetings was the United Nations, designed to replace the already crippled League of Nations, and be an effective peace-keeping body. That it is still in existence, despite its early problems, may be some tribute to its success.

The War left a terrible legacy. Over all lay the appalling shadow of the mushroom cloud and the obscene brutality of the Nazi regime in Europe. Although America alone possessed nuclear weapons all were aware that it was only a matter of time before the Soviet Union also had equivalent power, and after Potsdam the alliance began to crack. As the War ended, premonitions of other future conflicts were beginning to appear. In China the Red Army and the Nationalists resumed hostilities; in Greece a Communist rising was suppressed by Allied troops; while in the Middle East fighting had again broken out between Jewish settlers and the Arab inhabitants of Palestine. Despite the bright hopes of peace and reconstruction, despite the apparent victory of democracy over the horrors of fascism, all was clearly not well with the world.

# The Outbreak of War

The war crisis of 1939 began on 21st August, with the announcement that Ribbentrop, German foreign minister, had been invited to Moscow by the Soviet government. Though the Nazi-Soviet Pact was not formally concluded until 23rd August, it was obvious that Ribbentrop would not go to Moscow unless agreement had already been reached in principle. Hence it was certain that the negotiations for an alliance between France, Great Britain, and Soviet Russia had broken down. This is what Hitler wished to establish. Soviet neutrality in itself was not enough for him. What he needed was public news of this neutrality so that he could shake the nerves of the British and French governments. Stalin, the Soviet dictator, exacted his price in return. Though he, too, like Hitler, probably expected British and French resolution to collapse, he wanted to keep the Germans far from the Soviet frontier if war occurred after all. Hence the Nazi-Soviet Pact drew a barrier in Eastern Europe which the Germans were not to cross.

The pact was neither an alliance nor a partition agreement. The Soviet government merely promised to stay neutral which is what the Poles had always asked them to do, and in addition they set a limit to German expansion. However, the immediate effect was certainly discouraging for the Western powers. Until the last moment they had gone on dreaming either that Hitler would be frightened by the Soviet bogeyman or that Soviet Russia would do their fighting for them. Now they had to decide for themselves, and Hitler was convinced that they would run away. On 22nd August he delivered to his generals a wild oration: 'Close your hearts to pity. Act brutally.' He boasted: 'I have got Poland where I wanted her,' and added cheerfully: 'The probability is great that the West will not intervene.' Hitler was play-acting in order to impress the German generals. He guessed that some of them would leak to the British, and sure enough some did. Almost at once the British embassy received an exaggerated version of Hitler's speech and was correspondingly alarmed.

*Left: In contrast to the scenes of August 1914, Britain and France went to war in September 1939 with a sense of weary foreboding, although their resolution to fight for Poland had not collapsed as Hitler had expected; appeasement had run its course. This newsvendor in London's Trafalgar Square tells his own story*

On 23rd August Hitler went a step further. He moved forward the attack on Poland, fixed for 1st September, to 4.40 a.m. on 26th August. This, too, was play-acting. The German preparations could not be complete before 1st September. Attack on Poland before then was possible only if she had already surrendered. Thus Hitler counted confidently on the collapse of the Western powers.

The French almost came up to his expectations. Georges Bonnet, the foreign minister, had always wanted to desert the Poles. He accepted the German case over Danzig. He had no faith in the Polish army. On 23rd August Daladier, the Premier, summoned the Committee of National Defence at Bonnet's request. Bonnet asked: should they push Poland into a compromise and postpone the war until they were stronger? Gamelin, the French commander-in-chief, would not admit the weakness of his army. He asserted that the Poles could hold out until the spring. By then, France would be 'impregnable'. There was no suggestion that France could aid Poland in any way. Nor did the French attempt to discuss the situation with the British. There were no Anglo-French meetings of ministers such as had marked the Czech crisis. Ideally, the French would have liked the British to force surrender on them. But they would not take the lead in abdication themselves. There was a choice between abandoning Poland and fighting a great war in which France would carry most of the burden. The French refused to choose. They sat by throughout the week when others decided the fate of Europe and of France.

### British obstinacy

The British government were apparently more resolute. On 22nd August they issued a statement that the coming Nazi-Soviet Pact 'would in no way affect their obligation to Poland'. There was nothing else to do. The British ministers were proud and obstinate. They were not going to have the Opposition crowing that their policy was in ruins. Besides, they feared to be swept away in a storm of public opinion if they showed weakness. Conservative backbenchers had disliked the negotiations with Soviet Russia. But many of them had fought in the First World War. They could not imagine that Great Britain was unable to impose her will on Germany if she determined to do so. As for the Opposition, they had championed the Soviet alliance. Now they were resolved to show that, unlike Stalin, they stuck to their principles.

Central Press

In secret, the British ministers wanted to give way. Chamberlain told Kennedy, the American ambassador: 'The futility of it all is frightful; we cannot save the Poles; we can only carry on a war of revenge that will mean the destruction of all Europe.' Chamberlain said he could not put pressure on Poland himself. Would President Roosevelt do it for him? Roosevelt refused. The only hope was to warn Hitler, or rather to plead with him. On 23rd August Nevile Henderson flew to Berchtesgaden. He delivered a warning that Great Britain would stand by Poland. But he also asserted that Hitler could get Danzig peacefully, and he spread out the delights of an Anglo-German alliance. Hitler appeared to be unimpressed. He stormed and ranted. When Henderson left, Hitler slapped his thigh and exclaimed: 'Chamberlain will not survive that conversation. His government will fall tonight.' Back in Berlin, Henderson told Lipski, the Polish ambassador, that the only chance was for Poland to start negotiations immediately. Lipski took no notice.

On 24th August the British Parliament met. It unanimously applauded what it supposed to be the government's firm stand. Hitler began to doubt whether the British government had yet reached the point of surrender. He flew to Berlin and held a conference with Ribbentrop and his leading generals. He asked: should they stick to 26th August as the date for the attack on Poland? He decided that he would make a further attempt to detach the Western powers from their alliance with Poland. This took the form of a 'last offer' which Hitler made to Henderson soon after midday on 25th August. He declared that the problems of Danzig and the Corridor must be 'solved'—though he did not say how. Once this was done, he would guarantee the British Empire, accept an agreed limitation of armaments, and renew his assurance that Germany's western frontier was fixed for ever. Henderson was impressed as usual and thought that Hitler spoke 'with apparent sincerity'. Henderson promised to take Hitler's offer to London the next morning. Hitler approved. What was he up to? By the time Henderson

*Jacques Duclos, French Communist leader, thrown into dilemma by Nazi-Soviet Pact*

left Berlin the German attack on Poland would presumably have begun. Did Hitler think that the British would abandon the Polish alliance on sight of his offer? Had he forgotten his own time-table? Or was advancing the date of attack to 26th August a bluff all along?

The last seems the most probable explanation. All afternoon on 25th August Hitler raged round the Chancellery. At 3 p.m. he ordered the attack to proceed. Three hours later Attolico, the Italian ambassador, brought the news that Italy could not enter the war unless she received vast quantities of raw materials which Germany was in no position to supply. Immediately afterwards Ribbentrop reported that the Anglo-Polish treaty had been formally signed in London. Hitler pulled back. He summoned Keitel, the chief-of-staff, and said: 'Stop everything at once. I need time for negotiations.' The attack on Poland was called off at the last moment.

The British government seemed to have committed themselves for good when they signed the alliance with Poland, particularly as it included a guarantee of Danzig. Their real attitude was quite different: they were still eager to sell out. The Foreign Office drafted terms for an offer to Hitler which stated that Danzig should have 'the right to determine its

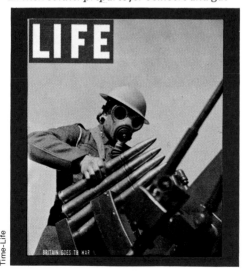

*US magazine cover on outbreak of war. British soldier prepares for bombers and gas*

political allegiance', and Halifax, the foreign secretary, told the Polish ambassador that the Polish government would make a great mistake if they ruled out 'peaceful modifications of the status of Danzig'. Hitler and the British government thus agreed how negotiations should end—with a Polish surrender. The problem was how to get negotiations started. The two sides circled round each other like wrestlers before a clinch. The British offered to arrange direct negotiations between Germany and Poland if Hitler promised to behave peacefully. Hitler answered that there would be no war if he got his way over Danzig.

Göring, who did not want war, now called in an unofficial intermediary, a Swedish businessman called Dahlerus. Dahlerus flew to London on 25th August and back to Berlin on 26th August; to London and back on 27th August; and the same again on 30th August. In Berlin he saw Göring and sometimes Hitler. In London he saw Chamberlain and Halifax. Each side felt that the other was weakening. Both wanted another Munich, but on favourable terms, and neither side knew how to push the Poles over the brink.

On 28th August Henderson delivered the British reply to Hitler's last offer. The British government urged that there should be direct negotiations between Germany and Poland. If these reached agreement, the way would be open for 'a wider and more complete agreement between Germany and Great Britain'. Hitler had repeatedly declared that, as his offers to Poland had been rejected in the spring, he would never negotiate directly with the Poles again. On the other hand, Henderson made no objection when Hitler said that negotiations must involve a Polish surrender over Danzig and the Corridor. Thus Hitler thought he would succeed either way. If the Poles yielded, he would get Danzig and the Corridor. If they refused, the British government would repudiate them. He decided to accept direct negotiations, but to do it in such a way that Germany would still seem to be dictating to both Great Britain and Poland.

On 29th August Hitler saw Henderson again and delivered his answer. He agreed to direct negotiations, but a Polish representative, with full powers, must arrive

VOILA CE QUI NOUS ATTEND, SI LE GOUVERNEMENT N'EST PAS CAPABLE DE SORTIR L'AVIATION FRANÇAISE DE LA SITUATION DRAMATIQUE OÙ L'A PLACÉE LE FRONT POPULAIRE!

Institute of Social History, Amsterdam

*The fears of 1939: French poster, 1939, urges the Daladier government to make good the inadequacies of the French air force. The Popular Front had underestimated the need for national defence and left France weak before the Nazi threat*

in Berlin within the next twenty-four hours. Henderson objected that this was an ultimatum. Hitler and Ribbentrop answered, with typical German pedantry, that the word 'ultimatum' nowhere appeared in the German note. Ultimatum or not, Henderson was eager to accept it. Hitler's offer, he telegraphed to London, was 'the sole chance of preventing war'. Henderson urged acceptance on everybody – on his own government, on the French, on the Poles. He hurried round to Lipski and urged immediate acceptance. Lipski was unmoved and did not even report Hitler's offer to Warsaw. The French were as resolute in the opposite direction. Bonnet telegraphed to Beck that he should go to Berlin at once.

Decision rested with the British government. Here was the proposal they had

*German cartoon. Death, to Churchill: 'Go on making trouble; we'll soon be in business'*

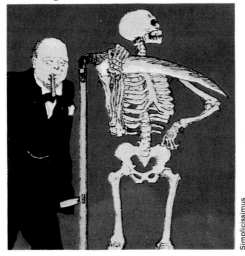

Simplicissimus

always wanted: direct negotiations between Germany and Poland. Hitler had agreed. Now they could not deliver the Poles. Chamberlain told Kennedy that he was 'more worried about getting the Poles to be reasonable than the Germans'. And with reason. Beck replied firmly: 'If invited to Berlin of course he would not go, as he had no intention of being treated like President Hácha.' (President Emil Hácha of Czechoslovakia had, five months before on 15th March, been forced by Hitler, Göring, and Ribbentrop to sign away his country's independence.) The British government had to make a temporizing reply, which Henderson delivered only twenty-five minutes after midnight on 30th August, that is after the German 'ultimatum' had run out. The British welcomed Hitler's proposal, but they asked him to wait a bit – they could not produce a Polish representative at such short notice.

Hitler meanwhile had prepared terms which he would present to the Poles. They were for him moderate: immediate return of Danzig and a plebiscite in the Corridor. Henderson thought that these terms were 'not unreasonable'. Back at the British embassy, he summoned Lipski and urged him to seek an interview with Ribbentrop at once. Lipski refused and went back to bed. The next morning Göring sent Dahlerus to Henderson with the German terms in writing. Henderson again summoned Lipski, and when he refused to come, sent Dahlerus round to him. Lipski was still obstinate. He declared that 'German morale was weakening and that the present regime would soon crack'. Dahlerus reported his failure to London and added that the German terms were 'extremely reasonable'. The British agreed. Henderson telegraphed to London that 'on German offer war should be completely unjustifiable', and Halifax telegraphed to Warsaw: 'I do not see why Polish government should feel difficulty about authorising Polish Ambassador to accept a document from the German government.'

Hitler's manoeuvre was succeeding. A breach was opening between Poland and her Western allies. But Hitler was trapped by his own time-table. He had repeatedly declared to his generals that he would either produce a Polish surrender by 1st September or go to war. He dared not face their contempt if he confessed failure. Besides, military action could not be improvised at a moment's notice. If the attack planned for 1st September were called off, it would have to be postponed for many weeks or even months. All the British messages had been intercepted, and Hitler knew how anxious the British government were to surrender. He had to gamble that they would surrender even if war against Poland had started. In this tight situation he had no choice if he were to maintain his prestige. Maybe too, he liked gambling. As he told Göring: 'I always call *va banque*. It is the only call I know.' At 12.40 p.m. on 31st August he ordered that the attack on Poland should proceed.

At 1 p.m. Lipski asked to see Ribbentrop. He was asked whether he was coming as a plenipotentiary. He replied: 'No, as ambassador.' This was enough for Hitler. The Poles were still obstinate. At 4 p.m. Hitler confirmed the order for war. At 6.30 p.m. Lipski at last saw Ribbentrop. Lipski said that the Poles were 'favourably considering' the idea of direct negotiations. Ribbentrop again asked whether he was a plenipotentiary. Lipski again said no. Ribbentrop did not communicate the German terms. If he had tried to do so, Lipski would have refused to receive them. The Poles had kept their nerve unbroken to the last moment. At 4.45 a.m. on 1st September the German forces attacked Poland without warning or pretext. At 6 a.m. German aeroplanes bombed Warsaw.

*Trapped into war*

The ally of Great Britain and France had been wantonly attacked. It only remained for them to declare war on the aggressor. They did nothing of the kind. The two governments merely 'warned' Hitler that they might have to go to war unless he desisted. Meanwhile they hoped that Mussolini would save them as he had done during the Czech crisis, and he duly did his best. He proposed a European conference to survey all causes of conflict, with the condition that Danzig should return to Germany at once. Hitler replied that he would answer on 3rd September. The British and French governments were therefore desperate to postpone any action until that day. But they, too, were trapped – by the indignation of British opinion. The French remained supine. The British were in an uproar. At the very least, German troops must be withdrawn from Poland before the proposal for a conference was accepted. Mussolini knew that this was hopeless and dropped his proposal. The British and French governments went on hoping for a conference which was already dead.

On the evening of 2nd September Chamberlain addressed the House of Commons. MP's expected to hear that war had been declared. Instead Chamberlain said that, if the German government would agree to withdraw their troops from Poland (not actually to withdraw them), the British government would forget everything that had happened, and diplomacy could start again. Chamberlain sat down in dead silence. Greenwood, rising to speak for Labour, was greeted with a shout from Amery: 'Speak for England, Arthur.' Afterwards Greenwood warned Chamberlain that there would be no holding the House if war were not declared. The cabinet met late at night and resolved that an ultimatum should be sent to Germany at once. Halifax, who regretted this decision, put off the ultimatum until the next morning.

The British ultimatum was delivered in Berlin at 9 a.m. on 3rd September. The German government made no reply, and the ultimatum expired at 11 a.m. The French trailed after their ally and declared war at 5 p.m. The Second World War had begun. It is possible that Hitler intended to conquer Europe at some time. It is also possible, though less likely, that the British government intended at some time to resist him. Neither of these intentions caused the actual outbreak of war. Then Hitler merely wanted Danzig and the Corridor, and the British government wanted to give them to him. These plans were wrecked first by Polish obstinacy and then by the indignation of Conservative backbenchers. The very men who had applauded Munich now insisted on war.

There was much talk later about a crusade against fascism. In fact most countries were pushed into war. The Poles had no choice. The French were dragged along by the British. Russians and Americans, mighty boasters both, waited supinely until Hitler chose to attack them. Only the British people and their dominions went to war of their own free will. They were not concerned about fascism. They did not even save Poland. They went to war out of national pride and for the sake of national honour. Ultimately they brought Hitler down, and this was something to be proud of.

*Relative strength of all major belligerents in Second World War. The number increased after the first blows: Italy entered in 1940 and Russia, Japan, and the USA the following year. Russia's apparent dominance was offset by the obsolescence of her land forces*

| | | Great Britain | France | USSR | USA | Poland | Germany | Italy | Japan |
|---|---|---|---|---|---|---|---|---|---|
| | Population (thousands)* | 47,692 | 41,600 | 167,300 | 129,825 | 34,662 | 68,424 | 43,779 | 70,590 |
| | National income ($m)* | 23,550 | 10,296 | 31,410 | 67,600 | 3,189 | 33,347 | 6,895 | 5,700 |
| | Reserves (millions) | 0.4 | 4.6 | 12.0† | ** | 1.5 | 2.2 | 4.8 | 2.4† |
| | Peacetime armies (millions) | 0.22 | 0.8 | 1.7† | 0.19 | 0.29 | 0.8 | 0.8 | 0.32† |
| | Aircraft (first line) | 2,075 | 600 | 5,000† | 800 | 390 | 4,500† | 1,500†† | 1,980 |
| | Destroyers | 184 | 28 | 28 | 181 | 4 | 17 | 60 | 113 |
| | Submarines | 58 | 70 | 150 | 99 | 5 | 56 | 100 | 53 |

*1938     **not available     †approximate     ††1940

# Blitzkrieg on Poland

The Polish Campaign opened in the early morning of 1st September 1939, when German forces crossed the Polish frontier shortly before 0600, preceded by air attacks which had begun an hour earlier. It was of great significance in the history of warfare because it was the first exposition of the theory, originated in Great Britain in the 1920's, of fast-moving mechanized warfare by armoured forces and aircraft in combination.

Britain's early protagonists of the theory depicted its action in terms of the play of 'lightning'. From now on, aptly if ironically, that simile came into world-wide currency under the German title of Blitzkrieg (lightning war).

Poland, with its far-stretching frontiers —3,500 miles in extent—was well fitted, all too well fitted, for the practice and demonstration of the Blitzkrieg theory. The stretch of 1,250 miles adjoining German territory had recently been extended to 1,750 miles by the occupation of Czechoslovakia. This also meant that Poland's southern flank had become exposed to invasion—even more than the northern flank, facing East Prussia, already was.

The Polish plain offered flat and fairly easy going for a mobile invader, though not so easy as France would offer because of the scarcity of good roads in the country, and the frequency of lakes and forests in some areas. But the time chosen for the invasion—when the terrain was dry and hard-surfaced—minimized these drawbacks.

In view of the geographical and strategical conditions, it would have been wiser if the Polish army had assembled farther back, behind the Vistula and the San. That, however, would have meant abandoning some of the most important industrial areas. The Silesian coalfields lay close to the frontier, and most of the main industrial area, although farther back, lay west of these river-lines.

The economic argument for delaying the enemy's advance was reinforced by national pride and military over-confidence, as well as an unrealistic idea of what Poland's allies in the West could do to relieve the pressure. A third of the Polish forces were concentrated in or near the 'Corridor', where they were exposed to a double envelopment from East Prussia and the west combined. This indulgence of national pride—in opposing Germany's re-entry into the piece of her pre-1918 territory for which she had been agitating —seriously reduced the forces available to cover the areas more vital to Poland's defence. Nearly another third of Poland's forces lay in reserve north of the central axis, between Łódź and Warsaw, under the Commander-in-Chief of the Polish Army, Marshal Smigły-Rydz.

The Poles' forward concentration in general forfeited their chance of fighting a series of delaying actions, since their foot marching army was unable to get back to man rear positions before they were overrun by the invader's mechanized columns. Lack of mobility was more fatal than incomplete mobilization.

On the other side the forty German infantry divisions used in the invasion counted for much less than their fourteen mechanized or partially mechanized divi-

*Right: The Panzer Mk IV. Cutting edge of the Panzer Divisions and the forefront of tank design in the period of Germany's early victories. The commander's black uniform with the soft beret changed after Poland.*
*Below: German Stukas (dive-bombers) over Poland (still from German newsreel). An hour before German troops crossed the Polish border the Luftwaffe began the systematic destruction of Polish air power, communications, and troop concentrations*

sions. These included six armoured divisions, four light divisions (motorized infantry with two armoured units), and four
motorized divisions. Their deep and rapid
thrusts decided the issue, in combination
with the attacks of the Luftwaffe—which
smashed the Polish railway system, besides knocking out most of the Polish air
force before it was able to come into action.

The Luftwaffe operated in a very dispersed way, instead of in large formations,
but it thereby spread a creeping paralysis
over the widest possible area. Another
weighty factor was the German radio
bombardment, disguised as Polish transmissions, which did much to increase the
confusion and demoralization of the Polish
rear. All these factors were given a multiplied effect by the way that Polish over-
confidence in the power of their men to
defeat machines led, on the rebound, to dis-
illusionment and disintegration.

In the north, the invasion was carried
out by Bock's Army Group, which comprised the III Army (under Küchler) and
the IV Army (under Kluge). The former
thrust southward from its flanking position
in East Prussia, while the latter pushed
eastward across the Polish Corridor to
join it in enveloping the right flank of the
Polish forces.

The principal role was given to Rundstedt's Army Group in the south. This was
nearly twice as strong in infantry, and more
in armour. It comprised the VIII Army
(under Blaskowitz), the X (under Reichenau), and the XIV (under List). Blaskowitz, on the left wing, was to push towards
the great manufacturing centre of Łódź,
and help to isolate the Polish forces in the
Poznań salient, while covering Reichenau's
flank. On the right wing, List was to push
for Kraków and simultaneously turn the
Poles' Carpathian flank, using Kleist's
armoured corps to drive through the
mountain passes. The decisive stroke was
delivered by Reichenau, in the centre, who
had the largest part of the armoured forces.

By 3rd September—the date Great Britain and France declared war—Kluge's
advance had cut the Corridor and reached
the lower Vistula, while Küchler's pressure
from East Prussia towards the Narew
was developing. More important, Reichenau's armoured forces had penetrated to
the Warta, and forced the crossings there.
Meanwhile List's army was converging

*Left: 1 Russian tanks move into Poland.
2 Motorized German infantry advances.
The leading car carries insignia plundered
from a Polish frontier post. **Right:** 1
Sarcastic German comment on Paderewski
playing while Warsaw burns. The famous
pianist and former Prime Minister was
invited to succeed Moscicki as President of
Poland after the latter fled to Rumania.
He declined because of ill health.
2 Cavalry—the pride of the Polish army
but hopelessly obsolete. 3 The campaign,
showing subsequent Russo-German
boundary. 4 'Luftwaffe' by the Polish
artist B.W.Linke portrays horror felt by
those who experienced the Blitzkrieg.
5 Hitler on a visit to the Polish front
stands before the bust of Piłsudski*

Ullstein

LITHUANIA
Kaunas •
Königsberg •
Danzig • E. PRUSSIA
Army
Group
North
IV Army.
II Army
Bydgoszcz •
Narew R.
Białystok •
Pinst •
Poznań •
Bug R.
Warsaw •
Brest Litovsk •
Łódź •
MANY
Pilica R.
Kielce •
Sandomierz •
Kraków •
Vistula R.
San R.
my VIII Army
oup X Army
uth XIV Army
Przemyśl •
Lwów •
Dunajec R.
Carpathian Mts.
80 | 120 MLS
160 | KM
HUNGARY
RUMANIA

M. B. Linke, Warsaw

from both flanks on Kraków, forcing the Poles in that sector to abandon the city and fall back to the Nida and the Dunajec.

On the following day Reichenau's leading forces had reached and crossed the Pilica, fifty miles east of the frontier. By 6th September his left wing was well in rear of Łódź, and his right wing had driven into Kielce. The other German armies had all gone far towards fulfilling their part in the vast enveloping operation planned by Halder, the Chief of the Army General Staff, under the direction of Brauchitsch, Commander-in-Chief of the Army. The Polish armies had begun to split up into unco-ordinated fractions, some of which were in retreat while others were delivering disjointed attacks on the enemy columns nearest to them.

Exploiting a gap, one of Reichenau's armoured corps drove through to the edge of Warsaw on 8th September—having covered 140 miles in the week. The next day the light divisions on his right wing reached the Vistula farther south, between Warsaw and Sandomierz, and turned north.

Near the Carpathians, List's mobile forces had swept across the Dunajec, and a series of other rivers in turn, to the San on either flank of the famous fortress of Przemyśl. In the north Guderian's armoured corps (which was in Küchler's army) had driven across the Narew and was attacking the line of the Bug, in rear of Warsaw. Thus a second and wider pincer-movement developed outside the inner pincers that were closing on the Polish forces in the bend of the Vistula near Warsaw.

This stage of the invasion had seen an important variation of plan on the Germans' side. Their view of the situation was momentarily obscured by the extraordinary state of confusion on the Poles' side, where columns appeared to be moving in many different directions, raising clouds of dust that obscured aerial observation. Under these circumstances the German High Command thought that the bulk of the Polish forces in the north had already escaped across the Vistula. On that assumption it gave orders that Reichenau's army was to cross the Vistula between Warsaw and Sandomierz, with the aim of intercepting the Poles' anticipated withdrawal into south-eastern Poland. But Rundstedt demurred, being convinced that the bulk of the Polish forces were still west of the Vistula. After some argument his view prevailed, and Reichenau's army was wheeled north to establish a blocking position along the Bzura west of Warsaw.

As a result the largest remaining part of the Polish forces was trapped before it could withdraw over the Vistula. To the advantage which the Germans had gained by their strategic penetration along the line of least resistance was now added the advantage of tactical defence. To complete the victory it had merely to hold its ground—in face of the hurried assaults of an army which was fighting in reverse, cut off from its bases, with its supplies running short, and increasingly pressed from the flank and behind by the converging eastward advance of Blaskowitz's and Kluge's armies. Although the Poles fought fiercely, with a bravery that greatly impressed their opponents, only a small proportion ultimately managed to break out, by night, and join troops of the Warsaw garrison.

On 10th September the Polish commander-in-chief, Marshal Smigły-Rydz, ordered a general retreat into the south-east of Poland and put General Sosnkowski in charge there, in the hope of developing a defensive position for prolonged resistance on a comparatively narrow front. By now the Germans were already penetrating deeply into the country beyond the Vistula, while they had also outflanked the line of the Bug in the north, and that of the San in the south. On the northern flank Guderian, with his armoured corps, swept southward to Brest Litovsk, while on the southern flank Kleist's armoured corps reached Lwów on 12th September. These mechanized spearheads were running short of fuel, after their deep drives, but the Polish command system was so badly disjointed that it was unable to take advantage of the Germans' diminishing pace, and increasing tiredness.

### Guerrilla resistance

Then on 17th September the forces of Soviet Russia advanced, and invaded Poland from the east, at a moment when there were scarcely any Polish troops left to oppose them. On the following day the Polish government and the Commander-in-Chief of the Army left Polish soil and took shelter in Rumania. Even after that, the garrison of Warsaw held out for a further ten days, under heavy bombardment both from the ground and the air. Indeed, the last large fraction of the Polish army fought on until 5th October before it surrendered, and many fragments continued resistance in a guerrilla manner throughout the winter.

The Russian forces met the Germans on a line mid-way through Poland, running south from East Prussia past Brest Litovsk, to the Carpathians. The fresh partition of Poland that followed was short-lived. It did not cement their temporary partnership but increased the friction that arose once the two countries were in close contact along a common frontier.

Meantime the French had merely made a small dent in Germany's western front. It looked, and was, a feeble effort to relieve the pressure on their ally. In view of the weakness of the German forces and defences it was natural to feel that they could have done more. But deeper analysis tends to correct the obvious conclusion suggested by the comparative figures of the opposing forces.

Although the French northern frontier was 500 miles long, in attempting an offensive the French were confined to the narrow ninety-mile sector from the Rhine to the Moselle—unless they violated the neutrality of Belgium and Luxembourg. The Germans, however, were able to concentrate the best part of their available forces on this narrow sector, and they sowed the approaches to their Siegfried Line with a thick belt of minefields, thus imposing delay on the attackers.

Marshal Smigły-Rydz, C-in-C of the Polish Army. He was quite unable to defend his country against the German Blitzkrieg

### The conscript mass

Worse still, the French were unable to start their offensive until about 17th September—except for some preliminary probing attacks. By that date, Poland was so obviously collapsing that they had a good excuse for countermanding it. Their incapacity to strike earlier arose from their mobilization system, which was inherently out of date. It was the fatal product of their reliance on a conscript army—which could not come effectively into action until the mass of 'trained reserves' had been called up from their civil jobs, and the formations had been made ready to operate. But the delay was increased by the French command's persistent belief in old tactical ideas—particularly the view that any offensive must be prepared by a massive artillery bombardment on the lines of the First World War. They still regarded heavy artillery as the essential 'tin-opener' in dealing with any defended position. But the bulk of their heavy artillery had to be brought out of storage, and could not be available until the last stage of mobilization. That condition governed their preparations to deliver an offensive.

For several years past one of France's political leaders, Paul Reynaud, had constantly argued that these conceptions were out of date, and had urged the necessity of creating a swift-moving mechanized force of professional soldiers ready for instant action—instead of relying on the old and slow-mobilizing conscript mass. But he had been a voice crying in the wilderness. French statesmen, like most French soldiers, placed their trust in conscription, and numbers.

The military issue in 1939 can be summed up in two sentences. In the East a hopelessly out-of-date army was quickly disintegrated by a small tank force, in combination with a superior air force, which put into practice a novel technique. At the same time, in the West, a slow-motion army could not develop any effective pressure before it was too late.

# Radar

Scientists had been aware of the principle of radar many years before they realized that a practical application was possible. Before 1920 it was known that radio waves produced echoes and in 1924 E.V. (later Sir Edward) Appleton used this phenomenon to prove the existence of the ionosphere and to discover the height of its various layers by measuring the time required for a radio echo to return to the ground.

Ten years elapsed before a system for the detection of aircraft in a radio beam was devised.

In June 1934 A.P.Rowe, an Air Ministry scientist uneasy about the way the situation in Germany was developing, on his own initiative leafed through the fifty-three available files on air defence. He found that hardly any effort had been made to tackle the whole problem scientifically. Rowe reported his findings to Wimperis, director of scientific research at the Air Ministry, who then proposed to the secretary of state for air, Lord Londonderry, that a Committee for the Scientific Survey of Air Defence should be set up. This became the celebrated committee under Henry (later Sir Henry) Tizard.

For many years inventors had submitted propositions for a death ray which would immobilize an aircraft or incapacitate the crew. Before the first meeting of the Tizard Committee Wimperis informally asked R.A. (later Sir Robert) Watson-Watt of the Radio Research Station, Slough, whether in fact enough radio energy could conceivably be transmitted to damage an aircraft sufficiently. Watson-Watt passed the problem to one of his staff, A.F.Wilkins, who in half an hour's work showed that, although damage to an aircraft could be dismissed, the detection of radio energy reflected from an aircraft and, therefore, the determination of its distance could be found.

## Discovery that saved Britain

This information was digested by the Tizard Committee when it first met at the end of January 1935. On 26th February the first test of radio detection was held. A van containing suitable radio receivers halted in a field about ten miles from the short-wave transmitters of the Daventry broadcasting station. A pilot was instructed to fly over a course near the radio station. The van's instruments detected the aircraft as it flew through the radio transmissions at a distance of eight miles. It has been written, not without cause, that this simple experiment determined in large measure the fate of Great Britain and even of the world.

The authorities speedily grasped the importance of the experiment and gave permission and funds for research to begin. A small team of scientists under Watson-Watt secretly developed the first practical radar

*Left: Painting of Type 16 fighter direction radar installation, by W.T.Rawlinson.*
*Below: The indicator of the ASV (air to surface vessel radar) Mark II. Operational from 1940, this meter equipment enabled bombers to detect and home on surfaced U-boats*

Imperial War Museum

Science Museum

*The radar plotting room aboard a US aircraft-carrier in the Pacific. Working on information provided by radar, the men plot the positions of hostile and friendly surface vessels and aircraft*

Keystone Press

equipment at Orfordness on the Suffolk coast. Rowe had given the cover name RDF to the experiments—R standing for radio (because the tall aerial masts could not be disguised) and DF because direction finding was external to the original proposal. RDF became 'radar' (RAdio Detection And Ranging) later in the war and by then included a number of devices not all of which made use of radio echoes. The radar researchers soon moved to Bawdsey Manor, south of Orfordness and Bawdsey became the prototype of a chain of coastal radar stations.

By the late 1930's radar had reached a similar state of development in Germany, France, Holland, and the United States. In Germany, although the equipment was technically in advance of the British, the Services, anticipating a short war, made no plans for long term research. They failed, moreover, to discover the purpose of the British radar chain and, when war came, failed to destroy the vital radar stations. In the United States there appeared to be no pressing need for radar. So the US Navy was caught napping at Pearl Harbour. France was the first country to devise a radio navigational system— for the liner *Normandie*—but little attention was paid to military uses.

### Fast and accurate information
Two factors were essential to the success of the warning system; one was the speed with which the radar information was despatched to the appropriate quarter by landline or radio; the other was the need to maintain the continuity of a hostile aircraft's track under a permanent reference

designation from Command Headquarters downwards to fighter groups and sectors.

The heart of the system was at Headquarters, Fighter Command, at Stanmore, Middlesex, where, in an underground filter room, the radar plots of the position, strength, height, and direction of the raiders were received, sifted, and reported when a track became discernible by specially selected and trained filter officers. In the early stages of the war the height-finding technique was liable to some degree of error and the filter officers had occasionally to resort to simple probability exercises. The tracks provided by the filter officers went to the adjoining operations room where the controller and his assistants sat on a raised dais and watched the airmen and WAAF plotters as they moved the counters on the glass-topped table, representing hostile and friendly aircraft, with their long croupier-like rakes according to the information received through their headphones. From here the air raid warning system was set in motion. The fighter groups and sectors, each equipped with identical operations and filter rooms, also received the raiders' tracks. In the early days of the war all the filtering was done at Stanmore, but after the deployment of German formations along the French coast information went directly to the appropriate groups.

As the coastal radar sets could not 'look' backwards, it was the responsibility of the Observer Corps to provide warning inland, and information on the approach of hostile aircraft was sent to the Observer Corps control rooms.

In the fighter sector operations rooms the controllers directed their squadrons to attack at the right place and time and afterwards brought them safely back to base. The medium of communication was the high frequency radio telephone. High frequency

direction finders situated in each sector provided the position of every aircraft and, in addition, every fighter aircraft was provided with an automatic device known as 'Pip-squeak' which switched on the pilot's high frequency transmitter for fourteen seconds in every minute. Each aircraft had IFF (Identification, Friend or Foe) which characterized its radar 'blip'.

At night, the fighter pilot and his observer had enough to contend with in the business of taking off and landing and of navigating in total darkness and trying to locate an enemy bomber without control from the ground was like looking for a needle in a haystack. It was necessary for the controller to know at one and the same time the position, track, speed, and height of both the night fighter and the bomber. Provided with this information the controller could radio to the pilot the direction and height at which the latter should fly and, if necessary, to reduce speed in order not to overshoot his target. Control by night was made practicable by the Plan Position Indicator (PPI). This device was used in conjunction with a rotating radar beam with which it was possible to estimate an aircraft's range (up to about ninety miles) and direction.

The PPI which next to shortwave radar was the most important radar development during the war, was incorporated in the Ground Controlled Interception equipment. This resembled a domestic TV set with a map of the area imposed on the screen. The controller was able to plot the position of the enemy bomber and the pursuing fighter from the bright spots on the tube face, and by calculating the speed and direction of flight of the enemy was able to direct the night fighter towards it by the shortest route. In the final stages of the pursuit the fighter homed onto its quarry using its own Aircraft Interception set (AI).

### Creation of the Magnetron
But the early AI sets had severe limitations as did the sets for detecting surface vessels, and particularly surfaced submarines. Very narrow radio beams were required which could detect small objects, like a surfaced submarine, from the air, and without interference from ground echoes or from enemy jamming. The Bawdsey scientists had long foreseen the need for microwaves, but at that time there was no valve adequate to generate the high power required. Again, Great Britain made a revolutionary step forward in radar history. Early in 1940, at the instigation of the Admiralty, J.T. (later Sir John) Randall, and his colleagues at Birmingham University, devised the magnetron—a valve no bigger than a child's fist, which eventually provided a reliable output of hundreds of kilowatts in short pulses.

When, in August 1940, it was decided to divulge to the Americans, sixteen months before they entered the war, the latest British scientific achievements, the magnetron was the most important item taken to the USA by the Tizard Mission. The Americans, who had not yet solved the problem of generating microwaves, were now able to produce short wave sets for the detection of night bombers and surface vessels from the air, and for the control of anti-aircraft fire.

# Churchill's Lonely Road

When Churchill became Prime Minister on 10th May 1940 – on the very day that Hitler ended the phoney war by invading France, Holland, and Belgium – the British people were much relieved. Not so the politicians. Whereas the man in the street saw Churchill as the one dynamic figure capable of rescuing the war from catastrophe, the average politician was aghast. As Neville Chamberlain's private secretary has recorded: 'In May 1940 the mere thought of Churchill as Prime Minister sent a cold chill down the spines of the staff at 10 Downing Street.' Nor was this feeling confined to Whitehall. Chamberlain himself would have preferred Lord Halifax, his foreign secretary, to succeed him as Prime Minister. This view was widely shared. On the very morning of 10th May *The Times* published as its principal letter an appeal from the Oxford historian and Labour candidate A.L.Rowse, urging Halifax as the most suitable national leader in time of crisis. At Buckingham Palace on that decisive day, King George VI accepted Neville Chamberlain's resignation; as he recorded that evening in his diary: 'We then had an informal talk over his successor. I, of course, suggested Halifax . . . I thought Halifax was the obvious man.'

To the Crown, and to the serried ranks of respectable politicians, Halifax was the discreet, unexcitable, remote aristocratic ideal; he was held in high esteem throughout the Tory Party. Churchill, by contrast, was distrusted personally and regarded with grave suspicion politically. As Lady Violet Bonham Carter, one of his few political friends, recorded: 'I have heard him called "erratic", "unreliable", "not a safe man". Not safe enough to fill the armchair of a humdrum office in safe days, but when all was at stake, when our own survival and the fate of civilisation were rushing towards the rapids, then we saw him as the one man strong enough to save.' In retrospect, perhaps, a majority now share Lady Violet's view. But on 10th May 1940 she was one of a bold minority of public figures for whom Churchill was acceptable as Prime Minister. He came to that office because the Labour Party refused to serve under Halifax, and because Halifax himself hesitated when faced with the thought of such responsibility. Neville Chamberlain's personal regard for Churchill, developed during nine months of increasingly intimate wartime collaboration, was decisive. It was some weeks before the vast Conservative majority in the House of Commons gave Churchill a spontaneous cheer. And in the higher echelons of the Tory Party there were some who never accepted his leadership, and throughout the war spoke, and wrote, and even intrigued against him.

## The lonely road

Churchill had plunged into the mainstream of British political life in the years before the First World War. From the outset of his career he roused strong – and predominantly hostile – emotions. On the outbreak of war in 1939 he was an isolated and discredited old man of sixty-five. His transformation within a year to the position, not only of war leader, but of national hero and saviour of his country, must not obscure the facts of his career. For forty years he walked a lonely road. Although holding high political office, and serving in the cabinets of four Prime Ministers, he never won the confidence or held the allegiance of a political party.

Four years after entering Parliament in 1900 he had left the Conservative ranks and turned to denouncing Conservative policies with almost unprecedented vigour, seeming to his contemporaries more bitter against wealth and property than even Lloyd George. Even when he rejoined the Conservative Party twenty years later, in 1924, and was given office as chancellor of the exchequer by Stanley Baldwin, he remained to most Conservatives a hated figure. He was the man who had played a leading part in smashing the power of the House of Lords in 1911; he had insisted in 1918 upon leniency to the defeated Germans; and even when back in the Tory fold he had as chancellor of the exchequer brought in social legislation, including widows' pensions, of a sort which Conservatives feared as the thin end of the socialist wedge. As a Liberal minister in 1909 Churchill had denounced 'the unnatural gap between rich and poor . . . the absence of any established minimum standard of life and comfort among the workers, and at the other end, the swift increase of vulgar, joyless luxury'; Conservatives did not easily forget, and seldom forgave such attacks upon themselves. When in 1916 Lloyd George had asked the leader of the Conservative Party, Bonar Law, whether he would rather have Churchill in the government as a colleague, or out of the government as an opponent, Bonar Law had replied: 'I would rather have him against us every time'; and five years later a leading Conservative newspaper, *The Morning Post,* described Churchill derisively as 'a floating kidney in the body politic'.

It was not the Conservative political machine alone which regarded Churchill with such distrust. The Liberals, whose ideals he had so ably championed, and whose social legislation he had magnificently enhanced before the First World War, were equally suspicious of this 'renegade' from the Tory camp, this advocate of equality from an aristocratic family, this energetic enigma who would bombard his colleagues with long, inquiring, and troublesome memoranda on every conceivable topic. The Liberals were all for social reform, but many hesitated when they discovered Churchill was its advocate. Even the Liberal Prime Minister, H.H. Asquith, found Churchill's unquenchable energy a strain, and did not believe that at base Churchill was sound. As Asquith wrote in the early months of the First World War: 'It is a pity that Winston hasn't a better sense of proportion, and also a larger endowment of the instinct of loyalty . . . I am really fond of him, but I regard his future with many misgivings . . . He will never get to the top in English politics, with all his wonderful gifts; to speak with the tongue of men and angels, and to spend laborious days and nights in administration, is no good if a man does not inspire trust.' Although he worked so hard for the Liberal government between 1906 and 1915, Asquith's verdict was indeed its verdict: he did not inspire trust. Just as Lloyd George's archive in 1916 is full of letters from Conservatives bitterly opposing Churchill's entry into the Lloyd George coalition, so Asquith's archive in 1915 abounds with the censure of his Liberal 'colleagues'. Thus one leading Liberal backbencher wrote to Asquith about Churchill in 1915, speaking on behalf of fellow Liberal MPs: 'We regard his presence in the Government as a public danger.' And when, having resigned from Asquith's government, and returning from the trenches of Flanders in the spring of 1916, Churchill dared to criticize the conduct of the war as lethargic (a view held by a growing number of people) Asquith's wife wrote in fury to the Conservative statesman A.J.Balfour: 'I have never varied in my opinion of Winston I am glad to say. He is a hound of the lowest sense of political honour, a fool of the lowest judgement, and contemptible.'

Such was the Liberal view. The Labour Party could hardly be more hostile, but it was not noticeably less so. In the rich fiction of Labour history Churchill was responsible for every hostile act against Labour. He had shot workers at Tony-

Imperial War Museum

Zionist Central Archives

Central Press

pandy in 1910; he had wheeled in armoured
vehicles against the strikers during the
General Strike of 1926. Historical research
has shown that neither belief is true. At
Tonypandy it was Churchill who exercised a *restraining* influence, and greatly
angered Conservatives by stating in the
House of Commons that 'it is a great object
of public policy to avoid a collision between soldiers and crowds of persons engaged in industrial disputes'. *The Times*
newspaper had censured Churchill for his
leniency; and it was the Tory rank and file
who objected to Churchill's statement that
'for soldiers to fire on the people would
be a catastrophe in our national life'.
Similarly, the story of 1926 is more complex and less discreditable to Churchill
than the legend. For it was Churchill who
wished to give the miners a decent wage,
and clashed with Baldwin on this very
point. Not only was Churchill never an
enemy of social reform; a glance at the
Statute Book both when he was a Liberal
minister before the First World War, and
when he was Conservative chancellor of
the exchequer from 1924 to 1929, show
that his sympathies were with the dispossessed, and that the actual legislation
which he piloted through the House of
Commons improved in many spheres the
conditions of life for the underdog. As a
vigorous politician in Liberal, and then
in Conservative administrations, Churchill
naturally attacked the Labour opposition
with fervour. No politician worth his salt
allows the opposition party a day of rest.
But the records show that he had a deep
admiration for the Labour chancellor of
the exchequer, Philip Snowden; and during the years when he was warning the
government and people of Hitler's intentions, some of his staunchest supporters
were Labour men. But, as Emanuel Shinwell, a leading Labour politician, has written: 'Nobody in British politics during
the early 'twenties inspired more dislike
in Labour circles than Winston Churchill.
His crowning sin was the fatuous declaration that Labour was unfit to govern, an
accusation that gave the gravest offence
to members of the Labour Party . . . The
mention of his name at Labour gatherings
was the signal for derisive cheers; when a
Labour speaker found himself short of
arguments, he only had to say "Down with
Winston Churchill". This never failed to
draw thunderous applause.' Yet Shinwell
saw Churchill's worth: 'One could, so it
seemed to me, dispose quite easily of his
arguments. Yet his resolution, his marshalling of the facts and his industry,
elevated him above his fellows, most of
whom were political midgets in comparison.'

Shinwell's comment provides the key
to Churchill's career. No man likes to be
overshadowed; and nothing upsets medi-
ocrities more than the presence of someone
of undoubted ability. The 'political midgets'—who are always present in large
numbers in all the political parties—disliked Churchill, not because his policies
were unsound, but because his abilities
were in such marked contrast to their own.
Churchill made many political mistakes.
He made errors of judgement, some of them
serious. His attempt to mobilize British
opinion against Bolshevik Russia in 1919
was ill-timed. His opposition to Indian independence in the 1930's was ill-judged.
But it was not these questions of policy
which made him enemies; they merely
enabled the enemies to reload their
weapons of scorn and malice with fresh
ammunition. A most remarkable feature of
Winston Churchill's career is the way in
which almost every action of his was interpreted by contemporaries in the worst
possible light. Few people were ever willing
to give him the benefit of the doubt. The
jealousies of the pigmies often deprived
Churchill of the right to be heard, to be
listened to with attention, to be accepted
at face value. It was always assumed that
something sinister lay behind each Churchillian proposal or explanation.

He came to political prominence long
before his thirtieth birthday and for this
precociousness it seems he could never be
forgiven; for the next thirty-five years of
his life he suffered on account of his early
achievements. Being a vigorous, forthright
person, he never attempted to disguise his
feelings or his opinions; this added in
every year of his life more enemies and
critics. By 1930 he was distrusted by Conservatives, Liberals, and Labour men alike;
and it was assumed by anyone considered
wise in the sphere of politics that his
active days were over. As a young National
Labour MP, the writer and historian
Harold Nicolson, wrote in 1931: 'How can
a man so versatile and so brilliant being
considered volatile and unsound?'
Yet Nicolson continued, prophetically: 'He
is a man who leads forlorn hopes, and when
the hopes of England become forlorn, he
will once again be summoned to leadership.'

### The voice in the wilderness
In 1931 most Englishmen regarded Nicolson's prophecy as close to lunacy. In that
same year a National Government was
formed, which was to govern Great Britain
until 1940, and from which Churchill was
excluded. He remained a back bencher,
while the leading Conservative politicians
returned to the cabinet. His opposition to
Indian independence had made him a

pariah to most Tories, and for all practical
purposes he was once again a politician
without a party.

On 1st November 1934, Churchill spoke
in his constituency against Home Rule for
India. But he spoke also of 'another issue
far larger than party'—the state of Great
Britain's defences. 'Germany,' said Chur-

*Top: Asquith in 1924. While Prime
Minister he had doubted Churchill's
chances of 'getting to the top'. Centre: Low
cartoon of 1920 shows Churchill surrounded by his 'blunders': 'He hunts lions
and brings home decayed cats'. Bottom:
British cartoon, 1939. Churchill and Eden,
both without office, urge an alliance with
Russia to deter German aggression*

chill, 'is arming, secretly, illegally, and rapidly.' Here was a further topic on which Churchill found himself at variance with his party. German rearmament did not worry Baldwin unduly. The government hoped to avoid war with Germany by timely concessions and a show of pro-German feeling. They refused to believe that Hitler might want war with Great Britain, or seek to dominate Europe by force. And when Churchill turned his powers of concentration and his mastery of language to criticizing the government's foreign policy, he was regarded with even greater hostility.

Churchill's detractors accused him of wanting war with Germany. This was not so: as Hitler had come to power in Germany and shown from the first days of his rule that he wanted to challenge both democratic government at home and moderate diplomatic procedure abroad, Churchill stressed the need for armaments not in order to wage war but in order to try to deter a potential aggressor.

Speaking in the House of Commons on 14th March 1933, Churchill urged the creation of an air force adequate to defend the civilian population; nine days later he begged the government not to press for French disarmament while Germany was busy rearming, and he pointed with a warning finger to 'the tumultuous insurgence of ferocity and war spirit, the pitiless ill-treatment of minorities, the denial of the normal protection of civilized society to large numbers of individuals solely on the ground of race.'

Churchill was not content to issue warnings. Nor did he consider rearmament the full answer to Great Britain's needs. On 13th July 1934, he asked the House of Commons to support the League of Nations, and to apply, where necessary, the sanctions authorized by the Covenant of the League: '. . . the League of Nations should be the great instrument upon which all those resolves to maintain peace should centre . . . I do not see how better you can prevent war than by confronting an aggressor with the prospect of such a vast concentration of force, moral and material, that even the most reckless, even the most infuriated, leader would not attempt to challenge these forces.'

Succeeding generations will ask how such wise counsel can have been so consistently ignored, and so rudely rebuffed. Yet, just as rearmament was abhorrent to the mass of the Labour Party, so many Conservatives saw the League as a forum for nothing but pettiness and futility.

Many people interpreted Churchill's call for collective security as a call for war. But contrary to popular belief, he was not a man who delighted in war; he knew its terrors and was convinced that the act of war between civilized states was a sign of the total failure of human reason. In November 1934 he declared: 'To urge preparation of defence is not to assert the imminence of war. On the contrary, if war were imminent preparations for defence would be too late.' Churchill's appeals were not heeded. Baldwin and his colleagues argued that the general mood of

the nation was pacifist; that rearmament would be a mistake politically and that they must accept the dictates of public opinion. On 22nd May 1935 Churchill challenged this view: 'I have been told that the reason for the Government not having acted before was that public opinion was not ripe for rearmament. I hope that we shall never accept such a reason as that. The Government have been in control of overwhelming majorities in both Houses of Parliament. There is no vote proposed for the national defence which would not have been accepted with overwhelming strength.'

Churchill wrote in retrospect, in the first volume of *The Second World War:* 'It would be wrong in judging the policy of the British Government not to remember the passionate desire for peace which animated the uninformed, misinformed majority of the British people, and seemed to threaten with political extinction any party or politician who dared to take any other line. This, of course, is no excuse for political leaders who fall short of their duty. It is much better for parties or politicians to be turned out of office than to imperil the life of the nation. Moreover, there is no record in our history of any Government asking Parliament and the people for the necessary measures of defence and being refused.'

On 16th March 1935, the German government introduced conscription. Seven months later the German Staff College was reopened. By the end of the year ten army corps had been set up. On 7th March 1936, Hitler sent German troops into the demilitarized Rhineland. This, said *The Times*, is the moment to be generous towards Germany. This answered Churchill, is the moment to insist on collective security: 'Do not let us be a rabble flying before forces we dare not resist. Let us negotiate from strength and not from weakness; from unity and not from division and isolation.'

A slight flutter of alarm ruffled the front bench. Baldwin was brought to believe that a new minister was needed who could co-ordinate the various departmental activities concerned with defence. Churchill was named, in most newspapers and in every pub, as the probable choice. Yet Baldwin feared a man of such energy at the cabinet table. Appeasement was still the desire of the majority of his ministers. They did not want to believe that war might be inevitable, or that the only way of averting it might be to rearm intensively and seek strong allies. The post was given to a man of no great energy or enterprise, Sir Thomas Inskip.

Churchill remained in the wilderness. Anthony Crossley, a young Conservative MP (who was killed in an aeroplane crash in August 1939) expressed the anger of Churchill's friends at his exclusion from office:

'Did you dare, Father Churchill, did you dare to expect
A summons to council again
In face of the feeling that haunts the elect
That they scoffed at your warnings in vain?...

You're polite to the small and you're rude to the great:
Your opinions are bolder and surer
Than is seemly today in an office of state —
You've even insulted the Führer.'

Crossley pictured the cabinet deciding finally against Churchill:

'But Winston were worst, with his logic accursed
For he'll scorn our impartial endeavour.
He'll make up his mind, right or wrong, with the first,
And how should we temporise ever?
Let's have soldier or sailor or peer or civilian,
Whatever his faults, so they be not Churchillian.'

But the wilderness had some advantages. Churchill could speak loudly and often. He did not have to worry about the sensitivities of ministerial colleagues, and he served as a focal point for the discontented of all parties; Stafford Cripps and Walter Citrine, stalwarts of the left wing and of the trade unions, supported his plea for a more broadly based National government. He devoted much time to his voluminous history of the life and times of the great Duke of Marlborough, who had sought to destroy the overweening power of France by a Grand Alliance of all the powers threatened by France. Churchill saw that a similar combination might deter, and if necessary defeat Germany.

### Eyes on the German danger
But the mental stimulus of work in the wilderness was no consolation for political or personal loneliness. Churchill was often downhearted. It was rumoured in the lobbies that he was ill, and that he was losing his powers of concentration. At sixty-two, even some of his friends expected and his enemies hoped, that he would retire altogether from public life. He himself had moments of severe depression, telling his American financier friend, Bernard Baruch, that he intended to abandon politics and take up stocks and shares. Baruch replied tersely — 'you don't know much about money; stick to politics and the prize will come your way'. For a politician to keep his head above water, when all around are hostile or apathetic forces, is a hateful prospect. But he never weakened in his fervent desire to serve his country; he never lost his grasp of detail; he never fell,

*Right: 1 In 1939 Churchill's continued exclusion from the cabinet prompted this poster in the Strand. To this day, no one knows who paid for it. 2 In a cartoon entitled 'The old sea-dog', Punch sees Churchill as a latter-day Sir Francis Drake in July 1939. 'Is there a telegram for me?' he asks. 3 Anthony Crossley, a radical Tory MP and Churchill's friend who poured scorn on the government for keeping Churchill out. 4 Harold Nicolson, the diarist, man of letters, and National Labour MP, who prophesied Churchill's return to office if danger were to threaten*

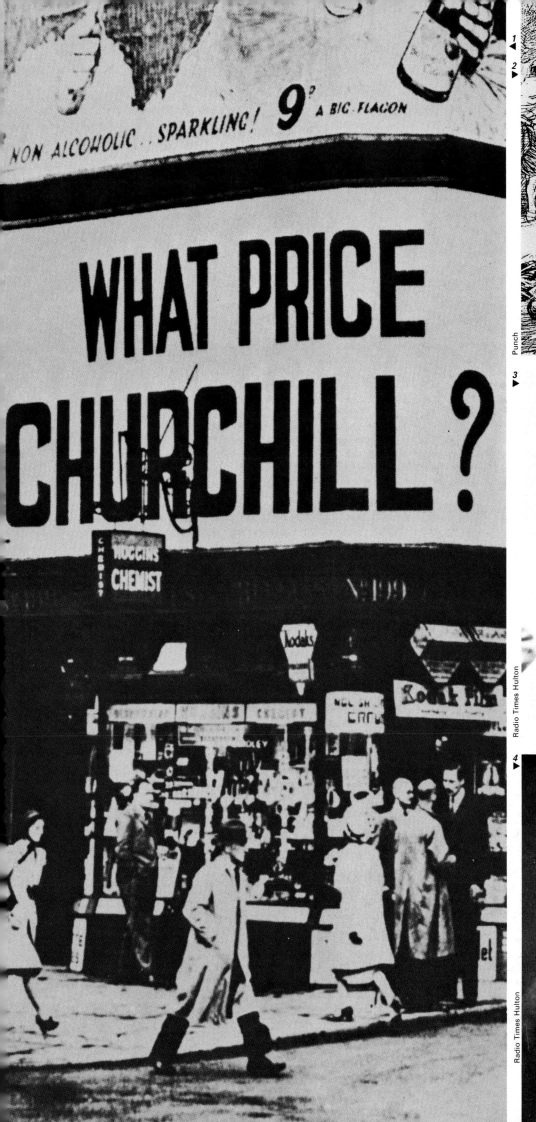

NON ALCOHOLIC..SPARKLING! 9ᴰ A BIG·FLAGON

# WHAT PRICE CHURCHILL?

WIGGINS CHEMIST

CHURCHILL WANTED

CALL UP WINSTON

in his own favourite phrase, 'below the level of events'.

Whether in conversation or in debate, by laughter or by stern words, Churchill's mind was fixed upon the German danger. Most men thought of foreign policy only in their spare moments; at rest after a hard day's work or at the breakfast table in the brief interval between waking and working. Churchill lived with the problems of Europe. He never grew weary of criticizing the government's slackness. 'Is there no grip, no driving force, no mental energy, no power of decision or design?' he appealed in the House of Commons on 21st May 1936. 'We are told that we must not interfere with the normal course of trade, that we must not alarm the easy-going voter and the public. How thin and paltry these arguments will sound if we are caught a year or two hence, fat, opulent, free-spoken – and defenceless.'

In March 1938 Hitler annexed Austria. The outward march of Nazism had begun. For a moment it seemed that, as Churchill's warnings were seen by many to be clearly justified, his fortunes would improve, and his advice be sought from within the government. But Chamberlain, who had succeeded Baldwin as Prime Minister, still hoped to abate German ambition by concessions. He doubted the value of collective security, of warnings, and of preparations for war publicized too openly. On 20th March 1938 he wrote to his sister: 'The plan for the "Grand Alliance", as Winston calls it . . . is a very attractive idea; indeed there is almost everything to be said for it until you come to examine its practicability. From that moment its attraction vanishes. You have only to look at the map to see that nothing that France or we could do could possibly save Czechoslovakia from being overrun by the Germans if they wanted to do it. I have therefore abandoned any idea of giving guarantees to Czechoslovakia, or to the French in connection with her obligations to that country.'

Churchill knew nothing of this dismissal of his much advocated plan.

Despite the logic of his arguments and the growing tensions in Europe, Churchill remained isolated. When, in protest against Chamberlain's refusal to speak sternly to Mussolini, Anthony Eden, the foreign secretary, resigned in February 1938, Churchill hoped to gain a recruit to his cause. But Eden held back and made no brave speeches against the government. He gathered around himself a small band of malcontents, but he stayed away from Churchill. Eden's group avoided Churchill's friends. It was said that Baldwin had warned Eden to keep away from Churchill and to be as loyal as he could to the government. Eden acted entirely in this sense. Critics of appeasement, liking him more than they liked Churchill, felt that Eden, not Churchill, was the future leader of the Tory Party and of the nation. They looked to Eden for guidance; but he gave none. He would not take the initiative himself in demanding a more vigorous foreign policy, nor would he throw in his lot with Churchill.

The Munich crisis found Churchill still without office. His plea to bring Russia into an anti-German alliance was much disliked. Part of Chamberlain's support for a four-power conference at Munich sprang from his desire to keep the matter away from the League of Nations, where Russia would be able to speak in Czechoslovakia's defence. While Chamberlain was at Munich, Churchill drafted a telegram warning him that if the Czechs were forced to sacrifice too great an area, the Munich agreements would be widely criticized in the House of Commons. Churchill sought other signatures for his telegram. Clement Attlee refused to sign, pleading that he must have the approval of the Labour Party before doing so. Eden refused on the grounds that such a telegram would be interpreted as a vendetta against Chamberlain.

When the Commons debated the Munich agreement, Churchill said: 'I find unendurable the sense of our country falling into the power, into the orbit and influence of Nazi Germany, and of our existence becoming dependent upon their goodwill or pleasure. It is to prevent that that I have tried my best to urge the maintenance of every bulwark of defence – first, the timely creation of an Air Force, superior to anything within striking distance of our shores; secondly, the gathering together of the collective strength of many nations; and thirdly, the making of alliances and military conventions, all within the Covenant, in order to gather together forces at any rate to restrain the onward movement of this power. It has all been in vain. Every position has been successively undermined and abandoned on specious and plausible excuses. I do not grudge our loyal, brave people, who were ready to do their duty no matter what the cost, who never flinched under the strain of last week, the natural, spontaneous outburst of joy and relief when they learned that the hard ordeal would no longer be required of them at the moment; but they should know the truth. They should know that there has been gross neglect and deficiency in our defences; they should know that we have sustained a defeat without a war, the consequences of which will travel far with us along our road; they should know that we have passed an awful milestone in our history, when the whole equilibrium of Europe has been deranged, and that the terrible words have for the time being been pronounced against the Western democracies: "Thou art weighed in the balance and found wanting". And do not suppose that this is the end. This is only the beginning of the reckoning. This is only the first sip, the first foretaste of a bitter cup which will be proffered to us year by year unless, by a supreme recovery of moral health and martial vigour, we arise again and take our stand for freedom as in the olden times.'

In March 1939 Hitler's troops marched into Prague, and Czechoslovakia became a German 'protectorate'. Chamberlain turned reluctantly from appeasement to resistance; a promise was made to defend Poland against aggression, and negotiations were begun with Rumania, Greece, and Turkey. But this new mood led to no

*Right: Poster issued by the Ministry of Information after Churchill became Prime Minister, May 1940. More than any single man, Winston Churchill brought about the recovery of the sense of national unity and purpose which had been absent for so long. The victory of the great air battle of 1940 known as the Battle of Britain broadened the sense of participation and shared danger*

improvement in Churchill's fortunes. In his own constituency, hostility led to strong words of censure. 'Mr. Churchill,' said Captain A.E.Jones, the chairman of the Epping Unionist Association, 'is a menace in Parliament. I admire his brains, his mental capacity; I decry his judgment. He has no judgment.' And Mr (now Sir) Colin Thornton-Kemsley, chairman of the Chigwell Unionists, insisted that 'his castigation of the National Government, which we returned him to support, is a mockery and a sham.'

In April 1939 there were cabinet changes. But no place was found for Churchill. In May a number of newspapers, led by the *Daily Telegraph* and the *Daily Mail*, began to urge upon Chamberlain that Churchill join the government. But Chamberlain was scornful of such advice. 'If I am asked,' he had told the House of Commons after Munich, 'whether judgment, the greatest quality of a statesman, is one of the qualities of the Right Honourable Member for Epping, I hope the House will not press me too far.' *The Times,* which under the editorship of Geoffrey Dawson had for six years done its utmost to stimulate pro-German feeling, informed its readers that Churchill's 'vigour does not make him an infallible guide on the more complicated issues of foreign policy'. Dawson refused to publish a letter signed, among others, by Lady Violet Bonham Carter, urging Churchill's inclusion in the government. Thus Churchill remained in the wilderness until Hitler invaded Poland. Chamberlain then offered him a choice between a place in the war cabinet, without portfolio, or the Admiralty, outside the war cabinet. Only when he had accepted the latter did Chamberlain have second thoughts, and bring him into the war cabinet.

As Churchill had himself written about one of his own ancestors, the great Duke of Marlborough's father: 'The frozen years were over. He had drunk to the dregs the cup of defeat and subjugation.' But although, in 1940, Churchill's fortunes changed so dramatically, and the outcast was transformed into the paragon, his reputation has never recovered from the forty years of mistrust. The historians have taken over the work of denigration so competently begun by contemporaries. Early in 1969 a distinguished British historian told an eager audience that 'Churchill contributed nothing to the politics of the 'thirties – except idiocy. He jumped from one lunatic policy to another'. The reader may quarrel with this confident verdict; but the fact that it is the verdict of the brilliant A.J.P.Taylor, underlines Churchill's dilemma. For many people, whatever Churchill did was wrong.

"LET US GO FORWARD TOGETHER"

# Dunkirk

'Dunkirk,' A.J.P.Taylor has written, 'was a great deliverance and a great disaster.' Yet it might simply have been a great disaster.

The German Blitzkrieg offensive in the West had whirled into the Low Countries on 10th May 1940 with its customary surprise, violence, ruthlessness, and treachery. As a counter-measure three days later 1st, 7th, and 9th French Armies together with the nine divisions of the British Expeditionary Force under Field-Marshal Lord Gort raced to join the Belgian army in defensive positions running along the River Dyle from Antwerp to Namur and south along the Meuse to Sedan. It was a trap. While General von Bock's Army Group B struck into Holland and Belgium in what seemed the primary German thrust, General von Rundstedt's Army Group A, its formidable armour to the fore, emerged from the Ardennes between Dinant and Montmédy in what was in fact the main German assault, and advanced against a front lacking permanent fortifications and manned by only two divisions of professional troops. On 14th May the avalanche broke. Preceded by waves of Stukas, General von Kleist's Panzer Group, comprising the armoured corps of Guderian and Reinhardt, forced a crossing of the Meuse at Mézières, Monthermé, and Sedan. Cutting a swath through the weak and ill-prepared 9th and 2nd Armies the mass of armour, unopposed by any French reserves, plunged towards the Channel threatening to isolate the British, Belgian and French armies in the north. On 21st May Kleist's Panzer Group reached the mouth of the Somme at Abbeville, captured Boulogne, enveloped Calais, and advanced within twelve miles of Dunkirk.

Thus between a formidable wedge of seven armoured divisions and Bock's advancing Army Group B lay the Belgian army, ten divisions of the French 1st Army, and the bulk of the BEF. They were trapped and Kleist was poised to hammer them against the anvil of the advancing VI and XVIII Armies which had just crossed the River Schelde after breaching the Dyle line. For the dazed Allied forces annihilation seemed inevitable. The final phase of the great encirclement battle appeared to be at hand. But suddenly, on 24th May, the bounding armour stopped dead in its tracks. For the reeling Allied armies disaster was about to be mitigated.

On Hitler's orders Kleist's Panzers were halted west and south of Dunkirk on a line from Lens, through Béthune, Aire, St Omer to Gravelines. It was the first of the German High Command's major mistakes in the Second World War. It reprieved the Allies and made possible the 'miracle' of Dunkirk.

The only hope the Allies had of extricating themselves from encircling German forces was for the armies in Belgium to disengage from VI Army attacking them there, turn south-west and fight their way through the German armoured wedge and link up with French forces pushing northwards from the Somme. But by 25th May Lord Gort realized that with the forces at his disposal such a break-out, with Belgian resistance crumbling fast and no evidence of a French attack northwards, stood little chance of success.

The British, French, and Belgian armies were by now confined to a triangle of territory with its base along the Channel coast from Gravelines to Terneuzen and its apex at Valenciennes. There could be no escape but by sea. On 27th May the British government, which on 19th May had insisted Gort attack southwards to Amiens, informed the Commander-in-Chief of the BEF that his sole task was 'to evacuate the maximum force possible'. It was a measure he had foreseen and for which contingency plans had been prepared.

Seven days earlier in the deep galleries below Dover Castle Vice-Admiral Bertram Ramsay had inaugurated a discussion on 'emergency evacuation across the Channel of a very large force'. In the following days the Admiralty began to amass shipping for a possible evacuation of the BEF and Allied forces from France. The desperate venture code-named 'Operation Dynamo' was in large part to be facilitated by the interruption of the German Panzer onslaught.

What was the reason for this apparently inexplicable order to arrest the progress of the armour on the threshold of what could have been one of the worst disasters in military history? Who was responsible for it? The generals led by Halder, the Chief of the Army General Staff and Rundstedt, commander of Army group A, have since put the blame exclusively on Hitler. The peremptory order, although emanating from the Führer in his capacity as Supreme Commander of the Armed Forces did, however, enjoy the support of both Rundstedt and Göring.

The Führer visited the former's headquarters at Charleville on the morning of 24th May where he listened to a report of the fighting and heard the intentions of Army Group Command. Rundstedt suggested that the infantry should attack to the east of Arras, where on 21st May the British had shown they were still capable of vigorous action, while Kleist's armour, which he knew had suffered serious losses, stood on a line west and south of Dunkirk in order to pounce on the Allied forces withdrawing before Army Group B. Hitler expressed complete agreement with the Army Group commander and underlined the need to husband the armour for the coming operations south of the Somme. Hitler and Rundstedt were thus in agreement in their judgement of the situation.

### Göring makes an offer

But the Führer had other reasons for issuing the apparently inexplicable order to restrain the armour. He recalled how in 1914 the low-lying Flanders plains between Bruges, Nieuport, and Dixmude had flooded and bogged down the German northern flank. The low-lying terrain to the west and south of Dunkirk was similarly intersected by thousands of waterways and was, Hitler believed, clearly unsuited for large-scale armoured operations. In view of Hitler's concern for Kleist's armour, Göring's characteristically flamboyant offer to the Führer on 23rd May was received enthusiastically.

From his mobile HQ in the Eifel mountains the Commander-in-Chief of the Luftwaffe telephoned Hitler to propose that 'his' air fleets which, after all, were 'to settle the fate of the German nation for the next thousand years' should destroy the British Army in northern France. After this had been accomplished Göring claimed the German army would only have to 'occupy the territory'. He further urged acceptance of his proposal by remarking that the final destruction of the enemy should be left to the 'National Socialist' Luftwaffe as Hitler would lose prestige to the army generals if they were permitted to deliver the coup de grâce.

It is clear that Hitler's plan, prompted by Göring and Rundstedt, was to let the Luftwaffe and Army Group B, which with very little armour was slowly driving back the Belgians and British south-west to the Channel, eliminate the troops in the Dunkirk pocket. It would, of course, be essential to halt Kleist's armour for fear of hampering Luftwaffe operations in the area. But neither the Luftwaffe nor Bock's Army Group were to prove capable of achieving their objectives.

Hitler, however, had yet further reason to

*Relics of a defeated army. German soldiers examine the debris of the BEF's hasty exit strewn along Dunkirk's promenade. The British Army lost most of its heavy equipment, tanks and artillery in the evacuation. All the soldiers could carry back were their rifles*

impose his own military leadership on the army for on 24th May a crisis of leadership had occurred. From 2000 on that day Field-Marshal von Brauchitsch, the Commander-in-Chief of the Army who was determined to see that Army Group B fought the last act of the encirclement battle, decided that Rundstedt should surrender tactical control of Kluge's IV Army and that together with all mobile units it should pass under the command of Army Group B. Whether Brauchitsch preferred to make the transfer rather than restore harmony between the two Army Groups and confront the organizational problems that their conjunction would pose or whether he was dissatisfied with the less dynamic Rundstedt is not clear. Knowledge of the transfer may have led Rundstedt to propose measures he knew the Führer would support when they met at Charleville, but what is clear, however, is that neither Hitler nor OKW, which had replaced the War Ministry and become Hitler's personal staff, knew anything about this Army High Command (OKH) transfer order. Hitler was highly indignant that Brauchitsch and Halder had re-organized command responsibilities without informing him. He promptly cancelled the order.

Thus in halting the armour Hitler sanctioned Rundstedt's proposal besides demonstrating that on the battlefield his position as Supreme Commander of the Wehrmacht was no mere formality. But Halder was not prepared to accept the Führer's order and on the same night issued a wireless message to both Army Groups stating that the continuation of the attack up to Dunkirk on the one hand and Ostend on the other was permissible. In an act unprecedented in German military history Rundstedt decided not to pass on the communication from his superiors to IV Army. Supported by Hitler, and assuming his observations on the morning of the 24th represented his own opinions, he could afford to hold a different view of the situation from that of OKH. In his opinion Army Group B would sooner or later subdue resistance in Flanders and it therefore appeared wiser to preserve the armoured forces for use at a later stage.

Although Hitler may have genuinely taken political objectives into consideration when he restrained the armour it is patently obvious that he did not intend to spare Great Britain a bitter humiliation and thereby facilitate a peace settlement by such action. Both the Luftwaffe and the German army had clear and definite instructions to destroy the entrapped enemy in Flanders and this was made unmistakably apparent in Führer Directive No. 13, signed by Hitler on the evening of 24th May 1940. Halder has since claimed that Hitler expressed his determination to fight the decisive battle in northern France rather than on Flemish soil for political reasons. The Führer, Halder maintains, explained that his plans to create a National Socialist region out of the territory inhabited by the 'German-descended' Flemish would be compromised if war was permitted to ravage the region. Therefore although Hitler was partially responsible for the decision to halt the armour he has undoubtedly been unjustly credited with the sole responsibility for the fatal error.

### The perimeter shrinks

'Operation Dynamo' was based on the assumption that three ports would be available but the fall of Boulogne, followed on 26th May by the collapse of British resistance in Calais left only Dunkirk. Yet the defence of Calais termed by Guderian 'heroic, worthy of the highest praise' gave Lord Gort time in which to elaborate his plan for evacuation. The Allies' predicament grew steadily worse. On 25th May the Belgians expended their last reserves and their front broke. On the following day Hitler rescinded the halt order in view of Bock's slow advance in Belgium and the movement of transports off the coast, authorizing the resumption of Rundstedt's advance by 'armoured groups and infantry divisions in the direction of Dunkirk'. However, for technical reasons sixteen hours were to pass before the armoured units were ready to move forward and assail the town. By 28th May the Allies had organized a tighter perimeter defence around Dunkirk stretching from Nieuport along the canals through Furnes and Bergues to Gravelines. Repeatedly assaulted by German tanks and without the support of the Belgian army which had capitulated the same day, the perimeter shrank. South-west of Lille, however, the Germans encountered spirited resistance from the French 1st Army which detained seven of their divisions from 29th May to 1st June thus preventing their participation in the assault on the Dunkirk pocket. The exhausted and bewildered Allies often fragmented into separate battalions or separate companies retreated steadily along congested roads into the perimeter and by midnight on the 29th the greater part of the BEF and nearly half of the French 1st Army lay behind the canal line, by which time the naval measures for evacuation had begun to demonstrate their effectiveness.

At 1857 on 26th May the Admiralty launched Operation Dynamo. Besides an inspiring example of gallantry and self-sacrifice it was to display what Hitler had always held to be one of Great Britain's greatest strengths—the genius for improvisation.

The first day of the evacuation, 27th May, proved disappointing. Only 7,669 troops were brought out by a motley assortment of destroyers, passenger ferry steamers, paddle steamers, self-propelled barges, and Dutch *schuiten* which Vice-Admiral Ramsay had collected. But after the loss of Boulogne and

*British soldier replies to German aircraft strafing him on Dunkirk's beaches. Though the British troops were dangerously exposed, the sand partially muffled the blasts of the German bombs*

*An orderly line of British troops wading out to a rescue steamer. The evacuation by larger boats was mostly well-ordered, though there was some panic in the rush to smaller vessels*

Calais only Dunkirk with its adjacent beaches remained in Allied hands. For the intrepid rescuers, entering the harbour, when not impossible, was a hazardous task. Not only had they to contend with fire from shore batteries and ferocious air attack but they had to negotiate the many wrecks that lay between them and the blazing town.

It became clear that the hungry, exhausted troops would have to be embarked from the sandy beaches on either side of the town, but as yet Ramsay had few small craft capable of embarking men in shallow water. He signalled urgently for more. The next day, 28th May, utilizing the beaches together with the surviving but precarious East Mole of the harbour 17,804 men were embarked for Britain. The losses in craft on that day, however, were very heavy. Ships that left the congested mole unscathed were frequently damaged or sunk by bombing as they steamed down the narrow offshore channel unable to manœuvre adequately for wrecks, debris, and corpses.

Despite the fact that 47,310 men were snatched from Dunkirk and its neighbouring beaches the following day, as soon as the wind had blown aside the pall of smoke obscuring the harbour and roadstead, the Luftwaffe wreaked fearful havoc with a concentrated bombardment of the mole, sinking three destroyers and twenty-one other vessels.

On 30th May smoother seas, smoke, and low cloud ceiling enabled the rescuers to remove 13,823 men to safety. Although a number of small craft had arrived off Dunkirk on 29th May they were only the vanguard of a volunteer armada of some 400 yachts, lifeboats, dockyard launches, river tugs, cockle boats, pleasure craft, French and Belgian fishing boats, oyster dredgers, and Thames barges which, with small craft called into service by the Royal Navy, ferried 100,000 men from the beaches to the

deeper draught vessels from the following day. Moved by the desperate plight of the Allies, the seafaring population of south and south-eastern England had set out in a spontaneous movement for the beaches of Dunkirk where in innumerable acts of heroism they fulfilled a crucial role in the evacuation.

On 31st May despite intense bombing and shelling, 68,014 troops were removed to safety but on the following day a furious artillery bombardment and strafing of the whole length of the beaches together with resolute dive-bombing of shipping out at sea and in the harbour effectively halted daylight operations.

The climax of the evacuation had taken place on 31st May and 1st June when over 132,000 men were landed in England. At dawn on 2nd June only 4,000 men of the BEF remained in the perimeter, shielded by 100,000 French troops. On the nights of 2nd and 3rd June they were evacuated along with 60,000 of the Frenchmen. Dunkirk was still defended stubbornly by the remainder who resisted until the morning of 4th June. When the town fell 40,000 French troops who had fought tenaciously to cover the evacuation of their Allied comrades marched into captivity.

'Let us remember,' wrote Churchill, 'that but for the endurance of the Dunkirk rearguard the re-creation of an army in Britain for home defence and final victory would have been gravely prejudiced.'

The British with French and Belgian assistance had evacuated 338,226 troops, of whom 139,097 were French, from a small battered port and exposed beaches right under the noses of the Germans. They had extracted every possible advantage from the valuable respite accorded them when the armour was halted, consolidating defensive positions in the west, east, and on the Channel front. Moreover they had fought tenaciously, upholding traditions that had so impressed the Germans in the First World War.

The primary German error was to regard the Dunkirk pocket as a subordinate front. In fact its strategic importance was not

recognized until too late largely because it was not clear until almost the last moment how many Allied troops were actually in the pocket.

Moreover, for the nine days of Operation Dynamo, the Luftwaffe, due to adverse weather conditions only succeeded in seriously interfering with it for two-and-a-half days—on 27th May, the afternoon of 29th May, and on 1st June. The Luftwaffe's mission, readily shouldered by the vain, ambitious Göring proved too much for it. If Rundstedt had made a mistake, Göring fatally miscalculated. His aircraft had failed to prevent the Allied evacuation because the necessary conditions for success —good weather, advanced airfields, training in pin-point bombing—were all lacking. Bombers and dive-bombers for the first time suffered heavy losses at the hands of British Spitfires and Hurricanes now operating from their relatively near home bases.

For Germany's military leadership Dunkirk was the first great turning point in the Second World War, for it was during the campaign that Hitler first forced OKH to accept his own military views, by short-circuiting it at a critical juncture of the fighting and transferring a decision of far-reaching importance to a subordinate command whose views happened to coincide with his own. OKH, the actual military instrument of leadership, was in future to be undermined, overruled, and with terrible consequences for the German people, finally abolished altogether.

### The grim realities

At Dunkirk instead of winning a battle of annihilation the German army had to content itself with an ordinary victory. Great Britain on the other hand could console itself with the knowledge that almost its entire expeditionary force had been saved. 'In the midst of our defeat,' Churchill later wrote, 'glory came to the Island people, united and unconquerable . . . there was a white glow, overpowering, sublime, which ran through our Island from end to end . . . and the tale of the Dunkirk beaches will shine in whatever records are preserved of our affairs.'

If the British people felt they had won a great victory the grim realities belied their euphoria. The BEF, no longer in any condition to defend the country had suffered 68,111 killed, wounded, and taken prisoner. It had been compelled to abandon 2,472 guns, 90,000 rifles, 63,879 vehicles, 20,548 motorcycles and well over 500,000 tons of stores and ammunition. Of the 243 ships sunk at Dunkirk, out of 860 engaged, six were British destroyers. A further nineteen British destroyers were damaged. In addition the RAF had lost 474 aircraft.

Dunkirk had been a catastrophe alleviated, not by a miracle, but by German miscalculation and Allied tenacity and improvisation. Yet the elation of victory pervaded Britain. A supreme effort had cheated Hitler of his prey and a little self-congratulation seemed appropriate. The British had been the first to confound the German military juggernaut and after Dunkirk they resolved with a wholehearted determination to defeat it.

# The Battle of Britain

Of all the innumerable battles fought during the last 2,500 years, no more than fifteen have been generally regarded as decisive. A decisive battle has been defined as one in which 'a contrary event would have essentially varied the drama of the world in all its subsequent stages'. By this reckoning, the Battle of Britain was certainly decisive.

To find another decisive battle fought so close to British homes we have to go back to the defeat of the Armada in 1588, when Drake's well-handled little ships, with some assistance from the weather, destroyed a vast array of Spanish warships. But a closer parallel is with the Battle of Trafalgar.

In 1805 Napoleon controlled the whole of Europe west of the Russian frontier, with the exception of Great Britain and some parts of the Iberian peninsula. He understood very well that if he could destroy British sea power he could invade and conquer that stubborn island kingdom, and the whole of Western Europe would fall under his sway. But at Trafalgar his own sea power was destroyed by Nelson's fleet, and with it disappeared his hopes of subduing Great Britain. The narrow waters of the Channel were an insuperable barrier to his invading armies. Thwarted in the west, he turned against Russia, and his Grande Armée was all but destroyed amid the ice and snow during the terrible retreat from Moscow in the winter of 1812.

In August 1940 Hitler had mastered all Western Europe, apart from Great Britain, Spain, and Portugal. Although most of the men of the British Expeditionary Force had been brought home—the miracle of Dunkirk—they had lost almost all their weapons and equipment. This disaster had left Great Britain without any effective land forces, for in the whole country it was scarcely possible to put into the field one division, fully armed and equipped.

Things had changed since the days of Napoleon. This time the Royal Navy could not save Great Britain, for its ships could not operate in the southern North Sea and the Channel against concentrated German air and submarine attacks. And many of its warships were absent, fully employed in guarding the convoys that brought in the vital supplies of food and raw materials.

The Germans knew that if they could destroy the Royal Air Force, they could invade and conquer Great Britain, and all military resistance in Western Europe would end. Hitler had every reason to feel

*Right: The much vaunted Me 110 which proved a failure in the battle. Below: The 'Battle of Britain' by Paul Nash, an artist during both wars*

confident of success. The German air force (Luftwaffe) had destroyed the Polish, Dutch, Belgian, and French air forces. Its Commander-in-chief, Reichsmarschall Hermann Göring, had no doubt that his powerful air fleets would make short work of the much smaller RAF.

In 1805 and again in 1940, Great Britain stood alone against a large continental army, flushed with success, and on both occasions, by a brilliant and decisive victory, she saved herself from invasion and Western Europe from military subjection.

But there the similarity ends. Trafalgar was fought and won in a day, but the Battle of Britain, the first decisive battle in the air, was a long drawn out battle of attrition. The daylight battle began in early August, and continued through a long fine autumn until the middle of October. After the day battle had died down, the struggle was carried on by night, through the winter of 1940-41. It ended only when Hitler, despairing of conquering Great Britain, turned, as Napoleon had done before him, against Russia. And, like Napoleon, Hitler was to see his great armies all but annihilated battling against the illimitable spaces and the bitter winter climate of Russia.

Looking back, the people of Great Britain may wonder why the battle had to be fought in their skies, over their heads, and why it was their towns and cities that were bombed and devastated by fire. The answer to this is to be found in the sequence of events between the two world wars.

After the Armistice in November 1918 the greatly expanded armed forces of the Allies were hastily and clumsily demobilized. Improvised war organizations were dismantled, and the watchwords of the British government were economy and retrenchment. The war had been won, there was no visible threat to Allied security, and Great Britain and France were swept by a wave of anti-war feeling, largely induced by the terrible casualties and intolerable conditions of trench warfare.

In 1925 the League of Nations had set up a Preparatory Commission to explore the ground for a general disarmament conference. Progress in this field is never rapid, and for many years the commission was involved in interminable difficulties and arguments. Eventually a Disarmament Conference was convened in Geneva in 1932, at which proposals for outlawing air bombardment and drastically limiting the loaded weight of military aircraft were discussed. Hoping for success in these negotiations, the British government declined to authorize the design and construction of any effective bomber aircraft. In addition, it had introduced in 1924 what became known as the 'Ten-year Rule', which postulated that there would be no major war for ten years. Unfortunately each successive year was deemed to be the starting point of this tranquil epoch, and so the period always remained at ten years.

The Disarmament Conference finally broke up in May 1934 without achieving any result whatsoever. But meanwhile Hitler had come to power in Germany, and was clearly bent on a massive pro-

gramme of rearmament. In 1933 the British government at last permitted the issue of Air Staff requirements for a high-performance multi-gun fighter, which in due course produced the Hurricane and Spitfire. It is often asserted that these two aircraft, and especially the Spitfire, were forced on a reluctant Air Ministry by a far-sighted aircraft industry and its capable designers. There is not a word of truth in this. Both aircraft were designed, ordered, and built to Air Ministry specifications.

Even after the collapse of the Disarmament Conference in 1934 the British government was reluctant to rearm. Alone among nations the British seem to think that if they rearm it will bring about an arms race. The result of this curious delusion is that they usually start when the other competitors are half-way round the course. The bomber force was therefore given a very low priority, but development of the fighters was allowed to proceed, though without any undue haste.

In 1935 two British ministers, Mr Anthony Eden and Sir John Simon, visited Germany. They reported that Hitler's rearmament in the air had proceeded much farther and faster than the British government had believed possible. This was because the Germans had made a secret agreement to train the Soviet air force, an agreement enabling them to keep in being a sizeable corps of expert pilots and technicians. The government was alarmed, and ordered quantity production of the Hurricanes and Spitfires before the prototype had even flown—the so-called 'ordering off the drawing-board'.

Lord Trenchard, chief of the Air Staff from 1919 to 1928, had always believed that in air defence the bomber was as important as the fighter. He maintained that the air war should be fought in the skies over the enemy's territory, and he therefore advocated a bomber force powerful enough to take the offensive, and attack an enemy's vital centres from the outset. He argued that this would rob an enemy of the initiative and throw his air force on to the defensive.

*The aces. 1 Squadron Leader 'Sailor' Malan. He was the third highest RAF scorer with thirty-five enemy aircraft shot down. The RAF's top scorers were M.T.St John Pattle with forty-one kills, and Johnny Johnson (thirty-eight). 2 Squadron Leader Stanford Tuck. Between May 1940 and January 1942 he shot down twenty-nine German aircraft making him the eighth highest RAF scorer for the war. In 1942 he was shot down over France and captured. 3 Major Adolf Galland, top German scorer in the Battle of Britain with fifty-seven kills. Although he was grounded for three years he shot down 103 aircraft in the West and was the Luftwaffe's fourth highest scorer in that theatre. Top German scorer in the West, Captain Hans-Joachim Marseille, shot down 158 aircraft. 4 Lieutenant Colonel Werner Mölders. In the Battle of Britain he scored fifty-five kills. He was shot down and killed in 1941. 5 and 6 Spitfires seen from the nose gun position of Heinkel 111 bombers*

Beat 'FIREBOMB FRITZ'

# BRITAIN SHALL NOT BURN

BRITAIN'S FIRE GUARD IS BRITAIN'S DEFENCE

Eventually Trenchard's views were accepted by the British government, and in the air defence of Great Britain two-thirds of the squadrons were to be bombers and one-third fighters. But because it was thought that the bombers were offensive while the fighters were defensive in character, it was judged that the building up of fighter strength would not be liable to trigger off an arms race. The seventeen authorized fighter squadrons were in existence by 1930, but at that date no more than twelve of the thirty-five authorized bomber squadrons had been formed, most of them equipped with small short-range day bombers. In 1935 the alarm caused by German rearmament in the air occasioned a further shift of emphasis in favour of the fighters. A system of radio-location, later called radar, which would provide invaluable early warning and make it possible to track incoming raids, was pioneered by Robert Watson-Watt, and given all possible encouragement.

The Munich crisis of 1938, when for a time war seemed unavoidable, brought home to the British government, though not to the British people, their appalling military weakness and almost total unreadiness for war. France, which was in no better shape, and Great Britain had to make the best bargain they could with Hitler. The British government now realized that war was likely in the near future, with no possibility of building up a bomber force that could carry the war into the enemy's skies. The opening phase of the war was therefore bound to be defensive, to gain the time needed to modernize and build up the armed forces. The Air Ministry had to switch all remaining priorities to the expansion and equipment of Fighter Command, at the expense of the development of the bomber force. It was also necessary to build, with great urgency, a chain of radar stations to provide early warning and controlled interception of incoming enemy raids. The most that could be hoped for was to foil any attempt at invasion, and survive the opening defensive phase in good enough shape to begin to build an offensive capacity. For it must be remembered that even the most successful defensive action cannot win a war; it can stave off defeat and buy time to create the right conditions for an offensive, but no more.

At the outbreak of war in September 1939 the odds against the RAF, in terms of

*1 German air reconnaissance photograph of oil installations at Purfleet on the Thames after the heavy air raid on London on 7th September 1940. 2 Poster issued by Ministry of Home Security calling for national solidarity against incendiary attacks. The first heavy incendiary attack was on 15th October 1940. To meet the new threat, the minister of home security, Herbert Morrison, organized a compulsory fire-watching service and consolidated local fire brigades into a single National Fire Service. 3 German fighter pilots relaxing but ready to 'scramble'. 4 Remains of a German bomber brought down in an English farmyard*

modern aircraft, were about four to one. Although money had been poured out like water during the years since the Munich crisis, it had been too late to redress the balance. It was only time—as much time as possible—would be able to do that.

Hitler's assault on the West began on 10th May 1940, and within two months Belgium, Holland, and France were defeated and prostrate, with Denmark and Norway already occupied by German troops and air forces. During these two months the RAF operated at maximum intensity, in a vain effort to stave off disaster, and later to give protective cover to the evacuation from the continent. Losses were very heavy, and in some ways these operations put just as great a strain upon Fighter Command as did the Battle of Britain.

At the beginning of July Great Britain stood alone, with no more than a narrow strip of sea separating her from the victorious armed forces of Hitler's Germany. The strategy and assumptions with which the Allies had begun the war lay in ruins all around them. Had the Germans been able to follow up their success by an immediate invasion across the Channel they might have succeeded, for Fighter Command was exhausted, and Great Britain's land forces were so disarmed and disorganized that effective resistance would scarcely have been possible. But fortunately the Germans were also in need of a breathing space. They needed time to regroup their armies, collect barges and stores, re-deploy their air forces on new airfields in captured territories, build up stocks of bombs, ammunition, fuel, and spare parts, and to give their aircrews a much needed rest.

It is sometimes forgotten that the object of the RAF in the Battle of Britain was not simply to defeat the German air attacks, but the destruction of Hitler's plan, code-named 'Sea Lion', for the invasion and conquest of Great Britain. This was to involve not only Fighter Command, but the whole of Bomber Command too.

The battle began on 8th August 1940. Rising production of fighter aircraft and intensive training of pilots had by this time reduced the odds against the RAF to about three to one. On the very day that Hitler launched his assault against the West, a new Ministry of Aircraft Production was set up, with Lord Beaverbrook at its head. He was especially charged with doing everything possible to increase the production

*1 Battle of Britain poster emphasizes importance of fighter aircraft for national survival. 2 Member of the Women's Voluntary Service carrying some of the aluminium pots and pans given in response to Lord Beaverbrook's appeal. The WVS drove mobile canteens, cared for the bombed-out, staffed rest centres and clothing depots, and helped with evacuation. 3 London street after an air raid in September 1940. 4 Ack-ack girls practise air raid drill. Women from the Auxiliary Territorial Service worked in anti-aircraft units and performed non-combatant duties, like plotting and ranging enemy aircraft, releasing men for active service*

**KEEP THEM BOTH FLYING!**

**SPEED IS *Vital!***

Imperial War Museum

Fox Photos

Imperial War Museum

Associated Press

of fighter aircraft and all of the equipment needed for air defence. He was a man of boundless energy, whose administrative methods were ruthless, improvised, and fluid rather than methodical or orderly. He spared no effort to make the people of Great Britain realize the vital importance of fighter production. Householders were asked to give every aluminium saucepan they could spare, and many did so in the belief that in the twinkling of an eye their household utensils would be turned into Hurricanes and Spitfires.

In sober fact there were only three ways in which the planned production of fighters could be accelerated during the next three months. Firstly, by convincing the aircraft industry and the trade unions of the vital need to increase production; secondly, by concentrating every available priority on air defence; and thirdly, by reducing the production of spare parts and using the capacity thus released to build aircraft instead. Beaverbrook used all three methods. The first two had only a marginal effect, and the third produced the most obvious result, though largely at the expense of serviceability in the field. It compelled squadrons to 'cannibalize'; that is, to rob unserviceable aircraft of spare parts to keep the others going. Though Beaverbrook assumed office too late to achieve much genuine increase in production until the

*The Battle of Britain—Hitler's first defeat. Germany lost twice as many aircraft as Great Britain*

day battle was over, it was generally believed that he had done so.

The German plan for the invasion of Great Britain required the destruction of the RAF, followed by the transport across the Channel of some 200,000 German troops and their impedimenta, conveyed in the huge barges used commercially on the Rhine and other great European rivers and canals. It was the task of Fighter Command to avoid destruction and to win the air battle, and that of Bomber Command to destroy the barges and dumps of war material collecting in the Channel ports.

At the beginning of the battle, Fighter Command consisted of fifty-four regular and auxiliary squadrons, of which twenty-seven were equipped with Hurricanes, nineteen with Spitfires, six with Blenheim night-fighters, and two with Defiants, a two-seater fighter which proved unsatisfactory in operations. Thus there was a total of forty-six effective day fighter squadrons, giving a front-line strength of about 820 aircraft. Against this, the Germans had deployed a total of some 2,600 aircraft, of which about 1,000 were day fighters, and the remainder bombers of various kinds.

The German fighters were the single-engined Messerschmitt 109, and the twin-engined Messerschmitt 110. The performance of the Me 109 was slightly better than that of the Hurricane, but not as good as the Spitfire. The Me 110 was regarded by the Luftwaffe as a destroyer rather than a fighter. It combined long range and a

powerful armament, but was relatively unmanoeuvrable, and no match for the British interceptor fighters.

The 1,200 long-range bombers were mainly Dornier 17s and Heinkel 111s, both good fast aircraft, but with inadequate defensive armament. The normal bomb load of the Dornier was 2,205 lb, and that of the Heinkel about 3,000 lb, with provision in the latter for a maximum of 5,512 lb for short ranges. They flew in well-drilled formations, with the Me 110s as close escort, and the Me 109s providing high cover.

Göring was confident that he could achieve his aim by smashing the fighter defences around London, and then extending his assault northwards and westwards.

### Fighter Command

Fighter Command, however, had immense confidence in its aircrews, its aircraft, and its well-developed system of ground-controlled interception. Its aircrews were as well-trained as any in the world, and second to none in courage and determination. They had inherited the great traditions of the gallant fighter pilots of the Royal Flying Corps in the First World War, and their morale was very high. They knew very well how much depended on their efforts, and they were obviously defending their homeland from a monstrous assault. Moreover, they had their parachutes and friendly territory beneath them. The Hurricanes and Spitfires were reliable and had an excellent performance. With

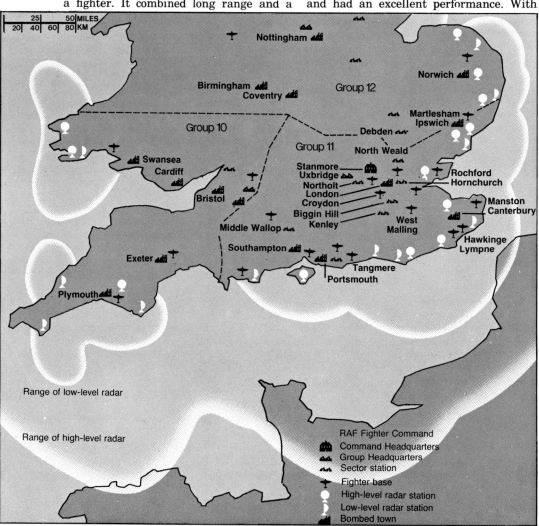

their eight machine-guns they were superior in armament to any other fighter in the world. And there had been time to build the chain of radar stations, and accustom the pilots and operations rooms staffs to the new techniques of interception. Finally, a simplified and very effective system of battle tactics had been worked out.

Fighter Command was ready—but only just ready—for battle.

Air Marshal Sir Hugh Dowding, the Commander-in-Chief of Fighter Command, was a shrewd and very experienced commander. He was generally held in more respect than affection, for he had a sharp tongue and a gruff and somewhat ungracious manner, which had earned him the nickname of 'Stuffy'. But those who knew him well realized that this manner concealed a humane and rather shy personality.

Dowding understood very well the magnitude and importance of his task. He also realized that the battle would be one of attrition and that, while the most vigorous and resolute tactical offensive against the Luftwaffe was essential, he would have to husband his resources. He had to guard against exhausting his pilots and ground crews by asking too much of them. Except for short spells in an emergency, he must keep his operations at a level that could be maintained for a long period.

The command, group, and sector operations rooms, placed underground, each had a large map in the form of a table. All incoming raids were plotted by radar, and counters were immediately placed on the map, indicating position, altitude, direction of flight, and approximate strength. Large numbers of officers and airwomen of the Women's Auxiliary Air Force were employed in the operations rooms on these duties, and in intelligence and codes and cyphers. The controller, in a gallery, could see all the information on the map at a glance, and issue orders to the appropriate squadrons. Once airborne, they could be given a course which would bring about an interception. Controllers had to be cool and experienced, to avoid being deceived by feints and to ensure that the main attacks were intercepted with maximum force. While delegating much to the group commanders, the command operations room retained general over-all control of the battle.

The first phase opened with a very intense attack on British shipping in the Channel. This was, however, a probing attack, involving but slight penetration of the defences. A few days later, on 12th August, orders were given for the full-

*Seen from behind the undercarriage of a British Hawker Hurricane, an RAF pilot adjusts his parachute before going into action. Hanging from the face mask are the oxygen line and the lead for the pilot's radio-telephone, which fed information from the chain of radar stations and plotting-rooms, and rapidly vectored the eight-gun Hurricanes and Spitfires on to the incoming enemy bomber streams*

scale offensive. On 15th August the pattern changed, and a widespread attack by 1,800 German aircraft was carried out against all sorts of objectives. That evening Göring gave orders that all further attacks were to be directed solely against the RAF – its bases and communications, and especially against the main strength of Fighter Command deployed in a ring of airfields around London.

This second phase was, from the British point of view, the most dangerous of the whole battle. Concentrated attacks severely damaged airfields at North Weald, Hornchurch, and Debden, and Biggin Hill was so wrecked as to be temporarily out of action. All the fighter airfields suffered varying degrees of damage. The defence of these airfields was vital, and so intense were the operations that the pilots and airmen were near to exhaustion. The worst hit squadrons were sent north to quieter sectors to recuperate, but all too soon the 'rested' squadrons would have to return to the south-east. The situation was becoming desperate, and had the Germans persisted in their policy for another fortnight the result might well have been disastrous for Fighter Command.

Soon, however, affairs were to take a new turn. On the night of 23rd August the Germans bombed London, and the Prime Minister ordered a retaliatory attack on factories in Berlin. The night was almost too short for such an operation, but Bomber Command successfully carried it out. Hitler reacted promptly. He ordered that German air attacks should in future be directed against British industrial cities and towns, with London as the primary objective. Göring had told him that the air battle was all but won, and that the RAF was at its last gasp. Hitler believed that these new attacks would shatter British morale and pave the way for his invasion.

### Invasion imminent

In fact, this change of emphasis in the third phase relieved the pressure on Fighter Command. Damaged runways and other airfield facilities were repaired, broken communications were quickly made good, and the Command's fighting capacity rapidly restored. On 7th September the Germans launched a tremendous attack, involving almost their whole strength. Wave after wave of bombers, escorted by hordes of fighters, crossed the coast. Many great fires were caused, especially in the London docks. Guided by the flames, the bombers continued the attacks through the hours of darkness. The damage and loss of life were grievous, but the British people were undaunted, and the over-all effect was far less catastrophic than the attack on the fighter airfields. An attempt to follow up these attacks on 8th September was repulsed with heavy losses.

There could be no doubt, however, that Operation Sea Lion was imminent, and on 7th September the British government issued a warning that invasion was probable during the next few days. That night the whole strength of Bomber Command was concentrated against the barges and military dumps in the Channel ports. The weather was good, and these attacks were highly successful. Night after night the bombers pounded the invasion ports. On 11th September Hitler postponed the date of Sea Lion to 24th September. But on the night of 13th September an especially successful bombing attack did enormous damage, sinking no less than eighty huge barges in the port of Ostend alone.

Göring remained optimistic. He assured Hitler that 'given four or five more days of good weather, the results would be decisive'. But another tremendous air assault on 15th September, which raged from dawn to dusk, suffered a severe defeat at the hands of Fighter Command. This day is generally regarded as the climax of the Battle of Britain.

On 17th September Hitler resolved to postpone Operation Sea Lion indefinitely. He realized, more clearly than did Göring, that the Luftwaffe had failed to defeat Fighter Command, and that he could no longer maintain his vast concentrations of barges, troops, and military stores in the Channel ports in the face of Bomber Command's devastating attacks. He gave orders for the remaining barges and stores to be dispersed, and the troops moved away from the danger areas around the ports.

Air reconnaissance soon confirmed that these German concentrations were melting away, and it was clear that the danger of immediate invasion was over. The supply of trained pilots had proved to be just sufficient, while the production of fighter aircraft just managed to cope with the wastage.

The German air force had failed utterly to achieve its aim of breaking Fighter Command, and had suffered severe losses in the attempt. It was not easy to assess these losses accurately. No doubt, at the time, the German losses were exaggerated, but this is inevitable in large-scale fighting in the air. But whatever the actual losses were, they were enough to call a halt to Göring's air attacks, while Bomber Command had destroyed a great part of the shipping and war material on which the invasion depended.

On 13th October Hitler postponed Operation Sea Lion until the spring of 1941, but in reality the plan was dead.

### The Blitz continues

As the battle by day slowly died away, the fourth phase began and the German bombers were switched to night operations. There had been a fair number of night attacks during the day battle period, but these were not very heavy and were usually follow-up attacks of targets bombed during the preceding day.

The problems confronting aircraft operating in darkness were at that time largely unsolved. The bomber's problems were those of navigation by night, often in poor weather conditions over a blacked-out countryside, of target identification, and bomb-aiming. For the fighter there were the problems of finding the bomber in the dark, and making an effective attack on it.

The German bomber crews were not well trained or experienced in night operations. Hence they used a radio beam technique, called 'Knickebein' (crooked leg), which enabled a pilot to navigate by radio signals. The system had the disadvantage of being vulnerable to radio counter-measures. It could be interfered with by jamming, but the most successful method was to bend or deflect the beam.

By day the fighters could be vectored on to incoming enemy formations located by radar, and interception made relatively easy. By night, against a swarm of individual bombers, such methods failed. A means of interception had to be carried in the fighter itself. This was the AI (aircraft interception), which was at first fitted to the Blenheim, a fast bomber aircraft converted, in default of anything better, to a night-fighter. After many initial set-backs and failures, it was found possible to vector a night-fighter close enough to a bomber to pick it up on its AI, and a sighting made. But progress was slow. The Blenheim was not fast enough or well enough armed to be very successful.

Later in the period a new night-fighter, the Beaufighter, appeared. This was an adaptation of a sea-reconnaissance aircraft, the Beaufort. With improved AI, and armed with four 20-mm cannon and four machine-guns, it proved a most useful night-fighter. But it was not available in sufficient numbers until the night-blitz was almost over.

Considerable success was in fact achieved by the night air defences, but not enough to provide a deterrent.

The attacks on British towns and cities killed and wounded many civilians, and caused serious, if temporary, losses of industrial output. Indeed these losses, due not so much to the actual destruction of factories as to the disruption of gas, electricity, and water supplies, communications, and above all to absenteeism caused by the destruction of workers' dwellings, gave the British a somewhat exaggerated idea of the effectiveness of such operations.

For centuries, except for a few civil wars long ago, the British people had been used to the idea that battles were fought on the high seas, or far away in other countries and were exclusively the business of the armed forces. The First World War disturbed, but did not destroy, these beliefs.

The direct attack from the air on their homes and places of work shocked and angered the British people, but they were not dismayed. A new spirit of neighbourly friendship and concern developed. Little had been known, in the absence of actual experience, of the behaviour of a civilized population under air attack, and on the whole the courage and endurance of the British people exceeded most official expectations.

With the coming of the shorter summer nights the night bombing attacks died down, and when in June 1941 Hitler began the invasion of Russia, his bombers were moved to the Eastern Front.

The Battle of Britain had been fought and won. But it was not the beginning of the end of the war, but the end of the beginning.

# Barbarossa

On 22nd June 1941 Nazi Germany attacked the Soviet Union. The eastern horizon had hardly begun to lighten when thousands of German guns opened fire across the Soviet border. Without warning German aircraft attacked airfields of the Soviet air force situated near the border, and German assault groups opened the way for the main forces of the Wehrmacht.

Hitler and his generals had not the slightest doubt that Germany would rapidly vanquish the Soviet state. They had carried out prolonged preparation, secretly concentrating on the Soviet frontiers a huge army, three million strong, which had experienced no defeat during two years of war and which had confirmed on the battlefields of Europe its doctrine of Blitzkrieg. They had worked out in detail a war-plan (Barbarossa) according to which the main forces of the Red Army were to be wiped out in a single gigantic operation, and Soviet territory right up to the Volga occupied by the autumn of 1941.

When the invasion began the Soviet forces guarding the 2,000-kilometre frontier were not ready. On 22nd June the Red Army in the western border districts of the Soviet Union were being deployed, and the only forces that faced the German tanks and infantry as they crossed the border were frontier guards and a small part of the covering force which had succeeded in getting to the frontier in response to the alarm. The principal forces guarding the western frontier were scattered over a large area up to 280 miles from the front. Despite all the indications that war with Germany was approaching neither the Soviet people nor the Red Army were expecting the German attack when it came. In the summer of 1941 everyone hoped that war might be avoided for a little longer.

Apart from the complete surprise of their attack the Germans had great superiority of forces in the areas where the main blows were struck.

The German armies broke through deep into Soviet territory, trying to surround and destroy concentrations of Soviet forces and prevent a retirement by the effective forces of the Red Army towards the east, behind the Dnieper and Dvina.

At 0715, Marshal Timoshenko, people's commissar for defence, ordered retaliation. Air attacks were to destroy German planes on the ground, and land forces were to throw back the German army to the frontier, without, however, crossing it. But the order was impossible to fulfil. Deep penetration by German tank units,

supported by aircraft, frequently resulted in the enemy appearing in the rear of Soviet troops, who were then surrounded.

The German armies were divided into Army Groups North, Centre, and South under the command of Field Marshals Leeb, Bock, and Rundstedt. Facing them were the Soviet troops of the north-western, western, and south-western fronts under Generals Kuznetsov, Pavlov, and Kirponos.

The situation became especially critical on the western front, in Belorussia. German Army Group Centre surrounded the principal forces of 3rd and 10th Armies of the western front near Białystok, broke through to Minsk with II and III Panzer Groups commanded by Generals Guderian and Hoth, captured Minsk (after it had first been largely destroyed by bombing), and then began to move towards the Dnieper. By the beginning of July there were wide gaps in the line of the western front, through which the German tank columns poured farther and farther eastwards. Meanwhile Army Group North invading from East Prussia had penetrated about 450 kilometres into the Baltic region by 10th July, and Army Group South was moving its main forces towards Kiev.

At Hitler's headquarters, the *Wolfsschanze* (wolf's lair), set in strong bunkers of reinforced concrete amid the forests of East Prussia, near Rastenburg, a triumphant atmosphere reigned. In a report to Hitler on 3rd July, General Halder, Chief of Army General Staff, concluded: 'The main forces of the Russian army in front of the Dnieper and Dvina rivers have been largely destroyed . . . it will be no exaggeration if I say that the campaign against Russia has succeeded in a single fortnight' – a view with which Hitler entirely agreed. There were even plans for the withdrawal of troops to concentrate on the conquest of Great Britain and the Near East.

Hitler's war on the Soviet Union had not finished, however; it had only just begun. The Soviet government and the Supreme Command of the Armed Forces carried out far-reaching mobilization of the country's resources for the fight against the invaders. On 30th June the State Defence Committee (GKO) was set up, with Stalin at its head. The GKO concentrated all power in its hands. The national economy

*Right: German troops move into the Ukraine. The secret and prolonged preparation for the attack found the Soviet Union totally unprepared for war*

Bundesarchiv., Koblenz

was reorganized and wholly geared to the production of war materials. Civilian factories were turned over to the production of weapons and equipment and more than 1,500 factories, with their entire plant and personnel, were moved bodily to eastern areas away from the western part of the country, where they were in danger of falling into enemy hands. This was a very large-scale operation, unprecedented in its complexity. All through the summer and autumn of 1941 trains ran in endless streams along all the main railway lines, carrying machine-tools and other factory machinery. On these same trains, some in carriages and some in open trucks, travelled the engineers and workers of these factories with their families and belongings. It was as though entire towns had been plucked up and were moving in a great migration to new lands. Having arrived at their new locations in the Urals, in Siberia, or in Central Asia, the war factories began production without delay. Often the workers and engineers got down to work on sites under the open sky, in rain and foul weather. In the opposite direction, towards the front, flowed another stream, carrying troops, tanks, guns, ammunition.

The Supreme Command of the Red Army did much to form fresh reserves. In the course of the summer of 1941 more than 324 divisions were sent to the front. It is interesting to note that, before the invasion, the German command estimated that the Soviet Union was capable of mobilizing a maximum of 140 divisions in the event of war.

In July 1941 the whole front was split into three strategic sectors: north-western, western, and south-western. Several fronts (army groups) came under the authority of each sector. Of decisive importance was the western sector commanded by Marshal Timoshenko, the Smolensk-Moscow axis. There, between 10th July and 10th September, the greatest battle of the summer and autumn of 1941 took place—the battle for Smolensk.

At the start of the battle the Germans outnumbered the Soviet forces on the western sector in men by 1.6 to 1, in guns by 1.8 to 1, in tanks by 1.5 to 1, in aircraft by 4 to 1. The Soviet reserves which had just arrived from the interior of the country could not be fully deployed. The gigantic battle at first went in the enemy's favour. Between 10th and 20th July II, IX, and IV German Armies and their II and III Panzer Groups strove, along a 500-kilometre front, to break the forces of the western front into isolated sections, to surround 19th, 20th, and 16th Armies protecting Smolensk, and to seize the city

*Top: German motorized infantry streams eastwards at the opening of Barbarossa. By the evening of 22nd June the forward units of the German armies had penetrated far into Soviet territory. Centre: Germans shell a Russian village. Bottom: Soviet supply train carrying guns to the front. Right: Two sequences from the German attack on Zhitomir—the artillery in action, and its effects*

Éditions Rencontre

which had long since been marked down by the invaders as the 'key to Moscow'.

The Germans, using powerful tank groups which they concentrated on narrow sectors of the front, and with massive air support, achieved a number of deep breakthroughs in the areas of Polotsk, Vitebsk, and Mogilev. Hoth's III Panzer Group succeeded in breaking through in the Yartsevo area and cutting the chief line of communication of the western front, the motor road between Minsk and Moscow. Farther south, Guderian's II Panzer Group penetrated the outskirts of Smolensk. On the right flank of the western front the Germans forced the Soviet troops to fall back on Velikiye Luki and Nevel, while on the left flank they captured Yelnya, establishing a salient extending far to the east. The German command began to consider this as the jumping off area for the next offensive, against Moscow.

The Soviet troops put up resistance all along the line. Step by step they slowed down the offensive of Army Group Centre and steadily counter-attacked. In order to divert the German forces from the Smolensk sector, an offensive by General Kuznetsov's 21st Army was launched in the direction of Bobruysk. The 20th Army, led by General Kurochkin, deeply enveloped on both flanks in front of Smolensk, tied down a number of German formations for several weeks.

The battle for Smolensk reached its climax between 21st July and 7th August. During this struggle the Red Army Supreme Command deployed several dozen additional fresh formations in three echelons in the western sector and established a new front, called the reserve front, in the rear of the western front.

The principal centres of fighting in this desperate battle were Smolensk, Yelnya, and Yartsevo. For several days troops of the 16th Army, led by General Lukin, put up a stubborn resistance in Smolensk. An extremely intense struggle went on for many weeks without a break around Yelnya. Here the Nazis suffered such heavy losses that they called it 'the bloody furnace'. The battle for Yelnya was crowned with success for the Soviet troops, who drove the Germans out of the town and occupied it themselves. Near Yartsevo, tanks and infantry of Hoth's III Panzer Group were halted by General Rokossovsky's troops. Yartsevo, burning and in ruins, changed hands several times. German reports from the front commented on the determined—even fanatical—Russian resistance; Halder was even beginning to doubt whether decisive victory was possible in these circumstances.

Bundesarchiv, Koblenz

Imperial War Museum

*Top: Russian prisoners. Trapped by the German advance, 3,000,000 were captured in 1941 — few survived. In their camps they were just left to die of starvation and disease. Knowing their fate if captured, the Russians fought fanatically. Centre: German soldiers survey the ruins of a Russian village. Bottom: SS troops resting. The speed of their advance exhausted the German troops*

# Barbarossa: the campaign

*Barbarossa was intended to occupy Russia well beyond Moscow by the autumn. But within two months it was clear that the plan was not going to succeed.*

**Army Group North:** the first major obstacle was the Dvina River, but by 2nd July all of Leeb's armour was across, ready to tackle the next problem: the northern strongpoints of the Stalin Line. Smashing a Soviet armoured challenge, Leeb's Panzer units pressed on to the Luga, under 100 miles from Leningrad itself, which they reached on 14th July. Trapping 20,000 prisoners in the Luga pocket, the Panzers cleared out Estonia by the end of August and were preparing to storm Leningrad. But Hitler had already decided to fence off the city, and to concentrate on Moscow. On 17th September all of Army Group North's armour except for one Panzer corps was switched to the centre under Hoepner and the siege of Leningrad was taken over by infantry.

**Army Group Centre** had two Panzer Groups poised north and south of the Bialystok salient. The Soviet frontier forces were surrounded in large pockets around Bialystok on 30th June, and Minsk on 9th July. Fending off counter-attacks from the south by Timoshenko, the Panzer forces loosely roped off another huge pocket of over 300,000 Russians by taking Smolensk on 16th July. Then Hitler switched Guderian's armour to the Ukraine to smash Budenny at Kiev, reprieving Moscow, and losing vital campaigning weeks. Operation Typhoon, the offensive against Moscow, began on 2nd October, with spectacular successes in the double battle of Vyazma/Bryansk. But within a week the mud of the Russian autumn and ever-stiffening Soviet resistance halted operations. A new offensive in mid-November, when the early frosts restored movement to the Panzers, took the Germans to within nineteen miles of Moscow, but they could do no more. Exhausted and badly equipped for the Russian winter, Army Group Centre now had to face Zhukov's counter-offensive which began on 5th December.

**Army Group South:** the target was Kiev and the Ukraine. Spearheaded by Kleist's Panzers, Army Group South battered through the southern Stalin Line forts by 9th July and the Rumanians moved on Odessa. Budenny, Soviet commander in the south-west, planned to concentrate at Uman and Kiev after the failure of his first counter-offensives. But Russian plans to defend the western Ukraine were shattered by the speed of the two German claws which pushed south-east between the Dniester and the Dnieper, sealing off the Uman concentration on 4th August and taking 100,000 prisoners. In the next three weeks Kleist pushed into the Dnieper bend. Then came the southward switch of Guderian's Panzers from Army Group Centre, which joined up with Kleist on 16th September. After the annihilation of the Kiev pocket in late September, in which over 500,000 were killed or captured, Rundstedt's forces drove for Kharkov and the Donets, trapping another 100,000 on 6th October. XI Army, now under Manstein, sealed off the Crimea and Kharkov fell on 24th October. The Moscow offensive by Army Group Centre was mirrored in the south by a drive on Rostov, which fell on 21st November; within a week the Wehrmacht suffered its first major defeat when the Russians recovered it.

**Leeb** — **Army Group North**
- XVIII Army Küchler
- IV Panzer Group Hoepner
- XVI Army Busch

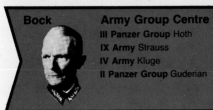

**Bock** — **Army Group Centre**
- III Panzer Group Hoth
- IX Army Strauss
- IV Army Kluge
- II Panzer Group Guderian

**Rundstedt** — **Army Group South**
- VI Army Reichenau
- I Panzer Group Kleist
- XVII Army Stülpnagel
- III Rumanian Army Dmitrescu
- XI Army Schobert
- IV Rumanian Army Ciuperca

The original plan

1 German attacks 22nd June–1st October

2 German attacks 2nd October–5th December

○ Major pockets of Soviet troops

At the beginning of August a balance of forces was achieved on the western sector. The German armies were pinned down and obliged to go over to the defensive.

Within two months Army Group Centre had penetrated 170-200 kilometres to the east of the Dnieper, but this was not the progress that the German High Command had expected. Whereas in the first days of the war the German troops had advanced on the average thirty kilometres in twenty-four hours, in July they had slowed down to six or seven kilometres. Smolensk, at the very centre of gravity of the German advance, had delayed the Blitzkrieg for two months and upset the schedule of Operation Barbarossa. Hitler was forced to change his plans, and, on 23rd August, rejected his generals' proposal to launch a concentrated attack on Moscow and made up his mind to attack the Ukraine and the Crimea. Economic factors obsessed Hitler; the wheatlands and industries of the Ukraine were of more importance than Moscow. And the Crimea, according to

Hitler, was 'a Soviet aircraft-carrier for attacking the Rumanian oilfields'. Guderian's II Panzer Group was therefore transferred from the Smolensk-Moscow sector to the Ukraine.

At the same time there was fierce fighting in the other sectors of the Soviet-German front as well, namely, the north-western and the south-western sectors.

The Nazi leaders calculated that the capture of Leningrad, Kronstadt, and the Murmansk railway would result in the Soviet Union losing the Baltic region and the far north, together with the Baltic Fleet. They also counted on acquiring a suitable area for a blow from the north-west at the rear of the Soviet forces protecting Moscow. Simultaneously, the Finnish army was to attack on the Karelian Isthmus and in the direction of Petrozavodsk. To the south of this they were to join up with the Germans who were attacking round Lake Ilmen, also in the Petrozavodsk direction. The XVIII Army was to occupy Estonia.

The Soviet people were determined to

defend Leningrad. As early as the end of June a plan was drawn up for making defensive fortifications round the city, and this task was put in hand at the beginning of July. Around Leningrad a system of defences was established, comprising several zones. The city's inhabitants worked on these fortifications alongside the soldiers. No fewer than 500,000 people went out every day during July and August to take part in the digging. Weapons for the front were being forged in the works and factories of the city. Home guard battalions were formed.

On 10th July the Germans attacked Novgorod. In a stubborn battle lasting four days, near the town of Soltsy, Soviet troops annihilated part of the German Panzer corps commanded by General Manstein. Field Marshal Leeb, commanding Army Group North, found himself obliged to halt the offensive of IV Panzer Group for a time.

After re-grouping, the Germans reached Krasnogvardeysk, a town situated less than ten kilometres from Leningrad. Their

*Soviet painting of an incident in the Crimea in 1941. A Black Sea sailor arms himself with grenades before throwing himself at a German tank*

XVIII Army occupied Estonia and arrived on the shores of the Gulf of Finland.

Before beginning to attack the defensive positions in front of Leningrad, the Germans subjected the city to a heavy artillery and air bombardment. Facing stiff opposition German troops got as far as the suburbs. From 8th September the city's communications with the outside world had to be kept up exclusively by air and across Lake Ladoga. However, the Germans' attempt to break into the city and link up with the Finnish army advancing over the Karelian Isthmus was decisively rebuffed by the Soviet forces directly defending Leningrad and those deployed along the northern bank of the Neva. The Germans were unable to move one step further forward. Army Group North was forced to abandon the offensive. Hitler decided to take the city by blockade.

In the Ukraine in July 1941 the Soviet troops of the south-western front waged great defensive battles to the south of Polesye and before Kiev and Korosten. The

southern front held the invading Germans and Rumanians in check in Moldavia.

Having great superiority of forces, German I Panzer Group, followed by VI Army, pressed towards Kiev, where they were halted. For seventy-two days the brave garrison of the Ukrainian capital defended the city, while to the south-west 5th Army, led by General Potapov, carried on a stubborn struggle, pinning down twelve German divisions and thereby easing the task of Kiev's defenders.

Farther south, the main forces of the south-western front were absorbed in great battles in right-bank Ukraine (the part of Ukraine to the west of the River Dnieper), which carried on until the first days of August 1941. Soviet 6th, 12th, and 26th Armies inflicted heavy losses on German Army Group South. Kleist's I Panzer Group lost fifty per cent of its tanks. But by means of a deep turning movement in early August the Germans surrounded 6th and 12th Armies near Uman and thus changed the course of the battle.

In view of the grave situation, the Red Army Supreme Command ordered the armies of the south-western and southern fronts, commanded by Generals Kirponos and Tyulenev, to retire behind the Dnieper and stand on its left bank, while holding Kiev, Dnepropetrovsk, and a number of bridgeheads on the right bank of the river. The Soviet forces carried out this retirement in the last days of August, and military operations were transferred to left-bank Ukraine (Ukraine to the east of the Dnieper).

Now Guderian's II Panzer Group and II Army were transferred from Army Group Centre near Smolensk to the Ukraine to help Army Group South encircle the Soviet armies near Kiev. Guderian's tank formations broke through the defence lines of the Soviet forces near Konotop and moved from the north into the rear of the main forces of the Soviet south-western front. Kleist's tank divisions pushed up from the south to meet Guderian, coming from the bridgehead on the Dnieper at Kremenchug. The two tank wedges met at Lokhvitsa. The four Soviet armies of the south-western front were now surrounded to the east of Kiev. On 18th September the Germans began to close in on the Kiev pocket of half a million trapped Red Army soldiers. On the next day the capital of the Ukraine fell to Hitler's armies. The battle of Kiev was the greatest disaster in the Red Army's history. The German forces advanced to the approaches to the Crimea.

At the same time Rumanian and German forces were blockading and besieging Odessa, one of the chief bases of the Black Sea Fleet. The city's inhabitants had constructed some defence lines around Odessa by the beginning of September. The enemy's attack on Odessa began on 10th August. The troops of the Special Black Sea Army and sailors of the Black Sea Fleet who were defending the city threw back the onslaught. Marine light infantry, supported by naval artillery, counter-attacked and smashed several Rumanian units.

On 20th August the enemy renewed the attack, with a five-fold superiority of forces over the defenders of the city. A bloody battle raged for a whole month. Very slowly, and with heavy losses, the attackers drew near the outskirts. Since the overall situation of the Soviet forces in the Ukraine and the Crimea in the autumn of 1941 had become extremely critical, the Supreme Command decided to evacuate the defenders of Odessa by sea and use them to strengthen the garrison of Sebastopol, the principal base of the Black Sea Fleet, which was also threatened.

By throwing in fresh reserves, the Soviet Supreme Command halted the German armies in the south in the late autumn. The Germans had suffered heavy losses. Nevertheless they were able, at the beginning of November, to get as far as Rostov, regarded as 'the gate to the Caucasus'. As a result, however, of transfers of Soviet troops to this area and a counter-offensive near Rostov, the shock force of Army Group South was smashed and thrown back from the town.

By the autumn of 1941 Hitler's plan for a Blitzkrieg against the Soviet Union had failed. Despite some resounding victories, Hitler and his strategists had proved unable to complete their eastern campaign before the autumn as they had hoped. The war was dragging on. The Soviet Union was still standing. The Red Army had repulsed the first and strongest blow of the aggressor, and had created the conditions for a turning point in the course of the war. This determined everything that followed. The main forces of Hitler's Wehrmacht were tied down for a long time on the Soviet-German front, and the danger of a Nazi invasion of Great Britain and of the Near East was finally dissipated.

*Top right: Reprisals. Bottom right: German machine-gunners*

Novosti

Bundesarchiv, Koblenz

On 5th December 1941 the Red Army counter-attacked the German armies threatening Moscow. Warmly-clad, well-equipped fresh troops from Siberia pounded the exhausted, ill-clad Germans in temperatures far below zero. The Germans retreated and Moscow was saved

Hitler and his generals had not achieved the victory they had expected. But the situation of the Soviet Union remained critical. The invaders were before the walls of Leningrad, were threatening Moscow, had occupied the greater part of the Ukraine, and held some of the most important economic areas of the country.

Hitler thought that victory over the Soviet Union was near. He now ordered the final blow against Moscow, so as to capture the Soviet capital and thereby terminate the eastern campaign.

The drive on Moscow was assigned to Army Group Centre, headed by Field Marshal Bock. Operation Typhoon, as it was called, envisaged the striking of three blows by tank and infantry groups in order to break up and surround the Soviet forces defending Moscow. After opening the road to the capital, Bock's forces were then to capture it by means of a headlong attack.

An army of a million men, comprising seventy-seven divisions (including fourteen tank divisions and eight motorized divisions with 1,700 tanks and assault guns) and 950 fighter aircraft assembled near Moscow. The preparations for the 'final blow' took more than a month.

The Soviet command entrusted the task of defending the approaches to Moscow to the troops of the western, reserve, and Bryansk fronts under the command of General Konev, Marshal Budenny, and General Yeremenko. The Nazis had twice as many tanks and guns as the defenders of the capital and three times as many aircraft. The offensive began on 2nd October. The defenders could not repulse the attack. By 7th October the main forces of the western and reserve fronts were surrounded near Vyazma. The roads to Moscow were open.

Extraordinary efforts now had to be made and measures taken by the Soviet command in order to prevent the fall of the capital. Above all it was necessary to gain time. By their stubborn resistance the surrounded troops tied down twenty-eight German divisions for over a week. The Supreme Command and the new commander of the western front, General Zhukov, began to concentrate all available forces in the Moscow area. First, a rapid redeployment of the troops stationed nearby succeeded in covering the main roads leading to the capital from the west and in holding the German units which were advancing from Vyazma. Meanwhile, from Siberia, the Volga region, the Far East, and Kazakhstan troop-trains flowed in bringing fresh forces. Soon it was possible to throw another fourteen divisions, sixteen tank brigades, forty artillery regiments, and other units into the battle for Moscow. A new defensive front was formed, along the Mozhaysk defensive line prepared by the people of Moscow.

On 10th October the Germans reached this line and attacked it. Desperate fighting went on for many days and nights without a break. The Germans succeeded in breaking through on a few sectors, capturing Kalinin, Mozhaysk, and Volokolamsk. They reached the close approaches of the capital.

At the end of October and the beginning of November the German advance was halted, thanks to the tremendous efforts of the Soviet troops. The German armies, which had made a 250-kilometre dash in October 1941, were forced to go over to the

*Graves of Germans who fell victim to 'General Winter' and Russian resistance*

*Russian peasants fleeing before the German advance on Moscow. By December 1941 70,000,000 people were living under German rule in Russia. The Nazi exploitation of occupied Russia was brutal. Millions were deported for slave labour, millions were arbitrarily executed*

Novosti

defensive along a line 70 to 120 kilometres from Moscow. There was a pause in the battle. The Soviet command had gained time for further strengthening of the approaches to the capital. The pause before Moscow enabled the Red Army Supreme Command to reinforce the western front with fresh troops and an anti-tank defence system was constructed in depth along the principal lines of approach to Moscow. In the first half of November the western front received an additional 100,000 men, 300 tanks, and 2,000 guns. The Muscovites dug defence-works in front of the entrances to their city.

The German command, after concentrating forces along the main roads leading to Moscow, began their second attack on the Soviet capital on 15th and 16th November. Again there was fierce and bloody fighting. Slowly, suffering heavy losses, the Germans drew nearer to Moscow, the capture of which they saw as their single and final aim, and their salvation. But the defences in depth held by the Soviet forces prevented them from penetrating the front. Guderian's II Panzer Army broke through to Tula, an important industrial centre and hub of communications. Numerous attempts to capture the town were successfully resisted by the troops under General Boldin, aided by detachments of Tula workers. Tula stood its ground, trans-

formed into the southern defence bastion of the western front. Then Guderian, leaving part of his forces to cover his right and left flanks, pushed on northwards with his main tank group, in order to come out to the east of Moscow and there join up with II and III Panzer Groups which were advancing from the north-west. The Germans were within a few kilometres of Moscow.

But the crisis of the German offensive had already come to a head. The staunch defence put up by the Soviet forces had worn out the shock troops of Army Group Centre. Having failed on the northern and southern approaches to Moscow, they tried to break through the defences in the centre of the western front. On 1st December the enemy succeeded in doing this in the sector to the north of Narofominsk (forty miles south-west of Moscow). Tanks and motorized infantry streamed along the highway as far as Kubinka, sixty kilometres from Moscow. But their further advance was held up by formations of 5th Army, commanded by General Govorov. After losing nearly half their tanks, the Germans turned eastwards into the area of Golitsyno station. Here the counter-blows of 33rd and 5th Armies descended upon them. The enemy's attempt to get through to Moscow had been frustrated. On 4th December, formations of these armies routed the Germans in fierce fighting and managed to

restore the front on the River Nara.

Thus concluded the last Nazi offensive against Moscow. The Soviet armed forces had won the defensive battle. The German shock groups had been bled white and deprived of power to continue their attack. Between 16th November and 5th December alone the enemy lost 55,000 dead and over 100,000 wounded and frostbitten.

The success of the defensive battle in front of Moscow was largely due to the fact that, at the most difficult period in the defence of the capital, Soviet forces went over to the counter-offensive south-west of Leningrad and in the Rostov area. The enemy was therefore unable to transfer forces from these areas to the Moscow sector. At the same time fresh Red Army reserves were assembled in the capital. The 1st and 20th Armies were deployed to the north of Moscow, and 10th Army to the south-west. The balance of forces gradually changed to the advantage of the Soviets.

On 5th December the Red Army began its counter-offensive before Moscow. The Germans were pushed back from the capital and were forced to assume the defensive, and were never again able to mount an offensive simultaneously along the entire strategic Soviet-German front. Their defeat at the walls of Moscow showed how much Hitler had under-estimated Soviet resistance.

# Pearl Harbour

America's decision to position her Pacific Fleet at a point covering Japanese lines of expansion was an event of great significance. Near Honolulu in the Hawaiian Islands, United States military authorities had dredged out a lagoon called Pearl Harbour, on which they located America's strongest outlying naval base before the Second World War and set up army and army air installations to protect it and the Pacific Fleet. Because of its location, Pearl Harbour came to be variously viewed as the Gibraltar of the Pacific, the defensive outpost of continental United States, a deterrent to Japanese aggressive intentions, or an encouraging inducement to Japanese to attack American forces and supplies situated in the East.

Pearl Harbour's destiny inevitably became involved in relations between Japan and the United States. These had been deteriorating badly since the previous year,

*Launch edges up to blazing* West Virginia *to snatch a survivor from the water. In fact, most ships damaged and even sunk were restored to fighting condition*

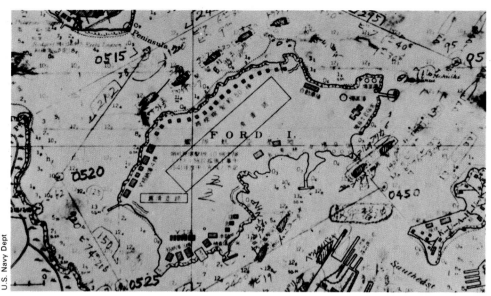

*Japanese chart supplied to Pearl Harbour strike pilots marks the supposed position of US Navy vessels in the base. It was not very accurate*

as disagreements arose over Japan's southward expansion on the Asiatic continent. During the 1930's the United States had limited its objections to efforts to impose moral sanctions.

By 1940 both countries began to examine their relationships in the light of the war in Europe. The Japanese took advantage of Nazi successes to make new advances down the coast of China. The hard pressures of war forced the French to acquiesce in the movement of Japanese troops into northern Indo-China and the British to agree to close the Burma Road, the last important supply line into China from Lashio to Kunming. By imposing a limited check on the export of war materials to Japan, the United States emerged as the principal obstacle to Japanese advance.

In May 1940 President Roosevelt changed the Pacific Fleet's main base from San Diego, California to Pearl Harbour despite the opposition of its commander, thus mak-

*Negotiations in Washington, October 1941.*
**Left to right:** *Admiral Nomura, Japanese ambassador, Cordell Hull, American secretary of state, and Saburu Kurusu, Japanese special envoy*

ing the force a pawn in the diplomatic manoeuvring between Japan and the United States.

But the Japanese had been making moves as well and in September 1940 secured a new alliance with Germany and Italy, known as the Tripartite Pact, which established spheres of influence, in effect giving Germany Europe, and Japan the Far East. In an obvious reference to the United States, the pact guaranteed mutual aid 'if attacked by a power at present not involved in the European war or in the Sino-Japanese conflict'.

Early in 1941, Japan fatefully started a dual course of action, one diplomatic and the other military, both aimed at removing American obstacles to Japanese expansion. The diplomats hoped to gain these ends peacefully by persuading the United States to stand aside. Meanwhile the militarists planned on war should the diplomats fail.

In January 1941 the American ambassador to Japan Joseph C. Grew reported a rumoured Japanese plan for a surprise attack on Pearl Harbour, but the report was discounted as 'fantastic'. Actually Admiral Isoroku Yamamoto was starting a study of the Pearl Harbour operation, convinced that the Pacific Fleet's destruction was essential to Japanese victory. In July, military and civilian leaders meeting before the Emperor decided to work for the 'establishment of the Greater East Asia Co-Prosperity Sphere and World Power', and declared that they would 'not be deterred by the possibility of being involved in a war with England and America'. The United States, too, hardened its position by freezing Japanese assets in the United States on 26th July 1941.

By this time the Washington government was being assisted greatly by intercepted and decoded messages. This 'Magic', as the decoding system was called, made it possible for the Americans, unknown to the Japanese, to be aware of Japanese diplomatic communications throughout the world. While it had limitations, including the fact that the information was diplomatic rather than military, the 'Magic'

*Above: Architect of the attack on Pearl Harbour: Admiral Yamamoto, C-in-C Combined Fleet. The approach to the operation was astonishingly successful and the shock enraged America, and turned the war into a world war. Right: Detail of illustration from American magazine* Fortune, *published after Pearl Harbour, depicting (from left) a Japanese soldier, Prime Minister Tojo, Admiral Nagumo, who delivered the raid, and Emperor Hirohito*

intercepts gave the American government at least an important diplomatic preview of things to come.

Another Japanese resolution on 6th September set in operation the advance to war. Only the successful achievement by diplomacy of three principal demands could halt the move. The United States and Great Britain should neither interfere with the settlement of the 'China Incident' nor strengthen their own forces in the Far East. Moreover, they should co-operate with Japanese efforts to obtain raw materials.

When a new, more militaristic government came into power in mid-October, the Japanese ambassador to the United States Kichisaburu Nomura felt out of touch and requested recall. Instead, the Japanese government sent Saburu Kurusu to Washington as a special emissary to work with Nomura.

On 5th November another Imperial Conference ordered one more diplomatic effort. If it failed, the question of war would go to the Emperor. Unable to persuade Tokyo to wait, its diplomats presented a new memorandum to Washington. Cordell Hull, the secretary of state, had no intention of accepting this proposal, which would have meant a reversal of the American position, but since he was under pressure from the military to delay, he and Roosevelt drafted a counter-proposal, including a short truce. They also learned through 'Magic' that Tokyo had set a final deadline for the diplomats – 29th November. 'After that, things are automatically going to happen,' said the message.

Discouraged by British and Chinese opposition to the temporary proposal, Washington dropped it and presented a ten-point memorandum to the Japanese, restating its original position. Nomura and Kurusu 'argued back furiously' against the proposal but had to forward it when Hull remained 'solid as a rock'. Two days later Tokyo told Nomura that the memorandum was unacceptable and that negotiations would be 'de facto ruptured', although Nomura was instructed not to reveal this fact to the Americans.

### Diplomatic efforts fail

After the war, Japanese leaders claimed that the American note forced Japan into war. True, the memorandum threatened Japanese expansion, but it did not menace Japan, its people, or its right to trade in the Far East. It challenged Japan's right to hold lands she had seized on the mainland but it did not threaten Japan in the sense that if Japan rejected the proposals the United States would declare war. The United States was not following a policy of dual initiative; it was not even planning to sever diplomatic relations. Nevertheless, Hull realized that the Japanese would not accept the proposals and that diplomacy was virtually at an end. On the 27th he told the secretary of war: 'I have washed my hands of it and it is now in the hands of . . . the Army and the Navy.'

Warnings had already been going out from time to time to outlying military commands. On 25th November, for ex-

*U.S. Navy Dept*

ample, Admiral Husband E. Kimmel in Hawaii heard that neither Roosevelt nor Hull 'would be surprised over a Japanese surprise attack'. On 27th November, military authorities decided to send new warnings to Admiral Kimmel and General Walter C.Short, the navy and army commanders in Hawaii. The note to Kimmel was the more explicit: 'Consider this dispatch a war warning.' It stated that diplomatic efforts had failed and that Japan might make an aggressive move 'within a few days'. Another message to Short on the same day, unfortunately, indicated sabotage as the principal threat, and he responded by issuing an alert, bunching aircraft against sabotage rather than dispersing them against air attack. Fortunately, no American aircraft-carriers were in Pearl Harbour on 7th December as the *Enterprise* and *Lexington* had been despatched to carry Marine fighter aircraft to Wake and Midway Islands.

Acting as if negotiations were still possible, the Japanese diplomats continued the farce, even while receiving orders to destroy codes and prepare to leave. On 6th December they received word that a fourteen-part memorandum was on the way, but were told, 'the situation is extremely delicate, and when you receive it I want you to keep it secret'.

The first thirteen parts of the memorandum were received first and, decoded by 'Magic', were ready for distribution about 9 p.m. on 6th December. When Roosevelt saw them, he reportedly said 'this means war', and discussed the matter with his

*Pearl Harbour seen on Japanese film.*
*Top: Still shows hilarity with which pilots of Pearl Harbour Task Force, en route for their objective, greeted a broadcast by the unsuspecting Americans on Oahu. Above: Carrier deck crews hold Zero fighters bound for Pearl Harbour until their engines have been revved up to take-off speed. Right: Oklahoma and West Virginia gush oil after the attack. Below right: Ford Island as the raid begins. A Kate peels off after scoring a direct hit on Oklahoma; the torpedoed Utah (arrowed) lists to port*

confidential assistant Harry Hopkins, without mentioning Pearl Harbour. Knox, the secretary of the navy, and some high military officials also saw the message but acted as if it had no military significance. Moreover, the despatch was not sent to General George C.Marshall, Chief-of-Staff, although he was at his home.

The fourteenth part was available by 7.30 or 8 a.m. on 7th December. Seeing it about 10 a.m., President Roosevelt commented that it looked as if Japan would sever diplomatic relations, for this part stated that it was 'impossible to reach an agreement through further negotiations'.

Meanwhile, another intercepted message from Tokyo was ready for distribution about 9 a.m. Referring to the longer memorandum, it asked: 'Will the ambassador please submit to the United States government (if possible to the secretary of state) our reply to the United States at 1 p.m. on the 7th your time.'

The officer in charge saw that the message was significant and got it to a presidential aide within twenty minutes. General Marshall returned late from a morning ride and did not read the message until almost 11.30 a.m. He immediately went into action and in longhand prepared a warning to key commands, including the Hawaiian Command:

'The Japanese are presenting at 1 p.m., Eastern Standard Time, today what amounts to an ultimatum. Also they are under orders to destroy their code machine immediately. Just what significance the hour set may have we do not know, but be on the alert accordingly.'

The message which went to Pearl Harbour met obstacles that appear almost comic in retrospect and did not arrive until after the bombs began to fall.

### Target Pearl Harbour
In Washington, the diplomatic game came to an anticlimactic end. The Americans decoded the Japanese messages faster than did the Japanese embassy, which had to ask for a delay in meeting Secretary Hull, and the diplomats did not arrive until shortly after 2 p.m. On his way to meet them, Hull received a telephone call from President Roosevelt, who said, 'there's a report that the Japanese have attacked Pearl Harbour'. He added that the report had not been confirmed. Hull then went to meet the ambassador and Kurusu and read quickly through the fourteen-point memorandum which, unknown to the Japanese, he had already seen. Coldly furious, he told them that in his fifty years of public life he had never seen a document 'more

crowded with infamous falsehoods and distortions on a scale so huge that I never imagined until today that any government on this planet was capable of uttering them'. He dismissed the diplomats and a few minutes later received confirmation of the Pearl Harbour attack.

All nations at this time had plans for possible war, and the United States was no exception. In 1924, American military planners prepared an 'Orange' plan in case of war with Japan. In the 1930's they replaced this with 'Rainbow 5' which envisaged war with the Axis, seeking particularly to enforce the Monroe Doctrine and protect the United States, its possessions, and its sea trade. By 1941 the United States had held discussions about the Far East with the British and the Dutch, but had not reached agreement. When war came each nation began fighting according to its own plan.

As war neared, American military leaders became increasingly concerned with fighting a defensive struggle in the Pacific against Japan and making the major effort in the Atlantic against Germany. Transfer of vessels from the Atlantic to the Pacific might 'well cause the United States to lose the battle of the Atlantic in the near future'. Consequently, the only plans recommended by General Marshall and Admiral Stark were 'to conduct defensive war, in co-operation with the British and the Dutch, for the defence of the Philippines and the Dutch East Indies'. Knowing that preparations were inadequate, they asked for more time.

Meanwhile, as we have noted, the Japanese had been carrying on their own war plans, in line with the policy of dual initiative. The nature of the nation's resources dictated a short conflict. Plans included early capture of oilfields in the East Indies, seizure of Singapore and the Philippines, and disabling the United States Pacific Fleet to keep it from interfering. Planners developed three phases of attack. First would be a blow at Pearl Harbour and an advance south in the Far East to seize lands and establish a perimeter extending from Wake Island through the Gilbert Islands, New Guinea, and the Dutch East Indies to Burma and the border of India. Second would be strengthening the perimeter, and third would be beating off attacks until the enemy tired of the effort. From the standpoint of the amount of territory to be occupied, the plan was aggressive and greatly expansionist. On the other hand, Japan apparently had no designs on either the United States or Great Britain.

Actual preparations for the Pearl Harbour attack began in August. The striking force consisted of six aircraft-carriers, screened by nine destroyers. A supporting force included two battleships, two cruisers, three submarines, tankers, and supply ships. Of the advance force of some twenty submarines, eleven bore small planes, and five were equipped with midget submarines, carrying two men and powered by storage batteries.

### The battleships devastated
Leaving Japan in mid-November, the Pearl Harbour task-force rendezvoused in utmost secrecy at Tankan Bay in the Kurile Islands. On 26th November, it left the Kuriles to approach the Hawaiian Islands from the north. The weather probably would be rough and refuelling difficult, but the chances of avoiding detection were best by this route. On the morning of 7th December, the force reached its predetermined launching site, some 230 miles north of Pearl Harbour, and at 6 a.m. the first aircraft took off: forty Nakajima B5N2 ('Kate') torpedo-bombers equipped with torpedoes adapted for dropping in shallow water, fifty more Kates for high-level bombing, fifty Aichi D3A2 ('Val') dive-bombers, and fifty Zero fighters (Mitsubishi Zero-Sens, officially codenamed 'Zekes' by the Allies). The second wave consisted of fifty Kates, eighty Vals, and forty Zeros.

There was no significant advance warning. In the fleet a so-called 'Condition 3' of readiness was in effect, in which one machine gun in four was manned, but it was a peacetime 'Condition 3' in which main and 5-inch batteries were not manned and even manned machine guns had their ammunition in locked boxes to which officers of the deck had the keys.

### The raid begins
At 7.30 a.m. a boatswain's mate saw twenty to twenty-five aircraft circling, but he did not identify them as enemy machines. At about 7.55 a.m. the Commander, Mine Force Pacific, on a mine-layer in the harbour, saw an aircraft drop

U.S. Navy Dept

a bomb but thought it was an accident until he saw the crimson sun insignia on the machine. He immediately called General Quarters and had the signal hoisted: 'All ships in harbour sortie.' A few minutes later Admiral Kimmel heard of the attack, and Rear-Admiral Bellinger broadcast: '*Air raid, Pearl Harbour—this is no drill.*'

Earlier, at 6.45 a.m., a midget submarine was detected and sunk, but the sole reaction was to send another destroyer to the area. Radar protection was primitive, poorly understood, and underrated. The one detection that was made by men practising on a radar set was disregarded by the watch officer as blips of approaching American bombers from the mainland.

Escaping detection and initial opposition, therefore, the Japanese aircraft swept in from over the sea. The first attack, starting at about 7.55 a.m., lasted for approximately half an hour. There were four separate torpedo-bomber attacks, with the first two directed at the main objectives, the battleships lined up in 'Battleship Row' on the south-east shore of Ford Island. The third attack was by a single aircraft on the cruiser *Helena,* and the fourth struck at ships on the north side of the island.

The second major attack came at about 8.40 a.m., after a brief lull, and consisted of a series of high-level bombing runs across the targets. Dive-bombers and fighters followed with a half-hour attack, and at 9.45 a.m. the aircraft withdrew.

The results were devastating. Among the battleships, *West Virginia* was hit by six or seven torpedoes, and quick counter-flooding alone prevented the vessel from capsizing. *Tennessee,* moored inboard of *West Virginia,* was protected by it from torpedoes and suffered relatively little damage or loss of life from bombings and fires. *Arizona* was the hardest hit. Torpedoes and bombs caused explosions and fires, and the vessel sank rapidly, carrying to their deaths over a thousand men trapped below decks. Although sustaining at least five bomb hits and one torpedo, *Nevada* managed to get clear and avoid sinking or capsizing. *Oklahoma* took three torpedoes and capsized until her masts stuck in the mud of the harbour bottom. *Maryland* was saved from torpedoes by *Oklahoma* and suffered the least damage of the battleships. *California,* struck by torpedoes, sank into the water and mud until only the superstructure showed. Aircraft attacking the north-west shore inflicted heavy damage on the light cruiser *Raleigh,* damaged the seaplane tender *Curtiss* and capsized the

*Above left: At the height of the attack on Pearl Harbour.* West Virginia *lies sunk but upright as a result of prompt counter-flooding. Inboard is the* Tennessee *which she protected from torpedoes and which consequently suffered relatively little damage.*
*Above right: Marines at Ewa Field fire at attacking Japanese aircraft. Men fought back against hopeless odds, at great personal danger and sacrifice, and with insufficient weapons. Below: A scene of devastation at Pearl Harbour's Naval Air Station after the attack*

old battleship *Utah* which had been converted to a target ship. Another light cruiser *Helena* was heavily damaged and *Oglala,* the minelayer alongside it, was sunk. Other vessels damaged included the light cruiser *Honolulu,* the destroyers *Cassin, Downes,* and *Shaw,* and the repair ship *Vestal.* The battleship *Pennsylvania,* in drydock, was hit but received no serious damage.

Although the battleships and other vessels were the prime targets, the Japanese did not forget airfields, and, relatively speaking, American airpower suffered more heavily than did sea power. The attackers strafed and bombed land-based aircraft and practically eliminated the seaplanes. Army Air Force aircraft at Hickam Field, bunched against sabotage, proved a perfect target for Japanese attackers.

By the end of the day, 'a date which will live in infamy' as President Roosevelt called it, the Americans had suffered 2,403 deaths, of which 2,008 were from the navy. Three battleships sank, and other vessels took varying degrees of punishment. The Japanese destroyed two-thirds of American naval aircraft and left only sixteen serviceable Army Air Force bombers. In contrast, Japanese losses were slight: besides five midget submarines only nine Zeros, fifteen Vals, and five Kates were lost out of an attacking force of 360 aircraft.

American reactions on the island ranged from an initial incomprehension through disbelief, shock, frustration, to displays of the utmost courage. Men fought back with all they had, in some cases successfully, as the twenty-nine downed planes attest, but more often against hopeless odds, at great personal danger or sacrifice, and with insufficient weapons.

### A tremendous blunder
Nearby Honolulu suffered little damage. The fires which started were determined later to have stemmed mainly from misdirected anti-aircraft fire from Pearl Harbour. Over a local radio, the governor proclaimed a state of emergency, and at 11.41 a.m. the army ordered commercial broadcasting stations off the air. Radio silence and the suddenness of the attack gave rise to uncertainties among the civilian population and the spreading of many unfounded rumours. Radio stations occasionally broadcast important messages, such as the announcement at 4.25 p.m. that the island had been placed under martial law.

Viewed from the level of high political policy, the Pearl Harbour attack was a tremendous blunder. It is difficult to conceive of any other act which could have rallied the American people more solidly behind a declaration of war on Japan. Generally speaking, Americans were not neutral; they favoured and gave aid to the nations fighting the Axis. However, without an incident such as Pearl Harbour, there would have been strong opposition to open participation in the war. Many people remembered the unsatisfactory aftermath of the First World War and they questioned what the Second World War could

accomplish. The Pearl Harbour attack ended all significant debate on such matters. The nation, in the eyes of Americans, had been attacked ruthlessly and without warning, and the only way out was to declare war on Japan.

The Japanese predicted American reactions but reasoned that strategic results would be worth it. Strategically, however, the Pearl Harbour attack was a blunder in that it was unnecessary. The Pacific Fleet could not have stopped or even checked the initial planned advance of the Japanese. American war plans envisaged defensive actions but reasoned that strategic results would be worth it. Strategically, however, the Pearl Harbour attack was a blunder in aircraft without the most careful preparations. The fate of the British ships *Repulse* and *Prince of Wales* early in the war is an indication of what would have happened.

Even tactically the Pearl Harbour attack was a blunder. Capital ships were no longer as effective a means of exercising sea power as aircraft-carriers, and the two carriers *Lexington* and *Enterprise* were out of harbour when the Japanese attacked. In fact, most of the ships that were damaged and even sunk were later restored to fighting condition. *Nevada*, for example, participated in the Normandy invasion and later helped bombard Iwo Jima. *California, Maryland, Pennsylvania, Tennessee,* and *West Virginia* all took part in the Philippines campaigns. It would have been more effective to blast permanent installations and oil supplies than ships. Destruction of the oil tanks would have delayed advance across the Pacific longer than damage to ships and aircraft. In fact, one of the reasons for surprise was the belief that the Japanese also recognized that such an attack would be unnecessary.

Pearl Harbour might have been more effective had it not been followed by a colossal blunder by Hitler. After the attack, Japan called on Germany to join in the fight against the United States. Had Hitler refused, the American administration would have been in a most difficult position. Its leaders viewed Germany as the principal enemy, but without any specific incident in the Atlantic they might have had difficulty gaining support for a declaration of war on Germany while launching into a struggle with Japan. Pressure would have been strong to fight the visible and open enemy and not deliberately to seek another foe. It is difficult to know what would have been the result in the Atlantic. One recalls that Marshall and Stark earlier had warned that withdrawal of American ships from the Atlantic might cause Great Britain to lose the Battle of the Atlantic. Fortunately for the American government, Germany forced the United States with a declaration of war. This action made it possible for the Allies to plan a coalition war that was world-wide.

*Painting by Japanese artist M.Susuki of newly qualified pilots at a passing-out ceremony — part of the militaristic ritual which reinforced the self-sacrificial fighting spirit of the Japanese*

U. S. Air Force

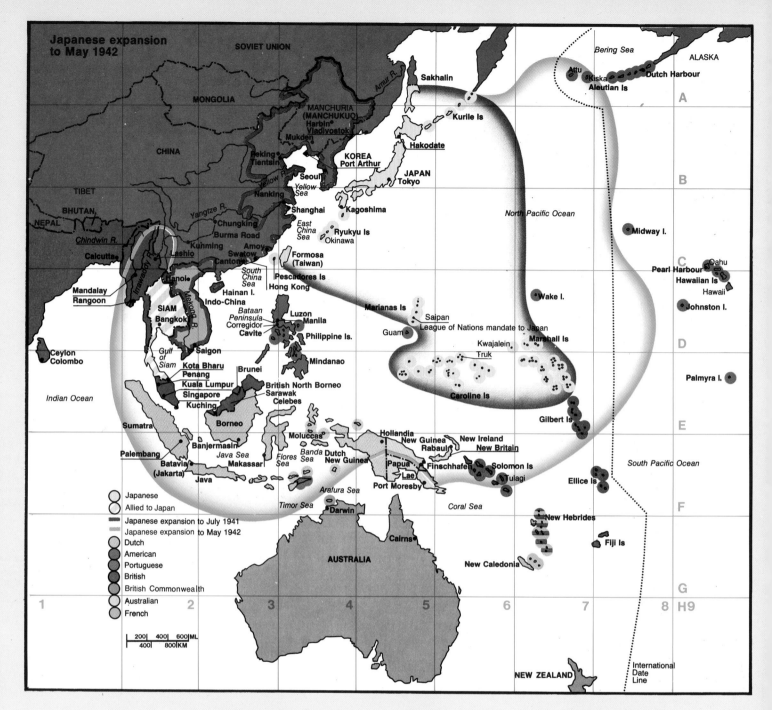

Japanese expansion to May 1942

**Legend:**
- Japanese
- Allied to Japan
- Japanese expansion to July 1941
- Japanese expansion to May 1942
- Dutch
- American
- Portuguese
- British
- British Commonwealth
- Australian
- French

Scale: 200 400 600 ML / 400 800 KM

# The Risen Sun

America's introduction to total war came on 7th December 1941, with the greatest naval defeat suffered by a first-class power since the Battle of Trafalgar. In an age in which the battleship was still the index of maritime power, nothing experienced by the Germans in the First World War or by the Italians in the Second World War compared with the blows delivered on the United States Pacific Fleet by Admiral Chuichi Nagumo's naval aviators.

The catastrophe of Pearl Harbour was made possible on the Japanese side by a combination of superb training and re- markable duplicity, and on the American by culpable negligence in both Hawaii and Washington, aggravated by unsatisfactory communication between them. Perhaps it could be said that the Americans had made an even more direct contribution to their own defeat, as Nagumo's airmen followed a plan of attack based on that executed successfully against the same target by Vice-Admiral Ernest J.King during manoeuvres carried out by the Pacific Fleet in 1938. But there was some excuse for American negligence. All parties concerned fully appreciated in the last months of 1941 that the Japanese were planning to attack the British and Dutch colonial empires in the Pacific. Few considered it rationally conceivable that they would add immeasurably to their difficulties by an attack on the United States at the same time.

Nor indeed did it prove to have been a rational decision. But there were certainly

*Japanese boys ape their soldier fathers. Young and old held the victorious military in great esteem in the early stages of the Pacific War*

few signs during the first six months of the Pacific War that the Japanese had over-extended themselves. The assault on Pearl Harbour itself did not nearly exhaust their offensive capacity. Seven other attacks were launched almost simultaneously against British, Dutch, and American positions in the Pacific. These developed into an enveloping march of conquest unmatched in military history. No soldiers or sailors had ever before won such victories against such enemies. In terms of human achievement, nothing compares with Japanese triumphs in the Second World War except Japanese economic recovery after it. On 8th December forty-two American aircraft were destroyed on the ground in the Philippines, for the loss of only seven Japanese. Two days later, *HMS Prince of Wales* and *HMS Repulse,* observed rather than escorted by one antique and two veteran destroyers, and under the command of an admiral resolutely disbelieving in air power, made history by becoming the first capital ships to be sunk in open sea by aerial bombardment. But the Japanese were to establish a number of records at British expense during the next few months. Hong Kong surrendered on Christmas Day 1941 after a resistance which cost the attackers some 2,754 casualties but involved the total loss of its uselessly exposed garrison of 12,000 British and Commonwealth troops. Meanwhile a numerically superior Commonwealth army, inadequately trained and inappropriately deployed, was hustled through Malaya into Singapore by a Japanese force less than half its size, and forced to capitulate on 15th February 1942. 138,708 British troops had become prisoners or battle casualties in the greatest defeat and most humiliating surrender in British history. General Yamashita's invaders had lost only 9,824 killed or wounded. The catalogue of disaster rolled on. In two days of fighting in the Java Sea on 27th-28th February, a combined American, British, Dutch, and Australian fleet lost eleven of its fourteen vessels, without managing to sink a single Japanese warship. And in four dreadful days in the Indian Ocean Admiral Nagumo's veteran fliers sank a British aircraft-carrier, two cruisers, two destroyers, and a corvette, and drove British naval power helplessly back to the Arabian Sea. Even the RAF itself was unable to match the attackers. In wild air battles over and around Ceylon, the British lost some forty-three aircraft, not counting those sunk with the carrier *Hermes*, against seventeen Japanese. And on 20th May the last British forces withdrew from Burma across the Indian border, after the longest retreat in British history, having suffered 13,463 casualties, against 4,597 Japanese.

The conquest of the Dutch East Indies presented the invader with even fewer problems. Borneo and Celebes were effectively overrun by 24th January; Ambon by the end of the month; Sumatra, Bali, and Timor by the third week of February; and Java by 9th March. The American colonies presented a rather different prospect, however. Almost undefended, Guam was over-

run easily on 10th December. But Wake Island repelled a first attack and held out until 23rd December, by which time its garrison of 520 Marines had sunk two Japanese destroyers and killed or wounded about 1,150 of the enemy. And American resistance in the Bataan Peninsula and Corregidor Island actually set back the Japanese time-table for the conquest of the Philippines by a whole four months, and resulted in the disgrace of the unfortunate Japanese commander, General Homma. The heroic tenacity of his fighting men managed to obscure the fact that MacArthur's generalship in the Philippines was distinguished by errors of optimism at least as serious as those which General Percival had been guilty of in Malaya, and that the number of American and Filipino troops put out of action by General Homma was about the same as that of the British and Commonwealth forces routed by Yamashita. But due to the fact that Wake, Bataan, and Corregidor held out for longer than anybody expected they have entered American mythology as symbols of defiant and inspiring resistance, while Singapore has become associated with disgrace, and Hong Kong with tragic futility.

## 'Victory disease'

There was no disputing the sweep and rapidity of the Japanese conquests or the relatively slight losses with which they were gained. But they were not without features ominous for the victors themselves. The most serious one was that they had clearly not achieved their basic purpose. Japanese grand strategy required the establishment of an island barrier behind which the conquerors could enjoy the fruits of their conquest while meeting the inevitable American counter-attack. But this required that American offensive capacity should first have been effectively destroyed. And this had not been done at Pearl Harbour. The battleship force of the Pacific Fleet had certainly been put out of action. But the fast aircraft-carriers had completely escaped the Japanese attack. *Saratoga* was still in California; *Lexington* was delivering Marine fighter aircraft reinforcements to Midway; and *Enterprise* was returning to Pearl Harbour from Wake Island having completed an identical mission there. This meant that the United States still possessed the means of striking against Japan with the same weapon of naval aviation which had been used so devastatingly against herself. Elementary prudence would thus have suggested that all the resources of the Imperial Navy should have been devoted to bringing the American carrier squadron to battle and destruction. But elementary prudence was the last quality to be considered in the Japanese plan of action. They, of course, had sufficient reason to be confident. Their fighting men had undoubtedly earned a reputation for invincibility; their only naval losses had been the five submarines lost at Pearl Harbour and the two destroyers sunk at Wake Island; and they still possessed a great numerical superiority in the air over the Americans, as well as in all classes of surface ships. But there was

reason to believe that this invincibility was incomplete, and that the numerical advantage could easily be lost. Air losses had turned out to be about equal at the end of the Burma campaign, but in the brief air battles over Rangoon the Japanese had shown a disquieting inferiority to the veterans of the American Volunteer Group, who were shooting them down for a time at the rate of four or five to one. This at least suggested that the Japanese might need all the air supremacy they could get. And it was clear that Japanese strategic planning seemed to discount the basic principle of the concentration of force.

It was not merely the case that the Japanese and their supposed German allies were fighting totally separate and unrelated wars. So, frequently, were individual Japanese commanders in the field. Their tendency to go off on wild hunts after easy conquests unrelated to any overall strategic plan was categorized by the Japanese themselves as the 'victory disease'. It was accompanied and aggravated by what might similarly be termed the 'octopus complex'. This took the form of a predilection for enormously ambitious and complex plans of campaign which merely compounded the possibilities for human error in situations where rational military direction should surely have sought to minimize them.

The victory disease and octopus complex appeared in full bloom in the crucial campaigns of May and June 1942. Conflicting factions in the Imperial Navy were unable to agree either with themselves or with the army whether immediate priority should be assigned to seizing Port Moresby, so as to neutralize Australia; to attacking the Aleutian Islands, to divert American strength from the central Pacific; or to a thrust at Midway Island, to force the remainder of the Pacific Fleet to accept battle, as should have been done as soon as possible after Pearl Harbour. It was effectively decided to proceed with all three. Even this did not satisfy the determination of the Japanese High Command to make things difficult for themselves. The ships assigned to the Port Moresby campaign were divided into no less than six separate forces, performing two quite distinct operations. By contrast Admiral Chester W. Nimitz, Commander-in-Chief of the US Pacific Fleet, boldly concentrated every available ship to meet the Japanese in the Coral Sea. The result was that the opposing forces were not too disproportionate. When battle was actually joined on 7th May, two American aircraft-carriers with 121

*Right: 1 Lieutenant-General Sakai heads triumphant Japanese entry into Hong Kong, Christmas Day, 1941. 2 Japanese troops on a British gun emplacement in Hong Kong cheer news of the garrison's surrender. 3 Japanese paratroops are dropped to seize oil installations near Palembang, Sumatra, 14th February 1942. 4 Sinking of small British aircraft-carrier Hermes off Ceylon, 9th April 1942. Attacked by ninety bombers and fighters, she was sunk in twenty minutes. Orders to British fighters to give her cover failed to get through*

aircraft and seven cruisers faced three Japanese carriers with about 180 aircraft and six cruisers. The odds were soon shortened in any case when bombers from both *Lexington* and *Yorktown* blew the carrier *Shoho* out of the water. *Lexington* was itself lost the following day, but in the meantime the Americans had put a further carrier, *Shokaku*, out of action.

The action in the Coral Sea might have seemed inconclusive as shipping losses were about equal and both fleets withdrew from the area, but in fact every advantage lay with the Americans. They had lost only eighty-one aircraft against 105 Japanese; the assault on Port Moresby was countermanded; and all the Japanese carriers had been immobilized, as the third, *Zuikaku*, had lost too many aircraft to be fit for action until its losses had been replaced. This weakening of the Japanese carrier strength at the Battle of the Coral Sea may well have determined the course of the Second World War.

It was not that the Japanese were even then seriously short of carriers. The enormous fleet available to Admiral Isoroku Yamamoto must have guaranteed him victory in any single enterprise he had committed it to. But Japanese naval power was dissipated in a futile attempt to confuse an enemy who could have been overwhelmed by a direct and concentrated attack. Yamamoto decided to proceed with the diversionary raid on the Aleutian Islands as well as the frontal assault on Midway, despite the failure of the Port Moresby bid. His plan of campaign resulted in the Japanese armada being scattered in ten separate groups all over the north and central Pacific. Two carriers were detached to cover the attack on the Aleutians, leaving the Midway force actually deficient in air power, although excessively strong in surface ships. Seven battleships, six heavy and light carriers, thirteen cruisers, and fifty destroyers challenged Nimitz's three carriers, eight cruisers, and fourteen destroyers. But Yamamoto brought with him only 325 aircraft, while Nimitz could assemble a motley collection of 348 land and sea-based machines. The Americans obviously could not offer battle at sea. Everything depended upon the prowess of the United States Naval Air Service — a glamourized body of fighting men, with their swashbuckling airborne admirals, their huge wooden-decked carriers, and years of experience in dive-bombing techniques.

And here two Japanese errors helped Nimitz decisively. The first was that Yamamoto still thought that two American carriers had been sunk in the Coral Sea engagement, and consequently quite underestimated the strike capacity of his opponent. The other was that the Japanese had not yet been forced to learn how to integrate their carrier squadrons with the rest of their fleet. The Americans had learned the hard way. Bereft of battleships, they had of necessity adopted their carriers as capital ships, and deployed their other craft as escorts around them. But the battle force which should have been in attendance to shield Nagumo's carriers with its

anti-aircraft batteries was 400 miles distant when the assault on Midway commenced.

However the Japanese nearly won. The initial air battles between their naval aircraft and American land-based planes were wholly in their favour. They wrecked everything above ground on Midway and shot down thirty-three American aircraft for a loss of only six of their own. Then retribution came. Rear Admiral Raymond A. Spruance on board *Enterprise* ordered strikes by his torpedo and dive-bombers at a time deliberately calculated to reach the Japanese carriers while they were still refuelling their aircraft. The torpedo bombers arrived first and flew on to destruction, losing three-quarters of their number without scoring a single hit. But the death-flight of the old Douglas Devastators drew the attention of the Japanese away from the upper air where Spruance's Douglas Dauntless dive-bombers were assembling. In less than five minutes three Japanese carriers, the *Kaga, Akagi* and *Soryu*, were on fire and out of action, and the great Pacific War had been won and lost. The surviving carrier *Hiryu* struck back, crippling *Yorktown,* but was itself destroyed by a further strike from *Enterprise*. By the end of the day, Yamamoto's air arm had been virtually eliminated. Twice on the following nights, he belatedly deployed his battle force in attempts to sink Spruance's carriers by gunfire. However, the Americans skilfully drew away at evening, returning with daylight to deliver more strikes, as a result of which a Japanese heavy cruiser was sunk.

Final casualty figures were four carriers, a cruiser, and 322 aircraft for the Japanese, against a carrier, a destroyer, and 147 aircraft for the Americans. The battle had been won on the American side by Spruance's almost faultless judgment and by the courage and technical skill of his aviators. It had been lost on the Japanese by the now familiar vices of over-confidence, over-complexity of planning, and unwillingness to concentrate on one objective at a time. This time they had been fatal. The margin of strength so brilliantly gained at Pearl Harbour had been squandered. The siege of the Japanese Empire had begun.

### Victims of success
There can be little doubt that at any time between 7th December 1941 and 4th June 1942 the Japanese might have secured the victory of the Axis powers, if only they had got their priorities right and been content to do one thing at a time. An all-out search-and-destroy operation against American naval power after Pearl Harbour, culminating in an air and sea bombardment of California, would have made it virtually impossible for the Roosevelt administration to have maintained its policy of 'Germany First'. It would have certainly inhibited the transfer of American tanks and artillery to Africa which made possible the British victories at El Alamein, and thereby prevented the Germans from outflanking the Russian defences from the south. Even a headlong drive across India might have achieved the same end result. But the Japanese were the victims of their

own military prowess. They had triumphed beyond all expectation. It was accordingly not surprising if they neglected the precautions necessary in a combat with an adversary whose economic capacity was some sixteen times as great as their own. But one need not be too critical of Japanese strategy. The outcome of the Pacific War, and effectively of the Second World War as a whole, was decided after all in less than five minutes over Midway. And there are many ways in which those minutes might never have happened.

### Japanese arms in action
In the wave of conquest which followed Japan's strike southward, four actions were of special significance. A detailed examination of these is important for an understanding of the nature of the Japanese successes and why they should have had such a stunning effect on the world. Two of these were British disasters: the loss of *Prince of Wales* and *Repulse*, and the fall of Singapore; two were tough, fruitless defensive actions by Americans in Wake Island and the Philippines.

The nature of the Japanese offensive which disguised its central objective and dazed ill-prepared opponents was dictated by a number of important considerations. The need to continue the war against China and protect Manchuria from Soviet incursions together with the shortage of merchant shipping necessitated the employment of the same units in successive operations and precluded protracted fighting. Fast moving, surprise attacks, moreover, were essential if the considerable oil, rubber, tin, and bauxite (aluminium ore) resources of South-East Asia and the south-west Pacific were to be seized undamaged at an early stage in the hostilities, which Japan's Naval and General Staffs had timed to avoid the north-east monsoon in the South China Sea and the violent gales in the north Pacific.

### Force Z detected
The first American possession to fall to a Japanese invasion force was Guam which capitulated on 10th December after half an hour's resistance. On the same day, the third of the Pacific war, the Japanese invaded the Philippines and seventy-five of their bombers from Saigon sunk the British capital ships *Prince of Wales* and *Repulse* seventy nautical miles south-east of Kuantan in eastern Malaya. At 1755 on 8th December the vessels, in company with the destroyers *Electra, Express, Vampire* and *Tenedos* under the command of Admiral Sir Tom Phillips, had slipped out of Singapore into the misty sunset to forestall further Japanese landings on the north-east coast of Malaya.

Later that evening at 2253, Phillips received a signal from Singapore informing him that fighter cover would not be available when he reached the area. The Japanese had taken Kota Bharu airfield, thus depriving the fleet (code-named Force Z) of one of the basic conditions on which the successful execution of its mission depended. But the British force had the advantage of surprise and Phillips decided

to proceed. The following day driving rain and thick, low cloud shrouded Force Z from Japanese air reconnaissance. But at 1700 the weather suddenly cleared to reveal three aircraft observing the fleet and Phillips, who had planned to alter course for Singora at nightfall to shell Japanese transports, was now robbed even of the advantage of surprise.

Although he was unaware that his ships had also been sighted by the Japanese submarine I 65 south of Poulo Condore at 1340, he promptly decided to abandon the mission and turn back. But to confuse the enemy he ordered Force Z, with the exception of *Tenedos*, to continue north until nightfall before altering course south. The heavy guns of the fleet, it appeared, would not be brought to bear on the vulnerable Japanese transports. But at 2400 as the fleet steamed for Singapore, *Prince of Wales* received a message which read: 'Enemy reported landing Kuantan, latitude 03 degrees 50 north.' Force Z, its commander hoped, would still have an opportunity of disrupting the Japanese landings in Malaya and fearful of sacrificing the element of surprise he once more enjoyed, Phillips maintained strict radio silence, assuming incorrectly that fighter cover would be provided when he reached his new objective.

At 0220 the following day, 10th December, a Japanese submarine, I 58, sighted Force Z and between dawn and 0930, seventy-five aircraft took off from Saigon in pursuit of the British fleet which had arrived off Kuantan at 0800 to discover it had answered a false alarm. The detonation of a number of mines in the vicinity of the town by straying water buffaloes had apparently prompted Indian troops to pass the information to Singapore that a Japanese landing was taking place.

Disappointed, Admiral Phillips ordered his fleet back onto a north-easterly course and proceeded to search for a suspicious tug and barges sighted earlier. Half an hour later *Tenedos*, which Phillips had ordered to Singapore when Force Z was discovered by Japanese reconnaissance aircraft, radioed that she was under air attack. Increasing their speed to twenty-five knots the ships of Force Z assumed first degree readiness and raced for base. But a patrolling Japanese reconnaissance aircraft sighted them and put out a general call.

At 1107 aircraft of the Japanese XXII Air Flotilla, which had strayed almost within sight of Singapore in quest of Force Z and which had bombed *Tenedos*, were sighted and at 1119 precisely the high angle guns throughout the fleet began firing at the attackers. Under a barrage of bombs and torpedoes *Repulse* sank at 1233 and as the

*Above: Seven of Wake Island's twelve Grumman Wildcats lie destroyed after a Japanese bombing raid on 8th December 1941. Left: An American soldier gives a dying Japanese captive a drink during bitter fighting on the Bataan Peninsula in the Philippines, March 1942. American and Filipino forces had withdrawn into the peninsula on Luzon for a last ditch stand*

Keystone Press

*Survivors scrambling over the sides of* HMS Repulse *as she settles into the waters of the South China Sea after being bombed by Japanese aircraft off Malaya on 10th December 1941*

eleven Buffalo fighters charged with the protection of Force Z arrived at 1320 in response to a belated distress call from Captain W.G.Tennant, commander of *Repulse*, *Prince of Wales* rolled over ponderously to port and sank with Admiral Phillips still on the bridge.

The loss of the two ships with 840 men on board sealed the fate of Malaya and confirmed Japan's command of the Pacific and Indian Oceans for the loss of three aircraft. 'Over all this vast expanse of water Japan was supreme, and we everywhere were weak and naked,' wrote Churchill. On the day after the action, a Japanese aircraft dropped a large bouquet of flowers over the sea in honour of the men who had died.

### Wake spits back

There was no respite for the Allies. The exultant Japanese kept on hitting. But for two weeks the defenders of a lonely, treeless atoll in the central Pacific held a powerful invasion fleet at bay, subjecting the victory-flushed Japanese navy to its only defeat in the opening months of the war. Wake Island, annexed by the United States in 1899 and later developed as an aircraft staging post, belonged with Makin and Tarawa in the Gilbert Islands to a group of objectives Japan required if she was to secure the eastern boundary of her defence perimeter. On the outbreak of war, the island's occupants comprised seventy civilian employees of Pan American Airways, 1,146 civilians employed by contractors and a garrison of 449 marines, sixty-eight sailors, and five soldiers. Major James Devereux of the United States Marine Corps who effectively commanded the garrison had at his disposal six 5-inch coast defence guns, twelve 3-inch anti-aircraft guns, a number of machine-guns, besides twelve obsolete Grumman Wildcats of Marine Fighting Squadron 211 flown in from the *Enterprise* on 4th December. Not only did the island lack two-thirds of its garrison, it had no radar, fighter control centre, or fire control equipment. There were, moreover, no mines, no barbed wire, and no revetments for aircraft.

On 8th December, under cover of rain squalls, thirty-six Japanese bombers swept in over Wake and destroyed seven Wildcats on the ground. Air attacks continued on the following two days and on the 11th at 0500 the invasion forces composed of the light cruisers *Yubari*, *Tenryu*, and *Tatsuta* with six destroyers and accompanying vessels under the command of Rear-Admiral Sadamichi Kajioka steamed in, guns blazing to assault the island. Major Devereux held his fire. Contemptuous of the atoll's defences, Kajioka took his invasion fleet to within 4,500 yards of the shore. Suddenly, Devereux's 5-inch guns opened up and with their second salvo damaged the flagship *Yubari*. Within the first few minutes the island's 5-inch batteries sank the destroyer *Hayate* and damaged several other ships. Four of the five surviving Wildcats then took off to bomb and strafe the fleet, damaging the light cruisers *Tenryu* and *Tatsuta* and sinking the destroyer *Kisavagi*. It was one of the most humiliating reverses the Japanese navy had ever suffered and soon after 0700 Kajioka retreated to Kwajalein six hundred miles away to lick his wounds. Wake Island's few guns and aircraft had repulsed a powerful amphibious attack, sunk two destroyers, damaged several other vessels and inflicted some 700 fatalities on the invaders for the loss of two Wildcats.

Alarmed by this ignominious rebuff at Wake, Admiral Yamamoto, Commander-in-Chief of the Combined Fleet, ordered reinforcements to assemble for a second landing attempt and on 15th December Rear-Admiral Tamon Yamaguchi's II Carrier Division with the aircraft carriers *Soryu* and *Hiryu* escorted by four destroyers proceeded to a position north of the island. Accompanying the carrier force was Rear-Admiral Abe's VIII Cruiser Division with the heavy cruisers *Tone* and *Chikuma*. While the powerful invasion fleet assembled off Wake, the island was subjected to a series of attacks by land-based bombers and on the 21st aircraft from the carriers lent their weight to the bombardments. On the same day Kajioka again sailed from Kwajalein and before dawn on 23rd December, with no preliminary bombardment, substantially reinforced troops of the naval landing force began to pour ashore at points on which the American 5-inch guns could not be brought to bear. The only gun trained on the two antiquated destroyers, which had been beached with companies of the landing force, put fifteen shells into the nearest one, breaking its back. Without air support, its last two Wildcats having been shot down the previous day, the island's defences were pounded by aircraft and naval guns and at 0730, heavily outnumbered, the garrison surrendered. Fifty-two American servicemen, seventy civilians and 820 Japanese soldiers were killed during the bitterly contested landings, and 470 officers and men and 1,146 civilians were captured. The navy had vindicated itself for its initial failure to take the island and the gallant American defenders, despite their defeat, earned the admiration of the world.

### Singapore surrenders

Yet Wake might have been saved and a naval victory scored had Rear-Admiral Frank Fletcher's carrier-borne aircraft intervened while the Japanese invasion force was still disembarking equipment and supplies. Fletcher, who left Pearl Harbour for Wake on 17th December with a relief force which included the aircraft-carrier *Saratoga*, lost his chance of preventing the Japanese landings by pausing to refuel his destroyers. Although he could have caught the invasion fleet at a disadvantage he was ordered back to base for fear of risking his vessels in an encounter with those units detached from the Pearl Harbour Striking Force which were believed to contain two battleships.

While Wake defied the wrath of the Japanese navy, and American and Filipino troops were being driven into the Bataan Peninsula, the Japanese invasion of Malaya was proceeding swiftly. Its extent, once appreciated, spread demoralization among the confused British and Commonwealth forces. Without either command of the sea or air they fell back down the west coast of Malaya before Lieutenant-General Yamashita's XXV Army until they reeled into Singapore on 31st January. At 1810 on 15th February 1942, Lieutenant-General Arthur Percival,

*Japanese troops land on Corregidor Island to reduce the last bastion of defence in the Philippines, 5th May 1942*

GOC Malaya, surrendered the town to Yamashita in a room in the Ford factory at Bukit Timah. It was the greatest disaster inflicted on the British Empire since Cornwallis surrendered Yorktown in the American War of Independence, and Churchill termed the fall of what was considered to be an impregnable fortress, 'the worst disaster and largest capitulation in British history'.

In the Malayan campaign, lost by the failure to provide adequate defence in the north, British, Indian and Australian forces lost a total of 138,708 soldiers of whom more than 130,000 were taken prisoner. The Japanese casualties in the seventy-three day campaign were 3,507 dead and 6,150 wounded.

It had been General Percival's misfortune, as James Leasor has written in *Singapore, The Battle That Changed The World*, to 'direct an ill-equipped and wrongly-trained army in a hopeless campaign; to defend a country for whose defence pre-war politicians influenced and activated by blind, petty motivations and crass ignorance, by indifference on the part of the voters who had elected them, had neglected to pay the insurance premium.' The humiliation of Great Britain at the hands of a numerically inferior Asiatic army that rode on bicycles and lived on rice was to have fateful consequences for the Far East. The capture of Singapore, 'the bastion of the Empire' and the consequent premature collapse of Europe's hegemony in South East Asia after the war created a power vacuum which Communism struggled desperately to fill.

### Bataan Death March

The fall of Malaya and Singapore led directly to the collapse of the Dutch East Indies. Burma was overrun within weeks and the Japanese tide swept on to the Indian frontier. For the United States, the military outlook was as bleak and on 6th May, after a desperate defence of the Bataan Peninsula and Corregidor Island, which humiliated General Homma's XIV Army and delayed Japanese victory for four

months, American and Filipino resistance ended. Morale among the diseased, undernourished men had slumped when with the departure of General MacArthur, Commander-in-Chief United States Army Forces in the Far East, on 12th March, it became evident that reinforcements could not be expected. However, before handing over his command and leaving for Australia at Roosevelt's insistence, MacArthur promised the Filipinos that one day he would return to redeem the pledge of complete independence by 1946 which the American government had given eight years earlier. Just over a month after he left, the 64,000 Filipinos and 12,000 Americans who had surrendered on Bataan, began a fifty-five mile march from Mariveles to San Fernando. Because the Japanese had only expected to take some 25,000 prisoners, their arrangements for transporting and feeding the captives broke down. Between 7,000 and 10,000 men, including 2,330 Americans died of disease, starvation, exhaustion or brutality on what became known as the Bataan Death March.

It revealed the contempt the Japanese reserved for enemy soldiers who had not fallen in battle and foreshadowed the barbarous treatment Allied prisoners would receive at Japanese hands throughout the Pacific War.

Japan was everywhere victorious and the Allies everywhere in defeat or disarray. Yet prior to the outbreak of the Pacific War the strength of Japan's armed forces had been gravely underrated, ignored or even disbelieved. It was popularly supposed that, preoccupied with China, she was unable to mount military operations elsewhere. But although the allocation of forty divisions and 800 aircraft to the defence of Japan, Korea, Manchuria, and occupied China only left eleven divisions and some 700 first-line aircraft for the other theatres of war, Japan was able to reduce the whole vast south seas region. The myth of Japanese inferiority was promptly and extremely forcefully replaced by the myth of Japanese invincibility.

# The Russian Patriotic War

Novosti

Russia's war against Nazi Germany was in a very real sense a patriotic war. From the start it was a war which intimately involved the whole Russian people. Within six months of the opening strikes of Barbarossa, Hitler's legions stood within fifteen miles of the gates of Moscow and one-third of European Russia lay prostrate under Nazi domination. Of the twenty million Russians who lost their lives during the war a great many were civilians and prisoners-of-war who were either massacred in cold blood or who perished under the barbarity of Nazi forced labour. There could be no doubt that this was a war which, in Hitler's words, threatened 'Russia's very power to exist', and it was this power which the Russian people fought to preserve, not only in the front line but equally on the home front. The story of their loyalty in the face of overwhelming hardship is a story of true patriotism.

It is also the heroic picture painted by Soviet historians which, although true, is not the whole truth. A question naturally arises in the Western mind: were the Russian peoples, by fighting for Russia, also fighting for the Stalinist regime, a political system which had already proved itself to be a ruthless and despicable tyranny? To an extent they were, for Stalin had seen that the focus of their sentiments was Russia and by emphasizing Russia and patriotism rather than Lenin and Bolshevism, he succeeded in projecting himself as a *national* leader. But there was another side to the coin. Many Russians at first welcomed the Germans as liberators, collaboration was rife, and Party members often met unmerciful treatment from their own peasantry.

*Model of Nevsky Prospect in Leningrad during the 900-day siege. People collect water from a hydrant, lower windows are sandbagged, a tram stands derelict*

As Russia fought for survival in 1941-42, and millions of Russian lives hung in the balance, it was natural that Soviet leaders should clamour for a 'second front' in the West to ease the pressure on the Red Army. That it was quite impossible to organize a second front until 1944 meant that millions of British and American lives were saved which would otherwise have been lost. Churchill admitted this when he said that it was the Russians who 'tore the guts out of the German army', with all the losses that this entailed. But the lasting scar which the memory of the war has left on the Russian consciousness has led Soviet historians to discount the British and American contribution to the Russian war effort. Between October 1941 and March 1946 Great Britain delivered military equipment to the value of 308 million pounds. Between March 1941 and October 1945 the United States delivered goods worth over 11,000 million dollars. Since the Russians did not provide ships, the task of transporting the goods fell to the suppliers (which meant Great Britain almost single-handed until June 1942). It was a bitter task. Out of 811 ships in convoy through Arctic waters to north Russia between 1941 and 1945 a staggeringly large total of 100 were lost.

It is true that during Russia's hour of greatest need, from the summer of 1941 to the autumn of 1942, the volume of Anglo-American supplies was small compared with Soviet needs, but American production could not be increased immediately and British supplies were generous in comparison to her own war production, already strictly rationed among commanders-in-chief in many theatres. Later much larger supplies were given. Little gratitude was ever shown by the Russians for these, nor for the skill and endurance of the men who worked the Arctic convoys. But conversely the Western powers too often forget the incomparably greater losses of their war-time Communist ally: the twenty million Russian dead.
(Simon Rigge)

*Left: 1 'We will fight hard, even desperately – descendants of Suvorov, children of Chapayev'. Soviet poster recalling Russian martial heroes – Alexander Nevsky, the medieval prince and saint, Count Suvorov, the 18th-century hammer of the Turks, Chapayev, the Red Army commander during the Civil War – inspire the Red Army. 2 People of Leningrad digging defence works outside their city before its hideous ordeal by siege. 3 'Father and Child' by Ben Shahn, American artist born in Lithuania. Expatriate view of havoc wrought by Germans in eastern Europe. 4 A wall in Leningrad during the siege. The notice on the right says: 'Citizens! During shelling this side of the street is extremely dangerous' – because it was exposed to the German shells coming in from the south. 5 A row of T34 tanks built in 1942 by Young Communists from Khabarovsk in eastern Siberia. Right, above: Collective farmers taking corn to a reception centre for the Defence Fund. Below: Russian orphans in the ruins of their village*

The years preceding the war saw a rapid development of the Soviet economy. Under the third Five-Year Plan the country's national income increased from 96·3 milliard roubles in 1937 to 128 milliard in 1940. Also, the number of office and manual workers in the national economy increased from just under 11 million in 1928 to just over 30 million in 1940. This harmonious development of the Soviet Union's productive forces was disrupted by the war. Millions of men between the ages of 23 and 36 were torn from peaceful labour. The classes of 1905 to 1918 were called up, and large numbers of volunteers were enrolled in the People's Militia in Moscow, Leningrad, Kiev, and other cities.

By November 1941 the enemy forces had occupied territory on which, before the war, about forty per cent of the population of the Soviet Union were living. Some of these, ten million people in all, were evacuated to the rear areas in the summer and autumn of 1941, but the majority were unable to leave. More important to the Russian war effort was the fact that the territory occupied by the Nazis had previously produced a very high proportion of vital materials: 63% of all coal, 68% of all pig-iron, 58% of steel, and 60% of the total aluminium output. It was also vitally important for food supplies, producing 38% of grain, 84% of sugar, 38% of beef and dairy cattle, and 60% of pigs.

Soviet transport workers did a tremendous job in moving industrial enterprises to new areas, mainly the Urals, Siberia, and the Central Asian republics. Between July and November 1941, over 1,500 industrial enterprises were evacuated by rail, many of them large-scale war factories, and 15 million truck loads of freight. Evacuation operations went on round the clock. Often workers, technicians, and engineers dismantled factories under enemy gunfire and air attack. After journeys of incredible hardship they arrived in the interior to find that there were no industrial complexes capable of supplying equipment, no houses for the workers, no adequate supplies of fuel and power. Frequently they had to work under open skies, in rain, snow, and frost, and live in tents and dug-outs. At the height of the Siberian winter such conditions taxed human endurance to the limit. But the technical personnel overcame these difficulties and rapidly got their enterprises into production again. In spite of these superhuman efforts war production was unable to meet the needs of the front for some time after the outbreak of war. In the second half of 1941 the economy went through a very difficult phase. The gross national product dropped by more than half. In November and December the USSR received not a single ton of coal from the Donets and Moscow basins, the output of rolled iron and steel was reduced to one third, and the production of ball-bearings, indispensable for the production of aeroplanes, tanks, and guns, fell to less than a twentieth. Production of non-ferrous metals fell 430 times. But the decline in industrial production was finally halted in December 1941 and in

March 1942 the economy began to show signs of improvement: in the unoccupied eastern parts of the country alone the output of war material in that month reached the level of production at the start of the war over the whole of the USSR. Broadly speaking, the economy was established on a war basis within twelve months after the German invasion.

One of the most complicated problems that had to be solved during the war years was the organization of labour. In accordance with a decree of June 1941, the managers of industry, transport, agriculture, and the distributive trades were given the right to compel manual and office workers to work overtime for between one and three hours a day. At the same time all holidays were abolished, financial compensation being provided in their stead. In the fight to produce, workers were transferred between different

industrial areas. Yet there was widespread enthusiasm among women and young people to take the places in industry which had been left empty by the men when they joined the army. In the second half of 1941 150,000 students entered industry, together with more than 500,000 housewives and 360,000 schoolchildren.

Yet even this great patriotic movement could not close the manpower gap. Other methods had to be used, and the Soviet people had to sacrifice a great deal during this period. All able-bodied people not engaged in social production were mobilized: manual and office workers were called up for regular work in the war industries and enterprises associated with them, universal labour service was introduced, the right to leave one's job was abolished, and in transport, military discipline was established.

By the end of 1942 the country had a

Imperial War Museum

*Above:* An RAF Hurricane fighter at Murmansk in northern Russia. Great Britain sent two Hurricane squadrons to Russia in September 1941. *Left:* German prisoners-of-war in Moscow 1944

well-organized and rapidly growing war economy. Enterprises which had previously produced goods to satisfy the people's needs had begun to turn out weapons, munitions, and military equipment. The factories evacuated from the west were producing at full blast and new enterprises had been brought into operation in the Urals, Siberia, and Central Asia.

The peasantry toiled staunchly alongside the industrial proletariat, but the loss of important agricultural areas in the west had an almost catastrophic effect on Russian food supplies. The number of able-bodied farm workers was greatly reduced since most of the men in the villages were called up and hundreds of thousands of collective farmers of both sexes were mobilized for factory work. For those that remained in the country life was hard. A considerable proportion of tractors, cars, and horses were handed over to the army and those vehicles which remained became badly worn out, often to the extent of being unusable. Spare parts were in short supply and it was hard to obtain fuel. As a result farm work and haulage were carried out by manual effort. Since the number of able-bodied men on the collective farms at the end of 1943 was less than a third of the number at the start of hostilities, almost the entire burden of agricultural production had to be carried by women and children. Yet in spite of enormous efforts to ensure adequate supplies of food, crop yields declined. Some help came from the USA, but the total amount of these supplies was very small.

### Hardship and sacrifice
Naturally the army had first priority. In order to make sure that its several million men were provided with all necessities, the entire system of supply to the civilian population was reorganized. In July 1941 rationing was introduced in Moscow and Leningrad and some surrounding areas. It covered bread, barley, sugar, confectionery, butter, meat, and fish and also soap, footwear, textiles, and all sewn or knitted articles. Outside the metropolitan areas rationing was introduced at different periods and by 10th November it was universal in all towns and workers' housing estates. Those inhabitants of rural localities who were not directly engaged in agriculture were supplied with bread according to standards laid down by the local soviets. In general the bread ration fell into two categories: workers in coal-mining, the iron and steel industry, and other heavy industries received between 800 grammes and 1·2 kilogrammes a day; engineering and technical staff received 500 grammes and office workers 400—450 grammes a day. Other foodstuffs were rationed monthly.

Although a large part of the country's population subsisted mainly on the rationing system, it was possible to buy extra food on the collective farm markets, but inevitably prices rose as a result of the war. In 1943 they were thirteen times higher than they had been before the war. Individual kitchen gardens and the cultivation of waste land by factories greatly helped the supply of food to the urban population. Nearly every urban family worked a small allotment of land, growing potatoes, cabbages, onions, and other vegetables. Although these measures considerably increased the quantity of provisions available, the personal consumption of Soviet citizens declined by between 35% and 40% during the war years. Although rationing was not applied to the collective farms, there was great hardship in the country. In 1944 and 1945 the collective farmers consumed two and a half times as many potatoes as before the war but received only 300 grammes of bread a day. Manufactured food products disappeared from the village tables, and there was no sugar.

Manufactured goods for mass consumption were also in short supply during the war years. What goods there were found their way into the hands of the peasants as 'payment' for state procurement levies of agricultural produce, and were made available to the workers according to a rationing system. Secondhand stalls selling old clothes and footwear were set up in town markets. Quilted jackets and caps with ear-flaps came to be worn by many and scarves became the principal headgear for women in both town and country. Nobody worried about fashion in those years—people wore whatever they could get; they were not ashamed of patches, and the peasants in many places went back to making their own clothes. In Moscow, department stores sold oddments such as barometers and curling-tongs, but nothing useful. For the most part, shop windows were sand-bagged or else displayed cardboard hams, cheeses, and sausages, all covered with dust. Chemists' shops were also nearly empty and dentists were reduced to pulling teeth without anaesthetics. Owners of cigarettes would charge passers-by two roubles for a puff—and, amazing as it may sound, they were able to do good business.

### The nation unbroken
As they retreated westwards the German armies systematically laid waste the territory they had occupied, adding to the destruction already brought about by the fighting. Perhaps a quarter of all Soviet property was destroyed in the war—17,000 towns, 70,000 villages, 31,000 factories, 84,000 schools, 40,000 miles of railway track, as well as nearly forty-five million horses, head of cattle, and pigs. Twenty-five million people were left homeless. They lived in huts, cellars, and dugouts—pits dug in the earth and roofed over with branches and earth, and quite unfit for human habitation.

The task of repairing these losses now fell to the Soviet people. Factories rose from the ruins and flooded mines were dried out, ruined power stations were restored and new ones built. The iron and steel works of the south returned to life. Gradually the general condition of the country improved and economic life picked up. The moral and political unity of the multi-national nation remained unbroken. The Soviet Union emerged from the war unweakened by the hard struggle against Nazi Germany—indeed it had become still mightier. The victory which had been achieved in the Great Patriotic War was the result of the efforts and sacrifices of the whole Soviet people.

*(A. V. Karasev, translation)*

# Alamein

General Sir Claude Auchinleck, Commander-in-Chief Middle East Land Forces, took over personal command of 8th Army from Lieutenant-General Neil Ritchie on 25th June 1942. There is little doubt that Auchinleck had been ill-judged in February 1942 when he confirmed Ritchie in what had been a temporary command, despite evidence and advice that Ritchie lacked the experience and capacity to command an army. Equally it would have been well if Auchinleck, as Prime Minister Churchill had urged, had taken personal charge of the Gazala battles at an early stage. However, the Western Desert was only one among the commander-in-chief's several cares. It was not so simple a matter to go off and look after a single front. For although the Middle East Command had shed East Africa since Wavell's time, it was still responsible for support of Turkey, a neutral state, and for the defence of the Persian Gulf oilfields from attack from the north, through the Caucasus. Auchinleck had lived with this latter danger ever since the German invasion of Russia had reached the Don the previous autumn.

Auchinleck, therefore, unlike his predecessors or his successor, bore the double burden of an army commander and of a theatre commander-in-chief.

For this reason it was Auchinleck's belief as commander-in-chief that 8th Army must not be exposed to the risk of a final defeat, but must at all cost be kept in being, in order to continue to defend the Gulf oil from Rommel. Whereas Ritchie had planned a do-or-die battle at Mersa Matruh, Auchinleck wished to retreat to El Alamein which would give him a little time to reorganize his forces and plan his own battle instead of fighting Ritchie's. But Rommel struck the day after Auchinleck assumed personal command. The Battle of Mersa Matruh (26th-28th June 1942), fought in decayed defences according to Ritchie's deployment, marked the climax of German moral domination in the desert. With handfuls of exhausted troops Rommel bluffed the British (including fresh, strong formations) into thinking they were broken through, surrounded, and beaten, while poor communications virtually cut Auchinleck off from the battle. As soon as he saw the compromised battle was lost, Auchinleck ordered the army back to Alamein. Both armies, units all mixed up, raced each other for the forty-mile-wide neck between the sea at Alamein and the impassable Qattara Depression. Alexandria lay only sixty miles beyond.

Although 8th Army narrowly won the race, the British still faced the possibility, in Auchinleck's words, of 'complete catastrophe'. 'No one,' he wrote later, 'least of all I, could say whether the Army could be rallied and re-formed soon enough to hold Rommel and save Egypt.' Auchinleck thus faced the greatest test of a general – the rallying of a beaten army and the redemption of a lost battle. Behind him in Egypt there was panic and defeatism. He told his soldiers: 'The enemy is stretching to his limit and thinks we are a broken army . . . He hopes to take Egypt by bluff. Show him where he gets off.'

In fact this was an accurate military appreciation. By failing to halt after Tobruk to allow Malta to be attacked, as agreed, Rommel had taken an immense gamble. For unless he managed to break through to the Delta very quickly, his army would be increasingly starved of supplies, reinforcements, and fuel, owing both to British naval action based on Malta and the length of his own communications. On 1st July, three days after Matruh, Rommel attacked 8th Army at Alamein.

The essential unity of all the fighting at Alamein from July to November 1942 has been obscured by the changes in the British command that took place in mid-August, when General Sir Harold Alexander replaced Auchinleck as commander-in-chief and Lieutenant-General B.L.Montgomery became the new 8th Army commander. It was one extended battle with pauses between the actions. It opened with Rommel's desperate attempts to shoulder his way past Auchinleck, his failure, and the failure in turn of Auchinleck to force him into retreat. This was the First Battle of Alamein (1st-26th July 1942). There followed a period of stalemate broken only by an unrealistic and vain second attempt by Rommel to break through: the Battle of Alam Halfa (31st August-3rd September). Finally came the British counter-stroke with massive fresh forces that swept Rommel out of Egypt. This was Montgomery's victory in the Second Battle of Alamein (23rd October-4th November 1942).

The commanding natural features of the Alamein battlefield (although so slight as to be discernible only to the military eye) were two east-west ridges, the Ruweisat Ridge, and farther to the south and well to the east, the Alam Halfa Ridge. These were the tactical keys to the neck of land between the sea and the Qattara Depression. At no time in the Alamein battles was this neck solidly held by the British. In July Auchinleck had lacked the troops,

and later he (and after him Montgomery) preferred to form a south-facing left wing that might entice Rommel into a trap.

Auchinleck's army at First Alamein was made up of survivors of the Gazala battles like 1st South African and 50th Divisions, survivors of Matruh like the New Zealand divisions and 9th Indian Brigade, together with fresh troops like 18th Indian Brigade from Iraq. Auchinleck was weakest in armour, for although 1st Armoured Division possessed 150 tanks, only two squadrons were Grants, and the division's skill, cohesion, and morale were not high. Nevertheless 8th Army heavily outnumbered Panzer Army Africa, now reduced to 60 German and 30 Italian tanks, some 5,000 Germans, and a similar number of Italians.

As a personal adviser and acting chief of staff in the field Auchinleck had brought with him from Cairo Major-General E.Dorman-Smith. He was not a member of the British army 'establishment' who had muddled the Gazala battles, but a man fertile in unorthodox ideas. These were reflected in some of the reforms Auchinleck attempted to carry out in the army's organization and tactics during First Alamein. Auchinleck believed that the standard British infantry division was too large, cumbersome, and lacking in hitting power for mobile desert warfare. He therefore extemporized brigade-groups or smaller 'battle-groups' on the German pattern – trucked infantry escorting guns. Instead of manning the static defences of the Alamein perimeter, he kept the brigade-groups of 1st South African Division mobile in the open desert to the south. After the first day's fighting he also evacuated two 'boxes' in the centre and extreme south of the Alamein neck, in order to keep his army mobile and concentrated. (Boxes were strongpoints surrounded by wire and minefields.) At the same time the heavy and medium artillery was transferred from corps to army command to provide massed firepower. Auchinleck also tried to diminish the sluggishness and rigidity of the stratified British command organization by demanding the energetic local initiative and flexibility evinced by the enemy. The course of the First Battle of Alamein was to show that orders or instructions in this spirit failed to have much effect on minds habituated to another military tradition.

*Right: A German Hanomag half-track of the Afrika Korps rolls across the soft sand of the desert. The number plate prefix means 'Wehrmacht Heer', indicating an Army vehicle*

Although First Alamein was a highly complicated and shifting battle on the ground, it was essentially a struggle of will between the opposing generals. The struggle lasted for the first two weeks of July and ended with Rommel's surrender of the initiative to Auchinleck.

On 1st July Rommel tried to repeat his triumph at Mersa Matruh with a similar plan and similar audacity. He proposed to drive through Auchinleck's centre and turn outwards in a double envelopment of Auchinleck's wings. Both envelopments stuck under heavy flanking-fire from British battle-groups. On 2nd July Rommel reduced his plan to a single envelopment of the Alamein perimeter. This too failed. On 3rd July he tried again in the centre, made some progress, and stuck again, despite his own personal leadership of the attack. On 2nd and again on 5th July Auchinleck counter-attacked elsewhere, forcing Rommel to re-group, but 8th Army proved a slow and hesitant instrument. However, Rommel was forced to deploy Italian infantry for the first time since he attacked at Gazala. Nevertheless he decided to attack again on 10th July, after a brief respite, and try to break straight through eastwards into the Delta. Instead, on 9th July Auchinleck launched a major-counterstroke in the coastal sector: a bombardment that reminded some Germans of the Western Front in 1917, followed by an assault by Auchinleck's personal reserve, the fresh 9th Australian Division. The Italians collapsed, the hill of Tel el Eisa fell, and Rommel had to abandon his own offensive in order to succour the Italians.

It was Auchinleck's plan (suggested by Dorman-Smith) to go for the Italians in one sector after another, thus forcing Rommel to run to and fro to their aid with his Germans. It worked brilliantly.

Between 9th and 16th July six such attacks on Italians were launched, and Rommel only prevented the total collapse of his front by using his last German reserves.

On 21st-22nd July and 26th July Auchinleck attempted to turn Rommel's defeat into his destruction or retreat. These counter-strokes were a total failure. The cause lay yet again in the gulf of misunderstanding between British armour and infantry, which were incapable of the supple and intimate co-operation of the German troops who were trained together on common lines. A further cause lay in a breakdown of radio communication. Either the infantry was massacred by German armour because the British armour failed to come up in time; or the armour was massacred trying to 'charge' German defences that should have been carefully assaulted in conjunction with infantry.

Although Rommel had not been forced to retreat, First Alamein saved Egypt and the Middle East. It was one of the decisive battles of the Second World War.

It was Dorman-Smith's prediction, expressed in a strategic appreciation of 27th July accepted by Auchinleck, that Rommel even after reinforcement would not be strong enough to launch another offensive except as a gamble. Auchinleck therefore looked ahead to a set-piece British offensive in strength some time in September.

Meanwhile the British and American governments had taken a major strategical decision. Instead of an invasion of France in 1942, deemed a hopeless undertaking with the available troops and landing craft, the Allies were to invade French North Africa in the autumn, and, in conjunction with 8th Army, clear the entire North African coast. This operation would both re-open the Mediterranean to through sea traffic and appease Stalin with some kind

of a 'second front' at not too great a risk of failure. The decision was made on 24th July, after Auchinleck had halted Rommel's offensive. It entirely changed the context of the war in the desert, for occupation of Algeria and Tunisia would directly threaten Rommel's own base at Tripoli and squeeze him between two armies.

### Churchill visits the front

On 3rd August Churchill and the Chief of the Imperial General Staff arrived in Cairo. On 6th August, after visiting Auchinleck at 8th Army Headquarters, Churchill decided to replace Auchinleck and his immediate staff. General Sir Harold Alexander was appointed commander-in-chief, and Major-General W.H.E. Gott, a corps commander with a legendary though not altogether justified reputation, was appointed to command 8th Army. In these decisions personal political considerations undoubtedly played a large part. There was mounting public criticism of Churchill's leadership in Great Britain, and by-elections had gone heavily against the government. There had been a long run of disaster: the loss of the *Prince of Wales* and *Repulse*, the fall of Singapore, the loss of Burma, the loss of Tobruk, the Gazala battles. Churchill needed a resounding victory as quickly as possible to preserve his own position. There can be little doubt that Auchinleck therefore sealed his fate when he stubbornly refused to promise to attack before mid-September, arguing that this was the earliest that 8th Army could be re-organized and re-trained, and the new equipment run in.

Churchill instructed the new Comman-

*Wreckage of a German Junkers 52.*
*Rommel's supply planes were shot down*
*in droves crossing the Mediterranean*

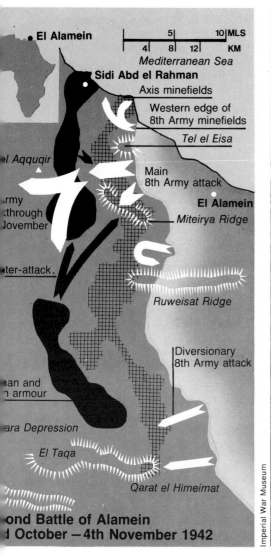

Second Battle of Alamein, 23rd October-
4th November 1942. It marked the beginning
of the Allied offensive to clear North
Africa of Axis troops. **Left:** Map showing
8th Army attack and breakthrough.
**Above:** Australians advance behind a
smoke screen during final phase of the
battle, 3rd November

der-in-Chief Middle East, General Alexander, that his primary task was 'to take and destroy the German-Italian army commanded by Field-Marshal Rommel.' The commander-in-chief was relieved of anxiety about the German threat from the Caucasus (the German offensive in Russia poured across the Don into the Caucasus on 24th July, in the last days of First Alamein), for Iraq and Persia were transferred to a new command. Thus in the end all the vast existing resources of the Middle East base, and the immense reinforcements and supplies now flowing into Egypt had come to be devoted to the single purpose of fighting four somewhat neglected German divisions and their Italian allies. It was a measure of the success of the German diversion in North Africa, and also of the usefulness of the British Empire's contribution to ground fighting in the third year of the war. The Red Army was currently engaging some 180 German divisions, including twenty Panzer divisions.

Alexander's sole responsibility was therefore to support his 8th Army commander. On 7th August, however, Gott was killed, when the aircraft flying him to Cairo was shot down, and Lieutenant-General Montgomery was appointed commander of 8th Army. Montgomery was a man of legendary eccentricity and ruthless professionalism. He had not commanded in the field since 1940, had never commanded large masses

of armour in battle, and was new to the desert. He compensated for these initial handicaps by a brilliant clarity of mind, iron willpower, and a bleak realism about the potentialities of individuals and units alike. He had an unrivalled power of piercing complex matters to the underlying simplicities. In August 1942 he enjoyed the advantage of the new broom, and he swept very clean indeed.

His first task was to meet the renewed German offensive which was expected soon. His plan, like that evolved by Auchinleck and Dorman-Smith, depended on forming a south-facing left wing along the Alam Halfa Ridge, and his main dispositions followed the existing defences and minefields. However, he brought up 44th Division, now available, to strengthen Alam Halfa. Although his general plan so closely resembled Auchinleck's, his style of fighting the battle was very different. He accurately took the measure of 8th Army's capabilities and enforced his own direct control right down to division level. It would be in his own words 'an army battle'. There would be no loose fighting, but a tight defence of tactical ground.

Rommel launched his offensive on 31st August 1942. It was, as Dorman-Smith had predicted in July, a gamble without much chance. Rommel had 203 tanks against 767 British; he himself and several senior officers were sick; and his army was so

short of fuel that it had to make a tight turn up to the Alam Halfa Ridge instead of outflanking it to the east. After four days of vain effort to pierce the British defences while under violent air attack he slowly withdrew. An attempt by the New Zealand Division to endanger his retreat broke down in the usual 8th Army muddles and misunderstandings. Except for this failure Montgomery's first battle had been entirely successful. He was free to continue preparing his own offensive.

Alexander like Auchinleck was strongly pressed by the Prime Minister for an early offensive. He and Montgomery, with the advantage of being new men who could not be sacked, also refused. They, like Auchinleck, realized that an immense amount of training and preparation was needed before 8th Army would be fit to attack. In fact the Second Battle of Alamein opened on 23rd October, and even then 8th Army was by no means up to German standards.

The chronic problem lay in the inability of the British armour and infantry to work closely together. It originated in peacetime, when the British failed to evolve a coherent doctrine of tank warfare, but instead divided ground war into two separate compartments—the infantry battle of positions, and the (almost) all-tank mobile battle. Just before his departure Auchinleck had proposed to re-model the whole 8th Army into German-style mixed tank-infantry divisions. Co-operation would be secured under a single divisional command. Montgomery and his advisers instead decided to form a special wholly armoured corps (10th) in addition to the existing 30th and 13th Corps, charged with fighting a tank battle and then exploiting in pursuit. Thus co-ordination of armour and infantry would not now be secured by divisional commanders, or corps commanders as hitherto, but by the army commander himself. The course of Second Alamein was to show that Montgomery also failed even by this scheme to solve the problem of armour and infantry.

### Second Battle of Alamein

In planning his offensive Montgomery faced what was for the desert a novel problem. Rommel had created a continuous defence system across the forty-mile-wide neck between the sea and the Qattara Depression. It was of the standard German pattern dating back to 1917—a maze of strongpoints and switchlines, protected by belts of wire, in minefields some $2\frac{1}{2}$ to $4\frac{1}{2}$ miles deep, and garrisoned by intermingled German and Italian infantry. Close behind lay the Panzer divisions. To this Western Front problem Montgomery produced a Western Front answer—a deliberate infantry attack under cover of a massive bombardment to drive a gap right through both the forward and main battle zones of the enemy defence system. The 10th Corps (armour) would then pass through this gap on to the enemy communications and fight and defeat the Panzer divisions. Montgomery recognized however that the skill and training of 8th Army was such that any 'mixing it' with the Panzer Army in the open would be risky. He therefore altered his plan to make it even more deliberate and methodical. The armour would merely defend the gap made in the enemy defences against counter-strokes, while behind its shield the defence system and its infantry garrison would be 'crumbled' away piecemeal. This Montgomery hoped would force the Panzer divisions to attack to try to save the infantry and expose themselves to defeat by British tanks and anti-tank guns fighting defensively.

For the battle Montgomery fielded 1,029 tanks against 496 (220 German); 1,451 anti-tank guns against 550 German and 300 Italian; 908 field and medium guns against 200 German and 300 Italian (plus 18 heavy howitzers); 85 infantry battalions against 31 German and 40 Italian. The overall odds were about two to one: 195,000 men against just over 100,000. For the first time the British anti-tank artillery was principally composed of powerful six-pounders, while the armour included 252 American Shermans, tanks at last really the equal of German equipment. The

1

3

Imperial War Museum

Search Ltd.

British enjoyed complete air superiority.

The Second Battle of Alamein fell into three phases. During 23rd-25th October the original plan of breaking clean through the German left centre failed. The infantry assault, instead of piercing the German defence system in one bound as ordered, spent its force in the German forward zone and stalled in the battle zone. Montgomery ordered 10th Corps (armour) to force its own breakthrough, then modified his order to one armoured regiment; but the armour too became bogged down in the German defences. The super-imposition of two corps (10th and 30th) on the same sector caused much confusion. In the second phase of the battle (26th-31st October) Montgomery re-made his plan of operations and got a stalled offensive on the move again by sheer force of will. In this phase divisional attacks 'crumbled' the Axis defences away, while Rommel's counter-strokes (he had returned from a hospital bed in Austria to take command) foundered under air attack and anti-tank fire. In the third phase (1st-4th November) Montgomery (who had patiently re-created a reserve) launched a second massive breakthrough attempt. After fierce fighting and heavy loss the British this time succeeded. An order from Hitler to stand fast delayed the Axis retreat for twenty-four hours, and then the Panzer Army streamed west in defeat.

Second Alamein, like the battles of 1917, had turned on the size of reserves available to both sides. Although the Panzer Army had consistently inflicted a higher rate of loss on the British throughout the battle (the British lost more tanks than the original total German strength), the British superiority in resources proved just too great. Yet it had been a near-run battle for the exhaustion and confusion of 8th Army prevented immediate and effective pursuit.

Nevertheless the Panzer Army had been shattered: most of the Italian infantry were captured (some 26,000) and only 36 German tanks remained in action.

Because of the late pursuit, the British failed to cut off and destroy the remnants of Rommel's army. There followed a long pursuit and retreat back to Rommel's old bolt-hole of El Agheila characterized by bluff on Rommel's part and caution on Montgomery's — perhaps understandable in view of Rommel's reputation.

Meanwhile the Anglo-American landings in North Africa (Operation Torch) had taken place on 8th November. 'This,' wrote Rommel, 'spelt the end of the army in Africa.'

*Left: 1 Montgomery, wearing Australian hat, discusses military situation with officers of 22nd Armoured Brigade in August 1942, soon after taking command of 8th Army. 2 Painting by British war artist Anthony Gross of desert casualties. 3 A barbed-wire fence is lifted to enable Rommel (striding ahead) to pass through to inspect units of the Afrika Korps. Rommel acquired a legendary reputation extending far beyond North Africa, among Germans and Allies alike*

Imperial War Museum

# Stalingrad

It has often been said that Stalingrad was the decisive battle, and the turning point, of the eastern campaign. And indeed a glance at the map, with some hindsight of the German plans for the summer of 1942, would seem to make this the obvious site. Yet the irony is that neither side intended, or foresaw, that the fight to the death should be there.

At the beginning of 1942 both the German Armed Forces High Command (OKW) and the Stavka (the Supreme Command of the Red Army) projected planning for the summer that grossly over-estimated their own capabilities. In spite of the punishment they had sustained during the Soviet winter offensives of 1941 the Germans were confident that they could master the Red Army when the weather no longer impeded their mobility. And indeed there was some substance in this, for the terrible battles of the deep winter had been fought by a quite small proportion of the German strength which the extreme temperatures had isolated from manoeuvre or relief. More than sixty-five per cent of the infantry had never been engaged in the winter fighting, and had spent the winter in training and re-equipment.

At the nadir of German fortunes there had been voices in the German Army High Command (OKH) which had favoured retreat to the line of the Dnieper and a sus-

*Russians contest a few yards of rubble in the shattered streets of Stalingrad*

pension of offensive operations for a whole twelve-month period. But with the milder weather this caution evaporated (helped, no doubt, by the wholesale dismissals which Hitler had implemented in the new year) and planning proceeded apace for the summer campaign.

In fact it was the Red Army which got off the line first, staging three separate offensives immediately after the spring thaw. The Soviet intention was to relieve Leningrad and Sebastopol, and to recapture Kharkov—objectives more ambitious even than those of mid-winter, and set, moreover, in a context of German recovery and Russian exhaustion. In the result all three failed, and with crippling casualties. The Kharkov offensive in particular had most serious consequences as it ran head-on into a strong enemy concentration deployed to eliminate the Lozovaya salient, which had been established by the Red Army in January. The Russians lost over 600 tanks and in this critical area, where the Germans had decided to concentrate their summer offensive, the ratio of armour swung dramatically from five to one in the Russian favour to nearly ten to one against them.

For the Germans then, an initial domination of the battlefield was a certainty. How they would exploit this was less definite. At least three separate operational plans existed. The most conservative, naturally, was that formulated by the OKH staff, which envisaged advancing as far east as was necessary to safeguard the mineral resources of the Donets Basin. Stalingrad was suggested as a final objective but with the escape clause that if its seizure was not possible it would be enough to 'expose it to our heavy fire, so that it loses its importance as a centre of communications'. The OKW toyed with two schemes; the first anticipated swallowing Stalingrad in the opening weeks, wheeling north up the left bank of the Volga and outflanking Moscow; the second, only slightly less grandiose, also presumed the city's early fall followed by its tenure as a 'blocking point' to cover a *southward* wheel into the Caucasus where the Soviet oilfields lay. General von Kleist, commanding I Panzer Group, had been personally told by Hitler as early as April that '. . . I and my Panzers were to be the instruments whereby the Reich would be assured of its oil supplies in perpetuity. Stalingrad was no more than a name on the map to us.'

### The southern offensive

Army Group South, commanded by Field-Marshal von Bock, launched its attack on 28th June. Three armies split the Russian front into fragments on either side of Kursk, and Hoth's eleven Panzer divisions fanned out across hundreds of miles of open rolling corn and steppe grass, towards Voronezh and the Don. Two days later the southern half of the army group went over to the attack below Kharkov, and Kleist took I Panzer Group across the Donets.

The Russians were outnumbered and outgunned from the start, and their shortage of armour made it difficult to mount even local counter-attacks. With each day the Russian disorder multiplied, their command structure degenerating into independent combat at divisional, then at brigade, finally at regimental level. Without even the protection of mass, which had characterized the Red Army's deployment in the Ukraine in 1941, or of swamp and forest, which had allowed small groups to delay the enemy in the battle of Moscow, these formations were at the German's mercy. Polarizing around the meagre cover of some shallow ravine or the wooden hutments of a *kolkhoz*, they fought out their last battle under a deluge of firepower against which they could oppose little save their own bravery. '. . . quite different from last year [wrote a sergeant in III Panzer Division]. It's more like Poland. The Russians aren't nearly so thick on the ground. They fire their guns like madmen, but they don't hurt us.'

Within a fortnight the Soviet command structure had disintegrated and on 12th July the Stavka promulgated a new 'Stalingrad front'. The title of this force (front was roughly equivalent administratively, though not necessarily in strength, to a German army group) showed that the Stavka, at least, appreciated where they must make their stand, and it was here that they were now directing their last reserves, which had been concentrated around Moscow. General Chuykov, who was to emerge as one of the vital personalities who inspired and directed the battle of Stalingrad, brought his reserve army of four infantry divisions, two motorized and two armoured brigades from Tula, a distance of 700 miles south-east. On his arrival Chuykov was given instructions so vague as to convince him that 'front HQ obviously possessed extremely limited information about the enemy, who was mentioned only in general terms'.

Chuykov has described how on his first day he was on a personal reconnaissance: 'I came across two divisional staffs . . . they consisted of a number of officers travelling in some three to five trucks filled to overflowing with cans of fuel. When I asked them where the Germans were, and where they were going, they could not give me a sensible reply. It was clear that to restore to these men the faith they had lost in their own powers and to improve the fighting quality of the retreating units would not be easy.'

This was the moment which offered the Germans the best prospect of 'swallowing' Stalingrad as postulated in the wide outflanking plans of the OKW. In fact the Russian troops, though thrown into battle piecemeal as they arrived, proved just adequate to slow the German advance guard, now outrunning its supplies after an advance of 300 miles in three weeks. It took Paulus's VI Army five days to clear the Don bend, and he did not have the strength to eliminate every Soviet position in the loop of the west bank—an omission which was to have catastrophic consequences in November.

Stalingrad now began to exercise its magnetism over the whole of Army Group B (the northern section of Army Group South) and up along the chain of command to the Führer himself who moved his headquarters from Rastenburg to Vinnitsa (120 miles south-west of Kiev) on 25th August, where it remained until the end of the year. The Germans were committing themselves to the one kind of battle where their adversary held the advantage, forsaking their own enormous superiorities in firepower and mobility for a mincing machine of close combat. Hoth's Panzers were swung north, out of the steppe into the brick and concrete of the Stalingrad suburbs, and for nearly four months the city was wracked by continuous hand-to-hand fighting.

The nearest historical parallel is with the Battle of Verdun in 1916. But there are significant differences. At Verdun the contestants rarely saw one another face to face; they were battered to death by high explosives or cut down at long range by machine-gun fire. At Stalingrad each separate battle resolved itself into a combat between individuals. Soldiers would jeer and curse at their enemy across the street; often they could hear his breathing in the next room while they reloaded; hand-to-hand duels were finished in the dark twilight of smoke and brick dust with knives and pickaxes, with clubs of rubble and twisted steel. General Doerr has described how 'the time for conducting large-scale operations was gone for ever; from the wide expanses of steppe-land the war moved into the jagged gullies of the Volga hills with their copses and ravines, into the factory area of Stalingrad, spread out over uneven, pitted, rugged country, covered with iron, concrete, and stone buildings. The mile, as a measure of distance, was replaced by the yard. GHQ's map was the map of the city. 'For every house, workshop, water tower, railway embankment, wall, cellar, and every pile of ruins, a bitter battle was waged, without equal even in the First World War with its vast expenditure of munitions. The distance between the enemy's army and ours was as small as it could possibly be. Despite the concentrated activity of aircraft and artillery, it was impossible to break out of the area of close fighting. The Russians surpassed the Germans in their use of the terrain and in camouflage and were more experienced in barricade warfare for individual buildings.'

In the first week of September Hoth's tanks, operating in the southern sector, broke through to the Volga bank and split the Russians into two. A critical four-day period followed, with the defenders of the northern half outnumbered three to one, and the Germans got close enough to bring the central landing stage (where the Volga ferries landed supplies for the defending forces) under machine-gun fire. But the sheer tenacity and individual courage of the Russian foot-soldier was the deciding factor. General Paulus's offensive subsided, fought to a standstill.

It was now plain that a major strategic revision was called for. But the Germans were prisoners of their own propaganda, which had steadily been building up the importance of the battle. Any misgivings that Paulus himself may have felt were quietened by a visit from General Schmundt, formerly Hitler's adjutant and now chief of the Army Personnel Office. Schmundt strongly hinted that Paulus was being considered for 'a most senior post' (in fact the succession to Jodl as Chief of the Armed Forces Operational Staff), but that the Führer was most anxious first to see the Stalingrad operations 'brought to a successful conclusion'. Paulus's awareness of his own interests was, at all times, keener than his tactical abilities. This time he decided to strike head-on at his enemy's strongest point—the three giant edifices of the Tractor Factory, the Barrikady (Barricades) ordnance plant, and the Krasny Oktyabr (Red October) steel works, which lay in the northern half of the city, ranged one after another a few hundred yards from the Volga bank. This was to be the fiercest, and the longest, of the five battles which were fought in the ruined town, and that which finally drained the offensive strength from the German armies in south Russia. It started on 4th October and raged for nearly three weeks. Paulus had been reinforced by a variety of different specialist troops, including police battalions and engineers skilled in street fighting and demolition work. But the Russians, though still heavily outnumbered, remained their masters in the technique of house-to-house fighting. They had perfected the use of 'shock groups', small bodies of mixed arms—light and heavy machine-gunners, tommy gunners, and grenadiers usually with anti-tank guns, who gave one another support in lightning counter-attacks; and they had developed the creation of 'killing zones', houses and squares heavily mined, to which the defenders knew all the approach routes, where the German advance could be canalized.

Slowly and at a tremendous price the Germans inched their way into the great buildings, across factory floors; around and over the inert machinery, through the foundries, the assembly shops, the offices. 'My God, why have you forsaken us?' wrote a lieutenant of XXIV Panzer Division. 'We have fought during fifteen days for a single house, with mortars, grenades, machine-guns, and bayonets. Already by the third day fifty-four German corpses lay strewn in the cellars, on the landings, and the staircases. The front is a corridor between burnt-out rooms; it is the thin ceiling between two floors. Help comes from neighbouring houses by fire escapes and chimneys. There is a ceaseless struggle from noon till night. From storey to storey, faces black with sweat, we bombard each other with grenades in the middle of explosions, clouds of dust and smoke, heaps of mortar, floods of blood, fragments of furniture and human beings. Ask any soldier what half an hour of hand-to-hand struggle means in such a fight. And imagine Stalingrad; eighty days and eighty nights of hand-to-hand struggles. The street is no longer

*1 The German advance. 2 The German assault on Stalingrad. 3 Red Army counter-attacks. 4 The crushing of VI Army*

measured by metres but by corpses . . . Stalingrad is no longer a town. By day it is an enormous cloud of burning blinding smoke; it is a vast furnace, lit by the reflection of the flames. And when the night arrives, one of those scorching, howling, bleeding nights, the dogs plunge into the Volga and swim desperately to gain the other bank. The nights of Stalingrad are a terror for them. Animals flee this hell; the hardest stones cannot bear it for long; only men endure.'

By the end of October the Russian positions at Stalingrad had been reduced to a few pockets of stone, seldom more than three hundred yards deep, bordering on the

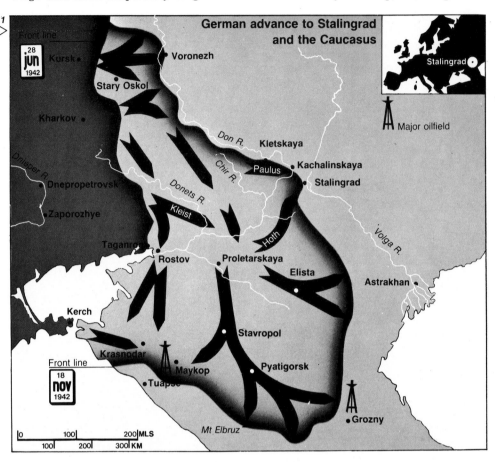

German advance to Stalingrad and the Caucasus

Major oilfield

Front line
.28 jun 1942

Front line
18 nov 1942

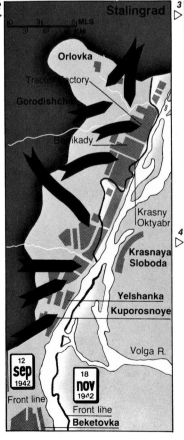

Stalingrad

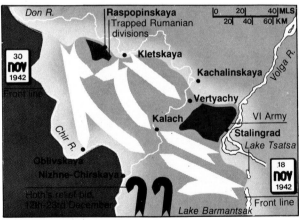

Raspopinskaya
Trapped Rumanian divisions
30 nov 1942
Kletskaya
Kachalinskaya
Vertyachy
Kalach
VI Army
Stalingrad
Lake Tsatsa
18 nov 1942
Front line
Oblivskaya
Nizhne-Chirskaya
Hoth's relief bid, 12th–23rd December
Lake Barmantsak

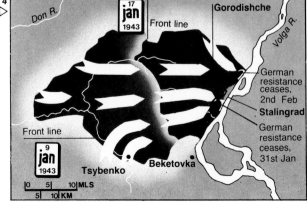

.17 jan 1943
Front line
Gorodishche
German resistance ceases, 2nd Feb
Stalingrad
German resistance ceases, 31st Jan
9 jan 1943
Front line
Tsybenko
Beketovka

right bank of the Volga. The Krasny Oktyabr had fallen to the Germans who had paved every metre of the factory floor with their dead. The Barrikady was half lost, with Germans at one end of the foundry facing Russian machine-guns in the extinct ovens at the other. The defenders of the Tractor Factory had been split into three.

### Zhukov counter-attacks

But these last islets of resistance, hardened in the furnace of repeated attacks, were irreducible. Paulus's VI Army was spent, as exhausted as Haig's divisions at Passchendaele had been exactly a quarter of a century before. And all the time, to the north and west, a terrible storm was gathering. Early in September the Stavka had sent Zhukov — architect of their winter victory at Moscow — to the southern theatre and with him Zhukov had brought his colleagues Novikov and Voronov, the artillery specialist. For two months Zhukov carefully built up his reserves on the German flank and reinforced the Don bridgeheads against the Rumanians defending the German northern flank. Of twenty-two fresh infantry divisions created during this period only two were committed in Stalingrad itself. Virtually the entire autumn tank production was held back for use in the counter-offensive.

Paulus's Intelligence had warned him that something was afoot, but both Luftwaffe and army had grossly under-estimated its scale. The XLVIII Panzer Corps, VI Army's sole mobile reserve, consisted of ninety-two Czech light tanks, with Rumanian crews, and the remains of XIV Panzer Division refitting after five weeks continuous action in the rubble of Stalingrad. Against this, on 19th November, Zhukov threw six fresh armies, 450 new T34 tanks, and an artillery barrage from over 2,000 guns, in a pincer movement that converged on either side of the German salient whose tip was at Stalingrad.

The staff of VI Army went sleepless for

two nights as they struggled to regroup the precious Panzers and pull back their infantry from the smoking maze of Stalingrad to protect the collapsing flanks. In the rear confusion was absolute: the western railway from Kalach had already been cut by Russian cavalry in several places; the sound of firing came from every direction, and periodically broke out between Germans going up to the front and ragged groups of Rumanians in leaderless retreat. The huge bridge at Kalach over which every pound of rations and every bullet for VI Army passed, had been prepared for demolition, and a platoon of engineers was on duty there all day on 23rd November in case the order to destroy the bridge should come through. At half past four that afternoon tanks could be heard approaching from the west. The lieutenant in charge of the engineers thought at first that they might be Russians but was reassured when the first three vehicles were identified as Horch personnel carriers with XXII Panzer Division markings; assuming that it was a reinforcement column for Stalingrad he instructed his men to lift the barrier. The personnel carriers halted on the bridge and disgorged sixty Russian tommy-gunners who killed most of the engineer platoon and took the survivors prisoner. They removed the demolition charges and twenty-five tanks from the column passed over the bridge and drove south-east, where that evening they made contact with the southern claw of the pincer, 14th Independent Tank Brigade from Trufanov's 51st Army. The first tenuous link in a chain that was to throttle a quarter of a million German soldiers had been forged, and the turning point in the Second World War had now, at last, arrived.

In the three days following their penetration of the Rumanian corps, the Russians had moved thirty-four divisions across the Don, twelve from Beketonskaya bridgehead and twenty-two from Kremenskaya. Their tanks had turned westward, defeating XLVIII Panzer Corps and probing dan-

*Above left: After the Soviet counter-attack — men of VI Army crouch in the snow. In November the Red Army surrounded a quarter of a million men at Stalingrad. By 2nd February half of them were dead. Above: Field-Marshal Paulus at his interrogation by the Russians. After his capture he became an active member of the anti-Nazi 'Free Officers' Committee' and broadcast from Moscow*

gerously into the confusion of stragglers, service and training units, and mutinous satellites who milled about in the German rear. Their infantry had turned east, digging with feverish energy to build an iron ring around VI Army. Zhukov kept the whole of the Stalingrad pocket under bombardment from heavy guns sited on the far bank of the Volga, but for the first few days he had exerted only a gentle pressure upon the surrounded Germans.

The Soviets' intention was to probe in sufficient strength to be able to detect the first signs of their enemy's actually striking camp, but to avoid any action which might precipitate this. For them, as for Paulus, these first hours were vital. All night on 23rd and during the morning of 24th November, men and tractors hauled and struggled with battery after battery of 76-mm guns across the frozen earth. By that evening Russian firepower on the west side of the pocket had trebled. Over a thousand anti-tank guns were in position in an arc from Vertyatchy, in the north, around to Kalach, then eastwards below Marinovka, joining the Volga at the old Beketonskaya bridgehead.

Field-Marshal von Manstein, the newly appointed commander of the German army group, set about preparing a relief operation, using the rump of Hoth's Panzers that had been left out of the encirclement, and some mobile units pulled back from the Caucasus. However, Russian pressure and administrative difficulties delayed the counter-attack (Operation Winter Tempest) until 12th December. Hoth's column was never strong enough to penetrate the Soviet ring on its own, and a simultaneous full-scale sortie by Paulus's force on the code signal *Donnerschlag*—'Thunderclap'—was to be vital to its success. When it came to the point Paulus refused to move, making a succession of excuses and finally referring Manstein to Hitler. Hitler, over the telephone, said he had to leave it to Paulus. With the overall position deteriorating daily it was impossible to keep Hoth's column poised in the steppe for long and over Christmas it withdrew, carrying with it the last prospects of relief for the beleaguered army.

Stalingrad was the greatest single defeat suffered by German arms since the Napoleonic Wars. To this day it is impossible to make a final assessment of the failure to relieve the surrounded army because all the surviving participants are inhibited, for one or another reason, from giving an impartial account. Russian strength was, of course, a primary factor. Also contributory was the misrepresentation by the Luftwaffe of its ability to supply VI Army (incredibly Göring assumed that the He 111, which could carry 2,000 kilogrammes of *explosive* could as easily load 2,000 kilogrammes of *cargo)*. But the real mystery is a strategic one. There was a widespread conviction that the Stalingrad garrison must stay where it was in order to cover the retreat of the rest of the army. Manstein himself is on record with the view that 'if the enemy siege forces had been released . . . the fate of the whole southern wing of the German forces in the East would have been sealed.' It was impossible to recommend that Paulus should be *sacrificed* to this end—easy to take comfort (as Paulus himself was doing) from the fact that many, weaker 'pockets' had held out through the previous winter until the thaw had brought relief.

At all events, the revictualling of so large a garrison was quite beyond the powers of the Luftwaffe even while its forward airfields were safe. Once these were lost to the Russian advance the garrison's life could be measured in weeks. VI Army rejected a surrender demand on 10th January and defeated the last Russian attack. On 2nd February the last remnants of the garrison were obliged by shortage of food and ammunition to surrender. Over 130,000 men went into the prison cages and German strength in the East was never to recover.

*Russian soldiers emerge from hiding in a ruined house, October 1942. The stubbornness of the Russian defence baffled the Germans—and as they became tied down in the savage hand-to-hand fighting, they chose to regard it as a 'battle of attrition' in which the Red Army would be bled white. But it was the Wehrmacht which had failed to understand tactics as well as strategic reality; it was the German Army which was being exhausted and forced to throw in all its reserves, while the Russians built up their strength, committing only enough troops to deny the Germans any chance of a breakthrough*

Novosti

# The Nazis at War

When Hitler ordered the attack on Poland on 1st September 1939, he thought he had only a localized campaign before him, yet he consciously risked its extension into world war. War for Hitler and the Nazi regime was not only a means to an end; with it was bound up the whole philosophy of Nazism. The Nazi dogma of the 'iron law' of struggle between races was nothing more than the naked spirit of warfare. And the preparation for the battle for 'Lebensraum' had defined all Nazi policy in Germany since 1933.

The First World War had shown what levels such a national fighting spirit was capable of reaching. Hitler consciously seized on this model. The desire to raise Germany from the 'disgrace' of 1918, the conviction that only treachery, stupidity, and weakness had caused defeat in the First World War, and the fanatical determination to resume once again – and this time more resolutely – the fight for Germany's greatness and her place in the world: all this was part of the special gospel of National Socialism. The Second World War was the decisive act of Hitler's regime. The total strength and the true nature of Nazism only came out fully in war, but so did its great weakness – its fanatical egocentricity, which was eventually to bring about its destruction.

Hitler's enormous military successes in the first years of the war – the eighteen-day war against Poland, the daring naval and air action to occupy Norway, and, above all, the swift victory over France which inspired Mussolini to come into the war on Hitler's side – spread Germany's hegemony over almost the whole continent and created a readiness practically everywhere for the creation of a 'new Fascist order in Europe'.

The sensational triumphs in the military field and in foreign policy also strengthened the Nazi position in internal affairs and lent conviction to the belief that Hitler was not a dangerous gambler but a divinely endowed genius. Now National Socialist propaganda in Germany itself, conducted by its talented leader Joseph Goebbels, could pull out all the stops in the creation of national euphoria. This included special radio broadcasts linked by resounding military marches, newsreels glorifying German successes put out by the army's propaganda unit, the composition and broadcasting of more and more new battle songs, the award of higher and higher decorations for bravery, and the popularization of individual war-heroes. Hitler himself contributed to the creation of this

mood with fifteen big speeches in the first two years of the war and so successful was Nazi 'education' that apparently only a minority in Germany preserved enough critical capacity to see the mania which spoke through Hitler's uncontrolled attacks.

It was true, however, that there was in the German population, as the confidential security service reports for 1940-41 show, an enduring and lively fear that Germany would, by over-extending her forces, run the risk of 'conquering herself to death'. But the full extent of Hitler's miscalculations, already visible in 1940, remained largely hidden. Thus only a few realized the importance of the RAF's success in the Battle of Britain and that Great Britain had by this time received the first reliable indication of active military support from the United States in the form of fifty destroyers.

But it was not only propaganda which served to conceal the seriousness of the situation. Food rationing, instituted in August 1939, guaranteed the nation a sufficient amount to eat in the first years of the war. Trusting in Hitler's Blitzkrieg strategy and the economic preparations for war which had been going forward since 1934, the Nazi regime thought that even in 1942 no radical switch in the economy to arms production was necessary and that it would be possible to preserve a relatively high standard of living for the civilian population. Nor did the military situation cause immediate alarm. The number of Germans killed in action up to the end of 1941 remained relatively low (about 200,000) and the RAF's night attacks, which had increased during 1940-41, did not at first cause great damage.

Military developments and Nazi propaganda also largely hid the changes in the state's power structure which were to have serious consequences in the future.

Although the army was potentially an important power-factor it had for some time shown itself to have feet of clay. The clearest signs of this were the forced resignations of Fritsch, the Commander-in-Chief of the Army, and General Beck, the Chief of the General Staff, and Hitler's

LA BELLE SIBERIE VOUS APPELLE!

Premier départ 3 semaines après la libération

*Mobilizing mass support for Nazism.*
*Above: One of a series of slides shown to women in the Nazi Labour Service, stressing the joys of working for Germany.*
*Right: 'Come to lovely Siberia': Nazi poster issued in Belgium equates Allied 'liberation' with terrors of Bolshevism – deportation and death*

Musée Royal de l'Armée, Brussels

setting up in February 1938 of the High Command of the Armed Forces (Oberkommando der Wehrmacht, OKW) which was directly answerable to him under the command of General Keitel. These developments showed that after the consolidation of Nazi power Hitler was not prepared to allow the armed forces any significant influence in making political decisions. After the outbreak of war he pursued the suppression of the forces' political influence even more rigorously (for instance, by strangling the truth about the sinking of the *Athenia*). From the first day of the war, it was not the military commanders but the highest-ranking Gauleiters who were appointed Reich defence commissioners and who were also entrusted with making the top decisions in all cases of civil emergency.

The army leaders took another fall — not without protests from individual generals — when in the autumn of 1939 commanding officers in occupied Poland tolerated the first systematic mass shooting of Poles and Jews by Special Action Units of the SS which claimed that they were acting under special secret orders from above.

The appointment of the Waffen-SS, under Himmler's supreme command, in the winter of 1939-40 also ended the army's monopoly as the only element allowed to bear arms, the monopoly which had been defended so successfully against the SA in 1934. The Waffen-SS, a direct rival to the army, amounted to only one division at the beginning of 1940, but towards the end of the war its numerous volunteer units comprised some 600,000 men.

As he had done on many different occasions since 1937 when he presented his expansionist aims, Hitler reproached the army leadership for being far too cautious and hesitant in applying his plan for the campaign in the West. This plan, which foresaw the violation of Dutch and Belgian neutrality, led to further deterioration in his relations with top officers on the Army General Staff (for example with Halder, Chief of the General Staff, and Canaris, head of the Abwehr, the OKW counter-intelligence department). The first cells of military opposition formed.

The success of the campaign in the West, however, once again justified Hitler's judgement and increased his prestige to the

detriment of that of the army leadership. In December 1941, after the first failures in Russia, Field-Marshal Brauchitsch resigned as Commander-in-Chief of the Army and Hitler took over this position himself.

As in Poland, moreover, Hitler took care to force the commanding army generals out of the administration of those occupied territories in which the Nazi regime was especially interested as soon as they had been overrun. Everywhere civilian rulers were installed. They were always high Party functionaries, usually Gauleiters, and all directly responsible to Hitler. There arose autocratically ruled satrapies in which control was wielded by Party favourites, the officials responsible for the carrying out of Göring's Four-Year Plan, and the security police and other SS organs under Himmler. It was this type of administrative irregularity that provided the basis for mass shooting, mass deportation, concentration camps, and ghettos, and finally, from 1941, the extermination camps — the means of achieving the 'final solution to the Jewish problem'.

### Revolutionizing the law

The shift of power in the occupied territories into the hands of Party officials and the security police had its effect on the constitution of the Nazi regime itself. A variety of measures, caused directly by the war, but which were principally ideological and political, altered the division of power between the Nazi leaders to the advantage of the extremists.

This was particularly true of the law. Demands by Hitler and other Party leaders for stiff war-time penal laws led in the autumn of 1939 to the passing of a mass of new laws covering, for example, listening in to enemy radio broadcasts, economic sabotage of the war effort, 'disrupting the armed forces', and 'crimes of violence'. Crimes which carried the death sentence rose to forty-six by 1944. Statistics on death sentences passed by the civil courts rose from 43 in 1938, to 2,015 from January to August 1944. Hitler was however not content with the draconian increase in the severity of legal sentences. In the autumn of 1939 he had already authorized Himmler to use the security police for immediate execution without a court death sentence in cases of anti-national acts and sabotage which seemed particularly serious. The executions were mostly carried out in concentration camps. The SS and security police officials who undertook these killings received formal protection from inquiries by the state prosecutors by the introduction of special SS and police tribunals in October 1939. The total number of concentration camp prisoners in Germany between 1934 and 1938, when the Nazi regime was relatively moderate, was around 7,000 to 10,000, but after the beginning of the war the imprisonment of those from occupied countries suspected of opposition and the erection of new camps pushed the figure up to some 100,000 by 1942. But the highest numbers are to be found in the last war years (1944-45) when, under the forced labour scheme for armaments production, some half a million

*The Nazis and German Youth.*
*Left: A poster of the 1930's*
*expressing the National Socialist*
*ideal of the young Nazi. The rival*
*youth organizations of the pre-Hitler*
*years, the red-scarved communists and*
*the socialists in berets flee with*
*their decadent mentors from the vision*
*of Aryan heroism. Goebbel's propaganda*
*reached to the cradle. Right: A Hitler*
*Youth at a hero commemoration ceremony.*
*The Nazi grip on the young was total,*
*from the Adolf Hitler Schools through*
*the ranks of the Hitler Youth, training*
*was for total obedience. Drafted into*
*the Civil Defence early in the war, by*
*1945 twelve-year-olds went into the*
*front line to face the advancing*
*Russian tanks*

Südd-Verlag

prisoners of all nationalities were crammed together in twenty main camps and 165 subsidiary camps.

From the start of the war, Hitler sought to link his fight against external enemies with the eradication of internal enemies and 'inferior' national elements. His aim was made quite explicit by his secret order of September 1939 to kill all the mentally ill. Under the euthanasia programme, for which a secretly selected commission of doctors was responsible, about 70,000 mentally ill were killed in hospitals in Bernburg, Hadamar, Hartheim, and elsewhere, until, in 1941, Hitler felt himself obliged to call a halt in response to various protests, especially from clergy.

### Calculation and hate
The more extreme nature of the Nazi regime in 1941-42 was directly connected with the critical military situation. The combination of rational calculation and pathological hate, which increasingly dominated Hitler's decisions the more he was dominated by the idea of his role in history, was especially apparent in his decision to attack Russia.

This decision had no necessity other than as an escape from the military dead-end Hitler had reached in the West over Great Britain. It was also, however, an attempt

*Victim of Nazi bestiality. Baby murdered by Germans in a Donbas village, Ukraine*

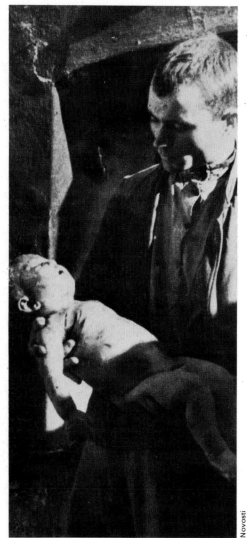

Novosti

to wage his own war, the war he had planned two decades before with the intention of conquering the Lebensraum of the East and destroying 'Jewish Bolshevism'.

His decision linked many elements: an obstinate determination to keep the initiative, if not against Great Britain, then against the last potentially dominant power on the continent, an impatient, half-blind impulse to take action (always a characteristic of Hitler and the Nazi movement as a whole), bitterness and anger that the Blitzkrieg strategy had not brought victory, increasing hate of the world-wide enemy, Jewry, on which he blamed his own miscalculations, and an increasingly fanatical desire for destruction.

Thus, significantly, it was in connection with the preparations for the Russian campaign that Hitler issued the brutal secret orders which were later to acquire such terrible infamy in the Nazi war crimes trials: the order for the 'final solution of the Jewish problem', the order that captured Soviet commissars should be shot (an order which the Wehrmacht did not oppose), and the 'Night and Fog' decree of September 1941, which as a deterrent against sabotage in the Western occupied territories laid down that those suspected of opposition should be seized by police and whisked away to German prisons without any information being given to their families as to their fate.

At the same time, the German police introduced a mass of oppressive new measures against the churches, mostly the Catholic Church, with tighter bans on church demonstrations and the seizure of some 100 monasteries.

### Failure and forced labour
The battle for Moscow during the winter of 1941-42 and the long drawn-out attacks of 1942 revealed what the battle of Stalingrad (October 1942 to February 1943) then confirmed: that victory in the East was no longer within reach. In the West, too, the initiative passed to the other side after the United States entered the war (December 1941). From 1942, 'area bombing' by the British and American air forces, which from 1943 possessed undisputed mastery of the air over Germany, had a disastrous effect on Germany's war economy and on the German population. Bombs killed some 400,000 civilians, and destroyed countless towns and industrial plants. The Anglo-American landing in Morocco and Algeria in November 1942 forced the capitulation of the Afrika Korps in May 1943. The Allied invasion of southern Italy in July 1943 also led to a German retreat. Mussolini's subsequent fall and the withdrawal of Italy from the Axis in August 1943 — which also brought into question the reliability of Germany's smaller allies (Hungary and Rumania) — threw the Nazi regime into its most severe political crisis to date.

This string of failures accelerated the growing extremism of Nazi policy inside Germany and caused further lasting changes in the Party's power structure in accordance with the 'total warfare' which

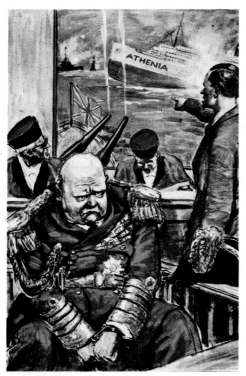

*German cartoon of 1940 accuses Churchill of sinking the* Athenia *to arouse anti-German feeling. The British liner was sunk a few hours after war started by a German U-boat, drowning 112 people, twenty-eight of them Americans. Mindful of how the sinking of the* Lusitania *helped bring America into the First World War, Hitler ordered a denial that a U-boat was involved and in October the official Nazi newspaper proclaimed: 'Churchill sank the* Athenia'. *The naval leaders who knew the truth were ordered to keep silent. Hitler had taken a further step towards total control of Germany and her people*

had now been instituted. Symptomatic of this were the innovations in armaments production and labour allocation in March 1942. Particularly successful was the appointment of Albert Speer as Reich minister for armaments and production; the energetic and talented direction of the former architect put Germany's armaments economy into high gear, and made possible a three-fold increase in arms production in 1943-44 compared with 1941, despite the Allied bombing raids. This brilliant technical and organizational feat was, however, closely bound up with the simultaneous massive extension of forced labour, for which responsibility was borne by Gauleiter Fritz Sauckel, named plenipotentiary general for the allocation of labour in March 1942, and — in the control of concentration camps — by Himmler. Millions of Russians — referred to derogatorily as *Ostarbeiter* (Eastern workers) — and Poles were forcibly brought to work in the Reich (as were French, Belgians, Dutch, Serbs, Czechs, Italians, and others). The building of the underground V-weapon production plant in the Harz mountains (transferred from Peenemünde after the RAF attack in 1943) was largely the work of 30,000 concentration camp prisoners. At least a quarter of them died of exhaustion before the end of the war.

## Instruments of the police state

The fact that the regime had become more markedly a police state was also shown by the appointment of the former president of the Nazi People's Court, Otto Georg Thierack, as minister of justice in August 1942. Until then the department had been under the control of Franz Gürtner, of the German National People's Party (DNVP), and after his death in January 1941, of his state secretary, Schlegelberger. Both had repeatedly intervened to uphold fundamental legal principles and at least partly preserve the competence of the law, even if they were unable to prevent the law adapting in some form to Hitler's political and ideological standards.

Thierack sought right from the very outset a close understanding with Himmler and undertook on his behalf the sell-out of the legal system, for instance by his readiness to transfer some 10,000 state prisoners into SS concentration camps and to allow the prosecution of certain groups (Jews, Poles, Eastern workers) to be pursued wholly by the security police. His successor as president of the People's Court was Roland Freisler, who took office in the summer of 1942. Under his direction, this tribunal became an exemplary dispenser of Party justice after the manner of Stalin's show trials, most notably in the sentencing of the July Plot conspirators in 1944. In fact Freisler had become a fanatical Bolshevik as a prisoner of war in Russia in the First World War; he turned Nazi in 1924 but remained a warm admirer of Soviet terror. 'Freisler is our Vishinsky' (who was prosecutor during the Purge) exclaimed Hitler in one of the first conferences after Stauffenberg's attempt on his life.

## An exotic Eastern court

Apart from Speer, who after 1942 replaced Göring as the leading power in economic policy (the Reichsmarschall's credit largely ran out with Hitler after the failure of the Luftwaffe), it was Goebbels, Himmler, and Bormann who held the most power and were the decisive influences from 1942–43. As Speer, the ablest and least corrupted member of Hitler's entourage, said: 'Relations between the various high leaders can only be understood if their aspirations are interpreted as a struggle for the succession to Adolf Hitler'. Hitler's last years reveal the steadily quickening breakdown of the machinery of government until his cabinet resembled an exotic Eastern court, with each vying with the other for the ruler's favours.

From 1942 onwards, Hitler tended to avoid public speeches and gatherings and seldom left his headquarters in East Prussia; the responsibility for the whole field of propaganda in the second half of the war thus fell increasingly on Goebbels. In contrast to the other Nazi officials, the propaganda minister, with an instinctive feeling for his job, saw that the turn of events after the first euphoric phase of the war demanded a completely new approach to propaganda. He knew that in the case of dire necessity, appeal to the suppressed readiness for self-sacrifice and participation, and to defiant national solidarity could be even more effective than delirious rapture. Thus Goebbels, in the famous demonstration in the Berlin Sportpalast on 18th February 1943, shortly after the Battle of Stalingrad was able even so to carry his listeners away into a fanatical affirmation of his own total commitment to sacrifice, an affirmation which later seemed merely to be an expression of mass hysteria.

In fact the attitude of a large part of the German population at this stage would be hard to understand without a knowledge of the psychological state of mind so successfully controlled by Goebbels. Certainly there was now growing doubt and criticism, and the war had brought considerable hardship—two million German soldiers dead by 1945. But recognition of the one who was truly responsible became more difficult the longer Hitler was relied upon and applauded. People managed to convince themselves that it was a precept of loyalty to hold out in the face of difficulties; they no longer really believed in 'final victory', but no-one dared think of defeat since in the present situation this would mean Russian victory and domination. This psychological mixture of panic, loyalty, self-pity, and self-deception also created a moral blindness to the spreading oppressiveness of the regime and the sufferings of the persecuted Jews, with whom contact had long been lost by discrimination and imprisonment in ghettos, even before the secret, but not unnoticed, deportations in 1941-42. It was the greatest failure that at this time those guardians of the nation who still held their posts—clergy, university professors, high-ranking officers—remained almost completely silent throughout the oppression and atrocities.

Goebbels' indispensability as propagandist of the total war effort greatly extended his influence in the last years. He remained true to the myth which he had served faithfully for so many years. At the end he had no thought of escape. He planned his death to mirror Hitler's. The high standing Goebbels won with the Führer was shown when Hitler appointed him future chancellor of the now non-existent Reich in his political testament dated 29th April 1945.

Himmler, too, had continually acquired new powers and responsibilities since the beginning of the war. Since 1936 joint SS-chief and head of the police, he was appointed Reich commissioner for the consolidation of German nationhood on 7th October 1939 and was given responsibility for the direction of the whole policy of deportation and Germanization of the East. Himmler's influence and that of individual SS departments spread increasingly to foreign policy through Himmler's control of relations with Germans living abroad, the enrolment of Germanic volunteers for the SS, and above all through his contacts with the security police and the intelligence services of allied and neutral countries. In addition, Himmler assumed control of the Reich Interior Ministry in 1943, and of the Reserve Army at home

*Young and old under arms. Goebbels inspects regular troops in Silesia, 1945*

after the July Plot. Göring, Ribbentrop, Frick, and other formerly very influential ministers were unequivocally outmanoeuvred by Himmler from 1941 onwards.

## Byzantine absolutism

Himmler's only competitor in the last years of the war was Martin Bormann, who was largely unknown even in 1939 but assumed the direction of the Party Chancery in May 1941 when Hitler's deputy Rudolph Hess flew to Great Britain on his peace bid. But what was more decisive for Bormann's rise was his position of confidence as Hitler's permanent attendant and secretary. He became the vital intermediary between Hitler and the outside world. He matched his master's eccentric hours and became the sole channel for his orders.

The more Hitler absented himself from Berlin, the more absolute his rule became. And, as it was impossible for his ministers to penetrate his headquarters for months on end, the more important became Bormann's position as king of the lobby, as executor and interpreter of Hitler's orders.

This Byzantine consequence of Hitler's absolutism was characteristic of the last phase of Hitler's rule; it meant that even Hitler's adjutants and the permanent representatives of the ministers in Hitler's headquarters became decisive figures. The almost permanent power struggle between personalities and groups for Hitler's favour and the increasing chaos in the definition of responsibilities—all this led to a process of growing self-destruction in the regime, which was only held together by more orders from the Führer. In the end, everyone who had the power to do so was playing the petty Führer to the full extent of his influence. With Hitler's suicide, dissolution was complete. Colossal energies had been unleashed, colossal crimes begun, colossal destruction risked —and nothing remained.

# SS:The Empire Within

The SS (Schutzstaffel meaning protection squads) first showed their strength in the Night of the Long Knives, the moment chosen by Hitler to eliminate the SA. With their violent and rowdy demonstrations the Brownshirts had dominated the streets of Germany and, indeed, Germany's political life, throughout the 1920's. They were to do so no longer. On 30th June 1934 the main leaders of the SA were arrested, executed on the spot, or handed over to improvised execution squads. The instrument of this savage purge was the SS, which now became the custodian of Party values.

Although created in 1923, the SS had less than 300 members when Himmler was appointed Reichsführer-SS in 1929. Under his leadership the SS greatly increased in size and importance but it remained, until 1934, a force within a force, nominally subordinate to the general organization of the SA. 'Made up of men at the peak of physical fitness, the most trustworthy and the most faithful to the Nazi movement', its role was to keep an eye on the Party and to guarantee the Führer's personal safety. The latter task was entrusted to a guard of 120 select men of absolute reliability under the command of Sepp Dietrich, a Bavarian ex-sergeant, former waiter and butcher's boy, who had made a veritable cult of the person of Hitler. At the end of 1933, the Führer gave his personal guard the official title of Leibstandarte (bodyguard regiment) SS Adolf Hitler.

The SS, in their elegant black uniforms, were the evil guardian angels of the Nazi regime. Recruited from a higher social class than the SA, they were more discreet and avoided rowdy demonstrations; they had other means of proving their terrible efficiency. Completely dominated by Nazi ideals their prime characteristic was absolute fidelity and blind obedience to Hitler's orders: 'On 30th June 1934,' Himmler said later, 'we did not hesitate to do the duty laid down for us and put guilty friends up against the wall and shoot them . . . . . . Each of us found it appalling, yet we are all sure that if such orders were ever necessary again, we would carry them out as we did then.'

On the eve of the war, the SS, with its 250,000 members, constituted the élite of the Party and of the Third Reich. Already the formidable organization created by Himmler was taking on its definitive form with its three main branches: the intelligence service of the Party, or SD (Sicherheitsdienst), which towards the end of the war absorbed the armed forces intelligence

services (Abwehr); the police, including the regular police (Ordnungspolizei or Orpo) and the security police (Sicherheitspolizei or Sipo), itself composed of the state criminal police (Kripo) and the state secret police (Geheimestaatspolizei or Gestapo); and finally the military section of the SS. When war broke out the latter consisted of four regiments: Leibstandarte Adolf Hitler, Deutschland, Germania, and Der Führer. Deutschland and Germania had been formed in 1936, and Der Führer in 1938 after the Anschluss. These four regiments were known as the Verfügungstruppe (troops at Hitler's disposal). After the Polish campaign, Deutschland, Germania, and Der Führer were brought together in the Verfügungsdivision, and two other divisions were raised: Totenkopf, from the concentration camp guard units, and Polizei, from the police. These three divisions, together with the Leibstandarte which remained an independent regiment until 1941 when it was raised to division strength, became known as the Waffen-SS (armed SS) in 1940. Together they constituted an autonomous branch of Himmler's organization.

Himmler planned to expand the military SS into a group of shock troops which would attract the greater part of German youth, become an army in its own right, and constitute the 'racial' élite of the Third Reich. But from 1938 onwards Hitler resisted these ambitions and the Waffen-SS thus remained a militarized police force, though very well armed. Its main task was to quell any attempts at a coup d'état and maintain law and order in occupied territories. To acquire the necessary prestige in the eyes of the German population, Waffen-SS members shed blood on the battlefield—in compliance with Hitler's orders—alongside regular army units. Limited to five per cent of the army's total strength, the Waffen-SS acted as a model, embodying the ideals which National Socialism intended to instil into the army.

In 1940 the SS organization already had its own characteristics: it was, for instance, independent as far as administration and recruitment were concerned. Until 1942 it only accepted volunteers who fulfilled strict moral and physical conditions, though as the Third Reich's 'stud' became weaker under the blows of the Allies and

*Portrait of Himmler, Reichsführer-SS. Under Himmler the SS became the custodian of Nazi values and the most dreaded force in Europe*

*Dutch civilians in a Gestapo jail*

the Red Army, the requirements became less demanding. 'Up until 1936,' Himmler was to write, 'we never took on anyone with the least physical defect, even if it was just a filled tooth. We were able to bring together in the SS the most superb elements of our race.'

The Waffen-SS cadres, recruited with the greatest care, were trained in special officer-schools — *Junkerschulen* — in Brunswick and Bad Tölz. Instruction was ideological, physical, and military. The future officers had to be convinced of the value of the Nazi racial theories. Did not they make up the ethnic élite of the Third Reich, destined to dominate a Europe no longer encumbered with the racial problem and to integrate within its frontiers all the

peoples of Germanic origin? They had to show themselves hard, pitiless, scorning their own lives and those of others. It was not in good taste to declare oneself an atheist, Protestant, or Catholic; the future officers were advised to be theistic. The whole liberal and Christian heritage of Western civilization was ruthlessly rejected. The training of the future Waffen-SS leaders adhered to the very roots of National Socialist doctrine: the cult of will, the attachment to 'blood and soil', the scorn of so-called 'inferior' peoples.

A very important place was given to sport as a means of toughening the body and mind of the volunteers. Finally, there was intensive military training: tank and infantry exercises of the greatest possible realism. There was one particularly demanding test: to prove his self-control, the

future officer had to prime a grenade, balance it on his helmet, and stand to attention until it exploded.

At the end of their ruthless training, the young Waffen-SS members had to take an oath of absolute obedience to Hitler: 'I swear to you, Adolf Hitler, as Führer and Reich Chancellor, loyalty and bravery. I vow to you, and to those you have named to command me, obedience unto death, so help me God.'

By 1942 the Waffen-SS had won a reputation for 'cold daring . . . , spirit in action . . . , unshakeable fortitude in tough moments . . . , comradeship,' and even for 'modesty', in the words of General von Mackensen.

But in 1942 the Waffen-SS was on the brink of profound changes. After Stalingrad, it underwent development in two directions. Its total forces doubled annually, reaching 300,000 at the end of 1943 and almost 600,000 in 1944-45. At the same time, foreign members were taken on until they made up more than half the total strength. These sudden changes followed from Hitler's realization that German forces would have to be reconstituted to undertake a longer war. The Waffen-SS was now to become a powerful and vigorous army.

### Revolution in recruitment

The enormous jump in membership naturally led to a revolution in its recruiting programme, which had scarcely been able to fulfil Himmler's demands. From the end of 1942, Himmler was authorized to draw on the Wehrmacht intake, despite its protests. Thenceforth, the majority of the SS recruits were members of the Hitler Youth and of the *Volksdeutsch*—foreign nationals of German race. This influx of new blood undoubtedly lowered the ideological level of the intake. There was no longer the time to devote to political indoctrination, but on the whole, the new Waffen-SS, at least the German formations, preserved their National Socialist 'purity', their intransigence, their scorn of life, and their effectiveness.

The Waffen-SS were military shock troops, but time and again they showed their importance as a political force. As

*Below: The Deputy Protector of Bohemia-Moravia and SS terrorist Reinhard Heydrich. On 5th July 1942, he was assassinated by two Czech paratroopers. Below right: The murder of Lidice: as a reprisal, all the men of the Czechoslovak town of Lidice were killed, the women sent to concentration camps, the children placed in appropriate institutes and the town levelled to the ground by the SS. Bottom right: Articles left behind by Heydrich's assassins who were killed by the SS*

the custodians of the regime, they had to prevent any attempt at internal subversion or at a putsch by generals sceptical of the outcome of the war. The Waffen-SS were also responsible for maintaining the dependence of Germany's allies on the Reich. One method of ensuring this was the massive intake of foreign volunteers. In 1943, of thirty-eight large SS units, some fifteen only had a German or *Volksdeutsch* origin. All the other units were composed of foreigners from Eastern or Western Europe. In 1944, the Waffen-SS presented the most extraordinary ethnic mixture that one could imagine: there were 'Westerners'—Scandinavians, Dutch, Walloons, Flemings, and French, together with 'Easterners'—Balts, Ukrainians, Bosnians, Croats, Serbs, Albanians, Hungarians, Rumanians, Bulgarians, Russians, not to mention British and Indian legions.

Only military necessity and ulterior political motives could have justified recruitment in such blatant contradiction of the ethnic principles which were the basis of the Waffen-SS. By appealing in particular to Eastern volunteers—a far remove from the pure Nordic ideal—Himmler played on the ethnic and religious antagonism which periodically embroiled Eastern Europe and the Balkans. Thus, to support the Prinz Eugen SS Division in action against Tito's partisans, the Handschar Division was created out of Muslim Bosnians, who nourished a more than secular hatred towards the Serbs. Wearing fezes, receiving special rations, and accompanied by their Imams, the Bosnian battalions received the blessing of the Grand Mufti in Jerusalem. This gave a considerable twist to Himmler's atheism and he was later to tell Goebbels that 'he had nothing against Islam because this religion assumes the task of instructing men, promising them heaven if they fight with courage and get

themselves killed on the battlefield; in short, it is a very practical and attractive religion for a soldier!' The creation of the Handschar Division was followed by other Muslim formations; the Skanderbeg Mountain Division, recruited in Albania, and the Kama Division of Croats.

The call for a Galician SS division met with extraordinary success; some one hundred thousand volunteers came forward, mostly Ukrainians. Two other divisions composed of Russians fought with the Germans or were set against General Vlasov's so-called Liberation Army. During the last months of the war, there appeared many other more or less bizarre formations of Serbs, Hungarians, Rumanians, Bulgarians, even Caucasians and Cossacks. And from 1942 each of the Baltic states undertook to provide one foot-division.

What motives could have prompted such diverse people to join the SS? Traditional hatreds certainly played a part: Muslims against Serbs, Ukrainians and Balts against Russians. Enrolment in the SS also meant for many—especially Russians—an escape from forced labour and the hell of prison camps ravaged by famine and typhus. There was in addition a higher motive among the Balts and Ukrainians: 'The volunteers from the East fought above all for the liberation and independence of their countries,' wrote Felix Steiner, a senior Waffen-SS leader. Most of the volunteers from the East did not join to defend Western civilization, still less to be part of the future of a Greater Germany.

There was no shortage of volunteers in the West either. There, the Waffen-SS recruitment drive had undeniable success, and more than 125,000 young people applied for membership. The Dutch headed the list with 50,000, followed by the Flemings and Walloons with 40,000; the French provided 20,000; the Danish and

r.10,000,000
ODMĚNY
ZA ZPRÁVY, KTERÉ BY VEDL
K DOPADENÍ PACHATELŮ
KDO ZNÁ ZDE VYSTAVENÉ
VĚCI ?

LÉON DEGRELLE

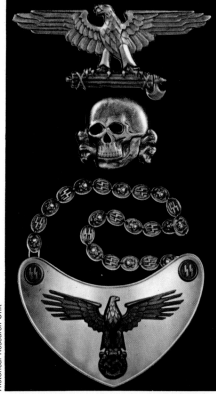

*Initially a German élite force, the SS was transformed to include men of numerous nationalities and races. The need for man-power and a desire to strengthen the Nazi hold over occupied Europe led to large-scale foreign recruitment. In 1943 only fifteen of the thirty-eight large SS units had a German or Volksdeutsch origin.* **Far left:** *Léon Degrelle, Belgian collaborator, whose volunteer unit was integrated into the Waffen-SS.* **Left:** *Italian officer's cap badge, death's head badge (common to all SS divisions), standard-bearer's gorget.* **Below left:** *Belgian SS division recruiting poster*

Norwegian contingents amounted to 12,000; there were 1,200 Swiss, Swedes, and Luxembourgers. Many were very close to the ethnic ideal of the SS. The avowed motive was to participate in a crusade against Bolshevism. The Waffen-SS might have been a multi-national, European army, the forerunner of a united Europe. This theme was developed copiously by Léon Degrelle, commander of the SS unit Wallonie, in his book *The Russian Campaign*: 'Whatever our views on the way in which the war has been waged, whatever regrets we have for the past, whatever bitterness there has been for our countries in foreign occupation, each of us knows that, above the satisfaction or disagreements experienced between 1939 and 1941 by the European nations, the fate of all Europe was in the balance. It is this which explains the extraordinary mood which has spurred countless young people to action, from Oslo, to Seville, from Antwerp to Budapest. They did not leave their homes . . . just to serve Germany's special interests. They were taking a part in defending 2,000 years of the highest form of civilization.'

### A Greater German Reich

The ideal of a Greater German Reich was the guiding light of the *Junkerschulen*. Himmler in 1943 told the officers of the SS armoured divisions: 'The Reich, the German Reich — nay, the German Reich within the German nation — will rightly find confirmation of its destiny in the fact that

*Fighting élite: crack SS unit Götz von Berlichingen, formed in December 1943*

WALLONIE

SS Viens à nous!

✠✠-Division blindée «WALLONIE»

henceforth we have an outlet to the East . . . Then, centuries hence perhaps, it will be possible to constitute a world-wide German Empire, which will be politically German . . . In this operation all the peoples which were formerly part of Germany, of the German Empire, and which belonged to us from 1606 or even 1648, that is, Flanders, Wallonia, the Low Countries, must be and will be incorporated into the German Reich. Furthermore, we must have the power to bring into our ranks by a second operation all the Germanic peoples and states which have not yet been part of the German Reich: Denmark and Norway, and their populations.'

The Reichsführer-SS envisaged the creation of a Western area called Burgundia, grouping the Netherlands, Belgium, and the north and east of France, which was to be the prototype SS state. In this new satrapy, Himmler intended to put his organizational talent to work. Whatever the appeal of this, there were many other reasons than the struggle against Bolshevism which dictated the entry of the young people into the SS. Many of the young – disorientated and out-of-work – were conscious of the prestige of the Waffen-SS, of a need for adventure, of the rewards of high office. In some measure, the Waffen-SS perhaps played the same role as the Foreign Legion before the war. The scorn for the Western regimes which had broken down in 1940 impelled a large number of men to don the SS uniform and to adhere to a system which had proved its superiority.

Certainly, political considerations were not far from their minds. Many had decided to back totalitarian style regimes in their own countries, subservient to Germany. Léon Degrelle admitted in 1943, when his volunteer unit was integrated into the Waffen-SS: 'An identical will united us all: to represent with brilliance our people among the twenty nations who had come running to the battle; to fulfil, without subservience, our duty as Europeans fighting against Europe's mortal enemy; to obtain for our country a choice place in the continental community which would result from the war . . .' This ideal of a European union was common among foreign members of the Waffen-SS. It envisaged a union of free and independent states with a common army.

But there was no question of a Europe of 'free states' nor of a European army. Himmler made this quite clear: 'From the start I told the volunteers: you can do what you want, but be certain of this: the SS will be organized in your country and there is in all Europe just one SS – the Germanic SS under the command of the Reichsführer-SS. You can resist, but that is a matter of indifference to me, for we will create it in any case . . . We do not ask you to turn against your country nor to do anything repugnant to anyone proud of his country, who loves it, and has his self-respect. Neither do we ask you to become Germans out of opportunism. But what we do expect of you is that you subordinate your national ideal to a superior racial and historical ideal, that of the German Reich.' In short,

in the minds of the Nazi leaders, the foreign Waffen-SS in occupied and satellite countries was to constitute a catalyst for the German cause.

### A way of life
How did this 300,000-strong mass of foreigners perform? On the whole, the Eastern volunteers were mediocre. Those from the Balkans, the Russians, even the Ukrainians were disappointments. Among the Balts, only the Letts displayed fortitude under fire. The Indians had a talent for making Hitler angry; he had never been favourable to the unlimited extension of the foreign Waffen-SS. 'The Indian Legion is a joke!' he once said. 'There are Indians who can't kill a louse, who would rather let themselves be eaten up. They won't kill an Englishman either. I consider it nonsense to put them opposite the English . . .'

The behaviour of the Western volunteers was on the whole better; they fought to the end with more desperation than many Germans. The Wallonie Division showed exceptional courage: of 6,000 volunteers, 2,500 died in the east. It was the same with the Viking Division, in which Germans, Dutch, and Scandinavians fought side by side. The French volunteers, first placed in the Wehrmacht, then, in 1944, in the Charlemagne SS Division with 2,000 militiamen and other Frenchmen of diverse origin, fought with gallantry near Moscow, in White Russia against the partisans, in Minsk and on the Vistula in 1944. The survivors took part in the last defence of the Reich Chancellery during the battle of Berlin.

Although SS units were under the tactical command of the Wehrmacht, they preserved administrative and legal independence and there was certainly no question of them applying the Wehrmacht code of honour. Their reputation for callousness and savagery could scarcely be surpassed. From May 1940, during the French campaign, a detachment of the Totenkopf unit distinguished itself by the summary execution at Paradis-Finistère of 100 British soldiers who had put up a particularly tough resistance. During the battle of Normandy, the Hitler Jugend units time and again slaughtered groups of Canadian or British prisoners in cold blood. Finally, during the Ardennes offensive, the Peiper group of the Leibstandarte unit machine-gunned seventy-one American prisoners. If the SS took great liberties in the West with normally accepted conventions, on the Eastern Front their excesses were far more numerous, though many of the atrocities imputed to them were committed by the regular army. At Taganrog, as a reprisal for the execution of six German soldiers, the SS killed in the course of three days all the soldiers who had fallen into their hands—more than 4,000 in all. When the SS fought against the partisans, they lost all restraint. During a 'pacification operation' in the Pripet region in 1941 the cavalry brigade Florian Geyer killed 259 Russian soldiers and 6,504 civilians. In northern Italy, in the antipartisan struggle, the Leibstandarte destroyed the town of Voves and massacred

its inhabitants. As it crossed the Massif Central to reach Normandy, the Das Reich Division left the hangings of Tulle and the bloody ruins of Oradour in its wake. The operation figures in the division records gives the balance as '548 enemy dead' at the price of 'two wounded'.

In the Balkans, where the war took on an unheard-of savagery, SS units like the Prinz Eugen Division won a notorious name for infamy. There too, where all the refinements of cruelty were practised, the German and Italian troops took reprisal for assassinations, sabotage, or the defeat of some of their units with atrocities. Specialized groups of the Waffen-SS undertook the extermination of racial minorities on a massive scale. The Polizei Division, composed mainly of policemen who in peace time were in control of traffic and noise abatement, was used in Russia in 1941 but not in the front line. It was mainly used against the partisans, with exemplary brutality. Most of the atrocities committed in the East by the SS were due to its activities. Transferred to Greece, it again committed heinous crimes, like the massacre of the inhabitants of a village of Klissoura. In certain cases SS units helped the Einsatzgruppen – Special Action units – charged with the mass execution of Jews in the Eastern territories – in their sinister task. Near Minsk, a company of Das Reich helped one of these Special Action units to shoot 920 Jews. The destruction of the Warsaw ghetto was in part the work of SS recruits.

Although Waffen-SS participation in the racial extermination policy was limited and often accidental, and although its members fought bravely on the battlefield as ordinary soldiers, it is impossible to forget their sinister ideology and the horrors they undoubtedly perpetrated. Himmler and his clique always claimed responsibility for these atrocities. The Waffen-SS became symbolic of an attitude, of a way of life, of policies against which the whole of the rest of the free world was fighting.

These 'soldiers like any others' – as Guderian once called the SS – may be exonerated by some, but nothing can ever change the significance of their double flash emblem as a symbol of the worst danger to life and civilization that humanity has ever faced.

*Opposite top: SS prisoners taken by British paratroopers, Normandy 1944. **Opposite centre:** Sauberzweig, commander of the Muslim SS Handschar Division. Political expediency caused Nazi views on race and religion to be relaxed. Himmler, an atheist, even regarded Islam, with its stress on courage, as a 'very practical and attractive religion for a soldier'. **Opposite bottom:** Sepp Dietrich, brutal commander of Hitler's bodyguard regiment. In 1946, he received twenty-five years for complicity in the murder of American prisoners-of-war. He was released after ten years. **Left:** Members of Der Führer SS regiment, predominantly Austrian, created after the Nazi invasion of Austria in March 1938*

Historical Research Unit

# Resistance

Wherever men have exercised power there have been others to offer resistance. A greater number are usually prepared to collaborate, even in war. But in the Second World War collaboration became a dirty word and resistance acquired a new dimension, a new sense of tragic dedication. Hitler's conquest of Europe was no simple matter of armies crossing national boundaries. As the peculiar atrocities of the Nazis and the vicious doctrines of their perverted ideology became evident, they provided an indisputable reason against collaboration. It was the argument against selling one's soul to the devil. Those who aided their Nazi overlords soon reaped the scorn of all self-respecting men and, when liberation came, the most violent reprisals. It was not only patriotism but the need to defend human decency which impelled many men and women to risk capture by the Gestapo, to suffer brutal torture, and to give their lives in the cause of a free Europe.

As Hitler's Panzers rolled up to the western coast of Europe in the fateful summer of 1940, representatives of the governments of eight defeated nations withdrew across the Channel to Europe's last bastion of democracy, Great Britain. There they provided a focus for the loyalty of their now subject peoples and a base for continuing the fight against Nazism. Already in the lands they had left spontaneous resistance was growing. In Holland, for example, the introduction of anti-Jewish legislation led to long queues outside Jewish shops and crowded waiting-rooms in the surgeries of Jewish doctors. Clandestine newspapers and pamphlets began to play an important role in psychological warfare. The underground Press in Belgium became so highly organized that in November 1943 100,000 copies of a fake edition of the German-controlled *Le Soir* were sold on newsstands throughout the country. But in the ultimate aim of freeing national territory the resistance was helpless without Allied aid.

In Western Europe this aid came from Great Britain, together with the émigré governments. Churchill showed an immediate interest in the European underground and, in keeping with his resolve 'to set Europe ablaze', he established in July 1940 the Special Operations Executive (SOE). Directed from a secret address in London, bankers, dons, lawyers, journalists, film directors, schoolmasters, wine merchants, and even women were trained to harass the enemy. This was to be done by setting up intelligence networks, organizing sabotage on a large scale, and training secret armies which would emerge when the Allied inva-

sion of Europe was mounted. New personalities were carefully fabricated, forged documents prepared, and special kits assembled. A whole new industry arose supplying false-bottomed suitcases and toothpaste tubes with special compartments. In 'Operation Lavatory' agents hid their radio sets in the cistern, set up a special chain as the aerial, and transmitted using codes in invisible ink written on men's shirt-tails and on women's pants and petticoats. There were new developments in sabotage: explosive 'coal lumps' destined for Gestapo offices, hand-painted explosive 'horse droppings' to be dropped in the path of German staff cars, and incendiary 'cigarettes'. Finally there was the 'L' pill which contained potassium cyanide. Held in the mouth during torture, its insoluble coating could be crushed between the teeth if the pain became too much for the agent to bear. Death would be almost instantaneous.

Agents were despatched to Hitler's Europe by parachute, by Lysander aircraft, submarine, or small fishing boat. The moment when they set off on their missions was likely to be the most solitary they had ever experienced. In the early days this was not purely subjective. The first agents were entirely on their own and 'parachuted blind', for British secret service links with all the occupied countries of Europe had virtually broken down. SOE therefore started from scratch, and by June 1941 little had been achieved and many lives tragically lost. It was the 'heroic' period of the resistance, characterized by lack of co-ordination, inexperience, and successful infiltration by V-men, informers working for the Nazis. But on 22nd June there was a turning point, for when Hitler attacked Soviet Russia Communists all over Europe ranged themselves wholeheartedly behind the Allies in a 'holy' war against Nazism. By the end of 1941 resistance was better organized and more efficient.

In Western Europe the Nazi tyranny never became as harsh as it was in Eastern Europe. Though exploiting to the full the occupied territories in the West, the Germans also attempted to win the allegiance of their new subjects. But even in partly German-speaking Luxembourg this policy failed. Everywhere resistance became the

*Top: Fake issue of the Nazi military magazine* Signal *printed by Belgian resistance, entitled: 'An outrage against humanity; after the Munich Putsch Mr Hitler was arrested.' Right: Fruits of resistance in Czechoslovakia. Freight train derailed by partisans in Moravia*

norm and in most countries proved its value in the struggle against Nazism. It was resistance which removed the possibility of a Nazi nuclear bomb. In March 1943 the Norwegian secret army, Milorg, co-operated with SOE in destroying the heavy water plant at Rjukan upon which the Nazi nuclear research programme depended. In Belgium, a vital staging-post for escape routes to Switzerland and Spain, underground engineers put all the high-tension lines in the country out of action simultaneously in January 1944, costing the Nazis vital man hours in repairs. In Denmark, however, resistance was slower to mature since the government, not officially at war with Germany, remained in Copenhagen. Until 1943, therefore, when the Nazis imposed direct rule, underground activity was hindered by the stigma of treason. And in Holland resistance suffered a catastrophe. The early capture by the Nazis of an SOE radio operator and the use of the secret code to deceive London condemned many Dutch agents to death and, by crippling the Dutch resistance, was ultimately responsible for the delayed liberation of the country after D-Day.

Radio, as the case of Holland suggests, was a vital element in resistance activities. It was underground Europe's chief contact with the outside world. On average two million words a week passed through SOE signals stations and on 5th June, the eve of D-Day, 500 signals were sent to alert agents and their secret armies. The German counter-measure was the Funkpeil Dienst (radio direction finding service) whose 'detection' vans constantly toured the darkened streets of occupied Europe in search of underground transmitters. The BBC had its own special war effort, broadcasting messages of hope and providing news for clandestine publications. Apparently meaningless sentences heard on overseas programmes, such as 'the cow will jump over the moon tonight', were in fact prearranged signals to herald the arrival of a new agent from London or to convince a sympathetic foreign banker of the *bona fides* of an agent in need of money.

Resistance was not only a revolt against Nazism; it was also a political movement. This was particularly true in France where the shattering of the Third Republic created a constitutional desert in which new institutions would have to be set up. As the dust settled, two architects appeared among the ruins. The first was the right-wing Marshal Pétain, victor of Verdun. To begin with the population rallied to his French State based on Vichy and collaboration became the order of the day. But as the Nazi tyranny became more oppressive the French turned to resistance—and therefore to Charles de Gaulle who as an unknown general had arrived in London in June 1940 as the self-appointed representative of the Free French. Progressively he established himself as the leader of the new republic which was to be constructed.

The road to victory was not an easy one. It was marred by bad relations between the general's BCRA (Bureau Central de Renseignements et d'Action), established with British credits, and SOE whose French

A sign of growing resistance to German rule: German captured by French maquis. Allied propaganda fanned the flames of resentment and hatred of the Germans

section under Colonel Maurice Buckmaster played a major part in organizing the resistance. In addition the Nazis infiltrated several important circuits. Through one such coup they were able to make full preparations to repulse the ill-fated Dieppe Raid in August 1943. However, after the union of disparate resistance groups under the National Resistance Council in November 1942, sabotage increased and by early 1944 100,000 underground fighters were organized to take part in the fight for liberation. With the founding of the French Forces of the Interior (FFI) the resistance war effort was linked directly to SHAEF (Supreme Headquarters, Allied Expeditionary Force) and played an important part behind the lines during the Allied landings in Normandy (Overlord) and Provence (Anvil). Alone the resistance could never have defeated the Nazis, but together with the Allied armies General Eisenhower considered that it 'played a very considerable part in our victory'.

Bearing the brunt of the worst Nazi barbarism, the peoples of Eastern Europe were quick to organize resistance. Help came from two sources, Soviet Russia and Great Britain, and it was to be politically motivated: once the Red Army was bearing down on Berlin, Stalin used the Communist elements of the resistance to install regimes congenial to himself. This pattern became evident in Czechoslovakia. President Beneš and his government in exile at first directed resistance operations from London. It was from London that the murder of 'Hangman' Heydrich, protector of Bohemia-Moravia, was arranged in cooperation with SOE in May 1942. But when Beneš saw that the Red Army would reach Prague before the Western powers, he established closer relations with Soviet Russia. Increasingly control passed from London to Moscow. The same occurred in Poland where the resistance, which ran the best radio communications system in occupied Europe, was at first directed by General Sikorski in London. But after the Warsaw Rising in August 1944, when Stalin stood by while the Germans ruth-

lessly crushed the uprising of the Polish Home Army and razed Warsaw to the ground, Poland fell under a Russian-directed Communist regime based on Lublin.

Resistance also brought Yugoslavia into the Communist camp, but for the less sinister reason that here the British supported the Communist partisans under Tito. But in Greece, where antagonism between the two wings of the resistance verged on civil war, monarchist elements triumphed—because Churchill sent British troops to crush the Communists.

Resistance in the Axis countries and their satellites was by far the weakest. In these countries it was resistance by citizens against their own governments and therefore treason. Against traitors the Reich proved to have all the trump cards, and since the Allies seemed not to believe in the possibility of 'good Germans', resistance in Germany was deprived of outside help. It was therefore condemned to failure as the July Plot demonstrated, but it is as well to remember the words of Moltke, leader of the Kreisau circle, in a letter to an English friend: 'Never forget that for us there will be a bitter, bitter end to all this. When you are through with us, try to remember, however, that there are still a few who earnestly want to help you win the war and the peace.' In Italy the anti-Fascists succeeded in toppling Mussolini from power in July 1943, but this was more a matter of coincidental rather than concerted action. Once Mussolini was re-established at Salò, resistance was no longer treason for he was merely the puppet of an external power. In German-occupied Italy, therefore, resistance took much the same form as elsewhere in Europe: sabotage and assassinations. It was at the hands of Italian partisans that Mussolini met his death in April 1945.

Was resistance worth it? Compared with the victories of the Allied armies its achievements were modest. It could never have played more than a supporting role but as an ancillary force it had many successes. As an instrument of destruction it rivalled and on occasion surpassed Bomber Command. The continuous strain imposed by sabotage and assassination in the interior tied down many divisions that could otherwise have been employed on the front lines against Allied troops. As a medium of intelligence the resistance performed a vital service. And in France FFI units liberated five departments unaided.

But the achievements of the resistance were won at great cost. The murder of Heydrich was avenged by the destruction of Lidice and the massacre of 3,000 hostages in Prague and Brno. In France the disabling by FFI units of the SS Division Das Reich on its way to Normandy in June 1944 led to the murder of ninety-nine hostages in Tulle and the massacre of the entire population of Oradour-sur-Glane. In Russia anti-partisan operations often turned into orgies of murder and destruction.

For the many unsung heroes who fought in the secret war the reward was to know that they had played their part in the destruction of National Socialism. For those in Eastern Europe it was to see a new tyranny imposed. And for a great many it was death.

# D-Day

To uninitiated Frenchmen the second half of a verse by Verlaine transmitted by the BBC at 2115 on Monday 5th June 1944 meant nothing. But to the resistance *'Blessent mon coeur d'une langueur monotone'* concealed a message they had longed to hear: more than three and a half million Allied troops were poised to invade and liberate France in one of the greatest amphibious operations in history.

Although Stalin had urged the creation of a second front in France ever since the German invasion of the Soviet Union, proposals for an attack on Brest or Cherbourg in 1942 and the liberation of France in 1943 never developed. In fact planning for a mighty cross-Channel assault on Hitler's *Festung Europa* (Fortress Europe) did not begin until the Casablanca Conference in January 1943 when it was resolved to set up a joint Anglo-American staff to attend to the multiplicity of problems involved in such a massive and hazardous venture. The conception of a full-scale invasion of France was confirmed at the Washington Conference in May 1943 and code-named 'Operation Overlord', it was set for 1st May 1944.

Three months later Lieutenant-General Sir Frederick Morgan, who led the Allied team with the designation Chief of Staff to the Supreme Allied Commander (COSSAC), submitted a tentative plan to the Quebec Conference, and although Churchill suggested a twenty-five per cent increase in the forces employed, its proposals were approved. At the end of the year the appointment of General Dwight D.Eisenhower as Supreme Allied Commander for Operation Overlord was announced. Within the space of one year a relatively unknown chief of staff of an American army training in Texas, whose promotion had been consistently slow, had become the Allied commander-in-chief of a daunting military array charged with striking into the heartland of Germany and destroying her armed forces. It was an inspired choice. The Supreme Commander may not have been a great soldier but the great soldiers of his day willingly served him. Universally trusted, he won the affection, respect, and loyalty not only of his men but of political and military leaders alike. But his greatest contribution to victory undoubtedly lay in his very real ability to allay inter-Service rivalry and

*Men of the 1st South Lancashire Battalion help wounded comrades ashore during their comparatively easy landing on Sword beach, 6th June 1944*

international prejudice among the forces under his command. It was a gift that enabled him to weld together the Allied armies in the field and forge a weapon which the Germans, distracted by their mortal struggle in the east, were unable to deflect.

The remainder of Eisenhower's team was speedily selected. Air Chief Marshal Sir Arthur Tedder was appointed as his deputy, and General Walter Bedell Smith became his chief of staff, with General Sir Frederick Morgan as his deputy. Admiral Sir Bertram Ramsay, the mastermind of Dunkirk and Air Chief Marshal Sir Trafford Leigh-Mallory had been appointed earlier as the commanders-in-chief of the Allied naval and air forces respectively. There was no parallel appointment of commander-in-chief for Allied land forces and although Eisenhower expressed a preference for General Alexander, 'a friendly and companionable type', Churchill felt he could not be spared as Commander in Chief Allied Armies in Italy and consequently Sir Bernard Montgomery handed over command of the 8th Army to assume command of the British 21st Army Group with operational control of all land forces during the initial phase of Operation Overlord. When he was first shown the COSSAC plan for the invasion of France and asked for his comments by Churchill, Montgomery replied that he considered the initial assault forces too weak and the proposed frontage of assault too narrow. The Supreme Commander thus requested the dynamic, and supremely confident general to make his first task the revision of the plan in co-operation with Ramsay, Leigh-Mallory, and Bedell Smith.

COSSAC had proposed the area between Grandcamp and Caen in the Bay of the Seine for the assault. The choice of location, confined by the effective range of the Spitfire to the coast between Flushing and Cherbourg, had to possess harbours capable of handling an immense concentration of men and materiel besides beaches across which the assault forces could be reinforced before ports could be captured. Although the Pas de Calais area offered many obvious advantages such as good air support and a quick turn round for shipping it was formidably defended and offered poor opportunities for an expansion out of the lodgement area. On the other hand, the relatively lightly defended Caen sector afforded a sheltered coastline and offered good terrain for airfield construction. In addition the region was suitable for the consolidation of the initial bridgehead

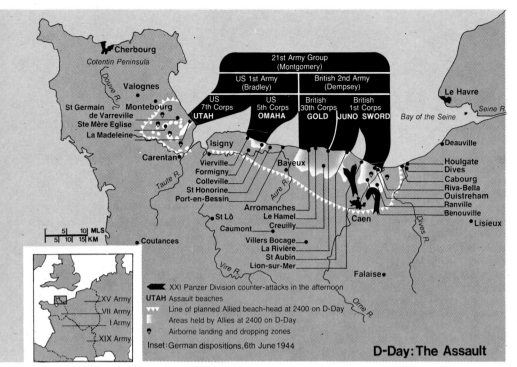

21st Army Group (Montgomery)

US 1st Army (Bradley) | British 2nd Army (Dempsey)

US 7th Corps UTAH | US 5th Corps OMAHA | British 30th Corps GOLD | British 1st Corps JUNO SWORD

D-Day: The Assault

◄▬ XXI Panzer Division counter-attacks in the afternoon
UTAH Assault beaches
▽▽▽ Line of planned Allied beach-head at 2400 on D-Day
▮ Areas held by Allies at 2400 on D-Day
⚲ Airborne landing and dropping zones
Inset: German dispositions, 6th June 1944

and discouraged the development of armoured counter-attacks. COSSAC's plan, limited as it was by resources, proposed the invasion of Normandy with three seaborne divisions and two airborne brigades in the assault, and although Montgomery accepted its proposals, he considered that the assault should be mounted in greater strength and on a wider front.

He therefore recommended the dropping of two, or, if possible, three airborne divisions before a seaborne assault on a five-divisional frontage. But it was easier to recommend these increases than to find

*Into France: US MP does some homework before invasion of Normandy, June 1944*

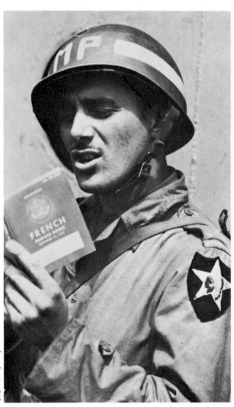

the means of implementing them. While Air Chief Marshal Leigh-Mallory envisaged no difficulties, Admiral Ramsay reported that the Admiralty was uncertain whether it could even meet COSSAC's demands for 'Operation Neptune' (the cross-Channel assault phase of Overlord) which called for 3,323 landing-craft (a generic term embracing landing-ships), 467 warships, and 150 minesweepers. Montgomery's amended plan would double the number of minesweepers and require a further 240 warships and 1,000 landing craft. The central problem was the provision of these craft and although a quantity could be obtained from other theatres of war, Ramsay and Montgomery proposed that the invasion should be postponed until early June to enable an additional month's factory production to be utilized. However, even with this extra production it was discovered that there would still be insufficient craft for the undertaking and it was suggested that additional resources be apportioned Overlord from the Mediterranean. Ever since the Casablanca Conference an invasion of southern France code-named 'Operation Anvil' had been under consideration. By the end of 1943 the Combined Chiefs of Staff decided that both assaults on France were to be 'the supreme operations for 1944'. But although Eisenhower regarded Anvil as an important adjunct to Overlord he advised the Combined Chiefs of Staff that he regarded Overlord as the first priority and that if insufficient naval resources were available for both operations, Anvil should be postponed or reduced. Therefore, despite the fact that he would have preferred to launch the invasion of Normandy in May, to obtain the longest campaigning season, he recommended to the Combined Chiefs of Staff that Overlord should be postponed for a month. They agreed to this on 1st February and at the same time General Eisenhower informed them that the exact date of the assault would depend on a detailed study

of moonlight and tidal conditions prevailing during the first week of June. On 24th March the American chiefs of staff, who had opposed any interference with Anvil, agreed to its postponement so that the landing craft of one division could be used for the invasion of Normandy. The craft for a further division would be obtained by the postponement of Overlord. As for the additional forces, Great Britain and the United States would each contribute one division to bring the total to five.

Apart from the question of shipping, the postponement of Operation Overlord afforded a longer period for the strategic bombing of Germany which had been accorded highest priority at the Quebec Conference and for the destruction of bridges and railways which had to be severed if German communications into the invasion area were to be disrupted. Moreover, weather conditions at the end of May would be more likely to favour the launching of a large-scale Russian offensive in conjunction with Operation Overlord.

The broadening and strengthening of the assault was only a partial solution to the problem of breaching the German Atlantic Wall. It was to take specialized equipment and new techniques to break out from the beaches and establish a lodgement. Fortunately the COSSAC planners and the War Office had paid close attention to lessons of the disastrous Dieppe raid which taught that a far stronger and closer fire support for the assaulting troops together with tank support from the moment of disembarking would be required of any future attempt to land in France.

The débâcle had a profound effect on the planning of Overlord and in March 1943 General Sir Alan Brooke, Chief of the Imperial General Staff, ordered the conversion of 79th Armoured Division into Specialized Armour and ordered its commander, Major-General Sir Percy Hobart, to devise and develop specialized armour and equipment for the invasion of France. As a brigadier, Hobart had commanded 1st Tank Brigade, evolving tactics and doctrines of armoured warfare which the Germans had eagerly assimilated. In 1938 he had created the celebrated 7th Armoured Division (the 'Desert Rats') but in the process so outraged orthodox thinkers with his pioneering concepts that he was relieved of his command and, driven into premature retirement in 1940, he became a corporal in the Home Guard. Happily he was rescued from oblivion on Churchill's personal intervention but it was not until Brooke became convinced of the need for specialized armour to eliminate beach obstacles that his exceptional ingenuity received full rein. By early 1944, despite numerous frustrations, he was able to reveal a range of vehicles to his brother-in-law, General Montgomery, and to the Supreme Commander, General Eisenhower. Tagged 'The Funnies', Hobart's creations presented a bizarre spectacle. There were Crabs, Sherman tanks fitted with flails to beat pathways through minefields; Bobbins, track-laying Churchill tanks; Churchill AVREs (Armoured Vehicles, Royal En-

Ullstein

U.S. Army Dept

*Opposite: The Normandy landings, 6th June 1944. With the exception of Omaha, where the Americans were delayed at the cost of 1,000 dead and 2,000 wounded, the Allies landed swiftly. Left: Rommel (left) inspects the Atlantic Wall, January 1944. He was given command of the two armies holding the most important sector of the invasion coast. Below: Eisenhower briefs paratroopers before take-off*

was destroyed in a violent storm from the 19th-22nd of June.

Faced with the inevitable destruction of port facilities, the provision of adequate fuel for vehicles and aircraft was another problem that had confronted COSSAC planners. Their solution was 'PLUTO' or Pipe-Line-Under-The-Ocean along which fuel was pumped first from the Isle of Wight to Cherbourg and later from Dungeness to Ambleteuse near Boulogne. But the pipeline only began functioning forty-one days after the invasion and by that time the Allies were moving through Belgium.

By the spring of 1944 all southern England had become a gigantic air base, workshop, storage depot, and mobilization camp. On 1st January American forces in Great Britain numbered three quarters of a million and in the following five months they increased to over one and a half million. While British and Canadian troops assembled in south-eastern England, the Americans gathered in the western and south-western coastal belt. Between Dorset and Cornwall, Sir Basil Liddell Hart observed wryly, lay 'occupied England'.

While the massive invasion force trained and rehearsed its tasks, constant reconnaissance, often involving daring landings on the enemy beaches, provided vital information on off-shore rocks, the geological formation of the beaches, beach obstacles, tidal conditions, and changes in the seabed. Great pains were moreover taken to persuade the enemy that the blow was to fall in the Pas de Calais. This was done by simulating concentrations of troops in Kent and Sussex, assembling fleets of dummy ships in south-eastern ports, staging landing exercises on nearby beaches, stepping-up wireless activity, and dropping more bombs on the Pas de Calais than in Normandy. Furthermore, the SD and Abwehr were deliberately swamped with 'secret information' which convinced them that the invasion was scheduled for July in the Pas de Calais. And they were no better served by the Luftwaffe. Its reconnaissance aircraft seldom managed to penetrate the formidable defences which ringed southern England from Falmouth to Harwich. The Germans were almost completely deceived — only Hitler guessed the correct location for the invasion and he was reluctant to back his hunch. The larger part of the German forces were thus deployed east of the Seine and even after D-Day, the Germans believed that the real attack was still to come.

In the last few months before the invasion, security dictated a severe restriction on civilian movement. Coastal areas from the Wash to Land's End were banned to visitors and innumerable ammunition

gineers), bridge-laying tanks; Churchill Crocodiles, flame-throwing Churchill tanks; Churchill AVREs which could hurl explosive charges against blockhouses; armoured bulldozers, and most significantly of all, amphibious or Duplex-Drive (DD) tanks which could swim ashore under their own power. Although the latter were the brainchild of Nicholas Straussler, a Hungarian-born engineer, Hobart's contribution was to adapt the canvas screen attachment, which enabled the tanks to swim, from obsolete British Valentines to American Shermans. Montgomery immediately recognized the significance of Hobart's 'Funnies' and while Eisenhower appreciated the value of the DD tanks, requesting a brigade's worth, he left the choice of other vehicles to General Omar Bradley, commander of the American assault forces. With fateful consequences, Bradley rejected the devices.

### 'Occupied England'

The Dieppe raid had made it clear that no major port could be captured quickly or intact and before Cherbourg could be cleared of mines and repaired, Overlord forces would have to be supplied across open beaches. The upshot was the production of two prefabricated harbours known by their code names as Mulberry A and Mulberry B which would be towed across the Channel and sunk or anchored in position off the Normandy coast northwest and north-east of Bayeux. However, only one was brought into use as the harbour on the American sector near Vierville

*Left: Picture by Robert Capa, who went in with the first wave of troops, shows a GI struggling through the surf to land on Omaha, the bloodiest of the landing-areas. Assault troops landed cold, sodden, cramped, and weakened by seasickness. Below left: American forces land on Omaha after dogged assaults and naval bombardment had breached the defences.*

counter attacks to drive small bridgeheads back into the sea.

Throughout the winter of 1943 Rundstedt had appealed repeatedly to OKW for reinforcements; but instead of the men he badly needed, Hitler sent him the hero of North Africa, Field Marshal Erwin Rommel. Initially appointed to inspect defences between Denmark and the Spanish border in November 1943, he was given command of the two armies holding the most important sector of the invasion coast from the Zuider Zee to the River Loire — VII and XV Armies — three months later. Rommel predicted that Allied air power would disrupt the movements of Rundstedt's reserve and that once Allied forces had secured a lodgement they would inevitably break out. He therefore insisted that the invasion would have to be broken on the beaches if it was to be broken at all.

The differing theories of how best to counter the invasion were to lead to a fatal compromise. While the armoured reserves were generally kept well back, the majority of the infantry divisions were committed to strengthening the coastline. In the event the Panzer divisions were forced into action prematurely and found it impossible to concentrate in order to deliver a co-ordinated blow until too late.

In February 1944 Rommel, who had come to share Hitler's view that Normandy would be the main Allied target, instituted an elaborate scheme for obstructing the coastline with underwater obstacles. It was hoped that the 'Czech hedgehogs', concrete tetrahedrons, and mined stakes would impale, cripple, or destroy landing-craft before they reached the beach minefields and that steel 'Belgian grilles' and 'Maginot portcullises' would disable any tanks that landed. To obstruct airborne assaults all open areas within seven miles of the coast were to be sown with booby-trapped stakes. In addition, low-lying areas were to be flooded and gaps between them mined. It was Rommel's intention that heavy coastal batteries immune to air attack should engage the Allied armada at sea. As they raced for the beaches the assault waves would be met by direct fire from fortified machine and anti-tank gun emplacements and from the indirect fire of inland mortars and artillery. Rommel believed that those craft which survived such a devastating concentration of fire and the forest of lethal underwater obstacles would shatter themselves on the mined beaches. Any troops or tanks which landed would have to contend with additional minefields, barbed-wire, anti-tank ditches, and the withering blast of flame-throwers. Immediately behind this belt Rommel proposed to deploy all armoured

dumps, airfields, camps, and vehicle parks became prohibited areas. Nothing was left to chance. The delivery of letters was postponed and foreign embassies were forbidden to send cipher telegrams. Even their diplomatic bags were delayed.

'The whole mighty host was tense as a coiled spring,' wrote Eisenhower in *Crusade in Europe*, 'and indeed that is exactly what it was — a great human spring, coiled for the moment when its energy should be released and it would vault the English Channel in the greatest amphibious assault ever attempted.' Immense force had been assembled: 1,200 warships, 4,000 assault craft, 1,600 merchant vessels, 13,000 aircraft, and over three and a half million men. They would shortly be pitted against the Atlantic Wall.

For several years the Germans had been developing this coastal defence complex,

primarily concentrating on the defence of ports and the Pas de Calais, and although by the end of 1943 a quarter of a million men, conscript workers, and garrison troops were toiling at its construction, it was only approaching completion between Antwerp and Le Havre. Field Marshal Gerd von Rundstedt, Commander in Chief West, had no faith in forts. He was acutely aware of the wall's weaknesses, observing after the war that it had been nothing but 'an illusion fostered by propaganda to fool the Germans as well as the Allies'. Committed to defending 2,000 miles of French coastline, Rundstedt believed that an actual landing could not be prevented and he planned, therefore, to hold strongly only key ports and the most vulnerable sections of the coast. By these tactics the Commander-in-Chief West hoped to delay any Allied build-up long enough for

divisions so that they could pour their fire onto the foreshore. It was imperative, he maintained, that the maximum force should oppose the invasion on the very day of the landings. 'The first twenty-four hours,' Rommel averred, 'will be decisive.'

The considerable variation in the quality of the sixty German divisions in the West gave Rommel further cause for concern, for while the equipment, training, and morale of the SS and Panzer divisions was superb, the infantry formations contained many low-quality, static, coast-defence troops. Many were too young or too old and many more were Armenian, Georgian, Azerbaijanese, and Tartar 'volunteers' who had

elected to wear a German army uniform rather than face a slow death in a prison camp. Rommel had few illusions about his task. The German armies in the West, deprived of training, transport, and their essential radar installations and harassed continually from the air, could only wait for the blow to fall. It was perhaps fortunate for the Allies that the dynamic hero of North Africa had not been appointed earlier and that his plans were neither wholeheartedly supported by his superiors nor thoroughly executed by his subordinates.

In essence, Allied mastery of the air (won by the introduction of the Mustang long-range escort fighter in December 1943) en-

*Left:* Survivors of a wrecked landing-craft are helped ashore on Utah. *Below:* Flail tank for clearing minefields. Had General Bradley provided such tanks on Omaha, assaulting American forces would not have suffered so grievously

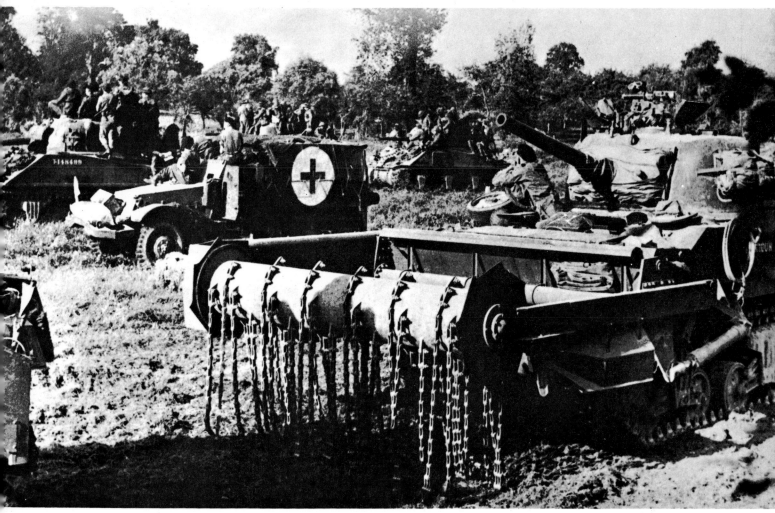

sured the success of Operation Overlord, but the interdiction of road and rail communications into the battle area was not achieved without prolonged and acute inter-Allied wrangling. The 'Transportation Plan', as the massive air offensive was code-named, concentrated on the scientific destruction of those control, repair, and maintenance facilities which were vitally necessary for the operation of railways in northern and western France, the Low Countries, and western Germany. By mid-May the German armies in France were cut in two for lack of communications.

On 17th May Eisenhower selected Monday 5th June as the tentative D-Day. A final decision would depend on the weather. But the weather was not favourable. Gales and high seas lashed the fog-bound Normandy beaches on Sunday 4th June and the Supreme Commander decided that the invasion would have to be postponed. At 4 a.m. the following day, promised a short period of good weather, Eisenhower announced 'OK, we'll go', and within two hours a mighty armada began emerging into a stormy Channel from Falmouth, Fowey, Plymouth, Salcombe, Dartmouth, Brixham, Torbay, Portland, Weymouth, Poole, Southampton, Shoreham, Newhaven, and Harwich. It was almost four years to the day that the BEF had escaped by the skin of its teeth at Dunkirk. Now with powerful Allies the British were going back to avenge their humiliation and liberate France.

Meanwhile Allied aircraft had been maintaining diversionary attacks on gun emplacements and beaches in the Pas de Calais and that evening the impression created by these attacks was reinforced. It was essential that the enemy should not discover the course of the invasion fleet and accordingly those radar stations between Cherbourg and Le Havre which had survived air attacks were jammed, while those between Le Havre and Calais were persuaded that the fleet was moving towards this section of the coast. As ships of the Royal Navy towed barrage balloons and produced 'big ship echoes' on the operative German radar sets, bombers circled nearer and nearer the French coast jettisoning bundles of metal foil known as 'Window' which appeared to German radar operators as a large convoy crossing the Channel.

On D-Day, 6th June 1944, the long months of preparation and planning for the most momentous amphibious operation in history came to an end. As the silent column of ships surged towards the Bay of the Seine through ten swept channels, waves of aircraft roared over them and at 0020 the first Allied troops to reach French soil, a *coup de main* force of the British 6th Airborne Division, landed by glider with extreme accuracy near Bénouville to seize the bridges over the Canal de Caen and the River Orne. Half an hour later 3rd and 5th Brigades began to drop east of the Orne to silence the Merville battery, destroy the bridges over the River Dives, and clear an area north of Ranville so that seventy-two gliders carrying guns, transport, and heavy equipment could land

at 0330. While 6th Airborne Division was securing the eastern flank of the beachhead, the US 101st and 82nd Airborne Divisions had landed in the south east corner of the Cotentin Peninsula near Ste Mère Eglise and Vierville to carry out the same task on the western flank. Despite losses and confusion arising out of the scattered nature of the landings they forced the enemy on the defensive and succeeded in capturing the causeways across the inundated areas behind the western-most landing area.

While the airborne landings were in progress, over 1,100 British and Canadian bombers attacked coastal batteries between Le Havre and Cherbourg and at daybreak, during the half hour before the first waves hit the beaches, a massive naval and air bombardment was delivered against coastal defences in the target area. The Germans were confident they could not be surprised, but blinded by the bombing and jamming of their radar installations they failed to intercept the airborne forces and only detected the invasion fleet when it was close enough to be heard.

At 0630 Force U, comprising the US 4th Infantry Division of the 7th Corps of the US 1st Army spearheaded by 8th Regimental Combat Team, made a swift and painless landing at the eastern base of the Cotentin Peninsula near the village of La Madeleine, on a beach code-named Utah. Through a navigational error the force had been deposited a mile too far south in a surprisingly weakly defended area and this fortunate error, together with the fact that late launching of the DD tanks ensured the survival of twenty-eight out of thirty-two, accounted for the ease of the landing achieved at the cost of only twelve dead.

### Bloody Omaha
Force O, however, landing between Vierville and Colleville on Omaha beach, was not to breach the Atlantic Wall with similar impunity. The plan on this beach provided for the US 1st Infantry Division of 5th Corps of the US 1st Army to assault with two regimental combat teams, supported by two battalions of the DD tanks and two special brigades of engineers. At 0300 the force boarded its assault craft and was lowered into heavy seas twelve miles offshore. Almost at once ten small craft were swamped and others were only kept afloat by troops who baled vigorously with their helmets. As the assault battalions lurched towards the shore beneath a protective barrage, limited in its effectiveness by poor visibility, twenty-seven prematurely-launched DD tanks foundered. There were no dry landings. The apprehensive men, cold, sodden, cramped, and weakened by sea-sickness, disembarked awkwardly to be raked with mortar shell and machine-gun fire. Three hours later the foreshore was littered with burning vehicles, shattered craft, dead, exhausted, and terrified men. For some hours the position on Omaha hung in the balance. Yet the outcome need never have given rise to such anxiety or the battle claimed so many lives had the commander of the American assault forces, Lieutenant-

General Omar Bradley, utilized more of Hobart's menagerie of specialized armour. As a consequence of his rejection of the Crabs, Crocodiles, and AVREs, Omaha rapidly became a bloodbath where the Americans suffered 1,000 dead and 2,000 wounded. Although they met a degree of resistance from a spirited infantry division whose presence they had discounted, their cruel losses from gunfire and mines would have been infinitely fewer had Crabs been available to flail the necessary exits. The failure to land the DD tanks – which Bradley had only grudgingly accepted – in advance of the infantry and the ineffectiveness of the naval and air bombardment left the infantry at the mercy of strongpoints they were expected to storm. Only a combination of sustained and accurate naval bombardment and dogged assaults broke the crust of the defences and prevented a local disaster from becoming a major crisis.

If it had not been for the specialized armour and the policy of preceding all British units by special assault teams of Hobart's 79th Armoured Division, progress on the British beaches, code-named Gold, Juno, and Sword, might have been as agonizingly slow and costly as it was on Omaha. But Forces G, J, and S, comprising British and Canadian troops of 1st and 30th Corps of the British 2nd Army under the command of Lieutenant-General Sir Miles Dempsey, landed swiftly between Le Hamel and St Aubin, and Lion-sur-Mer and Riva-Bella.

'Apart from the factor of tactical surprise, the comparatively light casualties which we sustained on all beaches, except Omaha, were in large measure due to the success of the novel mechanical contrivances which we employed and to the staggering moral and material effect of the mass of armour landed in the leading waves of the assault,' the Supreme Commander stated in his report, adding, 'it is doubtful if the assault forces could have firmly established themselves without the assistance of these weapons.'

By nightfall on 6th June 1944, 156,000 Allied troops had landed in Normandy and, although Caen had not been carried in the first onslaught as was planned, the vaunted Atlantic Wall had been breached on a front of thirty miles between the Vire and the Orne at the cost of 11,000 casualties of whom not more than 2,500 lost their lives.

With no reserves behind the thin beach defences and no heavy artillery to challenge the naval bombardment squadrons, Rommel had failed to smash the invasion on the beaches and by 9th June, despite an attack by XXI Panzer Division, the Allied bridgeheads had been safely consolidated. The previous year Churchill had expressed hopes for the liberation of France 'before the fall of autumn leaves'. The liberation had not come and the Germans scattered green paper leaves in French streets bearing the mocking inscription: 'I have fallen, Oh Churchill! Where are your soldiers?' They were here now. Rommel had insisted that the first twenty-four hours of the invasion would be decisive. They had been.

# The Bombing of Germany

At the outset of the war in September 1939 Bomber Command went into action with such stringent instructions to avoid causing civilian casualties that there was even doubt about the advisability of attacking German warships at their bases in case civilian dock staff should be on or near them. Less than three years later, in May 1942, Bomber Command launched a thousand bombers against the centre of Cologne. In late July and early August 1943 about 40,000 German civilians were killed in a series of Bomber Command operations against Hamburg. In February 1945 even greater casualties were caused by a catastrophic attack on Dresden, which was of doubtful strategic importance, crowded with refugees and virtually undefended.

In September 1939 Bomber Command was small in size, inadequate in equipment, and defective in technique. For operations against Germany it could muster about 280 aircraft. Bomber Command was not only much smaller than the corresponding German force but it was also equipped with less reliable high explosive bombs than the German equivalents. In addition, Bomber Command, surprisingly, had no proper system of navigation.

By the end of the war Bomber Command could regularly despatch more than 1,500 aircraft on a single operation. More than a thousand of these were four-engined Lancasters which, with their great range, their huge bomb loads of up to ten tons, and their remarkable durability, were, as heavy

bombers, internationally in a class of their own. Of the rest, some 200 were Mosquitoes which, owing to their performance, had a versatility perhaps exceeding that of any other aircraft which saw service in the Second World War. The bombs available ranged from the 4lb incendiary which chiefly accounted for the firestorms in Hamburg and Dresden, to the 22,000lb Grandslam designed by Dr Barnes Wallis which, with the smaller version, the 12,000lb Tallboy, brought down the Bielefeld viaduct.

Nor was this the whole, or even in terms of numbers of aircraft the greater part, of the bomber forces which, in the last year of the war, could be brought to bear upon Germany. Other than Great Britain, the United States was the only power which before the war had evolved a doctrine of strategic bombing and during it had worked up a force to carry it out. This working up began in 1942 when US 8th Air Force, having established bases in the United Kingdom for its B-17 Flying Fortresses and B-24 Liberators, both of which were four-engined bombers, began experimental daylight operations against targets in France and other parts of German-occupied Europe. In January 1943 these operations were extended to Germany but it was not until the end of the year that 8th Air Force had enough bombers to mount regular operations from 600 to 700 strong.

Meanwhile, another US bomber force, the 15th, was formed on Italian bases and

in January 1944 these two formations were placed under unified command to compose the United States Strategic Air Forces in Europe. By June 1944 the American bomber forces so combined could despatch more than 1,500 aircraft on operations in a single day. Thus, within two years of their initial bombing attacks in August 1942 involving only a dozen aircraft, the Americans were ranging over all Europe from England and Italy in greater strength than RAF Bomber Command.

Because their aircraft carried lighter loads than the British, the Americans were in the last year of the war still inferior to the British in bombing power. All the same, American 8th and 15th Air Forces were in some other respects more significant fighting formations than Bomber Command. In particular, the Americans made a more important contribution to the winning of command of the air than the British, and command of the air was decisive in making bombing a really effective and ultimately conclusive way of waging war.

This paradox arose from the different bombing policies which the two forces followed. In the last three years of peace, when the bombing offensive was planned, and in the first year of the war, when it began to be attempted, the main idea of the British was the selection of key points in the German war machine such as power stations, oil plants, railway junctions and marshalling yards, dams, and other sensitive points destruction of which would impede or even dislocate the German war effort. This policy, to be effective, depended upon accurate intelligence since the whole idea of 'key point' attack would only work if the target really was a key point. It also depended upon a high degree of bombing accuracy and destructiveness.

Marching with this selective key point theory was another which owed its origin not only to its own merit but also, perhaps, to a fear in anticipation that key point bombing might be hard to realize in practice. It was that bombing, even if it lacked the accuracy and destructiveness to dispose effectively of key points, might, through its moral effect upon the people who lived and worked in their neighbourhood, nevertheless achieve important and possibly even decisive effects upon the enemy's capacity to continue the war. After all, the bombing

*Veteran Lancaster bomber about to make its 100th operational trip, May 1944. The base commander watches as the ground crew write a message on an 8,000-lb bomb to be loaded on the aircraft*

of London in June 1917 by a mere handful of primitive Gothas had caused a panic. The merit of this idea was that it could seemingly be realized with a considerable bombing inaccuracy, such as for example would be produced in night operations, and by a force lacking the power to destroy major installations like concrete dams. The difficulty was that it might be considered improper to attack towns rather than installations and there had, indeed, been a furore about the bombing of people rather than things in the Spanish Civil War.

By Christmas 1939 Bomber Command had sufficient experience of war to know that it could not carry on major operations against Germany in daylight. The reason was simply that an aircraft able to go the distance and carry a worthwhile load of bombs could not achieve the performance to survive in combat with an enemy fighter which could do its work with a much smaller load and duration. By the autumn of 1941, Bomber Command had proved photographically that oil plants and even large railway

marshalling yards were much too small to be found and hit in night operations against defended areas.

### Area attack on major cities

Thus, at the end of 1941, Bomber Command was presented with the alternatives of being withdrawn from its strategic offensive against Germany or of concentrating upon much larger targets. At a time when British arms on land and at sea were defeated almost upon appearance, at a time when the Germans were advancing rapidly into the heart of Russia, and the Japanese, having struck down the American fleet at Pearl Harbour, were on the verge of the conquest of an empire, it is not to be wondered at that the British, despite some disagreement in their inner councils, refused to put Bomber Command into voluntary liquidation. Instead the policy of area attack upon major German cities was instituted as the prime one to be followed.

Though this did not initiate area bombing, which had already been practised both

by the British and the Germans, it did make it the main theme of the Bomber Command offensive, which it remained for the duration of the war. From this, and in particular from an important directive of February 1942, there flowed the great offensive of 1942-45 embracing the Battles of the Ruhr, Hamburg, and Berlin.

This was not wanton or indiscriminate bombing. It was an organized attempt to destroy German military power, which nothing else seemed able to check, through the systematic destruction of its greatest industrial and administrative centres. But to be effective, area bombing had to be concentrated, sustained, and very heavy. In the Thousand Bomber attack upon Cologne in 1942 only about 400 Germans were killed and this attack was only made possible by calling into action the whole front line of Bomber Command and the whole of its operational training organization as well. Clearly Bomber Command had to be greatly expanded and its operations had to be made much more concentrated.

This latter requirement found expression in the creation of the Pathfinder Force and accompanying techniques and equipment ranging from marker bombs to radar devices for navigation and target finding. By these means more and more bombers were brought over smaller and smaller areas in shorter and shorter times and in 1943 Bomber Command became more and more able to 'rub out' towns. These greater concentrations of bombers which emitted more and more radar emanations and pyrotechnics, however, offered the German night-fighter force easier targets for interception and the bombing offensive at night became a grim race between the destruction of towns by Bomber Command and the destruction of Bomber Command by the German night-fighter force.

In the summer of 1943 when the Battle of Hamburg was over, Albert Speer, the German minister for armament and war production, thought that six more blows on that scale would end the war. In the four and a half months of the Battle of Berlin from November 1943 to March 1944, Bomber Command lost the equivalent of the whole of its front line, mostly to German fighters, and it became obvious that a continuing offensive on that scale would end, not the war, but Bomber Command.

As the fortunes of Bomber Command and the German night-fighter force see-sawed with each tactical shift and technical innovation, the constant factor was the inability of Bomber Command to deal directly with its scourge. Lancasters could not fight Junkers 88s or even Messerschmitt 110s. Their only hope was to dodge them. Nor could they bomb their airfields and factories. The area bombing offensive, for all its destructive and terrifying powers, could only achieve incidental or indirect effects against 'key' targets. Whatever else it may have done in diverting German effort and pinning it down, area bombing up to March

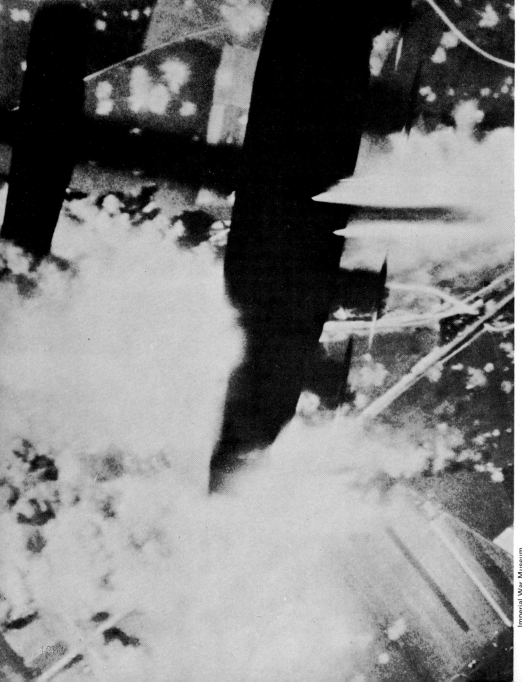

Imperial War Museum

*Left: Flares illuminate German V1 flying bomb launching site for RAF Halifax bomber, July 1944. V1s killed some 6,000 people, mainly in London*

1944 had not resulted in a significant reduction in essential German war production nor had it prevented the German armed forces from continuing their operations in Russia and Italy or against Bomber Command itself.

The Americans had expected as much. They had refused to be diverted by British warnings from their plan of daylight precision attacks against selected key point targets. Throughout 1942, however, they had not felt strong enough in numbers to carry their determination into operational effect over Germany. In 1943 they began to do so. Believing that night area bombing was a blunt and ineffective tactic and possessing aircraft unsuitable for and crews untrained in night-flying, they massed their Flying Fortresses and Liberators in tight highly-disciplined formations and operated at very high altitudes. At high altitude they hoped to escape the worst of the flak and in their formations they hoped to bring such concentrated fire-power to bear that the formations would successfully fight their way to and from their targets in daylight.

One difficulty was that at altitude over Germany the bombers often found themselves over dense cloud so that the best they could do was to deliver approximate or area attacks. Another was that the formations were regularly shot to pieces by the German fighters. The Americans therefore gave higher priority to bombing Germany's aircraft industry. But the aircraft industry in Germany was divided into small units, well dispersed, and often at extreme range from England. So the Americans were given no alternative to the policy of seeking to make a dangerous and difficult task possible by undertaking a more dangerous and more difficult one. The result was disaster. Two-thirds of a force despatched to Schweinfurt on 14th October 1943 was destroyed or damaged. Within six days and from four attacks the Americans lost 138 bombers.

This was comparable to, and indeed, even more decisive than the fate which at that time was approaching Bomber Command in the Battle of Berlin and in incurring it the Americans had done much less damage to Germany than the British had achieved. So in the winter of 1943-44 it seemed that the strategic air attack on Germany had been a costly failure. The indications, however, were misleading. The break-through in the air was imminent and the heavy bombers of Great Britain and America were on the verge of achievements which were not only important but decisive for the war.

The reasons for this, one of the most extraordinary and abrupt changes in military fortune in the Second World War, are

*The Allied bombing of enemy cities gave the Germans good material for propaganda. Between 1939 and 1945 nearly 600,000 German civilians were killed in bombing raids. The total British civilian losses for the same period were 65,000. **Above:** Posters issued in Holland and Belgium stress civilian suffering. **Right:** Germans salvage belongings after an air raid*

ROTTERDAM
PARIJS - ANTWERPEN

Musée Royal de l'Armée, Brussels

Les femmes et les enfants d'Europe accusent!

Par la R.A.F.

C'est l'Angleterre qui a jeté les premières bombes le 12 janvier 1940 sur la population civile

Bundesarchiv, Koblenz

*German bomb victim, the result of controversial British bombing of enemy cities at a desperate cost to civilians*

chiefly to be found in three singular developments: first, the introduction of an effective long-range fighter, secondly, the advance of Allied armies across France, and thirdly, the development by Bomber Command of heavy precision-bombing techniques.

After Schweinfurt, the Americans realized that their survival depended upon the introduction of a machine with the range of a bomber and the performance of a fighter. The answer was found in the hybrid P-51 Mustang, a North American aircraft with a Rolls Royce engine and hitherto chiefly in service with the RAF, which, with droppable long-range tanks, was rushed into action with US 8th Air Force from December 1943. By March 1944, it had developed the capacity to fight over Berlin from British bases. Moreover, it could take on any German fighter in service on at least equal and, in most respects, superior terms. These aircraft swept into action in such force — 14,000 were produced before the end of the war — and to such effect that the day-fighter force of Germany in the air was rapidly smashed and the way opened for a major resumption of the daylight bombing offensive. From February 1944 onwards 8th and 15th Air Forces seized their opportunity with growing confidence and rapidly diminishing casualties. The command of the daylight air over Germany and German Europe passed from the Germans to the Americans. In May 1944, the Americans began an offensive against German synthetic oil production.

### To prepare for the invasion

During this period, Bomber Command still had to face severe casualties in maintaining what it could of the area offensive against Germany and in conducting a night precision offensive against the French railway system. The latter was to open the way for the invasion of Europe by the American and British armies. And it did. So accurate and so destructive were these Bomber Command attacks that the Germans lost the sovereign advantage which had previously made ideas of invasion academic, namely, an efficient interior system of communications which would enable them rapidly to concentrate a superior force against whatever invasion areas were selected.

The Bomber Command attacks, however, did even more than that. They showed the way to heavy precision bombing. They were the link between the vast destructive power which the needs of the area offensive had demanded and generated and the almost surgical accuracy of the Möhne Dam raid of May 1943. In June 1944, Bomber Command began to reinforce the American attacks on German oil plants. By September the Germans were confronted with an oil crisis so serious that they were compelled to restrict flying and the Allied air superiority became even more pronounced. As the armies advanced towards the German frontier, greatly aided by this superiority, the Germans lost the forward bases of their fighter defences and the Allied bomber forces were able to push their radar transmitters nearer the German targets upon which a greater and more and more accurate rain of bombs therefore descended.

Differences of opinion as to the best tar-

gets, together with weather and tactical considerations, divided the aim of the bombers between support of the armies, the oil offensive, the destruction of communications, naval bombing, and the continuing area offensive. But in late 1944 and early 1945, the huge destructive power of bombing was liberated by the attainment of command of the air. The great German synthetic oil plants were ruined beyond repair and the oil crisis became a famine. The communications system of Germany was rendered chaotic and eventually unworkable to the point where administration began to break down.

As the German armies retreated from the East and the West, they fell back not upon a heartland but upon a national disintegration which proved incapable of mounting even an underground resistance. The British and American bombers played a vital role in assisting the advance of the armies. They also produced a situation in the interior of Germany which guaranteed the collapse of the war machine.

The surviving paradox of the final triumph of strategic bombing is this: if the British had not adopted the policy of night area bombing, which in itself produced disappointing results, it is difficult to see how the power of heavy destruction of 1944-45 could have been generated. If the Americans had not persisted with the policy of daylight self-defending formation-bombing tactics, which produced poor results and terrible casualties, it is hard to see how command of the air could have been won. It was, in the last resort, the combination of command of the air and very heavy bombing which made a critical contribution to Germany's defeat.

# From Normandy to the Baltic

The Allied liberation-invasion of Normandy, in June 1944, was the most dramatic and decisive event of the Second World War. The cross-sea move of the Anglo-American expeditionary force, based on England, had been delayed by bad weather. It was launched when the wind was still strong enough to make the move hazardous—but also unlikely. General Eisenhower's decision to take the risk was not only justified by the outcome of the Normandy invasion but contributed to its surprise effect.

The Allied landings were made on the morning of 6th June in the Bay of the Seine between Caen and Cherbourg and were immediately preceded by the moonlight dropping of strong airborne forces close to the two flanks. The invasion was prepared by a sustained air offensive of unparalleled intensity, which had been particularly directed against the enemy's communications, with the aim of paralysing his power of moving up reserves.

Although many factors had pointed to this sector as the probable scene, the Germans were caught off their balance—with most of their reserves posted east of the Seine. That was due partly to the ingenuity of the plans for misleading them, and partly to an obstinate preconception that the Allies would come not only direct across the Channel but by the shortest route. The effect of this miscalculation was made fatal

*Troops of Cheshire Regiment land on east bank of the Rhine during opening phase of 21st Army Group's drive across the Rhine towards the heart of the Ruhr, March 1945*

by the action of the Allied air forces in breaking the bridges over the Seine.

By deductions drawn from the lay-out of the Anglo-American forces in England prior to the invasion, and contrary to the views of his military staff, Hitler had, in March, begun to suspect that the Allies would land in Normandy. Rommel, who was put in charge of the forces on the north coast, came to the same view. But Runstedt, who was commander-in-chief in the West, counted on the Allies landing in the narrower part of the Channel between Dieppe and Calais. That conviction was due not only to the Allies' past fondness for maximum air cover, and the effect of their present deception plans, but even more to his reasoning that such a line was theoretically the right line since it was the shortest line to their objective. That was a characteristic calculation of strategic orthodoxy. Significantly, it did not credit the Allied command with a preference for the unexpected, nor even with an inclination to avoid the most strongly defended approach.

The invaders' actual plan secured more than the avoidance of the best prepared defences. In choosing the Normandy route, the Allied command operated on a line which alternatively threatened the important ports of Le Havre and Cherbourg and was able to keep the Germans in doubt until the last moment as to which was the objective. When they came to realize that Cherbourg was the main objective, the Seine had become a partition wall dividing their forces, and they could only move their reserves to the critical point by a wide detour. The movement was lengthened by the continued interference of the Allied air forces. Moreover, when the reinforcements reached the battle-area, they tended to arrive in the sector farthest from Cherbourg—the Caen sector. The British lodgement here became, not only a menace in itself, but a shield for the development of the American operations farther west, in the Cotentin Peninsula. That double effect and alternative threat had a vital influence on the success of the invasion as a whole.

The vast armada achieved the sea-passage without interference, and the beaches were captured more easily than had been expected, except where the American left wing landed, east of the Vire Estuary. Yet the margin between success and frustration, in driving the bridgehead deep enough, was narrower than appeared. The invaders did not succeed in gaining control of the keys to Caen and Cherbourg. Fortunately, the .wide frontage of the attack became a vital factor in redeeming the chances. The Germans' natural concentration on preserving these keys on either flank left them weak in the space between them. A quick exploitation of the intermediate landings near Arromanches carried the British into Bayeux, and by the end of the week the expansion of this penetration gave the Allies a bridgehead nearly forty miles broad and five to twelve miles deep between the Orne and the Vire. They had also secured another, though smaller, bridgehead on the east side of the Cotentin Peninsula. On the 12th, the Americans

*Dutch SS poster predicts end of European culture from brutalized US 'liberators'*

pinched out the intermediate keypoint of Carentan, so that a continuous bridgehead of over sixty miles span was secured.

General Montgomery, who was in executive command of the invading forces as a whole, under Eisenhower, could now develop his offensive moves more fully.

The second week brought a marked expansion of the bridgehead on the western flank. Here American 1st Army developed a drive across the waist of the Cotentin Peninsula, while British 2nd Army on the eastern flank continued to absorb the bulk of the German reinforcements by its pressure around Caen.

In the third week, having cut off Cherbourg, the Americans wheeled up the peninsula and drove into the port from the rear. Cherbourg was captured on 27th June, though not before the port itself had been made temporarily unusable. Around Caen, British thrusts were baffled by the

enemy's skilful defensive tactics in country favourable to a flexible defence, but their threat continued to distract the German command's free use of its reserves.

Under cover of this pressure, the build-up of the invading forces proceeded at a remarkably rapid rate. It was aided by the development of artificial harbours, which mitigated the interference of the weather and also contributed to surprise—by upsetting the enemy's calculations.

July was a month of tough fighting in Normandy, with little to show for the effort except heavy casualties. But the Germans could not afford such a drain as well as the Allies could, and behind the almost static battle-front the Allied resources were continually growing.

On 3rd July American 1st Army, having regrouped after the capture of Cherbourg, began an attempted break-out push southward towards the base-line of the peninsula.

But the attackers were still short of room for manoeuvre, and progress was slow. On the 8th, General Dempsey's British 2nd Army penetrated into Caen, but was blocked at the crossings of the Orne. Successive flanking thrusts were also parried. On the 18th a more ambitious stroke, Operation Goodwood, was attempted—when a phalanx of three armoured divisions, one behind the other, was launched from a bridgehead north-east of Caen—through a narrow gap created by a terrific air bombardment by 2,000 aircraft on a three-mile frontage—and drove across the rear of the Caen defences. A break-through was momentarily in sight, but the Germans were quick in swinging a screen of tanks and anti-tank guns across the path. After that missed opportunity, fresh British and Canadian attacks made little headway. But they kept the enemy's attention, and best troops, fixed in the Caen sector. Seven of the eight Panzer divisions were drawn there.

At the western end of the Normandy bridgehead, the American forces under General Bradley advanced their front five to eight miles during the first three weeks of July. Meantime, General Patton's American 3rd Army had been transported from England to Normandy, in readiness for a bigger thrust.

### Operation Cobra

Operation Cobra was launched on 25th July, initially by six divisions on a four-mile frontage, and was preceded by an air bombardment even heavier than in Operation Goodwood. The ground was so thickly cratered that it aided the sparse and dazed defenders in putting a brake on the American drive. On the first two days only five miles was covered but then the breach was widened, and progress quickened—towards the southwest corner of the peninsula. The decisive break-out took place on 31st July. It was helped by a sudden switch of the weight of British 2nd Army from east of the Orne to the central sector south of Bayeux, for an attack near Caumont, the previous day. While the enemy were reinforcing this danger-point with such troops as they could spare from Caen the Americans forced the lock of the door at Avranches, near the west coast of the Cotentin Peninsula.

Pouring through the gap, Patton's tanks surged southward and then westward, quickly flooding most of Brittany. Then they turned eastward and swept through the country north of the Loire, towards Le Mans and Chartres. The cramped seventy-mile front of the bridgehead had been immediately converted into a potential 400-mile front. Space was too wide for the enemy's available forces to impose any effective check on the advance, which repeatedly by-passed any of the road-centres where they attempted a stand.

The one danger to this expanding torrent was that the enemy might bring off a counter-thrust to cut the Avranches bottleneck, through which supplies had to be maintained. On Hitler's insistence, the Germans attempted such a stroke on the night of 6th August, switching four Panzer divisions westwards for the purpose.

The approach, chosen by Hitler on the map at his remote headquarters in the east, was too direct, and thus ran head-on into the Americans' flank shield. Once checked, the attack was disrupted by the swift intervention of the Allied air forces. And when the thrust failed, it turned in a fatal way for the Germans—by drawing their weight westward just as the American armoured forces were sweeping eastward behind their rear. The American left wing wheeled north to Argentan, to combine in a pincer move with General Crerar's Canadian 1st Army, pushing down from Caen upon Falaise. Although the pincers did not close in time to cut off completely the two armies within their embrace, 50,000 prisoners were taken and 10,000 corpses found on the battlefield, while all the divisions which got away were badly mauled. Their vehicles were even worse hit than their men by the continuous air-bombing they suffered in an ever-narrowing space. The Germans' losses in the 'Falaise Pocket' left them without the forces or movement resources to meet the Allies' continued easterly sweep to the Seine, and past the Seine.

The rapidity of this wide flanking manoeuvre, and its speedy effect in causing a general collapse of the German position in France, forestalled the need of the further lever that was inserted by the landing of General Patch's American (and French) 7th Army in southern France on 15th August. The invasion was a 'walk-in', as the Germans had been forced to denude the Riviera coast of all but a mere four divisions, of inferior quality. The subsequent advance inland and up the Rhône Valley was mainly a supply problem, rather than a tactical problem. Marseilles was occupied on the 23rd, while a drive through the mountains reached Grenoble the same day.

On the 19th, the French Forces of the Interior had started a rising in Paris, and although their situation was critical for some days, the scales were turned in their favour by the arrival of Allied armoured forces in the city on the 25th. Meantime Patton's army was racing towards the Marne, north-east of Paris.

The next important development was an exploiting thrust by British 2nd Army, which crossed the Seine east of Rouen, to trap the remnants of German VII Army, which were still opposing Canadian 1st Army west of Rouen. Dempsey's spearheads reached Amiens early on the 31st, having covered seventy miles from the Seine in two days and a night. Crossing the Somme, they then drove on swiftly past Arras and Lille to the Belgian frontier—behind the back of German XV Army on the Pas de Calais coast. To the east, Hodges' American 1st Army had also leapt forward to the Belgian frontier near Hirson.

Farther east, Patton's army made an even more dazzling drive through Champagne and past Verdun, to the Moselle between Metz and Thionville, close to the frontier of Germany. And although it had begun to lose impetus through the difficulty of maintaining adequate petrol supplies and its armoured spearheads were halted by lack of petrol, its strategic importance

was increasing daily. For Patton's army was hardly eighty miles from the Rhine. When they received sufficient fuel to resume their advance, opposition was stiffening. Patton's thrust had produced a decisive issue in the Battle of France, but the supply position checked it from deciding the Battle for Germany in the same breath. The strategic law of overstretch re-asserted itself, to impose a postponement. On this sector it proved a long one, as Patton became drawn into a direct approach to Metz, and then into a protracted close-quarter battle for that famous fortress-city to the forfeit of the prospects of a by-passing manoeuvre.

In the early days of September the pace grew fastest on the left wing, and it was thither that a bid for early victory was now transferred. British armoured columns entered Brussels on the 3rd, Antwerp on the 4th, and then penetrated into Holland. By this great manoeuvre, Montgomery had cut off the Germans' remaining troops in Normandy and the Pas de Calais—their principal force in the West. American 1st Army occupied Namur and crossed the Meuse at Dinant and Givet.

### German recovery

At this crisis the executive command of the German forces in the West was taken over by General Model, who had gained the reputation on the Russian front of being able 'to scrape up reserves from nowhere'. He now performed that miracle on a bigger scale. On any normal calculation it appeared that the Germans, of whom more than half a million had been captured in the drive through France, had no chance of scraping up reserves to hold their 500-mile frontier from Switzerland to the North Sea. But in the event they achieved an amazing rally which prolonged the war for eight months.

In this recovery they were greatly helped by the Allies' supply difficulties, which reduced the first onset to a lightweight charge that could be checked by a hastily improvised defence, and then curtailed the build-up of the Allied armies for a powerful attack. In part, the supply difficulties were due to the length of the Allies' own advance. In part, they were due to the Germans' strategy in leaving garrisons behind to hold the French ports. The fact that the Allies were thus denied the use of Dunkirk, Calais, Boulogne, and Le Havre, as well as the big ports in Brittany, became a powerful indirect brake on the Allies' offensive. Although the Allies had captured the still greater port of Antwerp in good condition, the enemy kept a tenacious grip of the estuary of the Schelde, and thus prevented the Allies making use of the port.

Before the break-out from Normandy, their supplies had to be carried less than twenty miles from the base in order to replenish the striking forces. They now had to be carried nearly 300 miles. The burden was thrown almost entirely on the Allies' motor transport, as the French railway network had been destroyed by previous air attacks. The bombing that had been so useful in paralysing the German counter-measures against the invasion became a boomerang when the Allies needed to maintain the momentum of their pursuit.

In mid-September a bold attempt was made to loosen the stiffening resistance by dropping three airborne divisions behind the German right flank in Holland, to clear the way for a fresh drive by British 2nd Army up to and over the lower Rhine. By dropping the airborne forces in successive layers over a sixty-mile belt of country behind the German front a foothold was gained on all four of the strategic stepping-stones needed to cross the interval – the passage of the Wilhelmina Canal at Eindhoven, of the Meuse at Grave, of the Waal and Lek (the two branches of the Rhine), at Nijmegen and Arnhem respectively. Three of these four stepping-stones were secured and passed. But a stumble at the third forfeited the chance of securing the fourth in face of the Germans' speedy reaction.

This check led to the frustration of the overland thrust and the sacrifice of 1st Airborne Division at Arnhem. But the possibility of outflanking the Rhine defence-line was a strategic prize that justified the stake and the exceptional boldness of dropping airborne forces so far behind the front. 1st Airborne Division maintained its isolated position at Arnhem for ten days instead of the two that were reckoned as the maximum to be expected. But the chances of success were lessened by the way that the descent of the airborne forces at these four successive points, in a straight line, signposted all too clearly the direction of 2nd Army's thrust.

The obviousness of the aim simplified the opponent's problem in concentrating his available reserves to hold the final stepping-stone, and to overthrow the British airborne forces there, before the leading troops of 2nd Army arrived to relieve them. The nature of the Dutch countryside with its 'canalized' routes, also helped the defenders in obstructing the advance, while there was a lack of wider moves to mask the

directness of the approach and to distract the defender.

After the failure of the Arnhem gamble, the prospect of early victory faded. The Allies were thrown back on the necessity of building up their resources along the frontiers of Germany for a massive offensive of a deliberate kind. The build-up was bound to take time, but the Allied command increased its own handicap by concentrating, first, on an attempt to force the Aachen gateway into Germany, rather than on clearing the shores of the Schelde to open up a fresh supply route. The American advance on Aachen developed into a too direct approach, and its progress was repeatedly checked.

Along the rest of the Western Front the efforts of the Allied armies during September and October 1944 amounted to little more than nibbling. Meantime the German defence was being continuously reinforced – with such reserves as could be scraped from elsewhere, with freshly raised forces, and with the troops which had managed to make their way back from France. The German build-up along the front was progressing faster than that of the Allies, despite Germany's great inferiority of material resources. The Schelde Estuary was not cleared of the enemy until early in November.

In mid-November a general offensive was launched by all six Allied armies on the Western Front. It brought disappointingly small results, at heavy cost; and continued efforts merely exhausted the attackers.

### Allied differences
There had been a difference of view between the American and British commanders as to the basic pattern of this offensive. The British advocated a concentrated blow, whereas the Americans chose to test the German defences over a very wide front. After the offensive had ended in failure, the British naturally criticized the plan for its dispersion of effort. But closer analysis of the operations suggests that a more funda-

mental fault was its obviousness. Although the offensive was wide in the sense of being distributed among several armies, it was narrowly concentrated within each army's sector. In each case the offensive effort travelled along the line where the defender would be inclined to expect it. For the attacks were directed against the natural gateways into Germany. Moreover, the main attacks were made in flat country that easily became water-logged in winter.

In mid-December the Germans gave the Allied armies, and peoples, a shock by launching a counter-offensive. They had been able to hold the Allied autumn offensive and slow it down to a crawl without having to engage their own mobile reserves. So from the time when the chances of an American break-through waned, the risk of a serious German riposte might have become apparent – and the more so, in view of the knowledge that the Germans had withdrawn many of their Panzer divisions from the line during the October lull, to re-equip them with fresh tanks. But the Allies' expectations of early victory tended to blind them to the possibility of any counter-stroke, so that this profited by unexpectedness in that respect.

The German command also profited by treating the problem of suitable ground in a way very different from their opponents. They chose for the site of their counter-offensive the hilly and wooded country of

*Right  1 Poster issued by the SS in Belgium depicting a profit-hungry Roosevelt riding to prosperity in war, exploiting the efforts of Churchill and Stalin. To the very end of the war Hitler hoped to split the Alliance. Ironically, while German propaganda depicted Roosevelt as the arch enemy – 'a Jewish Bolshevik' – Hitler still hoped to break his partnership with Stalin. 2 The vice tightens. Map shows the armies of the Allies advancing into Germany.* **Bottom:** *Crowds greet General de Gaulle as he walks down the Champs Elysées from the Arc de Triomphe on 26th August, 1944, the day after Paris's liberation*

# Entente cordiale!

1 △   2 ▽

Russian and East
European forces

| | |
|---|---|
| 1 | Malinovsky |
| 2 | Tolbukhin |
| 3 | Rokossovsky |
| 4 | Konev |
| 5 | Zhukov |
| 6 | Chernyakhovsky |
| 7 | Zakharov |

Western Allied
forces

Montgomery
Bradley
Patton
Patch
De Lattre
Devers

Yugoslav partisan
forces, Tito

— · — · —   1937 boundaries

50  100  150 ML
100   200  KM

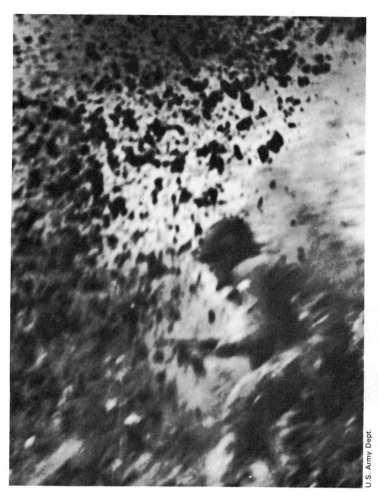

Imperial War Museum

U.S. Army Dept.

*Dropping forces behind the front at Arnhem, September 1944, was part of a bold plan to outflank the Rhine defence-line. The gamble failed and hope for an early victory faded.* **Left:** *British Horsa glider used to land troops.* **Right:** *American paratrooper at Arnhem*

the Ardennes. Being generally regarded as difficult country, a large scale offensive there was likely to be unexpected by orthodox opponents. At the same time, the thick woods provided concealment for the massing of forces, while the high ground offered drier ground for the manoeuvre of tanks.

Their chief danger was from the speedy interference of Allied air-power. Model summed up the problem thus: 'Enemy No. 1 is the hostile air force which, because of its absolute superiority, tries to destroy our spearheads of attack and our artillery through fighter-bomber attacks and bomb carpets, and to render movement in the rear impossible.' So the Germans launched their stroke when the meteorological forecast promised them a natural cloak, and for the first three days mist and rain kept the Allied air forces on the ground. Thus even bad weather was converted into an advantage.

### High stakes on limited funds

The Germans needed all the advantage that they could possibly secure. They were playing for high stakes on very limited funds. The striking force comprised V and VI Panzer Armies, to which had been given the bulk of the tanks that could be scraped together.

An awkward feature of the Ardennes from an offensive point of view was the way that the high ground was intersected with deep valleys, where the through roads became bottle-necks. At these points a tank advance was liable to be blocked. The

German command might have forestalled this risk by using parachute troops to seize these strategic defiles. But they had allowed this specialist arm to dwindle and its technique to become rusty since the coup that captured Crete in May 1941. Only a few handfuls were used.

The aim of the counter-offensive was far-reaching—to break through to Antwerp by an indirect move, cut off the British army group from the American as well as from its supplies, and then crush the former while isolated. V Panzer Army, now led by Manteuffel, was to break through the American front in the Ardennes, swerve westward, then wheel north across the Meuse, past Namur to Antwerp. As it advanced, it was to build up a defensive flank-barricade to shut off interference from the American armies farther south. VI Panzer Army, under an SS commander, Sepp Dietrich, was to thrust north-west on an oblique line, past Liège to Antwerp, creating a strategic barrier astride the rear of the British and the more northerly American armies.

Aided by its surprise, the German counter-offensive made menacing progress in the opening days, creating alarm and confusion on the Allied side. The deepest thrust was made by Manteuffel's V Panzer Army. But time and opportunities were lost through fuel shortages, resulting from wintry weather and growing Allied air-pressure, and the drive fell short of the Meuse, though it came ominously close to it at some points. In that frustration much

was due to the way in which outflanked American detachments held on to several of the most important bottle-necks in the Ardennes, as well as to the speed with which Montgomery, who had taken charge of the situation on the northern flank, swung his reserves southward to forestall the enemy at the crossings of the Meuse.

In the next phase, when the Allied armies had concentrated their strength and attempted to pinch off the great wedge driven into their front, the Germans carried out a skilful withdrawal that brought them out of the potential trap. Judged on its own account, the German counter-offensive had been a profitable operation, for even though it fell short of the objectives, it had upset the Allies' preparations and inflicted much damage at a cost that was not excessive for the effect—except in the later phase, when Hitler hindered the withdrawal.

But viewed in relation to the whole situation, this counter-offensive had been a fatal operation. During the course of it, the Germans had expended more of their strength than they could afford in their straitened circumstances. That expenditure forfeited the chance of maintaining any prolonged resistance to a resumed Allied offensive. It brought home to the German troops their incapacity to turn the scales, and thereby undermined such hopes for victory as they might have retained.

Since the summer of 1944 the main Russian front had been stationary along a line

*American column delayed whilst moving up to meet the German retaliation in the Ardennes, December 1944. The German counter-offensive inflicted some damage but it cost the Germans the chance of maintaining any prolonged resistance to a resumed Allied advance*

past Warsaw through the middle of Poland. But in mid-January 1945 the Russian armies launched another and greater offensive, making longer bounds than ever before. By the end of the month they reached the Oder, barely fifty miles from Berlin, but were there checked for a time.

### A new Anglo-American offensive

Early in February 1945, Eisenhower launched another offensive by the Anglo-American armies, aimed to trap and destroy the German armies west of the Rhine before they could withdraw across it. The opening attack was made by Canadian (and British) 1st Army on the left wing, wheeling up the west bank of the Rhine to develop a flanking leverage on the German forces that faced American 9th and 1st Armies west of Cologne. But the delay caused by the enemy's Ardennes stroke meant the attack was not delivered until the frozen ground had been softened by a thaw. This helped the Germans' resistance. They improved their dangerous situation by blowing up the dams on the River Roer, thus delaying for a fortnight the American attack over that waterline. Even then it met tough opposition. As a result the Americans did not enter Cologne until 5th March. The Germans had gained time to evacuate their depleted forces, and much of their equipment, over the Rhine.

But the Germans had been led to throw a high proportion of their strength into the effort to check the Allied left wing. The consequent weakness of their own left

wing created an opportunity for American 1st and 3rd Armies. The right of 1st Army broke through to the Rhine at Bonn, and a detachment was able to seize by surprise an intact bridge over the Rhine at Remagen. Eisenhower did not immediately exploit this unexpected opening, which would have involved a switch of his reserves and a considerable readjustment of his plans for the next, and decisive, stage of the campaign. But the Remagen threat served as a useful distraction to the Germans' scanty reserve.

A bigger advantage was gained by 3rd Army's breakthrough in the Eifel (the German continuation of the Ardennes). 4th Armoured Division—once again the spearhead as in the break-out from Normandy—dashed through to the Rhine at Koblenz. Patton then wheeled his forces southward, over the lower Moselle into the Palatinate and swept up the west bank of the Rhine across the rear of the forces that were opposing Patch's 7th Army. By this stroke he cut them off from the Rhine, and secured a huge bag of prisoners, while gaining for himself an unopposed crossing of the Rhine when he turned eastward again. This crossing was achieved on the night of the 22nd, between Mainz and Worms, and was quickly exploited by a deep advance into northern Bavaria. That unhinged the Germans' whole front, and forestalled the much-discussed possibility that the enemy might attempt a general withdrawal into their reputed mountain stronghold in the south.

### Assault on the Rhine

On the night of the 23rd the planned assault on the Rhine was carried out, far downstream near the Dutch frontier, by Montgomery's 21st Army Group. The great river was crossed at four points during the night, and in the morning two airborne divisions were dropped beyond it, to loosen the opposition facing the newly gained bridgeheads. The Germans' resistance began to crumble everywhere, and this crumbling was soon to develop into a general collapse. The outcome was therefore inevitable.

When the British advance developed, much the most serious hindrance came from the heaps of rubble created by the excessive bombing efforts of the Allied air forces, which had thereby blocked the routes of advance far more effectively than the enemy could. For the dominant desire of the Germans now, both troops and people, was to see the British and American armies sweep eastward as rapidly as possible to reach Berlin and occupy as much of the country as possible before the Russians overcame the Oder line. Few of them were inclined to assist Hitler's purpose of obstruction by any form of action which might lead to self-destruction.

Early in March Zhukov had enlarged his bridgehead over the Oder, but did not succeed in breaking out. Russian progress on the far flanks continued, and Vienna was entered early in April. Meanwhile the German front in the West had collapsed, and the Allied armies there were driving

eastward from the Rhine with little opposition. They reached the Elbe, sixty miles from Berlin, on 11th April. Here they halted.

On the 16th, Zhukov resumed the offensive in conjunction with Konev, who forced the crossings of the Neisse. This time the Russians burst out of their bridgeheads, and within a week were driving into the suburbs of Berlin – where Hitler chose to remain for the final battle. By the 25th the city had been completely isolated by the encircling armies of Zhukov and Konev, and on the 27th Konev's forces joined hands with the Americans on the Elbe. But in Berlin itself desperate street by street resistance was put up by the Germans, and was not completely overcome until the war itself ended, after Hitler's suicide on 30th April, with Germany's unconditional surrender.

In Montgomery's 21st Army Group the advance across the Elbe by British 2nd Army began in the early hours of 29th April. It was led by 8th Corps, employing DD (swimming) tanks, while the infantry were conveyed in amphibian vehicles, as in the crossing of the Rhine. On its right it was also aided by US 18th Airborne Corps (of three divisions) operating on the ground, which crossed the Elbe on the 30th. Progress now became swift, and on 2nd May British 6th Airborne Division, also operating on the ground, meeting no opposition, occupied Wismar on the Baltic coast after a forty mile drive. (A few hours after its arrival Russian tanks appeared and made contact with the British troops.) British 11th Armoured Division entered the city of Lübeck, on the Baltic, without opposition, after an exploiting drive of thirty miles. The American troops on its right likewise made rapid progress. Meanwhile, British 12th Corps had passed through 8th Corps' bridgehead with the task of capturing Hamburg, but the German garrison commander came out to surrender the city, and as a result of this, the British troops were able to enter it without any further opposition on 3rd May.

The war in Europe came to an end officially at midnight on 8th May 1945, but in reality that was merely the final formal recognition of a finish which had taken place piecemeal during the course of the previous week.

*Left: 1 German soldier during the Ardennes counter-offensive. The chief danger to the Germans came from the Allied superiority in air-power. The attack was not launched, therefore, until the meteorological forecast promised rain and low cloud, which would ground the Allied air forces. 2 Moment of weariness for US soldier in Bastogne, Belgium, one of the vital bottlenecks which held out against the German assault. Bastogne was weakly defended until the US 101st Airborne Division ('the Screaming Eagles') raced in from Reims one day ahead of the Germans. On 22nd December the German commander demanded surrender. McAuliffe, commanding the 101st, replied with just one word: 'Nuts!' 3 Painting by Canadian Alex Colville of infantry near Nijmegen, Holland*

# Victory in the Pacific

By August 1943 it was clear that the tide had turned in the Pacific and that American naval and air power was beginning to force the Japanese from the outer ring of their early conquests. Plans for continuing the war against Japan were discussed and broadly settled that month at the Quadrant Conference between Churchill, Roosevelt, and the British and American chiefs of staff. There was some fear in British minds that the Americans

were concentrating excessive forces in the Pacific at the expense of the European theatre, where the build-up for the Allied invasion of Normandy in the summer of 1944 was now starting, and where operations against the Germans in Italy promised well. However, the balance of American forces between Europe and the Pacific was not allowed to endanger the principle of the overriding need of destroying Germany first.

*A painting of* Kamikaze *suicide pilots by S.Awata.* Kamikaze *or 'Divine Wind' was a reference to the typhoon that destroyed an invading Mongol armada in 1281. The Japanese first resorted to the use of these fliers, who dived their explosive-laden aircraft on to American warships, in January 1945 in the Philippines. By May 1945, however, it was apparent to the Allies that there was not much likelihood of further serious resistance in the air*

## Tarawa — bitter resistance

By December 1943, the situation in the Pacific was tense. In New Guinea, the Australian and American divisions under General MacArthur were closing in on the Huon Peninsular which was to fall that month. Further east, Admiral Nimitz's forces, with the Solomon Islands safely secured, had taken Tarawa Atoll in the Gilbert Islands in late November after a bitterly contested landing and were preparing for the next amphibious attack on the Marshall Islands in the central Pacific. As the two prongs of the Allied advance — MacArthur in New Guinea and Nimitz in the Solomons — had struggled forward in the summer of 1943, it had been thought necessary to capture Rabaul, the big Japanese naval airbase in New Britain. But as American air power began to overwhelm the Japanese, it was decided to bypass Rabaul and let it wither away through lack of supplies. During 1944 Nimitz's amphibious forces were to advance to the Marshalls, within bombing range of the great Japanese base at Truk which would be bypassed, and thence to Ponape in the Caroline Islands. Meanwhile MacArthur, supported by the 7th Fleet, was to work westward along the New Guinea coast, capturing Manus and its fine harbour in the Admiralty Islands en route. Thus by the end of 1944, the two prongs of the advance would meet for an attack on the Philippines which MacArthur was determined should be the next objective. But since Admiral King preferred that Nimitz's forces should swing north to the Marianas Islands and Formosa, no decision was taken at the Quadrant Conference and the argument continued for many months.

On 1st February 1944, the 4th Marine Division landed on Kwajalein Atoll. The lesson of Tarawa had been well learned. Area bombardment which had failed to neutralize Japanese resistance there was replaced by close-range gunfire at selected targets. Small islands were captured to provide flank artillery support. Amphibious DUKWs were introduced for the first time in the Pacific. The results were good: the northern islands of Roi and Namur were taken on 2nd February by the marines and Kwajalein itself on 4th February by the army. Six weeks ahead of programme, Eniwetok Island was assaulted by the reserve which had not been required at Kwajalein and its capture was complete by the 23rd February.

The next objective was the Marianas Islands from which B-29 bombers would be able to reach the Japanese homeland. Saipan was to be attacked first on 15th June, followed by Tinian and Guam as soon as conditions allowed. Two vast assault forces, the northern comprising 71,000 troops for Saipan and Tinian and the southern of 56,000 men for Guam, were formed and the preliminary pounding from the air was allotted Task Force 58 of Admiral Spruance's 5th Fleet. This task force now contained no less than four separate aircraft-carrier groups and each had its own escort of battleships or cruisers and destroyers and carried about 250 aircraft. On 11th June, the air attack started, the first targets being Guam, Saipan, and Tinian, with a diversion by two of the groups to neutralize Chichi Jima and Iwo Jima on the 12th. By 13th June, air supremacy was complete and on 15th June the first Americans landed in Saipan, supported by a bombarding group from Task Force 58.

## A death-blow

But the Japanese had suspected that the Marianas or Palau in the western Carolines would be the next target and had prepared an elaborate plan to lure the American fleet within range of shore-based aircraft after which carrier aircraft from the Japanese main fleet would deliver the coup de grâce. The result was the Battle of the Philippine Sea on 19-20th June — the greatest carrier battle of history. Neither fleet sighted the other but during the action American air-strikes virtually destroyed remaining Japanese air strength at small loss. Although only two of the eight Japanese carriers were sunk (three were seriously damaged), there can be little doubt that the battle dealt the Japanese navy a blow from which it never recovered. The subsequent assaults were severe and long drawn out, but the issue was never in doubt. Saipan was secured by 9th July, Tinian by 1st August, and Guam by 15th August.

We must now turn to the left-hand prong. In the last weeks of December 1943, the 7th and 1st Marine Divisions, the latter a veteran of Guadalcanal which had been resting and re-training in Australia, landed on Cape Gloucester at the western end of New Britain and quickly established themselves ashore. Despite appalling terrain — the intelligence reports had been too optimistic — and bitter Japanese resistance, the airfield was captured on 1st January 1944, and thereafter the marines pushed steadily eastwards against a skilful and determined enemy retiring through easily defended jungle. The 5th Marine Division landed on Willaumez Peninsula on 6th March, and the airfield at Talasea was quickly taken; the western part of the island was now secure and the straits between New Britain and New Guinea were safe. By the end of April an army division, the 45th, arrived to replace the marines who were released for further amphibious attacks. Meanwhile, on 29th February, units from the 1st Cavalry Division had made a recon-

*Right: Top: Two highly romanticised views of the Pacific war. 1 'Fighter in the Sky' by Tom Lea. A grimly determined American pilot in combat with Japanese Zeros. On 19th June 1944, 891 American aircraft shot down 330 aircraft out of a 430-strong Japanese force. It was dubbed 'the Marianas turkey shoot'. 2 In a painting by T.Ishikawa American and Japanese carrier-borne aircraft duel over the south Pacific. 3 Chinese coolies unloading ammunition from Dakotas at Kweilin in south China painted by Samuel D.Smith. The aircraft supplied the American 14th Air Force based there*

U.S. Army Photo Dept

3

U.S. Army Photo Dept

U.S. Air Force Dept

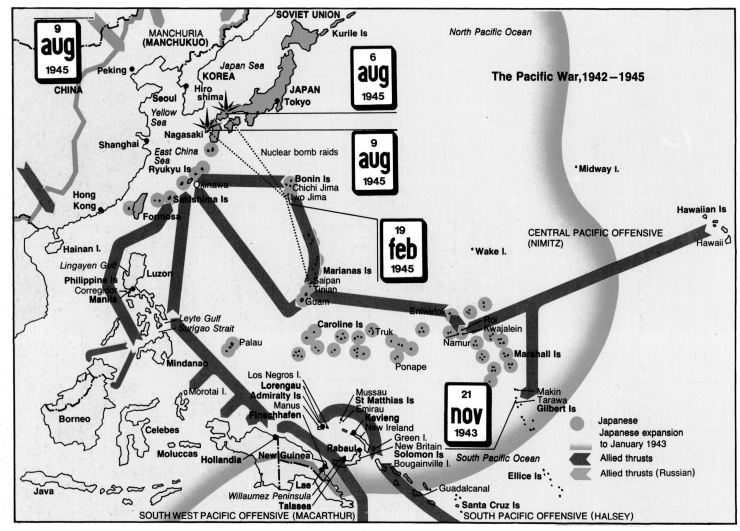

The Pacific War, 1942-1945

| | |
|---|---|
| ● | Japanese |
| (shaded) | Japanese expansion to January 1943 |
| ▶ (dark arrow) | Allied thrusts |
| ⊳ (light arrow) | Allied thrusts (Russian) |

naissance in force on Los Negros Island in the Admiralties. MacArthur himself came ashore on the first day to assess the strength of the defences and it was soon evident that more forces would be needed. During the next two weeks, units from the 7th, 8th, and 12th Cavalry Divisions landed, both at Los Negros and on Manus Island itself near the airfield at Lorengau. By the end of March, the main resistance had ended, though sporadic fighting continued during May. A fine natural harbour was now available—it was used later by the British Pacific Fleet—and two large airfields were quickly constructed. The defence, as always, had been determined to the point of suicide and no Japanese prisoners were taken. A comparison of the American casualties—329 killed and 1,189 wounded—with those of the Japanese —3,280 killed—reflects the tenacity of the Japanese and the skill and weapon superiority of the Americans.

Concurrently, on 20th March, an unopposed landing by the 4th Marine Division on Emirau in the St Matthias Islands led to the speedy construction of a fine airfield. A glance at the map will show that both Rabaul and Kavieng, another Japanese base on New Ireland, were now surrounded by airfields at Manus, Emirau, Talasea, and Green Island, and the usefulness of the Japanese garrisons was rapidly nullified. Amphibious attacks were now unnecessary and both bases were eventually 'mopped up' in 1945.

## The strategic possibilities

Having followed the fortunes of the two main thrusts, we should turn to other parts of the Pacific theatre and to British strategic plans in particular. One of the key factors—always a difficult one to evaluate—was the position of China. Although the Japanese, with an army of one million men, held the whole Chinese coastline and some inland areas, General Chiang Kai-shek, with his headquarters at Chungking, still controlled the hinterland with a large but rather disorganized army of a nominal 300 divisions. The only access for the Allies was over the famous 'Hump' to north-east India; and much effort was devoted to flying supplies to the small American 14th Air Force under General Chennault, which operated from the Kweilin area, and to sending essential items to the Chinese army. The only sure route to China was along the Burma Road which the British campaign in Burma sought to free from Japanese hands. The Americans, in particular, placed much importance on keeping China in the war and they planned to build up a force of B-29 bombers to operate against the Japanese homeland from the Kweilin airfields.

Further north in Manchuria, the Japanese Kwantung Army of three-quarters of a million men faced the Russian frontiers where an uneasy peace prevailed. Again the Americans were anxious that the Russians should enter the war as soon as possible and attack the Kwantung Army.

*Allied forces—largely American, but including Australian units in the south-west Pacific—bound towards Japan in an island-hopping campaign which began with landings on Guadalcanal on 7th August 1942 and ended in June 1945 on Okinawa*

Both in China and Manchuria the Japanese retained high quality troops, which included armoured divisions, and one of their worst mistakes was to delay the removal of these troops to more important areas in the Pacific until it was too late.

In Great Britain there was an acrimonious debate between Churchill and his chiefs of staff about future strategy. By the summer of 1944, some people, though not Churchill, believed that the war in Europe would be over by the end of the year. The defeat of Italy had released strong naval forces which could be sent eastwards, and the employment of the British fleet and, later of the army and air force released by the defeat of Germany, became a controversial question in London.

There were three main strategic possibilities—the first to defer the dispatch of the British fleet to join Nimitz in the central Pacific and to concentrate all available Commonwealth forces in South-East Asia with an object of completing the conquest of Burma, Sumatra, Malaya, and possibly Indo-China; the second to reduce the effort in South-East Asia and to form a British Commonwealth Task Force of all arms in the south-west Pacific under

Imperial War Museum

MacArthur. In this case, the British fleet could be detached to join Nimitz in the central Pacific if necessary. The third possibility was to send the British fleet to the Pacific as soon as possible and to adopt a modified effort in South-East Asia.

Eventually it was decided at the Octagon Conference at Quebec in September 1944 to adopt the third course, with the addition of a bomber force of forty squadrons of Lancasters to join in the air attack on Japan when Germany had been defeated. President Roosevelt accepted this course in the face of a reluctant Admiral King, who would have preferred to finish off Japan unaided, and in the event, the coming of the *Kamikaze* suicide attacks made the contribution of the British fleet most welcome.

We must now return to the Pacific in the autumn of 1944. Admiral Halsey, with his 3rd Fleet (the Fleet was called the 3rd under Halsey and the 5th under Spruance; the ships were the same but the staff and command changed) was attacking the Philippines with his aircraft in mid-September, when, finding opposition unexpectedly light, he suggested that the invasion of Leyte Gulf be brought forward two months and that the operations against Yap, Palau, and Mindanao be abandoned. This was at once agreed by the Joint Chiefs of Staff, then meeting at Quebec, and so the shape of future strategy was decided. MacArthur's 'Philippines first' concept had won.

The operations which centred on Leyte

Gulf involved the greatest number of warships ever engaged in battle at sea, while the land and air force units which took part were also very powerful. Again, the Japanese navy had planned to lure away the main American fleet, leaving the amphibious forces to be destroyed by two powerful surface forces attacking from the west. The plan at first succeeded admirably and on 24th October, Halsey with the whole of the 3rd Fleet, was drawn northwards by the Japanese aircraft carrier force under Ozawa. Ozawa had few aircraft in his carriers and his mission was suicidal; he lost all four carriers, but the beachhead in the Leyte Gulf was left very lightly defended – by a few escort-carriers and destroyers. However, the main Japanese surface force under Kurita, which had lost a battleship and two cruisers from air and submarine attacks en route, hesitated, and so reached the beachhead via the San Bernardino Straits too late. By then the second surface force under Nishima had already been destroyed in the Surigao Straits by Admiral Ollendorf's battleships, cruisers, and destroyers, and Kurita's nerve seemed to fail. He mistook the escort carriers and destroyers at the beachhead, which fought very bravely, for a 'gigantic task force', and after a short engagement he turned back, so losing a perfect opportunity of causing extensive damage to the assault forces. The Japanese navy had failed, and so ended its last great battle of the war for it never succeeded in getting into action again.

*In a painting by L.Cole an orderly makes his rounds in Changi Gaol, Singapore, attending prisoners suffering from starvation and beri-beri. The Japanese exploited and neglected their prisoners with a haphazard ruthlessness*

### The price of Iwo Jima

Ashore, the fighting was hard and there were delays in setting up the airfields, but after heavy losses Leyte Island was secured by 25th December.

The next step was the invasion of Luzon which started on 9th January 1945. Again, the fighting was bitter and involved the largest scale land operations of the Pacific War. Admiral Kreuger's 6th army contained over 200,000 men, and the Japanese defenders over 250,000 men. The approach to Lingayen Gulf was made most disagreeable by the first *Kamikaze* air attacks, which succeeded in hitting several American and Australian ships, but the landing itself was unopposed and the serious fighting started well away from the beachhead. Corregidor, MacArthur's former headquarters, was taken on 21st February and Manila was secured by the end of March; after this the operation became that of 'mopping up' a desperate and fanatical enemy, but by April the main battle was over and the key points captured.

Almost at once, Nimitz took over the headlines by the attack on Iwo Jima, which was needed as an airbase for fighter planes to escort the bombers over Japan, and as a

refuge for damaged aircraft. After several weeks of aerial bombardment from the Marianas and several days battering by ships, the 4th and 5th Marine Division landed on 19th February 1945. The 3rd Marine Division was in reserve, but was soon committed to the fight. Spruance's 5th Fleet was in support and made sure that no reinforcements reached Iwo Jima. The island was small—only eight square miles —but it had three airfield sites and the volcanic hills had been made into defensive warrens with many disguised weapon sites.

Serious fortification did not start till December 1944, and the full plan was not completed by the day of the landing but the garrison had been reinforced to a total of 21,000 men. The initial landing was not strongly opposed and the Americans were first attacked when about 200 yards from the beach, when they met a murderous fire from the island's caves, pillboxes, and blockhouses. But they had been able to land much engineering equipment as well as tanks and guns and were well prepared for a tough battle. Co-operation with the bombarding ships and aircraft was excellent and gradually the most important defence positions were destroyed, but the honeycombs were difficult to subdue and the island was not declared secure until 18th March, while fighting continued spasmodically until 26th March. Even so, the first damaged B-29 landed safely on 4th March (the first of 850 emergency landings in three months) and on 7th April the first fighters left to escort a daylight bombing raid on Tokyo. The Americans lost about 7,000 marines and sailors.

The next operations quickly followed with the invasion of Okinawa by Buckner's 10th Army, which included three marine divisions for the initial landings. At this point the Royal Navy came into action in the Pacific with the task of neutralizing the airfields on the Sakishima Islands, through which the Japanese hoped to fly reinforcements to Okinawa.

*Left: 1 An American transport, its decks crammed with supplies, including petrol and trucks, heads for Cape Gloucester in New Britain where Allied forces landed on 26th December 1943. Rabaul, the key Japanese base on New Britain, was virtually encircled and isolated by thrusts through the Solomons and Bismarck Archipelago. 2 Rather death than dishonour: a dead Japanese soldier lies in the sand of Namur islet, Kwajalein, in the Marshalls after squeezing the trigger of his rifle with his foot. Although Namur received a heavy preliminary bombardment, marines who assaulted the islet met stiff resistance from an intricate system of blockhouses. 3 US marine on Guadalcanal in the Solomons. Although landings on the island were unopposed, the Japanese soon reacted violently, and for nine months Guadalcanal was the scene of bitter battles. Right: End of a Kamikaze off the Philippines, June 1945. Under the force of the guns of an American carrier a suicide bomber is transformed into a fireball*

Keystone Press

U.S. Defence Dept

U.S. Navy Dept

Keystone Press

*Fanaticism on Okinawa*
After a bombardment of Palembang in Sumatra, the British fleet had arrived in Australia on 4th February 1945. By April when Okinawa was attacked, its main elements were four aircraft-carriers, two battleships, four cruisers, eleven destroyers, and a large 'fleet train' of supply ships which enabled operations to continue for many weeks without putting in to harbour. Admiral Fraser was in overall command, Admiral Rawlings the commander at sea, and Admiral Vian in charge of the carriers. It is enough to say that the British force acquitted itself well and in particular that its armoured deck aircraft-carriers were able to survive the *Kamikaze* attacks whereas the lighter decked Americans had to retire when struck.

The attack on Okinawa was on an enormous scale. During the campaign, which lasted eighty-two days, over half a million Allied troops took part and the initial assault was carried out by 183,000 soldiers and marines. The ships at sea suffered severely from the *Kamikaze* attacks and many were sunk or damaged during their long ordeal. Again, the troops landed without opposition, but soon came up against a fanatical defence. The campaign was long and bitter but the island was finally secure by 21st June, by which time the Japanese had lost 110,000 men, while the Americans had suffered nearly 8,000 killed and the ships afloat nearly 5,000—the latter almost all victims of *Kamikaze* attacks.

Although it was not known at the time, the last great operation of the Pacific War was over, though in July and August Halsey's 3rd Fleet, of which the British contingent formed part, cruised freely off Honshu, attacking the enemy with aircraft and bombarding him.

While these arduous battles were being fought, a brilliant campaign of attrition against Japanese merchant shipping had been maintained and it proved to be an extremely important factor in Japan's eventual decision to surrender. Waged

*Left: 1 Marines burn out Japanese resistance with a flame-thrower, Guam, July 1944. 2 Marines hug the beach after landing on Iwo Jima in the Bonin Islands, 19th February 1945. During the month that it took to break organized resistance on the formidably fortified island the Americans suffered 26,000 casualties of whom 6,800 were killed and when all resistance ceased on 26th March the 21,000-man garrison had been virtually annihilated. By the end of the war emergency landings had been made on the island by 2,251 B-29s which might otherwise have been forced to ditch in the Pacific. 3 Jubilant marines with a souvenir of war, Leyte Island, Philippines, December 1944. Right: 1 Incendiary bombs rain from the bellies of American B-29s over Yokohama, Japan, May 1945. Forty per cent of the built-up area of more than sixty Japanese cities and towns was destroyed in these incendiary raids. 2 Kobe receives its third incendiary bomb raid on 5th June 1945. 3 View of railway yards near Osaka after American air raid*

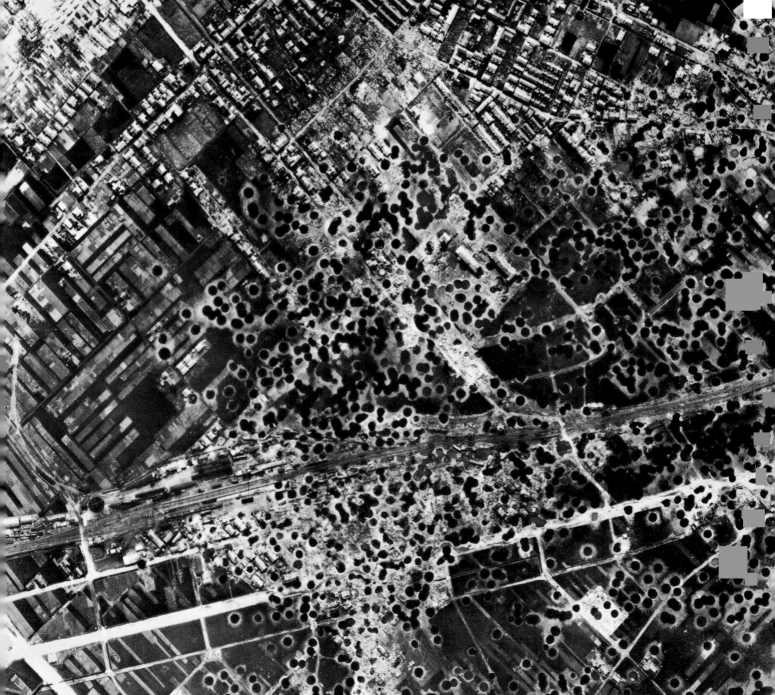

*Ecstatic Allied prisoners of war at a camp near Yokohama celebrate their liberation by American forces, August 1945. A formal surrender ceremony was held on 2nd September*

mainly by submarines, almost all American, and by B-29 bombers which dropped mines in Japanese coastal waters, it started to gather strength in early 1944, by which date the Americans had gathered no less than seventy-five modern 'fleet' submarines of great endurance, each armed with eighteen torpedoes. These torpedoes ran true and exploded on impact, unlike the American torpedoes used earlier in the war. Radar was also fitted, which gave the Americans a great advantage at night.

The success of the American submarine campaign was helped by the blindness of the Japanese navy, almost to the last, both to the seriousness of the situation and to the methods of retrieving it. To the Japanese, the protection of merchant shipping was 'defensive' and therefore smacked of the dishonourable. As a result they allocated far too few resources—surface and air—to the defence of merchant shipping and when they did eventually adopt the convoy system, the convoys were too small and the escorts woefully weak.

Moreover, the Japanese homeland—its industries and its people—relied almost entirely on shipping for the raw materials of war and for the rice to feed its population. Oil had to be carried from the Netherland's East Indies, iron-ore from the Asian mainland, and slowly but steadily the war economy was reduced until, by the summer of 1945, it was grinding to a halt.

It is now time to consider the internal situation in Japan. By the middle of 1944, a number of thoughtful politicians and serving officers had come to the conclusion that defeat was inevitable and that it was in the interest of the country to negotiate a settlement of the war as soon as possible. Otherwise, it was argued, Communism would follow the inevitable chaos.

## The Emperor broadcasts

After the fall of Saipan in July 1944, the government of General Tojo, who had been Prime Minister since 1941, fell and a coalition took over with a mandate to continue to prosecute the war. Tojo had accumulated much power over the years and he ended up as his own Chief of the Army General Staff as well as being Prime Minister. He refused to consider the possibility of defeat and believed, like many of the Japanese generals, that honour demanded the destruction of the whole Japanese people rather than voluntary submission. By early 1945, the Emperor was extremely worried and he consulted many elder statesmen, most of whom advised the continuation of the war. Prince Konoye, a former Prime Minister, declared roundly, however, that the war had been lost and that it was vital that peace must be made as soon as possible.

The loss of Iwo Jima during April 1945 brought the fall of the coalition government: almost simultaneously the Russians announced that they would not renew the neutrality pact with Japan which was due to expire in April 1946. After much discussion, an elderly Admiral, Suzuki, was nominated as Prime Minister with a clear mandate to bring the war to an end as soon as possible. The shipping situation was disastrous, heavy air-raids were destroying Japanese cities one by one, and production of war materials was coming to an end. Suzuki's task was not easy—most of the generals were fanatically determined on resistance to the bitter end and the Japanese people had relapsed into fatalistic despair. After the end of the war in Europe, it was decided to ask the Russians for mediation and talks were held with the Russian ambassador to Japan Jacob Malik. But the Russians did not answer and it was not until 12th July that the Japanese ambassador in Moscow was ordered by cable to approach the Russian government. On 21st July he made a formal request for Soviet mediation to bring the war to an end. The Potsdam Conference was then in session, and Stalin informed Roosevelt and Churchill of this approach

(of which the Americans were already aware through their reading of the Japanese cyphers), but nothing was done because the Japanese had not yet agreed to surrender unconditionally. Behind all these discussions loomed the atomic bomb, which was successfully tested during the conference. The first bomb was dropped on 6th August, and the second on 9th August, on the same day as the Russian invasion of Manchuria. On 15th August the Emperor broadcast his rescript which ended the war.

The Russian invasion was swift and successful and the whole of Manchuria and north Korea was in their hands by the end of August. Elsewhere, Hong Kong was re-occupied by British naval forces in early September, and in many Pacific islands surrenders were being arranged. On 2nd September a formal surrender ceremony was held aboard the American battleship *Missouri* in Tokyo Bay. General MacArthur signed as Supreme Commander of the Allied Powers, and he was followed by representatives of all the powers which had taken part in the war against Japan.

Thus, happily, the great invasion of the Japanese homeland, which had been planned during the summer of 1945, was unnecessary. 'Operation Olympic' against Kyusho was due to take place on 1st November, and the main operations against Honshu in March or April of 1946 ('Operation Coronet'). Both invasions would have been on an enormous scale. A British Commonwealth force of two or three divisions was planned to join Coronet and by then British bombers would also have been taking part in the strategic air attack on Japan.

## Miracles of production

While there can be no doubt as to the eventual outcome, the operations would have been tough and losses high. The Japanese armies were still intact and they had good supplies of ammunition, while the remaining aircraft would have been used in suicide attacks which could cause great damage. The prospect of last-ditch resistance making necessary scores of operations like those on Iwo Jima and Okinawa was a depressing one to the Allied commanders. The American High Command was divided on the problem of whether the invasion would be ultimately necessary and some high officers believed that capitulation would come through the air and sea blockade alone. Historians are similarly divided, though the full knowledge of the underground work of the peace party in the summer of 1945 has only been widely known comparatively recently, and thus the evidence against invasion has been somewhat strengthened. It is too soon for a certain judgement to be made—the issue is still fogged by inter-service rivalry. Whatever the decision of history, however, nothing can alter the superb achievements of the American forces nor of the industry which worked miracles of production to support them. Nor can the story of the fanatical bravery and skill—however misguided—of the Japanese fighting men ever be diminished.

# The Bomb

The history of the birth of the atomic bomb has something to offer everyone. To the nuclear physicist, it is a tale of scientific research on an unprecedented scale, completed successfully in spite of appalling handicaps imposed by secrecy and wartime shortages of men and materials. To the engineer it is an epic of technological enterprise, in which 1,400 million dollars worth of productive resources were staked on four largely untested industrial processes, each one of which came perilously close to failure. To the political historian, it is a saga of machinations in the corridors of power, set against a backcloth of international hostility and suspicion. To the moral philosopher it is a study in conflicts of loyalty—the competing claims made upon a scientist or politician by his own instincts and ambitions, his friends, his country, and mankind. To the man in the street it is like other stories of war—a drama at once thrilling and disgusting which is played by an enormous cast, with characters ranging from the most

*The fateful mushroom cloud billows up over the Japanese city of Nagasaki. It was here that the second atomic bomb was dropped on 9th August 1945*

dedicated patriot to the most perfidious secret agent.

How do nuclear weapons work? The basic facts of nuclear physics had been established by 1940. To explain briefly, the nuclei of atoms consist of a mixture of protons and neutrons. The number of protons can be anything from one to 105 and this number determines the chemical element of the atom. Thus hydrogen nuclei have one proton, iron 26, uranium 92, and plutonium 94. The number of neutrons is variable, and nuclei differing only in the number of neutrons are called 'isotopes'. Thus there are three known isotopes of hydrogen with zero, one, and two neutrons, known colloquially as hydrogen, deuterium, and tritium respectively, and fourteen isotopes of uranium, of which the most abundant on earth are $U^{235}$ and $U^{238}$ with, respectively, 143 and 146 neutrons. The existence of these isotopes, and the non-existence of other isotopes with different numbers of neutrons, is a consequence of the rather peculiar laws governing the forces which hold nuclei together. Roughly speaking, protons and neutrons attract each other strongly when very close together and otherwise ignore or (in the case of protons) repel each other. Nature has had some difficulty in building stable units with this rather uncompromising material, and it turns out that the only viable combinations are those in which the nucleus has more neutrons than protons, but not many more. The most stable nucleus is that of iron (with 26 protons and 32 neutrons), and as a rule any nuclear reaction (that is a re-arrangement of protons and neutrons to form a new nucleus or nuclei) which leads to a nucleus in which the number of protons is closer to 26 than previously, results in a release of nuclear energy. Consequently one can obtain nuclear energy either by fusing together two nuclei which are much lighter than iron (for example, deuterium and tritium which both have one proton) or by fissioning (splitting into two roughly equal halves) nuclei which are much heavier than iron (for example, uranium 235 which has 92 protons). The hydrogen bomb is based on the former option, the atomic bomb on the latter.

Fortunately for the stability of the material world, both fusion and fission only occur under exceptional circumstances. Fusion only occurs when nuclei collide very violently, and until recently the temperature required (around 100 million degrees Centigrade) could only be reached on earth with the help of an atomic bomb. Fission, on the other hand, is an exceptional phenomenon only because the universe is many millions of years old, and during its evolution most of the nuclei capable of spontaneous fission have already done so, and the few that are left (for example radium) fission so slowly as to be useless as sources of energy. However, since certain heavy nuclei are only just stable, the addition of one more neutron is sufficient to tip them over the edge. The uranium isotope $U^{235}$ and plutonium are examples of this. Since each fission releases two or more neutrons, it is possible to

induce a chain reaction: a first neutron is captured by a heavy nucleus which fissions, releasing two neutrons which are captured by two more nuclei and so on.

Such a chain reaction can be thought of as a population explosion in neutrons, and it leads to the enormously rapid release of nuclear energy which occurs in every atomic explosion. However, like all population explosions, it depends upon maintaining a 'reproduction rate' of more than one neutron per neutron captured. Two adverse factors can prevent this. First, if the lump of material containing the fissile nuclei is too small, too many neutrons can escape from its surface, rather than undergo capture by other nuclei within it and thus lead to fission. Second, if the nucleus which captures a neutron is of the wrong kind, it may not undergo fission at all, or not fast enough. The first factor is not crucial – it simply shows that the lump of material must exceed a certain critical size, and atomic bombs are in practice ignited by bringing together two lumps of uranium, each slightly less than the critical size. However, the second factor is crucial, for uranium 238 is not fissile. Thus even a fairly small proportion of $U^{238}$ in a lump of $U^{235}$ is sufficient to prevent an explosive chain reaction from occurring within it. In fact, natural uranium consists of 99·3% of $U^{238}$ and a mere 0·7% of $U^{235}$, so before $U^{235}$ can be used as a nuclear explosive it is necessary to separate it from a much larger quantity of $U^{238}$. The other fissile material, plutonium, does not exist in nature at all; however, if one bombards $U^{238}$ with *slow* neutrons (obtained by passing fast neutrons through a 'moderator' made of heavy water or graphite in a nuclear reactor) it slowly becomes transmuted into plutonium which can then be separated off and used as an explosive. The first option ($U^{235}$) was used in the bomb exploded at Hiroshima, the second at Nagasaki.

Virtually all the physical ideas described above were familiar to the nuclear physi-

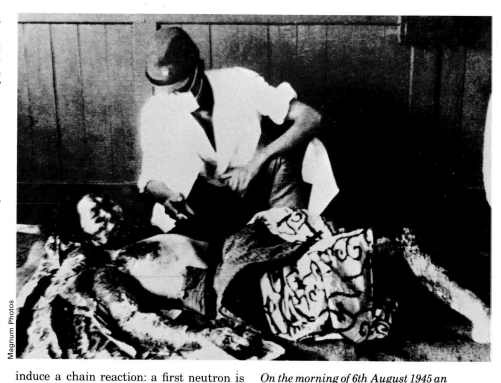

On the morning of 6th August 1945 an American bomber named Enola Gay *dropped the first atomic bomb on Hiroshima. Here, a doctor tends a burnt victim*

cists of all nations by September 1939, and it is hardly surprising that every scientifically advanced country took steps to explore the military potential of nuclear energy. But progress in the various countries concerned was very uneven. In France nearly all work stopped with the German occupation and most of the principal nuclear physicists fled to England (and later transferred to Canada), including two who were to make a considerable impact, Halban and Kowarski. In the Soviet Union the Academy of Sciences formed a 'special committee on the uranium problem', but its plans were frustrated by the German invasion which led to the evacuation of the bulk of Soviet industry and research establishments beyond the Urals. This delayed their nuclear programme until the end of 1942, by which time they were already receiving regular communications about the British and American work from their agent Klaus Fuchs. But it seems they did not give high priority to producing their own bomb until 1945.

In Germany, work was impeded from the outset by the loss of many of the most gifted nuclear physicists during the anti-Jewish purges of the academic community immediately before the war, and by factional disputes among those who remained. Nevertheless, by mid 1940 a powerful group of physicists, including Bothe, Weizsäcker, and Heisenberg, had set up a research institute in Berlin which was given the code name 'The Virus House'. Until about 1942 their work was at a level roughly comparable with that of America. However, in April 1942, an Anglo-Norwegian sabotage team wrecked the heavy water plant at Rjukan, upon which their programme heavily depended, and from then on their fortunes declined. Nevertheless, the possibility of an imminent German weapon continued to serve as a spur to Allied physicists until the discovery of Weizsäcker's papers in Strasbourg (captured in 1944) revealed how far behind they then were.

In Great Britain, most of the nation's scientists were initially occupied in other war work and in the early months the nuclear effort depended largely upon refugees who were prevented by their nationality from being incorporated into secret military projects! Nevertheless, during the early years, Great Britain made most of the main contributions to nuclear weapons development. The first serious indication that it was possible to build an atomic bomb was given in February 1940 by Professors Peierls and Frisch, then working at Birmingham University. In their outstanding *Memorandum* (which has since been published) they set out in three pages the main problems in designing a bomb, and the possible solutions. They pointed out for the first time that it was vital to separate $U^{235}$ from $U^{238}$ and indidated a method by which this could be done – 'thermal diffusion'. They calculated the 'critical mass' of $U^{235}$ and obtained a figure of 600 grams, an answer which was subsequently revised upwards to nine kilograms as more accurate nuclear measurements were made. The resulting explosion, they estimated, would be equivalent to about 1,000 tons of TNT, and they commented on the lethal effects of the radiation which would be produced.

With the stimulus provided by the Peierls-Frisch memorandum, research on isotope separation was given steadily increasing support during 1940, chiefly under the direction of Professor Simon at Oxford University. By the end of the year it was clear that a different separation process – gaseous diffusion – was better than thermal diffusion and that a plant capable of separating enough $U^{235}$ for a bomb would cost over five million pounds and would require materials for its construction which only considerable research and development effort could produce. In the meantime, the French physicists Halban and Kowarski, who had joined Cambridge University, had shown that a slow chain reaction could be maintained in natural uranium, producing plutonium, provided that heavy water was used to moderate the speed of the neutrons, and their colleagues Bretscher and Feather suggested that the plutonium could indeed be used as a nuclear explosive. Finally, at Birmingham University, Oliphant was working on a third technique for separating isotopes – the electromagnetic method. However, neither this approach nor the Cambridge plutonium approach appeared very hopeful at this stage, and when the Maud Committee (set up by the Air Ministry to investigate nuclear weapons) finally reported in mid-1941, it came down in favour of the gaseous diffusion method.

By this stage, it was clear to most British scientists that the larger scale work which was now required could only be carried out in America where the necessary productive resources were still available. Until 1942, the American effort had been less intense,

and less successful, than the British; indeed they had repeatedly pressed for closer co-operation with Britain. By the summer of 1942, however, as a result of the impact of Pearl Harbour and the strongly favourable report by the Maud Committee on the feasibility of nuclear weapons, the American effort had at last acquired momentum. Their programme, which for security reasons was known as the 'Manhattan Project', was now put under the control of the army, in the person of the formidable General Groves, and expenditure which had hitherto been measured in thousands of dollars was now to be measured in millions. The timing of this major expansion was such that Great Britain graciously consented to co-operate with America in a development programme at precisely the moment when the American scientific leaders Conant and Bush had decided they were no longer dependent upon British help. The resulting breakdown in co-operation was a disastrous episode in Anglo-American relations, and the resentment and suspicion on both sides were only slowly removed even after the quarrel had been officially resolved by direct discussions between Churchill and Roosevelt which led to the Quebec agreement in August 1943. In the meantime, work progressed in America on all the approaches described above – gaseous diffusion isotope separation under Urey and Dunning at Columbia University, electromagnetic separation under Lawrence at California, thermal diffusion separation under Abelson at Anacostia, and plutonium breeding with slow neutrons under Fermi at Chicago. The fluctuating fortunes of these four approaches were the despair of General Groves and his scientific advisers. The gaseous diffusion method required the manufacture of literally acres of 'membrane' – thin metal sheets with millions of fine holes in them through which uranium hexafluoride gas diffused – and the construction of a vast industrial plant consuming enough electricity to supply a large city. This plant, at Oak Ridge, Tennessee, was largely completed (at a cost of 280 million dollars) by July 1944 but technological difficulties with the 'membrane' were still proving so formidable that there was a serious possibility that the entire investment would be wasted. The electromagnetic method depended on scaling up a delicate laboratory instrument to industrial dimensions. The electromagnet used in Lawrence's early experiments had measured a few inches across: in the electromagnetic separation plant (also at Oak Ridge) it was a massive 122 feet long and 15 feet high with electrical windings made of 86,000 tons of pure silver, borrowed from the Treasury bullion reserves for the purpose. Here again there were repeated setbacks: the plant began to operate in February 1944, but by July it was clear that there was no hope of relying upon this method alone to produce enough $U^{235}$ before the end of the war. The thermal diffusion process proved useless as a means of enriching $U^{235}$ by a large amount, though good for small improvements. Finally there was the plutonium approach, which ap-

peared very hopeful after the success of Fermi's first experimental pile, built in Chicago in December 1942. This pile, which was the brilliant forerunner of all subsequent nuclear reactors, led to the construction of several enormous plutonium breeding reactors at Hanford on the Columbia river. The first of these was set into action by Fermi in September 1944, but within a few hours it shut itself down, as a result of a totally unexpected 'nuclear poisoning' phenomenon.

In the end, all four approaches were used. The thermal diffusion method was used to raise the $U^{235}$ content of uranium from 0.7% to 0.9%. This slightly enriched material was then fed into the gaseous diffusion plant, which took it up to about 20% $U^{235}$, and finally the electromagnetic plant was used to produce material with over 90% $U^{235}$. As a result, enough $U^{235}$ for a weapon was available by August 1945 at a total cost of about 1,000 million dollars. Plutonium production proved more difficult to plan, since the amount required to produce a weapon remained uncertain until the last minute, and there were doubts at one stage whether it could be made to work at all. For this reason, it was decided to test a plutonium weapon as soon as enough became available. This test was carried out in the Alamogordo desert in New Mexico on 17th July 1945, under the scientific direction of J. Robert Oppenheimer, the physicist who was responsible for the top secret weapon design laboratory at Los Alamos. The explosion, which comfortably exceeded the calculations of the theoreticians, had an impact which was not to be measured only in kilotons equivalent of TNT. For a number of the scientists who witnessed the test, the horror of the experience convinced them that the weapon must never be used against men. However the majority (at least of the senior scientists whose voices carried weight in government circles) had no serious doubts that nuclear weapons should be used against Japan if by so doing the war could be shortened. In spite of strenuous protests by Szilard and other leading scientists, the final decision to use it was taken by Truman, with the concurrence of Churchill, and the bombs were dropped on Hiroshima on 6th August and on Nagasaki on 9th August. The Japanese Emperor communicated his decision to surrender on the 10th. How events would have developed if the bombs had not been dropped is one of the great unresolvable uncertainties of history. A strong though not watertight case can be made that the Japanese would shortly have surrendered in any case, without further major bloodshed. At a different level it has been argued that the use of the weapons then has given them the credibility upon which their role as deterrents to world warfare now depends. It is impossible to be certain about such imponderables: what is certain is that the events of August 1945 initiated a debate about the morality and efficacy of these weapons of destruction which will continue at least until general and complete disarmament has become a practicable means of ordering human affairs.

# Disruption and Disillusion 1945-1976

## INTRODUCTION

The greatest single factor shaping world politics since 1945 has been what was called the 'Cold War': the rivalry between the United States and her allies and Russia and hers. This has set the scene in which all other problems have had to be tackled. In 1945, linked by the overriding need to destroy Germany, the Allies had agreed at Yalta on the partition of the post-war world, but when victory came, Russia's obsession for security in the West divided them into two hostile camps, and laid the foundations of the Cold War. Allied unity had covered up grave divergences of principle and interest.

By the end of 1945, fighting had stopped almost everywhere (although the Greek Civil War was not finally over until 1949), and men took stock of the ruins. One of the more subtle kinds of damage done by the war was moral, and the atrocities of Nazism had dealt a heavy blow to confidence in European civilization. The Nuremberg trials of the remaining leaders of the Nazi state caused enormous controversy over the wisdom and morality of attempting to bring to justice the men who had caused so much suffering. In retrospect it is hard to see what good the trials achieved, but at the time the demand for punishment could not be resisted.

Some people were able to feel hopeful about the future, gloomy as the present was, because a positive step had been taken

*One year of running the Berlin airlift: US airmen celebrate with baptism of 'Coke'*

towards the foundation of a new world order: the United Nations was established in San Francisco in 1945. Although some of the weaknesses of the old League of Nations had been avoided, time was to show that the UN, too, would fail to satisfy all the hopes of its founders.

Already in 1945 some of the problems of the next thirty years were apparent. Four major nations had suffered grievous defeat. Italy, France and Germany were never to recover their previous military standing. In both Italy and France the traditional state had been gravely compromised by military failure and ideological alienation. The future of Japan was not so obvious, but she, too, was crippled as a great military power.

Britain's predicament was different. She still had the trappings and commitments of a great power, and had not suffered the devastation and destruction which had virtually reduced France and Italy to ruins by 1944. Britain was one of the victorious allies, with an empire and strong armed forces. Time would show, however, that the war had in fact strained the foundations of British world influence beyond repair. The beginnings of internal readjustment came under the first post-war Labour government, and with it the initial legislation creating the Welfare State which followed the Beveridge Report.

After 1945 a new division was imposed on Europe, between East and West, between Communist and non-Communist peoples. Roughly speaking, the division between East and West in Europe is still the boundary between the victorious armies of 1945, for Russia had recovered her borderlands and the Red Army had occupied huge areas of Eastern and Central Europe. Russian presence and influence were the essential determinants of the Communist takeovers in Eastern Europe. Although the Red Army had originally come to Eastern Europe as liberators, it soon became the instrument of Stalinist expansion. In June 1948, the Czech socialist Beneš resigned as head of the coalition of 'progressive' forces which had governed Czechoslovakia since its liberation, and was replaced by the Communist, Gottwald. In December of the same year, Rákosi became Deputy Premier of Hungary, and this put the Communists in a position of real power there too. By mid-1950, Albania, Bulgaria, Rumania and Poland were also

under Communist control—an Iron Curtain had come down across Europe, as Churchill described it.

In the Far East, European political hegemony was virtually at an end. Japanese occupation and the resistance movements it provoked had been the detonator of the major changes which showed this. Face had been lost by the colonial powers, war and occupation had led to a revolution of Asian ideas and aspirations. The stirrings towards independence before 1941 had been held in check; the war and the way the war had been won now made them irresistible. The days of the Raj in India were now over. This de-imperialization and decolonization surprised and distressed both those who had always accepted India's eventual evolution to self-rule, and also those who had opposed it. As in the former Dutch possessions, like Indonesia, the realities of the post-colonial experience were often to prove terrible. Yet a vast historical change was carried out in each of these two countries with great rapidity and completeness.

Their achievement of formal independence, however, important as it was, did not match the significance of the establishment of the People's Republic in China in 1949. Although China had never been formally a colonial territory, she had long been a client and a victim both of the West and of Japan. Now she was ready to move towards the distant, though clearly discernible, status of the world's third super-power.

For the moment, the core of world politics was to be the relationship between the two unquestioned super-powers, Russia and the United States. This situation was likely to continue so long as a more united Europe failed to emerge. The battered structure of the liberated countries of the West provided the Russians with a quick opportunity for subversion. Only the United States could sustain these states, yet she was curiously slow to act. After the First World War America had withdrawn into isolation, leaving Europe to sort out her own problems. There seemed a danger that she might do so again now. However, America's recognition that Britain could no longer bear the burden of police duties in Greece and military aid to Turkey gave rise to a historic change in her policy. The Truman Doctrine which ensured that she would not leave Europe open to

Sudd-Verlag

# The United Nations

### The General Assembly

Administrative Tribunal

UN Emergency Force, UN Relief and Works Agency

Committees, Subsidiary Bodies

**International Court of Justice**

**Trusteeship Council**

**Security Council**

**Economic and Social Council**

Special Bodies: UN Children's Fund (UNICEF), Commissioner for Refugees

Military Staff Commission

Regional Economic Commissions, Functional Commissions

Disarmament Commission

**Secretariat**

International Atomic Energy Agency

Commission on Co-ordination, Technical Assistance Board

Responsible to
independent after election
autonomy of action

Specialized Agencies

**1945**     **1968**

In 1945 slightly more than half the world's population was represented in the UN

In 1968 slightly more than three-quarters of the world's population was represented in the UN

Countries with no representation:

Switzerland
West Germany
East Germany
North Korea
South Korea
North Vietnam
South Vietnam
Communist China

Proportion of world population represented in the UN

**General Assembly**
The General Assembly discusses all matters pertaining to peace and security, welfare of mankind, and the promotion of human rights. It receives reports from other organs, approves the budget, and elects the ten non-permanent members of the Security Council, the twenty-seven members of the Economic and Social Council and those members of the Trusteeship Council which are elected. It also takes part with the Security Council in the election of judges of the International Court of Justice and, on the recommendation of the Security Council, appoints the Secretary-General. Voting on important questions, such as recommendations on peace and security, election of members to organs, admission, suspension and expulsion of members, trusteeship questions and budgetary matters, is by a two-thirds majority. On other questions it is by a simple majority. Each member has one vote.

**Security Council**
The Security Council is composed of five permanent members—China, France, the USSR, Great Britain, and the United States—and ten non-permanent members elected by the General Assembly for two-year terms. Originally it consisted of eleven members but it was enlarged to its present fifteen in 1965 in accordance with an amendment to the Charter. It functions continuously and investigates any dispute or situation which might lead to international friction. It can propose peaceful settlement, take non-military measures or adopt military sanctions. The Security Council acts on behalf of all the members of the United Nations, all of which agree to carry out its decisions and to undertake to make available to the Security Council, at its request, armed forces, assistance and facilities necessary for the maintenance of international peace and security.
Voting in the Security Council on all matters other than questions of procedure is by an affirmative vote of nine members, including the concurring votes of the permanent members. However, any member, whether permanent or non-permanent, must abstain from voting in any decision concerning the pacific settlement of a dispute to which it is a party.

**Trusteeship Council**
The Trusteeship Council is composed of members of the United Nations administering trust territories, permanent members of the Security Council who do not administer trust territories, and enough other members (elected by the General Assembly for three-year terms) to make an equal division between countries which administer trust territories and countries which do not.

**Secretariat**
The Secretariat is the permanent international civil service and major administrative organ of the UN. It functions under the direction of the Secretary-General. The first Secretary-General was Trygve Lie of Norway who was appointed for a five-year term on 1st February 1946. On 1st November 1950 his period of office was extended by three years and on 10th November 1952 he tendered his resignation, to be succeeded by Dag Hammarskjøld of Sweden on 10th April 1953. On 26th September 1957 Hammarskjøld was appointed for a further five-year term beginning on 10th April 1958. After his death in an aircrash in September 1961, U Thant of Burma was appointed Acting Secretary-General on 3rd November 1961 to complete Hammarskjøld's unexpired term. In November 1962, U Thant was appointed Secretary-General on a five-year term beginning with his assumption of office on 3rd November 1961.
On 1st November 1966 the General Assembly extended the appointment of U Thant as Secretary-General until the end of the Assembly's twenty-first session, and on 2nd December 1966 he was appointed Secretary-General for another term ending on 31st December 1971.

**International Court of Justice**
The International Court of Justice is the principal judicial body of the United Nations. It is composed of fifteen judges from different nations elected by the General Assembly and Security Council. The judges are completely independent. The court settles all legal disputes between nations submitted to it and gives advisory opinions to the UN on legal questions. Permanent headquarters are at The Hague.

**Economic and Social Council**
The Economic and Social Council is composed of twenty-seven members, nine of which are elected each year by the General Assembly for a three-year term of office. Originally consisting of eighteen members, the Economic and Social Council was enlarged to its present membership in 1965 in accordance with an amendment to the Charter.
The council studies and prepares recommendations on economic, social, educational, health, human rights, and other matters related to the welfare of mankind. It establishes special commissions, specialized in any of the subjects under its competence, and co-ordinates the activities of various inter-governmental agencies. It also co-operates with private organizations.

---

Soviet expansion marked the true beginning of the Cold War. ('I believe that it must be the policy of the United States to support free peoples who are resisting attempted subjugation by armed minorities or by outside pressure,' President Harry Truman declared on 12th March 1947.) This was the first landmark in the movement towards Western acceptance of a divided world. Its corollary was the Marshall Plan: they were, as Truman said, 'two halves of the same walnut'. This great scheme helped to strengthen the economic security of the 'free world'. The blockade of Berlin in 1948 was the most important encounter of the Cold War, for it emphasized the division of Europe, and reiterated the United States' determination to maintain its position in Europe, by force if necessary.

Meanwhile a new international military alliance of unprecedented complexity and far-reaching political implications—the North Atlantic Treaty Organization (NATO) —was brought into existence in 1948. This 'shield of the West' embodied a commitment by its signatories to assist each other in the event of attack, and established an organization designed to join the defences of its members into a single integrated system.

The basic divisions of post-war inter-national life which seemed so rigidly fixed in the early 1950's—Russia and America and the groups of satellites and allies which clustered round them—also brought into being the concept of 'The Third World'. This was a phrase which began to be used frequently after the Bandung Conference (in Indonesia) of April 1955. The conference was unique in the sense that for the first time in modern history a group of twenty-nine former colonial nations, once under the aegis of European domination, met to discuss their mutual interests and, as it turned out, their differences.

Neutrality in the Cold War conflict or at least an aspiration to it was the main standpoint of the original Third World. Later the Third World became, in some eyes, a 'second world' roughly co-terminous with the poor (against the rich), the coloured (against the white), with those who needed economic aid (as against those who could supply it). Among the Asians, Sukarno and Nehru embodied the concept of political neutralism. But the most successful practitioner of obtaining support first from one Cold War camp and then recognition from the other, was Tito in Yugoslavia. He was able to resist Stalin's pressure, relying on the strong nationalist feeling of the

*Diagram showing structure of the United Nations: the organs and the relationship, in terms of responsibility, between the six main ones*

only group of peoples in Europe which had achieved a Communist revolution as a result of their own efforts.

Troubles within the Third World were soon to prove that it had little political cohesion. It was already apparent in the late 1940's how easily some new nations could make enemies of others. The birth of Israel is an example of this; when the British resigned their mandate in Palestine in 1948, they left behind them an unresolved conflict between the Jews and Palestinians and other Arabs which still shows no signs of abating, as four Wars of 1948, 1956, the Six-Day and Yom Kippur have demonstrated. Only an unimaginable concession on one side or the other, or the co-operative intervention of the super-powers seems likely to divert this conflict from developing into yet another conflict.

On the other side of the world Japan was beginning her post-war evolution. Under American occupation, she moved towards a uniquely successful and individual democratic system which, spared the burden of

*Mercenary in action in Congo. Political
unrest bedevilled independent Africa*

*Example of apartheid, established after
Nationalists took power in South Africa*

heavy arms expenditure, was soon to tap
traditional Japanese skills and attitudes and
produce the most spectacular economic
growth of the century.

Elsewhere too, the repair of damage
wrought by the war was virtually completed
during the 1950's, and the possibilities of a
new abundance and a new affluence first
began to be widely seen. They were symbolized everywhere by very visible signs—
shiny tall buildings, jet airliners, better cars,
television. But at the same time people on
both sides of the Iron Curtain, with the rising
tensions of the Cold War, also began to live
with the thought of another world war—
this time a far more terrible one, for it became
clear that such a war might be nuclear.

The first major international armed
struggle after 1945 was the Korean War,
which looked, at one moment, as if it might
develop into the first nuclear war. Post-1945
attempts to work out Korean independence
proposals had broken down by 1947, when
the US handed the problems over to the UN.
The role of the UN was too influential for the
control of events to be completely in Russian
or American hands. One of the results of the
Korean War was increasing tension in
Eastern Europe with new and heavy economic
problems being imposed on Russia's new
sphere of domination. The Russians brooked
no opposition; but their ruthlessness inevitably created the very opposition they
sought to destroy and pressures appeared
below the surface.

The death throes of colonialism in one
form or another have been among the most
frightening of the war's legacies. In 1945
France, in common with Britain, faced the
difficulty of resuming direct government of
areas in the Far East which had undergone
Japanese occupation. In addition, France
had never been as ready to accept evolution
towards self-government as the Labour
Government of Britain. (It may be argued
that much of the subsequent history of
Indo-China—and what came to be known as
Vietnam—was as much shaped by deep-
rooted nationalism as by the appearance
of an expanding Communist revolutionary
movement.) The humiliating defeat of the
French expeditionary corps at the hands of
the 'Vietnamese peasants' at Dien Bien Phu

in the spring of 1954 shattered the confidence
of the French in their conventional forces.
The imbalance left behind in Vietnam was
to lead directly to American intervention.
The Algerian war of 1958–1962 was even more
damaging to French national life than had
been the long struggle in Indo-China. In the
end it brought the collapse of the Fourth
Republic and the establishment of de Gaulle's
decade of presidency.

The difficulties of the Algerian situation
also played a part in persuading French
statesmen to join in what was probably the
greatest single act of folly on the part of
colonial powers in the entire post-war period.
This was later known as the Suez Crisis
of 1956; Nasser's nationalization of the Suez
Canal was the catalyst. Arguably the British
government had even less excuse than the
French, for it had more to lose in circumstances in which there was little possibility
of gain. In an illusory attempt to safeguard
the canal for economic and strategic reasons,
Britain jeopardized the American alliance,
the unity of the Commonwealth and even,
potentially, the balance of payments.

Within the United States an enormous
increase in wealth after 1945 transformed
her society and made possible a world role
unthinkable before the war. The only state
which could and did challenge its supremacy
was the Soviet Union, and this threat has
exerted a profound influence both abroad
and at home. Senator Joseph McCarthy's
relentless attack on 'Un-American Activities'
epitomized American anti-Communist feelings. The new affluence brought a spreading
conservatism expressed in the Republican
return to power in the 1950's under the
presidency of Eisenhower. With its accent
on materialism, the Eisenhower era was not
marked by any radical movements in politics
or ideas. American commitment to Europe
and the poorer nations continued: between
1945 and 1965 the United States gave more
than 40,000 million dollars-worth of non-
military aid to the rest of the world.

The gift was not without strings, however.
It was in America's interests that pro-
American regimes should be established
throughout the Third World—an increasingly important source of raw materials as
well as crucial political support in the UN.
To this end, a series of often corrupt and
brutal regimes, as much satellites of America
as the Eastern European nations were of the
Soviet Union, were created and supported.
In cases where local movements emerged
to counter these regimes, as in Vietnam,
Cambodia, the Lebanon and Cuba, America
used all her powers from diplomatic and
economic pressure through to armed intervention, to ensure the continuance of her
influence.

American action was directed most consistently against the governments of independent states of Latin America. This
came to its height in the 1960's. In 1959 the
guerrilla forces of Fidel Castro entered
Havana and dealt the death blow to the
almost-universally hated regime of Batista.
For a brief period, the US attempted to work
with Castro, using the traditional offers of
aid and advisers. By mid-1960, however, it
had become clear that Castro was not
prepared to offer an ounce of Cuban in-

dependence in return for this aid. In addition
Castro began to lead his country along 'the
Cuban road to socialism', which included
widespread nationalization and appropriation of American-owned property. In March
1960, therefore, Eisenhower instigated the
secret training of Cuban refugees for an
invasion of Cuba on similar lines to that
which had overthrown the left-wing Guate-
malan regime in 1958.

The new President, Kennedy, authorized
their arming with American weaponry and
financial support from the CIA and the group
landed at the Bay of Pigs in April 1961. The
venture was a complete disaster as the
White House lost its nerve at the last
moment and cancelled USAF support. The
invaders were defeated within two days;
diplomatically, this venture was to push
Castro even more firmly in the direction of
the Soviet Union. Following her expulsion
from the Organization of American States
in January 1962 Cuba became increasingly
isolated from Latin America, and therefore
accepted the Russian demands for missile
bases on Cuba. In the last weeks of October
1962, the US Navy imposed a blockade on
Cuba to prevent Russian ships carrying the
missiles to the partially completed sites there.
Over the weekend of 25th–27th October 1962
the world watched. Then on 28th October
Khrushchev, in line with the change in
Soviet foreign policy, backed down. But
American hostility to Cuba remained, and
remains a feature of American foreign policy.

It is mainly based on Cuba's insistence on
exporting revolution. Cuba has seen herself,
since the early 1960's, as a base from which
the revolution in the Third World could
begin. During the 1960's, Cuba supported
guerrilla movements in Venezuela, Guatemala and Bolivia, as well as almost certainly
giving aid to left-wing movements in most
other Latin American countries. Moreover,
its concern to spread socialism has not been
limited to the American hemisphere. Cuban
advisors have been present in Syria, Congo-
Brazzaville, Somalia, and crucially in Angola,
where Cuba's military intervention in the
first two months of 1976 on the side of the
Marxist MPLA ensured their victory over
the superior forces of UNITA and the South
African-backed FPLA.

Although the Bay of Pigs was a disastrous failure for the CIA and American foreign policy, they had nonetheless scored a number of notable successes in Latin America and elsewhere. On 21st April 1967, the Greek Army led by a group of right-wing officers, who later composed what came to be known as the Colonels Junta, took power on the classic excuse that they were saving Greece from a communist takeover. The role of the CIA in the Colonels' takeover and their regime remains unclear; however, since the collapse of the Colonels (due to their disastrous handling of the Cyprus crisis), it seems likely that American involvement in the Colonels' Greece was considerable.

There is no doubt of CIA involvement in other European countries. Since the mid-1950's, millions of American dollars have been poured into supporting right-wing political parties, like the Christian Democrats in Italy, as well as encouraging a variety of ventures to act as a front for covert US policy. Outside Europe, CIA involvement in the internal affairs of other countries has also been evident.

In the autumn of 1970, Salvador Allende, a Marxist, was elected president of Chile at the head of a popular front dominated by his own Socialist Party and the Chilean Communist party, but also including sections of the revolutionary left. Allende was a moderate who had started a wide-ranging programme of reform, while remaining committed to the ideals of democratic socialism. On the night of 10th–11th September, 1973, Chilean troops led by General Pinochet staged an armed uprising against the Chilean Government. Allende fell, fighting in the rooms of the presidential palace, and the country was taken over by a violent and repressive military dictatorship, headed by Pinochet. Although the CIA cannot solely be held responsible for Allende's overthrow, recent evidence indicates that America encouraged the coup and financed and supported the 'strike' of the middle classes which had preceded it.

At home, the Democrats narrowly won the presidential election again in 1960. Some of the ambiguities of their victory were overlooked, for America was swept along by John F. Kennedy's brand of youthful idealism; but this was to end with the

tragedy of Kennedy's assassination in November 1963. Kennedy's successor, Lyndon Johnson, achieved far more, but was far more unjustly treated by his countrymen. He was to reap the crop of the Vietnam War sown by his predecessor, and his reforming legislation was dwarfed by the internal conflict over Vietnam and the riots and bitterness of America's urban and racial problems which erupted in the mid-1960's.

In the Soviet Union, the death of Joseph Stalin in March 1953 marked the end of an epoch in Russian history. For nearly thirty years he had held personal power and had given the word Stalinism to the language of every country which had a socialist movement. Stalin was replaced at the head of the Communist Party of the Soviet Union in due course by Khrushchev and Bulganin. Of the two, Khrushchev was the dominant figure. He made an indelible mark on the history of the world communist movement by his famous speech at the secret session of the Twentieth Party Congress in February 1956, when he launched an attack on 'the cult of personality', a harsh criticism of Stalin and Stalinism. It was greeted throughout the Communist world as the beginning of a great era of 'liberalization'. For a brief moment, a new and critical socialism flourished, particularly among Western intellectuals, but also in the communist states of Eastern Europe. 'De-Stalinisation' was short-lived, however. In October 1956 reform movements began in both Hungary and Poland. The Polish movement was soon crushed, though the appointment of Gomułka to secretaryship of the party was a definite concession to the anti-Stalinist faction. Hungary was more serious. On 24th October 1956, Imre Nagy, an anti-Stalinist Communist, was elected to the premiership and anti-Soviet rioting began. For a few days all seemed in the balance, then, on 4th November, Soviet troops entered Hungary to 'restore socialist legality'. By the end of the month the rising, blamed on 'imperialist agents' and 'fascist elements' was over.

Russia's departure from the 'orthodoxy' of Stalinism has had far-reaching effects outside Eastern Europe. To the Chinese, Khrushchev's attack on Stalin seriously undermined the unity of the world communist movement. However, Chinese support

*Federal soldier forces Biafran to surrender*

for the Soviet invasion of Hungary patched up disagreements for a time. But the continuation of Khrushchev's 'revisionism', particularly the policy of coming to terms with the West, was seen by China as a direct threat to the Sino-Soviet alliance. In April 1960 *Red Flag* (the Chinese party journal) published a lengthy attack on Khrushchev. In less than three years, what had begun as mere polemic had degenerated into a total split duplicated in the national Communist Parties of the free world. By the late 1960's Russia and China faced one another not as fellow Communists, but as rivals in a series of border disputes which threatened the stability of Asia. The mid-seventies seem to show slight signs of change. Despite the feting of Nixon in China in early 1976, the anti-Soviet tone of Chinese pronouncements has moderated a little, and rapprochement between the two great Communist powers no longer seems totally impossible.

Hungary did not mark the end of Soviet problems in Europe. In 1958 the Rumanians were able to force the withdrawal of Soviet troops, and by 1964 Rumania was able to go as far as discussing Sino-Soviet relations with the Chinese. Czechoslovakia, however, presented a more serious problem. In January 1968 the essentially Stalinist Novotny was replaced as First Secretary of the Party by the more liberal Alexander Dubček. There followed the so-called 'Prague Spring'—a period of liberalization. In spite of all the changes that had taken place in the Soviet Union's policies since the death of Stalin, the reaction in 1968 was much the same as in 1956. On 20th–21st August 1968 the armies of the Soviet Union and other Warsaw pact countries invaded Czechoslovakia at the 'request of the Czech government' to restore order. What 'order' meant was clear and the replacement of Dubček by the pro-Soviet Husak in April 1969 merely underlined true Russian policy.

Russia's acquisition of atomic weapons gave the world its third nuclear power after the US and Britain. In the years that followed France, China and India have joined the league. However, during the 1960's, the apparently wasteful 'space race' dwarfed the importance, in the public eye, of nuclear weapons as the major area of Soviet/US competition. Begun soon after the Second World War as a minor adjunct of the weapons' programme of both countries devoted to scientific research, it

*Left: Fidel Castro, the Cuban revolutionary leader. Right: Windows in the hall of the Organization of African Unity in Addis Ababa symbolize a free, united Africa, unhappily not a reality*

developed after the launching of Sputnik 1 in October 1957 into an often bizarre spectacular that Hollywood would have been proud of. In May 1961, following the first manned space flight by Yuri Gagarin, President Kennedy committed the US to landing a man on the moon by 1970; this goal was achieved on 21st July 1969, when Neil Armstrong set foot on the moon. Since then, the race seems to have become less important to both nations, and signs of co-operation in 'real' scientific research seem to be appearing. The future of this co-operation must rest with the future of detente—still very much an unknown quantity.

Since the war, Europe has been moving slowly towards realizing its industrial strength and wealth. In May 1951, the Paris treaty created the European Coal and Steel Community between France, West Germany, Italy, and the three Benelux countries. The Rome treaties of 1957 set up two more communities—the European Atomic Energy Community (Euratom) and the European Economic Community (the Common Market). Europeans on the continent worked steadily towards a united Europe which has made it difficult for Britain (who joined the Common Market in 1973) to become integrated after such a long period of isolation.

There have been other obstacles, too, towards the realization of a post-war ideal, the creation of a United States of Europe. The Fourth Republic in France—with twenty-four governments during twelve years—seemed undependable. The uncertainty ended with the republic's collapse and the era of de Gaulle, but the latter, ironically, was for a time to create new obstacles to real European unity. However, a divided Germany no longer represented the traditional threat to France, which was now able to develop within the Community.

Although Europe was moving towards a new era of economic and social unity, culture in the Western world was still largely influenced by the United States. Throughout the 1940's and the 1950's, Hollywood continued to dominate the screens of the cinema, though from the mid-1950's onwards there were definite signs of the emergence of a new European cinema, particularly in France (the New Wave), and Italy and Scandinavia, where individual directors—Bergman, Antonioni and Fellini—were producing a new kind of essentially non-romantic film. More important, was the development of television. By the 1940's, television had become a part of the American way of life; like so many aspects of American culture, it spread rapidly into Europe, although there was widespread resistance to the purely commercial channels which dominated American T.V.

Musically, America also made the running, at least until the early 1960's, with Rock and Roll. This mixture of poor white 'country music' and black urban blues came to represent the rebellion of a whole generation of white youth on both sides of the Atlantic, who were benefiting from the increased prosperity of the 1950's. Gradually it became clear that the American music industry could no longer produce original material and a number of British groups, notably the Beatles and the Rolling Stones,

NASA

*Homo lunaris? Aldrin photographed by Armstrong at 'Tranquillity base'. The portable life support system, carried on the astronaut's back, plugs into sockets in his spacesuit and supplies oxygen for breathing and water to keep him cool as it circulates through a network of tubes next to his skin. The controls for the life support system and radio are carried on his chest.*

both of whom turned to black music for their inspiration, temporarily toppled American domination of popular music.

Indeed, for a short time British popular culture spread its influence over a wide area. The 1960's became the era of Britain. Increasing consumer purchasing power led to a blooming in fashion and interior design as well as music. The increased purchasing power of the young led to demands by youth for independence and control of their own lives. Encouraged by establishment liberalism, this youth culture became the vanguard of social and sexual permissiveness which so characterized at least the outward show of the 1960's.

The transformation of London to the 'swinging' capital of the world was linked to a number of other movements. In America, resistance to the Vietnam War had led to the development of a 'counter culture', at once political and artistic. The student riots of Berkeley linked into the music of Bob

Dylan and then the new West Coast rock groups like Jefferson Airplane and Country Joe. In Europe, again influenced by the Vietnam War, a new rebellious generation of students and young workers challenged the orthodoxy of the Western European Communist parties and took to the streets of Paris, Rome, Berlin, and eventually London. For a moment, traditional stability was in doubt. In Paris a general strike was called in support of the students as they occupied the Latin Quarter, while de Gaulle called his generals together. However, the status quo was reasserted. The European Communist parties stifled the student revolt as effectively as the Right-wing had emasculated the counter culture.

In Africa, a new history was being generated after Europe's decolonization. For a variety of reasons, the new African states have tended towards authoritarian regimes. The colonial past and new foreign influences must bear much of the responsibility for African troubles. This is clearly borne out in the example of the post-colonial war in the Congo, one of the most tragic episodes in recent African history. Equally shocking, though quite distinct in origin and motivation was the merciless civil war in Nigeria against Biafra, a struggle between two rival groups of élite for the patrimony of the country. As well as anti-colonialism, the continental politics of Africa are also bedevilled with racial tension. No-one is more responsible for this than the Afrikaaner population of South Africa, whose racial policies represent, in many Africans' eyes, the essence of white domination. The problems and hatred these policies have caused remain ominous for the future of Africa.

The ebbing of the British Empire was followed by the evolution of a new organization, the Commonwealth. In the 1950's, it seemed for a time that a new political entity, containing different races, creeds, and ideologies, might be viable. The Rhodesian UDI of November 1965 produced widespread revulsion and showed up Britain's weaknesses as no other change in the Commonwealth had done. The old white Commonwealth, Australia, New Zealand and Canada, each of them politically and economically stable and imbued with confidence in their great

*1968—flood-tide of the New Left. Memories of 1871—on the barricades of Paris*

Keystone Press

economic potential, began to look to the US for a complexity of reasons. The most important of these was the change in Britain's position as a world power.

Suez had also shown up the pointlessness of one survival of imperial days—the belief in the strategic value of Cyprus. This led to bloodshed and communal strife, which ended in discredit. (Cyprus was granted independence in 1960.) On the other hand, Malaysia demonstrates a happier survival of the old imperial policing power. The use of British forces had almost entirely beneficial effects on world stability in the area, and the successful crushing of the Communist attempt to take over Malaya during the twelve-year Emergency was welcomed by the Malays and Chinese alike.

Many surprises and disturbances followed the withdrawal of Western imperial powers from Asia, for when the colonial powers went away the problems did not go with them. Indigenous Asian hostilities and religions were major obstacles to the peaceful development of the continent. The situations in India and Pakistan are striking examples of this; neither country has yet succeeded in creating conditions in which the future can be confidently faced.

In China, the Communists realized that to consolidate their hold they must win over the country village by village; Mao Tse-tung and his advisers showed much more flexibility in dealing with the possibilities and difficulties facing them than was often recognized by foreign observers.

The 1960's had in some ways been a period of hope and change, and of economic prosperity in the West at least; the 1970's were to prove very different, for the legacies of the previous decade were bloody ones. The war in South-East Asia dragged on, with America becoming ever more deeply involved, despite mounting pressure against the war at home. By mid-1974 American withdrawal was stepped up, and in January 1975 the South Vietnamese and Cambodian puppet regimes faced internal guerrilla war and intervention from North Vietnam. Although the American-backed regimes had superior arms and equipment, they both collapsed in the early summer of 1975.

In the Middle East, the uneasy peace following the Six Day War was shattered by the outbreak of the Yom Kippur War in October 1973. The combined Arab forces gained initial advantages, but Israeli counter-attacks struck deep into Egyptian territory. At the truce, however, it was clear that any peace settlement was bound to push the Israelis back across Sinai beyond the Mitla Pass. Final disengagement was completed in February 1976 on these terms, and an uneasy new balance of power was achieved. The Middle East was not yet completely at peace, for in the summer of 1975 fighting broke out between the Christian and Muslim factions in the Lebanon which engulfed the Lebanese in a serious internal war. Peace was made after the Syrian military intervened early in 1976. This peace was soon proved fragile. By mid-March fighting broke out again, and there seems little hope for a long-term settlement in the immediate future.

Another legacy of the 1960's was international terrorism. The Palestinian Liberation Organization and its various associated organizations began a campaign of terror against Israel and her supporters in the late 1960's, which culminated in the massacre of Israeli athletes at the Olympic Games in Munich in 1972. The campaign embraced individual acts of terrorism, armed raids, the taking of hostages and hijacking aircraft. The recognition of the PLO by the UN in 1975 may be a hopeful sign, yet so many splinter organizations exist which are not prepared to recognize the more moderate leadership of the PLO that the continuation of the campaign seems inevitable.

Britain has had her share of terrorism. In 1969 British troops were sent into Northern Ireland to restore order and to protect the Catholic population against increasing Protestant violence. What was seen as a short-term problem has proved to have worldwide implications, particularly in America with her large Irish population. Early in 1976, the Provisional IRA restarted its campaign of bombing civilian targets in England. In the tragic cities and villages of Northern Ireland, it had never ceased, the figure of 1,000 dead having long been passed. Solutions suggested by the various groups involved seem so far to have come to nothing.

The rest of Europe has also seen major upheavals during the 1970's. Only Germany and France remain substantially unaltered in their political course, yet even France, with a strong Communist Party strengthened by the abandonment of 'proletarian dictatorship', seems set for change. In southern Europe Italy remains almost ungovernable while Communist strength grows. In Spain, the death of General Franco has so far brought little change, since King Juan Carlos seems to be firmly under the control of the 'bunker'. The Communist Party, though still outlawed, represents a real alternative, especially in an alliance with the Socialists.

The example of Portugal is quite clear. In the spring of 1974 a 'democratic juncta' of Army officers overthrew the Caetano dictatorship. This was followed by a swift move to the left, with the Communists and the Socialists emerging as the leading parties. An abortive left-wing coup in the autumn of 1975 arrested this movement and enabled

*The long-standing bitterness in Northern Ireland explodes—riots in Newry, January 1969*

Associated Newspapers

the centre parties to gain ground.

The Portuguese revolution had far-reaching consequences in her ex-colonial territories. Angola was torn by civil war, as were the tiny islands of Timor where the Indonesians seem ready to move in in the face of a local movement. Mozambique, on the other hand, had a relatively peaceful transition to independence after many years of underground war. Elsewhere in Africa the 1970's has seen the end of some potentates and the appearance of others. On 12th September 1974 Haile Selassie, 'the Lion of Judah', was overthrown by a popular movement led from within the army in Ethiopia, while in Uganda, 'General' Amin came to power on 26th January 1971. His approval by the British government was short-lived, for in 1972 Amin proceeded to expel all the Ugandan Asians, who were compelled to come to Britain. In Nigeria 1975 saw a 'peaceful revolution' in which General Gowon was demoted (*in absentia*) from head of state to politics student.

The early 1970's saw the continued emergence of China as a world power. In 1972 following the visit of President Nixon to China the US removed its veto and allowed China to take its seat at the UN, the reversal of twenty-five years of policy. In other ways, too, the people of the US were forced to open their eyes in the 1970's. A sordid burglary of the Democratic Party headquarters in Washington led to the exposure of a major scandal. In the summer of 1973 the details were released following the trial of the Watergate burglars. President Nixon remained in office despite the forced resignation of his vice-president Spiro Agnew in the autumn of 1973. Finally, on 8th August 1974 Nixon resigned following the revelation of massive corruption within his administration. He was replaced by Gerald Ford, one of America's least auspicious presidents.

Two other major world powers suffered constitutional crises in the mid-1970's. In India, Mrs Gandhi's increasingly autocratic rule was given quasi legality in the summer of 1975 by the effective banning of opposition and the imposition of press censorship. In Australia, Gough Whitlam, the flamboyant Labour Party leader, found himself forced into a General Election after the Governor General had dissolved Parliament. Surrounded by financial scandal and faced with an economic crisis he lost the election to the Liberal and Country Party under Michael Fraser.

The 1940's were austere, the 1950's saw some improvement, and the 1960's had hope—yet the underlying feeling of the 1970's is of a terrible crisis even worse than that of the 1930's. Most western currencies have been in trouble since 1973, there is serious widespread inflation due in part to a shortage of raw materials triggered off by the Yom Kippur War; unemployment rises and public morale seems low. The 1970's have seen a flowering of nostalgia and escapism. In the arts and in politics a turn away from the search for an alternative to a more sombre acceptance of the old traditional parties. So far the decade has been a grim and colourless one in which many of the hopes of the 1960's in the Western world particularly have been dashed.

# Europe in Ruins

The Second World War, like its predecessor a generation earlier, brought destruction and exhaustion to Europe. The goal of a belligerent society is not economic growth, nor a rising standard of living, nor the promotion of human welfare, but the destruction of the population and resources of the enemy. In the European war destructive capacity had been developed to an unprecedented level, without the war being shortened thereby. To pay for destruction, government savings were realized, money was borrowed, and civilian needs were met at the minimum possible level.

Paradoxically the war also had the effect of increasing economic efficiency. The concentration of effort on war production called forth unused resources of labour and capital; technology developed faster than it ever did in peace-time; medical knowledge was advanced; in Britain the very shortage of food meant fairer distribution, through rationing and welfare foods.

These advances had their impact on the post-war world. But when the fighting ended Europe lay under a pall of physical and human devastation. The pattern of destruction differed in one substantial respect from that of the First World War: France and the Low Countries, although badly scarred by invasion and liberation, had been spared the ravages of prolonged trench warfare; while Germany, virtually unscathed in the First World War, had suffered continuous and increasing aerial bombardments. Only in pockets, where the

Allied invasion was held up, as at Caen or in the Ardennes, were French towns bombarded by artillery, aircraft, and tanks. The communications system suffered most heavily, the whole network of road and rail being broken into pieces by the systematic attacks of the French resistance and the invading armies. Across the Rhine, the streets of the great industrial complex of the Ruhr were but canyons bulldozed through the rubble; six months after the end of the war the ruins still smelled of fire and death. Some six hundred thousand German civilians are believed to have been killed by bombing in the course of the war.

Eastwards the toll of destruction continued. Warsaw was methodically destroyed by the Germans in 1944. In the Soviet Union, western Russia, Belorussia, and the Ukraine had been ravaged, and Stalingrad, Minsk, Kiev, and Smolensk

*Radio Times Hulton*

*In the chaos after defeat, many Germans faced severe hardship. Children clamber on to a refuse lorry for pick of the spoils—firewood, cigarettes, and even food*

**1914-18**

**1939-45**

17,000,000 WW II

Ru[...]

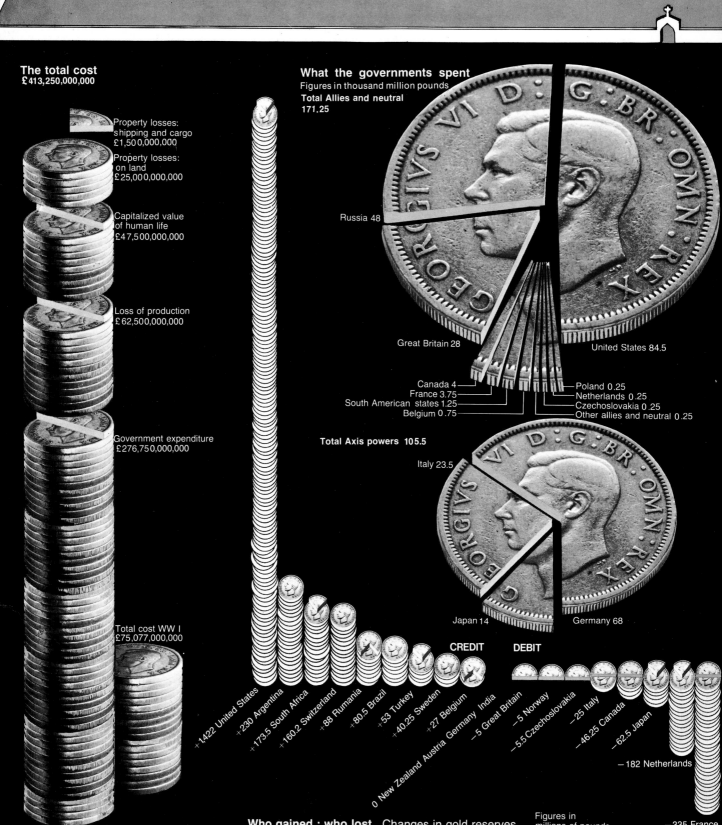

## The total cost
£413,250,000,000

Property losses:
shipping and cargo
£1,500,000,000

Property losses:
on land
£25,000,000,000

Capitalized value
of human life
£47,500,000,000

Loss of production
£62,500,000,000

Government expenditure
£276,750,000,000

Total cost WW I
£75,077,000,000

## What the governments spent
Figures in thousand million pounds
**Total Allies and neutral
171.25**

Russia 48

Great Britain 28

United States 84.5

Canada 4
France 3.75
South American states 1.25
Belgium 0.75

Poland 0.25
Netherlands 0.25
Czechoslovakia 0.25
Other allies and neutral 0.25

**Total Axis powers 105.5**

Italy 23.5

Japan 14

Germany 68

CREDIT        DEBIT

+1,422 United States
+230 Argentina
+173.5 South Africa
+160.2 Switzerland
+88 Rumania
+80.5 Brazil
+53 Turkey
+40.25 Sweden
+27 Belgium
0 New Zealand Austria Germany India
−5 Great Britain
−5 Norway
−5.5 Czechoslovakia
−25 Italy
−46.25 Canada
−62.5 Japan
−182 Netherlands
−335 France

**Who gained : who lost** Changes in gold reserves

Figures in
millions of pounds

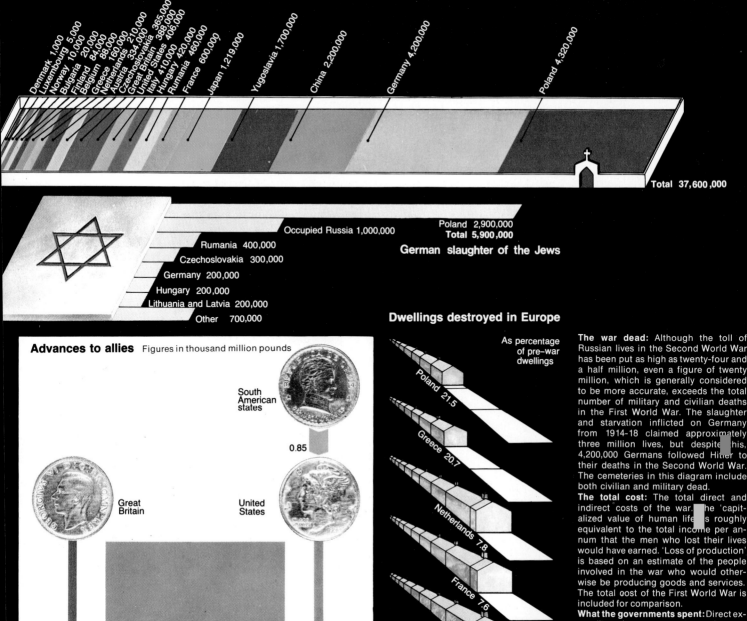

Denmark 1,000 · Luxembourg 5,000 · Norway 10,000 · Bulgaria 20,000 · Finland 84,000 · Belgium 88,000 · Greece 160,000 · Netherlands 210,000 · Austria 334,000 · Czechoslovakia 365,000 · Great Britain 388,000 · United States 406,000 · Italy 410,000 · Hungary 420,000 · Rumania 460,000 · France 600,000 · Japan 1,219,000 · Yugoslavia 1,700,000 · China 2,200,000 · Germany 4,200,000 · Poland 4,320,000

**Total 37,600,000**

Occupied Russia 1,000,000

Poland 2,900,000
**Total 5,900,000**

## German slaughter of the Jews

Rumania 400,000
Czechoslovakia 300,000
Germany 200,000
Hungary 200,000
Lithuania and Latvia 200,000
Other 700,000

## Dwellings destroyed in Europe

As percentage of pre-war dwellings

Poland 21.5
Greece 20.7
Netherlands 7.8
France 7.6
Great Britain 6.5
Belgium 6.2
Italy 4.9
Hungary 3.9
Norway 3.6
Czechoslovakia 3.4

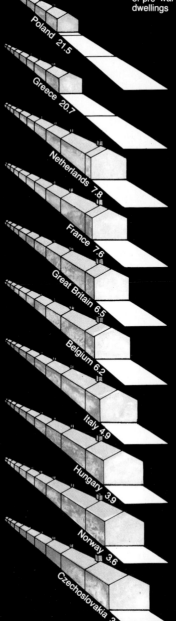

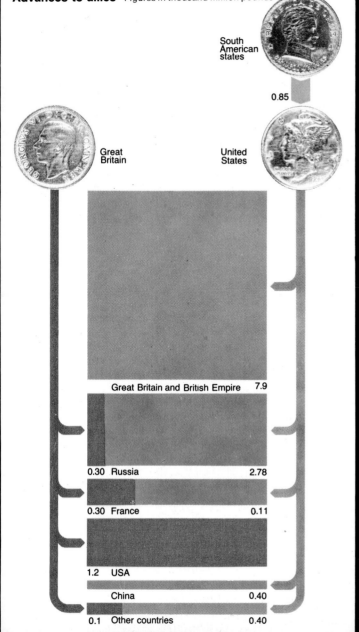

**Advances to allies** Figures in thousand million pounds

South American states

Great Britain

United States

0.85

Great Britain and British Empire 7.9

0.30 Russia 2.78

0.30 France 0.11

1.2 USA

China 0.40

0.1 Other countries 0.40

**The war dead:** Although the toll of Russian lives in the Second World War has been put as high as twenty-four and a half million, even a figure of twenty million, which is generally considered to be more accurate, exceeds the total number of military and civilian deaths in the First World War. The slaughter and starvation inflicted on Germany from 1914–18 claimed approximately three million lives, but despite this, 4,200,000 Germans followed Hitler to their deaths in the Second World War. The cemeteries in this diagram include both civilian and military dead.

**The total cost:** The total direct and indirect costs of the war. The 'capitalized value of human life' is roughly equivalent to the total income per annum that the men who lost their lives would have earned. 'Loss of production' is based on an estimate of the people involved in the war who would otherwise be producing goods and services. The total cost of the First World War is included for comparison.

**What the governments spent:** Direct expenditure by governments on the war, excluding loans to allies. Not all of this should be regarded as loss. It includes military pay and the creation of assets like merchant ships.

**Who gained, who lost:** Some significant changes in gold in reserve and in circulation between the end of 1938 and the end of 1945, indicating some nations who profited from the industrial demands of the war, such as the USA, the 'arsenal of democracy', and minerally-rich South Africa and Brazil.

**German slaughter of the Jews:** The decimation of Polish Jewry is self-evident. Only 100,000 survived the extermination camps. 'Other' comprises Denmark, Holland, Belgium, France, Italy, Bulgaria, Yugoslavia, Austria, and Greece. Some Jews saw the danger in time: 280,000 left Europe for the United States, South America, Great Britain, and Japan from 1933–40.

**Advances to allies:** Loans by the United States and Great Britain to their allies. British advances to the United States were termed 'reciprocal aid' and consisted of raw materials.

**Dwellings destroyed in Europe:** For some countries—including Russia and Germany—there are no exact figures. Rough estimates put the dwellings destroyed or damaged in these areas at about 7,500,000.

were the best known among some 1,700 towns and cities destroyed. Moreover, the retreating Germans had torn up some 39,000 miles of railway track with great drag-hooks fitted to special trains.

In some places towns and monuments were preserved. In Copenhagen a squadron of RAF Mosquitoes succeeded in picking off the Gestapo headquarters while leaving the surrounding houses intact; in Cologne the spires of the cathedral still rose triumphantly from a sea of rubble; in Italy the efforts of a few officers, German and British, saved the monuments of Florence and Ravenna's 6th-century basilica of Sant'Appolinare in Classe. But where the fighting was harshest, on the Eastern Front, the landscape was laid waste.

More was destroyed than buildings, towns, farms, and monuments. For millions, the war meant the destruction of the whole civilized community in which they had lived. Great Britain was the exception. There society and government remained intact, flexible enough to accommodate the social changes which modern war brings about — the increased strength of organized labour, the extension of the government's regulation of economic and social life, the opening of careers and jobs to women. Elsewhere the political framework which had guaranteed an ordered life for citizens had been swept away.

The keystone of this society had been the nation-state — sovereign government over a defined territorial area, unchallenged by private armies or subversive forces, framing laws and ensuring obedience to them, providing protection for property, and permitting the development of industry and trade. Ironically the glorification of the nation-state, the strident excess of nationalism, and the denial of the rights of the individual vis-à-vis the state had been one of the root causes of the war. The fact remains that no better means than the nation-state had been devised for the provision of security for the citizen — and all that goes with it in the arts of peace.

In Eastern Europe this framework was, for a major part of the population, utterly destroyed. It was there that the nation-state had been planted with the least success and the fewest guarantees for the citizen, and partly for this reason proved most vulnerable. In the great northern plain of Europe there were few fixed boundaries formed by geographical features. The peace settlement of 1919 — the much-maligned Treaty of Versailles — was the only attempt in modern history to create a division between Germany and Poland based on ethnic lines, regard for minorities, and plebiscites. Yet, in spite of the thought and consideration, it was here, over the Polish Corridor and Danzig, that the immediate cause for another war was found.

So as the war ended the frontiers were once again decided by *force majeure*. The short-lived states of the Baltic — Estonia, Lithuania, and Latvia — had been taken over by the Soviet Union in 1940 and large sections of their populations carried off to Siberia. Now the whole of Poland was moved westwards; the Soviet Union itself acquired Königsberg (renamed Kaliningrad) and part of East Prussia; some German territory became Polish; and east Germany was occupied by Russia.

This movement of frontiers, coupled with the establishment of Communist rule — Russian, Polish, or East German — over the whole of north-eastern Europe, made the biggest addition to the stream of refugees who had already been torn from their homes by the war and by the Nazi onslaught on the Jews. Long after political order, whatever its shortcomings, had been re-established in Europe as a whole the

remnant of this mass of people remained, institutionalized, in camps established to care for them. In the immediate aftermath of the war they could be seen trudging along the roads of Germany. They were not only homeless but stateless, lacking the protection of their own government which citizens normally take for granted.

The state of Germany was shattered by Hitler's choice of destruction for Germany as well as himself, and by the decision of the war-time Allies to accept nothing less than unconditional surrender. Sovereign authority in Germany passed into the hands of the Allied commanders and their governments. But it was more than a government and a state which Nazism had destroyed. For the German people were now cut off from their own immediate past. The Nazi leaders would be tried, executed, or imprisoned; the lesser members of the Party struggled to escape from their Nazi past; and those who had succeeded in remaining as free as possible from the taint of the regime wished they could suppress part of their collective past. The sense of past glories—which is always a major component of national self-respect—was temporarily destroyed by the immediacy of Nazism.

### Cigarettes as currency

The essentials of life—food and clothing—were in desperately short supply and the value of the currency was destroyed. Only the occupying armies were well provided with food, drink, and such basic luxuries as cigarettes and chocolate. The ordinary values of a society based on property were thus turned upside down. Occupying troops who, as civilians, no doubt led faultless suburban lives, now indulged in petty looting—strictly forbidden but impossible to prevent. Cigarettes became currency, more sought after than paper notes—and Germans, smoking them, knew they were smoking their money away. British and American soldiers were ordered not to fraternize with the Germans but when an ordinary German girl sold her virtue for a carton of cigarettes was it 'fraternization'?

Germany, the occupied country after the war, provided an extreme example of the collapse of political order, a collapse also felt by all countries which had been under Nazi occupation. Hitler's so-called 'New Order' in Europe meant that the legal identity, the sense of honour, and the personality of occupied countries were sustained by governments-in-exile and resistance forces. Effective authority was divided

*Hope for the future. 'Europe after the rain', by Surrealist painter Max Ernst. He sees signs of new life even amidst war-time ruin and decay*

between them, and the armed force of the Nazis. So French society was torn between 'resisters' and 'collaborators'—the division made more cruel by the fact that a French government had signed an armistice with the Germans. The very identity of France was threatened as men whom ordinary Frenchmen had accepted as the legal government of their country were now brought to trial and condemned to death or imprisonment. *Incivisme*—a less than perfect respect for laws, especially tax laws —had always been a problem for French governments; but during the war it was patriotic to cheat; and when the Germans retreated, the black market, with all that it meant in terms of disrespect for the legal framework of society, continued to flourish.

The problems of France were not peculiar to that country; as always it was a microcosm of the conflicts of Europe. In every country there were citizens now disowned by society for their collaboration—tried and then summarily executed by the resistance. Men and women who in civilized

Südd-Verlag

*When the war ended, cigarettes were of greater value than German paper currency. Germans smoking cigarettes were well aware that they were smoking their money away*

society regard arrest as a matter for the police, and justice as the work of law courts, now shaved the heads of girls who had consorted with the occupying forces, to shame and humiliate them.

This was primitive vengeance. But Europe was not a primitive society. If it had been, the passage of time and change of seasons would slowly have restored its life, as the corn grew on the old battle-fields and the stock of cattle was slowly replaced. But in the complex industrial community which had grown up this was only part of recovery. The prosperity of Europe was dependent upon a trading relationship founded on efficient communication and relatively free exchange, sound banking and the confidence necessary for investment.

The war and its aftermath destroyed the basic patterns of European trade and economy. The division of Germany and Europe meant that trade between East and West—the purchase of the agricultural produce of the East in return for the industrial exports of the West—could not be renewed. Germany itself, which Keynes had described as the kingpin of the European economic system, was laid waste, divided, and occupied.

Initially it was not the intention of the occupying powers to hasten German recovery. The Soviet Union, with Lend-Lease ended, removed capital equipment as reparations to speed its own recovery; while the level of industrial agreement between the four powers was intended to keep German production to fifty-five per cent of the 1938 level. Eighteen months after the war ended the cost of such restriction on German production was obvious and, in different ways, the policy was abandoned by Russia as well as by the Western powers. But by that time the division of Germany and Europe had solidified. In Eastern Europe recovery was fettered by the political aims of the Soviet Union in establishing its control over countries that were fast becoming its satellites, with their economies subordinated to its own.

In Western Europe trade was caught in a descending instead of an ascending spiral. The problem of the balance of payments was endemic. Imports into Great Britain in the first half of 1945 were 66·5% of their pre-war level; by the end of the year they were held to 53%. As each country imposed restrictions and limitations to safeguard its own position others suffered as a result. It was an unstable position; but upward movement could not be achieved without outside aid: the imminent danger was a degeneration into increasing national self-sufficiency at a far lower standard of industrial production.

### The rubble of Europe

The major efforts of reconstruction in the five years following the war grew out of these conditions. The ideology of the European movement owed much to the failure of nation-states to provide the most basic of all needs of the citizen – protection from invasion. The Marshall Plan to speed European economic recovery was born from the imaginative realization of the United States government that Europe needed help to help itself. Once this was provided an ordered society could re-emerge.

Yet even when this happened Europe did not regain its place in the world. In Europe nationalism was, for the time being, discredited by the excesses of Nazism and the failures of the nation-state; outside Europe the tide of nationalism was reaching its full flow and it was impossible for the European powers to re-establish their imperial dominion over the rest of the world. The war had destroyed their prestige, which for so long had made it unnecessary for them to exercise coercive force. Once prestige had gone coercive force was inadequate – and morally unacceptable to the conscience of Europe.

At the same time the supremacy of Europe was destroyed by the growth in power and wealth of the United States and the emergence of the Soviet Union, stretching from the Baltic to the Pacific and from the Himalayas to the Arctic Circle, as a second super-power. The rubble of Europe was cleared away and the ruins rebuilt; but a generation after the end of the war Eastern Europe could not escape from the domination of the Soviet Union, while Western Europe, owing its initial recovery to aid from the United States, still sought to understand its new personality in a world of two major powers and a multitude of new states.

*Above left: Aerial view of ruined houses in Hanover, 1945. During the city's heaviest bombing raid, on 19th October 1943, some 2½ square miles had been destroyed. Left: Sculpture by Ossip Zadkine in Rotterdam symbolizing the recovery of this city from the destruction of war. Above right: A collaborator is shot in a wood after the liberation of Rennes, August 1944. Civilians frequently took justice into their own hands as the Germans withdrew. Right: The ruins of the past look out on the ruins of the present – snow-covered casts of Greek sculptures in ruined Munich academy*

B.N.-Est.

Photo: Herbert List

# Exhausted Britain

On 5th July 1945 the British people voted for the government that they wanted to lead them through the post-war years of reconstruction, and on 26th July, after a delay to allow the soldiers' votes to be collected from all over the world, the results were declared. In other countries people had refused to believe that a government which had had the ballot-boxes in its care for three weeks could be defeated.

But defeated it was—routed would be a better word. Churchill the great war leader was overthrown; his triumphal tours during the election campaign were revealed as an expression of gratitude for past services rather than any confidence that he was the man to deal with the new problems ahead. He was dragged down by his party; memories of unemployment, of appeasement, of Dunkirk had convinced the electorate that the Conservatives should not be entrusted with power again.

The Labour Party had campaigned on a programme of putting into effect Beveridge's scheme for social insurance, of building houses, and of nationalization— this last point probably did not help the Labour Party much except by raising the enthusiasm of committed supporters, but it had very little negative effect; people were used to the government running things after six years of war, and saw no need to think it would do any worse than private industry had done in the 1930's.

Clement Attlee—a modest little man with a great deal to be modest about, as Churchill once put it—formed a powerful government, and then went back to the crucial Potsdam Conference with Truman and Stalin. Only a few days later nuclear bombs were dropped on Hiroshima and Nagasaki, and the war was over.

It was a merciful deliverance for the soldiers in the Far East and for their families, but it raised an unexpected and deep-seated problem for the government and for everybody in Britain. The war had been expected to last for another eighteen months, and it had been arranged that during this period Great Britain would continue to receive Lend-Lease help from the United States. This would enable her to reconvert her industries from war to peace. But when the war ended suddenly, Lend-Lease ended equally abruptly, in accordance with the original legislation.

The period of reconstruction could only be bridged by a loan, and Lord Keynes went to Washington to negotiate it. In a great masterpiece of exposition he explained how Great Britain's economic position had suffered during the war. Over

£1,000 million of foreign investments sold; about £1,000 million of industrial depreciation to be made up; over £1,000 million of destruction by bombing; £3,000 million of debts in Egypt and India, and other countries—the 'sterling balances', as they became known. To pay its way in the post-war world, Great Britain would have to export one-and-three-quarter times as much as before the war; this could not be achieved for three or four years, and to cover imports in this period about £1,250 million would be needed.

The survey was accurate. The actual loan made by the United States gave a little less than was asked for, and the 'sterling balances' were a constant source of worry, but the balance-of-payments problem was kept under control. Until 1949 the pound remained at its 1939 value of $4·03. In 1947 there was the first of many sterling crises, but this really had very little to do with the performance of the British economy; when granting the loan the United States had insisted that the British government must prepare to pay for its imports in money that could be converted into dollars. When this obligation fell due, every country in the world wanted dollars. The British government could not meet the demand, and after a fair amount of the loan had been spent trying to do so, sterling had to be made unconvertible again.

At this stage Great Britain could sell abroad all that she produced. But by 1949 this was no longer the case. It was now time to bring down the value of the pound to a level that recognized the changes of the past ten years. Natural pride, a desire not to disrupt the pattern of trade, and a desire not to part too readily with a symbol of Great Britain's pre-war greatness led the British government to fight against the change for longer than made sense, but in September the pound was devalued to $2·80. A great many other currencies were brought down at the same time, but the British took their devaluation much more seriously than anyone else.

At the end of the war Great Britain had stood as one of the three great powers. Less important than the USA or Russia, no doubt, but still her position was to be compared to theirs rather than to that of any other country. Devaluation was one of the first clear signs that this pre-eminence could not be retained. The government had already seen for various reasons the need to withdraw from some of its imperial commitments.

The British largest withdrawal was from India. Independence was in fact inevit-

Paul Popper

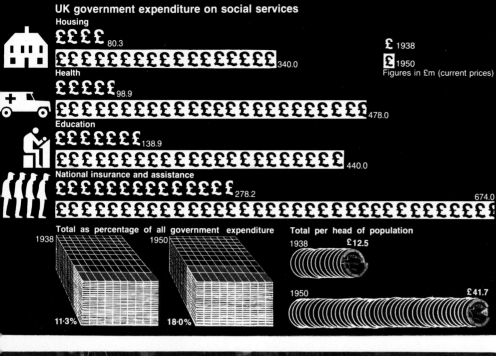

## UK government expenditure on social services

**Housing**
££££ 80.3
£££££££££££££££££ 340.0

**Health**
£££££ 98.9
££££££££££££££££££££££££ 478.0

**Education**
££££££ 138.9
££££££££££££££££££££££ 440.0

**National insurance and assistance**
£££££££££££££ 278.2
£££££££££££££££££££££££££££££££££ 674.0

£ 1938
£ 1950
Figures in £m (current prices)

**Total as percentage of all government expenditure**
1938    1950
11·3%     18·0%

**Total per head of population**
1938   £12.5
1950   £41.7

Paul Popper

Fox Photos

able; fortunately it was a part of the Labour programme, and the government could carry it out with all the air of men who were of their own free will making a magnanimous sacrifice. Hindu and Muslim might hate each other, but in August 1947 they both parted with the British on good terms.

In Palestine the process of withdrawal was less happy. By the time the British left in 1948 the Arabs believed that Israel had been set up as a British outpost in the Middle East, the Israelis believed that the British had hoped that the Arabs would sweep Israel into the sea, and the British believed that both Arabs and Israelis had treated the British and their soldiers in Palestine abominably. So the conflicting and irreconcilable promises of the First World War worked themselves out.

British troops had also to withdraw from Greece and from Turkey, though this was for more directly financial reasons. Americans took their place, the first sign that the United States was going to commit its strength to maintaining the European boundaries of 1945. Despite this withdrawal to save money, the British government spent a lot on defence. Attlee and his foreign minister Bevin were not imperialists or war-mongers, but they began the policy of spending a larger proportion of the national income on defence than any country of comparable size.

Some of this money went into preparing an atomic bomb. Scientists had already acquired the knowledge needed; all that had to be done was to provide the equipment and this, at very great expense, the government proceeded to do. A good deal of the expense could be presented as part of the programme of developing atomic power stations; a good deal more had simply to be hidden in the government's financial estimates until it was announced some years later that an A-bomb had been prepared and would be tested.

While it was pursuing a dream of world greatness, the government was also carrying out its domestic programme despite the appearance of some unforeseen disadvantages. The Labour legislation is sometimes called a social revolution; it would be more reasonable to call it legislation to prevent a counter-revolution. In 1945 there were still people who thought it would be pleasant and possible to get back to 'before

*With the war in Europe over, the British chose their leaders for the years of reconstruction. Far left: Churchill during the election campaign. As the overwhelming Conservative defeat showed, his popular reception stemmed from gratitude for past services, not confidence in his party's ability to handle the problems ahead.*
*Left: 1 Diagram showing increased expenditure on social services after Labour's legislation. 2 Employees at Littlewoods, Liverpool, try to keep warm whilst checking the pools. Nationalization of the coal industry on 1st January 1947 was unjustly blamed for the fuel shortage in the cold months that followed. 3 Attlee, with his wife and daughters, watches 1950 general election results come in at Labour HQ*

*Sir William Beveridge arriving at the House of Commons in February 1943, two months after the publication of his report. He was a man of great conceit and indefatigable political determination. In February 1941, when the trade unions were pressing for a comprehensive reconstruction of the social services Beveridge was made chairman of the investigatory committee, and began work on the blueprint for a complete welfare state*

the war'. By 1950 nobody thought it was possible, though there were still people who thought it would be pleasant.

The central feature of the reforms was the national insurance legislation which established the welfare state, along the lines Beveridge had proposed in his wartime report.

During the war great concern with social reform had been aroused, and during 1942 the deliberations of the Beveridge committee, established to investigate the social services, gave rise to considerable speculation. However, Churchill felt strongly against the diversion of energies away from the war effort, and the recommendations of the report were not acted upon until after the war was over.

Early in the committee's sitting, Beveridge had decided that instead of concentrating simply on 'social insurance and allied services' he would, by introducing 'various assumptions', deal with the whole sweep of social policy: not with, as he put it the 'giant want' alone, but with all five giants on the road to reconstruction: 'want, disease, squalor, ignorance and idleness'. He thus provided the blueprint for a complete welfare state.

A single national insurance scheme, financed partly by a weekly purchase of a single insurance stamp, would provide financial protection against all the usual economic crises of life: family allowances payable to a mother with more than one child; health insurance; unemployment insurance; pensions for widows and orphans; and old age pensions. The insurance benefits were meant to be large enough to make it possible to abolish the Poor Law, but a temporary national assistance scheme for people who needed more than the fixed benefit was set up; and still survives.

Most of this was a simple matter of arranging financial transfers. But the National Health Service was harder to set up; in 1911 the doctors had protested at the idea of an insurance scheme, and in 1946 they protested just as vehemently at the setting up of a health service. Aneurin Bevan, the minister of health, was a skilful negotiator but he saw no reason to be conciliatory; the secretary of the British Medical Association, Dr Charles Hill (who later went into politics and became a Conservative cabinet minister), was equally determined to keep up the morale of his troops by the vigour of his denunciation. By degrees the two sides came together, and more and more doctors withdrew from their originally expressed determination to go on strike rather than work the scheme. In July 1948 the National Health Service began as scheduled.

Horror stories appeared about the immense demand for wigs, spectacles, and false teeth, and about an invasion of foreigners who were eager to take advantage of a scheme that was free to all the world. But it seems that most of the people who took part in the sudden rush to get things on the national health at the beginning of the service had simply been too poor to buy them previously— the sample budgets of the poor drawn up in the 'thirties all show that very little

money was spent on health except for the panel doctor and for patent medicines.

There may well have been people who came from abroad, but they came to admire rather than to take advantage of the National Health Service. The British idea of the welfare state was taken up in several other countries and while many of them, during the 'fifties, arranged higher scales of benefits and pensions, very few of them were prepared to face the initial argument with the doctors that seemed to be an inevitable part of setting up a comprehensive health service.

Another, less explicit but quite definite aspect of the welfare state was full employment. The wartime government had accepted a commitment to full employment in its 1944 white paper, and its successors interpreted full employment in the sense laid down by Beveridge in his book criticizing the white paper for its timidity. In this book Beveridge stated that there should at all times be more jobs available than there were workers out of work. Prices were almost certain to go up as a result; Beveridge was right in assuming that most people would prefer a little inflation to any return to unemployment on the scale of the 'thirties. The Labour government benefited from this; at the end of the 'forties full employment was a positive vote-winner, though during the 'fifties people began to take it for granted and to blame the government when unemployment appeared.

### Nationalization

On the other hand there was much to make people dissatisfied with the government. The great programme of nationalization went through Parliament, and a good deal of it—the Bank of England, gas, and electricity—went more or less unnoticed. But coal and transport were a different matter. Both industries were in an unsatisfactory condition when they were taken over; the railways had been cutting their dividends for many years past, and the mine-owners were in no position to find the large sums of money needed to mechanize the pits to maintain the level of coal production.

Naturally enough, nationalization worked no miracles in either industry. All the complaints about slow and dirty trains that had been heard before the war were heard once more, but this time with the implication that nationalization was to blame. And within a few weeks of the nationalization of the coal mines on 1st January 1947 the country was hit by a disastrous fuel shortage. The bleak winter of 1947, when over a million men were at one time out of work because factories had to close down, and when housewives found that cooking a simple meal took hours because electric current was weak and gas pressure ran low, was the moment at which the Conservatives first became convinced that the Labour government was not invincible.

And undoubtedly government forecasting of the country's need for fuel was at fault. It was not reasonable to blame the National Coal Board for this, but blamed it was and for ten years to come there were complaints that coal was in short supply.

National Archives, Washington

School of Slavonic Studies Library

ЭВОЛЮЦИЯ АНГЛИЙСКОЙ МОДЫ

In the late 1950's the complaint changed: there was now too much coal, because oil had come forward so rapidly that coal was no longer needed in such large quantities.

Rationing of food went on all through the period of the Labour government, and undoubtedly contributed to its unpopularity. Clothes came off the ration in 1949, and petrol in 1950, though the waiting-list to buy motor-cars was so long that this concession did not make as much difference as might have been hoped for. The personalities of the Labour ministers of food did not help: during the war Lord Woolton had always managed to convince housewives that he was on their side and was solving their problems, but Dr Edith Summerskill's remark that very few people could tell the difference between butter and margarine gave the impression that really she did not care which they had.

Also unpopular was the government's scheme for growing groundnuts in East Africa; in principle it was a splendid proposal that would build up the African economy and would provide oils and fats for the British market, but in practice the site was ill-chosen and the whole scheme came to a miserable end. The public was not yet accustomed to the idea of the government spending large sums of money on experimental projects that eventually had to be written off; the Conservatives later were to have plenty of experience of this when they had to cancel expensive weapons-systems, but in the late 1940's they pointed at the government and said that nothing like this had ever happened before. This was true: governments were less active before 1939.

The spirit of the Labour government in its later years was personified for many people by Sir Stafford Cripps. His ebullient predecessor as chancellor of the Exchequer, Hugh Dalton, had had to resign after telling a newspaper what would be in his autumn 1947 budget a few minutes before he announced it to the House of Commons. Sir Stafford was a man of unbending rectitude — 'there,' Churchill said, 'but for the grace of God, goes God' — and in his teetotal and vegetarian habits he seemed to personify the policy of 'austerity'. His moral exhortations had some effect in making British businessmen go out into the export market, and from 1948-50 he managed to induce the trade union leaders to co-operate in composing a wage freeze.

Despite the difference in personality, Sir Stafford's actual economic policy was not very different from Dalton's. Both men were determined to make sure that there should be no return to the conditions of the 'thirties, and they agreed that low interest rates would safeguard full employment. The bank rate was kept down to two per cent. Naturally this led to a very active economy; house-building, new investment, replacement of depreciation, increased exports, and high consumer demand for all unrationed goods meant that the whole system was under great pressure. This pressure was restrained by a system of licences and controls which meant that the government had to decide what should be done next. As Aneurin Bevan put it, 'the religion of socialism must be preached in the language of priorities'.

Translated into practical policy, this came rather closer to saying, in the words of Douglas Jay, 'the man in Whitehall knows best'. This was not a conciliatory way to put it, though there was something in what he said. In the 1930's the means of production — capital and labour — had been available in profusion, but had not been used because there was no possibility of using them at a profit. In the conditions of high demand in the late 1940's there were all sorts of opportunities for making things at a profit, and businessmen felt bitter at

*Left: Cripps, chancellor of the Exchequer who personified austerity. Above: Cartoon from Russian satirical magazine* Krokodil, *1952, depicts the decline of British power. The majestic, confident lion has been replaced with a drab, gloomy beast*

the system of controls which restrained them. Of course, if everybody had tried to make use of these opportunities at once, the economy would have suffered an uncontrollable inflation, possibly followed by a return to the depressed conditions of the 1920's; this was what the government was trying to hold in check, and the man in Whitehall was probably the best judge of the overall pressure of demand which might explode if left unchecked. High demand coupled with strict controls did not make for comfortable running of the economy, though it did produce a faster rate of peace-time growth than the country had had for almost a century.

The businessmen were joined in their anger against the government by the people who wanted to get back to the days before the war. In retrospect this latter group may look like a collection of mean-minded people who wanted to get their servants back, and it was true that servants did not re-emerge in great numbers after 1945 as they had after 1918. But there is no doubt that this section of the middle and upper class really thought a social revolution was upon them.

People like this, who looked back to 1936 as if to some far-off golden age, were obviously likely to be an electoral handicap to the Conservative Party, and in the party reorganization under Lord Woolton that followed the 1945 defeat one objective of the reformers was to weaken the impact of this sort of thinking. The Conservatives presented their appeal in terms of freedom — freedom from rationing, freedom to make

money without the restraint of government controls, and freedom to build and develop land without the need for government permission.

Labour defended its position with the slogan 'Fair shares for all', and in the 1950 election it still polled two and a half per cent more of the popular vote than the Conservatives. But in the House of Commons its margin was down to six, and a new election was clearly going to come soon. As the siege tightened, the older defenders fell away; Cripps had to retire from the Exchequer in October 1950 and Bevin had to leave the Foreign Office in March 1951—both men had been in government posts for the last ten years, and could not go on any longer.

By this time another strain was growing increasingly important. Great Britain was not immediately concerned to any great extent in the Korean War which broke out on 25th June 1950, though the British contingent was, next to the American, the largest in the United Nations force that went to defend South Korea. But the general effect on the economy was much larger than the fifty million pounds spent directly on the war.

Part of this was unavoidable; as the United States began rearming, the prices of a great many raw materials shot up, and this meant that goods imported by Great Britain inevitably went up in price and the balance-of-payments suffered accordingly. As the United States became more deeply involved in Korea, the American government became more and more eager that its European allies should rearm themselves so that they could hold their own even though some United States forces had to be withdrawn from Europe to the Pacific. As Great Britain showed every sign of having recovered from the war much better than

the other European countries, a large contribution was expected from her.

The Labour government had already gone some way towards military preparedness by introducing conscription in time of peace under the National Service Act of December 1948, and by spending about seven per cent of the national income on armaments. But under the stress of Korea the period of conscription was extended, and the amount of national income devoted to defence was increased, first to ten and a half per cent and then—at least on paper—to fourteen per cent. This second step increased the strain on the government; Aneurin Bevan resigned in protest against the imposition of charges on national health prescriptions, and Harold Wilson resigned on the grounds that it was not possible to transfer resources to the armaments industries without crippling the engineering industries that provided so large a part of the country's exports. Whatever might be thought about Bevan's resignation, events certainly seemed to bear out Wilson's criticism, and the blow was particularly serious because German and Japanese manufacturers were re-emerging in the world market to take up the opportunities being abandoned by British manufacturers.

For the coming election the Conservatives developed the promise of an end to rationing—'good, red meat' as they said—and appealed to the Liberals not to waste their votes by putting up impossibly large numbers of candidates as they had in 1950. The Conservatives also promised to build 300,000 houses a year. Housing had suffered because Bevan had been in charge of it as well as health; he had been too busy with the National Health Service, and too concerned with getting money from the

*Passengers on the London underground read of increased food prices. High demand coupled with strict government controls cost Labour many supporters*

Treasury for it, to be able to find either time or money for housing. The result was a shortage of houses that led to discomfort, overcrowding, and great difficulty for people who wanted to change jobs, so the Conservative promise to do something about it was well-received.

The Korean War had provided one issue that helped the Labour Party. When General MacArthur seemed to be on the point of extending the war into China, Attlee had flown to Washington, and shortly afterwards Truman had dismissed MacArthur. It is not possible to say how much effect Attlee had on this decision, but it enabled the government to stand as the defender of the peace and to suggest that Churchill would not be safe as Prime Minister. 'Whose finger on the trigger?' asked the *Daily Mirror*, and the implication was clearly that Attlee had a steadier hand.

The government fought its rearguard action skilfully and with determination. When the election came on 25th October 1951 the Labour Party once more polled more votes than the Conservatives (and more votes than any party has polled in any other election), but too many of them were concentrated in Labour strongholds. The Conservatives had a small but adequate majority; and everybody could relax. The age of high expenditure on social services, high expenditure on armaments, and an impossible dream of continued British world leadership was over. Under the Conservatives people could enjoy themselves and Great Britain could face the fact that she was not a great power any more.

# Marshall Aid: Rebuilding Europe

Although Winston Churchill observed that the Marshall Plan was 'the most unsordid act in history' it was not, despite the magnitude of its conception and the extent of its generosity, a policy devoid of self-interest for the United States. It is doubtful whether a vague, altruistic programme geared to a general spirit of benevolence would have found the necessary popular or political acceptance; the relevance and function of the plan, as a realistic instrument of policy based on a rational analysis of the European situation, contributed directly to its success. Historic ties between the United States and Europe were strong. Isolationism within the United States had been weakened, if not entirely destroyed, by the Second World War. Growing awareness of the nature and power of the Soviet system brought about a recognition that the United States could not meaningfully survive alone in a hostile world. To many Americans it seemed to make excellent sense to divert part of their national wealth to assist European recovery.

European national economies were in chaos. Large parts of the continent had been devastated by war, and the imperial powers had largely exhausted their overseas reserves in the struggle against Nazism. They lacked capital for rebuilding industry and converting to peace-time production. Shortages were acute, particularly of food, fuel, and raw materials. The situation in Great Britain was serious: despite a net Lend-Lease inflow of $21,000 million, overseas investments worth $4,500 million had been liquidated to pay for war supplies, and external debts amounted to some $14,000 million at the end of the war. The special American loan of $3,750 million in 1946 provided valuable short-term relief, but did little to stabilize the long-term situation.

From the end of the war to the beginning of Marshall Aid in 1948, the United States supplied Western Europe with $4,500 million in grants and extended a further $6,800 million in credits, but the European dollar deficit in 1947 was still $8,000 million and the position looked dangerous.

Descent of the Iron Curtain across Europe aggravated post-war problems, for the European economy was severed into two artificial units, symbolized by divided Germany. In both 1946 and 1947 industrial and agricultural production in all European countries fell below pre-war levels and was inadequate for the needs of a population that, despite the appalling losses of the war years, was greater than before. The forces of nature also seemed to be con-

spiring against recovery. The terrible winter of 1946-47 was followed first by floods and then by drought. A major consequence of economic dislocation was political instability, and the circle was completed when political weakness contributed to economic tensions: insecure governments were unable to take the rigorous measures which were necessary to bring about economic restoration.

At the time when the Truman Doctrine was taking shape the Council of Foreign Ministers was meeting in Moscow, and despite high hopes of positive achievements it was unsuccessful. The four great powers failed to agree on the future of Germany, and after private conversations

with Stalin on 15th April, the secretary of state, George Marshall, became convinced that the Soviet Union was playing for time and awaiting a European economic collapse. He saw the only solution was immediate American action. Positive planning of an aid programme had already begun in the Department of State under the direction of the under-secretary, Dean Acheson. In a speech on 8th May Acheson publicly advocated such a programme in

*Below: In a Czech cartoon, 1952, Truman and Acheson are depicted as card sharps who have cynically cheated their allies. In fact they helped to preserve the tottering status quo in Western Europe*

Dikobraz

*George Marshall during the war when he was US Army Chief of Staff*

Paul Popper

the interests of the American economy, the survival of democratic institutions in Europe, and general humanitarian concern. Marshall's speech at Harvard University on 5th June 1947 forcefully expressed American interest in the rehabilitation of Europe, and is generally regarded as the official launching of the Marshall Plan.

From the beginning it was assumed that positive initiatives must come from Europe, and that participation in the plan would be opened to all countries in Europe, including the Soviet Union, although there was little expectation that the Russians would join. The leading European nations established a Committee for European Economic Co-operation, and on 22nd September 1947 CEEC presented to the United States government a report advocating a four-year programme for economic recovery embracing sixteen countries of Europe and western Germany. Four objectives were outlined: an increase in industrial and agricultural productivity at least up to prewar levels, the establishment of financial stability, economic co-operation between the participating countries, and a solution of the problem of dollar deficits through the expansion of exports. Members pledged co-operation, reduction of tariffs, and ultimate convertibility of currencies.

Parallel with the work of the CEEC, study groups in the United States were drafting plans to meet the emergency. The Council of Economic Advisers made detailed analyses of the general situation; the President's Committee on Foreign Aid, under the chairmanship of the secretary of commerce, Averell Harriman, explored the ramifications of a wide ranging aid programme; and a third committee under the guidance of Julius Krug, secretary of the interior, explored the capacity of the

United States, in terms of resources, to service a vast economic aid programme. When the committees reported in the autumn of 1947 each supported the Marshall Plan concept, and each based its arguments on the ways in which American national interests would be served by such a programme. All agreed that the security of the United States would be endangered should Europe collapse. The Council of Economic Advisors reported that without a large aid programme American exports would decline sharply, with consequent problems for the domestic economy. The Harriman committee estimated that between 12,000 and 17,000 million dollars would be required for European recovery and that such aid would be not charity but expenditure in the public interest. All groups defined the American national interest broadly, and took care to stress the economic, political, strategic, and humanitarian factors that were involved.

A constant theme was that the United States should not direct operations from across the Atlantic but rather co-operate in a programme inspired from Europe. The Harriman committee specifically rejected the proposal that the aid programme should be used to persuade European countries to establish or maintain an economic system on the American model.

Within five months of Marshall's Harvard speech the preparatory work on Marshall Aid had been done, and on 19th

*Vyshinsky, the Russian foreign minister (1), welcomes Marshall (2) and Dulles (3) through an interpreter (4) at Moscow, March 1947*

Keystone Press

December President Truman sent a message to Congress on American support to European recovery. Hearings on the European Recovery Program began in January 1948. Quite apart from discussion in governmental and congressional committees the policy had already been the subject of vigorous public debate. The most important publicist for its aims was the Committee for the Marshall Plan, composed of prominent citizens from all walks of life, which conducted an important and influential campaign. Although the hearings on the plans were by no means a formality, much of the ground work had already been done. The Communist coup in Czechoslovakia in February 1948 helped to confirm belief in the aggressive and expansionist nature of Communism, and the congressional committees reported unanimously in favour of the plan at the end of the month. The tone of the Senate debate on the bill was set by Senator Vandenberg of Michigan, chairman of the Senate Foreign Relations Committee. In an impressive speech this former isolationist related the aid programme to the Truman Doctrine, spoke 'in the name of intelligent American self-interest', emphasized that the legislation sought peace and stability for free men in a free world by economic rather than military means. 'It sustains Western civilisation. It means to take Western Europe completely off the American dole at the end

of the adventure.' The debate that followed Vandenberg's speech was characterized by a sincere desire to understand the full implications of the recovery legislation, rather than by die-hard opposition to such a far-reaching American commitment. The bill was ratified on 3rd April 1948.

The act envisaged a four-year plan to implement the recovery programme, and authorized an appropriation of some $4,300 million for the first year. Bilateral agreements were to be made with participating countries, and each foreign government was to deposit local currency, 'counterpart funds', equivalent to the amounts received in grants, to be used to assist recovery. Each participating country was required to assist the United States to accumulate stocks of strategic materials, and a number of particular requirements were designed to protect American shipping and other interests. To implement the programme the Economic Co-operation Administration was established, headed by an administrator responsible to the President and of equal status to heads of the executive departments. In April 1948 Paul G. Hoffman, president of the Studebaker Corporation, became administrator.

The working concept of the European Recovery Program remained that with which early planning had begun. Hoffman himself declared: 'I had a strong belief that no pattern imposed by a group of planners in Washington could possibly be effective

. . . the responsibility must be given to the Europeans themselves.' Averell Harriman was appointed special representative in Europe, and worked in close collaboration with the Organization for European Economic Co-operation (OEEC) that developed out of CEEC. Although the member countries retained economic autonomy, they agreed to take decisions in the light of the possible consequences for other participating countries, to reduce tariff barriers, and to work towards a multilateral system of payments. As the programme developed, different priorities, were found to be necessary in different parts of Europe and planning proceeded on a country by country basis. Procurement of supplies was handled directly by the participating countries, thereby obviating the need for ECA, unlike UNRRA (United Nations Relief and Rehabilitation Administration), to establish an extensive bureaucracy of procurement agencies. The procurement authorization requests submitted by individual governments were referred to the Economic Co-operation Administration in Washington, where they were checked to ensure that they fitted within authorized allotments and had no adverse implications for the domestic American economy.

During the life of the Marshall Plan between 1948 and 1952 Congress appropriated a total of some $13,150 million for the recovery programme, with the highest

*Diagram showing amounts extended by United States to Western Europe under Marshall Aid. Great Britain received the lion's share*

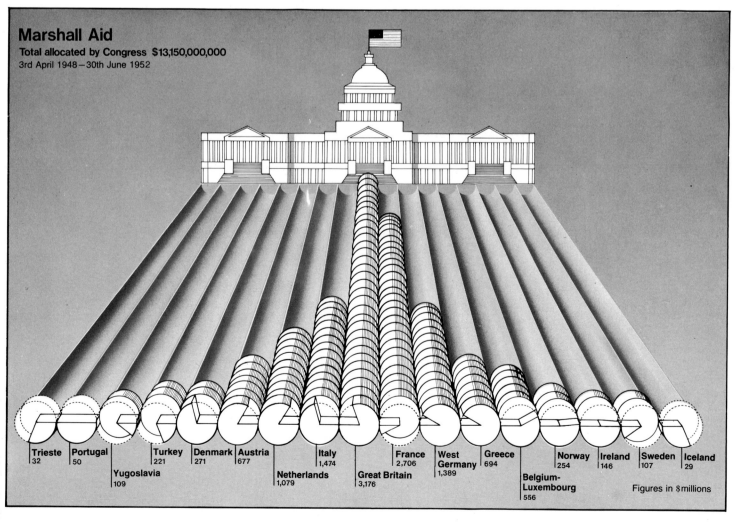

**Marshall Aid**
Total allocated by Congress $13,150,000,000
3rd April 1948 – 30th June 1952

Trieste 32
Portugal 50
Yugoslavia 109
Turkey 221
Denmark 271
Austria 677
Italy 1,474
Netherlands 1,079
France 2,706
Great Britain 3,176
West Germany 1,389
Greece 694
Belgium-Luxembourg 556
Norway 254
Ireland 146
Sweden 107
Iceland 29

Figures in $millions

annual appropriation coming in the first year. Initial emphasis was placed upon the provision of food, animal feedstuffs, and fertilizers to relieve immediate shortages in Europe and increase agricultural productivity. Later emphasis shifted to industrial raw materials and semi-finished products, with machinery, vehicles, and fuel also forming significant proportions of the total volume of supplies. 69.7% of all goods were procured in the United States, including 98% of the vehicles and machinery, with consequent benefits for the American domestic economy. The lion's share of aid, $3,176 million, went to Great Britain. France came second with $2,706 million, while West Germany, fourth in the line, received only $1,389 million which was slightly more than half the aid given to France.

The effects of the programme were quickly felt in all recipient countries and in all branches of industry and agriculture. It contributed to land reclamation projects in Italy, shipbuilding in Britain, agricultural improvements in Germany, and introduced maize to Benedictine monks in the Pyrenees. In addition to the aid itself, production began to rise under the stimulus of investment of counter-part funds. During the first two years of Marshall Aid industrial production in Western Europe as a whole rose by more than 25%, and in all countries advanced above 1938 levels. This progress in industry and agriculture continued during 1951 but began to taper off the year after.

By then Marshall Aid had accomplished its primary objectives and the general environment of international politics had changed. This was to be expected. The problem of European recovery was a short-term one. Although the war had left the economies of Western Europe shattered, it had not destroyed the capacities for self-help. These only needed stimulation in order to achieve their own momentum. The new vitality which quickly appeared found expression in a European Payments Union in 1950 and the European Coal and Steel Community, composed of six continental countries, in 1952. Another genuinely European movement was the tendency to discard the concept of confederation that was inherent in OEEC and the European Recovery Program and to transfer elements of national sovereignty to supra-national authorities. After the ratification of the NATO treaty in 1949, there was a change of emphasis away from economic recovery to military security. The Marshall Plan had ensured that the countries of Western Europe could now play their part in the defence of their own territory. It could not return Europe to her former greatness. It did prevent the shadows of the Kremlin from darkening the entire continent.

*Left: German workmen erect a crane financed from Marshall Aid, of which West Germany received the fourth largest share of $1,389 million. Marshall Aid ensured West Germany's incorporation in the economic structure of Western Europe after the end of the war*

Südd-Verlag

# Truman and Eisenhower

In the spring of 1945 the Allies were on the crest of victory. In Germany, British and American troops were racing each other and the Russians to Berlin; in the Pacific, American forces were reducing Okinawa while American bombers were pounding the Japanese mainland. Then, without warning, the news fell on stunned America that Franklin D.Roosevelt, the leader of his people and of the whole Allied coalition, had died of a cerebral haemorrhage. The longest, most storm-tossed presidency in American history had come to an end.

On no one did this news break with more shattering impact than on Harry S.Truman, the vice-president. Born in the small town of Lamar, Missouri, in 1884, he appeared to be the typical small-town American, who after a succession of unimpressive jobs had passed into the backwaters of Missouri politics. But with his election to the Senate in 1934 a more impressive figure began to emerge. During the war years he headed a notable Senate committee which kept a very effective eye upon the government's handling of munitions production and it was his success in this which no doubt recommended him to Roosevelt as a running-mate in 1944. But as vice-president he had virtually no share in responsibility or power; he was a spare wheel on the chariot of state. Consequently he was totally unprepared for the office so suddenly thrust upon him; he felt, he said, as if 'the moon, the stars, and all the planets' had fallen on him. But he brought to his task unshakable courage, stout common sense, and a profound belief in the principles that had guided Roosevelt's policies at home and abroad. His first official acts were to invite the members of Roosevelt's cabinet to stay in office and to announce that the conference at San Francisco for setting up the United Nations would proceed as planned.

Not all his immediate decisions were so uncontroversial. When victory came in Europe and Asia Truman's instinct was to bring the boys back home and pick up the threads of Roosevelt's New Deal where the advent of war had broken them off. But the war had induced a revulsion against any kind of government interference. Truman found Congress unwilling to give him powers to control prices and restrain wage increases. 1946 saw considerable inflation and formidable strikes in every sector of American industry. Though a friend of labour, Truman had to force the leaders to back down by seizing control of the railways and coal mines and threatening to

induct the railwaymen into the army. Fortunately the phenomenal level of production attained during the war years was largely kept up and provided the basis upon which a generally high level of consumption at home could be combined with the shipping of surpluses abroad for relief and rehabilitation, in Europe and Asia.

In November 1946 the wave of post-war conservatism showed its strength at the ballot box. In the elections to Congress the President's supporters lost heavily and the Republicans won a majority in both houses. Even among the Democrats, Truman's own party, it was the conservatives, not the New Dealers, who came off best. A legislative alliance of Republicans and conservative Democrats went into action, under the leadership of Senator Robert Taft of Ohio, to pass the Taft-Hartley Law in June 1947 over Truman's veto. The act reflected a widespread sentiment that the gains the trade unions had won under the New Deal were excessive. Though it permitted a union shop where a majority of workers desired it, it forbade the closed shop and jurisdictional strikes, it required a sixty-day 'cooling-off' period for strikes, and authorized the President to seek court injunctions which would provide for an eighty-day 'cooling-off' period in relation to strikes which affected the national interest—a procedure which Truman and Eisenhower were to employ on no less than seventeen occasions. Moreover, it debarred unions from making political contributions and required them to register and file reports on their finances. The unions bitterly opposed and resented what they called a 'slave labour act', but it turned out to be much less hampering than they feared; even the ban on political contributions could be evaded by establishing so called 'political education committees'. In the end the measure undoubtedly helped the Democrats by convincing organized labour that the Democrats were their friends and the Republicans their enemies.

1947 saw the open emergence of the Cold War, the outright split over Germany, the launching of the Truman Doctrine and its twin the Marshall Plan, and the first wave of Communist witch-hunting inside the USA itself. To one old New Dealer, Henry Wallace, all this was anathema; having resigned from Truman's cabinet in protest against his foreign policy, he allied himself in 1948 with extreme left-wing elements to challenge Truman's renomination. In a convention of self-styled 'Progressives' he was nominated as a presidential candidate. Meanwhile, on the other

wing of the Democratic Party southerners were disgruntled by the President's proposals for outlawing poll taxes and discriminatory legislation. When the young liberal mayor of Minneapolis, Hubert Humphrey, induced the Democratic convention to incorporate these civil rights proposals in the party's official platform, this was too much for extreme 'Dixiecrats', as they were called. Seceding under the banner of the 'States' Rights Party', they nominated a notorious white supremacist, Governor Thurmond, of South Carolina, as their presidential candidate.

Under fire from both these flanks of his own party, Truman was faced directly with a confident challenge from the Republicans who had nominated the competent, if colourless, Governor Dewey of New York, the man who had had the thankless task of opposing the invulnerable Roosevelt in 1944. In 1948 his chances seemed much brighter. Truman's programme had become bogged down in a hostile Congress and so many of his own party had lost faith in him that at one stage they seriously contemplated nominating General Eisenhower, the popular commander-in-chief

*Below: Harry S.Truman sets off with a full head of steam on his 'whistle-stop', 'give 'em hell' election tour. His dynamic campaign for the presidency against the Republican governor Dewey of New York in 1948 took America by surprise. This cartoon was one contemporary reaction.*

**1** in Europe, whose political attachments were unknown. However, when it came to the crunch Truman won his renomination easily enough; what came as a surprise was his ensuing, dynamic, 'whistle-stop', 'give 'em hell' campaign. The little man from Missouri called back what he called 'the do-nothing eightieth Congress' in a special session, ostensibly to consider price control, housing, social security, and civil rights legislation, but in fact to dramatize his own stand on all these issues.

As election day approached, the public opinion polls echoed the general opinion in giving Governor Dewey a clear lead. The Republican *Chicago Daily Tribune* went so far, on the basis of early returns, as to print the banner headline: 'Dewey defeats Truman.' The final results, however, gave Truman over twenty-four million votes to Dewey's less than twenty-two million, an impressive tribute to Truman's campaigning courage and conviction. The breakaway candidates scored little more than a million each, but Governor Thurmond did carry four states in the south. In Congress the President's victory brought back Democratic majorities in both houses.

However, although the new Congress accepted the President's leadership in foreign policy, notably in endorsing the Marshall Plan and NATO, it was still too conservative to accept all of what he called his 'Fair Deal' proposals, the unfinished agenda of its predecessor. It gave him money for housing and higher social security benefits and it extended old New Deal programmes in conservation and rural electrification. But repeal of the Taft-Hartley Act and passage of health insurance and a fair employment practices act were denied him. Much of Congress's energies were absorbed by a neurotic obsession with the menace of Communist subversion.

The outbreak of war in Korea in 1950 was met by Truman with characteristic resolution and common sense, but the Republicans both blamed the administration for the war and simultaneously demanded its more vigorous prosecution. They linked it up with what they called the 'loss of China' to Communism and they made General MacArthur, the commander-in-chief in Korea, into a national hero and a party totem. Thus the President's firm refusal to involve the United States with China, either by accepting aid from Chiang Kai-shek, or by allowing MacArthur to strike beyond the Yalu River,

*Left: 1 Truman gets the last laugh on the Republicans' 'kept Press'. After his 1948 election victory over Dewey, he displays a headline that jumped the gun. 2 Republican convention, 1952: Nixon-Ike partnership for presidential elections. 3 Democratic convention, 1956. From left: former President Truman and defeated protégé Harriman, Stevenson, presidential candidate, and Kefauver, running mate. Right: President Eisenhower arrives in Minneapolis during his election tour in 1956. He looked healthy and fit for a second term in spite of a heart attack the previous year*

caused fierce controversy, MacArthur tried to rouse Congress and the public against the President by openly criticizing this policy. Such conduct raised the whole question of the subordination of the military to the civilian arm. Faced with this challenge, Truman did not hesitate. In April 1951 he announced that since MacArthur was 'unable to give his whole-hearted support' to the government's policies he would be 'relieved of his commands at once'. The general's return was marked by a hero's welcome in Washington, New York, and Chicago, but public opinion remained on Truman's side. The Senate conducted an exhaustive investigation of the frustrating course of the war which ended in a virtual demonstration that the MacArthur strategy would involve the USA, as General Bradley said, 'in the wrong war, at the wrong place, at the wrong time, and with the wrong enemy'.

The country supported the war but it did not always accept its consequences. When the President, to check the inflation caused by huge war expenditure, proposed a 'freeze' on wages and prices, labour refused to collaborate with the Wages Stabilization Board until revisions were made to allow substantial wage increases. The producers' lobbies were similarly hostile to price controls and prevented the passage of really effective legislation. Congress reluctantly agreed to extend the President's powers to call up young men for military service by the Military Manpower Act of June 1951.

The Korean War was becoming increasingly burdensome. The hopes raised by the truce negotiations in the summer of 1951 were cruelly frustrated; neither victory nor peace came nearer while the suffering and the casualties mounted. Thus 1952, Truman's last year in the White House, was clouded with disappointments and irritations. The Democrats seemed debilitated by their long rule and, on the evidence of several scandals, corrupted by power. Hopes of liberal legislation were dashed as Congress became increasingly obsessed by McCarthyism and even flirted, under Senator Taft, with dreams of a new American isolationism.

This risk stimulated liberal and world-minded Republicans to persuade General Eisenhower to leave his post as Supreme Allied Commander in Europe and accept the party's nomination for the presidency. The party 'regulars' would have preferred Senator Taft, but the general's broad appeal was irresistible. It owed nothing to party but everything to his role as a national hero, an unmilitaristic but triumphant organizer of the Allied coalition, the victor in war who was also a man of peace. It mattered not that Eisenhower had no previous party affiliation, nor even that he had no defined set of political objectives. He had a generally liberal image and an immensely broad appeal.

To oppose him the Democrats selected a man who was a striking departure from the conventional model of an American politician, Adlai Stevenson. Though he had displayed vote-winning ability by his election as governor of Illinois in a year of

*Above: British view of 1956 Republican convention. X-ray shows Ike's 'Dicky' heart, a comment on Nixon's importance as second man for a President in ill health*

Republican successes, he was a man of intellectual rather than popular tastes, a wit with a tendency to self-depreciation, an advocate of liberal policies but on most social issues a Whig at heart. His campaign against the all-popular 'Ike' was marked by its honesty, its eloquence, and its amateurism. It won him many hearts but few votes. Eisenhower and his running mate, a young crusading anti-Communist senator, Richard Nixon, won a crushing victory: they carried every northern state and, by winning Florida, Tennessee, Texas, and Virginia, proved that the new Republicanism could seduce even the once solidly Democratic south.

No campaign pledge of Eisenhower's enlisted a more enthusiastic response than his undertaking, if elected, to go to Korea. In December 1952 he went, with the implied purpose of hastening the war's end, but it took the death of Stalin, with its moderating effect on Communist policy, before a compromise armistice was signed at Pammunjon on 27th July 1953. By then the United States had suffered 140,000 casualties including over 54,000 dead.

In foreign affairs Eisenhower placed great confidence in his secretary of state, John Foster Dulles, who incarnated the east coast Republicans' policy of accepting the USA's responsibilities in Europe and Asia and adopting a hard line towards Communism everywhere. However, Eisenhower's own influence was always thrown on the side of compromise and a policy of co-existence whenever this was at all possible. At home he delegated authority to his cabinet members, who tended for the most part to be conservative business leaders, like George Humphrey, the secretary of the treasury, and Charles Wilson, the president of General Motors who became his secretary of defence. However, he disappointed those Republicans who expected him to reverse the achievements

of the New and Fair Deals. He saw himself as ideally a President above party and faction, a kind of benevolent and tolerant elected monarch who would run the executive branch by the same rules of order and hierarchy as he had run the army, while leaving the legislature a free hand to frame financial and legislative policy. This sometimes exposed him and his administration to embarrassment and even humiliation at the hands of Congress, especially in his first two years. Thus he found himself at odds with the Senate over McCarthy and at odds with the Senate and House of Representatives because they wished to cut taxes while the economy was in recession. Against his better judgment he had to allow the oil interests to obtain access on very favourable terms to oil lands under the sea within the coastal boundaries of the USA. The desire to economize led, in foreign policy, to too ready a reliance on what Dulles, the secretary of state, called 'massive retaliation'—i.e. air power and the threat to use the atomic bomb—and too little attention to diversified means of warfare, particularly the use of light and mobile land and sea units.

Paradoxically when the Republicans lost control of both the House of Representatives and the Senate in Eisenhower's first mid-term elections in November 1954 his task became easier. This was because all the pressures that bear down upon the presidency are for positive government action and such action was more acceptable to Democrats than it was to Republicans. In addition two Texas Democrats, Lyndon Johnson, majority leader of the Senate, and Sam Rayburn, speaker of the House of Representatives, kept the Democrats in line behind the President, who for his part gradually revealed himself to have more in common with middle-of-the-road Democrats than with conservative Republicans.

### Negro rights
However, it was not in the White House or in Congress that the most important domestic action of Eisenhower's first term was taken, but in the Supreme Court. The American negro's slow progress towards equality had always been frustrated in Congress by the determined opposition of the southerners who either talked out or emasculated whatever civil rights legislation was proposed. But in 1954 the Supreme Court heard the case of Brown v. the Board of Education of Topeka in which the whole question of the segregation of the races was raised in the crucial context of education. Previously the court had been content to interpret the Constitution's guarantees of 'equality' as being compatible with segregation, under the formula 'separate but equal'. This enabled the south, in particular, to maintain separate public facilities so long as it could sustain the fiction that the black man's schools, waiting rooms, or other places of public resort were as good as the white man's. Now the court ruled that enforced separation was intrinsically unequal and it called on the south to integrate its public school system (and by implication everything

else) 'with all deliberate speed'. The fact that the court was unanimous, that the chief justice, Earl Warren, had run for vice-president on Dewey's conservative ticket in 1948, and that the three southern justices voted with their six non-southern colleagues – all this lent additional weight to the court's momentous decision.

Although a few of the border states sought to comply with the court's ruling, it met with opposition elsewhere in the south, which was the more determined because Eisenhower's attitude of being above the struggle prevented the Department of Justice from throwing its full weight behind enforcement. Consequently the open defiance by Governor Faubus at Little Rock, Arkansas, in 1957 obliged the President eventually to send federal troops to enforce a court order for the desegregation of the public schools. Even after that the process of desegregation in Arkansas and elsewhere in the south remained disappointingly slow.

Even so the court's decision is deservedly regarded as a landmark. It gave an endorsement and a fillip to the negro's claim in every area. Congress was induced, in 1957 and 1960, to pass two civil rights measures which for the first time gave the federal government effective power to promote and protect the negro's right to vote. Meanwhile, the negro himself, encouraged by this and stimulated by his experiences as a conscript in the desegregated armed forces, became vastly more assertive of his rights. Sit-ins, protest marches, and organized boycotts were his weapons, generally employed with an impressive show of non-violence. However, the gains thereby secured were accompanied, in general, by an increased tension between the races, as a great wave of negro migration developed from the poor, rural south to the great urban centres of the

*Eisenhower's homespun image: photograph of Ike with his mother, taken in 1938 and released in 1955*

north-east and middle west, where overcrowding and high unemployment made the negro sections little better than black 'ghettos'. Crime rates mounted and white residents increasingly left the cities proper and migrated to the suburbs. Thus the quality of city life and city government declined as over-population and impoverishment went hand in hand.

In all this Eisenhower's main contribution was not that of a creative reformer, like Roosevelt, but that of a peace-maker, a non-partisan spokesman for the American tradition of live and let live. His critics called him lazy, and pointed to the hours he spent on the golf course; his many admirers found in him the kind of tolerant, decent, non-ideological American they sought in themselves. Those who worked closely with him deplored his reluctance to exploit the full resources of his presidential office – except at election times. One thing was certain; the American public liked him. In their eyes his heart attack in 1955 and his operation for ileitis in 1956 were no bar to his enjoying another four years in the White House. So he was renominated by acclamation, in company with Richard Nixon. With peace, prosperity, and personal popularity all working for him he was able to campaign from an Olympian height. Adlai Stevenson, for all his charm and talent, could not compete. He succeeded initially in winning the primaries from Senator Kefauver, and then the nomination from Averell Harriman. (In the process the young senator from Massachusetts, John F. Kennedy, narrowly missed the vice-presidential nomination which went as a consolation prize to Kefauver.) In the ensuing campaign Stevenson did not hesitate to broaden his appeal, by offering extravagantly high guaranteed prices to farmers and holding out the bait of an end to conscription. But Eisenhower had the dual crises of Suez and the Russian rape of Hungary working for him, for emergencies always favour the incumbent. His victory was even greater than in 1952.

In 1957 the Russian achievement in launching Sputnik I provoked a widespread concern that in the successful pursuit of prosperity the United States had neglected not only its defences but also the educational base without which the necessary scientists and technologists could not be produced. For the first time a substantial amount of federal money was put into education, hitherto a matter for the states or private sources. At the same time federal expenditure on missiles and space exploration was increased. Opinion differed on whether the rate of public expenditure was too high; 1958 saw a marked economic recession which might have been averted if the President had been willing to resort to some vigorous deficit financing. In 1959 the Democrats, heartened by further congressional gains in the mid-term elections of 1958, made political capital out of what they called a budget which 'put pocketbook before people'. But they themselves persisted in a policy of curtailing expenditure on foreign aid. This change of mood from a Congress which ten years earlier had launched Marshall Aid reflected concern

over a new phenomenon, an imbalance in the country's overseas payments. Imports were exceeding exports and the gold which had so long been piling up at Fort Knox was having to be paid out by the United States Treasury to make up the deficit. As another consequence there was a revival of protectionist sentiment; quotas were imposed on oil imports and the British wool exporter, not for the first time in his history, had to face a higher duty on his products.

From one point of view the American economy was still a fabulous success story. In his last year in the White House Eisenhower saw the national product pass the annual rate of $500,000 million for the first time in history and by 1959 half the families in the United States had an annual income of over $5,400 (£1,930). The enormous strength of this productive and distributive mechanism enabled it to ride out a 116-day steel strike in 1959 estimated to have cost $6,000 million. However, two weaknesses were indisputable. This remarkable productivity involved high and continuing inflation; thus the cost of living index at the end of 1960 was a record 127·4 compared with 100 in 1947-49. Furthermore unemployment was high: in 1960 there were almost $4\frac{1}{2}$ million unemployed, 6·8% of the labour force.

These weaknesses provided the Democrats with ammunition in their quadrennial campaign for the White House. They depicted Eisenhower as an exhausted President who had been too long in office. He also had the misfortune in May 1960 to see his long-nurtured hopes of a 'summit meeting' at Paris with Khrushchev turn to ashes when the US secret reconnaissance aircraft, the U2, was shot down over the Soviet Union. The talks with the Russians broke up before they had properly begun and the administration was caught in a web of denials and admissions, disavowals and blusterings which were largely of its own making. Against this image of a tired and muddled administration young John F.Kennedy projected the picture of a dynamic young challenger. After an efficiently organized and lavishly financed campaign across the country he won the Democratic nomination from his principal rival, Senator Humphrey, and, at the Democratic convention at Los Angeles, selected as his running-mate Lyndon Johnson who had run a poor third in the nomination for President.

The Republicans, as expected, chose Mr Nixon as their champion. He started off with the advantage of Eisenhower's implicit endorsement, since he was his vice-president, and he was able to negotiate an agreement with Governor Rockefeller of New York, his only serious rival, by which the governor stood down in return for a reasonably liberal Republican platform.

Kennedy won the ensuing contest but only by a hair. For weeks it seemed the Republicans would find enough voting irregularities in Illinois and Texas to put those states back in the Republican column and reverse the national verdict. Never in the history of the USA had so striking a change in the White House been effected by so minute a margin of the popular vote.

# India: Independence and Partition

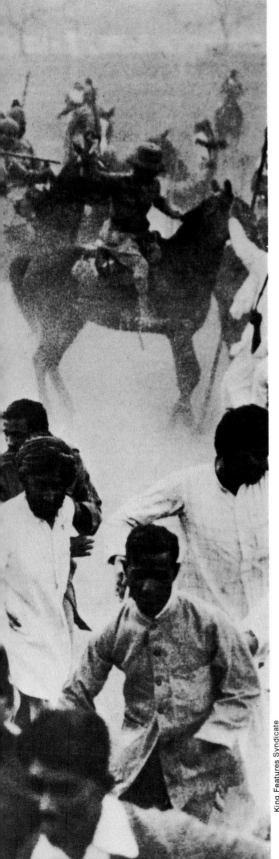

*Police disperse anti-British demonstrators, Calcutta, about 1940. As demands for independence grew, it was increasingly hard to control anti-British feeling — and to suppress the growing violence between Hindu and Muslim communities*

The Government of India Act 1935 proved to be the last constitutional milestone along the road to India's independence. Some people, prominent among whom was Sir Maurice Gwyer, the first chief justice of India, who had been responsible for a good deal of the drafting of the act, had always thought that this would be so. He firmly believed that the working of it would give rise to political conventions whereby imperceptibly, but quite quickly, India would become virtually independent so that her final constitutional release from any sort of subordination to Great Britain would be little more than a mere formality.

Part 1 of the act of 1935 established almost complete parliamentary self-government in the provinces. The governors, still usually British, retained some reserve powers, but Sir Maurice rightly foresaw that they would be loth to use them and that they would become in effect 'constitutional' governors.

The act also provided for a federal government for the whole of India including the princely states which were thus for the first time brought into close constitutional relationship with British India. Ministers responsible to the federal legislature were to be in charge of all subjects except defence and external affairs which were to continue to be the responsibility of the governor-general. But Sir Maurice and others predicted that it would be difficult to conduct the federal government in water-tight compartments and that in practice the governor-general would largely share his responsibility with the popularly elected ministers. Thus the federal government would also soon insensibly become in effect a popular government.

These views were not universally accepted even by the British. For instance, Lord Linlithgow, Viceroy from 1936-43, considered that the end of British rule was not in sight and would not be so for many years to come. As for Indian nationalist politicians, they were naturally distrustful of the Act and thought that it would fasten the British yoke firmly on their shoulders for an indefinite period.

These divergent views were never put to the test; for the act in its entirety was never brought into operation. The part of it that was concerned with the provinces came into effect in 1937, and the Congress Party, recognizing the very real measure of self-government that the act conferred, consented, after some initial show of hesitation, to form ministries in the seven provinces (out of a total of eleven) in which they commanded a majority. But the projected federation, provided for in part II of the act, could not come into being until a specified number of princely states had formally 'acceded' to it; and they never did so. Attempts to coax them into it failed to achieve success by the outbreak of war in September 1939, after which they were suspended.

By this time, however, the princes' reluctance to 'accede' was no longer the only obstacle to the introduction of the federation. During 1937-38 the attitude of the Muslim community towards it had undergone a rapid and revolutionary change. The creation of a federation for India, with wide powers allotted to the provinces, had always been a Muslim demand; for in certain provinces they were in a majority and could hope to dominate the government, and they felt, therefore, that a federal structure would mitigate their disadvantage as a minority community in the country as a whole. During the discussions that preceded the passing of the 1935 act most of the Muslim representatives, particularly those from the large provinces of Bengal and the Punjab where the Muslims constituted just over fifty per cent of the population, had seemed quite content with the constitutional proposals. Only the more nationalist section of Muslim opinion, represented by Jinnah and the Muslim League, had been critical of them, and they, like Congress, objected to them on the ground that they did not concede full self-government. There was little or no complaint that Muslims would be subjected to the tyranny of a Hindu-dominated federal government.

This was the position at the beginning of 1937. Within two years it had been completely transformed and Muslims all over India were ranged under the banner of the League, with Jinnah as their acknowledged leader, to fight the threat of a Congress (Hindu) Raj which, they claimed, a federal government would entail. Federation, the League declared in 1939, was an objective to which they were irrevocably opposed, and in March 1940, at a session in Lahore, they came out with the drastic demand that India be partitioned and that the Muslim majority areas of the north-west and north-east be formed into separate 'independent states'. Only so could

Muslims escape coming under the heel of a Hindu Raj.

What had suddenly excited these Muslim apprehensions? Why had Jinnah, the erstwhile keen nationalist and Congress sympathizer, led the demand for the partition of the country and the creation of 'Pakistan' which only a few years earlier he had himself regarded as 'only a student's scheme . . . chimerical and impracticable'? The change in attitude was largely the result of events in the United Provinces. Jinnah had drafted the League's election manifesto for the provincial elections under the new constitution so as to be in broad accord with that of Congress. He and his lieutenants certainly expected that in the Hindu-majority provinces the Congress, if successful at the polls, would join with the League in forming coalition governments. They were, therefore, rudely disappointed when in the United Provinces, where the League was strongest, the Congress refused to give League members places in a Congress ministry, unless they joined the Congress and 'ceased to function as a separate group'. Since the Congress had won an absolute majority at the elections, parliamentarily it was in no way incumbent on them to enter into a coalition with the League. Yet it would have been wise to do so, for this would have reassured the minority community; and it was most unwise to suggest that the League should merge itself in Congress and give up its separate identity. Nothing was better calculated to alarm and antagonize the Muslims.

The immediate effect was to alert Muslims in the Muslim-majority provinces to the dangers of the projected federation. The example of the United Provinces seemed to show that when a federal government came to be formed, Congress, as the dominant party, would only admit to some share of power those prepared to surrender themselves to Congress, and would exclude altogether those belonging to independent minority parties. There would be no place for Muslims who stood squarely for Muslim interests.

So throughout India Muslims began to question the federal proposals and a dangerous chasm opened between the Congress and the Muslim League. If the federal part of the act of 1935 could have been introduced in 1937 almost concurrently with the provincial part, the Muslims would have been swept into the federation before they had had time for second thoughts about it. But the princes' hesitations prevented this happy outcome, and on the outbreak of the Second World War the introduction of federation was adjourned indefinitely and, as it proved, for ever. Failure to introduce federation at this time must be reckoned among the causes of the eventual partition.

This failure might have been repaired if, to secure the unity of the country in the

Fox Photos

India House

*Above: Sir Stafford Cripps (left), who proposed safeguards for the Muslims in an independent India, and Jinnah, Muslim leader who demanded a separate Muslim state. Below: Nehru, the first Prime Minister of independent India*

prosecution of the war, the Congress and the League could have been induced to form coalition governments in the provinces and to nominate members to represent them on the Viceroy's Executive Council. Moderate men in both camps would have welcomed such a move; but the attitude of the British and of the Congress made it impossible. The British, on the outbreak of war, declined to declare unequivocally that at the end of it India would be granted independence; and in the absence of such an assurance the Congress refused to co-operate in any way in the war effort and directed the Congress provincial ministries to resign. Reluctantly they complied.

The Congress leaders were at this time strangely blind to the menacing turn that Muslim opinion had taken. They ridiculed the demand for 'Pakistan' and despite the fact that it was publicly put forward by the League in March 1940, they clung to the belief that Jinnah was bluffing and that when it came to the point he would be neither willing nor able to break up the unity of India. So they made no serious attempt to come to terms with him.

This attitude was short-sighted, for even if the demand for Pakistan was at first partly bluff, it would have been prudent to seek a settlement with the Muslims before they became fully committed to extreme courses. It is probable that in 1940 Jinnah was to some extent using 'Pakistan' as a bargaining counter and would have been prepared to interpret it as meaning a good deal less than an absolutely independent Muslim state. And at this stage the majority of Muslims would probably have been satisfied by a looser federation than that envisaged by the act of 1935 or by one in which there were more built-in safe-guards for the Muslims.

But now that the League had accepted as its ostensible goal the creation of an independent Muslim state, it would be difficult to abandon this goal or render it innocuous. A very real threat to the unity of India had appeared.

The British authorities, conscious of this threat, did nothing to encourage the demand for Pakistan; but they did not positively reject it. Congressmen asserted that if only the British would give a firm 'No' to it, the Muslims would very soon abandon their demand. At best, however, positive rejection would have been a doubtful gamble; and in time of war, with the Congress already aloof, if not hostile, the British could not run the risk of driving the Muslim League also into open hostility by outright rejection of the demand for Pakistan. So they temporized and for the first two and a half years of war were content to leave unreconciled the conflicting aims of the Congress and the League.

At last, however, in March 1942, in the hope of rallying India to repel the threat of a Japanese invasion, they made an imaginative attempt to effect a political settlement. Sir Stafford Cripps was sent out from England with proposals designed both to satisfy Congress and to allay the fears of the Muslims. Now for the first time the British gave an unequivocal promise of independence, not indeed immediately,

but as soon as hostilities ended and a new constitution had been framed. To meet the Muslim objection that the Hindus, being in a majority, would frame a constitution to suit themselves and would override Muslim interests, it was proposed that individual provinces and princely states, unwilling to accept the new constitution, should be entitled to stay out of the projected Indian union and form separate unions of their own. Thus while Pakistan was not explicitly conceded, the possibility of its coming into being through the non-accession of some of the Muslim-majority provinces was for the first time publicly acknowledged by the British government.

The Cripps offer afforded the Congress a golden opportunity of coming to terms with the British and seeking an accord with the Muslims. Very foolishly they rejected it; whereupon Jinnah and the Muslim League did likewise. In retrospect it can be seen that with the rejection of this offer the last chance of preserving the unity of India was thrown away.

Soon after this the Congress embarked on the senseless 'Quit India' movement and most of its leaders were put in prison where they remained till near the end of the war. Jinnah took full advantage of their absence to indulge in anti-Congress propaganda and to consolidate the position of the League by crushing the considerable elements of opposition to his leadership and to the demand for Pakistan that still existed in the key provinces of Bengal and the Punjab. When the war came to an end and fresh elections were held, Jinnah and the League won almost all the Muslim seats. Muslim parties other than the League were virtually eliminated.

The Labour government, which assumed office in Great Britain at the end of July 1945, announced that it sought 'an early realization of self-government in India'. It seemed to mean business, and even Congress politicians began to think that at last independence might really be at hand. But the Muslim League's triumph at the elections worsened the prospects of avoiding partition. If the Muslims really wanted Pakistan, as the elections seemed to prove, how could it be denied to them?

Did they really want it? If so, in what form? The Pakistan of Jinnah's conception comprised six provinces – Sind, Baluchistan, the Punjab, the North-West Frontier Province, Bengal, and Assam. But in Assam the Muslims were not in a majority, and in Bengal and the Punjab, though they were in a slight overall majority, non-Muslims considerably predominated in the western half of Bengal and in the eastern half of the Punjab. Logically, therefore, the very principle on which Jinnah demanded Pakistan would justify the non-Muslims in demanding the partition of these two Muslim-majority provinces.

There was small chance, therefore, of the Muslims getting the six-province Pakistan of Jinnah's conception, and if they insisted on having Pakistan in some form, then the most that they could hope to get would be contiguous areas in the north-west and the north-east of India in which they they were

in an absolute majority. These would comprise Sind, the North-West Frontier Province, and Baluchistan, but only about half Bengal and half the Punjab and a small fragment of Assam. Jinnah had described this as a 'maimed, mutilated, and moth-eaten Pakistan', and had rejected it with scorn. Did he and the Muslims really want Pakistan, if this was all they could get? It seemed that they might be prepared to accept a loose all-India federation in preference to a moth-eaten Pakistan.

It was in this hope that the Labour government now made a last supreme effort to preserve the unity of India while granting independence. In March 1946 a trio of cabinet ministers, of whom Sir Stafford Cripps was the moving spirit, flew out to India to assist the Viceroy, Lord Wavell, in bringing the political parties to an agreement both on the framing of a constitution and on the formation of a new Executive Council, that would function as an interim government.

After several weeks of discussion the cabinet mission put forward an ingenious scheme for a three-tiered federal constitution consisting of an all-India union (comprising both provinces and princely states) limited to foreign affairs, defence, and communications; three groups of provinces and states (two of which comprised the provinces claimed by Jinnah for Pakistan) dealing with such common subjects as the groups themselves might decide; and the individual provinces and states in which all residuary powers would be vested. For framing a constitution on these principles, there was to be a constituent assembly which would meet to settle the union constitution, but which would be divided into three sections, corresponding to the three groups of provinces, for drawing up constitutions for the provinces and for deciding what subjects should be dealt with at group level.

To everyone's relief Jinnah persuaded the Muslim League to accept this elaborate plan. Though the mission had not conceded Pakistan – indeed they expressly rejected it – Jinnah perceived that the plan did not exclude its ultimate establishment, if the two groups of Pakistan provinces later elected to secede. With the League's acceptance of the plan, it really did seem that the partition of India could be avoided. It was also known that Jinnah was willing to accept proposals that had been formulated by the Viceroy for a new Executive Council, that would constitute an interim government.

The Congress had not yet spoken, but there were high hopes that they, too, would accept. Bitter, therefore, was the disappointment when, on Gandhi's intervention, they rejected outright the proposals for an interim government (on the ground that no Muslim belonging to Congress had been selected to be a member) and accepted the constitutional plan only with some qualification. For they said that they adhered to their view – which the mission had repudiated – that it should be optional for a province to join the group in which it had been placed.

Jinnah complained that the Congress's

acceptance of the constitutional plan was
disingenuous; but the mission, anxious to
save something from the wreck of all their
hopes, preferred to assume, without too
much scrutiny, that it was genuine, and returned to England, expressing their happiness that constitution-making could now
proceed with the consent of the two major
parties.

A fortnight later Jinnah's complaint was
shown to be correct. Nehru at a press conference said that the Congress had agreed
to go into the Constituent Assembly and
had agreed to nothing else; and in regard
to grouping, which was an essential feature
of the mission's plan, he volunteered the
view that there would be no grouping at all.
Jinnah and the League promptly retaliated
by withdrawing their acceptance of the
plan and declaring that they would say
goodbye to constitutional methods and take
'direct action' to achieve Pakistan.

Jinnah had all his life been strictly law-
abiding and a stickler for constitutional
methods. He had strongly disapproved of
Gandhi's non-cooperation and civil dis-
obedience movements. His call for 'direct
action' was a startling and unfortunate innovation; for already the situation in the
country was explosive. Many months of
violent, venomous, and unscrupulous propaganda, especially on the Muslim side,
had engendered in the two communities
such mutual hatred, hostility, and fear that
in many places they were ready to fly at
each others' throats at the slightest provocation. The League's celebration of 16th
August as 'Direct Action Day' provoked in
Calcutta a fearful outbreak of communal
rioting, far exceeding in scale and intensity
anything of the kind that had been known
before. It is estimated that at least 4,000
people were killed and 15,000 injured.

The frenzy soon spread to east Bengal,
first to Dacca and then to the remoter
districts of Noakhali and Tipperah. Muslim
gangs went about killing or forcibly converting Hindus, destroying and pillaging
Hindu property, and abducting Hindu
women. Numbers of Hindus fled in terror
to west Bengal and Bihar. The tales of woe
carried by these refugees provoked reprisals in Bihar where at the end of
October thousands of Muslims were but-
chered by Hindus with horrible savagery
and many others driven from their homes.
There was no knowing where the chain
reaction would end. Gandhi declared that
the country was nearing civil war.

Lord Wavell had by this time succeeded
in drawing both Congress and League representatives into an interim government.
But it soon proved to be not a genuine
coalition government but a government of
two bitterly hostile blocs, each trying to
thwart the other and to consolidate its own
power. And agreement about constitution-
making remained as remote as ever. Vainly
Lord Wavell, and later the British government, strove to extract from the Congress
an unqualified acceptance of the cabinet
mission plan and to persuade Jinnah and
the League that they had done so. Though
some progress was made, the Congress
always entered some qualification, and
Jinnah, unconvinced that their acceptance

**The partition of India**

India and Pakistan: the frontier and the distribution of Hindu and Muslim populations

was genuine, stubbornly refused to take
part in the Constituent Assembly.

At last in February 1947 the British
government, despairing of bringing the
parties to an agreement and fearing that
further communal clashes would lead to
chaos and civil war, boldly announced that,
whether there was any agreement or not,
they would definitely transfer power to
responsible Indian hands not later than
June 1948, 'either as a whole to some form
of central government, or in some areas
to provincial governments or in such other
way as might seem reasonable'. They also
announced that Lord Mountbatten would
replace Lord Wavell.

This meant partition, for owing to the
Congress-League feud there could be no
central government capable of exercising
power over the whole of British India to
which power could be transferred. The
Congress leaders were aware of this and,
except for Gandhi, were by this time reconciled to partition. Their experience in the
interim government had convinced them
that it would be impossible in conjunction
with the League to build up the strong
united India that they desired, and they
thought that rather than to acquiesce in a
loose federation it would be better to let
Jinnah and the Muslims take away altogether those areas that they could indisputably claim—the maimed, moth-eaten
Pakistan that he had previously spurned.

Jinnah, too, on his side realized that the
Congress would not accept a loose, easily
breakable federation and that he would
have to be content with the mutilated
Pakistan to which alone on a population
basis the Muslims were entitled.

This was the solution of the problem to
which all parties were now shepherded by
Lord Mountbatten with great speed and
skill. Fearing that delay would lead to
further disorders, he advanced the date
for the transfer of power from June 1948
to 15th August 1947. His fears were justified. Early in March communal rioting of
unprecedented severity had broken out in
the principal towns of the Punjab and had
spread in some places to the rural areas.
Several thousand people were killed or
seriously injured and Sikhs in Rawalpindi
and other neighbouring districts in the
north-west of the province were driven
from their homes.

Lord Mountbatten's plan for the partition
of India (involving the partition of both
Bengal and the Punjab) and the creation
of two separate dominions of India and
Pakistan was accepted in India with remarkable unanimity and acclaimed
throughout the world. In the circumstances it was perhaps the best that could be
devised; but for all the parties most
directly concerned it was very much of a
last resource. The Congress and the
British government had to see the unity

Fox Photos

*Lord Mountbatten and his wife, August 1947. Mountbatten supervised the partition of India and Pakistan, and remained there afterwards as governor-general*

King Features Syndicate

*After independence – internal opposition. Communist student rallies mob, Bombay, August 1948. Communists have provided the only real opposition to Congress*

of India broken; Jinnah and the League had to rest content with a moth-eaten Pakistan; while the Sikhs of the Punjab, a small community of about six million, had to face the disaster of being about equally divided between India and Pakistan.

The hard choice before the Sikhs had long been clear. Concentrated as they were mainly in the central districts of the Punjab, they had to submit either to inclusion as a whole in Pakistan or to being split between the two new dominions. Inevitably, perhaps, they chose the latter. For the Sikhs, originally only a religious sect, had emerged as a distinct and militant community as a result of Muslim rule and oppression; and for fifty years before the coming of the British, having got the better of the Muslims, they had been the rulers of the Punjab. They recoiled, therefore, from the thought of incorporation in a Muslim state.

Some of the Sikh leaders had canvassed the idea of an entirely separate Sikh state; but since the Sikhs were not in an absolute majority in even a single district, this was not a practical proposition. Others for a while nursed the illusion that the line dividing the Punjab might be pushed so far to the west that the majority of the Sikh population would fall on the Indian side of it. But this could not be done without grave injustice to the Muslims. It would mean including in India the Muslim city of Lahore and large tracts of country in which Muslims were in a majority. On a population basis the line of division was bound to run down the centre of the Punjab between Lahore and Amritsar. When the Mountbatten plan was put forward, the exact boundary line was still to be decided. But the Sikhs were aware of their fate.

The leaders of the Congress, the League, and the Sikhs agreed publicly to the Mountbatten plan early in June. In order to give it the seal of democratic approval, diverse and somewhat complicated arrangements were made for recording the popular will in the Muslim-majority provinces which either had to be separated as a whole from India or, in the case of Bengal and the Punjab, had to be themselves partitioned. Except in the North-West Frontier Province where a referendum was held, the vote of the provincial legislatures was taken. The legislators duly met and those of Bengal and the Punjab duly cast their votes in favour of the division of these two provinces.

Law and order had never been fully restored in the Punjab after the March disturbances and communal rioting continued sporadically on a small scale throughout the months of April to July. The partition of this province, involving as it did the division of the Sikhs, would have been fraught with danger at the best of times. How could it be peaceably effected when communal passions were so inflamed? The Sikhs in particular were blazing with anger and thirsting for revenge. The few of them who lived in the north-west of the province had been attacked by the Muslims in March and hounded from their homes amid taunts and ridicule. It was impossible that the Sikhs should take these insults and injuries lying down. They had not struck back immediately, but they were simply biding their time.

About a week before 15th August, the date for the transfer of power, they began their long-meditated revenge. In Amritsar armed gangs of Sikhs went about setting fire to Muslim villages and butcher-

ing the inhabitants, and soon throughout most of eastern Punjab the Muslims were being massacred and forced to flee from their homes. These atrocities had immediate repercussions in western Punjab where the Muslims, repeating on a much larger scale their March exploits, began murdering and expelling the Sikhs and Hindus. By the second half of August long columns of bewildered refugees were trekking in opposite directions across the Punjab, Muslims from the eastern part seeking to escape into Pakistan and Sikhs and Hindus from the western part seeking to escape into India.

A boundary force under a British commander had been created to deal with possible trouble in the districts bordering on the line of division, but both in size and composition it was quite inadequate to cope with such serious and widespread disorders. At the end of August it was dissolved and the two new governments of India and Pakistan were left to deal with the situation with their own resources. Massacres and migrations continued throughout September largely uncontrolled; but in October the communal frenzy began to die down. Attacks on refugee trains by bloodthirsty mobs, which had been a fearful feature of the disturbances, were gradually checked and the evacuation of the minority communities was organized under proper protection. By the end of November there had been an almost complete exodus of Muslims from eastern Punjab and of Sikhs and Hindus from western Punjab. During the ensuing winter nearly all the Sikhs and Hindus who were still left in the other areas of West Pakistan were evacuated to India; virtually no Sikhs remained and only a few hundred thousand Hindus. Altogether about five million of them migrated from West Pakistan to India, while six to seven million Muslims migrated from India to West Pakistan. Casualties have been variously estimated, but probably did not exceed 250,000.

The partition of Bengal gave rise to similar migrations, but they were on a smaller scale, more long-drawn-out, and unaccompanied by such violence. There was not such a complete exodus of Hindus from East Pakistan and about nine million of them are living there to this day.

Lord Mountbatten did not foresee the disasters that occurred in the Punjab; even if he had foreseen them, he could have done nothing to avert them. They could have been averted only by the deployment in the central Punjab of about 100,000 wholly reliable troops. Such troops were not available and could not have been provided. It was certainly not creditable to the British that the ending of their rule in India should have involved a hurried, last-minute division of the country with attendant massacres and migrations; but neither Lord Mountbatten nor his predecessor, Lord Wavell, nor Mr Attlee's Labour government were to blame. These disasters were the outcome of a failure of statesmanship, not on the part of the British alone, over a fairly long period of time.

# The Birth of Israel

The association of the Jewish people with Palestine has existed for over 3,500 years, at a conservative estimate. Since the age of Joshua there has always been a 'Jewish presence' there, though after the second century AD it declined to minority status. In the 19th century persecution of Jews in Russia provoked a revival of Jewish national feeling there which looked to a modern Jewish state in Palestine. It became known ultimately as the Zionist movement.

Influenced by various considerations of policy (all based on misinformation) and prompted by genuine idealism, the British government issued a declaration in November 1917. It was signed by Arthur Balfour, the foreign secretary, who had been influenced in the matter by the Zionist leader in Britain Dr Chaim Weizmann. The central statement ran as follows: 'His Majesty's Government view with favour the establishment in Palestine of a national home for the Jewish people . . . it being clearly understood that nothing shall be done which may prejudice the civil and religious rights of existing non-Jewish communities in Palestine. . . .'

The Balfour Declaration had surprisingly little effect at the time on the Arabic-speaking world in general, but was the cause of great commotion within Palestine. However the worst fears were not realized and in 1921 the country, ruled by the League of Nations through the British mandate, settled down to an uneasy peace which persisted till 1928. From then on Arab-Jewish tension increased. It was helped by the rise of a new Arab leader, Haj Amin el Husseini, the Mufti of Jerusalem. He was an extreme nationalist and he gave his fellow Palestinians a simple and fanatic cause: Holy War against non-Muslims. Thus when anti-Semitism was revived in Europe by Hitler, Jewish refugees to Palestine found Arabs waiting with murderous hostility.

The British government found itself in a jam. It realized that a large proportion of the oil Britain would need in the event of war lay in the Arabic-speaking world, and could not risk a major quarrel there. In the summer of 1939 it summoned an Arab-Jewish conference which quickly broke down. The government then imposed its own 'solution'. The new policy permitted a Jewish immigration of 75,000 over five years, after which further Jewish immigration would depend on Arab agreement (of which there was no likelihood). The white paper succeeded in taking the sting out of Arab hostility to Great Britain, and the British armies in the Middle East never lacked for oil. But the paper caused lasting Jewish embitterment.

During his war-time premiership Winston Churchill, a passionate sympathizer with Zionism, tried in vain to reverse the white paper policy. Opposition to him by British Middle East administrators was always too strong. As the war went on it became evident that his attitude was out of date. The Zionists of Palestine had become suspicious of or indifferent to British overtures. Two events were chiefly responsible.

One was the gradual loss of Weizmann's moderate leadership to the more ruthless leadership of Ben Gurion. Weizmann remained effectively the chief in negotiations abroad with Great Britain and the USA, but among the Jews in Palestine Ben Gurion was the man who counted.

The second event was the change in the character of on-the-spot Zionism. It was

*Above: Postcard of Jerusalem sent by Herzl, one of the founders of Zionist movement.*
*Left: Herzl with members of a Zionist delegation aboard ship en route to meet the Kaiser in Jerusalem in 1898, in an effort to win support for the establishment of a Jewish national home in Palestine*

JNF Publicity

fully nationalist now, prepared to accept only statehood as a permanent solution, and this aim became more and more associated with violence. There had been Zionist terrorists before and their activities had been looked on with great repugnance by the Jewish population, but the mental climate was changing now. There were two main terrorist organizations among the Zionists: Irgun Tsva'i Leumi, meaning the National Military Organization, and the Stern gang, the followers of a terrorist who was killed in 1942 named Abraham Stern.

The Jews, by 1944, had borne more than men can, and they sought a solution to their problem in revenge. There was a new sympathy for Irgun and the Sternists. The terrorists saw the British administration in Palestine as an actively anti-Jewish organization, and they persuaded many. The last slender hope of an accommodation in Palestine lay in a private agreement reached between Winston Churchill and Chaim Weizmann on 4th November 1944. Two days later Lord Moyne, the British minister of state in the Middle East, on whom the agreement largely depended, was murdered by Jewish terrorists. The Jews condemned the crime half-heartedly. Such was the new climate.

In the meantime the foreign secretary, Anthony Eden, had made an imaginative proposal in which many believed that a solution could be found. In 1941 and again in 1944 Eden assured the Arabic-speaking world that the British government would 'give their full support' to an Arab union enjoying popular approval. As a result, on 22nd March 1945, after much vacillation, the Arab League was established.

The British hope seems to have been that a coalition of Arab states friendly to Britain, having recreated something like the ancient Arab empire of the Omayyads, would look on the Jewish national home as a small thing. The hope was to solve the problem by thinking big. All such hopes were rudely disappointed. This was no age of big-thinking but of narrow nationalism.

All member states and delegates of the Arab League were determined on one thing: not to appear as servants of Great Britain. From the beginning the Arab League was united in being anti-British in varying degrees. As they believed that Zionism was the obedient slave of Great Britain, the member states found another element of unity in extreme anti-Zionism. They had little other unity. League activity consisted chiefly in rousing anti-Zionist hatred throughout Islam. An explosion was inevitable.

The difficulties of the Palestine situation

*Left: 1 The Mufti of Jerusalem, leader of the Palestinian Arabs, visits Muslim SS units in Yugoslavia during the war. 2 The Exodus in Haifa harbour after her interception by the Royal Navy. Right: 1 Poster, in Hebrew, issued by the British in Palestine, 1942. It offers rewards for information leading to the arrest of the Stern gang. Abraham Stern is pictured top right. 2 British troops arrest an illegal Jewish immigrant. 3 Orthodox Jews till the stony soil of Palestine*

Jewish Agency, Jerusalem

Central Zionist Archives, Jerusalem

# פרסים

ממשלת הארץ הקציבה את הפרסים דלקמן חלף ידיעות שיביאו לידי
כל איש יאיש דלקמן מחברי הארגון האחראי להתפצצות שארעה
עשרים בינואר, 1942, ברחוב יעל, 8 תל-אביב.

| נחמן שולו | יעקב פולני | אברהם בן מרדכי |
|---|---|---|
| | נודע בשם פוליאקוף | שמרן |
| | | נודע בשם יאיר |

| פרס 200 ל | פרס 400 לא"י | פרס 1000 לא"י |
|---|---|---|

| אהרן צוקר | חנוך סטרליץ | זרוני בנימין |
| נודע בשם א | | נודע בשם בן-צבי |
| | | ינניאל |
| | | אבני |
| | | קרנר |

Jewish Agency, Jerusalem

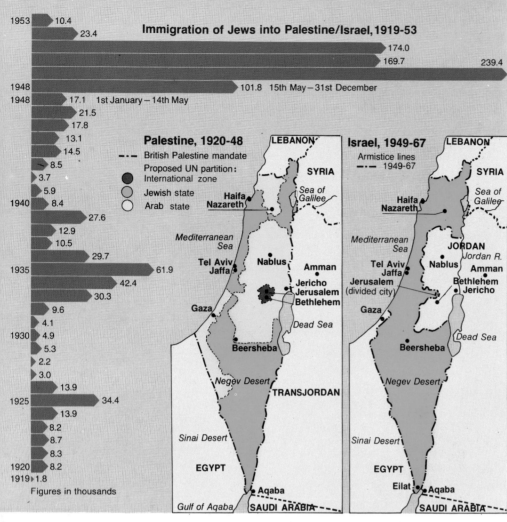

**Immigration of Jews into Palestine/Israel, 1919-53**

Figures in thousands

| Year | Figure (thousands) |
|---|---|
| 1953 | 10.4 |
| | 23.4 |
| | 174.0 |
| | 169.7 |
| | 239.4 |
| 1948 | 101.8 (15th May – 31st December) |
| 1948 | 17.1 (1st January – 14th May) |
| | 21.5 |
| | 17.8 |
| | 13.1 |
| | 14.5 |
| | 8.5 |
| | 3.7 |
| | 5.9 |
| 1940 | 8.4 |
| | 27.6 |
| | 12.9 |
| | 10.5 |
| | 29.7 |
| 1935 | 61.9 |
| | 42.4 |
| | 30.3 |
| | 9.6 |
| | 4.1 |
| 1930 | 4.9 |
| | 5.3 |
| | 2.2 |
| | 3.0 |
| | 13.9 |
| 1925 | 34.4 |
| | 13.9 |
| | 8.2 |
| | 8.7 |
| | 8.3 |
| 1920 | 8.2 |
| 1919 | 1.8 |

**Palestine, 1920-48**

- – · – British Palestine mandate
- Proposed UN partition:
  - ● International zone
  - (shaded) Jewish state
  - ○ Arab state

LEBANON · SYRIA · Sea of Galilee · Haifa · Nazareth · Mediterranean Sea · Tel Aviv · Jaffa · Nablus · Amman · Jericho · Jerusalem · Bethlehem · Gaza · Dead Sea · Beersheba · Negev Desert · TRANSJORDAN · Sinai Desert · EGYPT · Aqaba · Gulf of Aqaba · SAUDI ARABIA

**Israel, 1949-67**

- Armistice lines
- – · – 1949-67

LEBANON · SYRIA · Sea of Galilee · Haifa · Nazareth · Mediterranean Sea · JORDAN · Jordan R. · Tel Aviv · Jaffa · Nablus · Amman · Jerusalem (divided city) · Bethlehem · Jericho · Gaza · Dead Sea · Beersheba · Negev Desert · Sinai Desert · EGYPT · Eilat · Aqaba · SAUDI ARABIA

Robert Capa—Magnum

were increased by a colossal political blunder made by the Labour Party. In December 1944, Clement Attlee announced on Labour's behalf that his party favoured massive Jewish immigration, the extension of Palestine's frontiers at the expense of its neighbours, and a transfer of the Arab population. When Attlee became Prime Minister a few months later he found the Arab League confirmed in a belief that Zionism was the British imperial weapon to be fought to the death, and the Zionists determined to make capital out of a pledge which could not be honoured. The new foreign secretary was Ernest Bevin. He said he would stake his political reputation on solving the Palestine problem.

In the meantime the United States had become deeply involved in Middle East politics. Over the past seven years they had acquired an immense oil interest in Saudi Arabia which their economy could not afford to jeopardize. Since 1933 the Jewish population of America had become progressively Zionist and their good will was wrongly believed in America to be of decisive electoral importance. President Roosevelt dealt with the predicament by giving cordial encouragement to both sides. His successor, Truman, was simpler and more honourable. He was determined to find a refuge, preferably in Palestine, for the surviving Jews of Europe, and to this aim he gave priority. In June 1945 he sent Earl G. Harrison to Europe to report on 'displaced persons' especially Jews. Harrison reported in August that 100,000 Jews should be allowed into Palestine. Mr Truman approved the findings and sent them to the British Prime Minister. Then in the same month, dealing with the same question, the Zionists put themselves in danger by making a serious and impetuous mistake. Their own researches had led to figures identical with those of Harrison, and Ben Gurion in person demanded 100,000 immigration certificates from the British Colonial Office. If the proposal had been accepted then it would have been very difficult for the Zionists to have asked for more, while retaining public sympathy; and an increase in population of 100,000 would have been inadequate for state-building. The British government saved them by a flat refusal.

As the disorder in Palestine grew, Truman urged the appointment of an Anglo-

*Opposite: above left: The figures for immigration up to 1948 do not include some 31,000 Jews who entered Palestine illegally. Above right: Jewish immigrant building a road in the desert, 1948. Below left: A burial in Israel for the ashes of the victims of Nazi persecution, 1948. Below right: Chaim Weizmann, president of the World Zionist Organization from 1920–30 and 1935–46, is sworn in as Israel's first President, February 1949. Right: Palestinian Arab officers before the war with the Jews. Standing left is General Abdel Khader el Husseini, cousin of the Mufti. Abdel Khader was killed during the battle of Qastel. The Mufti controlled two Palestinian Arab military organizations — but they were no match for Haganah*

Robert Capa–Magnum

*November 1948, Israeli troops move up to the front. The Jewish army or Haganah (self-defence) was first organized in the 1920's to protect Jewish settlers from Arab attacks, and remained an illegal, underground organization up to the end of the British mandate*

American Committee of Enquiry, and Bevin promised he would support any unanimous recommendation of the committee. The committee urged the continuation of the mandate and the admission of 100,000. Bevin on receiving the report in April 1946 repudiated his word. He rejected the report and considered himself the victim of a Russian plot. When three months later the British government itself proposed the immigration of 100,000 it was too late.

One inevitable result of incompetent policy was a breakdown in British military morale. There was a descent into brutality. Apparently ignorant of the history of Ireland, the British government sent in commandos to meet terror with terror. The results were sordid and ineffective – as in Ireland. There was no lack of provocation: one of the most appalling acts was in 1946 when Irgun blew up the King David Hotel in Jerusalem with heavy loss of life.

Then in 1947 Bevin did a sensible thing. Seeing clearly (but only for a moment) that Great Britain could not continue as the guardian of Palestine, he announced on 14th February that the British government would hand back the mandate to the UN. This was done, but with immediate second thoughts. The government was divided in mind. From 1947 onward Great Britain both sought UN help and thwarted it.

A Special Committee on Palestine was appointed by the UN. Its delegates fol-

lowed the weary path of the Anglo-American Committee arriving in Palestine in June 1947. They, unlike their predecessors, saw Palestine in the throes of terrorism and repression, and, also unlike their predecessors, gave in to the blandishments of Zionist propaganda, notably in the celebrated affair of the immigration ship *Exodus*. (The ship, carrying 4,500 Jewish refugees from Europe, was intercepted by the Royal Navy and its passengers were transported to displaced persons' camps in Germany.) Unlike the preceding committee they recommended a partition scheme. This was aptly described by Professor George Kirk as a 'fighting serpents plan', for the wavering lines of the proposed frontiers would have ensured a state of perpetual guerrilla warfare between Jew and Arab. Yet, strange to relate, the Zionist leadership accepted this plan. They may have counted on the Arab boycotting habit. If so they were proved right. The Arabs immediately rejected the plan while, in well-meaning ignorance, the UN General Council accepted the plan as a just solution.

It is painful for an Englishman to tell of the last phase of the Palestine mandate. It is like recalling a case of mass lunacy. The main facts are these: in December 1947 the colonial secretary, Arthur Creech Jones, announced that Britain would withdraw totally from Palestine on 15th May 1948. The UN then asked that a cadre

administration from the UN might enter Palestine to arrange an orderly transfer of authority. This was emphatically refused. A secret agreement concluded between Bevin and King Abdullah of Transjordan in late 1947 ensured that the well-disciplined Arab Legion would take over the military positions in the non-Jewish area, in accordance with the recommendations of the UN special committee. But the agreement was not honoured. In April 1948, the British, seeking to placate King Farouk of Egypt, who saw Abdullah as his rival for the domination of the Arab world, ordered the legion to withdraw. At the same time Arab guerrilla bands were entering the country from Syria, with British acquiescence.

British policy seemed determined to end the mandate in the most disorderly way possible.

One explanation can be offered from the evidence. The British government had reason to believe that there would in fact be no Arab-Jewish war. The conferences of the Arab League had all ended with ferocious declarations of hostility to Zionism, but these were deceptive. Only the Mufti was intent on war, but his leadership was not what it had been. Outside Palestine it was questioned. What the optimists overlooked was that no Muslim leader could now withdraw without a fatal loss of prestige.

It is difficult to say exactly when the first

*Ben Rothenberg/Israel Publishing Co*

*Palestinian refugees — the terrible result of Arab-Jewish enmity. Nearly a million Arabs fled from Palestine out of fear of reprisals from the Israelis. Their continuing plight twenty years after the first Arab-Israeli war was the main obstacle to peace in the Middle East*

Arab-Jewish war began. The battle of Qastel near Jerusalem, one of the fiercest and most fateful of the whole war, was fought from 31st March to 9th April 1948 while the mandate still ran. The official date of the opening of hostilities is presumably 14th May, when the last high commissioner left and the state of Israel was proclaimed. The Jews now had a state at war with other states, namely Lebanon, Syria, Iraq, Transjordan, and Egypt. The same day, however, Israel received a welcome boost in morale from Truman's decision to recognize Israel. On 18th March 1948 Truman had secretly promised Doctor Weizmann that when the Zionist leaders decided to proclaim a state of Israel he would recognize it. The oil-conscious American representatives at the UN under-estimated Truman and pursued a non-Zionist policy without consulting him. Indignant at their conduct, the President took the initiative and recognized Israel as soon as the state was proclaimed.

The war fell into three phases. The first lasted till 11th June 1948. By a narrow margin the Jews had a superiority in arms gained by secret negotiations in Czechoslovakia. They repelled the five-fold onslaught with astounding firmness, though they nearly lost their line of communication with Jerusalem and had to surrender the Jewish quarter in the old city. They were defeated in the south where the

Egyptian army approached the suburbs of Jerusalem. On 11th June the UN 'mediator', Count Bernadotte, imposed a month's truce.

In Palestine Bernadotte attempted to prolong the truce. All were willing to agree except Syria and Egypt who could not, having already announced their total victory over Israel. There followed the 'ten-day war' from 8th to 18th July which sealed the Jewish victory. In the north almost all of the pre-1967 territory of modern Israel was conquered, though the situation in the south remained unchanged. On 18th July a second truce was imposed.

During five months or so of war, there had begun a continuing flight of Arabs from Israel territory. It turned into a mass-movement after 8th April. On this day a combined force of Irgun and Sternists seized the village of Dir Yassin and, believing it to be an Arab headquarters, they massacred the inhabitants. News of this atrocity increased the flight of the Arabs a hundredfold. Later, Arab leaders asserted that the flight was a deliberate act of Arab policy, but the claim seems baseless. The movement had obvious advantages for Israel and in the ten-day war the Jewish army increased Arab flight by terrorizing, though not descending to the bestialities of the Jewish terrorists. By the end of the war most Arabs within Israel had gone.

The second truce was stained by another

terrorist crime. On 17th September 1948 Sternists murdered Bernadotte. He was succeeded as mediator by Dr Ralph Bunche. The new shape of Palestine began to emerge. The Mufti declared himself ruler of the remaining Arab area but he was deposed by Abdullah who incorporated the area in his kingdom. Three years later the Mufti had his revenge when Abdullah was assassinated by his agents.

The second truce broke down on 14th October. It was soon restored but broke down again after four days. In late December there was fought the last campaign of the war which resulted in a final Israeli victory in the south. Armistices were signed in the course of 1949, but no peace treaty followed. An opportunity for peace came in 1952 when King Farouk of Egypt was forced to abdicate in favour of his infant son, who in turn was deposed the following year. Farouk was heavily involved in a wholly unrewarding anti-Zionist war policy and this could have been repudiated by the new leader General Neguib, or his successor Gamal Abdel Nasser, without loss of prestige. However, they elected to continue the conflict, as did Nasser's successor, Anwar Sadat. It was not until January 1974 and the signing of the first Egyptian-Israeli disengagement agreement, which was followed by the signing of a second agreement in September 1975, that some hope of permanent peace for Israel became possible.

# Communist Takeovers in Eastern Europe

During the inter-war years Stalin's Russia was the only state in the world organized on Marxist principles. To the politicians who gathered at Munich in September 1938 the Soviet Union seemed potentially menacing but comfortably remote. Ten years later all had changed: Berlin and Vienna were islands of joint control within Soviet zones of occupation; the Russian sphere of influence had been pushed to the River Elbe; and Communist governments had come to power in seven Eastern European countries – Albania, Bulgaria, Czechoslovakia, Hungary, Poland, Rumania, and Yugoslavia. Not since Napoleon had Europe experienced such a dramatic toppling of an existing social order.

Marxism was not a powerful revolutionary force in any of these seven countries between the wars. In the early 1920's Communists had gained successes in municipal elections in Yugoslavia and Poland but had been forced underground soon afterwards. There had been a very short-lived Bolshevik regime under Béla Kun in Hungary during the summer of 1919, an abortive insurrection in Bulgaria in 1923, a muddled conspiracy among junior Yugoslav army officers in 1932, and a number of assassinations which were blamed, rightly or wrongly, on the Communists by the various right-wing governments of those days. Most of the universities had secret Marxist cells among the students but the only effective parliamentary group had been in Czechoslovakia where the Communist Party polled a million votes in 1925 and retained the support of some ten per cent of the electorate in 1929 and 1935. This contrast between relative success in Czech lands and general failure elsewhere was hardly surprising. In the 1930's two-thirds of the population of Czechoslovakia depended for their livelihood on industry or commerce, while two-thirds of the people in the other six countries lived directly off the land. Marxism was too sophisticated and too dogmatic for peasants, with their obstinate traits of individualism and their simple religious faith. Revolution in these lands could never come as a spontaneous explosion of the labouring classes against the established economic system. It required the catalyst of war and invasion.

When Churchill, Roosevelt, and Stalin

*Czech Stalinist painting. Czechoslovaks, young and old, throng around Stalin in adulation. In fact Stalin never visited any of the satellite states he created and was morbidly afraid of crowds*

met in conference at Tehran in November 1943 it was agreed by them that Soviet military strategy would determine the destruction of the Nazi forces in Eastern Europe, leaving the western and southern periphery of the continent to the British and Americans. The Red Army therefore entered the Vistula and Danube basins in 1944-45 as a liberating force, but its political role varied according to local circumstances. In Yugoslavia and Albania, for example, the Communist partisan organizations of Tito and Enver Hoxha had been genuinely unifying movements of patriotic resistance to the Axis invaders, and by the end of the war their leaders were almost legendary heroes with substantial popular support. The Russian contribution to the liberation of Yugoslavia was far less than in the other Danubian lands and in Albania it was non-existent. On the other hand, in the Czech provinces the Red Army was welcomed as a means of both national salvation and regeneration, for the legitimate Czechoslovak government of the pre-war President, Eduard Beneš, returned to Prague only five days after Marshal Konev's troops had reached the city.

Rumania and Bulgaria had abandoned their Axis connections in August and September 1944 when the Russians reached their frontiers. The Rumanians subsequently lost 150,000 men fighting their way through the Carpathians as allies of the Soviet Union in the winter of 1944-45, and Bulgarian troops similarly participated in the advance up the Danube and the Sava. The Rumanians had little enthusiasm for their Soviet ally and even less for Communism: they fought to recover the parts of Transylvania ceded to Hungary, on Hitler's insistence, in 1940. Bulgaria had never declared war on the Soviet Union and its people were traditionally pro-Russian; a lingering sentiment of Panslavism made them more inclined to accept the Soviet way of life than their northern neighbours. It was in Poland and Hungary that the Russians were least welcome; and in both countries the Soviet military had to intervene in what were essentially matters of domestic concern.

The Communist parties did not immediately assume exclusive control of the government machine in any of these seven states apart from Albania, where the withdrawal of the Germans in October 1944 left an administrative vacuum swiftly filled by Enver Hoxha's Liberation Front in the absence of any other organized political body. Elsewhere the movement towards one-party rule followed a regular

pattern: a coalition government in which the Communists shared power with other 'democratic' and 'progressive' parties; the acquisition by the Communists of the most important posts, giving them control of the armed forces and the police; and the discrediting of any independently-minded leaders of the non-Communist parties as a preliminary to the establishment of a monolithic people's democracy in which policy was determined by a Politburo whose members had, literally, been schooled in Moscow. Although the timing of these stages varied from country to country, the pattern was followed in Bulgaria, Rumania, Hungary, Poland, and Czechoslovakia. In Yugoslavia, on the other hand, the initial period of coalition was succeeded, after only six months, by a People's Front government in which all power was held by the former partisan leaders and no Moscow-trained puppets challenged their authority.

The transition to a people's democracy went most smoothly in Bulgaria. In September 1944 a coup d'état had brought to power a Fatherland Front government which was headed by Kimon Georgiev, who had been Prime Minister ten years earlier and was associated with a non-Communist progressive group known as the Zveno, from the name of its periodical. He was supported by representatives of the Social Democrats and the principal peasant party (the Agrarians) as well as by the Communists. The Fatherland Front took harsh measures against the supporters of the old regime and any whom it believed to have collaborated with the Germans. In a general election, held in November 1945, three-quarters of the voters supported the Fatherland Front, although British and American observers protested that the election had been preceded by intimidation and that the results were blatantly falsified. A referendum held in the following autumn indicated that ninety-two per cent of the Bulgarian people were opposed to monarchy. King Simeon, who was only nine years old, left the country and Bulgaria was proclaimed a people's republic on 15th September 1946.

All effective power in Bulgaria rested with the Communist leader, Georgi Dimitrov, who flew in from Moscow in November 1945 after twenty-two years of exile. Dimitrov had gained international renown in 1933 by the courageous way in which he had won acquittal for himself and two colleagues charged by the Nazis with complicity in setting fire to the Reichstag in Berlin. The Communist Party made full use of this legendary reputation in building him up as a Bulgarian Lenin, a wise leader who could achieve miracles for his country. Cautious land reforms, based on co-operatives rather than the detested collectivization of agriculture, wooed the peasantry, and by the end of 1946 Dimitrov felt sufficiently strong to oust the Zveno ele-

ment from the Fatherland Front. He himself became Prime Minister and Communists controlled the nine most important ministries. In August 1947 he risked a clash with the peasants by staging a show trial of the Agrarian leader, Nikola Petkov, on trumped-up charges of treason. Petkov's execution on 23rd September shocked opinion in the non-Communist world but there were no repercussions from the peasants. It was clear that the Communists were unchallenged masters of Sofia. Significantly, in December all Red Army units were withdrawn from Bulgaria. Stalin had every reason to be satisfied with his protégé.

It took the Communists longer to carry through their takeover bid in Rumania. King Michael, the twenty-three-year-old ruler of the country, had himself seized the initiative in overthrowing the pro-German government in August 1944 and was duly presented with one of the highest Soviet decorations, the Order of Victory. But this improbable marriage of King and Communists lasted only seven months. In March 1945 Michael was induced by the Soviet deputy foreign minister to appoint a National Democratic Front government. At first the Communists held only three posts, the Ministries of the Interior, of Justice, and of National Economy. The Prime Minister was a former member of the Agrarian Party, Petru Groza, and he continued to head successive governments until 1952. The King accepted a land reform but thereafter withdrew from Bucharest, refusing royal assent to any measures until the government became more representative. In January 1946 Groza broadened the coalition slightly and the royal strike ended. It made the Communists determined to get rid of the monarchy.

The Communist Party itself grew only slowly in Rumania. It was built up by Emil Bodnaras, a former Rumanian army officer who had become a Soviet citizen and returned to Bucharest with the 'liberators'. But Bodnaras (who is still in 1976 a vice-president of the Rumanian Republic) has always worked behind the scenes. The pacemakers were Ana Pauker, a remarkably able Jewess who had become well-known as a broadcaster to Rumania on the Soviet radio, and Gheorge Gheorghiu-Dej, a former tramway engineer. While Gheorghiu-Dej concentrated on restoring Rumanian industry, Ana Pauker took charge of foreign affairs. It was she who forced King Michael to abdicate on 30th December 1947, shortly after he had announced his engagement to Princess Anne of Bourbon-Parma. The Communists could not risk a royal wedding in Bucharest, it would increase the popularity of the monarchy. Rumania duly became a people's republic early in 1948.

At the time of the King's abdication the Communists were still a minority party in the Bucharest parliament: only one deputy in six was technically a Communist Party member. But the other groups in the National Democratic Front had been intimidated by a series of trials in which two of the most distinguished veterans of Rumanian political life, Maniu and

*Left: A pro-Soviet crowd cheers a Red Army parade in Bucharest, Rumania.*
*Right: French anti-Communist poster sees France as the next victim of Stalin's takeovers. French Communist leaders accompany Stalin's 'Caucasian dance'*

Pictorial Press

Mihalache, had been sentenced to savage terms of imprisonment. The willingness of the National Democratic Front to follow the Communist line was shown in the spring of 1948 when the government promulgated a new constitution based upon the 1936 Soviet model. Elections held soon afterwards gave the National Democratic Front 405 seats in parliament, with nine opposition members. The Communists thereupon consolidated their hold on the republic: Bodnaras became minister of defence and Gheorghiu-Dej announced the establishment of long-term economic planning, another Russian importation. Communists held the five most important cabinet posts: by controlling the army, the police, and all civil administration they made it certain that Rumania would become a Soviet satellite no less than Bulgaria. Joint Soviet-Rumanian companies saw to it that the country's petroleum products and cereals were sold to the USSR at ridiculously low rates. The Rumanian people seemed cowed and obedient; but the Red Army remained in Rumania, and it was not until the summer of 1958 that they were withdrawn.

The Communists moved at first with caution in Hungary. A provisional coalition government established at the end of 1944 under Soviet auspices contained a number of distinguished veterans of the Horthy era and only two Communists. It guaranteed democratic rights and decreed extensive land reforms, breaking up the huge estates of the Magyar gentry and thus making it possible for some 640,000 peasants to acquire smallholdings in a matter of eighteen months. This agrarian revolution was initiated by the Communist minister of agriculture, Imre Nagy; but it was by no means a Socialist programme, and in the first months of peace the Smallholders' Party rapidly gained support in the country.

This development was reflected in the election returns of November 1945 which gave the Smallholders sixty per cent of the parliamentary seats and a combined list of Communists and Social Democrats only seventeen per cent. Although the reactionary parties of the Right were proscribed, the election was freer than any other held in territory under Soviet occupation. But the head of the Allied Control Commission in Budapest, Marshal Voroshilov, had no intention of permitting the Smallholders to form a government, even though they possessed a clear majority. Their party leader, Zoltán Tildy, became Prime Minister of a coalition: his two deputies were a left-wing socialist and the Communist, Mátyás Rákosi. The Ministry of the Interior was also in Communist hands, giving the Party control of the civil police and eventually of the sadistic Security Police, the AVH (first organized in

1947). When Hungary was formally proclaimed a republic in January 1946 Tildy became President and was succeeded as Prime Minister by another Smallholder spokesman, Ferenc Nagy (who was no relation to Imre Nagy, the 'liberal' Marxist). Soon afterwards the Soviet military authorities put pressure on the government

to appoint one of Rákosi's nominees minister of defence and by the summer of 1946 all security forces were directly under Communist orders.

Throughout 1946 and the early months of 1947 Ferenc Nagy and the Smallholders fought a losing battle with the Communist Party machine, under Rákosi's sinister

Communist takeovers in Eastern Europe, 1945-1955

- - - 1937 frontiers

⊚ Under four-power control

● to USSR by 1945

● Areas which fell under Communist control, 1945–48

*Above: Rákosi, the Hungarian Communist leader (right), with Szákásits, a Socialist, after announcement of fusion of their two parties into Hungarian Workers' Party – last stage in the establishment of a Communist dictatorship.* **Below:** *Divided Europe*

control. Such 'dangerous nests of reaction' as the Roman Catholic youth movements and the Boy Scouts were dissolved and a number of 'conspiracies' were discovered, all of which seemed to implicate the Smallholders. At the end of February 1947 Béla Kovacs, who was general secretary of the Smallholders' Party and a close friend of Ferenc Nagy, was secretly tried on charges of espionage and sent to Siberia. The Prime Minister, in bad health and alarmed by the fate of Kovacs, took a holiday that spring in Switzerland. While there, he was informed that the Communists had evidence linking him with yet another conspiracy; and in May he resigned without returning to Budapest. He was succeeded as head of the government by a pliant Smallholder, Lajos Dinnyés, but all major decisions were henceforth taken by Rákosi. The Smallholders were split into so many factions that they were unable to check the Communists. The Social Democrats remained nominally independent until June 1948 when their movement was taken over by the Communists in a formal fusion which established a Hungarian Workers' Party; but the Communists were in control long before then.

Events in Poland followed a similar pattern. The long contest between the Polish government-in-exile in London and the Russian-sponsored administration in Lublin was formally ended in June 1945 with the establishment of a Government of National Unity. The Communists held only six posts in this coalition—although, as elsewhere in Eastern Europe, they included the ministries responsible for internal security. The former head of the émigré government, Stanisław Mikołajczyk, became a vice-premier and by the start of 1946 his Peasant Party had more than 600,000 registered members. The Communist strongholds were in the former German lands, extending westwards to the Oder and the Neisse.

### Western protests
It had been understood at the crucial Potsdam Conference of 1945 that the Poles would have free elections within a year. But it was not until January 1947 that any election took place and, at the time, the procedure shocked Western observers into protests. Mikołajczyk estimated that a sixth of his party workers were imprisoned during the campaign and he was himself smeared as a 'Western agent'. The combined Communist-Socialist list gained 394 seats and Mikołajczyk's Peasant Party only twenty-eight. The Socialist Cyrankiewicz became Prime Minister of Poland in February 1947 and held that office, apart from a brief interlude in the early 1950's, until 1970. Mikołajczyk, anticipating arrest, escaped to the West in the following October. A Soviet-style constitution was adopted and the Russian and Polish economic systems closely integrated. The only oppositional force in Poland (as in Hungary) was the Roman Catholic Church and every effort was made to lessen its hold.

The fate of Czechoslovakia, from which Russian troops had voluntarily withdrawn in December 1945, was tragically unique.

Scrupulously fair elections in May 1946 gave the Communist Party thirty-eight per cent of the votes and 114 out of the 300 seats in parliament. President Beneš invited the Communist leader, Klement Gottwald, to form a coalition government. His cabinet consisted of nine Communists (who controlled, as usual, the main interior ministries) and seventeen non-Communists. For over a year the coalition worked well. In July 1947, however, Soviet pressure induced the Czechs to withdraw their earlier acceptance of Marshall Aid; and thereafter friction developed within the coalition.

On 12th February 1948 the non-Communist ministers demanded that the Communist minister of the interior should cease packing the police force with his nominees. On 20th February most of these non-Communists resigned hoping this would enforce the dissolution of the government. Meanwhile, a Soviet deputy foreign minister, Zorin, had arrived to co-ordinate the coup. Communist pressure increased. The Communists controlled the radio and the printing unions, and their action committees in the factories and universities gave vociferous support to Gottwald. For a week the Czech lands seemed on the verge of revolution. President Beneš, fearing civil war and possible intervention from the Red Army poised on the borders, felt compelled to accept the immediate formation of a Communist-controlled government with Gottwald as Prime Minister. The ever-popular Jan Masaryk, the son of the first Czechoslovak President, remained as foreign minister out of loyalty to Beneš.

A fortnight later Masaryk was found dead. His death had the effect of removing the last active campaigner against Communist dominance in Prague. Gottwald's power thereafter knew no restraint. The 1948 election marked a complete breach with Czechoslovak precedent. There was no opposition party; the voters opted for or against a combined Communist-Socialist list of candidates; and eighty-eight per cent of those who went to the polls gave Gottwald their support.

It was all too much for President Beneš. Sick at heart for the democratic republic which he had twice sought to build in Czechoslovakia, he resigned his office and died three months later. Gottwald became President and the trade-union leader Zápotocký Prime Minister. The universities and civil service were purged and forced labour camps established for those who deviated from the Party line. Even without the presence of the Red Army, Czechoslovakia had become as integral a part of Communist Europe as her neighbours to the north and south.

In March 1948 Stalin's mastery of Eastern Europe seemed total and complete. It was an illusion, but liberalization was to prove a bitterly frustrating process.

*Some of the ten million refugees who fled to West Germany from the territories incorporated into Russia, from East Germany, Czechoslovakia and Austria*

Südd-Verlag

# China: Communist Victory

In 1937 only a very few far-sighted people, in China or outside, would have forecast that ten years later the Chinese Communist Party would be on the eve of a triumphal campaign which would bring all China under their rule.

Mao Tse-tung may have been one of those few, for he undoubtedly did foresee, more clearly than most, that war between China and Japan was inevitable, and unlike most others, he believed that the course of that conflict would favour his Communist movement and would lay the foundation for its victory. The prospect seemed remote. The Communist forces had regrouped in north Shensi province after the famous Long March of 1935 and in December 1936 they had taken advantage of a mutiny of the Manchurian army, which was confronting them in Shensi, to negotiate with Chiang Kai-shek (whom the mutineers had made prisoner at Sian, the capital of the province) for an end to the civil war and a national union to resist Japanese encroachments. Chiang, to save his own life, had had to agree. This outcome of the Sian Incident, as it was called, was one cause of the Japanese militarists' decision to pro-voke a full-scale conflict with China the next year. Chiang, by making an agreement with the Communists to end his war against them, was no longer in Japanese eyes a sufficiently reliable anti-Communist to merit any further consideration. Japan feared the strength which a united China would soon develop and decided to strike the first blow while there was still time.

On 7th July 1937 the blow was delivered ('The Double Seventh' as the Chinese call it) in the north of China, near Peking. Hitherto Chiang had negotiated when Japanese encroachments occurred, yielding control of outlying provinces, to the indignation of Chinese patriots. Now he had to stand firm and accept the position of leader of a national resistance; very probably he expected large-scale defeats, but he had one solid hope. The progress of Japanese aggression in China would sooner or later involve the interests of the Western powers, above all the USA, to the point where they would be drawn into the conflict. China would in the end gain powerful allies and with their aid China would win. Mao Tse-tung also had his hopes: the Japanese assault would destroy the Nationalist government and armies and in the vacuum so created the Communist Party would thrive to gradually take over the burden of national resistance and reap the ultimate rewards. Both were to be in part justified, in part disappointed.

The first years of the war, while China fought alone, saw sweeping Japanese advances. North China was fully overrun by the end of 1937. The Chinese defence of Shanghai held up the Japanese from August until November when, outflanked by new landings, the Chinese had to fall back on Nanking. The city fell in December and the event was marked by the disgraceful sack and massacres in which the Japanese army was permitted to indulge. The Japanese had advanced south into Shentung in December 1937, but their westward movement in north China was held up by the vast floods which the cutting of the Yellow River dykes by the Nationalist army placed in their path. This was the equivalent of a 'scorched earth' policy

*Chinese Nationalist troops surrendering an entrenched position to their Communist adversaries, May 1949*

which the Chinese had adopted. In March 1938 a Japanese corps which was advancing on Nanking from the north was heavily defeated at the village of Taierhchuang in Shentung. This was the only victory in the field which the Chinese could claim. In October the temporary capital, Wuhan, fell to the Japanese advancing up the Yangtze. In the same month another Japanese army landed along the south-east coast and took Canton and other seaports. China was now without any outlet to the sea. The government retired beyond the Yangtze gorges to Chungking in Szechuan, which became the war-time capital. This region is almost impenetrable if defended, and the Japanese halted at the eastern end of the great gorges.

In the huge areas of north China which the Japanese had overrun, but not fully occupied, organized government collapsed, and the Communist guerrilla armies based on Yenan in Shensi, began the work of infiltration and the organization of guerrilla resistance and 'liberated areas'—enclaves which they fully controlled. By the end of 1939 this development was in full swing, and soon proved embarrassing to the occupying Japanese forces. Throughout 1939 and 1940, indeed up to the outbreak of the Pacific War with the Japanese attack on Pearl Harbour on 7th December 1941, the main military effort of the Japanese was spent on trying to suppress and destroy the growing guerrilla resistance. Campaigns of 'three alls' ('Burn all, slay all, loot all') were launched against guerrilla areas. They did terrible damage, but they also convinced the rural population that their only hope was to support the Communist guerrilla armies. Japanese field officers, as wartime papers have since revealed, recognized the fatal consequences of the policy they were ordered to carry out. Their views were ignored by the high command, which persisted in its extermination campaigns. This was to remain the pattern of the war even after the attack upon Pearl Harbour and on the British and Dutch colonies had brought the Western powers into the war against Japan.

While the Communist movement and its guerrilla armies grew and spread throughout north China, the Nationalist armies remained inactive behind the barrier of the Szechuan mountains and the Yangtze gorges. They still controlled north-west and south-west China; across the former a thin trickle of Soviet war supplies reached the Nationalists, and across the latter, by the famous airlift from India, after the British loss of control in Burma in 1942, a substantial but still inadequate flow of essential supplies was maintained.

### A major clash
Meanwhile relations between the Communists and Nationalists had deteriorated. Even before Pearl Harbour there had been in January 1941 a major clash when Nationalist forces attacked and partly destroyed the Communist New 4th Army which was trying to organize guerrilla warfare against the occupying Japanese in the middle Yangtze region. Part of the New 4th Army escaped northwards, but the in-

cident left ill feeling between the two parties. In the latter years of the war Chiang stationed some of his best troops along the southern perimeter of the Communist base area in Shensi, to prevent Communist infiltration, and also to deny the Communists any outside supplies. It was already evident that Chiang counted the ultimate defeat of the Communists as more important than the defeat of the Japanese. Of the latter development he was supremely confident; no nation which was opposed in arms by the USA could hope to win a war; all the Nationalists needed to do was to hold on to their western fortress areas, wait till America had defeated Japan, and then move in to forestall and eliminate any Communist attempt to seize power, whether locally or nationally. But he could not prevent the steady growth of Communist power, both in terms of armed forces and in territory. By 1944 the 8th Route Army numbered 328,000 men and the New 4th Army 150,000. Of 914 county towns (*hsien*) in so-called Japanese occupied territory in March 1945, no less than 678 were in Communist hands.

In the last year of the war the Japanese had made a further major advance in south-west China to destroy the American air bases from which raids upon Japanese shipping were mounted. They occupied much of Kweichow province, but failed to penetrate the Yunnan mountains, or reach Szechuan. As elsewhere, one consequence of further Japanese occupation was to implant Communist guerrillas in a countryside where they had not been active since before the Long March.

The surrender of Japan in August 1945 took the Chinese combatants of both parties by surprise. No one had known of the atomic bomb. It had been expected that in 1946 a massive American invasion would land in eastern China to capture Shanghai. The Communist-liberated areas behind the Japanese lines, to the north of Shanghai, would have come under intense pressure so as to clear Japanese communications from Manchuria to the Yangtze. The Nationalists hoped that Japanese defence in the middle Yangtze would crumble under the threat in the east, and the Nationalist forces could then advance with slight risk down the river to reoccupy the richest region in China. It was also to be hoped that, following an American advance northward, the Nationalist forces could reoccupy the northern provinces also, and drive the Communists out. The atomic bombs on Hiroshima and Nagasaki altered everything. Still in partial occupation of two-thirds of China, with all the major cities, Japan surrendered. Manchuria, the puppet empire of Manchukuo, had been overrun by a brief but massive Russian invasion in the last six days of the war. Thus the greatest prize of Japanese defeat was neither in the hands of the Americans, the Nationalists, nor the Communist Chinese; it was occupied by the Russians. A most urgent question now arose: which army was to accept the surrender of the Japanese forces in various regions of China, and by doing so acquire great stocks of weapons and many of the great cities.

*On Chinese poster Mao is feted as leader of his country and international Communism*

Chiang claimed that as head of the Chinese government, a major war ally, and recognized Commander-in-Chief of the China War Zone, he could call upon the US Air Force to airlift his own men to the Japanese garrisons, take their surrender, and occupy the cities. But these Japanese garrisons were in most cases surrounded by Communist guerrilla armies, now in full control of the countryside. They claimed that in the areas which they dominated, they should take the Japanese surrender. This claim was denied; the US Air Force carried in Chiang's troops, to whom the Japanese surrendered, often at Chiang's orders, resisting Communist attacks until Chiang's men arrived. For answer, the Chinese Communists cut all the land communications and closed rail and road traffic through the regions they controlled. Already at the end of 1945 the spectre of civil war loomed over the Chinese scene. Every political effort was made by the US government to avert this disaster. General George Marshall came to China as mediator. But American assistance to Chiang under wartime agreements continued uninterrupted, both in the supply and training of his forces. The Communists pointed to this and declared that America spoke with two voices: one sought peace, the other prepared the Nationalists for war. This dichotomy was to prove fatal to all efforts to avert civil war.

### An invitation to suicide
American military opinion, although not deeply impressed with the quality of the Nationalist forces, saw that they were more than four times as numerous as those of the Communists and that the Nationalists had a total monopoly of air power. The Communists had no aircraft. It therefore appeared inevitable that the Communists as the weaker side must make concessions, which should take the form of entering a coalition government in which their role would be subordinate, and accepting a limitation to the forces under their control far below that of the Nationalists. The Communists saw this programme as an invitation to suicide. With difficulty General Marshall contrived a

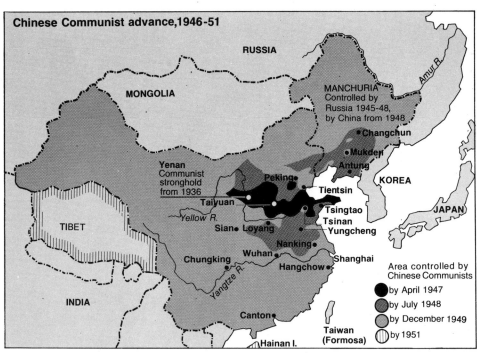

**Chinese Communist advance,1946-51**

RUSSIA

MONGOLIA

MANCHURIA
Controlled by
Russia 1945-48,
by China from 1948

Amur R.

Changchun

Mukden

Antung

Yenan
Communist
stronghold
from 1936

Peking

KOREA

JAPAN

Tientsin

Taiyuan

Yellow R.

TIBET

Sian Loyang

Tsingtao
Tsinan
Yungcheng

Wuhan

Nanking

Chungking

Shanghai

Hangchow

INDIA

Yangtze R.

Area controlled by
Chinese Communists

by April 1947

by July 1948

by December 1949

by 1951

Canton

Taiwan
(Formosa)

Hainan I.

*Left: Antithesis of old and new China. Aged Confucian scholar and Communist recruits taken in 1948 by Henri Cartier-Bresson, one of the masters of photo-reportage. Right: Map of China, showing Communist territorial gains in the war with the Nationalists, 1947-50*

truce and an agreement preserving the status quo so as to permit negotiations to continue. Even this was often violated by both sides, and soon the Manchurian question made it abortive. The Russians had declared their intention of evacuating Manchuria, after disarming the Japanese forces and carrying off the bulk of the industrial equipment and much other 'war booty', by May 1946. Chiang thereupon concentrated three of his best armies in the Peking area ready to occupy Manchuria as the Russians left it. But meanwhile, as the Russians withdrew from the Manchurian countryside the Communist guerrillas from north-west China entered the country, and at once activated the long clandestine local Communists and rapidly expanded their strength. Japanese war material dumps in the remoter areas fell to them.

In the early months of 1946, although the Marshall truce nominally held in China within the Great Wall, it had no effect in Manchuria. The Nationalist forces had occupied Jehol province (in western Manchuria) in November 1945. This was a move to block communications between Manchuria and Yenan. In March 1946 Communist and Nationalist forces clashed at Mukden (Shen-yang) when the Russians left. In April, the Communist armies seized Changchun, the former capital of Manchukuo, when the Russians departed and in the same month they quietly succeeded the Russians in the whole huge area of northern Manchuria, the provinces of Heilungkiang and Kirin. Next month, in May, the Nationalists advancing tardily but in strength, drove the Communist forces from Changchun and Kirin, but they never penetrated the most northerly region. By June 1946 civil war was open and spreading in Manchuria; at the same time the truce in China proper collapsed, and a general civil war began which soon engulfed every region.

In the opinion of his American military advisers, General Wedemeyer and his successors, Chiang Kai-shek made a fatal error in trying to occupy Manchuria while he still did not control land communications between Nanking and the north of China. Nationalist communications with the Peking region and with Manchuria were by sea or by air. Chiang should first have cleared the Communists out of north China, and then moved into Manchuria. This may be sound strategy but it would undoubtedly have been bad politics. Once in full control of Manchuria, a huge rich country, contiguous with the USSR it is more than doubtful whether Chiang could ever have driven the Communists out of it. Nor is it certain or even probable that with Manchuria in Communist hands Chiang would have been strong enough to drive the Communists out of north China. Mao Tse-tung would have become the head of a rival government controlling nearly half China; no prospect of peace or compromise could have emerged from this situation. Chiang felt he must have Manchuria, and north China too; he tried to win both at once; his forces were too badly led and organized to succeed in either attempt, and thus he lost the war.

Immediately after the break-down of the truce, full scale civil war had resumed in June 1946. The Nationalists attempted to conquer Shentung province and open the rail link from Nanking to Peking. The effort was sustained, but failed to gain these objectives. The Communists, commanded by General Ch'en Yi (foreign minister of China from 1958 to 1966), evaded major battles, abandoned empty cities, continued to keep communications cut, and ground the Nationalist offensive to a halt. Elsewhere the Nationalists were able to claim victories which seemed impressive; they advanced north-west of Peking into Inner Mongolia, and in March 1947 captured the war-time Communist capital, Yenan. This was acclaimed as a major victory, and as

the outside world had heard much of Yenan, it was duly impressed. But in fact it was not defended; the Communists had shifted their administration and main forces to Honan and Shentung, where they blocked the only railways leading from the Yangtze to Peking and Manchuria. The Nationalist advance in the north-west was a decoy which drew off their strength to a region not then of strategic importance.

From January to June 1947 the Nationalists were engaged in violent battles with the Communists in northern Manchuria, around Kirin. In May they suffered a severe defeat, and in June the Communists occupied the south-eastern part of Manchuria, the Liaotung Peninsula with the cities of Antung and Liao-yang. It was estimated that the Nationalists lost fifty per cent of their forces in this area. By the end of 1947 the Nationalist armies in Manchuria had been brought to a standstill in the major cities; they no longer were able to dispute the countryside, which was passing wholly under Communist control. By the same period the second attempt of the Nationalists to conquer Shentung had failed completely, and the Communists had occupied almost the whole province of Shansi except its capital Taiyuan. In August 1947 the Communist armies launched a counter-offensive in central China, which drove through to the Tapieh Shan mountains which divide Honan from Hupeh, where they established a new base. They also advanced south-eastward towards Nanking, and they drove the Nationalists out of Shentung. The attempt to reopen land communications with north China had wholly failed; the Nationalists had lost territory which they had controlled in 1946, and their armies in Manchuria were being surrounded in the two great cities of Changchun and Mukden. Rail links with Peking were cut, and all communication was by air. Under the cover of the spurious Nationalist victories in the

*Left: Mao Tse-tung, 1943. He hoped the Japanese would destroy the Nationalists, thus enabling him to assume the burdens of resistance and reap the rewards. Right: Chiang Kai-shek on stamp, 1945. He was more concerned with defeating the Communists than the Japanese*

north-west the war had changed radically in favour of the Communists. In spite of great losses the Nationalist forces at the end of 1947 were still twice as numerous as their opponents, and still had total control of the air. On the other hand the inept political actions of the Nationalists, the economic mismanagement, the corruption of the army and civil service, the growing, disastrous inflation of the currency, had greatly undermined morale. Everyone already knew that whereas the Communist forces were superbly disciplined, and treated the population with scrupulous honesty and fairness, the Nationalist forces, their men ill-paid, and cheated of even that, were allowed and encouraged to loot and plunder so as to live off the country. In 1946 every observer believed that the civil war must be settled by a compromise peace, enforced by American intervention if necessary. By the end of 1947 the belief that the end would be an outright Communist victory was rapidly growing.

Chiang Kai-shek's American military advisers were now also deeply concerned at the deteriorating situation. It was constantly represented to Washington that only swift and drastic reforms in the Nationalist regime and army could avert disaster. But there was no means of enforcing these policies upon Chiang Kai-shek and his supporters, who were dedicated to the maintenance of the Nationalist dictatorship and still hoped for victory. Chiang seems to have believed, as he had in the war with Japan, that if the situation became really perilous, America would intervene on his side, with all her power, to redress the balance. But America had disbanded her armies, put much of her air force out of commission, and was in no mood to embark on another major war in Asia. The apparent control of all the major cities by the Nationalists and the fact that few journalists could penetrate or work in the Communist areas blinded opinion to the

realities. Chiang still seemed to rule in every area of China. In fact his position was threatened by corruption, infiltration, and declining morale. Only a strong push was needed to send the whole rickety edifice tumbling.

### The last conclusive blows

Lin Piao, until his death in 1971 the declared heir to Mao, was then the Communist commander-in-chief in Manchuria. Early in January 1948 he opened his main offensive against the remaining Nationalist strongholds, and soon took Kirin and the important railway junction of Szupingkai. With the loss of these places the Nationalist forces were besieged in their two main garrison cities, Changchun and Mukden. The forces so confined throughout the summer were very large and as their supplies could only be brought in by air it became clear that unless relieved before winter they would be starved into capitulation. Chiang Kai-shek must make a supreme effort to free them while the weather remained suitable, for the Manchurian winter is very severe. His only means of doing so was to land troops on the south-west coast of Manchuria at the small port of Hulutao and seek, with the co-operation of the Mukden garrison, to re-open rail communications from that city to Hulutao. He could also use the port of Ying-kou on the other side of the gulf of Liaotung which was connected by rail with Mukden. The distance was no greater, but the Nationalist command preferred to put its main effort into the western sector in the hope of reopening direct rail connections between Peking and Mukden. This plan required that the Nationalist forces hold the important city of Chinchou, between Hulutao and Mukden. In the summer Chiang began to build up a force of eleven divisions at Hulutao, some of which were the American trained and equipped élite corps which had served in Burma.

Meanwhile the spring of 1948 within the Great Wall saw the rapid decline of the Nationalist position in central China. In March the Communist forces retook Yenan and drove the Nationalist forces south-westward, but failed to advance into Szechuan. In April, crossing into Honan from their base in Shansi province, they took Loyang, capital of Honan, and in May inflicted a severe defeat on the Nationalists at K'ai-feng, capital of eastern Honan, which they temporarily occupied. In these months the Communists, no longer concerned with Nationalist power in the upper Yellow River valley provinces, shifted their main strength eastwards to Central China, where they expected to confront and destroy the large Nationalist forces north of Nanking. On 24th September they took the capital of Shentung, Tsinan, by assault; this was the first really large city taken and held by the Communists, who were now clearly passing from guerrilla warfare to set battles between major formations. The fall of Tsinan heralded this change of tactics and was everywhere recognized as a significant portent. It was believed in Peking that it followed a conference of Communist leaders held at Shihkiachwang, their headquarters in Hopeh, which had rejected Russian advice to continue guerrilla warfare, and decided that the time had come to strike the last conclusive blows.

As autumn advanced the Nationalists still held Mukden and Changchun in Manchuria, Peking and Tientsin and the country connecting them in Hopeh, and most of China south of the Lung Hai railway and Huai River, which formed an east-west line from the sea to the Peking-Hankow railway in Honan. Nationalist forces of poorer quality also still held the western and north-western provinces. Early in October Lin Piao attacked Chinchou in Manchuria, held off the forces sent to relieve it, and forced the garrison of 100,000 men to surrender with all their equipment.

Chiang now realized that unless a last attempt was made to force a passage to Mukden the fate of his Manchurian armies, 400,000-strong, was sealed. Changchun had already fallen, on 20th October, and the five Nationalist divisions there with all their equipment had surrendered to the Communists. On 27th October and the next two days, Lin Piao, placing his forces between the Mukden garrison, which had sortied to meet the Nationalist army based on Hulutao, and the Nationalist forces along the line from Mukden to Ying-kou, attacked the Mukden army from front, flank, and rear. In seventy-two hours the Communists totally destroyed and eliminated the entire Nationalist army from Mukden, killing its commander, and forcing Mukden to surrender two days later. Only the eleven divisions landed at Hulutao, who had played so tardy and useless a role in the battle, were withdrawn by sea. Including the losses at Changchun, Mukden, and the battles around Chinchou, the Nationalists had lost over 400,000 men, mainly as prisoners, and all their weapons, one third of which were American made. They also lost the arsenal of Mukden, the best in China.

Nothing could now prevent the Communist forces in Manchuria, now 400,000 strong, from pouring southward into China within the Great Wall. By the end of October they were approaching Tientsin and closing in on Peking. Further south it was obvious that the last strength of the Nationalist armies must be gathered along the Lung Hai railway to defend the approaches to Nanking and the Yangtze valley. The Communist armies of the central front were concentrating in this region, and Lin Piao's huge Manchurian army could move south to reinforce them. Isolated Peking and Tientsin could be left blockaded without hope of relief. The battle of Huai Hai, as it is called in China (a shortening of Lung-Hai railway and Huai river) opened in November, on ground which throughout Chinese history has been the site of great decisive battles. Armies defending the south, or invading it, must clash here, where the terrain is flat. Huai Hai was only

the last of many decisive battles fought in this region. The forces were now about equal, 600,000 on each side. By any standard Huai Hai is one of the major battles of the modern age. From the opening stages it became clear that the Communists, moving from east, north, and west and not tied to rail communications, were at an advantage over the Nationalist forces which had been told to hold the railway junction of Suchou at all costs, and adopted fixed positions, which were progressively outflanked and surrounded. Bad leadership on the Nationalist side, inflexible tactics, and poor morale contributed to the débâcle. At first the Nationalist forces fought well, but as their supply position deteriorated and the tactics of their generals were so manifestly at fault, morale collapsed. Several divisions surrendered, or even changed sides. Suchou fell on 1st December, and members of its garrison retreating to another walled town, Yungcheng, were surrounded and cut off. On 15th December the eastern group of Nationalist armies, also surrounded since the fall of Suchou, surrendered. Tu Yu-ming, the Nationalist commander-in-chief, held out with his now starving army in and around Yungcheng until 6th January 1949 when the Communist armies stormed the perimeter and brought the whole force to surrender. Tu Yu-ming attempted escape in disguise but was recognized and made prisoner. The Nationalist armies lost 600,000 men in the battle of Huai Hai, of which no less than 327,000 were made prisoners. It was the end; Chiang retired from the presidency, the Communist armies advanced to the banks of the Yangtze.

*Above right: Heroic painting shows Communist forces crossing the Yangtze, 20th April 1949. Four days later they took Nanking. Below right: Peasant denouncing landlord, 1949. The Communists were accepted as liberators by the oppressed peasantry, whereas the ill-paid Nationalists, who looted and pillaged, were regarded with fear and loathing. Below: Unit of the People's Liberation Army marches into Nanking, 24th April 1949*

For nearly four months in the late winter and spring of 1949 there was a lull. The Nationalist government under provisional President Li Tsung-jen tried to negotiate, in Peking, with the Communist leaders. Peking had fallen in January after an inactive siege of six weeks. Tientsin had been taken by assault on 12th January. Had these negotiations succeeded the Communists would have taken over the dominant role in the government of China, and the question of recognition and China's seat at the United Nations would never have been open to question. But the talks were ended by strong intervention by the supporters of Chiang Kai-shek, now busy installing some remnants of his army in Taiwan. The Communists then crossed the Yangtze in force, took Nanking on 24th April 1949, Shanghai on 25th May, and by the end of the year had occupied all the southern and western provinces where many of the local military commanders supported them without offering resistance. Canton, where the fugitive Nationalist government had briefly established itself, was taken on 14th October. In December the last Nationalist cities in distant Szechuan surrendered. In April 1950 the island of Hainan off the coast of south China was occupied. Only Taiwan and some small offshore islands remained in Nationalist hands, to prove, as has since become plain, an abiding difficulty in finding any permanent solution to the problem of peace in the Far East. When the People's Republic was proclaimed in Peking on 1st October 1949 only a few mopping-up operations remained to bring all China under Communist control. By the end of the year these operations were completed. In two and a half years, since large-scale civil war resumed in June 1946, the Communists had risen from a guerrilla army only occupying country districts to a vast well-equipped conventional army which had conquered one of the largest countries in the world. Within a year of victory, the Communists exercised their power further by occupying Tibet. The huge armies which Chiang had at his disposal in 1946 had melted to a remnant and withdrawn to safety in Taiwan.

The Nationalists lost the war because they were badly led, followed wrong strategy, were corrupt, and lost the support of the people, including that of their own ill-treated conscripts. The Communists won because they had a disciplined and dedicated army, were accepted as liberators by the peasantry, conceived their strategy on sound principles, and executed their operations with brilliant tactics. They had no air cover or any air force at all; the Nationalist superiority in equipment and American supplied weapons remained intact until the end, as did their command of the air. It availed them nothing.

*Above left: Detail from propaganda poster. Left: Tibetan lamas (Buddhist priests) gaze apprehensively at the Chinese invader—some play instruments in welcome. Right: During celebrations to mark Shanghai's liberation on 1st August 1949, youths parade Communist star symbol and Mao banner*

毛澤東主席

# The Korean War

The Korean War, which broke out on 25th June 1950, dominated international relations in the early 1950's. Its roots were in the events immediately following the Japanese surrender in August 1945 which ended the Pacific war. At that time the United States and the Soviet Union had agreed on a purely military demarcation of Korea along the line of the 38th parallel in order to facilitate the surrender of enemy forces.

However, the war-time Cairo declaration of December 1943, signed by the US, Great Britain, and China, had promised that 'in due course' Korea would become free and independent, and this pledge was underwritten by the Russians on their entry into the Pacific war. Nevertheless, post-war attempts by the occupiers to work out Korean

independence proposals had broken down by September 1947, when the US turned the Korean problem over to the UN. By this time the issue of Korean independence had become involved in the rivalry on the world stage between America and Russia, and events now moved towards the creation of two Korean states separated by the already fortified line of the 38th parallel.

A majority at the United Nations favoured all-Korean elections to unite the country but the Russians refused to co-operate and claimed that Korea remained a four-power matter. Voting was therefore held only in the south, supervised by the UN, and led to the establishment of the Republic of Korea (ROK) in August 1948 under the presidency of the veteran Korean nationalist Dr Syngman Rhee. In Septem-

ber the Democratic People's Republic of Korea was created at Pyongyang, capital of the northern zone, under the premiership of Kim Il Sung, a former Korean guerrilla leader. The ROK was recognized by many Western countries while North Korea exchanged ambassadors with Moscow and the Soviet bloc. Three years after Japan's defeat two mutually antagonistic Korean states, each claiming jurisdiction over the whole country, and each backed by one of the opposing super-powers, faced one another over the 38th parallel.

Soon, sporadic fighting broke out along the 38th parallel which continued into the spring of 1950. The South Korean army lacked tanks, aircraft, and heavy weapons, while the extent of the Soviet build-up in North Korea of these necessities of modern

*'Rubble in Korea' by David Hall. Although South Korea was devastated as a result of the war, a comprehensive programme of American economic assistance, amounting to $500,000,000 between 1953 and 1955, did much to rehabilitate the country and restore its economy*

war during the winter of 1949-50 was not fully appreciated in the South. Given the political instability of the South, it was expected that psychological warfare, terrorism, and guerrilla attacks would be the chief threat. As Dean Acheson, the US secretary of state, put it later, while the responsible agencies of the US government were in agreement that an invasion of the ROK was possible, 'its launching in the summer of 1950 did not appear imminent'.

Nevertheless, there were understandable reasons why the North Koreans, and presumably their Soviet allies who supplied and supervised much of their equipment, might have calculated that an invasion of the South would not be contested from outside. US troops had been withdrawn from the South by June 1949, and South Korea was considered of peripheral importance by the US Joint Chiefs of Staff who assumed that any future conflict would be a global one. Both General Douglas MacArthur, Supreme Commander for the Allied Powers in Japan, and also American Commander-in-Chief, Far East, and Dean Acheson had publicly stated during 1949-50 that South Korea was outside the US defence perimeter in the Pacific. Strategically, a successful invasion of the South would greatly strengthen the Russians' own defence perimeter in the Pacific. Moreover, a successful takeover of South Korea would no doubt influence anti-American forces in Japan as the US prepared to negotiate a far-reaching peace treaty with its former enemy during 1950. It is in this general Asian context that the ebb and flow of the war in Korea during 1950-53 is best understood.

Whatever the precise calculations in Pyongyang, the North Koreans achieved complete strategic surprise with the timing as well as the scale of their dawn invasion on 25th June 1950. Altogether, seven infantry divisions and one armoured division, equipped with Russian-built T-34 tanks, struck south over the 38th parallel. Simultaneously, a series of amphibious landings took place on the east coast, and North Korean Yak fighters attacked targets over a wide area around Seoul. Pyongyang radio claimed that South Korean troops had attacked North Korea which had then gone over to the counter-offensive. 'The bandit traitor' Syngman Rhee, the broadcast went on, would be arrested and executed. Later, Kim Il Sung stated that the war was a just one for the unification and independence of Korea, and that the North was fighting for freedom and democracy. By 28th June, North Korean forces had captured Seoul, and by the beginning of July their armour was already across the Han River, moving south towards Taejon and Pusan.

But US combat troops were already in Korea. They had been sent from Japan as a result of a series of decisions taken by President Truman and his advisers between 25th and 30th June, in close consultation with the UN and America's allies. Reacting swiftly to the news of the invasion, Truman had immediately ordered MacArthur to send arms to South Korea, while the UN Security Council called for the withdrawal of the North Koreans behind the 38th parallel. On 26th June, as the South Korean position deteriorated, American air and naval support had been promised to the South Koreans. Then, on the 27th, the Security Council, in the continued absence of the Soviet member, and after hearing from the UN commission in Seoul that the Communists were carrying out 'a well-planned, concerted, and full scale attack', recommended that all members 'furnish such assistance to the ROK as may be necessary to meet the armed attack'. By 30th June, US naval and air operations against North Korea had been sanctioned and MacArthur had been given 'full authority' to use all the ground forces under his command.

The first US combat troops had been airlifted into Korea on 1st July, and on the 7th, two days after clashing in a desperate skirmish with the invaders near Osan, the Security Council voted to set up a 'unified command' under the US in Korea. Next day, MacArthur was appointed Commander-in-Chief of the United Nations Command (UNC), and soon all South Korean forces were assigned to his control. Eventually fifteen nations, including most of the Atlantic allies, sent armed forces to fight under the UN flag in Korea.

In effect, Truman's decision to fight a localized, conventional war in Korea reversed the global, atomic preoccupations of US strategy. But the US was determined, if possible, to keep the fighting limited, in view of its responsibilities to the Atlantic allies. Yet, aggression had to be met, the administration argued, if the drift to general war was to stop, and Truman regarded the Korean situation as a symbol 'of the strength and determination of the West'. The President was to write that the Korean decision was the 'toughest decision' of his entire presidency.

The Korean crisis had now become the Korean War, and the world watched with suspense the race between the advancing North Koreans and the desperate build-up of US reinforcements in South Korea. The crucial objective for both sides was Pusan, the deep-water port in the south-east, a hundred miles from Japan. North Korean tanks smashed through the US defences at Taejon on 19th July and advanced towards the Naktong river. This was the last major natural obstacle guarding the Pusan perimeter which had been organized by Lt-Gen Walton Walker, commanding US 8th Army in Korea, despatched from Japan by MacArthur. Another Communist motorized column, advancing through south-west Korea, was within forty miles of Pusan at the beginning of August. But in heavy fighting Walker managed to check the North Korean Blitzkrieg and to hold the perimeter intact. US tanks, artillery, and soldiers flowed into the beachhead through Pusan, and United Nations aircraft attacked the North Korean supply lines.

By September 1950 a strategic deadlock existed on the Pusan perimeter. MacArthur had already decided to break this impasse by the daring manoeuvre of landing the hastily organized 10th Corps at

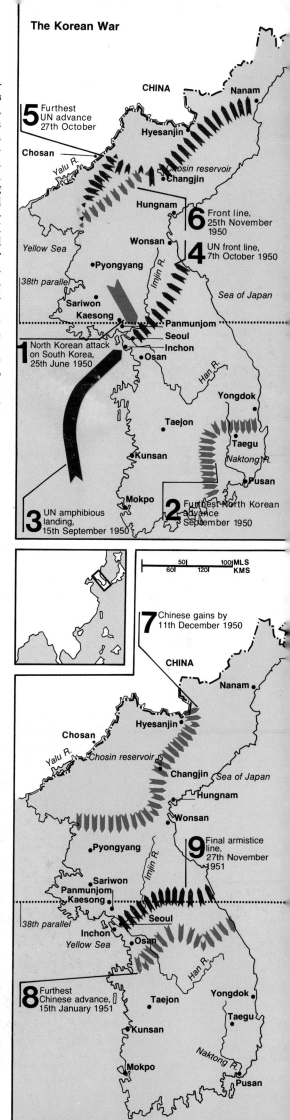

The Korean War

5 Furthest UN advance 27th October

6 Front line, 25th November 1950

4 UN front line, 7th October 1950

1 North Korean attack on South Korea, 25th June 1950

2 Furthest North Korean advance September 1950

3 UN amphibious landing, 15th September 1950

7 Chinese gains by 11th December 1950

9 Final armistice line, 27th November 1951

8 Furthest Chinese advance, 15th January 1951

50 100 MLS
60 120 KMS

Inchon, the west coast port of Seoul, two hundred miles behind the North Korean front lines. If successful, the landing would completely outflank the North Koreans. On 15th September 1950 the Marines went ashore at Inchon, as 8th Army launched an offensive from the Pusan perimeter. By the end of the month the North Korean army had disintegrated, Seoul had been recaptured, and the UNC stood on the 38th parallel after one of the most dramatic victories in military history.

Carried away by victory, the US administration, together with its allies and many in the UN, saw an opportunity to create the united Korea which had always been a formal UN objective. MacArthur was given authority to extend operations north of the 38th parallel, and on 7th October 1950 the UN General Assembly recommended that 'all appropriate steps' be taken so that elections could be held to set up a 'united, independent, and democratic' Korea. The limited objective of June 1950, a defence of the 38th parallel, had been abandoned, and on 15th October, a few days before UNC troops entered Pyongyang, Truman conferred with MacArthur on Wake Island to discuss post-war plans for the new Korea. The battle for North Korea seemed over when on 24th October 1950 the first men under MacArthur's command reached the Yalu river boundary of Korea and Manchuria at Chosan.

Yet on the very weekend that MacArthur was assuring Truman on Wake Island that there was 'very little' chance of Chinese intervention in Korea, the first men of the massed armies of the Chinese Communist forces were entering Korea, undetected, over the Yalu bridges at Antung and Manpojin. These regular troops, numbering altogether over 300,000, had been designated the 'Chinese People's Volunteers' in Korea and were directed by General Peng Teh-huai during this initial crossing of the Yalu from a joint Chinese-North Korean headquarters staff at Mukden, Manchuria. Later, in early 1951, Peng became the commander of the Chinese forces in Korea, under the technical control of Kim Il Sung's 'combined headquarters' to preserve the appearance of 'volunteer' status.

The prospect of Chinese intervention had been contemplated in Washington and Tokyo from the very beginning of the war. As a part of his Korean decision, Truman had also 'neutralized' Formosa on general strategic grounds, by interposing the US 7th Fleet in the straits between the mainland and Chiang Kai-shek's garrison on the island. But the Truman administration had also calculated that the new regime in Peking, proclaimed in October 1949, was more nationalist than Communist, and that frequent assurances of American goodwill, combined with the President's statement in July 1950 that the neutralization of Formosa was 'without prejudice' to the political future of the island, would be accepted by the Chinese Communists.

However, the presence of US forces near the Manchurian border, following the placing of the 7th Fleet in the straits, was unacceptable to Peking on both strategic and ideological grounds. There was no common ground between the two positions. On 2nd October, after several public assurances of solidarity with North Korea, Chou En-lai summoned the Indian ambassador, K.M.Panikkar, to a dramatic midnight conference at the Foreign Affairs Ministry, declaring that if US forces entered North Korea, China would resist them. The warning was ignored in the US and the UN, where MacArthur's prestige was never higher. By the end of October 1950 the UNC had already clashed with elements of the Chinese forces south of the Manchurian border, but these 'hostiles' soon faded away into the mountains as the Korean winter set in.

MacArthur was still confident that his command could advance to the Yalu by Christmas, so completing his mission in Korea. On 24th November, an 'end-the-war' offensive was launched across the Chongchon river by the 8th Army, and in north-east Korea, where 10th Corps had been re-deployed after Inchon, the Marines moved north from the Chosin reservoir. But unknown to the allies, two armies were on the move south of the Yalu. Two days later the Chinese launched their own mighty counter-offensive, almost outflanking the 8th Army and surrounding the Marines at Chosin. Rapid withdrawal from North Korea was now the only way to preserve the UN Command, and by the end of the year MacArthur's forces were back at the familiar starting point, the 38th parallel. Carrying on with their offensive, the Chinese took Seoul in early January 1951, eventually coming to a halt later in the month about sixty miles south of the parallel as they outran their supply lines.

But as the heavily reinforced divisions of the 8th Army, including a strong British contingent, and now commanded by Lieutenant-General Matthew Ridgway, slowly pushed their way back to the 38th parallel, it was obvious that the allies faced what MacArthur called 'an entirely new war'. In its turn the Chinese incursion had brought about three important developments on the international scene. In the first place, Truman and Clement Attlee, the British Prime Minister, meeting in Washington during December 1950, had decided to abandon the objective of uniting Korea by force of arms. Korean unity, the leaders agreed, would have to come about 'by peaceful means' as they reverted to the original, pre-Inchon objective of defending South Korea.

Secondly, alarmed that the Chinese incursion into Korea presaged a policy of world military conquest by the Sino-Soviet powers, the Truman administration embarked on a major rearmament drive that was followed in varying degrees by the other Atlantic allies. The US armed forces were to be increased from 1·5 to 3·5 million men, the United States Air Force was to be doubled, its overseas base structure greatly enlarged, and the production of nuclear devices, including hydrogen weapons, was to be accelerated on a crash basis. Altogether annual US defence expenditure was to be increased from $13,000 million to $60,000 million. But the US emphasised that the defence of Western Europe remained its primary objective and in fact four divisions were sent to Germany in the spring of 1951, and not to Korea.

The third result of the Chinese intervention was to bring about the 'great debate' in the US on the entire basis of American foreign policy, with special emphasis on the Korean War. The conflict of opinion was dramatized by the fate of MacArthur, who with the withdrawal from North Korea demanded that he be authorized to win the war by attacking the 'privileged sanctuary' of Manchuria. When he publicly carried his case to the American people by stating that 'there is no substitute for victory', Truman dismissed his over-mighty subject on 11th April 1951, replacing him in all his pro-consular commands by General Ridgway. The debate continued with MacArthur's speech to a joint session of Congress after a tumultuous welcome in the United States. Here the old soldier outlined his victory strategy in which he advocated an economic and naval blockade of Communist China, use of Formosan troops against the mainland, and extended aerial surveillance of China's coastal areas with the implied threat that this would lead to air attack against the Manchurian airbases from which MiG fighters were increasingly harassing UN aircraft over North Korea.

However, the general's strategy (and rhetoric) was effectively deflated in a subsequent Senate inquiry on Korea which aroused world-wide interest. The legendary General George Marshall, secretary of defence, emphasised that US operations in Korea were only part of a foreign policy designed to check aggression 'in different fashions in different areas', with the objective of avoiding the incalculable cost of another general war. General Bradley, the chairman of the Joint Chiefs of Staff, reminded his listeners of the classical precept that the most dangerous enemy was the strongest enemy, and that the US should not allow itself to be bogged down in the Far East by the Chinese. In a particularly telling phrase, Bradley described the MacArthur programme as 'the wrong war, at the wrong place, at the wrong time, and with the wrong enemy'. Secretary Acheson summed up on the advantages of combining rearmament with the revised, status quo objectives of the allies in Korea: 'Time is on our side if we make good use of it.' The risks of the MacArthur programme appeared much too great, and there seemed no alternative to the administration's strategy.

Fortunately for the defenders of the Truman administration, military events in Korea during the MacArthur hearings seemed to bear out its case. In April and May 1951, the Communists launched two mass offensives aimed at destroying the 8th Army, now commanded by General James Van Fleet. In both offensives the Chinese were thrown back with appalling casualties as the UNC used its firepower to maximum advantage. Going over to the counter-offensive, and with the Chinese surrendering in their thousands, Van Fleet advanced to slightly north of the 38th

begin an 'active defence', became the scene of artillery duels and infantry engagements up to regimental level. Simultaneously, the sea and air war waged against North Korea by the United Nations Command went on without respite. UN warships continued to blockade and bombard North Korea, as the air forces worked on the Communist supply lines south from the Yalu, sometimes opposed from the MiG fighter bases in Manchuria. Yet during this period political developments were as important as the events on the battlefield which were directed during 1952-3 by General Mark Clark who had replaced Ridgway as UN commander in Tokyo in May 1952. The UN allies were eager to end the war, as South Korea had been successfully defended, while their adversaries, through charges of atrocities, aggression, and above all germ warfare, were attempting to erode the resolution that still kept the UNC in the field and at the truce talks. The allies faced a test of their staying power, Acheson told the UN in October 1952, as the General Assembly passed a resolution affirming the stand on voluntary prisoner repatriation.

### 'Land of the morning calm'

Events outside Korea now led to a final signing of the armistice. In the US presidential election of November 1952, in which the Democratic administration was on the defensive for failing to end the war, General Eisenhower had been triumphantly elected after his promise to bring an early and honourable end to the conflict. After a visit to Korea before his inauguration in January 1953, Eisenhower decided to warn the Chinese that unless an armistice was agreed at Panmunjom the US would enlarge the war, attacking the Manchurian bases with atomic weapons to gain a decision. The second external factor which helped to bring about an armistice was the death of Stalin in March 1953, bringing about a subsequent thaw in international relations which was soon noticed in Panmunjom when the Communists decided to resume discussion on the deadlocked prisoner issue. Soon an agreement on this issue was reached in June 1953, in which the UNC maintained its stand as the non-repatriated prisoners were to be turned over to a neutral nations repatriation commission for disposal as they wished.

Eventually, the final armistice agreement bringing about a ceasefire that day was signed at Panmunjom on 27th July 1953. It incorporated the above agreement on the prisoner repatriation as well as the earlier accords on a joint military armistice commission, a neutral nations supervisory commission, and provided for a four-kilometre demilitarized zone separating the armies, centred along the demarcation line when the shooting stopped. On the same day, the 'Declaration of Sixteen' signed in Washington by the countries participating in the UN Command stated that in the event of the armistice being broken, in all probability it would not be possible 'to confine hostilities within the frontier of Korea'. Following the recom-

*Innocent sufferers: caught between cross fire, a wounded Korean girl carries her more seriously wounded sister to safety. A dead South Korean soldier lies in the road. It is thought that a million civilians from both sides died in the violent oscillations of the Korean War*

parallel, and then in June and July began to fortify the commanding terrain of the easily defensible 'Kansas-Wyoming Line'. During these operations, on 23rd June, Jacob Malik, the Soviet ambassador to the UN, had suggested that a ceasefire could be negotiated in Korea. After an exchange of radio messages and liaison officers, these 'strictly military' talks, with no political content, began between the two delegations on 8th July, at Kaesong, near the 38th parallel. Both sides were now willing to abandon the search for 'victory' and to negotiate on the basis of a divided Korea. Again the war seemed to be coming to an end.

Yet it soon became clear that the armistice negotiations, so far from bringing the war to a quick end, were but another, political, front of the fighting which went on for another two years. However, agreement was reached on an agenda within the first two weeks, before the truce site was moved from the Kaesong tea-house to the more convenient nearby hamlet of Panmunjom on the highway to Seoul. Basically, the two delegations, led by Admiral Joy, US Navy, and General Nam Il, North Korean army, had to agree on arrangements for a demarcation line and demilitarized zone as a basic condition for ending hostilities; arrangements for supervising the truce; and arrangements relating to prisoners of war.

On the first item, following numerous angry exchanges of charge and counter-charge which characterized the entire proceedings at Panmunjom, both sides had agreed by November 1951 on the establishment of a demarcation line, in the centre

of a demilitarized zone, following the truce. This line would be based on the firing line at the end of hostilities, and would be supervised, like the zone, by a joint military armistice commission. By the following April, tentative agreement on the supervision of the truce had been reached with the plan for setting up a neutral nations supervisory commission and deploying observer teams to prevent a new military build-up in the two Koreas. There remained the intractable problem of the Communist prisoners held by the UNC, which was to prolong the war for another fifteen months. As only 6,000 of the 20,000 Chinese prisoners, and 76,000 of the 112,000 North Koreans wished to be repatriated, the Communist side at Panmunjom alleged that the prisoners had been coerced and insisted on compulsory repatriation. At the same time the UNC found it equally impossible to yield on such an issue on grounds of both principle and expediency, for if it could be shown that large numbers of Chinese and North Koreans preferred the camp of imperialism to the camp of peace, then that would be a major political victory. The UNC position therefore remained one of voluntary prisoner repatriation.

The deadlock at Panmunjom was therefore as complete as that on the highly fortified main line of resistance slashed across the peninsula from coast to coast by the UN Command. This line, based on the Kansas-Wyoming Line, incorporating local advances up to November 1951, when Ridgway ordered Van Fleet to dig in and to

US Army Photograph

Il Mondo △ Camera Press ▷

mendation of Article 60 of the armistice agreement which looked forward to a political conference on Korea, the Geneva Conference of 1954 failed to agree on the problems of the divided country, and thus the armistice remains in force, with the country still in a state of formal belligerency.

The cost of the war, which in spite of the ideological barrage had been fought for crucial political-military objectives, was heavy to all concerned.

The wider political effects of the war were considerable. South Korea today is a relatively prosperous and stable community, and the authority of the UN was upheld in a crisis that could have accelerated the drift to general war in the early 1950's. As far as the US and its allies were concerned, their rearmament, combined with the consolidation of the Atlantic alliance, deterred further adventures of the Korean pattern. At the same time, under the impetus of the Korean War, West Germany was brought into the Atlantic community with the virtual ending of the occupation regime, and the Japanese peace treaty had been successfully negotiated – hardly objectives of Soviet policy.

Whilst the USSR gained some political capital from the fact of Western rearmament, combined with UN military activities in an Asian country, the Korean War, with its heavy industrial demands on the Soviet bloc, greatly aggravated internal stresses leading to disturbances in Eastern Europe.

Although China was unable to gain Formosa and a UN seat, she prevented the unification of Korea under Western auspices and established herself as a major power in her own right inside the Communist bloc. At Panmunjom, the military armistice commission still meets regularly to exchange insults over the numerous infringements of the truce. There is still no prospect that 'the land of the morning calm' will ever become united.

In the mid-1970's, despite the American setback in Indochina, South Korea's defence continues to be underwritten by the United States. For three of the world's largest countries, China, USSR and Japan, surround Korea, and the US remains closely involved in the country for the strategic reasons noted above.

The wider historic factors which underlay the Korean War of 1950–53 thus remain essentially unchanged.

*1 In a cartoon from the Russian satirical magazine* Krokodil *entitled 'Darwin Corrected' the ape, brandishing a grisly picture of Himmler, insists that the American officer in Korea is descended from 'this butcher of Auschwitz and Majdanek'.*
*2 UN and North Korean liaison officers initial the demarcation line at Panmunjom on 27th November 1951 after provisional agreement had been reached. 3 ROK soldier stands guard over North Korean prisoners. They have been stripped to deter escape attempts. 4 Using a periscope, an American military policeman maintains surveillance of North Korean territory at Panmunjom*

# The Suez Crisis

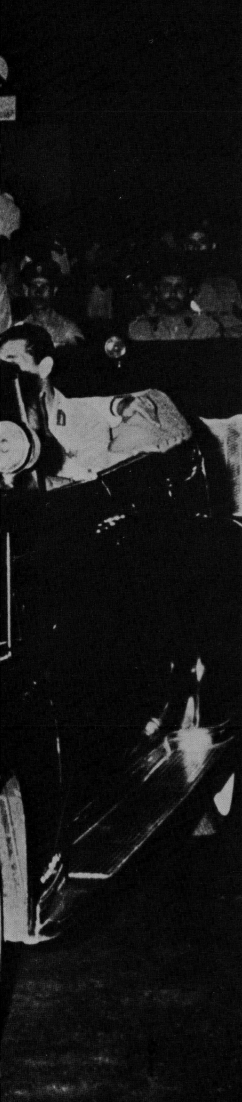

The Suez crisis was the outcome of three different but related power struggles in the Middle East. The first was the struggle between Israel and its Arab neighbours which had been going on ever since the formation of the Jewish state in 1948. The second was the struggle between Arab nationalism and the colonial powers, Great Britain and France, which were seeking to preserve their influence in the area and the third was the Cold War between the Soviet Union and the United States.

At the centre of all three power struggles was Egypt under its militant leader, Colonel Gamal Abdel Nasser. It was Egypt which, in April 1955, set up the *fedayeen* ('self-sacrificers'), or special guerrilla units designed to sabotage and kill inside Israeli territory, and which blockaded the Straits of Tiran against Israeli shipping in September of the same year. It was Egypt which compelled the British to evacuate their Suez base in 1954, which organized Arab opposition to the British-sponsored Baghdad Pact in 1955 and 1956, and which sought to undermine the British position throughout the Middle East and Africa, even to the extent of putting out broacasts in Swahili to the people of Kenya. It was Egypt too which gave aid and encouragement to the Algerian nationalists, who had launched their rebellion against France in November 1954. Finally, it was Egypt which, in September 1955, announced a huge arms deal with the Communist bloc, causing American secretary of state, John Foster Dulles, to tell a cabinet meeting that 'for the first time the Russians were making a determined effort to move into the Middle East, where two-thirds of the world's known oil reserves were located.'

Egypt's actions helped to forge new alignments. Israel moved closer to France, seeking to buy modern armaments, particularly aircraft, to offset Nasser's purchases from the Communists. Great Britain and France, whose rivalry in the Middle East went back to the Second World War and beyond, began to patch up their differences. But even though Great Britain's Prime Minister, Anthony Eden, had decided by March 1956 that Nasser posed such a threat to British interests that he had to be 'destroyed', the Egyptian leader's enemies were a long way from a co-ordinated plan of action designed to bring him down.

It was the nationalization of the Suez Canal in July 1956 which acted as the catalyst. This in turn arose out of the withdrawal of the British and American offer to help finance the Aswan Dam. In December 1955 it was announced that the World Bank would provide a loan of $20 million, which, together with an American grant of $56 million and a $14 million one from Great Britain, would give the Egyptian government sufficient capital to begin constructing a high dam at Aswan in upper Egypt, which was intended to improve irrigation in the Nile valley and to supply hydro-electric power for industrialization. But the offer contained strings designed to weaken Egypt's growing ties with the Soviet bloc and Colonel Nasser denounced this attempt to influence his government's foreign policy by financial means. Over the next few months, he sought to obtain a relaxation of the conditions by threatening to turn to Russia for the full cost of the project while, at the same time, making no effort to lessen British and American hostility to his regime in other ways. His intransigent attitude made it highly unlikely that Congress would have agreed to put up the American share of the money in any case and, on 19th July 1956, Dulles told the Egyptian ambassador in Washington that the deal was off. Although the British government would, in Eden's words, have preferred to 'play it along', it followed suit.

*Left: President Nasser receives the plaudits of the crowd in Alexandria after making the speech in which he announced the nationalization of the Suez Canal. It was this action which convinced Anthony Eden that the crunch had come and he observed that Nasser could not be allowed 'to have his thumb on our windpipe'. Right: Nasser announces nationalization of Suez Canal to crowd of 50,000, 26th July 1956*

AFP

United Press International

There is evidence that Colonel Nasser expected this outcome and had already worked out a contingency plan to meet the situation. At any rate, it was not long before he unveiled one. In a speech at Alexandria on 26th July, he announced that Egypt had nationalized the Suez Canal and that the revenue from it would be used to finance the Aswan Dam.

### 'Thumb on our windpipe'

Eden was convinced that the crunch had come. It was true that full compensation was promised to the canal's owners and that no attempt was made to restrict its use, but, in the British Prime Minister's view, 'a man with Colonel Nasser's record' could not be allowed 'to have his thumb on our windpipe'. Moreover, as he wrote to President Eisenhower, 'my colleagues and I are convinced that we must be ready, in the last resort, to use force to bring Nasser to his senses. For our part we are prepared to do so.' He soon found that the French were no less determined and joint military planning began in London on 10th August.

The attitude of the United States was crucial in any attempt to use force. It was not that the British and French wanted any direct help in their efforts to 'bring Nasser to his senses', but, as Eden put it to Robert Murphy 'we do hope you will take care of the Bear'—in other words, prevent the Soviet Union from coming to the aid of its Egyptian protégé. Moreover,

when Dulles told Eden on 1st August that 'a way had to be found to make Nasser disgorge what he was attempting to swallow', the British Prime Minister felt that he had won over the Americans to his point of view. 'These were forthright words,' he wrote later. 'They rang in my ears for months.'

But Eden was deluding himself. There were at least three reasons why the United States would not condone the use of force to settle the Suez dispute. In the first place, 1956 was an election year and President Eisenhower and his administration had no intention of becoming embroiled in any kind of conflict at such a time. Secondly, American interests were not so much at risk as were those of Great Britain and France. The United States, for example, imported less than four per cent of its crude oil requirements from the Middle East, whereas the same area provided three-quarters of western Europe's needs. Finally, there was the age-old American suspicion of European 'colonialism'. As Sherman Adams, one of President Eisenhower's closest advisers, put it, 'our firm opposition to colonialism made us sympathetic to the struggle which Egypt and the other Arab states were making to free themselves of the political and economic control that the British felt they had to maintain in the Middle East in their own self-interest.'

For the moment, however, the funda-

mental incompatibility between the British and French position on the one hand and that of the United States on the other was concealed by the fact that, as it would take time to mount a military operation, Great Britain and France were prepared to try and justify it by showing that all attempts to reach a peaceful solution had failed. All three countries were therefore able to agree on the summoning of a conference of canal users in London in mid-August. The conference produced a plan for international control of the canal which Egypt rejected on 9th September. Dulles then came forward with a proposal for a Suez Canal Users' Association, which was even less acceptable to the Egyptians, and finally, on 23rd September, Great Britain and France referred the matter to the Security Council of the United Nations.

'If John Foster Dulles ever was actually convinced of the possibility of organizing a Canal Users' Association to operate the Suez canal,' Robert Murphy has since written, 'I was not aware of it. . . . It seemed to me that he was skilfully working

*Below: Building in Port Said set alight by Anglo-French naval bombardment which began at dawn on 6th November. At 4.30 British commandos went ashore and tanks followed. Right: British troops in action during the Suez operation. The Anglo-French advance ended at El Cap, twenty-five miles south of Port Said, but advance patrols penetrated within twenty-five miles of Suez*

for time in the hope that public opinion in western Europe would harden against a military adventure.' By September, indeed, it became clear that the United States was not prepared to support a military solution. 'I must tell you frankly,' President Eisenhower wrote to Eden on 2nd September, 'that American public opinion flatly rejects the thought of using force' and, on the 13th, Dulles publicly told a press conference, 'we do not intend to shoot our way through [the canal]. It may be we have the right to do it but we don't intend to do it as far as the United States is concerned.' On 2nd October he denied reports that the teeth were being taken out of the plan for a Canal Users' Association. 'I know of no teeth,' he said. 'There were no teeth in it, so far as I am aware.' One of the British Prime Minister's closest advisers has observed that 'this was for Eden the final let-down'.

### Paratroops swoop down

The French had always been much less sanguine about American intentions. Throughout the summer they had been in close touch with Israel and had even informed the latter in general terms of the Anglo-French plan to invade Egypt. The Israelis were quick to see that such an action would provide them with a splendid opportunity to break out of the stranglehold which the Egyptian blockade of both the Suez Canal and the Straits of Tiran represented for them, and, at the same time, to strike a decisive blow at the source of the *fedayeen* raids upon their territory. The French, for their part, were eager to involve the Israelis in the Anglo-French attack and, in a top secret meeting at Chequers on 14th October, raised the matter with the British. In the words of one of those present, 'the plan . . . was that Israel should be invited to attack Egypt across the Sinai peninsula and that France and Britain, having given the Israeli forces enough time to seize all or most of Sinai, should then order "both sides" to withdraw their forces from the Suez canal, in order to permit an Anglo-French force to intervene and occupy the canal on the pre-text of saving it from damage by fighting.'

Utterly disillusioned and exasperated by what he felt to be American indifference to Great Britain's plight, Eden was only too happy to accept the French proposal, overruling the warnings of some of his advisers to the effect that participation in what one described as a 'sordid conspiracy' with Israel would irretrievably prejudice Great Britain's relations with its remaining Arab friends, such as Iraq and Jordan. After further discussions with the French and the Israelis, the British cabinet accepted the plan on 25th October. Under its terms, the Israelis attacked across the Sinai desert on 29th October. The Anglo-French ultimatum was issued on the 30th and, when Egypt predictably rejected it; British and French aircraft began bombing Egyptian airfields on the 31st. On the same day, the invasion fleet set off from Malta. It arrived off Port Said on 6th November, twenty-four hours after British and French paratroops had begun dropping in the region of the town.

It is likely that when the British and

Burt Glinn – Magnum

*Above:* Israeli soldier mounts guard over captured Egyptian troops. Israel was quick to see that an Anglo-French invasion of Egypt would provide her with an opportunity to break the Egyptian stranglehold on the Straits of Tiran and the Suez Canal and strike a decisive blow at the source of the fedayeen raids. *Right:* Map of the Suez operation, the cost of which the Labour Party assessed at £328 million, taking into account the loss of exports and the increased cost of imports. The British lost 22 killed, the French 10, the Israelis 200, and the Egyptians between 2,650 and 3,000

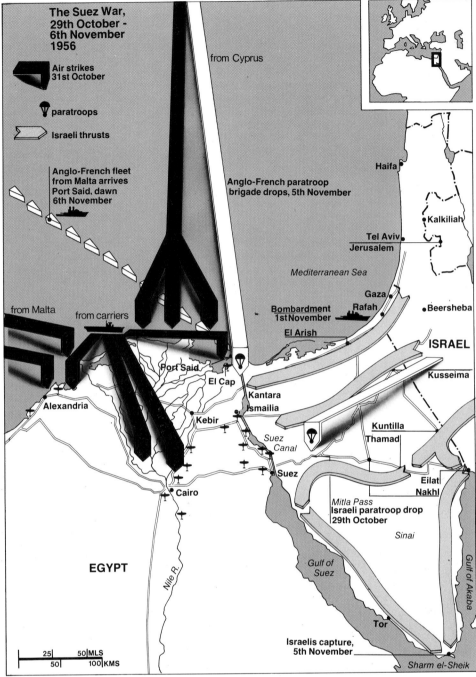

French governments finally decided to resort to force, they reasoned that the United States, which they had deliberately kept in the dark about their plans, would at least maintain a neutral attitude in public. If so, they were doomed to disappointment, for it was the American representatives who led the attack at the United Nations against the British, French, and Israeli action, both in the Security Council on 30th October and in the General Assembly on 2nd November. As President Eisenhower wrote later: 'We could not permit the Soviet Union to seize the leadership in the struggle against the use of force in the Middle East and thus win the confidence of the new independent nations of the world.'

### Threat of nuclear attack

While the Soviet Union did support the Egyptians throughout the Suez crisis, it was careful not to get too closely involved. The Russian advisers in Egypt were in-

structed not to take part in the fighting and some of them were even flown home. In addition, the Egyptians were denied the use of a force of forty-five Ilyushin IL-28 bombers which had recently been supplied by the Russians. The aircraft were moved, first to upper Egypt and later to Syria, presumably to prevent them from falling into British or French hands. Soviet caution was prompted by two considerations. In the first place, the Anglo-French attack upon Egypt coincided with the climax of the Hungarian rebellion and the USSR was more concerned with events in Eastern Europe than those in the Middle East. Secondly, the Soviet Union was not quite sure what attitude the United States would adopt when fighting actually broke out. It was only on 5th November, after the crisis in Hungary had been surmounted and the United States had openly displayed its opposition to the British and French action, that Russia felt free to inform Britain, France, and Israel that they were

'fully resolved to use force to crush the aggressors and to restore peace in the Middle East.' There was even a hint that London and Paris might be the object of a nuclear strike if the British and French did not call off their attack and the United States government had to make it clear that, whatever its feelings about its behaviour over Suez, it would respond to a nuclear attack upon its allies in kind.

The day after the dramatic Soviet intervention, the British and French governments agreed to the UN's demand for a cease-fire. It would be a mistake, however, to see in the juxtaposition of these two events a simple case of cause and effect. The invasion of Egypt had split British public opinion wide open. The Labour Party—under the slogan 'Law not War'—was in full cry against Eden's policy and there was opposition in the ranks of the Prime Minister's own Conservative Party and inside the government itself. Even more serious, there had been a run on the

On the cartoon:

Cummings

3

by permission of M^r Nehru

O.K. by IKE

With permission of Liberace

With TITO's permission

Permission from M^r POLLITT

Licensed by Mao

LICENSED TO WIELD TWO STROKES OF THE FEATHER BY M^r KRUSHCHEV

Licensed by D^r Adenauer

Permission of Col. Grivas

Permission of Mau-Mau

With Col. Nasser's Permission

O.K. by FRANCO

Cummings and the Daily Express

Kukriniski/SCR

*Left:* A Russian comment on the Suez fiasco: the British lion and the French cockerel, bedraggled and woe-begone, escape from Suez, tail and tail-feathers tweaked off by an angry Sphinx. In fact, it was international pressure, expressed through the UN, which forced withdrawal. *Above:* Daily Express cartoon entitled 'The circumstances in which Mr Gaitskell (the leader of the Opposition) would approve of Eden protecting our interests . . .' The invasion of Egypt split British public opinion wide open and there was even opposition to it among the Prime Minister's own Conservative Party. In the circumstances, Eden had no alternative but to resign

pound, and the United States, which was the only power in a position to help, intimated that no assistance would be forthcoming unless the invasion was brought to a halt. In the circumstances, Eden felt he had no alternative but to agree to a cease-fire and, as they were unable to carry on alone, the French too were forced to comply. Having achieved all their aims in the Sinai peninsula, the Israelis had already stopped fighting.

### Humiliation and disaster

The Suez invasion was a failure on almost every count. Intended to safeguard the canal, it resulted in the Egyptians closing it by sinking block-ships. Intended to maintain the uninterrupted flow of oil to Western Europe, it resulted in not only the closure of the canal to tankers but the sabotage of nearly all the direct pipelines to the Mediterranean which soon compelled Great Britain, for one, to introduce petrol rationing. Intended to topple Nasser,

it resulted in his acquiring more prestige than ever in the Arab world, having successfully defied the 'imperialists'. Britain's staunchest friend in the Middle East, Nuri as-Said of Iraq, was placed in an impossible position and perished in a bloody coup some twenty months later, while the Algerian nationalists went from strength to strength and eventually won their independence in 1962. Intended to keep the Russians out of the Middle East, its failure created a power vacuum in the area which only encouraged them further and compelled the United States, at the beginning of 1957, to intervene with the 'Eisenhower Doctrine' of assistance to any Arab state which felt threatened by Communist intrigues. However, American influence, because of her support of Israel, became overshadowed by that of the Soviet Union, who, in the wake of the Suez War, became the chief supplier of arms to the militant Arab states, including Egypt.

In the long term, the 'collusion' between

Great Britain, France, and Israel at the time of Suez immeasurably strengthened the Arab myth that Israel is a springboard of Western imperialism in the Middle East, a sentiment which came out into the open at the time of the 'six-day war' in June 1967. Even that war itself can be partly blamed on Suez, for Nasser was able to fool both himself and the Arab world that he could have beaten Israel in 1956 had it not been for the British and French, thus tempting him to try again in 1967. Great Britain's decision to agree to a ceasefire against French wishes provided one more example of 'perfidious Albion' to French Anglophobes, including General de Gaulle, while the relations between Western Europe and its American ally have never been quite the same since. Indeed, perhaps the only positive result of Suez was that, by showing the individual European states that their ability to act independently of the two super-powers was strictly limited, it gave them added impetus to unite.

**1**

1% OF THE PEOPLE OWN
NEARLY HALF THE
NATION'S WEALTH

CAN THIS BE RIGHT?

*VOTE LABOUR*

Labour Party

**2**

MAKE NO MISTAKE
THIS TIME

LABOUR

TWO BIRDS

TORY

LIBERAL VOTE

ONE STONE

VOTE LIBERAL

Liberal Publications Dept

**3**

DOWN
WITH
STATE
CONTROL

Vote
CONSERVATIVE

Conservative Research Dept

**4**

AND NOW—
WIN THE PEACE

VOTE LABOUR

Labour Party

*1 The class struggle still dominated Labour's electioneering in 1959. But after defeat, the party worked hard to establish a new image of efficiency, class-lessness, and pragmatism. 2 1955 – Liberals hoped to capitalize on voters' disgust with both major parties. 3 1964 – the Tories hammered away at the bogy of state control. Yet in office they had dismantled few of the controls established by Attlee's government. 4 1945 – with a thumping majority over the Conservative Party of 180 parliamentary seats, it seemed the dawn of a brave new world for Labour. 5 But a 1946 cartoon invites voters to take a 'second look' at Labour's election promises. 6 1955 – Hugh Gaitskell pictured in photographer Philippe Halsman's* Jump Book

# Tories and Socialists

When the votes were counted after the 1945 general election, David Low published a cartoon in the *Evening Standard* entitled 'Make Way!' It showed a heroic, vaguely proletarian figure striding purposefully towards the dawn over a heap of cringing, black-coated city gents along a road labelled 'To the Socialist Era'. Better than any other comment, it summed up the mood which had produced the greatest left-wing landslide in British politics for forty years.

Among Labour Party activists, and to a remarkable extent among working-class Labour voters, the mood of enthusiasm and determination persisted. The 1945 Labour government faced appalling problems. Before the war, the British had lived on the achievements of their ancestors. They had exported less than they imported, and had made up the difference with the income from foreign investments made in the days of Great Britain's industrial supremacy before 1914. Now most of her foreign assets had been sold to pay for the war against fascism. Her income from foreign investments was less than half the figure in 1938, and the price of her imports had multiplied four-fold. It was calculated that to fill the gap she would have to surpass her pre-war level of exports by seventy-five per cent.

After six years of hardship, followed by the most decisive military victory in their history, the British people could be forgiven for hoping for easier times. These hopes had to be disappointed if the government was to overcome the problems that faced it. War-time austerity continued into peace; in some ways it even intensified. Yet Labour's morale remained high, and its hold on the working-class electorate was unbroken. When the country went to the polls in 1950 Labour won the largest popular vote ever received by a British political party (though it was smaller than that achieved by the coalition National government in 1931).

The reason seems clear. After the First World War a short-lived boom was followed by a disastrous slump; ex-servicemen who had fought for their country found themselves on the scrapheap. The Second World War had a very different sequel. Full employment continued – and by continuing vindicated Labour's claim to power. Socialism, Labour candidates declared proudly, worked after all. And the fact that it worked after the war proved that it would have worked before the war, if it had been tried. The poverty and unemployment of the inter-war years were not

acts of God: they were the result of Conservative selfishness and stupidity. If the Conservatives came to power again, they would turn the clock back.

### The party of the workers
Labour's working-class supporters in 1945 and 1950 often disagreed with the party's policies and underlying philosophy. But that made no difference to their political loyalties. They voted Labour because they believed, as a result of their experiences during and after the war, that the Labour Party was 'their' party: that their interests were by definition opposed to middle-class interests, and that they would only be safe under a Labour government.

Labour's appeal to working-class solidarity went hand in hand with an appeal to socialist ideology. This too was of long standing. For nearly thirty years the Labour Party had been committed to the public ownership of the means of production, distribution, and exchange. Before the war its commitment had been expressed more often in uplifting generalities than in concrete proposals. Between 1945 and 1950 it was expressed in legislative action. Coal, gas, electricity, steel, the railways, and the Bank of England were all nationalized. And although the government approached the end of its term of office with no clear idea of what to nationalize next, there was little doubt that nationalization was the essence of its creed.

Labour's nationalization measures were fought tooth and nail by the Conservative opposition. So too were the establishment of the National Health Service, the withdrawal from India, and the continuation of war-time rationing and controls. In 1950 and 1951 the Conservatives campaigned on the slogan 'Set the People Free!'; and it seemed clear that whatever else might follow a Conservative victory, it would undoubtedly lead to a rapid diminution in the role of the state. In 1950, in other words, the two main parties appeared to be divided by an impassable gulf of ideology and class interest. Labour was essentially a more successful version of the party it had been in 1918, standing for the same beliefs and appealing to the same social groups. It was opposed by a Conservative Party dominated by the traditional governing class, and appealing to the traditional Conservative principles of patriotism, order, and private enterprise.

The next fifteen years were to see the virtual disappearance of this gulf, as technological and economic change transformed the social basis of British politics and

*Sir Alec Douglas-Home, the rather remote aristocratic leader of the Conservative Party from 1963 to 1965*

forced politicians of both parties to appeal to new groups in a new way. The Conservatives were the first old dogs to learn new tricks. In 1951 they were returned to power in a close election. But Labour warnings that a Conservative government would lead Great Britain back to the bad old days did not come true. Despite their vigorous, free-enterprise rhetoric in opposition, the only nationalized industry which the Conservatives returned to private ownership was steel. They made no attempt to dismantle the welfare state, and went out of their way to keep on good terms with the trade unions.

The same was true of foreign and colonial policy. Since the 19th century, the Conservatives had been pre-eminently the party of empire. Yet the Conservative governments of the 'fifties and early 'sixties proceeded to liquidate the British Empire at least as rapidly as the post-war Labour government had done. Similarly, Conservative Prime Ministers were at least as anxious as Attlee had been to exercise a moderating influence in the Cold War, and to act as honest brokers between East and West.

### 'You've never had it so good'

Above all, the Conservatives maintained full employment. The techniques of economic management which had been worked out by J.M.Keynes before the war, and which had been applied in practice by the war-time coalition and the post-war Labour government, remained in use under successive Conservative chancellors—as they did throughout the Western world. In Great Britain, as in the United States and Western Europe, post-war capitalism was a triumphant success. So far from returning to the dole queues of the 'twenties and 'thirties, the working class enjoyed a dramatic rise in personal living-standards.

All this produced a crisis on the Left. Labour's commitment to public ownership had rested on two main pillars: the belief that capitalism and the profit motive were immoral, and the belief that it was impossible to regulate the economy, and prevent recurrent booms and slumps, while

the means of production were privately owned. It was the second of these two beliefs which gave the Labour Party its political cutting edge in 1945; and in the light of the experience of the 'fifties it became increasingly untenable. For although the 1945 Labour goverment had greatly extended the frontiers of public ownership, large areas of the economy still remained in private hands. Yet this did not prevent even Conservative governments from controlling the economy with a precision and completeness undreamed of before the war.

Rising working-class living standards also undermined Labour's claim to be the sole guardian of working-class interests. Working-class voters still saw the Labour Party as 'their' party, and still believed that it would defend their interests more energetically than the Conservatives. But their reasons for believing this underwent a subtle change. At the beginning of the period, working-class Labour voters tended to see politics as the expression of a class war in which the working class could only gain at the expense of the middle class, and vice-versa. This belief grew more and more difficult to sustain in the face of growing prosperity, and although a majority of the working class continued to vote Labour, its attachment to the Labour Party grew less and less intense.

Meanwhile, technological and economic change gradually eroded Labour's old working-class base. Its greatest strength had always lain in the traditional heavy industries—coal, steel, shipbuilding, the railways, the docks—where the workers were most strongly unionized. But these industries were steadily shrinking, and in the new industries which replaced them the trade unions were weaker and the workers less likely to identify themselves automatically with the Labour Party.

These social changes were reflected in a shrinking Labour vote. The Labour Party lost ground at every general election in the 1950's; in 1959 the Conservatives achieved the unprecedented feat of increasing their parliamentary majority for the third time in succession. Commentators began to speculate about the possibility of permanent Conservative rule, and it was seriously suggested that since modern governments could always manipulate the economy to produce a boom in time for the next election, Great Britain had become in practice a one-party state.

### A faltering economy

These predictions proved wide of the mark. The prosperity of the 1950's was based on insecure foundations. Great Britain's share of world trade was steadily shrinking, and her balance of payments position became increasingly unhealthy. The government reacted to successive balance of payments crises by deflationary measures, which hit investment and still further weakened the industrial structure. Meanwhile, rising living standards produced rising social aspirations. New car owners demanded new roads to drive on; a more prosperous working class demanded

better education for its children. By the early 'sixties, the complacent atmosphere of the 'fifties had given way to a mood of national anxiety, as the British looked across the Channel and saw their European neighbours overtaking them.

Meanwhile, the Labour Party had reluctantly begun to modify its old appeal. Hugh Gaitskell, who had been elected as party leader when Attlee retired in 1956, tried to persuade his followers to abandon their formal commitment to public ownership. He failed, and for a while it looked as though the party might be torn apart in an internecine battle between Left and Right. But although the party made no formal repudiation of public ownership, it adopted a programme in which public ownership played only a minor part. In 1963 Gaitskell died suddenly after a short illness. His successor, Harold Wilson, led the party into the 1964 election on a platform of pragmatic social and economic reform, in which its traditional socialist ideology was subordinated to an increasing concern with faster growth and greater efficiency.

Wilson's strategy was triumphantly successful. Labour narrowly won the 1964 election, and in 1966 increased its majority to nearly 100. In both elections, it held its ground in working-class areas, but made its greatest gains among the middle class. It still drew most of its support from the working class, and a majority of the working class still supported it, but it was no longer a class party of the kind it had been in 1950.

Labour's ties with the trade unions had grown weaker too. The party had been founded in 1900 as a result of a vote at the Trades Union Congress. Yet in the 'fifties and early 'sixties, the trade unions still kept their entrée to government, even though their party was in opposition. They still provided the Labour Party with most of its income, and they still controlled a majority of the votes at the party conference. But their influence in its councils had steadily waned. By 1970 the Wilson cabinet contained no former trade union leaders at all.

By the mid-'sixties, then, the gulf between the two main parties in Great Britain seemed narrower than it had been for fifty years. Once again, however, there were surprises in store—only this time they came from the Right rather than from the Left. The characteristic economic approach of the Wilson government was indicative economic planning on the French model (which involved negotiations with the various interest groups rather than state dictation), and deliberate government interference with the movement of prices and incomes. Both had been foreshadowed under the Conservatives between 1960 and 1964. After 1966, however, the Conservatives rapidly turned their backs on the policies they had followed when in power. In 1965 Sir Alec Douglas-Home, who had become leader of the Conservative Party when Harold Macmillan resigned in 1963, was himself bullied into resigning. His successor was Edward Heath—a grammar school boy from Broadstairs, totally lacking

*The young, down-to-earth Harold Wilson*

in patrician airs and graces, and with no affiliations with the traditional governing class. And, for a while, it looked as though Heath and his supporters would give the Conservative Party a more coherent—and a much more distinctively Conservative—ideology than it had had since 1945.

Economic planning was denounced, not on the grounds that the Labour Government's plans did not succeed, but on the grounds that planning was, by its very nature, bound to fail. Discriminatory state aid to industry was opposed, not on the grounds that the Government discriminated in favour of the wrong firms or the wrong industries, but on the grounds that state interference with the market was bound to be wasteful and inefficient. Sweeping cuts were advocated in public expenditure, not only on the grounds that taxpayers in the higher income groups would be better off as a result (though that argument undoubtedly lurked in the background), but on the grounds that high levels of state spending were *ipso facto* incompatible with a high rate of economic growth. Above all, the Government's attempts to control the rate of wage and salary increases were attacked, not on the grounds that ministers had chosen the wrong 'norm' or tried to enforce its policies in the wrong way, but on the grounds that the whole experiment was unnecessary and misconceived. The Labour

*Mrs Margaret Thatcher, the first woman leader of a major political party in Europe*

Party was presented as the party of high taxation and bureaucratic interference: the Conservatives as the party of free choice and the market mechanism.

Alas for the simplicities of opposition! In June 1970, much to the discomfiture of the opinion pollsters, who had, virtually without exception, predicted a Labour victory, the Conservatives won the general election and Edward Heath found himself in Downing Street. For a while, he and his colleagues made a heroic effort to put their pre-election slogans into practice. Public spending and direct taxation were both cut, though not by much. The Labour Government's Industrial Reorganization Corporation, which had channelled state aid to firms in need of assistance, was summarily abolished. So was the Prices and Incomes Board, which had policed the Government's successive incomes policies.

However, the new Government's ideological zeal soon faltered. Early in 1972, the mining industry was convulsed by a great strike, which ended in a massive pay award to the miners. The rate of wage inflation speeded up, as workers in other industries pressed for comparable increases. The Government's attempts to reach agreement with the unions on a voluntary wages policy broke down, and by the autumn of 1972 ministers found themselves, to their visible astonishment, travelling the same road which their predecessors had travelled six years before. A Counter-Inflation Act was passed, establishing more comprehensive controls over wages and prices than Britain had ever had before, and for the rest of the Government's term of office wage levels and profit margins were determined, not by the laws of the market, but by the *fiat* of Whitehall.

Meanwhile, the Labour opposition had swung to the left in much the same way that the Conservatives had swung to the right between 1966 and 1970. In office, Harold Wilson and his colleagues had tried unsuccessfully to take Britain into the European Economic Community (Common Market). In opposition, however, opinion in the party moved more and more strongly against entry; and by the summer of 1971, when the Conservatives finally succeeded in negotiating terms for British membership which most

*James Callaghan, elected leader of the Labour Party, 5th April 1976*

dispassionate observers considered to be at least as good as any which a Labour Government could have obtained, the 'pro-marketeers' in the Labour Party were unmistakeably in a minority. In October, the party conference voted overwhelmingly against entry on the Government's terms; and when the House of Commons voted at the end of the month, the parliamentary Labour Party imposed a three-line whip against the Government's motion approving the terms agreed upon during the summer.

Sixty-nine Labour MPs, however—led by the deputy leader and former chancellor of the exchequer, Roy Jenkins—defied the party whip and voted in the Government lobby. Another twenty abstained. The result was that the Government motion was carried, and that the right-centre coalition, which had dominated the Labour Party since the early 1950's was torn in two. Partly because of this, and partly because the left had gained ground in a number of big trade unions in the middle and late 1960's, the party turned away from the pragmatic, revisionist line it had followed in office. Wage controls were denounced, though on grounds of class solidarity rather than of free-market economics. Sweeping measures of nationalization were promised. In a phrase more reminiscent of continental Marxism than of British reformism, the Labour Party was declared to stand for a 'fundamental and irreversible' transfer of wealth and power to the workers.

Once again, however, opposition rhetoric proved a poor guide to ministerial action. Early in 1974, the Heath Government found itself embroiled in another potentially crippling dispute with the miner's union, this time over the application of its counter-inflation legislation. Partly because of its own ham-fistedness, and partly because of the miners' intransigence, attempts to reach an accommodation with the union failed; and in February 1974 the Conservatives held a general election on the cry: 'Who governs?'. Neither party won a majority in the House of Commons, but—to its obvious astonishment—Labour came ahead of the Conservatives, and at the beginning of March Harold Wilson returned to Downing Street at the head of a minority Government. Seven months later, he called a second general election; and in October 1974, Labour won a tiny majority over all other parties combined.

In June 1975, a referendum was held on British membership of the Common Market. The Labour Government recommended continued membership, on terms indistinguishable from those obtained by the Conservatives, and the electorate voted by more than two-to-one to accept the Government's recommendation. A month later, the Government introduced a new form of statutory wages policy. The wheel had come full circle, not once but twice. Again the heady ideologies of the past had proved irrelevant to the practical problems of governing a complex, modern industrial society.

On the morning of 16th March 1976, Harold Wilson shook the country by announcing that he would resign as Labour Party leader as soon as a new leader had been elected and, on 5th April, James Callaghan became the new Prime Minister.

# Eastern Europe: Hopes and Realities

The Hungarian Revolution of 1956, and its tragic outcome, brought together in a concentrated form all the main themes of the history of Soviet Eastern Europe. The mounting demands of the Hungarian people for a higher standard of living, for a less rigidly-centralized economic system, and for a greater degree of independence from the Soviet Union, expressed in an extreme form the feelings shared by most of the satellite peoples. Again, the savage response of the Soviet Union – the invasion by armoured might in which about 20,000 Hungarians were killed – showed with horrifying clarity the limits of Soviet toleration of the new demands.

Eastern Europe took care to heed the lesson of these limits for a decade. But even the restrained moves of the Czechs in early 1968, when they took the greatest care to avoid the mistakes made by the Hungarians twelve years earlier, turned out to be more than the Russian rulers would stand for.

There were several reasons for the broad spread and the deep bitterness of anti-Communist and anti-Soviet feeling in Hungary in the 1950's. In the first place the Hungarians, not being a Slav people, lacked the historic ties with Russia which had under certain circumstances made a pro-Russian alignment relatively acceptable in Czechoslovakia, Bulgaria, and even Poland. Again, the recent political tradition in Hungary had been strongly anti-Communist: the short-lived Hungarian Communist government of 1919, which was led by Béla Kun, had provoked a violently reactionary response from the Hungarian right wing, and the resulting right-wing government had gone so far as to lead the country into war at Hitler's side against the Soviet Union. This in turn meant that Hungary was treated by the invading Red Army as an occupied Nazi satellite, which naturally kept alive the anti-Communist sympathies of much of the population.

Almost sufficient as an explanation for anti-Communism in itself, however, was the nature of the Stalinist regime which was built in Hungary by Mátyás Rákosi, the veteran Communist who became first secretary of the Hungarian Communist Party in 1945 and also Prime Minister in 1952. Rákosi, a hardliner of the most

*Far left: Hungarians burn portraits of Rákosi outside the secret police building in Budapest, a day before Soviet tanks moved in. Left: Walter Ulbricht, Head of State of the Communist regime of East Germany until his death in 1973*

ADN/Zentralbild

cynical sort, returned from the Soviet Union after the war and imposed on his country a Stalinist tyranny in which no criticism or opposition was permitted to exist. At the end of the 1940's a wave of purges removed many of his leading opponents, notably László Rajk who was executed after a phoney trial, and in fact of the ninety-two members of the Hungarian Workers' Party's Central Committee elected at the party congresses of 1948 and 1951, no less than forty-six – exactly half – had been removed by 1954.

Rákosi's two principal lieutenants, Ernö Gerö and Mihály Farkas, made themselves just as hated as their leader: and the dreaded Communist secret police, known by its initials AVH, had a large number of prisons and concentration camps into which opponents of the regime disappeared. It is estimated that during the Rákosi period about 150,000, or perhaps even 200,000, people were arrested, of whom about 2,000 were executed – mainly without trial – while many more died after torture and ill-treatment in prison.

As well as the atmosphere of terror and persecution in which they lived, the Hungarians were becoming increasingly dissatisfied with their material conditions. Life for the ordinary Hungarian before the war had not been luxurious, but the standard of living had been above the average for Eastern Europe: now, an increasing gap developed between the standard of living of the privileged party bosses and AVH men on the one hand, and on the other the mass of the people who found that their index of real wages fell by more than five per cent between 1949 and 1955.

In these conditions of latent revolt against the Rákosi dictatorship, it is not surprising that a change had to be made during the months of general disturbance in the Communist world which followed the death of Stalin in March 1953. In July of that year, Rákosi was summarily removed from the prime ministership by the Russians, who replaced him by one of his few surviving critics, Imre Nagy. Nagy, a much more liberal figure, held views similar to those of the new Soviet Prime Minister Malenkov on the need for greater priority to be given to consumer goods as against heavy industry, and he tried to introduce this more flexible economic policy in Hungary. He was, however, seriously handicapped by the fact that Rákosi still retained his post as first secretary of the party, and by 1955 Nagy was condemned as a 'rightist deviationist', expelled from the prime ministership, also from his party offices, and even from the party itself.

Rákosi appeared to have triumphed, but Nagy's moment was to come in 1956: in the climate of agitation and self-criticism that followed Khrushchev's denunciation of Stalin and the Twentieth Soviet Communist Party Congress in 1956. Hungarian workers and intellectuals became more outspoken in their demands. While the workers pressed for better material conditions and the right to a greater say in the management of their factories through workers' councils, the writers and artists of Budapest began to hold increasingly subversive meetings in the newly-founded Petöfi Circle, named after a Hungarian hero of the revolution of 1848. Faced with mounting criticism of the ultra-Stalinist Rákosi, the Russians did not hesitate to ditch him in July 1956 (Mikoyan made a special visit to Budapest for the purpose), and to replace him as party secretary by his former loyal assistant Gerö. Gerö attempted to hold back the rising tide of Hungarian demands for a higher standard of living, more freedom of speech, and greater contacts with the West, but it soon engulfed him. In October, after a long campaign, the Hungarian Workers' Party accepted the rehabilitation of the 'traitor' Rajk, executed in 1949: his reburial with full public honours was the occasion of a general demonstration against Stalinism.

This was followed on 21st October by the news of Gomułka's return to power in Poland, and this event appeared to symbolize a general return to liberalism. The Hungarian protestors adopted this as their slogan, and Imre Nagy as their hero; he was reinstated as a member of the party, and after widespread rioting against the Gerö government by students and workers, he became Prime Minister on 24th October.

Nagy's return to power was the signal for an enthusiastic release of emotions – as well as for the release of thousands of the political prisoners of the previous regime. The radio and press began to give fuller and more honest reports of home and foreign news; there was talk of founding new political parties, to break the monopoly of the one-party Communist system; and Hungarians in large numbers were permitted to travel abroad.

It is a matter for debate whether the Russians would have felt it necessary to intervene if Nagy had been able to limit the reform movement to domestic economic and libertarian changes, and had suppressed talk of a new alignment in foreign policy. (The evidence of what happened to Czechoslovakia in 1968 suggests that the Russians probably would have intervened even if he had done so.) What made Russian intervention virtually certain was the evident desire of the majority of Hungarians to break away from the Soviet-dominated Warsaw Pact and to acquire a neutral international status like that won by Austria the previous year.

After several complicated manoeuvres in which Russian military forces first withdrew from Budapest, then pretended to negotiate an agreement with representatives of the Nagy government (including the minister of defence General Pál Maléter, whom they in fact treacherously arrested), the Soviet tanks came rumbling back into Budapest on 4th November.

A period of a few delirious days of liberty, symbolized by the smashing of the vast bronze statue of Stalin that had dominated Budapest – a period during which freedom of speech had been possible, and the workers of Hungary had arisen in justified anger and lynched hundreds of the hated AVH men who tried to defend themselves by machine-gunning innocent crowds – came to an end with the shelling of Budapest by the Red Army.

### The Revolution betrayed

The material destruction was enormous – the streets of Budapest still bear the marks – and so were the human losses. As already mentioned, as many as 20,000 are estimated to have been killed, 20,000 were rapidly imprisoned as counter-revolutionaries (the AVH, restored to its previous power, sent its men through the streets accompanied by Soviet troops to round up suspects), and as many as 200,000 Hungarians went into exile.

The fate of Nagy himself was a tragic reminder of how little the Russians could tolerate the sort of revolt he stood for: betrayed by one of his former colleagues, János Kádár, who became the new Prime Minister after returning to Budapest with the tanks of the Red Army, Nagy took refuge in the Yugoslav embassy in Budapest. After the fighting was all over, and the last groups of young Hungarian resisters had been shelled into submission by the Russians, Nagy and some of his colleagues surrendered to the Kádár government which had promised that they would be allowed to go free. They were in fact immediately kidnapped and taken under close arrest to Rumania, where almost two years later – in June 1958 – Nagy was executed after a secret trial, along with several other Hungarian leaders including General Pál Maléter.

In a brave speech after being sentenced to death – a speech which was only published ten years later – Nagy predicted 'I know that there will one day be another Nagy trial, which will rehabilitate me' – but the day of his rehabilitation in the eyes of the Hungarian rulers has still not come.

After the brutal suppression of the Hungarian Revolution, and the accompanying implication that the leaders of revolt in Poland had only narrowly escaped a similar fate, Eastern Europe was quiet – at least on the surface. The popular demands for economic decentralization and for more attention to the wishes of the consumer, which had been powerful ingredients of discontent both in Poland and in Hungary, continued, though in a lower key: the new governments, both in Poland and in Hungary and elsewhere throughout the Soviet world, wisely took account of these pressures and bought off popular discontent by making consumer goods more readily available. It was only in the later 1960's that the ideas of economic decentralization and of re-emphasizing the profit motive both in the management of individual factories and in the decisions to be made by each socialist country about its foreign trade, again reached explosive proportions – this time in the case of Czechoslovakia – which helped to provoke a new Soviet intervention. In the meantime the economists whose ideas would later prove so subversive – men like the Czechoslovak Ota Sik and the the Russian Liberman – were unknown to the public at large, and the standard economic policy continued to be only a slightly modified version of Communist orthodoxy.

In foreign policy again, there were few open stirrings among the Soviet satellites. It is true that the new Gomułka government of Poland put forward – through the mouth of its foreign minister Adam Rapacki – a series of proposals that both blocs in the Cold War should remove nuclear weapons from the advanced zones in which they confronted one another: this would have meant the West removing nuclear weapons from West Germany, and the Russians removing them from East Germany, Poland, Hungary, and Czechoslovakia. Despite a general atmosphere of *détente* in the Cold War, these proposals were never taken seriously by the West – partly because they implied the virtual neutralization of West Germany, regarded as too high and too risky a price to pay, and partly because Khrushchev's pressure on Berlin from 1958 onwards created suspicion of Russian motives.

Poland, in any case, had very little freedom of action in her foreign policy, because of her constant need for Soviet support against any revival of German strength. The part of Eastern Europe where states gradually developed more independence was in fact the Balkans, where the pressure of powerful neighbours was not so great. Yugoslavia under Tito continued her independent course, both in pursuing a broadly non-aligned foreign policy between the Cold War blocs and in insisting on her right to develop her domestic economic pattern – agricultural reform and workers' control of industry – in her own way. Khrushchev continued in the path of conciliating Tito which he had begun to tread in 1955, and it was this conciliation of one deviant which led – paradoxically – to the stirring up of another form of deviation within the Soviet bloc, this time of a quite different character. The liberal, revisionist deviation of Yugoslavia was now followed by the neo-Stalinist deviation of Albania.

Albania, the smallest and most isolated of the Communist satellites, squeezed between Yugoslavia and the Adriatic Sea, had always been in fear of Yugoslav domination or even, so she alleged, of Yugoslav designs for a takeover. By 1960, Khrushchev's *rapprochement* with Tito had gone so far that the Stalinist dictator of Albania, Enver Hoxha, seriously feared for his position: he claimed it was because Russian support of Tito would embolden the latter to invade Albania, but the more immediate threat was that Tito's more liberal brand of Communism in Yugoslavia might be imitated by Hoxha's enemies at home.

Albania, deeply alarmed by Khrushchev's actions in denouncing Stalin at home and supporting Tito abroad, looked around for support against Russia. There was of course no hope of support from the capitalist West, but within the Communist bloc Albania found one possible protector —China. The huge and complicated story of the transformation of Sino-Soviet partnership into a deadly rivalry, between the mid-1950's and the mid-1960's, would take us right away from the history of Soviet Eastern Europe: but it is worth recalling that one of its contributory causes was the purely Balkan tension between Yugoslavia and Albania, and that for several years the leaders in Moscow and Peking uttered their maledictions and condemnations of one another in terms of criticism of Albania and Yugoslavia respectively. When Khrushchev condemned Albania, he meant China: when Mao Tse-tung denounced the revisionism of Yugoslavia he had Russia in mind.

By the early 1960's, the split between the two major Communist powers had come out into the open: at a series of meetings of the member parties of the world Com-

munist movement. Moscow and Peking laid out their accusations against one another in full. The Chinese accused the Russians of revisionism, of giving up such basic principles of Marxism-Leninism as the inevitability of war with the capitalist world, and of neglecting the revolutionary potential of underdeveloped and exploited parts of the world, such as Algeria and Cuba; the Russians retaliated by accusing the Chinese of dogmatic adherence to outworn concepts, of readiness to plunge the world into nuclear war in the name of world revolution, and of underestimating the chances of spreading world Communism by exploiting the obvious splits in the capitalist world, such as the split between Paris and Washington.

The effect of these resounding arguments in the satellites of Eastern Europe was considerable. On the whole the satellite governments supported Russia (and Yugoslavia) against the Chinese (and Albanian) attacks; but it was obvious to all of them that the Russians were now on the defensive against Chinese attacks, and that they

could expect to be rewarded for supporting Moscow—the reward would be greater independence. Gradually, and for some time mainly in economic and trade matters, the states of Eastern Europe began to reassert their right to run their affairs in their own way. China, by her policy of supporting Albania had in fact contributed to supporting the kind of general move towards national independence in the Communist world which she had begun by condemning.

The Soviet satellites were in no position to attempt an open revolt in the diplomatic or military sphere—to try to pursue a neutralist foreign policy, or to organize their defence policies outside the framework of the Warsaw Pact. The area in which greater independence was possible was that of economics, where the Russians still attempted to impose conformity to

*Novotny (left) and Gomuɫka, the Czech and Polish leaders. Novotny fell from power in 1968 amid demands for liberalization; Gomuɫka was ousted in 1970*

their own wishes through the Comecon. This organization, officially entitled the Council for Mutual Economic Assistance, was in fact a device by which the Soviet rulers imposed a unified plan for the economic development of the whole Soviet bloc on a group of states who wished increasingly to plan their own economies.

Whereas it might be reasonable on grounds of overall economic rationality for the countries of the Soviet bloc to specialize – for Czechoslovakia, for instance, to push ahead with her already advanced industrial development, while Rumania remained a source of raw materials and agricultural produce – the prospect clearly had little appeal to the Rumanians. Again, the Czechs themselves began to question whether, for instance, it was really in their best interests for their steel industry to process low grade and expensively transported ore from Siberia, instead of higher grade ore from Sweden.

It was the Rumanians who took the lead in challenging the Soviet form of economic integration – a challenge which soon developed political overtones. The Rumanian Communist Party embarked in the late 1950's on a series of economic plans designed to overcome the economic backwardness of their country. These national plans were criticized by the Russians at an increasingly bitter series of meetings of the Comecon in the early 1960's, cul-

minating in a formal condemnation in February 1963. The Rumanian leaders in return asserted their right to develop their economy in their own national interests, and argued that the Comecon should restrict its activities to arranging bilateral or multilateral co-ordination between the national economic plans of member countries, rather than trying to impose an overall pattern of integration.

This declaration of economic independence by the Rumanian government won for it considerable support among the Rumanian people—the notions of national pride and independence, ingrained through long centuries of European history, had triumphed over the Russian principle of the 'international socialist division of labour'.

Rumania now began to evolve an increasingly neutralist foreign policy, by which – while remaining a member of the Warsaw Pact – she developed increasingly friendly relations with a number of Western countries. She gradually achieved the remarkable situation of being able to make agreements on economic and commercial matters with France, West Germany, and Great Britain, at the same time as with Yugoslavia, and even with the Chinese who, though flatly disagreeing with much of what the Rumanians said, recognized their nuisance-value in the struggle against the Russians.

The tendency described by the veteran Italian Communist Togliatti as 'polycentrism' appeared to be steadily gaining the upper hand by the time Khrushchev fell from power at the end of 1964. The open revolts of Poland and Hungary had been overcome, but the successful claims to independence by dogmatist Albania and neutralist Rumania could not be withstood, and the whole Communist world appeared to be in a state of disarray. The Communist states of Eastern Europe were increasingly following the Rumanian example not just in doing more of their economic planning in national terms, but also in flexing their muscles for a more independent foreign policy. They were also insisting, more strongly than they could conceivably have done under Stalin, on rediscovering and developing their own national cultural traditions, on publishing the facts about their own national historical development, and on rehabilitating the victims of the Stalinist purges. In economics, diplomacy, literature, history,

and politics, the nationalisms of Eastern Europe were reasserting themselves.

The limits of reassertion, however, remained fairly clear: anything amounting to the sort of challenge to Russia which the Hungarians had issued in 1956 – a demand to leave the Warsaw Pact and adopt a fully neutralist position – was ruled out. This was fairly clear by the later 1960's both to the leaders of the Western world who were trying to open up new relations with the states of Eastern Europe (this is particularly true of the West German coalition government whose new Eastern policy developed during 1967 and early 1968) and to the leaders of Eastern Europe themselves. Even the most enterprising and adventurous of these Eastern European nations, the Czechoslovaks under Alexander Dubček and his colleagues, took the utmost care to refrain from provoking the Soviet Union. Although their economic policy borrowed from the West such concepts as profitability, and came to depend increasingly on trade relations with Western countries, they made it quite clear that they had no intention of deserting the Warsaw Pact for neutralism. Again, although the abandonment of censorship brought freedom of expression in Czechoslovakia during the spring and early summer of 1968, open criticism of Russia's policies did not occur until after the Soviet leaders' attack on Czechoslovak policies.

Nonetheless, the Russians took fright: in August 1968 the Red Army marched into Prague, this time accompanied by the satellite armies of Hungary, Bulgaria, and East Germany, and the city appeared likely to suffer the same fate as Budapest twelve years before. This time, however, there was no armed resistance, and the experiment of the Czechs with freedom was ended practically without bloodshed.

The Russian invasion of Czechoslovakia in 1968 appeared to set back for several years the prospects of more freedom, economic and political, for Eastern Europe. It certainly showed that this freedom was not to be won by nations striving independently and impetuously for more than the Russians would grant. Peaceful co-existence, it now appears, must be based on the co-existence of the two blocs, rather than their early dissolution. This means that the first step in the process must be for the two super-powers to overcome their mistrust of each other and come together in a series of negotiations about the limitation of strategic weapons, and the procedures for preventing the Middle East and other non-European trouble spots from erupting into world war. Only when the understanding between the super-powers has reached a certain level of intensity will closer co-operation between the European states be able to progress very far: at that stage there will certainly be a prospect of greater economic transactions between the two halves of Europe, as well as probably a security system which will supersede NATO and the Warsaw Pact.

This prospect of gradual change may not be an exciting one for the Eastern Europeans: but it is the best they have.

*Left: Kádár of Hungary. Betrayer of the 1956 revolution he took over from Nagy when the Red Army rolled in. Opposite: Above left: Enver Hoxha, Stalinist dictator of Albania, in 1962. He broke with the Soviets in 1961. Centre: Alexander Dubček, First Secretary of the New Communist Party in Czechoslovakia, until the Russian invasion in August 1968. Top right: Antonin Novotny, the Czech dictator whose power rested on his command of the Communist Party apparatus. Above right: Gustav Husàk, Dubček's successor, presided over the dismantling of the reform. Below: Prague, 20th January 1969. A procession in honour of Jan Palach who burned himself to death in protest against the Soviet-led invasion of Czechoslovakia*

Keystone Press

Paul Popper

Camera Press

Camera Press

# South-East Asia in Turmoil

The term South-East Asia is a recent one, dating only from the Second World War, and is today used to refer to those countries lying in the area between the Indian subcontinent and China. But its use suggests a homogeneity which does not exist, for some of the countries are island states and some mainland, they share no common culture, language, or religion, and are inhabited by ethnically different peoples. Their populations range from Laos's 2,700,000 to Indonesia's 129 million. Yet common factors do exist, and the countries of South-East Asia have undergone remarkably similar historical experiences. In the early decades of this century all of them, with the single exception of Thailand, were ruled by Western colonial powers, and all have today achieved national independence. The departure of the colonial regimes, earnestly desired over a long period by the subject peoples, has left in its wake a host of problems and difficulties which few of these newly independent countries had fully anticipated. During the colonial period, for example, external security had caused them no concern since it was assured by the colonial powers, whose presence in the region produced a high degree of political stability. The tasks of government, administration, and ensuring the harmonious coexistence of different ethnic groups in the several multi-racial societies which exist there were all carried out by the colonial governments. The local economies were, to a greater or lesser extent, geared to those of the ruling countries, which provided the necessary capital and expertise for economic development, purchased exports, and supplied manufactured goods. These responsibilities have now devolved on the independent governments of South-East Asia.

The ending of colonial rule was unquestionably the most important factor bearing on the subsequent course of events in South-East Asia because the circumstances in which this was achieved, and the persons who achieved it, determined to a very high degree the attitudes, policies, and conduct of affairs in each country. During and after the Second World War two major influences affected the independence movements: Japan, and international Communism. The Japanese occupation

*Federation of Malaysia is proclaimed in Singapore, 16th September 1963. The federation—of Malaya, Singapore, Sabah and Sarawak—was an attempt to find political stability in a troubled area after Great Britain granted independence*

forces fostered, trained, and armed South-East Asian nationalist groups with a view to preventing the return of Western colonial rule to the area. Communism, still dominated at that time by Stalin and the Soviet Union, ordered its adherents in the region to engage in armed conflict against the Japanese and to make ready for later struggle with the colonial powers after Japan had been defeated. Japan created local puppet governments in a number of the countries, and in Burma, Malaya, Laos, and the Philippines anti-Japanese resistance forces were formed in which Communists played a leading part. During the last two years of the war an uneasy alliance of convenience developed between the local Communists and nationalists, and the British and Americans, who clandestinely supplied them with arms. Many of these arms were carefully stored for use, not against the Japanese, but against the Western colonial powers who would subsequently return. Thus the stage was set for the tumultuous happenings of the post-war period.

The Second World War ended on 15th August 1945, and two days later the Indonesians, headed by Sukarno, proclaimed their country's independence. On 2nd September Ho Chi Minh established the Communist-controlled Democratic Republic of Vietnam. Troops of the former colonial powers returned to both these countries to restore their lost authority, but the Philippines received her independence in July 1946 with the blessing of her colonial power, the United States. Burmese nationalists negotiated their country's independence late in 1947 and formally proclaimed it on 4th January 1948. In only one case, Vietnam, did the Communists contrive to dominate the independence movement, but Communism's main effort to seize control of the whole region was not long delayed. Plans completed in the Soviet Union were transmitted to South-East Asian Communist Parties during the World Youth Conference which met at Calcutta during February 1948 and, shortly afterwards, almost simultaneous Communist-directed insurrections began in Burma, the Philippines, Indonesia, and Malaya. Since the first two countries were already independent and the third had proclaimed itself so, the rebellions had little relevance to the local situation. Only in Malaya did the movement have any semblance of reason, but even there it was confined to the Chinese population and failed to attract any support from Malays or Indians. The Communists explained

*427*

their uprisings in ideological terms, arguing that bourgeois nationalist revolutions had to be completed by proletarian revolutions.

Despite Mao Tse-tung's victory in China in 1949, which established a Communist giant on the fringe of South-East Asia, the four Communist insurrections ultimately failed to achieve their objective, though not all for the same reasons. Meanwhile the process of de-colonization went on, with the Netherlands transferring sovereignty to Indonesia in December 1949, and Great Britain to Malaya in 1957 and Singapore in 1959. In French Indo-China developments had followed a different course, for it was there that the Communist Ho Chi Minh had early taken control of the anti-French struggle, in which the establishment of Communist rule in China marked the turning point. Viet Minh soldiers occupied the area adjacent to the Chinese border in 1950, after which China provided military and economic aid and permitted her territory to be used as an inviolable sanctuary which afforded facilities of every kind to the Vietnamese. The movement became overtly Communist and the declared aims of the insurgency were duly modified, which persuaded the United States to conclude that this was not an independence war after all but armed Communist expansionism. American aid began to flow to the French, but to no avail, for they had their heaviest defeat at Dien Bien Phu, coinciding with the opening of an international conference at Geneva in May 1954, convened to seek a peace settlement of the war in Indo-China. The conference whose membership included the United States, the Soviet Union, China, Great Britain, and France as well as delegations from Cambodia, Laos, and Vietnamese Communists and nationalists, reached agreements which ended the fighting and divided Vietnam at the 17th parallel, entrusting all territory to the north of that to the Communists and the rest to the nationalists. Cambodia remained intact but two northern provinces of Laos were ceded temporarily to the Communist Pathet Lao.

Alarmed at this Communist accretion of territory in South-East Asia, the American secretary of state, Dulles, worked to create a defensive alliance which would contain Communism within its existing frontiers and serve to defend the rest of the region. The result was the South-East Asia Treaty Organization (SEATO), which lost much of its intended force when, as a result of bitter criticism from India, it was boycotted by all Asian countries save Pakistan, Thailand,

*Colonial power crumbles—Communism threatens.* **Top:** *A Chinese peasant is questioned in hunt for Communists, Malaya, 1949. Communist-directed insurrections occurred generally in South-East Asia, but only in Vietnam did Communists dominate the independence movement.* **Centre:** *The French pull out— a farewell parade, Saigon, 14th April 1956.* **Bottom:** *President Diem of South Vietnam (second from right) and his family. Political chaos followed his assassination in 1963*

and the Philippines. The non-Asian members were the United States, Great Britain, France, Australia, and New Zealand. Because SEATO military intervention could be undertaken only by agreement of all its members, the growth of Sino-Pakistan friendship and Gaullist France's antipathy towards the United States and Great Britain made such unanimity impossible to achieve, and the organization became militarily impotent.

Having passed through a phase of militancy, which witnessed the Korean War and the capture of Tibet, China moved into one of reasonableness, which produced marked effects on South-East Asia. By beguiling Pandit Nehru into a mood of childlike trust—the extent of his gullibility was revealed only by later events—she undermined SEATO's effectiveness from its inception, and then went on to organize the Afro-Asian Conference at Bandung, Indonesia, in April 1955. There Chou En-lai disarmed the suspicions of many South-East Asian leaders in two brilliant speeches and created an atmosphere far more cordial and accommodating towards China than had existed in the past. Conversely, South-East Asian attitudes towards the United States, which China has consistently regarded as her principal enemy, became noticeably more guarded.

For a time South-East Asia enjoyed a period of relative peace. By 1955 the French Indo-China War had ended and the former member states had settled down to confront the initial problems of independence within the frontiers laid down by the Geneva conference. The Communist rebels in the Philippines had been defeated and Malaya was unmistakably mastering the rebellion there. Burma was still troubled by Communist guerrillas, who showed every sign of continuing their subversion indefinitely, but was learning to live with them and to conduct the normal business of the country in spite of them. August 1957 saw the granting of independence to Malaya, the last of the major South-East Asian states to receive it.

But the potential dangers to South-East Asian security and stability remained legion. China, the world's most populous nation, now united under a single government, was modernizing herself with Soviet aid and guidance. Not only did she subscribe to the notion of 'spheres of influence'—plainly she feels that South-East Asia lies within hers—but she was energetically exporting and sustaining Communist revolution abroad. Large Chinese communities in the countries of South-East Asia constituted an excellent vehicle for

*Keystone Press*

*Central Press*

*Top: Anti-SEATO demonstration by Indonesian students, 1958. Set up in 1954, SEATO was intended to check the spread of Communism; in fact internal disagreements made it militarily impotent. Centre: Jubilant supporters carry Lee Kuan Yew after the 1959 elections which made him Prime Minister of Singapore. Bottom: British troops with captured rebels in Brunei, December 1962. The revolt was soon put down, but the rebels got their way —Brunei did not join Malaysia*

*Central Press*

that purpose. North Vietnam, temporarily quiescent, made no secret of her determination to annex the South, and Communist Party documents, captured during the French Indo-Chinese War, revealed her intention of taking over Laos and Cambodia too when circumstances permitted. With her powerful army, by far the strongest in mainland South-East Asia, she posed a considerable threat to future peace. Indonesia's President Sukarno dreamed of reconstituting the former empire of Madjapahit, which implied that he wished to extend his rule over Malaya, New Guinea, and possibly the Philippines as well. In Malaya, where the overseas Chinese population was only slightly less numerous than the Malays themselves, there was an ever present danger of inter-racial conflict.

Laos and Vietnam were the places in which these potential dangers first materialized and shattered the short-lived calm. Directed, trained, armed, and reinforced by Communist North Vietnam, the Pathet Lao refused integration with the central government and embarked on a protracted guerrilla war during 1959. An already complex situation there was further confused in 1960 by the emergence of a third faction, the neutralists, led by Kong Le, and hostilities continued until another international conference was convened at Geneva in 1961. This dragged on for fourteen months and the agreements it concluded in July 1962 were never carried out. The United States, which had earlier aided the central Laotian government, withdrew its uniformed forces as demanded by the agreements, but North Vietnam did not. Instead she increased her military and political intervention and secured control of the eastern region running alongside her own frontier and that of South Vietnam. This was to serve as a supply corridor through which men and supplies were moved from North to South Vietnam and was given the nickname 'The Ho Chi Minh Trail'.

1959 was also the year the war commenced in South Vietnam. When that country was divided in 1954, the South Vietnamese segment of the Communist Party cached its arms and the members returned to their towns and villages. Party organization went underground and 80,000 guerrillas, all South Vietnamese and none of them Communists, went to North Vietnam for further training. With arms and a Communist Party concealed inside South Vietnam, and seasoned South Vietnamese guerrillas who might be re-infiltrated, North Vietnam could commence military operations in the South whenever she wished. Nor would North Vietnam be directly involved, for all the personnel fighting there would be Southerners. Hostilities began slowly but steadily gathered momentum, using the techniques of people's revolutionary warfare. South Vietnam's army, trained and equipped for conventional warfare, floundered ineffectually against such elusive adversaries and the government lost popularity both for its lack of success against the enemy and for the irksome restrictions imposed on the people by new security regulations. Following popular demonstrations in 1963 the government was overthrown by a military coup, but President Ngo Dinh Diem's successors fared even worse. By restoring total freedom in war-time, they opened wide the defences to the enemy, who seized the opportunity and occupied large areas of the country.

The ensuing political chaos was finally ended by a committee of senior generals, but military collapse could not be staved off without massive external aid. The United States, which had throughout provided South Vietnam with economic and military assistance, faced the choice of committing American soldiers to the fighting or withdrawing quickly before the collapse came. President Johnson chose the former course early in 1965 and sent in a force which was ultimately to exceed half a million

*The Duke of Gloucester hands the scroll of independence to Malaya's new head of state, Tunku Abdul Rahman, Kuala Lumpur, August 1957*

Keystone Press

men. To impede North Vietnamese reinforcement of the insurgents, systematic bombing of North Vietnam's communications and military installations began at the same time. Australia, South Korea, New Zealand, and Thailand also contributed smaller forces. To counter the military build-up, North Vietnam committed large numbers of her own army units and the scale of the conflict increased. The Communists were driven back in the field but their international political struggle, showing the United States as an aggressor, a bully, and guilty of every atrocity, achieved total success. In every part of the world anti-war protest movements denounced America ceaselessly, while the American people developed a guilt complex and grew increasingly impatient of its government's failure to win a rapid victory. A massive Communist assault in February 1968, known as the Tet Offensive, proved a military disaster, but the world-wide publicity it achieved forced President Johnson to halt the bombing of North Vietnam, to open peace talks with the Communists in Paris, and to announce his own retirement from politics. Later that year, during his presidential election campaign, Richard Nixon stated that any president who could not end the Vietnam conflict in his first term did not deserve re-election, thereby serving notice that the United States would win or quit the Vietnam war before 1973.

Meanwhile events no less important for South-East Asia's future were taking place elsewhere. Profound differences between the Communist leaderships of the Soviet Union and China broke into the open about 1960 and grew increasingly embittered, passing through successive stages of withdrawal of Soviet aid to China, mutual recrimination, and, later, border clashes. Malaya's leaders, anxious to amalgamate Singapore with their country but fearful of the effects upon the racial balance of the accretion of so many Chinese, hit on the solution of incorporating as well the three territories of British Borneo, Sabah, Brunei, and Sarawak, into a single state. In the event, Brunei's ruler declined, but the remainder fused to become the new state of Malaysia in September 1963. Indonesia's President Sukarno, who raised no objection when the idea was first proposed in 1961, attacked it furiously early in 1963. Failing to prevent the state's formation, he assailed it with military force in a campaign which became widely known as 'confrontation', employing subversion and guerrilla warfare against the Borneo territories, attacking Malaysian shipping, and landing saboteurs in Malaya and Singapore.

President Sukarno's growing reliance upon the Indonesian Communist Party (PKI) became a matter of concern to the army and the people. Matters came to a head on 30th September 1965 when the PKI attempted to seize power. Its attempted assassination of the senior army generals was only partly successful and provoked an army massacre of the PKI. The Party was decimated and most of its leaders were killed. Step by step General Suharto, who had led the army reaction, reversed Sukarno's earlier policies (Sukarno's popularity precluded his immediate dismissal from office)—confrontation was finally abandoned in August 1966—until he eventually replaced him as President. Under Suharto's leadership Indonesia concentrated upon overcoming the economic chaos resulting from Sukarno's impractical extravagance and adopted a policy of greater co-operation with her South-East Asian neighbours.

Malaysia continued to encounter difficulties, but none assumed unmanageable proportions. Personality clashes between the Malaysian leader Tunku Abdul Rahman and Singapore's Prime Minister Lee Kuan Yew, as much as any other factor, persuaded the former to force Singapore out of Malaysia, and a dispute arose between Malaysia and the Philippines over the Borneo territory of Sabah, to which both lay claim. Following the 1969 elections, cracks appeared in the political alliance between the Malays and Chinese, and inter-racial disturbances broke out. Though violence was quickly brought under control, the danger of renewed clashes remains very real and could disrupt Malaysian unity in the future.

Cambodia's ruler, Norodom Sihanouk, was overthrown during his absence abroad in March 1970 and the successor government pledged itself to drive the Vietnamese Communists from its land, but military resources were lacking and it appealed for help to the United States and South Vietnam. In May soldiers of the two crossed the Cambodian frontier and destroyed many Communist installations, but the popular outcry around the world forced their premature withdrawal and the Communist forces survived to fight on. Under Chinese and North Vietnamese tutelage, an indigenous armed resistance was formed to fight the new Cambodian government, and the third country of Indochina found itself engaged in war.

Thereafter the United States progressively reduced her commitments in the countries of Indochina, withdrawing troops, cutting military aid, and preparing for the end which would come when President Nixon faced re-election in November 1972. Throughout long secret negotiations with Le Duc Tho of North Vietnam, Dr Kissinger made one concession after another in his quest for American disengagement, eventually demanding only a cosmetic form of settlement which would save American face by concealing the full extent of her military failure. The Watergate scandal and mid-term elections, which returned large anti-war majorities in Congress, further weakened President Nixon's position and made early withdrawal imperative. A Vietnam ceasefire agreement was belatedly signed in Paris at the beginning of 1973, followed immediately by an American military withdrawal, which left South Vietnam at the mercy of Northern Communists. American military aid to both South Vietnam and Cambodia was progressively cut, with the result that, early in 1975, the Communist resistance movements were able to make their final bid for victory. The Cambodian capital, Phnom Penh, fell

*Stamp, 1952, shows Nam-Phuong, wife of Bao Dai, Emperor of Vietnam until 1955*

only days before Saigon was taken, and the two states were brought under Communist rule. In neighbouring Laos, where the position of the Royal Government had been steadily eroded while the strength of the communist Pathet Lao continued to grow under the patronage of North Vietnam, the Communist victory came, not through war but through irresistible political pressure. By the end of the year, Laos, Cambodia, and the whole of Vietnam were communist ruled; the United States had withdrawn her military forces from the whole of South East Asia, and in circumstances that made their return virtually impossible; Britain, Australia and New Zealand had ended their military commitment too, and South-East Asia was without foreign forces for the first time in three centuries. In Thailand, where successive military governments had for many years given the appearance of stability, power had passed to the political parties, whose large number made transient coalitions the only possible form of government.

By 1976 a profound change had taken place in the situation of South-East Asia. The United States, Europe, Australia and New Zealand had effectively withdrawn from the area and were unlikely to return. Japan had established an economic presence there, but lacked military power to sustain this if it should be challenged. Mutually hostile China and Soviet Union watched developments with intense interest from the sidelines, but meanwhile the region was left to its own devices. Foreign military withdrawal had created a power vacuum, yet had left Vietnam with the strongest armed forces Asia had ever seen. Never before had the future of South-East Asia been more uncertain. Individual states sought regional co-operation through such organizations as the Association of South East Asian Nations (ASEAN), while the world awaited imminent change in China's long established leadership and watched to see what use Communist Vietnam would make of her great military strength. This region of the world has reached a crossroads, yet none can tell which of the turnings it will elect—or be forced—to take.

# Sino-Soviet Relations

China and Russia, to use a well-known adage, are two nations separated by one common ideology. Both claim to be the true inheritor and representative of Marxist-Leninist orthodoxy, and each abuses the other for its deviations from true socialism. The general rule that the heretic is always more evil and more dangerous than the non-believer may explain the vehemence of this polemic war. What is more difficult to understand is why the two great Communist powers should have become so opposed to each other by the 1970's. Understanding of the radically differing natures of the Russian and Chinese revolutions helps to clarify the situation. In their separate and distinctive conceptions of the road to socialism lies much of the explanation of the modern development of Sino-Soviet relations.

The urban-based Russian revolution was born out of war, and was followed by a cruel and brutal civil war. The imperatives of that situation demanded the suppression of any dissenting voices within the Party. Subsequently, Stalin was able to strengthen the conception of the monolithic Party both in Russia and abroad, through his control over its machinery. His influence extended abroad on the wave of the prestige of the successful revolution. Because the Russian Communist Party was the first to succeed in revolution it automatically assumed leadership of all Communist revolutionary movements. Communism became totally identified with the Russian experience. Loyalty to a Communist party came to mean loyalty to Stalin. To oppose Stalin was to excommunicate oneself from the body of true Communism—the Third International. The real threat to Stalin's system came not from Khrushchev's secret speech at the Soviet Party's Twentieth Congress, but from the Chinese revolution which reached its successful climax in 1949 after twenty-eight years of struggle.

China was the first country to establish its own revolution without reference to the Russian experience. It was one of the Chinese Communist grievances against the Soviet Union that the latter either hindered the revolution or gave bad advice that was both expensive, and yet difficult to ignore because of the immense authority the Russians wielded on account of their arguable claim to revolutionary leadership.

That Mao Tse-tung had developed an independent and successful revolution, whose emphasis was substantially different from the Stalinist one, was a fundamental stumbling block to good Sino-Soviet relations. In effect, it meant that the Chinese would

*Chinese frontier guards argue with Russian troops (facing) on the frozen Ussuri River, 1969. Border disputes have been one of the clearest indications of the break-down of Sino-Soviet relations*

not remain subservient to the Russians. The Russians were too used to the idea of their own monolithic position to tolerate the concept of an independent and equal socialist state.

Stalin's politics were based on two concepts: the indivisibility of the Communist Party and socialism in one state. Mao began from the opposite direction: a theory of contradictions and a belief in the interdependence of socialist movements. The disparate Russian and Chinese views on foreign policy were built on these bases; the profound discrepancy between them eventually led to an unbridgeable rift.

Mao wrote a famous essay *On Contradictions* in his Yenan cave headquarters in 1937 during a lull in the fighting against the Japanese. Although it was intended as a political orientation lecture to cadets, its principles remain the basis of Chinese interpretation of Marxist dialectic to this day. In brief, it asserts the universality of the law of contradictions. 'Internal contradictions exist in every single thing', Mao wrote, 'hence its motion and development'. A realization of that truth leads to differentiating the primary from secondary contradictions, and finally one can act upon that knowledge. During the war against Japan, for example, the primary contradiction was between Japanese imperialism and Western neo-colonialism in China, and not, as some left-wingers in the Party had indicated, between Chiang Kai-shek's Nationalists and the Communists. Since 1945, the primary contradiction has been seen as that between American imperialism and national liberation movements; and in recent years, the primary contradiction has focussed on the Soviet Union and what the Chinese called the Second (developed countries excluding the super-powers) and Third Worlds. To combat the Japanese, the Communists were willing to join forces with Chiang Kai-shek. To combat the Americans, the Chinese, at various times, have shown a willingness to unite with the secondary, capitalist countries as well as the socialist ones. To combat the Soviet Union, the Chinese have been willing and eager to develop closer relations with the Americans.

In effect, Mao's theory of contradictions allowed for a flexible *tactical* approach to domestic and foreign policy. One could and should, he argued, unite with non-Communists in the struggle against a greater evil. The *strategic* consideration, however, remained unchanged: the defeat of 'imperialism' and the victory of the peoples of the world as represented by the advance of socialism. This policy was embodied in his dictum 'Isolate the main enemy', and demonstrated clearly in his alliance first with the Kuomintang under Chiang Kai-shek to defeat the Japanese, and later his turning against the Kuomintang to establish his own supremacy.

As far as strategy was concerned, the Chinese continually asserted the relevance of Mao's way to other 'liberation' struggles. Only a month after the establishment of the People's Republic of China, Liu Shao-chi addressed a conference of Asian Trade Unions with the reminder that 'the path taken by the Chinese people in defeating imperialism and its lackeys and in founding the People's Republic of China is the path that should be taken by the peoples of many colonial and semi-colonial countries in their fight for national independence and people's democracy.'

Whether ideological fervour or nationalist sentiments of aggrandisement lay behind this claim was irrelevant to the Russians. It clearly appeared to them nothing less than a bare-faced attempt to undermine Russian leadership of the Communist world. The Chinese as yet could not afford to offend their Russian comrades, and such statements were toned down; but they were never forgotten.

Against Stalin's advice the Chinese made their revolution. They achieved their goals, however, within a cold war world that left them isolated and threatened. More than a quarter of a century of fighting had left the country weak and exhausted, and China desperately needed friends in order to allow her to reconstruct. Overtures of peace and friendship to the Americans in 1946 (and earlier) had been brusquely dismissed. They had no choice then but, in Mao's words 'to lean to one side'—towards the Soviet Union. Not that the Soviet Union had proved herself to be the most reliable of allies. In 1945 Stalin had concluded a treaty of alliance with Chiang Kai-shek's Nationalist government. In 1949 the Russian ambassador was the last to withdraw from the Nationalist capital as the victorious Communist forces advanced. At no time had Stalin given wholehearted support to the Communist struggle. On the contrary he urged them to caution and compromise in the face of the Americans and the threat of the atomic bomb. Mao scorned the advice and labelled both the Americans and the bomb 'paper tigers'. Yet he was careful not to offend Russian sensibilities. The Soviet Union was cited as the 'defender of world peace'. In 1948, the Chinese Communist Party loyally endorsed the expulsion of Tito from the Comintern, for they were trying to reassure Stalin that he had nothing to fear from them. Although the Chinese were very much aware of Russian prevarication, they nevertheless respected the Soviet Union's pre-eminent position in the Communist world, in some part because of an awareness that the existence of Soviet Russia had paved the way for the Chinese revolution, but mainly because of the pressure of the plain, hard facts of life. China needed aid badly, and the only source was the Soviet Union. So, in the interests of security and economic development, China had to compromise her revolutionary purity—but then she had always been ready to play, often conflicting, power games in the interests of her long term objectives.

However, she based this compromise, and the resultant bond with the Soviet Union, on one very important principle: the Soviet Union's capability and willingness to defend the socialist revolution. Once the Soviet Union began to show signs of abdicating her role, as she seemed to in the 1950's and 1960's with the so-called detente policy, then the Chinese felt free, not to revert to their brand of socialism—they had always followed their own minds in that direction—but to challenge the Soviet Union for the leadership of the international Communist movement.

## Developments after 1956

Until 1956 Sino-Soviet relations flowed more or less smoothly. In February 1950, after nearly three months of long and arduous negotiations, Stalin and Mao signed a treaty of friendship, alliance and mutual assistance, though Mao certainly did not achieve all that he had wanted. The Russians continued to hold important concessions in Manchuria, including the two important ports of Port Arthur and Darien. Economic aid, in addition to long term credits amounting to US $300 million, contained provisos for the establishment of Joint Stock Companies which gave the Russians control of important industries. The essential point, however, was granted—the promise of mutual assistance in the event of foreign aggression, even if the clause was not worded quite the way the Chinese would have wished. The Chinese would have liked to see the United States named in the treaty as a potential aggressor. The Russians refused. As leaders of the Communist world it was important for them to conclude a treaty with the Chinese, but they would not allow that to endanger their relations with the United States. The threat of nuclear warfare was a daunting one, especially after the devastation wreaked upon Russia during the Second World War. War must be avoided and therein lay the crux of the problem between the Russians and the Chinese. The Chinese felt that the threat of war was much less important than the Russians did—indeed they saw it as inevitable given the contradictions of the world, and hoped that it would be the force to unleash revolution in the world. What mattered to the Chinese was whether the Russians could be relied upon. Events seemed to indicate that they could not.

The first test came a mere four months after the signing of the Sino-Soviet Treaty. In June 1950, North Korean troops advanced across the 38th parallel. Within days United Nations' troops, mainly Americans, were fighting the Communists and pushing them back. As MacArthur advanced towards the Manchurian border the Chinese mobilized. In the autumn they threw themselves into the struggle. Although the Russians supplied arms, they remained aloof, for Stalin was quite happy to see the Americans and Chinese bogged down in Korea. In fact, resolution of the Korean conflict was only achieved after Stalin's death in March 1953.

The Korean War showed the Americans that they must consider the Chinese serious adversaries. It showed the Russians that the Chinese were trustworthy. But it did not allay Chinese misgivings about Soviet policy. Nothing was conclusively proved one way or the other but there were signs of Russia's dangerous penchant for maintaining the *status quo*.

Stalin's death marked the end of an epoch in Sino-Soviet relations. No one could again assume the power that Stalin had possessed. Even the Chinese had had to bow to his leadership. With Khrushchev matters were different. He had to prove himself, and the Chinese could afford to take a tougher stand with him. Khrushchev visited Peking on the fifth anniversary of the founding of the Chinese People's Republic. His purpose was to gain support for his struggle for power, for he had to have the Chinese behind him.

This is perhaps one of the reasons why he did not protest more vigorously against Chinese bombarding of the offshore islands held by the Nationalists. Khrushchev, like Stalin, feared being drawn into armed confrontation with the United States. On the other hand, the Chinese based their actions on the 'paper tiger' analysis. Imperialism met by force would retreat.

The bombardments were a direct response to the American policy of containment in the Far East: the Manila conference on SEATO and the announcement of plans for a Mutual Defence Treaty with Taiwan. Once again the Russians refused to be involved. The policy of detente was already in its formative stages. Detente was the rock on which Sino-Soviet relations stumbled, and Taiwan was but another stepping stone on the road to the split. Khrushchev's concessions to the Chinese—the return of Port Arthur, increased long-term credit and aid, the dissolution of the Joint Stock Companies in China's favour —were forgotten, but the sense of betrayal of

the socialist alliance could not be easily wiped away.

A year later, at the first post-war summit, the Russian leadership openly told their Western counterparts that they were uneasy about Chinese intentions—'they (the Russians) look ahead and wonder whether China may not be a danger', concluded Britain's Harold Macmillan.

Meanwhile China continued to press for an independent foreign policy, regardless of whether it agreed with that of the Soviet Union. Chinese delegations headed by Chou En-lai attended both the Geneva conference on Indochina in 1954 and the Bandung conference of Afro-Asian nations in 1955. China was endeavouring to break out of her isolation, and to establish connections with the Third World of which she considered herself a part.

The task had some urgency, for the Soviet Union's participation in the Four Powers Geneva summit conference in 1955 alarmed the Chinese. China was being left out in the cold and she did not like it. Her fears were

heightened by Khrushchev's dramatic denunciation of Stalin at the Twentieth Party Congress in 1956.

The danger of de-Stalinization, as the Chinese saw it, was that it tended to undermine all authority in the Communist movement. The linking of Stalin and Communism was of such long standing that it could not be sundered without serious effects on international socialism both internally and externally. Stalin had legitimacy because of the success of the Russian revolution; Khrushchev had no such basis for his authority. So his attack on Stalin rocked to the core the most cherished conceptions of the nature of Communism. With one stroke he invalidated the root truths of Communism and laid it open to destructive dissension and attack. It was this that so appalled the Chinese.

### Basic differences

This episode indicates the basic differences in Russian and Chinese Communism. The Russians, immured in a monolithic mentality, could not conceive of an approach that reflected diversity in unity. The Chinese had long been aware of the value of diversity and Mao's theory of contradictions gave it a limited legitimacy. But, and this must be emphasized, contradictions could only be accepted within the framework of a Communist unity; this is why the Chinese strongly demanded of the Russians that they bear the burden of their leadership responsibilities. The Russians were materially the strongest of the Communist countries; the Chinese view was that they must be so morally as well.

The consequences of the Chinese position emerged clearly in their response to the Polish and Hungarian uprisings of 1956. In Poland, where the revolt remained under the aegis of the Communist Party, China supported Gomulka against Khrushchev. In Hungary the situation was reversed. The rebellion moved out of the accepted bounds, and the Chinese urged Khrushchev to send in the troops to save the revolution at a time when Khrushchev vacillated on the proper course of action to take.

In another direction, the Eastern European debacle proved a watershed in Sino-Soviet relations. For the first time, the Chinese claimed a right to involve themselves in traditional Soviet spheres of influence. This was a natural extension of the Chinese belief in the interdependence of all Communist movements. At the time the Russians were rather relieved to have Chinese support in a messy situation, but the potential controversy was obviously great.

Ultimately more damaging to Sino-Soviet relations than Khrushchev's de-Stalinization programme was his outline of the direction of Soviet external relations at the Twentieth Party Congress. Khrushchev's proposals

*Camera Press*

*H. Cartier-Bresson—Magnum*

*Cooperation—with tension not far beneath the surface. Above: Khrushchev and Mao after signing a joint declaration in Peking, August 1958. Left: 1958 Independence Day parade in Mongolia. Russian-style uniforms testify to strong Russian influence in this buffer state which before 1919 was part of China*

became the basis of his and his successors' foreign policy and the source of enormous contention and friction with the Chinese. The main elements of Khrushchev's speech were a belief in the possibility of peaceful co-existence with the capitalist countries, a reappraisal of Lenin's theory of imperialism, which held that war was inevitable as long as capitalism-imperialism existed (Khrushchev denied its modern validity), and an acknowledgment that there were means other than violent revolution to attain socialism, for instance, parliamentary elections.

The Chinese did not respond immediately to the Khrushchev doctrine, for they were still too dependent on Russian military and economic aid to cause an open breach, and they still believed that the Russians could be brought back into line by the dialectical process of criticism.

The Chinese had the opportunity to express their views at the Moscow conference of World Communist Parties in 1957. The aim of the conference was to establish a core of Communist orthodoxy to which all members of the socialist camp could adhere. In substance it followed the Khrushchev line, but it also contained references to the Chinese reservations. The compromise achieved in the Moscow Declaration of November 1957 was reiterated three years later in the Moscow Statement of November 1960, agreed to by eighty-one Communist Parties.

Although compromise was agreed to, friction between the Russians and the Chinese continued to build up. In the final analysis the Chinese could never agree to the rejection of the Leninist theory of imperialism implied in the Khrushchev doctrine. War was, in the Maoist view, inevitable. But in war lay the seeds of hope—revolution. The Chinese never abandoned the doctrine of revolutionary struggle. It was unlikely, they stated, that revolution could be achieved except by violent means. Given the truth of Lenin's theory of imperialism, peaceful co-existence was impossible. And it was on this point that the Russians and the Chinese radically diverged. Khrushchev had a healthy respect for nuclear arms. Mao was conspicuously indifferent to its threat. In a celebrated comment at the 1957 Moscow conference, Mao declared that even in the event of a nuclear war half the world's population would survive and socialism would triumph.

So it was with more than misgivings that the Chinese viewed Khrushchev's detente policies in the late 1950's. They grew increasingly wary of Russia's 'great-power chauvinism', as they labelled it. On their part the Russians saw the Chinese as wild, reckless men, unaware of the dangers of war in their efforts to extend their hegemony in the world.

**Right:** *Diagram shows economic development of Communist China. The exaggerated grain-production claims shown for 1958 and 1959 in fact no longer seem to be accepted in Peking. Trade figures clearly reflect changing Sino-Soviet political relations, with a build up in reciprocal trade from 1949 to 1959 followed by a steep decline*

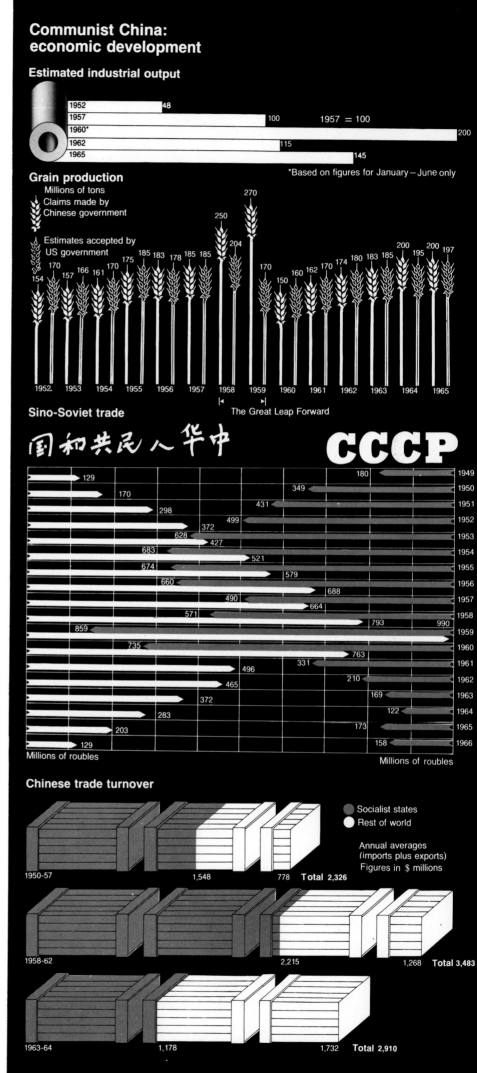

Musée Royal de l'Armée, Brussels

## СЛАВА ВЕЛИКОМУ КИТАЙСКОМУ НАРОДУ, ЗАВОЕВАВШЕМУ СВОБОДУ, НЕЗАВИСИМОСТЬ И СЧАСТЬЕ!

*Before the big rift—Russian poster, 1949, commemorates Communist victory in China: 'Glory to the great Chinese people who have gained freedom, independence, and happiness'*

The 1958 crises in the Middle East and in the Taiwan Straits only served to reinforce the entrenched opinions of both sides. In mid-July at the invitation of their respective governments American troops landed in Lebanon and British troops in Jordan. Khrushchev, without consulting the Chinese, proposed to Eisenhower a great power conference consisting of the USSR, the US, Britain, France and India. Eisenhower replied that such a meeting should take place within the framework of the United Nations Security Council. Khrushchev agreed. Then, at the end of July, he made a hurried visit to Peking for consultation with the Chinese

leaders. The result was a cancellation of the Security Council meeting and a communiqué condemning British and American aggression.

What irritated the Chinese was not merely the lack of consultation in the initial stages of the crisis. It was more Khrushchev's readiness to drop China in the interests of great power summitry. The Chinese had always insisted on their status as one of the five Great Powers recognized as such by permanent membership of the United Nations Security Council. United States policy meant that China could not actively undertake her duties as a great power but on no account did

or would the Chinese relinquish their status. The Chinese were thus naturally affronted when Khrushchev suggested substituting India for China in dealing with crucial affairs of world politics.

In late August 1958 the Chinese commenced bombardment of Nationalist-held Quemoy island. Once more the Russians were threatened with being drawn into direct confrontation with the United States, and again they gave reassurances to the Chinese while remaining essentially aloof from the conflict.

### Detente and its consequences

Chinese apprehension and resentment over Russian policy increased in direct proportion to the latter's success with detente. They saw a situation in which Russian-American rapprochement would totally debilitate the Sino-Soviet alliance. Soviet readiness to talk disarmament clinched the argument as far as the Chinese were concerned. The 'nuclear club' and its protection was to be closed to them. This was confirmed by the Soviet repudiation in 1959, at the height of the 'Camp David spirit', of a secret agreement of 1957 to supply aid to China in the manufacture of nuclear weapons.

The Chinese retaliated by attacking Khrushchev in his most vulnerable spot—his authority as Communist leader. The first polemical shot was fired in the Chinese party journal *Red Flag*. The first of a series of articles entitled *Long Live Leninism*, which forcibly attacked the Khrushchev doctrine, was published on 16th April 1960. The dispute was finally out in the open, and degenerated with an amazing rapidity into an open split within three years.

Throughout 1960 the ideological dispute raged—at the World Federation of Trade Unions in Peking, at the Bucharest conference in Rumania and at the Moscow conference of the eighty-one Communist Parties. The lines of argument had been clearly drawn in 1956 by Khrushchev. The old debates were elaborated but nothing new was added. The Moscow statement in November unanimously adopted by the conference mechanically integrated the Russian and Chinese versions of Marxist-Leninist orthodoxy; in other words, the question had not been resolved. Neither the Chinese nor the Russians had given an inch. The worsening of the dispute was signalled by the mass exodus of Russian technicians from China in August 1960. From then on trade between the two countries decreased rapidly, until it reached minimal levels.

Two years later the final blows to the Sino-Soviet alliance were delivered. The first was the Soviet-Yugoslav rapprochement. Hitherto Yugoslavia had been excluded from the functions of world Communism and anathematised as that ultimate Communist horror—the revisionist. The Chinese, in particular, had been vehement in their denunciation of Tito and Titoism. Tito's cardinal sin had been the breaking of socialist solidarity. The Russian's sudden about turn on the Yugoslav question could only mean one thing to the Chinese—a shaft directed against themselves.

Secondly, Soviet military aid to India at a time of tense Sino-Indian relations enraged the Chinese. Only a few months later the Sino-Indian war broke out. Russia remained neutral. The Soviets, it seemed, were deliberately breaking up the line of socialist solidarity.

The Cuban missile crisis provided a further focus of criticism on the Soviet Union. By introducing missiles to Cuba, argued the Chinese, the Russians had acted rashly. But once this had been done, to withdraw was to do world Communism a grave disservice, for every appeasement was a defeat.

The Soviet Union's primacy in the socialist world, based on her capability and willingness to defend that world, was rapidly becoming undermined as far as the Chinese were concerned. Incidents, such as those in 1962, seemed to prove Soviet reluctance to take up the cudgel on behalf of international socialism.

In the early months of 1963 a call went out for a meeting between the two super-powers to try and heal the growing rift between them. It was agreed to hold discussions in July. In June the central committee of the Chinese Communist Party sent to Moscow and published in the *People's Daily* a 60,000 word statement listing twenty-five points to be covered in the Moscow talks. Without actually naming Khrushchev, the 'Twenty-Five Points' was the most comprehensive attack on him and Soviet policies to date. Point by point, it repudiated the main Russian policy statements issued since 1956. The Soviet Union was critized for destroying the unity of the socialist bloc, for advocating peaceful co-existence with imperialist countries, for placing undue emphasis on disarmament, for asserting that revolutions were possible without war, for denying class struggle, for maintaining unequal relations with fraternal countries, and for 'taking a passive or scornful or negative attitude towards the struggles of the oppressed nations for liberation'. Naturally, the Russians refused to accept the 'Twenty-Five Points'.

The tenuous alliance was finally ruptured when Moscow signed the 1963 Nuclear Test-Ban Treaty, for this was decisive proof to the Chinese that the Soviet Union had abandoned socialist solidarity. An essential quality of Russian Communism had been destroyed, and the Russians had become revisionists. The treaty symbolized for each the moral turpitude of the other, and both launched readily into a hostile war of propaganda. The Chinese, said Moscow, recklessly hoped for a nuclear war which would leave them dominant while the other major powers destroyed themselves. The Russians, said Peking, wished to maintain an exclusive nuclear club so that they could divide up the world between themselves and the Americans. The open breach allowed the outpouring of years of accumulated bitterness and irritation earlier suppressed in the interests of a common front. Chief among

*With Communism has come an aggressive militarism.* **Above:** *Chinese troops advance during the campaign in which China seized Tibet, 1951.* **Right:** *The break made public. The USSR, newly converted to coexistence, accused of complicity with USA. 'The new Munich agreement': Chinese cartoon of 1966 depicts Kosygin selling out to Johnson*

these was the border problem.

Since 1962 there has been sporadic trouble at both ends of the Sino-Soviet land frontier. In the west, where minority tribes outnumber ethnic Chinese, 60,000 of the former fled in 1962 from Chinese Sinkiang to Soviet Kazakhstan. The Chinese accused the Russians of fomenting rebellion among the ethnic tribes and closed down the Russian

consulates in the area. Similar movements of population later on led to frontier clashes between Chinese and Soviet border guards.

In the east, where the Amur and Ussuri rivers mark the frontier, there were frequent disputes over contested fishing grounds and islands. The 1964 border negotiations collapsed. China insisted upon a Soviet admission that the various treaties of the 19th

Keystone Press

Camera Press

Camera Press

*Above left:* Brezhnev, who has recently been re-elected a chief of the Politboro. *Left:* Kosygin. With Brezhnev, he has carried on Khrushchev's policy of co-existence. *Above:* Former US President Nixon in Peking. Chinese rapprochement with the US conforms with Maoist teaching

century which had determined the boundaries (and had enlarged the territory of Tsarist Russia at China's expense) were 'unequal', although Peking made it clear that she was prepared to accept them as the basis for a new settlement.

The Soviet Union, however, was only prepared to discuss those sections of the border where specific disagreements had arisen—the 'unequal treaties' should stand as a historical legacy which had been sanctioned by the passage of time.

Relations between the two countries sank to a new low when severe border clashes over the Ussuri river broke out in March 1969. The Damansky/Chenpao battle led to the serious possibility of full scale war between China and Russia. However, for the time being the hawks on both side of the fence were quieted.

Border negotiations were reopened in Peking in 1970. They fell through on the same stumbling blocks as the 1964 meetings. The Chinese proposed a two-part agreement that would bind the interested parties to maintain the *status quo* in disputed areas, and to withdraw armed forces from those areas. These proposals were not acceptable to the Russians who feared that the *status quo* boundary would become the *de facto* one.

In 1971, and again in 1973, the Russians suggested that the two countries sign a treaty renouncing the use or the threat of force against each other. The Chinese rejected the Russian initiative on the grounds that the 1950 Treaty of Alliance was still intact and, that such a treaty would be meaningless until the Soviet Union agreed to withdraw its forces from the disputed areas.

From the break in 1963 a propaganda war was unleashed which soon reached unprecedented proportions. The aim was, and is, to discredit and, as far as possible, isolate the other side. Both sides had their successes and failures: the Russians over the Vietnam War and the Cultural Revolution; the Chinese over the Czechoslovak crisis of 1968 and, generally, over the inroads they made in the Third World where, quite often, they supplanted Soviet influence. The effect, however, was to hasten the drift towards national autonomy in the international Communist movement.

In one particular area the Russians seriously failed in their anti-Chinese policies. This was in keeping her isolated from the world community. By the early 1970's most Western nations had recognized China. In 1971 she was at last admitted to her rightful place in the United Nations, at Taiwan's expense. But the supreme victory of Chinese diplomacy must be President Nixon's visit to Peking in February 1972.

The Chinese had opened the path for Nixon's visit by a significant shift in their analysis of the world situation. From 1969 Russia replaced the United States as the main enemy. Thus the rapprochement with the States was completely in line with Maoist doctrine and practice of 'contradictions'. For, once the Chinese accepted the Soviet Union as the 'primary contradiction', then alliances became possible and necessary with former enemies. This is why, in 1976, the spectacle of a disgraced American President being feted in China was seen.

It was not the first time that the Chinese had shown their support for an ousted Western leader. Only a few years earlier, Edward Heath of Britain made that trip to Peking. The Chinese did not forget their friends. Heath was a friend because he had steered Britain into the Common Market. For the Chinese a strong EEC was another bulwark against the Russian threat.

A few months prior to his death in January 1976 Premier Chou En-lai summed up the Chinese view of the international situation. 'The capitalist world is facing the most serious economic crisis since the war and all the basic contradictions in the world are sharpening. On the one hand, the trend of revolution by the people of the world is actively developing. . . . On the other hand, the contention for world hegemony between the two super-powers is becoming more and more intense. The focus of contention is Europe. The Soviet Union makes a feint to the East while attacking the West. The two super-powers are the source of a new world war.' And of the two super-powers the Russians more than the Americans. Today, the Chinese fear most the Russian grab for power, and they will support anyone, in the West or East, who will fight against Soviet expansionism.

# India since Independence

Over the last twenty-eight years, from 1947 to 1975, India has been ruled almost continuously by the Nehrus—father and daughter. During the brief interregnum, from the summer of 1964, when Jawaharlal Nehru died, to January 1966 when his daughter Indira Gandhi was elevated to the Prime Ministership, a little, self-effacing man, Lal Bahadur Shastri, presided over the affairs of the country. Shastri's rule, however, was cut short by his sudden death.

Leaders are important in every society but they are particularly crucial in the developing world where there are fewer institutional restrictions on the exercise of their individual powers, and more room, in spite of the written constitutions, for their policies and public conduct to be motivated and moulded by their personal zeal and prejudices. In this way, both Nehru and his daughter, in their different approaches, have influenced India.

The years from 1947 to 1951 were the years of statesmanship for Nehru, during which he formulated an independent foreign policy, evolved a democratic and secular political structure, and devised a system of mixed economy. He succeeded in achieving these in spite of fierce opposition internally and internationally.

Nehru believed in a foreign policy of non-alignment and peaceful co-existence. At the time of India's independence the world was divided into two power blocs, the Soviet and the American. They were arrayed against each other armed with pacts and alliances. For the decolonized and developing countries of Asia and Africa there seemed little alternative but to join one or the other bloc. To Nehru, neither system contained the totality of truth and justice. He was wedded to the Anglo-American democratic way of life, yet repelled by the brutality and vulgarity of competition and profiteering that characterized American capitalism. The socialism of the Soviet system attracted him, but he was shocked by its totalitarianism. It was thus out of the question for India to join either bloc. Not only must India have an independent foreign policy, Nehru believed, but it should also play an active role in preventing a third world war, towards which the super-powers appeared to be heading, and in stopping the

*India's Shastri, Pakistan's Ayub Khan and Soviet Prime Minister Alexei Kosygin, in Tashkent, 10th January 1966, during negotiations to try and end the Indo-Pakistan war over Kashmir*

cold war which they were already waging against each other. This, Nehru believed, could be achieved by enlarging what he called 'the area of peace'. In adopting a non-aligned policy, he hoped that the other countries of Asia, and possibly of Africa, would follow India's example.

Nehru reasoned that an area of non-aligned nations could be turned into an area of peace by keeping the super-powers out of that area, for if one super-power intervened on some excuse, the other was bound to follow. With these objectives in view Nehru launched a three-dimensional foreign policy. First, he commenced a vigorous campaign against defence pacts and alliances. He condemned America's indirect intervention in the Middle East through the Bagdad Pact of 1955, and the direct intervention in South-East Asia through the South-East Asia Collective Defence Treaty of 1954. Nehru feared that American intervention in these areas of Asia would inevitably bring the Russians in, and the very purpose the Americans wanted to achieve through these pacts, which was to stop Soviet advancement in the Middle East and Sino-Soviet infiltrations in South-East Asia would be frustrated. His fears were well founded.

Secondly, Nehru campaigned for the recruitment of new members to his non-aligned league. In this task he was considerably aided by Red China's acceptance, in 1954, of the principle of peaceful co-existence. This diminished the fear of Red China which the new nations of South-East Asia had been nourishing since the Communist victory in 1949. In 1955 twenty-nine Afro-Asian nations met at Bandung in Indonesia to proclaim the legitimacy of non-alignment as a basic concept of international behaviour.

Thirdly, Nehru attempted to bring about a rapprochement between the US and the Soviet Union. Throughout the 1950's, when the tension between the super-powers was high, Nehru continually pointed out the need for friendship. He pleaded with them to discard their mutual suspicion of each other and to meet at a summit conference. In 1963, when his life was drawing to a close, Nehru drew some satisfaction from the signing of a partial Nuclear Test Ban Treaty, which to him symbolized the opening of a new chapter in international relations.

Nehru's independent foreign policy was to some extent, and much to his dislike, tainted by India's deep involvement in Kashmir and her border problems with China. India's claim on Kashmir as an integral part of her territory was openly supported by only one country in the world— the Soviet Union—a factor which tended to influence Nehru in favour of the Soviet Union. Consequently, in 1956, he was more restrained in condemning Soviet military intervention in Hungary than he was in attacking Anglo-French belligerency in

Egypt. The Chinese occupation of Tibet in 1950 brought China onto the entire length of India's 2,600 miles of northern frontiers and raised the problem of undefined borders between them. From 1950 to 1958, Nehru tried to contain China by befriending her. In 1958, however, China took a hard line on the frontier question and the Sino-Indian friendship reached its breaking point. From 1959 to 1962, therefore, Nehru tried to establish what he considered should be India's internationally recognized boundary with China's Tibet, by occupying or repossessing many posts and barren patches in the mountainous region; at the same time he relied on the belief that the Chinese would not opt for open war. His expectations were to be frustrated. China went to war in October 1962; but she renounced the lost posts she recovered after the declaration of a unilateral ceasefire on 20th November 1962. A number of reasons have been offered for China's action; it is possible that the Chinese wanted to teach the hostile Tibetans a lesson, and to show them the futility of looking to India for help. The Chinese showdown obliged Nehru to accept military aid from the US and Britain, and it was expected that he would shift his allegiance towards the Anglo-American bloc. But this was not to be. Anglo-American aid brought with it a plea to India to settle her dispute with Pakistan about Kashmir. On the other hand, Russia, by disapproving of Chinese action and expressing her sympathy and promises of help to India, not only retained her attraction for Nehru but also enabled him to proclaim that, in spite of China's desperate attempt to destroy her neutral status, India would remain non-aligned, retaining the friendship of both the US and the Soviet Union. This was Nehru's way of turning defeat into victory.

## Mrs Indira Gandhi

Although the framework of Nehru's foreign policy remains outwardly intact its basis has changed from moral to physical power. To Indira Gandhi, nothing makes a system look more ethical than the physical power to support it. In acquiring that power for India through a much closer association with Russia (embodied in the Indo-Soviet Friendship Treaty of August 1971), and by turning India into a nuclear power (as demonstrated by India's exploding its first nuclear bomb in May 1974) Mrs Gandhi has departed from her father's moorings. She did not show her father's hesitancy in using India's military power during the Bangladesh war of December 1971, and inflicted a total defeat on Pakistan.

While Nehru's foreign policy has been modified, the mixed economic structure he devised for India in 1948 has undergone fewer changes during his daughter's rule. Nehru had devised for India a mixed economic structure based on both public and private enterprise. Indian industry was divided into three categories: those which were to be exclusively owned and managed by the state, those which could be run by both state and private enterprise, and those which could be left in the hands of the private industrialists but subjected to some official control. This system was geared to a long-term planning programme, formulated in India's Five-Year Plans. Considerable progress was made in all aspects of the country's economic life, though the industrial output was not matched by agricultural development, because all of the land, upon which three-quarters of the Indian people still depend, is privately owned, and much-needed reforms (like consolidation and collectivization) could not be introduced as the peasants were opposed to such innovations. In this they

*The age-old curses of hunger and disease still afflict India. But great efforts are being spent on developing a sound and progressive economic structure. **Right:** Indira Gandhi, minister of atomic energy as well as Prime Minister, makes a speech beside the Bombay nuclear reactor*

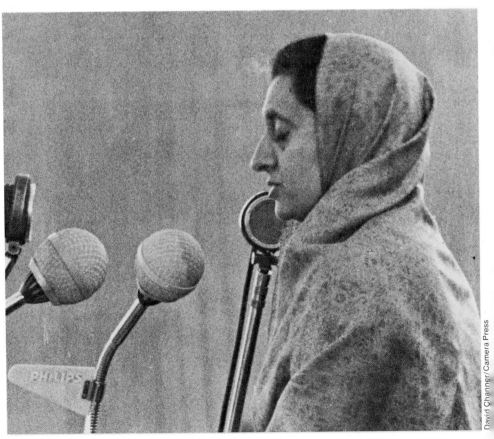

David Channer/Camera Press

*A Kashmir village after shelling by Indian forces in the 1965 India-Pakistan War*

Keystone Press

fighting her, joined the leaders of other opposition parties in a grand alliance. Mrs Gandhi accepted the challenge, and held India's fifth election early in 1971, a year earlier than scheduled. She triumphed, winning 350 seats.

## The Struggle for Power
Mrs Gandhi now had power but she lacked charisma. Even her victory in Bangladesh could not give her personality the aura of charismatic power of Nehru and Gandhi. She was feared, obeyed, appeased and even styled as *Kali*, the Hindu goddess of destruction, but she was not, even by the illiterate masses of the country, adored and respected as India's noble soul. When the excitement over her accomplishments of 1971 subsided, the opposition leaders began their campaign against her, accusing her of corruption, nepotism and abuse of power. Having exhausted all constitutional means of overthrowing her, the leaders of various opposition parties gathered round J. P. Narayan, who had started a Gandhian style non-co-operation movement against Mrs Gandhi's regime. Throughout his long political career, Narayan has been an honourable politician but his followers and collaborators, who gathered around him in 1975, had been in opposition for many years and were angry, bitter and impatient, with very little sense of discretion and responsibility. In June 1975, at the end of a long drawn out case in which Mrs Gandhi was accused by an opposition leader of corrupt election practices in the 1971 election, the High Court verdict went against her and she was disqualified from elective office for six years. The opposition were carried away by their sense of victory and marched on Delhi demanding her immediate resignation. At this point Mrs Gandhi gained the sympathy of many, for the world knew that the verdict was based on a legal technicality, that it was unduly severe, and therefore most likely to be annulled by the Supreme Court of India.

If Mrs Gandhi had stepped down from her office until her appeal was heard and she was acquitted by the Supreme Court, she might have returned to office with added power and glory. But she feared that once she quitted office, even for a temporary period, everyone might turn against her—even the judges of the Supreme Court and her cabinet colleagues— and she might never return to office. Mrs Gandhi, therefore, did not stoop to conquer. She decided to fight her opponents from her present position. On 26th June 1975, she declared a State of Emergency under the Indian Constitution. All her opponents were put into jail, a number of communal organizations were banned, and India's sixth General Election which was due to be held in March 1976 was postponed for a year. Mrs Gandhi has suspended the working of the world's largest democracy in order to fight most effectively, as she proclaims, the anti-democratic and anti-national forces in the country. Now it is up to her alone to decide when it would be safe for democracy to return to India. She may even decide that her father's form of democracy is not suited to India.

were supported by the right-wing politicians, who during Nehru's era dominated all the state governments and the Congress party organizations.

During her decade of rule, Mrs Gandhi has forced the right-wing members out of her Congress, and she has been more vigorous than her father in the adoption of socialist programmes for her government. No structural change has yet been made; the implementation of a number of agrarian reforms, which stand as approved on the statute books, has been, as in the past, delayed or obstructed by the slow moving and corruptible Indian bureaucracy. Apart from the nationalization of the banks in 1969–70—to enable the peasants and other needy to borrow money from the banks for investment—Mrs Gandhi has so far done nothing spectacular to support her image of a leader determined to banish poverty from India.

However, she has made some radical alterations to her father's political system. A dedicated democrat and secularist, and an ardent guardian of Indian unity, in the crucial years from 1947 to 1951, Nehru successfully fought the communists, communalists and regionalists. The communists did not pose any immediate threat to democracy but the militant Hindu communalists demanded a Hindu Raj for India and challenged Nehru's secularism which, in their eyes, had failed to prevent the partition of the country and therefore must be abandoned. The regionalists agitated for linguistic and ethnic divisions of India, and as most of them belonged to non-Hindu speaking areas, they were also opposed to the adoption of Hindi as the national language of India. In combatting these forces, and Hindu orthodoxy in particular, Nehru was aided not only by the power of his charisma but also, indirectly, by the assassination of Gandhi by a Hindu fanatic (which turned the tide against the Hindu communalists), and the accession to India of the predominantly Muslim State of Kashmir (which strengthened the case for India remaining secular). In 1950, India adopted a constitution which made her

political structure democratic, secular and republican. Having laid the foundation for the world's largest democracy (the Indian electorate rose from 173 million in 1951 to 210 million in 1962), Nehru nourished it through three general elections (1951, 1957 and 1962), and maintained his Congress Party in power at the centre and in all the Indian States except one.

With his death the struggle for power began—in the Congress party itself between the right- and left-wing elements, and between Congress and all the opposition parties. In 1966, Mrs Gandhi was the only leader in Congress who had acquired some national stature though she lacked her father's charisma. She was also suspected of lacking integrity and administrative skill and abounding in arrogance and conceit. The Congress had put her on the throne, hoping that they would be able to exercise the real power. While Mrs Gandhi was finding her feet, the fourth general election took place in 1967; it went badly for the Congress Party. Although they were not fully routed as the opposition parties had predicted, their strength in Parliament was reduced to a bare majority of 279 in a House of 525, and they lost eight of the seventeen States of India to opposition parties or their coalitions. Instead of losing heart and leaning on the Congress leaders at this point, Mrs Gandhi emerged determined to stand in her own right, to win popular support by appealing directly to the people, and to destroy the image in the people's mind that she held the highest executive office just because she was the daughter of the great Nehru. It became her obsession to acquire full power through a continuous display of skill, courage, ruthlessness and strategy. First, she asserted her supremacy within Congress against the party chiefs who had put her in power. In 1969 Congress was split up between the 'old' Congress of the right and the 'new' ruling Congress of Mrs Gandhi. With her own election to the Presidency of India she defeated the old faction of the Congress Party. The leaders of the old Congress, determined to continue

# Spain: Franco and After

On 19th July 1936, when the European press reported that a group of Spanish generals had risen against the 'weak' Second Spanish Republic, little was known about General Franco except that he was the brother of a famous aviator. Yet he was soon to become the leader of Nationalist Spain. Very few Spaniards—other than the military conspirators who knew his character and merits—could have predicted that he would rule Spain as *Caudillo* (leader). He was known as a studious regimental officer who had won a reputation for extreme bravery as commander of the Foreign Legion in the terrible campaigns which the Spanish army fought in Morocco in the 1920's.

Like many a statesman, General Franco's political actions were founded on a vision of his country's historical destiny. Born in 1892 of a family of naval administrators, his youth was passed under the shadow of 'the Disaster': the total defeat of Spain and the destruction of the Spanish fleet by the United States in 1898. How was this defeat to be explained? To Franco the fault lay with the ineptitude of the party politicians of a debased parliamentary state. Party politics were, therefore, an anti-Spanish conception.

To this dislike of parliamentary politics General Franco added the conventional political theory elaborated over the previous century by Spanish army officers to justify their constant interventions in politics. When politicians neglected the 'true' interests of Spain, when they could not even preserve public order and government lay 'in the gutter', then it was the duty of the army to defend national honour and save the nation by taking a direct hand in government.

To the irritation of some of his brother generals Franco was in no hurry to put military political theory into practice. The Second Republic of 1931-36 with its army reforms, its concessions to Catalan nationalism, was distasteful to those generals who did not seek a career in republicanism. After the Popular Front victory in the elections of February 1936 which made the socialists a power in the state, it became intolerable. General Franco had no objections to a republican form of government provided it was right of centre, trusted the army, and kept order: thus he had co-operated with the republic in the period 1934-36 and had played a major planning role—he was exceptionally able as a staff officer—in the suppression of the Asturian miners' rising in October 1934. But he disapproved intensely of the popular

street pressure in 1936 and was prepared to back a government that would resist it.

Once he had failed to secure a 'strong' government he moved inescapably towards conspiracy to overthrow what he considered a 'weak' government. He hesitated only because, unlike other conspirators, he wanted to be certain of success before unleashing a rising which might turn into a civil war. The government had sent him to the Canary Islands out of harm's way, and the details of the military rising were planned by General Mola. But Franco's ability and prestige made his participation essential to success. The Moroccan army rose on 17th July; Franco left the Canaries in mufti in a hired aircraft to take over the leadership of the troops he knew so well.

With the help of German and Italian aircraft Franco ferried his African army to Spain. By September he had 13,000 men, the best trained fighting force in the Civil War. Cutting through the Republican militia regiments his troops arrived on the outskirts of Madrid in the first week of October. Partly because he delayed to relieve the Alcázar of Toledo, partly because he had under-estimated the Republican resistance, Franco stuck in the suburbs. The failure to take Madrid altered the whole character of the uprising. It would be a long struggle, not a military take-over as the generals had hoped. Hence Franco was bound to depend on German and Italian aid; he fought to preserve his own independence as a commander and to his foreign advisers he appeared a 'slow coach'. This criticism was unjustified. He was cautious and like all generals he made mistakes. But he was a highly competent commander and he could scarcely have fought a Blitzkrieg when he never had more

*1 Franco's traditionalist Spain: a policeman's cap badge shows the eagle of St John holding the yoke and arrows which were the insignia of Isabella the Catholic.*
*2 Major Franco (he was known as the 'little major') in Morocco with his legionaries, 1922. 3 Supreme power. Franco invested as Head of Government of the Spanish State by General Cabanellas (far right) in a Burgos palace, October 1936.*
*4 Neutrality. Franco and Hitler inspect a German guard of honour, Hendaye station, 1940. Then for ten hours Hitler tried to make Franco join the Axis—in vain. Afterwards he jumped on his hat in rage. 5 Franco, his wife (left), and daughter at a Catholic ceremony in Madrid, 1948. Much of his support derived from his Catholicism*

3 △  ▽ 4  5 ▽

than 200 tanks. By the final battle of the Ebro his army was relatively so well equipped that final victory was inevitable.

It was his position as commander of the strongest Nationalist army—that of Africa —and his prestige in the army that made him the choice of his fellow generals as generalissimo and head of state. As a politician he was, and remained, ruthless. Nationalist Spain was an amalgam of radical nationalist Falangists, rightist Falangists, traditionalist Carlists, and conservatives—monarchical and otherwise. In the spring of 1937 the Carlists, supporters of the claim to the Spanish throne of the descendants of Don Carlos, brother of Fernando VII who died in 1833, were showing signs of independence and the radical Falangists distrusted generals and conservatives who did not share the Falangist dream of winning over the working classes to nationalism. By April 1937 Franco had mastered these nascent oppositions. The sole political force recognized in Nationalist Spain was the 'Movement', a combination of Falangists and Carlists, of which Franco was leader; he had attained a political mastery of Nationalist Spain that he kept until his death in 1975.

### Stubborn independence

Victor in the Civil War, he became effective ruler of Spain at a most difficult time—April 1939. Spain was exhausted by civil war and dangerously dependent on her German and Italian allies. When the Second World War came they sought their pound of flesh: the active co-operation of Spain, which became of great importance once the war came to North Africa. Franco had no sympathy with the Allies and his foreign minister, Serrano Suñer, believed in the advent of a 'New Order'; but the Caudillo knew Spain was exhausted, and by 1943 was no longer certain that the Allies would lose. He hedged in such a determined fashion that Hitler compared an interview with him to a visit to the dentist. Alone among the war leaders Churchill was willing to acknowledge the advantages Franco's stubborn independence had brought to the Allies. The victors, however, were determined to ostracize him as a fascist; in December 1946 the United Nations voted to exclude Spain from all UN agencies.

Franco, on receiving the news, continued with his newly adopted hobby of painting. He knew that ostracism by foreigners could only strengthen his position at home.

How did Franco maintain himself in power? Partly because memories of the Civil War and the hungry 'forties, when Spain could hope for no aid from abroad, encouraged support for the existing government as the only alternative to disaster. Partly because his undisputed control of the army and the ruthless action of the police subdued political opposition. Partly because his skill in balancing the forces supporting his regime prevented any single force from becoming too strong.

When the Civil War ended the Falangists were in a strong position. They controlled the new trades union organization—in which both employers and workers were officially represented; they controlled the press censorship and university unions. But they were disliked by Carlists and conservative monarchists. Increasingly Franco used the Falange, not as the axis of his new state, but as one force among others.

Camera Press

"Gaceta Illustrada", Madrid

*Top: No longer an outsider: Franco and Eisenhower part with a spontaneous embrace after meeting in Madrid, December 1959.*
*Centre: Problems at home: Basque secessionists stick up a poster in their own language saying: 'Long live the Basques'.*
*Bottom: The succession: Franco with Juan Carlos, installed as Prince of Spain in 1969, at a march past in Madrid, 1965*

EFE (Spanish News Agency)

Increasingly, too, the ideology that had sustained the Civil War became less usable. The Falangists, for instance, believed in a self-sufficient economy closed against the outside world and controlled by the state. By the 1950's autarchy had failed to produce growth; after fifteen years of a controlled economy the per capita income in 1954 had only climbed back to the level of 1931.

### Growing economy
If the economy was to be opened up and liberalized it needed an injection of foreign capital to buy the capital equipment for industrial growth. The possibility of such an injection came in 1953. The demands of the Cold War drove the United States to seek an agreement that would give her military bases in return for economic aid to Spain. The American embrace did not merely give Spain international respectability; it gave her the foreign exchange to re-equip her industry. But by 1957 the economy was in crisis: exports did not pay for imports and inflation brought a rash of strikes. The economy was put into the hands of the 'technocrats' of the Catholic lay organization Opus Dei; the Stabilization Plan of 1959 (devaluation, a wage freeze, the encouragement of foreign investment) was designed to lay the basis for steady growth.

After a period of recession, growth was spectacular, equalled only by that of Japan. The later 1960's were the years of the economic miracle; this growth was dependent on the availability of foreign exchange, and was fuelled by the remittances of workers in Europe and the profits of a tourist boom. It probably owed little to the various development plans. By the 1970's Spain had altered out of all recognition; from a country that ended the Civil War with 42 per cent of its active population in agriculture, by 1970 only 25 per cent remained. Vast numbers of Spaniards had left the impoverished countryside for industrial cities; those who could not find work in Spain found it abroad. Spain had become a semi-industrialized country with the problems of a consumer society: parking problems and pollution in its cities; television and refrigerators in a growing number of its homes.

The problem of the later 1960's and 1970's was that economic growth had not been accompanied by political change. In all essentials, in spite of some 'democratic'

window dressing, the regime remained as it had been in 1939. There was no democratically elected parliament to which ministers were responsible; ultimate power still rested with Franco. It was he who chose ministers and dismissed them. There were no political parties, no free press; those who did not accept the system were repressed or ostracized, for they had no power to develop an alternative government.

The acute question of the 1960's was that of the succession. If Franco died, who would succeed? This was settled unilaterally by Franco when, in 1969, he chose Prince Juan Carlos, son of the pretender Don Juan, as future King. The title to rule of Juan Carlos did not derive from the secular claims of the Bourbon monarchy (the heir was Don Juan who supported a constitutional monarchy) but from Franco's appointment. Juan Carlos swore allegiance to the 'Principles of the Movement', and his legitimacy came therefore from the victory of the Nationalists in the Civil War.

In the 1970's the regime was under pressure. The workers no longer accepted the 'official' unions and set up their own workers' commissions; there were serious strikes. The middle classes were attracted by the new prosperity over which the regime had presided, yet increasingly conscious of the political and social gap between Spain and the rest of Europe. There was unrest among students.

However, it was the older, intractable problems of Spanish history which created most difficulties for the regime. The Basque provinces and Catalonia enjoyed a measure of self-government under the Second Republic; this autonomy vanished in the period after the Civil War. Catalans and Basque nationalists sought to recover their lost liberties and their efforts to do so were suppressed. Basque nationalism has developed an extremist terrorist wing, the ETA. It was the ETA which, in December 1973, succeeded in assassinating the Prime Minister, Admiral Carrero Blanco, the main supporter of continuismo—the survival 'after Franco' of the regime more or less in its existing form.

### The Future
Carrero Blanco's successor was a civilian, Arias Navarro. During the first months of his premiership a division developed between

*Left: The lying-in-state and funeral of General Franco caused scenes of widespread grief in Spain, after nearly 40 years of personal rule. Right: The inauguration of King Juan Carlos, Franco's heir, with whom lies the hope for a peaceful transition to full democracy in Spain*

two philosophies of survival for the regime. The aperturistas wanted an 'opening', a quasi democratization which would bring a greater degree of participation and therefore 'institutionalize' some of the conflicts in Spanish society. 'The men of the bunker' believed any liberalization of the regime would lead to its destruction. The aperturistas failed and left the ministry in October 1974. So, when Franco died after a long illness in November 1975, the regime had not changed very substantially.

It was no longer supported by the forces that had welcomed the victory of Franco in 1939. The Church felt uneasy about its alliance with the state. In the Basque Provinces the local clergy were sympathetic to Basque demands. A considerable proportion of the episcopacy still clung to the old view of the Church as one of the pillars of the regime, but the younger priests in particular believed that the Church should free itself from its alliance with the existing state. They lent their vestries to meetings of the workers' commissions, and criticized the police action of the government. The Falange, in its original form, was an historic memory; the business community was nervous and many of its members were eager for entry into the European Economic Community, the price for which would be liberalization of the regime. The opposition had always been weakened by splits (largely between the Communists and other parties, between the exiles and the internal opposition); it now sought unity on a programme of democracy and amnesty for political prisoners.

It will fall to King Juan Carlos to preside over the transition to full democracy for, in the end, there is no alternative. The transition will be opposed by those now in power who fear the vengeance of the opposition. It will be difficult if there is a collapse of public order. In the last instance the peaceful transition to democracy will depend on the army, for, now, as before, the army is the ultimate arbiter of public life in Spain.

# West Germany: Post-War Prodigy

*Above: A German cartoon of 1964 comments on West Germany's importance in any attempted East-West détente. Johnson tries to break down Erhard's stubborn unwillingness to approach a grumpy Khrushchev: 'Go on, be nice to Uncle Niki,' he says. Below: Erhard and Adenauer — two major architects of post-war West Germany. Erhard's 'economic miracle' in the 1950's provided a firm base from which Adenauer could pursue his policy of reconcilation with France and the rest of Western Europe. Bottom: Karl Schiller, the economics minister from 1966 to 1969. His youthful brilliance guided the country through a critical period of economic development*

The Federal Republic of Germany is a progeny of the Cold War, one expression of the post-war deterioration of the relations between the USA and Russia and their respective satellites or allies. It bore all the birthmarks of improvisation. The victorious allies decided neither to eradicate Germany as a nation by vast annexations, nor to allow it a government of its own with which to conclude a peace treaty. Instead they assumed the internal and external sovereignty of the defeated country.

This was inevitably a temporary solution and the need for an alternative was soon felt as the cleavage between the two major world powers widened. The development of the three Western zones went along on an ad hoc basis. Only the 'spectre of Communism', created by Russian action in Czechoslovakia and in Berlin in 1948, provided the climate of opinion conducive to setting up the German Federal Republic in 1949. By 1955 it had become constitutionally sovereign.

In contrast to the first German Republic, the Federal Republic so far has been remarkable for its political stability. Other factors apart, political stability has been a consequence of the considerable simplification of the Federal Republic's parliamentary life. Whereas Weimar, under the impact of internal and external events, had its democratic Centre eroded to the benefit of the extremes of both Right and Left, the Federal Republic in successive elections since 1949 has demonstrated a remarkable consolidation of its democratic forces. West German voters have increasingly given their support to the Christian Democrats (the Christian Democratic Union [CDU] with its Bavarian wing, the Christian Social Union [CSU]) and the Social Democrats (SPD). In 1949 the two together polled 60·2% of the vote; twenty years later that share of the poll had increased to 88·8%. In 1949 the margin between the two major parties was still 8·3%. By 1969 it had narrowed to 3·4%—not enough to prevent the formation of a Socialist-Liberal coalition. Slowly but steadily the SPD caught up and overtook the CDU, due to the increasing dominance of the urban SPD vote and the influence of urban patterns of behaviour upon the immediately surrounding countryside, as well as to the increasingly moderate image of the SPD. By the time of the election of 1972, the SPD with 45·9% of the vote, overtook the CDU/CSU, which polled 44·8%. It was still necessary for Brandt's party to renew the coalition with the FDP (which increased its share to 8·4% of the vote), so that the

FDP leader Walter Scheel, as Vice-Chancellor and foreign minister, continued to win a share of the credit for the Government's achievements in foreign policy. In 1974, Brandt was replaced by Helmut Schmidt as Chancellor, and Scheel's place as foreign minister was taken by his FDP colleague, Hans-Dietrich Genscher, and the popularity of the governing coalition appeared to increase. As the election of October 1976 approaches, it appears likely that seven years' effective exercise of power will give the present coalition the advantage over a divided and indecisive CDU opposition. In any case, 'coalitionitis' is likely to persist in the future.

There is no harm in this, providing there exists a strong parliamentary opposition, be it the Christian Democrats or the Socialists. One of the main factors for the re-emergence of extreme right-wing radicalism under Adolf von Thadden and his NPD at a provincial level in 1966-67 was the protest vote against the 'Grand Coalition' of CDU/CSU-SPD—a coalition for which there was no pressing need and which left particularly the younger voter frustrated. It seemed that the only possible alternatives were the NPD or the 'extra-parliamentary opposition'· (APO). The SPD's firm commitment on the eve of the elections not to enter again into any Grand Coalition provided the electorate with an acceptable alternative and as a result pushed the NPD back into the political wilderness.

But the political stability of the past twenty years could hardly have been achieved had it not been based on an expanding economy. What the Federal Republic's first minister of economics Dr Ludwig Erhard called the 'social market economy' was, until 1966, no more than the dogma of an economic liberalism of a specifically German brand. Free competition was encouraged, as was the free play of all economic forces; yet at the same time the federal government retained a role which would allow it to control and if necessary to direct them as well as absorb all economic and social conflicts associated with a traditional liberal society.

### The 'economic miracle'

West Germany's economic recovery was heralded by the monetary reform of 20th June 1948. In 1946 the index of industrial production had been thirty-three in relation to a level of 100 in 1936. Three years later when the Federal Republic came into being the index figure had already risen to ninety. 'Full employment' was achieved during its first four years of existence. To the world outside it appeared a 'miracle'. The miracle is explicable in terms of hard work and the existence of a pool of highly skilled industrial workers, mainly those expelled from Germany's lost eastern territories. Their economic and social integration into the Federal Republic is one of the main reasons accounting for the 'economic miracle'.

The desire for a stable currency was sufficient incentive for an endeavour to make up the material losses of the war. But America's Marshall Plan was of vital importance, for although Western Europe as a whole needed help, West Germany needed it more: only an economically prosperous country would constitute a politically viable unit.

Dr Ludwig Erhard's 'social market economy' allowed free production, made available a vast range of consumer goods, and established a price level determined in part by the law of supply and demand. In order to limit the amount of money in circulation, prices were also kept relatively stable during the early years of the Federal Republic. Production increased, as did wages and of course profits. The Federal Republic's GNP in constant prices increased by ninety-two per cent between 1949 and 1969. Though the balance of payments was in the red up to 1951, from 1952 higher exports led to increasing surpluses. And by 1956 the gold and foreign currency reserves amounted to DM17,580 million. As reserves continued to increase, the Federal government carried out in March 1961 a five per cent revaluation of the DM, to be followed eight years later by one of eight-and-a-half per cent. The general tendency was for capital to be reinvested for further expansion of home industries rather than for investment abroad. But even so the Federal Republic occupies seventh position in the list of countries which invest abroad. At the head of this list is the USA, followed by Great Britain and France. West German investments in Europe are heavily concentrated in EEC countries, and those overseas in North and South America.

Naturally external events such as the Korean War did much to stimulate the growth of West Germany's economy, but even after 1953 extremely favourable economic growth continued, interrupted by a minor recession in 1966 which was overcome twelve months later.

The Federal Republic's foreign policy was for the first fourteen years effectively determined by the man who was also the republic's first Chancellor: Konrad Adenauer. His two major objectives were the restoration of West Germany's position within the framework of a politically and economically integrated Western Europe, and secondly, the reconciliation between the ancient contenders for mastery in Europe: Teuton and Gaul. German reunification seems to have come a poor third. None of his two major objectives was achieved fully, though they were objectives which could hardly be attained within fourteen years. The actual measure of achievement was nevertheless substantial.

Adenauer envisaged that the military integration of West Germany in Europe would be within the European Defence Community. The rejection of this plan by France in 1954 was one of his most severe setbacks since it brought back a new German national army which, though part of NATO, might become an instrument of power which could serve a different political bloc and ends other than those he envisaged. What Adenauer wanted was a secure rather than a strong state. He endeavoured to avoid subjecting fifty-five million Germans, many of whom were still not completely integrated during the Federal Republic's first decade, to any serious political temptations. Personal happiness and a reasonable standard of living were preferential to questionable greatness – therefore 'no experiments'. Those who have looked on Adenauer as a 'revanchist' as a man whose primary aim was to fan East-West tensions, may well have done him wrong. Adenauer knew too well that any careless weakening of the West's guarantees for the Federal Republic could have a devastating effect upon its population.

Perhaps Adenauer's vision of the Europe of the future throws into relief the limitations of his political vision. He underestimated the national forces which determine the policies of Germany's Western neighbours. The suggestion that for the sake of integration they should forego part of their political sovereignty also shows a lack of empathy. They had no reason to say goodbye completely to their history: they had remained nations and emotionally were in accord with their past. Little wonder that among those inclined to be more hostile to Adenauer, he is credited with aiming at the establishment of another 'Mitteleuropa'.

### Deep suspicion of the East
Adenauer regarded the East with deep suspicion, Prussians and Russians alike, the former particularly because they were 'red' Prussians. Moulded by an urban, Rhenish, Roman Catholic environment, anything east of the Elbe was suspect to him. Hence 'liberty' meant more to him than German 'unity', much to the despair of his great opponent Kurt Schumacher, leader of the SPD. Had Adenauer had a free choice it seems plausible that he might well have written off East Germany entirely – but on this issue the electorate determined his position. His one great legacy is, as one of his obituaries put it in 1967, that he taught Germans that it was possible to walk tall and straight even without wearing a uniform.

The Federal Republic's claim to be the sole representative of the German nation brought immediate advantages but in the long run also considerable disadvantages. Whereas Adenauer claimed continuity, Ulbricht could ignore the obligations of the past by pointing to an explicit discontinuity and a new beginning. The federal government's position was put to the West German parliament on 22nd September 1955 when Adenauer stated that 'in our relation with third states we shall main-

tain the present position with regard to the so-called German Democratic Republic. I must emphasize that the federal government will also in future consider the establishment of diplomatic relations with the "DDR" by third states with which we have diplomatic relations as an unfriendly act, since it would further deepen the division of Germany.' A year later this statement was qualified in the sense that the 'federal government would in a case of this nature examine its relations with the state concerned'. How and when these declarations obtained the name 'The Hallstein Doctrine' is not clear. In any case this description is misleading, for it suggests a personal interpretation by Professor Hallstein, the secretary of state. And it placed unnecessary doctrinal shackles upon Germany's foreign policy.

In fact the statement was no more than an amplification of the attitude of not accepting Germany's permanent division, and of defending the principle of German unity against Russia's attempt to establish a second German state. Such an amplification was thought necessary particularly since free elections did not and still do not exist in the DDR – as long as it was possible for East Germans to vote against their government with their feet, they did so most demonstratively. But the so-called Hallstein Doctrine was being eroded even before Chancellor Willy Brandt implied a de facto recognition of the DDR in his first policy statement of 30th October 1969. Perhaps the DDR's new constitution of 1968 provided him with one by its first paragraph, according to which the DDR is a socialist republic 'of the German nation'.

The issue of German reunification is still officially alive and will remain so until the people in the DDR are given the opportunity to express their opinion freely. But hopes in West Germany that reunification would only be a matter of a few years, though common in the 1950's, have largely been abandoned not only at the official level but, according to a recent public opinion poll, by over seventy per cent of the West German electorate.

Against this background of public support, the Brandt-Scheel government embarked on a dynamic new policy towards the East. It is in many ways ironical that the Eastern policy should have become the main element in the programme of the new government, since both the SPD and the FDP, during the 1969 election campaign, had emphatically stated that their main objective was internal reform within West Germany. The Ostpolitik acquired prominence only through a number of accidents, including the fact that the two coalition partners could not agree on some of the details of domestic reform. By the end of 1970 Brandt had laid what appeared at the time to be firm foundations for a new relationship between the Federal Republic and its eastern neighbours. The Oder-Neisse frontier had been recognized as the permanent frontier between Germany and Poland, and the division of the German nation into two states had also been tacitly accepted by Brandt's readiness to hold discussions with his East German counter-

*Aspects of the new German affluence. 'Girlie' magazine shop (the proprietor still tries to preserve old-fashioned respectability as a 'Dr')*

Photo: David Brinson

part, Willi Stoph. Brandt's visits to Moscow and Warsaw, in August and December 1970, led to the signing of non-aggression pacts which, it was hoped, would help to normalize West Germany's relations with the Soviet Union and Poland. As far as the difficult question of Berlin was concerned, an international agreement between the Soviet Union and the Western powers, signed in September 1971, recognized the continuing right of West Berlin to maintain links with West Germany. The whole complex of East-West treaties was completed by the Basic Treaty between the two German states, signed at the end of 1972. However, the fact that the SPD/FDP coalition was under immense pressure to produce results, caused the negotiations between West Germany and Russia, as well as those with East Germany, to be carried out rather quickly, leaving behind a number of ambiguities in the interpretation of the treaties. Naturally this left the coalition highly vulnerable to the charges of the CDU/CSU opposition, especially important in 1976, the election year.

This accomplishment in establishing a new relationship between the Federal Republic and its eastern neighbours depended, of course, on the agreement of the Soviet Union. In 1968, alarmed by the early development of a more flexible West German policy towards the East during Willy Brandt's period as foreign minister, the Russians had invoked the threat of this policy as one of their reasons for invading Czechoslovakia. A little more than a year later, deprived of the NPD bogey and with Brandt as Chan-

cellor, Leonid Brezhnev declared that 'We are against the division of Europe into military blocs confronting one another. We support collective European security and the easing of tensions, the establishment of good relations with all nations including the Federal Republic.'

Walter Ulbricht, the powerful leader of the German Democratic Republic ever since its establishment in 1949, was deeply alarmed by the prospect of an understanding between Moscow and the West Germans. He was, in his way, as tenacious as Adenauer, and his regime had risen to a position of great influence in the Warsaw Pact during the years of the Cold War. He was particularly alarmed at the prospect of being forced into a closer relationship with West Germany, because he was aware that many sectors of the East German population were eager for closer links with the West. This applied not only to older Germans with memories of a united Reich, but also to the rising generation of young technicians and administrative experts who were not by any means committed to the ideological aims of the East German State. Ulbricht therefore used all possible means to perpetuate the tension arising from the Berlin problem, and to convince the Russians that the differences between East and West Germany were irreconcilable. By 1971, when Brezhnev was determined to achieve a more stable relationship with West Germany, the time had come for Ulbricht to be removed from power. The Russians replaced him by Erich Honecker, a loyal East German party official who could be relied on to accept the Russian

line. The German Democratic Republic thus signed the necessary agreements with the West German State—though Honecker insisted obstinately that the establishment of diplomatic links with the Federal Republic only underlined the East German viewpoint that there were now two German nations, and that the notion of reunification must be abandoned for ever. The East German doctrine of 'demarcation', by insisting on a relationship of competitive coexistence between the two German rival states, ensured that the problem of German reunification would continue to preoccupy Europeans for the 1970's and beyond.

### NATO's major conventional land power

The Federal Republic entered the 1970's as Europe's economic giant as well as being Western Europe's and NATO's major conventional land power. In 1976 its military forces reached 495,000, the level stipulated by NATO, for the first time, and during the NATO manoeuvres in autumn 1975 displayed a degree of efficiency and effectiveness which had not been thought possible six years earlier.

At the outset, the basis for this West German army was extremely precarious. During the 1950's NATO's strategic concept, although committed on the public platform to forward defence, consisted of plans designed to meet and halt any Russian advance west of the Rhine. In other words, the first task of a German 'national' army would have been to retire beyond the borders of its own territories in order to defend its western neighbours. Only if a counter-

*Left: Düsseldorf head office of Alfred Thyssen's huge industrial complex.* **Right:** *Reactor, part of the commercial nuclear energy plan*

attack was possible could it hope to recover its own national territory. For an army in its infancy this was hardly helpful in building up morale, or inspiring the German tax-payer with any great confidence in it.

One of the first tasks of Franz-Josef Strauss, when appointed minister of defence in 1956, was to persuade the western allies to accept forward defence in principle, i.e. at West Germany's eastern zonal frontier. Though successful in this, he encountered difficulties at home where the demands for manpower by the armed forces clashed with the demands of a rapidly expanding economy. The economy won and West Germany had to inform its allies that it would not be able to meet its NATO obligations for some time to come. As an alternative Strauss espoused the Eisenhower administration's concept of massive nuclear retaliation. The nuclear threshold was lowered and the response to a 'conventional' attack would be the immediate use of nuclear weapons. In 1958 it was planned to set up a total of thirty NATO divisions by 1963, each equipped, as would be their air forces, with tactical nuclear weapons. Atomic warheads began to be stockpiled in Western Europe including the Federal Republic, guarded jointly by Americans and Germans. This step also took into account what was then Bonn's attitude, that only participation in the access to nuclear weapons would give it an equal and decisive voice in the councils of the West in general and the German question in particular.

This alternative also determined Strauss's choice of the American Starfighter for the

Luftwaffe. One of its several versions was to be a nuclear-strike craft, capable of bombing targets as far east as Minsk. Together with subsequent abortive projects, such as the MLF and the ALF, it gave the Bundeswehr a potentially offensive character, a feature duly exploited by Eastern propaganda.

In effect, according to 'war games' and manoeuvre results, only since late 1967 has the Bundeswehr been able to overcome its teething troubles and fulfil its role as a defensive force on land as well as in the air. Only its navy appears to have reached a high degree of proficiency at a very early stage and in the decade from 1960–70 could be expected to succeed in its task of effectively aiding its NATO allies in containing the Russian fleet in the Baltic. But since the Russian naval build-up in the Baltic, NATO's naval forces have not been able to keep up the pace set by the Russians, and the West German navy in particular has been allowed to develop serious defi-ciencies which are not likely to be remedied before the end of the 1970's.

Since 1967 the Bundeswehr has also adopted a much more flexible concept of defence, placing much greater reliance on conventional forces. The aim is to defeat any conventional attack with limited aims primarily by anti-tank defence relying on what is now considered NATO's best battle tank, the Leopard Panzer, which is clearly superior to the Russian T-62 used by all the Warsaw Pact powers. In addition to the Leopard there are also self-propelled anti-tank guns operating to a depth of

approximately seventy miles and—as a result of the lessons learned from the Six-Day War in the Middle East—an array of anti-tank missiles, primarily of the *Milan* and *Hot* type, mounted on self-propelled carriers and helicopters. But the crisis affecting in varying degrees the economies of the western countries has had its effects on NATO also. The attempts to cut national budgets drastically has affected the defence sector seriously, so much so that West Germany's allies, including the US, are no longer capable of meeting their NATO obligations. According to General Steinhoff, until April 1974 chairman of NATO's defence committee in Brussels, NATO forces in 1976 and for several years to come will not be in a position to hold up any attack from the East for longer than a few days.

Paradoxically the economic crisis has also affected the Bundeswehr favourably. Whereas between 1956 and 1969, the Federal Republic had the highest rate of officially approved conscientious objectors to military service in the world (40,000 cases), this rate has dwindled into insignificance. 'Job security' has made the German army attractive again, together with its extensive programme of further education. This makes it compulsory for regular officers to acquire an academic degree, while NCO's and other ranks, be-cause they serve a minimum of four years, become skilled craftsmen and engineers and if they wish to leave the armed forces they are snapped up by industry immediately, despite an unemployment rate of more than one million.

Several features distinguish the officer

corps of the Bundeswehr from its predecessor, the Wehrmacht. The most important of these being, perhaps, the radical difference in the social origins of its officer corps. Sons of skilled workers and artisans (23%) outnumber the sons of industrial managers (20%), with the sons of civil servants coming third (16%) and those of professional soldiers fourth (12%).

At the beginnings of the Bundeswehr, armaments production had very little effect on the German economy, but since the late 1960's with the introduction of the Leopard tank, followed in the early 1970's with the highly sophisticated Marder Armoured Personnel Carrier, international demand has been heavy. Demand is in excess of supply, the supply being limited by the German government's self-denying ordinance not to supply military hardware to any but NATO countries. However, as a result of the economic depression, the SPD as well as the German trade union movement are demanding increased export in order to secure jobs threatened by the government's pruning of its own defence budget.

Nor has scientific and technological research been encroached upon in the Federal Republic by military demands. In 1954 the Federal Republic signed an agreement in which she undertook not to manufacture atomic, bacteriological, or chemical weapons. But, as in any highly industrialized country, the scientific and technological potential to do so is there. This has been underlined by the financial support given by the Federal government to the atomic energy programme which in turn is part of the EEC's atomic energy programme under the auspices of EUR-ATOM. West German scientists have succeeded in developing a new type of nuclear reactor in which the energy of neutrons is not curbed or neutralized through breaking down substances such as heavy water or graphite. Energy is released by means of a gas centrifuge, simultaneously converting uranium 238 into plutonium.

The development of the gas centrifuge eliminates dependence upon the supply of enriched uranium from the USA. The upshot of this scientific and technological development has been Anglo-Dutch-German approval of a proposed agreement of December 1969 for the construction of plants using the gas centrifuge process. Theoretically the way is open for the manufacture of atomic weapons, but from a practical point of view it can be argued that even the possession of nuclear weapons by the Federal Republic is a non-issue. Given her small geographic size and position, as in the case of any other Western and Central European nation, dabbling in 'atomic power' politics would be tantamount to suicide. Proceeding from the absurd hypothesis that the Federal Republic would succeed in getting in a first strike against Eastern Europe, Russia's remaining counter-strike capacity would turn Germany into an uninhabitable desert.

While the Federal German government has heavily subsidized the atomic energy programme, other sectors have been completely neglected. Pure and industrial chemistry – in which Germany once led the world – have fallen to a level which, if allowed to remain, would over the next decade reduce the Federal Republic in these fields to the status of an under-developed nation. Since 1966, however, the West German government has made it a cardinal point of policy to encourage both these types of research.

## The furor teutonicus

West Germany's economic strength in Europe has been politically neutralized by Germany's division and by her economic and military integration in the EEC and NATO respectively. But within the EEC countries the fear of the *furor teutonicus* can still be quickly whipped up. This was shown during the monetary crisis of 1968. It is evident in the memorandum which eight former Gaullist ministers submitted to President Pompidou before his departure to The Hague conference in December 1969. In it they expressed their opinion that 'the establishment of solid guarantees against any German hegemony represents the precondition of a lasting system of security'. Gaullist ministers were not the only Frenchmen to express sentiments of this kind. *Les Echos* insisted that 'the industrial confrontation with Germany is more important than that with America'. Suffering from their own domestic crises, the rise of the phoenix from the ashes inevitably caused a good deal of ill feeling among some of the victorious allies.

These fears were voiced again on several occasions when the Federal Republic's power became apparent, for instance during a Franco-German disagreement about the level of price increases under the European Community's agricultural policy in September 1974. By now the British Government, hoping vainly for large German subsidies for regional development through the EEC, had also become fully aware that Germany's economic might entailed political power.

In May 1974, after a period as Chancellor in which he had vastly contributed to confirming Germany's high standing in the world, Willy Brandt resigned after an undignified scandal involving his relationship with an East German spy. Perhaps the greatest of his achievements was the Eastern policy, by which he reconciled West Germany with Poland and the Soviet Union in a way comparable to the reconciliation with France and Israel achieved by his great predecessor, Adenauer. Under Brandt's successor, Helmut Schmidt, power passed to a new generation of German politicians, and the moral standing which Brandt had conferred on Germany was used in a more pragmatic and hard-headed way. Although the Federal Republic remained deeply committed to the construction of a strong European Community, there were now clear limits on the extent to which Germany would hand out financial subsidies to her partners. The Federal Republic fully adopted the new and less high-flown objectives of the European Community – a Community in which national interests would henceforth be more carefully calculated. With one-third of the total economic strength of the nine-member European Community, the Federal Republic could afford as well as anyone else to place national interests higher on its list of priorities.

Konrad Adenauer, a European Christian Democrat, set his imprint upon the first phase of the life of the Second German Republic. His successor Willy Brandt, a European Socialist, helped to consolidate Adenauer's achievement by leaving a Federal Republic which was strong economically, politically, and morally: a Federal Republic which would continue to play a leading part in the affairs of the Western world, although it would never forget the problem represented by the other part of the German nation still living under the rule of the German Democratic Republic.

*Left: Willy Brandt, Chancellor of the Federal Republic from 1969–1974. He was forced to resign from office after a scandal involving an East German spy. **Right:** Helmut Schmidt, Brandt's successor, one of the new generation of German politicians*

# France: The Fifth Republic

If the French revolution of 1958 was a revolution, then it was a very prolonged one. The immediate crisis, which had begun on 13th May with the rising of the students and settlers of Algiers, seemed to be resolved by 1st June when de Gaulle received the approbation of the Assembly and when he was voted full powers to produce a new constitution. But this constitution had to be worked out. It had to be approved by a referendum held throughout the overseas territories as well as in metropolitan France. A general election had to be held. And then a presidential election had to take place, in which the two chambers, together with some 80,000 notables (mayors and municipal councillors, more or less the same people who elected the Senate) formed an electoral college and voted General de Gaulle as President of the Republic. In January 1959 he installed himself at the Elysée Palace and invited M. Michel Debré to be the first Prime Minister of the new republic.

During these months there had been a good deal of speculation about de Gaulle and about the policies that he would follow. A number of politicians, led by Mendès-France (who lost his seat in the elections of 1958), refused to have anything to do with the General. They believed that he was indelibly marked by the circumstances of his coming to power, which meant that he owed his position to the military. The regime could only become a military dictatorship. On the other hand, there were other politicians who believed that the period of Gaullism could only be a short one. De Gaulle had a mission, that of resolving the Algerian crisis. Once this was accomplished and once some solution had been found to the war that had been dragging on since 1954, then there would be no further need for de Gaulle and normal political life would be resumed. They were encouraged in this belief by the General's age (he was sixty-nine when he became President) and by his apparent reluctance to break with the politicians of the Fourth Republic, since M. Pinay for example, a man whom de Gaulle was reputed to dislike, remained minister of finance in Debré's government. If other politicians believed de Gaulle might be in power for a long time, no one foresaw eleven years of Gaullist rule.

De Gaulle himself was more skilful than he had been earlier in the days of the Liberation or the Rally of the French People. The referendum, the general election, and the presidential elections showed that he had overwhelming support, and

that there was no opposition, whether Communist or non-Communist, capable of appealing to the population as a whole. De Gaulle had all the prestige of great patriotism; he could not be held responsible for the mistakes and the agonies of the Fourth Republic; he was very obviously both a world figure and an historical personality, and he exploited his position in two deliberate ways. Firstly, he demonstrated that, apart from himself, there was no one who could be expected to offer any solution to the Algerian problem. All sides looked to him, and by prolonged silences as well as by a deliberate ambiguity of phrase, he encouraged widely divergent ideas of what he would do. But the emphasis was always on de Gaulle. There was no other statesman who was prepared to offer a policy or to take the responsibility for the affair. Secondly, de Gaulle realized the advantages of personalizing power. The Fifth Republic coincided with the spread of television in France and de Gaulle showed a mastery of television technique. His television appearances, a series of carefully stage-managed press conferences (which were also televised), and a number of tours through the provinces, were an essential part of Gaullism. He became a version of Bagehot's definition of monarchy, an interesting man doing interesting things. He dramatized his position. He spoke of his country and himself being together again; he called upon the French people to help him; he claimed that it was he who incarnated the sovereignty of France since 1940. It was always he who chose the moment, and the manner, of these utterances. There were no airport interviews, no kerb-side press conferences, no parliamentary questions. He therefore used the capital of his words carefully. And he always suggested that, for Frenchmen, this was a period which could become one of greatness.

But one should not make the mistake of seeing de Gaulle alone. Those who claimed that de Gaulle was an illusionist usually meant that de Gaulle was pretending to a power that France did not possess. In reality, it could be said that he was pretending to a power that he himself did not possess. He was forced to feel his way much

*Paris, May 1968.* **Above right:** *Demonstrators depict the President hitch-hiking home to Colombey. The following April de Gaulle fell from power, but for a time after the May riots most Frenchmen continued to support him.* **Right:** *Gaullist rally*

451

more than he allowed it to appear. His changes of policy, broken promises, the ambiguities of many of his statements, arose from an awareness of what was possible rather than from any Machiavellian mastery of affairs. And it is difficult to see how de Gaulle would have succeeded had a Gaullist party not been formed that was to win the elections of 1958 and 1962. It was part of the myth of Gaullism that de Gaulle was above political parties. It is undoubtedly true too that this new Gaullist party, the UNR (Union pour la Nouvelle République) put fidelity to the General as its first principle. But its very success made de Gaulle dependent on it. The officials, the technocrats, the administrators also grew in number and in importance. Through them, as through the UNR, some sections of the patronat, and of the banks, exerted their influence.

The period from 1958 to 1969 can best be described in a number of phases. The first is the institutional phase, which began in 1958 and which was to be continued in a number of subsequent reforms. The second, which also began in 1958 and which was concluded in 1962, was the Algerian phase. The third, stretching from 1962 to 1966, can be described as the climax of Gaullism, while a fourth phase marks the decline of de Gaulle, and is particularly apparent from 1967 to his resignation on 28th April 1969. It is important to note that none of these periods is completely uniform. Perhaps one of the characteristics of de Gaulle's method of government was to allow things apparently to drift, and then, suddenly, to animate the situation by some intervention. Such an intervention was not always successful, and the fortunes of de Gaulle's regime therefore varied. Nevertheless these phases can be discerned.

There can be little doubt that de Gaulle gave prime importance to the need to create a new constitution. If the world thought that his major preoccupation was with Algeria, then the world was wrong. When de Gaulle visited Algiers on 4th June 1958, his confrontation with the crowd in the Forum was one of the major episodes of his career. His opening words to them showed his ability to find the right phrase. 'I have understood you' he said ('Je vous ai compris'). But he did not say what he had understood. And he went on to speak about the renovation of France. While everyone waited for de Gaulle to opt for or against Algeria remaining French, it was a typical Gaullist tactic that he should refuse to choose either of the alternatives, since whatever his choice he was bound to lose support somewhere. It was tactically wiser to elevate the issue, and to move to a ground where he had more freedom of action. And compared to the Gaullist principle that the state should be strong, the problem of Algeria was only a secondary issue. In this sense Algeria provided the opportunity for de Gaulle to force his constitutional ideas on a political community that would otherwise have been reluctant to accept them.

The basis of Gaullist constitutional ideas was formed by two contradictory principles. The first was that there was a basic unity in France and that no great issue could be decided without the consent of the French people. That was democratic. The second was that there were basic divisions amongst the French people and if these were given free expression in a regime dominated by political parties, then they would paralyse any effective government. Therefore there had to be an authority which was above parliament. Such a principle was clearly authoritarian. Both these principles were incorporated in the constitution of 1958. The Chamber of Deputies, elected in single-member constituencies on a double-ballot system, and the Senate, remained as the legislature. The government, headed by the Prime Minister, was responsible to parliament, and although a number of procedural devices made it difficult, it was possible for the government to be overthrown by a hostile majority. The President of the Republic, elected by the small number of notables, had considerable powers in normal conditions and had the possibility of enlarging these powers in an emergency. There seemed therefore to be some sort of a balance between the powers of parliament and the powers of the President; possibly the compromise centred around the position of the Prime Minister. There was the suggestion, made on one occasion by Chaban-Delmas, the president of the Assembly, that there was one domain reserved for the President (essentially that of foreign affairs and defence), and one for the Prime Minister and the rest of the government.

But de Gaulle changed this compromise, both in practice and in principle. He soon showed that presidential decisions could be taken in all fields of government, and that the President was the force that predominated. Then in 1962, disregarding the opinion of those who believed his action to be unconstitutional, a referendum approved his scheme to have the President elected by universal suffrage. The relationship between the President, thus elected, and the Assembly, also elected by universal suffrage, became difficult to understand. The system, first employed in 1965 when de Gaulle was elected on the second ballot, worked because there was a loyal Gaullist party with a majority in the Assembly.

Like so many things, it is not certain what de Gaulle's opinions on Algeria were in 1958. Almost certainly he was sensitive to the argument that the possession of Algeria was an essential part of France's greatness. But he had never been a colonial general, and he had shown some doubts as to whether the French had succeeded in establishing viable communities in their colonies. He had no liking for the French settlers who, in the past, had been partisans of Pétain and of Giraud and who had shown no enthusiasm for de Gaulle. In particular, he must have been aware of the way in which the war in Algeria was weakening France. In international organizations such as the United Nations, a certain French isolation was created and demonstrated. The French army, instead of being a modern army, equipped for modern warfare in the vital centres of the world, was stuck in the role of an old-fashioned colonial army. Finally, as an acute politician, de Gaulle was aware of the dangers to his own position if those who had organized the 13th May rising, and who were therefore the leading partisans of keeping Algeria French, were allowed to remain powerful.

At first de Gaulle seemed to have some idea of a compromise solution. In the summer of 1958 he said that if any part of the French Union, the association of French overseas possessions and metropolitan France established in 1946, wished for independence, then all they had to do was to oppose the referendum on the new constitution. Only one territory, Guinea, voted against it. De Gaulle therefore seems to have thought that a substantial body of Muslim opinion in Algeria would favour remaining associated with France. He believed that the Muslims, like the French and the Africans, would rally round his prestige and his person. To encourage these Muslims he announced a massive policy of investment in Algeria. To discourage the rebel extremists military activities against them were intensified.

But the failure to adopt integration, and to make Algeria completely and irretrievably French, which had been thought to be de Gaulle's intention, caused a rising by some settlers in Algiers (January 1960). This rising was a failure; the army did not give any support; the weakness of the settlers' position was emphasized, while metropolitan opinion hardened against them. De Gaulle was able to speak of 'Algérie algérienne', of the future existence of an Algerian republic, and started tentative negotiations with certain rebel leaders. Attempts to assassinate him, the creation of a secret army, l'Organisation de l'Armée Secrète (OAS), to fight for French Algeria, and the attempt by four generals, Salan, Challe, Zelter, and Jonhaud, to seize power in Algiers in April 1961, only served to isolate the cause of the French settlers still further.

De Gaulle attends execution of French liberty. Cartoon on referendum of 1969

*Left: De Gaulle inspects the Chelsea Pensioners during his state visit to London, in 1960.*
*Right: Giscard D'Estaing, elected President of France in May 1974. He is committed to the*
*progressive liberalization of French society, but the pace of reform has been slowed by the*
*conservative Gaullist element in the governing coalition*

At what point de Gaulle decided to accept complete independence for Algeria and to abandon his expectation that Algerian Muslims would choose to remain in some sort of association with France is not clear. He had accepted rather easily the break-up of the French Union in 1958 and its supersession by the French Community, and during 1960 a great many African territories became independent. It seems probable that by the end of 1960 (and some would say earlier) he had accepted Algerian independence as inevitable. What remained was to find a solution which would be acceptable to the French, which the rebels would also be able to accept, and which would not appear as a humiliation for the French army. It took more than a year for such an agreement to be found, and de Gaulle was obliged to make concessions (for example, he had stated that the Sahara should remain French). He was assisted, rather than hindered, by the terrorist activities in France of the OAS. In March 1962 the Evian agreements ended the war and prepared the way for Algerian independence, with some paper guarantees for a continued French presence. In April this solution was approved by a huge majority in a referendum. Out of all the bitterness of the Algerian War a national unity had been created after all.

The third phase of Gaullism was marked by the emphasizing of presidential power and prestige. Michel Debré was replaced as Prime Minister by Georges Pompidou, which was very much a personal choice. A referendum was organized to approve the constitutional change whereby the President of the Republic was to be elected by universal suffrage. And the press conference of May 1962, which was almost entirely preoccupied with questions of Europe, showed that General de Gaulle intended to insist upon his own conception of how Western Europe should be organized.

### An important world power

Throughout this period the emphasis was to be on foreign affairs. De Gaulle found scope for affirming his belief in the nation-state as the principal reality of political life and for making France appear to be an important world power. He insisted that the defence of France must be controlled by the French government, and after some attempts to persuade the Americans to reform the North Atlantic Treaty Organization he began a gradual process whereby France disengaged herself from it. He was equally determined that the organization of Europe should not become dominated by any supra-national organization. 'Dante, Goethe, Chateaubriand,' he said in May 1962, 'belong to Europe in the degree to which they were respectively and eminently Italian, German, and French. They would not have been of use to Europe had they been stateless and had they thought or written in some integrated Esperanto or Volapuk.' He considered that the European Economic Community as it existed was convenient for France and he was averse to any modifications. In January 1963 he announced that he did not consider that Great Britain was ready to join Europe, and he thus ended the British application for membership of the Common Market. It was undoubtedly significant that soon after the loss of Algeria the French were able to see their President behaving as the spokesman of Europe.

Like Bismarck, de Gaulle was devoted to diplomacy. He was ready to use all sorts of diplomatic pressures in order to achieve his ends. He made diplomatic overtures towards Soviet Russia and the Communist states of Eastern Europe; he established a special relationship with West Germany; he recognized Communist China; he toured Latin America. And all this was carried out, as he never ceased to explain, on the basis of domestic political stability. A speech of April 1964 in particular emphasized the contrast between the economic stagnation of the past and the vitality of the Fifth Republic. This was *le miracle français* – the French system of economic planning was said to be the best in Europe.

But even at the height of his success, de Gaulle was never altogether secure. In the first ballot of the presidential elections in 1965, de Gaulle only received about forty-three per cent of the votes, and although he won on the second ballot (with nearly fifty-five per cent of the votes cast when the candidates were reduced to two), a majority of the population had clearly voted against de Gaulle.

This movement was to grow. The period of economic expansion came to an end, and de Gaulle began to emphasize the need for France to save gold. This deflationary policy, while popular with the bankers, offended those who believed in the need to modernize. It emphasized the conservative nature of much of the Fifth Republic's activities and gave support to Communist complaints that the working class was not getting its share of the general prosperity. This undoubtedly assisted the opposition to organize itself more effectively. In the general elections of 1967, Communists, socialists and other groups worked together to defeat many Gaullist candidates. For the first time since the Fifth Republic had been formed the government had such a slender majority that the possibility of it being defeated in the Assembly seemed quite real. The Gaullist threat that France would dissolve into anarchy should the Gaullists be defeated seemed to have lost its force. There was increasing speculation about *'après-Gaullisme',* and certain of the General's actions in foreign policy (as when he appeared to encourage the separatists of French Canada) aroused alarm.

The student rebellion of May 1968 therefore took place in an atmosphere of crisis. The student agitation preceded an extraordinarily extensive movement of strikes, and the government appeared powerless. De Gaulle considered resignation. However on 30th May he announced that he would not resign and that the Chamber would be dissolved. This time the threat of anarchy should de Gaulle disappear from the scene seemed real enough. The elections saw a considerable Gaullist majority (de Gaulle replaced Pompidou with Couve de Murville, a faithful official who had been a loyal foreign minister since 1958), and the regime seemed to have emerged strengthened from its worst crisis.

But this was not the case for de Gaulle. He wanted to finish his work of equipping France with institutions. He attempted to introduce a profound modification of the system of centralization and he asked that this should be approved by referendum. But the reform was slow in being prepared; it was complicated and confused; it offended a whole series of interests, many of which would normally have voted for de Gaulle. The result was a majority of those voting 'No' on 27th April 1969. De Gaulle's resignation was immediate, and just over a year later, on 9th November 1970, he died.

Despite de Gaulle's abrupt retirement there was no sign of confusion. The Gaullist Georges Pompidou was elected as President and he held office from 20th June 1969 until his death on 2nd April 1974. He was replaced by Valéry Giscard D'Estaing, who, after a very close contest with the Socialist François Mitterand, took office on 27th May 1974.

# Europe: The Struggle for Survival

The European Community is the first practical attempt to make a dream come true — the age-old dream of uniting Europe not by the force of arms but by the free choice of its governments and peoples. Though great strides have been made, the Community is still far from giving its peoples the single voice in world affairs which it was intended to bring. That is because it has not yet succeeded in creating constitutional machinery capable of formulating common policies, resolving deadlock, and taking and implementing decisions speedily, effectively and democratically.

In May 1944, from the war-torn countries of Europe, there converged on Geneva in neutral Swiss territory, a motley and unlikely band—members of the Resistance movements of Europe, representing all shades of political opinion. They came to see how, out of the slaughter, division and destruction of war, a new Europe could be built—a united Europe, where differences would be resolved by discussion rather than war, and where the bonds between peoples would

*Three problems were to afflict the Common Market: British entry, French nationalism, and agricultural policy. 1 German cartoon (1962) sees Great Britain's concern for the ramshackle Commonwealth as an obstacle to her entry. Kennedy urges Macmillan to move into Europe, compact and functional. 2 'But, my dear Charles, why can't we have a ménage à trois?' says Adenauer to de Gaulle—British cartoon, 1963. De Gaulle feared for France's dominance if Great Britain joined. 3 French farmers protesting against EEC farm policy burn their Prime Minister in effigy. 4 'Witch-hunt' 62'—angry farmers chase sorcerous Europa (German cartoon)*

be so close that further civil war between the peoples of Europe would be not only unthinkable but impossible. The following July they issued a joint declaration in which they set out their belief that 'federal union alone could ensure the preservation of freedom and civilization on the Continent of Europe, bring about economic recovery and enable the German people to play a peaceful role in European affairs.'

In their lives, in their homes and their places of work, most of the peoples of the Continent had known the degradation of defeat and occupation. The meeting of the Resistance leaders in Geneva reflected their determination that such a situation should never arise again, and that the excesses of nationalism which in two world wars had brought Europe to economic chaos and the verge of ruin should be banished from the Continent.

In their aim of uniting Europe, they were joined by an ally of unparalleled prestige. In 1946 Winston Churchill made a triumphant tour of Western European cities, urging a 'sovereign remedy' which would make all Europe, or the greater part of it, 'as free and happy as Switzerland is today. . . . It is to re-create the European family, or as much of it as we can, and provide it with a structure under which it can dwell in peace, in safety and in freedom. We must build a kind of United States of Europe.'

The United Nations and its agencies had already been set up to permit the peoples of the world to co-operate, and the Bretton Woods monetary structure—the International Monetary Fund and the International Bank for Reconstruction and Development (the World Bank)—were in place to see that world trade did not begin to contract because of shortage of funds and that there was a channel for investment funds to flow from the richer to the poorer nations. The weaknesses of the world institutions were already apparent, however: the world had divided into two blocs, and the United Nations suffered from this division. In the Security Council, decisive action on crucial questions of peace and security was made virtually impossible by the veto which each member wielded.

## The years of disappointment

In Europe, Czechoslovakia was taken over in 1948 by a coup d'état engineered by the Russians, and the whole of Europe east of the Oder-Neisse line and north and east of Greece and Yugoslavia was, to all intents and purposes, under Soviet military occupation. In 1948, too, the Soviet siege of West Berlin was overcome only by means of a massive Allied airlift.

The drive towards unity in Western Europe had received a new impulsion from the Marshall Plan for the Continent's economic reconstruction. The Marshall Plan offered American aid to all European countries, but Poland and Czechoslovakia had to withdraw their acceptance of it after the receipt of instructions from the Russian dictator, Stalin. The Western European continental states, and the United States too, had hoped that from the Marshall Plan would emerge a federal structure able to avoid the veto and to move at last towards the peaceful unification of that part of Europe not subject to Soviet orders. Britain was adamant, however, that national sovereignty should prevail and that the basis of the Marshall Plan organization should be intergovernmental co-operation, in which each member state would have a veto over all policy and action. The Organization for European Economic Co-operation (OEEC) and the European Payments Union, which came into being originally to administer Marshall Aid funds, to remove quantitative restrictions on trade, and to provide a clearing account for payments between European states, made excellent progress as they were carrying out these vital, but limited, tasks. As soon as they tried to move beyond them, to the removal of other trade barriers for example, the veto of one or other of the member states blocked progress.

Meanwhile, on the political side, groupings in favour of a United Europe had formed on both Right and Left in all the European countries where the formation of such groups was still permitted. In May 1948 the first Congress of Europe was held in The Hague, and from it emerged the Council of Europe. In the summer of 1949, its Consultative Assembly held its first meeting, in Strasbourg. Unfortunately, that first meeting was to be the high point of its European faith and endeavour. Notions that the Assembly could itself undertake the unification of Europe soon vanished. It had no real powers, and the Council of Ministers rarely met. The year was not out before a British journalist referred to the Assembly as a talking shop. The Council of Europe did indeed become a useful discussion forum and meeting place, whose main achievement was the European Convention on Human Rights. But it was soon clear that it was not destined for great achievements. Its Committee of Ministers could not take decisions binding on the member governments, and even its recommendations were few and of secondary importance, since in practice it sought unanimity before making them. Those numerous federalists and others who still believed in unification rather than traditional inter-governmental co-operation were deeply disappointed with the new economic and political organizations, and with the role the British Government had played in making sure that they had no teeth. Yet, as the menacing clouds of Stalinism loomed in the East, the desire to find a practical means of unifying and strengthening Europe and of bringing Germany back into the European comity of nations became greater than ever.

### The Schuman Plan

On 9th May 1950, France's Foreign Minister, Robert Schuman, launched the plan—assembled by France's chief planner, Jean Monnet—which reversed French policy towards Germany (till then harsh and repressive) and re-charted the course of European history. He proposed that Europe should be united through a series of concrete achievements, which would first create a real basis of solidarity, and then lead to 'the European Federation which is indispensable to the preservation of peace'. The first step would be to pool Franco-German production of coal and steel under a common High Authority, within the framework of an organization open to the other countries of Europe. Thus were spun in the Schuman Declaration the twin threads of pragmatism and idealism which ever since have marked the development of Community Europe.

Out of the Schuman Plan arose the first of the concrete steps—the European Coal and Steel Community (ECSC). It was set up by the Treaty of Paris, signed on 18th April 1951, and its executive body, the High Authority, of which Jean Monnet became the first president, started work in Luxembourg in August of the following year. The member countries were the Six who had responded to Robert Schuman's call in May 1950—France, the Federal Republic of Germany, Italy, Belgium, the Netherlands and Luxembourg. The ECSC established the first common market—for coal, steel and iron ore—by abolishing price and transport discriminations, customs duties, quota restrictions and other trade barriers across the 1,700 miles of land frontiers within the six-nation area. It also enforced the first European anti-trust policy and levied the first European tax—a levy on the value of coal and steel production.

### The high point of federalism

The early 1950's were the high point of European federalism. The structure of the ECSC institutions was unashamedly federalist; it comprised the High Authority, a Council of Ministers whose task it was to reconcile the High Authority's policies for coal and steel with the general economic policies of the member governments, a parliamentary assembly (the Common Assembly of seventy-eight members), and a Court of Justice to ensure the rule of law. The outbreak of the Korean War in July 1950 had reminded an ill-equipped Europe once again of the threat of Communist aggression. The federalists now attempted to move rapidly towards their final goal—political unification of the Six—through a European Defence Community (EDC) and a European Political Community (EPC). In October 1950 the French National Assembly approved the Pleven Plan for a Defence Community, negotiations went ahead, and in May 1952 the Six signed the EDC Treaty, which provided for a European Army, to be controlled through institutions modelled closely on those of the ECSC. Four months later the ECSC Council of Ministers asked the members of its Common Assembly to transform itself into an ad hoc Assembly and draft a Treaty for a European Political Community. The draft, which provided for incorporation of the ECSC and the EDC into the Political Community, was rapidly completed, and approved by the Assembly in March 1953. The EDC Treaty was quickly ratified in Germany, the Netherlands, Belgium and Luxembourg.

The federalist tide was already ebbing, however. Stalin died, and the threat from the East seemed to diminish; the absence of Britain from the EDC raised grave doubts in many minds, particularly in France, about the advisability of rearming Germany; NATO seemed better equipped to face aggression than it had done in 1950. The French and Italian Governments hesitated to put the Treaty to the vote in their National Assemblies, and in June 1954 its fate was sealed by the arrival in power in France of a Gaullist-Radical coalition headed by Pierre Mendès-France. On 30th August the EDC Treaty was rejected by the French National Assembly by 319 votes to 264. The vote signalled the end not only of EDC, but also of the Political Community—and of the attempt to move, in one decisive leap, to full political union of the Six.

### The European Economic Community

Henceforth, the lines of development were to be less spectacular. The 'Europeans', who were in a majority in all six member countries of the ECSC, were not ready to stop there. If the main line was blocked, then a new route must be found. Two were in fact chosen: a customs union, with elements of closer economic union, and an atomic energy Community. The hopes of the federalist, or 'supranational', Europeans reposed in the more supranational European Atomic Energy Community (EAEC, but better known as Euratom) for that was still the time of the post-war energy shortage, and the development of nuclear energy for peaceful purposes seemed an imaginative as well as worthwhile task. But it was along the other route—that of the European Economic Community (EEC), which proved to be slower and more pedestrian, that the Europeans came in sight of their goal of unification. That it proved to be much more distant and elusive than imagined in the first federalist wave was only to be expected.

The EEC and Euratom Treaties were signed in Rome on 25th March 1957. As in the ECSC Treaty, the Six voluntarily delegated certain of their sovereign powers to common or Community institutions, to be exercised jointly by them for the general gain. Under the ECSC Treaty, many powers were delegated directly to the executive body, the High Authority; they were, however, limited to the industrial sectors of coal, steel and iron ore. The EEC Treaty involved a much wider transfer of powers, since the Common Market which it envisaged covered the whole economy of the member states not subject to the ECSC and Euratom Treaties. This explains why the major powers of decision were delegated, by and large, not to the EEC Commission, which represents the general Community interest, but to the Council of Ministers, in which are represented the national interests of the member states.

Both Treaties also provide written constitutions for the Communities they set up.

*Right: The signing of the Rome Treaties, 25th March 1957. Great Britain had refused an invitation in 1955 to take part in negotiations for setting up an economic community—but soon relented. In August 1961 a British application to join the Community was lodged in Brussels. A delegation, headed by Edward Heath, started negotiations*

Keystone Press

The ECSC Treaty, however, set out detailed rules for 'governing' the coal and steel industries; the EEC Treaty merely set out a series of objectives, with deadlines by which they must be reached and the institutional procedure which must be followed in reaching them and in carrying out the policies which are worked out in the process.

The EEC Treaty struck a clear balance between the interests of its member countries. In exchange for granting Germany free access for her industrial exports, France insisted on an agricultural policy which would permit free trade in farm products throughout the Community. The Benelux countries knew that their role as entrepôt traders must benefit. For Italy, special measures were taken, in the shape of the European Investment Bank, the Social Fund, and provision for a common policy on occupational training, to deal with her particular regional problems of under-development and chronic unemployment.

The EEC Treaty also strikes a delicate constitutional balance between the Community interest, represented by the Commission, and the interests of the member states represented in the Council of Ministers. The complex interaction between the Commission and the Council, together with the possibility of majority voting in the Council, was also intended to avoid deadlock, resolve disputes and safeguard national interests, particularly those of the smaller countries.

## De Gaulle and the enlargement of the Community

The attitude of General de Gaulle towards the European Communities had always been contemptuous. He regarded them as an American inspiration, and their supranational pretensions as an affront to the nation state, which for him was the highest form of human organization. When he gained power in 1958 he did not, however, destroy the Communities, but was determined to use them as an instrument of French policy. At the same time, he conducted an unremitting doctrinal war against supranationalism, and in particular the powers of the 'stateless technocrats' of the EEC Commission and their 'pretension' to political status, and the majority vote in the Council of Ministers. Once he had achieved the formulation of a common agricultural policy early in 1965, from which France stood to benefit greatly as the Community's main agricultural producer, the doctrinal war became an over-riding priority, and the attitude of France became obstructive in most fields. Paradoxically, it was de Gaulle's attitude towards the Community, and towards British membership, which effectively stifled progress towards the strong and independent Europe which he would have liked to bring into being. The other five were prepared to have a supranational Europe without Britain or an intergovernmental Europe with Britain, but an intergovernmental Europe without Britain could, for them, mean only French domination. And that the Benelux countries were not ready to accept.

When the Commission in 1965 put forward proposals for providing the Community with its own financial resources and increasing the budgetary powers of the European Parliament, de Gaulle used them as a pretext for a seven-month boycott of the Community institutions. France returned to the fold in January 1966, but only after making it clear that she would accept no further decisions on very important matters by majority vote, but expected the Council of Ministers to go on discussing such matters until agreement was reached. From 1965 to 1969, the Community experienced its leanest years: progress towards economic union was limited to the strict minimum, and Euratom ceased to have any real importance.

De Gaulle's other noteworthy intervention in Community affairs had been his personal veto of British membership in January 1963, after negotiations had been in progress since October 1961. His veto also put paid to applications for membership from Denmark, Ireland and Norway. On 11th May 1967, Britain and Denmark again submitted formal applications for membership, to be followed once more by Ireland and Norway. De Gaulle repeated his veto, but the applications remained 'on the table', overhanging every aspect of Community activity.

## The summit conference of The Hague

The turning point in the Community's development came following the departure of de Gaulle from the French presidency in April 1969. His successor, President Georges Pompidou, adopted a cautious policy of 'continuity' and 'ouverture' which nevertheless held promise of important changes in policy towards the European Community. At a conference held in The Hague in December 1969, the six Community heads of government decided to complete the tasks still remaining under the EEC Treaty, and to set about the twin new tasks of 'deepening' and 'widening', or 'enlarging', the Community. They set July 1970 as the possible date for opening membership negotiations with a Britain still sceptical that the change had really taken place.

The Council of Ministers, under the chairmanship of Belgium's Foreign Minister Pierre Harmel, speedily reached a joint Community negotiating position, and the negotiations opened ahead of schedule on 30th June. The Association Treaty was signed on 22nd January 1972, and on 1st January 1973, Britain, Denmark and Ireland entered the three European Communities. Norway had fallen by the wayside, a referendum to approve membership having given an unfavourable answer; referenda in Denmark and Ireland both gave strongly favourable votes.

## Britain's referendum

The saga of British membership was by no means over, however. In February 1974, Edward Heath's Conservative Government, which had negotiated British entry, was replaced by a Labour Government pledged to 're-negotiate' Britain's terms of accession and submit the results to the British people. In fact, the so-called re-negotiation turned out to be a limited operation which did not involve any actual re-negotiation of Treaty terms. Britain merely requested changes in Community policies (the common agricultural policy, co-operation with developing countries, and regional and industrial policies) a corrective mechanism to ensure that Britain did not pay an unfair share of the Community budget, and guaranteed access for New Zealand butter and cheese to the Community after 1977.

These relatively minor adjustments, regarded by many as pure window-dressing to placate the Labour Party's left wing, were obtained without real difficulty, and the British Government duly declared itself satisfied with them. In a referendum on 5th June 1975, the British people voted overwhelmingly, by 67.2 per cent to 32.8 per cent, to remain in the Community.

## The Community achievement

The core of the European Community's achievement to date has been the creation of a customs union, within which trade barriers have largely been removed and around which a common customs tariff is in force. By July 1968 customs duties among the Six had been abolished, and by July 1977 they were due to be eliminated between the three new members, Britain, Denmark and Ireland, and the Six. Quantitative restrictions among the Nine are already a thing of the past. However, many other forms of trade barrier exist, and not all of them have been eliminated, even among the Six. Tax barriers remain; though a uniform value-added tax system is in force in all the member countries, it still needs a common basis of assessment and, eventually, if the tax barrier at internal frontiers is to be eliminated, harmonized rates. The Commission also plans to remove some of the more glaring differences between the national systems of excise duties, company taxation, and the withholding tax on dividends and interest. Substantial progress has been made with technical barriers to trade under a programme, adopted in 1969, to replace varying national standards by Community standards; goods which meet these standards can be traded freely throughout the Community. Some progress has also been made in opening up public works contracts to Community-wide public tender, but supply contracts are not yet open.

One of the characteristics of all three Community Treaties is the insistence on competition as a means of raising efficiency and living standards and keeping prices down. The Treaties ban cartel agreements and practices which restrict or distort competition in trade between member countries, and the abuse of dominant or monopoly positions. A substantial body of case-law has been built up, and the possibility—utilized on many occasions—of imposing heavy fines ensures that firms take Community competition law into account. The Commission has also been particularly insistent that firms do not use patents and trademarks to carve up the market and artificially increase profit margins.

Nationals of Community countries can now move freely to any country in the Community without having to obtain a work permit. The task of ensuring that individuals and companies can establish businesses or factories, or offer their services without restriction, in Community countries other than their own, is well under way, though hampered by the difficulty of deciding on the equivalence among the vast numbers of different degrees, diplomas and other qualifications issued in the different trades and professions in the nine member states. Some progress has been made in getting rid of exchange controls, so as to enable capital to flow freely to the areas of the Community where it can be most useful, economically and socially; but many of the member states have failed to meet the targets set.

### The battle for Community policies

The EEC Treaty provided for common policies for agriculture, transport and external trade. Subsequent summit meetings—notably those of The Hague, in December 1969, and Paris, in October 1972—have extended the Community's role, though without always setting the specific targets and deadlines which are an important part of the Treaties and of 'the Community method'. The Paris summit of October 1972 formally extended the Community's purview to regional and industrial policy and gave new emphasis to social, environmental and energy policies. It re-affirmed the intention to go ahead with the second stage of economic and monetary union and invited the Nine to adopt an 'overall policy of development co-operation'.

In practice, the Community by 1976, was still at the stage of a largely completed customs union, with a fully developed but much criticized common agricultural policy; a virtually complete external trade policy under fairly frequent attack from assertions of national particularism; some, but not many, of the elements of a common transport policy; and rudiments, but little more, of economic, monetary, regional, industrial, energy, environmental and social policies. The great years of progress of the EEC were 1958–64, when the agricultural policy was formulated and adopted, and 1969–72, when the log-jam of the Gaullist era was broken and the completion, deepening and enlargement of the Community agreed on and achieved.

Those were also the years in which the world was still experiencing a period of sustained growth and technological development unprecedented in the world's history, supported by the relative stability of the Bretton Woods monetary system. In these conditions the added stimuli of the removal of trade barriers, increasing competition and the challenge and opportunities of a greatly enlarged home market helped to make the European Community an area of high investment, rapidly expanding trade, and fast economic growth, in agriculture and services as well as industry. By the end of the 1960's the Six were devoting 24–25 per cent of their gross national product (GNP) to gross investment, compared with $17\frac{1}{2}$–18 per cent in Britain and $16\frac{1}{2}$ per cent in the US (Japan 35 per cent). From 1958 to 1972, the Six increased their trade with each other more than eightfold—from £3,536 million to £29,120 million; they also increased their trade with the rest of the world much faster than the world average, and twice as fast as Britain. Over the 1960's (from 1960 to 1970) gross national product in the Community of Six grew at an annual average

rate of 5.3 per cent, compared with 2.8 per cent in Britain and 4.0 per cent in the US (Japan 11.1 per cent).

The years following the enlargement of the Community in January 1973 were in many ways years of disappointment. From February 1974 till the referendum in June 1975, the British Labour Party sent no members of parliament to Strasbourg and her trade unions were unrepresented in the Community's consultative body, the Economic and Social Committee. The development of Community policies was blocked. Subsequently, the Labour Government showed that its reticence about European unification had not ended with the referendum. Within a few months of the referendum it had asked for derogation from the terms of the Accession Treaty on transport, refused to approve the principle of control of discharge of highly toxic substances into rivers and seas, been less than co-operative in the formulation of a common energy policy, and insisted—alone of the Nine and against all her partners, and in the end without success —on having a separate seat additional to that of the Community at the Conference on International Economic Co-operation.

Enlargement had also give the Community a new breadth of view, even if it had not enabled it to devise a global international strategy. There were now regular European Councils at summit (heads of government) level, and much more effective co-ordination of the action of the ambassadors of the Nine in the capitals of non-member countries. On certain matters such as aid to Portugal and the execution of terrorists in Spain—though not in any crucial foreign-policy development—the Community was able to act as a unit. The Lomé Convention between the Community and forty-seven countries in Africa, the Caribbean and the Pacific (the ACP countries) with a population of 270 million created one of the most complete and effective forms of co-operation in existence between industrialized and developing countries. It has been greatly extended in comparison with its predecessors, the two Yaoundé Conventions, which covered only eighteen countries and eighty-eight million people. It provided 3.39 billion units of account (some £1.7 billion) of aid, including outright grants of 2.1 billion units of account, over a five-year period; set up a highly original export stabilization scheme guaranteeing the forty-seven against loss of export income through fluctuations in commodity prices; and provided for duty-free entry into the Community of all industrial products, and 96 per cent of exports of agricultural products, from the forty-seven, without requiring reciprocity for Community exports.

It is true that this form of aid to a select group of countries constitutes a 'special relationship', and that the Community as such does relatively little, apart from providing food aid, for certain very poor and highly populated areas—the Indian subcontinent, Burma and Indonesia. Much bilateral aid goes from the individual member countries to these areas, however, and in trade the Community has already begun to globalize its help to developing countries through the generalized scheme of preferences (GSP) which it put into force in

1971 and has since greatly improved. Under this scheme the Community has abolished tariffs for its imports of manufactures and semi-manufactures (up to a given ceiling) from all developing countries, and created duty-free or low-tariff quotas for processed foodstuffs.

The Community had worked out before enlargement a trade and co-operation policy for the Mediterranean, under which it planned to sign preferential agreements aiming at free trade with virtually all the countries bordering the Mediterranean, backed up by aid for the poorer developing countries. In 1975 and 1976 it was able to sign the first agreements—with Israel, Morocco, Tunisia and Algeria—under its new policy, and to open negotiations with Egypt, Syria, Jordan and Lebanon. Enlargement also brought with it a vast extension of free trade with the former European Free Trade Area countries: a free trade area in industrial goods with Norway, Sweden, Iceland, Finland, Austria, Switzerland and Portugal came into being on 1st April 1973 to be largely completed by 1st July 1977. It seemed as if trade and economic agreements would be signed by the Community with Comecon, China and Canada.

### A balance sheet

There could be no question in the second half of the 20th century of the Community being unified by an individual 'federator'— a new Napoleon. The Community has, however, tried two 'federations' of a different kind—the common agricultural policy (CAP), and economic and monetary union (EMU). In the early 1960's, the Six were to be pushed rapidly towards a single currency by means of fixing the prices of farm products throughout the Community in terms of a gold-pegged unit of account. In the late 1960's, however, this particular 'conjuring trick' broke down because of the devaluation of the French franc and the revaluation of the Deutschmark and the Dutch guilder, which meant that compensatory payments had to be made at frontiers if free trade in farm products was to continue. EMU was chosen to repair the damage and bring the Six back towards a single currency by gradually locking together the parities of their currencies. Both attempts failed, because the realities of economic government, which determined the course of growth rates, prices, employment levels and the balance of payments, were still almost entirely in the hands of the national governments. There was no Community body with the power to ensure that the member countries' economies moved together rather than apart.

The sudden quadrupling of oil prices by the Organization of Oil-producing Countries (OPEC) in October 1973, aided by the inflationary boom which had preceded it, threw the economies of the Community countries into confusion and emphasized their dependence on the oil-producing countries. Throughout 1973, 1974 and 1975, the gap between the economies of economically viable members and the ailing economies of Britain and Italy widened alarmingly. At the beginning of 1976 the currencies of these two countries were still floating downwards at a

*Meeting of the Council of Europe in Luxemburg on 1st–2nd April, 1976. From left to right: Helmut Schmidt, Chancellor of West Germany; Aldo Moro, Prime Minister of Italy; Léo Tindemans, Prime Minister of Belgium; J.M. Den Uyl, Prime Minister of the Netherlands; Valéry Giscard d'Estaing, President of the French Republic; HRH the Grand Duke Jean of Luxemburg; Gaston Thorn, Prime Minister of Luxembourg; Harold Wilson, former Prime Minister of Great Britain; Anker Jørgensen, Prime Minister of Denmark; Liam Cosgrave, Prime Minister of the Republic of Ireland; François-Xavier Ortoli, President of the European Community*

somewhat alarming rate, while those of the other member states floated jointly against the dollar in the Community 'snake', in company with those of Norway, Sweden and Austria. Britain's inflation in 1975 reached 25 per cent—double the Community average—and Britain alone among the major Community countries still had a massive payment deficit, of some £1.75 billion, in that year. Britain alone still faced a continued increase in unemployment in 1976. The Italian Government crisis early in 1976 brought a sharp fall in the lira and increased doubts about the country's ability to solve its political and administrative problems. The division of the Community into first-class and second-class economies seemed complete, and EMU very far away. The attention of those who believed EMU fundamental to closer union turned to the creation of a parallel European currency co-existing with national currencies and forming the basis of a Community reserve.

## Farm policy survives
The CAP had long been under attack because of its high cost—5.49 billion units of account were allocated to it for 1976, or nearly three-quarters of the total Community budget. The CAP also has the effect of subsidizing efficient as well as inefficient farmers, of tending to push prices upwards, and consequently to produce surpluses and to reduce consumption. But the great agricultural 'stocktaking' of 1974–75 rejected as too expensive any general move to replace price support by direct income aid to farmers, and recommended only some general principles for dealing with points at which the CAP was not working properly—notably the accumulation of surpluses. Despite the defects of the CAP, the Community's agriculture had been transformed since 1950; productivity had risen spectacularly and the proportion of the workforce of the Six occupied in farming had fallen from 30 per cent in 1950 to 11.6 per cent in 1972.

Little progress was made in industrial policy, despite the accumulation of evidence that American industry was again sweeping ahead in the high-technology sectors. The Commission in 1975 submitted to the Council of Ministers proposals for revitalizing the Community's aerospace industry, for example, whose share in world civil aircraft

sales had fallen by 1974 to 6.3 per cent, while that of the US had risen to 93.7 per cent. In the computer industry, Commission hopes of forming a strong European grouping were dashed when Europe's Unidata association broke up following the withdrawal of the French partner, CII, in May 1975 and its merger with the US firm of Honeywell. Regional policy made some advances with the long-postponed creation of a Regional Development Fund in 1975 and its distribution of the first £150 million worth of Community regional aid. But there was no hint so far of a genuine Community regional policy to supplement those of the national governments.

OPEC's quadrupling of oil prices in 1973 following the Yom Kippur War, and the cutting-off of supplies to some Community countries—but not others—by the Arab oil-producing countries, produced a grave crisis during which the Community almost fell apart. France and Britain in particular attempted to solve their own problems separately, without seeking Community solutions, and the Community countries quarrelled bitterly with the US over the appropriate methods for overcoming the crisis. Only gradually did the Nine start putting together the beginnings of a policy to reduce dependence on imported energy from 63 per cent in 1973 to 50 per cent, and if possible to 40 per cent, by 1985, by reducing consumption and developing new sources of energy.

Whenever it had come to a testing time, the Community had failed to speak with a single voice or to have any significant influence. During the energy crisis of 1973, and the Soviet/Cuban intervention in Angola in 1976, its role was limited to issuing somewhat pathetic statements. Rather than act jointly, they—or some of them—rushed to seek whatever individual advantage they could. In both these examples, France led the rush. The notion that the Community had come to be 'a civilian power' was shown to have as little foundation in fact as when the Soviet Union occupied Czechoslovakia in 1968. Major decisions were taken by the two super-powers, and in both the Cyprus and Middle East crises Europe was unable to play any useful part; the role of peacemaker was played by the US. The failure of EMU to date caused increased emphasis to be placed on foreign policy as a means of

unification, but achievements in that field were bound to be very slow until the Community was ready to place foreign policy, and later defence, under a joint institutional system such as that of the Community, with powers to take and implement binding decisions and the instruments of speedy and effective action. That would mean, above all, placing foreign policy within the purview of the Community institutions rather than inter-governmental co-operation, and an increasing use of the majority vote in the Council of Ministers.

## Direct election of the European Parliament
Such a strengthening of the Community institutions could not be envisaged without effective democratic control. That was why the strongest emphasis in Community development in 1976 was placed on the election of the European Parliament by direct suffrage, rather than the system of nomination by and from the national parliaments used so far. The first direct elections were planned for May or June 1978. It was hoped that a directly elected parliament would in time obtain greater powers over legislation and provide a spur to more rapid progress in unification. It was also beginning to be clear that further enlargement of the Community by the entry of Greece, whose application to join was accepted in principle by the Community in 1976, and possibly Spain, whose government had expressed its interest in membership following General Franco's death, together with some smaller Mediterranean countries, would make it all the more necessary to streamline the decision-making process. For the Community's outstanding successes had all been achieved where the member states had the obligation to act as a single entity—in the Kennedy Round of world trade negotiations in GATT (General Agreement on Tariffs and Trade) from 1963 to 1967, in the Lomé Convention with the forty-seven ACP countries, and in the generalized scheme of preferences. It was beginning to be understood that there was little point in proclaiming that Europe must speak with a single voice and regain influence in world affairs, unless the Community was equipped with the constitutional means of taking decisions and of acting speedily, effectively, and democratically.

# The Middle-East Wars

The early 1950's were a period of reassessment for the Arab world. While Israel had become a Jewish state which discriminated against Arabs still left in it, hundreds of thousands of Arab refugees, many of whose families had lived in Palestine from time immemorial, fled from Israel to parts of Palestine still unoccupied by Israeli armies; the Gaza Strip, belonging to Egypt, and the west bank of the Jordan River, which belonged to the Hashemite Kingdom of Jordan. This flight was encouraged by the Israelis, who burned Arab homes and killed many civilians in the intensity of their struggle for independence.

Hatred of Arabs in Israel intensified, and the feeling was mutual. Treatment of Palesttinian Arabs became the *cause célèbre* of Muslim nations all over the world, but few other than those immediately affected—Syria, Jordan and Egypt—paid more than lip service to the cause of those displaced by the Jews. European sympathies were on the side of the Jews. After all, Western Europe and the United States could have allowed emigration of Jewish refugees into their countries after the war, but they had refused. Zionism was championed by the Western nations because of the guilt they shared in covert anti-semitism, which was the cause of Zionism in the first place, and because their propaganda in the Second World War directed against Germany largely centered around German overt racism and anti-semitism. In America it was politically expedient to champion the Jewish cause, since the most populous state at the time, New York, had about four million Jews, and the nation itself had five and a half million, most of whom regularly gave donations to Israel through charities, buying Jewish bonds, and pressuring the US government by various means to supply arms and grants to Israel.

The revolution in Egypt in 1952 which overthrew the corrupt regime of King Farouk eventually brought Gamal Abdel Nasser to power, a superb orator and a man who aspired to becoming the leader of all Arab peoples. Egypt had been within the British sphere of influence since 1882, and even after independence had been granted to Egypt, British troops still policed the Suez Canal and British interests remained paramount in Cairo and Alexandria. It was precisely this influence which Nasser hoped to challenge and break.

In 1954 Nasser negotiated a deal with the United States to have them finance the building of an Aswan Dam, which was

*Humiliation in Sinai, June 1967—an Egyptian soldier captured by Israelis*

Charles Harbutt-Magnum

with the US and the Soviet Union in agreement.

Whatever the motivation, the threats from Washington and Moscow, the cutoff of oil, the hostility of virtually every country in the world, as well as intense hostility from the opposition parties within their countries and significant parts of the parties in power, Britain and France decided to call it a day. A ceasefire and eventually a withdrawal was agreed on the 7th. Britain and France had suffered an unprecedented humiliation, and it took more than a year before relations with the US were put on a firm footing. Anglo-French forces withdrew from the hostilities by December.

The whole affair might have succeeded if Britain and France had taken Eisenhower and Dulles into their confidence, but it was the manner and secrecy in which the invasion was carried out that caused the US to abandon its European allies.

During the years after the Suez War British and French influence in the Middle East rapidly declined, as the British continued to wind up their imperial operations in Africa and Asia and the French under de Gaulle rid themselves of virtually all of theirs,

*Israel's victory over Jordan in June 1967 gave the Israelis full possession of the city of Jerusalem.* **Below:** *Israelis flock to worship at the Wailing Wall, won back by force of arms*

Keren Hayesod/United Israel Appeal

supposed to bring prosperity and power to large parts of Egypt. John Foster Dulles scotched the deal, and Nasser turned to the Soviet Union, which welcomed Nasser and the opportunity to build the dam with open arms. Although British forces left the Suez in 1954, they still maintained a base in Ismailia, so they could re-enter Egypt if they so desired. When the US refused to give Nasser military aid without strings in 1955, Nasser began to encourage guerrilla activity inside Israel and moved closer to the Soviet bloc, which was anxious to become involved in the Middle East in order to fill the obvious power vacuum that the US and the UK were leaving. The arms deal which Nasser struck with Czechoslovakia convinced the new British Prime Minister, Anthony Eden, that Nasser was an evil force who had to be checked early. Invidious comparisons were made between Nasser and Hitler. Eden likened Nasser to the German dictator, who had been encouraged by appeasement in the 1930's. Thus, Nasser's power had to be checked at once in case he seized further influence in the Middle East.

This comparison, in retrospect, seems absurd. Nasser repeatedly tried to buy arms or obtain arms grants from the US and UK, but was refused because of their support of Israel. If Nasser was to appear as a credible champion of Arab interests, and latterly the interests of the Palestinian Arabs, he needed to challenge Israel. The US took a more sanguine view of Nasser, which infuriated both Eden and the Israelis. Israel, in order to stop an increase in Nasser's military strength, considered invading the Sinai peninsula, part of Egyptian territory, late in 1955. By 1956, however, they were able to get support for this pre-emptive strike from Britain and France, who collaborated with Israel in a plot to invade Egypt. Nasser nationalized the Suez Canal, which had been owned by an Anglo-French company, in 1956 and Britain and France, which had already lost parts of their vast colonial empires, wanted to regain lost prestige and assert their independence from the Americans by consorting with

Israel. The US was having an election in November 1956 and wanted no part of anything which smacked of a neo-colonialist display of force, particularly since the United States was trying to maintain and increase its position in the Middle East, above all in Saudi Arabia and the oil-producing states of the Persian Gulf.

The Polish and Hungarian revolutions of October 1956 were an unexpected fillip to the Anglo-French-Israeli plans. The Soviet Union would be tied down with these events, and was obliged to send troops into Hungary in November. All of these dramatic occurrences would allow the invasion forces to continue their preparations in secret with most of the world's press concerned with events in Eastern Europe. Feeling that neither the US nor the USSR would interfere, hopes rose in London and Paris that a swift slapping down of Nasser would be able to proceed successfully.

## The Suez War

On 29th October 1956 the Israeli part of the invasion began. Border posts were quickly seized, and with the help of 36 Mystères of the French Air Force, Israel started to plunge across the Sinai Desert toward Suez. President Eisenhower, astonished by the attack, asked Britain and France to condemn this aggression in the UN, which they, of course, refused to do. Britain began to activate its plans to retake the Suez Canal 'temporarily', the same phrase used by Gladstone when Egypt was occupied by Britain in 1882.

American infuriation with the Anglo-French attack rose dramatically. Eisenhower asked Britain and France to stop in no uncertain terms, and for a few days a diplomatic revolution took place. For a change, America and Russia were on the same side, both demanding that the invasion cease. By the following day fighting between Israel and Egypt had virtually come to a halt, and British and French armoured columns had progressed to within 75 miles of the city of Suez. The United Nations called for a ceasefire,

Daily Telegraph

**Left:** *Some of the greatest tank battles in history were fought in the Sinai Desert and the Golan Heights during the 1973 Yom Kippur War.* **Right:** *Israeli tanks cross the Suez Canal on dam-like bridges during the final withdrawal of their forces as agreed in the Kilometre 101 talks after the Yom Kippur War. Similar bridges were constructed during their break-through across the Canal during the war*

including Algeria, after a vicious guerrilla war which, in fact, continued for almost twenty years.

American influence was greatest outside Israel in the conservative oil-rich sheikdoms of the Persian Gulf and above all in Saudi Arabia, which was threatened by Nasser's growing influence in Yemen. King Hussein of Jordan was perhaps closest to Britain, despite the fact that British control of the famed Arab Legion had long since passed. Nasser forged a union with Syria, the United Arab Republic, but it soon broke up when Syria realized that it would be the junior partner. By 1966 Syria, of all the Arab states, had drawn the closest to Russia, which supplied her with tanks, planes and all sorts of military equipment and economic aid. But despite border activity on the part of Palestinian liberation groups which were loyal to no state and only to their own cause, the situation in the Middle East remained relatively quiet.

Israel's economic growth, thanks to American aid, was phenomenal, and immigration of Jews to Israel from the Afro-Asian world was stepped up to the point where oriental Jews almost outnumbered Jews of European origin in Israel. But skirmishes along Israel's borders with Syria and Egypt increased in the spring of 1967, and finally Nasser asked the UN forces within his territory to leave forthwith. This was a warning to Israel that Egypt might try out the heavy Russian armour and aircraft she now had in her possession. When Nasser announced the closure of the Straits of Tiran to Israeli ships and ships carrying strategic goods to Israel on 23rd May 1967, Israel began to make extensive and well-organized preparations for another pre-emptive strike against her neighbours.

## The Six-Day War

With Jordan, Syria and Egypt ranged against Israel, all with powerful air forces and ground troops, and the latter two well equipped with Russian tanks (Jordan had mostly US and UK armour), Israel faced a real problem in deployment. If she waited for war to come, and she felt that this was inevitable, she would be faced with an attack on three sides. If, however, Israel struck first, where would the first strike come? For the first hours of the pre-emptive strike would bring the might of the other two states upon her. Israel was outnumbered on every count; men, planes and armour. The plan devised by the Israeli General Staff, under the leadership of General Moshe Dayan, was very like that which Hitler used to attack Holland in 1940. Destroy the Egyptian air forces on the ground by attacking them from their blind side—the west—rather than across the Sinai Desert where an attack would be expected. The time of 0845 Egyptian time (0745 Israeli) was perfect, as it was the moment after the usual dawn readiness alert. Egyptian flight crews would be breakfasting, and the ground mist, which was normal for that time of year, would have cleared by 0800. Under a cover of 40 Mirages, the first wave of attacking Israeli Mystères hit nine Egyptian airfields in small groups on the morning of 5th June 1967. The Israeli aircraft flew very low over the sea to avoid the radar screen. Just at the moment of attack the aircraft climbed so as to be visible on the Egyptian radar, so that the pilots would scramble to their planes, just in time to be destroyed on the ground. The Israelis allowed for about four runs at the airfields in the ten minutes allotted to them, for their fuel consumption dictated that they could have no more than ten minutes in the attack. Furthermore, anti-aircraft fire would become too intense after the first strikes were made.

## Destroyed on the Field

After the first attack, the anti-aircraft fire appeared with each successive wave. But the damage was done. Only eight MiG-21s of the Egyptian Air Force reached the skies, and only two Israeli Mirages were lost in the attack. But further waves of Israeli aircraft, each following the other at ten-minute

intervals, descended from the cloudless skies. This kept up for 80 minutes, and at 1000 hours three more Egyptian airfields were hit. By 1035 the job had been done. The Egyptian Air Force had been wiped out. All 17 Egyptian airfields had been attacked, and over 300 planes destroyed. Israel gambled everything on this surprise attack and it had paid off. With command of the skies in Israeli hands, Israel could now turn her air forces toward Syria and Jordan, while panzer groups swept aside demoralized Egyptian armour as they moved across the Sinai Desert to the Suez Canal. By 1145 the Syrian Air Force began its attack on Israeli territory while Israeli bombs pounded Jordanian air strips. The attack on Jordan began at 1215, and within twenty minutes the Jordanian Air Force was wiped out. Israel lost only one plane over Jordan. As Iraqi troops pushed into Jordan to help their reluctant Arab ally, Israeli planes pounded away at them for the balance of the day. Meanwhile Syrian airfields were hit at 1215, the same time as the attack on Jordan. In 25 minutes most of the Syrian Air Force had met with a similar fate. It had been a busy day. In the first four hours of the Six-Day War Israel had won by her daring gamble in the skies.

On the second day of the war Israel was briefly surprised by a Lebanese air attack, but it was insignificant and Lebanon, reluctant to make war anyway, did not fight thereafter. Mopping up operations occurred over Egyptian territory when the remainder of their air forces challenged the Israelis, and after the second day there was hardly any opposition to Israel in the air. The victory in the air was the key to victory on land, as it gave the Israeli tanks and troops sufficient air cover and reconnaissance to proceed without difficulty. On the first day Israeli tanks crossed into Sinai on three major fronts. The Russian T-34's, T-54's and T-55's used by the Arabs were excellent weapons, and these faced the Israeli tank commanders, Israel Tal, Ariel Sharon and Avraham Yoffe, who had Centurions, Pattons and Shermans at their disposal. However, supported by paratroop brigades, these Israeli *Ugdas* or task groups swept through the disorganized and unprotected opposition.

The Gaza Strip was sealed off and taken

Popperfoto

on the first day. By the end of the second day of fighting, thanks to the Centurions of the Yoffe *Ugda*, the Egyptians had withdrawn to the central ridge in Sinai, which meant that half the desert had been relinquished. This advance continued into the third and fourth day, and although the Egyptians made some counter-attacks against the force crossing the desert near the sea and another near the Mitla Pass, Israeli air power smashed the Egyptian armoured units so that Egypt had the choice of withdrawing across the Suez Canal, which some one hundred tanks did, or being attacked by Israeli tanks and planes in the desert and destroyed. By the end of the fourth day the whole of the Sinai Desert up to the Suez Canal, including Sharm el Sheikh, was in Israeli hands. Although Egypt started the war with twice the number of tanks and men Israel possessed, air power and the element of surprise won the day.

*Fight for Jerusalem*
On the Jordanian front things went almost as well. The worst fighting took place in Jerusalem, half of which was controlled by Jordan. Fierce building by building, hand-to-hand combat took place. By the third day not only Jerusalem but the entire West Bank of the Jordan River had fallen to Israel. Jordanian troops, deprived of air cover, fought bravely, unlike so many of the Egyptian units which in the chaos of retreat quickly capitulated, but the leadership of Jordanian General Riad is open to question. His retreat across the Jordan was mismanaged, but the loss of Jerusalem was a mortal one to Jordan and the entire Arab cause. In three days King Hussein had lost the richest part of his kingdom, and he was relieved when Israeli forces stopped at the Jordan River, which they could easily have crossed.

On the Syrian front Israel was prepared to hold the line as their troops advanced elsewhere, but after the first four days when Egypt and Jordan had clearly lost, Israel turned her attentions to the strategic Golan Heights, which commanded both the approaches to Damascus as well as Israeli territory, held by Syria since 1948. Brigadier Elazar started the advance on the fourth day,

but on the fifth, when most of the Israeli Air Force was freed from duties on the other two major fronts, it pounded away at Syrian field positions. By the end of the day, after heavy fighting, much of the territory on the heights had been taken. But many Israeli tanks were lost on the fifth and sixth days. Syrian lines held despite the severe air attacks upon their positions, and Israeli high command admitted later that it lost more men in the two major days of fighting in Syria than on the other two fronts combined. But the Golan Heights belonged to Israel, and her air force declined to press further when the Syrians retreated to defend their capital, Damascus.

After six days of fighting Israel had more than doubled its territory. It had won on every front with apparent ease, with the loss of only 778 soldiers and 26 civilians. Many of the Palestinian Arabs were now within Israeli territory, although 150,000 of them fled across the Jordan. Taking into account Israel's Arab population before the war of some 300,000, Israel now had about 1,385,000 Arabs under her flag. There were only 2,365,000 Jews in Israel. The Jews of European origin who helped found the country in 1948 and who, by and large, ruled it, were now outnumbered by roughly a 3:1 ratio. Israel had stunned the world with its resounding victory, but the problems imposed by the magnitude of that victory in the Six-Day War were to prove a heavy burden in the years to come.

Egypt and Syria were drawn even closer to the USSR in the years after the Six-Day War. Their armour and air forces were re-equipped, and new missiles were installed near the Suez Canal, now the border between Egypt and Israel. Nasser, because of the loss of a good deal of his territory and all of the prestige of his armies, offered to resign, but the Egyptian people rallied behind him. The UN and the US tried to force Israel to withdraw as they had done in 1957, but without success. A war of attrition began on Israel's new frontiers with Egypt and, to a lesser degree, Syria in 1969, which grew in intensity with each passing year. Israeli hopes that the death of Nasser on 28th September 1970 would bring a new policy and a detente were soon dashed by Egypt's new President, Anwar Sadat. In order to maintain his credibility as Egypt's leader, Sadat could ask no less than an Israeli withdrawal, which Israel was unwilling to make. As time went on Sadat could not remain in power without challenging Israel at the first opportunity. Until then the war of attrition continued, and the sporadic fighting was often intense, costing many lives.

*The uneasy truce*
By 1973 the uneasy truce was not expected to last much longer. Most observers expected another Israeli pre-emptive strike as more missiles and other arms flooded into Egypt and Syria. The United States was unwilling to allow Israel to lose the superiority which she had proven in 1967, but conversely the US was anxious to make a lasting peace in the Middle East which could only be accomplished by Israel's relinquishing some of her newly-won territory. It was an impasse, which the Soviet Union exploited in

her favour by rushing more arms to the Arabs, placing the US in a position in which she had to increase her arms to Israel or face the ultimate collapse of her protégé. After the riots in Cairo in 1972, Sadat knew that he could not wait too long if he was to maintain his support among his people.

Meanwhile the Palestinian Arab situation was getting worse. There were now something like two million of them, 600,000 of whom were lodged in refugee camps. The Israelis began to incorporate parts of formerly Arab Palestine into their country. The annexation of the Old City of Jerusalem, until the Six-Day War part of Jordan, was especially provocative to all Muslim states, as the Holy Places of Islam were now officially part of Israel, along with the Wailing Wall, which has equally emotive connotations to Jews all over the world. Palestinian guerrilla groups of varying degrees of fanaticism attacked Israeli athletes at the Munich Olympics in 1972. Israeli planes all over Europe and Israeli tourist and airline offices and embassies were threatened, and Israeli citizens or prominent Jews living abroad were kidnapped, killed or menaced. The desperation of the Palestinian Arabs' plight was obvious. They were pawns to the national interests of the various Arab states. Their cause, which was ostensibly championed by these Arab countries, was secondary to them, and the Palestinians knew it. Now the whole of Palestine was in Israeli hands. The problem between Jew and Arab would not be settled until the situation of the Palestinians was resolved.

Meanwhile the Russian presence in Egypt continued to increase. Some 40,000 Russians, advisers and their families, were present in Egypt along with the missiles they installed. After realizing that neither Russia nor America was keen to have another war break out in the Middle East, and knowing that his position in Egypt depended on another war soon, Sadat ordered all Soviet military personnel to leave Egypt at once on 17th July 1972. Egypt took over the SAM sites and the airfields rebuilt by the Russians. Dissatisfaction with Sadat in the army and among the students was stilled by this dramatic announcement. But Sadat's diplomatic initiatives in the following months were as inconclusive as ever. By spring 1973 Sadat made it clear that only another war could help clear the diplomatic obstacles which made concessions on either side of a significant nature virtually impossible.

Israel was complacent in the years after 1967. Always contemptuous of the Arabs, the Israelis were convinced of their invincibility. The victory in the Six-Day War was, in a way, their undoing. Overconfidence led to inadequate preparations for a pre-emptive strike on the Arabs' part, which was by now considered an unthinkable possibility. By the summer King Hussein was won over to a policy of an attack against Israel, which the Syrians had never opposed. This time Egypt would be supported to the full by the conservative members of the Arab bloc, including Saudi Arabia and the Gulf States. As Egyptian armour, now equipped with T-62 tanks, massed near the Suez Canal in September, the Israelis were not worried. Manoeuvres were held every autumn. Al-

Popperfoto

though Dayan issued warnings that similar build-ups were occurring on the Syrian frontier near the Golan Heights, Israeli attentions were turned towards Vienna, where a Jewish refugee agency had been closed after it had been threatened by Palestinian Arabs. The last Cabinet meeting before the holiest day in the Jewish calendar, Yom Kippur, dealt with this Schonau incident.

## The Yom Kippur War

Yom Kippur, the Day of Atonement, 6th October 1973, found most Jews in Israel in their synagogues. Over 700 Syrian tanks attacked the Golan Heights while Egyptian units swept across the Suez Canal into Sinai, taking the Israelis totally by surprise on the day when even most Israeli soldiers were not on duty. The afternoon of the 6th and that evening, Egyptian forces crossed the Canal at three key points, bringing with them heavy armoured units. The first line of Israeli defence, the Bar-Lev Line, was soon taken. As air raid warnings were heard in Jerusalem, a stunned Israeli public became aware that the fourth Arab-Israeli War was in progress. The radio broke its traditional holy day silence at 1440, and soldiers on leave were pulled from their synagogues to return to the fronts. Syrian thrusts on the Golan Heights threatened to cut Israeli forces in half, and their early capture of Mount Hermon enabled the Syrians to range their artillery against Israeli positions. By the third day of the war the Golan front seemed to stabilize, but Egyptian forces continued to pour into Sinai. This was to be no Israeli rout as in 1967. Complacency had given way to terror, as Israeli civilians feared that this time their presumed armed superiority might be in doubt. By 12th October, the sixth day of the war, the three Egyptian bridgeheads across the Suez Canal had widened into a broad front controlling the whole west bank of the canal.

When Israel swept across Sinai in 1956 and 1967 there were only three ways to get through to the Suez Canal: the Mitla Pass, the Gidi Pass, and the Khatmia Pass. The alternative was the northern route across the top of the desert between the Sea of Sand, impossible for tanks to penetrate, and the Mediterranean. The Egyptian armoured legions faced the same choice if they were to drive Israel out of Sinai. Saad Shazli, the Egyptian Chief of Staff, urged a further push into Sinai, preferably along the northern route, since the three key passes were heavily defended. As Russia airlifted new supplies to the Syrians, they began to fall back from their newly-won positions, but when the Israelis penetrated Syria as far as Saasa, the second line of Syrian defence held fast, protecting the road to Damascus.

The first week of the war ended inconclusively, with Syria on the defensive in the north, but Egypt holding their western bank of Suez. On Sunday, 14th October, one of the greatest tank battles in history took place near the Israeli defensive position guarding the Gidi and Mitla Passes. Something like 2,000 tanks fought bitterly, compared with the 1,600 which fought at El Alamein in 1942. Super-Shermans, similar to those used by Montgomery at Alamein, were used by the Israelis, while the Egyptians were equipped

with T-34's, used at Kursk in 1943, and the more modern T-55's and T-62's. But the Centurions and Pattons which the Israelis also had were superior in desert warfare to the Russian equipment because of their range of fire. The greater comfort the American tank gave to the crew in comparison with the Russian models became an important factor in the torrid heat of the Sinai Desert. By the evening of 14th October the major Egyptian thrust had been broken. Israeli lines held. It was now time to move to the counter-attack.

## Battle of Chinese Farm

General Arik Sharon discovered a gap between the Egyptian Second and Third Armies west of the canal, and on 15th October decided to try to break through this gap, while one of his three armoured brigades made a diversionary move to the west. His Third Brigade pressed the advantage, and then swung north of the Great Bitter Lake, around it, and then southward to expand the bridgehead. On the night of 16th October, the Egyptians moved down to cut off this daring thrust in the Battle of Chinese Farm. They were too late. The Israeli forces withstood this assault, and were not cut off. The bridgehead held, and with this battle the tide of the war turned in favour of Israel. Meanwhile the oil-producing countries, encouraged by Egypt, decided to raise the price of oil by 70 per cent, using petroleum as a lever to force the United States and Western Europe to wring concessions from their protégé. Nixon responded by putting his troops in Europe on full alert and sent massive military aid to Israel, some of it airlifted from Europe. Russia, seeing her policy of detente with the West crumbling, urged Egypt to quit while they were still ahead. While Israeli ground troops continued to destroy the missile sites west of the canal which had hampered her ability to knock out the Egyptian air force as she had done in 1967, the Egyptian Third Army found itself trapped near the town of Suez by the Israeli sweep around the Great and Little Bitter Lakes.

When the final ceasefire came into effect on 24th October, Israeli forces were deep into Egypt, only 60 miles from Cairo. But the Egyptians still held part of the area east of the canal. Henry Kissinger, President Nixon's Secretary of State, had forged a truce, but the Yom Kippur War ended inconclusively. Although Israeli armed forces held more territory on the Syrian front than they ever had before, and now had territory west of Suez, some territory east of Suez had been forfeited to Egypt. It was a victory for Arab morale. The Western World had discovered its dependence on Arab oil. The Arab states, after 25 years and four wars, had achieved unity and with it, impressive strength. Above all, it became clear to Arab and Jew alike that wars of this kind could never bring about the desires each of them harboured. On Egypt and Syria's part, revenge for past defeats; for Israel, security for her ever-expanding frontiers.

In the uneasy peace which followed the Yom Kippur War, Sadat and his Persian Gulf supporters who embargoed the shipment of oil to the United States, realized that in the

final event Russia would never help the Palestinian Arabs, nor would she allow Israel to be utterly destroyed if this meant nuclear confrontation with the United States. In the months after the war, Russian influence in the Middle East waned, as Henry Kissinger successfully brought all the Arab states, including a reluctant Syria, perhaps the most militant and anti-Israeli of all, into the American camp. It looked as if the Yom Kippur War might be the last in the series of wars plaguing the Middle East ever since Israel's creation. But until the vexing problem of the Palestinian Arabs was solved and the Israelis retreated to more realistic frontiers, no permanent peace in the Middle East could be reached.
*(S.L. Mayer)*

## Disengagement

In Sinai the uneasy peace saw the beginning of the complex manoeuvres to disengage the forces of Israel and Egypt in a manner acceptable to both sides. Israel had undoubtedly suffered a serious defeat and stood to lose the considerable gains made in Sinai in 1967 while the Egyptians clearly would not accept the presence of Israeli forces in Egypt or on the east bank of the Suez Canal. The working out of the settlement was difficult and fraught with the danger that extreme groups on either side might make the working of any such agreement impossible.

The conference on disengagement finally began in December 1973 and was sponsored by the US and USSR. It was marred at the beginning by the refusal of Syria to negotiate with Israel while 'any Israeli troops remained on Arab soil'. However, on 17th January it was announced that an outline agreement had been reached and that this would be signed on 18th January at Kilometre 101 on the Suez/Cairo road. The agreement provided for Israeli withdrawal to a line behind the Mitla Pass and although this meant abandoning a considerable amount of territory gained in 1967 it still left Israel in a strong position of natural defence. The withdrawal and disengagement was to be supervised by UN troops who would remain in the area. Although the agreement took nearly two years before it was finally worked out it was carried through with no serious renewal of hostilities.

Meanwhile, on Israel's northern border disengagement presented more problems be-

*Far left: General Moshe Dayan, the main architect of Israeli policy in occupied areas during the Six-Day and Yom Kippur Wars. Centre left: President Sadat of Egypt, who realized that, in the final event, the Russians would never help the Palestinian Arabs nor would they allow Israel to be completely destroyed. Left: Former Israeli Premier, Mrs Golda Meir*

At the moment the Middle East seems relatively peaceful, but a number of serious problems remain unresolved. The most serious of these is undoubtedly the position of the Palestinian Arab refugees. While they remain in camps it is difficult to see how real detente can be achieved between Israel and her Arab neighbours. Secondly, the problem of the Muslim majority (as they now are) in the Lebanon remains unsolved, though on the 19th February 1976 the Syrian foreign minister issued a statement from Beirut which seemed to suggest that a settlement might be possible. Certainly the guerrilla war against Israel will continue both in the Middle East and elsewhere, especially while Colonel Gaddafi supports any action, no matter how barbaric, against Israel and while the hardened right-wingers within Israel continue to insist on keeping the Arab inhabitants in subjection. At the moment the vicious circle, despite Kissinger's diplomacy, remains essentially unbroken.
*(Alun Howkins)*

*Below: Militant Lebanese appeal for Arab solidarity with the refugees from the Israeli-occupied territories*

cause of Syria's intransigence. Their continued refusal to negotiate meant that on a number of occasions through 1974 it seemed that serious fighting might be renewed on the northern front. For instance, there was a serious outbreak of fighting around Mount Hermon in February and March 1974. However, under considerable diplomatic pressure from the US and USSR the Syrians and Israelis finally agreed on disengagement on 31st May 1974, and on 5th June fighting on the Golan Heights, which had continued since the end of the Yom Kippur War, ended.

The period of the fourth Arab-Israeli War had seen the Arab states more united, and thus a good deal more powerful, than in the past. This was shown particularly by the Arab oil boycott of countries which supported Israel, which began in the autumn of 1973 and continued against the US and the Netherlands until July 1974. However, it seems that the enormous price increases and the boycott may not be such a powerful weapon in the future with increasing use of off-shore oil supplies and a general cut in domestic consumption of oil in Western Europe.

The disengagement did not mean the complete cessation of fighting in the Middle East. Since the end of the 1967 War various Palestinian guerilla groups and their supporters had carried out a terrorist campaign against Israel and her friends both in the Middle East and elsewhere. The attacks, although usually small-scale, had a particular horror especially when carried out overseas on apparently innocent civilians. Although these attacks outside Israel caused outcry in the West, especially the attack on the Israeli team at the 1972 Olympic Games, the attacks into Israel from the Lebanon and Syria were, from the Israeli point of view, more serious. These attacks were (and are) mostly carried out from refugee camps in Lebanon and Syria by well-trained and armed members of the Palestine Liberation Organization and its various splinter groups. From 1967 onwards the battle between these Arab 'infiltrators' and Israeli forces and the subsequent retaliatory attacks by Israeli forces and aircraft on the refugee camps became an almost weekly occurence.

However, 1976 saw the PLO in action inside one of its 'host countries', the Lebanon. The Lebanese give a permanent advantage to the Christian groups within the country by assigning to one of them the powerful office of President and there is a 6:5 ratio of Christians to Muslims in Parliament and the Civil Service. But in the last twenty years the population balance has swung in favour of the Muslims, especially since the creation of the refugee camps, and the political structure has become unrepresentative of the reality of the political situation. The dissatisfaction came to a head in mid-April 1975 when fighting broke out between the extreme right-wing Christian Phalangist Party and various Muslin groups. By July 1975 23,000 people had been killed or injured in the most serious disorders since the Yom Kippur War. One ceasefire after another broke down, the Christians refusing to negotiate until order had been restored and the Muslims persisting in their demands for reforms. The climax came in January 1976 when the PLO threw its full weight behind the Muslims after a series of Christian attacks on refugee camps and Muslim ghettos. At the peak of the fighting, troops of the well-organised and disciplined Palestine Liberation Army crossed the border from Syria and, by simple armed presence, restored order. How long this tenuous peace will last is difficult to say. The casualties of the war are appalling. The UN estimated in February 1976 that 12,000 had died in the fighting, up to 40,000 were injured and some 400,000 had been affected in some way. Further, 20 per cent of the houses in Beirut had been destroyed and over 50 per cent of the businesses had been destroyed or looted. Worst of all, no formula has yet been derived which will satisfy the Muslim demand for reform which is also an acceptable compromise for the Christians.

Since the end of the Yom Kippur War a period of stabilisation seems to have begun in most of the Middle East. Egypt, under the leadership of Sadat, has become noticeably less aggressive in her policies and has moved into a non-aligned position which is bound to be more favourable to the West in the long term. Only Gaddafi's Libya still echoes the Arab militancy of ten years ago. By embracing both the extremes of Islam and a curious form of 'Arab socialism' Gaddafi remains the most anti-Israel and anti-Western of all the Arab leaders and the only one to openly support the most extreme elements of the Palestinian guerrillas.

465

# The Vietnam War

Of all the types of war fought by men over the centuries, two, guerrilla war and civil war, are the most terrible. The war that has been going on continuously in Vietnam and Indo-China since the Second World War has the worst aspects of both. A civil war between hill tribesmen and lowland agriculturalists, country versus town, Christian against animist against Buddhist, Communist versus bourgeois opportunist, the hope for freedom against the promise of dictatorship—the war in Vietnam is all of these. Sinicised for over two thousand years, Vietnam has felt the heel of the Chinese and European invader and has adjusted its way of life to both. Conquered by Imperial France under Napoleon III, a conquest which was completed by the Third Republic, Indo-China kept largely to its indigenous, langourous and individual life style during the French occupation. Some industry was built up in the north along the Red River; rubber plantations were created by the French, and in Saigon, (now Ho Chi Minh City), great tree-lined boulevards and smart clubs and restaurants reminded settlers and planters on a spree that a French presence endured in Vietnam. But this atmosphere, pleasant and decadent, was superficial. Behind the sophisticated French mask lay the faces of millions of peasants and hill tribesmen virtually untouched by European civilization. When Japan conquered Indo-China after France itself fell to the Wehrmacht, the French presence remained, while Japanese soldiers called the tune. But when the conquest of Japan appeared imminent in 1945, jockeying for power by the Vietnamese themselves ensued. Ho Chi Minh, a long-time Communist, an ascetic and enigmatic figure, had organized a guerrilla organization during the war for this purpose. His dream was a unified, independent Indo-China under Vietnamese Communist domination. He hoped for American support for his cause. It was not forthcoming, as the French supported his rival, the aristocratic and indolent Bao Dai, who tried to set up an alternative government before the Japanese troops were evacuated.

The situation became confused after the Japanese capitulation. Vietnam had two rival governments as the British and Nationalist Chinese forces moved into coastal Vietnam to take the Japanese surrender. Within a few months they slowly withdrew in favour of the French, who hoped to reconquer their colony while paying rather transparent lip service to Vietnamese ideals of nationalism and independence *(doc-lap)*. The Viet Minh, the army of Communist Vietnam, was led by a brilliant strategist, Vo Nguyen Giap, who correctly assessed the dilemma facing France: 'The enemy will pass slowly from the offensive to the defensive. The blitzkrieg will transform itself into a war of long duration. Thus, the enemy will be caught in a dilemma: he has to drag out the war in order to win it and does not possess, on the other hand, the psychological and political means to fight a long, drawn-out war...'

Giap's assessment of how the war in Vietnam would be fought was right on the mark. The French grossly underestimated the strength of will of the Communists to fight for Vietnamese independence, and they discounted the degree to which nationalist sentiments would attach themselves to the Viet Minh when a credible, non-Communist nationalist alternative failed to appear. Bao Dai was not a credible nationalist figure. A former Emperor of Annam under French protection before the war, amiable enough and a charming ladies' man, Bao Dai had the taint of European influence on him which he was unable to shake off. He was fond of French ambiance and the Côte d'Azur in particular. The French played Bao Dai off against Ho Chi Minh, who initially was prepared to do a deal with the French to gain some degree of legitimacy, but Ho Chi Minh tired of this game when the French began to reassert their authority over Indo-China in 1946. By the end of that year Giap's forces numbered some 50,000 armed largely with equipment begged, borrowed or stolen from the Chinese, French, British and Americans. The French military authorities considered this motley army with irregular equipment to be no match for the trained, well-equipped legions of the French Empire, many of whom had considerable combat experience in the Second World War. They were too strong not to be used; but not strong enough to prevent the Viet Minh from trying to solve the problem by force. Perhaps compromise was impossible. All that was needed was a spark to set Vietnam alight for decades.

## The Haiphong Incident

The Haiphong Incident, 20th November 1946, provided that spark. A French naval boat, having stopped a Chinese junk loaded with contraband, brought it to the port of Haiphong. Local Vietnamese forces opened fire as both ships anchored. The sound of gunfire caused the Viet Minh in the port to cross barricades erected by the French, thereby cutting off French units from each other. About 23 French soldiers were killed. On 22nd November a French burial detail was ambushed by the Viet Minh, and

*Left:* General Vo Nguyen Giap, victor at Dien Bien Phu, and master of guerrilla warfare during both the French and American phases of the war. *Right:* Ho Chi Minh, an enigmatic and a long-time Communist, whose object was the conquest of the whole of French Indo-China

*US marines arriving in Da Nang, 1967—
part of the million-dollar-a-day US
military aid programme which halted
Communist success after 1965*

Marc Riboud/Magnum

six more French soldiers were killed. The French commander in the area, General Valluy, decided that Viet Minh ought to be taught a lesson, and French troops issued an ultimatum to the Viet Minh to evacuate the Chinese quarter of Haiphong which they occupied. The French moved in, and fighting broke out, as thousands of Vietnamese civilians streamed out of Haiphong to the surrounding countryside. The French cruiser, the *Suffren*, anchored offshore, noticed the fighting, and opened fire on the city. Over 6,000 Vietnamese were killed by the gunfire, the street fighting, or were trampled to death in the panic. On 19th December, despite conciliatory moves by both sides to avoid a general war, a rumour was spread among French circles that an uprising was about to take place in Hanoi. At 2000 hours the electric power plant was blown up, and waves of Viet Minh militia killed or abducted nearly 600 French civilians in the northern capital. Within hours every French garrison in the country was under attack. The Vietnam War had begun.

The Viet Minh, which launched this all-out war, were greatly provoked by French arrogance, but they hoped for a quick victory. All major cities in the country were under Communist fire. The coup was meticulously planned and executed. The French turned to Bao Dai as a nationalist alternative to Ho Chi Minh, and the Americans supported him as a Western puppet. But Bao Dai was unwilling to play this role, as he wanted an independent if European-oriented Vietnam as much as Ho Chi Minh wanted a Communist and neutralist, independent Vietnam. The French wanted to re-establish their colony, an aim which the Americans opposed. In the confusion, Ho Chi Minh and the French turned to armed conflict as the only way to solve this dilemma. The French cleared the cities of the Viet Minh, but it took months before Hué, the old imperial capital of Vietnam, was cleared of the Communists. Ho Chi Minh's popularity in the country increased as the French came to realize that a purely military solution to their problem was impossible. Too late they decided to create a quasi-independent Vietnam under French influence, and Bao Dai played along with them when France officially recognized the independence of Vietnam in 1948. But the French definition merely meant autonomy, as France still retained some measure of control and, of course, continued to fight the Viet Minh. But the military initiative had passed into the hands of Ho Chi Minh just as the political initiative already had done. Ho Chi Minh seemed to be the true representative of Vietnamese independence, as he was tied to no foreigner. It seemed as if the mistake made by the Americans in tying Chiang Kai-shek too closely to them in China after the war was being repeated by the French in Vietnam.

## De Lattre arrives

As guerrilla warfare intensified, the French maintained their control over the cities and the chief railways and ports, while the Viet Minh began to tighten their net in the northern countryside. French morale was flagging, and to support it, a new High Commissioner and Commander-in-Chief of Indo-China was appointed: General Jean de Lattre de Tassigny, who combined the political and military roles. Autocratic, an aristocrat to his buttonholes, he shored up French morale by preventing the withdrawal of French families from Indo-China and by taking a strong and spirited hand at a moment when spirit was lacking on the French side. The French having gone into the struggle over-confidently, Giap had defeated them badly in early 1950 and the whole area of northern Tonkin from the coast to the Laotian border, as well as the territory adjacent to China, except for the enclaves of the major cities was under Communist control. The French army was despondent, having been beaten in battle by an ill-trained and poorly equipped guerrilla force. The politicians in Paris blamed the soldiers. The soldiers blamed the politicians. De Lattre was sent to end this bickering. He was a born leader of men, a man not to be questioned easily and his arrival in Saigon on 17th December 1950 restored confidence almost at once.

Giap, flushed with recent success and reinforced with arms from Communist China, decided to strike in the Red River Delta, the heartland of what territory remained to France in northern Tonkin. If the link between Hanoi and Haiphong could be severed, the war in the north was won. The French built up their forces in the north and repelled this attack in early 1951. The French victory was due entirely to de Lattre, whose authority was unquestioned and whose resolve was iron. De Lattre asked the hill tribes to wage counter-insurgency against the Viet Minh. His use of napalm against the enemy surprised them and threw them back throughout the north. De Lattre was convinced he was leading a crusade against Communism, in line with NATO policy and the war in Korea. He was also keen to protect the huge French investments still extant in Indo-China. They owned all the rubber plantations, all the mines, the shipping, two-thirds of the rice and most of the banks. French finance backed the war, but the French public was tiring of it. Victories were needed, and victories were provided by de Lattre.

Giap, defeated in the Delta, turned to consolidating the Viet Minh hold over the northwest, especially the area close to the Laotian border. By 1952 the Viet Minh were once again on the road to victory. De Lattre, deathly ill, had to return to France in December 1951, and he died of cancer in Paris in January 1952. If anyone could have won for France it was he. Now he was gone and the Viet Minh moved to the offensive once more. US aid began to pour into Vietnam, which the French both needed and resented, while a native Vietnamese force was being created to fight the Viet Minh as French financial resources and public patience wore thin. Henri Navarre was appointed C-in-C in Indo-China to replace de Lattre, and he issued a report which indicated that French forces were over-extended and tied down in hopelessly defensive positions. The local Vietnamese forces were being trained to take over these defensive positions, while America urged France to take action or make a truce, as US aid since 1950 amounted to about $500 million annually. The US reluctantly agreed to supply more material so that the French forces could take the offensive while the Vietnamese took over the static positions. One string attached to American aid was the promise of real independence to Laos, Cambodia and Vietnam, which the French set into motion. In order to block a Viet Minh incursion into Laos, and to defeat them in their strongest area, Navarre decided to seize and hold a forward base near the Laotian frontier, Dien Bien Phu, as a sign of strength which was necessary to maintain morale among his troops and to show Paris and Washington that the French were capable of winning.

## Dien Bien Phu

The gamble to hold Dien Bien Phu was the undoing of France in Vietnam. Of little strategic significance in itself, Dien Bien Phu controlled routes into China and Laos and had two airfields in the area surrounding it so supplies could be airlifted to the fortress. The French controlled the hills around the plain. Giap felt that if he could win a victory there, the heart would go out of the French

*America's losses mount. Unwilling to extend the war or to back down on commitments, America seemed caught in a war which brought a steady drain on men and supplies. **Left:** Helicopter wheels over dump after a guerrilla attack.*

determination to stay in South-East Asia. In the second week of March 1954, Giap began his attack on Dien Bien Phu. First, he planned to overrun the three outlying French defensive areas, and then begin an all-out assault on the positions surrounding the airstrip and the village. The first phase began on 13th March, and the three outlying posts were soon lost, at a great cost in lives to the Communists. But the French did not count on the ability of the Viet Minh to transport heavy artillery and anti-aircraft guns across the mountainous terrain of northwest Tonkin. The Viet Minh were able to concentrate their fire, and many French planes bringing in supplies were brought down. Giap surrounded the French redoubt, and while the French were hungry for more ammunition, the Viet Minh brought up more of their own. The Communist guns died down on the 26th, lulling the French into a false sense of security. On the afternoon of 30th March, the massive Communist assault began. The major assault had taken further territory at a great cost in lives to the Vietnamese, and French defences around Dien Bien Phu held. By mid-April 50,000 Viet Minh were in place around the village, and more artillery was brought in through the mountains. The 16,000 French troops, including units from the élite Foreign Legion, were hopelessly trapped. The French begged the Americans for more aid, which was not forthcoming. Giap began his final assault on Dien Bien Phu on 1st May at all points along the perimeter, and regardless of casualties, the Communists advanced. Navarre realized that he had miscalculated, but all too late. On 7th May at about noon the Viet Minh 308th Division broke through into the heart of the French defences. Soon after this the French raised their white flags. The news of the fall of Dien Bien Phu reached Geneva where the international conference to discuss the future of Indo-China and Korea had just begun. The Vietnamese National Army, on which so much hope had been placed, was starting to break down. The French day in Indo-China, after almost a hundred years of interrupted occupation, was done.

At Geneva the French had to accept the inevitable, and began to make plans for their withdrawal from Indo-China. The ball was placed firmly in the Americans' court. Would they replace the French and continue the struggle, or allow the whole of Indo-China to fall into Communist hands? Their decision was to permit a partition of Vietnam, giving the territory above the 17th Parallel to the government of Ho Chi Minh, while South Vietnam would be reconstructed along with an independent Laos and Cambodia, the three successor states being protected by the newly-formed SEATO Pact. Ngo Dinh Diem was chosen as the leader of South Vietnam, a Catholic mandarin of aristocratic and authoritarian bearing. Bao Dai was summarily dropped, and elections were promised to unite the whole of Vietnam under one government by 1956. As the Americans began to pour aid into their new protégé's capital, Saigon, they realized what the French already knew. If elections were held Ho Chi Minh, the acknowledged nationalist leader, would win hands down. The elections were never held. Instead, while Giap re-equipped his forces and began to send men into South Vietnam down the Ho Chi Minh Trail through the mountains and jungles of Laos, the South Vietnamese Army was built, retrained and re-equipped with American arms and advisers.

*Escalation in the South*
By 1958 infiltration of the South had reached a dangerous point. The hard core of guerrillas in the South numbered perhaps 5,000, but this figure was soon to double. The threat to major cities in the South was growing. By 1959 about a third of the countryside in the South was controlled by the Viet Cong, the guerrilla organization equivalent to what had been the Viet Minh in the North. While Diem's forces outnumbered the Communists by seven or eight to one, the quality of government forces was poor. The Communists held the initiative, even more so because they were Southerners themselves, not North Vietnamese regulars sent into help, although obviously there were even a

few of these at this stage acting in an advisory capacity to the Viet Cong. By late 1960, after the American Presidential election which put John F. Kennedy in power, a major attempt to overthrow Diem was launched. On the morning of 11th November three paratroop battalions of the South Vietnamese forces seized key government centres in Saigon and prepared to attack Diem's palace. The Americans knew of the coup plan but did nothing to warn Diem. That evening Diem agreed to step down but secretly moved troops loyal to him around the capital, and they retook the city's strong points. The failure of the coup and the flight of its leaders to Cambodia did nothing to dispel the feeling, widespread in Washington and Saigon, that Diem was simply not the man to champion Vietnamese nationalism or to prevent a Communist takeover of the South. When President Kennedy took office the US still had only a small number of advisers assisting the efforts of the Army of the Republic of Vietnam (ARVN). Kennedy urged Diem to undertake land reform while immediately increasing the American presence in Saigon.

Kennedy began to lose his nerve about events in Indo-China almost as soon as he took office. The situation in Laos had deteriorated to the point where large parts of the country, chiefly the highlands along the Vietnamese border, had fallen to the Communists in Laos, the Pathet Lao, aided and abetted by North Vietnam. Kennedy went on television to prepare the American people for a possible US military intervention on the part of the so-called democratic forces in Laos, but changed his mind soon after, when he accepted the fact that the logistics of supplying a non-government in a non-country with weapons and men hundreds of miles from a major port made a defence of Laos unrealistic. His recent failure in the Bay of Pigs fiasco in Cuba made it obvious that yet another blunder of an interventionary nature would be disastrous for his presidency. It was at this point that the US decided to help create a 'neutralist' government in Laos, abandoning Eisenhower's policy of resisting the Communists obdurately. This meant that if the US was to take a stand in support of pro-Western elements in Indo-China, it would have to be in South Vietnam. And the US seemed to be stuck with Diem. Vice-President Lyndon B. Johnson's visit to Saigon convinced the South Vietnamese that some attempt at land reform was the only way to pacify the Americans. It was, in fact, the only realistic way to help the South Vietnamese help themselves to remain independent of Hanoi.

*The Fall of Diem*
But whatever land reform took place was done halfheartedly. The guerrillas continued to make progress, while organized opposition to Diem faded for a time. The US increased its aid and its advisers, who numbered some

United Press International

*Americans in command: marines lead captured Viet Cong. But conventional forces could find no lasting answer to guerrilla tactics*

16,000 by 1963, while Buddhist and other opposition to Diem began to be felt. The South Vietnamese had the choice between the rigours of Communist terrorism and the decadent hand of French-educated élitism represented by Diem which was only less stultifying because of its inefficiency. The most far reaching land 'reform', if that is the operative word, was the concept of strategic hamlets. This plan, inspired by the Americans after a model used by the British to defeat Communism in Malaya, forced the evacuation of the people in certain parts of the countryside into fortified villages which were defensible. In a Vietnamese context the village, the people living in the village and on the produce of the land were inextricably entwined. Although the plan had some military merit, it displaced too many people, creating disorientation among the peasants and a decided disinclination to support those who moved them out of their traditional homes. Only middle-class elements actively supported the strategic hamlet idea, since their position was shored up by it. But the vast majority of people in Vietnam were cultivators; peasants. Although a good idea from a short-term military standpoint, this scheme did more to undermine Diem's and therefore the Americans' position than any other. By 1963 opposition to Diem and his brother, Ngo Dinh Nhu, a megalomaniac and drug addict to whom Diem had given considerable power, was massive, even in pro-Western circles in Saigon. On 1st November Diem and Nhu were overthrown with American concurrence, and both were killed by their captors. Now Kennedy was faced with an even more difficult problem. Which South Vietnamese leader had the charisma to save the demoralizing situation in Saigon? For all his faults. Diem had been respected by many peasants, and had had the wholehearted support of the Christian community, some 15 per cent of the population. Those who were to step in his place—Duong Van Minh, Air Vice-Marshall Nguyen Cao Ky, and General Nguyen Van Thieu—were military men. Diem, at least, had been a tradi-

tional mandarin and held in some esteem if only for that reason. He had been an integrative factor in a disintegrating society. He would not be replaced easily.

President Kennedy was assassinated only three weeks after Diem, and the new President, Lyndon Johnson, a rough Texan imbued with the Hispanic obsession with *machismo*, had long felt that Kennedy should not 'play around' with the Communists in Vietnam. Johnson could not accept the fact that the United States were unable to handle the North Vietnamese. Immediately on taking office, Johnson began to take steps to escalate the war dramatically. The military situation in Vietnam was deteriorating badly, but America, stunned by the death of Kennedy, was unready for full commitment to a war in Vietnam in an election year. Barry Goldwater, Johnson's Republican opponent in the 1964 election openly declared that the US should intervene fully. Johnson covered his real intentions until the election, in which he won a landslide victory, was over. General Nguyen Khanh ruled Vietnam for a time, backed by General William Westmoreland. They would have to hold the line until after the elections. Meanwhile Johnson started to convince his Cabinet and advisers, mostly old Kennedy hands, that the US should enter fully into the Vietnam War.

## The Tonkin Gulf Incident

His opportunity came during the election campaign when the USS *Maddox*, actually some thirteen miles from a North Vietnamese island in the Tonkin Gulf, was attacked by North Vietnamese PT boats, returned the fire and hit one of them. Johnson claimed the ships were thirty miles offshore, and therefore had a right to be there. Johnson ordered that the *Maddox* and its companion ship, the USS *C. Turner Joy*, return to the area four days later on 3rd August 1964. The ships were challenged again. What actually happened in the Tonkin Gulf is still not altogether clear, the obfuscation a deliberate gesture on the administration's

part. Later Johnson suggested the incident may never have taken place. But the immediate result of the incident was LBJ's request to the Congress that they give him the power to wage aerial war on North Vietnam and a blank cheque to increase massively the numbers of American troops in Vietnam. This Tonkin Gulf Resolution was passed by Congress, which thereafter relinquished its power to curb the President's war-making capacity.

Under pressure from men like General Curtis LeMay, who believed that wide-scale bombing won the war for the Allies in the Second Word War, Johnson began massive bombing of military targets on both South and North Vietnam, and later stepped up this campaign in Operation Rolling Thunder which was supposed to bomb North Vietnam into the Stone Age. Hanoi and Haiphong were carefully excluded from this saturation bombing effort although these were, perhaps, the only two targets worth destroying.

Saturation bombing had even less effect on Vietnam than it had had on Germany, a far more highly industrialized and urbanized country and therefore more susceptible to strategic bombing attacks. By the end of President Johnson's Administration more bombs had been dropped on Vietnam than the US dropped in the Second World War, and under Nixon's first four years two and a half million tons more were dropped. (The US dropped about two million tons of bombs in the years 1941–45). But all of this came to nothing. The war in Vietnam could not be won in the air, despite the fact that for the most part North Vietnam had no air cover and until the end little in the way of effective anti-aircraft artillery. Communist infiltration was a matter of subversion of confidence in the South, so that peasants would acquiesce in the takeover of their villages. The only way to track down these infiltrators was by going out into the village, the jungle, the trails and the hills of Vietnam and winkling them out. Once the American elections were over Johnson began to increase troops in Vietnam to do just that.

## The US intervention

The fear that the regime in the South would crumble in the autumn of 1965 caused Johnson to increase American involvement. LBJ felt that if he allowed Vietnam to go the way of China and Eastern Europe his entire domestic programme would never pass Congress. 'They won't be talking about my civil rights bill, or education or beautification. No sir, they'll push Vietnam up my ass every time', Johnson elegantly put it. But it turned out that they (the Congress) and the country did that anyway, and hundreds and hundreds of thousands of Americans were sent to defend a country which wouldn't defend itself and fight for a cause which never seemed clear even to those who supported it.

But how many combat troops were needed, Johnson asked General Maxwell Taylor. In early 1965 75,000 was considered the right figure. By July it was 125,000. Johnson told the American people that some 50,000 might be required, but at the time he said it he had already increased his private estimate .to 200,000. As Marine and regular army units poured into Vietnam in 1965, Johnson re-

*Below: Nguyen Cao Ky, who was the southern military ruler from 1965 until 1968*

Camera Press

luctantly accepted the fact that the US was taking over the war, not merely helping out an ally. The analogy of appeasement and Munich and Hitler was again raised, despite the fact that even Ho Chi Minh in his wildest imagination only thought of taking over Indo-China, not Asia or the world. The question of Vietnam's value to the United States was not asked in Cabinet circles. Paramount in the minds of Johnson's advisers—McGeorge Bundy, Walt Rostow, Robert MacNamara and the rest—was the domino theory, once mooted by Eisenhower.

The domino theory held that if South Vietnam fell to the North, then so would Laos and Cambodia, then Thailand, Malaysia, Indonesia and so on, until, at the very least, the Communists would be in Australia or San Francisco. If Communism were a monolithic international conspiracy, this might have been the case. But Communism had never been monolithic, and with Russia and China competing for North Vietnam's favour, while Ho Chi Minh tried to play each off against the other to maintain his own independence from both, the domino theory seemed only to make sense in Indo-Chinese terms. If Ho Chi Minh won in the South, surely Laos and Cambodia would fall under North Vietnam's influence. Whether or not this mattered to American and Western interests was never seriously debated at the time. For Johnson it was a matter of pride to win in Vietnam where Kennedy had failed to win; to prove that his own *macho* (or masculinity) was stronger than his predecessors, his critics, or his opponents in Hanoi. This was Johnson's, and America's, tragedy.

## In too deep

By 1967 the Communists were closer to victory than ever. American bases proliferated on the coast of South Vietnam and the US presence there neared 500,000. At each stage of the escalation General Westmoreland kept talking about 'the light at the end of the tunnel' and repeated that his last request would be sufficient, only to later argue that only 100,000 more men would be enough. As Johnson repeated these platitudes and examples of wishful thinking to the American public, they began to seriously question the wisdom of going into Vietnam in the first place. But too late, far too late. America found herself in a similar position to France in the early 1950's stepping up the war effort while the political position of her leadership crumbled under criticism of the war at home. North Vietnam began to send regular troops into the South to support the insurgency. As the ratio between guerrillas and their opposition narrowed, Johnson felt obliged to keep the ratio at between eight and ten to one, the ratio required for victory. Russia and China supplied North Vietnam with arms, and many American weapons found their way into Communist hands through pilfering of US supplies or, more often than not, the South Vietnamese selling the weapons the US gave them to the Communists through the black market.

Black market activities and the very presence of so many Americans in a poor, underdeveloped country torn by decades of war played a major role in subverting the entire societal structure and economy of South Vietnam. A prostitute could make more in a good day than a professor could make in a month. A hawker of stolen PX goods in a street stall could make more money than a worker or farmer. As Communist activity in the country stepped up, a mass flight to the cities occurred which broke up families and sapped the will of the Vietnamese people to care who won the war. Vietnamese currency became so inflated by the introduction of comparatively rich Americans with their PX's, NCO clubs and R and R (Rest and Recreation) centres that the most profitable business in the South was catering to their needs. Bars on Tu Do Street in Saigon thrived, teeming with GI's, prostitutes and pushers of marijuana and other, more lethal, drugs. In 1968 alone an estimated $250 million went into the black market. Meanwhile, the US balance of payments deficit soared as the US had the only economy in the Western world that was on anything like a wartime basis. US inflation was exported to Europe and Japan as the vicious spiral escalated with every increase of the war effort. As government platitudes to the public masked a growing despair in circles surrounding Johnson, riots and demonstrations of all kinds spread from American campuses to the streets, where anti-war manifestations were joined by civil rights riots which grew in ferocity and destruction. The US was losing the Vietnam War at home.

## The Tet Offensive

But in the jungles and villages of steaming South Vietnam, the Communists needed another decisive victory, another Dien Bien Phu, to put an end to American determination to remain in the war. At three o'clock in the morning of the first day of the Vietnamese New Year, Tet, 31st January 1968, the American Embassy in Saigon was invaded by Viet Cong. In those early morning hours almost every important American base was under attack by the National Liberation Front, the South Vietnamese Communists. Eleven NLF battalions entered Saigon, while simultaneously around the country some 84,000 troops moved on major cities and bases.

The ARVN and the Americans were taken completely by surprise, and while the Communists tried to seize the South and destroy the American sense of security in the cities, measures to counter-attack were launched. At the same time North Vietnamese forces crossed the so-called demilitarized zone at the 17th Parallel and pushed south to the US Marine outpost at Khe Sanh. The American military reckoned that Khe Sanh would be their Dien Bien Phu and reinforced it, while the North Vietnamese simply went past the coastal town and moved into Hué, the old imperial capital. Like a wounded animal, the US and ARVN forces responded with a ferocity not yet experienced in the war. American planes strafed and bombed large population centres indiscriminately, destroying whole cities like Kontum City, My Tho and Ben Tre. Hué suffered the worst of all, the beautiful city on the Perfume River reduced to rubble as US Marines fought for weeks to drive out the Viet Cong. Communist forces were soon pushed out of Saigon and other major centres, but the fight for Hué riveted American public attention to Vietnam as never before in the war. Civilian dead in the Tet Offensive numbered 165,000; two million more refugees streamed into the ruined cities. By March Hué was also cleared and the results of Tet became clear to both sides. As a military venture, a go-for-broke gesture to win the war at a stroke, the Communist offensive was a dismal failure. Their best units destroyed, their carefully hoarded supplies near exhaustion, the Viet Cong and NLF were in no position to mount another offensive for years. But as a political gesture, the Tet attack was a stunning success.

President Johnson's credibility reached a new low at the moment when he planned to launch his re-election campaign. Although the US had ironically won a great victory over Communist forces, the US had been humiliated. Pressure to step down as President mounted in the country as anti-war demonstrations continued. In a primary election in New Hampshire, Senator Eugene McCarthy, an anti-war Democrat, did surprisingly well, and the popular brother of President Kennedy, Robert Kennedy, belatedly announced his intention to run for the Democratic nomination for President against Johnson. On 10th March Westmoreland informed Johnson that he would need 206,000 more men in Vietnam, when the American presence already stood at over half a million. Johnson was then told that America would be forced to devalue the dollar if a further escalation were contemplated.

On 31st March Johnson decided not to run again. He knew he was beaten, not so much on the battlefield as politically. No candidate could run and hope to win on the promise of four more years of war. The public, disillusioned with Democratic war policies for the past eight years and shattered by the assassinations of Martin Luther King, the black leader, and Robert Kennedy, turned reluctantly to the familiar Richard Nixon, Eisenhower's Vice-President and candidate for President in 1960. Rioting by blacks, anti-war riots and the usual political demonstrations common to an American election year vied for headlines, as US and ARVN forces tightened their grip in South Vietnam. For the first time in memory the Communists were on the defensive, just at the moment when America lost its will to fight.

## Vietnamization

But the war was far from over. Nixon announced a policy of 'Vietnamization' of the war, which was a cover word meaning a slow American withdrawal from Indo-China while the ARVN was trained and equipped to maintain its newly-won positions. General Creighton Abrams, Westmoreland's successor, cleared villages once under NLF control; dangerous roads were cleared of snipers and ambushers. Under US pressure President Thieu ordered a full mobilization of South Vietnamese youth for the first time in the war. Some 400,000 more men were recruited for the ARVN, which by 1970

*Tanks seal off the Cho Lon district, scene of heavy fighting in the battle for Saigon*

Popperfoto

stood at over a million. About half the young able bodied males of the South were in the armed forces. The US gave the ARVN the new M-16 rifles, rocket launchers, helicopters, tanks and F-5 bombers which previously had been kept in American hands. But the Vietnamization policy accelerated the social upheaval of South Vietnam which the war and the American intervention had brought, thereby creating conditions in the long run which would play into the Communists' hands.

Despite continuing American troop withdrawals, after the overthrow of neutralist Norodom Sihanouk in Cambodia, Nixon gave in to the Pentagon's request to attack North Vietnamese bases in Cambodia in April 1970. Although thousands of tons of North Vietnamese equipment was destroyed in the Cambodian incursion, the public reaction in the US to this raid was violent. Congress opposed this apparent re-escalation of the war and Nixon was obliged to withdraw US troops from Cambodia in July. The attack probably set the Viet Cong back about a year, but it also encouraged the American public and the Congress to urge Nixon to step up the American withdrawal from Indo-China.

A similar and less successful operation against Viet Cong bases in Laos was launched in February 1971, but ARVN casualties were so great that the operation was halted later in the spring. Meanwhile the US Air Force continued to bomb targets south and north of the 17th Parallel. By 1972 the US still had over 100,000 men in Indo-China; the Viet Cong and Pathet Lao position in Laos had strengthened to the point where about three-quarters of the country was in Communist hands. Communist activity in South Vietnam began to increase once more. It was another election year. Nixon had to extricate the US from the war or face electoral defeat. Just before the November elections, after Henry Kissinger had forged a detente with Russia and China which involved their promises not to support North Vietnam, the Presidential adviser, subsequent Nobel Prize winner and Secretary of State announced that the end of the war was 'at hand'. Nixon won an overwhelming victory at the polls and in 1973 the last American troops left

Indo-China with the South Vietnamese government still in control of the situation. (S. L. Mayer).

## The End of the War

The war in Vietnam continued without American troops though massive American aid continued to pour into the country right up to the end. However, the actual withdrawal of American troops heightened the contradictions within the regime of President Thieu. In September and October 1974 there was, for instance, widespread popular agitation, led and directed by Roman Catholics against the corruption and military inefficiency of South Vietnam. This took the form of demonstrations throughout the country, some of which ended in armed clashes between Government forces and demonstrators. Although Thieu made some concessions to the demonstrators and dismissed some of the more openly corrupt of his cabinet the main result was further curbs on individual freedom and the arrest and imprisonment of three newspaper editors who had published the demands of the anti-corruption group in full.

The corruption of the Thieu regime and the internal problems of South Vietnam were soon to be completely overwhelmed by more serious concerns when, at the beginning of 1975, the forces of the North Vietnamese Army and the Provisional Revolutionary Government of South Vietnam began their final attack on the South.

Although American troops had left, the forces of South Vietnam still enjoyed an overwhelming superiority, at least on paper, over those of the North. The South Vietnamese Army, before the March 1975 offensive, had a strength of about 450,000 regulars plus some 2 million irregulars organized into local para-military units. The South Vietnamese Air Force had about 60,000 men and over 500 aircraft. The actual size of the North Vietnamese forces is difficult to estimate exactly but it seems that at that time the combined forces of the North and the Provisional Revolutionary Government amounted to some 350,000 consisting of about 150,000 North Vietnamese regulars plus 100,000 support troops and 100,000 guerrillas. However, it was not simply a

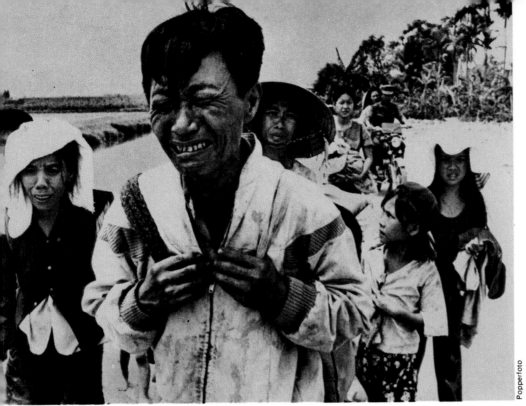

*Part of the 'convoy of tears' from the abandoned central highlands, March 1975; carrying only a few things on his back, the weeping head of a family leads the way along Highway One towards Nha Trang. At that time an estimated 1.5 million were feared trapped in Da Nang*

matter of strength. The South Vietnamese regime, riddled with corruption and inefficiency, deserted by its allies and rapidly losing any popular support in the South, was simply in no position to fight the war. As Paul McCloskey, a Republican member of the House of Representatives wrote to President Ford in March, 'The North continues to acquire additional territory although outgunned, outnumbered and suffering at least double the casualties of the South. The aggressiveness, will and sense of purpose of the North, its leaders, its soldiers, presently far exceed the aggressiveness, will and sense of purpose of the bulk of their South Vietnamese counterparts.'

In December 1974 the forces of the Provisional Revolutionary Government supported by the North Vietnamese Army began their move South. The end of bombing had enabled them to create a network of metalled roads to replace the old Ho Chi Minh Trail and greatly increased the speed and effectiveness of their advance. On 7th January 1975 they overran the provincial capital of Phuoc Binh. Thieu, faced with declining morale in his army (there were about 24,000 desertions a month in the first months of 1975) and the revival of opposition at home was forced to withdraw his troops from the Central Highlands to defend the coast road and Saigon in the hopes of reversing the advance of Northern forces as he had done in the Tet Offensive.

Although the North Vietnamese Army and the forces of the PRG did not seriously pursue the South Vietnamese forces through the Central Highlands they were constantly harried by local units comprised of Montagnard tribesmen. They had previously been among Thieu's strongest supporters and their desertion to the PRG was a bad omen. As *Le Monde* wrote 'the local population played an essential part in expelling the Government troops from the Central Highlands'.

As the South Vietnamese Army withdrew through the Central Highlands the combined forces of the North began to press home their attack on other fronts. In the Saigon sector in the region of Tay Ninh the district town of Tri Tam fell on 11th March and on 17th March the units in that sector began a concerted attack on Saigon. To combat this threat Thieu withdrew troops from the northern front which seriously weakened the forces in that sector who were now under heavy attack.

On 25th March Hué, on the northern front, fell without any resistance and Thieu announced that a new line would be established at Da Nang which would be 'defended to the death if necessary'. But in Da Nang itself chaos prevailed with thousands of refugees, particularly those who had grown rich in Thieu's corrupt regime, fighting for places on any plane or boat leaving. The *New York Times* reported that 'most of the rest of the population of Da Nang seems content to stay....'

On 29th March Da Nang fell amidst a complete collapse of Army morale. As Northern forces entered the city they issued a series of orders, which were to be repeated in Saigon. Private property was not to be seized or attacked. Historic buildings and churches, as well as works of art, were to be protected but, above all, all workers were to return to work immediately.

Meanwhile the US attempted to organise relief for civilians in Vietnam and launched an international appeal for aid to get refugees out; a move denounced by the North Vietnamese as 'forced evacuation of the population'. But the concern was not only for the civilian population. On 28th January 1975 President Ford asked Congress to authorize an extra $300 million loan to Vietnam and $222 million for Cambodia. His proposal was opposed by both sides of Congress and despite a passionate appeal on 6th March, it was clear that Congress would no longer be at all willing to support any kind of military intervention whatever in Vietnam from now on.

In South-East Asia the American-supported regime in Cambodia was entering its last months. The overthrow and arrest of Prince Norodam Sihanouk in 1970 had started five years of civil war between the Government and the National United Front of Cambodia (the Khmers Rouges). The Khmers offensive had been aimed from the beginning at isolating the Cambodian capital, Phnom-Penh, and by mid-1974 all roads to the city had been cut. On 1st January 1975 the Khmers Rouges launched a major attack on Phnom-Penh advancing into the suburbs of the city itself. Their attacks eventually cut the vital supply route along the Mekong River, which meant that all supplies had to be brought in by air. Although various American agencies flew in food supplies of up to 600 tons a day most of this went to the army. However, increasingly heavy attacks by the Khmers Rouges on the vital air bases and the refusal of Congress to allow any more funds for Cambodia ensured the Government's defeat. During the night of 14th–15th April the Khmers Rouges began their final assault on Phnom-Penh and by the dawn of 17th April the city was in their hands.

Meanwhile Thieu's regime was tottering in South Vietnam. From the fall of Da Nang onwards the combined forces of the North Vietnamese Army and the P.R.G. pushed on down the coast road. Many positions were given up without fighting as morale in the South Vietnamese Army deteriorated still further. In Saigon increased pressure was put on Thieu to resign so that a truce could be made, and on 21st April he finally resigned his position as head of state to his deputy Tran Van Huong. Huong held office for only seven days and was replaced on 28th April by General Duong Van Minh. But it was all too late. On 28th April the Americans began the final withdrawal of their remaining personnel and the more prominent supporters of the Thieu regime. (Thieu himself had already fled on 26th April).

On 30th April 1975 the longest war of the 20th century ended as the victorious troops of the P.R.G. and the North Vietnamese Army entered Saigon. On 29th April Saigon was renamed Ho Chi Minh City as a tribute to the original leader of the Vietnamese.

Since that time both Cambodia and South Vietnam have settled into their own versions of Communism. Vietnam now seems to be moving towards unity and despite some clashes between Government troops and Thieu supporters in early 1976 a relatively liberal regime seems to have emerged. Cambodia has followed a much more rigid system taking the Chinese example of sending town dwellers into the fields and supporters of the former Lon Nol regime to corrective labour.

The real legacy of the Vietnam War is this: would the United States now face *any* enemy, fight *any* foe, if America's needs were at stake? If the United States was overcommitted in the 1950's what is her real commitment now? North Vietnam proved that a great power *can* be defeated in a guerilla war. Vietnam has crucially altered American foreign policy to one of non-intervention—as in the case of Angola—at least for the time being.

*(Alun Howkins)*

# USA: Kennedy and After

On a bitterly cold day in January 1961 John F. Kennedy took office as President of the United States. Although the Democratic Party had secured majorities in both the House of Representatives and the Senate, these were by no means a guarantee for the easy passage of the President's programmes. There were—and are—many powerful Democratic members of Congress who are even more conservative than right-wing Republicans on certain issues. A liberal, forward-looking President, anxious to introduce legislation on civil rights for ethnic minorities, determined to improve social security and medical welfare payments for the needy, could therefore expect strong opposition from both Republicans and Democrats in the Congress.

Nevertheless there were some successes, and during his two years and ten months in the presidency John F. Kennedy used all the powers of his office to secure legislation aimed at improving the welfare of the poorer sections of American society.

Overall, however, President Kennedy's legislative programme on those domestic issues he held to be vital to the health of the nation—both its economic and its spiritual health—did not meet with success. If he had served for another term in the presidency, perhaps his rare qualities of dynamism, energy, and leadership would have persuaded the Congress to pass his legislation. But his tragic death on 22nd November 1963 makes this merely speculative. Kennedy's brief term had inspired a period of vigorous, though moderate reformism, and his assassination profoundly shattered the confident mood of the people of the United States. In retrospect, it seems as if the tragedy may have unleashed dark furies in the American soul which have yet to be curbed.

Vice-President Lyndon Johnson's sudden accession to power was, however, at first auspicious. At fifty-five, he had accumulated an unprecedented amount of experience as a legislator: twenty-three years in the House and Senate, including a period as the Democratic leader in the Senate. He was a moderate liberal, steeped in New Deal ideals. Despite being the first Southern president since Andrew Johnson a century before, he had genuine compassion for minorities. He was also a man of restless drive, who was often criticized for 'bullying' people and for reacting harshly to dissent.

Johnson seized the Presidency with fervour. He quickly appointed a commission led by the Chief Justice of the US Supreme Court, Earl Warren, to investigate Kennedy's death. In 1964, the Commission concluded that Lee Harvey Oswald alone had shot Kennedy, because he had become embittered by a life of failure. Criticizing Warren's report soon became one of the nation's major industries—inspiring hundreds of books, films, plays and songs all of which cast doubt on the theory of the lone assassin.

The new President rapidly became involved in legislation. He presided over the passage of two Kennedy-sponsored bills: the $11.5 billion tax-cut bill which soon stimulated an era of economic growth, and the Civil Rights Act of 1964, the first major pro-black legislation in Congress for decades. The act prohibited discrimination in the use of federal funds and in places of public resort, and established an Equal Employment Opportunity Commission. Subsequently, under Johnson's leadership, a voting rights act passed in 1965 authorized the federal government to register those whom the states refused to put on the voting lists; the bill led to a new black electorate in the South, and brought an end to overt racism in politics.

In the 1964 presidential contest between Johnson and Republican Senator Barry Goldwater, a conservative from Arizona, Johnson introduced his approach to social change in America called the 'Great Society'. He argued for greater government involvement in fighting poverty and providing for the needs of the citizens. Goldwater attacked this idea of government help; he advocated selling the Tennessee Valley Authority, a government agency which had brought power, electricity, water and prosperity to the ailing backlands of several Southern states. He proclaimed that 'extremism in the defence of liberty is no vice', which rather shook Americans concerned about their prospective president, whose trigger finger would rest on the nation's nuclear button. Johnson's idea of social reform carried the day. He won over sixty-one per cent of the popular vote, taking all but six states. He also obtained a working liberal majority in the House of Representatives, the first time any president had done so since 1938.

Johnson quickly turned to his Great Society programme. In 1965–66, he pushed through Congress bills designed to give Federal aid to education, underwrite medical benefits for the old (Medicare), create a new cabinet position, the Department of Housing and Urban Development (to which he appointed the first black Cabinet officer), control water pollution, liberalize immigration laws, provide more money for the arts, subsidize the rents of low-income Americans, and help attack city slums through agencies like the Model Cities Programme. His most controversial enactment was the creation of the Office of Economic Opportunity (OEO), which stood at the forefront of the American 'war on poverty'. The OEO educated dropouts from high schools, employed the jobless, funded a domestic Peace Corps, taught pre-school children, and organized ghettos to fight poverty. Federal spending under Johnson for health, education and social purposes rose dramatically from $54 billion in 1964 to $98 billion in 1968. Coupled with the 1964 tax cut, the new appropriations for social reform helped reduce the percentage of people living on poverty income from 22.4 per cent in 1959 to 12.5 per cent in 1969. However, many of Johnson's experimental ideas sowed confusion, and it is possible that they aroused more expectations than they satisfied; nonetheless they represented the most far reaching domestic changes in American life since the New Deal.

## Vietnam

Lyndon Johnson, whose instinct appeared to be so unerring in matters of domestic legislation, was less able when dealing with foreign policy. A product of the Cold War of the 1950's, he judged events overseas as a continual conflict between the Free World and Communism. This led him to send 22,289 United States Marines into the midst of a murky civil war in the Dominican Republic in 1965, to combat what he called 'Communist infiltration'. Ultimately he settled the conflict by compromising between the loyalists and the rebels, when he could find no Communist leaders. The instinct to attack first and ask questions later took him rapidly into Vietnam.

Originally, President Kennedy had com-

*Rivals for the presidency, 1960: Kennedy and Nixon after television confrontation*

United Press International

473

mitted 16,300 'advisers' to support the authoritarian regime of President Ngo Dinh Diem against an indigenous movement of Viet Cong guerillas, partly supported by the North Vietnamese. Johnson, who genuinely desired peace (though this meant peace arranged on his own terms) claimed, during the 1964 presidential campaign, that he would not send more American 'boys' to Asia. Nonetheless, because he was loath to 'lose' a war against Communists, he took the country increasingly deeper into the conflict. Early in 1964, he authorized hit-and-run military operations against North Vietnam; then, in August 1964, taking as a dubious pretext a North Vietnamese attack on two US destroyers engaged in electronic surveillance in the Gulf of Tonkin, he ordered air strikes on North Vietnam, and rushed through Congress the famous Tonkin Gulf resolution which broadly authorized the President to 'take all necessary steps' to assist South Vietnam.

From now on, Johnson began to accede to the demands of the US military for more weapons and troops for Indo-china. After several Americans were killed at Pleiku early in 1965, Johnson began the Rolling Thunder campaign, which gradually escalated the air war against North Vietnam. He also increased the number of American troops in South Vietnam: by 1965 there were 184,300; 385,300 at the end of 1966; by the close of 1968, 536,100. Johnson justified his massive involvement first to revive morale in South Vietnam, and second to break the will of the North. In the meantime, he directed the CIA into a secret war against the Pathet Lao in Laos. Soon he had expanded his rationale for the war from protecting the 'freedom' of South Vietnam to preventing Chinese expansionism all over Asia. In this Johnson tended to forget both the corruption and unpopularity of the South Vietnamese government, and Vietnam's historic enmity with China.

The Americanization of the war intensified the debate at home over its value. Americans reacted with growing outrage to the rise in US combat casualties; 1,130 in 1965, 4,179 in 1966, 7,482 in 1967, and 12,588 in 1968. As the bombing increased—by the end of 1968, American planes had dropped 3.2 million tons of explosives on the Vietnamese landscape (as against a total of two million tons on all fronts in the Second World War)—and as television conveyed the destruction in vivid reports, a moral revulsion against the fighting spread through a large segment of the country. Students at the universities, professionals, middle-class parents with sons being drafted, intellectuals, dissidents on the streets, all began to protest against the government. The furious outcry soon reached the ears of Senators and Congressmen who reacted in many cases by breaking publicly with Johnson over his conduct of the war.

The war was even destroying Johnson's masterpiece, the Great Society. The Democrats had lost their working liberal majority in the Congress in the 1966 elections. Johnson could no longer go to Congress for help on social programmes, with the cost of the Indo-China venture reaching over $20 billion in 1967. His underestimates of military spending were creating inflation at home and a balance of payments problem abroad. And the Vietnam fighting was going badly. In February 1968, the Viet Cong suddenly launched the destructive Tet offensive, which was followed by an invasion of the US embassy in Saigon by South Vietnamese dissidents. At this moment, the US military demanded 206,000 more American troops. Political reality finally forced Johnson to refuse the request, and from then on he worked solely towards a negotiated peace.

However, the passions aroused by the war had already created fatal political opposition within the Democratic party. Eugene McCarthy, a Democratic Senator from Minnesota, challenged Johnson in the New Hampshire primary and almost beat him. Later, Senator Robert Kennedy joined the fray, and fought in the primaries until he was assassinated in June 1968, after winning the California contest. Johnson

Larry Schiller-Magnum

*Left: The Watts riots—guarded by soldiers, firemen fight blazes in Los Angeles' negro ghetto. On the night of 11th August 1965 the attempt by white policemen to arrest a Watts youth for a traffic violation sparked off a six-day riot which resulted in thirty-four deaths and property damage of forty million dollars. But an equally staggering statistic is that unemployment in Watts before the riots had reached a total of about thirty per cent*

*Above: Riots in Harlem, July 1964, sparked off by the killing of a fifteen-year-old negro by a white policeman*

an idealism in universities across the country. Students joined the Peace Corps and travelled South to fight racism through lunchcounter sit-ins and the 'Freedom Rides' on segregated buses. The social activists sometimes even swept ahead of their political inspiration, Kennedy. In 1963, they helped organize the famous black 'March On Washington' for civil rights which the Kennedy Administration had privately admired but failed to endorse publicly.

The murder of Kennedy, however, marked the beginning of a change in attitude toward American democracy. With the extraordinary double killings five years later, in 1968, of Kennedy's brother, Senator Robert Kennedy, in the midst of his presidential drive, and of the Reverend Martin Luther King, the most eloquent and well-known of the nation's black leaders, the unthinkable suddenly seemed to be normal. The deaths of idealistic leaders began to engender a spirit of cynicism and alienation among young Americans who repeatedly saw every chance of political change in the United States being wantonly destroyed.

The spirit of reform soured along with the loss of idealism. The onrushing campaign for civil rights gradually lost its biracial character and momentum as more militant leaders came to the fore and the pace of school and economic integration remained modest. In 1967, thirteen years after the Supreme Court decision desegregating public schools, only sixteen per cent of the three million blacks attending school in the South were in integrated educational institutions. The one-time black student leader, Stokely Carmichael, caught the angry mood of the blacks with his slogan, 'Black Power'. Militancy by the Black Muslim religious sect and the Black Panthers, a radical black political group led by Bobby Seale and Eldridge Cleaver, reinforced a nationalist fervour among the Negro minority. By now the Negro population in major American cities was near to a majority (in 1970, for example, seventy-one per cent of Washington, D.C., was black; fifty-four per cent of Newark; forty-four per cent of Detroit). Still ghetto conditions remained terrible. Suddenly blacks erupted in a series of destructive riots: Watts, California (1965); Chicago (1966); Tampa, Florida, Cincinnati, Ohio, Atlanta, Georgia, Detroit, Michigan, and Newark, New Jersey (1967); in 1968, Martin Luther King's assassination set off riots in 172 cities resulting in forty-three deaths and 27,000 arrests. Yet this wave of violence brought about very little reform.

Just as the civil rights movement was crumbling into mob disturbances, the Vietnam war was generating a new level of passionate opposition. In October 1967, some 200,000 people, led by literary figures like novelist Norman Mailer and the poet Robert Lowell, marched on the Pentagon. Colleges across the land were organizing petition drives, draft card burnings, demonstrations against Army recruiters and other forms of protest. The student protest was unlike anything that had ever happened in American education. This was partly the result of increased college enrolment, which more than doubled from 1960 to 1970 (3.8 million to 8.5 million).

had already in April 1968 withdrawn from the race for renomination. With Kennedy's death, the way was open to nominate Vice-President Hubert Humphrey, who was publicly identified as an apologist for Johnson's Indo-China policy.

The 1968 Democratic Convention in Chicago was a disaster for Humphrey. The defeat of the McCarthy and Kennedy forces at the convention and Humphrey's refusal to break with Johnson over Vietnam led to a bloody riot in Chicago between police and anti-war demonstrators. Humphrey refused to criticize the actions of the police and did not, until too late in the campaign, suggest that the war had been a mistake—thereby losing his opportunity to attract dissident

Democrats back to the fold before election day. The Republican candidate, Richard Nixon, once Eisenhower's Vice-President, defeated Humphrey narrowly, 31.8 million votes to 31.4 million votes, with former Governor George Wallace of Alabama receiving 9.9 million votes. With only 43.4 per cent of the total vote, Nixon was a minority President. The Democrats retained control of Congress, making Nixon the first President since Zachary Taylor in 1849 whose party on his election did not control at least one chamber.

## The Counterculture

The 1960's had opened in a glow of hope. John Kennedy's 'New Frontier' had awakened

However, for a long time the anti-war demonstrations did not seem to have much influence on the government's Vietnam policy. As a result, some disillusioned young people turned to drugs, or joined communes, or sought out anonymous, non-threatening life-styles in hippie areas like Haight-Ashbury in San Francisco, where feelings of love and community briefly predominated. Others, angered over the betrayal of their government, dived into political rebellion, joining the 'New Left' which argued for various forms of civil disobediance, or even violence (the belief of the revolutionary Weathermen) to bring down the government.

All of this protest culture became loosely known as 'the Movement'. It was a mood rather than a coherent collection of ideas. The singer Bob Dylan, the English group the Beatles, the pop festival at Woodstock, movies like *Easy Rider* and novelists like Ken Kesey *(One Flew Over The Cuckoo's Nest)* all were shapers and prophets of this separate society. But a number of forces gradually began to shatter the movement. First, self-destructive impulses from within the counter-culture, like the satanic Charles Manson 'tribe', members of which killed actress Sharon Tate and six others, broke the romantic image of the movement. Then government trials of leaders of the New Left like Dr Benjamin Spock, accused of assisting students in draft evasion, and the Chicago 7, charged with conspiracy to incite a riot after the troubles in Chicago during the Democratic Convention there in 1968, distracted the rebels from protest demonstrations. As the war slowly wound down, the anti-war fervour abated further. Finally, the worsening economy drove many people to seek stability in regular jobs and to desert anti-establishment activities.

## Nixon's First Term

The election of Richard Nixon was an unlikely even for this time. Defeated in 1960 by John Kennedy, defeated again in 1962 for the California governship, widely scorned as a political 'loser' and manipulator (hence the nickname 'Tricky Dicky'), Nixon was also a man totally in opposition to the rebellious mood of the 1960's. Yet, in spite of this, at the age of fifty-six, he became the leader of the United States at one of the most turbulent times in its history.

His first term focussed mainly on foreign affairs. He appointed Henry Kissinger, a Harvard intellectual, to serve as his special assistant for National Security affairs. Together they began a policy of rapprochement with Communist powers, which repudiated much of Nixon's previous record of obdurate anti-Communism. Nixon quickly adopted Kissinger's thesis that American foreign policy should be based on a classical balance of power politics. This approach opened up new negotiating possibilities with Cold War enemies, but at the same time appeared to neglect human values of freedom in

*Above: Larry Edwards, leader of Californian drop-out group. The young were dis-illusioned with politics. Left: After their landslide victory in 1964 President Johnson entertains Vice-President-elect Hubert Humphrey at his ranch in Texas*

favour of stable, authoritarian governments, whether they were Marxist (Russia) or Fascist (Greece, Brazil).

Nixon's most audacious move was to establish contact with the Chinese People's Republic. In his early political years, he had denounced American leaders for 'losing' China to the Communists; now, as President, he reversed his position and, responding to the urging of Chinese leaders who felt threatened by nearly fifty divisions of Russian troops on their border, sent Henry Kissinger to Peking in July 1971 for talks. In February-March 1972, Nixon himself visited China for a week and met Mao Tse-tung. In the Shanghai Accord, the two leaders agreed to exchange diplomats, and the US also recognized that Taiwan was part of mainland China. Nixon later visited Moscow in May 1972, the first American President ever to do so. He concluded an agreement with the Russians on the Strategic Arms Limitations Talks (SALT), which had begun in 1969. The compact froze the number of offensive missiles and restricted the development of anti-ballistic missile systems on both sides, in an attempt to try and ensure the cooling down of the arms race for a few years.

In dealing with the Vietnam War, however, Nixon was unable to shed his fundamental anti-Communism. In fact, during his first term, he dramatically enlarged the fighting in Indo-China. While he continued the peace talks in Paris, he never dropped his basic condition for settlement—that the North Vietnamese accede to the continuance of the government of President Nguyen Van Thieu. The North Vietnamese, who had been fighting in Indo-China for thirty years, showed no willingness to accept this condition. Nixon grew more belligerent as the North refused to put down arms. He accelerated the bombing of Vietnam—by the end of 1971, his administration had dropped 3.3 million tons of bombs on the country, as well as Laos and Cambodia (more in three years than President Johnson had dropped in five). He poured new funds into the fighting: by 1972, the war had cost the United States more money than any conflict since the Second World War, about $120 billion from 1965–71. More significantly, Nixon expanded the war into Cambodia. Shortly after a coup in Cambodia in March 1970 supported by the CIA, which ousted Prince Norodom Sihanouk, a neutralist, Nixon approved an 'incursion' by US troops into the country to clean out North Vietnamese units operating from neutral Cambodian 'sanctuaries'. The dispatch of American forces without statutory or treaty authorization or Congressional consultation retriggered the anti-war movement in the US and set off college protests involving 1.5 million students. The worst incident occurred at Kent State University in Ohio when the National Guard killed 4 students demonstrating against the invasion.

As a result of Nixon's actions, Congress began to reassert its powers over foreign policy. To prevent another Vietnam, for example, Congress immediately repealed the Gulf of Tonkin Resolution and banned funds for American ground troops in Laos, Thailand and, after the invasion, Cambodia. Two years later, in August 1973, Congress

ended all American bombing of Indo-China and, over Nixon's veto, passed the War Powers Act, an attempt to limit the authority of the President to commit American troops to battle overseas without Congressional approval. The bill, however, permitted the President ninety days before he was obliged to ask for Congressional backing; by then, of course, US troops might be so deeply committed to a foreign war that public opinion would not permit Congress to cut off aid. The legislation was therefore somewhat ineffective.

Nixon denounced these events, but stuck to his policy of 'Vietnamizing' the war. He reduced American troops from 543,000 in April 1969 to 60,000 in September 1972. Just before the 1972 election, he almost concluded peace with North Vietnam, but

*Right: 1969 cartoon reflects current US disenchantment with interventionist foreign policy. Early in the 1960's angry demonstrations in several US cities opposed the 1961 CIA-backed invasion of Cuba. Below: Negroes pay last respects to Martin Luther King, assassinated in Memphis on 4th April 1968. His attempts to find a peaceful solution to US racial problems had won him the 1964 Nobel Peace Prize*

Dallas Notes/LNS

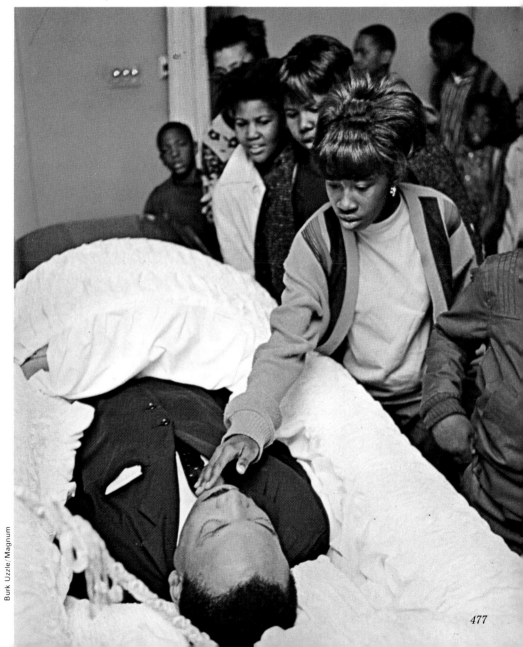

Burk Uzzle/Magnum

*Clouds of tear gas hang over the campus of Kent State University as national guardsmen attempt to disperse rioting students. Four people were killed on 4th May 1970, on the fourth day of rioting against President Nixon's South-East Asian policies*

President Thieu repudiated it, and Nixon then broke off his talks with the Communists. In late December 1972, Nixon launched a savage bombing of North Vietnam in an attempt to force the Communists to agree to new US conditions; but early in 1973, the US and the North finally signed a second peace treaty which was virtually the same as the one reached before the US elections. The war was now over, but it had severely damaged the economic and psychological state of US society. Events like the American massacre at My Lai in March 1968, and US government lies about the war had, according to Gallup Polls, made many Americans distrustful of their governmental institutions.

Nixon showed scant interest in domestic programmes during this period. He considered the introduction of a minimum income plan for the poor to replace the archaic welfare system, but he later discarded the idea. Then he adopted a Keynesian economic philosophy in the summer of 1971, accepting the largest peace-time deficit in American history—$38.8 billion in 1972. He instituted wage and price controls, but these had little impact on high inflation and increasing unemployment, primarily because they were allowed to lapse after Nixon had won the 1972 election. For the most part, Nixon practised a policy of confrontation at home—making conservative appointments to the Supreme Court, proclaiming law and order as the Republican standard in the 1970 Congressional elections (in which the Republicans lost nine seats in the House of Representatives), and denouncing busing, job quotas, and the permissive society symbolized by the protest culture known as 'the Movement'. Nixon's appeal, bolstered by his triumphant trips to China and Russia, as well as the winding down of the Indo-China war, enabled him to defeat the Democratic nominee, Senator George McGovern, in the 1972 presidential election by an overwhelming popular vote—Nixon received 46 million votes against McGovern's 28.5 million.

## Watergate

Nixon started his second term in triumph, but the victory soon turned sour. During the summer before the 1972 election, a burglary occurred at the Democratic National Headquarters at the Watergate Office Building in Washington, D.C. The police arrested five men, one of whom was the head of security for the Republican Committee to Re-Elect the President, known as CREEP. Hard-nosed investigative reporting by two young reporters on *The Washington Post* led to disclosures which indicated that the Nixon Administration might have been involved in the planning of the break-in as well as in a number of other unexplained 'dirty tricks' played on Democratic candidates during the presidential primaries.

After his election, Nixon attempted to play down the Watergate 'incident' and to focus attention on his electoral landslide. Through a new series of legislative proposals, he tried to dismantle Johnson's Great Society and much of Roosevelt's New Deal. He began to impound monies authorized by Congress for environmental and social programmes. In a post-election interview, he remarked that the average American citizen was like a 'child' who must be given responsibility. Nixon attempted to aggregate to the Chief Executive the three fundamental powers of Congress: the war-making power (the invasion of Cambodia without Congressional consultation or approval); the power of the purse (impoundment of monies authorized by Congress for social reforms); the power of oversight and investigation (the doctrine of unreviewable executive privilege which was used to ward off Watergate investigators). But, like Canute, Nixon could not stop the rising tides of Watergate.

At the beginning of 1973, Nixon's popularity was sixty-eight per cent. Less than seven months later, a Gallup Poll showed that it had dropped to thirty-one per cent, the lowest of any president in twenty years. A series of revelations about Nixon's morals, his staff, his politics and his possible criminality virtually destroyed any belief in him as a leader. These disclosures came tumbling out first in the trial of the Watergate burglars in Judge John Sirica's court in early 1973, and then in the testimony of Nixon's top aides from the White House before the Senate Select Committee on Presidential Campaign Activities in the summer of 1973. Both forums provided information on presidential misuse of power including the following illegal practices: the use of Federal agencies like the Internal Revenue Service, the Small Business Administration and the Attorney General's office to reward those

*British cartoon shows the embarrassment of President Nixon over the Watergate scandal and other doubtful revelations about his administration—all of which combined to shatter his standing*

'He that is without sin among you, let him first cast a stone . . .'
[St. John, Chapter 8, verse 7]

London Express Service

*Dr Henry Kissinger, Harvard intellectual and US Secretary of State, with President Nixon*

people who supported Nixon and to punish those who opposed him; the unreported collection of millions of dollars in campaign contributions through doubtful means; the expenditure of certain campaign donations to finance the Watergate break-in; the use of political malpractice in 1972 against Democratic politicians, the president's cover-up of these crimes which violated his oath of office faithfully to 'preserve, protect and defend' the constitution of the US.

The turning point came in the summer of 1973, when one of Nixon's aides revealed to the Senate Watergate Committee that Nixon had kept a taping system in the White House. Archibald Cox the Special Prosecutor appointed by Nixon under popular pressure early in 1973, immediately subpoenaed the tapes. Nixon resisted, ultimately firing Cox (the Attorney General and Assistant Attorney General also resigned) in the 'Saturday Night Massacre' in the autumn of 1973. The 'firestorm' which ensued forced Nixon to give up incriminating tapes, and led to the start of impeachment proceedings in Congress. The resignation in the autumn of 1973 of Nixon's Vice-President, Spiro Agnew, for corruption unrelated to Watergate; the revelation that Nixon owed $450,000 in back taxes because one of his lawyers falsely backdated a deed; the fact that by June 1974, seventeen members of Nixon's Administration had either confessed to or had been found guilty of criminal acts; and finally Nixon's repeated television appearances in which he proclaimed his innocence of the Watergate cover-up—all combined to shatter the President's standing. Then, on 25th July 1974, the US Supreme Court ordered Nixon to surrender more tapes. One of these revealed that he had impeded a FBI investigation and directed that criminal evidence be covered up. Now even his own Republican Party urged him to go. On 8th August, Nixon resigned; a month later in early September, the new President, Gerald Ford, pardoned him for all crimes committed while in office.

## Ford in office

Gerald Ford is an amiable, conservative Congressman in the Republican Party from Grand Rapids, Michigan, who has served for some twenty-five years in the House of Representatives; he achieved the position of Republican minority leader in 1965. Richard Nixon originally selected him to be Vice-President during the Watergate tribulations (he was sworn in on 6th December, 1973)

because he needed somebody well known to Congress who would win approval there quickly. Ford brought to the presidency a somewhat limited view of the national interest. In twenty-five years, he loyally supported all Republican presidents as a Congressman and Minority Leader but showed little independence of thought as a legislator.

However, Ford's pleasantness as a person at first seemed more important than his qualities as a leader. He took office bathed in enormous popularity (seventy-one per cent in the Gallup Poll); but soon after he pardoned Nixon his popular acceptance dropped to fifty per cent, and people began to examine more closely what Ford really represented. After this it was difficult for him to recover the confidence of the American people.

From the beginning, he was in a position of unusual weakness. He was the country's first un-elected President with no natural following. In November 1974, the Democrats won the Congress in overwhelming numbers, gaining forty-nine seats in the House of Representatives and five seats in the Senate. Ford had virtually no power to influence events in Congress except by the veto—which he used with great frequency. In his first three months in office, Ford vetoed more bills (fifteen) than Nixon had in his first eighteen months (twelve), though Ford had a higher percentage of them overridden (four out of fifteen) than any President since Franklin Pierce in the 1850's. By December 1975, Ford had used the veto forty-two times and Congress overrode him seven times in that period.

Stalemate has characterized his leadership so far. After prices of imported oil rose, Ford called for higher tariffs on the oil to force Americans to use less petrol, but Congress blocked the plan. Ford faced 5.3 per cent unemployment in August 1974; a year later, after pursuing tight money policies, vetoing most government-financed employment programmes, and displaying a generally *laissez-faire* attitude toward the American economy, unemployment had risen to 8.3 per cent. He seemed alarmed at the millions of workers out of jobs, but was more concerned about high inflation damaging American business. Nonetheless, despite his conservative precepts, Ford tolerated a large tax-cut bill and the largest peace-time deficit in the nation's history in his 1976 budget—$51.9 billion.

Despite Watergate and the need for ending

secrecy in government, Ford has opposed a Freedom of Information bill (which allowed Americans to obtain files on themselves held by government agencies). Congress passed the bill over his veto. In addition, Ford battled against Congressional investigations of the FBI and the CIA. Congress went ahead and probed the two intelligence units in the autumn of 1975, and proposed far-reaching reforms in the powers of both agencies. Finally, despite Vietnam's lessons, Ford fought to supply the pro-West faction in the Angolian civil war with secret CIA aid, but Congress finally opposed the assistance.

## The Future

The 1976 presidential election—which occurs exactly 200 years after the original thirteen colonies declared their independence from England—centres, as ever, on the great question in American history: was the nation prepared to embark on new major, economic and social reforms, or was it content to maintain the present situation? The growth of new political movements among various minorities in US society like the blacks, the Puerto Ricans, the Chicanos, the progressive labour unions, the middle-class liberals in the cities and the suburbs, and the women (who were actually a majority of the population) suggested that the tide of reform was running strongly in American politics. The popularity of economic reformers like Ralph Nader seemed to indicate that the giant economic configurations in the US were likely to bear the brunt of change. There was strong sentiment in the nation against bigness—in the 1960's the top eighty-seven corporations with assets of more than $1 billion—less than one per cent of all manufacturing firms—increased their share of total assets of industrial corporations from twenty-six per cent to forty-six per cent, concentrating more and more wealth in the hands of fewer and fewer firms.

However the resolution of the reform versus the status quo issue seems to remain very much in doubt because neither political party has yet produced a leader with enough influence to sway public opinion decisively in one direction or another.

*President Gerald Ford, who became the first unelected president of the United States*

# Epilogue

## INTRODUCTION

We have now entered the last quarter of the 20th century. Behind us lie 75 years of unparalleled violence, destruction and waste. The hordes of Ghengis Khan did less damage in ten years than his 20th century equivalents, of whatever nation, have achieved in one. But these have also been years of enormous advance. Technology has swept forward, the fight against disease and famine has gained great victories and all over the world inequalities are gradually being abolished. But what of the future? Prophesying is a notoriously difficult task—all we can really do is review the events of the recent years and try and point to some of the areas in which significant change may come.

The economic prosperity of the Western world in the 1950's and 1960's came to an abrupt end in the 1970's. By September 1974 the London *Times* while seeing depression as a short-lived phenomenon ending probably in 1976 or 1977 also predicted that the subsequent boom would be a short-lived phenomenon at the end of which 'it can be expected that the financial structure of major countries will break down, and the financial calamity which we have probably narrowly avoided in the last boom will really hit us.' Only the Far East, especially Hong Kong and Japan (and increasingly Singapore), with a vast army of cheap labour, have been able to weather the storm. Against a background of spiralling inflation and rising unemployment the politics of the Western world have taken on a new and grimmer tinge. Gone was the liberal excitement and flamboyance of the 1960's as the curtain was raised on the scene of depression.

Although there are some signs of economic recovery, the face of capitalism has been changed, particularly in Britain where the government has continued to intervene in industry with varying degrees of success. This has also been coupled with an agreed anti-inflation policy with the Trade Unions— a remarkable demonstration of the sobering effects of unemployment on Union militancy. Not only Britain has been affected. Both France and Italy found themselves with serious currency problems early in 1976. Here the potential political effects are more far-reaching. Since the mid-1960's both countries have seen a decisive swing to the Left, and particularly to the Communist parties, which shows no signs of abating. Indeed, the French departmental elections which ended on the 14th March 1976 saw the Left gain more than 250 seats from supporters of the presidential coalition, including the seat in the department of Pay de Dome where the president, Valéry Giscard d'Estaing, is a departmental councillor. In Italy three interlocked crises— monetary, economic and political—have enormously increased the Italian Communist Party's chance of reaching the 'historic compromise'—membership of a coalition government.

The hopes of both the French and Italian Communist Parties were considerably raised by the 25th Congress of the Soviet Communist Party. This congress, which may well turn out to be as significant for the Western Parties as the 20th Congress was for the Soviet Union, saw the rejection of the traditional line of the 'proletarian dictatorship' by the French, Italian and British Parties. This has enabled the Italian Communists to announce that if elected to power they would remain within NATO and guarantee individual freedoms, including the right to form opposition parties. Even though this pronouncement may not be taken seriously by the Italian extreme right-wing, it must to some extent ease suspicion of the national Communist parties.

However, there remains deep antagonism to any European Communist government. On the 1st March 1976 Russian novelist Alexander Solzhenitsyn, interviewed on BBC television, issued a grave warning that continuing detente with the Soviet Union, let alone any Western European Communist government, would mean the end of Western democracy; 'the West is on the verge of collapse created by its own hands.' Solzhenitsyn's warning, especially his insistence that he is a defender of democracy, lost some of its impact when, later that month, on a visit to Spain he praised that country's regime.

Other attacks on the fragile detente of recent years have less justifiable origins. Following the election of President Nixon in 1968, the United States adopted a more liberal policy towards the non-capitalist world. Led by Dr Henry Kissinger, a Harvard intellectual, American foreign policy moved towards what became known as *detente*, a foreign policy based on classical balance-of-power politics. Most spectacularly, it led to the US recognition of the People's Republic

*The advance of military technology has placed yet another stumbling block in the way of SALT negotiators—the cruise missile. Small and compact it can carry both conventional and nuclear multiple warheads up to 6,000 miles. Its space age micro-circuitry enables it to fly below radar range and to avoid obstacles in its path. The missile is virtually undetectable by existing monitoring techniques. And that is SALT's latest headache*

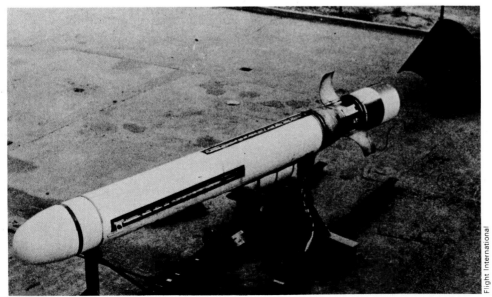

Flight International

*Far left: Portuguese marines in Angola during an early native rebellion. Left: San Francisco hippy peddles 'underground' newspapers*

The future of Latin America seems uncertain. In Argentina, Señora Peron's 'non-government' collapsed in the face of massive inflation and opposition from both Right and Left as well as a wide spectrum of the Peronist movement, with the inevitable military coup. The Right-wing regimes in Chile, Brazil and Uruguay appear to be unchallenged, although with inflation at around 300 per cent in these countries it is difficult to predict what may happen. Cuba alone seems stable although detente with the US is increasingly unlikely.

In Africa the future of the white-minority regimes is uncertain. With the end of the former Portuguese occupation of Mozambique and Angola, the illegal Smith regime in Rhodesia and the South Africans are isolated even further. The final collapse of talks on the move towards majority rule in March 1976 seems to leave no option but bloodshed in Rhodesia. If that happens, South Africa will stand alone.

In the Middle East the temporary peace established by Israel's final withdrawal after the Yom Kippur war has again been shattered, this time by internal problems in the Israeli occupied West Bank of the Jordan but more seriously in the Lebanon. Here Syria intervened once again in an attempt to restore order but any long-term peace prospect seems remote.

And so we enter the last quarter of the 20th century—and we cannot but enter it with pessimism. There seems to be little gained from the foolish nostalgia which pervades much of the world. Film, theatre and fashion all constantly look back to 'a better time' or 'the good old days'. Many major exhibitions in the last five years have looked backwards—at a 'golden age' which was in reality a thousand times worse than the present. For we should not underestimate the achievements of the 20th century, and we should never forget that life now, for the majority of the world's population, is better than it was 76 years ago.

*The overlords of today's international monetary system—the 'gnomes of Zurich'. The trust they command and their consequent huge reserves make them the world's most important bankers*

of China in 1972, and Nixon's visits to Peking and Moscow in that year. It also led to the SALT (Strategic Arms Limitation Talks) in 1969 and a general easing of the US-Soviet relations.

However, detente seems to be losing credibility. President Ford has even repudiated the word and now talks of 'peace through strength'—a decidedly chilling concept. Recent changes in the US have indeed gone far to show just how fallacious the concept was in some senses in that it now seems to have fallen victim to internal US politics. During the presidential campaign President Ford seemed increasingly to be vying with the right wing of his party in his attacks on the Soviet Union. Encouraged by Kissinger's speculation of Europe being predominantly Communist by 1984, he has launched a number of attacks against the Soviet Union and Cuba which seem to prefigure a return to the excess of the Cold War. Only time can tell whether this manoeuvring will lead to a long-term change in Soviet-American relations. If it does, the fragile peace which dominated the world since 1945 will be increasingly at risk.

This shift in American policy is a direct result of the climate in which the 1976 election has been fought. The withdrawal of the Americans from South-East Asia was felt to be undoubtedly a serious blow to American prestige. Since then a definite move to the Right has been noticeable in American politics, a move hastened by the collapse of the American-backed forces in Angola in the face of Cuban aid to the Marxist-orientated MPLA.

American life in general seems to be becoming more and more cynical and violent. The failure of the counter-culture to seriously affect the American system and the upsurge of radicalism centred around the McCarthy/Kennedy campaign of 1968 have led to an increasing hardening of attitudes. The Left are more and more isolated into tiny quasi-terrorist groups like the Symbionese Liberation Army bent on individual acts of terrorism while the right-wing element has come to the forefront of both major political parties. Violence in the major cities shows little sign of decreasing. With massive expenditure cuts engendered by the economic crisis (particularly in New York), the reform programmes begun so hopefully a decade ago seem doomed. What will replace them

can only be guessed at, but we must sincerely hope that it will be a simple capitulation to the cry of law and order. Like so much of the Western world America's future ultimately depends on the defeat of the economic crisis and thus radical and effective government. Tragically, none of the contenders to the White House throne seem like a potential 'F.D.R.'.

British politics saw the resignation of Prime Minister Harold Wilson in March 1976, the longest serving peace-time prime minister of the 20th century. His replacement by James Callaghan marks no significant change in the direction of British politics as Callaghan is likely to continue the Wilson anti-inflation policy with its strong links to voluntary trade union wage restraint.

Elsewhere in Western Europe, particularly in Spain and Portugal, significant change seems imminent. In Portugal the Armed Forces Movement which took power in a virtually bloodless revolution in April 1974 guaranteed that free elections will be held on 25th April 1976, the second anniversary of the revolution. The future of Spain seems less secure. Juan Carlos has proved considerably less democratic than his more optimistic supporters had hoped. As long as the Communists remain excluded from legitimate politics the underground war against Franco's heirs is bound to continue—and to be marked by increasing violence.

The position of America is shifting to the right, but the other two super-powers, China and the Soviet Union, show little sign of change. Russia seems to have accepted the insistence of both Rumania and Yugoslavia at the 25th Party Congress that they should follow their own lines. The same Congress saw Brezhnev re-elected as the head of the Politburo. China, as ever, is a more difficult situation to evaluate. Following the election of Hua Kuo-feng as 'acting prime minister' at the death of Chou En-lai an ideological struggle directed at Teng Hsiao-ping, the former vice-premier, developed. Teng was accused of being a 'Capitalist roader' and was succeeded by Hua Kuo-Feng early in April 1976. Although there have been signs of *rapprochement* between the Soviet Union and China there has been no significant change in the Soviet attitude, while ex-President Nixon's visit to China shows continuing Chinese interest in detente with the West.

# The International Monetary System since 1945

During the Second World War the British and the American governments drew up independent proposals for international monetary reform. The experience of the inter-war period had convinced them that the world's monetary problems could only be solved through close international co-operation. There was to be no repetition of the devaluation cycles which followed the collapse of the gold standard in 1931. Competitive devaluations, bilateral trading arrangements, and uncontrolled movements of 'hot money' should not disrupt international trade as they had done in the 1930's. At the same time it was necessary to avoid the rigidity of the gold standard which had led to its own collapse and which had required Britain to pursue deflationary policies during the 1920's.

The British plans were prepared by J.M. Keynes in 1943 and were concerned primarily to provide sufficient international means of payment and exchange rate flexibility to enable countries to achieve the domestic objective of full employment. Keynes recommended that an International Clearing Union be set up which could act as a world bank. It could create a new paper currency, Bancor, to be used by Central Banks to settle accounts through the Union. Members would accept payment in Bancor and would enjoy overdraft facilities within certain limits. The basic idea was to apply at an international level the principle of a closed banking system. When the Union granted an overdraft to a country which had a balance of payments deficit, it could be used to make payments to countries with a surplus, who would then receive a credit in Bancor. This could not be withdrawn in the form of gold or foreign currency so that the Union would not experience difficulty in meeting claims arising from the granting of overdrafts. The total amount of Bancor would depend on overdrafts granted and on sales of gold to the Union, since gold could be paid in but not withdrawn from the Union.

The Clearing Union could bring pressure to bear on members who were persistent debtors and could require depreciation of their exchange rates. Surplus countries could remain in credit at the Union although they might be encouraged to increase their imports or to re-value their currencies. If a country was a substantial creditor it could accumulate a credit balance equal to the combined quotas of all other members. The upper limit to a member's debit balance would depend on the size of its quota, which would be related to the volume of its trade. The Keynes Plan did not require members

to maintain fixed exchange rates, parities might be adjusted by five per cent per annum. Thus countries with persistent balance of payments difficulties would be provided with loans and be permitted to adjust their exchange rates to restore equilibrium.

The American proposal, known after its author as the White Plan, was less ambitious than the Keynes Plan. The proposed Fund was to be smaller than the Union ($5 billion against $26 billion) and it could only make available to deficit countries gold and national currencies which had been subscribed by its members. On exchange rates the White Plan proposed a system of highly rigid, if not fixed, parities. The International Monetary Fund which was discussed at Bretton Woods in New Hampshire in 1944 and started operating in 1947, was a compromise between the British and American proposals. But the final scheme was much closer to the American concept. Members were required to subscribe quotas (25 per cent in gold and 75 per cent in their national currency) and in return received rights to borrow gold and foreign currencies from the Fund, which started with total resources of $9.2 billion. Subject to the approval of the

IMF, a country may borrow, or strictly purchase, foreign exchange up to 125 per cent of its quota. Access to the Fund's resources is conditional upon appropriate domestic policies being followed and is not automatic as in the Keynes Plan. A surplus country receives payment in gold or its national currency and does not accumulate credit balances at the Fund. The maximum amount of accommodation which it must extend is limited to the size of its own subscription and not the combined quotas of other members as in the Keynes Plan. As the largest potential creditor, the United States was naturally concerned to limit the amount of unrequited exports which it could be required to deliver. It is not surprising that this feature of the Keynes Plan was regarded as objectionable by the Americans.

The British achieved some recognition of the problems of deficit countries, although both points were elements of the White Plan and could not, therefore, be regarded

*Angry crowds protest outside 10 Downing Street, 19th November 1967, as the cabinet meets to discuss devaluation of the pound announced the previous day*

as a major shift in the American position. First, a country was to be permitted to change its parity in the event of 'fundamental disequilibrium' in its balance of payments and second, a surplus country might become liable to exchange discrimination should its currency become 'scarce' within the Fund. Scarcity would occur when a number of countries wanted to use their quotas to purchase a surplus country's currency so exhausting the Fund's holding of the currency concerned. In such circumstances the Fund was prepared to sanction discrimination against the surplus country. Since the Americans attached great importance to free multilateral trade, the 'scarce currency' clause was a notable concession. However, unless the clause was activated the contribution which the Fund could give only limited assistance to relieve a worldwide payments problem.

## The Return to Convertibility

The IMF made little contribution to the finance of post-war reconstruction. This was hardly surprising since it was intended to facilitate international payments under normal conditions and not to cope with the acute structural problems of war-torn economies. The Fund started to give assistance in 1947 but this virtually ceased when European countries receiving Marshall Aid were not permitted to draw dollars from the Fund. The American government insisted that provision of dollars by the Fund would lead to reductions in Marshall Aid and so the decision of the Fund to husband its dollars until the aid ceased was understandable. This did, however, produce a paradoxical situation. At a time when the world demand for American goods created an acute dollar shortage, dollars were not a 'scarce currency' within the Fund and so the 'scarce currency' clause was not invoked. Restrictions on the use of dollars were generally recognized to be necessary, particularly after the sterling crisis of 1947, which resulted from a premature attempt to remove exchange restrictions. Both the European Payments Union and the Sterling Area used payments restrictions to make the best use of dollars. The IMF acquiesced in such discrimination against the dollar and did not have much say in the major round of post-war parity adjustments, which included the devaluation of sterling by 30 per cent in September 1949.

The Korean War eased the dollar shortage and rapid industrial recovery made Western Europe less dependent upon the United States. In February 1952 the IMF authorities relaxed the somewhat rigid attitude which they had adopted to the use of their resources. They recognized that the twenty-five per cent of a member's quota which was subscribed in gold (the gold tranche) could be withdrawn automatically. It should, therefore, be included in members' reserves beside holdings of gold and foreign currencies. Members could also count upon being able to withdraw an additional twenty-five per cent of their quotas, which was subscribed in their national currency. The Fund also introduced 'stand-by-credit' facilities which could be made available to a member but need not be taken up immediately. It was

providing members with a source of secondary reserves. The first major use of the Fund's resources was made by Britain and France during the Suez Crisis of 1956. Assistance was given in the form of both conditional drawing rights and 'stand-by-credits'. This intervention showed that the IMF could play a useful role in international finance and it was followed by a decision to increase member's quotas by fifty per cent in 1959 raising the resources of the Fund to $14 billion.

By 1958 the dollar shortage of the immediate post-war years had disappeared and there were even signs of a dollar glut because of deficits in the US balance of payments. The deficits arose from the outflow of private long-term capital which exceeded the continuing trade surplus. The ending of the dollar shortage led to the dismantling of regional payments arrangements which had served to discriminate against the dollar. The European Payments Union ceased operations in 1958 and there was a general movement toward making currencies freely convertible. Overseas holders of sterling had been granted increasing freedom to use their balances provided they did not make purchases from the dollar area. However it proved increasingly difficult to prevent sterling from being used in this way; a fact which was recognized by the Bank of England's decision in 1955 to support the rate at which Transferable Account sterling could be exchanged for dollars on the unofficial market. Sterling became convertible *de facto* at that time although it was not until late in 1958 that the pound was officially declared convertible. The removal of restrictions on international payments was accompanied by reductions in trade barriers under the auspices of the General Agreement on Tariffs and Trade (GATT) and regional trading arrangements, such as the EEC and the European Free Trade Association (EFTA). The international mobility of short-term capital increased as restrictions on payments were relaxed. Activity developed in borrowing and lending of dollar balances held outside the United States, giving rise to the Euro-dollar market. Euro-dollars furnished convenient assets for an international market in short term capital. The linkage of national money markets was also facilitated by the system of rigid exchange rates which emerged after the devaluations of 1948–49.

## The Gold-Exchange Standard

As world trade expanded rapidly the growing demand for an internationally acceptable means of payments was met primarily by increased holdings of dollars. From 1956 to 1969 world monetary reserves consisting of gold, foreign exchange and the gold tranche at the IMF rose from $56 billion to $78 billion, an increase of thirty-nine per cent. During the same period holdings of foreign exchange (mainly dollars) went up from $18 billion to $32 billion, a rise of seventy-eight per cent. Reserve positions at the IMF rose from $2.3 billion to $6.7 billion and gold holdings from $36 billion to $39 billion. This indicates the growing importance of the contribution of the dollar to world monetary reserves, the small contribution made by the IMF and the stagnant role of gold. The dollar was

acceptable because of the underlying strength of the US economy and the adequacy of US gold holdings to support growing external liabilities. An additional factor was the moderate rate of inflation in America due to restrained monetary and fiscal policies. Dollars were readily available because of continuing US balance of payments deficits and they were also generally acceptable as means of payments. The position of the dollar was not unlike that of sterling under the international gold standard before 1914.

This international monetary system has been described as the Gold-Exchange Standard. Dollars were held by countries as reserve assets because their convertibility into gold was assured by the adequacy of US gold reserves. There was, however, an inherent instability in the system, as noted by Professor Triffin, the American economist, in 1960. The addition to the world's liquidity depended on increased holdings of dollars, since the contribution of other reserve assets, such as gold, sterling and reserve positions at the IMF was slight. If the United States met the world's demand for liquidity by running a continuing balance of payments deficit, there would be a deterioration in its reserve/liability ratio, as dollar liabilities increased relative to US gold reserves. This would sooner or later provoke a crisis of confidence as the acceptability of the dollar was questioned and foreign holders of dollars sought to convert them into gold. If, however, the United States restricted its balance of payments deficit and reduced the extent of dollar liabilities, the world's growing need for liquidity would not be satisfied.

Triffin proposed that the world's monetary problems be tackled by reforming and enlarging the IMF. His proposal was in some respects a development of the Keynes Plan. Members would hold deposits at the IMF as under the Keynes Plan, but the deposits could be exchanged for gold and foreign currencies provided members held a minimum proportion of their reserves (about twenty per cent) at the IMF. The Fund would be able to expand its deposits through undertaking open market purchases of the assets of member countries. The expansion of the IMF's resources through open market operations would enable it to maintain a steady ratio of international liquidity to world trade. This would ensure that the world's need for growing reserves would be satisfied. The role of the dollar in the gold exchange standard would be ended and Britain would be relieved of the burden of outstanding sterling liabilities. Holders of both dollars and sterling would receive in exchange deposits at the IMF.

Triffin was followed by a host of imitators, who did little but call attention to the problems which he had observed. Mention may be made of the Stamp Plan, which proposed that provisions for additional liquidity be linked to aid to developing countries and Sir Roy Harrod's case for raising the price of gold. Since this had been fixed by the US Treasury at $35 per ounce since 1934, it was hardly surprising that the relative importance of gold in the world's monetary reserves was diminishing. The situation could be rectified by a rise in the official price.

## Ad Hoc Measures and Official Proposals for Reform

The official reaction to Triffin's analysis was muted. No schemes were hurriedly prepared for world monetary reform. Rather Central bankers and IMF officials sought to deal with the situation by a series of ad hoc expedients. Concern about the US balance of payments deficit prompted an upsurge in the London gold market in late 1960. The market price of gold rose well above the maintained price of $35 per ounce, so threatening the US gold reserves. In October 1961 a group of central banks formed a 'Gold Pool' which would intervene in the market to stabilize the price of gold at the official level.

One of the weaknesses of the system of fixed parities sanctioned by the IMF was the scope which it gave for speculation over probable changes in exchange rates. A reserve currency, such as sterling, which had a low ratio of reserves to liabilities was quite clearly going to be particularly vulnerable to such speculation.

Speculators would gain in the event of a devaluation of sterling but would lose little if the parity were maintained. It was the one-way option offered by an exchange rate which would move downwards, if it moved at all, which made speculation appear both profitable and riskless. Speculative flows of short-term capital had become more serious since the advent of convertibility. In March 1961 eight European central banks agreed to give mutual assistance to offset speculative currency movements under the Basle Agreement. The arrangement was put to the test in the sterling crisis which occurred later in the year. Recycling of funds among central banks to offset flows of 'hot money' was very soon to become a regular feature of international monetary management.

Sterling was not the only reserve currency to come under pressure. In May 1962 the Federal Reserve began operations to protect the dollar through intervention in foreign exchange markets. Later in the year holders of dollars were encouraged to take up 'Roosa bonds', which were non-marketable securities bearing a guarantee against the risk of a devaluation of the dollar. The bonds were an attempt to fund foreign dollar holdings and so to reduce the pressure on US gold reserves due to European countries switching from dollars to gold. Currency swaps among central banks were also introduced to bolster the dollar.

The IMF itself was in need of support because of the danger of exhaustion of holdings of the currencies of surplus countries. According to the Bretton Woods rules a situation might arise in which the 'scarce currency' clause would be invoked. In October 1962 the Group of Ten was formed; its members were Belgium, Canada, France, Germany, Italy, Japan, Netherlands, Sweden, Great Britain and the United States. Under the General Arrangements to Borrow (GAB) the Group of Ten agreed to make loans to the IMF of up to $6 billion which carried a gold guarantee. The IMF would then have the resources to give assistance in the event of a major currency crisis. A further step in this direction was the

twenty-five per cent increase in quotas which was proposed in 1964 and became effective two years later.

The Basle Agreement, 'Roosa bonds', currency swaps and the GAB were piecemeal attempts to sustain the gold exchange standard without undertaking a comprehensive review of the system. By 1963 there was growing recognition in official circles that something should be done about providing for the growth of world liquidity. But progress was slow because of fundamental disagreements among the major countries. The United States, as the main provider of international means of payment, would not benefit from any reform which dethroned the dollar. Such would have been the result of the acceptance of the Triffin plan or any proposal which centralized reserves in the IMF. Continental countries with a strong balance of payments and growing dollar holdings were in a good position to influence proposals for reform. Since they were likely to be creditors in a reformed IMF, they were concerned that unconditional assistance should not be made available to countries with persistent balance of payments deficits. France pressed for a return to a system based on gold which would end the predominance of the dollar in international finance and also require the US government to recognize the existence of a balance of payments constraint.

The discussions over monetary reform were prolonged and involved the examination of a number of alternative schemes as set out in the Ossola Report of 1965. Eventually agreement was reached in 1967 on the creation of a new reserve asset known as the Special Drawing Right (SDR). SDRs are unconditional drawing rights like the gold tranche of IMF quotas and therefore included in members' reserves. They are allocated among members in proportion to their quotas and are international money because they must be accepted by other members within agreed limits. A country can use its SDRs to acquire foreign currency from other members whose account is then credited. The aggregate amount of SDRs is decided by collective agreements among members. The initial issue made in 1970 was of $9.5 billion over three years, which was a rather larger amount than had been envisaged in the earlier discussions. SDRs appear to be intended to provide for the growth of world liquidity and not to contribute directly to the problem of the composition of reserves.

## The Disintegration of the Bretton Woods System

The decision of the United States government to finance the Vietnam war, without imposing severe taxation aggravated the American balance of payments deficit. It was also worsened by a growing American taste for foreign goods and a higher level of US private overseas investment. The international monetary system became subject to greater strain after 1965 when it became obvious that the United States was using its position as provider of the world's monetary reserves to draw resources from its trading partners. Between 1965 and 1971 world monetary reserves increased from $71 billion

to $130 billion, an increase of eighty-three per cent, while the foreign exchange component increased from $23 billion to $79 billion, an increase of 243 per cent. Thus of the aggregate increase in world reserves of $59 billions, ninety-five per cent was in the form of greater holdings of foreign exchange, principally dollars. It is hardly surprising that the rapid growth of dollar holdings created problems for the rest of the world. Governments found difficulty in insulating their countries from the American economy which was bent on a path of accelerating inflation. The situation became particularly acute by 1970–71 when balance of payments surpluses and inward capital flows could not be prevented from expanding the domestic money supply in some countries. Measures to insulate the money supply were made less effective by the high degree of mobility of short-term capital in a system with inflexible exchange rates.

The ratio of US gold reserves to dollar liabilities continued to decline after 1965 and concern about the dollar was reflected in the growing private demand for gold. The Gold Pool ceased to sell gold early in 1968 when a two-tier market for gold was established. Gold transactions between central banks continued to take place at the official price but they were separated from the private gold market. In this way the United States gold reserves were protected since it was no longer necessary to make sales in the private market. But the change did not restore confidence in the dollar.

After the initial post-war adjustment of exchange rates parities became relatively rigid. The rigidities caused strains which became worse with the passage of time. Despite its slow rate of growth of productivity and declining competitive ability in world markets, Britain struggled to maintain an over-valued pound. Devaluation was finally forced on the British authorities in November 1967. The fall of the pound undermined the IMF system of fixed exchange rates. France devalued in 1969 when there was no evidence of a 'fundamental disequilibrium' in its balance of payments. Expectations of an appreciation of the Deutschmark led to a large inflow of speculative funds which forced the German authorities to revalue. European governments continued to add to their dollar balances but the American government finally became so concerned about the size of its liabilities that it suspended the convertibility of the dollar into gold in August 1971. The suspension of dollar convertibility has been seen by most observers as the collapse of the Bretton Woods system and has threatened the future of the dollar as the world's leading reserve asset.

In December 1971 a new set of fixed exchange rates was announced after a meeting at the Smithsonian Museum in Washington. The price of gold was raised to $38 per ounce and the IMF announced that currencies could fluctuate within slightly wider margins than the previous limit of one per cent. This was a small step in the direction of exchange rate flexibility. However, the new arrangements did not restore confidence. Speculation against the pound led to the decision to float sterling in June

*French magazine cover, November 1968, draws attention to de Gaulle's fight to defend the franc as gold reserves dwindled. The battle was lost: France devalued on 8th August 1969*

1972. There was also a move towards floating by both Switzerland and Italy. Such changes increased anxiety about the dollar, which was devalued by ten per cent. In March 1973 five EEC countries announced a joint float against the dollar while keeping their currencies within a narrow band. Even this degree of co-ordination did not last for long. Since 1973 the world has been operating a system of flexible exchange rates with some official intervention in exchange markets, commonly described as 'dirty floating'.

### Flexible Exchange Rates

During the discussions on monetary reform in the 1960's central bankers and finance ministers were reluctant to accept the arguments for flexible exchange rates. But there was growing support for exchange flexibility among academics. Freely floating rates with no government intervention have been urged by the American economist, Professor Milton Friedman. This arrangement would not be accepted by officials who were not prepared to entrust the determination of exchange rates to purely market forces. A proposal which in the course of time won a measure of official support was for a 'crawling peg' exchange rate which would permit a gradual adjustment of parities at a pre-determined rate. The suggestion was an extension of Keynes' recommendation for adjusting exchange rates under the Clearing Union.

The collapse of the Bretton Woods system led to an enforced experiment with flexible rates. The experiment has been reasonably successful and saw no repetition of the allegedly chaotic experience of the inter-war years. Exchange rates have shown considerable movement and businessmen have had to accept greater exchange risks since facilities for forward cover have been imperfect. However, the freedom of rates to move in either direction has removed the easy gains to be made by speculation under the previous 'adjustable-peg' system.

Flexible rates have been better able to cope with a situation in which countries have had widely differing rates of inflation. It appears that since 1971 currencies have depreciated against the Deutschmark broadly in line with relative movements in domestic price levels. The association between the decline in the exchange rate and the rise in the internal price level has been notable for both Britain and Italy. Although flexible rates have given governments greater scope for independent stabilization policies it is possible that depreciating exchanges gave an extra twist to the inflationary spiral through increasing the cost of imports. The greater degree of autonomy permitted by flexible rates has been much needed in view of the quadrupling of oil prices which followed the Arab-Israeli war of 1973. Governments have had a measure of choice between letting rates depreciate or seeking to support rates by running down reserves or borrowing.

The sharp rise in oil prices implied a substantial redistribution of income in favour of members of the Organisation of Petroleum Exporting Countries (OPEC). This was a potentially deflationary influence in that the purchasing power transferred was saved rather than being spent on increased imports. The savings were held mainly in the form of liquid assets in established financial centres. The massive accumulation of these claims by members of OPEC did not cause a major monetary disturbance and there was no repetition of the draining of gold and dollars from Europe which contributed to the breakdown of the gold standard in 1931. But there remained the problem of financing the balance of payments deficits of individual oil importing countries. Fortunately industrial countries agreed to finance deficits by mutual accommodation rather than to attempt to eliminate them by deflation.

The final collapse of the Bretton Woods system did not lead to serious disruption of international trade. The consequences have been much less disturbing than the events which followed the abandonment of the gold standard. But the question of the reconstruction of the international monetary system remains unsettled. As individual countries bring inflation under control there will be both a decline in rate of increase of prices and less variation among countries. Flexible rates will be subject to less fluctuation and the case for a return to fixed parities may be revived. There are signs of such a revival in the Report of the IMF Committee of Twenty which was presented in 1974. Even if free floating is ruled out, it will be necessary to allow for a greater degree of flexibility of rates than was permitted under the Bretton Woods system. As to the problems of monetary reserves, SDRs provide a useful means of augmenting the world's liquidity but their future role is uncertain until agreement is reached on the composition of reserve assets. These could include gold, dollars or SDRs alone or in combination. The future of the massive holdings of dollars outside the United States, known as the 'dollar overhang', also remains unsettled.

# The Decline of Liberalism

*The 19th century was the hey-day of liberalism. Parliament was the hub of power, the mechanism for settling group conflict.*
*1 19th-century painting of the British House of Commons crammed with the political élite, the land-owning gentry. The absence of a strong monarchy supported by army and bureaucracy aided the smooth development of the British 'liberal model'.*
*2 King John signs the Magna Carta. Victorians idealized it as the first 'bill of rights'. 3 John Locke, the 17th-century liberal political theorist: the legitimacy of government derives only from the consent of the governed. 4 John Wilkes MP, the 18th-century reformer who was at the centre of storms about the protection of individual liberty against parliamentary or ministerial privilege*

At the beginning of the 20th century, the 'liberal model' of the state, in one form or another, seemed to command the assent of most people in the more developed countries. In the less advanced countries, many of them under foreign rule, the politically vocal elements aspired to it. Even on the Left it was not entirely shunned. Although their ideologies looked forward to the advent of a classless, socialist society which would make much of the apparatus of the parliamentary system unnecessary – and would in particular make political parties superfluous – the more left-wing movements had largely accepted the view that countries such as Russia would have to pass through the liberal phase. They also agitated for such well understood liberal institutions as freedom of speech, press, and association.

At that time there were of course variants of the liberal model: the constitutional parliamentary monarchies of northern Europe with Great Britain (and her dominions) as the most conspicuous example; the European republican model of which the French Third Republic was the typical instance; and finally the presidential system of the United States. All of them were considered respectable, and all commanded different degrees of admiration outside the European and North Atlantic world. Since then, there have been two significant developments: the model itself has been subject to increasingly severe strains in all three of its forms; and second, the majority of newly independent Asian and African countries have either begun by discarding the model, or have found it impossible to sustain for any length of time.

## 1919: a rebirth for liberalism?

These developments were somewhat masked by the outcome of the First World War. The defeated powers were the four great empires – Russian, Austrian, German, and Ottoman – in which the liberal model had been either rejected altogether, or accepted only to a very limited degree. This seemed to bestow on the liberal democracies which had triumphed over them the aura that always accompanies military success. President Woodrow Wilson's talk of making the world safe for democracy seemed to have retrospectively conferred upon the struggle an ideological content absent from its beginnings. More than that, the League of Nations, founded in 1920, looked like an application of the liberal model to a new area – international relations. Finally, and

perhaps most important of all, while Russia passed rapidly through the only liberal phase in its history – the provisional government of 1917 – to a new and much harsher tyranny, both Germany and the new national states that arose on the ruins of the old empires adopted liberal republican constitutions on the basic French model. Weimar Germany, for example, represented one of the most systematic attempts to codify the prescriptions of liberal democracy. Its collapse before the combined onslaught of Communism and National Socialism between 1930 and 1933 is one of the main turning-points in the story. Italy, a victorious power in 1918, but with some of the resentments of the defeated, had passed through a similar experience earlier, when the Fascist regime was set up under the cover of monarchical constitutionalism. With few exceptions, of which Czechoslovakia was the most notable, the new states of Central and Eastern Europe as well as the Balkan monarchies also succumbed to one form of totalitarian rule or another.

The Second World War could only by stretching language and truth be regarded as another liberal or even democratic triumph, since the Soviet Union, as well as the United States and Great Britain, was among the victors who were to set the pattern of the post-war world. The effect of this Soviet victory was to impose Communist forms of government upon most of Eastern and Central Europe. Where the Nazi yoke was broken by the Anglo-American armies the liberal model was applied, but right-wing totalitarianism of the inter-war period long survived in the Iberian peninsula. Although the new West German Federal Republic, with a constitution modelled to avoid some of the most patent weaknesses of the Weimar Republic, has proved to have more democratic staying power than its ill-fated predecessor, a perceptible if perhaps temporary shift towards a more authoritarian style of government in France, the instability of the regime in Italy, and the triumph for some time of a military dictatorship in Greece all cast new doubt on the viability of liberalism.

In the only other major industrial country – Japan – the course of events has also been only partially encouraging. Japan acquired parliamentary institutions along with the other trappings of Western industrial society at the end of the 19th century, and even the elements of a party system. But the powers retained by the Emperor, the special role of the armed forces, and the authoritarianism carried over into industrial life from the country's quasi-feudal past, made the working of the Japanese system very unlike that of its models. Increasing economic and external difficulties in the inter-war period enhanced the authoritarian and militaristic nature of Japanese government. After Japan's defeat in 1945, the American occupation authorities exerted their influence to secure the passage of a new Western-style constitution in which the Emperor played only a constitutional role. This has survived, but as Japan's independence of the United States becomes more marked, the emergence of new anti-liberal trends on both the Left and the Right of the political spectrum is bound to raise some disquieting reflections.

### The liberal model rejected

Surprise at the failure of the liberal model to implant itself in the basically non-Western societies of Africa and Asia in the post-imperial phase should have been moderated by the reflection that most Latin American countries had long had constitutions based upon that of the United States, and that in nearly all cases these had either been abandoned altogether or had become merely the cover for military or single-party domination. It is curious that experience in the Western hemisphere seems to have had so little influence on American policy, either in Europe in Woodrow Wilson's time, or in Asia and Africa under President Franklin Roosevelt and his successors. Not until the respect shown by Americans for their own institutions faltered—a by-product of the Vietnam imbroglio and of set-backs in race relations—was serious consideration given to the view that the liberal model may have been a response to quite special conditions in the North Atlantic world in the 18th and 19th centuries, and that its durability under quite different circumstances can nowhere be taken for granted.

For this reason the dissatisfaction now expressed in Great Britain with the British parliamentary system, even though it has not so far been very widespread or very urgently expressed, is worth dwelling upon. The common complaints are that Members of Parliament are little more than the delegates of mass party organizations, that political opinions are formed by the impact of the mass media and are thus subject to manipulation by those in control of them, that independence of judgement is increasingly rare, and that government is remote from the individual and increasingly impersonal. There is obviously something to this. It is less often said that the causes of these phenomena may lie principally in developments of which most of the complainers explicitly or implicitly approve.

### The changing nature of politics

In retrospect it looks as though the British version of the liberal model—with the importance it attached to the House of Commons and its political debate, and to a serious press—depended upon a number of preconditions: the existence of a recognized political class many of whose members enjoyed financial independence, the restricted character of the franchise, the habit of deference to authority among many of the non-enfranchised, and above all the spontaneous limitation of the scope of central government.    19th-century thinkers often understood these preconditions and were aware of the distinction that their successors chose to blur, the distinction between liberalism and democracy. They were well aware of the pressure to bring more and more citizens within the pale of the constitution, making universal franchise the only ultimate conceivable goal. They saw that larger and larger electorates would demand more and more and that the state would become a welfare organization intent upon the redistribution of wealth; they knew that such electorates would more and more demand that their representatives should act as a channel through which their demands for legislative action were given direct effect. Liberalism talks of representatives, democracy of delegates. They could see that as electorates grew, and politics became more and more impersonal, national party machines would develop whose patronage would be essential for a new political class, a class increasingly divorced in membership and ethos from the social élite with which in the 19th century it was largely identical. These changes, many of them prefigured in American experience in the first half of the 19th century, made rapid strides on the British scene between the Second Reform Act of 1867 and the giving of votes to eighteen-year-olds in 1969—the measure that finally snapped the historic link between some economic and social responsibility and the wielding of political power, since political power without a property commitment is a new thing. Though it was reasonably argued that if youth were responsible enough to serve in the forces, they were responsible enough to vote.

Only one advantage that the liberal model enjoyed in 19th-century Great Britain persisted: as an island, the country had either a very small military force or one largely based overseas. For this

*Until the 19th century the British Parliament was totally unrepresentative of the people who 'had nothing to do with the laws but obey them'. The industrial revolution spawned a new middle class which demanded a place in the political system. This set in motion the movement towards a wider franchise which had its first success with the Reform Bill of 1832. But the reformers wanted more than a broader franchise; they wanted to clean up elections.* **Right: 1 and 2** *The 18th-century satirist Hogarth jibes at the corruption of politics—bribery and vote-buying were the norm. The secret ballot was only introduced in 1878. 3 Cartoon attacks the rotten boroughs, constituencies with only a handful of voters, since most of the population had migrated to urban areas. The MP was left 'sitting pretty'. They were abolished in 1832. 4 An idealized view of 'The county election' by the American C.G. Bingham. American negroes are no longer denied access to the polls*

reason, the fear of the 'man on horseback', the advent of a military saviour to redress the excesses of democracy, was always largely absent. Law and order could be left to a civilian police. The exception that proved the rule was Ireland, and again more recently Northern Ireland. It was only here that Great Britain did not enjoy the advantage of a relatively homogeneous population. And it is clear that neither the liberal nor the democratic model can sustain itself where the population is so divided by permanent ties of race, religion, or language that voting patterns are objectively determined and that minorities will not willingly and permanently accept being outvoted. While liberal forms of government, like all other forms of government, rest ultimately upon force, the liberal model is one in which force can be kept in the background. Indeed, when it is compelled to use its ultimate coercive power for political purposes, it has automatically suffered a defeat, for it is no longer liberal. It remains to be seen if Scottish and Welsh nationalism can be satisfied within the liberal model.

As the scope of government widens and new powers are taken on which intimately affect the citizen's social and economic life, bureaucracy necessarily grows—to administer the rules and regulations that government makes. If arbitrariness and corruption are to be avoided the bureaucracy must act according to prescribed formulae. For good or evil, the citizen cannot expect from the local office of some far-away ministry or even of his own local authority the same personal treatment for good or ill which the pre-industrial villager might have received from the lord of the manor or the parish priest. Parliament, also, cannot act as a forum for individual complaints when the ministers who are accountable to it are so much more numerous and rule over bureaucratic empires which are too vast for them to oversee in any detail.

## Continuity and survival

What is surprising about Great Britain is not the degree to which the liberal model has been abandoned but the extent to which it has endured. Habits of action formed, and procedures in the courts and Parliament established during the liberal era have largely survived. The mass media may or may not have an undue influence on voting patterns, but individuals are not bribed or bullied and ballot-boxes are not stuffed. The government controls the parliamentary time-table but does not use it to stifle minority voices. Controls of various kinds exist over the press and still more over television and radio, but these are not used to deprive the government's opponents of their say. Indeed, some of the facile observations about the subservience of Members of Parliament to the party whip have hardly applied to the Parliaments elected in 1966, 1970 or 1974. It is debatable whether the reasons for Great Britain's ability to run a democracy in the liberal style are due to the high degree of continuity of the country's institutions— the absence of revolutionary breaks and

From *Straight Herblock* (Simon & Schuster 1964)

Shelter

Novosti

purges — or whether something can be attributed to national character, to a British respect for procedural forms irrespective of content. But the reality is too often noted by external observers for anyone to deny it altogether.

Whether by the 1970's this observation can hold for the future rests upon two opposing trends. The liberal model depends upon the willingness of those with grievances to seek remedy through the processes of representative government, and above all through orderly discussion. It assumes that until the law is changed, the law will be obeyed. In the 1960's and early 1970's some sections of society developed the view that if the democratic process did not produce the right answer soon enough, self-help was allowable, whether through unofficial strikes, demonstrations, or other means. Furthermore, there was some unwillingness on the part of government to use its legal powers to the full, or to seek to strengthen them where they seemed insufficient to deal with the tactics of direct action. Similar trends appeared in very many countries in the Western world. The social consensus was breaking down.

Connected with this phenomenon, but distinct from it, was the recrudescence of doctrines that repudiated the liberal model itself, that dismissed government through representative institutions and reform through ordered discussion, and favoured direct and even violent action by groups who were considered to have right on their side: oppressed racial minorities, underpaid workers, students, and so on. The glorification of direct action and the repudiation of reasoned argument had of course formed the staple of much of the nationalist ideology that gave rise to Italian Fascism, German Nazism, and their lesser imitators and heirs. The at-

*The liberal model wears thin.*
**Left: 1** *'You're out of order,' blasts the Rules Committee, hitting 'representative government' on the head. Congress has been described as the 'broken mirror in which America can not see its face'. 2 Supporters of Shelter demonstrate. Shelter exists to help the homeless where government action has either failed or is absent. Such extra-parliamentary pressure groups attempt to influence government by gaining public support and lobbying MP's. They can be happily accommodated in modern democracies, but their existence indicates a basic change in the nature of Western politics, when group interests can no longer be effectively represented from within parliament. 3 Russians vote during an election to the Supreme Soviet. The Stalin Constitution (1936) pledged universal adult suffrage, secret elections, and other basic elements of the liberal system — but theory and practice are at odds. The Party controls elections since only Party-approved candidates can stand. The liberal model is now widely regarded as impractical and possibly as quite undesirable, yet even the Soviet Union pays lip-service to many of its ideals and principles*

titude of some left-wing groups, particularly among the young, now bore a striking similarity to that of earlier right-wing movements, and were of course very easy to exploit by those who had quite different and perhaps even sinister political purposes to serve.

### The authoritarian menace
The mass media, by their constant flattery of youth, by the praise they gave to anything that could be called spontaneous or sincere, and by their adamant refusal to give full support to the values that underpinned the liberal model played their full part in building up the menace that overhung liberal societies in the West, and not least in Great Britain. By repudiating the lessons of history, by refusing to face the fact that an orderly society is not something that can be taken for granted but is the product of constant work and conscious self-control, the accredited intellectual leaders of Great Britain in the mid-20th century made a poor showing by comparison with their predecessors in the age of Mill and Gladstone, and of the early Labour leaders. The danger was perhaps not so much that anarchy would triumph, as that the reaction against anarchy would produce a demand for authoritarian solutions more rigorous than necessary. If in Great Britain natural kindliness and a deep-seated tolerance on the part of the older, if not the younger, generation made this perhaps unlikely, in the United States and in some continental countries the danger was quite real.

If the liberal model found it hard to cope with some of the new demands placed upon it by affluent societies, it is not surprising that it had little prospect of survival in poor countries whose political leaders relied upon their capacity to keep abreast of the 'revolution of rising expectations'. How, indeed, could there be government through discussion when it was hard to keep government going at all, and when the transistor radio arrived before the school-slate? In such a situation, any plea for patience and moderation was bound to be regarded as pusillanimous. When the 19th-century thinkers looked at the future of countries then under imperial rule, they certainly thought that they would one day achieve self-government, but they envisaged first a long period of apprenticeship, during which new élites would be trained, the infrastructure of ordered government established, the minimum conditions of internal peace and security guaranteed. None of these conditions was fulfilled. The decolonization of Asia and Africa in the quarter century after the Second World War took place at breakneck speed with little but lip-service paid to any of these preconditions. Countries usually achieved independence without the benefit of their traditional élites and without the services of a sufficiently large or well-trained élite of the Western kind. The existence of this kind of élite largely depended on the length of time they had been under European rule. The Indian subcontinent appeared to have the best chance of coming through more or less un-

scathed, although the ability of India itself to maintain the liberal model has recently been called into question. Sri Lanka (Ceylon) (and one or two Caribbean countries) were the only former British possessions which had successfully undergone the supreme test of the liberal model — changing the government through the ballot-box. Elsewhere, the best that could be hoped for was that the original nationalist movement to which power had been handed over would stay sufficiently united to maintain at least the outward show of parliamentary institutions, even if as the vehicle for a legally or factually one-party regime.

### Homogeneity: a key to success
Even this degree of success depended, as the liberal model always must, on a sufficient degree of homogeneity in the population. The partition of the Indian subcontinent was the precondition of India's partial ability to apply the liberal model, but perhaps the country is still too heterogeneous to work it effectively at the centre. In Africa, the civil wars in Nigeria and the Congo, and in muted fashion in the Sudan, provide ready indicators of the difficulty of applying Western models of government to countries whose boundaries do not contain identifiable national groups with any pronounced sense of solidarity. The independent countries of East Africa have all been at different times on the brink of similar conflicts. In these circumstances the cultivation of a national mystique seems the only way of providing the government with the backing it needs if it is to take important decisions. And this can often best be aroused by fanning animosity towards minorities: the persecutions of the Indians in East Africa, of the Chinese in Indonesia, and the unwillingness of the Malays to admit the full equality of the Chinese. These are only some of the reasons why the prescriptions of the liberal model seem to make so little sense outside the geographical area in which the model first came into existence.

### Lip-service: a consolation
Nevertheless, if the facts of the case show that the model is often disregarded in action, the lip-service paid to it by the leaders of many of the states is perhaps some consolation. If they, even theoretically, give it preference over its competitors — the Soviet and Chinese versions of Communism or the anarchical utopianism of the so-called New Left in Europe and North America — perhaps they can hold the fort long enough for some part of the model actually to work. For the model does not carry with it every nuance of British mid-Victorian society: other forms of representative government, other models of rational discussion are conceivable. A more collectivist accent may be inevitable. The 20th century has seen much hope dissipated, but the belief that the material conditions for a liberal society may come to exist in many parts of the world gives the appearance of being far better founded today than could have been thought a century ago.

During the 19th century the attitude that poverty arose from thriftlessness and crime from sinfulness gradually changed. Public organizations were set up to better social conditions, supplanting the private charity of previous ages. **1** Nuns tending a sick man—14th-century painting. Private charity still exists to complement the welfare state. **2** A spick and span living-room on the Millbank estate—one of London's first council blocks, 1900. **3** Lloyd George election poster, 1911. The start of British medical insurance. **4** Cleanliness in a Highgate dispensary. Free post-natal care dramatically lowered the infant mortality rate. **5** The poor house—a reminder of the horrors of poverty before the welfare state

Mansell Collection

Mansell Collection

GLC Photo Library

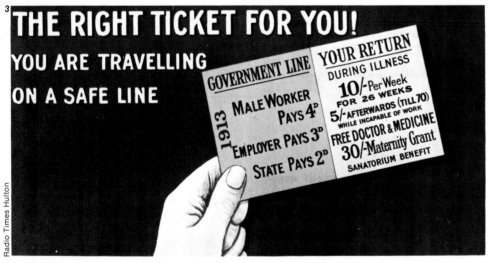

THE RIGHT TICKET FOR YOU!

YOU ARE TRAVELLING
ON A SAFE LINE

GOVERNMENT LINE

1913

MALE WORKER PAYS 4ᴰ

EMPLOYER PAYS 3ᴰ

STATE PAYS 2ᴰ

YOUR RETURN
DURING ILLNESS
10/- Per Week
FOR 26 WEEKS
5/- AFTERWARDS (TILL 70)
WHILE INCAPABLE OF WORK
FREE DOCTOR & MEDICINE
30/- Maternity Grant
SANATORIUM BENEFIT

Radio Times Hulton

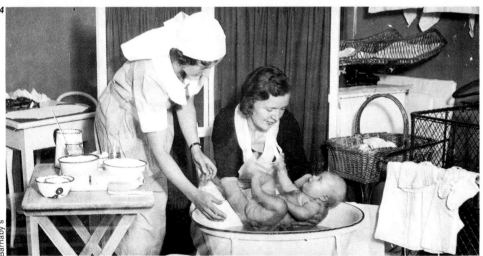

Barnaby's

# The Welfare State

The role of the state has always been a central issue of politics, but in modern times it has become the linchpin on which political debate turns. How much should social life be regulated by law, and how much by private and voluntary action? This is the question at the heart of the divide between Right and Left. Certainly no modern man could fail to be aware of the extension of state regulation since the late 19th century: vast increases in the volume of legislation, large and permanent bureaucracies, greater spending by public authorities, the extent to which nearly all discontent is ultimately converted into a demand for legislative action – all these are signs that collectivism is here.

Few states have remained unaffected by these tendencies, and the historical factors at work have been the same nearly everywhere. In the first place, the two world wars of the 20th century gave a great impetus towards collectivism. The administrative machinery and political practices necessary to mobilization for 'total war' both strengthened the claims of those who saw state intervention as a practicable possibility, and weakened the resistance of those who saw it as unnecessary. Second, the democratic idea of government – of and for (if not always by) the people – has created a world in which those who are economically underprivileged occupy politically a position of central importance. And it is from such quarters that the demand for equality through state action has most often come. Third, the technological changes basic to modern industrial life have required a degree of social co-ordination and direction which private and voluntary actions could not provide. Fourth, the contemporary claims of technology have reinforced the views of those who believe that men ought to use their knowledge to control their lives in a rational way. State regulation can thus be represented as scientifically planned control of the social environment, in contrast with the impersonal, arbitrary, and mysterious workings of 'the market'.

## 'Interference' – a liberal view

Yet although collectivism has triumphed in the modern world, the views of preceding ages have not been obliterated. To describe state action as 'intervention' is to imply that collectivism may sometimes resemble 'interference' with more respectable mechanisms. In this way state regulation is seen as the negative business of mitigating the worst consequences of private and voluntary action. This is the 'liberal' view, the view which watches with concern the increase of state regulation.

19th-century European liberalism regarded the government as a neutral referee in a game of social players. The referee had an obligation to enforce the rules equally upon all players and to prevent cheating, but once equality of political rights had been achieved, it was up to the players rather than the referee to decide the result of the game. This sort of liberalism derived its suspicion of state action from the characteristics of coercion and uniformity which it saw as inseparable from legal regulation. State action meant the enforcement of one solution instead of the variety of experiments and solutions of voluntary activity: the state playing in society the same role as monopoly did in industry. Moreover, since laws ultimately involve policemen, state action was coercive upon all, whereas voluntary action was by definition imposed upon none.

## Collectivism: extension of liberal view

It might seem natural that those who were concerned with political rights such as the suffrage and freedom of speech and association should suspect state action. Indeed, they assumed that men would use these rights to veto state intrusion into their private affairs. Yet the history of state intervention in the 20th century reveals that the relationship between political rights and the degree of collectivism is more complex than this type of liberalism could allow. Before we can read the history of the modern world as the rejection of liberal, individualist, and voluntarist assumptions, we face the problem that some aspects of state intervention are not as inconsistent with these assumptions as they might appear. In the first place, few European governments of the 19th century ever pursued liberal arguments to their logical conclusions. Laissez-faire liberalism was always an intellectual artifact rather than a realistic description of the limits observed by practising politicians. Second, liberalism always allowed for state intervention where the common interest was demonstrably unattainable by voluntary means: defence and police functions were obvious examples. In the present century enormous extensions of state activity have been justified by reference to this criterion. Keynesian economics could be represented as the argument that mass unemployment benefited no one, unemployment could not technically be solved by voluntary action, and therefore state intervention to maintain full employment could be justified on liberal grounds.

A third extension of the liberal view was that if the role of the state was to maintain a balance between different social interests, then the bargaining power of relatively weak 'players' could legitimately be raised by, for example, income redistribution and welfare programmes. If liberalism conceded that state action to prevent one social group from coercing another (as in the case of anti-trust legislation) was justifiable, and if coercion of one group by another was faciliated by great inequalities of income, was not the redress of such inequalities a condition of a 'fair game'?

*Applying liberal principles*
Finally, it is often forgotten that a considerable proportion of modern government intervention is accounted for not so much by new kinds of intervention, such as public ownership of industry, and state provision of welfare, but rather by extensions of older and universally accepted functions. Most of the above examples could in fact be represented as attempts to bring in new areas of government control under old liberal principles, but even established areas have been dramatically extended. Consider, for example, transport. Political supervision of private schemes for building roads, canals, and railways had always been accepted as a condition of a rational system of national communications. The invention of the internal combustion engine has meant that even if the state confines itself to its traditional function of regulation and supervision, then the quantity of state action is dramatically increased. And this characteristic is to be found in every area where the state has traditionally exercised functions of regulation or inspection. The United States, for example, has not proceeded as far along the road to state ownership or provision as have most European states. Yet the growth and complex organization of government institutions concerned with regulating, controlling, and supervising (as opposed to owning or providing) social activities and services has greatly expanded: witness the activities of the significantly-named Federal Regulatory Commissions.

Another example is government concern with public health. In this sphere, liberalism has never been interpreted to imply that freedom is the right to spread contagious diseases; and state regulation and inspection have thus been accepted. Even if the state had confined itself to the regulation, rather than the direct provision, of public health the growth of medical knowledge would have involved, in the present century, a considerable expansion of state activity (as measured, for example, in terms of the numbers of personnel employed).

The interventionist state has thus been as much the product of attempts to apply liberal principles as it has been a conscious rejection of them. Even in those cases where liberal ideology has played little conscious part, state intervention has often been the unintended consequence of 'doing what seems to be the appropriate thing'. And such consequences have arisen in all relatively advanced countries. If the extent of state regulation is to be the criterion, then both Great Britain and the USSR have more in common with each other than with the United States and Franco's Spain. And even if differing political liberties are allowed for, we still have to recognize that modern democratic socialism has everywhere attempted to persuade and encourage people to use their political rights to demand more, not less, state action.

*The welfare state*
Societies have always accepted an obligation to aid those who fall below a tolerable minimum standard of material comfort; inarticulate humanitarianism, rather than ideology or principle, has often been at work. Before the end of the 19th century, such an obligation was usually discharged by voluntary, rather than state action: the church, the landowner, and the charitable society were regarded as the obvious sources of relief. But suppose, as was the case, that statistical techniques and tender consciences combine to reveal that the dimensions of unacceptable poverty are vastly greater than have commonly been imagined. Are the resources of private charity sufficient to deal with the problem? Even then, the kind of state action required could be (and was) open to argument. State relief could (and initially did) take the form of subsidizing incomes rather than directly providing welfare services — the traditional obligation to aid the poor may not initially lead to the conclusion that massive state intervention is necessary. Compelling individuals to insure against their old age does not necessarily require the state to act as their insurance company. The British system of motor-car insurance is an example of this: it leaves the individual to decide which private insurance company will receive his custom. But suppose (as was again the case) that it becomes widely accepted that unemployment is a major cause of poverty, and that unemployment is a consequence of the prevailing economic *system*, and cannot therefore be remedied by voluntary action. This switches the argument from the question of welfare to the question of unemployment, but the consequences for the role of the state are considerable. It is in this sense that the logic of the argument has seemed obvious to modern politicians: poverty must be relieved; unemployment is a prime cause of poverty; unemployment can only be relieved by state action. In this way, an inarticulate humanitarian assumption can combine with the growth of knowledge about society to produce a very strong case for state action.

*Where the state has withdrawn*
Although the increase of state intervention is undeniable, considered as a total quantity, in some areas it has gone side by side with state withdrawal from others. Perhaps this is nowhere more obvious than in the field of moral conduct. There has been a considerable decrease in state regulation concerning the content of books, plays, and films, the questions of religious observances, sexual conduct, and the rights of women and young people. The coercive or punitive element in the treatment of criminals has also been diminished. It is in these areas, above all, that 'classical' liberalism has secured important victories. Historically, then, the relevant question is not only the extent to which the 'volume' of collectivism has increased, but also the extent to which the areas of social life which are now subject to legal regulation have changed.

*Welfare: alternative forms*
In the 20th century, state action on a considerable scale has come to be accepted, in democracies no less than in totalitarian states, as a fact of life. Those who believe that state action is inherently undesirable are no longer at the political centre of gravity. The debate now focuses on what precise form intervention should take, and what the relationship between collectivism and political liberty should be.

Assuming that the state can, and should, accept the obligation to maintain at least minimal standards of social welfare and full employment, and that it has an important part to play in the stimulation of economic growth, a variety of alternative forms of intervention have been debated and introduced. The state's role in economic planning can be discharged through direct controls such as licensing schemes or public ownership of 'key' industries; through voluntary co-operation between government and industry (for example the French Commissariat au Plan and the Swedish system of national wage-fixing); through indirect changes in the economic framework which alter incentives (such as tariffs, taxes, export bounties, government contracts); or a combination of all three. Similarly, state welfare schemes can be financed through contributions on the 'insurance principle' (which is to regard the state as a giant monopoly insurance company), or from progressive taxation, or a combination of both.

It is, however, on the question of the distribution rather than the financing of welfare benefits that most controversies have occurred. Should benefits be confined to those in need, leaving the rest to make private provision, or should benefits be available to all? Much of this debate turns upon the problems of deciding what constitutes 'need' (a level-of-income criterion is usually the most convenient for the purposes of administration) and whether the welfare state should be regarded as a

*The all-caring state intervenes in every aspect of life. **Right: 1** Education: children in a London council school learn the first steps in dancing, 1908. **2** Keep-fit class at the Central Lenin Stadium, Moscow. A healthy body makes for a disciplined mind. **3** After-work exercise for office clerks in a Shanghai square*

GLC Photo Library

Novosti

Keystone Press

guarantor of minimum material standards, or as a positive engine of social equality. The second belief is likely to produce an all-inclusive welfare state, on the grounds that to permit the well-off to contract out of state welfare benefits will necessarily produce unequal standards of health, education, living conditions, and so on. Need, not income, should on this view determine the amount of welfare to which the individual is entitled.

Another difficult question is the extent to which the various accepted ends of state action are compatible with one another, and what the relative priorities should be. Is long-term economic growth compatible with full employment and high welfare expenditure in the short-run? Is it possible to have full employment, stable prices, and a balance of payments surplus – all at the same time? Is economic growth to be calculated in terms of material improvement, or are social costs such as pollution, deterioration of the physical environment, and psychological strain to be counted? Is it more important to have consistent and continuous government action (irrespective of *which* policies and priorities are selected) rather than continual debate, change, and uncertainty about what future policy will be?

### The criteria of good government
The political implications of the interventionist state are subject to similar disagreements. Briefly, the attitude of the modern progressive is that good government consists of state intervention to secure adequate welfare, full employment, and economic growth while at the same time preserving the traditional political virtues: the right to vote, genuine participation in the legislative process, the rule of law, and so on. It is for this reason, perhaps, that Western intellectuals have often regarded autocracies – for example Spain, Greece, South Africa – with more disfavour than they have shown to Russian totalitarianism. The Soviet state may 'intervene' to curtail political freedoms but it is also a recognizable sort of welfare state, whereas the autocracies are seen to have neither adequate welfare nor political liberty.

Yet to reconcile 'big government' and political freedom is by no means a simple matter. The inconsistencies are obvious enough. The state may treat individuals as members of an administrative category: it may lack the selectivity, flexibility, and individuality of voluntary associations. On the other hand, if the state is to take account of individual differences or needs, public administration inevitably loses the predictability and clarity which are basic to the idea of the rule of law. The choice may thus lie between an impersonal rigid, and unselective bureaucracy on the one hand, and a 'human', flexible, and hence unpredictable governance on the other. Moreover 'big government' may have a 'ratchet effect' on bureaucratic power; bureaucracies are necessary to administer the interventionist state, but does the indispensability of bureaucrats provide them with power which can be misused for per-

sonal or non-welfare ends? In other words, how can the interventionist state be rendered accountable to those whom it is designed to serve? Does the size, complexity, and discretionary power of the modern state render older forms of judicial control irrelevant? Or can legal arrangements be amended to take account of new circumstances? On the whole, the states of Western Europe and the United States have opted for legal change, while Great Britain has relied heavily on political control. But if legal control is diminished, what sort of political controls can provide a counterweight? In this respect, the proposed remedies are of a traditional kind, ranging from the reform of Parliament, through reliance on the checking powers of organized interests, to hopes for a better informed electorate.

### The crucial balance

The experience of nearly a century of the interventionist state has resulted in widespread agreement that the crucial issue is how to preserve both collective welfare and individual liberties. The experience has also shown that neither the 'liberal' nor the 'socialist' ideologies provide entirely satisfactory solutions. First, 'laissez-faire liberalism' has historically failed as an acceptable argument against increasing state intervention, and has overlooked the fact that the state may be welcomed as a saviour (rather than resisted as an intruder) and that whether state intervention is desirable depends ultimately upon what sort of state is in question. It is not laws in themselves that present problems, but rather the political constraints under which the laws are made. Second, the more naïve assumptions of socialism have proved of limited relevance. Legal regulation cannot of itself guarantee success; statesmen and bureaucrats are not necessarily less foolish or wicked than the voluntary institutions they have often replaced; and state control has often meant not the removal of uncertainty, insecurity, and inconsistency from social life, but rather the transfer of such age-old burdens from the private to the public sphere.

### The issue to be faced

There is, in fact, some sign that modern politicians have not been blind to the lessons of the past: that state and voluntary regulation are alternatives neither of which can be pursued to the exclusion of the other; that the appropriateness of each is usually a matter of circumstance; and that the desirability of state regulation is a question which cannot be decided in isolation from the question of how the state is to be controlled.

**Left:** *A government poster gives stern advice to the motor-bike brigade. This advice was made law in Britain in 1973.*
**Right:** *Modern man is besieged by the demands of state bureaucracy.*
*The welfare state is a hall-mark of 20th-century life. Political debate no longer centres round the desirability of state control but on its application*

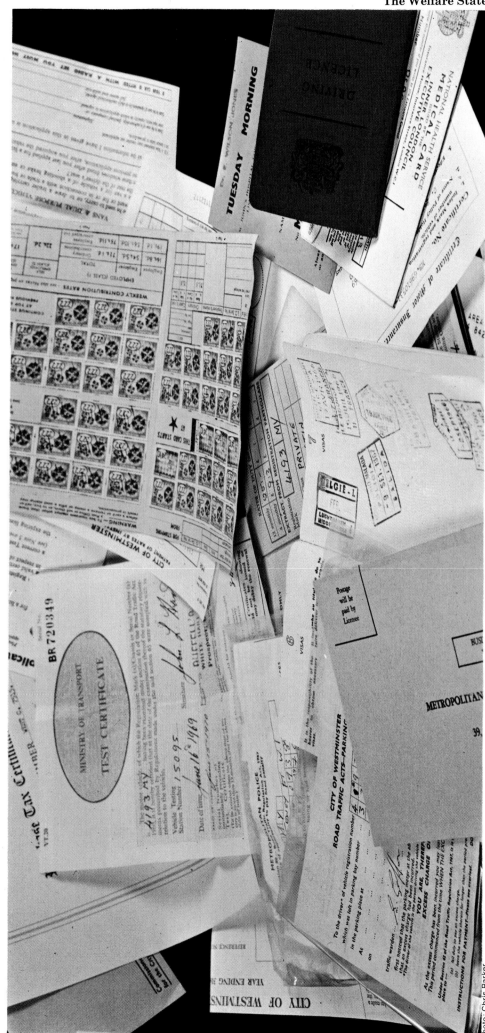

Photo: Chris Barker

2

# The Communist World

*Revolutionary vigour is kept at fever pitch in China by Mao's policy of permanent revolution. In the USSR, by contrast, more attention is paid to economic management and great power politics. 1 Festivities after the completion of the vast Ming Tombs dam, near Peking, 1958.*
*2 The military might of the USSR: May Day parade in Moscow, 1967. In 1950 the Chinese had cast in their lot with the USSR. 3 'Eternal friendship': in a Chinese cartoon of 1950 Stalin and Mao dwarf Churchill and Truman. But by the 1960's the alliance had split. 4 Chinese cartoon accuses Brezhnev of singing the same tune as Johnson. 5 Duet by the Chinese duck and the French cockerel — Soviet comment after these powers refused to sign the 1963 Test-Ban Treaty*

There is not a single state in the world today which claims to be Communist. Those countries which are conventionally thought of as Communist in the Western world would only call themselves people's democracies — that is, states in which power has passed into the hands of the working masses. One or two of the more ambitious style themselves socialist — that is, states in which class distinctions have gone because the people control all wealth. Communism is their common goal, but officially Communism means that all exploitation will have disappeared, and that there will therefore be no state at all — since the state is an instrument of coercion in the hands of the exploiting classes. In Marx's words, the state will have withered away. But there is no sign of when this might happen.

The theory might not seem to matter much, but in fact it is vitally important. For if Communism means the abolition of the state, it follows that it provides no theory of government. Unfortunately Communism — or Marxism-Leninism to give it a more accurate name — has turned into a *system*, but its practitioners still regard it as a *strategy*: to change the world. Until the world has been changed, they are stuck with a system, but do not know what to do with it — and have therefore become concerned primarily with maintaining their own power.

This is obviously an over-simplification, but it is not fundamentally misleading. The maintenance of power demands more than a secret police or an efficient military machine. Since no country can remain in complete isolation, Communist governments share many of the normal preoccupations of governments everywhere; and quite clearly this goes beyond a simple determination to remain in power. But it is the context that is different. In 1968, for example, the Dubček government in Czechoslovakia was prevented by the Soviet Union from carrying out its experiment, not because anyone could show that liberalism was leading to inefficiency, but because liberalism itself threatened the system which had been developed in Eastern Europe. On a smaller scale, in Russia, some of Khrushchev's attempts to divorce the administration from the Party came to nothing — although it was almost demonstrable that they would make the Soviet economy more efficient — simply because they threatened the power of the Party. The custodian of history and midwife of the future is the supremacy of the Party, and 'maintaining the leading role of the Party' is official doctrine.

In this sense, then, the chief task of every ruling Communist Party is to remain in power. Its secondary task is to prepare for the day when the state is no longer necessary and can be abolished. But that is now such a distant prospect that it has almost become a myth. Its importance is not that it is happening, or is ever likely to, but that in Communist countries it turns all actual policies into different forms of transition. Obviously, every society is living through transitions, but in most Western countries, for example, it is generally expected that the system will last. There will still be governments, still responsible to parliaments. But in Communist countries, the system is itself transitional; and at the same time, the future is more indeterminate than elsewhere, because short of real Communism nobody knows what to expect. And it is this state of perpetual transition towards a totally indefinable future which makes the politics of the Communist world so difficult to understand from outside, and which leads to such bitter disputes within it.

But two other factors have done much to shape the character of these politics and disputes, neither of which was foreseen by the Bolsheviks in 1917. The first was the failure of the revolution in the industrialized world; the second was the emergence of the Soviet Union as one of the world's two greatest powers. Originally, the revolution in Russia was regarded as the prelude to a much wider revolution throughout Europe, and especially in Germany. When this did not happen, Stalin defined the formula of 'socialism in one country'. This meant first that Soviet foreign policy would be directed toward normal state relations with other countries until they were ready for the revolution; and second that the problem of defining what socialism actually was became more acute. For obviously the Soviet Union would have to continue as a state like other states while it survived in a hostile world: indeed, far from preparing for the transition to Communism, the Soviet state apparatus was strengthened and increased in scope. So Stalin's victory over Trotsky's attempts to spread the revolution meant that at home the state concentrated on building up its power and turning the most backward of European powers into a highly industrialized country, while abroad the effort and activity of other Communist parties were ruthlessly sacrificed to the interests of Soviet foreign policy. The revolution became synonymous with industrialization; and the Soviet Union with great power politics. Both these policies bore fruit after the Second World War.

Instead of attempting merely to survive, the Soviet Union was now one of the world's leading powers. Ever since, the Soviet leaders have behaved with a mixture of ruthlessness in the exercise of their power and awed anxiety at their vast responsibilities—especially in the avoidance of nuclear war. In consequence, the Soviet Union is the centre of the Communist world, but is at the same time the state which works most closely with the United States in many of the questions which determine world peace or world war.

### Tito and Mao

But there were two countries, after the Second World War, where there was an authentic revolution, and where the victory of the Communist forces owed nothing to Soviet intervention. These were China and Yugoslavia. And they are the only two countries where the Communist system is significantly different today from that which dominates all the other countries. Both have successfully defied Soviet power. China, indeed, has begun to gather protégés in Asia, though Vietnam under Communist rule has moved closer to the Soviet Union. Apart from this, however, the two countries have nothing in common. When Tito first defied the Soviet Union in 1948, he was almost as much a dictator as Stalin himself. But in the past few years, he has done much to dismantle the apparatus of orthodox Communist rule. He has stripped the secret police of much of their power; he has begun to give the workers a voice in the running of their factories; he has moved towards decentralization in the government of Yugoslavia; and he has introduced considerable flexibility in economic planning. Mao, on the other hand, has attempted to revive the revolution all over again. It is noteworthy that the two countries which owe nothing to the Soviet example have attempted to do something about fulfilling the ideas of the revolution—though in opposite ways, and with much hatred and contempt for each other. One other country, Cuba, has attempted an original Communist model, but the results still depend on hidden foreign support.

In Russia the Revolution has almost died out, and has given way to a series of problems about the new industrial revolution—based on electronics and nuclear power. The Soviet state, though dictatorial in Eastern Europe, is much less anxious to fan the flames of revolution elsewhere in

*The Chinese now accuse the USSR of collaborating with the West, but attacks on the 'capitalist imperialists' are common in the propaganda of both. 1 Victory over capitalism for China's Red Guards— woodcut from the Cultural Revolution. 2 Under the make-up of the Western imperialist are the horrors of violence and famine—Soviet magazine cover. 3 Soviet cartoon—no vacancies for imperialist governesses in Africa, the Near and Middle East, and Asia. 4 Soviet cartoon ridicules US President Johnson's attempts to cast himself in the role of peace-maker in Vietnam. 5 Chinese poster calls for Third World solidarity to drive out US imperialists*

the world than it is to avoid a war with the Western powers.

There are two main problems in the Communist world, the first about economics and advanced technology, the second about the Sino-Soviet conflict. They have a continuous effect on each other.

### The failure of planning

First, economics. There is one central difficulty with Communist planning. It is easy to define and almost impossible to solve. The argument goes like this: if all the means of production—or practically all of them—are controlled centrally, it is certainly possible to draw up plans for the development of the economy, such as the various five-year plans. At first sight that is a sensible thing to do, since it shows exactly what resources a country will have available over the next few years and should eliminate all waste. (Capitalism on the other hand depends on waste: if Americans did not throw away their cars, it would not take long for the whole system to collapse.) But it also means that *every* nut and bolt over the five-year period has to be planned and foreseen. And that in turn means that there is never going to be any scope for innovation. Every factory manager who has to fulfil his quota will actively discourage new techniques or new materials because, though they might be more efficient in the long run, they will disrupt production—for a month or a year—and he will be in serious trouble. And not only he, but the manager of the next factory up the line, which depends on his product, and so on right round the economy.

Thus, total centralized planning is geared to inertia and old-fashioned methods; while capitalism, precisely to ensure that products become obsolete and that people will therefore buy new ones and so keep the profits going, is geared to ceaseless innovation. While, heaven knows, this produces evils of its own, it does mean that a Communist economy, so long as it obeys the rules, is bound to fall further and further behind an efficient capitalist economy. And this has been happening. In Czechoslovakia, previously the most advanced industrial country in Eastern Europe, and indeed one of the leading countries of the world, the effects have been disastrous. In the Soviet Union itself, most machinery and most methods are far behind the standards of Western Europe, let alone those of the United States. There is, of course, always some scope for innovation: the Soviet economy has not prevented space developments, or fundamental scientific research in half a dozen fields. But these are taken out of the economy, as it were: products are fed to them, and they do not pay them back in any economic sense of the word. They remain isolated pockets of achievement. Otherwise, even in agriculture, where techniques change more slowly than elsewhere, the Soviet Union is now humiliatingly dependent on imports of American grain for years ahead. And in the production of motor-cars, for instance, the government has now invited Fiat to come and do much of the work for them.

These are fairly abject remedies for a

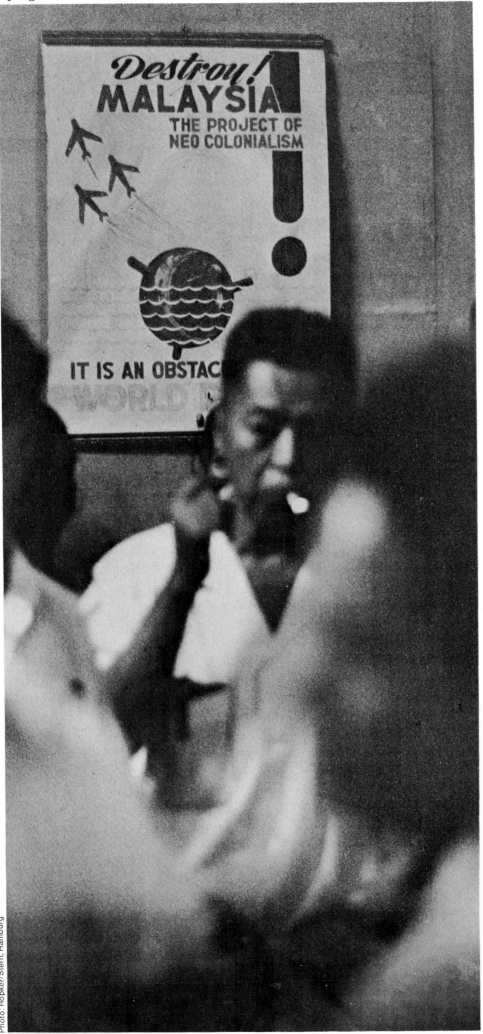

system which claimed to have all the answers; and they are not permanent remedies. Not only that: the system of centralized planning was set up at an unspeakable human cost (Stalin killed five million peasants alone), and now the people are beginning to expect some benefits. This has become an important political fact. So, for the past ten years or so, the leaders in the different Communist countries have tried to find an answer; and they have done so by bending the rules in different ways. The political relations between the European Communist states have been very largely determined by this attempt – both on a formal level, in the Council of Mutual Economic Aid (Comecon), and in less direct ways. The difficulty has always been that economic reform is bound to have certain political implications. For example, if planning is no longer quite so centralized and factory managers are given more power of decision, they are inevitably given more power and it must be expected sooner or later that some members of the Party will ally themselves with these other forms of power to challenge the ruling group. So, on the formal level, Rumania's policy of defying the Soviet Union in the name of its own national interest began in Comecon because Rumania still insisted on Stalinist planning when the Soviet leaders were anxious to break away from it; but the Rumanian example encouraged other East European states to challenge the USSR in the name of more liberal economic and social policies.

The case of Czechoslovakia was the most dramatic, and it failed; but that was not the end of the story. Today, in Comecon, there are severe conflicts between the different national Parties. The Soviet Union has tried to use the machinery of the Warsaw Pact to overcome these. In what has come to be known as the Brezhnev Doctrine it announced that it would feel free to intervene with military force whenever it decided that the interests of 'socialism' (i.e. the Soviet Union) were being threatened by the national policies of another socialist country. But this attempt has been only partially successful. It has inhibited some internal changes, but now accepts that many countries must seek closer association with the West, in order to encourage capital investment from abroad. Indeed, since the Helsinki Conference of 1975, such agreements are officially encouraged everywhere in Europe; and in other ways these countries still try to pursue their own interests whatever the Soviet government decrees. The country where reforms are still going on – in a canny, experimental, but still fairly radical manner – is Hungary. In East Germany the ruling group has so far managed to achieve the best of both worlds – economic reform without serious political trouble. In other countries,

*Indonesian Communist poster calls for the destruction of Malaysia, created in 1963. Indonesia pursued a policy of 'confrontation' with Malaysia but in 1965, following an attempted coup d'etat, the Communist party was charged with trying to set up a Peking-orientated regime and was officially banned*

there is a process of slow and cautious experiment. So the attempt to call in the Warsaw Pact to control relations between them has done no more than slow down a process which can not be stopped entirely. And inside the various Parties there are fundamental cleavages between the bright young technocrats who want to get things moving and the old Party faithful who still assert that the main task is to stay in power. This applies even in the Soviet Union, and has led recently to a creeping political crisis whose outcome it is impossible to foresee.

### The end of the Communist bloc

In all Communist countries economic policy is far more important than foreign policy. Indeed, questions of relations with the Western world very often arise through economic necessity, and are important only insofar as they affect the economy. But in two areas foreign policy is vitally important to the Soviet government. The first is a matter of world security, and turns largely on relations with the United States. Here, even while it was trying to lay down the law in Eastern Europe, it has concentrated on improving Soviet-American relations. The attempts were of course reciprocal, and have now culminated in the Strategic Arms Limitation Talks. As they have continued, these talks have become the mainstay of super power detente today. Simultaneously, the Soviet government has been cultivating better relations with West Germany, and its example has been followed by Poland (willingly) and by East Germany (most reluctantly). In this way, the Soviet government seems to be anxious to eliminate the two chief problems in the West, and drastically reduce the dangers of war. But the price is that ideological conflicts in the East have intensified, for developments in the West affect the second chief problem of the Soviet Union and the Communist world—relations with China.

The Chinese government openly scorns the Soviet system in Eastern Europe, and avers that it is based on bourgeois methods. Mao is anxious in the extreme to prevent any such development in China. He is most afraid that after his death China could either break up as it has done many times before, or else become an ordinary modern state. His answer, however, has not been Stalinist planning but an attempt to galvanize the youthful masses of the country to prodigies of revolutionary fervour and, now, production. This also means, of course, that China must continue to set a world-wide example in revolutionary purity, and in fact the Maoist policy is twofold. Internally, it has meant the deliberate re-creation of a revolutionary situation—which is now coming to an end. Externally, it has meant that China claims to lead the world in revolution, accuses the Soviet Union of collaboration with the imperialist powers, and takes pride in being threatened by both at once.

The Chinese programme was summed up before his death in 1971 by Lin Piao, in his declaration that the countryside of the world would overcome the cities of the world—that the underdeveloped countries would triumph in revolution over the advanced technologies of the West, including Russia. China, in fact, is dedicated to continuous revolution both inside and outside. And although they split with Russia, in the name of loyalty to Stalin whom the Russians had denounced, the Chinese are, in fact, very much nearer to being Trotskyists than Stalinists in their programme. The difference is the degree of internal coercion held to be necessary—and here they are Stalinist indeed.

But they have attracted considerable support in revolutionary movements elsewhere, and bid fair to become the leaders of many Communist parties. Soviet relations with friendly states, such as those in the Arab world, are conducted at the state level, and are based upon common interest; Chinese relations with states, though formally correct for the most part, are only one aspect of Chinese foreign policy. At least equally important is Chinese interest in revolution. In parts of India, for instance, the pro-Chinese Communists ran a campaign for some years against state governments, in which the chief mode of operation was killing landlords. Meanwhile, India and the Soviet Union become more friendly, but it is hard to foresee how much authority the Indian government will enjoy if it ever restores democratic rules. And while the traditionally anti-Chinese people of Vietnam have become more pro-Soviet since the war, the reverse is the case in Cambodia, where the revolutionary Khmers Rouges hate and despise the Russians.

Throughout the Third World, in fact, China poses a serious challenge to Soviet power and Soviet prestige, and this challenge has made the position of the Soviet government even more difficult. The Soviet leaders have clearly felt trapped between the demands of their relations with China and those of their relations with the United States; and it is for this complex of reasons that the recent Sino-Soviet disputes are a matter of concern for all the world.

But even the thoughts of Chairman Mao cannot protect his people against nuclear radiation. The Chinese have in fact been more cautious than their enemies believed, both in their dealings with the Soviet Union, and with the West. They have also suffered their reverses, such as the total destruction of the Communist Party in Indonesia, once the biggest in the non-Communist world. Indeed, the successes of recent years, whether in Soviet technology or Soviet or Chinese foreign policy, appear increasingly to have led nowhere. The future is entirely unpredictable, but it is clear that the transition to Communism is nowhere in sight. A Yugoslav critic of Marshal Tito, a brilliant writer and intellectual, has summed it up. Instead of Communism, said Milovan Djilas, all they have succeeded in creating is a 'new class'. A class of privileged bureaucrats ignorant of what to do next. And can the Chinese really manage without one?

*Fidel Castro makes a fiery speech in 1959, the year in which he led the revolution which overthrew the government of General Batista. Cuba is economically dependent on the USSR, but Castro has often taken his own line politically*

United Press International

# Index